AMERICA ON WHEELS

Great Lakes & Midwest

ILLINOIS, INDIANA, MICHIGAN,

MINNESOTA, OHIO, AND WISCONSIN

MACMILLAN • USA

Frommer's America on Wheels: Midwest & Great Lakes

Regional Editor: Sylvia McNair
Inspections Coordinator: Laura Van Zee
Associate Editors: Anna Idol, Patricia Lewis
Editorial Assistants: Allen McNair, Shirlee Taraki

Contributors: Catherine Wells Bentz, Amy Boerman-Cornell, William Boerman-Cornell, Marygael Cullen, Joan Dunlop, Erin Gibbons, Elizabeth Granger, Fred Granger, Joe Haag, Joyce Harms, Martin Hintz, Steve Hintz, Mary Lee Hopkins, Kiki Johnson, Virginia Johnson, Blair Laden, Paula Martin, Mike Michaelson, Irene McMahon, JoAnn Milivojevic, Polly Mills, Fred Nofziger, Nelda Pake, Mary Ann Porucznik, Mary Pittis, Arnie Raiff, Bill Roberts, Ted Ryan, Ruth Schoenbeck, Eloise Smith, Lynda Stephenson, Rita Stevens, Janice Urion, Phil Urion, Kathy Usitalo, Robin Veenstra

Frommer's America on Wheels Staff
Project Director: Gretchen Henderson
Senior Editor: Christopher Hollander
Database Editor: Melissa Klurman
Assistant Editor: Marian Cole
Editorial Assistant: Tracy McNamara

Design by Michele Laseau
Driving the State maps by Raffaele DeGennaro

Macmillan Travel
A Simon & Schuster Macmillan Company
1633 Broadway
New York, NY 10019

Find us online at **http://www.mgr.com/travel** or on America Online at keyword **Frommer's**.

MACMILLAN is a registered trademark of Macmillan, Inc.

Manufactured in the United States of America

ISSN: 1082-0884
ISBN: 0-02-860935-2

SPECIAL SALES
Bulk purchases (10+ copies) of Frommer's and selected Macmillan travel guides are available to corporations, organizations, mail-order catalogs, institutions, and charities at special discounts, and can be customized to suit individual needs. For more information write to Special Sales, Macmillan General Reference, 1633 Broadway, New York, NY 10019.

Contents

Minnesota

Ohio

Wisconsin

Introduction

America on Wheels introduces a brand-new lodgings rating system—one that factors in the latest trends in travel preferences, technologies, and amenities and is based on thorough inspections by experienced travel professionals. We rate establishments from one to five flags, plus a unique rating we call Ultra, a special award reserved for only a handful of outstanding properties in each category. Our restaurant selections represent the ethnic diversity of today's dining scene and are categorized with symbols according to their special features, ambience, and services available. In addition, the series provides in-depth sightseeing information, including driving tours and best-of-the-state highlights.

State Introductions

Coverage of each state in the *America on Wheels* series begins with background information that will help familiarize you with your destination. Included is a summary of the state's history and an overview of its geography, followed by practical tips that we hope you will find useful in planning your trip—what kind of weather to expect, what to pack, sources of information within the state, driving rules and regulations, and other essentials.

The "Best of the State" section provides you with a rundown of the top sights and attractions and the most popular festivals and special events around the state. It also includes information on spectator sports and an A-to-Z list of recreational activities available to you.

Driving Tours

The scenic driving tours included guide you along some of the most popular sightseeing routes. Every tour is keyed to a map and includes mileage information and precise directions, refreshment stops, and, for longer tours, recommended places to stay.

The Listings

The city-by-city listings of lodgings, dining establishments, and attractions together make up the bulk of the book. Cities are organized alphabetically within each state. You will find a brief description or "profile" for most cities, including a source to contact for additional information. Any listings will follow.

TYPES OF LODGINGS

Here's how we define the lodging categories used in *America on Wheels*.

Hotel
A hotel usually has three or more floors with elevators. It may or may not have parking, but if it does, entry to the guest rooms is likely to be through the lobby rather than directly from the parking lot. A range of lodgings is available (such as standard rooms, deluxe rooms, and suites), and a range of services is available (such as bellhops, room service, and a concierge). Many hotels have a restaurant or coffee shop open for breakfast, lunch, and dinner; they may have a cocktail lounge/bar. Recreational facilities may be available (such as a swimming pool, fitness center, and tennis courts).

Motel
A motel usually has one to three floors, and many of the guest rooms have doors facing the parking lot or outdoor corridors. A motel may only have a small, serviceable lobby and usually offers only limited services; the nearest restaurant may be down the street. A motel is most likely to be located alongside a highway or in a resort area.

Inn
An inn is a small-scale hotel or lodge, usually in an older building that may or may not have been designed for lodgings, and it is often located in scenic surroundings. An inn should have a warm,

welcoming atmosphere, with a more homelike quality to its furnishings and facilities. The guest rooms may be individually decorated in a style appropriate to the inn's age and location, and the rooms may or may not have telephones, televisions, or private bathrooms. An inn usually has a lounge or sitting room for guests (with parlor games and perhaps a television) and a small dining room that may or may not be open to the public. Breakfast, however, is almost always served.

Lodge

A lodge is essentially a small hotel in a rural, remote, or mountainous location. The atmosphere, service, and furniture may be more casual than you'd find in a regular hotel, and there may not be televisions or telephones in every guest room. The facilities usually include a coffee shop or restaurant, bar or cocktail lounge, games room, and indoor or outdoor swimming pool or hot tub. In ski areas, the lounge usually has a fireplace and facilities for storing ski gear.

Resort

A resort usually has more extensive facilities and recreational activities than a hotel, and offers three meals a day. The atmosphere is generally more informal than at comparable hotels.

HOW THE LODGINGS ARE RATED

Every hotel, motel, resort, inn, and lodge rated in this series has been subjected to a thorough hands-on inspection by our team of accomplished travel professionals. We ask the kinds of questions that readers would ask if they could inspect the rooms in advance for themselves (How good is the sound-proofing? How firm is the bed? What condition are the room furnishings in?). Then all of the inspection reports are reviewed by regional editors who are experts on their territories. The top-rated properties are then rechecked by a special consultant who has been reviewing and critiquing luxury hotels around the world for almost 25 years. *Establishments are not charged to be included in our series.*

Our ratings are based on *average* guest rooms— not lavish suites or concierge floors—so they're not artificially high. Therefore, in some cases a hotel rated four flags may indeed have individual rooms or suites that might fall into the five-flag category; conversely, a four-flag hotel may have a few rooms in its lowest price range that might otherwise warrant three flags.

The detailed ratings vary by category of lodgings

—for example, the criteria imposed on a hotel are more rigorous than those for a motel—and some features that are considered essential in, for example, a four-flag city hotel are relaxed for a resort that offers alternative attractions, sporting facilities, and/or beautiful and spacious grounds. Likewise, amenities such as telephones and televisions—essential in hotels and motels—are not required in inns, whose guests are often seeking peace and quiet. Instead, the criteria take into account such features as individually decorated rooms and complimentary afternoon tea.

There are, of course, several basic attributes that apply to all lodgings across the board: the cleanliness and maintenance of the building as a whole; the housekeeping in individual rooms; safety, both indoors and out; the quality and practicality of the furnishings; the quality and availability of the amenities; the caliber of the facilities; the extent and/or condition of the grounds; the ambience and cleanliness in the dining rooms; and the caliber and professionalism of the service in relation to the rates and types of lodging. Since the *America on Wheels* rating system is highly rigorous, just because a property has garnered only one flag does not mean it is inadequate or substandard.

WHAT THE INDIVIDUAL RATINGS MEAN

≣ One Flag

These properties have met or surpassed the minimum requirements of cleanliness, safety, convenience, and amenities. The staff may be limited, but guests can generally expect a friendly, hospitable greeting. Rooms will have basic amenities, such as air conditioning or heating where appropriate, telephones, and televisions. The bathrooms may have only showers rather than tubs, and just one towel for each guest, but showers and towels must be clean. The one-flag properties are by no means places to avoid, since they can represent exceptional value.

≣ ≣ Two Flags

In addition to having all of the basic attributes of one-flag lodgings, these properties will have some extra amenities, such as bellhops to help with the luggage, ice buckets in each room, and better-quality furnishings. Some extra services may include availability of cribs and irons, and wake-up service.

≣ ≣ ≣ Three Flags

These properties have all the basics noted above but also offer a more generous complement of amenities, such as firmer beds, larger desks, more drawer space, extra blankets and pillows, cable or satellite TV, alarm clock/radios, room service (although hours may be limited), and dry cleaning and/or laundry services.

☰☰☰☰ Four Flags

This is the realm of luxury, with refinements in amenities, furnishings, and service—such as larger rooms, more dependable soundproofing, two telephones per room, in-room movies, in-room safes, thick towels, hair dryers, twice-daily maid service, turndown service, concierge service, and 24-hour room service.

☰☰☰☰☰ Five Flags

These properties have everything the four-flag properties have, plus a more personal level of service and more sumptuous amenities, among them bathrobes, superior linens, and blackout drapes for lightproofing. Facilities normally include a business center and fitness center. Generally speaking, guests pay handsomely to stay in these properties.

♔ Ultra

This crème-de-la-crème rating is reserved for those rare hotels and resorts, possibly also motels and inns, that are truly outstanding in every or almost every department—places with a "grand hotel" presence, an almost flawless level of service, and a standard of dining equal to that of the finest restaurants.

UNRATED

In the few cases where an inspector was not able to make a detailed inspection, the property is listed as unrated. Also, in some cases where a property was in the process of changing owners or managers, or if the property was undergoing the kind of major renovations that made formal evaluation impossible, then, again, it is listed as unrated.

TYPES OF DINING

Restaurant

A restaurant serves complete meals and almost always offers seating.

Refreshment Stop

A refreshment stop serves drinks and/or snacks only (such as an ice cream parlor, bakery, or coffee bar) and may or may not have seating available.

HOW THE RESTAURANTS WERE EVALUATED

All of the restaurants reviewed in this series have been through the kind of thorough inspection described above for lodgings. Our inspectors have evaluated everything from freshness of ingredients to noise level and spacing of tables.

Unique to the *America on Wheels* series are the easy-to-read symbols that identify a restaurant's special features, its ambience, and special services. (See the inside front cover for the key to all symbols.) With them you can determine at a glance whether a place is a local favorite, offers exceptional value, or is "worth a splurge."

HOW TO READ THE LISTINGS

LODGINGS

Introductory Information

The rating is followed by the establishment's name, address, neighborhood (if applicable), telephone number(s), and fax number (if there is one). Where appropriate, location information is provided. In the resort listings, the acreage of the property is indicated. Also included are our inspector's comments, which provide some description and discuss any outstanding features or special information about the establishment. You can also find out whether an inn is unsuitable for children, and if so, up to what age.

Rooms

Specifies the number and type of accommodations available. If a hotel has an "executive level," this will be noted here. (This level, sometimes called a "concierge floor," is a special area of a hotel. Usually priced higher than standard rooms, accommodations at this level are often larger and have additional amenities and services such as daily newspaper delivery and nightly turndown service. Guests staying in these rooms often have access to a private lounge where complimentary breakfasts or snacks may be served.) Check-in/check-out times will also appear in this section, followed by information on the establishment's smoking policy ("No smoking" for properties that are entirely nonsmoking, and "Nonsmoking rms avail" for those that permit smoking in some areas but have rooms available for nonsmokers). This information may be followed by comments, if the inspector noted anything in particular about the guest rooms, such as their size, decor, furnishings, or window views.

Amenities

If the following amenities are available in the majority of the guest rooms, they are indicated by symbols (see inside front cover for key) or included in a list: telephone, alarm clock, coffeemaker, hair dryer, air conditioning, TV (including cable or satellite hook-up, free or pay movies), refrigerator, dataport (for fax/modem communication), VCR, CD/tape player, voice mail, in-room safe, and bathrobes. If some or all rooms have minibars, terraces, fireplaces, or whirlpools, that will be indicated here. Because travelers usually expect air conditioning, telephones, and televisions in their guest rooms, we specifically note when those amenities are not available. If any additional amenities are available in the majority of the guest rooms, or if amenities are outstanding in any way, the inspector's comments will provide some elaboration at the end of this section.

Services

If the following services are available, they are indicated by symbols (see inside front cover for key) or included in a list: room service (24-hour or limited), concierge, valet parking, airport transportation, dry cleaning/laundry, cribs available, pets allowed (call ahead before bringing your pet; an establishment that accepts pets may nevertheless place restrictions on the types or size of pets allowed, or may require a deposit and/or charge a fee), twice-daily maid service, car-rental desk, social director, masseur, children's program, babysitting (that is, the establishment can put you in touch with local babysitters and/or agencies), and afternoon tea and/or wine or sherry served. If the establishment offers any special services, or if the inspector has commented on the quality of services offered, that information will appear at the end of this section. Please note that there may be a fee for some services.

Facilities

If the following facilities are on the premises, they are indicated by symbols (see inside front cover for key) or included in a list: pool(s), bike rentals, boat rentals (may include canoes, kayaks, sailboats, powerboats, jet-skis, paddleboats), fishing, golf course (with number of holes), horseback riding, jogging path/parcourse (fitness trail), unlighted tennis courts (number available), lighted tennis courts (number available), waterskiing, windsurfing, fitness center, meeting facilities (and number of people this space can accommodate), business center, restaurant(s), bar(s), beach(es), lifeguard (for beach, not pool), basketball, volleyball, board surfing, games room, lawn games, racquetball, snorkeling, squash, spa, sauna, steam room, whirlpool, beauty salon, day-care center, playground, washer/dryer, and guest lounge (for inns only). If cross-country and downhill skiing facilities are located within 10 miles of the property, then that is indicated by symbols here as well. Our "Accessible for People With Disabilities" symbol appears where establishments claim to have guest rooms with such accessibility. If an establishment has additional facilities that are worth noting, or if the inspector has commented about the facilities, that information appears at the end of this section.

Rates

If the establishment's rates vary throughout the year, then the rates given are for the peak season. The rates listed are EP (no meals included), unless otherwise noted. We'll tell you if there is a charge for an extra person to stay in a room; if children stay free, and if so, up to what age; if there are minimum stay requirements; and if AP (three meals) and/or MAP (breakfast and dinner) rates are also available. The parking rates (if the establishment has parking) are followed by any comments the inspector has provided about rates.

If the establishment has a seasonal closing, this information will be stated. A list of credit cards accepted ends the listing.

DINING

Introductory Information

If a restaurant is a local favorite, an exceptional value (one with a high quality-to-price ratio for the area), or "worth a splurge" (more expensive by area standards, but well worth it), the appropriate symbol will appear at the beginning of the listing (see inside front cover for key to symbols). Then the establishment's name, address, neighborhood (if applicable), and telephone number are listed, followed by location information when appropriate. The type of cuisine appears in boldface type and is followed by our inspectors' comments on everything from decor and ambience to menu highlights.

The "FYI" Heading

"For your information," this section tells you the reservations policy ("recommended," "accepted," or "not accepted"), and whether there is live entertainment, a children's menu, or a dress code (jacket required or other policy). If the restaurant does not have a full bar, you can find out what the liquor policy is ("beer and wine only," "beer only," "wine only," "BYO," or "no liquor license"). This is also where you can check to see if there's a no-smoking policy for the entire restaurant (please note that smoking policies are in flux throughout the country; if smoking—or avoiding smokers—is important to you, it's a good idea to call ahead to verify the policy). If the restaurant is part of a group or chain, address and phone information will be provided for additional locations in the area. This section does not appear in Refreshment Stop listings.

Hours of Operation

Under the "Open" heading, "Peak" indicates that the hours listed are for high season only (dates in parentheses); otherwise, the hours listed apply year-round. If an establishment has a seasonal closing, that information will follow. It's a good idea to call ahead to confirm the hours of operation, especially in the off-season.

Prices

Prices given are for dinner main courses (unless otherwise noted). If a prix-fixe dinner is offered throughout dinner hours, that price is listed here, too. This section ends with a list of credit cards accepted. Refreshment Stop listings do not include prices.

Symbols

The symbols that fall at the end of many restaurant listings can help you find restaurants with the features that are important to you. If a restaurant has romantic ambience, historic ambience, outdoor dining, a fireplace, a view, delivery service, early-bird specials, valet parking, or is family-oriented, open 24 hours, or accessible to people with disabilities (meaning it has a level entrance or an access ramp, a doorway at least 36 inches wide, and restrooms that are on the same floor as the dining room, with doorways at least 36 inches wide and properly outfitted stalls), then these symbols will appear (see inside front cover for key to symbols).

ATTRACTIONS

Introductory Information

The name, street address, neighborhood (if located in a major city), and telephone number are followed by a brief rundown of the attraction's high points and key attributes so you can quickly determine if it's worth a full day of exploration or just a brief detour.

Hours of Operation & Admission

Service information includes hours of operation ("Peak" indicates that the hours listed are for high season only) and the cost of admission. The cost is

	ABBREVIATIONS
A/C	air conditioning
AE	American Express (charge card)
AP	American Plan (rates include breakfast, lunch, and dinner)
avail	available
BB	Bed-and-Breakfast Plan (rates include full breakfast)
bkfst	breakfast
BYO	bring your own (beer or wine)
CC	credit cards
CI	check-in time
CO	check-out time
CP	Continental Plan (rates include continental breakfast)
ctr	center
D	double (indicates room rate for two people in one room (one or two beds))
DC	Diners Club (credit card)
DISC	Discover (credit card)
EC	EuroCard (credit card)
effic	efficiency (unit with cooking facilities)
ER	En Route (credit card)
info	information
int'l	international
JCB	Japanese Credit Bureau (credit card)
ltd	limited
MAP	Modified American Plan (rates include breakfast and dinner)
MC	MasterCard (credit card)
Mem Day	Memorial Day
mi	mile(s)
min	minimum
MM	mile marker
refrig	refrigerator
rms	rooms
S	single (indicates room rate for one person)
satel	satellite
stes	suites (rooms with separate living and sleeping areas)
svce	service
tel	telephone
V	Visa (credit card)
w/	with
wknds	weekends

indicated by one to four dollar signs (see inside front cover for key to symbols). It's a good idea to call ahead to confirm the hours.

SPECIAL INFORMATION

DISABLED TRAVELER INFORMATION

The Americans with Disabilities Act (ADA) of 1990 required that all public facilities and commercial establishments be made accessible to disabled persons by January 26, 1992. Any property opened after that date must be built in accordance with the ADA Accessible Guidelines. Note, however, that not all establishments have completed their renovations to conform with the law; be sure to call ahead to determine if your specific needs can be met.

TAXES

State and city taxes vary widely and are not included in the prices in this book. Always ask about the taxes when you are making your reservations. State sales tax is given under "Essentials" in the introduction to each state.

A DISCLAIMER

Readers are advised that prices fluctuate in the course of time, and travel information changes under the impact of the varied and volatile factors that affect the travel industry. The publisher cannot be held responsible for the experiences of readers while traveling. Readers are invited to send ideas, comments, and suggestions for future editions to: *America on Wheels,* Macmillan Travel, 1633 Broadway, New York, NY 10019-6785.

TOLL-FREE NUMBERS/WORLD WIDE WEB SITES

The following toll-free telephone numbers and URLs for World Wide Web sites were accurate at press time; *America on Wheels* cannot be held responsible for any number or address that has changed. The "TDD" numbers are answered by a telecommunications service for the deaf and hard-of-hearing. Be sure to dial "1" before each number.

LODGINGS

Best Western International, Inc
800/528-1234 North America
800/528-2222 TDD

Budgetel Inns
800/4-BUDGET Continental USA and Canada

Budget Host
800/BUD-HOST Continental USA

Clarion Hotels
800/CLARION Continental USA and Canada
800/228-3323 TDD
http://www.hotelchoice.com/cgi-bin/res/
webres?clarion.html

Comfort Inns
800/228-5150 Continental USA and Canada
800/228-3323 TDD
http://www.hotelchoice.com/cgi-bin/res/
webres?comfort.html

Courtyard by Marriott
800/321-2211 Continental USA and Canada
800/228-7014 TDD
http://www.marriott.com/lodging/courtyar.html

Days Inn
800/325-2525 Continental USA and Canada
800/325-3297 TDD
http://www.daysinn.com/daysinn.html

DoubleTree Hotels
800/222-TREE Continental USA and Canada
800/528-9898 TDD

Drury Inn
800/325-8300 Continental USA and Canada
800/325-0583 TDD

Econo Lodges
800/55-ECONO Continental USA and Canada
800/228-3323 TDD
http://www.hotelchoice.com/cgi-bin/res/
webres?econo.html

Embassy Suites
800/362-2779 Continental USA and Canada
800/458-4708 TDD
http://www.embassy-suites.com

Exel Inns of America
800/356-8013 Continental USA and Canada

Fairfield Inn by Marriott
800/228-2800 Continental USA and Canada
800/228-7014 TDD
http://www.marriott.com/lodging/fairf.html

Fairmont Hotels
800/527-4727 Continental USA

Forte Hotels
800/225-5843 Continental USA and Canada

Four Seasons Hotels
800/332-3442 Continental USA
800/268-6282 Canada

Friendship Inns
800/453-4511 Continental USA
800/228-3323 TDD
http://www.hotelchoice.com/cgi-bin/res/
webres?friendship.html

Guest Quarters Suites
800/424-2900 Continental USA

Hampton Inn
800/HAMPTON Continental USA and Canada
800/451-HTDD TDD
http://www.hampton-inn.com

Hilton Hotels Corporation
800/HILTONS Continental USA and Canada
800/368-1133 TDD
http://www.hilton.com

Holiday Inn
800/HOLIDAY Continental USA and Canada
800/238-5544 TDD
http://www.holiday-inn.com

Howard Johnson
800/654-2000 Continental USA and Canada
800/654-8442 TDD
http://www.hojo.com/hojo.html

Hyatt Hotels and Resorts
800/228-9000 Continental USA and Canada
800/228-9548 TDD
http://www.hyatt.com

Inns of America
800/826-0778 Continental USA and Canada

Intercontinental Hotels
800/327-0200 Continental USA and Canada

ITT Sheraton
800/325-3535 Continental USA and Canada
800/325-1717 TDD

La Quinta Motor Inns, Inc
800/531-5900 Continental USA and Canada
800/426-3101 TDD

Loews Hotels
800/223-0888 Continental USA and Canada
http://www.loewshotels.com

Marriott Hotels
800/228-9290 Continental USA and Canada
800/228-7014 TDD
http://www.marriott.com/MainPage.html

Master Hosts Inns
800/251-1962 Continental USA and Canada

Meridien
800/543-4300 Continental USA and Canada

Omni Hotels
800/843-6664 Continental USA and Canada

Park Inns International
800/437-PARK Continental USA and Canada
http://www.p-inns.com/parkinn.html

Quality Inns
800/228-5151 Continental USA and Canada
800/228-3323 TDD
http://www.hotelchoice.com/cgi-bin/res/
webres?quality.html

Radisson Hotels International
800/333-3333 Continental USA and Canada

Ramada
800/2-RAMADA Continental USA and Canada
http://www.ramada.com/ramada.html

Red Carpet Inns
800/251-1962 Continental USA and Canada

Red Lion Hotels and Inns
800/547-8010 Continental USA and Canada

Red Roof Inns
800/843-7663 Continental USA and Canada
800/843-9999 TDD
http://www.redroof.com

Renaissance Hotels International
800/HOTELS-1 Continental USA and Canada
800/833-4747 TDD

Residence Inn by Marriott
800/331-3131 Continental USA and Canada
800/228-7014 TDD
http://www.marriott.com/lodging/resinn.html

Resinter
800/221-4542 Continental USA and Canada

Ritz-Carlton
800/241-3333 Continental USA and Canada

Rodeway Inns
800/228-2000 Continental USA and Canada
800/228-3323 TDD
http://www.hotelchoice.com/cgi-bin/res/
webres?rodeway.html

Scottish Inns
800/251-1962 Continental USA and Canada

Shilo Inns
800/222-2244 Continental USA and Canada

Signature Inns
800/822-5252 Continental USA and Canada

Super 8 Motels
800/800-8000 Continental USA and Canada
800/533-6634 TDD
http://www.super8motels.com/super8.html

Susse Chalet Motor Lodges & Inns
800/258-1980 Continental USA and Canada

Travelodge
800/255-3050 Continental USA and Canada

Vagabond Hotels Inc
800/522-1555 Continental USA and Canada

Westin Hotels and Resorts
800/228-3000 Continental USA and Canada
800/254-5440 TDD
http://www.westin.com

Wyndham Hotels and Resorts
800/822-4200 Continental USA and Canada

CAR RENTAL AGENCIES

Advantage Rent-A-Car
800/777-5500 Continental USA and Canada

Airways Rent A Car
800/952-9200 Continental USA

Alamo Rent A Car
800/327-9633 Continental USA and Canada
http://www.goalamo.com

Allstate Car Rental
800/634-6186 Continental USA and Canada

Avis
800/331-1212 Continental USA
800/TRY-AVIS Canada
800/331-2323 TDD
http://www.avis.com

Budget Rent A Car
800/527-0700 Continental USA and Canada
800/826-5510 TDD

Dollar Rent A Car
800/800-4000 Continental USA and Canada

Enterprise Rent-A-Car
800/325-8007 Continental USA and Canada

Hertz
800/654-3131 Continental USA and Canada
800/654-2280 TDD

National Car Rental
800/CAR-RENT Continental USA and Canada
800/328-6323 TDD
http://www.nationalcar.com

Payless Car Rental
800/PAYLESS Continental USA and Canada

Rent-A-Wreck
800/535-1391 Continental USA

Sears Rent A Car
800/527-0770 Continental USA and Canada

Thrifty Rent-A-Car
800/367-2277 Continental USA and Canada
800/358-5856 TDD

U-Save Auto Rental of America
800/272-USAV Continental USA and Canada

Value Rent-A Car
800/327-2501 Continental USA and Canada
http://www.go-value.com

AIRLINES

American Airlines
800/433-7300 Continental USA and Western Canada
800/543-1586 TDD
http://www.americanair.com/aahome/aahome.html

Canadian Airlines International
800/426-7000 Continental USA and Canada
http://www.cdair.ca

Continental Airlines
800/525-0280 Continental USA
800/343-9195 TDD
http://www.flycontinental.com

Delta Air Lines
800/221-1212 Continental USA
800/831-4488 TDD
http://www.delta-air.com

Northwest Airlines
800/225-2525 Continental USA and Canada
http://www.nwa.com

Southwest Airlines
800/435-9792 Continental USA and Canada
http://iflyswa.com

Trans World Airlines
800/221-2000 Continental USA
http://www2.twa.com/TWA/Airlines/home/
home.html

United Airlines
800/241-6522 Continental USA and Canada
http://www.ual.com

USAir
800/428-4322 Continental USA and Canada
http://www.usair.com

TRAIN

Amtrak
800/USA-RAIL Continental USA
http://amtrak.com

BUS

Greyhound
800/231-2222 Continental USA
http://greyhound.com

The Top-Rated Lodgings

FIVE FLAGS

Four Seasons Hotel, Chicago, IL
Grand Hotel, Mackinac Island, MI
The American Club, Kohler, WI
The Ritz-Carlton Chicago, Chicago, IL

FOUR FLAGS

Akron Hilton Inn at Quaker Square, Akron, OH
Amway Grand Plaza Hotel, Grand Rapids, MI
Atheneum Suite Hotel and Conference Center,
Detroit, MI
Canterbury, Indianapolis, IN
Chicago Hilton and Towers, Chicago, IL
The Cincinnatian Hotel Downtown,
Cincinnati, OH
The Fairmont, Chicago, IL
Herrington Inn, Geneva, IL
Hotel Inter-Continental Chicago, Chicago, IL
Hotel Nikko Chicago, Chicago, IL
Hyatt Regency, Milwaukee, WI
Hyatt Regency Minneapolis, Minneapolis, MN
The Lowell Inn, Stillwater, MN
Marquette Hotel, Minneapolis, MN
Oak Brook Hills Hotel & Resort,
Oak Brook, IL

Omni Netherland Plaza, Cincinnati, OH
Park Hyatt Chicago, Chicago, IL
Pfister Hotel, Milwaukee, WI
Radisson Plaza Hotel Minneapolis,
Minneapolis, MN
Renaissance Chicago Hotel, Chicago, IL
Renaissance Cleveland Hotel, Cleveland, OH
The Ritz-Carlton Cleveland, Cleveland, OH
The Ritz-Carlton Dearborn, Dearborn, MI
The Saint Paul Hotel, St Paul, MN
Sofitel Hotel, Bloomington, MN
Sutton Place, Chicago, IL
Swissôtel, Chicago, IL
The Townsend Hotel, Birmingham, MI
The Tremont, Chicago, IL
The Westin Hotel Indianapolis, Indianapolis, IN
The Whitney Hotel, Minneapolis, MN

ILLINOIS

One State, Many Faces

Natives of Illinois are too busy, too pragmatic, and perhaps too proud to give much weight to what doesn't directly concern them. Tending to business, and doing it well, seems to preoccupy most of the folks here, whether it's farming, sports (who else has Michael Jordan?), education, medicine, music (the Chicago Symphony Orchestra, perhaps the world's finest), manufacturing, or entertainment. Oddly, visitors and newcomers who have moved here are amazed at how friendly and helpful people are, even in the cities. There is a general "live and let live" mind-set as well, perhaps generated by the fact that the people here are accustomed to the different looks, lifestyles, and value systems that have always been part of the culture of this state.

Along with a basic unpretentiousness is an assumption that Illinois is not only Midwestern (and therefore centrally important to the United States), but also "mid-world," with travelers coming from everywhere. The products, services, and people of this energetic state reach into the farthest corners of Europe, South America, and Asia. Visitors to Chicago are usually surprised to discover that this world-class city is also downright beautiful—clean, open, and with miles of unobstructed parkland along the lakeshore. Chicago's obvious prosperity, pride, and exuberance is a popular draw for visitors to Illinois.

And while the US census shows that 91% of Illinois residents are native born, it seems that everyone's roots and cultural heritage go back for two or three or more generations. You can come here—whoever you are—and find your favorite food (whether Afghan, Polish, Caribbean, or Japanese) and someone to converse with in your native language, all within the context of down-home middle America.

A Brief History

Mound Builders & Canadian Trappers

Over 10,000 mounds, scattered in the central and southern parts of what is now Illinois, attest to the works of the area's early residents. These silent earthworks came from the Hopewellians, who built burial mounds over 9,000 years ago, and from the Mississippians, who built religious mounds during the period 800–1500. By the late 16th century these people were gone, and the Illiniwek ("the men"), a confederation of Potawatomi, Cahokia, Kaskaskia, Michigamea, Moingwena, Peoria, and Tamaroa, held sway in this fish- and game-filled territory. By the mid-17th century, intimations of trouble came as the Iroquois intruded on these lands in search of fur-bearing animals to trade with the Europeans in the East.

When French traders Louis Jolliet and Père Jacques Marquette came down from their Canadian post in 1673 to explore this part of what was then French-held Louisiana, they were welcomed by the Illiniwek, who hoped for help against the Iroquois. The French built forts and missions (Sieur de La Salle set up forts in both Peoria and Starved Rock); settled with their French wives and children or married Native American women; and shortened the name of this area to "Illinois."

Fun Facts

• The Illinois Territory was so sparsely populated in the early 19th century that it had to count many Illinoisans twice—and even travelers just passing through—to claim the 60,000 residents required of a territory applying for statehood.

• In 1881, a flood moved the course of the Mississippi River, leaving Kaskasia as the only town in Illinois on the western shore of the great river.

• Mrs O'Leary's cow didn't really start the great Chicago fire of 1871: the story was fabricated by Chicago newspaper reporter Michael Ahern.

• The first McDonald's restaurant opened in Des Plaines, a suburb of Chicago, in 1955.

From British Rule to Statehood In 1763, the British gained nominal title to Illinois after defeating the French in the Seven Years' War. Setting up a few posts in this far-flung land, the British used them to harass the rebelling colonists in the American Revolution. In short order, Kentuckians crossed the Ohio and captured these outposts, and Illinois was ceded by the British at the end of the Revolution as part of the Northwest Territory (which comprised present-day Ohio, Indiana, Illinois, Michigan, Wisconsin, and part of Minnesota).

In the late 1770s, a Haitian immigrant named Jean Baptiste Point du Sable set up a trading post up north along Lake Michigan in a marshy area called "Checagou." His post was just west of present-day Michigan Avenue, an area where Chicago merchants still prosper today.

In 1787, the US Congress passed the Northwest Ordinance, which gave such guidelines for the territory—freedom of religion and no slavery—as to encourage settlement. In 1794, Indiana's Gen "Mad Anthony" Wayne gained US possession of Checagou from the Native Americans in the Battle of Fallen Timbers. In the southern part of the Illinois lands, settlers began trickling in from the south and southeast while in the northern part, only the area of du Sable's trading post had non-Native residents. In 1800, du Sable closed up business and left Checagou.

In 1803, the US Army built Fort Dearborn just south of the Chicago River, and a merchant named John Kinzie took over du Sable's trading post the following year. This small enclave of 70 soldiers and approximately 40 civilians lived among the much larger Native American populations until the War of 1812, when the British enlisted the help of some of the Native Americans to attack the US outpost. Against the advice of Chief Black Partridge, the small contingent from Fort Dearborn set off for Indiana. Within a mile, what came to be known as the Fort Dearborn Massacre occurred: more than half of their number were killed by the Pottawatomie, and Fort Dearborn was burned. Chief Black Partridge was able to stop the slaughter, but this event discouraged white settlement of Illinois for some time to come.

When Illinois was granted statehood in 1818, only the southern part of the state had settlers, so the state capitol was established in the south, first at Kaskaskia (1818); then at Vandalia (1820); and finally at Springfield (1837), which remains the seat of Illinois government.

Growth & Conflict The majority of early settlers to Illinois came via the Mississippi River or the Cumberland Road and settled in the southern and central parts of Illinois. It was not until 1825, with the building of the Erie Canal, that there was an easy route from the Northeast for settlers from New England and immigrants from Europe to come to the northern tier of Illinois. By 1831, the US government asked, and then forced, the Sauk and Fox tribes to move west across the Mississippi. The following spring, Chief Black Hawk recrossed the

Mississippi with 400 people in order to plant corn. The fearful settlers asked the army to intervene, and the army massacred Black Hawk and his followers in one of the territory's last, and most shameful, organized conflicts between Native Americans and whites.

In 1837, the invention of a polished steel plow—one that prairie sod wouldn't break and the black soil wouldn't stick to—changed the fortunes of a blacksmith named John Deere in Moline and opened the riches of black dirt of Illinois to settlers. In the 1840s, immigrants from two countries dominated the great influx of people to Illinois: Germans, escaping from the restoration of the Bund in their homeland, and Irish fleeing the Great Potato Famine (1845–49). By 1857 (20 years after its incorporation), Chicago was the largest city in the state, having had a four-fold increase in population from 1830 to 1850. While the northern part of Illinois was most heavily antislavery, the strongest voices for emancipation came from farther south: an Alton newspaper editor named Elijah Lovejoy and a little-known country lawyer named Abraham Lincoln, in Springfield. The editor was killed, but Lincoln's views became nationally known during his unsuccessful run for senator. The Lincoln-Douglas debates were published and distributed, and when Lincoln won the presidency in 1860, it was with the strong support of his fellow Illinoisans.

DRIVING DISTANCES

Chicago

93 mi S of Milwaukee, WI
157 mi NE of Peoria
177 mi SE of Dubuque, IA
184 mi N of Terre Haute, IN
199 mi NE of Springfield
296 mi NE of St Louis, MO

Rockford

83 mi SE of Madison, WI
88 mi NW of Chicago
92 mi SE of Dubuque, IA
96 mi NW of Joliet
97 mi SW of Milwaukee, WI
195 mi NE of Springfield
292 mi NE of St Louis, MO

Springfield

69 mi S of Peoria
77 mi N of Vandalia
85 mi SW of Champaign
96 mi NE of St Louis, MO
199 mi SW of Chicago
209 mi W of Indianapolis, IN
224 mi NW of Evansville, IN
230 mi NW of Paducah, KY

brick buildings were in place and the city was bustling again. Within twenty years, Chicago's industrial strength made it the second-largest city in the country.

In 1893, "the first time cosmopolitanism visited the Western World," it did so in Chicago at the World's Columbian Exposition, a massive endeavor that gave Chicago a first-class debut among world cities. Not only were the latest scientific, technological, and consumer goods exhibited, but daring ideas were given a formal introduction. Congresses on social reform, women's progress, philosophy, religion, literature, education, and commerce were held in conjunction with the Exposition, as was the first Council for a Parliament of the World's Religions.

Violence in the Streets
With the growth of mining and manufacturing, the miseries of Illinois's low-paid workers came to light. The Knights of Labor formed, and strikes occurred in the Illinois coal fields. Labor troubles in Illinois had worldwide significance. On May 4, 1886, during a peaceful rally in Haymarket Square in Chicago, the police attacked: in the melee that ensued, seven police officers and two demonstrators were killed. In the aftermath, four labor leaders were hanged and another committed suicide. (The events of that day continue to be commemorated in the massive May Day celebrations of some socialist countries.) In 1889 Jane Addams opened Hull House to help the poor immigrants, and in 1891 Illinois passed safety laws for coal miners and child-labor laws.

Northern growth continued with the arrival of more Germans and Irish, along with Poles, Scandinavians, and Italians. The first influx of African Americans occurred during World War I. They came to work in the factories on the south side of Chicago and in East St Louis, but they entered into many of the same miseries of the previous workers, who had temporarily gone away to war. After the war, when

Chicago Comes of Age After the Civil War, Chicago's growth continued apace, reaching 300,000 people by 1870. Transporting of goods by rail and boat and processing the riches from the countryside underlay the increasing wealth of the city, while attracting more people to work in the factories. The city's infrastructure was itself an astonishingly flimsy affair, built mostly of wood. On October 8, 1871, the Great Chicago Fire stormed the city, leaving 300 dead and 100,000 homeless. Yet the vitality of the city was such that by 1874, new

the workers returned, competition for jobs and housing periodically erupted into ugly racial conflicts.

Then came the Roaring Twenties, and Chicago had the loudest roar of all. With Al Capone calling the shots—literally—Chicago's corrupt politicians and police put up little objection to the gang wars raging in the city's streets. The most sensational of the conflicts was the St Valentine's Day Massacre, in which Capone's gang killed seven of Bugs Moran's gang. Oddly, this very short chapter in the city's history has made a strong and lasting imprint on Chicago's image.

Because of the highly industrialized economy of Illinois, the Great Depression that followed hit the state like a sledgehammer. About the only good that came of that period was from the Civilian Conservation Corps, which put some people to work on such long-lasting facilities as the lodge at Starved Rock and other parkland improvements. But the outbreak of World War II in 1941 snapped the economy out of the doldrums almost immediately. There was work enough for everyone: Caterpillar in Peoria made tanks; Rock Island made ammunition and artillery; and Chicago made aircraft engines. And very quietly, war work of earth-shattering significance was being carried out at the University of Chicago by a team led by Enrico Fermi: the theoretical basis for the development of the atomic bomb.

Postwar Decades Without question, the political figure that dominates the state's modern history is Richard J Daley, the mayor of Chicago from 1955 to 1976. Known as a kingmaker, Daley, with his all-powerful political machine, ruled the city as no mayor had before. Though a popular mayor during his long tenure, he achieved notoriety in some quarters from his handling of the riot at the 1968 Democratic Convention, during which Vietnam War protesters were left to the not-so-tender mercies of the Chicago Police Department—with no intervention from Daley. Other mayors since Daley have been "firsts" for Chicago: the first woman mayor of Chicago, Jane Byrne, and the first African American, Harold Washington.

During the 1970s and 1980s, rising farm debt and falling land prices hit Illinois's farmers with force, and many family farms were auctioned off. Chicago, Rockford, and East St Louis—all highly industrialized—suffered high unemployment. The crashing savings and loan industry swept with it the Chicago-based US League of Savings Institutions and all the jobs associated with it. But the 1990s have seen better times arrive. Chicago's renovated Navy Pier hosted several World's Cup soccer matches and is a textbook example of urban beautification; meanwhile, Champaign has become a creative gathering place for new music. The exuberance continues, and Illinois goods pour out to the world; the universities produce top-ranked professionals; and O'Hare International Airport, the world's busiest, hums with the excitement of people on the move. Illinois is a dynamic state, embracing new ideas—the bigger, the better.

AVG MONTHLY TEMPS (°F) & RAINFALL (IN)		
	Chicago	Carbondale
Jan	26/3.8	33/6.8
Feb	24/0.8	32/3.3
Mar	34/4.5	41/2.6
Apr	45/4.6	51/5.1
May	60/1.8	64/4.0
June	66/10.0	72/7.6
July	74/4.5	80/3.8
Aug	73/5.7	77/2.3
Sept	59/4.5	65/9.5
Oct	46/2.2	54/3.6
Nov	39/1.5	42/8.1
Dec	30/1.0	36/2.4

A Closer Look
GEOGRAPHY

On the east, the magnificent shoreline of Lake Michigan; on the west, the palisades on the Mississippi River, watched over by soaring bald eagles; and cradled on the south by the wooded forests along the Ohio River, Illinois is a beautifully encircled gem of some of the richest farmland in the world.

"Black gold" here comes in three basic forms: the earth itself, bituminous coal, and petroleum. Over 90% of the state is almost flat, with miles and miles of corn, wheat, barley, and soybeans covering the rural pastures. The richness of Illinois soil—deposits left by the Ice Age, overlaid by thousands of years of prairie grass decomposing and regenerating—is a renewable, priceless resource. As farmers like to say about this foot-and-a-half deep deposit of black, soft earth, "All you have to do is look at it funny, and it'll grow something at you."

Coal and oil have also been strong factors in the economy of this state. Father Louis Hennepin made the first discovery of coal in North America in 1679, about 80 miles southwest of present-day Chicago alongside the Illinois River. About two-thirds of the state is underlaid by bituminous deposits. The oil of Illinois is mainly in the south central part of the state. With the availability of water and rail transportation, coal and oil still play a role in the economy. Fortunately, extraction of these resources has not led to the degradation of the state's natural beauty.

In the southern part of the state, the Ozark Plateau lends some more typically scenic terrain, with forests, real hills (up to 1,000 feet above sea level), and deep canyons. The Shawnee National Forest in this territory is a great place to visit, camp, exercise your body, and refresh your spirit. The delta land where the Mississippi and Ohio Rivers meet is popularly known as Little Egypt due to its similarity to the Nile delta.

Water defines much of the boundary and development of Illinois: the Mississippi on the west, the Ohio on the South, and the 63-mile Lake Michigan shoreline to the north. Water links Chicago with the Atlantic Ocean and the Gulf of Mexico, a connection forged through harbor improvements, canal building, and the St Lawrence Seaway. As a railroad hub and an air hub (O'Hare Airport is the busiest in the world), Chicago continues to keep Illinois connected to the rest of the world.

CLIMATE

In whatever season you choose to visit Illinois, the weather is likely to surprise you. Any particular day can fall so far outside expectations, even of the day before, that preparedness and a certain alertness to changing circumstances will be beneficial. Yes, it does snow, heavily, in April and sometimes in May, every 10 years or so. And winter temperatures can linger at −25°F. And the wind is sometimes so strong in Chicago that ropes are strung up so that pedestrians can hang on instead of skittering along icy sidewalks. While many people shudder to think of Illinois in winter, seeing Michigan Avenue in Chicago during a heavy snowstorm in the holiday season —with the tiny white lights in the trees and the stores glittering with their ever-so-luscious wares— should rank as one of the most soul satisfying experiences of a trip. Indeed, cold weather in Illinois, with a knife-sharp wind, can be invigorating. Warm clothes will resolve any difficulties, even for the timid.

Illinois summers are most often hot, hazy, and humid, with frequent thunderstorms. The drama of weather here even brings in "storm watchers,"

tourists who want to experience these awe-inspiring events. Midwestern thunderstorms are so renowned for their vigor, light shows, and magnificent thunder. The only real weather-related problem that cannot be anticipated, easily evaded, nor overlooked is that of tornadoes. These can come any time from spring through early fall.

WHAT TO PACK

Because temperatures change rapidly from day to night and sometimes many times within a day, layers work best for comfort. Even on a hot summer's day, you may want a light jacket if you'll be out on Lake Michigan, for example. Casual clothes work well in most places; in Chicago and in some of the better resort areas, you'll feel most comfortable in your upscale casual clothes.

TOURIST INFORMATION

The **Illinois Bureau of Tourism** (tel 800/223-0121) publishes the *Illinois Visitors Guide and Events Calendar* as well as road maps and various brochures; these are available by calling the above number or writing to the bureau's main office c/o the James R Thompson Center, 100 W Randolph St, Ste 3400, Chicago 60601. For a very useful packet of information, including a state parks brochure and information on canoeing, camping, and fishing, call or write to Illinois Department of Conservation, Lincoln Tower Plaza, 524 S 2nd St, Springfield 62701-1787 (tel 217/782-7454). The State of Illinois maintains a World Wide Web page (http://www.state.il.us) with links to general information about Illinois. To find out how to obtain tourist information for individual cities and parks in Illinois, look under specific cities in the listings section of this book.

DRIVING RULES AND REGULATIONS

On interstates, speed limits vary within the state from 65 mph to 55 mph. Radar detection devices are illegal and will be confiscated. Right turns are permitted on red after stopping, unless otherwise indicated. No matter what time of day, or what lighting conditions exist, if you have your windshield wipers on, you must have your headlights on. Drivers must wear their seat belt and children must either be in car seats (if under four years old) or be wearing a seat belt (if over four years old). There is zero tolerance for alcohol for drivers under 21, who will immediately lose their licenses. There is a helmet law for motorcyclists.

RENTING A CAR

For the time that you are planning on spending most of your time in Chicago, you may be better off without a car. Parking is difficult and expensive, taxicabs are plentiful, and the public transportation system is ranked among the best in the United States. If you need a car to tour the rest of the state, the companies below have offices in Illinois.

- **Alamo** (tel 800/327-9633)
- **Avis** (tel 800/831-2847)
- **Budget** (tel 800/527 0700)
- **Dollar** (tel 800/800-4000)
- **Enterprise** (tel 800/325-8007)
- **Hertz** (tel 800/654-3131)
- **National** (tel 800/227-7368)
- **Rent-a-Wreck** (tel 800/535-1391)
- **Thrifty** (tel 800/367-2277)
- **Value** (tel 800/327-8281)

ESSENTIALS

Area Codes: The explosive growth of the Chicago-land area has led to the establishment of several new area codes: Chicago's central commercial area (the Loop) is still in **312,** but the rest of the city is now in the **773** area code. The north and northwest Chicago suburbs are in the new **847** area code; the northeast suburbs remain in **708;** and Du Page County, southern Kane County, and portions of Kendall County have been moved to **630.**

In northwestern Illinois, the area code is **815.** In the western section (encompassing such towns as Moline, Bloomington, and Macomb), the area code is **309.** A broad east/west swath across the state at the latitude of Springfield and Champaign has the area code of **217,** and the entire southern section is in **618.**

Emergencies: For police, fire, or ambulance, dial **911.**

Liquor Laws: The legal age for alcohol consumption or purchase is 21.

Road Info: Call 800/452-4368 for updated information on road conditions.

Smoking: Rapidly changing laws are adding more and more smoking restrictions. O'Hare International Airport, for example, is smokefree throughout. Restaurants are becoming more controlled also.

Taxes: There is quite a variation in taxes within the state, depending upon the municipalities. Overall, a sales tax of 8.25% is fairly common, but in Springfield, the tax is 7.25% and in Chicago, the tax is 8.75%. Hotel taxes, which include the sales tax, are 14.9% in Chicago and 10% elsewhere. For car rentals you can expect to pay taxes ranging from 12% to 18%. The airport tax for O'Hare International is $3 for either arriving or departing flights.

Time Zone: Illinois is in the central time zone, and the entire state observes daylight saving time.

Best of the State

WHAT TO SEE AND DO

Below is a general overview of some of the top sights and attractions in Illinois. To find out more detailed information, look under "Attractions" for individual cities in the listings portion of this book.

Parks & Recreation Areas In southern Illinois, see the Garden of the Gods in the **Shawnee National Forest. Père Marquette State Park,** the state's largest, offers every kind of outdoor opportunity. The **Mississippi Palisades State Park** offers one of the most scenic drives in the state. In the **Apple River Canyon State Park,** limestone cliffs loom above the Apple River. **Starved Rock State Park** commemorates the sad fate of a band of Native Americans in the 1700s; for the visitor today, there are plenty of trails for exploring.

Wildlife Bird watching is a popular activity throughout the state. Along the Mississippi River, eagles flock to the Quad Cities area and hundreds of bald eagles winter among the bluffs near Collinsville. At Crab Orchard Lake, in the Shawnee National Forest, hundreds of thousands of Canada geese spend the winter.

Historic Sites & Monuments Springfield is definitely a "must see" for visitors to the state. Here is Abraham Lincoln's restored home; the Old State Capitol Building is now a museum of state government. Just outside of the city is **New Salem Village,** a fully restored 1830s settlement. For earlier history, the **Illinois State Museum** concentrates on Native American life before the arrival of white settlers. Then visit **Cahokia Mounds State Historic Site,** near Collinsville. Here Monk's Mound, the largest prehistoric earthwork in the world, is over 900 years old. Take another giant step back in time at Kampsville, the site of the **Modoc Rock Shelter,** over 9,000 years old.

Galena's restored homes pay tribute to more recent history. **Nauvoo** was founded by Joseph Smith, the Mormon prophet. After Smith was murdered in his cell at nearby Carthage Jail, Brigham Young led the Mormons west to Utah. Nauvoo commemorates this early history and is an interesting town to visit. Writers are honored in Illinois, too. In Galesburg is the home of Carl Sandburg; and in Lewiston, the home of poet Edgar Lee Masters.

Chicago Outdoors The beauty of the lakefront, with its 29 miles of parkland interspersed with the magnificent buildings originally built for the 1893 Columbia Exposition, is unparalleled in urban design. Take any of the boats leaving from Michigan Avenue and the river for a wondrous view of this beautiful city; sightseeing, architectural, and dinner cruises are available. Wandering the downtown in search of public art is also a richly rewarding experience. You'll find Marc Chagall's softly colored mosaic *The Four Seasons* at One First National Plaza; Picasso's untitled 50-foot-tall sculpture graces Richard J Daley Plaza; a massive Claes Oldenburg baseball bat is outside Social Security Administration Plaza; and a grand statue of Native Americans on horseback sits on Congress Plaza. Along the lakefront north via winding Sheridan Road is some of the premier housing in the United States as well as the spectacular **Bahai'i Temple** in Wilmette.

Museums Chicago is the epicenter of museumgoing in the state, offering a little bit of everything. For an up-close look at dinosaurs, try the **Field Museum of Natural History.** At the **Museum of Science and Industry,** many hands-on exhibits are educational and downright fun. Or see the feeding of the fish at **Shedd Aquarium. Newberry Library** houses one of the best Americana collections; and

the **Du Sable Museum of African-American History** honors the contributions of African Americans. Of course, the **Art Institute of Chicago** has one of the finest collections of French Impressionist and Asian works. **Adler Planetarium** for star gazers; and for the curious, the **Museum of Holography.** In the archives of the **Chicago Historical Society** is the rich story of Chicago's past. Another informative exhibit can be found at the **Museum of Broadcast History** at the Cultural Center.

Performing Arts How can anyone overlook the world's finest orchestra? Certainly visitors should treat themselves to the best, and **Chicago Symphony** is it. The performing arts flourish here, from the classical beauty of **Lyric Opera** to cutting edge comedy. Check out the action at the **Blackstone, Steppenwolf, Auditorium, Drury Lane, Goodman,** or a host of others. Chicago may be the Second City, but its theater is advancing it to top billing.

Family Favorites In Chicago, **Navy Pier** juts out 3,000 feet into Lake Michigan and is the place for everything from a Ferris wheel to bike riding, as well as the site of major and minor events. Whenever you choose to wander there, you're sure to find fun and action. North of Chicago in Gurnee, you'll find **Six Flags Great America,** a 300-acre theme park with roller coasters, stage shows, and rides for children and adults.

Shopping In Chicago, State Street, that "great street," still has that magic; and on Michigan Avenue, the Magnificent Mile gleams with the latest high-fashion, high-quality elegance. In Gurnee, you'll find the world's largest outlet mall, **Gurnee Mills,** with bargains and more bargains. In Arlington Heights, you'll find a massive Japanese shopping area: **Yaohan Plaza.** Fresh Japanese foods of all sorts are sold in the grocery store, and there's a handy luncheon area for light meals too. For antiques, try towns such as Galena, Alton, Grafton, and Elsah, all of which have steamboat-era artifacts.

Architecture On a clear day, the panoramic view from Chicago's **Sears Tower** is breathtaking. The bold and beautiful skyline carries on the innovation developed here: the world's first skyscraper was completed in 1885 by the founder of the Chicago School of Architecture, William Le Baron Jenney. Chicago Architecture Foundation has walking, boating, and bus tours. Be sure to visit the Wintergarden skylighted top floor of Harold Washington Library, the world's largest public library, and one of the new additions to the striking architecture Chicago is known for. In the city, you'll see the works of Mies van der Rohe and Helmut Jahn. And of course, for examples of Frank Lloyd Wright's Prairie School of horizontal design, see the **Robie House** at the University of Chicago and his many buildings in Oak Park.

EVENTS AND FESTIVALS

CHICAGO AND ENVIRONS

- **St Patrick's Day Parade.** The Chicago River turns green and everyone in the city turns Irish. Marching bands and floats galore. March 17. Call 312/744-3315.
- **Viva Chicago Latin Music Festival,** in Grant Park. Big stars from Mexico, South America, and the Caribbean join local groups to make this a truly international celebration of music. May. Call 312/744-3315.
- **At Home With Wright,** Oak Park. A showcase of architecturally significant Frank Lloyd Wright structures. You can wander inside more than 10 buildings and shop in the galleries and studios for Wright-related arts and crafts. May. Call 708/848-1500.
- **Chicago Blues Festival,** in Grant Park. A weekend to hear the true blues greats—and some promising up-and-comers—in the town that nurtured this American art. June. Call 312/744-3315.
- **Venetian Night,** on the Chicago lakefront. Beautifully lighted boats of many sizes parade along the shoreline, bringing delight to onlookers. "Viewing parties," from ad hoc vantages on the street to full-dress affairs from balcony suites, lend gaiety to the occasion. June. Call 312/744-3315.
- **The Ravinia Festival,** Highland Park. A full panoply of performances from the Chicago Symphony to jazz to pop music. Picnic in the park and rest on a blanket during the performance or sit under the pavilion. June through September. Call 312/RAVINIA.
- **Chicago Symphony and Chorus Summer Season,** in Grant Park. International guest artists and conductors, music under the stars. Mid-June through late August. Call 312/294-2420.
- **Taste of Chicago,** in Grant Park. Highlights the great food available from over 70 fine restaurants in Chicago. Free entertainment includes top national stars as well as great local talent. Late June through July 4. Call 312/744-3315.
- **Fiesta de Hemingway,** Oak Park. Ernest Hemingway's Spanish adventures are celebrated with the "Running of the Bulls" in his home town. The food, wine, and music are authentically Spanish, but the bulls are handmade artist's conceptions. July. Call 708/848-2222.
- **Chicago Air and Water Show.** Come early and stake out a good vantage point along the North Avenue Beach for superb demonstrations on the water and in the air. International experts in aviation and water maneuvers come and show their precision skills. August. Call 312/744-3315.
- **Chicago Jazz Festival,** Grant Park. Three days of performances from the jazz greats. September. Call 312/744-3315.
- **Chicago Marathon,** starting at Daley Plaza, Washington and Dearborn Sts. A highly competitive field with thousands of runners, national and international. Late October. Call 312/527-2200.
- **Annual American Indian Powwow,** Chicago. Thousands of Native Americans, from over 30 tribes, come from all over the United States and Canada for competition dancing during this powwow. Native foods, arts and crafts. November. Call the American Indian Center at 312/275-5871 for specific time and place.

ELSEWHERE IN THE STATE

- **Steamboat Days,** Peoria. Boat races, concerts, carnival rides, and parades celebrate the city's river heritage. June. Call 309/676-0303.
- **Illinois Shakespeare Festival,** Bloomington. Selections from the Bard's repertoire are supplemented by madrigal music and other Renaissance entertainments. July through early August. Call 309/438-2535.
- **Illinois State Fair,** Illinois State Fairgrounds in Springfield. Held for 10 activity-filled days. This is serious business to the participants, who are competing in everything from raising prize-winning cattle to making the best apple pie in the state. August. Call 217/782-6661.
- **Central States Threshermen's Reunion,** Pontiac. Thousands of people gather here to see the antique tractors, farm equipment, tractor pulls, parades at this all-American celebration of the farm life. There's also country music and quilt-

judging, along with lots of food. Late August through early September. Call 815/844-3474 or 835-2055.

- **Abraham Lincoln National Railsplitter Contest and Crafts Festival,** Lincoln. Contestants compete to see who can swing the ax fastest and who can chop the most wood. Food, arts and crafts, flea market. Call 217/732-7146.
- **Festival of the Gnomes,** Joliet. Costumed gnomes roam the grounds of Bicentennial Park, as performances of gnome legends are acted out on stage. Arts and crafts, food. Early December. Call 815/740-2298.

SPECTATOR SPORTS

Baseball   Join some of the most devoted fans in the world at Wrigley Field, the home of the **Chicago Cubs** (tel 312/404-2827) and one of the most scenic—not to mention one of the most adored—ballparks in the country. The **Chicago White Sox** (tel 312/831-1769) play at the new Comiskey Park, which was constructed across the street from the old stadium.

Basketball   At the recently dedicated United Center, with its statue of Michael Jordan at the entrance, you can see the NBA's **Chicago Bulls** (tel 312/455-4000) in action. The Bulls have won four world championships in the last six years. Meanwhile, the **Chicago Rockers** (tel 312/595-1222) hold court at the UIC Pavilion.

Football   The **Chicago Bears** (tel 708/615-2327) of the NFL play at Soldier Field. "Da Bears," the oldest surviving professional football team, have won a combined eight league titles and Super Bowls.

College Football   The **Northwestern Wild Cats** (tel 708/491-2287), play at Dyche Stadium in Evanston, while the **Fighting Illini** (tel 217/333-3470) of the University of Illinois do battle at Memorial Stadium in Champaign. The **Northern Illinois University Huskies** (tel 800/332-HOWL) play at Huskie Stadium in De Kalb.

Hockey   One of the original six National Hockey League teams, the **Chicago Blackhawks** (tel 312/943-7000), play at the United Center in Chicago.

Horse Racing   Arlington **International Race Course** (tel 708/255-4300), located at Euclid and Wilke Rds in Arlington Heights, is a lovely newer facility with state-of-the-art Jumbotron, interactive videos for learning, and a tasteful ambience.

ACTIVITIES A TO Z

Antiquing   For adventuresome antiquers, there's a bounty to be found in the towns along the Mississippi as well as scattered throughout the state. Geneva, St Charles, Long Grove, Crete, and Beecher offer opportunities to take a treasure home. The **Kane County Flea Market** is fun for the whole family. You can get information by calling 800/74-RIVER.

Backpacking   All of the larger park and recreation areas have trails numerous enough to keep you exploring for a long time. The Ozark-Shawnee Trail, much of which is in the **Shawnee National Forest** (tel 618/253-7114), runs from Battery Rock on the Ohio River to Grand Tower on the Mississippi River. You can do all or just part of the 115-mile trek, as there are plenty of access points on this trail.

Biking   Along the Metra train tracks, beginning in Winnetka and extending north to Glencoe, is the Green Bay Trail, an excellent path for biking. Another railroad, the Chicago Aurora and Elgin Railway, abandoned their track from Elmhurst to Aurora. This right-of-way is now the Illinois Prairie Path. To traverse the Salt Creek Trail, within Cook County, you can enter from near Brookfield Zoo and continue to just west of La Grange. Or, you can travel the North Branch, a 20-mile trail, from Caldwell and Devon Avenues in Chicago to Lake County's Chicago Botanic Gardens.

Boating   With Lake Michigan, natural and man-made lakes, and 500 rivers within the state, a boater can find the ideal spot for launching. For those who wish to have the experience, but didn't bring their boat along, excellent boat rides can be taken from Chicago along the lakefront. An easy place to board is at Michigan Avenue and the Chicago River.

Camping   The **Shawnee National Forest** (tel 618/253-7114) in the south of Illinois and the over 200 state parklands offer camping from near luxury to completely primitive. At **Starved Rock State Park** (tel 815/667-4726), for example, you can hike and camp to your heart's content, while maintaining the option of having a gourmet meal in the lodge. The **Illinois Department of Conservation** (tel 217/782-2965) has complete information and contact points for you.

Canoeing   Of course, if you have your own canoe, the lakes and rivers of Illinois offer tremendous opportunities. If you don't have a canoe, you can call

815/939-2486 in Aroma Park to arrange for trips of up to two days duration.

Eagle Watching In Albany, Thomson, and Savanna, you're in Eagle country. These magnificent birds will be watching you as much as you're watching them, as they have a lot of territory to protect.

Fishing Throughout the state fishing is popular at every level of sophistication, from the old pole plus worm to serious sport fishing on Lake Michigan. To find out how the fish are biting in any area of the state, call the **Division of Wildlife Resources** (tel 800/ASK-FISH); for a booklet on all fishing regulations, contact the **Illinois Department of Conservation** (tel 217/782-2965).

Gambling Gambling on the horse races is available at the Arlington Park International Race Course, Arlington in Peoria, North Aurora Off-Track Betting, Balmoral Park Racetrack. Riverboat gambling is becoming increasingly popular; Aurora, Elgin, and Joliet already have facilities, and more are coming on line.

Golfing Wherever you are in Illinois, you're near a golf course. There are more than 150 courses in the Chicagoland area alone, including the prestigious **Kemper Lakes Golf Club** (tel 708/540-3450), home of the 1989 PGA Championship and the 1992 US Women's Amateur Championship. The **Spencer T Olin Community Golf Course** (tel 618/465-3111) in Alton was designed by Arnold Palmer; Robert Trent Jones Sr designed the **Rail Golf Course** (tel 217/525-0365) in Springfield.

Hiking All of the natural areas offer opportunities for hiking. All you need is comfortable footgear and you're set. A different sort of trail that might interest you runs along the Mississippi, through gardens, picnic areas, and playgrounds. Called the **Great River Trail,** this route is pretty civilized. You can find out more by calling 309/793-6300.

Hang Gliding Commercial hang gliding outfits are located throughout the state, and a listing of contact points and telephone numbers is available in the *Illinois Calendar of Events,* which you can get free from the **Illinois Bureau of Tourism** (tel 800/223-0121).

Kiting Along the shores of Lake Michigan, kiting is an inexpensive and popular sport. You're almost always sure to have a breeze, and there's plenty of public parkland for launching. **Illinois Beach State Park** (tel 708/662-4811), midway between Chicago and Milwaukee, is a popular spot to try your luck.

SELECTED PARKS & RECREATION AREAS

- **Lincoln Home National Historic Site,** 426 S 7th St, Springfield 62701 (tel 217/492-4150)
- **Apple River Canyon State Park,** 8763 E Canyon Rd, Apple River 61001 (tel 815/745-3302)
- **Big River State Forest,** RR1, Box 118, Keithsburg 61442 (tel 309/374-2496)
- **Cave-in-Rock State Park,** PO Box 338, New State Park Rd, Cave-in-Rock 62919 (tel 618/289-4325)
- **Clinton Lake State Recreation Area,** RR1, Box 4, DeWit 61735 (tel 217/935-8722)
- **Dixon Springs State Park,** RR 2, Golconda 62938 (tel 618/949-3394)
- **Giant City State Park,** PO Box 70, Makanda 62958 (tel 618/457-4836)
- **Goose Lake Prairie State Natural Area,** 5010 N Jugtown Rd, Morris 60450 (tel 815/942-2899)
- **Horseshoe Lake State Park,** 3321 IL 111, Granite City 60240 (tel 618/931-0270)
- **I&M Canal State Trail,** PO Box 272, Morris 60450 (tel 815/942-9501)
- **Illinois Beach State Park,** Zion 60099 (tel 708/662-4811)
- **Kaskaskia River State Fish and Wildlife Area,** 10981 Conservation Rd, Baldwin 62217 (tel 618/785-2555)
- **Lincoln Trail State Park,** RR1, Box 117, Marshall 62441 (tel 217/826-2222)
- **Mississippi Palisades State Park,** 4577 Rte 84 N, Savanna 61074 (tel 815/273-2731)
- **Moraine View State Park,** RR 4, Crosby Rd, Leroy 61752 (tel 309/724-8032)
- **Nauvoo State Park,** PO Box 426, Nauvoo 62354 (tel 217/453-2512)
- **Père Marquette State Park,** PO Box 158, Grafton 62037 (tel 618/786-3323)
- **Rock Cut State Park,** 7318 Harlem Rd, Loves Park 61111 (tel 815/885-3311)
- **Shelbyville State Fish and Wildlife Area,** RR1, Box 42, Bethany 61914 (tel 217/665-3112)
- **Starved Rock State Park,** PO Box 116, Utica 61373 (tel 815/667-4726)
- **Trail of Tears State Forest,** RR1, Box 1331, Jonesboro 62952 (tel 618/833-4910)
- **White Pines Forest State Park,** 6712 W Pines Rd, Mount Morris 61054 (tel 815/946-3717)

Spelunking The caves of Illinois offer the opportunities from safe, guided tours all the way to exploring wild caves. Whatever you comfort point in balancing claustrophobia and spelunking expertise, you can add a "cave experience" to your travels here. Some possibilities include **Cave-in-Rock State Park** (tel 618/289-4325); Ava Cave; Cave Spring Cave (Alto Pass); and Illinois Caverns in Monroe County.

Tennis Even in downtown Chicago, you can keep your game up at the **McClurg Sports Center** (tel 312/944-4546). Throughout the state, you'll find that open courts are readily available. Your hotel or motel personnel can usually tell you where the nearest court is, and some lodgings work out special discounts with nearby sports facilities.

Driving the State

Start	Oak Park
Finish	Glencoe
Distance	55 miles
Time	From two hours to two days
Highlights	Chicago's oceanlike lakefront and magnificent skyline; Frank Lloyd Wright's Prairie School of Architecture with an urban backdrop; bright, new Navy Pier chocked full of attractions and shopping opportunities; the opulent mansions of the northern suburbs

In a metropolitan area with so many buildings, it seems important to view at least some of them up close. We will start this tour in the Chicago suburb of Oak Park, for an intimate look at the work of Frank Lloyd Wright. From the west, the tour swoops into town the back way and then curves along the well-known Chicago lakefront, where the beaches draw big crowds at all times of the year for sunshine and fun times. You'll also see some of the most popular museums of the area. (They look so magnificent from the outside perched along Lake Shore Dr, you don't necessarily need to go inside to enjoy them.) Once you pass through the hubbub of the city, Sheridan Rd curls through the northern suburbs, hugging close to the lake and sweeping through some of the wealthiest areas of Chicagoland. The final stop is Chicago Botanic Gardens, 300 acres of quiet, colorful nature less than an hour away from the steel, brick, and glass of the Loop.

You can make this just a driving trip, never get out of your car, and get an eyeful of everything (except the best of what the Botanic Gardens has to offer) and get through it in less than two hours. Or you can stop at every stop, walk through every museum (quickly), ride the Ferris wheel at Navy Pier, sit in the grass at the Botanic Garden, and be done in about two days. Either way, you will get a good idea of the diversity of Chicago and its suburbs.

For additional information on lodging, dining, and attractions in the region covered by the tour, refer to specific cities in the listings portion of this chapter.

The tour begins in Oak Park, a suburb on the west side of Chicago, accessible by the Eisenhower Expwy (I-290). Take the Harlem Ave exit (IL 43 N). Go north on Harlem Ave about a mile to Lake St and turn right (east). You will be in the business center of our first stop:

1. Oak Park. One of the oldest suburbs of Chicago,

Oak Park is known as the birthplace of Ernest Hemingway and of many of Frank Lloyd Wright's architectural innovations. The **Oak Park Visitors Center,** 158 N Forest Ave, at Lake St and Forest Ave (tel 708/848-1500), provides an orientation program about the **Frank Lloyd Wright Prairie School of Architecture National Historic District** and has admission tickets for **Frank Lloyd Wright Home and Studio.** The home was built in 1889, when Wright was just 22 years old and beginning to create his low-slung, earth-hugging style of architecture. Most of the Wright structures are within walking distance of one another, and the stroll through this section of Oak Park is tree-lined and peaceful.

After the walk, drive back west on Lake St to Harlem Ave. Take Harlem Ave south a mile to the Eisenhower Expwy (I-290) and head east toward the Chicago Loop. You are coming into Chicago "the back way," since most photos and movies are shot from the lake. In just over 8 miles, exit onto the Dan Ryan Expwy (I-90/I-94) south. While you are on the Dan Ryan, you will pass by **Comiskey Park** (35th St exit), the practically brand-new stadium that serves as home to the Chicago White Sox. Take I-90/I-94 about 6 miles to the Garfield Blvd exit and take Garfield east toward the lake. (Note: This part of the trip, less than a mile along Garfield, passes through an area of the city that is rather run down. An alternate route that skips to a point further along the tour is listed below.) Follow Garfield as it curves right through Washington Park and take a left (east) on 57th St. At the corner of 57th St and Cottage Grove Ave is the:

2. DuSable Museum of African American History, 740 E 56th Place (tel 312/947-0600). This museum displays a variety of African and African American art objects, as well as many historical and cultural exhibits.

From the DuSable, continue east on 57th St through the main campus of the **University of Chicago,** with its mix of grand old buildings of higher learning and solid, urban residences. The **Frederick C Robie House,** 5757 Woodlawn Ave (tel 312/702-8374) is another Frank Lloyd Wright building, thought by some to be one of his finest. Tours are given at noon daily.

Less than a mile east on 57th St and you are at the:

3. Museum of Science and Industry (tel 312/684-

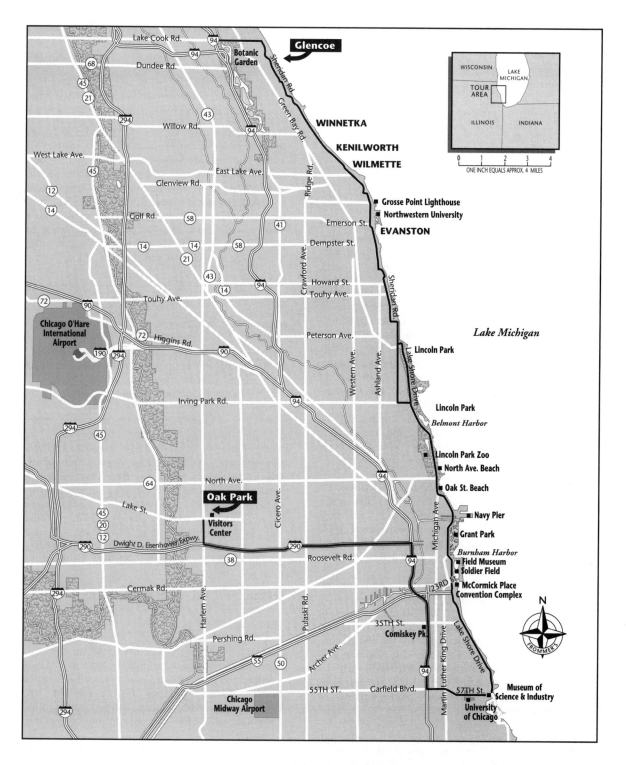

Glencoe

Botanic Garden

Lake Cook Rd.

Dundee Rd.

Willow Rd.

West Lake Ave.

East Lake Ave.

Glenview Rd.

Golf Rd.

Touhy Ave.

Chicago O'Hare International Airport

Higgins Rd.

Irving Park Rd.

North Ave.

Lake St.

Oak Park

Visitors Center

Dwight D. Eisenhower Expwy.

Roosevelt Rd.

Cermak Rd.

Pershing Rd.

Chicago Midway Airport

55TH ST.

Garfield Blvd.

Sheridan Rd.

Green Bay Rd.

Ridge Rd.

WINNETKA

KENILWORTH

WILMETTE

Grosse Point Lighthouse
Northwestern University

EVANSTON

Emerson St.

Dempster St.

Howard St.
Touhy Ave.

Crawford Ave.

Western Ave.

Ashland Ave.

Peterson Ave.

Sheridan Rd.

Lake Shore Drive

Lake Michigan

Lincoln Park

Lincoln Park
Belmont Harbor

Lincoln Park Zoo
North Ave. Beach

Oak St. Beach

Navy Pier

Grant Park

Burnham Harbor
Field Museum
Soldier Field

McCormick Place
Convention Complex

Michigan Ave.

123RD

35TH St.
Comiskey Pk.

Archer Ave.

Pulaski Rd.

Harlem Ave.

Cicero Ave.

Martin Luther King Drive

Lake Shore Drive

57TH St.
Museum of
Science & Industry

University
of Chicago

WISCONSIN

LAKE
MICHIGAN

TOUR
AREA

ILLINOIS

INDIANA

0 1 2 3 4
ONE INCH EQUALS APPROX. 4 MILES

N

1414). This is one of Chicago's hottest attractions with its coal mine, walk-in human heart replica, miniature circus, and 334-seat Omnimax Theater (extra fee required).

Outside the museum, along famous Lake Shore Dr, you'll get your first glimpse of **Lake Michigan.** It's so huge, with no sight of land on any other side of it, it could almost pass as an ocean. From the museum, take the drive about 3 miles north past **McCormick Place Convention Complex** at E 23rd St and Lake Shore Dr, the nation's largest exposition center.

You have the option of getting to this point directly from Oak Park. To do this, follow the same directions from I-290 to I-90/I-94, but exit onto I-55 N (about 3 miles on I-90/I-94) to Lake Shore Dr. I-55 zips past McCormick Place, which surrounds it on both sides, before it spills out onto Lake Shore Dr.

At press time, Lake Shore Drive is undergoing an extensive relocation and construction project designed to make getting around this area of Chicago more convenient. The directions listed below are current, but are subject to change due to this project. All attractions will continue to be open during the project, and detours will be clearly posted. For more information, call the Chicago Office of Tourism (tel 312/280-5740).

As you continue about a mile north on Lake Shore Dr, you will pass **Soldier Field,** the current home of the Chicago Bears. Just beyond that, on the same side of the drive, is the:

4. **Field Museum of Natural History,** Lake Shore Dr at Roosevelt Rd (tel 312/922-9410). This is the home of some of the most magnificent dinosaur bones in the country. The museum traces life on earth back to prehistoric times through extensive exhibits, lectures, films, and special demonstrations and performances.

As Lake Shore Dr curves past the museum, the **John G Shedd Aquarium,** 1200 S Lake Shore Dr (tel 312/939-2438), and **The Adler Planetarium,** 1300 S Lake Shore Dr (tel 312/322-0304), pop up against the spectacular backdrop of Lake Michigan. Heading north on Lake Shore Dr, you are surrounded by breathtaking sights. The lake—with its harbors, tour boats, and yacht club—spreads away from the city on the east, while on the west side of the drive is:

5. **Grant Park.** This big green area is where Chicago hosts many of its annual festivals like Taste of Chicago, Blues Fest, and Jazz Fest. The landscaped grounds are ideal for strolling, lounging, or picnicking. **Buckingham Fountain** (operational May

through September) cannot be missed as it shoots its 130-foot sprays in the air. At night the fountain is bathed in colored lights and can be seen from quite a distance.

Lake Shore Dr continues to skirt the fabulous Chicago skyline as it curves east. Keep driving for just over a mile until you can exit at Grand Ave for

6. **Navy Pier,** at 600 E Grand Ave. The old pier underwent a $150-million renovation project in 1995 that included construction of brand new facilities and attractions. There's 50 acres of fun here, including an IMAX Theater; a six-story, glass-enclosed, botanical garden; the Skyline Stage; and lots more. The brave may want to take a ride on the 15-story-tall Ferris wheel. You will also want to check out the open air market of vendor carts between Memorial Day and the first of October.

Take a Break

Widow Newton's Tavern, 700 E Grand Ave at Navy Pier (tel 312/595-5500). This medium-priced restaurant has a tasty menu to choose from. Try one of the appetizers, like baked goat cheese or the gazpacho cocktail, or dive into one of the heartier fish, chicken, beef, or vegetarian entrees.

Another mile or so down Lake Shore Dr and you will see some of Chicago's most popular beaches. **Oak St Beach** and **North Ave Beach** are filled with bodies in-line skating, biking, jogging, playing volleyball, or just plain soaking up the sun all summer long. The winter months change the bright blue lake to a frothy—sometimes steaming—border along the edge of the drive, but there are always people around, even in the cold. West of the drive here is:

7. **Lincoln Park.** This is Chicago's largest park, reaching along most of the north lake side of the city. At one corner of the park (take the North Ave exit off the drive to Clark St) is the **Chicago Historical Society,** where you can find out about the development of the city and its many cultures. Further north in the park you will come upon the **Lincoln Park Zoological Gardens** and the **Lincoln Park Conservatory.** Both of these attractions are open daily and provide lots of opportunities to get close to nature.

Past the conservatory you can get back on Lake Shore Dr at Belmont. You'll get a good sight of **Belmont Harbor,** which is teeming with boats in the summer. From there, continue north to the end of the drive, about 3 miles. Stay in one of the right lanes as the drive ends and turn right (north) on Sheridan Rd.

Take a Break

Sesi's Seaside Cafe and Gallery, 6219 N Sheridan Rd (tel 312/764-0544). This pleasant little place is inexpensive and offers a combination of American and Turkish cuisine. Breakfast, sandwiches, salads, hummus; good for a quick stop or a long, pretty, sit-down. You're right on the lake here, and when weather permits, outdoor seating is available.

Sheridan Rd goes through the north side of Chicago and curves close to the lake again at the border of **Evanston.** Follow the signs marking Sheridan Rd and you will soon come upon:

8. **Northwestern University,** Clark St at Sheridan Rd. This is a beautiful lakefront campus that has its own beach (admission charged on weekdays to use the beach facilities) and many grand old buildings. Guided walking tours leave from 1801 Hinman Ave (tel 708/491-7271) daily.

Another mile down Sheridan Rd, at Central St, you'll find **Grosse Point Lighthouse.** Tower tours and lighthouse film can be attended in the historical center.

As you follow another mile along the winding ways of Sheridan Rd from the lighthouse, you'll pass a sign welcoming you to Wilmette, and just a blink past that, on your left (west), look for:

9. **The Baha'i House of Worship,** Sheridan Rd and Linden Ave (tel 708/256-4400). You can't miss this nine-sided structure that looks almost as though it's made of white lace. Its sloping 200-foot-tall dome is surrounded by nine gardens and fountains. A visitors center offers slides and other exhibits about the temple and the Baha'i faith.

From here the drive is an eight-mile feast of small, beachside parks; luxurious residences with extensively landscaped gardens; and dips and curves through wooded, mostly posh suburbs. Along Chicago's North Shore, Wilmette gives way to Kenilworth (sometimes deemed to be Chicago's richest suburb per capita) and Kenilworth to Winnetka. Keep going through Glencoe, and at its edge, Sheridan Rd curves away from the lake (west) and meets with Lake-Cook Rd. Stay on Lake-Cook Rd for about one mile. On the left (south) you will find:

10. **Chicago Botanic Garden** (tel 708/835-5440). You'll find 300 acres of specialty gardens, lakes, lagoons, and woods here. Nature trails, an English walled garden, a Japanese garden, and a sensory garden for the visually impaired are just a few of the many things to visit. Take a tram tour or get around on foot. The Education Center houses an auditorium, museum, greenhouse, and gift shop.

From the Botanic Garden, it is an easy trip back to the city. Continue west on Lake-Cook Rd less than a mile to US 41 S to I-94 E back to Chicago. If you have had enough of the city for one day, I-94 can take you east or west to any number of places in the state or in the country.

Driving the State

LINCOLN LAND

Start	Vandalia
Finish	Springfield
Distance	Approximately 250 miles
Time	2 days
Highlights	The restored village where Abraham Lincoln lived and worked, the only home he ever owned, and his final resting place

Illinois was settled from south to north. The state's first capital was Kaskaskia, on the banks of the Mississippi River. Cairo, at the southernmost tip of the state, was a thriving, bustling river port in the early 19th century, when businessmen from the north were denied loans at the State Bank because "Chicago was too far from Shawneetown to ever amount to anything." But the people kept moving forward and northward, often coming from Indiana as the Thomas and Sarah Lincoln family did. The state's founding fathers moved the capital in 1820 about 90 miles northeast to Vandalia, where it remained until 1839. Largely due to the efforts of a young legislator named Abraham Lincoln, the capital again moved north, to the center of the state in Springfield. While Chicago has grown larger than the early pioneers could have imagined, the state capital remains in central Illinois.

The topography of the tour route varies. The southern quarter offers winding, hilly roads flanked by fields of sunflowers, sorghum, wildflowers, and prairie grass. The central section stretches for miles in every direction with fields of corn and beans, and horizons that deliver spectacular evening sunsets. The seemingly spare Illinois prairie landscape hides the rich black earth that yields much of the nation's food supply.

This tour assumes a south to north route toward Chicago with numerous stopping points, not all connected with the 16th president, but interesting none the less. Should you wish to follow his life in the order he lived it, you can contact the Springfield Convention and Visitors Bureau (tel 217/789-2360) or the Central Illinois Tourism Council (tel 217/525-7980). The city of Springfield contains the majority of historic sites connected to Abraham Lincoln. Plan to stay there overnight and start fresh for a second full day of touring.

For additional information on accommodations, restaurants, and attractions in the region covered by the tour, look under specific cities in the listings portion of this chapter.

From St Louis, MO, take I-70 E to the center of town in Vandalia, IL, your first stop.

1. **Vandalia Statehouse,** 315 W Gallatin (tel 618/283-1161), is the oldest statehouse still standing in Illinois. The legislature met in this gracious, Federal-style building from 1836 to 1839. Prior to that, two other buildings in Vandalia, now destroyed, served as the official seat of state government. Abraham Lincoln assumed the first statewide office of his career at Vandalia in 1834 in "the dilapidated second statehouse, " and he began his second term in 1836 in the capitol that stands today in Springfield. Lincoln led the charge to move the capital to Springfield as a legislator from New Salem and part of a group of Sangamon County representatives known as the "Long Nine." Before he left, he delivered his first speech against the injustice of slavery in this building. Located on the town square, the site is now surrounded by four blocks of storefront boasting five different antique shops. A delightful urban garden with piped-in music offers a quiet summertime place to reflect on the town's history and the rest of your trip through Lincoln Land.

A historical marker and an unusual statue, *Madonna of the Prairie,* featuring a pioneer mother and two children, pay tribute to the strength of women settlers who came here with their families over the famous Cumberland Trail.

Take US 40 E out of Vandalia for an interesting, rather hilly (at least by Illinois standards), two-lane drive through small rural towns and open fields to Effingham. At this point, get on I-70 E for approximately 27 miles to exit 119 toward Charleston. Follow the signs to Lincoln Log Cabin for approximately 17 miles on IL 130 N. (If it's open, you might want to stop at the **Lost Creek Orchard** roadside stand for seasonal fruits and vegetables.) Watch carefully for the sign to Lincoln Log Cabin approximately 6 miles down IL 130 and turn left on the road between a farmhouse and a grain bin. Note the abandoned one-room schoolhouse on the left about a mile down, which means you are closing in on the next stop:

2. **Lincoln Log Cabin,** RR 1 in Lerna (tel 217/345-6489), preserves the last home of Abraham Lincoln's father and stepmother, Thomas and Sarah Bush Lincoln. Abraham said goodbye to his family before they left their first Illinois homestead near Decatur and moved to the farm called Goosenest Prairie. He went to seek his fortune on the flatboats between New Salem and New Orleans. His family intended to return to Indiana but when they

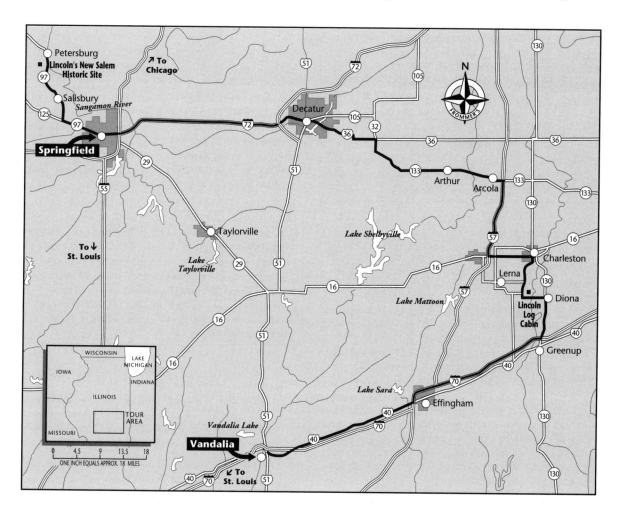

stopped to visit relatives here, they decided to stay. By 1845, there were as many as eighteen people (many of them from Sarah's extended family) living in the small two-room cabin. Abraham's visits were seldom. He did not come home for his father's funeral but visited the grave site in Shiloh Cemetery (one mile from cabin) with Sarah in 1861 on his way to Washington as President-elect. Today, all site staff adopt the persona of a Lincoln family member or neighbor and speak as though they lived in 1845. The site includes the log cabin, large log barn, smokehouse, root cellar, and a garden and orchard filled with 19th-century crop varieties. The nearby **Sargent Farm,** in marked contrast to the Lincoln farm, shows a wealthier lifestyle of the same period.

The next Lincoln-related historic site is not for another 125 miles, so sit back and enjoy the sights of Illinois Amish country. When leaving the Lincoln Log Cabin site, turn right and head for Rte 16. This country road will lead you through a portion of the town of Charleston for approximately 8 miles. Take the I-57 exit north toward Champaign. At Exit 203 head west for the Amish communities of:

3. Arcola and Arthur. Known as the broomcorn capital of the world, **Arcola** is home to three companies that still make brooms. In addition to brooms, shops all over town sell Raggedy Ann and Andy dolls, in tribute to the town's native son, Johnny Gruelle, the doll's creator. If you stop here, you'll likely notice the townsfolk's dress (women in white gauze bonnets and plain dresses, men in dark suits or bib overalls) and the horse and buggies on the side of the road.

Arthur was settled in 1865 by four families of the Old Order Amish Faith and has since grown to 300 families, making it the fifth-largest Amish community in the country today. The Amish way of life is exemplified by plain living (including no electricity), strength of faith, family bonds, and commit-

---

Take a Break

If your trip brings you to or near Arcola at dinner time, plan to stop at the area's finest restaurant. The **French Embassy,** at 112 W Springfield in Arcola (tel 217/268-4949) It may be hard to believe, but Chef Jean-Louis Ledent has combined a highly unlikely pair—a fine French restaurant and a bowling alley—in the same building. Positively elegant dining and atmosphere are combined with mouth-watering entrees and desserts. Dinner entrees cost $11–$18.

---

ment to community. Although agriculture remains the main industry of the Amish, there are nearly 100 Amish country businesses in the area offering beautifully handcrafted wood furniture, crafts, quilts, and antiques. Tours of the area and home businesses can be arranged at the Visitor Center in downtown Arthur. If you simply want to drive through the area, you'll still enjoy views of the well-kept fields, houses, and rows of freshly-washed clothes drying on the line.

Take Rte 133 toward Decatur, the site of the first Lincoln family homestead, which is marked today with a simple plaque. From Decatur, take I-72 west toward and through Springfield and head for Petersburg and Lincoln's New Salem before returning to Springfield for the night. Twenty miles northwest of Springfield on Rte 97, turn left at the entrance to the next stop:

4. **Lincoln's New Salem** (tel 217/632-4000), where Abraham Lincoln lived between 1831 and 1837. Here he worked as a store clerk, postmaster, deputy surveyor, and legislator. It was from New Salem that he enlisted in the Blackhawk War and, later, studied law. Timber houses, shops, and stores reconstructed by the Civilian Conservation Corps in the 1930s replicate the 1830s village, where costumed interpreters go about their daily chores of gardening, spinning wool, or tending the animals. Don't miss the wonderful gift shop at the end of the village. During the summer, on the nearby Sangamon River (where Lincoln once piloted a flatboat), the Talisman Riverboat offers leisurely trips to tourists for a small fee.

One last stop on your way back to Springfield: The primitive folk art shop and home of George Colin in Salisbury on Rte 97. Bright, colorfully painted Lincolns, alligators, watermelon benches and tables, and cows grace the front lawn of this unique place on the main road through town. Colin's art is on display (and for sale) in his Chicago

showroom, but the best place to see it is here in its natural surroundings.

If you've planned on spending the night in Springfield, you might want to try the **Mansion View Inn and Suites** (tel 217/544-7411 or toll free 800/252-1083). Located across the street from the Governor's Mansion and near the historic district, this is a good bet for couples or families. The **Holiday Inn East** (tel 217/529-7171) is about 10 minutes from downtown and offers a large Holidome area for active families with children. Both offer moderately priced rooms.

Take a Break

Gumbo Ya Yas, 700 E Adams St (tel 217/789-1530), offers the best view of the city from the 30th floor of the downtown Springfield Hilton Hotel. The Cajun-inspired menu lists a variety of bronzed or blackened fish entrees that are superb. Cajun caesar salad is the house specialty. Entrees cost $9–$15.

Springfield is called "the city Lincoln loved," and justifiably so. When he left, he said "No one, not in my situation, can appreciate my feelings of sadness at this parting." It is the perfect place to contemplate the life and legacy of Illinois's most famous son. Start your second day of touring early at:

5. **The Lincoln-Herndon Law Offices,** at the corner of 6th and Adams (tel 217/785-7289). This is the only surviving structure in which Lincoln maintained working law offices. Lincoln and partners Stephen Logan (1843–1844) and William Herndon (1844–1865) practiced law in offices located above Seth Tinsley's store and local post office and across the street from the new capitol he worked so hard to bring to this emerging frontier town. Guided tours of the offices are available.

From the law offices, walk out the front door and across the square to the:

6. **Old State Capitol** (tel 217/785-7961) where Lincoln delivered his famous "House Divided" speech in the turbulent days preceding the Civil War. Today, visitors can take guided tours of the building where Lincoln tried over 200 cases in the Supreme Court, borrowed books from the State Library, served as legislator, and spent time with the other lawyers and politicians of the day. An original copy of the Gettysburg Address is on display.

From here, walk two blocks south on 6th St and east one block to 7th St, where you will find the visitors center for our next stop:

7. **The Lincoln Home,** 8th and Jackson Sts (tel 217/492-4150). The Abraham Lincoln family resided in this Quaker-brown house for seventeen years. It has been meticulously restored to its 1860s appearance, and the Park Service rangers do a good job of giving visitors a real sense of Lincoln's family life on the guided tours. You'll see the parlor where Lincoln learned that he had been nominated as the Whig Party's candidate for president, as well as the Lincolns' bedrooms. The home is located in the midst of a restored four-block historic neighborhood managed by the National Park Service. It is a good idea to stop by the Visitor Center early in the day to get your free tickets to tour the home. Tours leave every fifteen minutes.

If you're visiting during the summer months, walk two blocks north and one block east to:

8. **Lincoln Depot,** 10th and Monroe (tel 217/788-1356), where Abraham Lincoln left as President-elect for Washington, DC. Today you can walk through the building's restored waiting rooms (one for the ladies, one for the luggage and the men) and view a slide show that recreates Lincoln's 12-day journey to his inauguration.

Take a Break

Maldaners Restaurant, 222 S 6th St, (tel 217/522-4313), is a great place for lunch or dinner. This local institution has been around since the 19th century, although Chef Michael Higgins is a relatively new, and welcome, addition. Lunchtime favorites on the seasonally changing menu include the turkey curry sandwich, fresh spinach salad, or chicken teriyaki salad. Lunch entrees cost $2–$7.

After lunch you can take a little break from the Lincoln sites and visit two unrelated attractions. Keep heading south to the next stop:

9. **State Capitol,** 2nd St and Capitol Ave (tel 217/782-2099), where the first legislative session was held in 1877. The continued growth of the state increased the need for more file, storage, and office space than the old capitol allowed. Today, visitors can watch politics in action from balcony-level seating when the legislature is in session.

10. **Dana-Thomas House,** 301 E Lawrence (tel 217/782-6776), designed by Frank Lloyd Wright and one of the finest and most complete of his Prairie-style residences. Built in 1902 for Springfield socialite Susan Lawrence Dana, it was his largest commission for many years. Tours offered Wednesday–Sunday.

The final stop on your tour of Lincoln Land was also Lincoln's final stop. Springfield's Oak Ridge Cemetery contains one of the state's most moving monuments to the Great Emancipator:

11. **The Lincoln Tomb,** 1500 N Monument Ave (tel 217/782-2717), is the final resting place for Abraham, Mary Todd, Tad, Eddie, and Willie Lincoln. Abraham was buried here at the request of Mrs Lincoln after his assassination in 1865. The statues surrounding the obelisk at the top of the Tomb depict the four military branches of the time and were made from melted down Civil War cannons. Also on site is the original receiving vault in which Lincoln's body was placed while the monument was built.

From Springfield, I-55 south will take you to St Louis, while I-55 north heads on to Chicago.

Illinois Listings

Altamont

Located in central Illinois on the Old National Road, midway between Lake Shelbyville and Carlyle Lake. **Information:** Altamont Chamber of Commerce, PO Box 141, Altamont, 62411.

MOTEL ▥

≣≣ Best Western Carriage Inn
I-70 and IL 128, 62411; tel 618/483-6101 or toll free 800/ 528-1234. Exit 82 off I-70. Three capped pyramids mark this clean, comfortable, country motel. **Rooms:** 38 rms, stes, and effic. CI 2pm/CO 11am. Nonsmoking rms avail. **Amenities:** ▥ A/C, cable TV w/movies. **Services:** ⌂ ⌂ **Facilities:** ▱ ▱ 1 restaurant, 1 bar. **Rates:** Peak (May–Sept) $29–$34 S; $42–$45 D; $48 ste; $55 effic. Extra person $3. Children under age 12 stay free. Lower rates off-season. Parking: Outdoor, free. AE, CB, DC, DISC, MC, V.

RESTAURANT ▥

★ Gilbert's Family Restaurant
Rte 2; tel 618/483-6288. Exit 82 off I-70. **American.** This cheerful blue and white diner—a local favorite—serves homemade soup with all deluxe sandwiches, including its "belly-buster" half-pound burger. Other options include chicken fried steak, meatloaf, shrimp basket, and a variety of salad plates. **FYI:** Reservations accepted. Children's menu. No liquor license. **Open:** Sun–Thurs 6:30am–9pm, Fri–Sat 6am–10pm. **Prices:** Main courses $5–$10. No CC. ▥

Alton

Located on the bluffs just above the confluence of the Mississippi and Missouri Rivers. Some of the older houses in town have rooftop platforms, from which Alton merchants once looked down the river to spot incoming steamboats laden with cargo for their stores. The final Lincoln-Douglas debate took place here in 1858. **Information:** Greater Alton/ Twin Rivers Convention & Visitors Bureau, 200 Piasa St, Alton, 62002 (tel 618/465-6676).

MOTEL ▥

≣≣≣ Holiday Inn
3800 Homer Adams Pkwy, 62002; tel 618/462-1200 or toll free 800/HOLIDAY; fax 618/462-0906. A cool white exterior and atrium lobby with fountains mark this Holidome, just minutes from Mississippi River casino boats, and halfway between Chicago, IL and Branson, MO. Golf, tennis, watersports, and boating available nearby. **Rooms:** 137 rms and stes. CI 2pm/CO noon. Nonsmoking rms avail. **Amenities:** ▥ ⌂ ▥ A/C, cable TV w/movies, dataport, VCR. Some units w/terraces. Refrigerator rentals available. **Services:** ✕ ▥ ▥ ⌂ ⌂ Babysitting. **Facilities:** ▱ ▥ ▥ ▱ 1 restaurant, 2 bars (1 w/entertainment), games rm, sauna, whirlpool, washer/dryer. Indoor pool has adjacent outdoor sun deck. Guests have access to local health club. **Rates:** $72– $82 S; $82–$92 D; $200 ste. Extra person $10. Children under age 18 stay free. Min stay special events. Parking: Outdoor, free. Golf, gambling, and family packages avail. AE, CB, DC, DISC, JCB, MC, V.

Arcola

Located in Amish country, where horse-pulled carriages run alongside the highways. Many Amish crafts shops can be found here. **Information:** Arcola Chamber of Commerce, PO Box 274, Arcola, 61910 (tel 217/268-4530).

MOTELS ▥

≣≣ Budget Host Arcola Inn
236 S Jacques St, 61910; tel 217/268-4971 or toll free 800/ BUD-HOST; fax 217/268-3525. Right off I-57 at exit 203, at the edge of Illinois Amish settlements. Syndicated columnist Dave Barry's chosen accommodations when participating in the local Lawn Ranger parade during Broom Corn festival. Close to business district and restaurants. **Rooms:** 30 rms. CI open/CO 11am. Nonsmoking rms avail. Clean, attractive rooms. **Amenities:** ▥ A/C, cable TV. **Services:** ⌂ ⌂ **Rates:** Peak (May–Oct) $29–$37 S; $34–$41 D. Extra person $5. Children under age 16 stay free. Lower rates off-season. Parking: Outdoor, free. AE, DC, DISC, MC, V.

≣≣ Days Inn

640 E Springfield Rd, 61910; tel 217/268-3031 or toll free 800/325-2525; fax 217/268-3144. Exit 203 off I-57. Easy access to I-57 and local attractions. Basic overnight accommodations. **Rooms:** 80 rms. CI 3pm/CO 11am. Nonsmoking rms avail. **Amenities:** 🛅 A/C, in-rm safe. **Services:** ⤴ ◁ Extra charge for pets. **Facilities:** ⛸ ᵹ **Rates (CP):** Peak (May–Oct) $37–$40 S; $48 D. Extra person $6. Children under age 14 stay free. Lower rates off-season. Parking: Indoor, free. AE, CB, DC, DISC, MC, V.

RESTAURANT 🍴

Dutch Kitchen

127 E Main St; tel 217/268-3518. Exit 203 (IL 133) off I-57, W ½ mi to Pine St, N 2 blocks. **Amish.** Cozy family restaurant in main shopping district features locally produced Dutch sausage, homemade pies, and other Amish specialties. Salad bar with every dinner, including kids menu. Buses and tour groups welcome with advance notice. **FYI:** Reservations accepted. Children's menu. No liquor license. No smoking. **Open:** Daily 7:30am–7pm. **Prices:** Main courses $7–$8. No CC. 👥

Arlington Heights

Now a bustling northwestern suburb of Chicago, Arlington Heights actually predates its larger neighbor. Its population has doubled in the past 30 years. **Information:** Arlington Heights Chamber of Commerce, 180 N Arlington Heights Rd, PO Box 6, Arlington Heights, 60006 (tel 847/253-1703).

HOTELS 🏨

≣≣≣ Arlington Park Hilton Conference Center

3400 W Euclid Ave, 60005; tel 847/394-2000 or toll free 800/HILTONS; fax 847/394-2049. 1 block E of Euclid exit off IL 53. Just west of Arlington Heights Int'l Racecourse. Newly renovated. **Rooms:** 421 rms and stes. Executive level. CI 3pm/CO 11am. Nonsmoking rms avail. **Amenities:** 🛅 ⓩ A/C, cable TV w/movies, dataport, voice mail. Some units w/minibars, 1 w/whirlpool. **Services:** ✕ ⊶ ⓥⓟ 🚗 ⊠ ⤴ Twice-daily maid svce, car-rental desk, masseur, children's program, babysitting. **Facilities:** ⛸ 🏊 2 🏓 1200 💻 ᵹ 2 restaurants (*see* "Restaurants" below), 1 bar (w/entertainment), basketball, volleyball, games rm, spa, sauna, whirlpool, washer/dryer. Extensive fitness center. Gift shop. **Rates:** Peak (Apr–June/Sept 15–Oct) $109–$149 S or D; $150–$500 ste. Extra person $15. Children under age 11 stay free. Lower rates off-season. Parking: Outdoor, free. AE, CB, DC, DISC, MC, V.

≣≣ Courtyard by Marriott

100 W Algonquin Rd, 60004; tel 847/437-3344 or toll free 800/321-2211; fax 847/437-3367. From I-90 E and W, exit N on Arlington Heights Rd to Algonquin Rd, go W 1 block. Set back from busy commercial street for quiet and privacy.

Rooms: 147 rms and stes. CI 3pm/CO 1pm. Nonsmoking rms avail. **Amenities:** 🛅 ⓩ ⓥ A/C, cable TV w/movies, refrig, voice mail. Some units w/terraces. **Services:** ✕ 🚗 ⊠ ⤴ Car-rental desk, babysitting. Complimentary hors d'oeuvres in bar area. Computer unit in lobby for guests to access information on nearby restaurants, health clubs, transportation, entertainment, etc. **Facilities:** ⛸ 🏓 90 ᵹ 1 restaurant (bkfst and dinner only), 1 bar, washer/dryer. **Rates:** Peak (Apr–Oct) $90–$100 S or D; $105 ste. Children under age 18 stay free. Lower rates off-season. Parking: Outdoor, free. AE, CB, DC, DISC, EC, ER, JCB, MC, V.

≣≣ Holiday Inn Express

2120 S Arlington Heights Rd, 60005; tel 847/593-9400 or toll free 800/HOLIDAY; fax 847/593-3632. N of IL 62 and I-90. Caters to corporate clientele. **Rooms:** 125 rms and stes. CI 2pm/CO noon. Nonsmoking rms avail. Oak-furnished rooms are spacious. Six suites are well designed for business meetings. **Amenities:** 🛅 A/C, satel TV w/movies, dataport. Some units w/minibars, some w/terraces. **Services:** ⊠ ⤴ Car-rental desk. **Facilities:** 80 ᵹ **Rates (CP):** $66–$89 S; $75–$92 D; $78–$92 ste. Extra person $7. Children under age 17 stay free. Parking: Outdoor, free. AE, CB, DC, DISC, ER, JCB, MC, V.

≣≣≣ Radisson Hotel Arlington Heights

75 W Algonquin Rd, 60005; tel 847/364-7600 or toll free 800/333-3333; fax 847/364-7665. Exit Arlington Heights Rd N off I-90 E or W. Popular with business people and families. Located just off interstate, convenient to Arlington International Racecourse. **Rooms:** 201 rms and stes. CI 3pm/CO noon. Nonsmoking rms avail. **Amenities:** 🛅 ⓩ ⓥ A/C, cable TV w/movies, dataport. **Services:** ✕ 🚗 ⊠ ⤴ ◁ **Facilities:** ⛸ 🏓 500 ᵹ 1 restaurant, 1 bar, games rm, sauna, whirlpool. **Rates:** $109 S or D; $195–$295 ste. Extra person $10. Children under age 18 stay free. Parking: Outdoor, free. AE, CB, DC, DISC, JCB, MC, V.

MOTELS

≣≣ Best Western Arlington Inn

948 E Northwest Hwy, 60004; tel 847/255-2900 or toll free 800/209-0009; fax 847/394-1093. 4 blocks E of Arlington Heights Rd; 2¼ mi E of IL 53. **Rooms:** 81 rms, stes, and effic. CI 3pm/CO noon. Nonsmoking rms avail. **Amenities:** 🛅 ⓩ ⓥ A/C, cable TV, refrig. **Services:** ✕ 🚗 ⊠ ⤴ **Facilities:** ⛸ 🏓 40 ᵹ 1 restaurant, 1 bar (w/entertainment), spa, whirlpool. **Rates:** Peak (May–Oct) $45–$65 S; $50–$74 D; $74–$81 ste; $74–$81 effic. Extra person $5. Children under age 12 stay free. Lower rates off-season. Parking: Outdoor, free. AE, CB, DC, DISC, MC, V.

≣≣ La Quinta Inn

1415 W Dundee Rd, 60004; tel 847/253-8777 or toll free 800/531-5900; fax 847/818-9167. Dundee Rd E exit off IL 53N, 1 block E. Fronts busy commercial road, but well set back. Bright, nicely furnished lounge area separated from check-in and lobby. Managed by husband-and-wife team who live on premises. **Rooms:** 123 rms and stes. CI 2pm/CO noon. Nonsmoking rms avail. Rooms larger than most in this price range. Recliner chairs. **Amenities:** 🔟 ☕ A/C, satel TV w/movies. **Services:** 🗻 🗭 Car-rental desk. Good personal attention to guests. **Facilities:** 🗔 🔟 🕹 Access and shuttle transportation (no charge) to nearby fitness center and health club. **Rates (CP):** $51–$72 S or D; $100 ste. Extra person $7. Children under age 18 stay free. Parking: Outdoor, free. Special rate benefits in frequent traveler program: Returns Club membership. AE, DC, DISC, MC, V.

📇 Red Roof Inn
22 W Algonquin Rd, 60005; tel 847/228-6650 or toll free 800/THE-ROOF; fax 847/228-6709. No-frills, but well-maintained motel. **Rooms:** 165 rms. CI 2pm/CO noon. Nonsmoking rms avail. **Amenities:** 🔟 A/C, satel TV, dataport. **Services:** 🗭 🗭 Local restaurant will deliver to room. Fax and copying machines available. **Facilities:** 🔟 🕹 **Rates:** Peak (May–Oct) $39–$51 S; $47–$59 D. Extra person $8. Children under age 18 stay free. Lower rates off-season. Parking: Outdoor, free. AE, DC, DISC, MC, V.

RESTAURANTS 🍴

Arlington Trackside Restaurant
2000 E Euclid Ave; tel 847/259-8400. 1 mi E of IL 53; at Wilke. **American.** Three large-screen and more than 75 small-screen televisions broadcast races from around the United States as patrons try their luck at the inter-track wagering windows. Outdoor patio, without broadcast races, offers quiet dining. Home-style jambalaya and meat loaf are lunch entrees. Dinner menu includes shrimp scampi and peppercorn-seared pork tenderloin. **FYI:** Reservations recommended. **Open:** Mon–Thurs 11am–10pm, Fri–Sat 11am–11pm, Sun 11am–5pm. **Prices:** Main courses $10–$19. AE, CB, DC, DISC, MC, V. 🍜 🏔 💲 🕹

Delaney & Murphy, A Steak House
In Arlington Park Hilton Conference Center, 3400 W Euclid Ave; tel 847/394-2000. 1 block E of IL 53. **American/Steak.** Offers pleasant decor with subdued lighting. Good variety of dishes, with beef tenderloin rolled in peppercorns a specialty. **FYI:** Reservations recommended. **Open:** Lunch Mon–Fri 11:30am–1:30pm; dinner Mon–Sat 5:30–10pm. **Prices:** Main courses $19–$28. AE, CB, DC, MC, V. 💗 🕹

♣ ✸ Le Titi de Paris
1015 W Dundee Rd; tel 847/506-0222. ⅜ mi E of IL 53. **French.** Award-winning upscale local favorite features Gallic architecture and elegant interior with art deco accents. For lunch, there's nut-crusted loin of veal with tapenade Niçoise and breast of free-range chicken with star anise, honey, and vinegar infusion. Dinner menu features most of the same entrees, including roasted pigeon with sweet garlic and pinot noir wine reduction and phyllo basket filled with sea scallops, sun-dried tomatoes, and saffron infusion. Specials change daily. Gratis treats at meal's end. Degustation menu available by arrangement with chef Pierre Pollin. No smoking on Sat.

FYI: Reservations recommended. Jacket required. **Open:** Tues–Fri 11:30am–9:30pm, Sat 5:30–10pm. **Prices:** Main courses $19–$24; prix fixe $39–$46. AE, CB, DC, DISC, MC, V. 💗 💌 🕹

The Rusty Pelican
10 E Algonquin Rd; tel 847/228-0040. IL 62 at Arlington Heights Rd, ⅛ mi N of I-90. **Seafood.** A smart dining room appropriate for business or special occasions. Fresh seafood is the draw here, but the menu also features meat and pasta. Lunch menu includes farm-bred Louisiana catfish with crab-meat coating, lobster sauce, and garlic mashed potatoes, or Hawaiian ahi with Chinese pesto and imported jasmine rice. Dinner menu features tequila-soaked shrimp, scallops, and crab in citrus cream sauce on savannah pasta, and prime rib. **FYI:** Reservations recommended. Children's menu. Additional location: 777 Butterfield Rd, Lombard (tel 708/573-0400). **Open:** Mon–Thurs 11:30am–10pm, Fri 11:30am–10:30pm, Sat 4:30–11pm, Sun 4:30–10pm. **Prices:** Main courses $14–$26. AE, DC, DISC, MC, V. 💗 💌 🕹

♣ ✸ Wellington of Arlington
2121 S Arlington Heights Rd; tel 847/439-6610. 1½ block N of I-90. **American/Seafood/Steak.** Set back from the road, this well-established, pleasantly decorated restaurant is favored by locals for special occasions. Beef Wellington is the star of the extensive menu. **FYI:** Reservations recommended. **Open:** Lunch Mon–Fri 11am–3:30pm; dinner Mon–Fri 5–11pm, Sat 4:30–11:30pm, Sun noon–10pm. **Prices:** Main courses $11–$26. AE, DC, MC, V. 💗 🕹

ATTRACTION 🏛

Arlington International Race Course
Euclid and Wilkie Rds; tel 847/255-4300. Popular facility offering special events and family entertainment, in addition to thoroughbred racing. Home of the Arlington Million, held every August. **Open:** May–Oct, daily 1–6pm. **$$**

Aurora

A Potawatomi village on the Fox River preceded this prosperous western suburb of Chicago. The Fermilab Particle Accelerator in nearby Batavia has attracted high-tech industry to the area. **Information:** Aurora Area Convention & Tourism Council, 44 W Downer Place, Aurora, 60506 (tel 630/897-5581).

MOTELS 🏨

📇📇 Best Western Fox Valley Inn
2450 N Farnsworth Ave, 60405; tel 630/851-2000 or toll free 800/528-1234; fax 630/851-2000 ext 115. White pillars and a colonial facade give a formal appearance to these comfortable lodgings. Located in a rural setting but with easy access to highway. **Rooms:** 107 rms and stes. Executive level. CI 2pm/CO noon. Nonsmoking rms avail. **Amenities:** 🔟

A/C, satel TV w/movies. 1 unit w/terrace. **Services:** 🛎 **Facilities:** 🏋 🖥 📼 ⅃ 1 restaurant (bkfst only), 1 bar (w/entertainment), washer/dryer. **Rates:** Peak (May–Oct) $52–$62 S; $60–$68 D; $75 ste. Extra person $5. Children under age 12 stay free. Lower rates off-season. Parking: Outdoor, free. AE, CB, DC, DISC, MC, V.

≣≣ Comfort Inn
4005 Gabrielle Lane, 60504; tel 630/820-3400 or toll free 800/221-2222; fax 630/820-3400. A sleek, clean motel located across from the Fox Valley Shopping Center. A step above basic accommodations. **Rooms:** 51 rms. CI 3pm/CO 11am. Nonsmoking rms avail. **Amenities:** 📺 A/C, satel TV w/movies, dataport. **Services:** ⅃ Complimentary *USA Today*. Fax machine in lobby. **Facilities:** 🏋 📼 ⅃ Spa, whirlpool. **Rates (CP):** Peak (May–Oct) $58–$65 S; $63–$70 D. Extra person $7. Children under age 18 stay free. Lower rates off-season. Parking: Outdoor, free. AE, CB, DC, DISC, ER, JCB, MC, V.

ATTRACTIONS 📷

Fermi National Laboratory (Fermilab)
Kirk Rd, Batavia; tel 630/840-3000. Named for Nobel Prize–winning physicist Enrico Fermi, this lab houses the world's largest energy particle accelerator, the Tevatron. Here scientists probe the fundamental structure of the universe. Free guided tours are available, by appointment, and consist of an orientation talk and slide presentation, a visit to various laboratory environments, and an opportunity to take in a panoramic view of the accelerator from the 15th floor of the lab's main building. The tour lasts about two hours, after which visitors are welcome to drive around the 6,800-acre site, to look at the distinctive architecture of the Fermilab buildings, and to see the buffalo and waterfowl that also occupy these lands. **Open:** Daily 8:30am–5pm. **Free**

SciTech—The Science and Technology Interactive Center
18 W Benton; tel 630/859-3434. More than 200 hands-on exhibits and demonstrations illustrate principles of astronomy, light and color, mathematics, sound and music, and magnets and electricity. Activity rooms, auditorium, solar telescope. **Open:** Wed, Fri and Sun noon–5pm, Thurs noon–8pm, Sat 10am–5pm. **$$**

Paramount Arts Center
23 E Galena Blvd; tel 630/896-6666. Old art deco movie theater and vaudeville house, designed in 1931 by noted architects Rapp and Rapp. The Paramount has been completely renovated and now hosts a variety of productions throughout the year. **Open:** Call for schedule. **$$$$**

Bedford Park

See Chicago

Belleville

Seat of St Clair County, in southwest part of state. Fine houses and shady streets justify its French name, which means "beautiful city." It is the financial center of southern Illinois and headquarters of Scott Air Force Base.

HOTEL 🏨

≣≣≣ Hyatt Lodge
2120 W Main St, 62223; tel 618/234-9400 or toll free 800/62-HYATT; fax 618/234-6142. Modernized facility with southwestern theme in lobby and rooms. Cool, tiled lobby has kiva fireplace. **Rooms:** 80 rms and stes. CI 2pm/CO noon. Nonsmoking rms avail. Rooms in rear addition are more modern, with larger baths. Two- and three-room suites available. **Amenities:** 📺 A/C, cable TV w/movies. Some units w/terraces. Some rooms have unstocked refrigerators. Suites have two phones, two television sets, coffeemakers, hairdryers; some have kitchens with microwaves and refrigerators. **Services:** ✉ ⅃ 🍴 Babysitting. VCR rentals. **Facilities:** 🏋 📼 ⅃ 1 restaurant, 1 bar. **Rates (CP):** Peak (May 15–Sept 15) $46 S; $54 D; $51–$100 ste. Extra person $6. Children under age 17 stay free. Lower rates off-season. Parking: Outdoor, free. Senior discount for guests age 55 and older. AE, CB, DC, DISC, MC, V.

MOTEL

≣ Imperial Inn
600 E Main St, 62220; tel 618/234-9670; fax 618/234-0177. Bright blue doors and attractive rock garden mark this in-town motel, just blocks from town center. Nothing fancy, but adequate. **Rooms:** 42 rms and effic. CI 11am/CO noon. Nonsmoking rms avail. **Amenities:** 📺 A/C, cable TV. **Services:** ⅃ 🍴 Small pets only; permission required. **Facilities:** Washer/dryer. **Rates:** $30–$35 S or D; $40–$45 effic. Extra person $5. Children under age 8 stay free. Min stay. Parking: Outdoor, free. Minimum one-week stay required for efficiencies. AE, DC, DISC, MC, V.

Bloomington

See also Normal

Seat of McLean County, in east-central part of state. The town site's gentle hill is part of the long ridge of drift left by the Wisconsin Glacier. Abraham Lincoln made his famous "lost speech" here in 1856 when the Illinois Republican party was formed. Illinois Wesleyan University (founded 1850) is located here. **Information:** Bloomington-Normal Area Convention & Visitors Bureau, 210 S East St, PO Box 1586, Bloomington, 61702 (tel 309/829-1641).

HOTELS 🏨

≣≣ Best Western Eastland Suites Lodge

1801 Eastland Dr, 61704; tel 309/662-0000 or toll free 800/528-1234; fax 309/663-6668. 3 acres. This parklike property consists entirely of suites in nine separate buildings arranged around a series of courtyards with grass, flowers, and shrubs. Comfortable yet elegant lobby with touches of brick, brass, and leather. Perfect for corporate meetings, seminars, or retreats, and for large families looking for something a little different. **Rooms:** 88 effic. CI 3pm/CO noon. Nonsmoking rms avail. **Amenities:** 🛁 🗄 A/C, cable TV w/movies, refrig, dataport. All units w/terraces, some w/fireplaces. Each suite has kitchen with refrigerator with ice maker, stove, sink, counter, dishes, cookware, toaster, coffeemaker, and table with chairs. Irons and ironing boards in rooms. **Services:** 🚐 📇 Express checkout available on request. Bellhop available until 11pm. Limo service available on-site. Complimentary cocktails daily 4:30–6pm. Muffins, juice, coffee, tea available Mon–Fri 6–10am. Very competent and professional staff. **Facilities:** 🖼 📇 ⓖ Sauna, washer/dryer. Pool has whirlpool jets at shallow end. Gas grills available in four picnic areas—one with gazebo. **Rates:** $78–$250 effic. Children under age 18 stay free. Parking: Outdoor, free. AE, CB, DC, DISC, JCB, MC, V.

≣≣≣ Jumer's Château Hotel

1601 Jumer Dr, 61704; tel 309/662-2020 or toll free 800/285-8637; fax 309/662-2020. Exit 167 off I-55. Truly lovely hotel with old-world exterior of French château complete with twin towers on either side of entrance plus elaborate canopy and stone water fountain with dancing cherubs. Lobby highlights include public phones in huge antique confessional, floral arrangements, a mix of antique-white and dark woods on furnishings, crystal chandeliers, gilded tables, and lobby fountain. **Rooms:** 180 rms and stes. CI 3pm/CO noon. Nonsmoking rms avail. **Amenities:** 🛁 A/C, cable TV w/movies. Some units w/fireplaces. **Services:** ✕ 🚐 📇 Babysitting. Box of Fannie Mae candy on arrival. **Facilities:** 🖼 📇 ⓖ 1 restaurant (see "Restaurants" below), 1 bar (w/entertainment), games rm, sauna, whirlpool. Excellent meeting facilities. **Rates:** $80–$91 S; $89–$98 D; $100–$150 ste. Extra person $9. Children under age 18 stay free. Parking: Outdoor, free. AE, CB, DC, DISC, JCB, MC, V.

MOTELS

≣ Hampton Inn Bloomington/Normal

604½ IAA Dr, 61701; tel 309/662-2800 or toll free 800/HAMPTON; fax 309/662-2811. Exit 167 off I-55. Rather average, with very nice, bright, open lobby area with tables, chairs, and TV. Located near College Hills Mall. **Rooms:** 108 rms. CI 2pm/CO noon. Nonsmoking rms avail. **Amenities:** 🛁 🗄 A/C, cable TV w/movies. Small TVs in rooms. **Services:** 🚐 📇 **Facilities:** 🖼 📇 ⓖ Convention/meeting center

adjacent to lobby/atrium area. **Rates (CP):** $65–$85 S or D. Children under age 18 stay free. Parking: Outdoor, free. AE, CB, DC, DISC, JCB, MC, V.

≣ Ramada Inn Fundome

1219 Holiday Dr, 61704; tel 309/662-5311 or toll free 800/385-0000; fax 309/663-1732. At Veterans Pkwy and IL 9. Older motel whose rooms, especially bathrooms, in the older section are very dated. However, all public areas and rooms around pool and atrium have been updated. Near shopping mall, restaurants, and bowling alley. **Rooms:** 209 rms and stes. CI 3pm/CO noon. Nonsmoking rms avail. **Amenities:** 🛁 A/C, cable TV w/movies. 1 unit w/whirlpool. **Services:** ✕ 🚐 📇 **Facilities:** 🖼 📇 ⓖ 1 restaurant, 1 bar, games rm, sauna, whirlpool, washer/dryer. **Rates:** $49–$70 S; $58–$80 D; $96–$150 ste. Extra person $9. Children under age 18 stay free. Parking: Outdoor, free. Business class rate is best deal at $59. AE, CB, DC, DISC, JCB, MC, V.

≣ Super 8 Motel

818 IAA Dr, 61701; tel 309/663-2388 or toll free 800/800-8000; fax 309/663-2388. Exit 167 off I-55. Typical Super 8 exterior. Larger than usual lobby area. **Rooms:** 62 rms and stes. CI 2pm/CO 11am. Nonsmoking rms avail. **Amenities:** 🛁 A/C, cable TV w/movies. **Services:** 📇 Free coffee/tea service counter and vending machines in lobby. **Facilities:** 📇 ⓖ **Rates:** Peak (May–Sept) $45–$53 S; $49–$57 D; $70 ste. Extra person $5. Children under age 18 stay free. Lower rates off-season. Parking: Outdoor, free. AE, CB, DC, DISC, JCB, MC, V.

RESTAURANTS 🍴

Central Station Cafe

220 E Front St (Downtown); tel 309/828-2323. **New American.** This interesting old building was the town's main fire station from 1902 until 1974. The warm and inviting interior—with touches like leaded glass and dark woodwork and a bar covered with an amazing large copper canopy—is the setting for casual, low-key dining on the likes of Jamaican jerk chicken with honey-jalepeño sauce, garlic-crusted prime rib, and honey-pecan pork chops cooked over mesquite. **FYI:** Reservations recommended. **Open:** Peak (Labor Day–Mem Day) lunch Mon–Sat 11am–3pm; dinner Mon–Sat 5–10pm. **Prices:** Main courses $10–$17. AE, CB, DC, MC, V. 🍽

Le Rodis Rouge

In Jumer's Château Hotel, 1601 Jumer Dr; tel 309/662-2525. Exit 167 off I-55. **Continental.** Well known for Jumer's fabulous miniature cinnamon rolls and breads served before every meal. Entree specialities include grilled Norwegian salmon and premium prime rib. Lighter fare, such as chicken daiquiri salad topped with a refreshing lime vinaigrette, is also available. **FYI:** Reservations recommended. Jazz. Children's menu. **Open:** Sun 7am–10pm, Mon–Thurs 6:30am–10pm, Fri–Sat 6:30am–10:30pm. **Prices:** Main courses $10–$20. AE, CB, DC, DISC, MC, V. 📇 ⓖ

Phil's Bar and Grill
In Eastland Commons Strip Mall, 401 N Veterans Pkwy; tel 309/662-9637. **Continental.** A fine dining establishment, surprisingly located in the middle of a strip mall. (Luckily, the lovely interior decor helps you forget that you just parked outside a supermarket.) The chef's pride is his many unusual sauces: ginger cream, avocado butter, fresh peach and pepper relish (for blackened tuna or swordfish), raspberry-dill butter (for the poached salmon). Larger parties may wish to try the lively paella Alfresco: a large platter of crab, lobster, shrimp, mussels, chicken, and andouille sausage, cooked together with saffron rice and peppers. **FYI:** Reservations recommended. Dress code. **Open:** Lunch Mon–Sat 11am–2pm; dinner Mon–Sat 5–11pm. **Prices:** Main courses $9–$26. AE, MC, V. ♿

ATTRACTIONS 🏛

Old Courthouse Museum
202 N Main St; tel 309/827-0428. Completed in 1903, this courthouse is listed on the National Register of Historic Places and now houses the headquarters of the McLean County Historical Society. Exhibits are organized into four galleries representing the people who settled the area, industries and occupations of the residents, the politics of the area (including famous local politicians Abraham Lincoln and Adlai Stevenson), and a farming gallery with prairie grass and farm implements. **Open:** Mon and Wed–Sat 10am–5pm, Tues 10am–9pm. **$**

Miller Park Zoo
1020 S Morris Ave; tel 309/823-4250. Small zoo featuring a tropical rain forest, red wolf exhibit, a wallaby walkabout area, and a children's petting zoo. Located in Miller Park, which offers swimming, fishing, picnicking, tennis, and miniature golf. **Open:** Peak (Mem Day–Labor Day) daily 10am–5pm. Reduced hours off-season. **$**

Carbondale

Surrounded by coalfields, lakes, and rivers, this small southern Illinois city is home to Southern Illinois University. **Information:** Carbondale Convention & Tourism Bureau, 1245 E Main St, #A-32, University Mall, Carbondale, 62901 (tel 618/529-4451).

MOTELS 🛏

≡≡ Best Inns of America
1345 E Main St, 62901; tel 618/529-4801 or toll free 800/237-8466; fax 618/529-7212. Exit 54B (IL 13W) off I-57, W to Giant City Rd, S to Frontage Rd entrance. Well-maintained accommodations. Fishing, golf, and boating nearby. **Rooms:** 86 rms. CI 1pm/CO 1pm. Nonsmoking rms avail. **Amenities:** 🖥 A/C, cable TV. **Services:** 🛄 ♻ ⇔ Extended "Special K" breakfast. Prior approval needed for pets.

Facilities: 🏋 ♿ Health center across the street. **Rates (CP):** $38–$46 S or D. Extra person $6. Children under age 18 stay free. Parking: Outdoor, free. AE, DISC, MC, V.

≡≡≡ Holiday Inn
800 E Main St, 62901; tel 618/529-1100 or toll free 800/465-4329; fax 618/457-0292. 18 mi W of I-57 (exit 54B) on IL 13. Clean, comfortable, newly remodeled motel. Boat rentals and marina nearby. Lakeshore beach approximately 1 mile away. **Rooms:** 118 rms and stes. CI 3pm/CO noon. Nonsmoking rms avail. **Amenities:** 🖥 🏷 A/C, cable TV w/movies. Some rooms have hair dryers. Suites have wet bars and refrigerators. **Services:** ✕ 🚐 🛄 ♻ ⇔ Twice-daily maid svce, car-rental desk. Complimentary toiletries, VCR and video rentals, and safe at front desk. **Facilities:** 🏋 [250] ♿ 1 restaurant, 1 bar, games rm, whirlpool, washer/dryer. Pool table and table tennis in atrium pool area. Free pass to local fitness center. **Rates (CP):** $59–$70 S or D; $132 ste. Children under age 12 stay free. Parking: Outdoor, free. Golf packages avail. AE, CB, DC, DISC, MC, V.

≡ Super 8 Motel
1180 E Main St, 62901; tel 618/457-8822 or toll free 800/800-8000; fax 618/457-4186. On IL 13, across from University Mall. Basic, clean, and comfortable accommodations. Across from University Mall and surrounded by restaurants. **Rooms:** 63 rms. CI 3pm/CO 11am. Nonsmoking rms avail. **Amenities:** 🖥 A/C, cable TV w/movies. **Services:** ♻ ⇔ **Facilities:** ♿ **Rates (CP):** $38–$41 S; $44–$46 D. Extra person $5. Children under age 13 stay free. Parking: Outdoor, free. AE, DISC, MC, V.

RESTAURANT 🍴

Larry's Pit BBQ
1181 Rendleman Rd; tel 618/549-1599. From IL-13, S on McKinney Dr to entrance, across from University Mall. **American/Barbecue.** A modern log cabin with wood siding and shingles houses this clean and friendly restaurant. No frills, but plenty of good food all day long, cooked to order. Try St Louis ribs, grilled chicken monterey, or "all-you-can-eat fish." Ideal for families. **FYI:** Reservations accepted. Children's menu. No liquor license. Additional locations: US 51S, Du Quoin (tel 542-3399); 608 N Victor, Christopher (tel 724-7115). **Open:** Mon–Sat 5:30am–midnight, Sun 6am–midnight. **Prices:** Main courses $6–$11. No CC. 👶 ♿

Carterville

See Marion

Centralia

Named for the Illinois Central Railroad. Centralia and its neighbors (Central City and Wamac) form a continuous urban trading center. **Information:** Greater Centralia Chamber of Commerce, 130 S Locust St, Centralia, 62801 (tel 618/532-6789).

MOTELS 🛏

⊫ Bell Tower Inn
200 E Noleman, 62801; tel 618/533-1300; fax 618/533-1461. Jct US 51 S/IL 161 E. Clean, comfortable rooms in centrally located motel. Across the street from the Centralia Memorial Carillon. **Rooms:** 58 rms, stes, and effic. CI 1pm/CO 1pm. Nonsmoking rms avail. **Amenities:** 🛗 🛁 A/C, cable TV w/movies. **Services:** 🖼 🍴 🍷 VCR and movie rentals available at front desk. Local car rental will deliver. Friendly staff. **Facilities:** 🏋 👤 Playground. Complimentary access to recreational complex with pool, indoor track, basketball courts, and more. **Rates (CP):** $42–$52 S; $47–$57 D; $52–$100 ste; $52–$100 effic. Extra person $5. Children under age 18 stay free. Parking: Outdoor, free. AE, CB, DC, DISC, MC, V.

⊫ Centralia Motel
215 S Poplar St, 62801; tel 618/532-7357; fax 618/533-4304. On US 51S across from City Hall. Well-maintained motel fine for business travelers. **Rooms:** 56 rms. CI open/CO 11am. Nonsmoking rms avail. Cheery rooms. **Amenities:** 🛗 A/C, cable TV. **Services:** 🍴 🍷 Free coffee and microwave in lobby. Pets $5. **Facilities:** 👤 **Rates:** $27–$30 S; $35–$39 D. Extra person $5. Children under age 12 stay free. Parking: Outdoor, free. Stay seven consecutive nights and the last night is free. AE, CB, DC, DISC, MC, V.

Champaign

Together with its sister city Urbana, Champaign is home to the University of Illinois. The main library is the third-largest academic library in the United States. **Information:** Champaign Urbana Convention & Visitors Bureau, 40 E University Ave, PO Box 1607, Champaign, 61824-1607 (tel 217/351-4133).

HOTELS 🛏

⊫ Chancellor Hotel
1501 S Neil St, 61820; tel 217/352-7891 or toll free 800/257-6667. Conveniently located just a few minutes from the University of Illinois campus. Provides special amenities for business travelers; familes enjoy on-site activities and entertainment. Popular for meetings. **Rooms:** 225 rms. Executive level. CI 3pm/CO noon. Nonsmoking rms avail. **Amenities:** 🛗 A/C, cable TV w/movies, voice mail. **Services:** ✕ 🖼 🚗 🖼 🍴 🍷 **Facilities:** 🏋 👤 📺 🖥 👤 2 restaurants, 1 bar (w/entertainment), sauna, steam rm, whirlpool. Large convention center. Sunshine Dinner Theater on premises. **Rates:** $61–$64 S; $69–$72 D. Extra person $8. Children under age 12 stay free. Parking: Outdoor, free. AE, DC, DISC, MC, V.

⊫ Fairfield Inn
1807 Moreland Blvd, 61820; tel 217/355-0604 or toll free 800/228-2800; fax 217/355-0604. Fairfield Inns are Marriott's answer to economy lodging, but the high standards associated with their more expensive properties are still applied. Modern, comfortable, and a good value. Near shopping mall and restaurants. **Rooms:** 62 rms and stes. CI 3pm/CO 11am. Nonsmoking rms avail. **Amenities:** 🛗 🛁 A/C, cable TV w/movies. **Services:** 🖼 🍴 🍷 **Facilities:** 🏋 📺 👤 Games rm, whirlpool. **Rates (CP):** $57–$60 S; $62–$66 D; $67–$85 ste. Extra person $6. Children under age 17 stay free. Parking: Outdoor, free. AE, CB, DC, DISC, MC, V.

⊫ Radisson Suite Hotel
101 Trade Center Dr, 61820; tel 217/398-3400 or toll free 800/333-3333. Exit 183 off I-74; 2½ mi S on Neil and Trade Center Dr. All-suite hotel conveniently located near university and interstates. **Rooms:** 128 stes. CI 3pm/CO noon. Nonsmoking rms avail. **Amenities:** 🛗 🛁 🖥 A/C, cable TV w/movies, refrig, dataport. **Services:** ✕ 🖼 🚗 🖼 🍴 Car-rental desk, children's program, babysitting. Morning newspaper. Extensive complimentary breakfast buffet. **Facilities:** 🏋 🍴 📺 👤 Whirlpool, beauty salon, washer/dryer. Complimentary use of nearby fitness facility. **Rates (CP):** $95–$105 ste. Extra person $6. Children under age 18 stay free. Min stay special events. Parking: Outdoor, free. AE, CB, DC, DISC, JCB, MC, V.

⊫ University Inn
302 E John St, 61820 (Campus Town); tel 217/384-2100 or toll free 800/332-8282. At 3rd St. Tall, circular building located in heart of University of Illinois campus; within walking distance of shopping, movie theaters, and university buildings. Guests may use pools, sauna, and exercise equipment at sister property, the Chancellor Hotel; complimentary shuttle provided. **Rooms:** 203 rms, stes, and effic. CI 3pm/CO 1pm. Nonsmoking rms avail. **Amenities:** 🛗 🛁 A/C, cable TV w/movies, voice mail. 1 unit w/minibar. **Services:** ✕ 🚗 🖼 🍴 **Facilities:** 📺 👤 1 restaurant, 1 bar. **Rates (CP):** $57–$62 S; $62–$70 D; $175–$275 ste; $57 effic. Extra person $8. Children under age 17 stay free. Parking: Indoor, free. AE, DC, DISC, MC, V.

MOTELS

⊫ Comfort Inn
305 Marketview Dr, 61820; tel 217/352-4055 or toll free 800/228-5150. Exit 182 off I-74 E; Neil St N. An economical choice for families. Nearby shopping mall and restaurants. **Rooms:** 67 rms and stes. CI 3pm/CO 11am. Nonsmoking rms avail. For a few dollars more, the extra space in the suite may be worth it, especially for multi-night stays. **Amenities:** 🛗 🛁 A/C, cable TV w/movies. **Services:** 🍴 🍷 **Facilities:** 🏋 👤 Whirlpool. **Rates (CP):** $49–$60 S; $55–$67 D; $60–$67 ste. Extra person $6. Children under age 12 stay free. Parking: Outdoor, free. AE, DC, DISC, MC, V.

≋≋ La Quinta Inn

1900 Center Dr, 61820; tel 217/356-4000 or toll free 800/531-5900; fax 217/352-7783. Exit 182 off I-74; N on Neil St. Cool Mexican tiling and southwest decor adorn lovely lobby. Located near large shopping mall and several restaurants. **Rooms:** 122 rms. CI 3pm/CO noon. Nonsmoking rms avail. **Amenities:** 🛏 ☕ A/C, satel TV w/movies, dataport. **Services:** 🛎 ⟲ ⟳ **Facilities:** 🏋 🎱 ♿ Washer/dryer. Complimentary privileges at nearby health club. **Rates (CP):** $51–$76 S; $58–$83 D. Extra person $7. Children under age 18 stay free. Min stay special events. Parking: Outdoor, free. AE, CB, DC, DISC, MC, V.

≋ Red Roof Inn

212 W Anthony Dr, 61820; tel 217/352-0101 or toll free 800/THE-ROOF. Exit 182 N off I-74. No-frills, economical lodging choice. Close to interstate; shopping mall and several restaurants. **Rooms:** 112 rms. CI 3pm/CO noon. Nonsmoking rms avail. **Amenities:** 🛏 A/C, cable TV w/movies. **Services:** ⟲ ⟳ **Facilities:** ♿ **Rates:** $33–$40 S. Extra person $6. Children under age 18 stay free. Parking: Outdoor, free. AE, DC, DISC, MC, V.

≋ Super 8 Motel

202 Marketview Dr, 61820; tel 217/359-2388 or toll free 800/800-8000. Exit 183 off I-74; W on Marketview. Modest accommodations, near shopping mall. Parking for semi-trucks. Plenty of restaurants nearby. **Rooms:** 61 rms. CI 1pm/CO 11am. Nonsmoking rms avail. **Amenities:** 🛏 A/C, cable TV. **Services:** ⟲ ⟳ **Facilities:** ♿ **Rates:** Peak (July–Aug) $40–$45 S; $50–$55 D. Extra person $4. Children under age 12 stay free. Lower rates off-season. Parking: Outdoor, free. AE, CB, DC, DISC, MC, V.

RESTAURANTS 🍴

Colorado Steak House

1805 S Neil St; tel 217/359-6776. At St Marys. **Burgers.** Its log cabin facade makes this place easy to find. The interior continues the country theme with cowboy boots and saddles adorning the walls. Specialties include aged sirloin, marinated and charbroiled, and Rocky Mountain rainbow trout, breaded and sautéed. Plenty of chicken and burger selections. **FYI:** Reservations accepted. Karaoke. Children's menu. **Open:** Mon–Thurs 11am–10pm, Fri–Sat 11am–11pm, Sun 11am–9pm. **Prices:** Main courses $8–$17. AE, CB, DC, DISC, MC, V. 📷 ♿

⑤ The Great Impasta

132 W Church St; tel 217/359-7377. **Italian.** Good food at a good price. Freshly made pasta, sauces, and soups are the highlight of this eatery. Heart Healthy foods are available, though you might want to indulge in the rich tiramisù or chocolate cannoli for dessert. **FYI:** Reservations accepted. Beer and wine only. **Open:** Daily 10am–10pm. **Prices:** Main courses $8–$13. AE, DISC, MC, V. ♿

Katy's Katsinas Restaurant

512 S Neil St; tel 217/356-6476. At Green St. **Greek.** Look for the large cat and "Katy's" printed on the outdoor sign and you'll have arrived at this busy, casual eatery serving Greek specialties like flaming saganaki, moussaka, and dolmades, along with many lighter and vegetarian dishes. **FYI:** Reservations recommended. Children's menu. **Open:** Mon–Fri 6am–10pm, Sat–Sun 7am–10pm. **Prices:** Main courses $8–$13. AE, DISC, MC, V. 📷 📺 ♿

Mountain Jack's Restaurant

1512 N Neil St; tel 217/359-8132. Neil St exit off I-74. **Seafood/Steak.** A popular, cozy place with dimly lit rooms, one with a fireplace. Broiled chicken breast with tomato pesto is served with wild rice and slivered almonds. Warm honey baked bread is delicious. **FYI:** Reservations recommended. **Open:** Mon–Thurs 4–10pm, Fri–Sat 4–11pm, Sun 4–9pm. **Prices:** Main courses $13–$19. AE, DC, MC, V. ♥ 📷 ♿

ATTRACTIONS 🖼

William M Staerkel Planetarium at Parkland College

2400 W Bradley Ave; tel 217/351-2446. Visitors sit in a 144-seat auditorium as images of the stars and planets are projected onto a 50-foot projection dome. The planetarium also presents big-screen movies, full-dome slide shows, and laser shows with musical accompaniment courtesy of a 4,000-watt audio system. **Open:** Fri–Sat. **$**

University of Illinois

Tel 217/333-0824. Established in 1867, this 56,000-student school is the largest in Illinois. Noted for its excellent physics and engineering departments, the university is one of only five in the country with a supercomputer on campus. Other highlights of the 200-building campus are the Illini Union Building; Allerton Park (a 1,500-acre woodland park), and the 75,000-seat **Memorial Stadium.** Guided campus tours are arranged through the visitors center at 919 W Illinois St. **Free**

Krannert Art Museum

500 E Peabody Dr; tel 217/333-1860. Known for its extensive collection of works of old masters, and for the Ewing Collection of Malaysian Art. Exhibits also highlight sculpture, photography, ceramics. **Open:** Tues–Sat 10am–5pm, Sun 2–5pm. **Free**

Channahon

See Joliet

Charleston

Seat of Coles County, in east-central part of state. Abraham Lincoln was an itinerant lawyer in the area and several members of his family (most notably, his father and stepmother) lived here. **Information:** Charleston Area Chamber of Commerce, 501 Jackson Ave, PO Box 77, Charleston, 61920 (tel 217/345-7041).

MOTEL

≝≝ Econo Lodge
810 W Lincoln Hwy, 61920; tel 217/345-7689 or toll free 800/424-4777; fax 217/345-7697. On IL 16, ½ block W of Douglas Drive. 10 minutes west of I-57, near Eastern Illinois University. A favorite spot for EIU parents and visiting teams. **Rooms:** 52 rms. CI open/CO 11am. Nonsmoking rms avail. Comfortable, nicely furnished rooms. **Amenities:** 🛎 �🍽 A/C, cable TV w/movies. **Services:** 🛄 ⟳ ⟲ **Facilities:** ⚹ **Rates (CP):** Peak (May) $35–$65 S; $45–$75 D. Extra person $5. Children under age 18 stay free. Lower rates off-season. Parking: Outdoor, free. Packages avail for graduation and track meets. AE, DISC, EC, JCB, MC, V.

ATTRACTION

Lincoln Log Cabin State Historic Site
4th St; tel 217/345-6489. Located 7 mi S of Charleston. Thomas and Sarah Lincoln (parents of Abraham) built this cabin in 1837 and they lived here until their deaths. The reconstructed cabin sits on an 86-acre site that also houses a re-created 1840s farm. Living history programs offered in summer. **Open:** Peak (Mar–Nov) daily 8am–dusk. Reduced hours off-season. **Free**

Chicago

See also Arlington Heights, Countryside, Downers Grove, Elmhurst, Evanston, Glen Ellyn, Glenview, Hillside, Hoffman Estates, Homewood, Itasca, Northbrook, Oak Brook, Oakbrook Terrace, Oak Lawn, Oak Park, Palatine, Skokie, Vernon Hills, Westmont, Wheeling, Willowbrook, Wilmette, Woodridge; for airport lodgings, see Chicago O'Hare Int'l Airport

The major metropolis of America's heartland—known in the past for its gangsters, stockyards, and cold, lake winds—is today a world business and cultural capital. Chicago is home to the world's tallest skyscraper (the Sears Tower) and one of the finest collections of French impressionist paintings in the world (the Art Institute of Chicago). The chic boutiques of Michigan Avenue, miles of Lake Michigan beaches, fascinating architecture, innovative theater, professional teams in every major sport, a plethora of ethnic restaurants, and a bustling nightlife are among Chicago's many assets. O'Hare International Airport is the busiest in the world. **Information:** Chicago Convention & Visitors Bureau, 2301 S Lakeshore Dr, Chicago, 60616 (tel 312/567-8500). Chicago Office of Tourism, Chicago Cultural Center, 78 E Washington St, 4th Floor, Chicago, 60602 (tel 312/744-2400).

PUBLIC TRANSPORTATION
The Chicago Transit Authority (CTA) operates four major **subway lines:** north–south, west–south, west–northwest (the O'Hare train), and a zigzag northern route called the Ravenswood line. A separate express line services neighboring Evanston, while a small local line in Skokie is linked to the north–south train. **CTA buses** operate citywide; PACE buses service the surrounding suburban areas. Fares, payable with exact change or tokens, are $1.50 during rush hours (Mon–Fri 6–10am and 3–7pm) and $1.25 (25¢ for transfers) during all other times. Children under age 7 ride free, while those 7–11 and senior citizens 65 and older pay 90¢ (15¢ for transfers) (call 312/814-0700 to obtain appropriate ID). For CTA schedule and route information call 312/836-7000 (4:45am–1am).

HOTELS

≝≝ Allerton
701 N Michigan Ave, 60611 (Magnificent Mile); tel 312/440-1500 or toll free 800/621-8311. Great location, casual and friendly. **Rooms:** 382 rms and stes. CI 3pm/CO 1pm. Nonsmoking rms avail. **Amenities:** 🛎 A/C, cable TV w/movies. 1 unit w/fireplace. **Services:** ✕ 🛄 ⟳ Masseur. Valet parking available next door. **Facilities:** 🔲 ⚹ 1 restaurant, 1 bar, beauty salon, washer/dryer. **Rates:** $109–$119 S; $119–$129 D; $125–$290 ste. Extra person $20. Children under age 16 stay free. AE, DC, MC, V.

≝≝ Best Western River North Hotel
125 W Ohio St, 60610 (River North); tel 312/467-0800 or toll free 800/727-0800; fax 312/467-1665. In a developing, hot new area where warehouses and factories have been reborn as hotels, art galleries, condominiums, and restaurants. Clientele includes many students and foreign travelers. Hallways have institutional feel—hard-painted walls and bright posters. **Rooms:** 148 rms and stes. CI 3pm/CO noon. Nonsmoking rms avail. Very large, high-ceilinged rooms; bathrooms, though, are cramped, with vanities outside. Ansel Adams photographs throughout rooms. **Amenities:** 🛎 ⚫ 🖭 A/C, cable TV w/movies, refrig, dataport, VCR. **Services:** ✕ 🆅🅿 🛄 ⟳ Babysitting. Hotel is on Airport Express route for pickup. **Facilities:** 🔲 🛝 🔲 1 restaurant, 1 bar, sauna. Exceptionally pleasant pool, with windows all around, tables, plants, and sun deck. **Rates:** $92–$122 S; $102–$132 D; $175–$181 ste. Children under age 12 stay free. Min stay wknds. Parking: Indoor, free. AE, DC, DISC, JCB, MC, V.

≝≝ The Bismark
171 W Randolph St, 60601 (Loop); tel 312/236-0123 or toll free 800/643-1500; fax 312/236-3177. At LaSalle. A popular site for weddings and conferences, the Bismarck dates from the 19th century—and remains lost in time. A grand staircase winds from street level up to the enormous lobby impressively done in art deco style. Giant, stained-glass, Frank Lloyd Wright–inspired windows dominate the entire front wall. The guest rooms, however, are a major disappointment.

Rooms: 500 rms and stes. Executive level. CI 3pm/CO noon. Nonsmoking rms avail. Dreary and dated rooms, with mismatched, flimsy furniture and windows that open directly onto brick walls. Bathrooms are spare and unattractive. **Amenities:** 🛏 🕹 🎨 A/C, cable TV w/movies, dataport, voice mail. **Services:** ✕ 🖥 VP 🚐 🖨 🍽 Twice-daily maid svce, babysitting. **Facilities:** [2000] 🕹 4 restaurants, 3 bars (1 w/entertainment), beauty salon. **Rates:** $120–$205 S; $140–$225 D; $205–$700 ste. Extra person $20. Children under age 12 stay free. Parking: Indoor/outdoor, $17/day. Entertainment Discount Cards accepted for 50% savings on rack room rates. Weekend bed-and-breakfast package $95/night. AE, CB, DC, DISC, JCB, MC, V.

⬛⬛⬛ Chicago Hilton and Towers
730 S Michigan Ave, 60605 (Grant Park); tel 312/922-4400 or toll free 800/HILTONS; fax 312/922-5240. Premiere convention hotel, which can handle up to 10,000 during special events. Extending a full block and marble end-to-end, loaded with crystal chandeliers, Oriental rugs, and original art and artifacts (the Normandy Room actually has the woodwork from the ship Normandy; the private art collection of Conrad Hilton is on display). Maintains the highest standards of guest services with remarkable efficiency and security. **Rooms:** 1,543 rms and stes. Executive level. CI 3pm/CO 11am. Nonsmoking rms avail. All rooms have cherry wood furniture; most have two bathrooms. **Amenities:** 🛏 🕹 A/C, cable TV w/movies, voice mail. All units w/minibars. Business and Tower floors have extra amenities in communications and extra housekeeping touches. **Services:** 🍽 🖥 VP 🖨 🍽 🍷 Car-rental desk, masseur, children's program, babysitting. Multilingual staff. On airport route for transportation. Small, domestic pets allowed. Good-humored attitude from staff, particularly when dealing with children. **Facilities:** 🎨 🏊 🍴 [1000] 🕹 4 restaurants, 2 bars (w/entertainment), sauna, steam rm, whirlpool. **Rates:** Peak (Apr 15–Oct) $99–$225 S or D; $325–$5,000 ste. Children under age 16 stay free. Lower rates off-season. Parking: Indoor, $17/day. Bounce Back Weekend packages avail. AE, CB, DC, DISC, EC, ER, JCB, MC, V.

⬛⬛⬛ Chicago Marriott
540 N Michigan Ave, 60611 (Magnificent Mile); tel 312/836-0100 or toll free 800/228-9290; fax 312/836-6139. At Erie. Modern high-rise hotel catering to business and convention travelers. Extended sports facilities and numerous shops and restaurants within the building make this a good choice for those who like everything on site. **Rooms:** 1,172 rms and stes. Executive level. CI 4pm/CO noon. Nonsmoking rms avail. **Amenities:** 🛏 🕹 📺 🎨 A/C, cable TV w/movies, dataport, voice mail. All units w/minibars. **Services:** ✕ 🖥 VP 🚐 🖨 🍽 🍷 Social director, masseur, babysitting. **Facilities:** 🎨 🏊 🍴 [1600] 🖥 🕹 4 restaurants, 2 bars (1 w/entertainment), basketball, games rm, spa, sauna, steam rm, whirlpool, beauty salon. **Rates:** $189–$219 S or D; $480 ste. Extra

person $30. Children under age 18 stay free. Min stay special events. MAP rates avail. AE, CB, DC, DISC, EC, ER, JCB, MC, V.

⬛⬛⬛ The Claridge
1244 N Dearborn Pkwy, 60610 (Gold Coast); tel 312/787-4980. A gracious and comfortable alternative to large hotels, this well-tended property is located in the heart of the Gold Coast, nestled in between brownstones on a tree-lined street. In summer and fall, a colorful and abundant farmer's market stretches an entire city block just around the corner. An amazing bargain for this neighborhood. **Rooms:** 168 rms and stes. CI 3pm/CO noon. Nonsmoking rms avail. Rooms are tasteful, immaculate, comfortable, and surprisingly spacious. **Amenities:** 🛏 🕹 A/C, cable TV w/movies, dataport, voice mail. All units w/minibars, some w/fireplaces, 1 w/whirlpool. **Services:** ✕ 🖥 VP 🚐 🖨 🍽 🍷 Babysitting. Personalized and efficient service. **Facilities:** [80] 🖥 🕹 1 restaurant, 1 bar. **Rates (CP):** $109–$175 S; $129–$175 D; $175–$550 ste. Extra person $20. Children under age 18 stay free. Parking: Indoor, $15/day. Weekday promotions of $89/room occasionally offered. AE, CB, DC, DISC, JCB, MC, V.

⬛⬛ Comfort Inn Lincoln Park
601 W Diversey Pkwy, 60614; tel 312/348-2810 or toll free 800/221-2222; fax 312/348-1912. Just E of Clark. The second-oldest hotel in Chicago, it has a lobby with fine brass furnishings, frosted glass windows, and bi-level comfortable seating with a wheelchair lift. Car rental and dry cleaning/laundry across the street. **Rooms:** 74 rms and stes. CI 2pm/CO noon. Nonsmoking rms avail. Some rooms have double bathrooms. **Amenities:** 🛏 🕹 🎨 A/C, cable TV w/movies, dataport. Some units w/whirlpools. Hot tub and sauna suites available. **Services:** 🍷 **Facilities:** 🍴 [50] Access to fitness center next door for fee. **Rates (CP):** Peak (May–Nov) $68–$84 S; $98–$103 D; $195–$250 ste. Extra person $10. Children under age 17 stay free. Lower rates off-season. Parking: Outdoor, $5/day. AE, CB, DC, DISC, JCB, MC, V.

⬛⬛⬛ Days Inn
644 N Lake Shore Dr, 60611; tel 312/943-9200 or toll free 800/DAYS-INN. Clean, economical hotel within walking distance of North Pier and Navy Pier. **Rooms:** 578 rms and stes. CI 3pm/CO noon. Nonsmoking rms avail. **Amenities:** 🛏 🕹 A/C, cable TV w/movies, dataport, voice mail, in-rm safe. **Services:** ✕ VP 🖨 🍷 Car-rental desk, babysitting. **Facilities:** 🎨 🍴 [100] 🕹 1 restaurant, 1 bar (w/entertainment), games rm, washer/dryer. **Rates:** $85–$95 S; $110–$115 D; $175–$600 ste. Extra person $15. Children under age 16 stay free. Parking: Indoor, $10/day. AE, DC, DISC, JCB, MC, V.

⬛⬛ Days Inn Near North
646 W Diversey Pkwy, 60614 (Near North); tel 312/525-7010 or toll free 800/DAYS-INN; fax 312/525-6998. At Clark; 1 mi S of Wrigley Field. A popular weekend spot for its proximity to Wrigley Field and other Near North neighbor-

hood attractions. Laura Ashley–styled lobby with long hall-way lined with tapestries and curtains. A favorite for local and touring bands, as well as travelers with disabilities. The 90-year-old building has been rated fireproof by the Chicago Fire Department. **Rooms:** 125 rms and stes. Executive level. CI 2pm/CO noon. Nonsmoking rms avail. Suites, hot tub suites, and spacious apartment-style rooms available for longer stays. Single rooms are rather small. **Amenities:** 🛏 ⚲ A/C, cable TV w/movies, in-rm safe. 1 unit w/whirlpool. **Services:** ⤸ ⬳ Young, energetic, and helpful staff. **Facilities:** ⚃ Washer/dryer. **Rates (CP):** $69–$84 S; $89–$104 D; $100–$150 ste. Extra person $10. Children under age 18 stay free. Parking: Indoor, $6/day. AE, CB, DC, DISC, JCB, MC, V.

≡≡≡ DoubleTree Guest Suites

198 E Delaware Place, 60611 (Magnificent Mile); tel 312/664-1100 or toll free 800/222-TREE; fax 312/664-9881. Just E of Michigan Ave. Used extensively by longer-term guests, such as government, medical, and academic people. Also good for families. **Rooms:** 345 stes. CI 3pm/CO noon. Nonsmoking rms avail. Suites have two smallish, comfortable rooms, with sofa bed in living room area. Separate vanity, wet bar. Very attractive. **Amenities:** 🛏 ⚲ 🖵 🍴 A/C, cable TV w/movies, voice mail, bathrobes. All units w/minibars. Ironing board and iron in rooms. **Services:** ⬩◯⬩ ⬤⎯ 𝖵𝖯 ⬛ ⤸ Babysitting. On airport transportation route for easy pickup. Friendly staff. **Facilities:** ⚃ ⬤⬤ ⬚300⬚ 💻 ⚃ 2 restaurants, 1 bar, games rm, spa, sauna, whirlpool, washer/dryer. Great views of Lake Michigan from pool area. Park Avenue Cafe ranked #1 new restaurant by *Chicago Magazine*. **Rates:** Peak (June–Dec) $160–$220 ste. Extra person $10. Children under age 18 stay free. Lower rates off-season. Parking: Indoor, $20/day. AE, CB, DC, DISC, JCB, MC, V.

UNRATED The Drake Hotel

140 E Walton Place, 60611 (Gold Coast); tel 312/787-2200 or toll free 800/55-DRAKE. At Michigan Ave. Landmark 1920s hotel. Lobbies are luxurious with lush plants and sparkling marble fountains. Famous Oak Street boutiques, including Giorgio Armani, Jil Sander, Sonia Rykiel, and Ultimo, are all within walking distance. **Rooms:** 535 rms and stes. Executive level. CI 3pm/CO noon. Nonsmoking rms avail. **Amenities:** 🛏 ⚲ 🍴 A/C, cable TV w/movies, refrig, dataport, bathrobes. All units w/minibars, 1 w/whirlpool. **Services:** ⬩◯⬩ ⬤⎯ 𝖵𝖯 🚐 ⬛ ⤸ Twice-daily maid svce, car-rental desk, masseur, babysitting. **Facilities:** ⬤⬤ ⬚600⬚ 💻 ⚃ 3 restaurants (*see* "Restaurants" below), 2 bars (1 w/entertainment), beauty salon. **Rates:** $195–$265 S; $205–$265 D; $495–$1,700 ste. Extra person $30. Children under age 18 stay free. AE, CB, DC, DISC, MC, V.

≡≡≡ Embassy Suites

600 N State St, 60610 (River North); tel 312/943-3800 or toll free 800/EMBASSY; fax 312/943-7629. At Ohio St. Comfortable for both business travelers and families. Gleaming, cheerful lobby with huge central urn of flowers

and comfortable seating areas. Just behind main lobby is central garden/waterfall/decorative pool—with loud splashing of water. Warm colors of Southwest are carried throughout decor. Car rental facility around the corner. **Rooms:** 358 stes. CI 5pm/CO noon. Nonsmoking rms avail. Biedermeier furniture; pinks, salmons, and sandstone colors; and tasteful appointments. Feather pillows, beds triple-sheeted. Vanities outside bathroom. Rooms face central courtyard and garden. **Amenities:** 🛏 ⚲ 🖵 🍴 A/C, cable TV w/movies, dataport, voice mail. All units w/minibars, all w/terraces. Nintendo, ironing boards, and irons in all suites. **Services:** ✕ ⬤⎯ 𝖵𝖯 ⬛ ⤸ Babysitting. Complimentary evening cocktails and snacks in garden area. VCRs, turndown service, and twice-daily maid service on request. Highly responsive staff. **Facilities:** ⚃ ⬤⬤ ⬚225⬚ 💻 ⚃ 1 restaurant (lunch and dinner only; *see* "Restaurants" below), 2 bars, sauna, whirlpool, washer/dryer. **Rates (BB):** $239–$299 ste. Extra person $30. Children under age 12 stay free. Min stay wknds. Parking: Indoor, $20/day. AE, DC, DISC, MC, V.

≡≡≡ Executive Plaza

71 E Wacker Dr, 60601 (Magnificent Mile); tel 312/346-7100 or toll free 800/621-4005; fax 312/346-1721. Just W of Michigan Ave on S side of Chicago River. On the south bank of the Chicago River, this hotel has a great location and beautiful views. The tiny, bustling lobby with wingback chairs is a modest entry for what turns out to be quite a lovely place. Very friendly, relaxed atmosphere. **Rooms:** 417 rms, stes, and effic. Executive level. CI 2pm/CO noon. Nonsmoking rms avail. Rooms are particularly spacious. Excellent views of Sun-Times Building, Wrigley Building, Tribune Tower, Lake Michigan. **Amenities:** 🛏 ⚲ 🖵 A/C, satel TV w/movies, dataport, voice mail. All units w/minibars. **Services:** ✕ ⬤⎯ 𝖵𝖯 🚐 ⬛ ⤸ Babysitting. VCRs, hair dryers available. Women's Traveler Program includes preregistration, rooms close to elevators, and escorts to rooms. Discount for Bally's fitness center across from hotel can be arranged through concierge. **Facilities:** ⬤⬤ ⬚150⬚ 💻 ⚃ 1 restaurant, 1 bar. **Rates:** $189 S or D; $289 ste; $800 effic. Children under age 18 stay free. Parking: Indoor, $19/day. Many special packages avail. AE, DC, DISC, JCB, MC, V.

≡≡≡≡ The Fairmont

200 N Columbus Dr, 60601 (Grant Park); tel 312/565-8000 or toll free 800/527-4727; fax 312/856-1032. Just E of Michigan Ave, S of Chicago River. With magnificent views of Lake Michigan, the Chicago River, and skyline, this luxury establishment is designed to please the discriminating traveler. **Rooms:** 692 rms and stes. CI 3pm/CO 1pm. Nonsmoking rms avail. Only 11 rooms per floor are accessible from each elevator, so there's minimal foot traffic. Most rooms have great views, and all furnishings are top of the line. **Amenities:** 🛏 ⚲ 🍴 A/C, cable TV w/movies, dataport, voice mail, bathrobes. All units w/minibars, some w/whirlpools. Every room has a fax, shoe buffing machine, and valet stand. Bathrooms have small TVs and a radio. Multiple phone lines

with call-waiting and modem accessibility. VCR on request. **Services:** 🍴 📠 VP 🚐 🖨 🔔 Twice-daily maid svce, car-rental desk, babysitting. Complimentary shoe shine. Foreign currency exchange. Multilingual staff. Hotel on route for regular airport transportation service. Very attentive service. **Facilities:** 1000 🖥 ♿ 2 restaurants (see "Restaurants" below), 4 bars (3 w/entertainment). The Sporting Club, connected to hotel, has fitness and spa center. Restaurants include Entre Nous, justly famed for fine French dining. **Rates:** Peak (May–June/Sept–Oct) $119–$289 S or D; $225–$2,750 ste. Min stay special events. Lower rates off-season. Parking: Indoor, $22/day. President's Club members enjoy discounts. AE, CB, DC, DISC, EC, JCB, MC, V.

⬗⬗⬗⬗⬗ Four Seasons Hotel

120 E Delaware Place, 60611 (Gold Coast); tel 312/280-8800 or toll free 800/332-3442; fax 312/280-9184. Like its sister hotel the Ritz-Carlton (two blocks away), the Four Seasons is deployed throughout a multi-use high-rise—doormen and bellmen at street level, reception on the 7th floor above a vertical shopping mall, guestrooms on the 30th–46th floors—but it makes for a quiet, uncluttered lobby awash in marble and crystal chandeliers. **Rooms:** 343 rms and stes. CI 3pm/CO 1pm. Nonsmoking rms avail. Traditional Four Seasons comfort, space, and efficiency, with real desks (leather-topped) and sitting areas with armchairs and ottomans. Six feet of windows afford city views. Suites are ideal for executives traveling with spouses or companions. **Amenities:** 🔒 ♨ ⦿ A/C, cable TV w/movies, dataport, voice mail, in-rm safe, bathrobes. All units w/minibars, some w/terraces. Two-line speakerphones. Door chimes. **Services:** 🍴 📠 VP 🖨 🔔 🐕 Twice-daily maid svce, masseur, children's program, babysitting. 24-hour concierge; overnight laundry; room service by white-gloved waiters. **Facilities:** 🔥 🍹 1200 🖥 ♿ 2 restaurants (see "Restaurants" below), 2 bars (1 w/entertainment), sauna, steam rm, whirlpool. Elegant indoor pool has wall of windows and big skylight (open 6am–9:30pm). Business center is staffed 9am–6pm, but equipment is available around the clock. **Rates:** $270–$295 S; $300–$325 D; $325–$2,500 ste. Extra person $30. Children under age 18 stay free. Parking: Indoor, $22/day. Rates vary by size rather than location. Special packages avail. AE, CB, DC, DISC, EC, ER, JCB, MC, V.

⬗⬗⬗ Holiday Inn Chicago City Centre

300 E Ohio St, 60611 (Magnificent Mile); tel 312/787-6100. 3 blocks past Michigan Ave. Connected to the McClurg Court Sports Center by interior hallway. **Rooms:** 500 rms and stes. Executive level. CI 3pm/CO noon. Nonsmoking rms avail. **Amenities:** 🔒 ♨ A/C, cable TV w/movies, dataport. **Services:** ✗ 📠 🚐 🖨 🔔 Masseur, babysitting. The bakery off the main lobby will prepare complete picnic lunches; their home-made bread and rolls have a local following. Friendly staff. **Facilities:** 🔥 🍹 1500 ♿ 2 restaurants, 1 bar, spa, washer/dryer. Guests may use the award-winning McClurg Court Sports Center, with indoor tennis courts, racquetball, swim-ming pool, whirlpool, free weight room, and aerobics classes. Children under 12 eat free in the main dining room. **Rates:** $145–$206 S; $161–$216 D; $350–$650 ste. Extra person $16. Children under age 18 stay free. Min stay special events. Parking: Indoor, $17/day. AE, CB, DC, DISC, JCB, MC, V.

⬗⬗⬗⬗ Hotel Inter-Continental Chicago

505 N Michigan Ave, 60611 (Magnificent Mile); tel 312/944-4100 or toll free 800/327-0200; fax 312/944-3050. Striking restoration of a 50-year-old landmark building that was once the exclusive Medina Athletic Club, including an indoor pool you'd expect to find in a sultan's palace rather than a hotel, and public rooms ornately decorated in Mesopotamian/Celtic motifs with hooded knights and Assyrian bulls. Spectacular meeting rooms make the hotel popular for conventions. **Rooms:** 844 rms and stes. CI 3pm/CO noon. Nonsmoking rms avail. "Superior" rooms in the north wing are contemporary and efficient but nothing to write home about, while "deluxe" rooms in the south wing (some with panoramic views on three sides) are furnished in Biedermeier style—they could almost be in two different hotels in terms of style and swank. **Amenities:** 🔒 ♨ 🔲 ⦿ A/C, cable TV w/movies, dataport, voice mail, bathrobes. All units w/mini-bars. Two-line speakerphones; voice mail. Irons and ironing boards in every closet. **Services:** 🍴 📠 VP 🖨 🔔 Twice-daily maid svce, masseur, babysitting. 24-hour concierge. Computer workstations for rent. **Facilities:** 🔥 🍹 450 🖥 ♿ 2 restaurants (see "Restaurants" below), 2 bars (1 w/entertainment), sauna. Olympic-size pool surrounded by blue majolica tiles, terra cotta fountain, and spectator tiers with wicker furniture (Johnny Weissmuller practiced here before the Olympics). **Rates:** $169–$249 S; $189–$269 D; $350–$1,600 ste. Extra person $20. Children under age 12 stay free. Min stay peak and special events. Parking: Indoor, $22.50/day. Rates (in two categories) do not vary by floor or view. Special packages avail. AE, CB, DC, DISC, EC, JCB, MC, V.

⬗⬗⬗⬗ Hotel Nikko Chicago

320 N Dearborn St, 60610 (River North); tel 312/744-1900 or toll free 800/NIKKO-US; fax 312/544-4455. Just N of Chicago River. Overlooks the river park and Chicago River. From the spacious, two-level black marble lobby, guests can look out on a Japanese garden. Attention to detail and beauty. Good for business travelers and families. **Rooms:** 422 rms and stes. CI 3pm/CO noon. Nonsmoking rms avail. Rooms and suites have marble fixtures in baths and highest quality furnishings, with either Western-style beds or tatami rooms with low tables and futon beds. **Amenities:** 🔒 ♨ ⦿ A/C, cable TV w/movies, dataport, voice mail, bathrobes. All units w/minibars, 1 w/whirlpool. Profusion of toiletries in the bathroom. **Services:** 🍴 📠 VP 🖨 🔔 🐕 Twice-daily maid svce, car-rental desk, masseur, children's program, babysitting. Domesticated animals allowed. Complimentary overnight shoe shine. Afternoon high tea served in lobby. VCRs available on request. Nikko Kids receive a welcome bag with luggage tag, games, small camera, and children's menus.

Facilities: 🛏 🏊 💻 ♿ 2 restaurants (see "Restaurants" below), 3 bars (1 w/entertainment), sauna. Overlooking the Chicago River, the Celebrity Cafe offers traditional American dishes subtly influenced by Asian and Mediterranean touches. Also overlooking the river, Benkay offers classic Japanese cuisine served in traditional style. At the small sushi bar near the entrance, visitors can enjoy a quiet cocktail. A unique import store for fine Asian artwork and furniture, Tobai International, is in the hotel. **Rates:** $235–$270 S; $260–$295 D; $300–$2,500 ste. Extra person $20. Children under age 18 stay free. Parking: Indoor/outdoor, $22/day. Several one- or two-night weekend packages avail. AE, CB, DC, DISC, ER, JCB, MC, V.

≡≡≡ Hyatt on Printers Row

500 S Dearborn St, 60605 (South Loop); tel 312/986-1234 or toll free 800/233-1234; fax 312/939-2468. At Congress. This mid-sized member of the Hyatt family is an excellent choice for business travelers who expect the service of a Hyatt, without the clamor of a giant business hotel. The property is actually three buildings purchased by Hyatt in 1991. The decor throughout is refined yet comfortable and hints of the Frank Lloyd Wright Prairie style. **Rooms:** 165 rms, stes, and effic. CI open/CO noon. Nonsmoking rms avail. Comfortable and clean. Extra high ceilings afford large windows, and thus plenty of light and a sense of spaciousness. **Amenities:** 📺 ☕ 🍴 A/C, cable TV w/movies. All units w/minibars. Full-size ironing boards and irons in each room. **Services:** ✕ VP 🚗 🏊 🐕 Twice-daily maid svce, children's program, babysitting. **Facilities:** 🛏 🍴 💻 ♿ 1 restaurant (see "Restaurants" below), 1 bar. Very bare-bones fitness facility; or pay $10 for elaborate Bally's Fitness Center in nearby River City. **Rates:** $99–$215 S or D; $750 ste; $1,000 effic. Extra person $25. Children under age 12 stay free. Parking: Indoor, $16/day. Hyatt Gold Passport Program (in which benefits are earned by paying with Visa card). Love Package costs $181 and includes room, champagne, and breakfast in bed. AE, CB, DC, DISC, EC, ER, JCB, MC, V.

≡≡≡ Hyatt Regency Chicago

151 E Wacker Dr, 60601 (Loop); tel 312/565-1234 or toll free 800/233-1234; fax 312/565-2966. Between Michigan Ave and Columbus Dr. Adjacent to Chicago River and near base of Magnificent Mile, this formidable twin-towered, 36-story hotel caters primarily to the business and convention crowd. Expansive and very busy lobby features sprawling one-story atrium complete with fountains, shimmering pools, and abundant greenery. Hotel is accessible via skyway to Illinois Center, a large, mixed-use urban facility offering retail arcades, restaurants, and convention facilities. **Rooms:** 2,019 rms and stes. Executive level. CI 3pm/CO noon. Nonsmoking rms avail. Rooms above fourth floor in each tower feature city, lake, or river views. **Amenities:** 📺 ☕ 📺 🍴 A/C, cable TV w/movies, dataport, voice mail. Some units w/minibars, some w/whirlpools. Hyatt Business Plan rooms feature personal work station and stocked refrigerators. **Services:** 🍽 🔑 VP 🚗 🏊 🐕 Babysitting. Hyatt Business Plan rooms include continental breakfast with morning newspaper. **Facilities:** 🏊 💻 ♿ 5 restaurants, 4 bars. Health club in Illinois Center available for a fee to hotel guests. **Rates:** $109–$199 S; $230–$350 D; $300–$2,000 ste. Extra person $25. Children under age 16 stay free. Parking: Indoor, $21/day. Room rates vary according to availability. Honeymoon packages and weekend getaway packages avail. AE, CB, DC, DISC, ER, JCB, MC, V.

≡≡≡ The Inn at University Village

625 S Ashland, 60607; tel 312/243-7200 or toll free 800/662-5233. A special place for weekend travelers and conference attendees, offering beautiful room furnishings and fantastic views. Located just off downtown area. **Rooms:** 113 rms and stes. CI 3pm/CO noon. No smoking. Egyptian art, fine linens, rich burgundy carpet. Patio views of Chicago's skyline from hospitality suite rooms. **Amenities:** 📺 ☕ A/C, cable TV w/movies, dataport. Some units w/minibars, 1 w/terrace. **Services:** ✕ VP 🏊 🐕 🍴 Only small pets allowed. Local round-trip transportation to downtown destinations. **Facilities:** 🛏 🍴 ♿ 1 restaurant, 1 bar (w/entertainment). **Rates (CP):** $99–$165 S; $99–$185 D; $175–$450 ste. Extra person $10. Children under age 18 stay free. Parking: Outdoor, $3–$6/day. Special children's package weekend rates as well as weekend and conference rates avail. AE, CB, DC, DISC, MC, V.

UNRATED Knickerbocker Hotel

163 E Walton St, 60611 (Magnificent Mile); tel 312/751-8100 or toll free 800/621-8140; fax 312/751-0370. Just E of Michigan Ave. Architectural gem opened in 1927, with the grand meeting rooms reflecting the elegance of that period; in fact, the main meeting room off the lobby is worth a visit just to look. Location is superb. **Rooms:** 254 rms and stes. CI 3pm/CO noon. Nonsmoking rms avail. Spacious, with two bathrooms. New bedspreads and couches. **Amenities:** 📺 ☕ A/C, cable TV w/movies, voice mail. **Services:** 🍽 🔑 VP 🏊 🐕 🍴 Babysitting. Dogs and cats up to 25 lbs permitted. Attentive service. **Facilities:** 🍴 💻 ♿ 1 restaurant, 1 bar. Access to nearby McClurg Court Sports Center $8 daily. **Rates:** $109–$185 S; $124–$200 D; $165–$225 ste. Children under age 17 stay free. Parking: Indoor, $21/day. AE, DC, DISC, MC, V.

≡≡ Lenox Suites

616 N Rush St, 60611 (Near North); tel 312/337-1000 or toll free 800/445-3669; fax 312/337-7217. At Ontario St; 1 block W of Michigan Ave. Quaint hotel with vaguely European feel is good choice for those with larger families and/or on extended stays. Convenient location near surrounding attractions and nightlife. **Rooms:** 325 rms, stes, and effic. CI 3pm/CO 11am. Nonsmoking rms avail. Lackluster yet very spacious room suites, some with queen-size sofa sleepers. Studio suites feature queen-size Murphy beds. **Amenities:** 📺 ☕ 📺 🍴 A/C, cable TV w/movies, refrig, dataport, voice mail. All rooms feature full kitchen with complimentary coffees and

teas. **Services:** ✗ ☎ VP 🚐 ⌷ ♪ Babysitting. **Facilities:** 🏊 ⟨30⟩ 🚻 Washer/dryer. Health club available nearby. **Rates (CP):** $119 S; $129 D; $149–$164 ste; $89–$129 effic. Extra person $10. Children under age 16 stay free. Parking: Outdoor, $15/day. Extended-stay programs avail. AE, DC, DISC, MC, V.

▤▤▤ Midland Hotel
172 W Adams St, 60603 (Loop); tel 312/332-1200 or toll free 800/621-2360; fax 312/332-5909. At LaSalle St. Fine, old hotel in heart of the Loop with lots of polished marble and brass, grand staircases and arches, and superb meeting facilites. Major renovations have kept beaux arts beauty intact, with recently regilded carved wooden ceilings vaulting up from balconied lobby. **Rooms:** 257 rms and stes. Executive level. CI 3pm/CO noon. Nonsmoking rms avail. Rooms are kept bright, cheerful, and up-to-date. **Amenities:** 🏰 ⌷ A/C, cable TV w/movies, dataport, voice mail. Some units w/whirlpools. **Services:** ✗ ☎ ⌷ ♪ VCRs can be rented through front desk. Cocktails in evenings. Hotel is on route for airport transportation buses and is close to trains to both airports. **Facilities:** 🍴 ⟨550⟩ 🖥 ⌷ 2 restaurants (see "Restaurants" below), 1 bar, beauty salon. Complimentary access to Chicago Health Club. Restaurants include Parisian 1920 bistro, with paintings à la Tamara de Lampke, and upscale dining room off balcony level. **Rates (BB):** $165–$220 S; $185–$240 D; $350–$575 ste. Extra person $20. Children under age 18 stay free. Min stay special events. Senior discounts are 25% off rack rate or 10% off weekend rate. Many weekend packages avail, such as comedy weekends with free tickets to Zany's and free cocktails. AE, CB, DC, DISC, JCB, MC, V.

▤▤ Motel 6
162 E Ontario St, 60611 (Magnificent Mile); tel 312/787-3580 or toll free 800/440-6000; fax 312/787-1299. E of Michigan Ave. This older hotel, just taken over by Motel 6, caters to young people in town and families. Right in the heart of the most elegant area of Chicago. **Rooms:** 192 rms and stes. CI 3pm/CO noon. Nonsmoking rms avail. Rooms beginning to show some neglect and mustiness, but adequate. **Amenities:** 🏰 A/C, cable TV w/movies, voice mail. **Services:** 🚐 ♪ Babysitting. Free local calls. **Facilities:** ⟨30⟩ 1 restaurant. **Rates:** $59–$79 S; $69–$89 D; $69–$99 ste. Extra person $10. Children under age 16 stay free. AE, CB, DC, DISC, MC, V.

▤▤▤ Palmer House
17 E Monroe St, 60603 (Loop); tel 312/726-7500 or toll free 800/445-8667; fax 312/917-1735. At State St. One of Chicago's oldest landmark hotels, it is reminiscent of an era of elegance and affluence—from its spectacular ballrooms to its opulent lobby. The restoration of the lobby's ceiling murals, painted by Louis Rigal, has recently been completed by the Florentine artist whose previous restoration projects included the Sistine Chapel. The unbeatable location makes a great base for exploring the city. **Rooms:** 1,639 rms and stes.

Executive level. CI 3pm/CO noon. Nonsmoking rms avail. Cheerful, cozy rooms feature antique reproductions of furniture and genuine marble bathrooms. Soundproofed windows have recently been installed in rooms on lower floors. **Amenities:** 🏰 ⌷ ♀ A/C, cable TV w/movies, refrig, dataport, voice mail. Some units w/minibars, 1 w/whirlpool. **Services:** ✗ ☎ VP 🚐 ⌷ ♪ ◁ Masseur, children's program, babysitting. Tower rooms, accessible by private elevator, offer extra services and amenities, including continental breakfast and cocktail-time hors d'oeuvres. **Facilities:** 🏊 🍴 ⟨2000⟩ 🖥 ⌷ 4 restaurants, 3 bars (1 w/entertainment), sauna, steam rm, whirlpool, beauty salon. Extensive fitness club features personal trainers, state-of-the-art exercise equipment, golf simulator, and three hitting areas. In Trader Vic's, Chicago's world famous Polynesian restaurant, you might rub shoulders with a visiting celebrity. Retail arcade includes airline ticketing office, travel agency and tour desk, barber shop, and other small shops in lower level. **Rates:** Peak (Apr–June/Sept–Oct) $135–$205 S; $160–$230 D; $225–$1,500 ste. Extra person $25. Children under age 12 stay free. Lower rates off-season. Parking: Indoor, $15–$22/day. Bounce-back weekend packages, romance packages, and occasional seasonal packages avail. AE, CB, DC, DISC, EC, ER, JCB, MC, V.

▤▤ Park Brompton Hotel
528 W Brompton Ave, 60657; tel 312/404-3499 or toll free 800/PARK-108; fax 312/404-3495. 1 block S of Addison St; 1 block W of Lake Shore Dr. The antique-filled setting comes complete with a drawing room. Located on a quiet, tree-lined street. **Rooms:** 52 rms and stes. CI 2pm/CO noon. All rooms decorated with antiques and fine furnishings, from beautiful wallpaper to embroidered luggage stands. Front rooms are sun rooms. Two-room suites and old-style bathrooms. **Amenities:** 🏰 ⌷ A/C, cable TV w/movies, refrig. Dataports available on request. **Services:** VP ♪ ◁ Pets allowed with prearrangement. **Facilities:** ⟨50⟩ Washer/dryer. Access to area fitness center for small fee. **Rates (CP):** Peak (June–Aug) $79–$85 S; $89–$99 D; $89–$99 ste. Extra person $10. Children under age 12 stay free. Lower rates off-season. Parking: Indoor, $6/day. AE, CB, DC, DISC, MC, V.

▤▤▤▤ Park Hyatt Chicago
800 N Michigan Ave, 60611 (Magnificent Mile); tel 312/280-2222 or toll free 800/233-1234. At the end of Michigan Ave. A quiet, tasteful hotel in a premiere location overlooking the original Water Tower and a small park. Attractive planters outside. Within walking distance of elegant stores, restaurants, and night spots. Multilingual staff. **Rooms:** 255 rms and stes. CI 3pm/CO noon. Nonsmoking rms avail. Live plants, fresh flowers, and high-quality furnishings and art. **Amenities:** 🏰 ⌷ ♀ A/C, cable TV w/movies, dataport, VCR, CD/tape player, bathrobes. All units w/minibars. Full ironing boards and irons included. Exercise equipment available for your room. **Services:** 🍽 ☎ VP ⌷ ♪ Masseur, babysitting. Maid service three times a day, complimentary newspapers,

packing assistance, complimentary car washing, 24-hour concierge, and seamstress. Special meals available, including Japanese breakfasts for groups. Afternoon tea served in lobby 2–5pm. **Facilities:** [200] ☐ & 1 restaurant, 1 bar (w/entertainment). **Rates:** $145–$229 S or D; $425–$650 ste. Parking: Indoor, $24/day. AE, CB, DC, DISC, JCB, MC, V.

≣≣≣ Radisson Hotel & Suites Chicago

160 E Huron St, 60611 (Magnificent Mile); tel 312/787-2900 or toll free 800/346-2591; fax 312/787-5158. ½ block E of Michigan Ave. Remarkable mural by Thomas Melvin in the lobby adds a "real Chicago" personal touch, and you're within walking distance of the most elegant shops and restaurants in the city. **Rooms:** 341 rms and stes. Executive level. CI 3pm/CO noon. Nonsmoking rms avail. Lovely views of the lake and the city shoreline from the eastern corner windows. **Amenities:** 🗗 & 🔲 🖘 A/C, satel TV w/movies, dataport, voice mail. All units w/minibars, some w/terraces, 1 w/whirlpool. **Services:** 🔟 🖛 VP 🖾 🖵 🖘 Babysitting. Pets allowed: common, domesticated, and under 30 lbs. **Facilities:** 🗗 🖢 [250] & 1 restaurant, 1 bar, games rm. **Rates:** Peak (Apr–Dec) $175–$195 S; $190–$210 D; $225–$240 ste. Extra person $15. Children under age 16 stay free. Min stay special events. Lower rates off-season. Parking: Indoor, $19/day. AE, CB, DC, DISC, JCB, MC, V.

≣≣ Ramada Congress Hotel

520 S Michigan Ave, 60605; tel 312/427-3800 or toll free 800/635-1666. At Congress. What used to be the flagship of the Pick Hotels is now co-owned by Ramada and Days Inn. Reminders of the past are the beautiful bronze elevator doors and the vaulted lobby with lovely tilework, gold beams, marble, and statuary. Odd accompaniment to this old elegance is the indoor/outdoor carpeting, leftover canopies with names of previous tenants, and the broken glass door on the south side; public areas have seen better days. Yet the service—and the clientele—have remained faithful to the good old days. **Rooms:** 820 rms and stes. CI 3pm/CO noon. Nonsmoking rms avail. Rooms in the newer, Days Inn section are pleasantly utilitarian; those in the older Ramada-owned section retain a certain elegance, with dark wood furniture, flowered bedspreads, and soft mauve carpeting. Many rooms have lake view. **Amenities:** 🗗 & 🔲 🖘 A/C, cable TV w/movies, dataport. **Services:** ✗ VP 🖾 🖾 🖵 Social director. Shoe shine service in lobby (shoes are returned to your room). **Facilities:** 🖢 [3000] & 2 restaurants, 1 bar, games rm, washer/dryer. **Rates:** $89–$145 S; $99–$165 D; $250–$700 ste. Extra person $20. Children under age 16 stay free. AP and MAP rates avail. Parking: Outdoor, $17/day. Weekend packages include parking and breakfast. Many special-interest packages in conjunction with Art Institute and museums. AE, CB, DC, DISC, MC, V.

≣≣ Ramada Inn Lakeshore

4900 S Lakeshore Dr, 60615; tel 312/288-5800 or toll free 800/2-RAMADA; fax 312/288-5745. 4 mi S of downtown. Quiet atmosphere and attentive staff. **Rooms:** 185 rms and stes. CI 3pm/CO 11am. Nonsmoking rms avail. Lakefront rooms have beautiful views. **Amenities:** 🗗 & 🔲 A/C, cable TV w/movies, dataport. Some units w/terraces. **Services:** ✗ 🖘🖾🖵🖘 Car-rental desk. Pets accepted with $50 deposit. Shuttle buses to downtown attractions. Transportation to and from UIC Hospital for outpatient surgery patients. **Facilities:** 🗗 [450] & 1 restaurant, 1 bar, washer/dryer. **Rates:** Peak (Apr–Oct) $89–$99 S; $99–$119 D; $150–$300 ste. Extra person $10. Children under age 17 stay free. Lower rates off-season. Parking: Indoor/outdoor, free. Outpatient surgery rates for UIC Hospital patients. AE, CB, DC, DISC, MC, V.

≣≣≣ The Raphael

201 E Delaware Place, 60611 (Gold Coast); tel 312/943-5000 or toll free 800/821-5343; fax 312/943-9483. 2 blocks E of Michigan Ave. Elegant, small hotel tucked away in quiet corner of historic Gold Coast area, yet still within walking distance of Michigan Avenue's Magnificent Mile and Watertower Place. European furnishings. **Rooms:** 172 rms and stes. CI 3pm/CO 1pm. Nonsmoking rms avail. **Amenities:** 🗗 & 🖘 A/C, cable TV, refrig, in-rm safe, bathrobes. All units w/minibars. **Services:** 🔟 🖛 VP 🖙 🖾 🖵 🖘 Twice-daily maid svce, car-rental desk, babysitting. Cordial, knowledgeable staff. **Facilities:** [40] & 1 restaurant, 1 bar (w/entertainment). **Rates:** $120–$140 S or D; $140–$175 ste. Extra person $20. Children under age 12 stay free. AE, CB, DC, DISC, MC, V.

≣≣≣≣ Renaissance Chicago Hotel

1 W Wacker Dr, 60601 (Loop); tel 312/372-7200 or toll free 800/HOTELS-1; fax 312/372-0093. At State St. A lovely hotel overlooking the Chicago River. Behind the marble reception desk is a mural of the Chicago city scene created by Zoia Chapovalova. Location is very handy for shopping on State Street and for river and lake boat trips. **Rooms:** 553 rms and stes. Executive level. CI 4pm/CO 1pm. Nonsmoking rms avail. Lovely, sound-proofed, ample rooms, with high-quality furnishings and bay windows. **Amenities:** 🗗 & 🔲 🖘 A/C, cable TV w/movies, dataport, voice mail, bathrobes. All units w/minibars, some w/whirlpools. Faxes in all rooms. **Services:** 🔟 🖛 VP 🖾 🖵 🖘 Twice-daily maid svce, masseur, babysitting. Small, domesticated pets allowed. Hotel on regular O'Hare Airport service run, and close to the Orange Line for Midway Airport. Concern for services extends to listing the general manager's home telephone number in the in-room services guide. **Facilities:** 🗗 🖢 [1200] ☐ & 2 restaurants, 3 bars (1 w/entertainment), sauna, whirlpool. 24-hour Kinko's business center in hotel. Great Street Restaurant and Bar serves American food, and Cuisines Restaurant and Cafe offers northern Italian fare. **Rates:** $230–$290 S; $250–$310 D; $450–$2,500 ste. Extra person $20. Children under age 18 stay free. Parking: Indoor, $22/day. AE, CB, DC, DISC, JCB, MC, V.

≣≣≣≣ The Ritz-Carlton Chicago

160 E Pearson St, 60611 (Gold Coast); tel 312/266-1000 or toll free 800/621-6906; fax 312/266-9498. Occupying 22 floors of the multi-use Water Place Tower (much like its skyscraper-ensconced sister hotel, the Four Seasons, two blocks away), with guestrooms on floors 15–31. Its 12th-floor lobby, with gilded swirls and conservatory-style windows, was a pacesetter when it opened a decade ago but now looks as much Donald Trump as Cesar Ritz. **Rooms:** 429 rms and stes. CI 3pm/CO 1pm. Nonsmoking rms avail. Plush, comfy, efficient rooms with fine period furnishings, leather-topped desks; armchairs with ottomans, and marble bathrooms. **Amenities:** 🛎 🅰 ⌨ A/C, cable TV w/movies, dataport, voice mail, in-rm safe, bathrobes. All units w/minibars. Two-line speakerphones. Lockable closets. **Services:** ⎇ ⚷ VP ⌸ ⌇ ⌸ Twice-daily maid svce, masseur, children's program, babysitting. 24-hour concierge. Unusually high level of service and quality control (one staffer spends most of his time just touching up the leather on the desks). **Facilities:** ⛲ ⛺ ▣500 💻 ⟨ 3 restaurants (see "Restaurants" below), 2 bars (1 w/entertainment), spa, sauna, steam rm, whirlpool. Elegant Carlton Club spa and fitness center with chilled towels, filtered water, and attractive swimming pool. **Rates:** $250–$350 S; $280–$380 D; $775–$2500 ste. Extra person $30. Children under age 18 stay free. Parking: Indoor, $25.25/day. Rates are among the highest in the city, but then so is the level of service. Weekend rates start at $195; special packages including breakfasts and dinners can be exceptional value. AE, CB, DC, DISC, EC, ER, JCB, MC, V.

≣≣≣ Sheraton Chicago Hotel and Towers

301 E North Water St, 60611; tel 312/464-1000 or toll free 800/233-4100; fax 312/464-9140. 3 blocks E of Michigan Ave. Sparkling new hotel in heart of downtown, within walking distance of North Pier, Magnificent Mile, and Art Institute. **Rooms:** 1,204 rms and stes. Executive level. CI 3pm/CO noon. Nonsmoking rms avail. Rooms are tastefully appointed with European-style, modern furniture. **Amenities:** 🛎 🅰 ⌨ ⌀ A/C, cable TV w/movies, dataport, voice mail, in-rm safe. All units w/minibars, some w/fireplaces, some w/whirlpools. **Services:** ⎇ ⚷ VP 🚐 ⌸ ⌇ Twice-daily maid svce, car-rental desk, social director, masseur, babysitting. **Facilities:** ⛲ ⛺ 💻 ⟨ 4 restaurants, 5 bars (1 w/entertainment), spa, sauna. **Rates (CP):** $119–$230 S or D; $350–$800 ste. Extra person $25. Children under age 18 stay free. Min stay special events. AP rates avail. Parking: Indoor/outdoor, $19/day. AE, CB, DC, DISC, MC, V.

≣≣≣ Summerfield Suites Hotel

166 E Superior St, 60611 (Magnificent Mile); tel 312/787-6000 or toll free 800/833-4353; fax 312/787-6133. Just ½ block E of Michigan Ave. Emphasis on corporate travel needs, but suitable for families. Great location for all the shopping, restaurants, nightspots, and cultural facilities. **Rooms:** 120 stes and effic. CI 4pm/CO noon. Nonsmoking rms avail. Newly renovated rooms in cheerful deep green or maroon with deep, marble window sills. East side rooms have lovely views of Lake Michigan and the shoreline. Suites and efficiencies have pull-out sofas. **Amenities:** 🛎 🅰 ⌨ ⌀ A/C, cable TV, refrig, VCR, voice mail. Iron and ironing board in closet. **Services:** ✗ VP ⌸ ⌇ Babysitting. Front desk personnel handle concierge duties. Benihana's Restaurant in the same building and Gino's Pizza provide room service for meals other than breakfast. **Facilities:** ⛲ ⛺ ▣65 💻 ⟨ 1 bar, games rm, beauty salon, washer/dryer. $10 daily passes available for nearby McClurg Court Sports Center. Full office setup available, including secretarial services. **Rates (BB):** $109–$179 ste; $119–$179 effic. Extra person $20. Children under age 16 stay free. Min stay wknds and special events. Parking: Indoor, $17/day. AE, CB, DC, DISC, MC, V.

≣≣≣ The Surf Hotel

555 W Surf St, 60657; tel 312/528-8400 or toll free 800/SURF-108; fax 312/528-8483. 1 block N of Diversey Pkwy at Broadway. Nestled between residential buildings on quiet, tree-lined street. Newly renovated lobby is beautiful, with touches of 19th-century Parisian ambience. **Rooms:** 55 rms and stes. CI 2pm/CO 11am. Nonsmoking rms avail. Each room decorated differently with antiques and fine furnishings. Cheval mirrors, embroidered luggage stands, beautiful wallpaper, Monet prints, and lush potted plants. **Amenities:** 🛎 🅰 A/C, cable TV w/movies. **Services:** ⌇ ⌸ Dry cleaning/laundry available by arrangement. Small pets allowed in cages. **Facilities:** ⟨ Washer/dryer. Access to nearby fitness center for small fee. **Rates (CP):** Peak (Apr–Oct) $79–$85 S; $89–$99 D; $89–$99 ste. Extra person $10. Children under age 12 stay free. Lower rates off-season. Parking: Indoor/outdoor, $7/day. AE, CB, DC, DISC, MC, V.

≣≣≣≣ Sutton Place

21 E Bellevue Place, 60610 (Gold Coast); tel 312/266-2100 or toll free 800/866-6888; fax 312/266-2104. Sophisticated Sutton Place personifies the Gold Coast neighborhood, with its sleek marble lobby, impeccably appointed rooms, and elegant international clientele. Snobbery, fortunately, does not make its way into the service. A great choice for the traveler who demands excellence and is willing to pay for it. **Rooms:** 246 rms and stes. CI 3pm/CO noon. Nonsmoking rms avail. Rooms are tastefully decorated in neutrals with soothing lighting and feature original artwork by Robert Mapplethorpe (commissioned when the hotel first opened—under another name—in 1986). Bathrooms glisten in striking black and white ceramic tile, with fine granite countertops. **Amenities:** 🛎 🅰 ⌀ A/C, cable TV w/movies, refrig, VCR, CD/tape player, voice mail, bathrobes. All units w/minibars, some w/terraces. Dataports available on request. **Services:** ⎇ ⚷ VP 🚐 ⌸ ⌇ Twice-daily maid svce, car-rental desk, masseur, babysitting. Wide selection of videos to rent. Genuinely friendly, knowledgeable staff. **Facilities:** ⛺ ▣250 💻 ⟨ 1 restaurant, 2 bars. Guests may also use nearby Gold Coast Multiplex Fitness Center for $12. **Rates:** $220–$255 S;

$245–$280 D; $650 ste. Extra person $25. Children under age 18 stay free. Parking: Indoor, $22/day. AE, CB, DC, DISC, JCB, MC, V.

≣≣≣≣ Swissôtel

323 E Wacker Dr, 60601 (East Loop); tel 312/565-0565 or toll free 800/654-7263; fax 312/565-0540. Between Columbus and Lake Shore Drs. This triangular, 43-floor monolith sports a distinctly European warmth and ambience for a hotel of its size. Its proximity to the Illinois Center (connected via underground walkway) appeals to the business and convention crowd, but it's a great place for anyone's jaunt into the city. Nine-hole golf course and driving range adjacent. **Rooms:** 630 rms and stes. CI 3pm/CO noon. Nonsmoking rms avail. Spacious and luxuriously appointed rooms with great city or lake views. Standard furnishings include sitting area, oversized furniture, and marble bathrooms. Deluxe corner rooms have both city and lake views. **Amenities:** 🕾 🕭 ☏ A/C, cable TV w/movies, dataport, voice mail. All units w/minibars, 1 w/fireplace. Mechanical doorbells, two-line phones with call waiting, bathroom scales. **Services:** |◎| 🗝 VP 🚐 🖎 🖵 Twice-daily maid svce, masseur, babysitting. VCRs available on request. Excellent service from pleasant and attentive staff. **Facilities:** 🔓 🛏 🔲 🖵 ㊗ 1 restaurant, 1 bar, spa, sauna, whirlpool. Extensive 42nd floor health club/spa with state-of-the-art equipment features sweeping views of lakefront. **Rates:** $205 S; $225 D; $420 ste. Extra person $20. Children under age 12 stay free. Parking: Indoor, $19/day. Weekend packages include Golf and Fitness, Celebration, Spa, Kidsotel, and Bed-and-Breakfast, and include overnight parking. AE, CB, DC, DISC, EC, ER, JCB, MC, V.

≣≣≣≣ The Tremont

100 E Chestnut St, 60611 (Magnificant Mile); tel 312/751-1900 or toll free 800/621-8133; fax 312/751-8691. Just W of Michigan Ave. An elegant hideaway, with a sense of old-fashioned privacy and personal service. For the discriminating traveler who wants to be near the action, but doesn't want to be disturbed. **Rooms:** 129 rms, stes, and effic. CI 3pm/CO noon. Nonsmoking rms avail. Fresh flowers and live plants in every room. Marble bathrooms. **Amenities:** 🕾 🕭 ☏ A/C, cable TV w/movies, VCR, CD/tape player, bathrobes. Some units w/minibars, some w/fireplaces, some w/whirlpools. Irons and ironing boards in closet. **Services:** |◎| 🗝 VP 🖎 🖵 ㊗ Twice-daily maid svce, masseur, babysitting. **Facilities:** 🔲 ㊗ 1 restaurant, 1 bar. **Rates:** Peak (May 1–May 24/June/Sept–Oct/Nov 20–Dec 4) $185–$225 S; $205–$245 D; $325–$950 ste; $75–$125 effic. Extra person $25. Children under age 10 stay free. Lower rates off-season. Parking: Indoor, $19.50/day. AE, CB, DC, DISC, ER, JCB, MC, V.

≣≣≣ The Westin Hotel

909 N Michigan Ave, 60611 (Magnificent Mile); tel 312/943-7200 or toll free 800/228-3000; fax 312/943-9347. 2 blocks S of Michigan Ave exit from Lake Shore Dr. Busy, friendly, large hotel right in the middle of Magnificent Mile. Two blocks from Oak St Beach. Families feel comfortable

here, yet celebrities often call this home, too. **Rooms:** 740 rms and stes. Executive level. CI noon/CO 3pm. Nonsmoking rms avail. **Amenities:** 🕾 🕭 ☏ A/C, cable TV w/movies, voice mail. All units w/minibars, 1 w/whirlpool. **Services:** |◎| 🗝 VP 🖎 🖵 ㊗ Twice-daily maid svce, masseur, children's program, babysitting. **Facilities:** 🛏 🔲 🖵 ㊗ 1 restaurant, 1 bar, beauty salon. **Rates:** $119–$220 S; $119–$245 D; $250–$1,600 ste. Extra person $30. Children under age 18 stay free. Parking: Indoor, $20.75/day. AE, CB, DC, DISC, ER, JCB, MC, V.

MOTELS

≣≣ Hampton Inn Midway

6540 S Cicero Ave, Bedford Park, 60638; tel 708/496-1900 or toll free 800/HAMPTON; fax 708/496-1997. Near Chicago's Midway Airport. On a slight rise above the busy commercial street, this sandstone-colored building offers a respite from the roar of trucks grinding through the area. The cheerful lobby captures the spirit of flight, with models of airplanes suspended from the ceiling, photos of classic planes, and an aerial photo of the Loop. Friendly, helpful staff. **Rooms:** 167 rms. CI 2pm/CO noon. Nonsmoking rms avail. **Amenities:** 🕾 🕭 A/C, cable TV w/movies, dataport. **Services:** ✕ 🚐 🖎 🖵 Airport/downtown shuttle service via colorful 1890s-style "trolley" van. **Facilities:** 🔲 🖵 ㊗ Fitness center in progress. **Rates (CP):** $89–$129 S; $99–$139 D. Children under age 18 stay free. Parking: Outdoor, free. "100% satisfaction guaranteed" or you don't pay. Park/sleep/fly package is very handy for those leaving for short trips from Midway. AE, CB, DC, DISC, JCB, MC, V.

≣≣ Holiday Inn Midway

7353 S Cicero Ave, 60629; tel 312/581-5300 or toll free 800/HOLIDAY. Standard, utilitarian facility; plans for major renovation may improve public areas. Exceedingly friendly staff. **Rooms:** 161 rms. CI 1pm/CO noon. Nonsmoking rms avail. **Amenities:** 🕾 🕭 ☏ A/C, cable TV w/movies. Direct link from room telephones for airport and airline information. **Services:** ✕ 🚐 🖎 🖵 Babysitting. Car rental arrangements can be made through front desk. **Facilities:** 🔓 🛏 🔲 ㊗ 1 restaurant, 1 bar. **Rates (BB):** $78 S; $88 D. Extra person $10. Children under age 18 stay free. Parking: Outdoor, free. AE, CB, DC, DISC, JCB, MC, V.

≣ Ohio House Motel

600 N LaSalle St, 60610 (River North); tel 312/943-6000; fax 312/943-6063. At Ohio St. Basic, two-story urban motel, steps away from Hard Rock Cafe, Michael Jordan's Restaurant, Planet Hollywood, etc. You won't beat the price for the location. **Rooms:** 50 rms and stes. CI 2pm/CO noon. Nonsmoking rms avail. Spacious rooms feature slightly funky yet pleasant decor with deep shag rugs. **Amenities:** 🕾 🕭 A/C, cable TV w/movies. **Services:** 🖵 No room service, but if tiny coffee shop isn't busy, one of the staff may walk your order to

your room. **Facilities:** 1 restaurant. **Rates:** $65–$72 S; $72–$80 D; $100 ste. Parking: Outdoor, free. Discounted senior citizen rates. AE, CB, DC, DISC, MC, V.

RESTAURANTS 🍴

🌹 Ambria
2300 N Lincoln Park West (Lincoln Park); tel 312/472-0076. **French.** This elegant restaurant with delicate art nouveau decor occupies several large rooms off the lobby of the Belden Stratford building. The menu changes frequently but always emphasizes natural juices and reductions to create lighter, flavor-filled food without excessive richness. Previous selections have included charred sirloin with zinfandel reduction, and venison with rice pancakes and root vegetables. **FYI:** Reservations recommended. Jacket required. No smoking. **Open:** Mon–Thurs 6–9:30pm, Fri–Sat 6–10:30pm. **Prices:** Main courses $20–$30; prix fixe $48–$64. AE, CB, DC, DISC, MC, V. ♥ VP &

⭐ Ann Sather's
929 W Belmont Ave (East Lakeview); tel 312/348-2378. **American/Swedish.** Founded in 1945 and situated on a busy thoroughfare, this local favorite—especially for breakfast—has somewhat of a faded old-world feel. Swedish-style banquet rooms upstairs are ornately decorated but nonetheless dowdy, and the place is a little run-down. But it's obviously the food that's the draw here, and the baked goods (in particular the cinnamon rolls) are practically fabled. The emphasis on good service and comfort food at comfortable prices makes this an excellent choice for families. **FYI:** Reservations accepted. **Open:** Daily 7am–10pm. **Prices:** Main courses $8–$12. AE, MC, V. 🖼

🌹 Arun's
4156 N Kedzie Ave (Albany Park); tel 312/539-1909. N of Irving Park Rd. **Thai.** Exquisitely prepared and presented Thai food, with seasonings savory, subtle, and sometimes surprising. The restaurant itself is a work of art and houses a gallery of vases, gold headdresses, lacquered chests, and ceramic pots. The new upstairs dining room adds an intimate atmosphere with blond wood, stark white trim, and pumpkin-colored walls. All this sets the scene for some of the finest Thai food in Chicago. Appetizers include spicy papaya salad, and lobster tails with roasted peanuts, coconut, spices, and tamarind juice. Main courses include such curries as chicken with taro stalks and kafir lime. **FYI:** Reservations recommended. **Open:** Tues–Sat 5–10pm, Sun 5–9pm. **Prices:** Main courses $14–$24. AE, CB, DC, DISC, MC, V. ♥

Avanzare
161 E Huron (Magnificent Mile); tel 312/337-8056. Just east of Michigan Ave. **Italian.** Very upscale casual for special occasions and business dining. Dishes include grilled salmon with Sicilian couscous and a carrot emulsion, pan-roasted Australian lamb chops, as well as homemade pastas and seafood. Sauces made with fresh herbs. Homemade gelatos and sorbets. Discounted parking across the street. **FYI:** Reservations recommended. **Open:** Lunch Mon–Fri 11:30am–2pm; dinner Mon–Thurs 5:30–10pm, Fri–Sat 5–11pm, Sun 5–9:30pm. **Prices:** Main courses $14–$26. AE, CB, DC, DISC, MC, V. ♥ &

🌹 Benkay
In the Hotel Nikko Chicago, 320 N Dearborn St (River North); tel 312/836-5490. **Japanese.** Named after a 15th-century warrior-monk, this find offers authentic Japanese delicacies and regional dishes in a stunning Japanese palace–style setting, complete with tatami rooms, lovely gardens, giant living bamboo stalks, and spectacular river views. Specialties include sushi, tempura, and teppanyaki. In private tearooms (tatamis), kimono-clad waitresses serve kaiseki (multicourse gourmet dinner), which includes at least one item from each of the traditional Japanese styles of cooking. **FYI:** Reservations recommended. Jacket required. **Open:** Breakfast Tues–Sat 7–10am; lunch Tues–Sat 11:30am–2pm; dinner Tues–Sat 5:30–10pm. **Prices:** Main courses $20–$40; prix fixe $45–$100. AE, CB, DC, DISC, MC, V. VP &

⭐ Berghoff's
17 W Adams St (Loop); tel 312/427-3170. At Dearborn St. **American/German.** This Chicago classic since 1898 is housed in a building that was one of the first constructed in The Loop after the Chicago fire. The dining rooms offer a warm turn-of-the-century ambience and a bustling, energetic atmosphere. The extensive menu maintains a host of traditional German dishes, such as sauerbraten, Wiener schnitzel, and smoked Thuringer sausage. Seafood, pasta, and other American-style entrees also offered. The place continues to brew its own beers and also produces its own bourbon. **FYI:** Reservations recommended. Children's menu. Dress code. **Open:** Mon–Thurs 11am–9pm, Fri 11am–9:30pm, Sat 11am–10pm. **Prices:** Main courses $9–$14. AE, MC, V. 🍺 &

⭐ The Big Bowl Cafe—An Asian Cafe
159½ W Erie St (River North); tel 312/787-8297. Between LaSalle and Wells Sts. **Asian.** You can choose your own vegetables to be stir fried in the wok, have Asian lemon chicken, or try some of the Szechuan chicken noodle soup. All foods are prepared in Asian style, and there are many low-calorie and vegetarian dishes. Signature drinks include homemade ginger ale and Thai ice coffee. **FYI:** Reservations not accepted. **Open:** Mon–Thurs 11:30am–10pm, Fri–Sat 11:30am–11pm, Sun 5–9pm. **Prices:** Main courses $5–$10. AE, CB, DC, DISC, MC, V. 🖼 🚗 VP &

⭐ Biggs Restaurant
1150 N Dearborn St (Gold Coast); tel 312/787-0900. At Elm St. **Seafood/Steak.** This award-winning restaurant housed in an 1874 mansion offers elegant continental dining, fine service, and an atmosphere that takes you back in time. This is truly a unique spot, with a fireplace in every room and even a carriage house in back. Menu items include roasted half-ducking grilled with sweet potatoes and green peppercorn sauce; classic beef Wellington with truffle sauce; and pheas-

ant breast lightly breaded and sautéed with grilled fresh pineapple and juniper berry sauce. A special appetizer is Russian beluga caviar with chilled Stolichnaya Chrystal vodka. **FYI:** Reservations accepted. Jacket required. **Open:** Daily 5–10pm. **Prices:** Main courses $13–$25. AE, DISC, MC, V. ♥ ▇ VP

Big Shoulders Cafe

1601 N Clark St (Lincoln Park); tel 312/587-7766. At the Chicago Historical Society. **Cafe.** Named for the "Big Shoulders" mentioned in Carl Sandburg's poem "Chicago," this cafe in the Chicago Historical Society offers simple, hearty fare prepared in imaginative ways. Bright posters and flowers greet patrons upon passing through a terra cotta arch (removed from the old Stockyard bank). Millet bread and cornbread sprinkled with flecks of jalapeño pepper is a nice way to start off. Soups include potato with roasted chicken; Sheboygan bratwurst is a favorite sandwich. **FYI:** Reservations accepted. Piano. Children's menu. Beer and wine only. **Open:** Mon–Fri 11:30am–3pm, Sat 11am–3pm, Sun 10:30am–3pm. **Prices:** Lunch main courses $3–$8. AE, DC, MC, V. &

Billy Goat Tavern

430 N Michigan Ave (Magnificent Mile); tel 312/222-1525. **Diner.** Famous Chicago diner that inspired a John Belushi routine on the original *Saturday Night Live*. Journalists have been known to frequent the place, and the walls are lined with famous names and photos. Cheeseburgers and roast beef are decent. Tacky, but worth a visit for those who enjoy a bit of kitsch. **FYI:** Reservations not accepted. **Open:** Mon–Fri 10am–2am, Sat 10am–3am, Sun 11am–2am. **Prices:** Main courses $2–$10. No CC. ▇

Bistro 110

110 E Pearson St (Magnificent Mile); tel 312/266-3110. Just W of Michigan Ave. **French/Provençal.** Inviting restaurant with outdoor cafe overlooking Water Tower Park caters to shoppers, couples on dates, and high-profile movers and shakers. Try the cassoulet Toulousain for a sturdy meal or watch calories with the salad Niçoise. **FYI:** Reservations accepted. **Open:** Mon–Thurs 11:30am–11pm, Fri–Sat 11:30am–midnight, Sun 10:30am–10pm. **Prices:** Main courses $15–$19. AE, DC, DISC, MC, V. VP &

★ Blackhawk Lodge

41 E Superior St (Magnificent Mile); tel 312/280-4080. Just W of Michigan Ave. **New American.** A North Woods atmosphere where regional American cuisine is celebrated. Outstanding interior design concept created by Marv Cooper, with log walls, wooden beams, oriental rugs, and antique tables. Menu includes meats, fish, and poultry, prepared for delicate to hearty palates. Try pan-roasted Pacific salmon with a ragout of Oregon morels and asparagus; or hickory-smoked baby back ribs with cottage fries. Screened-in sidewalk area is downright festive, and during brunch a Bluegrass band completes the pleasures. Great for families or romance.

FYI: Reservations recommended. Children's menu. **Open:** Lunch Mon–Fri 11:30am–3pm; dinner Sun–Thurs 5–10pm, Fri–Sat 5–11pm; brunch Sat–Sun 11:30am–3pm. **Prices:** Main courses $12–$23. AE, DC, DISC, MC, V. ♥ ▇ 🍴 👥 VP &

The Bongo Room

1560 N Damen Ave (Wicker Park); tel 312/489-0690. At Milwaukee Ave. **Cafe/Continental.** This tiny, funky storefront almost under the el train has a strong following among both young and old. Breakfast burritos; generous vegetarian croissant sandwiches; Mediterranean sandwiches of artichoke hearts, roasted red peppers, roasted mozzarella, garlic, and olive oil; and eclectic American and continental cooking attest to the training of recent Kendall Culinary School graduate John Latino. **FYI:** Reservations not accepted. No liquor license. **Open:** Breakfast Mon–Fri 7:30–11am, Sat–Sun 9:30–11am; lunch Mon–Fri 11am–3pm, Sat–Sun 11am–2:30pm; dinner Mon–Thurs 5–9pm. Closed 2 weeks in Jan. **Prices:** Main courses $6–$10. No CC.

Bossa Nova

1960 N Clybourn Ave (Lincoln Park); tel 312/248-4800. Just S of Racine. **Pan-Asian.** Billed as the supper club of the '90s, this multilevel, multicultural phenomenon specializes in "retro fusion" music of the '70s and modern Latin dance music. The food too, trips lightly from tapas (on each table is a multicolored assortment of small plates for your use in choosing tapas) to full dinners. Entrees include pan-roasted salmon, island spiced pork tenderloin, grilled chicken served with black beans, and wok-fried whole fish. But it would be a shame to pass up the tapas: The Bossa Nova spring roll (Vietnamese-style spring roll filled with mushrooms, bean sprouts, chiles, cucumbers, and carrots) and the papaya-marinated baby back ribs served with Venezuelan barbecue sauce are exemplary. Early in the evening, families and small groups of singles gather to enjoy this marvelous panoply of world foods in a festive atmosphere; the "clubbier" crowd comes after 10pm. **FYI:** Reservations accepted. Dancing/guitar/singer. **Open:** Tues–Thurs 5:30pm–midnight, Fri 5:30pm–2am, Sat 5:30pm–3am. **Prices:** Main courses $8–$16. AE, CB, DC, DISC, MC, V. ♥ VP

The Boulevard Restaurant

In Hotel Inter-Continental Chicago, 505 N Michigan Ave (Magnificent Mile); tel 312/944-4100. **New American/Mediterranean.** Part of a historic men's athletic club dating from 1927 and now a historic landmark, it incorporates grand architectural flourishes, ornately decorated ceiling beams, and terra-cotta carvings that conjure up visions of ancient Babylon. Tables are widely spaced, with twosomes getting prime locations by the windows overlooking Michigan Ave. The Mediterranean-inspired cuisine (gazpacho, grilled veal chop Alpina with morel cream sauce) is commendable, but the service can sometimes outfumble Fawlty Towers. **FYI:** Reservations recommended. **Open:** Breakfast Mon–Fri 6:30–

10:30am, Sat–Sun 7am–noon; lunch Mon–Fri 11:30am–2:30pm; dinner Mon–Sat 6–10pm. **Prices:** Main courses $21–$38; prix fixe $55. AE, CB, DC, DISC, MC, V. 🏛 VP &

Bridgeport Restaurant

3500 Halsted St; tel 312/247-2826. At 35th St. **American/Greek.** A classic Chicago diner where the waitstaff knows the customers by name. Folks from all walks of life stop in for Greek dishes, beef stew, and dessert. **FYI:** Reservations not accepted. Children's menu. No liquor license. **Open:** Daily 7am–9pm. **Prices:** Main courses $4–$11. No CC.

Bub City Crabshack & Bar-B-Q

901 W Weed St; tel 312/266-1200. 1 block S of North Ave; just N of Clyborn Ave. **Barbecue/Seafood.** A down-home, Texas-style eatery located in an old warehouselike garage. Decorated with everything from mounted marlins to buffalo heads, this place has an authentic Southern feel. Known for its Texas brisket and ribs, and crabs and fresh fish. Large aquariums let you preview your Dungeness crab and lobster. **FYI:** Reservations accepted. Blues/country music/rock. **Open:** Mon–Thurs 11:30am–10pm, Fri–Sat 11:30am–11pm, Sun 4–10pm. **Prices:** Main courses $7–$19. AE, DC, DISC, MC, V. VP &

Bukhara

2 E Ontario St; tel 312/943-0188. 2 blocks W of Michigan Ave. **Indian.** Authentic northwest Indian ambience with Indian brass service plates and cups, Persian rugs, and heavy wooden furniture from India. Calm, lovely restaurant. Chefs are visible behind glassed-in area. "Napkins" are colorful bib/aprons, and food is served family style. Specialty is tandoori-style cooking (clay pot over charcoal). Good for business meetings, family gatherings, couples. Children can eat as much or little of each dish as they like. **FYI:** Reservations recommended. **Open:** Lunch Mon–Fri 11:30am–2:30pm, Sat–Sun noon–3pm; dinner Sun–Thurs 5:30–9:30pm, Fri–Sat 5:30–10:30pm. **Prices:** Main courses $10–$25. AE, CB, DC, DISC, MC, V. ♥ 🖼 &

★ Busy Bee

1546 N Damen Ave (Wicker Park); tel 312/772-4433. Just S of North Ave, near Damen el stop on Blue Line. **American/Polish.** Old, very informal, family-run Polish restaurant with all recipes from home cooking of founder Sophie Madej. Decor is early Chicago, with photos of landmark buildings on walls. Everything is made fresh daily, and portions are ample. The Polish plate has stuffed cabbage, three pierogis (stuffed dumplings with buttered bread crumbs), a hamburger, sausage and sauerkraut, and mashed potatoes and gravy. Other specialties are kiszka (blood sausage with barley), cznarnia (duck blood soup), and flaczki (tripe soup). **FYI:** Reservations accepted. **Open:** Mon–Sat 7am–9pm, Sun 7am–7:30pm. Closed week of July 4. **Prices:** Main courses $5–$9. DISC, MC, V. 🖼

Cafe Ba-Ba-Reeba!

2024 N Halsted St (Lincoln Park); tel 312/935-5000. 3 blocks S of Fullerton. **Spanish.** Tapas are definitely the hot finger food of the moment in Chicago, and this "in" place does them as well as any restaurant in town. A glass of sherry makes the right complement to tasty tidbits such as marinated octopus with peppers, red onion, fennel, and citrus juice, or the bacalao and crab cakes with mango-lime vinaigrette, which can make you an aficionado of all things Spanish. Full entrees (such as paella) are available or you can easily make a meal out of the tapas. **FYI:** Reservations recommended. **Open:** Lunch Tues–Thurs 11:30am–2:30pm, Fri–Sat 11:30am–2pm, Sun noon–2pm; dinner Mon–Thurs 5–11pm, Fri–Sat 2pm–midnight, Sun 2–10pm. **Prices:** Main courses $12–$21. AE, CB, DC, DISC, MC, V. VP &

★ Cafe Bernard

2100 N Halsted St (Lincoln Park); tel 312/871-2100. **French.** A local favorite, this building served as a speakeasy in the 1920s for Al Capone and company. Now it is an intimate, romantic bistro serving country-style French food. Chef Bernard, a member of the prestigious Bocuse Chef Competition in France, takes pride in the careful preparation of his offerings. Specialties include bouillabaisse and cassoulet Toulousian, a casserole of white beans, pork, duck, lamb, and sausage. White chocolate mousse is served with mixed berries and a velvety chocolate sauce. **FYI:** Reservations accepted. **Open:** Mon–Thurs 5–10:30pm, Fri–Sat 5–11:30pm, Sun 5–10pm. **Prices:** Main courses $10–$18. AE, CB, DC, MC, V. ♥ &

Cafe Bolero

2252 N Western Ave (Bucktown); tel 312/227-9000. **Cuban.** An exciting find for those yearning for zesty meals served in an atmosphere that is at once immaculate and warm and inviting. Obvious pride is taken in the preparation and presentation of each dish. Specialties include stuffed fried plantains, grilled seafood kebabs, Cuban-style chicken with rice, grilled butterfly shrimp, and roasted pork with yucca. Desserts include a variety of rich custardlike flans made with coconut or other tropical fruits. Warm, friendly waitstaff. **FYI:** Reservations recommended. **Open:** Sun–Thurs 10am–10pm, Fri–Sat 10am–midnight. **Prices:** Main courses $5–$13. DISC, MC, V. 🍴 🖼 &

Cafe Escada

In Plaza Escada, 840 N Michigan Ave (Gold Coast); tel 312/751-2121. At Chestnut St. **Cafe/Eclectic.** Located on the fourth floor of the Escada boutique, with magnificent views of Michigan Ave and the lake. Light fare includes caesar salad, baguette sandwiches, and vegetable frittata. Daily specials of pasta and fish. Informal modeling on some days for the fashion-conscious. **FYI:** Reservations recommended. Dress code. Beer and wine only. No smoking. **Open:** Mon–Sat 11:30am–3pm. **Prices:** Lunch main courses $6–$10. MC, V. 🖼 &

★ **The Cape Cod Room**

In the Drake Hotel, 140 E Walton Place; tel 312/787-2200 ext 25. At the end of the Magnificent Mile. **Seafood.** Dark, cozy, complete with red-checkered tablecloths, wooden beams, and a seafarer's port atmosphere. Fine food, great service. Perfect for business dinners and quiet conversations. Great seafood flown in daily, an award-winning chef, and superb soups and sauces. Specialties include bookbinder soup, bouillabaisse, and lobster—from steamed to thermidor. Good selection of other shellfish. Also steak, veal, and lamb chops. All breads baked in original 1933 oven. **FYI:** Reservations recommended. **Open:** Daily noon–11:30pm. **Prices:** Main courses $19–$35. AE, CB, DC, DISC, MC, V. ♥ ▮ VP ⅛

Carlucci

2215 N Halsted St (Lincoln Park); tel 312/281-1220. Just S of Fullerton. **Italian.** From the faux-marble entry to the vaulted-atrium dining room and outdoor patio, this restaurant projects elegance and class. Chef Jonathan Harootunian brings creative flair (and an Italian accent) to his training in classic French cuisine. Seasonally available entrees include roasted duck breast with grilled onions and fig sauce, and pasta filled with leeks, zucchini, and carrots, and topped with prawns. This is the place to take important business contacts, people you want to impress, and anyone you love. (There have been so many marriage proposals here that the staff has champagne and flowers at the ready.) Groups of four to six can order a *dégustation* prix-fixe dinner with advance notice. **FYI:** Reservations recommended. Additional location: 6111 N River Rd, Rosemont (tel 708/518-0990). **Open:** Mon–Sat 5–11pm, Sun 5–10pm. **Prices:** Main courses $10–$20. AE, DC, DISC, MC, V. ♥ ⇑ VP ⅛

♥ **Charlie Trotter's**

816 W Armitage Ave (Lincoln Park); tel 312/248-6228. 1 block W of Halsted St. **New American.** Chef Charlie Trotter may be young, but he has gained an enviable reputation in the last few years because of the complicated, showy, and delicious dishes he creates from rather ordinary ingredients. The tasting menu at his namesake restaurant changes frequently (there are no à la carte items) and always includes a vegetarian option. Rabbit and braised-turnip lasagna with sweet pea sauce, seared salmon in a sesame crust, and spit-roasted free-range veal with zucchini are a few examples of his culinary artistry. Guests can even reserve a table (for an extra fee) so they can watch the artist at work. Most of the produce used is organic, and most of the meat is pasture-raised. The quiet, elegant ambience of the dining room, located in a turn-of-the-century townhouse, is accentuated by lavish floral arrangements. **FYI:** Reservations recommended. No smoking. **Open:** Tues–Thurs 5:30pm–close, Fri–Sat 5:15–11pm. Closed 2 weeks in Mar. **Prices:** Prix fixe $65–$85. AE, CB, DC, MC, V. VP ⅛

♥ **Chez Paul**

660 N Rush St (Magnificent Mile); tel 312/944-6680. Just W of Michigan Ave. **French.** Located in a historic 1875 mansion, this very special restaurant offers unique and intimate dining in rooms with fireplaces. Menu features light modern French cuisine, including grilled salmon tournedos with asparagus and brown sauce; grilled aged strip loin with button mushrooms and green peppercorn sauce; and fillet of beef grilled with Brie, oysters, and mushrooms. The whitefish is arguably the best in Chicago. **FYI:** Reservations recommended. Jacket required. **Open:** Lunch Mon–Fri 11:30am–2:30pm; dinner daily 5:30–10pm. **Prices:** Main courses $20–$30. AE, DC, DISC, MC, V. ♥ ▮ VP

♥ **The Chicago Chop House**

60 W Ontario St; tel 312/787-7100. **Steak.** Located in an 1887 Victorian brownstone filled with 1930s Chicago gangster photos and beautiful wood antiques. The main specialties are steaks—large, dry-aged, and flavorful cuts—chicken, and broiled and sautéed seafood. If you've left room for dessert, a good bet is Eli's rich cheesecake. **FYI:** Reservations recommended. Piano. Dress code. **Open:** Mon–Thurs 11:30am–11pm, Fri 11:30am–11:30pm, Sat 5–11:30pm, Sun 5–11pm. **Prices:** Main courses $16–$60. AE, CB, DC, DISC, MC, V. ▮ VP ⅛

★ **Club Lucky**

1824 W Wabansia Ave (Bucktown); tel 312/227-2300. 1 block N of North Ave; between Ashland and Damen. **Italian.** A favorite spot for locals to eat before or after a Bulls game. The decor is that of a Fifties-style supper club, with Naugahyde banquettes and Formica tables. The cuisine, however, is much more nouvelle, with grilled octopus, calamari, lasagna, and filet oreganatore among the menu specialties. **FYI:** Reservations recommended. **Open:** Mon–Thurs 11:30am–11:30pm, Fri 11:30am–midnight, Sat 5pm–midnight, Sun 4–10pm. **Prices:** Main courses $8–$19. AE, DC, DISC, MC, V. ⚏ 🚗 VP

Coco Pazzo

300 W Hubbard (River North); tel 312/836-0900. At Franklin. **Italian.** A spacious, beautifully finished loft space, with simple modern decor, colorful glass bottles, and paintings. An antique bar faces an open wood-burning oven of Spanish tiles. Interesting pastas such as penne alla Siciliana (quill pasta with tomato, garlic, capers, eggplant, black olives, and topped with aged ricotta cheese) are the backbone of the menu, which is rounded out by fresh seafood soups and meat entrees like raw, thinly sliced filet mignon topped with julienne vegetables and Parmesan. **FYI:** Reservations recommended. Dress code. **Open:** Lunch Mon–Fri 11:30am–2:30pm; dinner Mon–Sat 5:30–10:30pm, Sun 5–10pm. **Prices:** Main courses $13–$26. AE, CB, DC, MC, V. ♥ VP ⅛

The Corner Bakery

516 N Clark (River North); tel 312/644-8100. At Grand. **Italian.** All breads and desserts at this charming Italian-style bakery are made on premises. The luncheon menu features

chicken pesto on a baguette, roasted vegetables on a caramelized onion bread, and focaccia. Shares bar with adjoining Italian restaurant. **FYI:** Reservations not accepted. No smoking. Additional location: 676 St Clair (tel 266-2570). **Open:** Mon–Thurs 7am–10pm, Fri 7am–11pm, Sat 7:30am–11pm, Sun 8am–10pm. **Prices:** Main courses $6–$10. AE, CB, DC, DISC, MC, V. 🚢 📽 VP ⚕

♣ The Dining Room

In the Ritz-Carlton Chicago, 160 E Pearson St (Gold Coast); tel 312/266-1000. At Water Tower Place. **Continental/French.** A circular-octagonal salon of polished oak and chandeliers whose widely spaced tables, two-tier floor plan, and fountained patio create an air of quiet refinement. (The adjoining bar, however, loses some of its elegance with a large-screen TV dominating one corner.) The Continental-French menu is masterminded by award-winning chef Sara Stegner; the pastry chef, Sebastien Canonne, was trained at Gaston LeNotre in Paris. Seasonal offerings might include Colorado rack of lamb stuffed with pesto, artichokes, and oven-roasted tomatoes; sautéed turbot with braised cabbage and potato cake; or Muscovy duck breast in molasses-mustard marinade with duck hash. The wine list is outstanding. On Sundays the patio is given over to a bounteous buffet brunch (seatings at 10am and 1pm) complete with a low table for children. **FYI:** Reservations recommended. Piano. Children's menu. **Open:** Dinner Mon–Sat 6–11pm, Sun 6–10pm; brunch Sun 10:30am–2pm. **Prices:** Main courses $28–$39. AE, CB, DC, DISC, ER, MC, V. ♥ VP ⚕

Ed Debevic's

640 N Wells St (North Loop); tel 312/664-1707. At Ontario St. **Burgers/Diner.** Crowds of people come here to eat classic Mom-style comfort food (burgers, chili, meat loaf, malted milk shakes, apple pie à la mode) in the midst of decor and loud music from the Fifties, Sixties, and Seventies. Servers are in period garb and treat customers with a fresh, funny, friendly manner. **FYI:** Reservations not accepted. Additional location: 660 W Lake Cook Rd, Deerfield (tel 708/945-3242). **Open:** Sun–Thurs 11am–11pm, Fri–Sat 11am–1am. **Prices:** Main courses $5–$7. AE, CB, DC, DISC, MC, V. 📽 VP ⚕

Edwardo's

2120 N Halsted St (Lincoln Park); tel 312/871-3400. 2 blocks N of Armitage Ave. **Italian.** In the windows near the entrance to this casual, friendly place is a maze of fresh basil plants. Thin and deep-dish pizzas are enhanced with fresh herbs, plum tomatoes, vegetables, elephant garlic, sausage, cheese, and many more choices. Salads and desserts round out the menu. **FYI:** Reservations not accepted. Children's menu. Beer and wine only. Additional location: 1937 W Howard St (tel 761-7040). **Open:** Sun–Thurs 11am–11pm, Fri–Sat 11am–1am. **Prices:** Main courses $4–$19. AE, MC, V. 📽 🚗 ⚕

★ Eli's the Place for Steak

215 E Chicago Ave (Streeterville); tel 312/642-1393. E of Michigan Ave; next to Galter Carriage House. **American/Steak.** Just a block from the famous Water Tower, Eli's is celebrated for its cheesecake as well as its steaks. This is the place to indulge in chateaubriand for two or to have a perfect calf's liver Eli. Stained-glass panels depicting city scenes decorate the dining room. **FYI:** Reservations recommended. Piano. **Open:** Mon–Fri 11am–11pm, Sat–Sun 4–11pm. **Prices:** Main courses $17–$50. AE, CB, DC, DISC, MC, V. VP ⚕

Ennui Cafe

6981 N Sheridan (Rogers Park); tel 312/973-2233. At Lunt Ave. **Cafe.** Small, step-down storefront with sidewalk tables in summer. Between Northwestern University and Loyola University, this relaxed gathering place attracts students, local writers, academics, and chess players. Oversized cups of many types of coffee, with one free refill. Sandwiches, quiches, salads, scones, and muffins. **FYI:** Reservations not accepted. No liquor license. **Open:** Sun–Thurs 7:30am–11pm, Fri–Sat 7:30am–1am. **Prices:** Lunch main courses $1–$5. No CC. 🚢

Entre Nous

In the Fairmont, 200 N Columbus Dr (Grant Park); tel 312/565-7997. At Lake St. **New American.** Dimly lit restaurant with a warm, intimate air enhanced by floral arrangements. Available is a variety of beef, poultry (including ostrich), and seafood dishes prepared in interesting ways: tuna with sesame crust, seafood stew simmered in chardonnay-saffron sauce. **FYI:** Reservations recommended. Dress code. **Open:** Lunch Mon–Fri 11:30am–2:30pm; dinner Mon–Sat 5:30–10:30pm. **Prices:** Main courses $20–$28; prix fixe $28. AE, DISC, MC, V. VP ⚕

♣ Everest Room

In Chicago Board of Options Building, 440 S LaSalle St (South Loop); tel 312/663-8920. **New American/French.** Atop the Board of Options building, with a spectacular 40th-floor view of the city, the Everest Room has elegant table settings and fresh flower arrangements. Chef Jean Joho creates dazzling Alsatian and nouvelle French dishes, served with equally fine Alsatian and American wines. Startling contrasts are key here, with such inventive entrees as Texas-bred saddle of venison with wild huckleberries and gray shallots. **FYI:** Reservations recommended. Jacket required. **Open:** Tues–Thurs 5:30–9pm, Fri–Sat 5:30–10pm. **Prices:** Main courses $27–$33. AE, CB, DC, DISC, MC, V. ♥ 🏔 ▼ VP ⚕

Foodlife

In Water Tower Place, 835 N Michigan Ave (Gold Coast); tel 312/335-3663. Between Pearson and Chestnut Sts. **Eclectic.** Located in the beautiful Water Tower Place Mall, this unique garden-style food court is home to 13 different kitchens serving a variety of cuisines to fit different tastes for families. The emphasis is on low-fat foods, and every kitchen has something for vegetarians. Particular favorites range from grain dishes and make-it-yourself stir fry to burritos and pastas. Gooey desserts and chocolates are available for dessert. **FYI:** Reservations not accepted. Beer and wine only. No smoking. **Open:** Sun–Thurs 8am–9pm, Fri–Sat 8am–10pm. **Prices:** Main courses $6–$10. AE, CB, DC, DISC, MC, V.

★ Four Farthings Tavern and Grill

2060 N Cleveland Ave (Lincoln Park); tel 312/935-2060. At Lincoln and Dickens Aves. **Eclectic.** Traditional American meats, seafood, and pastas served in an English pub atmosphere. Try the sautéed Cajun shrimp and Andouille sausage served over angel-hair pasta and topped with a Cajun cream sauce. A place for fun, with a pool table, juke box, and satellite and cable sports broadcasts. **FYI:** Reservations recommended. Children's menu. **Open:** Mon–Thurs 11:30am–11pm, Fri–Sat 11:30am–midnight, Sun 11am–10pm. **Prices:** Main courses $11–$18. AE, CB, DC, DISC, MC, V.

★ Frontera Grill

445 N Clark St (River North); tel 312/661-1434. Between Illinois and Hubbard Sts. **Mexican.** Usually crowded, this casual joint is popular for its authentic Mexican food and beers. Colorful folk art decorates the walls while the open kitchen allows diners to watch the cooks at work. Menu specialties include chicken breast in a sauce of smoky chipotle chiles, herbs, and tangy thick cream. For lighter appetites, try the gazpacho poblano or enchiladas in red mole. **FYI:** Reservations accepted. Beer and wine only. **Open:** Lunch Tues–Fri 11:30am–2:30pm, Sat 10:30am–2:30pm; dinner Tues–Thurs 5:30–10pm, Fri–Sat 5–11pm. **Prices:** Main courses $9–$15. AE, CB, DC, DISC, MC, V.

Galans Ukrainian Cafe

2210 W Chicago Ave (Ukrainian Village); tel 312/292-1000. Between Damen and Western. **Ukrainian.** *Bitaemo!* The house specialty at this ultra-authentic ethnic cafe is the Kozak Feast. For $15.95, diners can fill up on borscht, salad, cabbage rolls, filled dumplings, Ukrainian sausage and sauerkraut, skewered beef tenderloin and pork, and potato pancake, plus coffee and dessert. **FYI:** Reservations accepted. Dancing. **Open:** Tues–Thurs 11am–10pm, Fri–Sat 11am–11pm, Sun noon–9pm. **Prices:** Main courses $7–$16; prix fixe $15.95. AE, DISC, MC, V.

★ Geja's

340 W Armitage Ave (Lincoln Park); tel 312/281-9101. At Lincoln Ave. **Fondue.** Named for a Moorish prince who established the forerunner of today's Geja's Cafe 30 years ago, it has been called Chicago's most romantic restaurant by the *Chicago Tribune*. The menu features the finest wines, cheeses, and spirits from all over the world. Guests prepare their own fondues at the table; fondue dinners include appetizers, salad, fresh vegetables with dipping sauces, and flaming chocolate fondue for dessert. **FYI:** Reservations

recommended. Guitar. **Open:** Mon–Thurs 5–10:30pm, Fri 5pm–midnight, Sat 5pm–12:30am, Sun 4:30–10pm. **Prices:** Prix fixe $19–$29. AE, CB, DC, DISC, MC, V.

★ Gibson's Steak House

1028 N Rush St (Gold Coast); tel 312/266-8999. At Bellevue. **Seafood/Steak.** A classic Chicago restaurant with a 1940s style and a long tradition. Photos of celebrities adorn the walls, and the busy dining room has booths and tables. Steak-lovers brag about this place, but it also serves fine seafood—chargrilled swordfish with peppercorns and brandy butter, and broiled Atlantic salmon with Nauvoo crumbs and cracked-mustard dressing. **FYI:** Reservations recommended. Piano. **Open:** Mon–Sat 5pm–midnight, Sun 4pm–midnight. **Prices:** Main courses $11–$29. CB, DC, DISC, MC, V.

★ Gino's East

160 E Superior St (Gold Coast); tel 312/943-1124. E of Michigan Ave; next to Neiman Marcus. **Italian.** A dark rathskeller with graffiti-strewn walls and funky decor. *People* magazine has written up Gino's as a mecca of deep-dish, Chicago-style pizza. Although it's a big place, it's so popular you may have to wait in line. Takeout available at the stand next door. **FYI:** Reservations recommended. Children's menu. Beer and wine only. **Open:** Mon–Thurs 11am–11pm, Fri–Sat 11am–midnight, Sun noon–10pm. **Prices:** Main courses $6–$10. AE, CB, DC, DISC, MC, V.

Gold Coast Dogs

418 N State St (River North); tel 312/527-1222. At Hubbard St. **Fast food.** A designer hot dog restaurant may seem like a contradiction in terms, but wait until you try these dogs covered in celery salt, fresh relish, hot peppers, and vegetables. The grilled chicken breasts are also a good bet, and there are homemade brownies for dessert. **FYI:** Reservations not accepted. No liquor license. Additional location: 325 S Franklin (tel 939-2624). **Open:** Mon–Fri 7am–midnight, Sat–Sun 10:30am–8pm. **Prices:** Main courses $4–$7. No CC.

★ Goose Island Brewing Company

1800 N Clybourn Ave (Lincoln Park); tel 312/915-0071. **Regional American.** Former car-wax factory turned into a polished warehouse pub with open brewery area and European-style bar. Specializes in microbrews, fish-and-chips, quesadillas. Pool table and darts complete the experience. **FYI:** Reservations recommended. Children's menu. **Open:** Mon–Thurs 11am–1am, Fri–Sat 11am–2am, Sun 11am–midnight. **Prices:** Main courses $8–$12. AE, DC, DISC, MC, V.

♥★ Gordon

500 N Clark St (River North); tel 312/467-9780. At Illinois. **New American/Continental.** For nearly 20 years, this restaurant has been a favorite with the chic and artsy crowd. The decor and food are elegant but the staff is down-home friendly. Fine food features "day-boat fish," roast loin of lamb with orange couscous, artichoke fritters, and a five-course "chef's special tasting." Dancing on Friday and Satur-

day nights. **FYI:** Reservations recommended. Jazz. Jacket required. **Open:** Sun–Thurs 5–9:30pm, Fri–Sat 5–11pm. Closed first week of Jan. **Prices:** Main courses $21–$29; prix fixe $55. AE, CB, DC, DISC, MC, V. 💟 📭 VP 🔙

✦ Greek Islands
200 S Halsted St (Greektown); tel 312/782-9855. At Adams St. **Greek.** The paintings on the walls will make you feel you're traveling in the Greek Isles, and the classic dishes will add to that impression. Saganaki is a favorite, partly because of its dramatic presentation. Family-style dinners include samples of a dozen different dishes—and there's plenty of good red Greek wine available to wash them down. **FYI:** Reservations not accepted. Additional location: 300 E 22nd St, Lombard (tel 708/932-4545). **Open:** Sun–Thurs 11am–midnight, Fri–Sat 11am–1am. **Prices:** Main courses $5–$20. AE, CB, DC, DISC, MC, V. 📭 VP 🔙

Green Door Tavern
678 N Orleans (River North); tel 312/664-5496. At Huron St. **American.** This historic frame structure was built just after the famed Chicago fire of 1871 (and before an ordinance prohibited the construction of wooden commercial buildings). In 1921 it was opened as a restaurant. The bar has many of its original fixtures, antique signs, and posters. Typical of the items on the sandwich menu are the Bearnaiseburger and the triple-decker grilled cheese. **FYI:** Reservations recommended. **Open:** Mon–Tues 7:30am–10pm, Wed–Sat 7:30am–11:30pm. **Prices:** Main courses $9–$11. AE, DC, DISC, MC, V. 🏛

✦ Harry Caray's
33 W Kinzie St (River North); tel 312/828-0966. At Dearborn. **American.** Sportscaster Caray is a Chicago institution, so it's only appropriate that his restaurant would be housed in a century-old converted warehouse. Museum-quality baseball memorabilia, photos, and a souvenir shop add to the All-American atmosphere and cuisine. Hearty, traditional fare—steaks, chops, chicken, fish, veal—and Italian favorites such as fettuccine Alfredo are served up in gigantic portions. **FYI:** Reservations accepted. Dress code. Additional location: 933 N Milwaukee, Wheeling (tel 708/537-2827). **Open:** Mon–Thurs 11:30am–10:30pm, Fri–Sat 11:30am–midnight, Sun noon–10pm. **Prices:** Main courses $9–$40. AE, CB, DC, DISC, MC, V. 🏛 📭 VP 🔙

Hat Dance
325 W Huron St (River North); tel 312/649-0066. At Orleans St. **Japanese/Mexican.** A number of the specialties at this hip Mexican/Japanese eatery go beyond the traditional—for example, the roasted pecan-crusted salmon and the tuna asada in sweet ginger-chive sauce. Margaritas are made with freshly squeezed fruits. **FYI:** Reservations recommended. **Open:** Lunch Mon–Fri 11:30am–2pm, Sat 11:30am–3:30pm; dinner Mon–Thurs 5:30–10pm, Fri 5:30–11:30pm, Sat 5–11:30pm, Sun 5–9pm. **Prices:** Main courses $8–$17. AE, CB, DC, DISC, MC, V. VP 🔙

✦ Heartland Cafe
7000 N Glenwood (Rogers Park); tel 312/465-8005. At Morse el stop; 1 block W of Sheridan Rd at Lunt. **Mexican/Vegetarian.** A funky Sixties-style coffeehouse offering "wholesome food for mind and body" (their motto). Chicken, turkey, fish, and farm-raised buffalo are on the menu alongside old vegetarian favorites like lentil burgers. There's a late night menu for late-daters; a gift shop sells books, T-shirts, and other souvenirs. **FYI:** Reservations not accepted. Additional locations: 1230 W Greenleaf (tel 274-6114); 25 N Stockton Dr (tel 935-7663). **Open:** Mon–Fri 7am–2am, Sat 8am–3am, Sun 8am–2am. **Prices:** Main courses $5–$13. AE, MC, V. ☕ 📭 🔙

✦ Ina's Kitchen
934 W Webster St (DePaul); tel 312/525-1116. 1 block S of Fullerton Ave. **New American.** A charming eatery serving up home-style breakfast and lunch dishes such as sour cream pancakes, oatmeal pancakes, and pasta frittata. **FYI:** Reservations not accepted. No liquor license. No smoking. **Open:** Tues–Fri 7am–3pm, Sat–Sun 8am–3pm. **Prices:** Lunch main courses $4–$9. No CC. ☕ 📭 🔙

Jada
1909 N Lincoln Ave (Lincoln Park); tel 312/280-2326. At Wisconsin St. **Thai.** Humble but highly regarded eatery. Offerings include *nam thok* (stir-fried spicy marinated beef) and chicken satay appetizers, lemongrass soup, and numerous traditional dishes like chili chicken and tomato squid. Vegetarian items also available. **FYI:** Reservations accepted. **Open:** Tues–Sat 5–11pm, Sun 4–10pm. **Prices:** Main courses $7–$9. AE, DISC, MC, V. 📭 🚗 🔙

✦ Jimmy's Woodlawn Tap
1172 E 55th St (Hyde Park); tel 312/643-5516. **Burgers.** A popular University of Chicago hangout marked by dark, grungy rooms, this is the only tavern within Hyde Park. A large selection of beers complements basic burgers-and-fries fare. "ABD" (all but dissertation) bartenders keep an encyclopedia handy to settle academic disputes. **FYI:** Reservations not accepted. **Open:** Mon–Fri 11am–2am, Sat 11am–3am, Sun 11am–2pm. **Prices:** Main courses $2–$5. No CC. 🔙

✦ Kiki's Bistro
900 Franklin St (River North); tel 312/335-5454. At Locust St. **French.** This rustic French inn is a little off the beaten path, but once you get there you will be welcomed by a large and comfortable bar and a very cozy dining room. The menu is heavy on culinary classics: escargots de Bourgogne, coquille St Jacques, and steak au poivre, for example. Pâtés and pastries are made fresh on premises daily. **FYI:** Reservations recommended. Dress code. **Open:** Lunch Mon–Fri 11:30am–2pm; dinner Mon–Thurs 5–10pm, Fri–Sat 5–11pm. **Prices:** Main courses $13–$17. AE, CB, DC, DISC, MC, V. 💟 VP 🔙

La Strada
155 N Michigan Ave (Loop); tel 312/565-2200. At Randolph St. **Italian.** A charming and elegant retreat in the middle of

busy Michigan Avenue and the Loop. Fine Italian cuisine includes scaloppine of veal Strada and pollo saltimbocca, as well as many pastas, steaks, and great desserts. **FYI:** Reservations recommended. Piano. Dress code. **Open:** Lunch Mon–Fri 11:30am–2:30pm; dinner Mon–Thurs 5–10pm, Fri–Sat 5–11pm. **Prices:** Main courses $18–$28; prix fixe $26. AE, CB, DC, DISC, MC, V. ⦿ ▣ VP ⌖

Lindo Mexico

2642 N Lincoln Ave (Lincoln Park); tel 312/871-4832. 3 blocks N of Fullerton Ave. **Mexican.** *Lindo* means "beautiful" in Spanish, and that certainly sums up the ambience here. Mariachi players stroll through the four dining rooms, as well as the garden, patio, and bar. If you are not in a hurry, order paella marinara—a spicy mixture of shrimp, scallops, clams, and squid that takes about a half-hour to prepare. Great variety of margaritas and other tropical drinks. **FYI:** Reservations accepted. Additional locations: 1934 Maple, Evanston (tel 708/475-3435); 8990 N Milwaukee, Niles (tel 708/296-2540). **Open:** Sun–Thurs 11am–2am, Fri–Sat 11am–3am. **Prices:** Main courses $6–$15. AE, CB, DC, DISC, ER, MC, V. 🚗 VP

★ Lou Mitchell's

625 W Jackson Blvd (Loop); tel 312/939-3111. W of Union Station. **American.** A popular spot for breakfast, so be prepared to wait. The wait, however, is usually short, and customers are offered a box of Milk Duds to pass the time until seating, usually at a long, communal table. Choose from fourteen different omelets, pancakes, waffles, and french toast. Orange marmalade, breads, and pastries are all made from scratch. Soups, salads, and sandwiches—as well as all breakfast items—available for lunch. **FYI:** Reservations not accepted. No liquor license. **Open:** Mon–Fri 5:30am–3pm, Sat 5:30am–3pm, Sun 7am–3pm. **Prices:** No CC. ⌖

Mambo Grill

412 N Clark St (River North); tel 312/467-9797. Between Hubbard and Kinzie Sts. **International.** A festive atmosphere heightened by rhythmic Latin music. The menu features dishes from Cuba, Mexico, Nicaragua, Ecuador, Argentina, Brazil, and Guatemala, in addition to a touch of Santa Fe cuisine. Specialties include grilled tuna with chayote relish, baby back ribs with spicy guava barbecue sauce, pork chops grilled with mango sauce, and chicken with chili–black bean sauce. **FYI:** Reservations not accepted. Dress code. **Open:** Mon–Sat 11am–1am, Sun 5–9pm. **Prices:** Main courses $6–$15. AE, DC, DISC, MC, V.

Mare

400 N Clark St (River North); tel 312/245-9933. Between Illinois and Hubbard Sts. **Italian/Seafood.** This place will make you feel like you're in an Italian villa by the sea. The interior features white and blue trim in the bar, frescolike murals of mermaids, mermen, and sea life on the ceiling, faux-stone walls, and fabric-draped ceilings. Choose from a variety of pasta, pizza, seafood, chicken, pork, lamb, and beef, plates. Complimentary antipasto in the bar Mon–Fri. **FYI:** Reservations recommended. **Open:** Lunch Mon–Fri 11:30am–2pm; dinner Mon–Thurs 5:30–10pm, Fri–Sat 5:30–10pm, Sun 5–9pm. **Prices:** Main courses $7–$19. AE, DC, MC, V. VP ⌖

★ Medici

1327 E 57th St (Hyde Park); tel 312/667-7394. **American.** Booths covered in student graffiti lend a collegiate atmosphere to this airy two-story restaurant serving pizza (both pan and thin-crust), hamburgers (including a half-pounder on black bread), sandwiches, salads, and milkshakes and malts. **FYI:** Reservations not accepted. No liquor license. Additional location: Harper Court (tel 667-4008). **Open:** Sun–Thurs 7am–midnight, Fri–Sat 9am–1am. **Prices:** Main courses $4–$9. MC, V. ⌖

Mekong

4953 N Broadway (Uptown); tel 312/271-0206. At Argyle Ave. **Vietnamese.** Anchor point of the new Chinatown on the north side,with authentic Vietnamese food ranging from satisfying rice and noodle dishes to burning charcoal fire-pot soup—shrimp, pork, chicken, mushrooms, bamboo shoots, and water chestnuts. Dishes are served family style, so guests can taste a variety of foods. Spices vary from mild to quite hot, and lemongrass is employed liberally. A good family place. **FYI:** Reservations accepted. Beer and wine only. **Open:** Sun–Thurs 10am–10pm, Fri–Sat 10am–11pm. **Prices:** Main courses $5–$19. AE, DC, DISC, MC, V. 👥

★ Michael Jordan's

500 N LaSalle St (River North); tel 312/644-DUNK. Between Illinois St and Grand Ave. **American.** Owned (and often frequented by) Chicago's most popular sports hero. (The upper-level dining room even has windows where diners can sneak a peak at Michael and his guests when he's around!) The bar/lounge/grill has space to spread out and play games, and there's a gift shop full of Bulls souvenirs and other sports memorabilia. For a theme restaurant, the food is surprisingly good—burgers, barbecue, and seafood entrees are complemented by tasty soups (chicken gumbo is a standout) and homey side dishes like macaroni and cheese. Michael's Own banana pudding makes a winning finish. **FYI:** Reservations not accepted. Children's menu. **Open:** Sun–Thurs 11am–10pm, Fri–Sat 11am–11:30pm. **Prices:** Main courses $7–$24. AE, CB, DC, DISC, MC, V. 👥 🚗 VP ⌖

★ Morton's of Chicago

1050 N State St (Gold Coast); tel 312/266-4820. ½ block N of Oak St. **Steak.** The first Morton's opened in Chicago in 1978 and rapidly built a reputation as a first-class steak house. The servers roll a cart to the table, where diners can pick their own fish, lobster, or cut of beef or veal. **FYI:** Reservations recommended. Dress code. **Open:** Mon–Sat 5:30–11pm, Sun 5–10pm. **Prices:** Main courses $16–$30. AE, CB, DC, DISC, MC, V. VP ⌖

Moti Mahal

1033 W Belmont Ave; tel 312/348-4392. At Kenmore St. **Indian.** A clean and simple setting for enjoying tandoor cooking. On display are pictures of ancient Indian statues from the Ajanta Caves. The best value is the moderately priced all-you-can-eat buffet, which offers many exotic Indian dishes, offered on weekends. The breads are recommended. **FYI:** Reservations accepted. BYO. Additional location: 2525 W Devon Ave (tel 262-2080). **Open:** Mon–Thurs noon–10pm, Fri–Sun noon–11pm. **Prices:** Main courses $5–$14. AE, MC, V.

Mrs Levy's Delicatessen

In Sears Tower, 233 S Wacker Dr (South Loop); tel 312/993-0530. **Deli.** This bustling delicatessen has an authentic look and feel to it. The decor features a spotless black-and-white tile floor and a gallery of celebrity photos. Sandwiches (including many triple-decker options) are well-packed with deli favorites, while staples such as knishes, blintzes, and soups are made daily. The cheesecake is a winner and the soda fountain is highly popular. **FYI:** Reservations accepted. Beer and wine only. **Open:** Mon–Fri 6:30am–3pm. **Prices:** Lunch main courses $4–$7. AE, CB, DC, DISC, MC, V. &

Nick's Fishmarket

One First National Bank Plaza (Loop); tel 312/621-0200. At Monroe and Dearborn. **Continental/Seafood.** Leave behind the bustle of Monroe St and step into the elevator that descends to the softly lit, hushed splendor of a very private sort of lair. The atmosphere here is anything but casual; this is a place for serious business and romance. Heavily padded leather banquettes provide exquisite comfort in the main dining room, and there is a wood-paneled private room and a black-marble bar area with pin spotlights. Seafood abounds, from oysters on the half shell and lobster bisque to lobster thermidor and Dover sole. Also available are roasted Amish chicken, filet mignon, and pastas. **FYI:** Reservations recommended. Dress code. Additional location: 10275 W Higgins Rd, Rosemont (tel 708/298-8200). **Open:** Lunch Mon–Fri 11:30am–3pm; dinner Mon–Thurs 5:30–11pm, Fri–Sat 5:30–11:30pm. **Prices:** Main courses $19–$50. AE, CB, DC, DISC, MC, V. ● VP &

Oo La La!

3335 N Halsted St (Lincoln Park); tel 312/935-7708. **French/Italian.** Located in Lakeview, Chicago's premier gay neighborhood, this place is popular with both gay and straight customers—including the occasional celebrity—in search of a very hip, young, LA-style ambience. In warm weather, guests can sit in the lovely, walled, ivy-lined terrace. After dinner, the restaurant transforms into a nightclub—really its true identity and a clue to why the food often takes a backseat to hipness. Popular choices are tomato-pumpkin ravioli, poulet balsamique, and tiramisù. Each week brings a different special. **FYI:** Reservations recommended. **Open:** Dinner Mon–Sat 5:30–11pm; brunch Sun 10am–3pm. **Prices:** Main courses $11–$16. AE, MC, V. VP

★ Orbit Restaurant & Cocktail Lounge

2948-54 N Milwaukee Ave (Avondale); tel 312/276-1355. At Central Park. **American/Polish.** Simple, traditional decor, with portraits of Polish kings hanging in the Royalty Room. Ethnic specialties include roast veal, sausages, sauerkraut, beef roll, cheese blintzes, and boiled whitefish topped with vegetables. **FYI:** Reservations accepted. **Open:** Sun–Fri 6am–midnight, Sat 6am–2:30am. **Prices:** Main courses $12–$21; prix fixe $11–$15. AE, CB, DC, DISC, MC, V. 👥 VP &

The Original A-1

401 E Illinois St (North Pier); tel 312/644-0300. **Barbecue.** A fun family place with a games room and pool table. The decor follows a cowboy motif, with saddles on the wall, hay stuffed into the ceiling, and vinyl cowhide tablecloths. The kitchen turns out ribs and traditional Tex-Mex. Side dishes include delicious baked beans, jalapeño mashed potatoes, corn bread, and tortilla soup. **FYI:** Reservations accepted. Children's menu. **Open:** Mon–Thurs 11:30am–4pm, Fri–Sat 11:30am–midnight, Sun 11:30am–9pm. **Prices:** Main courses $6–$17. AE, CB, DC, DISC, MC, V. 👥

Palette's

1030 N State St; tel 312/440-5200. At Oak St. **New American.** Colorful murals and whimsical metal furnishings mixed with antiques create a charming atmosphere in which to enjoy great seafood, chicken, steaks, and pasta entrees. Escolar fish from the Gulf of Mexico—seared, sautéed, and served with avocado relish—is one of the popular items. Double-breasted chicken stuffed with asparagus and mushrooms, herbs, and bread crumbs makes a hit as well. **FYI:** Reservations recommended. Piano. **Open:** Lunch Mon–Fri 11am–2:30pm; dinner daily 5pm–2am. **Prices:** Main courses $8–$28. AE, CB, DC, DISC, MC, V. ● VP &

Pane Caldo

72 E Walton St (Gold Coast); tel 312/649-0055. **Italian.** This charming Italian cafe just across the street from Bloomingdale's provides an ideal shopping break. Generous portions of grilled double lamb chops, salads, and pastas are a hit at lunch; Sunday brunch features live jazz. Validated parking. **FYI:** Reservations recommended. Dress code. **Open:** Lunch daily 11:30am–2:30pm; dinner Sun–Thurs 5–10pm, Fri–Sat 5–10:30pm. **Prices:** Main courses $10–$19. AE, DC, DISC, MC, V. VP

Papagus Greek Taverna

In the Embassy Suites, 620 N State St (River North); tel 312/642-8450. Between Ontario and Ohio Sts. **Greek.** Hearty, traditional Greek food served in warm, friendly surroundings reminiscent of a rustic taverna, with stone floors and walls, and wood and canvas ceilings. **FYI:** Reservations recommended. **Open:** Sun–Thurs 11:30am–10pm, Fri–Sat 11:30am–midnight. **Prices:** Main courses $9–$25. AE, DC, DISC, MC, V. VP &

★ **Paul Zakopane Harna's Restaurant**
2943 N Milwaukee Ave; tel 312/342-1464. Just S of Belmont Ave. **American/Polish.** In the center of Polish Chicago, this very friendly, upbeat, family place offers a full array of Polish delicacies. Beet soup, apple-stuffed duck, beef tongue, sausage and sauerkraut, and duck blood soup are offered along with American sandwiches and entrees. Free parking across street in Avondale bank lot. **FYI:** Reservations accepted. **Open:** Daily 7am–10pm. **Prices:** Main courses $5–$11. AE. 👥 ♿

Piccolo Mondo Cafe
1647 E 56th St (Hyde Park); tel 312/643-1106. Across from Museum of Science and Industry. **Italian.** Features traditional family-style Italian cuisine in an urbane but casual atmosphere. Its food shop stocks a selection of imported cheeses, meats, coffees, and other deli foods. **FYI:** Reservations recommended. **Open:** Mon–Thurs 11:30am–9pm, Fri–Sat 11:30am–10pm, Sun 3–9pm. **Prices:** Main courses $9–$15. DISC, MC, V. 💟 ♿

★ **Pizzeria Due**
619 N Wabash Ave (Navy Pier District); tel 312/943-2400. At Ontario St. **Italian/Pizza.** Classic Chicago pizza parlor located in the restaurant that claims to be the inventor of the deep-dish style. A dark wood bar, paneled walls, and red and white checked tablecloths help create a publike ambience. The pizza is scrumptious; other Italian specialties include antipasti, lasagna, and ravioli. **FYI:** Reservations not accepted. **Open:** Sun–Thurs 11am–1am, Fri–Sat 11am–2am. **Prices:** Main courses $10–$20. AE, CB, DC, DISC, MC, V.

Prairie
In Hyatt on Printers Row, 500 S Dearborn St (South Loop); tel 312/663-1143. At Congress Pkwy. **Regional American.** Fresh flowers on tables and a polished, professional waitstaff make for pleasant dining. Popular not only with hotel guests, but also with patrons of the nearby ballet, theaters, and opera. Menu specialties have included buffalo steak and grilled swordfish. **FYI:** Reservations recommended. Children's menu. **Open:** Breakfast Mon–Fri 6:30–10am, Sat–Sun 7–11am; lunch daily 11am–2pm; dinner Sun–Thurs 5–10pm, Fri–Sat 5–11pm. **Prices:** Main courses $15–$26. AE, CB, DC, DISC, ER, MC, V. 💟 VP ♿

♥ **Printer's Row**
550 S Dearborn St (South Loop); tel 312/461-0780. At Harrison Ave. **New American.** Wood walls, ceiling lamps over tables, half-curtains on the windows, and flowers on tables produce a warm ambience. Imaginative and intriguing combinations of ingredients characterize the frequently changing menu. Recent entrees have included spiced, roast pork chop; marinated, grilled lamb chop with Caribbean flavorings; and salmon with curry and dill. Venison offered regularly. **FYI:** Reservations recommended. **Open:** Lunch Mon–Fri 11:30am–2:30pm; dinner Mon–Thurs 5–10pm, Fri–Sat 5–11pm. **Prices:** Main courses $15–$25. AE, CB, DC, DISC, MC, V. ♿

Pump Room
In the Omni Ambassador East Hotel, 1301 N State Pkwy (Near North/Gold Coast); tel 312/266-0360. At Goethe St. **New American.** The glamorous fun starts when you walk through the famous entrance lined with hundreds of photos of some of the celebrities who have dined here over the years. The elegant room itself is topped with a net ceiling glittering with tiny lights. Prime rib and crispy roast duck are the house specialties. **FYI:** Reservations recommended. Piano. Jacket required. **Open:** Breakfast Mon–Thurs 7–11am; dinner Mon–Thurs 6–10pm, Fri 6pm–midnight, Sat 5pm–midnight, Sun 5–10pm; brunch Sun 10:30am–2:30pm. **Prices:** Main courses $18–$32. AE, DC, DISC, MC, V. VP ♿

Ranalli's Pizzeria, Libations & Collectibles
1925 N Lincoln Ave; tel 312/642-4700. 1 block S of Armitage Ave. **Italian.** This neighborhood eating and drinking spot has a large sports bar and an even larger beer garden featuring well over 100 beers from around the world. Food favorites are specialty pizzas, succulent ribs, and calamari. **FYI:** Reservations recommended. Additional locations: 337 S Dearborn (tel 922-8888); 24 W Elm (tel 440-7000). **Open:** Sun–Fri 10:30am–2am, Sat 10:30am–3am. **Prices:** Main courses $7–$14. AE, DC, DISC, MC, V. VP

★ **Reza's**
5255 N Clark (Andersonville); tel 312/561-1898. N of Foster Ave. **Persian.** Garage-size double doors open to the street in good weather lend a cafelike atmosphere to this well-established Persian restaurant. Broad selection of foods include lamb, beef, poultry, seafood, and vegetarian dishes. Seasonings are mild, and dishes can be served family style, making this an ideal place for children or for groups. The vegetarian eggplant steak or the maust museer—a dip for the pita bread—are especially good. **FYI:** Reservations accepted. Additional location: 432 W Ontario (tel 664-4500). **Open:** Daily 11am–midnight. **Prices:** Main courses $7–$13. AE, MC, V. 👥

⑤★ **Rose Angelis**
1314 W Wrightwood Ave (Lakeview/Wrightwood); tel 312/296-0081. **Italian/Seafood.** Friendly, hospitable neighborhood trattoria, tucked away on a quiet street. Offers generous helpings of pastas, chicken, and seafood. **FYI:** Reservations not accepted. **Open:** Tues–Thurs 5–10pm, Fri–Sat 5–11pm, Sun 4:30–9pm. **Prices:** Main courses $8–$10. DISC, MC, V. ♿

Rosebud's on Rush
55 E Superior St (Magnificent Mile); tel 312/266-6444. Just W of Michigan Ave. **Seafood/Steak.** Popular, always-busy restaurant with a small art deco bar downstairs and several dining rooms with rather close seating. Entrees include award-winning pasta, chicken Vesuvio Chicago-style (white wine, olive oil, garlic, peas and potatoes), peppercorn steak, lamb chops. **FYI:** Reservations accepted. Piano. **Open:**

Lunch Mon–Fri 11am–3pm; dinner Mon–Thurs 5–10:30pm, Fri–Sat 5–11:30pm, Sun 4–10pm. **Prices:** Main courses $10–$30. CB, DISC, MC, V. VP

The Saigon Vietnamese Restaurant & Shabu Shabu

232 W Cermak Rd (Chinatown); tel 312/808-1318. **Pan-Asian.** A simple, clean pan-Asian restaurant with a large selection of dishes borrowing from Vietnamese, Chinese, Thai, and Malaysian cuisine. The Vietnamese-style spring rolls go nicely with the Chinese beer. Shabu shabu is a kind of Chinese fondue where the diner adds shrimp, fish, and veggies to a steaming bowl of hot broth. **FYI:** Reservations not accepted. Beer and wine only. **Open:** Daily 11am–3am. **Prices:** Main courses $6–$12. AE, DC, DISC, ER, MC, V. ⛾ &

The Saloon Steakhouse

In the Seneca Hotel, 200 E Chestnut St (Magnificent Mile); tel 312/280-5454. Just E of Michigan Ave. **American.** Simplicity tinged with big-city chic is a good way to describe this particularly friendly, relaxing place, where neighbors in this upscale area stop in and chat with out-of-town visitors. The full-service steak house offers down-home meals like meat loaf and mashed potatoes as well as classics like oysters Rockefeller. **FYI:** Reservations recommended. **Open:** Mon–Sat 11am–11pm, Sun 4–11pm. **Prices:** Main courses $10–$25. AE, CB, DC, DISC, MC, V. ⛾ &

★ Schulien's Restaurant and Saloon

2100 W Irving Park Rd (North Center); tel 312/487-2100. Just W of jct Lincoln, Damen, and Irving Park. **American/German.** In business since 1877, this restaurant has a wealth of artifacts, old photos and newspapers, and family heirlooms. Tiffany lamps provide a warm glow. The food is no nonsense, ample, and tasty. Wiener schnitzel, bratwurst, rack of lamb, steaks, and chops have been joined by such lighter fare as pastas and salads. **FYI:** Reservations accepted. Magician. Children's menu. **Open:** Tues–Fri 11:30am–midnight, Sat 4–11pm, Sun 4–9pm. **Prices:** Main courses $14–$21. AE, DISC, MC, V. ▮ ⛾

★ Scoozi!

410 W Huron St (River North); tel 312/943-5900. At Sedgwick St. **Italian.** The gigantic red tomato atop the entrance announces this contemporary but rustic restaurant serving country Italian food in a boisterous atmosphere. The menu offers a wide variety of antipasti, traditional Italian thin-crust pizzas, salads, pastas, and other entrees, with many selections available in both small and large portions. Impressive selection of Italian wines. **FYI:** Reservations accepted. **Open:** Lunch Mon–Fri 11:30am–2pm; dinner Mon–Thurs 5–10:30pm, Fri–Sat 5–11:30pm, Sun 5–9pm. **Prices:** Main courses $12–$20. AE, DC, DISC, MC, V. ♥ ⛾ VP &

♣ The Seasons

In Four Seasons Hotel Chicago, 120 E Delaware Place (Gold Coast); tel 312/280-8800. **New American.** One of three dining spots on the seventh floor, or lobby level, above a shopping mall, this is a gracious, high-ceilinged room with widely spaced tables and elegant Schonwald china and place settings. Lunchtime dishes, like organic farmhouse greens with wild huckleberry vinaigrette and Lake Superior whitefish with vine-ripened tomatoes, are meticulously presented. At dinner, prices double but the offerings are even more tempting—Maryland crab–shiitake mushroom cake with charred papaya relish, roasted Walla Walla onion soup with smoked duck, roasted Atlantic salmon fillet with horseradish crust. A mostly American wine list complements the New American cuisine. Service is knowledgeable but could be more attentive (don't assume that the maitre d' will stop by to see how things are). The ambience in The Cafe in the next room is equally gracious and the dishes come from the same kitchen, but the prices are a notch lower. **FYI:** Reservations recommended. Piano. Children's menu. **Open:** Breakfast Mon–Sat 6:30–10:30am, Sun 6:30–10am; lunch Mon–Sat 11:30am–2pm; dinner daily 6–10pm; brunch Sun 10:30am–1:30pm. **Prices:** Main courses $15–$40. AE, CB, DC, DISC, ER, MC, V. VP &

Sesi's Seaside Cafe & Gallery

6219 N Sheridan Rd; tel 312/764-0544. 1 block N of Granville Ave. **International/Mediterranean.** A charming cafe and gallery located in a quaint two-story building right off a small park on Lake Michigan. Patio dining offers beautiful views of the lake, while the cozy, more formal dining area upstairs features a fireplace, full bookshelves, artwork on easels, and couches. The interesting international menu emphasizes Mediterranean fare. Moderately priced favorites include Mediterranean-style vegetarian dishes, Turkish kofta kebab and kadayif, and delicious homemade pastries like quince bake. **FYI:** Reservations not accepted. Folk/guitar. No liquor license. **Open:** Peak (June–Aug) Sun–Thurs 10am–11pm, Fri–Sat 9am–11pm. **Prices:** Main courses $5–$6. DISC, MC, V. ⛾ &

Shaw's Crab House and Blue Crab Lounge

21 E Hubbard St (Near North/Magnificent Mile); tel 312/527-2722. At State St. **Seafood.** This seafood house is really two restaurants in one. The Crab House, the main dining room that resembles a 1950s-style, East Coast seafood restaurant, serves more than 40 fresh seafood entrees as well as chicken, beef, and pasta dishes and its trademark key lime pie. The Blue Crab Lounge, with high stools and brick walls, is an oyster bar featuring oysters on the half shell, clams, lobster, and crab dishes. **FYI:** Reservations recommended. Blues/jazz. Dress code. **Open:** Lunch Mon–Fri 11:30am–2pm; dinner Mon–Thurs 5:30–10pm, Fri–Sat 5–11pm, Sun 5–10pm. **Prices:** Main courses $13–$19. AE, CB, DC, DISC, MC, V. VP &

♣ The Signature Room at the 95th

In John Hancock Building, 875 N Michigan Ave (Magnificent Mile); tel 312/787-9596. Between Chestnut St and Delaware Place. **American.** Located atop the John Hancock Building on the 95th floor, this elegant restaurant offers a spectacular view of the city skyline and Lake Michigan. The romantic, sophisticated ambience is heightened by large chandeliers and exquisite flower arrangements. Marinated and grilled ahi tuna with whipped potatoes, turnips and Barolo sauce, is one of the fine contemporary American dishes. Known as "the restaurant Chicago looks up to" for more than one reason. **FYI:** Reservations accepted. Jacket required. **Open:** Breakfast Mon–Fri 7–10:30am; lunch Mon–Fri 11am–2:30pm, Sat 11:30am–2:30pm; dinner Mon–Thurs 5:30–10pm, Fri–Sun 5:30–11pm; brunch Sun 10:30am–2pm. **Prices:** Main courses $22–$30. AE, DC, DISC, MC, V. ♥ ▲ &

65 Seafood Restaurant

2414 S Wentworth (Chinatown); tel 312/225-7060. S of Cermak Rd. **Chinese.** A Chinatown mainstay, this inviting bi-level establishment with a tastefully decorated lobby has a charming ambience. Family and group dinner specials allow plenty of sampling. Seafood choices range from shark fin soup to crab, oyster, clam, and lobster dishes. Friendly service. **FYI:** Reservations recommended. Additional locations: 336 N Michigan (tel 372-0306); 225 S Canal St (tel 474-0065). **Open:** Sun–Thurs 11:30am–10pm, Fri–Sat 11:30am–11pm. **Prices:** Main courses $8–$23. AE, DC, DISC, MC, V. &

★ Sole Mio

917 W Armitage Ave (Lincoln Park); tel 312/477-5858. Between Halsted and Sheffield; ½ block from Armitage el. **French.** Friendly, cozy, but casually elegant neighborhood bistro, reportedly favored by Robert De Niro when he's in town. Menu specialties include crispy duck and soft shell crab, prepared with a French flair. **FYI:** Reservations accepted. **Open:** Lunch Mon–Fri 11:30am–2pm; dinner Mon–Thurs 5:30–10:30pm, Fri–Sat 5:30–11pm, Sun 5:30–10pm. **Prices:** Main courses $10–$19. AE, DC, MC, V. ♥ ▲ VP

♥ Spiaggia

In One Magnificent Mile, 980 N Michigan Ave; tel 312/280-2750. At the end of the Magnificent Mile. **Italian.** Elegant, upscale, modern decor with most tables overlooking Oak Street Beach or Michigan Ave. Authentic regional dishes from chef Paul Bartolotta. All pastas and sauces are homemade. Specialties include wood-roasted salmon with sautéed spinach and black olive sauce, baked red snapper with artichokes and fresh oregano. **FYI:** Reservations recommended. Piano. **Open:** Lunch Mon–Sat 11:30am–2pm; dinner daily 5:30–10pm. **Prices:** Main courses $26–$29. AE, CB, DC, DISC, MC, V. ♥ ▲

★ Ticker Tape Bar & Bistro

In the Midland Hotel, 172 W Adams St (Loop); tel 312/332-1200. Between Wells and LaSalle Sts. **Eclectic.** Charming art deco bistro near the Financial Exchange, in the historic Midland Hotel. Entrees run the gamut from meat loaf and mashed potatoes to linguine with sausage, mushrooms, basil, and marinara sauce, and chicken curry with rice, almonds, raisins, and coconut. You might even hear a "big deal" being consummated at the next table. **FYI:** Reservations not accepted. **Open:** Daily 11am–11pm. **Prices:** Main courses $8–$17. AE, CB, DC, DISC, MC, V. ■ &

★ Topolobampo

445 N Clark St (River North); tel 312/661-1434. At Hubbard St. **Mexican.** A colorful restaurant in the same building as the Frontera Grill, featuring a more elegant atmosphere and regional recipes from all parts of Mexico. The fresh Gulf shrimp with toasted garlic, roasted duck with chile ancho, and rainbow trout stuffed with squash blossoms and poblano chiles all redefine American conceptions about Mexican cooking. Excellent margaritas. **FYI:** Reservations recommended. Beer and wine only. **Open:** Lunch Tues–Fri 11:30am–2:30pm; dinner Tues–Thurs 5:30–9:30pm, Fri–Sat 5:30–10:30pm. **Prices:** Main courses $18–$21. AE, CB, DC, DISC, MC, V. VP &

Trattoria Gianni

1711 N Halsted St (Lincoln Park); tel 312/266-1976. Near Steppenwolf and Royal George Theaters. **Italian.** Family-owned trattoria specializing in regional Italian food. Popular entrees include spaghetti with eggplant; Italian rice with seafood; chicken cooked with olives, rosemary, and hot peppers; and salmon baked with capers and white wine. Tiramisù for dessert. **FYI:** Reservations accepted. **Open:** Dinner Tues–Thurs 5–11pm, Fri–Sat 5–11:30pm, Sun 4–10pm; brunch Sun noon–3pm. **Prices:** Main courses $9–$19. AE, DC, MC, V. VP &

Tucci Benucch

900 N Michigan Ave (Magnificent Mile); tel 312/266-2500. **Italian.** The restaurant is segmented into rooms decorated to resemble an old Italian house: there's a sun room with a draped ivy canopy, a bedroom, dining room, and a kitchen next to the real kitchen. The menu features thin-crust pizza and interesting salad combinations (spinach goat cheese salad with oven-dried tomatoes and pine nuts); roasted garlic chicken, which is prepared in several different ways, is the main entree. **FYI:** Reservations accepted. Children's menu. No smoking. **Open:** Mon–Thurs 11:30am–10pm, Fri–Sat 11:30am–11pm, Sun noon–9pm. **Prices:** Main courses $8–$12. AE, CB, DC, DISC, MC, V. &

Tucci Milan

6 W Hubbard St (River North); tel 312/222-0044. At State St. **Italian.** The open kitchen, original artwork, and floor-to-ceiling walls create a comfortable and sophisticated atmosphere. The antipasto is mostly vegetarian, with vegetables from organic farms in Illinois. Fish is flown in daily from Boston. Fish and other meats are grilled over oak and cherry wood. **FYI:** Reservations recommended. **Open:** Mon–Thurs 11:30am–10pm, Fri 11:30am–11pm, Sat noon–11pm, Sun 5–9pm. **Prices:** Main courses $5–$20. AE, CB, DC, DISC, MC, V. VP &

Tuttaposto
646 N Franklin St (River North); tel 312/943-6262. Between Ohio St and Grand Ave. **Mediterranean.** A Mediterranean taverna with lively colors, warm woods, and concrete slab floors. A great place for nibbling on appetizers, it offers a 10-item, pan-Mediterranean antipasto platter. The frequently changing menu also includes distinctive selections like salt cod with truffle oil, wood-roasted rabbit with pancetta, and grilled calamari with smoked tomato, arugula, and garlic pita. Large selection of pastas and pizzas. **FYI:** Reservations recommended. Children's menu. **Open:** Lunch Mon–Fri 11:30am–2pm; dinner Mon–Thurs 5–10pm, Fri–Sat 5–11pm, Sun 5–9pm. **Prices:** Main courses $12–$22. AE, DC, DISC, MC, V. VP &

★ **Urbis Orbis**
1934 W North Ave (Wicker Park); tel 312/252-4446. 1 block E of Milwaukee. **Coffeehouse/Vegetarian.** Artsy, friendly, and slightly funky atmosphere in which to enjoy good light fare and coffees. The menu includes soups (Cuban black bean, tomato-zucchini, cold gazpacho), salads, vegetarian lasagna, curried chicken pie. An irregular schedule of entertainment is offered in a separate theater space **FYI:** Reservations not accepted. No liquor license. **Open:** Mon–Thurs 9am–midnight, Fri–Sat 9am–1am, Sun 10am–midnight. **Prices:** Main courses $3–$6. MC, V.

★ **Valois**
1518 E 53rd St (Hyde Park); tel 312/667-0647. **Cafeteria.** Acclaimed as one of the top greasy spoons in Chicago, this is where Hyde Park residents go for wholesome cafeteria food. Soups, salads, sandwiches, regular entrees. **FYI:** Reservations not accepted. No liquor license. **Open:** Daily 6am–10pm. **Prices:** Main courses $1–$7. No CC.

Viennese Kaffee Haus Brandt, Inc
3423 N Southport; tel 312/528-2220. Just N of Roscoe. **Cafe.** From the antique glass showcases filled with delicious homemade pastries to the hand-cut, polished marble tables and floors, this charmingly restored cafe will make you feel as if you've traveled in time to another era. The owner, a former professional opera singer, sometimes serenades customers. Coffees are roasted and ice cream and Italian ice are made in house. Vegetarian dishes, meatloaf, tuna steak available. Generous lunch portions. **FYI:** Reservations not accepted. Harp/piano. **Open:** Tues–Thurs 7am–10pm, Fri 7am–11pm, Sat 9am–11pm, Sun 9am–6pm. **Prices:** Main courses $7–$8. No CC. &

★ **Vinny's**
2901 N Sheffield Ave (Lincoln Park); tel 312/871-0990. 2 blocks N of Diversey. **Italian.** A prototypical trattoria, right down to the red-checkered vinyl tablecloths. Meals are served family-style, with huge platters of pastas for people to share. The basics—spaghetti with meat sauce, with meatballs, or with sausage—are supplemented by "fancy" pastas like shrimp tricolor rottini (red, white, and green pasta with creamy seafood sauce) and penne campagnole (with arugula,

yellow peppers, tomatoes, garlic, and anchovies). A full array of pizzas, soups, salads, and appetizers is available, too. **FYI:** Reservations recommended. Children's menu. **Open:** Lunch Mon–Fri 11:30am–2:30pm; dinner Sun–Thurs 5–10pm, Fri–Sat 5–11pm. **Prices:** Main courses $8–$13. AE, DC, DISC, MC, V. 👥 VP &

⑤ **Vivo**
838 W Randolph St (Old Market District); tel 312/733-3379. **Italian.** Stylish, elegant, yet casual Italian eatery that attracts a celebrity crowd. Bare brick walls, high, black, painted ceiling, and exposed ductwork characterize the decor (celebrities often request the table atop the bricked-in elevator shaft). Excellently prepared, imaginative fare is a good value. Don't miss the wonderful gazpacho studded with shrimp, or the artfully prepared antipasto filled with tempting items. **FYI:** Reservations recommended. **Open:** Mon–Thurs 11:30am–10pm, Fri 11:30am–midnight, Sat 5:30pm–midnight, Sun 5:30–10pm. **Prices:** Main courses $8–$19. AE, DC, MC, V. ❤ VP &

Widow Newton's Tavern
In Navy Pier, 700 E Grand Ave; tel 312/595-5500. **American.** Filled with antiques, stained glass, ceiling murals, fireplace gargoyles, and a stunning, carved 110-year-old bar, this place is vaguely reminiscent of a Gothic cathedral and a little like dining in a funky art museum. The cuisine consists of inspired creations like baked goat cheese with roasted red pepper and toasted crostini; mixed greens with a no-fat orange-balsamic dressing; and rotisserie half-chicken with mashed sweet potatoes and rosemary-corn relish. **FYI:** Reservations accepted. Children's menu. **Open:** Peak (June–Aug) lunch Mon–Sat 11:30am–4pm; dinner Mon–Thurs 5–11pm, Fri–Sat 5pm–midnight. **Prices:** Main courses $10–$23. AE, CB, DC, DISC, MC, V. ▮ VP &

★ **Wikstrom's**
5247 N Clark (Andersonville); tel 312/275-6100. N of Foster Ave. **Deli.** For over 35 years, this Swedish deli has been providing the real thing in fine Scandinavian foods. Beautiful Norwegian rosemaling around the door and cheerful murals of Swedish scenes on the walls combined with sparkling cleanliness make the tiny eating area particularly inviting. Authentic items include limpa bread, Swedish candies, lefse, imported cheeses, herrings of all types and seasonings, and lutefisk. On holidays, the mail orders are staggering, and the waiting time in the store can be up to three hours. A selection of T-shirts, coffee mugs, and books in the back relate to things Scandinavian. **FYI:** Reservations not accepted. No liquor license. No smoking. **Open:** Peak (Oct–June) Sun 11am–4pm, Mon–Sat 9am–6pm. **Prices:** Lunch main courses $2–$6. MC, V.

⑤ ★ **Yoshi's**
3257 N Halsted St; tel 312/248-6160. N of Belmont Ave. **Eclectic.** Critics and in-the-know diners proclaim this reasonably priced dinner spot in Chicago's North Side one of the

premiere restaurants in the city and region. Yoshi and Nobuko Katsumura have been impressing diners for 14 years with their unique blend of the best of the East and the West. Favorite dishes include the tuna tartare appetizer and the fresh fish of the day. Yoshi's also offers a health conscious menu with selections such as steamed fresh fish of the day with bonito broth or ginger infused oil and tofu steak with shrimp and shiitake mushrooms in a sweet sake, soy sauce, and sesame oil sauce. **FYI:** Reservations recommended. **Open:** Tues–Thurs 5–10:30pm, Fri–Sat 5pm–midnight, Sun 5–9:30pm. **Prices:** Main courses $7–$23. AE, CB, DC, MC, V. 🆅🅿 ⅃.

Zum Deutschen Eck

2924 N Southport Ave; tel 312/525-8389. 1 block N of Diversey, 2 blocks E of Ashland Ave. **American/German.** This busy, popular restaurant serving fine German and American cuisine is a heavy favorite among conventioneers, local businessmen, and banquet-goers, who are likely drawn by the German atmosphere, weekly sing-alongs, and Wiener schnitzel, seafood, and steak. **FYI:** Reservations recommended. Folk. **Open:** Mon–Thurs 11:30am–10:30pm, Fri 11:30am–midnight, Sat noon–midnight, Sun noon–10pm. **Prices:** Main courses $13–$20. AE, DC, DISC, MC, V. ⅃

REFRESHMENT STOP ☕

Swedish Bakery

5348 N Clark (Andersonville); tel 312/561-8919. North of Foster Ave. **Desserts.** Full assortment of fine European baked goods, with Swedish delicacies emphasized. Favorites include the traditional Princess Torte, a marzipan wrapped cake; a gorgeous fruit glaze cake; and limpa bread (fennel and rye). Visitors can stand at a window counter to enjoy their goodies. Self-serve, free coffee. Preordering recommended at holiday times. **Open:** Mon–Thurs 6:30am–6:30pm, Fri 6:30am–8pm, Sat 6:30am–5pm. Closed July 1–10/Dec 24–Jan 4. AE, DISC, MC, V.

ATTRACTIONS 🏛

TOP ATTRACTIONS

Art Institute of Chicago

Michigan Ave at Adams St (Loop); tel 312/443-3600. One of the world's major art collections, housed in an elegant Italian Renaissance–style palazzo constructed for the World's Fair of 1893. Some of the Institute's most famous holdings include Caravaggio's *Resurrection,* El Greco's *Assumption of the Virgin,* Delacroix's *Lion Hunt,* Seurat's *Sunday on the Isle of Grande Jatte,* van Gogh's *The Bedroom,* and Grant Wood's *American Gothic.* Other highlights include stained glass by Marc Chagall, and fine collections of Chinese sculpture and pre-Columbian art. Another popular attraction is the original trading room of the old Chicago Stock Exchange, salvaged

when the original building was demolished in 1972. **Open:** Mon and Wed–Fri 10:30am–4:30pm, Tues 10:30am–8pm, Sat 10am–5pm, Sun noon–5pm. **$$$**

Field Museum of Natural History

Roosevelt Rd and Lake Shore Dr (Grant Park); tel 312/922-9410. One of the largest museums of natural history and ethnology in the world, with 200,000 exhibits ranging from dinosaur skeletons to meteorites to a Pawnee earth lodge. The "Inside Ancient Egypt" exhibit is the Field's showcase, with 23 actual mummies, an ancient royal barge, and the entire tomb of the pharaoh Unis. Another permanent exhibit employs hundreds of artifacts from the museum's oceanic collection to re-create scenes of island life in the South Pacific. Instead of the traditional cafeteria found in most museums, there's a McDonald's. **Open:** Daily 9am–5pm. **$$**

Sears Tower

233 S Wacker Dr (Loop); tel 312/875-9696. The tallest skyscraper in the world, at 1,454 feet and 110 stories high. More than 17,000 employees work in this huge, vertical ant's nest serviced by 102 elevators. Designed by the same team of architects who built the John Hancock Center (see below), it's still the property of Sears Roebuck and Company. There are two observation decks, one on the 100th floor, the other on the 103rd. The lobby boasts a giant Alexander Calder mobile called *Universe.* **Open:** Peak (Mar–Sept) daily 9am–11pm. Reduced hours off-season. **$$$**

John Hancock Observatory

875 N Michigan; tel 312/751-3681. Three high-speed elevators carry passengers to the 94th floor of the John Hancock Center in 40 seconds. The observatory offers an excellent panorama of the city and an intimate view over nearby Lake Michigan and the various shoreline residential areas. (On a clear day you can even see portions of Michigan, Indiana, and Wisconsin.) The view up the North Side is particularly dramatic, stretching from the nearby Oak and North Street Beaches, along the green strip of Lincoln Park and the line of high-rises up the shoreline. **Open:** Daily 9am–midnight. **$$$**

Chicago Board of Trade

141 W Jackson (Loop); tel 312/435-3590. The largest futures and options exchange in the world is housed in a 44-story Art Deco building topped by a giant statue of Ceres, the Roman goddess of the harvest. Viewing galleries on the fifth floor allow guests to watch the trading action. **Open:** Mon–Fri 9am–1:15pm. **Free**

John G Shedd Aquarium

1200 S Lakeshore Dr; tel 312/939-2438. The largest aquarium in the world, with more than 8,000 fish and marine animals, from the dolphin to the piranha, and its own artificial coral reef. The 460,000 gallons of seawater required for the tanks is hauled by truck and rail from the Atlantic. The **Oceanarium** gives Midwesterners the experience of walking along an ocean coastline and shows off marine life rarely seen outside major aquariums on either coast. **Open:** Peak (summer) daily 9am–6pm. Reduced hours off-season. $$$

ART MUSEUMS

Terra Museum of American Art

666 N Michigan Ave (North Side); tel 312/664-3939. Opened in 1987, the Terra is one of the newest museums of American art in the country. A strange blend of modern architectural idioms (large bay windows, white Vermont marble) have been adapted to older structures. The internal ramps are somewhat reminiscent of the Guggenheim in New York. The permanent collections boasts over 800 major works by such artists as Edward Hopper, Jamie Wyeth, John James Audubon, Mary Cassatt, and John Singer Sargent. Free admission on Tuesdays. **Open:** Tues noon–8pm, Wed–Sat 10am–5pm, Sun noon–5pm. $$

The David and Alfred Smart Museum of Art

5550 S Greenwood Ave at University of Chicago (Hyde Park); tel 312/702-0200. Named for two of the founders of *Esquire* magazine, who established the foundation that funded this museum on the University of Chicago campus. The impressive permanent collection contains more than 5,000 works ranging from classical antiquity to the contemporary. Recent temporary exhibitions have included "Selected Works from the Prinzhorn Collection of the Art of the Mentally Ill," and "The Earthly Chimera and the Femme Fatale: Fear of Woman in Late Nineteenth Century Art." **Open:** Tues–Fri 10am–4pm, Sat–Sun noon–6pm. **Free**

Museum of Contemporary Art

220 E Chicago Ave (Magnificent Mile); tel 312/280-2660. Recently relocated to enormous new headquarters (seven times the size of the original location), the MCA is a great place to see innovative modern art of the past five decades. Among the highlights of the permanent collection are works by René Magritte, Andy Warhol, Franz Kline, and Alexander Calder. Special exhibitions run the gamut from Swiss video artist Pipilotti Rist to surrealist painter Meret Oppenheim. The state-of-the art audio tour is narrated by movie critics Siskel and Ebert. In addition, the museum features a sculpture garden, theater, restaurant, and a unique gift/book store. **Open:** Tues and Thurs–Sun 11am–6pm, Wed 11am–9pm. $$$

The Museum of Contemporary Photography

600 S Michigan Ave at Columbia College (South Loop); tel 312/663-5554. The permanent collection focuses on American photography produced since 1959, starting with Robert Frank's series *The Americans*. In addition, the museum presents lectures, video and film presentations, and traveling exhibitions. **Open:** Mon–Wed and Fri 10am–5pm, Thurs 10am–8pm, Sat noon–5pm. **Free**

Martin D'Arcy Gallery of Art

6525 N Sheridan Rd; tel 312/508-2679. A treasure trove of medieval and Renaissance art. All the rich symbolism of Catholicism through the baroque era is embodied in such works as a gem-encrusted sculpture in silver and ebony of Christ's scourging, a head of John the Baptist on a silver platter, golden chalices, rosary beads carved with biblical scenes, and many other highly ornamented ritual objects. **Open:** Sept–May, Mon–Fri noon–4pm. **Free**

CULTURAL MUSEUMS

DuSable Museum of African American History

740 E 56th Place (Hyde Park); tel 312/947-0600. Bears the name of Chicago's first settler, a black businessman from Haiti. The bulk of the collection dates from the WPA period in the late 1930s and the Black Arts movement of the 1960s, although some exhibits deal with earlier aspects of African and African-American art and history. **Open:** Mon–Wed and Fri–Sun 10am–5pm, Thurs 10am–6pm. $

Morton B Weiss Museum of Judaica

1000 E Hyde Park Blvd (Hyde Park); tel 312/924-1234. Among the artifacts of Jewish culture that visitors will see are some of the findings unearthed at digs in the Holy Land by amateur archeologist Gen Moshe Dayan. Also of note are the medieval marriage contracts (illustrated and written on parchment) and the Byzantine-style synagogue itself, built in 1924. **Open:** Mon–Thurs 9am–5pm, Fri 9am–3pm, Sun 9:30am–noon. **Free**

Spertus Museum of the Spertus Institute of Jewish Studies

618 S Michigan Ave; tel 312/922-9012. Rich collection of 5,000 years worth of Jewish manuscripts, religious objects, textiles and costumes, jewelry, coins, paintings, sculpture, and graphics. Zell Holocaust Memorial. ARTiFACT Center allows visitors to "dig," with authentic archeological tools, for pottery and other Middle Eastern artifacts. Past temporary exhibitions have included "GIs Remember: World War II and the Liberation of the Concentration Camps" and a collection of photographs of the Jewish community in war-torn Sarajevo. Free admission on Fridays. **Open:** Sun–Thurs 10am–5pm, Fri 10am–3pm. $$

Balzekas Museum of Lithuanian Culture

6500 S Pulaski Rd (Southwest Side); tel 312/582-6500. Permanent exhibits of antique weapons, armor, dolls, fine and folk art, rare maps and prints spanning more than 1,000 years of Lithuanian history. **Open:** Daily 10am–3:30pm. $$

Polish Museum of America

984 N Milwaukee (Milwaukee Avenue Corridor); tel 312/384-3352. Chicago has the largest ethnic Polish population of any city in the world after Warsaw. This museum is devoted to Poland and its art, culture, and folklore, as well as to contribution of the Poles to Chicago and to America. Rotating exhibitions, films, lectures. **Open:** Daily 11am–4pm. $

Ukrainian National Museum

721 N Oakley Blvd; tel 312/421-8020. Throughout the two upper stories of this converted brownstone are displays including decorative Easter eggs, fine embroidery, wood

carvings, artwork, crafts, and folk costumes, all of which reflect Old World craftsmanship. **Open:** Tues–Sun 11am–4pm. **$**

Mexican Fine Arts Center Museum

1852 W 19th St (Pilsen); tel 312/738-1503. The city's newest ethnic museum—and the only one of its kind in the Mid-west—highlights art and performances from Mexican and Mexican-American artists. **Open:** Tues–Sun 10am–5pm. **Free**

SCIENCE MUSEUMS

Museum of Science and Industry

57th St and Lake Shore Dr (Hyde Park); tel 312/684-1414. World's largest science museum, with some 2,000 exhibits spread over 14 acres in 175 exhibition halls. Highlights include a 15-foot-tall working model of a human heart, an authentic German U-boat from World War II, and a re-creation of a working southern Illinois coal mine. Popular permanent exhibits include "Colleen Moore's Fairy Castle," "Earth Trek," and "Ships Through the Ages"; the "Trans-portation Zone" houses old locomotives, cars, and planes by the dozen. There are a number of robots that can be operated by visitors, and an entire wing devoted to space research. Omnimax Theater offers Friday and Saturday eve-ning showings for an additional fee. **Open:** Peak (Mem Day–Labor Day) daily 9:30am–5:30pm. Reduced hours off-sea-son. **$$$**

Chicago Academy of Sciences, the Nature Museum

435 E Illinois St (North Pier); tel 312/871-2668. The oldest science museum in the Midwest with excellent dioramas on the variety of ecosystems surrounding Chicago. Examples include a 350-million-year-old forest with wildlife displays, as well as a "walk-through" cave and canyon. The Children's Gallery features puzzles, games, live animals, fossils, artifacts, and more for kids to explore. **Open:** Mon–Thurs 9:30am–4:30pm, Fri 9:30am–8pm, Sat 10am–4:30pm, Sun noon–4:30pm. **$**

Adler Planetarium

1300 S Lakeshore Dr; tel 312/322-0304 or 922-STAR (re-corded info). Space shows and telescope observation in summer; exhibits on space exploration—including the *Voyag-er* and *Apollo II* flights—are on display year-round. Entry plaza features a bronze sundial by sculptor Henry Moore. **Open:** Sat–Thurs 9am–5pm, Fri 9am–9pm. **$$**

International Museum of Surgical Sciences

1524 N Lake Shore Dr (Gold Coast); tel 312/642-6502. Housed in a 1917 mansion, the museum has a collection of surgical instruments, paintings, and sculpture depicting the history of surgery from prehistoric times to the present. A turn-of-the-century apothecary shop and dentist's office are re-created in a historic street exhibit. Donation suggested. **Open:** Tues–Sat 10am–4pm, Sun 11am–5pm. **Free**

OTHER MUSEUMS

Chicago Historical Society

1601 N Clark St (Lincoln Park); tel 312/642-4600. Exhibits are dedicated to American history—and the Civil War and the life of Abraham Lincoln in particular—as well as to the evolution of Chicago from its founding to the present. Temporary exhibitions, demonstrations of old trades. **Open:** Mon–Sat 9:30am–4:30pm, Sun noon–5pm. **$**

Chicago Children's Museum

600 E Grand Ave (Navy Pier); tel 312/527-1000. The perma-nent exhibit, "Amazing Chicago," is a mini-version of Chica-go represented by playhouse-size constructions of several well-known Chicago buildings. In the miniature "Art Insti-tute," children can draw and hang up their own art; in the "Sears Tower" they can learn about architecture and play with decorating materials. "Touchy Business" is a tactile tunnel for kids aged three to seven, where a labyrinth leads through a Lighted Forest to the pretend house of the Three Bears, with lots of stuff to touch and learn about along the way. **Open:** Tues–Fri 12:30–4:30pm, Sat–Sun 10am–4:30pm. **$$**

Museum of Broadcast Communication

78 E Washington St (Loop); tel 312/629-6000. Housed in the Chicago Cultural Center, the museum includes both the Radio Hall of Fame and the Kraft TeleCenter. Visitors can listen to or watch the classic programs of yore; there's even a "newsroom" where visitors can anchor their own newscast and take a video home as a souvenir. **Open:** Mon–Sat 10am–4:30pm, Sun noon–5pm. **Free**

American Police Center and Museum

1717 S State St; tel 312/531-0005. This unusual museum strives to create a spirit of cooperation between law enforce-ment officers and the general public through exhibits and special programs. Public service programs include informa-tion on how con artists operate and how burglars work their way into a locked home. Exhibit areas feature an Al Capone "Gangster Alley," drug displays, and shields and uniforms. **Open:** Mon–Fri 9am–5pm. **$$**

The Peace Museum

350 W Ontario (River North); tel 312/440-1860. The only museum of its kind in the United States. Dedicated solely to the role of the arts and sciences, and labor and ethnic minorities, regarding issues of war and peace. Recent shows have focused on South African artists, the life and times of Martin Luther King Jr, and the Vietnam Veterans Memorial. **Open:** Tues–Wed and Fri–Sat 11am–5pm, Thurs noon–8pm. **$$**

HISTORIC BUILDINGS & ARCHITECTURE

Pullman Historic District

111th St exit off I-94; tel 312/785-8181. Built as a planned housing community in 1880 by George Pullman, of the Pullman Palace Car Company, for his employees. Even though his workers would rebel and strike soon afterwards, "the village that Pullman built" still stands near the Calumet Expressway between 111th and 115th Sts. Guided tours of this fascinating community are conducted on the first Sunday of the month from May through October by the Historic Pullman Foundation. At all other times, visitors may pick up a free walking tour map at the foundation's headquarters in the **Florence Hotel**, 11111 S Forestville Ave. The hotel, built in 1881 in the Queen Anne style, was the showcase of the Pullman community. Other highlights of the tour include the nondenominational Greenstone Church and the Market Hall, where community members shopped for food and dry goods. **$$**

University of Chicago
59th St (Hyde Park); tel 312/702-8374 or 702-9559 (recorded info). Founded in 1890 by John D Rockefeller, this is one of the most respected of American universities, with a total enrollment of 8,000 students. There are a number of interesting buildings here by Frank Lloyd Wright, Mies van der Rohe, and Eero Saarinen, among others. On **Stagg Field** (S Ellis Ave between E 56th and E 57th Sts), a bronze composition by British sculptor Henry Moore marks the exact spot below which history's first controlled nuclear chain reaction took place in 1942. Campus tours are organized by the university's Office of Special Events and begin at 10am Monday to Saturday at Ida Noyes Hall (1212 E 59th St). Free campus maps and copies of a calendar of events are available at several locations on campus. **Free**

Robie House
5757 S Woodlawn Ave (Hyde Park); tel 312/702-2150. Said to be one of Frank Lloyd Wright's finest works and considered among the foremost masterpieces of 20th-century American architecture. A tour takes visitors to the first-floor living/dining room only (the other rooms serve as administrative offices for the University of Chicago). The open layout and craftsmanship are typical of a Wright design. Its institutional-looking exterior, though, may make Robie House less satisfying for some observers than some of the homes he designed in Oak Park. **Open:** Daily noon–1pm. **$**

Rockefeller Memorial Chapel
5850 S Woodlawn Ave (Hyde Park); tel 312/702-7000. On the University of Chicago campus grounds, just across from Robie House. John D Rockefeller was a generous patron. He founded the university (in cooperation with the American Baptist Society), built the magnificent mini-cathedral that now bears his name, and gave an additional $35 million in donations to the institution over the course of his lifetime. The Memorial Chapel's outstanding feature is the circular stained-glass window high above the main altar. **Open:** Daily 9am–4pm. **Free**

Hull House Museum
800 S Halsted St; tel 312/413-5353. Located on the campus of the University of Illinois–Chicago. This pioneering center for social work was founded in 1889 by Jane Addams, whose work among the immigrant poor in this Chicago neighborhood won her the Nobel Peace Prize. Inside the restored mansion are the original furnishings, Addams's office, and numerous settlement maps and photographs. Rotating exhibits re-create the history of the settlement and the work of its residents. Guided tours offered Sun–Fri. **Open:** Peak (summer) Mon–Fri 10am–4pm, Sun noon–5pm. Reduced hours off-season. **Free**

Chicago Fire Academy
558 W De Koven; tel 312/744-6666. Built on the site of Patrick O'Leary's stable, the legendary starting point of the fire that totally ravaged Chicago on October 8, 1871 and left a third of the city's population homeless. Tours available Monday through Friday at 10am, 11am, 1pm, and 2pm. **Free**

The Newberry Library
60 W Walton St; tel 312/943-9090. Dating from 1887 and boasting more than 1.4 million books, 5 million manuscripts, and 75,000 maps. The Newborn is most famous for its works on the Renaissance, Native Americans, and music history. **Open:** Reading rooms: Tues–Thurs 10am–6pm, Fri–Sat 9am–5pm. Exhibits: Mon, Fri, Sat 8:15am–5:30pm, Tues–Thurs 8:15am–7:30pm . **Free**

Our Lady of Sorrows Basilica
3121 W Jackson Blvd; tel 312/638-5800. This 1890 Italian Renaissance church features an 80-foot-high barrel vaulted ceiling, marble floors, and 1,100 separate gold panels. It is the national shrine of Our Sorrowful Mother and the national shrine of St Peregrine (patron saint of those with cancer). A special mass for the sick is held the third Saturday of every month. When the church is locked, visitors may enter through the monastery next door. **Open:** Mon–Sat 8am–4pm, Sun 9am–1pm. **Free**

PARKS & GARDENS

Lincoln Park
Lake Shore Dr, from North Ave to Hollywood Ave (Gold Coast). Located along the shores of Lake Michigan, this is the largest park in the city, extending for nearly five miles. In addition to numerous statues, the park contains several beaches, a bird sanctuary, playgrounds, and tennis courts. **Open:** Daily 24 hours. **Free**

Lincoln Park Conservatory
Fullerton Dr at Stockton Dr (Gold Coast); tel 312/294-4770. Inside are four great halls filled with thousands of plants, the closest thing (other than several smaller conservatories scattered in a few neighborhood parks) that Chicago has to a botanical garden within the city limits. The Palm House features giant palms and rubber trees, the Fernery nurtures the plants that grow close to the forest floor, and the Tropical House is a symphony of shiny greenery. A fourth environment is aptly named the Show House, for here the seasonal flower shows are held. **Open:** Daily 9am–5pm. **Free**

Lincoln Park Zoo

2200 N Cannon Dr (Gold Coast); tel 312/935-6700. Spread over 35 acres, the zoo is imaginatively designed with animals occupying separate habitats appropriate to their species. The more than 1,200 animals, birds, and reptiles who call the zoo home include seals, apes, rhinos, bears, camels, elephants, zebras, and big cats. Adjoining children's zoo. **Open:** Daily 8am–5:15pm. **Free**

Grant Park

Between Randolph St, Roosevelt Rd, Columbus and Lake Shore Drs. This downtown park contains the Petrillo Music Shell, which hosts live music performances throughout the summer. Also within the park is the Buckingham Memorial Fountain, with a central column of water which rises 280 feet into the air. A covered outdoor sports plaza features 12 tennis courts and an ice skating rink. Also cross-country ski trails, yacht basin, and rose and formal gardens. **Open:** Daily 24 hours. **Free**

Garfield Park Conservatory

300 N Central Park (Garfield Park); tel 312/746-5100. Historic glass-enclosed conservatory featuring an international array of tropical and subtropical plants such as ferns, palms, orchids, cactus, and aroids. Flower shows held November to May. **Open:** Daily 9am–5pm. **Free**

Chicago Botanic Garden

1000 Lake Cook Rd, Glencoe; tel 847/835-5440. Located 25 mi N of Chicago. This 300-acre preserve contains a variety of distinct botanical environments, ranging from Illinois prairie to a garden filled with English perennials. A designated bike path provides a pleasant route through the complex. Cafe, library, and garden shop also on grounds. **Open:** Daily 8am–sunset. **$**

Bergen Garden

5050 S Lake Shore Dr (Hyde Park); tel 312/288-5050. Located on the roof of an apartment building's parking garage, this one-acre formal garden is a unique urban oasis featuring lagoons, ducks, fountains, walkways, and more than 30,000 plants. Self-guided public tours available. **Open:** Mem Day–Labor Day, Mon–Fri 10am–7pm, Sat–Sun 10am–5pm. **Free**

Brookfield Zoological Park

1st Ave and 31st St, Brookfield; tel 708/485-0263. Located 14 mi W of the Loop. The Chicago area's largest zoo, Brookfield has an incredibly varied cast of residents from all branches of the animal kingdom. Visitors make the rounds from one habitat to another, encountering polar bears, Kodiak bears, walruses, and great apes along the way. **Open:** Peak (Mem Day–Labor Day) daily 10am–6pm. Reduced hours off-season. **$$**

ENTERTAINMENT VENUES

Auditorium Building and Theatre

50 E Congress Pkwy (Loop); tel 312/922-4046. National landmark designed and built in 1889 by Louis Sullivan and Dankmar Adler. The theater's interior—a glittering display of mirrors and stained glass—is renowned for its excellent acoustics and sight lines. The Auditorium Building was the first building to be wired for electric light in Chicago, and the theater was the first in the country to install air conditioning. Today the Auditorium attracts major Broadway musicals, such as *Miss Saigon* and *Les Misérables*. **Open:** Call for schedule. **$$$$**

Fine Arts Building

410 S Michigan Ave (Loop); tel 312/427-7602. Built as a showroom for Studebaker carriages in 1885, the landmark Fine Arts Building was converted at the turn of the century into a concert hall. Its upper stories sheltered a number of well-known publications (*Saturday Evening Post, Dial*) and provided offices for such luminaries as Frank Lloyd Wright, sculptor Lorado Taft, and L Frank Baum. Movie buffs should take note that the two original ground-floor theaters have been converted into an art cinema with four separate screening rooms. Visit the top floor (10th) to see the spectacular murals. **Open:** Daily 8am–6pm. **Free**

Chicago Cultural Center

78 E Washington St (Loop); tel 312/744-6630. Built in 1897 as the main branch of the Chicago Public Library, this sumptuous Renaissance-style building now hosts an eclectic array of arts programs. Most of the building's first floor houses the Museum of Broadcast Communications (see above); there are also numerous gallery spaces, performance halls, and a cafe. A film series offers children's films every Saturday; call for details. The interior is adorned with Carrara marble, mosaics, and Tiffany-style windows. **Open:** Mon–Thurs 10am–7pm, Fri 10am–6pm, Sat 10am–5pm, Sun noon–5pm. **Free**

Arie Crown Theatre

2301 S Lake Shore Dr; tel 312/791-6190. A showcase for road companies of traveling Broadway musicals. This gigantic house, despite casts that often feature big-name stars, has a reputation for tinny acoustics and poor sight lines in all but the first few rows. **Open:** Call for schedule. **$$$$**

ARENAS & STADIUMS

Wrigley Field

1060 W Addison St; tel 312/404-2827. Home of the Chicago Cubs. This vintage (some would say quirky) baseball field is a favorite with fans due to its ivy-covered outfield walls, hand-operated scoreboard, and views of the lake from the upper deck. **$$$**

Comiskey Park

333 W 35th St; tel 312/924-1000. Home of the Chicago White Sox. This new baseball field (opened in 1991) was built directly across the street from the original landmark ballpark where the Black Sox scandal—in which eight White Sox players allegedly threw the 1919 World Series—took place. **$$$**

Soldier Field

425 E McFetridge Dr; tel 312/663-5408. Giant, open-air football stadium where "da Bears" play. Concerts are also held here in the summer. **$$$$**

United Center

1901 W Madison St; tel 312/455-4500. Home base of the NBA's Chicago Bulls and their star player, Michael Jordan. (There's even a statue of Jordan out front.) The United also hosts concerts and other special events. **$$$$**

Rosemont Horizon

Mannheim St, between Higgins and Touhy Sts, Des Plaines; tel 847/635-6600. On the periphery of O'Hare Airport is the 18,000-seat Rosemont Horizon, which holds big events such as rock concerts, the circus, and important college basketball games. **Open:** Call for schedule. **$$$$**

OTHER ATTRACTIONS

Here's Chicago!

163 E Pearson; tel 312/467-7114. A 45-minute sound-and-sight show located in the Water Tower Pumping Station. Both the Pumping Station and the Water Tower across the street were among the only buildings in the path of the great fire of 1871 that survived.

The show begins with a brief tour of the Pumping Station's machinery. Next, patrons are treated to a few minor exhibits, one on the Chicago Fire, another a tableau of life-size figures representing the denouement of the St Valentine's Day massacre. The remainder of the show is visual. First comes a computerized slide show showing the varied scenes and human faces of Chicago, and finally a 70mm film entitled *City of Dreams* simulates a helicopter ride over the city. **Open:** Daily 9:30am–6pm. **$$$**

Untouchable Times and Tours

Tel 312/881-1195. Chicago's only bus tour of gangland landmarks from the 1920s and 1930s, from Al Capone's headquarters to the site of the so-called St Valentine's Day Massacre. The driver and tour guide dress as gangsters, pack plastic pistols in shoulder holsters, and spice up the commentary with hoodlum argot and their own sound effects. Tours depart from the corner of Michigan Ave and Pearson St, and from Clark and Ohio Sts. Call for reservations. **Open:** Daily, hours vary. **$$$$**

Navy Pier

600 E Grand Ave; tel 312/595-PIER. Built during World War I, Navy Pier has been a ballroom, a training center for Navy pilots during World War II, and a satellite campus of the University of Illinois. It has just undergone yet one more transformation, one that has returned it to its original intended purpose—a place for Chicagoans to come to relax and to be entertained. Developers have resurrected the ballroom, and they also have installed a winter garden, an ice rink, a concert stage, and a 15-story Ferris wheel. Navy Pier also hosts an annual art show. **Open:** Call for schedule. **Free**

North Pier

435 E Illinois St; tel 312/836-4300. A two-block-long complex fronting the Chicago River's Ogden Slip. Having outgrown its mercantile role (it was built as warehouses around 1910), North Pier has been converted into an all-purpose entertainment center. Now it houses nightspots, museums, restaurants, and nearly four dozen specialty shops, boutiques, and galleries. **Open:** Mon–Sat 11am–9pm, Sun noon–8pm. **Free**

Chicago O'Hare Int'l Airport

HOTELS 🏨

📗 Best Western at O'Hare

10300 W Higgins, Rosemont, 60018; tel 847/296-4471. Appropriate for all travelers. Restaurant and sports bar nearby. **Rooms:** 142 rms and stes. CI 3pm/CO noon. Nonsmoking rms avail. **Amenities:** 🛁 ⚙ 🔲 A/C, cable TV w/movies. Some units w/whirlpools. **Services:** 🚐 🖼 🛏 Car-rental desk. Many movies available. **Facilities:** 🔲 🔲 🖥 **Rates (CP):** $79–$95 S; $89–$105 D; $145–$175 ste. Extra person $10. Children under age 12 stay free. Parking: Outdoor, free. AE, CB, DISC, JCB, MC, V.

📗📗 Holiday Inn Airport

5440 N River Rd, Rosemont, 60018; tel 847/671-6350 or toll free 800/HOLIDAY. Across from the Rosemont Convention Center. Provides all the basics for the business or family traveler at reasonable rates. Atrium lobby has pleasant sitting area. The Rosemont Theater is next door. **Rooms:** 507 rms and stes. CI 3pm/CO noon. Nonsmoking rms avail. **Amenities:** 🛁 ⚙ 🔲 A/C, cable TV, voice mail. All units w/minibars, 1 w/whirlpool. **Services:** ✕ 🖼 🔲 🚐 🖼 🛏 🔲 Car-rental desk, masseur. Shuttle service available to nearby restaurants. **Facilities:** 🔲 🔲 🖥 2 restaurants, 2 bars (1 w/entertainment), games rm, spa, sauna, whirlpool, washer/dryer. **Rates:** $75–$119 S or D; $175 ste. Extra person $10. Children under age 12 stay free. Parking: Indoor, free. AE, DISC, MC, V.

📗📗📗 Hotel Sofitel

5550 N River Rd, Rosemont, 60018; tel 847/928-6955 or toll free 800/SOFITEL; fax 847/678-4244. A first-class hotel with classic comfort and a French accent. **Rooms:** 304 rms and stes. CI 3pm/CO noon. Nonsmoking rms avail. **Amenities:** 🛁 ⚙ 🔲 A/C, cable TV w/movies, voice mail, bathrobes. Some units w/minibars, 1 w/whirlpool. **Services:** 🍽 🖼 🔲 🚐 🖼 🛏 🔲 Car-rental desk, masseur, babysitting. Roses, chocolates, and champagne are some of the extras given to guests. Loaf of French bread presented at checkout. **Facilities:** 🔲 🔲 🔲 🖥 1 bar, sauna, beauty salon. Indoor walkway to Rosemont Convention Center.

Rates: $99–$175 S or D; $145–$280 ste. Extra person $10. Parking: Indoor/outdoor, free. In summer, kids get room next door free, if available. AE, DC, DISC, MC, V.

≣≣≣ O'Hare Hilton

Box 66414, Rosemont, 60666; tel 312/686-8000 or toll free 800/HILTONS; fax 312/601-2873. A favorite airport hotel of meeting planners, this hotel is located within O'Hare Airport, accessible from all terminals through an underground moving sidewalk. Also located underground is the O'Hare train, which can zip you to the Loop easily. Particularly popular with business travelers, who utilize the more than 35 conference rooms and the grand ballroom, this hotel offers excellent accommodations to all travelers. **Rooms:** 859 rms and stes. CI open/CO noon. Nonsmoking rms avail. Modern, tasteful decor. **Amenities:** 🛏 ₫ 🖥 ☎ A/C, cable TV w/movies, dataport, voice mail. All units w/minibars, 1 w/whirlpool. Fax machines in some rooms. **Services:** 🍽 VP 🚐 ⊠ 🖨 ↻ Twice-daily maid svce, masseur. **Facilities:** 🗋 ᴳᵘ 1500 💻 ⅙ 1 restaurant, 1 bar, games rm, sauna, steam rm, whirlpool. **Rates:** $95–$145 S or D; $225–$295 ste. Parking: Outdoor, $20/day. AE, DC, DISC, MC, V.

≣≣≣ Ramada Inn Airport

6600 N Mannheim Rd, Rosemont, 60018; tel 847/827-5131; fax 847/827-5659. 1 mi from airport. The third-largest convention hotel in the O'Hare area, appropriate for both families and business travelers. **Rooms:** 723 rms and stes. CI 3pm/CO noon. Nonsmoking rms avail. Some two-level penthouse suites. **Amenities:** 🛏 ₫ 🖥 ☎ A/C, cable TV w/movies, dataport. Some units w/minibars, some w/terraces. **Services:** ✗ 🚐 ⊠ ↻ Car-rental desk. **Facilities:** 🗋 ᴳᵘ 4000 💻 ⅙ 2 restaurants, 2 bars (1 w/entertainment), games rm, sauna, whirlpool. Popular Italian restaurant. Bar has "ladies night," with karaoke. **Rates:** $89–$113 S; $99–$123 D; $150–$500 ste. Children under age 12 stay free. Parking: Outdoor, free. AE, DISC, MC, V.

≣≣≣ Sheraton Suites O'Hare

6510 N Mannheim Rd, Rosemont, 60018; tel 847/699-6300. 1 mi from airport. All-suite hotel with sunny atrium lobby. Excellent for families who need to be near O'Hare. **Rooms:** 299 stes. CI 3pm/CO noon. Nonsmoking rms avail. **Amenities:** 🛏 ₫ 🖥 ☎ A/C, cable TV w/movies, refrig, dataport. All rooms have stocked refrigerators, irons, and ironing boards. **Services:** 🍽 🚐 ⊠ ↻ Car-rental desk, babysitting. **Facilities:** 🗋 ᴳᵘ 300 💻 ⅙ 1 restaurant, 1 bar, spa, sauna, whirlpool, washer/dryer. $7 passes to nearby health club and tennis facilities. **Rates:** $89–$205 ste. Extra person $10. Children under age 18 stay free. Parking: Outdoor, free. AE, DISC, MC, V.

≣≣≣ Westin Hotel O'Hare

6100 N River Rd, Rosemont, 60018; tel 847/698-6000 or toll free 800/228-3000; fax 847/698-4591. 2 mi from airport. Fully equipped for large conferences and conventions, this Westin won the Pinnacle Award for meeting facilities in 1994. **Rooms:** 525 rms and stes. CI 3pm/CO 1pm. Nonsmoking rms avail. Conference suites available. **Amenities:** 🛏 ₫ 🖥 ☎ A/C, cable TV w/movies, refrig, dataport, voice mail, bathrobes. Some units w/minibars, some w/whirlpools. Office Rooms have fax machines and copiers. **Services:** 🍽 VP 🚐 ⊠ ↻ Twice-daily maid svce, car-rental desk, masseur, children's program, babysitting. United Airlines passengers can check their baggage on site. Children get membership in Westin's Kids Club and receive special gifts. **Facilities:** 🗋 ᴳᵘ 4000 💻 ⅙ 3 bars (2 w/entertainment), sauna, whirlpool. Family plan allows kids to eat free in summer (mid-May–Aug). **Rates:** $79–$180 S; $205 D; $215–$1000 ste. Extra person $25. Children under age 18 stay free. Parking: Outdoor, free. AE, CB, DC, DISC, MC, V.

RESTAURANTS 🍴

★ Carlucci

6111 N River Rd, Rosemont; tel 847/518-0990. **Italian.** Close to the Expo Convention Center and Rosemont Theater, this restaurant, decorated with ceiling murals, is known for its fine antipasto, pizza, pasta, steaks, seafood, salads, and specialty dishes such as pollo alla romana (herb-marinated chicken with roasted potatoes, garlic, and olive oil). Cigar smokers are welcome in the cantinetta, a cozy bar. **FYI:** Reservations recommended. **Open:** Lunch Mon–Fri 11am–2:30pm; dinner Mon–Thurs 5–10pm, Fri–Sat 5–11pm, Sun 4:30–9pm. **Prices:** Main courses $10–$22. AE, CB, DISC, MC, V. ♥ ⅙

★ Morton's of Chicago

9525 W Bryn Mawr Ave, Rosemont; tel 847/678-5155. Across from the Rosemont Convention Center. **Seafood/Steak.** The classic steakhouse, popular with sports and media personalities as well as business travelers and locals. The dining room has dark oak walls and the sounds of Frank Sinatra wafting throughout. Entrees include shrimp Alexander and lemon-oregano chicken, as well as all kinds of steaks. Large wine and champagne selection. **FYI:** Reservations recommended. **Open:** Mon–Sat 5:30–11pm, Sun 5–10pm. **Prices:** Main courses $20–$30. AE, CB, MC, V. ♥ VP

Nick's Fishmarket

10275 W Higgins Rd, Rosemont; tel 847/298-8200. At Mannheim Rd. **American.** Low lighting, good service, and wall racks with hundreds of wine bottles characterize this well-regarded place. Offerings include chicken Vincenzo with arugula, asparagus, and mozzarella cheese; blackened lobster tail in Cajun butter sauce; and California abalone. A special salad is the Maui Wowie: chopped tomatoes, avocado, Maui onion, feta cheese, and bay shrimp. **FYI:** Reservations accepted. Piano/singer. Additional location: One First National Bank Plaza, Chicago (tel 312/621-0200). **Open:** Sun–Thurs 6–10pm, Fri–Sat 6–11pm. **Prices:** Main courses $20–$50. AE, DISC, MC, V. ♥ ⅙

Pine Grove Restaurant

6580 Mannheim Rd, Rosemont; tel 847/298-5110. At Higgins Rd. **American.** Convenient to the airport and hotels, this roomy, full-service restaurant serves until late at night. Entrees include broiled orange roughy, Grecian chicken, shish kabob, and steaks. **FYI:** Reservations not accepted. **Open:** Daily 6am–1am. **Prices:** Main courses $5–$14. DC, MC, V.

Rosewood

9421 W Higgins Rd, Rosemont; tel 847/696-9494. **Seafood/Steak.** A spacious restaurant with a piano bar. The menu features unusual appetizers such as yellowfin tuna, escargots, and smoked salmon cured with tequila, cilantro, and jalapeño peppers. A house specialty is filet à la Tuscany, lightly breaded and stuffed with buffalo mozzarella cheese, sun-dried tomatoes, and fresh spinach, served with Merlot wine sauce and cavatelli pasta. **FYI:** Reservations accepted. Piano. **Open:** Mon–Sat 11am–11pm. **Prices:** Main courses $18–$30. AE, MC, V.

Collinsville

This important manufacturing and coal center is populated mostly by people of Italian descent. Nearby Monks Mound is the largest prehistoric earthen construction in the New World. **Information:** Collinsville Convention & Visitors Bureau, One Gateway Dr, Collinsville, 62234 (tel 618/345-4999).

MOTELS

Best Western Bo-Jon Inn

I-55/70 and IL 159, 62234; tel 618/345-5720 or toll free 800/528-1234; fax 618/345-5721. A quiet, country motel located outside of town, but just minutes from several restaurants and area attractions. A fine choice. **Rooms:** 40 rms. CI 2pm/CO 11am. Nonsmoking rms avail. King rooms available. **Amenities:** A/C, cable TV w/movies. **Services:** Small pets allowed with permission. **Facilities:** **Rates (CP):** Peak (May–Sept 15) $40–$46 S; $47–$55 D. Extra person $5. Children under age 12 stay free. Lower rates off-season. Parking: Outdoor, free. Senior discounts avail. AE, DISC, MC, V.

Best Western Heritage Inn

2003 Mall Rd, 62234; tel 618/345-5660 or toll free 800/528-1234; fax 618/345-5660. Adobe walls and yucca plants accentuate the southwestern style of this comfortable lodging. Located near highways, restaurants, and movie theater. **Rooms:** 81 rms and stes. CI 3pm/CO noon. Nonsmoking rms avail. **Amenities:** A/C, cable TV w/movies. 1 unit w/whirlpool. **Services:** VCRs can be rented. Liquor sold at front desk. Toiletries available at front desk. Guests receive discount at 10 local restaurants. Copy machine in lobby for guest use. **Facilities:** Games rm, whirlpool,

washer/dryer. **Rates:** Peak (May 15–Sept 15) $49–$64 S; $55–$74 D; $120 ste. Extra person $7. Children under age 12 stay free. Lower rates off-season. Parking: Outdoor, free. AE, CB, DC, DISC, ER, MC, V.

Drury Inn

602 N Bluff Rd, 62234; tel 618/345-7700 or toll free 800/325-8300. Exit 11 (IL 157) off I-55/70; N ¼ mi to entrance. Sunken lobby and bright atrium in conveniently located lodging, just 10 miles from downtown St Louis. **Rooms:** 123 rms. CI 3pm/CO noon. Nonsmoking rms avail. All rooms have interior access. **Amenities:** A/C, cable TV, dataport. King deluxe rooms have microwaves and refrigerators. **Services:** Safety deposit boxes and toiletries available at front desk. Free local calls. Adjacent Bob Evans restaurant will deliver to rooms during restaurant hours. Pets must be under 25 lbs. **Facilities:** Meeting facilities available only during off-season (Dec–May). Guests have access to local health club at reduced rate. **Rates (CP):** Peak (June–Nov) $59–$64 S; $69–$74 D. Extra person $10. Children under age 18 stay free. Lower rates off-season. Parking: Outdoor, free. AE, CB, DC, DISC, MC, V.

Holiday Inn

1000 Eastport Plaza Dr, 62234; tel 618/345-2800 or toll free 800/551-5133; fax 618/345-0136. Exit 11 (IL 157) off I-55/70. Sunken seating surrounds a gas fireplace in the large lobby of this modern facility. Easy access to highways and multiple dining choices in immediate area. An excellent choice. **Rooms:** 230 rms and stes. CI 3pm/CO noon. Nonsmoking rms avail. **Amenities:** A/C, cable TV w/movies, dataport, in-rm safe. Some rooms available with unstocked refrigerator. **Services:** Babysitting. One week advance notice required to arrange airport transportation. Sales office provides business center services, such as copying and faxing. Service-oriented staff. **Facilities:** 1 restaurant (see "Restaurants" below), 1 bar, basketball, volleyball, games rm, sauna, whirlpool, washer/dryer. Half-court basketball, horseshoes, and sand volleyball. **Rates (CP):** Peak (Apr–Oct) $85–$95 S; $95 D; $75–$200 ste. Extra person $10. Children under age 18 stay free. Min stay special events. Lower rates off-season. Parking: Outdoor, free. AE, CB, DC, DISC, MC, V.

Pear Tree Inn

552 Ramada Blvd, 62234; tel 618/345-9500 or toll free 800/AT-A-TREE; fax 618/345-9500. Halfway up a hill, this comfortable lodging delivers service and value. Easy access to highway, adjacent to 24-hour restaurant. **Rooms:** 105 rms. CI 3pm/CO noon. Nonsmoking rms avail. **Amenities:** A/C, cable TV w/movies, dataport. **Services:** Safety deposit boxes, toiletries, and fax service available at front desk. Free local calls. Pets must be under 40 lbs. **Facilities:** **Rates (CP):** Peak (May–Oct) $53–$64 S or D. Extra person $6. Children under age 18 stay free. Lower rates off-season. Parking: Outdoor, free. Senior discounts avail. AE, CB, DC, DISC, MC, V.

RESTAURANTS 🍽

Char's of Collinsville

In Days Inn Collinsville, 1803 Ramada Blvd; tel 618/345-6004. Exit 11 (IL 157) off I-70/55. **American.** On a clear day, you can see the Gateway Arch of St Louis from this hilltop restaurant, but no matter where you're seated, you'll enjoy the view as much as you'll savor the steak and seafood. Dinner choices include pasta con broccoli, jumbo shrimp stuffed with crab and baked in a puff pastry shell, and the special 8-oz sirloin (marinated and grilled to order). **FYI:** Reservations accepted. Children's menu. **Open:** Lunch Mon–Fri 11am–2pm; dinner Mon–Thurs 5–11pm, Fri–Sat 5pm–midnight, Sun 4–11pm; brunch Sun 9am–2pm. **Prices:** Main courses $6–$23. AE, DISC, MC, V. 🔺 🍸

Porter's Steakhouse

In Holiday Inn, 1000 Eastport Plaza Dr; tel 618/345-2400. Exit 11 (IL 157) off I-55/70. **Seafood/Steak.** There is a clublike atmosphere in this contemporary dining room, with its wood-paneled fireplace, brass railings, and bookkeeper lamps. House specialty is grilled pepperloin (whole beef tenderloin marinated for 48 hours then rolled in cracked peppercorns and herbs, chargrilled to order, and served with house mustard). Other menu options include honey-coconut shrimp, a 22-oz chargrilled beef chop, and several mixed-grill and surf-and-turf offerings. **FYI:** Reservations accepted. Children's menu. Dress code. **Open:** Breakfast Mon–Fri 6:15am–2pm, Sat–Sun 7am–2pm; dinner Mon–Sat 4:30–10:30pm, Sun 4:30–10pm; brunch Sun 10am–2pm. **Prices:** Main courses $14–$30. AE, CB, DC, DISC, MC, V. ♿

Countryside

MOTEL 🏨

▤▤ Best Western Inn of La Grange

5631 S La Grange Rd, 60525; tel 708/352-2480 or toll free 800/528-1234; fax 708/354-0998. Set back from the highway with a spacious, parklike courtyard. **Rooms:** 47 rms. CI 1pm/CO noon. Nonsmoking rms avail. **Amenities:** 📺 🍽 A/C, cable TV w/movies. **Services:** 🍽 Complimentary daily newspaper. **Facilities:** 🔧 **Rates (CP):** Peak (June–Sept) $49–$54 S or D. Extra person $5. Children under age 12 stay free. Lower rates off-season. Parking: Outdoor, free. AE, CB, DC, DISC, MC, V.

Danville

Seat of Vermillion County, in eastern Illinois. French records maintained that this site was once the center of several trails used by Native Americans. Abraham Lincoln maintained a law office here during the 1850s, and by the late 19th century the area was a major coal center. Today, agriculture and small industry predominate. **Information:** Danville Area Convention & Visitors Bureau, 100 W Main, #146, PO Box 992, Danville, 61834 (tel 217/442-2096 or toll free 800/383-4386).

MOTELS 🏨

▤▤ Best Western Riverside Inn

57 S Gilbert St, 61832; tel 217/431-0020 or toll free 800/528-1234. Exit 215 off I-74. Economy lodging with easy highway access. The adjacent McDonald's boasts the state's largest "play palace," a good diversion for the kids. **Rooms:** 42 rms and stes. CI 2pm/CO noon. Nonsmoking rms avail. **Amenities:** 📺 A/C, cable TV. 1 unit w/whirlpool. **Services:** 🏊 🍽 🚗 **Facilities:** 🔧 **Rates (CP):** $47 S; $57 D; $112 ste. Extra person $5. Children under age 12 stay free. Parking: Outdoor, free. AE, CB, DC, DISC, MC, V.

▤▤ Comfort Inn

383 Lynch Rd, 61832; tel 217/443-8004 or toll free 800/228-5150. Exit 220 (Lynch Rd) off I-74. Basic, economy lodging conveniently located near interstate. Off-track betting facility across the street. **Rooms:** 56 rms. CI 2pm/CO 11am. Nonsmoking rms avail. **Amenities:** 📺 A/C, satel TV w/movies. **Services:** 🏊 🍽 🚗 **Facilities:** 🔧 🏊 ♿ Games rm, whirlpool. **Rates (CP):** Peak (June–Aug) $40–$55 S; $45–$60 D. Extra person $5. Children under age 18 stay free. Min stay special events. Lower rates off-season. Parking: Outdoor, free. AE, DC, DISC, JCB, MC, V.

▤ The Glo Motel

3617 N Vermillion, 61832; tel 217/442-2086. Economy lodging at no-frills, mom-and-pop establishment. **Rooms:** 22 rms. CI 2pm/CO 11am. Nonsmoking rms avail. **Amenities:** 📺 A/C, cable TV w/movies. **Services:** 🚗 **Facilities:** 🔧 **Rates:** $28–$45 S or D. Parking: Outdoor, free. AE, CB, DC, DISC, MC, V.

▤▤▤ Ramada Inn

388 Eastgate Dr, 61832; tel 217/446-2400 or toll free 800/628-6718. Exit 220 off I-74. Conveniently located to interstate, it offers several diversions, including Danville's only off-track betting facility. Good value for the price. **Rooms:** 131 rms and stes. CI 4pm/CO noon. Nonsmoking rms avail. **Amenities:** 📺 🍸 🎁 A/C, cable TV w/movies, dataport. **Services:** ✕ 🚗 🏊 🍽 🚗 Babysitting. **Facilities:** 🔧 🏊 ♿ 2 restaurants, 2 bars, games rm, whirlpool, washer/dryer. **Rates (BB):** $52–$70 S or D; $99 ste. Extra person $6. Children under age 18 stay free. Min stay special events. Parking: Outdoor, free. AE, V.

Decatur

Seat of Macon County, in central Illinois. This prairie town was founded on a bend of the Sangamon River. A young Abraham Lincoln took up residence just west of town and made his first political speech in what is now Decatur's

Lincoln Square. **Information:** Decatur Area Convention and Visitors Bureau, 202 E North St, Decatur, 62523 (tel 217/423-7000).

MOTELS

▣ Best Western Shelton Motor Inn
450 E Pershing Rd, 62526; tel 217/877-7255 or toll free 800/528-1234; fax 217/875-4085. Although dated and worn, it's on the upswing. New owner is in process of renovating—lobby and restaurant are finished and very nice, and doors to restaurant off lobby have elegant leaded glass. However, outside hallways and stairs are very rundown and dirty. **Rooms:** 150 rms and stes. CI 1pm/CO noon. Nonsmoking rms avail. Clean but worn. Bedspreads soft from washings. **Amenities:** 🛁 A/C, cable TV w/movies. **Services:** ✕ 🚐 🖇 🖐 Bellhop 24 hours. Deposit required for pets. **Facilities:** 🗔 250 ⅊ 1 restaurant, 1 bar, washer/dryer. **Rates:** $42–$44 S; $44–$47 D; $65–$85 ste. Extra person $3–$5. Children under age 12 stay free. Parking: Outdoor, free. AE, CB, DC, DISC, ER, MC, V.

▣ Budgetel Inn
5100 Hickory Point Frontage Rd, 62526; tel 217/875-5800 or toll free 800/428-3438; fax 217/875-7537. Exit 141B off I-72. Small, generic motel tucked away at the back of frontage road just across the street from shopping area. Small but pleasant, and nicely done lobby/front desk area. Next to Cracker Barrel restaurant. **Rooms:** 105 rms and stes. CI 1pm/CO noon. Nonsmoking rms avail. **Amenities:** 🛁 🕭 📺 A/C, cable TV w/movies, dataport. Microwave and/or refrigerator available on request. **Services:** 🖇 🖐 🖐 **Facilities:** 🔟 ⅊ **Rates (CP):** Peak (May 28–Sept 5) $40–$54 S; $47–$54 D; $52–$59 ste. Children under age 18 stay free. Lower rates off-season. Parking: Outdoor, free. AE, CB, DC, DISC, MC, V.

▣ Fairfield Inn
1417 Hickory Point Dr, 62526; tel 217/875-3337 or toll free 800/228-2800; fax 217/875-3337. Exit 141B off US 51 N. Freshly painted white exterior with slightly worn, older interior. Located in commercial area next to shopping mall. **Rooms:** 62 rms. CI 2pm/CO noon. Nonsmoking rms avail. **Amenities:** 🛁 🕭 A/C, cable TV w/movies. **Services:** 🖇 🖐 🖐 Most accommodating staff and manager. **Facilities:** 🗔 15 ⅊ Games rm, whirlpool. Pool area simple, bright, and cheery. **Rates (CP):** $49–$65 S or D. Extra person $5. Children under age 18 stay free. Parking: Outdoor, free. AE, CB, DC, DISC, EC, MC, V.

RESTAURANT

Taters Family Grill
2981 N Main St; tel 217/877-1111. At Pershing. **American.** The fun and festive decor at this roadside eatery includes a variety of wall hangings, a large stuffed shark, reproductions of old road signs, and sports memorabilia. As for eats, there are down-home meals of white meat loaf (made with a spicy blend of turkey and pork), ham and beans, and chicken and noodles. More "nouvelle" offerings (orange-almond salad with raspberry vinaigrette) are available, too. Kids eat for 99 cents on Mondays and Tuesdays. **FYI:** Reservations not accepted. Children's menu. Dress code. **Open:** Mon–Thurs 10am–11pm, Fri–Sat 10am–midnight, Sun 11am–10pm. **Prices:** Main courses $5–$14. MC, V. 👥 ⅊

De Kalb

Barbed wire was invented here in 1873 by local resident Joseph Glidden. De Kalb is perhaps best known today as the home of Northern Illinois University. **Information:** De Kalb Chamber of Commerce, 127 E Lincoln Hwy, De Kalb, 60115 (tel 815/756-6306).

MOTELS

▣ HoJo Inn
1321 W Lincoln Hwy, 60115; tel 815/756-1451 or toll free 800/654-2000; fax 815/756-7260. Annie Glidden exit off I-88; 1¼ mi W on IL 38. Exterior corridors. Northern Illinois University and Huskie Stadium are half-mile away. **Rooms:** 60 rms. CI open/CO noon. Nonsmoking rms avail. Luxury king-size and water beds available. **Amenities:** 🛁 A/C, cable TV w/movies. **Services:** 🖇 Wide selection of top-rated movies in office. Toiletries on request. **Facilities:** ⅊ Playground. **Rates (CP):** $39–$40 S; $45–$46 D. Extra person $2. Children under age 17 stay free. Parking: Outdoor, free. Special group rates. Special awards for members of Business Traveler and Golden Years Travel Clubs. AE, CB, DC, DISC, JCB, MC, V.

▣ University Inn
1212 W Lincoln Hwy, 60115; tel 815/758-8661; fax 815/758-2603. On IL 38. Conveniently located across from Northern Illinois University. Hosts college teams. Brochures available for food delivery from outside restaurants. **Rooms:** 114 rms. CI 2pm/CO noon. Nonsmoking rms avail. **Amenities:** 🛁 A/C. **Services:** 🖇 🖐 Will cater meals for groups. Complimentary newspaper. **Facilities:** 🗔 🛉 200 1 bar, games rm, washer/dryer. **Rates (CP):** $50 S or D. Extra person $5. Children under age 18 stay free. Parking: Outdoor, free. Special corporate rate avail. AE, DC, DISC, MC, V.

RESTAURANT

★ The Country Inn
2496 De Kalb Ave, Sycamore; tel 815/756-8110. **American.** This restaurant with French country decor and a wood-burning fireplace is noted for its lunch and dinner buffets. Ribs, steak, shrimp dishes. **FYI:** Reservations recommended. Children's menu. Beer and wine only. **Open:** Lunch Mon–Fri

11am–2pm; dinner Mon–Sat 5–8:30pm; brunch Sun 10am–3pm. **Prices:** Main courses $8–$12; prix fixe $8. AE, DISC, MC, V. ▪ ▫ ▫ ▫ ◦

Dixon

Seat of Lee County, in northern Illinois. A city of light industry and agriculture on the banks of the Rock River, best known today as the boyhood home of former US President Ronald Reagan. The first self-scouring steel plow was invented in 1837 in nearby Grand Detour. **Information:** Dixon Area Chamber of Commerce & Industry, 74 S Galena Ave, Dixon, 61021 (tel 815/284-3361).

MOTELS ▥

≣≣ Best Western Brandywine Hotel

443 IL 2, 61021; tel 815/284-1890 or toll free 800/528-1234; fax 815/284-1174. Nestled in a quiet country setting in the heart of the scenic Rock River Valley. By all standards it's a motel, despite the name. There is a Presidential Suite in which former President Ronald Reagan stayed during a 1984 birthday visit to his hometown. Nearby golf (5 miles), parks, boating, fishing, and nature trails. Sledding on hills. **Rooms:** 90 rms and stes. CI 2pm/CO noon. Nonsmoking rms avail. **Amenities:** ▥ ◦ A/C, cable TV w/movies, dataport. Some units w/whirlpools. Presidential Suite has whirlpool, conference room, wet bar, refrigerator, microwave, and two cable televisions. **Services:** ✕ ⤶ ⤷ Car-rental desk, babysitting. Snacks served around the pool. **Facilities:** ▥ ▲ ▫ ▫ ◦ 1 restaurant, 1 bar, whirlpool. **Rates:** $53–$130 S; $60–$160 D; $67–$160 ste. Extra person $7. Children under age 12 stay free. Parking: Outdoor, free. Special senior rates and Gold Crown Club benefits. AE, CB, DC, DISC, MC, V.

≣≣ Super 8 Motel

1800 S Galena Ave, 61021; tel 815/284-1800 or toll free 800/800-8000; fax 815/284-1800. Jct I-88 and IL 26. Small, clean, privately owned motel near a John Deere historical site and the boyhood home of former President Ronald Reagan. Also near historic Nachusa House and Lowell Park. Surrounded by cornfields. **Rooms:** 41 rms and stes. CI 2pm/CO 11am. Nonsmoking rms avail. **Amenities:** ▥ A/C, satel TV w/movies, dataport, in-rm safe. 1 unit w/whirlpool. **Services:** ⤶ ⤷ VCR rentals available. Coffee offered in lobby all day. **Facilities:** ◦ **Rates (CP):** Peak (Apr–Sept) $37–$45 S; $45–$65 D; $75–$85 ste. Extra person $5. Children under age 12 stay free. Lower rates off-season. Parking: Outdoor, free. AE, CB, DC, DISC, MC, V.

Downers Grove

The Downer Monument marks the site where Pierre Downer settled, in 1832, at the intersection of two Potawatomi trails. This western suburb of Chicago has quiet shaded streets, and is the hometown of baritone Sherill Milne. **Information:** DuPage Convention & Visitors Bureau, 2001 Butterfield Rd, #1320, Downers Grove, 60515-1047 (tel 630/241-0002 or toll free 800/232-0502).

HOTEL ▥

≣≣≣ Marriott Suites

1500 Opus Place, 60515; tel 630/852-1500 or toll free 800/228-9290; fax 630/852-6527. Landscaped grounds and large inviting lobby. Ideal for the business traveler. **Rooms:** 254 stes. CI 3pm/CO 1pm. Nonsmoking rms avail. **Amenities:** ▥ ◦ ▪ ◦ A/C, cable TV w/movies, refrig, dataport, voice mail. Some units w/terraces. **Services:** ✕ ▬ ▫ ⤶ ⤷ **Facilities:** ▥ ▫ ▫ ◦ 1 restaurant, 1 bar, spa, sauna, whirlpool. Indoor/outdoor pool for year-round swimming with adjacent fitness area. Separate, exceptional boardroom, plus regular meeting rooms. **Rates:** Peak (Mar–Nov) $109–$125 ste. Extra person $10. Children under age 12 stay free. Lower rates off-season. Parking: Outdoor, free. AE, CB, DC, DISC, MC, V.

MOTELS

≣≣ Comfort Inn

3010 Finley Rd, 60515; tel 630/515-1500 or toll free 800/221-2222; fax 630/241-1153. Impressive high vaulted lobby. Yorktown Mall and Oak Brook Mall are short drive away. **Rooms:** 121 rms and stes. CI 2pm/CO noon. Nonsmoking rms avail. **Amenities:** ▥ ◦ A/C, satel TV w/movies. **Services:** ▫ ⤶ ⤷ Neighboring restaurants will deliver. **Facilities:** ▥ ▫ ◦ Whirlpool, washer/dryer. **Rates (CP):** $59–$69 S; $69 D; $79–$89 ste. Extra person $5. Children under age 18 stay free. Parking: Outdoor, free. AE, DC, DISC, JCB, MC, V.

≣≣ Holiday Inn Express

3031 Finley Rd, 60515; tel 630/810-9500 or toll free 800/HOLIDAY; fax 630/810-0059. Winner of 1995 Holiday Inn Quality Award. Lobby features sunken lounge area with fireplace and separate television/coffee area. Restaurants are steps away. Location convenient to College of Dupage, Yorktown Mall, and Oak Brook Mall. **Rooms:** 123 rms and stes. CI 2pm/CO noon. Nonsmoking rms avail. **Amenities:** ▥ ◦ A/C, cable TV, dataport. Some units w/terraces. **Services:** ▫ ⤶ Babysitting. **Facilities:** ▫ ◦ **Rates (CP):** $65–$71 S or D; $79–$85 ste. Extra person $6. Children under age 18 stay free. Parking: Outdoor, free. AE, DC, DISC, ER, JCB, MC, V.

≣ Red Roof Inn

1113 Butterfield Rd, 60515; tel 630/963-4205 or toll free 800/THE-ROOF; fax 630/963-4425. Newly decorated, economical, and well-kept motel with restaurants and malls nearby. **Rooms:** 135 rms. CI open/CO noon. Nonsmoking rms avail. **Amenities:** ▥ A/C, cable TV. **Services:** ▫ ⤶ ⤷ Complimentary coffee. **Facilities:** ▫ ◦ **Rates:** Peak (June–

Aug) $35–$42 S; $45–$54 D. Extra person $7. Children under age 21 stay free. Lower rates off-season. Parking: Outdoor, free. AE, DISC, MC, V.

RESTAURANT 🍴
Copperfield's Restaurant/Lounge
1341 Butterfield Rd; tel 630/852-2424. 3 miles W of US 83. **American.** Located near a number of hotels and large corporate buildings across from the Finley Square Shopping Center, Copperfield's offers casual dining in a somewhat dated atmosphere. The bar and dining room are fairly cramped; service can be curt. It's certainly not the best option in the area, but it probably has the shortest wait. **FYI:** Reservations accepted. Children's menu. Additional locations: 6814 Windsor Ave, Berwyn (tel 708/749-1095); 795 Golf Rd, Schaumburg (tel 708/843-1956). **Open:** Sun 10am–11pm, Mon 11am–11pm, Tues–Thurs 11am–midnight, Fri–Sat 11am–1am. **Prices:** Main courses $5–$27. AE, CB, DC, DISC, MC, V.

ATTRACTION 🏛
The Downers Grove Museum
831 Maple Ave; tel 630/963-1309. Located in the Victorian-style Blodgett House, this museum contains a collection of objects significant to Downers Grove history housed in 10 period rooms. In the Museum Annex are 19th century agricultural tools and transportation artifacts, including an original plank from the Southwest Plank Road. **Open:** Wed 1–4pm, Sun 2–4pm. **Free**

Dundee
This quaint town on the Fox River was named for Dundee, Scotland.

RESTAURANTS 🍴
Duran's of Dundee
8 S River St, East Dundee; tel 847/428-0033. ½ block S of IL 72. **Continental/Seafood.** Housed in a historic 1892 building, Duran's has operated as a restaurant since 1984. A live fir tree grows through the roof of one of the rooms. Most of the menu consists of classic, hearty fare—veal, filet mignon, steaks—although a light menu is also available. **FYI:** Reservations recommended. Dress code. **Open:** Lunch Mon–Fri 11am–2:30pm; dinner Mon–Thurs 5–8:30pm, Fri–Sat 5–10pm, Sun 4–8pm. **Prices:** Main courses $9–$19. AE, DC, DISC, MC, V. ♥

$ ★ The Milk Pail
14 N 630 IL 25; tel 847/742-5040. 1 mi N of I-90 on IL 25; ¾ mi S of IL 72. **American.** A down-home local favorite. Birds are big on the menu—chicken, turkey, wild pheasant, duck—and an on-site bakery turns out freshly baked rolls and breads. Luncheon and dinner musicals are presented twice

weekly; call ahead for schedule. **FYI:** Reservations recommended. Children's menu. **Open:** Mon–Fri 11am–9pm, Sat 9am–9pm, Sun 9am–8pm. **Prices:** Main courses $7–$16. AE, CB, DC, DISC, MC, V. 🍷 🏔 🎿 ♿

ATTRACTIONS 🏛
Racing Rapids Action Water Park
Jct IL 25/72, East Dundee; tel 847/426-5525. Ten-acre water park featuring four water slides, a lazy river tube ride, and a special children's area. Also bumper boats and go-carts. **Open:** Mem Day–Labor Day, hours vary. $$$$

Santa's Village
Jct IL 25/72, East Dundee; tel 847/426-6751. A 55-acre theme park with more than 40 rides, shows, and attractions. Highlights include Old McDonald's Farm with 50 animals, pony rides, and petting zoo; the Galaxi Roller Coaster; a live magic show; and, of course, a visit with Santa. **Open:** Mem Day–Sept, hours vary. $$$$

Du Quoin
Southeast of St Louis, it is named for Jean Baptiste Du Quoigne, a Native American of French extraction who later became chief of the Kaskasia tribe. Du Quoin is in a fertile agricultural and mining region, with many substantial homes of retired farmers. **Information:** Du Quoin Chamber of Commerce, 20 N Chestnut, PO Box 57, Du Quoin, 62832 (tel 618/542-9570 or toll free 800/455-9570).

MOTEL 🏨
🏨 The Hub Motel
423 W Main St, 62832; tel 618/542-2108. On IL-152, 2 blocks W of US 51. No frills, basic motel. Fine for overnight stay for business travelers, but no more. **Rooms:** 26 rms. CI open/CO 11am. **Amenities:** 🛁 ⚙ A/C, TV. **Rates:** $25 S; $35 D. Extra person $2. Children under age 12 stay free. Parking: Outdoor, free. AE, DISC, MC, V.

Effingham
Seat of Effingham County, in southeast part of state. This small prairie town, settled in 1853 along the Old National Road, was profoundly shaped by German immigration. **Information:** Effingham Convention & Visitors Bureau, 508 W Fayette, PO Box 643, Effingham, 62401-0643 (tel 217/342-4147).

MOTELS 🏨
🏨🏨 Best Inns of America
1209 N Keller Dr, 62401; tel 217/347-5141 or toll free 800/237-8466; fax 217/347-5141. Exit 160 off I-57/70, N on Keller Dr (IL 32/33). Clean, comfortable accommodations. Fine for business traveler or overnight stay. Near several

restaurants and across street from factory outlet mall. **Rooms:** 83 rms. CI open/CO 1pm. Nonsmoking rms avail. **Amenities:** 📺 A/C, cable TV w/movies. **Services:** 🍴 🛎 **Facilities:** 🏊 & **Rates (CP):** Peak (Apr–Oct) $36–$42 S; $45–$48 D. Extra person $6. Children under age 18 stay free. Lower rates off-season. Parking: Outdoor, free. Senior discounts avail AE, CB, DC, DISC, MC, V.

≡≡ Hampton Inn

1509 Hampton Dr, 62401; tel 217/342-4499 or toll free 800/426-7866; fax 217/347-2828. Exit 160 off I-57/70; S on IL 32/33 to Hampton Dr. Newer motel with easy access to highway. Good for short stays. Near factory outlet mall and off-track betting parlor. **Rooms:** 62 rms. CI 3pm/CO 11am. Nonsmoking rms avail. Clean, comfortable rooms. **Amenities:** 📺 🕭 A/C, cable TV w/movies. Some units w/whirlpools. **Services:** 🛄 🍴 🛎 Weekly manager's wine and cheese reception. Permission required for pets. **Facilities:** 🏊 🏋 & Sauna. Free passes to local health club. **Rates (CP):** Peak (May–Sept) $51–$53 S; $56–$58 D. Extra person $7. Children under age 18 stay free. Lower rates off-season. Parking: Outdoor, free. AE, CB, DC, DISC, MC, V.

≡≡ Holiday Inn

1600 W Fayette Ave, 62401; tel 217/342-4161 or toll free 800/465-4329; fax 217/342-4161. Exit 159 off I-57/70; W on Fayette to 1st light, left to Frontage Rd entrance. Basic, clean, and comfortable accommodations. Golf and horseback riding nearby. **Rooms:** 135 rms and stes. CI 2pm/CO noon. Nonsmoking rms avail. **Amenities:** 📺 🕭 A/C, cable TV w/movies. 1 unit w/whirlpool. **Services:** ✕ 🚗 🛄 🍴 🛎 Twice-daily maid svce. **Facilities:** 🏊 🏋 & 1 restaurant, 1 bar, volleyball. Sneakers Restaurant, and sand volleyball on premises. **Rates:** $49–$59 S; $54–$64 D; $95 ste. Extra person $5. Children under age 18 stay free. Parking: Outdoor, free. AE, CB, DC, DISC, JCB, MC, V.

≡≡ Howard Johnson

1606 W Fayette Ave, 62401; tel 217/342-4667 or toll free 800/446-4656; fax 217/342-4645. Exit 159 off I-57/70. Nothing fancy, just good, clean, overnight accommodations. **Rooms:** 55 rms. CI 1pm/CO 11am. Nonsmoking rms avail. **Amenities:** 📺 A/C, cable TV w/movies, VCR. 1 unit w/whirlpool. **Services:** 🛄 🍴 🛎 One free movie/VCR rental with each night's stay. Extra charge for pets. **Facilities:** & **Rates (CP):** Peak (May–Oct) $30–$50 S; $42–$50 D. Extra person $5. Children under age 18 stay free. Lower rates off-season. Parking: Outdoor, free. AARP, corporate, and government discounts. AE, CB, DC, DISC, ER, JCB, MC, V.

≡≡≡ Keller Ramada Inn

N IL 32/33, PO Box 747, 62401; tel 217/342-2131 or toll free 800/535-0546; fax 217/347-8757. At exit 160 off I-57/70. The first Ramada Inn east of the Mississippi. Three antique European storefronts grace the beautifully appointed lobby and convention center. Floral decorations and upholstery. Great for families. Boating and waterskiing avail-able at nearby Lake Sara. Near factory outlet stores. **Rooms:** 169 rms and stes. Executive level. CI 2pm/CO noon. Nonsmoking rms avail. Most rooms have entrances to both the outside and to an indoor corridor. Even-numbered rooms face interior courtyard and pool. **Amenities:** 📺 🕭 🖥 A/C, cable TV w/movies, voice mail. Some units w/terraces, some w/whirlpools. Newer rooms have two phones, full-length mirrors, fans and heat lamps in bath, and grab bars in tub. **Services:** ✕ 🚗 🛄 🍴 🛎 Social director, masseur, babysitting. **Facilities:** 🏊 🛋 🍽 & 2 restaurants (see "Restaurants" below), 2 bars, games rm, spa, sauna, steam rm, whirlpool, playground. Coffee shop, Greenhouse Lounge, pizzeria, off-track betting, gift shop, bowling alley, miniature golf, batting cage, Thelma's Restaurant, and Keller Convention Center all on grounds. **Rates (CP):** $49–$109 S; $57–$109 D; $79–$109 ste. Extra person $7. Children under age 18 stay free. AP and MAP rates avail. Parking: Outdoor, free. AE, CB, DC, DISC, EC, MC, V.

RESTAURANTS 🍴

Niemerg's Steak House

1410 W Fayette Rd; tel 217/342-3921. Exit 159 off I-59/70; W on IL 32/33. **Seafood/Steak.** Country-style decorations, curtained booths, pressback spindle chairs, and a separate party room create a homey atmosphere. Dinner choices include country fried chicken, fried catfish, and a pork filet mignon, as well as a variety of steaks. A coffee shop and the Brass Rail lounge are attached to this popular eatery. **FYI:** Reservations recommended. Children's menu. **Open:** Daily 6am–2am. **Prices:** Main courses $6–$13. AE, DC, MC, V. 🖼

★ Thelma's

In Keller Ramada Inn, N IL 32/33; tel 217/342-2131. Exit 160 off I-57/70. **American/Seafood.** Somewhat formal dining room, decorated with crystal and bronze chandeliers, original oil paintings, and an immense fireplace. Nightly specials complement a menu that includes Cajun chicken fettuccini, broiled scallops, sautéed veal marsala, and the house specialty, roast standing ribs of beef. No reservations accepted for Tues night ("family and friends" night), when five people can enjoy an all-you-can-eat spaghetti dinner for just $10. **FYI:** Reservations accepted. Children's menu. Dress code. **Open:** Daily 6am–10pm. **Prices:** Main courses $4–$17. AE, CB, DC, DISC, MC, V. &

Elgin

This small town on the Fox River is famous for the Elgin watch and for the invention of condensed milk by local dairyman Gail Borden in 1856. **Information:** Elgin Area Convention & Visitors Bureau, 77 Riverside Dr, Elgin, 60120-6425 (tel 847/695-7540).

HOTEL 🏨

▤▤▤ Holiday Inn Elgin

345 W River Rd, 60123; tel 847/695-5000 or toll free 800/HOLIDAY; fax 847/695-6556. Exit IL 31 S off I-90. Holidome Recreation Center plus a five-story tower. Location just off interstate offers easy access to Chicago and western suburbs, nearby Medieval Times Dinner Tournament, Woodfield Mall, and Elgin. Semi-rural area. Activities for family and business travelers. **Rooms:** 203 rms and stes. CI 3pm/CO noon. Nonsmoking rms avail. Some rooms adjacent to Holidome and pool area. Rooms with king-size beds have sleeper couches. **Amenities:** 🛁 💧 🕹 A/C, cable TV, dataport. Suites have hair dryers. **Services:** ✗ 🗄 🛎 Car-rental desk. **Facilities:** 🏊 🏋 🛗300 🖥 ⚕ 1 restaurant, 1 bar, games rm, sauna, whirlpool, washer/dryer. **Rates:** Peak (Mar–Nov) $65 S or D; $125–$175 ste. Extra person $8. Children under age 19 stay free. Min stay special events. Lower rates off-season. Parking: Outdoor, free. Bed-and-breakfast package avail. AE, DC, DISC, JCB, MC, V.

RESTAURANT 🍴

⑤ ✦ Dieterle's

550 S McLean Blvd; tel 847/697-7311. Just S of IL 20. **German.** This family-owned and -operated rathskeller has been serving German cuisine for 22 years. Wiener schnitzel is the most popular dish, although some surprises (duck, seafood) show up on the menu as well. Carryout available. **FYI:** Reservations recommended. Children's menu. Dress code. **Open:** Lunch Tues–Fri 11:30am–4pm, Sat 11:30am–2:30pm; dinner Tues–Thurs 5–10pm, Fri–Sat 5–11pm, Sun noon–8pm. **Prices:** Main courses $9–$20. AE, CB, DC, DISC, MC, V. 🎦 ⚕

Elmhurst

This western suburb of Chicago was named for a majestic double row of elms that once extended for nearly a mile through town. **Information:** Elmhurst Chamber of Commerce & Industry, 105 Maple Ave, PO Box 752, Elmhurst, 60126 (tel 630/834-6060).

MOTEL 🏨

▤▤▤ Courtyard by Marriott

370 IL 83 N, 60126; tel 630/941-9444 or toll free 800/321-2210; fax 630/941-3539. A typical Courtyard by Marriott. **Rooms:** 140 rms and stes. CI 6pm/CO 1pm. Nonsmoking rms avail. **Amenities:** 🛁 💧 🕹 A/C, cable TV w/movies, dataport, VCR. Some units w/whirlpools. **Services:** 🗄 🛎 Videos for rent and various convenience items available at front desk. Polo Lounge serves hors d'oeuvres 4–10pm. Food can be delivered from large selection of local restaurants. Library on second floor has hundreds of books. **Facilities:** 🏊 🏋 🛗50 ⚕ 1 restaurant (bkfst only), 1 bar, sauna, steam rm, whirlpool, washer/dryer. Free admission to local health club. **Rates (BB):** $79–$84 S or D; $99–$109 ste. Extra person $10. Children under age 18 stay free. Parking: Outdoor, free. AE, CB, DC, DISC, MC, V.

ATTRACTION 🏛

Lizzardo Museum of Lapidary Art

220 Cottage Hill; tel 630/833-1616. The word "lapidary" refers to the art of stone cutting, and this repository of that art displays hard-stone carvings, gemstones, mineral specimens, and such oddities as an ivory carving of the Last Supper. The museum's jade collection is internationally renowned, a fact that is punctuated by the presence of a chunk of jade weighing over half a ton that greets visitors at the entrance. **Open:** Tues–Sat 10am–5pm, Sun 1–5pm. $

Evanston

Abuts Chicago to the north along Lake Michigan. Once home to the Women's Christian Temperance Union, Evanston is now world famous as the site of Northwestern University. **Information:** Evanston Chamber of Commerce, One Rotary Center, 1560 Sherman Ave, #860, Evanston, 60201 (tel 847/328-1500).

HOTELS 🏨

▤▤▤ Evanston Holiday Inn & Conference Center

1501 Sherman Ave, 60201; tel 847/491-6400; fax 847/328-3090. Off Dempster. On south end of downtown, it attracts traveling students and families. The lovely glassed-in art niches, with beautiful vases and flowers, lend tranquility amid the exuberance of the youngsters. Across the street from and within easy walking distance of some interesting Evanston restaurants. **Rooms:** 159 rms and stes. Executive level. CI 3pm/CO noon. Nonsmoking rms avail. **Amenities:** 🛁 💧 🕹 🍴 A/C, satel TV w/movies, dataport. **Services:** ✗ 🚐 🗄 🛎 Car-rental desk, babysitting. Bottled water available on three floors. **Facilities:** 🏊 🏋 🛗600 ⚕ 1 restaurant, 1 bar, sauna, washer/dryer. **Rates:** Peak (Apr–Oct 28) $92–$102 S; $102–$112 D; $139–$159 ste. Extra person $10. Children under age 18 stay free. Lower rates off-season. Parking: Indoor/outdoor, free. AE, CB, DC, DISC, JCB, MC, V.

▤▤▤ Omni Orrington Hotel

1710 Orrington Ave, 60201; tel 847/866-8700 or toll free 800/THE-OMNI; fax 847/866-8724. Off of Davis or Church. Gracious collonaded entrance on quiet, tree-lined downtown street. Only two blocks from Northwestern University and the parks and beaches. Caters to visiting parents, faculty, and business travelers. **Rooms:** 277 rms, stes, and effic. CI 3pm/CO noon. Nonsmoking rms avail. Elegant, old-fashioned (but newly remodeled), and comfortable. Upscale home atmosphere rather than hotel ambience. **Amenities:** 🛁 💧 A/C, cable TV w/movies. Some units w/terraces. **Services:**

✕ VP 🚗 🖼 🎧 Babysitting. **Facilities:** 🏊 ⅃ 1 restaurant, 3 bars (1 w/entertainment), games rm, beauty salon. The indoor/outdoor cafe, Cooking with Jazz, adds a festive note. **Rates:** $135–$145 S; $145–$155 D; $240–$500 ste; $350–$500 effic. Extra person $15. Children under age 12 stay free. Parking: Indoor, $8/day. AE, CB, DC, DISC, EC, ER, JCB, MC, V.

RESTAURANTS 🍴

Ⓢ ★ bistro 1800 & my bar
In 1800 Sherman Building, 1800 Sherman Ave; tel 847/492-3450. N side of town; 4 blocks W of Lake Michigan. **Eclectic.** Tucked into the back of a modern office building you'll find this delightful jewel of a restaurant. Two dining rooms, along with an outdoor patio, offer colorful, contemporary European bistro atmosphere and a jazz motif. Beautifully prepared food comes in surprising combinations that delight the senses. Feta cheese baked with onions and tomatoes, rainbow trout in a lemon-butter-wine sauce, and the fruit and cheese plate are a few favorites. **FYI:** Reservations recommended. Jazz/piano. No smoking. **Open:** Sun–Thurs 11am–midnight, Fri–Sat 11am–1am. **Prices:** Main courses $8–$14. AE, DISC, MC, V. ♥ 🍽 ⅃

★ Jilly's Cafe
2614 Green Bay Rd; tel 847/869-7636. Just N of Central St. **New American.** An intimate bistro with a decadent and whimsical atmosphere. The food is state of the culinary art, and the clientele from the surrounding area is likely to be comparing the escargot with what they had last week in Paris. Chef Kevin Shikami melds many cultures in this new American food, with pastas such as lemon linguine served with chicken, mushrooms, roasted peppers, broccoli, and goat cheese; and entrees such as grilled medallions of pork in pecan-mustard crust, served on polenta with peach chutney. Fine homemade pastries finish the meal. Pre-theater prix-fixe dinner available. **FYI:** Reservations recommended. Beer and wine only. No smoking. **Open:** Lunch Tues–Fri 11:30am–2pm; dinner Tues–Thurs 5–9pm, Fri–Sat 5–10pm, Sun 5–8pm; brunch Sun 10:30am–2pm. **Prices:** Main courses $9–$17. CB, DC, MC, V. ♥ 🟦

Kuni's
511 Main St; tel 847/328-2004. ½ block E of Chicago Ave. **Japanese.** A favorite gathering spot for medical and academic professionals. Excellent use of light wood for tables, chairs, and partitions creates attractive Japanese decor. Separate sushi bar and sushi kitchen. More than 20 appetizers are available, like deep-fried eggplant with sweet sauce, and cold, steamed spinach. Main courses include shrimp, beef, and chicken teriyakis, and sukiyaki. Japanese beers, hot or cold sake. Reservations requested for parties of six or more. **FYI:** Reservations accepted. Beer and wine only. **Open:** Lunch Mon 11:30am–1:45pm, Wed–Sat 11:30–1:45pm; dinner Sun–Mon 5–9:45pm, Wed–Sat 5–9:45pm. **Prices:** Main courses $15–$28. AE, MC, V. ⅃

★ Las Palmas
1642 Maple Ave; tel 847/328-2555. At Church, just W of train tracks. **Mexican.** A delightful, family-run neighborhood place with several rooms and a small outdoor patio. The northern Mexican decor includes serapes, large pots, and wooden parquet tables, and the menu encompasses a full array of traditional and inventive dishes. Tacos, burritos, enchiladas, and steaks (from carne asada to bistec Oaxaca) are well prepared and delicious. Especially marvelous are the fish dishes, such as red snapper prepared in the styles of Merida, the Yucatan, Campeche, or *al ojo*. The chicken soup—a large bowl with whole pieces of chicken, potatoes, corn on the cob and served with rice and tortillas—can be a complete meal all by itself. **FYI:** Reservations recommended. Harp. Children's menu. Additional locations: 1773 W Howard St, Chicago (tel 312/262-7446); 311 W Oakton, Westmont (tel 708/963-9999). **Open:** Sun–Thurs 11am–11pm, Fri–Sat 11am–midnight. **Prices:** Main courses $7–$16. AE, CB, DC, DISC, MC, V. ♥ 🍽 ⅃

Lindo Mexico
1934 Maple St; tel 847/475-3435. From downtown Evanston, take Chicago Ave N to Foster, left to Maple, left ½ blk. **Mexican.** Down-home Mexican cooking in a small, gaily decorated place. Bright oranges and pinks, stucco, and brick. Complete selection of northern Mexican dishes, good choice of imported beers. Very friendly staff. **FYI:** Reservations accepted. Additional locations: 8990 N Milwaukee Ave, Niles (tel 708/296-2540); 2638 N Lincoln Ave, Chicago (tel 312/871-4832). **Open:** Sun–Thurs 11:30am–10pm, Fri–Sat 11:30am–midnight. **Prices:** Main courses $8–$15. AE, V. 🍽

Nevin's Pub
1450 Sherman Ave; tel 847/869-0450. 2 blocks S of downtown. **Irish/Pub.** Convivial good cheer is the spirit at this Irish pub. Country dishes range from corned beef and cabbage and shepherd's pie to traditional Irish stew (on Sunday); side orders like Irish sausage roll and brown bread and butter can be ordered as well. The pub prides itself on its status as the number one Guinness distributor in Illinois. **FYI:** Reservations accepted. Folk. Children's menu. **Open:** Mon–Thurs 11am–1am, Sat–Sun 11am–2am, Sun noon–midnight. **Prices:** Main courses $8–$17. AE, DC, MC, V. 🍺 🍽 ⅃

New Japan Restaurant
1322-24 Chicago Ave; tel 847/475-5980. ½ block N of Dempster St. **Japanese.** Pristinely clean and simple. Table setting is a napkin and chopsticks in a basically white room with blond furniture. Even the bathroom sparkles, and has fresh, flowering plants. Full array of delicious sushi, tempuras, teriyakis, sukiyaki, as well as the generally less available dishes, such as chawan mushi. Popular with professionals from the hospital and university and couples. **FYI:** Reservations recommended. No smoking. **Open:** Lunch

Tues–Sat 11:30am–2:15pm; dinner Tues–Thurs 5–9:15pm, Fri–Sat 5–10:15pm, Sun 4:30–8:45pm. **Prices:** Main courses $12–$16. AE, CB, DC, MC, V.

Oceanique
505 Main St; tel 847/864-3435. ½ block E of Chicago Ave. **Seafood.** Chef Mark Grosz shows off his originality and delicate touch in this attractively decorated restaurant. Dishes include organically grown lettuces with vinaigrette; smoked salmon with cucumbers and horseradish crème fraîche; and farm-raised rabbit confit with morels. Special ales available. **FYI:** Reservations recommended. **Open:** Mon–Thurs 5:30–9:30pm, Fri–Sat 5:30–10pm. Closed June 26–July 6. **Prices:** Main courses $17–$28; prix fixe $24. AE, DC, MC, V.

Siam Square
622 Davis St; tel 847/475-0860. **Thai.** Authentic Thai artifacts and artwork. Special area created for Thai traditional service. Patrons must remove shoes on entering area and sit at special low banquette. Special luncheon buffet daily 11:30am–3:30pm for $6.95. In June and July on Fri and Sat evenings, Thai musicians and classical dancers perform in the patio dining area. Validation stamp available for two hours free parking at City Garage (two blocks away). **FYI:** Reservations recommended. Beer and wine only. **Open:** Fri 11am–10:30pm, Sun 11am–9pm, Mon–Thurs 11am–10pm. **Prices:** Main courses $6–$10. AE, DC, DISC, MC.

♣ Va Pensiero
In Margarita Inn, 1566 Oak Ave; tel 847/475-7779. 1 blk east of Ridge between Davis and Grove. **Italian.** Critically acclaimed regional Italian cooking under chef Peggy Ryan's top-notch standards sets this delightful place in a class by itself. Intimate, romantic, impressive, and beautiful, with a Greco-Roman decor. Homemade smoked veal sausages with basil and black olives sauced with fresh fennel, lemon, and olive oil; delicate pastas; garlic crusted lamb shank roasted with rosemary vinegar on a bed of white beans; and fresh and attractive salads. Definitely a place for that special date, family celebration, or important business deal. **FYI:** Reservations recommended. Dress code. **Open:** Lunch Mon–Fri 11:30am–2pm; dinner Mon–Thurs 5:30–9pm, Fri–Sat 5:30–10pm. **Prices:** Main courses $14–$19. AE, DC, DISC, MC, V.

★ Verdi & Puccini Opera Cafe
1458 Sherman Ave; tel 847/332-2742. 2 blocks S of downtown. **Italian.** A great place for opera lovers, as the waitstaff (music majors from nearby Northwestern University) regularly gives recitals of popular Verdi and Puccini arias. Authentic Italian fare features Italian wedding soup (orzo, spinach, and meatballs in a lemon-chicken broth) and basil fettucine, plus a full range of gourmet salads and sandwiches. The pastries and tartuffo are recommended for dessert. **FYI:** Reservations accepted. Beer and wine only. No smoking. **Open:** Tues–Thurs 11:30am–10:30pm, Fri–Sat 11:30am–11:30pm, Sun 11:30am–10:30pm. **Prices:** Main courses $7–$10. DISC, MC, V.

ATTRACTIONS

Northwestern University
Clark St and Sheridan Rd; tel 847/491-7271. Founded in 1851, the lakefront campus contains the Dearborn Observatory, the Pick-Staiger Concert Hall, with a variety of music programs, and the University Library, with a collection of rare books and art exhibits. Campus tours are conducted during the academic year by student guides. **Free**

Mitchell Indian Museum
2408 Orrington Ave; tel 847/866-1395. Informative and unusual museum with a collection ranging from pre-Columbian stoneware tools and weapons to the work of contemporary Native American artists. **Open:** Tues–Fri 9am–4:30pm, Sat–Sun 1–4pm. **$**

Willard House
1730 Chicago Ave; tel 847/864-1397. Evanston was the home of Frances Willard, founder of the Woman's Christian Temperance Union. Her home is still the headquarters of the Temperance Union and is open to visitors. Nine of the 17 rooms in this old Victorian "cottage" have been converted into a museum of period furnishings and memorabilia from the temperance movement. Donation requested. **Open:** Mon–Sat 9am–3pm. **Free**

Fairview Heights

HOTEL

≡≡≡ Ramada Inn Fairview Heights
6900 N Illinois Ave, 62208; tel 618/632-4747 or toll free 800/947-0317; fax 618/632-9428. Exit 12 (IL 159 N) off I-64. Easily seen from the highway, this five-story hotel has all the features business and family travelers will want. Working fireplace in lobby. Close to shopping, restaurants, golf, tennis, and jogging path. **Rooms:** 160 rms and stes. Executive level. CI 3pm/CO noon. Nonsmoking rms avail. **Amenities:** A/C, satel TV w/movies. 1 unit w/whirlpool. **Services:** Safety deposit boxes at front desk. Pets $10. **Facilities:** 2 bars (1 w/entertainment), games rm, washer/dryer. Free access to local Vic Tanny health club. Picnic tables and shelters around pool. Bar with pool table and comedy club on premises. **Rates:** Peak (June–Aug) $60–$70 S or D; $165 ste. Extra person $6. Children under age 12 stay free. Lower rates off-season. Parking: Outdoor, free. AE, CB, DC, DISC, MC, V.

MOTEL

≣≣ Super 8 Motel Fairview Heights

45 Ludwig Dr, 62208; tel 618/398-8338 or toll free 800/800-8000; fax 618/398-8158. Exit 12 (IL 159) off I-64. Easy access to highway and proximity to several restaurants make this no-frills lodging a good choice for business travelers. **Rooms:** 81 rms. CI 4pm/CO 11am. Nonsmoking rms avail. Executive singles have recliners. **Amenities:** 🛏 A/C, cable TV w/movies. **Services:** 🛎 🍽 Car-rental desk. **Facilities:** 🔲16 🚳 **Rates (CP):** Peak (Apr–Sept) $46–$50 S or D. Extra person $5. Children under age 12 stay free. Lower rates off-season. Parking: Outdoor, free. AE, CB, DC, DISC, MC, V.

Freeport

Seat of Stephenson County, in northern Illinois. First settled in 1835 by William "Tutty" Stephenson, whose wife disagreed with his generous sharing of meals with all comers. According to legend, she told him the place was getting to be a regular "free port." **Information:** Stephenson County Convention & Visitors Bureau, 2047 AYP Rd, Freeport, 61032 (tel 815/233-1357 or toll free 800/369-2955).

MOTELS 🏨

≣≣ Holiday Inn

1300 E South St, 61032; tel 815/235-3121 or toll free 800/HOLIDAY; fax 815/235-4946. Off of US 20. On a high bluff on the edge of town surrounded by country and screened from the highway by plantings. One third of the rooms are around a pool. A golf course is within 4 miles, and a nearby YMCA has racquetball and tennis courts. **Rooms:** 85 rms. CI 2pm/CO noon. Nonsmoking rms avail. Half of the rooms are nonsmoking. **Amenities:** 🛏 🅰 A/C, satel TV w/movies. Half of the bathrooms have hair dryers. Refrigerators and toiletries can be requested. **Services:** ✗ 🚗 🖼 🛎 🍽 Car-rental desk, babysitting. Federal Express and UPS boxes are in front of hotel for corporate clientele. **Facilities:** 🔲 🏋 🔲625 🚳 1 restaurant, 1 bar, games rm, sauna, whirlpool, playground. An atrium dining room is off the lobby; during the summer, children eat free with adults. **Rates:** $59 S; $65 D. Extra person $6. Children under age 19 stay free. Parking: Outdoor, free. AE, CB, DC, DISC, JCB, MC, V.

≣≣ Super 8 Motel

1649 Willard Dr, 61032; tel 815/232-8880 or toll free 800/800-8000; fax 815/232-8907. Off US 20. A small, clean, adequate motel. Management has received Super 8's Certificate of Excellence. Adjacent to numerous restaurants and a shopping mall. **Rooms:** 52 rms. CI 2pm/CO 11am. Nonsmoking rms avail. **Amenities:** 🛏 A/C. **Services:** 🆅🅿 🛎 🍽 **Facilities:** 🚳 **Rates (CP):** $41 S; $44–$62 D. Extra person $5. Children under age 12 stay free. Parking: Outdoor, free. 10% discount for VIP Club Members. AE, CB, DC, DISC, MC, V.

ATTRACTION 🏛

Silvercreek and Stephenson Railroad

Lamm and Walnut Sts; tel 815/235-2198 or toll free 800/369-2955. A 1912, 36 ton Heisler steam logging locomotive. The engine pulls three antique cabooses and a covered outdoor passenger flat car. Visitors embark on a four mile ride through Illinois farm land and native virgin timber. **Open:** May–Oct, Sat–Sun 11am–5pm. **$**

Galena

Seat of Jo Daviess County, in northwest corner of state. This quaint town has stood still in time, looking much as it did more than a century ago. More than 90% of its buildings are listed on the National Register of Historic Places, including the Italianate house given to Gen Ulysses Grant upon his victorious return from the Civil War. **Information:** Galena/Jo Daviess County Convention & Visitors Bureau, 101 Bouthillier St, Galena, 61036 (tel 815/777-3557 or toll free 800/747-9377).

HOTEL 🏨

≣≣≣ The DeSoto House Hotel

230 S Main St, 61036; tel 815/777-0090 or toll free 800/343-6562; fax 815/777-9529. In the center of town. Authentically restored hotel that has hosted such notables as Ralph Waldo Emerson, Abraham Lincoln, Susan B Anthony, Mark Twain, and Theodore Roosevelt. A sweeping staircase rises from the lobby with its velvet couch, large wooden reception desk, and at least one gaslight. The sitting rooms and library showcase fine antiques. Opened in 1855, it served as the presidential campaign headquarters for Ulysses S Grant. **Rooms:** 55 rms and stes. CI 3pm/CO 11am. Nonsmoking rms avail. Comfortably furnished rooms. **Amenities:** 🛏 🅰 A/C, cable TV w/movies. Some units w/fireplaces. **Services:** 🛎 Social director, babysitting. **Facilities:** 🏃 📺 🔲120 🚳 2 restaurants, 1 bar. **Rates:** Peak (Apr–Oct) $95–$115 S; $105–$150 D; $140–$175 ste. Extra person $10. Children under age 12 stay free. Lower rates off-season. AP and MAP rates avail. Parking: Indoor, free. AE, CB, DC, MC, V.

MOTEL

≣≣≣ Best Western Quiet House Suites

9923 US 20 E, 61036; tel 815/777-2577 or toll free 800/528-1234; fax 815/777-0584. A gray shingle structure with white trim, set back from the road. The lobby is comfortable with a gas fireplace. Recipient of the Best Western Directors Award for service and maintenance. Nearby golfing, Mississippi riverboat gambling, and dog racing. **Rooms:** 42 rms and stes. CI 2pm/CO 11am. Nonsmoking rms avail. Some rooms overlook rolling hills. Theme suites. **Amenities:** 🛏 🅰 A/C, cable TV w/movies, dataport. Some units w/terraces, some w/whirlpools. Most rooms have balconies or patios. The

Oriental Suite has a whirlpool for two. **Facilities:** 🏠 👤 📺 Whirlpool. **Rates:** $80–$170 S; $109–$190 D; $149–$169 ste. Extra person $10. Children under age 2 stay free. Min stay special events. Parking: Outdoor, free. AE, CB, DC, DISC, ER, MC, V.

INNS

UNRATED **The Aldrich Guest House**

900 3rd St, 61036; tel 815/777-3323. N of US 20. Guests may relax on screened porch overlooking side yard where General Grant's troops once drilled or enjoy double front parlor where Lincoln and Grant were often entertained. Built by an Illinois State representative who later became a Senator from Minnesota, the Greek Revival and Italianate-style house has had numerous additions. Christmas trees and decorations displayed Thanksgiving–Jan. Unsuitable for children under 18. **Rooms:** 5 rms and stes (1 w/shared bath). CI 4pm/CO 11am. No smoking. Brightly furnished with antique beds, handmade quilts, and tapestries. **Amenities:** 🛁 A/C, cable TV w/movies. No phone. 1 unit w/terrace, 1 w/fireplace. Robes with the room that has a shared bath. **Facilities:** 👤 📺 🗓 Guest lounge w/TV. VCR in library. **Rates (BB):** $70 S; $75 D; $110 ste. Extra person $15. Min stay wknds. Parking: Outdoor, free. DISC, MC, V.

UNRATED **Belle Aire Mansion Guest House**

11410 US 20 NW, 61036; tel 815/777-0893. US 20 W of Galena. 11 acres. A pre–Civil War, Federal-style home furnished with antiques and reproductions. Located only 2½ miles from Main Street Galena, yet in the country. There are two verandas; the one off the top floor has a porch swing. Children welcome. Nearby horseback riding, golf, and hiking. **Rooms:** 5 rms and stes. CI 4pm/CO 11am. No smoking. Antiques in rooms include king-size brass bed, sofa, white-eyelet canopy bed, clawfoot tub, antique trunk, and ice cream table. Back views from house overlook farm fields. **Amenities:** 🛁 A/C, TV w/movies. No phone. 1 unit w/terrace, some w/fireplaces, 1 w/whirlpool. One suite has a bedside double whirlpool. **Services:** ☕ Early morning coffee. **Facilities:** 👤 📺 Guest lounge w/TV. **Rates (BB):** $60–$130 S; $65–$135 D. Extra person $10. Children under age 13 stay free. Min stay wknds. Parking: Outdoor, free. Closed Dec 24–25. DISC, MC, V.

UNRATED **Captain Gear Guest House**

1000 S Bench St, 61036; tel 815/777-0222 or toll free 800/794-5656; fax 815/777-3210. Off US 20, S on Bench St ⅓ mi. 4 acres. This handsome guest house is on a high bluff overlooking Galena River Valley. Captain Hezekiah Gear, of the Blackhawk War, made his fortune by discovering one of the area's largest lead mines and built this Italianate mansion in 1855. Restored to its former elegance with museum-quality antiques from three centuries, the mansion has eight restored fireplaces and is on the National Register of Historic Places. Worth a splurge. Unsuitable for children under 18. **Rooms:** 3 rms and stes. CI 3pm/CO 11am. No smoking.

Rooms have views of either the garden or the valley. **Amenities:** 🛁 A/C, TV w/movies, VCR. No phone. All units w/fireplaces, 1 w/whirlpool. **Facilities:** 👤 📺 Whirlpool, guest lounge. **Rates (BB):** $125–$135 S or D; $155 ste. Extra person $10. Min stay wknds. Parking: Outdoor, free. DISC, MC, V.

UNRATED **Park Ave Guest House**

208 Park Ave, 61036; tel 815/777-1075 or toll free 800/359-0743. Off US 20, go N on Park for ¾ mile. This historic landmark is a three-story, Queen Anne, "Painted Lady" of seven colors with a turret and screened wraparound porch. Behind the lace curtains are such treasures as a Victrola with a horn, a Montgomery Ward pump organ, and "general store" collectibles. In the yard is a gazebo built from the elevator gates of the Marquette Building in Chicago. The century-old Victorian showplace is only a short walk to Grant Park and Water Park pool, and across the footbridge of the Galena River to Main Street shopping and restaurants. Nine Christmas trees decorated with hand-blown ornaments on display Thanksgiving–Jan 15. Unsuitable for children under 12. **Rooms:** 4 rms and stes. CI 4pm/CO 11am. No smoking. **Amenities:** 🛁 A/C, cable TV w/movies. No phone. 1 unit w/terrace, some w/fireplaces. **Facilities:** 👤 📺 🗓 Guest lounge w/TV. **Rates (CP):** $75–$85 S or D; $105 ste. Extra person $10. Min stay wknds. Parking: Outdoor, free. DISC, MC, V.

RESORTS

≣≣ **Chestnut Mountain Resort**

8700 W Chestnut Rd, PO Box 328, 61036; tel 815/777-1320 or toll free 800/397-1320; fax 815/777-1068. Exit US 20 S on 4th St, S on Blackjack Rd. 220 acres. Swiss-style chalet located high atop a wooded palisades overlooking the Mississippi River with 3,500 feet of scenic ski slopes and a 475-foot vertical drop—one of the Midwest's steepest. Two new trails and a new quad lift. Snow-making capacity. River cruises stop here. **Rooms:** 120 rms; 18 cottages/villas. CI 3pm/CO noon. No smoking. Almost all guest rooms have recently been remodeled. **Amenities:** 📺 🛁 A/C, satel TV w/movies. **Services:** ◻ ☕ 🍷 Children's program, babysitting. **Facilities:** 🏠 🚴 📷 👤 📺 ⚓² 🏊 👶 1 restaurant, 3 bars (1 w/entertainment); basketball, volleyball, games rm, sauna, whirlpool, playground. **Rates:** Peak (Dec–Mar/May–Sept) $82–$112 S or D; $65 cottage/villa. Extra person $5. Children under age 10 stay free. Lower rates off-season. AP rates avail. Parking: Outdoor, free. AE, CB, DISC, MC, V.

≣≣≣ **Eagle Ridge Inn and Resort**

444 Eagle Ridge Dr, PO Box 777, 61036; tel 815/777-2444 or toll free 800/892-2269; fax 815/777-0445. On US 20; 8 mi E of Galena. This hotel centers on 6,800 acres of golf courses and wooded, rolling hills. Acclaimed as one of the top golf resorts in the country. Ongoing exhibit of local artists in lobby. Perfect for families or groups. **Rooms:** 80 rms and stes; 330 cottages/villas. Executive level. CI 4pm/CO noon.

Nonsmoking rms avail. Rental homes are privately owned, different sizes, and nicely decorated. **Amenities:** 🛋 🗄 📺 🍽 A/C, cable TV w/movies, refrig, VCR, bathrobes. All units w/minibars, all w/terraces, some w/fireplaces, some w/whirlpools. Homes have fully equipped kitchens, washers and dryers, and woodburning fireplaces. **Services:** ✕ 🗝 🚗 📠 🛎 Car-rental desk, social director, masseur, children's program, babysitting. Programs for children half day or full day, $17–$25. **Facilities:** 🛗 🚴 ⛰ 🛥 🚣 ▶63 ⚓ 🎿 🧗 🛶 📷 ⛳ 🏇 🍽750 🖥 ♿ 3 restaurants, 1 bar (w/entertainment), 1 beach (lake shore), volleyball, games rm, lawn games, sauna, whirlpool, playground. The new golf course, designed by architect Roger Packard and championship golfer Andy North, will be the fourth course within this golfing mecca. A trail system renowned for its plants and wildlife winds around 220-acre Lake Geneva. Ice skating and sledding. **Rates:** Peak (Apr–Oct) $185–$225 S or D; $245 ste; $215–$420 effic. Extra person $10. Children under age 18 stay free. Lower rates off-season. AP and MAP rates avail. Parking: Outdoor, free. AE, CB, DC, DISC, MC, V.

RESTAURANTS 🍴

★ Cafe Italia
In Logan House, 301 N Main St; tel 815/777-0033. Center of Galena. **American/Italian.** Located in the town's oldest hotel, constructed in 1855. Red brick arches and tile floors project a Mediterranean ambience to this popular restaurant that specializes in pasta and dishes from northern, central, and southern Italy. A specialty is veal or chicken amore with asparagus. Lower level open in summer. **FYI:** Reservations recommended. **Open:** Peak (June–Sept) lunch daily 11am–3pm; dinner Mon–Fri 5–10pm, Sat–Sun 4:30–10pm. **Prices:** Main courses $11–$19. AE, CB, DC, DISC, MC, V. ♥ ♿

★ Eldorado
219 N Main St; tel 815/777-1224. **Seafood/Southwestern.** Can hold its own with good restaurants in downtown Chicago. Sophisticated Southwestern decor in the two-story historic building features adobe architecture and large photos of canyons. Much of the organically grown produce and the wild game is local. The cuisine is defined by owner Tracey Roberts as "contemporary gourmet." Fresh trout is prepared in wine sauce with lemon butter, while Cassoulita, a spicy vegetarian casserole, combines organic corn, Anasazi beans, and vegetables braised in chilaca sauce and baked with local white cheese. **FYI:** Reservations recommended. **Open:** Sun–Mon 5–9pm, Wed–Thurs 5–9pm, Fri–Sat 5–10pm. **Prices:** Main courses $11–$32. DISC, MC, V. ♥ 🍽

Fried Green Tomatoes
1301 Irish Hollow Rd; tel 815/777-3938. **American/Italian.** One of Galena's newer restaurants, this picturesque spot is in the original Jo Daviess County Poor House, which has been completely renovated (though it still retains its original wooden floors, red brick walls, and encircling porches). Many Italian dishes, steaks, chops, local fish. **FYI:** Reservations

recommended. Piano/singer. **Open:** Lunch daily 11am–2:30pm; dinner daily 5–10pm. Closed Jan 1–14. **Prices:** Main courses $10–$20. AE, MC, V. ♥ 🍽 🏞 👥

Silver Annie's
124 N Commerce; tel 815/777-3131. Center of Galena. **Regional American.** Turn-of-the-century decor is set by a series of Gibson girl prints hung on the walls of this small, 40-chair restaurant. Sheer curtains and satin valances give a feeling of intimacy. Specialties are pork chops stuffed with cheese and spinach, fettuccine Alfredo, and homemade desserts. Chef's Choice Champagne Dinner featured Sun nights. **FYI:** Reservations recommended. Guitar/piano. No smoking. **Open:** Tues–Thurs 5–9pm, Fri–Sun 5–10pm. **Prices:** Main courses $9–$18. AE, CB, DC, DISC, MC, V. ♥

ATTRACTIONS 🏛

U S Grant Home State Historic Site
500 Bouthillier St; tel 815/777-0248. This brick home was presented to Grant by the citizens of Galena in 1865, after Grant returned triumphant from the Civil War. Today the building has been beautifully restored and it is decorated with authentic period furnishings and Grant family memorabilia. **Open:** Daily 9am–5pm. **$**

The Old Market House State Historic Site
Market Sq–Commerce St; tel 815/777-2570. When it was built in 1845, the Market House served as the center of community life in Galena and sheltered both vendors and shoppers. The building remained an active office for the city council and fire department until 1938. Today the market has been fully restored and houses historical exhibits. **Open:** Wed–Mon 9am–5pm. **Free**

Belvedere House
1008 Park Ave; tel 817/777-0747. An Italianate villa built in 1857 for steamship owner and ambassador to Belgium J Russell Jones. Galena's largest mansion is furnished with Victorian furniture and period appointments. Guided tours. **Open:** June–Oct, daily 11am–5pm. **$**

Galesburg

Seat of Knox County, in western Illinois. Founded in 1837 by Presbyterian settlers from New York. Knox College, founded the same year as the town, was the site of a Lincoln-Douglas debate. Carl Sandburg was born and grew up in a three-room cottage here. **Information:** Galesburg Area Convention & Visitors Bureau, 154 E Simmons St, PO Box 631, Galesburg, 61402 (tel 309/343-1194).

MOTELS 🏨

≡≡≡ Jumer's Continental Inn
260 S Soangetaha Rd, 61401; tel 309/343-7151 or toll free 800/285-8637; fax 309/343-7151. Exit 48 off I-74. Well-appointed motel version of Jumer's Lodges, with antiques in

the spacious lobby. **Rooms:** 147 rms, stes, and effic. CI 3pm/ CO noon. Nonsmoking rms avail. **Amenities:** 🔒 ⚲ A/C, cable TV w/movies, dataport, voice mail. Some units w/terraces, 1 w/whirlpool. First-floor rooms facing the landscaped inner court have patios. **Services:** ✕ 🍽 🖼 🗣 🛎 Children's program. Limousine provides transportation to downtown locations. Secretarial service available. **Facilities:** 🏌 🏊 500 ♿ 1 restaurant (*see* "Restaurants" below), 1 bar (w/entertainment), sauna, whirlpool, washer/dryer. Tavern of the Pheasant is elegant restaurant. Indoor swimming pool was completely refurbished in 1995. **Rates:** $63–$73 S; $73–$83 D; $130 ste; $120 effic. Extra person $6. Children under age 18 stay free. AP and MAP rates avail. Parking: Outdoor, free. Special packages avail Thurs, Fri, Sat, or Sun night. AE, CB, DC, DISC, MC, V.

≣≣ Ramada Inn

29 Public Sq, 61401; tel 309/343-9161 or toll free 800/2-RAMADA; fax 309/343-0157. Conveniently located on Public Square. **Rooms:** 90 rms. CI 2pm/CO noon. Nonsmoking rms avail. Doubles have two queen-size beds; singles have king-size beds. **Amenities:** 🔒 ⚲ A/C, cable TV. All units w/terraces. **Services:** 🍽 🖼 🗣 🛎 Free coffee in lobby 24 hours. Video rentals in lobby. **Facilities:** 🏌 🏊 🍺 150 ♿ 1 restaurant, 1 bar, games rm, whirlpool. **Rates:** Peak (Apr–Oct) $50–$60 S; $60–$65 D. Extra person $5. Children under age 12 stay free. Lower rates off-season. Parking: Outdoor, free. AE, DC, DISC, EC, ER, JCB, MC, V.

UNRATED Relax Inn

565 W Main St, 61401; tel 309/343-3191; fax 309/343-5649. Soon to be a Day's Inn, it has an on-site manager. Steep driveway places you above Main St. **Rooms:** 60 rms. CI 3pm/CO 11:30am. Nonsmoking rms avail. One room has a waterbed, and two have triple queens. Second floor has balcony on east side. **Amenities:** 🔒 A/C, cable TV. Some units w/terraces. **Services:** 🗣 Free local calls. **Facilities:** 🏊 **Rates (CP):** $38 S; $48 D. Children under age 12 stay free. Parking: Outdoor, free. AE, DC, MC, V.

RESTAURANTS 🍴

Landmark Cafe & Creperie

62 S Seminary St; tel 309/343-5376. 1 block S of Main St. **American/French.** Housed in a turn-of-the-century building that was the first site designated by the local landmark commission. The original pressed-tin ceiling and hardwood floor, along with brick walls and antiques (including a "seven sisters" quilt), create a distinctive aura. Crepes, sandwiches, and potato dishes are frequent top choices. **FYI:** Reservations recommended. **Open:** Mon–Thurs 11am–9pm, Fri 11am–10pm, Sat 9am–10pm, Sun 9am–9pm. **Prices:** Main courses $5–$9. AE, CB, DC, DISC, MC, V. ▪

The Packinghouse Dining Company

441 Mulberry St; tel 309/342-6868. **American.** In 1979, a Swift & Company meat-packing plant was converted into this unique restaurant. The outside entrance ramp, decorated with old barrels, leads to an original refrigerator door through which you enter the dining room, once a huge walk-in cooler. Original overhead refrigeration lines and meat rails are still intact. Choose from a wide selection of steaks, prime rib, chops, chicken, pasta, and seafood. On your birthday get a free dinner when accompanied by another paying guest who orders an entree of equal value. **FYI:** Reservations recommended. Children's menu. **Open:** Lunch Mon–Sat 11am–2pm; dinner Mon–Thurs 5–9pm, Fri–Sat 5–10pm, Sun noon–8pm. **Prices:** Main courses $9–$19. AE, CB, DC, DISC, MC, V. ▪

Risco's Italian Restaurant

41 S Seminary; tel 309/341-4141. 1 block S of Main St. **Italian.** Green and white decor, original, pressed-tin ceiling, and etched-glass windows provide an interesting setting for quality dining. Extensive menu. **FYI:** Reservations recommended. **Open:** Lunch Tues–Sat 11am–2pm; dinner Tues–Thurs 5–9pm, Fri–Sat 5–10:30pm. **Prices:** Main courses $7–$17. AE, MC, V.

Tavern of the Pheasant

In Jumer's Continental Inn, 260 S Soangetaha Rd; tel 309/343-7151. **Continental.** Elements of the famous Jumer's Hotel remain here: etched-glass partitions, privately made china, grapevine ceiling, oil paintings, and elegant woodwork crafted in Jumer's own shop. Steaks, gourmet seafood, European and American favorites, and salads can be enjoyed in a lavish setting. **FYI:** Reservations recommended. Jazz. Children's menu. **Open:** Sun–Thurs 6:30am–10pm, Fri 6:30am–10:30pm, Sat 6:30am–11pm. **Prices:** Main courses $7–$18. AE, CB, DC, DISC, MC, V. ♥ ▽ ♿

Geneva

Seat of Kane County, in northeast part of state. Geneva was a major supply point for westward pioneers. More than 200 of its buildings are listed on the National Register of Historic Places. **Information:** Geneva Chamber of Commerce, 8 S 3rd St, PO Box 481, Geneva, 60134 (tel 630/232-6060).

HOTEL 🏨

≣≣≣ Herrington Inn

15 S River Lane, 60134; tel 630/208-7433 or toll free 800/216-2466; fax 630/208-8930. On Fox River off IL 38 at bridge. Beside the Fox River Bridge in downtown Geneva, this new, small, luxury hotel has the romantic ambience of an inn and the amenities of a first-class hotel. Natural stone building, riverside setting. **Rooms:** 40 rms. CI 3pm/CO noon. Nonsmoking rms avail. All rooms have river views; lavish bathrooms with full whirlpool baths and oversized marble showers; and a plush, beautiful decor. **Amenities:** 🔒 ⚲ 🖥 ☏ A/C, cable TV, bathrobes. All units w/minibars, some w/terraces, all w/fireplaces, all w/whirlpools. **Services:** ✕ 🔑 🚐 🖼 🗣 **Facilities:** 🏊 🍺 12 💻 ♿ 1 restaurant, 1 bar,

games rm, spa, whirlpool, beauty salon, day-care ctr, playground, washer/dryer. Atwaters, the fine-dining restaurant, offers lunch and dinner. Drinks and lunch can be served in riverside courtyard at shady umbrella tables. Riverside gazebo in courtyard houses full sauna-like whirlpool. **Rates (CP):** $125–$185 S or D. Children under age 18 stay free. Parking: Outdoor, free. Rates based on size of room and view, not number of persons in room. AE, DC, DISC, MC, V.

MOTEL

⊫⊨ Geneva Motel
33W209 Roosevelt Rd, PO Box 183, 60134; tel 630/232-7121. On IL 38, ½ mi E of Kirk Rd. This two-story motel in a country setting offers the lowest rates in the area. Owners live on premises. **Rooms:** 26 rms. CI 3pm/CO 11am. Nonsmoking rms avail. Ask for recently remodeled room. Ramp to room available for guests with disabilities; call in advance. **Amenities:** 🛏 A/C, TV. **Rates:** $35 S; $40–$46 D. Extra person $5. Children under age 12 stay free. Parking: Outdoor, free. AE, CB, DC, DISC, MC, V.

RESTAURANTS 🍴

⑤ Inglenook Pantry
11 N 5th; tel 630/377-0373. At State St. **Pennsylvania Dutch.** An Amish-style buggy outside the building serves to announce this family-owned eatery's hearty Pennsylvania Dutch cuisine. The huge buffet varies from day to day, but often includes such favorites as oven-baked chicken, baked ham, and dried corn. Sunday brunch—usually featuring scrapple—is an especially good value. Their bakery is next-door. **FYI:** Reservations accepted. Children's menu. Beer and wine only. No smoking. **Open:** Lunch Tues–Sat 11:30am–2pm; dinner Fri–Sat 5:30–8pm; brunch Sun 11am–2pm. **Prices:** Prix fixe $10.95. AE, CB, DC, DISC, MC, V. 🍴 🅿

★ Mill Race Inn
4 E State St; tel 630/232-2030. On the SW corner of IL 38 and IL 25. **American.** Surrounded by a park, offering lunches, dinners, and Sun brunch in rustic decor filled with historic ambience. Five restaurants housed in converted 1837 mill on banks of Fox River: Country Inn (main dining room); Duck Inn (English pub with sandwiches and hors d'oeuvres); Mallards (lunch and cocktails); Mill Grill (carvery sandwiches); and Gazebo (open deck outdoor grill). **FYI:** Reservations recommended. Piano. Dress code. **Open:** Breakfast Sun 9am–1:30pm; lunch Mon–Sat 11:30am–3pm, Sun 11:30am–9pm; dinner Mon–Thurs 5–9pm, Fri–Sat 5–10pm. **Prices:** Main courses $14–$22. AE, CB, DC, MC, V. 🍴 🏔 🆅🅿 &

Riverwalk on the Fox
In Geneva on the Dam Shopping Center, 35 N River Lane; tel 630/232-1330. IL 38, just W of Fox River. **Continental.** Casual dining overlooking the Fox River. Outdoor terrace is screened and climate controlled. Booth and table seating available; banquet rooms upstairs. Something for every pal-

ate, from vegetarian to seafood to chargrilled meats. Lighter luncheon fare. **FYI:** Reservations recommended. Children's menu. Dress code. **Open:** Lunch daily 11am–4pm; dinner Mon–Fri 5–10pm, Sat–Sun 5–11pm; brunch Sun 10am–2:30pm. **Prices:** Main courses $11–$22. DC, DISC, MC, V. 🍴 &

Glen Ellyn

Thomas E Hill named the picturesque glen at the foot of Cooper Hill for his wife Ellyn. This western suburb of Chicago has a number of houses more than 100 years old. **Information:** Glen Ellyn Chamber of Commerce, 500 Pennsylvania Ave, Glen Ellyn, 60137 (tel 630/469-0907).

MOTELS 🏨

⊫⊨ Best Western Four Seasons
675 Roosevelt Rd, 60137; tel 630/469-8500 or toll free 800/528-1234; fax 630/469-6731. At Park Blvd. Set off the road and backed by a local park and pond, this multi-building complex includes a variety of rooms, suites, and kitchenettes available on a daily, weekly, or monthly basis. **Rooms:** 122 rms, stes, and effic. CI 1pm/CO noon. Nonsmoking rms avail. **Amenities:** 🛏 A/C, TV w/movies. **Services:** 🛎 🚗 Car-rental desk. VCR provided with movie rentals at desk. Prior approval and desposit required for pets. **Facilities:** 🏊 🚻 & Washer/dryer. **Rates (CP):** $44–$47 S; $48–$51 D; $69–$88 ste; $51–$63 effic. Extra person $4. Children under age 18 stay free. Parking: Outdoor, free. Children stay free on overnight stays, not for weekly or monthly rentals. AE, CB, DC, DISC, MC, V.

⊫⊨⊨ Holiday Inn
1250 Roosevelt Rd, 60137; tel 630/629-6000 or toll free 800/HOLIDAY. On IL 38 at Finley Rd. Contemporary hotel with comfortable accommodations and amenities. **Rooms:** 121 rms. CI 3pm/CO 1pm. Nonsmoking rms avail. **Amenities:** 🛏 🗄 📺 A/C, cable TV w/movies, dataport. **Services:** ✕ 🚗 🧺 🛎 🚗 Twice-daily maid svce, car-rental desk. $25 pet fee. **Facilities:** 🏊 🚻 & 1 restaurant, 1 bar, washer/dryer. Complimentary access to local health and racquetball club. **Rates:** $63 S or D. Children under age 18 stay free. Parking: Outdoor, free. AE, CB, DC, DISC, ER, JCB, MC, V.

Glenview

This northern suburb of Chicago is the site of the Glenview Naval Air Station. Civil War Living History Days takes place on the last weekend of July, while Grovefest (a re-creation of a typical mid-1800s afternoon) is held in early October. **Information:** Gleview Chamber of Commerce, 2320 Glenview Rd, Glenview, 60025 (tel 847/724-0900).

HOTELS

⫴⫴⫴ Courtyard by Marriott Glenview

1801 N Milwaukee Ave, 60025; tel 847/803-2500 or toll free 800/228-9290; fax 847/803-2520. Willow Rd W exit off I-294 to Sanders Rd, S on Sanders. **Rooms:** 149 rms and stes. CI 3pm/CO 1pm. Nonsmoking rms avail. **Amenities:** 🛅 🌊 A/C, satel TV w/movies, dataport. All units w/terraces. **Services:** 🛏 🍸 🍷 **Facilities:** 🏋 🍴 ⟦35⟧ 🕭 1 restaurant (bkfst only), 1 bar, whirlpool, washer/dryer. **Rates:** Peak (Apr–Oct) $62–$80 S or D; $89 ste. Children under age 12 stay free. Lower rates off-season. Parking: Outdoor, free. AE, DISC, MC, V.

⫴⫴⫴ DoubleTree Guest Suites, O'Hare North

1400 Milwaukee Ave, 60025; tel 847/803-9800 or toll free 800/222-TREE; fax 847/803-8026. Willow Rd W Exit off I-294 to Sanders Rd, left at Sanders. **Rooms:** 251 stes. CI 3pm/CO noon. Nonsmoking rms avail. **Amenities:** 🛅 🌊 🖭 A/C, satel TV w/movies, refrig, voice mail. Some units w/minibars. **Services:** ✕ 🚗 🛏 🍸 Car-rental desk. **Facilities:** 🏋 🍴 ⟦400⟧ 🕭 1 restaurant, 1 bar, volleyball, sauna, whirlpool, washer/dryer. **Rates:** $79–$154 ste. Extra person $10. Children under age 17 stay free. Min stay special events. Parking: Outdoor, free. AE, CB, DC, DISC, JCB, MC, V.

⫴⫴ Fairfield Inn Glenview

4514 W Lake Ave, 60025; tel 847/299-1600 or toll free 800/228-2800; fax 847/299-1600. Located 10 miles north of O'Hare International Airport, in the shadow of I-294. **Rooms:** 138 rms. CI 3pm/CO noon. Nonsmoking rms avail. **Amenities:** 🛅 🌊 A/C, cable TV w/movies. Dataports on request. **Services:** 🛏 🍸 **Facilities:** 🏋 ⟦10⟧ 🕭 Games rm. **Rates (CP):** Peak (May–Sept) $60 S or D. Children under age 18 stay free. Lower rates off-season. Parking: Outdoor, free. 10% discount for group of more than 10 rooms. AARP discount avail. AE, DC, DISC, MC, V.

MOTELS

⫴⫴ Budgetel Inn

1625 Milwaukee Ave, 60025; tel 847/635-8300 or toll free 800/4-BUDGET; fax 847/635-8166. Willow Rd W Exit off I-294. **Rooms:** 150 rms and effic. CI 1pm/CO noon. Nonsmoking rms avail. **Amenities:** 🛅 🌊 🖭 A/C, satel TV w/movies, voice mail. **Services:** 🛏 🍸 🍷 **Facilities:** ⟦10⟧ 🕭 Washer/dryer. **Rates (CP):** $42–$61 S; $49–$66 D; $55–$65 effic. Extra person $7. Children under age 18 stay free. Parking: Outdoor, free. AE, CB, DC, DISC, MC, V.

⫴ Motel 6

1535 Milwaukee Ave, 60025; tel 847/390-7200 or toll free 800/466-8356; fax 847/390-0845. Clean, fairly recently remodeled motel offers basic accommodations at reasonable rates. A few restaurants are within walking distance. **Rooms:** 111 rms. CI open/CO noon. Nonsmoking rms avail. Rooms are small but tastefully decorated. Connecting rooms available on request. **Amenities:** 🛅 A/C, cable TV w/movies.

Services: 🍸 🍷 **Facilities:** 🕭 Washer/dryer. **Rates:** $32 S; $38 D. Extra person $3. Children under age 17 stay free. Parking: Outdoor, free. Discounts for AARP members. AE, CB, DC, DISC, MC, V.

RESTAURANTS 🍽

Dapper's North

4520 W Lake Ave; tel 847/699-0020. E of Milwaukee Ave. **American.** A family-style eatery with pleasant art deco–style decor. Sandwiches, salads, and soup are available in addition to daily specials. Homemade cheesecake is locally famous. Takeout available. **FYI:** Reservations not accepted. Children's menu. **Open:** Mon–Thurs 5:30am–1am, Fri–Sat 5:30am–2am, Sun 5:30am–midnight. **Prices:** Main courses $7–$12. AE, DC, MC, V. 🍴 🕭

Joe & Giuseppe Italian Chop House

1615 N Milwaukee Ave; tel 847/635-7707. **Italian.** Family photos and artifacts decorate the walls at this old-world–style trattoria. Southern Italy specialties; variety of steaks. **FYI:** Reservations recommended. **Open:** Mon–Fri 11am–10pm, Sat 4pm–midnight, Sun 4–10pm. **Prices:** Main courses $12–$24. AE, DISC, MC, V.

Grayslake

RESTAURANT 🍽

★ The Country Squire

IL 120 W at US 45; tel 847/223-0121. **Continental/Seafood.** Luminaries from Carl Sandberg to Marlon Brando have dined at this historic, romantic place occupying the former country home (1938) of Wesley Sears. Gardens and two gazebos add charm to the property's 13 acres. The original wood-paneled library is now the bar. Some popular entrees are shrimp DeJonghe and veal Oscar (sautéed cutlets of veal tenderloin, topped with crabmeat, asparagus spears, and hollandaise). Key lime pie for dessert. **FYI:** Reservations accepted. Children's menu. **Open:** Tues–Fri 11am–10pm, Sat 11am–11pm, Sun 10am–9pm. **Prices:** Main courses $9–$20. AE, CB, DC, DISC, MC, V. ♥ ▋ ☑ 🕭

Greenville

Seat of Bond County, in southwest part of state. This hilly rural community is the site of Greenville College. **Information:** Greenville Chamber of Commerce, PO Box 283, Greenville, 62246 (tel 618/664-9272).

MOTEL 🏨

⫴⫴ Best Western Country View Inn

IL 127 and I-70, 62246; tel 618/664-3030 or toll free 800/528-1234; fax 618/664-3030. Exit 45 off I-70, N on IL 127 to entrance. Several unassuming brown brick buildings comprise this neat, comfortable lodging with easy highway access. **Rooms:** 83 rms and stes. CI 1pm/CO noon. Nonsmoking rms avail. **Amenities:** 🛗 A/C, cable TV w/movies, VCR. **Services:** ✗ 🛎 🍽 Twice-daily maid svce. Movie rental includes VCR. Complimentary coffee always available. Prior approval required for pets. **Facilities:** 🏊 🚐250 ♿ 1 restaurant, 1 bar. Parking with electrical hook-ups available for RVs and semis. **Rates:** Peak (May–Sept) $39–$42 S; $47–$50 D; $70–$99 ste. Extra person $6. Children under age 18 stay free. Lower rates off-season. Parking: Outdoor, free. AE, CB, DC, DISC, MC, V.

ATTRACTION 🏛

Richard W Bock Sculpture Garden

311 E College Ave; tel 618/664-2800. Sculptor Richard W Bock worked with Frank Lloyd Wright from 1895–1915. This collection of Bock's sculpture, drawings, and photographs is supplemented by a selection of glass and drawings by Wright. **Open:** Sept–May, Mon–Fri 2–5pm, Sat 10am–noon. **Free**

Gurnee

Located a half-hour's drive north of Chicago, Gurnee is best known as the home of Six Flags Great America. **Information:** Lake County, Illinois Convention & Visitors Bureau, 401 N Riverside Dr, #5, Gurnee, 60031-5906 (tel 847/662-2700; 800/LAKE-NOW).

MOTELS 🏨

🏩 Adventure Inn

3732 Grand Ave, 60031; tel 847/623-7777 or toll free 800/373-5842; fax 847/623-3606. Exit IL 132 off I-94 E. This property is divided into three separate buildings: two are theme buildings, Jail Motel and Fantasy Sweets, and one is a standard motel. The Jail Motel lobby resembles an old western jail, and the theme is repeated through the rooms and halls. In Fantasy Sweets, the Heart to Heart Room has a heart-shaped bed and heart-shaped hot tub in the center of the room; there are about 20 other rooms with themes, such as Caesar's Palace and Prehistoric Love Nest. **Rooms:** 230 rms, stes, and effic. CI 3pm/CO 11am. Nonsmoking rms avail. The theme rooms are larger than the standards, and some have dining areas. Certainly not for everyone's taste. The rooms and hallways have a musty odor. **Amenities:** 🛗 🕭 A/C, cable TV w/movies, refrig. Some units w/whirlpools. Rooms equipped with microwaves and Nintendo. **Services:** 🛎 Car-rental desk. **Facilities:** 🎮70 Games rm. **Rates:** Peak (June–Aug) $76 S or D; $130 ste; $50–$70 effic. Extra person $6. Children under age 14 stay free. Lower rates off-season. Parking: Outdoor, free. Special packages offered with Six Flags Great America. AE, CB, DC, DISC, MC, V.

UNRATED **Fairfield Inn**

6090 Gurnee Mills Blvd E, 60031; tel 847/855-8868 or toll free 800/228-2800. Exit IL 132 off I-94 W. The motel has received Marriott Corporation's top recognitions for cleanliness and courteous staff. It's a good basic motel with no frills, adjacent to Gurnee Mills Mall and close to Six Flags Great America and Lipizzan Horses. Several corporations within three miles. Many nearby restaurants. **Rooms:** 63 rms and stes. CI 3pm/CO 11am. Nonsmoking rms avail. **Amenities:** 🛗 🕭 A/C, satel TV w/movies. **Services:** 🖨 🛎 🍽 Babysitting. Pets that weigh 10 pounds or less are allowed. **Facilities:** 🏊 🌀15 Whirlpool. **Rates (CP):** Peak (Apr–Dec) $93–$98 S; $109–$129 D; $139 ste. Extra person $5. Children under age 18 stay free. Lower rates off-season. Parking: Outdoor, free. AE, CB, DC, DISC, MC, V.

≣≣ Holiday Inn

6161 W Grand Ave, 60031; tel 847/336-6300 or toll free 800/HOLIDAY; fax 847/336-6303. Exit I-94 at IL 132 W. Full-service motel near Six Flags Great America, Dairyland Dog Track, and Gurnee Mills Mall. Public facilities are unkempt. Clientele in winter is mostly business and in summer, families. Golf and tennis nearby. **Rooms:** 223 rms and stes. Executive level. CI 4pm/CO 11am. Nonsmoking rms avail. Standard rooms have double beds, king leisure rooms have king-size beds and sleeper sofas. **Amenities:** 🛗 🕭 📺 A/C, satel TV w/movies, dataport, voice mail. Some units w/whirlpools. **Services:** ✗ 🖨 🛎 Car-rental desk, babysitting. **Facilities:** 🏊 🏋 🍽400 ♿ 1 restaurant, 1 bar, games rm, whirlpool, washer/dryer. Pool in separate glass-walled building. Meeting rooms have state-of-the-art equipment. **Rates:** Peak (June 15–Sept 9) $99 S or D; $115 ste. Children under age 18 stay free. Lower rates off-season. Parking: Outdoor, free. Advanced reservations can be made for bed-and-breakfast. AE, CB, DC, DISC, MC, V.

ATTRACTION 🏛

Six Flags Great America

542 N IL 21; tel 847/249-2133. Located midway between Chicago and Milwaukee, this is described as the Midwest's biggest theme/amusement park. More than 100 rides offer something for everyone; for the brave, there are nine roller coasters including the Shock-Wave (billed as the tallest and fastest steel roller coaster in the country). Live shows, theme areas, gift shops, and restaurants round out the experience. **Open:** Apr–Sept, call for schedule. **$$$$**

Highland Park

This northern Chicago suburb was built on the site of two Potawatomi villages. Lake shore, bluffs, woods, and ravines draw many nature lovers. The Chicago Symphony Orchestra, guest soloists, and chamber music and jazz artists perform at the summertime Ravinia Festival. **Information:** Highland Park Chamber of Commerce, 600 Central Ave, #205, Highland Park, 60035 (tel 847/432-0284).

MOTEL 🏨

≡≡≡ Courtyard by Marriott

1505 Lake Cook Rd, 60035; tel 847/831-3338 or toll free 800/321-2211; fax 847/831-0782. At jct I-94, Lake Cook Rd, US 41, and Skokie Blvd. The expected pleasant ambience of a Courtyard, located within a mile of Northbrook Court Shopping Mall, Chicago Botanic Garden, and Ravinia Music Park. **Rooms:** 149 rms and stes. CI 3pm/CO noon. Nonsmoking rms avail. Soft pastel prints complement rooms' colors. **Amenities:** 🛁 🌊 🖥 A/C, cable TV w/movies. All units w/terraces. Only suites have refrigerators and hair dryers. **Services:** 🚗 ⛵ 🍹 Car-rental desk. Honor bar 5–10pm where guests make their own drinks and charge them to their room. **Facilities:** 🏋 🛎 🔲 🏊 ⅃ 1 restaurant (bkfst only), 1 bar, whirlpool, washer/dryer. **Rates:** Peak (May–Oct) $89 S; $95 D; $109–$115 ste. Children under age 17 stay free. Lower rates off-season. Parking: Outdoor, free. AE, CB, DC, DISC, MC, V.

RESTAURANTS 🍴

♣ Carlos'

429 Temple Ave; tel 847/432-0770. E of Green Bay Rd. **French.** A plain storefront and canopy conceal one of the country's best restaurants. The elegant 55-seat dining room features dark wood, mirrored walls, and glass shelves, all softened with sheer-white swags of lace. Magazine awards cover one wall, including several recent Grand Awards from the *Wine Spectator*. French chef Jacky Pluton prepares such delicacies as poached halibut with seaweed risotto and spiced red wine sauce, and sautéed venison chop with pearl onions. **FYI:** Reservations recommended. No smoking. **Open:** Peak (summer) Wed–Mon 6–10:30pm. Closed Jan 1–15. **Prices:** Main courses $22–$31. AE, CB, DC, DISC, MC, V. ❤ 🔲 🆅🅿
⅃

Las Palmas

474 Central Ave; tel 847/432-7770. **Mexican.** A newish Mexican restaurant in the former Chi-Lin Court. Murals of Mexico decorate the long, narrow space. Favorite dishes are the fajitas (tender skirt steak served with Spanish onions, green pepper, mushrooms, and tomatoes) and camarónes à la plancha (grilled jumbo shrimp with garlic). **FYI:** Reservations accepted. Harp. Children's menu. Additional locations: 1773 Howard St, Chicago (tel 312/262-7446); 1642 Maple St, Evanston (tel 708/328-2555). **Open:** Mon–Thurs 11am–10pm, Fri–Sat 11am–midnight, Sun noon–10pm. **Prices:** Main courses $8–$14. AE, DC, MC, V. 🔳 ⅃

★ Morton's of Chicago

1876 1st St; tel 847/432-3484. **Steak.** This is the only Morton's still owned by the restaurateur of 50 years, Arnold Morton. In 1981 he sold his other eight restaurants, and

today 31 of these eminent steakhouses are owned by others. The Sunday brunch is a special event. **FYI:** Reservations recommended. No smoking. **Open:** Tues–Sat 5:30–9pm, Sun 10:30am–2pm. **Prices:** Main courses $15–$25. AE, DC, MC, V. ❤ ⅃

Panda Panda

1825 2nd Ave; tel 847/432-9470. **Chinese.** Pink and turquoise art deco with large panda hangings. Extensive menu features over 100 entrees, including orange beef sautéed with orange peel and hot peppers in sweet hot sauce, and the Panda Three Delicacies—beef, chicken, and jumbo shrimp with Chinese black mushrooms, bamboo shoots, red pepper, and broccoli. **FYI:** Reservations recommended. Dress code. **Open:** Mon–Thurs 11:30am–9:30pm, Fri–Sat 11:30am–10:30pm, Sun 11:30am–9:30pm. **Prices:** Main courses $9–$24; prix fixe $13. AE, MC, V. 🔳 🔲

Timbers Char House

In Crossroads Shopping Center, 295 Skokie Valley Rd; tel 847/831-1400. W off US 41 at Clavey Rd turn-off. **American/Seafood.** A large bi-level restaurant with an open kitchen and rustic decor reminiscent of a Rocky Mountain lodge. Ten varieties of fresh fish are offered each day. A surf-and-turf dish offers a small filet mignon, breast of chicken, and fillet of salmon with sauces. Entrees come with freshly baked bread, salad, and side dish. **FYI:** Reservations recommended. Children's menu. **Open:** Lunch Mon–Sat noon–4pm; dinner Mon–Thurs 5–10pm, Fri–Sat 5–11pm, Sun 4:30–8:30pm. **Prices:** Main courses $8–$23. AE, CB, DC, MC, V. 🔳 ⅃

Highwood

Fort Sheridan, founded in 1887, is a National Historic Landmark, with 94 buildings and structures. Recently closed, much of the land, including a golf course, is becoming public domain. **Information:** Highwood Chamber of Commerce, 17 Highwood Ave, #201, PO Box 305, Highwood, 60040 (tel 847/433-2100).

HOTEL 🏨

≡≡≡ Hotel Moraine

700 N Sheridan Rd, 60040; tel 847/433-5566 or toll free 800/433-4101; fax 847/433-9368. At N end of town, opposite Fort Sheridan. Previously part of a major chain, this hotel still has an undistinguished exterior; inside, however, the lovely, old-fashioned, elegant lobby has an open curved staircase, a 100-year old Ben Franklin clock and antique piano, and subdued, tasteful appointments. Patronized by visiting parents of students attending nearby schools. Top-flight catering service for receptions. **Rooms:** 100 rms and stes. CI 3pm/CO noon. Nonsmoking rms avail. Murphy beds in small suites, so the two rooms can be used as hospitality suite when required. Old-English, dark wood furniture motif, with paintings of hunting scenes. **Amenities:** 🛁 🌊 🍴 A/C,

cable TV w/movies, refrig. **Services:** ✕ 🚐 🖴 Car-rental desk, babysitting. Hotel is on Airport Express route from O'Hare International Airport ($15–$16). VCRs available through front desk. Catering will stock suites with most any request—personal service is highly valued here, and many special arrangements will happily be made. **Facilities:** 🏃 🍹 600 3 restaurants (dinner only), 1 bar, sauna. Natural light from large windows overlooking patio area by pool. **Rates (CP):** $85 S; $95 D; $130–$160 ste. Extra person $10. Children under age 18 stay free. Parking: Outdoor, free. Many special rates and packages avail. AE, DC, DISC, MC, V.

RESTAURANTS 🍴

The Bistro in Highwood

440 Green Bay Rd; tel 847/433-5600. Just W of Metra tracks at N end of town. **New American.** With its fireplaces in both dining rooms, bare wooden floors, and wood-beamed ceilings, this delightful bistro offers good cheer in addition to an array of fine dishes. Snails with artichokes, peas, tomato garlic broth and extra virgin olive oil; sautéed Idaho lake trout with portobello mushrooms, ginger broth, and crispy potatoes; and grilled New York strip steak with caramelized onions and homemade Worcestershire sauce are just a few. **FYI:** Reservations recommended. No smoking. **Open:** Sun–Thurs 4:30–10:30pm, Fri–Sat 4:30–11:30pm. **Prices:** Main courses $13–$19. AE, CB, DC, DISC, MC, V. 💟 🖼 🎦 💟 ♿

★ Del Rio's

228 Green Bay Rd; tel 847/432-4608. Just W of Metra tracks at S edge of town. **Italian.** Fine, classic Italian food from one of the oldest restaurants in town—a good place for a special dinner with family or friends. Green, sculpted-metal ceiling and rich, dark carpeting help set the scene. Veal del rio, lightly breaded and baked in lemon butter, plus chicken and eggplant parmigiana and pastas of many types are some of the hearty dishes. Good service. **FYI:** Reservations accepted. **Open:** Sun–Thurs 5–10pm, Fri–Sat 5–11pm. **Prices:** Main courses $14–$23. AE, DC, DISC, MC, V. 💟 🖼

Froggy's

306 Green Bay Rd; tel 847/432-7080. Just W of Metra tracks. **Continental.** Well-established in Highwood as a touchstone for fine French food. The distinctive, intimate dining room, filled with impressionistic oil paintings, makes an ideal setting for family, business, or romantic occasions. Entrees include breast of chicken grilled with Dijon mustard and seasoned bread crumbs; confit of duck surrounded by sliced breast meat with green peppercorn sauce; and fresh Atlantic salmon braised with a mussel cream sauce. **FYI:** Reservations accepted. Children's menu. **Open:** Lunch Mon–Fri 11:30am–2pm; dinner Mon–Thurs 5–10pm, Fri–Sat 5–11pm. **Prices:** Main courses $12–$16; prix fixe $26–$35. DC, DISC, ER, MC, V. 💟 💟

♣ Gabriel's

310 Green Bay Rd; tel 847/432-0031. Just W of Metra tracks. **French/Italian.** By taking its food and wine very seriously, this small, sparkling, very French eatery has attracted a devoted clientele. Special dining rooms downstairs offer privacy for family celebrations or private tastings. Specialties change seasonally and can include roasted langoustines with sautéed fennel and coriander; roasted venison with chanterelle mushrooms and port wine; or whole roasted trout wrapped in pancetta with mushrooms. Small outdoor cafe for summer dining. **FYI:** Reservations recommended. No smoking. **Open:** Tues–Thurs 5–10pm, Fri–Sat 5–10:30pm. **Prices:** Main courses $21–$28; prix fixe $35. AE, CB, DC, DISC, MC, V. 💟 ♿

★ Pappagallo's

246 Green Bay Rd; tel 847/432-6663. Just W of Metra tracks. **Italian.** Fronted by a long, narrow, green-canopied porch, where a parrot whose colors resemble those of the interior rests on its perch, this restaurant has an exuberance and richness that will please the senses. Specialties include lasagna and chicken Vesuvio, piccata, and parmigiana, as well as some interesting steak dishes, topped with porcini mushrooms, tomatoes, or Romano cheese. **FYI:** Reservations recommended. Children's menu. **Open:** Mon–Thurs 11am–10pm, Fri–Sat 11am–11pm, Sun 11am–9pm. **Prices:** Main courses $9–$23. AE, DC, DISC, MC, V. 💟 🖼 💟 ♿

Hillside

RESTAURANT 🍴

La Perla

2135 S Wolf Rd; tel 708/449-1070. ½ block N of Cermak (22nd St). **Mediterranean.** The unique setting created by larger-than-life wall murals along with the pan-Mediterranean cuisine and live entertainment make this a memorable restaurant. Roma pizza may seem familiar (spinach, plum tomato, oregano, garlic, mushrooms, fontina, and mozzarella), but the Moroccan pizza is definitely different (lamb sausage, eggplant, tomato, and goat cheese). Entrees range from beef or chicken shish kebab to grilled beef tenderloin with caramelized onions and casserole Marseilles. The tapas are very popular. **FYI:** Reservations accepted. Big band/blues/jazz. Dress code. **Open:** Mon–Thurs 11:30am–11:30pm, Fri 11:30am–12:30am, Sat 5pm–1am, Sun 4–9pm. **Prices:** Main courses $8–$22. AE, MC, V. 💟 🍽 ♿

Hoffman Estates

RESTAURANT 🍴

⑤ ★ Dover Straits

1149 W Golf Rd; tel 847/884-3900. 5 mi W of I-290/IL 53; at Gannon. **Seafood/Steak.** Nautical theme restaurant serving fresh seafood, including whitefish, trout, and Dover sole. **FYI:** Reservations recommended. Children's menu. Dress code. **Open:** Mon–Fri 11am–11pm, Sat 4pm–midnight, Sun 2–11pm. **Prices:** Prix fixe $12–$20. AE, CB, DC, DISC, MC, V. 🎨 🏊 📺 ♿

Homewood

This quiet town 24 miles south of Chicago's Loop was incorporated in 1892. **Information:** Homewood Chamber of Commerce, 1154 Ridge Rd, PO Box 1698, Homewood, 60430 (tel 708/957-6950).

HOTEL 🏨

🏨🏨 Best Western Homewood Hotel

17400 S Halsted St, 60430; tel 708/957-1600 or toll free 800/528-1234; fax 708/957-1963. From I-80/294 exit Halsted St, S ½ mi. Recently renovated. **Rooms:** 189 rms and stes. Executive level. CI 3pm/CO 11am. Nonsmoking rms avail. Four floors of enclosed open space above pool create balcony effect for rooms surrounding it. **Amenities:** 🔒 ♨ A/C, cable TV w/movies. **Services:** ✗ 🚐 📠 Car-rental desk. Super Nintendo. **Facilities:** 🏋️ 800 ♿ 1 restaurant, 1 bar (w/entertainment), games rm, beauty salon. Circle Restaurant features elevated dining circle above rest of dining room. **Rates:** Peak (May–Sept) $60–$80 S; $65–$85 D; $150–$300 ste. Extra person $5. Children under age 18 stay free. Lower rates off-season. Parking: Outdoor, free. AE, DC, DISC, MC, V.

RESTAURANT 🍴

★ Aurelio's Pizza

18162 Harwood Ave; tel 708/798-8050. 2 blocks S of Homewood train station at Ridge Rd. **Pizza.** A local favorite for more than 30 years that has spawned 28 other restaurants. Impressive blend of stained glass, brick, and large wooden beams that section restaurant off. Over 5,000 baby pictures of tots wearing Aurelio's shirts grace entryway. Aurelio's makes dough and sauce, and sausage arrives fresh daily from local source. Since they serve nearly 2,000 people on Fri night, expect to wait. **FYI:** Reservations not accepted. Additional location: 8000 Roberts Rd, Bridgeview (tel 594-3030). **Open:** Mon–Thurs 11:30am–10:30pm, Fri 11:30am–midnight, Sat 4pm–midnight, Sun 4–10:30pm. **Prices:** Main courses $4–$8. AE, DISC, MC, V. 🏊 ♿

Itasca

Pleasant western suburb of Chicago and gateway to the Busse Forest Preserve. **Information:** Itasca Chamber of Commerce, 100 N Walnut St, Itasca, 60143 (tel 630/773-0835).

HOTEL 🏨

🏨🏨🏨 Wyndham Hotel Northwest Chicago

400 Park Blvd, 60143; tel 630/773-4000 or toll free 800/WYNDHAM; fax 630/773-4087. Large, atrium lobby in 12-story hotel surrounded by acres of landscaped grounds. **Rooms:** 408 rms and stes. CI 3pm/CO noon. Nonsmoking rms avail. **Amenities:** 🔒 ♨ 📺 🍷 A/C, cable TV w/movies, dataport, voice mail. All units w/minibars. **Services:** ✗ 🗝️ VP 🚐 📠 Car-rental desk, masseur, babysitting. Manager on duty 24 hours. Sun brunch served in lobby. **Facilities:** 🏋️ 🏊 🎾 1200 💻 ♿ 3 restaurants, 2 bars, basketball, volleyball, racquetball, sauna, steam rm, whirlpool, beauty salon. Indoor pool has outdoor sun deck. Golf driving range. **Rates:** $89–$149 S; $89–$169 D; $275 ste. Extra person $20. Children under age 12 stay free. Parking: Outdoor, free. Senior discount avail. AE, CB, DC, DISC, MC, V.

RESORT

🏨🏨 Nordic Hills Resort & Conference Center

Nordic Rd, 60143; tel 630/773-2750 or toll free 800/334-3417; fax 630/773-3667. 100 acres. Twin nine-story buildings connected by sprawling single-story building, in a country setting. Resort built more than 20 years ago; new owners plan major renovations. **Rooms:** 220 rms and stes. Executive level. CI 3pm/CO noon. Nonsmoking rms avail. **Amenities:** 🔒 ♨ A/C, cable TV w/movies, dataport. Some units w/minibars, all w/terraces, some w/fireplaces, some w/whirlpools. Refrigerator in room on request. Suites equipped with coffeemaker, VCR, stereo, CD/tape player. **Services:** ✗ 🚐 📠 Car-rental desk, social director, masseur, children's program, babysitting. **Facilities:** 🏋️ ⛳18 🎾 🏊 🎾 800 ♿ 2 restaurants, 2 bars (1 w/entertainment), basketball, volleyball, games rm, lawn games, racquetball, spa, sauna, steam rm, whirlpool, beauty salon, playground, washer/dryer. Indoor pool is one of the largest in the Midwest. Many lounges and informal meeting spaces—some indoors, some outdoors. **Rates:** Peak (May–Oct) $95–$120 S; $110–$130 D; $150–$400 ste. Extra person $10. Children under age 5 stay free. Lower rates off-season. MAP rates avail. Parking: Outdoor, free. Senior discount avail. AE, CB, DC, DISC, MC, V.

Jacksonville

Seat of Morgan County, in west-central part of state. Jacksonville was an important station on the Underground Railroad, and both Stephen A Douglas and William Jennings Bryan began their practice of law here. Home to Illinois College (founded in 1829, it is the oldest college west of the Alleghenies) and MacMurray College (founded in 1846). **Information:** Jacksonville Area Convention & Visitors Bureau, 155 W Morton Ave, Jacksonville, 62650 (tel 217/243-5678).

RESTAURANT 🍽

★ Lonzerottis Italia Restaurant

In Old Chicago & Alton RR Depot, 600 E State St; tel 217/243-7151. **Italian/American.** Located in an old train station with an well-restored exterior and active railroad tracks nearby. Favorites include pork chops, broccoli-cheese lasagna, and broiled boneless catfish covered with Italian seasoning and mozzarella. Wine list astounds for its quality, variety, and price. **FYI:** Reservations recommended. **Open:** Lunch Mon–Sat 11am–2pm; dinner Mon–Thurs 5–9pm, Fri–Sat 5–10pm. **Prices:** Main courses $6–$16. AE, DISC, MC, V.

Joliet

See also Lockport

Seat of Will County, in northeast part of state. The Chicago Sanitary and Ship Canal carries millions of tons of barge traffic through the city and the Brandon Road Locks, south of Joliet, are among the largest in the nation. **Information:** Heritage Corridor Visitors Bureau, 81 N Chicago St, Joliet, 60431 (tel 815/727-2323 or toll free 800/926-2262).

MOTELS 🏨

🏮🏮 Comfort Inn North

3234 Norman Ave, 60435; tel 815/436-5141 or toll free 800/221-2222; fax 815/436-5141 ext 400. Exit 257 off I-55. Near interstate and major highways. What this place lacks in flash, it makes up for in personality of the employees. Lots of guests are return business travelers, and some are long-term guests in the process of relocation. **Rooms:** 64 rms and stes. CI 3pm/CO 11am. Nonsmoking rms avail. Queen-size and king-size beds. One-room suites available. **Amenities:** 🛗 🗘 A/C, cable TV w/movies, refrig. Suites have microwaves and refrigerators. **Services:** 🚗 🖵 🐦 Television and microwave available for use in lobby. Staff tries to know guests' names and to treat them like friends. Guest of the Day Program provides one randomly chosen guest with basket of goodies. **Facilities:** 🛗 🗘 Games rm, whirlpool. **Rates (CP):** Peak (June–Sept) $60–$70 S or D; $70–$80 ste. Extra person $10. Children under age 18 stay free. Lower rates off-season. Parking: Outdoor, free. Ask about the 13th Night Free and Travel Club programs. AE, DC, DISC, JCB, MC, V.

🏮🏮 Comfort Inn South

135 S Larkin Ave, 60436; tel 815/744-1770 or toll free 800/221-2222. Exit 130 B off I-80. Right off interstate, convenient to discount department stores and fast food chains. Travelers who like the reliability of multi-property hospitality groups will feel at home here. **Rooms:** 67 rms and stes. CI 2pm/CO 11am. Nonsmoking rms avail. Beds are either queen-size or king-size. Some rooms showed some wear. **Amenities:** 🛗 A/C, cable TV w/movies. Suites have micro-

waves and refrigerators. **Services:** 🖵 🖵 🐦 Guest of the Day Program—one guest chosen at random to receive basket of treats, coupons, and other surprises. **Facilities:** 🛗 🏊 🗘 Games rm, whirlpool. **Rates (CP):** Peak (May 1–Sept 15) $50–$116 S; $65–$125 D; $70–$125 ste. Extra person $6. Children under age 18 stay free. Lower rates off-season. Parking: Outdoor, free. AARP discounts. AE, CB, DC, DISC, ER, JCB, MC, V.

🏮🏮🏮 Fairfield Inn

3239 Norman Ave, 60435; tel 815/436-6577 or toll free 800/228-2800; fax 815/436-6577. Exit 257 off I-55. Bright new lodging located right off interstate. Comfortable for overnight stop or longer. Fine for business travelers or families. **Rooms:** 63 rms and stes. CI 3pm/CO 11am. Nonsmoking rms avail. Furnishings are fresh and stylish. One-room suites available with king-size bed and queen-size convertible couch. **Amenities:** 🛗 🗘 A/C, cable TV w/movies. Suites have microwaves and refrigerators. **Services:** 🚗 🖵 🖵 🐦 **Facilities:** 🛗 🏊 🗘 Games rm, whirlpool. Breakfast room off lobby can be used for small meetings. **Rates (CP):** Peak (May–Sept) $60–$69 S; $65–$74 D; $73–$81 ste. Extra person $6. Children under age 18 stay free. Lower rates off-season. Parking: Outdoor, free. AE, DC, DISC, MC, V.

🏮🏮🏮 Holiday Inn Joliet

411 S Larkin Ave, 60436; tel 815/729-2000 or toll free 800/HOLIDAY; fax 815/729-4231. Exit 130B off I-80. A comfortable place not overburdened with glitzy extras, this motel is big enough to accommodate many guests and functions, but small enough to treat each guest with highly individualized care. Provides many support services to business travelers. The Heritage Bluffs Golf Course, rated in the top ten Illinois new courses in 1995 by the *Chicago Tribune*, is 10 minutes away. **Rooms:** 200 rms. CI 3pm/CO noon. Nonsmoking rms avail. Bathrooms have been totally redone, and now feature skid-proof porcelain in the bathtubs. King-sized beds available. **Amenities:** 🛗 🗘 A/C, cable TV w/movies, dataport. **Services:** ✗ 🖵 🖵 Up to four children accompanied by adult eat free during summer season. Airport transportation can be arranged through an outside service, and requires a fee. **Facilities:** 🛗 🔲 🛢 🔲 🗘 1 restaurant, 1 bar, basketball, washer/dryer. **Rates:** $69–$79 S or D. Children under age 19 stay free. Parking: Outdoor, free. Weekend rates higher than weekday rates. AARP discounts avail. Reunion, relocation, and family packages are just a few of the packages avail. AE, CB, DC, DISC, MC, V.

🏮 Manor Motel

23926 W Eames Rd, Channahon, 60410; tel 815/467-5385; fax 815/467-1617. Exit 248 off I-55. Solid, older, multi-winged lodging adorned with cupolas and flagstone. The Kowalski family has owned and run this motel for more than 17 years, and their love for the business and concern for their customers is evident. **Rooms:** 76 rms. CI noon/CO 11am. Nonsmoking rms avail. Rooms are quite large and feature brick walls (good for soundproofing), deep closet areas, big bathrooms, and built-in luggage racks and vinyl benches. One two-room suite available. **Amenities:** ☎ A/C, satel TV w/movies. **Services:** ⌂ ⌂ Mrs Kowalski is usually at or near the front desk and is eager to provide information about restaurants and attractions. **Facilities:** ⛴ ᕕ **Rates:** $34–$45 S; $45–$53 D. Extra person $9. Children under age 10 stay free. Parking: Outdoor, free. Discounts for stays of more than two weeks. AE, CB, DC, MC, V.

🛏 Super 8 Motel Joliet South

1730 McDonough St, 60436; tel 815/725-8855 or toll free 800/800-8000; fax 815/725-8855 ext 237. Exit 130B off I-80. A typical Super 8, located right off the interstate, functional and convenient for overnight stays. **Rooms:** 64 rms and stes. CI 2pm/CO 11am. Nonsmoking rms avail. Some rooms have new carpeting and upgraded furnishings. Queen-size beds available. Single-room suites. **Amenities:** ☎ A/C, cable TV w/movies. **Facilities:** ⟨20⟩ ᕕ **Rates (CP):** $43–$60 S; $50–$65 D; $70 ste. Extra person $5. Children under age 16 stay free. Parking: Outdoor, free. AARP discounts avail. AE, DC, DISC, MC, V.

RESTAURANTS 🍽

★ Al's Steak House

1990 W Jefferson St; tel 815/725-2388. Exit 130 off I-80; N on Larkin Ave to Jefferson St; W to restaurant. **Seafood/Steak.** Owned and operated by the Karnezis family, who say their food is "as good as Mother's, better than others." The dining room is darkly elegant, with gas lamps, double tablecloths, and candlelit table settings. The menu lists dozens of entrees, including broiled mahi mahi, veal à la Oscar (veal topped with asparagus, crabmeat, and Mornay sauce), Cajun chicken breast, pork chops, Grecian pan-fried steak, charbroiled ribs, and an armload of steak choices. A salad bar provides ten or twelve items. Brunch is served all day Sunday, and includes items from eggs to red meat to fresh fish to a wide selection of pastries and deserts. Lighter menu available for early and late seatings in the bar or in the dining room; there's also a seniors' menu. **FYI:** Reservations recommended. Children's menu. Dress code. **Open:** Mon–Sat 11am–11pm, Sun 10am–4pm. **Prices:** Main courses $8–$38. AE, CB, DC, DISC, MC, V. ᕕ

Secrets Ribs & More

2222 W Jefferson St; tel 815/744-3745. Exit 130 off I-80; N on Larkin Ave to Jefferson St; W 1 mi. **Seafood/Steak.** Some say these ribs can't be beat—including the judges of Philadelphia's 1995 Backyard BBQ and Music Festival. The dining room has solid tables and chairs and comfortable booths for a settle-in-and-enjoy type of repast. Seafood and continental-style dinners like Alaskan snow-crab legs and chicken champagne (chicken simmered in a champagne wine sauce) are featured alongside the ribs. A Heart Healthy menu lists low-fat and low-sodium pasta, chicken, and fish dishes. **FYI:**

Reservations accepted. Karaoke. Children's menu. **Open:** Sun–Thurs 3:30–10pm, Fri–Sat 3:30–11pm. **Prices:** Main courses $8–$35. AE, CB, DC, DISC, MC, V. ᕕ

♥ Tallgrass

1006 S State St; tel 815/838-5566. ½ block S of jct IL 7 and State St. **French.** Intimate, modern restaurant in historic, renovated 1890s building nestled in group of unassuming, small-town buildings. Decor features original tin ceilings, carefully coordinated block prints on walls, and fresh flowers. Chef Robert Burcenski flavors his award-winning menu from his herb garden just outside the kitchen door. Specialties are breast of duck with portobello mushrooms and ginger sauce; peppered prime New York steak with mustard sauce; and seared ahi tuna with purple rice and wasabi butter. **FYI:** Reservations recommended. Jacket required. **Open:** Wed–Sun 6–10pm. Closed 2 weeks in Jan. **Prices:** Prix fixe $45–$55. AE, MC, V. ■ ᕕ

ATTRACTIONS 🎦

Will-Joliet Bicentennial Park

201 W Jefferson St; tel 815/740-2491. This city park hosts concerts during the summer. Its riverwalk and picnic benches provide a pleasant setting at any time of year. **Open:** Mon–Thurs 8am–4:30pm, Fri 8am–noon, and during scheduled events. **Free**

Rialto Square Theatre

102 N Chicago St; tel 815/726-6600. Built in 1926 with an interior designed after the Hall of Mirrors in the Palace of Versailles near Paris, this 1,900 seat performing arts center today plays host to a variety of top-name entertainment such as the actor Gregory Peck, vocal group Little Texas, comedienne Rita Rudner, and the Broadway musical *Beauty and the Beast.* **Open:** Mon–Fri 11am–5pm, plus show evenings. $$$$

Kankakee

Seat of Kankakee County, in northeast part of state. Once an extension of Bourbonnais, Kankakee became a separate community in 1855, around the newly constructed Illinois Central Railroad. The nearby Kankanee River is popular for canoeing and kayaking. **Information:** Kankakee Area Chamber of Commerce, 101 S Schuyler Ave, PO Box 905, Kankakee, 60901-0905 (tel 815/933-7721).

MOTEL 🏨

🛏 Days Inn

1975 E Court St, 60901; tel 815/939-7171 or toll free 800/DAYS-INN. Exit 312 off I-57. Modest establishment conveniently located off interstate. Extensive renovations have freshened things up quite nicely. **Rooms:** 98 rms. Executive level. CI 3pm/CO noon. Nonsmoking rms avail. Renovations to rooms included new carpeting, 25″ televisions, and bathroom countertops. **Amenities:** ☎ A/C, cable TV w/movies, in-rm safe. **Services:** ✗ 🖼 **Facilities:** 🄵 🕹 🕺 1 restaurant, 1 bar. "Relaxing" by pool means enduring buzz of traffic and air conditioners. **Rates:** Peak (Apr–Sept) $50–$60 S; $54–$64 D. Extra person $6. Lower rates off-season. Parking: Outdoor, free. Special packages with area sports providers (canoeing, fishing, and horseback riding) avail. MC, V.

RESTAURANT 🍴

★ Homestead
1230 Southeast Ave; tel 815/933-6214. **Italian/Steak.** Family-owned for nearly a century, this establishment features hand-cut meats and Italian specialities. The decor is a bit kitschy—reminiscent of the 1970s—but the room is clean and comfortable. Excellent burgers come on lightly-toasted buns with home fries. A good choice for family dining. **FYI:** Reservations recommended. Children's menu. **Open:** Sun–Thurs 11am–11pm, Fri–Sat 11am–midnight. **Prices:** Main courses $10–$20. MC, V. 🖼

Kewanee

Begun by Protestants from Connecticut in 1835 to "promote the cause of piety and education in Illinois." **Information:** Kewanee Chamber of Commerce, 113 E Second, Kewanee, 61443-2205 (tel 309/852-2175).

RESTAURANT 🍴

★ Andris Waunee Farm
US 34 and IL 78; tel 309/852-2481. **American.** Local gathering place for wholesome, unabashed fun and down-home cooking. Seats 700 in the complex of banquet areas, main dining room, and the Aku-Tiki Room. Farm supplies tomatoes, corn, and apples. Custom-cut steaks and homemade applesauce and chocolate puddings. Small shop sells farmer's hats and souvenirs. Senior discounts. **FYI:** Reservations accepted. Dancing/piano. Children's menu. **Open:** Mon–Sat 5pm–midnight. **Prices:** Main courses $5–$20. No CC. 💚 🍷 🖼 🕺

La Salle

See Peru

Libertyville

Native Americans often camped here when they came to visit the nearby mineral springs. Adlai Stevenson, Helen Hayes, and Marlon Brando once called this north suburb of Chicago home. **Information:** Libertyville Mundelein Vernon Hills Area Chamber of Commerce & Industry, 731 N Milwaukee Ave, Libertyville, 60048 (tel 847/680-0750).

MOTEL 🏨

≡≡ Best Inns of America
1809 N Milwaukee Ave, 60048; tel 847/816-8006 or toll free 800/BEST-INN; fax 847/816-8006. Jct IL 137/21. Attractive motel is 5 miles south of Great America amusement park. **Rooms:** 90 rms. CI open/CO 1pm. Nonsmoking rms avail. **Amenities:** 🛁 A/C, cable TV w/movies, dataport. **Services:** 🛎 🍷 **Facilities:** 🄵 🕹 🕺 **Rates (CP):** Peak (mid-May–mid-Sept) $48–$53 S; $50–$59 D. Extra person $6. Children under age 18 stay free. Lower rates off-season. Parking: Outdoor, free. Senior First discount for guests 50 years and older. AE, CB, DC, DISC, MC, V.

RESTAURANTS 🍴

★ Ann's Bavariahaus
114 W Peterson Rd; tel 847/367-5933. Jct IL 21/US 137. **Deli/German.** A local draw, this bustling establishment combines a German deli, restaurant, and grocery store. Many fine, imported Bavarian goods for sale line the deli's walls; available are various German meats, including bratwurst and schnitzel, as well as pastries. Over 35 imported beers. **FYI:** Reservations not accepted. **Open:** Tues–Thurs 5:30am–9pm, Fri–Sat 5:30am–10pm, Sun 7am–8pm. **Prices:** Main courses $5–$11. AE, DISC, MC, V.

Ⓢ ★ Lambs Country Inn
In Lambs Farm, Jct I-94/IL 176; tel 847/362-5050. **American.** Located at entrance to Lambs Farm. Daily luncheon specials include country favorites like fried chicken and barbecued ribs. Homemade soup; salad bar. **FYI:** Reservations recommended. Children's menu. **Open:** Lunch Mon–Sat 11am–4pm; dinner Mon–Sat 4–8pm, Sun 4–7pm; brunch Sun 10:30am–2:30pm. **Prices:** Main courses $8–$14; prix fixe $9. AE, CB, DC, DISC, MC, V. 🍷 🖼 🕺 🕺

Milwaukee Road House Bar & Grill
In Hill Top Executive Center, 1590 S Milwaukee Ave; tel 847/680-9330. On IL 21, ¾ mi N of IL 60. **American.** Charming suburban restaurant with unusually attractive surroundings. Several tables are located outdoors near a pond. The hearty menu fare includes steak, ribs, and local seafood. Salad bar. **FYI:** Reservations accepted. Children's menu. **Open:** Peak (mid-May–Sept) Mon–Fri 11am–10pm, Sat–Sun 8am–10pm. **Prices:** Main courses $8–$19. AE, CB, DC, DISC, MC, V. 🍴 🖼 🕺

Raffaelli's Italian Cafe
1765 N Milwaukee Ave; tel 847/367-8088. Jct IL 21/US 137. **Italian.** Casual, old-world-style eatery noted for its dark, cavernous main dining room with murals and exposed brick walls. Offers sturdy Italian meals and tiramisù and freshly filled cannoli for dessert. **FYI:** Reservations recommended. Dancing/singer. Children's menu. **Open:** Mon–Sat 11am–10pm, Sun 11am–2pm. **Prices:** Main courses $9–$16. AE, DC, DISC, MC, V.

Lincoln

Seat of Logan County, in central Illinois. A replica stands on the site of the original Postville Court House, where Lincoln practiced law. In mid-September, the Abraham Lincoln National Railsplitter Contest and Crafts Festival takes place at the fairgrounds. **Information:** Abraham Lincoln Tourism Bureau of Logan County, 303 S Kickapoo, Lincoln, 62656 (tel 217/732-8687).

MOTEL 🏨

≣ Comfort Inn
2811 Woodlawn Rd, 62656; tel 217/735-3960 or toll free 800/221-2222; fax 217/735-3960. Exit 126 off I-55. Small, generic motel located next to country dance barn and fast food restaurants. Clean and simple. **Rooms:** 52 rms and stes. CI 1pm/CO 11am. Nonsmoking rms avail. **Amenities:** 🛏 ⚕ A/C, cable TV w/movies. Refrigerator and microwave in suites only. **Services:** 🛆 🖉 🖏 **Facilities:** 🛍 🔲 ⅖ ᕕ Games rm, whirlpool. **Rates (CP):** Peak (Apr–Sept) $50–$70 S or D; $58–$75 ste. Extra person $5. Children under age 18 stay free. Lower rates off-season. Parking: Outdoor, free. AE, CB, DC, DISC, EC, ER, MC, V.

RESTAURANT 🍴

★ Tropics
1007 Hickox Dr; tel 217/732-6710. At jct IL 10/Lincoln Pkwy. **American.** A Lincoln fixture for more than 40 years. The original Tropics sign, located on old Route 66, is an area landmark and a welcome reminder of bygone days. The bar has been restored to its original 1950s look, with barstools in alternating turquoise and bright yellow. The typical Midwestern menu offerings include Swiss steak, meat loaf, chicken-fried steak, and roast turkey and trimmings. The ever-present buffet presents fried chicken every day, plus fish on Friday, roast beef on Sunday, and over 20 different salads, sides, and, soups. **FYI:** Reservations accepted. Children's menu. Dress code. **Open:** Daily 6am–11pm. **Prices:** Main courses $7–$25. AE, DC, DISC, MC, V. 👥 💟 ᕕ

ATTRACTIONS 🏛

Postville Courthouse State Historic Site
914 5th St; tel 217/732-8930. A 1950s reconstruction of the 1840 courthouse where young Abraham Lincoln visited as a circuit-traveling lawyer. (In 1929, auto magnate Henry Ford bought the original building and moved it to Greenfield Village in Michigan.) Today, the site houses a recreated mid-19th-century courtroom, and a law office furnished as it might have been when Lincoln was here. Call ahead to confirm hours; suggested donation. **Open:** Peak (Mar–Oct) daily noon–5pm. Reduced hours off-season.

Mount Pulaski Courthouse State Historic Site
City Square; tel 217/732-8930. Constructed in 1848 and restored in the 1930s, this two-story brick Greek Revival structure is listed on the National Register of Historic Places. The twice-yearly circuit court met here from 1848 to 1855; a restored courtroom and law offices are furnished with period antiques from the 1840s, when Abraham Lincoln practiced law here after his first Congressional term. **Open:** Peak (Mar–Oct) daily noon–5pm. Reduced hours off-season. **Free**

Lockport

See also Joliet

Macomb

Seat of McDonough County, in western Illinois. Named for Alexander Macomb, a general in the War of 1812. The town has two public squares, separated by a short block, and is the home of Western Illinois University. **Information:** Macomb Area Convention & Visitors Bureau, 118 N Randolph, Macomb, 61455 (tel 309/833-1315).

MOTELS 🏨

≣≣≣ AmeriHost Inn
1646 N Lafayette St, 61455; tel 309/837-2220; fax 309/837-1720. On US 67 N of Macomb. Opened in 1995, this sparkling new property is north of downtown and one mile from Western Illinois University. **Rooms:** 60 rms and stes. CI 3pm/CO 2pm. Nonsmoking rms avail. Rooms have two double beds or king-size beds. **Amenities:** 🛏 ⚕ A/C, cable TV w/movies, dataport, in-rm safe. Some units w/terraces, some w/whirlpools. Suites have refrigerator and microwave. **Services:** 🛆 🖉 **Facilities:** 🛍 🔲 ᕕ Sauna, whirlpool. **Rates (CP):** $48–$55 S; $58–$65 D; $75 ste. Extra person $6. Children under age 17 stay free. Parking: Outdoor, free. AE, CB, DC, DISC, MC, V.

≣≣≣ Holiday Inn
1400 N Lafayette St, 61455; tel 309/833-5511 or toll free 800/HOLIDAY; fax 309/836-2926. On US 67 N on N edge of town. Well-maintained motel located immediately north of town. **Rooms:** 147 rms. CI 3pm/CO noon. Nonsmoking rms avail. Waterbed room available. **Amenities:** 🛏 ⚕ 🖥 A/C, cable TV w/movies. **Services:** ✗ 🛆 🖉 🖏 Coffee available in lobby. **Facilities:** 🛍 🔲 ᕕ 1 restaurant, 1 bar. Bar has DJ booth and small dance floor. **Rates:** $47–$80 S; $53–$85 D. Extra person $6. Children under age 19 stay free. Min stay special events. Parking: Outdoor, free. AE, CB, DC, DISC, JCB, MC, V.

≣ Super 8 Motel
313 University Ave, 61455; tel 309/836-8888 or toll free 800/800-8000; fax 309/833-2646. Functional motel near Western Illinois University due for exterior renovation; interior is warm and friendly. **Rooms:** 40 rms. CI 2pm/CO 11am. Nonsmoking rms avail. Basic rooms. **Amenities:** 🛏 A/C,

cable TV w/movies. **Services:** ⌐ Free local calls. Fax and copy machines. **Facilities:** ⅄ ⅊ **Rates (CP):** $44 S; $49 D. Extra person $6. Children under age 12 stay free. **Parking:** Outdoor, free. AE, DC, DISC, MC, V.

RESTAURANT 🍴

Macomb Dining Company

127 E Carroll St; tel 309/833-3000. **American.** Originally a Montgomery Ward department store (1928–1973), the property was restored and converted to a restaurant in 1982. The original 14-foot, pressed-tin ceiling is complemented by art deco antiques, tall, wooden columns, and chain-suspended, glass light fixtures. There's a wide variety of dishes, but regulars are particularly fond of the prime rib and the cinnamon rolls. **FYI:** Reservations recommended. Piano. **Open:** Lunch Mon–Sat 11am–2pm; dinner Mon–Thurs 5–9pm, Fri–Sat 5–10pm. **Prices:** Main courses $7–$16. AE, DISC, MC, V. 🛢 ⅊

Marion

Seat of Williamson County. Marion has long been known as the agricultural and coal-mining center of southern Illinois; it is also a gateway to Crab Orchard National Wildlife Refuge. **Information:** Williamson County Convention & Visitors Bureau, PO Box 1088, Marion, 62959 (tel 618/997-3690).

MOTELS 🏨

≣≣ Best Inns of America

2700 W DeYoung (IL 13), 62959; tel 618/997-9421 or toll free 800/237-8466; fax 618/997-9421. Well-maintained, clean, and comfortable accommodations. Adjacent to Illinois Centre Mall. Meeting facilities, fishing, golf, tennis, fitness center, and boating nearby. **Rooms:** 104 rms. CI open/CO 1pm. Nonsmoking rms avail. **Amenities:** 🛎 A/C, cable TV w/movies. **Services:** ⌐ ⌐ ⌐ Complimentary expanded "Special K" breakfast. **Facilities:** ⌐ ⅊ **Rates (CP):** $37–$48 S or D. Extra person $6. Children under age 18 stay free. **Parking:** Outdoor, free. AE, CB, DC, DISC, MC, V.

≣≣ Best Western Airport Inn

Rte 8, Box 348-1, 62959 (Williamson County Regional Airport); tel 618/993-3222 or toll free 800/528-1234; fax 618/993-8868. Walk to your flight from this clean, modern facility that also has easy access to the Illinois Centre Mall and IL-13. Suitable even if you're not flying. Golf, fishing, and boating within five miles. **Rooms:** 34 rms. CI noon/CO 11am. Nonsmoking rms avail. **Amenities:** 🛎 A/C, satel TV w/movies, dataport. Some units w/whirlpools. **Services:** ⌐ ⌐ ⌐ Car-rental desk. **Facilities:** ⌐ 15 ⅊ **Rates (CP):** $43–$58 S; $48–$63 D. Extra person $5. Children under age 12 stay free. **Parking:** Outdoor, free. AE, CB, DC, DISC, MC, V.

≣≣≣ Comfort Suites

2608 W Main St, 62959; tel 618/997-9133; fax 618/997-1005. At exit 53 off I-57. Two-story cream stucco with green trim. Easy access from interstate and adjacent to restaurant and laundromat. Golf, fishing, and boating nearby. **Rooms:** 64 stes. CI 3pm/CO noon. Nonsmoking rms avail. All rooms are mini-suites. Rooms with sleeper sofas available on request. **Amenities:** 🛎 ⌐ ⌐ A/C, cable TV w/movies, refrig, dataport, VCR. All units w/whirlpools. All rooms have microwaves and wet bars. **Services:** ⌐ ⌐ ⌐ Car-rental desk. Guests receive 10% discount at 20's Hideout Steakhouse. **Facilities:** ⌐ 15 ⅊ Outside sun deck adjoins pool. **Rates (CP):** $65–$85 ste. Extra person $6. Children under age 18 stay free. **Parking:** Outdoor, free. Senior and corporate rates avail. AE, CB, DC, DISC, ER, JCB, MC, V.

≣≣≣ Holiday Inn

I-57 and IL 13, PO Box 609, 62959; tel 618/997-2326 or toll free 800/648-4667; fax 618/993-6984. Exit 54B off I-57. Holidome recreation and comfortable accommodations make this an excellent choice for longer stays. **Rooms:** 200 rms and effic. CI noon/CO noon. Nonsmoking rms avail. Some rooms have coffeemakers, VCRs, and/or refrigerators. Rooms on first floor facing pool have mini patios. **Amenities:** 🛎 ⌐ A/C, cable TV w/movies, dataport. Some units w/terraces. **Services:** ✕ ⌐ ⌐ ⌐ ⌐ **Facilities:** ⌐ ⌐ 500 ⅊ 1 restaurant, 2 bars (1 w/entertainment), games rm, sauna, whirlpool, washer/dryer. Pool tables and table tennis in Holidome. **Rates:** Peak (Mar–Oct) $64–$68 S; $68–$73 D; $68–$73 effic. Extra person $5. Children under age 12 stay free. Lower rates off-season. **Parking:** Outdoor, free. Corporate discounts avail. Golf, hunting, and fishing packages avail. AE, CB, DC, DISC, ER, JCB, MC, V.

RESTAURANTS 🍴

The Pioneer's Cabin

1325 Main St, Carterville; tel 618/985-8290. **American.** Family restaurant in a log cabin (built from a kit) with an immense fireplace at either end. Antique farm implements hang from the rafters and table decorations change monthly. Family-style specials include fried chicken, chicken and dumplings, fish, baked ham, meatloaf, and barbecue pork steaks. Children under 3 eat free; half-price for those ages 4–12 on family-style specials only. No reservations accepted on weekends. Gift shop attached. **FYI:** Reservations accepted. Children's menu. No liquor license. Additional location: RR1, Box 126, Percy (tel 497-2380). **Open:** Tues–Sat 6:30am–9pm, Sun 10:30am–4pm. **Prices:** Main courses $3–$7. DISC, MC, V. 🍴 👨‍👩‍👧

20's Hideout Steakhouse

2606 W Main St; tel 618/997-8325. Exit 53 off I-57, adjacent to Comfort Inn. **American/Burgers.** There's a speakeasy feel to this trendy steak house, decorated with pictures of Elliott Ness and John Dillinger. The menu is laced with gangster lingo, from the Scarface fried onion rings to Ma Barker's apple pie. Entrees include a 20-ounce porterhouse steak, grilled shrimp on wild rice, and a combo plate of baby back ribs and Cajun chicken breasts. **FYI:** Reservations not accepted. Children's menu. **Open:** Mon–Thurs 4–10pm, Fri–Sat 4–11pm, Sun 11am–8pm. **Prices:** Main courses $5–$18. AE, CB, DC, DISC, MC, V. &

Mattoon

This industrial town and agricultural market center was named for William Mattoon, an Illinois Central official instrumental in the town's development. Fishing and boating are available at nearby Lake Mattoon. **Information:** Mattoon Chamber of Commerce, 1701 Wabash Ave, Mattoon, 61938 (tel 217/235-5661).

MOTELS

≡≡≡ Ramada Inn & Conference Center
300 Broadway Ave E, 61938; tel 217/235-0313 or toll free 800/272-6232; fax 217/235-6005. On IL 16, ⅘ mi W of I-57 (Exit 190B). Access via Frontage Rd along IL16. Newly remodeled pink stucco. **Rooms:** 124 rms and stes. CI 2pm/CO noon. Nonsmoking rms avail. Odd number rooms face parking lot; even numbers face enclosed atrium/courtyard with indoor pool. **Amenities:** A/C. **Services:** Twice-daily maid svce. **Facilities:** 1 restaurant, 1 bar (w/entertainment), games rm, sauna, whirlpool, washer/dryer. Indoor and outdoor pools. Pool table, table tennis, basketball hoop game located in atrium. C W Dandy's restaurant/bar is local gathering place good for business lunches. Banquet facilities. **Rates:** Peak (May–Sept) $53–$58 S; $59–$71 D; $76–$81 ste. Extra person $5. Children under age 18 stay free. Lower rates off-season. Parking: Outdoor, free. AE, CB, DC, DISC, JCB, MC, V.

≡≡ Super 8 Motel
205 McFall Rd, 61938; tel 217/235-8888 or toll free 800/800-8000; fax 217/258-8808. Exit 190B off I-57. Basic overnight accommodations at intersection of IL 16 and I-57. Access through Frontage Rd. **Rooms:** 61 rms and stes. CI 4pm/CO 11am. Nonsmoking rms avail. Two suites (oversized rooms) available, with unstocked refrigerators. **Amenities:** A/C, cable TV. **Services:** Vending machines and microwave in lobby. **Facilities:** Rates (CP): $41 S; $45–$47 D; $55–$59 ste. Extra person $3. Children under age 12 stay free. Parking: Outdoor, free. Senior, military, and corporate discounts. AE, CB, DC, DISC, MC, V.

RESTAURANT

Alamo Steak House & Saloon
In Cross County Mall, 700 E Broadway Ave; tel 217/234-7337. Exit 190B (IL 16 W) off I-57; W to 3rd stoplight, N side. **Tex-Mex.** Noisy but fun family restaurant. Steaks, chicken, chops, seafood, burgers, and sandwiches made to

order and served charbroiled to Cajun style. The "Dynamic Duos" are a good value for two people to split. **FYI:** Reservations accepted. Children's menu. **Open:** Sun–Thurs 4–9pm, Fri–Sat 4–10pm. **Prices:** Main courses $5–$17. AE, DC, MC, V.

McHenry

Northwest suburb of Chicago. McHenry is set on a vast deposit of earth and stones left over from the last Ice Age. **Information:** McHenry Area Chamber of Commerce, 1257 N Green St, McHenry, 60050 (tel 815/385-4300).

MOTEL

≡≡ Tamara Royale Inn
4100 Shamrock Lane, 60050; tel 815/344-5500; fax 815/344-5527. 2 mi S of IL 120 on IL 31. 8 acres. Home-like atmosphere in quiet, country setting. Nearby Fox River and Lake Geneva recreation areas offer year-round outdoor sports. Numerous golf courses nearby. **Rooms:** 56 rms and stes. CI 3pm/CO 11am. Nonsmoking rms avail. **Amenities:** A/C, cable TV. Some units w/whirlpools. **Services:** Happy hour with free hors d'oeuvres in Foxes Den Lounge. Suburban passenger train service to Chicago. O'Hare limo service available. Complimentary shuttle service to Lake Geneva, Wisconsin. **Facilities:** 1 restaurant, 1 bar, whirlpool. Terrace for sunbathing. Live DJ every Fri night. Sun Champagne Brunch and special events, such as a luau. **Rates:** $60 S; $70 D; $175–$225 ste. Extra person $10. Children under age 17 stay free. Parking: Outdoor, free. Fri–Sat rates are $78 single, $88 double, $99 suite. AE, CB, DC, DISC, MC, V.

RESTAURANT

★ Jenny's Restaurant
2500 N Chapel Hill Rd; tel 815/385-0333. **American.** Adjacent to the historic Chapel Hill Country Club, opened in 1899. The restaurant and bar are have good views of the 18-hole golf course. Rib and chicken buffet, Black Forest chicken, veal and scallops with champagne sauce, and pan-fried lake perch are specialties. **FYI:** Reservations recommended. Children's menu. **Open:** Wed–Sat 4:30–10pm, Sun 10am–2pm. Closed Jan. **Prices:** Main courses $8–$24. AE, DISC, MC, V.

Moline

See also Rock Island

Moline and Rock Island in Illinois comprise half of the Quad Cities metropolitan area, along with Bettendorf and Davenport in Iowa. Moline is filled with tree-shaded blocks of Victorian homes overlooking the Mississippi and Rock Rivers.

The administrative center of the John Deere Company was designed by Eero Saarinen, the architect of the St Louis arch. **Information:** Quad-City Convention & Visitors Bureau, 2020 3rd Ave, Moline, 61265 (tel 309/788-7800).

MOTELS

Best Western Airport Inn

2550 52nd Ave, 61265; tel 309/762-9191 or toll free 800/528-1234; fax 309/762-9191 ext 101. Clean lodging, built in 1992, with comfortable lobby. **Rooms:** 48 rms. CI 1pm/CO 11am. Nonsmoking rms avail. **Amenities:** A/C, cable TV. VCRs available on request. **Services:** Motel pays for cab to airport. **Facilities:** Whirlpool. **Rates (CP):** $65–$85 S. Extra person $5. Children under age 12 stay free. Parking: Outdoor, free. AE, CB, DC, DISC, MC, V.

Comfort Inn

2600 52nd Ave, 61265; tel 309/762-7000 or toll free 800/221-2222. Airport exit off I-280. Convenient to airport, basic, pleasant. Families and corporate business. **Rooms:** 63 rms and stes. CI 1pm/CO 11am. Nonsmoking rms avail. **Amenities:** A/C, satel TV w/movies. 1 unit w/whirlpool. **Services:** Fax and copy machines at front desk. **Facilities:** Games rm, whirlpool. Attractive pool. **Rates:** Peak (May 28–Oct 14) $50–$55 S; $60–$90 ste. Extra person $5. Children under age 18 stay free. Lower rates off-season. Parking: Outdoor, free. Rates $5 higher on weekends. AE, DC, DISC, MC, V.

Exel Inn

2501 52nd Ave, 61265; tel 309/797-5580 or toll free 800/356-8013; fax 309/797-1561. Airport exit off I-280. Very clean property conveniently located near the airport. **Rooms:** 102 rms. CI noon/CO noon. Nonsmoking rms avail. **Amenities:** A/C, dataport. 1 unit w/whirlpool. **Services:** Personable and hospitable staff. **Facilities:** Games rm, washer/dryer. **Rates (CP):** $34–$39 S; $40–$52 D. Extra person $4. Children under age 17 stay free. Parking: Outdoor, free. Mid-week specials and senior discounts avail. AE, CB, DC, DISC, MC, V.

Hampton Inn

6920 27th St, 61265; tel 309/762-1711 or toll free 800/HAMPTON. Off I-74 and I-280. Just off busy street in a handy location. President and Mrs Bush stayed here. Fitness center, spa, and Holidome available at next door Holiday Inn. **Rooms:** 138 rms, stes, and effic. CI noon/CO noon. Nonsmoking rms avail. **Amenities:** A/C, satel TV, dataport. Some units w/whirlpools. **Services:** Room service available from next door Holiday Inn. **Facilities:** Rates (CP): $46–$51 S; $50–$56 D; $99–$150 ste; $99–$150 effic. Children under age 18 stay free. Parking: Outdoor, free. AE, CB, DC, DISC, MC, V.

Holiday Inn

6902 27th St, 61265 (Quad City Airport); tel 309/762-8811 or toll free 800/HOLIDAY; fax 309/762-3393. I-74 E to airport exit. Conveniently located near airport exit, about seven miles from Mississippi River gaming boats. Renovated in late 1995. **Rooms:** 216 rms, stes, and effic. CI 2pm/CO noon. Nonsmoking rms avail. **Amenities:** A/C, cable TV, voice mail. Some units w/whirlpools. **Services:** **Facilities:** 1 restaurant, 1 bar, games rm, sauna, steam rm, whirlpool, washer/dryer. Huge pool area, indoor miniature golf, table tennis. **Rates:** $62 S; $69 D; $140–$225 ste; $225 effic. Extra person $7. Children under age 18 stay free. Parking: Outdoor, free. AE, CB, DC, DISC, JCB, MC, V.

RESTAURANT

C'est Michele

1514 5th Ave (Heritage Block); tel 309/762-0585. ½ mi W of I-74, 7th Ave exit. **French/Mediterranean.** Built in 1894 as a jewelry store, this intimate, unusual establishment offers fine cuisine and personal attention. The original safe now guards the wine, early presses are used for the rolls, and herbs are grown in the roomy basement. Heavily used by local corporations for private parties, the restaurant is open to the public by reservation only (one to two weeks advisable). Call 309/762-8055 to discover the menu for the week. Doors open at 6:30pm, dinner is served at 7:15pm. You'll find your place card and matches engraved with your name at your table. Classic dishes: filet mignon, salmon with asparagus, grilled duck with raspberry sauce, saddle of lamb. **FYI:** Reservations recommended. Piano. **Open:** Thurs–Sat 6:30–9:30pm. **Prices:** Prix fixe $30–$37. AE, CB, DC, MC, V.

ATTRACTION

Niabi Zoological Park

13010 Niabi Rd, Coal Valley; tel 309/799-5107. 10 mi SE of Moline. Niabi is an Oswego word meaning "young deer spared from the hunter's arrow." In keeping with this principle, this 30-acre zoo is home to more than 300 animals and is surrounded by an additional 200 acres which act as a preserve for native flora and fauna. Making their home at Niabi are Bengal tigers, cougars, macaws, and pygmy goats, as well as an Asian elephant, reptiles, bears, and wallabies. A miniature railroad takes guests around the complex. **Open:** Apr–Oct, Wed–Fri 9:30am–7pm, Sat–Tues 9:30am–5pm. **$**

Monmouth

Seat of Warren County, in western Illinois. The town was named in honor of a Revolutionary War battle at Monmouth, NJ. Corn, soybeans, cattle, and hogs are the chief products of the area. Lawman Wyatt Earp was born here in 1848. **Information:** Monmouth Area Chamber of Commerce, 620 S Main St, PO Box 857, Monmouth, 61462 (309/734-3181).

MOTEL 🏨

≣ ≣ Meling's Motel
1129 N Main St, 61462; tel 309/734-2196; fax 309/734-2127. At US 67. This well-established motel with a policy of constant refurbishing provides comfortable lodging at a convenient location. The Meling's Family Restaurant with bar is in an adjacent building. **Rooms:** 55 rms. CI 2pm/CO 11am. Nonsmoking rms avail. **Amenities:** 🕿 A/C, cable TV w/movies, voice mail. **Services:** 🖵 **Facilities:** 🚣 🛏 1 restaurant, 1 bar. **Rates:** $41–$46 S or D. Extra person $5. Children under age 12 stay free. Parking: Outdoor, free. AE, CB, DC, DISC, EC, MC, V.

RESTAURANT 🍴

Meling's Family Restaurant
US 34 and US 67; tel 309/734-7965. **American.** Adjacent to Meling's Motel, this spacious facility offers hearty fare and "heart smart" options. Daily specials. Takeout available. **FYI:** Reservations accepted. **Open:** Mon–Sat 5:30am–9:30pm, Sun 7am–8pm. **Prices:** Main courses $6–$13. AE, CB, DC, DISC, MC, V. &

Morris

Seat of Grundy County, in northeast part of state. The Illinois & Michigan Canal, completed in 1848, linked Lake Michigan with the Illinois River at La Salle. **Information:** Grundy County Chamber of Commerce & Industry, 112 E Washington St, Morris, 60450 (tel 815/942-0113).

MOTEL 🏨

≣ Comfort Inn
70 W Gore Rd, 60450; tel 815/942-1433 or toll free 800/221-2222; fax 815/942-1433. At the end of a commercial strip, this motel is close to every kind of shopping, including a 24-hour adult bookstore right next door. The property is secure, though, with video cameras at the lobby entrance, and locked public entrances. The suite is a real value for a small group. **Rooms:** 50 rms and stes. CI 2pm/CO 11am. Nonsmoking rms avail. Large, two-room suite has kitchen, dining area, and sitting area, and can sleep up to six adults; fine for a family. **Amenities:** 🕿 🖨 A/C, cable TV w/movies. **Services:** 🖵 🐾 Twice-daily maid svce. **Facilities:** 🕿 🚣 🛏 & Games rm, whirlpool. **Rates (CP):** Peak (May 15–Sept 15) $50–$58 S; $60 D; $70–$83 ste. Extra person $6. Children under age 18 stay free. Lower rates off-season. Parking: Outdoor, free. AE, DC, DISC, MC, V.

RESTAURANTS 🍴

Drakes By The Lake
Pine Bluff Rd; tel 815/942-5580. **American.** Nestled in the countryside, this restaurant offers a good view of Goose Lake. Popular menu items include ribs, Grecian steak, and colossal shrimp. A large patio with tables and a bar overlooks the lake. Sunday buffet runs 11am–3pm. **FYI:** Reservations recommended. Children's menu. **Open:** Tues–Thurs 5–9pm, Fri 5–10pm, Sat 5–11pm, Sun 11am–8pm. **Prices:** Main courses $9–$22. AE, DC, MC, V. ⛰

★ Rockwell Inn
2400 US 6 W; tel 815/942-6224. Exit 112 off I-80. **Seafood/Steak.** Surrounded by farmlands and nature, this countryside eatery is off the beaten path but is well worth the trip. Don't expect kitschy gingham and needlepoint decor; the interior is actually quite elegant, with tablecloths, linen napkins, and staff dressed in impeccable uniforms. Folks come for the chicken piccata, prime rib, and chateaubriand bouquetière for two. For those willing, there's a super-sized banana split that comes with a kitchen band (staff on tambourines, clapping and singing). Surprisingly long wine list. **FYI:** Reservations recommended. Children's menu. **Open:** Mon–Sat 4–10pm, Sun 1–8pm. **Prices:** Main courses $10–$34. AE, MC, V. 💚 🛋 &

Mount Vernon

Seat of Jefferson County, in southern Illinois. Settled by Southerners, the city retains its Southern charm and traditions, despite industrial development. Site of the Sweetcorn-Watermelon Festival, held in late August. **Information:** Mount Vernon Convention & Visitors Bureau, 200 Potomac Blvd, PO Box 2580, Mount Vernon, 62864 (tel 618/242-3151).

HOTEL 🏨

≣ ≣ ≣ Ramada Hotel
222 Potomac Blvd, 62864; tel 618/244-7100 or toll free 800/243-7171; fax 618/242-8876. Exit 95 off I-57/64, E to Potomac Blvd, N to entrance. Large lobby opens onto atrium area with cafe. Fine for extended stays. Near horseback riding, city park, and outlet mall. Golf, boating, and fishing at Rend Lake. **Rooms:** 236 rms and stes. Executive level. CI 3pm/CO 1pm. Nonsmoking rms avail. **Amenities:** 🕿 🖨 🎛 A/C, cable TV, voice mail. Some units w/terraces, 1 w/whirlpool. **Services:** ✕ 🖨 🖾 🖵 🐾 Safe at front desk. **Facilities:** 🕿 🏊 🖥 & 2 restaurants (*see* "Restaurants" below), 1 bar, sauna, whirlpool. Outdoor sun deck adjoins indoor pool surrounded by greenhouse windows. **Rates (BB):** Peak (May–Oct) $39–$59 S or D; $75 ste. Extra person $9. Children under age 12 stay free. Lower rates off-season. AP and MAP rates avail. Parking: Outdoor, free. Golf packages avail. AE, CB, DC, DISC, MC, V.

MOTELS

≣ ≣ Best Inns of America
222 S 44th St, 62864; tel 618/244-4343 or toll free 800/237-8466; fax 618/244-4343. From I-57/64, exit 95 to IL

15, E to Frontage Rd entrance. Easy access to highway, gas stations, and restaurants. Bike rentals, golf, fishing, and boating available at Rend Lake. **Rooms:** 153 rms. CI open/CO 1pm. Nonsmoking rms avail. Basic rooms are clean and comfortable. **Amenities:** 📞 A/C, cable TV w/movies, dataport. **Services:** 🍽 🍷 Complimentary "Special K" breakfast. Complimentary toiletries available at desk. **Facilities:** 📷 ⚲ **Rates (CP):** Peak (May–Sept) $38–$42 S; $46–$48 D. Extra person $6. Children under age 18 stay free. Lower rates off-season. Parking: Outdoor, free. AE, DC, DISC, MC, V.

≣≣ Comfort Inn
201 Potomac Blvd, 62864; tel 618/242-7200 or toll free 800/221-2222; fax 618/242-9800. Exit 95 off I-57/64, E to light, N to entrance. New facility with clean, modern accommodations. **Rooms:** 64 rms. CI 2pm/CO 11am. Nonsmoking rms avail. **Amenities:** 📞 A/C, cable TV, dataport. Some units w/whirlpools. **Services:** 🍷 Safe available at office. **Facilities:** 📷 🛏 ⚲ Whirlpool. **Rates (CP):** Peak (Apr–Nov) $45 S; $50 D. Extra person $5. Children under age 18 stay free. Lower rates off-season. Parking: Outdoor, free. Corporate, military, and AARP discounts avail. AE, DC, DISC, MC, V.

≣≣ Drury Inn
I-57/64 and IL 15, PO Box 805, 62864; tel 618/244-4550 or toll free 800/325-8300. Exit 95 off I-57/64. Updated motel with easy access. **Rooms:** 82 rms. CI 3pm/CO noon. Nonsmoking rms avail. **Amenities:** 📞 ⚲ A/C, cable TV w/movies, dataport. **Services:** 🛄 🍷 🍷 Complimentary toiletries available at front desk. **Facilities:** 📷 🛏 ⚲ **Rates (CP):** Peak (May–Sept) $47–$53 S; $54–$66 D. Extra person $7. Children under age 18 stay free. Lower rates off-season. Parking: Outdoor, free. AE, CB, DC, DISC, MC, V.

≣ Thrifty Inn
100 N 44th St, 62864; tel 618/244-7750 or toll free 800/325-8300; fax 618/244-7750. Exit 95 off I-57/64. Nothing fancy about these basic accommodations. Fine for overnight, but not longer. **Rooms:** 41 rms. CI 3pm/CO noon. Nonsmoking rms avail. **Amenities:** 📞 ⚲ A/C, cable TV w/movies, dataport. **Services:** 🛄 🍷 🍷 Complimentary toiletries available at desk. **Facilities:** ⚲ **Rates:** Peak (May–Sept 15) $40–$48 S or D. Extra person $7. Children under age 18 stay free. Lower rates off-season. Parking: Outdoor, free. Corporate rates avail. AE, CB, DC, DISC, MC, V.

RESTAURANT 🍴
Caroline's
In Ramada Hotel, 222 Potomac Blvd; tel 618/244-7100. Exit 95 off I-57/64. **American/Southwestern.** Popular eatery with a southwestern flair. Large dining room is divided by several levels for a more intimate feel. Menu includes stew in a sourdough bowl, chimichangas, seafood quesadilla, and seafood linguine. **FYI:** Reservations accepted. Children's menu. Dress code. **Open:** Mon–Sat 11am–10pm, Sun 4–10pm. **Prices:** Main courses $6–$15. AE, CB, DC, DISC, MC, V.

Naperville

This fast-growing southwest suburb of Chicago retains some of the atmosphere of a small town, despite its growing reputation as a center of high-tech industry. A number of Victorian houses are maintained in a historic district downtown. **Information:** Naperville Area Chamber of Commerce, PO Box 832, Naperville, 60566 (tel 630/355-4141).

HOTELS 🏨

≣≣≣ Courtyard by Marriott
1155 E Diehl Rd, 60563; tel 630/505-0550 or toll free 800/321-2211; fax 630/505-8337. ½ mile off Naperville Rd and I-88. An intimate, quiet atmosphere is the goal here. **Rooms:** 147 rms and stes. CI 3pm/CO 1pm. Nonsmoking rms avail. Ask for room facing landscaped courtyard; outer rooms have sliding doors facing parking lot. **Amenities:** 📞 ⚲ 📺 📞 A/C, satel TV w/movies, refrig, dataport, voice mail. Some units w/terraces. **Services:** 🚐 🛄 🍷 Babysitting. **Facilities:** 📷 🏋 🛏 ⚲ 1 restaurant (bkfst and dinner only), 1 bar, whirlpool, washer/dryer. Small, cozy lounge area set off from lobby. Small pool, but pool area is spacious and part of courtyard. **Rates:** Peak (May–Oct) $89 S or D; $99–$109 ste. Children under age 12 stay free. Lower rates off-season. Parking: Outdoor, free. AE, CB, DC, DISC, MC, V.

≣≣≣ Holiday Inn Select
1801 N Naper Blvd, 60563; tel 630/305-4900 or toll free 800/531-6147; fax 630/505-8239. Off I-88. Excellent location off I-88 Naperville exit. Chosen as a Holiday Inn 1994 Torchbearer Award winner, one of Holiday Inn's top 24 properties. Now one of Holiday Inn's new Select hotels with special business emphasis, although they love families too. **Rooms:** 295 rms, stes, and effic. Executive level. CI 3pm/CO noon. No smoking. Nonsmoking rms avail. Recently renovated in pleasing decorator touches. **Amenities:** 📞 ⚲ 📺 📞 A/C, satel TV w/movies, refrig, dataport, voice mail, bathrobes. 1 unit w/whirlpool. **Services:** ✕ 🚐 🛄 🍷 Car-rental desk. **Facilities:** 📷 🏋 📞 🖥 ⚲ 1 restaurant, 1 bar, games rm, sauna. **Rates:** $89–$119 S; $99–$129 D; $150–$250 ste; $250–$250 effic. Extra person $10. Children under age 18 stay free. AP and MAP rates avail. Parking: Outdoor, free. AE, CB, DC, DISC, JCB, MC, V.

MOTELS

≣≣ Chicago/Naperville Travelodge
1617 Naperville-Wheaton Rd, 60563; tel 630/505-0200 or toll free 800/255-3050; fax 630/505-0501. Pleasant suburban location with easy access to highways, businesses, and tourist attractions. **Rooms:** 103 rms. Executive level. CI

3pm/CO noon. Nonsmoking rms avail. **Amenities:** 🔲 🔳 A/C, satel TV w/movies. Club rooms equipped with refrigerators. **Services:** 🔲 🔳 **Facilities:** 🔲 Games rm, washer/dryer. **Rates (CP):** Peak (Apr 1–Sept 15) $45–$58 S or D. Extra person $5. Children under age 16 stay free. Lower rates off-season. Parking: Outdoor, free. AE, CB, DC, DISC, MC, V.

≡≡ Days Inn

1350 E Ogden Ave, 60563; tel 630/369-3600 or toll free 800/325-2525; fax 630/369-3643. On IL 34, just E of Naperville-Wheaton Rd. Basic, no-frills accommodations. **Rooms:** 121 rms. CI 2pm/CO noon. Nonsmoking rms avail. **Amenities:** 🔲 A/C, cable TV w/movies, dataport, in-rm safe. **Services:** 🔲 🔳 🔲 🔳 Twice-daily maid svce. Complimentary toiletries at front desk. **Facilities:** 🔲 Washer/dryer. **Rates (CP):** Peak (Apr–Oct) $45–$51 S; $51–$57 D. Extra person $6. Children under age 13 stay free. Lower rates off-season. Parking: Outdoor, free. AE, CB, DC, DISC, JCB, MC, V.

≡≡ Exel Inn

1585 N Naperville-Wheaton Rd, 60563; tel 630/357-0022 or toll free 800/856-8013; fax 630/357-9817. Brick columns tower over the entrance to these basic lodgings. Adjacent to several restaurants. **Rooms:** 123 rms and effic. CI noon/CO noon. Nonsmoking rms avail. **Amenities:** 🔲 🔳 A/C, satel TV w/movies, dataport. 1 unit w/whirlpool. **Services:** ✗ 🔲 🔳 🔲 🔳 Car-rental desk. Selected restaurants will deliver and bill to room. No more than two pets, limited to 25 pounds each, permitted in smoking rooms only. **Facilities:** 🔲 Games rm, washer/dryer. Free health club passes to guests. **Rates (CP):** $48–$55 S; $58–$63 D; $53–$63 effic. Extra person $4. Children under age 18 stay free. Min stay special events. Parking: Outdoor, free. AE, CB, DC, DISC, MC, V.

≡≡ Hampton Inn

1087 E Diehl Rd, 60563; tel 630/505-1400 or toll free 800/426-7866; fax 630/505-1416. ½ mile from Naperville Rd and I-88. Dependable chain quality built in corporate area off I-88 tollway. Fine for overnight stay. **Rooms:** 130 rms. CI 3pm/CO noon. Standard for chain—clean and comfortable. **Amenities:** 🔲 🔳 🔳 🔳 A/C, satel TV w/movies, dataport. **Services:** ✗ 🔲 🔳 **Facilities:** 🔲 🔳 🔲 🔲 Rates (CP): $61–$72 S; $67–$75 D. Extra person $6. Children under age 18 stay free. Parking: Outdoor, free. AE, CB, DC, DISC, MC, V.

≡≡ Red Roof Inn

1698 W Diehl Rd, 60563; tel 630/369-2500 or toll free 800/THE-ROOF; fax 630/369-9987. Comfortable, basic accommodations for short-term stays. **Rooms:** 119 rms. CI 2pm/CO noon. Nonsmoking rms avail. **Amenities:** 🔲 A/C, satel TV w/movies. **Services:** 🔲 🔳 🔲 Separate check-in for groups available on request. **Facilities:** 🔲 **Rates:** Peak (May–Oct) $42–$52 S; $49–$52 D. Extra person $7. Children under age 18 stay free. Lower rates off-season. Parking: Outdoor, free. AE, CB, DC, DISC, MC, V.

RESTAURANTS 🍴

Casa Lupita

1633 N Naper Blvd; tel 630/505-7037. 2 blocks S of I-88. **Mexican.** Basic, authentic fare in a happy courtyard ambience. International Sunday brunch, $9. Spacious, lively, comfortable bar with nightly complimentary taco buffet, big screen TV, business crowd. **FYI:** Reservations recommended. Reservations accepted. Singer. Children's menu. **Open:** Mon–Thurs 11am–12:30am, Fri–Sat 11am–1:30am, Sun 10am–11:30pm. **Prices:** Main courses $6–$12. AE, CB, DC, DISC, MC, V. ♥ 🍽 🔲 🔲 🔲

Emilio's Meson Sabika

1025 Aurora Ave; tel 630/983-3000. 1½ mi W of downtown. **Spanish/Tapas.** This expansive historic mansion with sprawling lawn is a unique setting for feasting on hip Spanish finger food. A wide variety of tapas can be mixed and matched on a big platter for sharing, larger portions can be ordered as entrees. Two types of paella—one chicken and pork, one seafood—easily feed a crowd. Special dinner events focus on different aspects of Spanish culture and cuisine. There's a grand old bar, too. **FYI:** Reservations recommended. Flamenco. Dress code. Additional locations: 14 S 3rd St, Geneva (tel 708/262-1000); 4100 W Roosevelt, Hillside (tel 708/547-7177). **Open:** Lunch Mon–Fri 11:30am–5pm; dinner Mon–Thurs 5–10pm, Fri–Sat 5–11pm, Sun 4–10pm. **Prices:** Main courses $4–$16. AE, CB, MC, V. ♥ 🔲 🍽 🔲 🔲

♣ Montparnasse

In 5th Ave Station, 200 E 5th Ave; tel 630/961-8203. 2 blocks E of Washington Ave, 3 blocks S of Ogden Ave. **French Contemporary.** Housed in an old factory renovated into an unusual mall, this suburban bistro rivals downtown Chicago's most upscale restaurants for quality and originality. The cuisine is light but classical, and it employs only the freshest of ingredients. Changing menus feature pheasant, roast meats, and a large choice of fish and seafood. **FYI:** Reservations recommended. Jazz. No smoking. **Open:** Lunch Mon–Fri 11:30am–2pm; dinner Mon–Sat 6–9pm. **Prices:** Main courses $22–$30. AE, CB, DC, DISC, MC, V. ♥ 🔲 🔲

ATTRACTION 🔲

Morton Arboretum

IL 53, Lisle; tel 630/968-0074. A nature showcase of flora from around the world (organized into both formal and natural settings) and a wildlife refuge for foxes, beavers, birds, and other forest creatures. There are 40,000 different tree specimens, classified into 4,000 species. Nine miles of roadways allow visitors to drive through the grounds, but the 25 miles of pedestrian pathways provide a more intimate view of the plant and woods life. **Open:** Peak (Apr–Oct) daily 7am–7pm. Reduced hours off-season. $$$

Nauvoo

Once the largest city in the state, Nauvoo became a ghost town after the Carthage Jail lynching drove the Mormons west to Utah. Many of the structures have been restored from the days when this was the heart of the Mormon Church. **Information:** Nauvoo Chamber of Commerce, 2010 E Parley, PO Box 41, Nauvoo, 62354 (tel 217/453-6648).

MOTELS ▥

≣≣ Motel Nauvoo
1610 Mulholland St, 62354; tel 217/453-2219. Clean, utilitarian motel located a short distance from uptown shops and services on IL 96. **Rooms:** 11 rms. CI 4pm/CO 11am. No smoking. **Amenities:** ▦ ⚲ A/C, cable TV. **Services:** ⊠ ⊘ **Facilities:** ⚴ **Rates:** $38 S; $45 D. Extra person $5. Children under age 12 stay free. Parking: Outdoor, free. Closed Nov 23–Mar 1. MC, V.

≣ Nauvoo Family Motel
150 N Warsaw St, PO Box 187, 62354; tel 217/453-6527 or toll free 800/341-8000; fax 217/453-6527. Functional motel. **Rooms:** 32 rms and stes. CI open/CO 11am. No smoking. Basic motel rooms, plus family suites with two bedrooms, living room, and kitchen. **Amenities:** ▦ ⚲ A/C, cable TV. For families, a communal supply of kitchen utensils operates on the honor system. **Services:** ⊘ **Facilities:** ⚴ Washer/dryer. **Rates:** $35 S; $41 D; $49–$82 ste. Extra person $5. Children under age 2 stay free. Parking: Outdoor, free. Stay three nights and get fourth one free. AE, DISC, MC, V.

RESTAURANTS ▦

Grandpa John's
1255 Mulholland St; tel 217/453-2310. **American.** Grandpa John Kraus opened this cafe in 1918. Homemade ice cream, sandwiches, sundaes, sodas, floats, blueberry muffins, and breads are among the goodies available at this cafe under third-generation management. Dinner means roast beef, turkey, Swiss steak, and meat loaf. **FYI:** Reservations accepted. No liquor license. No smoking. **Open:** Peak (June–Aug) daily 7am–7:30pm. Closed Jan–Feb. **Prices:** Main courses $3–$8. No CC. ▦

Ⓢ Hotel Nauvoo Historic Inn
1290 Mulholland St; tel 217/453-2211. **American.** The building, built in 1840, is now primarily a restaurant, though there are still eight guest rooms upstairs. Downstairs there are six contiguous dining rooms; the Nauvoo Room features a restored front of a French Icarian house and brick walls, as well as the famous overflowing buffet tables. Choices include carved roast beef, turkey, ham, catfish, chicken, shrimp, vegetables, and homemade cinnamon rolls. Local wines from the Nauvoo Winery. **FYI:** Reservations accepted. Children's menu. **Open:** Tues–Thurs 5–8:30pm, Fri–Sat 5–9pm, Sun 11am–3pm. **Prices:** Main courses $10–$14. No CC. ⚴

ATTRACTIONS ▥

Brigham Young Home
Kimball St; tel 217/453-2237. Restored brick home of the second president of the Church of Jesus Christ of Latterday Saints. The house contains Young's office complete with period furnishings. **Open:** Daily 9am–5pm. **Free**

Carthage Jail
307 Walnut St, Carthage; tel 217/357-2989. 12 mi SE of Nauvoo. It was here on June 27, 1844 that the Mormon prophet Joseph Smith and his brother Hyrum were killed by a mob. It was after this event that Brigham Young led the Latterday Saints from Illinois in 1846. The jail has been restored to its original 1844 condition. Movie and visitors center. **Open:** Mon–Sat 9am–5pm, Sun noon–5pm. **Free**

Joseph Smith Historic Center
Water St; tel 217/453-2246. The center presents a film about the life of the founder of the Mormon church. From the center visitors can take walking tours of the **Homestead,** the log building on the banks of the Mississippi that served as Smith's first residence in Nauvoo, as well as the **Mansion House** (circa 1842) which has been restored as it was when the Smith family moved here from their log house. **Open:** Daily 9am–5pm. **Free**

Printing Office
Main and Kimball Sts; tel 217/453-2237. Served as the Church's chief comunication center and published the periodicals *Times and Seasons,* the *Nauvoo Neighbor,* and the *Nauvoo Wasp.* The building has been fully renovated and features the original 19th-century printing presses. **Open:** Daily 9am–5pm. **Free**

Historic Nauvoo Visitors Center
Main and Young Sts; tel 217/453-2233 or toll free 800/453-0022. Houses an extensive historical exhibit about The Church of Jesus Christ of Latterday Saints. Artifacts, documents, and a scale model of the Nauvoo of 1846 are on display. Free guide service for other sites in Nauvoo can be arranged at the center. **Open:** Mon–Sat 9am–5pm, Sun noon–5pm. **Free**

Normal

See also Bloomington

HOTEL ▥

≣≣ Holiday Inn Bloomington/Normal
8 Traders Circle, 61761; tel 309/452-8300 or toll free 800/HOLIDAY; fax 309/454-6722. Exit 165A off I-55. Very pleasant facility in a somewhat pastoral setting at the end of a frontage road. Open lobby extends into bar area in center of atrium and has large screen TV. Close to highway exits. **Rooms:** 160 rms and stes. CI 3pm/CO noon. Nonsmoking rms avail. **Amenities:** ▦ ⚲ ▤ A/C, satel TV w/movies,

dataport, VCR. **Services:** ✕ 🚐 🖼 🛏 🐕 Children's program, babysitting. Candies and toiletries in basket in each room. Small pets only. Holiday Inn's Official Fun & Games program allows children to take games and toys to their room. Very pleasant and professional staff. **Facilities:** 🏌 ⛳ 🏊₆₀₀ 💻 ♿ 1 restaurant, 1 bar, games rm, sauna, whirlpool, washer/dryer. Glassed-enclosed pool area has sun deck. Business center limited to pay phones, pay fax, and stamp machine. Small glass-enclosed restaurant looks elegant and is located in lobby/atrium area. **Rates:** $69–$80 S or D; $175–$275 ste. Extra person $9. Children under age 19 stay free. Parking: Outdoor, free. AE, CB, DC, DISC, MC, V.

MOTELS

🏨 Fairfield Inn

202 Landmark Dr, 61761; tel 309/454-6600 or toll free 800/228-2800; fax 309/454-6600. Exit 167 off I-55. Well-managed motel located near College Hills Mall. Small lobby area with TV. **Rooms:** 128 rms. CI 3pm/CO noon. Nonsmoking rms avail. **Amenities:** 🛗 🔥 A/C, cable TV w/movies, dataport. **Services:** 🖼 🛏 **Facilities:** 🏌 🏊₇₅ ♿ **Rates (CP):** Peak (May–Oct) $50–$70 S or D. Extra person $7. Children under age 17 stay free. Lower rates off-season. Parking: Outdoor, free. AE, DC, DISC, MC, V.

🏨🏨 Signature Inn

101 S Veterans Pkwy, 61761; tel 309/454-4044 or toll free 800/822-5252; fax 309/454-4044. Exit 167 off I-55. Lovely mid-range property perfect for corporate travelers. Lobby is bright and cheery with the signature winding glass and brass stairway leading up to business center and interview areas. **Rooms:** 124 rms and stes. CI 2pm/CO noon. Nonsmoking rms avail. **Amenities:** 🛗 🔥 A/C, cable TV w/movies, dataport. **Services:** 🖼 🛏 VCR and Nintendo available at front desk. **Facilities:** 🏌 ⛳ 🏊₁₀₀ 💻 ♿ **Rates (CP):** $65–$75 S or D; $100–$125 ste. Extra person $7. Children under age 17 stay free. Parking: Outdoor, free. AE, CB, DC, DISC, MC, V.

Northbrook

Several forks of the Chicago River run through this northern Chicago suburb, which was originally settled by Germans working on the Erie Canal. **Information:** Northbrook Chamber of Commerce & Industry, 2002 Walters Ave, Northbrook, 60062 (tel 847/498-5555).

HOTELS 🛏

🏨🏨🏨 Northbrook Hilton

2855 N Milwaukee Ave, 60062; tel 847/480-7500 or toll free 800/HILTONS; fax 847/480-0827. Willow Rd W exit off I-294. Impressive landscaping includes fountain and pond. Located 15 minutes from O'Hare International Airport, two minutes from Palwaukee Airport. Adjacent to and owned by Allgauer's Restaurant. **Rooms:** 274 rms and stes. Executive

level. CI noon/CO 3pm. Nonsmoking rms avail. Half of the nicely furnished rooms overlook the forest preserve and the Desplaines River. Small baths and dressing rooms, but rooms with whirlpools and hot tubs have larger baths. **Amenities:** 🛗 🔥 🖥 🍴 A/C, satel TV w/movies, refrig, dataport, voice mail, bathrobes. All units w/minibars, some w/whirlpools. **Services:** ✕ VP 🚐 🖼 🛏 Twice-daily maid svce, car-rental desk, social director, children's program, babysitting. Shuttle service to and from O'Hare available every hour on the hour 7am–10pm, $10. Special transportation services, when available, within a 5-mile radius of the hotel may be arranged at transportation desk for a small fee. Charge for valet service. Friendly and pleasant staff. **Facilities:** 🏌 🎾 ⛳ 🏊₉₀₀ 💻 ♿ 2 restaurants (see "Restaurants" below), 1 bar (w/entertainment), spa, sauna, steam rm, whirlpool. Frank's Place offers music, dancing, snacks, games, and complimentary hors d'oeuvres Mon–Fri afternoons. **Rates (CP):** Peak (Apr–Oct) $115–$140 S; $130–$155 D; $135–$375 ste. Extra person $12. Children under age 12 stay free. Lower rates off-season. Parking: Outdoor, free. AE, CB, DC, DISC, JCB, MC, V.

🏨🏨 Sheraton North Shore Inn

933 Skokie Blvd, 60062; tel 847/498-6500 or toll free 800/535-9131; fax 847/498-9558. Exit IL 68 W off US 41. Busy commercial property that lacks a special ambience. Good shuttle services to nearby attractions. **Rooms:** 375 rms and stes. Executive level. CI 3pm/CO noon. Nonsmoking rms avail. Rooms are more pleasant than lobby. Those on the east side view the forest preserve and get traffic noise from Edens Highway. **Amenities:** 🛗 🔥 🖥 🍴 A/C, cable TV w/movies. 1 unit w/fireplace. Some rooms have whirlpool, hot tub, and robes. **Services:** 🍴 🚐 🖼 🛏 Car-rental desk. Free shuttle service to nearby Chicago Botanic Garden, Ravinia, and O'Hare Airport, which is about 15 miles away. **Facilities:** 🏌 ⛳ 🏊₄₀₀ 💻 ♿ 1 restaurant, 2 bars, games rm, spa, sauna, whirlpool, washer/dryer. A large meeting space for this suburban area. **Rates:** $71–$126 S; $71–$156 D; $225–$450 ste. Extra person $12. Children under age 12 stay free. Parking: Outdoor, free. AE, CB, DC, DISC, EC, JCB, MC, V.

MOTEL

🏨 Red Roof Inn

340 Waukegan Rd, 60062; tel 847/205-1755 or toll free 800/843-7663; fax 847/205-1891. IL 68 W exit off I-94 to IL 43. A basic, adequate, seven-year-old motel. There has been no remodeling and all is beginning to look worn. Located right off highway, adjacent to Deerbrook Mall and Chicago Health Club. Several restaurants nearby. **Rooms:** 118 rms. CI 3pm/CO noon. Nonsmoking rms avail. No drawer space, but shelves. Rooms on the south side get noise from the highway. **Amenities:** 🛗 A/C, satel TV w/movies, dataport. 1 unit w/minibar, some w/terraces. **Services:** 🛏 🐕 **Facilities:** 🏊₂₂ ♿ **Rates (CP):** Peak (June–Sept) $42–$55 S;

$51–$63 D. Extra person $8. Children under age 18 stay free. Lower rates off-season. Parking: Outdoor, free. AE, CB, DISC, MC, V.

RESTAURANTS 🍴

★ Allgauer's On The Riverfront

In Northbrook Hilton, 2855 N Milwaukee Ave; tel 847/480-7500. Exit Willow Rd W off I-294; turn left on IL 21. **Continental.** Situated picturesquely on Desplaines River and forest preserve, adjacent to Northbrook Hilton Hotel, this 60-year-old family-owned restaurant is a local favorite. Under spacious high-vaulted ceiling of glass-walled dining rooms, enjoy steak Diane prepared table-side, daily buffet, or extravagant Sunday Champagne Brunch. **FYI:** Reservations recommended. **Open:** Mon–Fri 6:30am–11pm, Sat–Sun 7am–11pm. **Prices:** Main courses $13–$30. AE, CB, DC, DISC, MC, V. 🏔 VP &

Claim Company

In Northbrook Court Shopping Mall, 2124 Northbrook Court; tel 847/291-0770. **Barbecue/Burgers.** A noted family dining spot. Gourmet burger, the "Motherlode," can be topped with a variety of cheeses, mushrooms, onions, and sauces at no extra charge. Salad bar. **FYI:** Reservations recommended. Children's menu. Additional locations: 232 Oakbrook Center, Oakbrook (tel 708/574-3077); 900 N Michigan, Chicago (tel 312/787-5757). **Open:** Mon–Thurs 11:30am–10pm, Fri–Sat 11:30am–11pm, Sun noon–8:30pm. **Prices:** Main courses $7–$13. AE, CB, DC, MC, V. 👥&

Stefani's

601 Skokie Rd; tel 847/564-3950. From US 41 exit IL 68 W. **Italian.** Sheer curtains draping a glass ceiling soften the light of this pleasant restaurant. Chicken Vesuvio and veal scaloppine complement the Northern Italian cuisine. Noted for its pasta and its own pastries. Large selection of Italian and German wines. **FYI:** Reservations recommended. **Open:** Lunch Mon–Fri 11:30am–3pm; dinner Mon–Thurs 5–10pm, Fri–Sat 5–11pm, Sun 4–9pm. **Prices:** Main courses $10–$24. AE, DC, MC, V. ♥

★ Tonelli's

1038 Waukegan Rd; tel 847/272-4730. On IL 43. **Italian.** Second-generation family-owned Northern Italian restaurant specializing in pastas, chicken and veal dishes, chicken piccanti, and veal parmigiana. **FYI:** Reservations accepted. Children's menu. **Open:** Mon–Fri 11am–10:30pm, Sat–Sun 4–10:30pm. **Prices:** Main courses $7–$14. AE, MC, V. 👥&

ATTRACTION 🏛

River Trail Nature Center

3120 N Milwaukee Ave; tel 847/824-8360. Created by the Cook County Forest Preserve District to provide a safe haven for native plants and animals away from the nearby urban environment. Self-guiding trails give visitors a close-up look at wild geranium and indigo, sugar maple trees, and waterfowl and songbirds. Seasonal programs offered. **Open:** Peak (Mar–Oct) Mon–Fri 8am–5pm, Sat–Sun 8am–5:30pm. Reduced hours off-season. **Free**

Oak Brook

HOTELS 🏨

🟰🟰🟰 Chicago Marriott Oak Brook Hotel

1401 W 22nd St, 60521; tel 630/573-8555 or toll free 800/228-9290; fax 630/573-1026. Unique semicircular shape characterizes this modern facility, located across from Oak Brook Shopping Center. Much outdoor recreation available nearby. **Rooms:** 347 rms and stes. Executive level. CI 4pm/CO noon. Nonsmoking rms avail. **Amenities:** 🛏 ⓐ ⓠ A/C, satel TV w/movies, dataport, voice mail. Suites equipped with refrigerators. **Services:** ✗ 🖭 🚗 🛄 🛎 ⓐ Car-rental desk, babysitting. Cash station in lobby. Safety deposit boxes at front desk. Small pets only. **Facilities:** 🏋 ⛳ ⊡ 🔄 ⓐ 1 restaurant, 1 bar, games rm, spa, sauna, whirlpool, washer/dryer. Kinkos business center in lobby. **Rates:** Peak (Apr 15–Nov 30) $59–$139 S or D; $160 ste. Children under age 18 stay free. Lower rates off-season. Parking: Outdoor, free. "Two for breakfast" weekend packages avail. AE, CB, DC, DISC, ER, JCB, MC, V.

🟰🟰🟰 The Drake Oak Brook Hotel

2301 S York Rd, 60521; tel 630/574-5700 or toll free 800/334-9805, 800/235-2230 in IL; fax 630/574-0830. Cermak Rd (22nd St) exit off I-294. Resort atmosphere in suburban hotel, adjacent to the Butler National Golf Course. Intimate and charming. Near shopping and theaters. **Rooms:** 168 rms and stes. Executive level. CI 3pm/CO noon. Nonsmoking rms avail. **Amenities:** 🛏 ⓐ ⓠ A/C, cable TV w/movies, dataport, bathrobes. **Services:** ✗ VP 🛄 ⓐ Car-rental desk. Office will provide business services. **Facilities:** 🏋 🎾 ⚫2 ⊡ & 2 restaurants, 1 bar, volleyball, lawn games, whirlpool. Complimentary access to off-site fitness center. Gift shop with upscale products. **Rates (CP):** Peak (Apr–Nov) $99–$121 S or D; $150–$300 ste. Extra person $10. Children under age 16 stay free. Lower rates off-season. Parking: Outdoor, free. Special gift packages avail. AE, CB, DC, DISC, MC, V.

🟰🟰🟰 Hyatt Regency Oak Brook

1909 Spring Rd, 60521; tel 630/573-1234 or toll free 800/233-1234; fax 630/573-1133. A 360° circular wall mural of Chicago and the surrounding Illinois countryside decorates the atrium lobby of this modern facility, just across the street from the Oak Brook Shopping Center. Near golf, tennis, and polo. **Rooms:** 423 rms and stes. Executive level. CI 3pm/CO noon. Nonsmoking rms avail. **Amenities:** 🛏 ⓐ ⓠ A/C, cable TV w/movies, dataport, voice mail. Some units w/terraces. **Services:** ✗ 🖭 VP 🛄 ⓐ Car-rental desk, babysitting. Business Plan rooms have on-floor access to printer, copier, and other business essentials. **Facilities:** 🖼️ 🎿 ⛳ 1000 🖥️ ♿ 1 restaurant, 2 bars, basketball, sauna, whirlpool. Barber shop on premises. **Rates:** $69–$149 S; $69–$174 D; $175–$525 ste. Extra person $25. Children under age 18 stay free. Parking: Indoor/outdoor, free. AE, CB, DC, DISC, JCB, MC, V.

≣≣≣≣ Oak Brook Hills Hotel & Resort

3500 Midwest Rd, 60522; tel 630/850-5555 or toll free 800/445-3315; fax 630/850-5567. 105 acres. Luxurious, with a formal lobby that opens to informal multi-level seating overlooking the golf course. **Rooms:** 382 rms and stes. Executive level. CI 4pm/CO 1pm. Nonsmoking rms avail. **Amenities:** 📺 🧊 A/C, cable TV w/movies, dataport. All units w/minibars, some w/terraces, 1 w/fireplace, 1 w/whirlpool. Concierge level and some suites have in-room safes, refrigerators, hair dryers, bathrobes. **Services:** 🍴 🔑 VP 🛏️ ↺ Car-rental desk, social director, masseur, babysitting. **Facilities:** 🖼️ ▶18 🎿 ⛷️ ⛳ ⛳ 1000 🖥️ ♿ 3 restaurants (see "Restaurants" below), 2 bars (1 w/entertainment), basketball, volleyball, games rm, lawn games, spa, sauna, whirlpool, beauty salon. Ascots, the main dining room, offers Sun brunch and daily buffets. Pro shop open Apr–Nov. **Rates:** Peak (June–Sept) $167–$207 S or D; $325–$700 ste. Extra person $10. Children under age 18 stay free. Lower rates off-season. AP and MAP rates avail. Parking: Outdoor, free. Peak season rate changes apply to weekend packages only. Meal plans available for weekend packages only. AE, DC, DISC, MC, V.

≣≣≣ Renaissance Oak Brook

2100 Spring Rd, 60521; tel 630/573-2800 or toll free 800/HOTELS-1; fax 630/573-7134. Immediately adjacent to Oak Brook Shopping Center, this posh hotel with its intimate lobby and luxurious atmosphere pampers its clientele. Near dinner theater, arboretum, polo club, and more than 15 challenging championship golf courses. **Rooms:** 166 rms and stes. CI 3pm/CO noon. Nonsmoking rms avail. **Amenities:** 📺 🧊 🍷 A/C, cable TV w/movies, refrig, dataport, bathrobes. All units w/minibars, some w/terraces. Some rooms equipped with VCRs. **Services:** 🍴 🔑 VP 🚗 🛏️ ↺ Car-rental desk, babysitting. Complimentary evening hors d'oeuvres reception. Safety deposit boxes at desk. **Facilities:** 🖼️ ⛳ 250 🖥️ ♿ 1 restaurant, 1 bar, spa, sauna. **Rates (BB):** $79–$179 S or D; $190–$360 ste. Extra person $15. Children under age 18 stay free. Min stay special events. Parking: Outdoor, free. AE, CB, DC, DISC, ER, JCB, MC, V.

RESTAURANTS 🍴

Braxton Seafood Grill

3 Oakbrook Center Mall; tel 630/574-2155. Off US 83. **Seafood.** A lively jazz bar on the weekends and a large dining room make for a wonderful combination. Located next to Marshall Fields, Braxton's is perfect for an after-shopping meal. Subtle shifts in decor create a more intimate and original atmosphere in the winding dining area. Note the live lobster tank and large wine list. **FYI:** Reservations recom-

mended. Jazz. Children's menu. **Open:** Peak (Nov–Jan) lunch Mon–Fri 11:30am–2:30pm, Sat 11:30am–4pm, Sun 11:30am–9pm; dinner Mon–Thurs 5:30–10pm, Fri–Sat 5:30–11pm. **Prices:** Main courses $9–$43. AE, CB, DC, DISC, ER, MC, V. 🍴 ♿

♟ Fond de la Tour

In Oakbrook Towers, 40 N Tower Rd; tel 630/620-1500. At Meyers and Butterfield Rds. **French.** Continental cuisine in an elegant setting, tucked away on the first floor of a residential high rise. Menu favorites include shrimp scampi, rack of lamb, chateaubriand, and a selection of daily specials prepared by Chef Javier Martin. The wine cellar contains over 100 selections, including 15 Bordeaux. Choice desserts include cherries jubilee. **FYI:** Reservations recommended. Piano/singer. Jacket required. **Open:** Lunch Mon–Fri 11:30am–2:30pm; dinner Mon–Sat 6–10pm. **Prices:** Main courses $20–$44. AE, DC, DISC, MC, V. 🍷 VP

♟ The Waterford Restaurant

In Oak Brook Hills Hotel & Resort, 3500 Midwest Rd; tel 630/850-5520. At 35th St. **Continental.** Elegant dining in an intimate romantic setting lit by crystal chandeliers and graced by floor-to-ceiling walnut pillars and half-paneled walls. Dine on swordfish Santa Fe, broiled and topped with yucca, red onions, garlic, oregano, and olive oil; rack of lamb crusted with peanuts; filet mignon. **FYI:** Reservations recommended. Harp. Jacket required. **Open:** Mon–Sat 5:30–10pm. **Prices:** Main courses $23–$29; prix fixe $35. AE, DC, DISC, MC, V. 🍷 VP ♿

Oakbrook Terrace

HOTELS 🏨

≣≣≣ Hilton Suites Hotel

10 Drury Lane, 60181; tel 630/941-0100 or toll free 800/HILTONS; fax 630/941-0299. Fountains and greenery decorate the atrium lobby of this all-suite hotel that is a home-away-from-home for business travelers and vacationers. Adjacent to Drury Lane Dinner Theater. **Rooms:** 212 stes. CI 3pm/CO noon. Nonsmoking rms avail. **Amenities:** 📺 🧊 📻 🍷 A/C, satel TV w/movies, refrig, dataport, VCR, voice mail. Some units w/terraces. All rooms equipped with microwave, wet bar, and two TVs. **Services:** ✗ 🚐 🛏️ ↺ ⌖ Children's program, babysitting. Complimentary evening beverage reception and late night snacks. Safety deposit boxes at desk. Free fax service in continental United States. Children's program offered during summer weekends. Atrium Market is mini-grocery with gifts, sundries, and movie rentals. **Facilities:** 🖼️ ⛳ 100 🖥️ ♿ 1 restaurant, 1 bar, games rm, sauna, whirlpool. **Rates (BB):** $99–$139 ste. Extra person $20. Children under age 18 stay free. Parking: Outdoor, free. AE, CB, DC, DISC, ER, JCB, MC, V.

≡≡≡ Wyndham Gardens

17 W 350 22nd St, 60181; tel 630/833-3600 or toll free 800/822-4200; fax 630/833-7337. ½ mi E of Midwest Rd. Luxurious, full-service hotel with a lobby "library." Conveniently located; several golf courses nearby. **Rooms:** 222 rms and stes. CI 3pm/CO noon. Nonsmoking rms avail. **Amenities:** 🛁 ⓐ 📺 🍴 A/C, satel TV w/movies, dataport, voice mail, bathrobes. Refrigerators available on request. **Services:** ✗ 🗦 🍹 Safety deposit boxes at front desk. Front desk provides business services. **Facilities:** 🔂 🛁 🟦 👥 1 restaurant, 1 bar, whirlpool. **Rates:** $89–$99 S; $99–$109 D; $109 ste. Extra person $10. Children under age 18 stay free. Parking: Outdoor, free. AE, CB, DC, DISC, JCB, MC, V.

MOTELS

≡≡≡ Comfort Suites

17 W 445 Roosevelt Rd, 60181; tel 630/916-1000 or toll free 800/221-2222; fax 630/916-1068. Condominium-style parlor and one-bedroom suites ideal for families or long-term stays. **Rooms:** 104 stes. CI 3pm/CO noon. Nonsmoking rms avail. **Amenities:** 🛁 ⓐ A/C, cable TV w/movies, refrig. Some units w/terraces. Two TVs in every suite. Dataports available on request. **Services:** ✗ 🗦 🍹 Car-rental desk. Twice-daily maid service on request. Front desk provides business center services. Two complimentary cocktails per adult guest weekdays 5–7pm. **Facilities:** 🔂 🛁 🟦 👥 1 bar, spa, sauna, whirlpool, washer/dryer. **Rates (BB):** $77–$87 ste. Extra person $10. Children under age 18 stay free. Parking: Outdoor, free. AE, CB, DC, DISC, MC, V.

≡≡ La Quinta Inn

1 S 666 Midwest Rd, 60181; tel 630/495-4600 or toll free 800/531-5900; fax 630/495-2558. ½ block N of Cermak Rd (22nd St). White, hacienda-style building with red clay tile roof. Located near shopping, restaurants. **Rooms:** 150 rms. CI 2pm/CO noon. Nonsmoking rms avail. **Amenities:** 🛁 ⓐ A/C, satel TV w/movies. Dataports in king rooms. **Services:** 🗦 🍹 🐕 Car-rental desk. **Facilities:** 🔂 🟦 👥 Complimentary passes to local health club. **Rates (CP):** $70–$77 S; $77–$84 D. Extra person $7. Children under age 18 stay free. Parking: Outdoor, free. AE, CB, DC, DISC, MC, V.

Oak Lawn

Founded as Black Oaks Grove in 1856. In 1879, an agreement was made with the Wabash Railroad to create a permanent village. Oak Lawn was officially established in 1882. **Information:** Oak Lawn Chamber of Commerce, 6060 W 95 St, Oak Lawn, 60453 (tel 708/430-0003).

HOTELS 🏨

≡≡≡ Hilton Hotel

9444 S Cicero Ave, 60453; tel 708/425-7800 or toll free 800/HIL-9333; fax 708/425-8111. From I-294 exit 95th St and go 3½ mi E; from I-94 exit 95th St and go 5.2 mi W.

Circular, 12-story building convenient offering comfortable and spacious rooms. **Rooms:** 180 rms and stes. Executive level. CI 3pm/CO noon. Nonsmoking rms avail. The 12th floor Tower Room offers impressive view. Several 12th-story suites also available. **Amenities:** 🛁 ⓐ A/C, cable TV w/movies, dataport, voice mail, bathrobes. Some units w/minibars. **Services:** ✗ 🗦 🚗 🗦 🍹 Twice-daily maid svce, car-rental desk, social director, babysitting. **Facilities:** 🔂 🛁 🟦 🖥 👥 1 restaurant, 1 bar (w/entertainment), spa, sauna, whirlpool. Whitney's Bar and Grill features fabulous brunches popular with locals. Attractive health club includes step machines, Nautilus, exercise bikes, and indoor pool. **Rates:** $89–$125 S or D; $299–$629 ste. Extra person $15. Children under age 12 stay free. Parking: Outdoor, free. AE, CB, DISC, MC, V.

≡≡≡ Holiday Inn Southwest

4140 W 95th St, 60453; tel 708/425-7900 or toll free 800/3OAK-LAWN; fax 708/425-7918. From I-294 exit 95th St, go E 3½ mi; from I-94 exit 95th St go W 5 mi. Holiday Inn has designated this suburban hotel, managed by the same family since it opened in 1968, as one of four Midwest conference centers. Easy access to downtown Chicago; also convenient to Midway Airport and local shopping. **Rooms:** 139 rms. Executive level. CI 3pm/CO noon. Nonsmoking rms avail. **Amenities:** 🛁 A/C, cable TV w/movies. Business and executive rooms have dataports, armchair recliners, hair dryers, and coffeemakers. **Services:** ✗ 🚗 🗦 🍹 **Facilities:** 🔂 🟦 👥 1 restaurant, 1 bar (w/entertainment). **Rates:** $84–$99 S; $94–$109 D. Extra person $10. Children under age 18 stay free. Parking: Outdoor, free. AE, CB, DC, DISC, EC, JCB, MC, V.

Oak Park

One of Chicago's oldest suburbs was settled in 1837 and named for its natural growth of oaks. Ernest Hemingway was born here in 1899 and Frank Lloyd Wright kept a studio here for 20 years. The town still boasts a high concentration of Wright's Prairie School–style buildings. **Information:** Oak Park-River Forest Chamber of Commerce, 1010 Lake St, #102, Oak Park, 60301-1106 (tel 708/848-8151).

ATTRACTIONS 🏛

Hemingway Museum

200 N Oak Park Ave; tel 708/848-2222. A portion of the ground floor of this former church, now the Oak Park Arts Center, is given over to a small but interesting display of Hemingway memorabilia. A six-minute video presentation sheds considerable light on Hemingway's time in Oak Park, where he spent the first eighteen years of his life, and is particularly good on his high school experiences. **Open:** Wed and Sun 1–5pm, Sat 10am–5pm. **$**

Frank Lloyd Wright Home and Studio

951 Chicago Ave; tel 708/848-1976. From 1899 to 1909, this structure served as Wright's private residence, studio, and architectural laboratory. The home began as a simple shingled cottage that Wright built for his bride, but it soon became a work in progress as Wright remodeled it constantly. It embraces many idiosyncratic features—molded to his own needs, rather than those of a client—with add-ons such as a barrel-vaulted children's playroom and a studio with an octagonal balcony suspended by chains. Guided tours of this National Historical Landmark are given Monday through Friday at 11am, 1pm, and 3pm, and Saturday and Sunday every 15 minutes from 11am to 4pm. **$$$**

Unity Temple

875 Lake St; tel 708/383-8873. Designed in 1905 by Frank Lloyd Wright for the Unitarian Universalist congregation of which he was a member. Often called Wright's "Little Jewel Box," Wright himself described it by saying, "Unity Temple is where you will find the first real expression of my idea that the space within the building is the reality of that building." Its principal chapel is grand in its simplicity, looking somewhat like the Roman Senate. Color is used sparingly, with pale, natural effects achieved by pigmented plaster rather than paint. Other noteworthy details (all covered on the guided tour) include the great fireplace, the pulpit, the skylights, and the clesterory. Weekday self-guided tours and weekend guided tours available. **Open:** Daily 1–4pm. **$$**

Ottawa

Seat of LaSalle County, in northern Illinois. Ottawa was founded in 1830 at the confluence of the Fox and Illinois Rivers. The first of the Lincoln-Douglas debates took place in the public square. **Information:** Ottawa Area Chamber of Commerce & Industry, 100 W Lafayette St, PO Box 888, Ottawa, 61350 (tel 815/433-0084).

MOTELS 🏨

≣≣≣ Ottawa Inn

3000 Columbus St, 61350; tel 815/434-3400 or toll free 800/244-ROCK in IL; fax 815/434-3904. Jct IL 23 and I-80. This independently owned property is a welcome sight in a sea of chain motels. A local radio station broadcasts from a glass booth in the lobby. Suites are a real value. **Rooms:** 110 rms and stes. CI 2pm/CO 11am. Nonsmoking rms avail. Functional furniture is nothing special, but the suites are custom designed. **Amenities:** 🛏 A/C, cable TV w/movies. Some units w/terraces, some w/whirlpools. Whirlpool suites have a full-sized tub for at least two people that takes the space of one full bathroom. **Services:** 🚗 ↵ ⇦ Corporate Club visitors are offered a complete breakfast daily. What is called a continental breakfast (really a buffet complete with eggs, breads, and more) is open to all guests. The owners encourage all comments and suggestions. **Facilities:** 🏕 🚌 ♿

1 restaurant, 1 bar, games rm, whirlpool. Grills and picnic tables in courtyard. **Rates (CP):** $39–$52 S; $47–$58 D; $58–$89 ste. Extra person $6. Children under age 12 stay free. Parking: Outdoor, free. Corporate discounts avail. AE, CB, DC, DISC, MC, V.

≣ Sands Motel

1215 N La Salle St, 61350; tel 815/434-6440 or toll free 800/675-2217. 5 blocks N of courthouse. This small, independent property is convenient to Starved Rock State Park and other natural attractions in the area. A railroad track runs parallel to the parking lot, so there is some noise from passing trains. Close to downtown, restaurants, shopping. For a motel in the middle of a highly traveled vacation area, this property is quite reasonable. **Rooms:** 45 rms. CI 11am/CO 11am. Nonsmoking rms avail. Rooms are simply functional and the furniture is somewhat worn, but clean. King-size beds available in some rooms. **Amenities:** 🛏 A/C. **Services:** ↵ ⇦ Free coffee in lobby. The owner/manager is usually on-site and is very eager to please. **Rates:** $27–$30 S; $35–$38 D. Extra person $4. Children under age 12 stay free. Parking: Outdoor, free. AE, CB, DC, DISC, MC, V.

RESTAURANTS 🍴

$ ★ Hank's Farm

2973 IL 71 N; tel 815/433-2540. Exit 93 off I-80. **American.** Established in 1941, the restaurant moved to its distinctive hilltop barn setting in 1985. Outside, a large farm pen holds guinea hens, peacocks, bantam chickens, turkeys, a pot-bellied pig, and other animals; inside, the open-beamed ceiling still has its hay loft doors. Fridays feature a seafood buffet, and Sundays offer a brunch selection of dishes like fresh shrimp, choice roast beef, roast turkey, egg dishes, and pastries, including homemade cheesecakes. Gift baskets with homemade bread are sold. **FYI:** Reservations recommended. Children's menu. **Open:** Dinner Mon–Sat 4:30–10pm, Sun 3:30–9pm; brunch Sun 10am–2pm. **Prices:** Main courses $7–$18. AE, DISC, MC, V. 🏖 🍴

★ Monte's Riverside Inn

903 E Norris Dr; tel 815/434-5000. Near downtown Ottawa; on the Fox River. **American/Italian.** A pleasant atmosphere prevails here, with comfortable seating, low lighting, and thick carpets that help keep the place quiet during busy times. Known for fine steaks and fresh seafood, Monte's also prepares a variety of Italian dishes. The children's menu has favorites like fried shrimp, spaghetti, and junior-sized steaks. Weekends are usually booked; call in advance. Extensive wine list. **FYI:** Reservations recommended. Children's menu. **Open:** Lunch Mon–Fri 11am–2pm; dinner Sun 11am–9pm, Mon–Thurs 5–9pm, Fri–Sat 5–10pm. **Prices:** Main courses $9–$40. AE, MC, V. ♥ ♿

Palatine

A primarily residential suburb of Chicago. William Rainey Harper College is located here. **Information:** Greater Palatine Chamber of Commerce and Industry, 17 E Northwest Hwy #4, Palatine, 60067 (tel 708/359-7200).

RESTAURANT

Angel's Diner & Bakery

1520 E Dundee Rd; tel 847/991-1957. 2 blocks W of IL 53 N. **Diner.** Bright, cheerful, friendly 1950s-style diner. Red-and-white tile walls are accented with neon lights and chrome; seating is at counter, tables, and booths—some with jukeboxes. Daily chalkboard specials. Bakery goods made on premises daily. Souvenirs available. **FYI:** Reservations accepted. Children's menu. Beer and wine only. **Open:** Sun–Thurs 7am–11pm, Fri–Sat 7am–12pm. **Prices:** Main courses $5–$7. AE, DC, DISC, MC, V.

Peoria

Seat of Peoria County, in northwest part of state. Discovered by Jolliet and Marquette in 1673, Peoria is the state's oldest settlement. Home to Bradley University, the University of Illinois-Peoria College of Medicine, and the world headquarters of Caterpillar. **Information:** Peoria Convention & Visitors Bureau, 403 NE Jefferson St, Peoria, 61603 (tel 309/676-0303).

HOTELS

Hotel Père Marquette

501 Main St, 61602 (Downtown); tel 309/637-6500 or toll free 800/447-1676; fax 309/637-5211. Exit 92 off I-74 E; exit 93A off I-74 W. One of Peoria's finest hotels with history and traditions dating to 1927. Elegant spacious lobby reminiscent of days gone by with crystal chandeliers, expansive murals of historic scenes, and oriental carpets. Long list of celebrities who have stayed here include President Gerald Ford and Liberace, who was the hotel's piano player for a time. Executive level rooms offer the best deal. Wheelchair lift in lobby for series of stairs. **Rooms:** 288 rms and stes. Executive level. CI 4pm/CO noon. Nonsmoking rms avail. **Amenities:** A/C, cable TV w/movies, voice mail. Some units w/whirlpools. Executive level rooms have hair dryers and dataports. **Services:** Babysitting. Executive level rooms include free full breakfast, two free cocktails, and newspaper delivered to room. **Facilities:** 2 restaurants (see "Restaurants" below), 2 bars (1 w/entertainment). **Rates:** $89 S; $99 D; $150–$500 ste. Extra person $15. Children under age 18 stay free. Parking: Indoor, free. Executive Level Frequent Stayer program has best rate at $75 per room. AE, DC, DISC, MC, V.

Mark Twain Hotel

225 Northeast Adams, 61602 (Downtown); tel 309/676-3600 or toll free 800/325-6351; fax 309/676-3159. Exit 93B off I-74 W; exit 93 off I-74 E. Nine-story building located near the riverfront. Nice, open, midsize lobby with small fireplace and lots of wood. **Rooms:** 110 rms and stes. Executive level. CI 3pm/CO 11am. Nonsmoking rms avail. **Amenities:** A/C, cable TV w/movies, dataport. Some units w/whirlpools. **Services:** Bellhop available 24 hours. Executive level offers services for corporate travelers. **Facilities:** 1 restaurant, 1 bar (w/entertainment), whirlpool. Health club currently consists of weight room and midsize whirlpool. **Rates (BB):** $72–$99 S or D; $185–$250 ste. Parking: Outdoor, free. AE, DC, DISC, MC, V.

MOTELS

Best Western Eastlight Inn

401 N Main St, East Peoria, 61611; tel 309/699-7231 or toll free 800/325-6088; fax 309/694-2382. Exit 95A off I-74. Located just a short drive across the river from downtown Peoria, it's a great place to stay if you're interested in gambling (a gambling riverboat is on the East Peoria side). Lots of amateur sports teams like it here. Also a great place for families. A second back building connects to the main building, but it's better to stay in the main one. Restaurant next to motel. **Rooms:** 199 rms and stes. CI 3pm/CO 11am. Nonsmoking rms avail. **Amenities:** A/C, cable TV w/movies. 1 unit w/whirlpool. Refrigerators available on request. **Services:** Free cocktails Sun–Thurs 5:30–7:30pm. Small pets only. **Facilities:** 2 bars (1 w/entertainment), games rm, sauna, whirlpool, washer/dryer. Business center only offers desk space and telephones. On-site pizza kitchen serves pizza, calzones, breadsticks, and drinks. **Rates (CP):** $51–$65 S; $59–$75 D; $185 ste. Parking: Outdoor, free. AE, DC, DISC, MC, V.

Comfort Suites

4021 War Memorial Dr, 61614 (North Peoria); tel 309/688-3800 or toll free 800/221-2222; fax 309/688-3800. Exit 89 off I-74. Rather generic motel. Tall ceiling with brick gas fireplace in small lobby; meeting room and breakfast room adjacent. **Rooms:** 66 rms. CI 2pm/CO 11am. Nonsmoking rms avail. **Amenities:** A/C, cable TV w/movies, refrig. All rooms have microwaves. **Services:** **Facilities:** Whirlpool. **Rates (CP):** $60 S; $65 D. Extra person $5. Children under age 18 stay free. Parking: Outdoor, free. AE, CB, DC, DISC, EC, ER, JCB, MC, V.

Holiday Inn Brandywine

4400 N Brandywine Dr, 61614 (North Peoria); tel 309/686-8000 or toll free 800/HOLIDAY; fax 309/682-8237. Exit 89 off I-74. Tucked away on the back of a frontage road just a short drive from a major shopping mall, this hotel caters to weddings, receptions, and large meetings. Lovely lobby opens to atrium area with landscaping. **Rooms:** 251 rms and stes. Executive level. CI 4pm/CO noon. Nonsmoking rms avail. **Amenities:** 🛏️👙📺 A/C, cable TV w/movies, refrig, dataport. **Services:** ✗🚗🖼️🍽️🛎️ Car-rental desk, babysitting. Concierge level includes business center, full breakfast, and free cocktails. **Facilities:** 🏋️⛳ 💻 ♿ 2 restaurants, 1 bar, games rm, sauna, whirlpool, washer/dryer. Very small whirlpool. **Rates:** $72 S; $82 D; $150–$250 ste. Extra person $10. Children under age 12 stay free. Parking: Outdoor, free. Ask for the "Great Rate" for best deal. AE, CB, DC, DISC, JCB, MC, V.

≡≡ Signature Inn Peoria
4112 N Brandywine Dr, 61614 (North Peoria); tel 309/685-2556 or toll free 800/822-5252; fax 309/685-2556. Exit 89 E off I-74. Very nice—perfect for business travelers year-round and families in summer. Exceptional lobby with lots of brass and winding staircase. **Rooms:** 124 rms and stes. CI 2pm/CO noon. Nonsmoking rms avail. **Amenities:** 🛏️👙A/C, cable TV w/movies, dataport. Some units w/whirlpools. **Services:** 🖼️🍽️ Seven local restaurants offer a variety of complimentary food and drinks to guests with Signature Inn room key. Top-notch professional staff with above average commitment to service. **Facilities:** 🏋️🚴⛳ 💻 ♿ Small, full-service business center with open but private interview areas, desk space, typewriters, adding machines, and phones. Complimentary passes to fitness center ¼-mile away. **Rates (CP):** Peak (Apr–Oct) $53–$63 S or D; $105 ste. Extra person $7. Children under age 17 stay free. Min stay special events. Lower rates off-season. Parking: Outdoor, free. AE, CB, DC, DISC, MC, V.

LODGE
≡≡≡ Jumer's Castle Lodge
117 N Western Ave, 61604 (West Peoria); tel 309/673-8040 or toll free 800/285-8637; fax 309/673-9782. At Moss Ave. Well-run, service-oriented, family-owned establishment. The first of a series of elaborate European-style hotels and lodges built in Illinois and Iowa. Enter grounds through grand wrought-iron and stone archway; facility is imposing and castlelike. Lobby filled with ornate antique furnishings, huge brick working fireplace, and massive chandelier. **Rooms:** 175 rms and stes. Executive level. CI 4pm/CO noon. Nonsmoking rms avail. **Amenities:** 🛏️👙 A/C, cable TV w/movies, voice mail. Some units w/fireplaces. Whirlpool suites available. Loft rooms have working fireplace and circular staircase leading to upstairs bed. **Services:** ✗VP🚗🖼️🍽️ Babysitting. Small box of Fannie Mae candy provided in each room on arrival. Limousine service to anywhere in city can be arranged. Charming staff is very service oriented and in costume. **Facilities:** 🏋️⛳ ♿ 1 restaurant (*see* "Restaurants" below), 2 bars (w/entertainment), games rm, sauna, whirlpool. Two sun decks. **Rates:** $76–$85 S; $84–$89 D; $78–$135 ste. Extra person $9. Children under age 18 stay free. Min stay special events. Parking: Outdoor, free. AE, DC, DISC, MC, V.

RESTAURANTS 🍽️
Carnegie's Restaurant
In Hotel Père Marquette, 501 Main St (Downtown); tel 309/637-6500. **Eclectic.** Elegant fine dining with superior service. Decorated in gray velvets with touches of burgundy, the dining room allows plenty of privacy for each table. The servers meet with Carnegie's German master chef daily for a staff tasting of the evening's specialities, so you can ask for recommendations with confidence. Seafood ranges from oven-roasted salmon covered in thinly sliced potatoes and a creamy Boursin sauce to walleye macadamia in mango-basil sauce. Also available are rack of lamb Provençale and tenderloin of beef with stuffed shrimp in béarnaise sauce. The daily prix-fixe five-course meal is the best value. **FYI:** Reservations recommended. Dress code. **Open:** Mon–Sat 6–10pm. **Prices:** Main courses $15–$25; prix fixe $25. AE, DC, DISC, MC, V. ♿

The Grill 456 Fulton
In Twin Towers Mall, 456 Fulton St (Downtown); tel 309/674-6870. At Madison St. **Californian.** Lots of brass, oak, and glass accent the dining room of this upscale eatery in downtown Peoria. Menu highlights include sea bass roasted in a horseradish crust and salmon baked in paper with herbs and white-wine broth. Pasta, steaks, chops, chicken, and salads also available. **FYI:** Reservations recommended. Jazz/piano. Dress code. **Open:** Mon–Thurs 11am–11pm, Fri 11am–midnight, Sat 5pm–midnight, Sun 5–9pm. **Prices:** Main courses $13–$18. AE, DC, DISC, MC, V. ♿

Jumer's Restaurant
In Jumer's Castle Lodge, 117 N Western Ave (West Peoria); tel 309/673-8181. At Moss Ave. **American/German.** Both decor and cuisine—heavy, dark, and very German—are evidence of owner James Jumer's family roots in the castles of Upper Bavaria. A stuffed black bear offers a stoic greeting to Jumer's guests. Peach-colored fabric lamps hang above each table in the dining room, which is filled with ornately carved antiques and floral-print fabric. Upstairs is the Balcon Lounge, whose high-backed chairs, silver candleholders, and old-world paintings make it the best seating choice for lunch or dinner. The menu focuses on hearty favorites such as fillet of cod, braised calf's liver and onions, fried chicken, and three varieties of schnitzel. **FYI:** Reservations recommended. Children's menu. Dress code. **Open:** Breakfast Mon–Fri 6:30–11am, Sat–Sun 7–11am; lunch Mon–Sat 11:30am–4pm; dinner Mon–Fri 4:30–10pm, Sat 5–11pm, Sun noon–10pm. **Prices:** Main courses $9–$17. AE, CB, DC, DISC, MC, V. ■💟♿

Katie Hooper Pub and Pasta Cafe
1 Main St; tel 309/673-2628. On the Illinois River at the Landing. **International.** Located in a 1950s riverboat, now permanently docked on the Illinois River. Most tables have a view of the river, and the funky decor includes tables made from bowling-alley lanes. The innovative cuisine features

homemade pasta: Black pepper fettuccine is prepared with spinach, tomatoes, mushrooms, broccoli, and Alfredo sauce; red-pepper linguine is served with large shrimp in a slightly spicy tomato sauce. Wide range of sandwiches, salads, appetizers, kabobs, and tenders; daily selection of cheesecakes. Over 50 imported beers and microbrews. **FYI:** Reservations not accepted. Blues/jazz/reggae/rock. **Open:** Tues–Sun 11am–10:30pm. **Prices:** Main courses $6–$14. MC, V. 🏞

★ **River Station**
212 Constitution Ave; tel 309/676-7100. At the foot of Liberty St on river front. **New American.** Once a warehouse and depot for the Rock Island Railroad, this interesting building now houses three separate dining areas and a fabulous bar with old train photos, massive chandeliers, and floor-to-ceiling windows. Lots of natural light and live plants make for a very warm and welcoming atmosphere. The kitchen is known for its prime rib; crab-stuffed mushrooms and cold meat-loaf sandwich are just right for lighter appetites. Great service. **FYI:** Reservations recommended. Children's menu. **Open:** Lunch Mon–Sat 11am–2pm; dinner Mon–Fri 5–10pm, Sat 4:30–11pm, Sun 4–9pm; brunch Sun 10am–2pm. **Prices:** Main courses $12–$19. AE, CB, DC, MC, V. &

Stephanie
1825 N Knoxville Ave (East Bluff); tel 309/682-7300. Exit 92A off I-74. **New American.** One of Peoria's best-kept secrets. Awards from *Wine Spectator* magazine line the walls of the entryway. Chef Pawula aims to prepare his dishes in a healthy way, using flavored olive oils and never deep frying. Menu changes daily but always has a distinctly Mediterranean flavor. Entrees range from grilled squab with fresh berries to braised young rabbit with fresh chanterelle mushrooms. Appetizers include a range of gourmet pizzas. Prix-fixe degustation menu is $45 with wine or $30 without. Wine Tasting Sundays are held once or twice a month. **FYI:** Reservations recommended. **Open:** Lunch Mon–Fri 11am–2pm, Sat 11am–1:30pm; dinner Mon–Fri 5:30–9pm, Sat 5:30–9:30pm, Sun 4–9pm. **Prices:** Main courses $10–$20; prix fixe $30–$45. AE, CB, DC, DISC, MC, V. &

ATTRACTIONS 🏛

Glen Oak Park
McClure and Prospect Aves; tel 309/686-3364. A variety of large cats, monkeys, reptiles, and fish call this 100-acre zoo their home. Conservatory, botanical garden, tennis courts, fishing lagoon, and picnic areas also available. **Open:** Daily 10am–5pm. $

Lakeview Museum of Arts and Sciences
1125 W Lake; tel 309/686-7000. Wide range of exhibits ranging from archeology to folk art to wildlife. Highlights include a decorative arts gallery, a children's discovery center, a planetarium, a natural science area, and a sculpture garden. **Open:** Tues–Sat 10am–5pm, Sun noon–5pm. $

Peoria Historical Society
942 NE Glen Oak Ave; tel 309/674-1921. The Society maintains two historic homes: the **Flanagan House** (942 NE Glen Oak Ave) and the **Petengill-Morton House** (1212 W Moss Ave). Both of these 19th-century homes are beautifully renovated and are filled with period furnishings. Bus tours of Peoria leave from the Society's main office. **Open:** Sun 2–4:30pm. $

Illinois River National Wildlife and Fish Refuges
19031 E Cty Rd 2110N, Havana; tel 309/535-2290. 38 mi S of Peoria. Located on the grounds is the 4,488 acre Chautauqua National Wildlife Refuge, a resting, breeding, and feeding area for waterfowl. Concentrations of shorebirds can be seen August through September, while bald eagles can be spotted from November through February. Nature trail with three overlooks and telescope provides view of birds on Lake Chautauqua. **Open:** Daily sunrise–sunset. **Free**

Pére Marquette State Park

This 7,895-acre preservation area overlooks the Illinois River and is located five miles from Grafton on IL 100. Among the wide range of year-round recreational opportunities are horseback riding on 12 miles of horse trails, camping, fishing and boating on the Illinois River, and hiking on 15 miles of marked trails.

The centerpiece of the park is the massive lodge and adjacent guest houses, recently restored by the Illinois Department of Conservation. Originally built by the Civilian Conservation Corps in the 1930s, the lodge has a distinctive flavor of native stone and rustic timbers. For more information contact Pére Marquette State Park, Rte 100, PO Box 158, Grafton, IL 62037 (tel 618/786-3323).

Peru

The name of nearby Starved Rock comes from an old Native American legend that a band of Illiniwek, isolated by their enemies, starved to death on a rock above the Illinois River.

MOTELS 🏨

🏨🏨 **Days Inn**
191 N 30th Rd, La Salle, 61301; tel 815/224-1060 or toll free 800/DAYS-INN; fax 815/224-1605. Exit 75 off I-80. Appealing decor with vibrant colors and attention to details. **Rooms:** 106 rms. CI 2pm/CO noon. Nonsmoking rms avail. Single rooms are same size as doubles, but with only one bed, which gives you quite a lot of space. Some king-size beds available. **Amenities:** 📺 A/C, satel TV w/movies. **Services:** 🛎 🐾 **Facilities:** 🗂 250 & 1 bar, games rm, washer/dryer. **Rates:** $46–$56 S; $56–$72 D. Extra person $6. Children

under age 17 stay free. Parking: Outdoor, free. Days Inn cards accepted for special rates. AARP rates avail. AE, DC, DISC, MC, V.

≣≣≣ Howard Johnson Lodge

I-80 and IL 251, La Salle, 61301; tel 815/224-2500 or toll free 800/I-GO-HOJO; fax 815/224-3693. Expansive parking lot surrounds a well-tended exterior. Undergoing cosmetic upgrades, including new carpeting and some new furniture. Pool privileges provided at the Days Inn across the street. **Rooms:** 104 rms. Executive level. CI open/CO noon. Nonsmoking rms avail. Some rooms are very large. The top floor has accessible balconies and high, sloping ceilings. King-size beds available in some rooms. Bathrooms are somewhat worn. **Amenities:** 📺 A/C, satel TV w/movies. Some units w/terraces. **Services:** 🚐 🗄 🛏 🍽 Children's program. Executive service provides newspapers daily. KIDS GO HOJO, a program that offers games and toys for children, is provided in the summer. The motel staff is very friendly and knowledgeable about the area. Although it's not part of Howard Johnson's services, there's a rental car concession located in the parking lot. **Facilities:** 🛗 📷💯 🦽 1 restaurant (lunch and dinner only), games rm. Shaky's Pizza parlor on the motel premises. **Rates:** $40–$48 S; $45–$52 D. Extra person $8. Children under age 18 stay free. Parking: Outdoor, free. AARP rates avail. AE, CB, DC, DISC, MC, V.

≣≣ Super 8 Motel

1851 May Rd, 61354; tel 815/223-1848 or toll free 800/800-8000; fax 815/223-1848 ext 405. Exit 75 off I-80. Very clean, typical chain motel. Close to I-80 and conveniences, such as restaurants, service stations, and sundries. **Rooms:** 62 rms and stes. CI 2pm/CO 11am. Nonsmoking rms avail. Two rooms are quite spacious doubles with pull-out couches; they can also be used as meeting/conference rooms. **Amenities:** 📺 A/C, satel TV w/movies. **Services:** 🛏 🍽 Microwave in lobby available for guests' use. Staff is very friendly and attentive. **Facilities:** 📷12 🦽 **Rates:** $32–$34 S; $47–$49 D; $50–$55 ste; $57–$68 cottage/villa. Extra person $varies. Children under age 12 stay free. Parking: Outdoor, free. AARP rates avail. AE, DC, DISC, MC, V.

Petersburg

Seat of Menard County, in central Illinois. Most of the residents of nearby New Salem moved to Petersburg after Abraham Lincoln surveyed it in 1836. A state historic site reconstructs the village as it would have looked in the 1830s, when Lincoln lived here. **Information:** Petersburg Chamber of Commerce, 125 S 7th, PO Box 452, Petersburg, 62675 (tel 217/632-7363).

ATTRACTION 🏛

Lincoln's New Salem State Historic Site

RR 1; tel 217/632-4000. A restored 1830s village which was the home of Abraham Lincoln from 1831 to 1837. Located on the 650 acre site are 12 timber houses, stores, the Rutledge Tavern, a saw and grist mill, a school house, and the Onstat cooper shop (the only original building at the site). The visitors center houses an auditorium and museum and numerous pieces of Lincoln memorabilia. Seasonal highlights include living history demonstrations, outdoor dramas, and cruises aboard the *Talisman* riverboat. **Open:** Peak (Mar–Oct) daily 9am–5pm. Reduced hours off-season. **Free**

Rockford

Seat of Winnebago County, in northern Illinois. The state's second-largest city, Rockford's residents are mostly of Swedish and Italian descent. The city, founded in 1834, was originally called Midway because of its location midway between Chicago and Galena. **Information:** Northern Illinois Tourism Council, 117 S 3rd St, #A, Rockford, 61104 (tel 815/963-8111 or toll free 800/521-0849).

MOTELS 🏨

≣≣≣ Courtyard by Marriott

7676 E State St, 61108; tel 815/397-6222 or toll free 800/321-2211; fax 815/397-6254. Exit I-90 at US 20 W. Terraced courtyard with gazebo, table, and chairs. The Rockford–Peoria Bus Line goes from here to Chicago's O'Hare Airport. **Rooms:** 147 rms and stes. CI 3pm/CO noon. Nonsmoking rms avail. Separate seating area in all rooms. Pleasantly furnished. **Amenities:** 📺 🛁 📱 A/C, satel TV w/movies, dataport, voice mail. Some units w/terraces. Suites have refrigerators. **Services:** ✕ 🗄 🛏 Babysitting. Dry cleaning, laundry only on weekdays. **Facilities:** 🛗 🏊 🍽 📷50 🦽 1 restaurant (bkfst only), 1 bar, whirlpool, washer/dryer. **Rates:** Peak (May–Sept) $87 S or D; $110 ste. Extra person $10. Children under age 12 stay free. Lower rates off-season. Parking: Outdoor, free. Lower rates on weekends. Special AARP and senior citizen rates on availability. AE, CB, DC, DISC, MC, V.

≣ Exel Inn

220 S Lyford Rd, 61108; tel 815/332-4915 or toll free 800/356-8013; fax 815/332-4915. Exit US 20 off I-90. No frills, but comfortable stay. Numerous restaurants nearby and convenient to Magic Waters, Cherry Vale Mall, Downtown Rockford, and the Greater Rockford Airport. **Rooms:** 101 rms, stes, and effic. CI 3pm/CO noon. Nonsmoking rms avail. **Amenities:** 📺 🛁 A/C, satel TV w/movies. **Services:** 🛏 🍽 **Facilities:** 🏊 🦽 Washer/dryer. **Rates (CP):** Peak (May–Sept) $40 S; $45 D; $95–$125 ste; $53 effic. Extra person $5. Children under age 18 stay free. Lower rates off-season.

Parking: Outdoor, free. Seniors receive a 10% discount, and with an Insider's card the 13th night is free. AE, CB, DC, DISC, MC, V.

▤▤ Fairfield Inn

7712 Potawatomi Trail, 61107; tel 815/397-8000 or toll free 800/228-2800; fax 815/397-8000. Exit US 20 off I-90. Friendly atmosphere. Often motorcoaches, soccer teams stop here. Weather report every day at the front desk. They remodel every five years. Fairfield Inns have been voted #1 for value by *Business Travel News*. **Rooms:** 135 rms. CI 2pm/CO noon. Nonsmoking rms avail. **Amenities:** 🚪 🅿 A/C, satel TV w/movies. Some units w/terraces. **Services:** 🖨 🛎 Free local calls. Fax service available. Food delivery service to room from Pizza Hut, Luigi's, and Aunt Mary's. **Facilities:** 🔁 👤 🔟 🛗 **Rates (CP):** Peak (Mar–Oct) $70 S or D. Extra person $10. Children under age 18 stay free. Lower rates off-season. Parking: Outdoor, free. Seniors receive 10% discount. AE, DC, DISC, MC, V.

▤▤ Hampton Inn

615 Clark Dr, 61107; tel 815/229-0404 or toll free 800/426-7866; fax 815/229-0175. Exit to US 20 off I-90. This well-managed motel has received a Hampton Certificate of Excellence for product and service. Numerous restaurants nearby in this cluster of hotels. Close to Magic Waters theme park, Clock Tower Museum, downtown, Sportscore Fields, 18-hole Elliot Golf Course, Belford Drive-In, Sinnissippi Gardens, Rock Cut State Park, and Cherryvale Mall. **Rooms:** 122 rms. CI 2pm/CO noon. Nonsmoking rms avail. **Amenities:** 🚪 🅿 A/C, cable TV w/movies. All rooms have ironing boards and irons. **Services:** 🖨 🛎 Car-rental desk. **Facilities:** 🔁 🔟 🛗 Whirlpool. **Rates (CP):** $59 S; $65 D. Extra person $5. Children under age 18 stay free. Parking: Outdoor, free. AE, CB, DC, DISC, MC, V.

▤▤ Red Roof Inn

7434 State St, 61108; tel 815/398-9750 or toll free 800/843-7663; fax 815/398-9761. Exit US 20 at I-90. Good-looking exterior with some stone. 10 miles east of downtown. Many restaurants nearby. Near the Time Museum, Magic Waters, Cherryvale Mall, and Rockford College. **Rooms:** 108 rms. CI noon/CO noon. Nonsmoking rms avail. **Amenities:** 🚪 A/C, cable TV w/movies. **Services:** 🛎 🖨 **Facilities:** 🛗 **Rates:** Peak (Apr–Oct) $40 S; $62 D. Extra person $2. Children under age 18 stay free. Lower rates off-season. Parking: Outdoor, free. AE, DC, DISC, MC, V.

▤▤▤ Sweden House Lodge

4605 E State St, 61108; tel 815/398-4130 or toll free 800/886-4138; fax 815/398-9203. Off I-90 and US 20. A touch of Sweden in a characterful chalet. Chicago O'Hare Airport bus stop—15 round-trips every day. **Rooms:** 105 rms and stes. CI 2pm/CO noon. Nonsmoking rms avail. Swedish blue carpets and linens in very clean rooms. Small baths with dressing rooms. **Amenities:** 🚪 🅿 A/C, cable TV. **Services:** ✕ 🚗 🖨 🛎 Car-rental desk. **Facilities:** 🔁 👤 🛗 🖥 Games rm,

whirlpool, washer/dryer. **Rates:** Peak (May 25–Sept 5) $37–$51 S; $43–$55 D; $56–$71 ste. Extra person $2. Children under age 17 stay free. Lower rates off-season. Parking: Outdoor, free. AE, CB, DC, DISC, MC, V.

RESORT

▤▤▤ Best Western Clock Tower Resort

7801 E State St, PO Box 5285, 61125; tel 815/398-6000 or toll free 800/358-7666; fax 815/398-0443. At Jct I-90 and US 20. 23 acres. Year-round recreation center identified by an imposing clock tower. Beautiful museum clocks decorate the public spaces of the resort. **Rooms:** 252 rms and stes. CI 4pm/CO noon. Nonsmoking rms avail. **Amenities:** 🚪 🅿 📺 🎙 A/C, satel TV w/movies, VCR, voice mail. Some units w/minibars, all w/terraces, some w/fireplaces, some w/whirlpools. Some rooms have safes. **Services:** ✕ 🛏 🚗 🖨 🛎 Car-rental desk, social director, masseur, children's program, babysitting. **Facilities:** 🔁 🖼 👤 🏊 🕹 📹 🎾 🏓 🖥 🛗 2 restaurants (*see* "Restaurants" below), 2 bars (1 w/entertainment), basketball, volleyball, games rm, racquetball, sauna, whirlpool, beauty salon, playground, washer/dryer. Time Museum (*see* "Attractions" below), shopping arcade, restaurants, and live dinner theater are all a part of this busy resort. Also picnic tables. **Rates:** Peak (May–Sept) $89–$120 S; $99–$130 D; $125–$350 ste. Extra person $10. Children under age 17 stay free. Min stay wknds. Lower rates off-season. Parking: Outdoor, free. AE, CB, DC, DISC, MC, V.

RESTAURANTS 🍴

★ Bellamy's

In Best Western Clock Tower Resort, 7801 E State St; tel 815/398-6000. At Jct I-90 and US 20. **American.** Voted the best of Rockford by a local magazine. A large antique clock from the adjacent Time Museum decorates one of the three small dining rooms. Artistically painted walls, cherry wood, and soft classical music set an ambience for fine dining. The varied menu features black angus beef, seafood, and vegetarian selections. Award winning menu and wine list. Sunday champagne brunch. No checks. **FYI:** Reservations recommended. Children's menu. Jacket required. No smoking. **Open:** Lunch Mon–Fri 11am–2pm; dinner Mon–Sat 6–10pm; brunch Sun 10am–2pm. **Prices:** Main courses $22–$42. AE, CB, DC, DISC, MC, V. ❤ 📼 🛗

Giovanni's Restaurant

610 N Bell School Rd; tel 815/398-6411. W of Jct I-90 and US 20. **Continental/Italian.** Understated elegance, with contemporary prints brightening dark wooden walls. Try sautéed lobster and shrimp cakes for starters and follow up with roasted rack of lamb Italiana. Noted for homemade desserts and pasta. Takeout available. Appetizers served at a cozy, wood-paneled bar decorated with large posters. **FYI:** Reservations recommended. Blues/folk/jazz. Children's menu.

Open: Lunch Mon–Fri 11:30am–2pm; dinner Mon–Sat 5:30–10pm. **Prices:** Main courses $13–$23. AE, DISC, MC, V. 🌑 ♿

Michael's at Perryville
601 N Perryville Rd; tel 815/226-8286. N off US 20. **American.** A large, lively, noisy, barn-like restaurant with adjacent banquet facilities. Specialties are steak and prime rib. On Friday cod is offered, fried or boiled; on Sunday prime rib is the special. Attractive wine and appetizer bar. Reservations recommended on weekends. **FYI:** Reservations recommended. Children's menu. **Open:** Lunch Mon–Fri 11:30am–2pm; dinner Mon–Sun 5–10pm. **Prices:** Main courses $12–$20. AE, DC, DISC, MC, V. 🖼 ♿

ATTRACTIONS 🖼

Midway Village and Museum Center
6799 Guilford Rd; tel 815/397-9112. Turn-of-the-century village complete with stagecoaches, law office, blacksmith shop, stone school, town hall, and sheriff's office. Onsite museum features aviation exhibits. **Open:** Mon–Fri 10am–4pm, Sat–Sun noon–4pm. **$$**

Tinker Swiss Cottage Museum
411 Kent St; tel 815/964-2424. Swiss chalet–style house built in 1865 by Robert Tinker. The offbeat decor includes such items as a 300-year-old painting, diamond-dust mirrors, and Lincoln memorabilia. **Open:** Wed–Sun 2–4pm. **$**

Discovery Center Museum
711 N Main St; tel 815/963-6769. Created especially for children, the museum features a two-story maze, and hands-on exhibits about the human body, electricity and magnets, and color and light. Special exploration area designed for children five and under. **Open:** Tues–Sat 11am–5pm, Sun noon–5pm. **$**

The Time Museum
In Best Western Clock Tower Resort, Jct I-90/IL 20; tel 815/398-6000. Collection of time keeping devices from ancient sundials to an atomic clock. Exhibits are divided into three categories: technical history, international clocks and watches, and American development of clocks and watches from the 18th century to present time. **Open:** Tues–Sun 10am–5pm. **$**

Rock Island

Part of the Quad Cities metropolitan area. A center of trade, transportation, and industry. Home to a large US government arsenal and Augustana College. **Information:** Quad City Convention & Visitors Bureau, 2020 3rd Ave, Moline, 61265 (tel 309/788-7800)

ATTRACTION 🖼

Rock Island Arsenal Museum
Rock Island Arsenal, Bldg 60; tel 309/782-5021. Arsenal Island has been in use since 1816, when Fort Armstrong was built here during the Black Hawk War. The arsenal is still an active US Army factory and has been since 1862. Inside the museum (established in 1905) are exhibits that depict the people involved in the Island's history, the manufacturing process, and the equipment that is produced here. In addition there is an extensive collection of more than 1,000 weapons and firearms.

Also on the island are the **Col Davenport House** (circa 1834), a **Confederate Cemetery,** and the **Rock Island Arsenal National Cemetery**. **Open:** Daily 10am–4pm. **Free**

Rosemont

See Chicago O'Hare Int'l Airport

St Charles

Statues of foxes guard the bridge across the Fox River in this verdant city. The Fox River Festival takes place here in mid-June, and the second full weekend of October sees a Scarecrow Festival. **Information:** St Charles Convention & Visitors Bureau, 311 N 2nd St, PO Box 11, St Charles, 60174 (tel 630/377-6161).

MOTEL 🏨

📧📧 Best Western Inn of St Charles
1635 E Main St, 60174; tel 630/584-4550 or toll free 800/528-1234; fax 630/584-5221. On IL 64, ½ block E of Tyler Rd. Colonial exterior. Good for families—near several family-style restaurants, shopping, one mile from Fox River. **Rooms:** 53 rms and stes. CI 2pm/CO noon. No smoking. Larger rooms in separate building connected by canopied walkway to main building. **Amenities:** 🗄 & 🍴 A/C, cable TV. **Services:** 🔌 **Facilities:** 🛗 📦 ♿ Whirlpool, washer/dryer. **Rates (CP):** $45–$65 S; $55–$70 D; $85–$95 ste. Extra person $5. Children under age 16 stay free. Parking: Outdoor, free. AE, DISC, MC, V.

Schaumburg

This burgeoning northwest suburb of Chicago is best known as the site of Woodfield Mall, one of the largest shopping malls in the Midwest. **Information:** Greater Woodfield Convention & Visitors Bureau, 1375 E Woodfield Rd, #100, Schaumburg, 60173-5424 (tel 847/605-1010).

HOTELS 🏨

☰☰☰ Embassy Suites Schaumburg/Woodfield

1939 N Meacham Rd, 60173; tel 847/397-1313 or toll free 800/EMBASSY; fax 847/397-9007. I-90 to IL 53 N to Algonquin Rd exit, W 1 mi. Atrium lobby with fountain, tables, and chairs; corridors open to atrium. **Rooms:** 209 stes. CI 3pm/CO noon. Nonsmoking rms avail. Two-room suites. Shower/tubs have glass sliding doors. **Amenities:** 🔋 ⓐ 📞 A/C, cable TV w/movies, refrig, dataport, voice mail. TV and phone in each room of suite. Dishes furnished on request for mini-kitchen. **Services:** ✕ 🚐 🖼 ↩ Car-rental desk. Complimentary full breakfast and afternoon cocktails served in atrium. **Facilities:** 🛗 📞 📦750 ⅙ 1 restaurant (lunch and dinner only), 1 bar, sauna, steam rm, whirlpool, washer/dryer. **Rates (BB):** $109–$160 ste. Extra person $10. Children under age 18 stay free. Parking: Outdoor, free. AE, CB, DC, DISC, JCB, MC, V.

☰☰ Hampton Inn Schaumburg

1300 E Higgins Rd, 60173; tel 847/619-1000 or toll free 800/HAMPTON; fax 847/619-1019. Exit Higgins Rd W off I-290. Lobby, though small, is friendly meeting place with TV, tables, chairs, and comfortable seating. **Rooms:** 130 rms. CI 2pm/CO noon. Nonsmoking rms avail. **Amenities:** 🔋 ⓐ A/C, cable TV w/movies. Some rooms have dataports. **Services:** ✕ 🚐 🖼 ↩ Babysitting. Free coffee in lobby. **Facilities:** 📞 📦25 ⅙ **Rates (CP):** $72–$75 S; $74–$77 D. Extra person $3. Children under age 18 stay free. Parking: Outdoor, free. Special rates for special area events. AE, CB, DC, DISC, JCB, MC, V.

☰☰☰ Holiday Inn Schaumburg/Hoffman Estates

1550 N Roselle Rd, 60195; tel 847/310-0500 or toll free 800/HOLIDAY; fax 847/310-0579. Roselle Rd S exit off I-90 E; IL 53 N exit off I-90 W to IL 62 W to Roselle Rd S. Off-street location, just down road from Medieval Times Dinner Tournament. Near restaurant and convenience store. **Rooms:** 142 rms. Executive level. CI 2pm/CO noon. Nonsmoking rms avail. **Amenities:** 🔋 ⓐ A/C, cable TV. Some units w/whirlpools. Heartbeat Suites feature heart-shaped whirlpool. **Services:** ✕ 🚐 🖼 ↩ Car-rental desk. VCR available on request. **Facilities:** 🛗 📦50 ⅙ 1 restaurant, 1 bar (w/entertainment). **Rates:** $69–$185 S or D. Extra person $10. Children under age 17 stay free. Parking: Outdoor, free. AE, DC, DISC, JCB, MC, V.

☰☰☰ Homewood Suites Schaumburg

815 E American Lane, 60173; tel 847/605-0400 or toll free 800/CALL-HOME; fax 847/619-0990. Complex consists of four buildings surrounding gardenlike area and pool: lodge, two buildings with private entrances to suites, and one building with hallway entrances to suites. Ideal for traveler or business person on extended stay. **Rooms:** 108 stes and effic. CI 3pm/CO noon. Nonsmoking rms avail. **Amenities:** 🔋 ⓐ 📞 📱 A/C, satel TV w/movies, refrig, dataport, VCR, voice mail. Some units w/fireplaces. **Services:** ✕ 🖼 ↩ 🍽 Car-rental

desk, babysitting. Complimentary social hour/reception in lodge Mon–Thurs 5–7pm. Complimentary grocery shopping at nearby markets (grocery list in kitchen of suite). **Facilities:** 🛗 🏊 📞 📦40 🖥 ⅙ Basketball, whirlpool, washer/dryer. Convenience store in lodge. **Rates (CP):** $75–$124 ste; $75–$124 effic. Children under age 18 stay free. Parking: Outdoor, free. Weekend rates and special rates for extended stays avail. AE, CB, DC, DISC, MC, V.

☰☰☰ Hyatt Regency Woodfield

1800 E Golf Rd, 60173; tel 847/605-1234 or toll free 800/233-1234; fax 847/605-0328. N of Woodfield Mall. Guests receive special rates at local golf course. **Rooms:** 469 rms and stes. Executive level. CI 3pm/CO noon. Nonsmoking rms avail. Lovely furnishings and paintings. Some rooms have view of lobby. **Amenities:** 🔋 ⓐ 📞 A/C, cable TV w/movies, dataport, voice mail. Some units w/terraces. Ironing board and iron in each room. **Services:** ✕ 📠 🆅🅿 🚐 🖼 ↩ Car-rental desk. VCR available on request. **Facilities:** 🛗 📞 📦1000 🖥 ⅙ 1 restaurant, 1 bar, spa, sauna, steam rm, whirlpool, washer/dryer. Barber shop. **Rates:** $79–$143 S; $79–$168 D; $250–$550 ste. Extra person $25. Children under age 18 stay free. Min stay special events. Parking: Outdoor, free. AE, CB, DC, DISC, JCB, MC, V.

☰☰☰ Radisson Hotel Schaumburg

1725 E Algonquin Rd, 60173; tel 847/397-1500 or toll free 800/333-3333; fax 847/397-0665. Hotel set back from road with green space between it and nearby office buildings. Tennis courts available next door. **Rooms:** 200 rms. CI 3pm/CO noon. Nonsmoking rms avail. **Amenities:** 🔋 ⓐ 📱 A/C, cable TV w/movies. All units w/terraces, some w/whirlpools. **Services:** ✕ 🚐 🖼 ↩ Car-rental desk, babysitting. Nintendo available in each room. Free transportation to Woodfield Mall and Arlington International Racecourse. **Facilities:** 🛗 🏊 📞 📦300 🖥 ⅙ 1 restaurant, 1 bar (w/entertainment), whirlpool, washer/dryer. **Rates (BB):** $59–$109 S; $69–$119 D. Extra person $10. Children under age 18 stay free. Parking: Outdoor, free. AE, CB, DC, DISC, JCB, MC, V.

☰☰☰ Summerfield Suites Hotel

901 E Woodfield Office Court, 60173; tel 847/619-6677 or toll free 800/833-4353; fax 847/619-9184. I-90 to IL 53; S on IL 53 to Higgins Rd; W on Higgins to Plum Grove Rd; N to hotel. Excellent choice for families as well as corporate travelers. One- and two-bedroom suites located in six separate buildings, plus Guesthouse. Buildings surround pool and sport court area. Guesthouse also has lobby, meeting rooms, etc. **Rooms:** 112 stes. CI 3pm/CO noon. Nonsmoking rms avail. **Amenities:** 🔋 ⓐ 📱 A/C, cable TV w/movies, refrig, dataport, VCR, voice mail. Some units w/fireplaces. Each suite has fully equipped kitchen, ironing board, and iron. **Services:** 🚐 🖼 ↩ 🍽 Car-rental desk. Self-service guest laundry, including laundry soap, and 24-hour convenience store in Guesthouse. Fax and copy machines available in Guesthouse. Complimentary social hour (Mon–Thurs) in Guesthouse. Grocery shopping service available. **Facilities:**

Basketball, volleyball, whirlpool, washer/dryer. **Rates (CP):** Peak (May–Oct) $149–$189 ste. Children under age 21 stay free. Lower rates off-season. Parking: Outdoor, free. AE, DC, DISC, JCB, MC, V.

Wyndham Garden Hotel Schaumburg
800 National Pkwy, 60173; tel 847/605-9222 or toll free 800/WYNDHAM; fax 847/605-9240. Higgins Rd/IL 72 W from I-290/IL 53 to National Pkwy. O'Hare International Airport 15 miles away. Walking distance to Woodfield Mall. **Rooms:** 188 rms. CI 4pm/CO noon. Nonsmoking rms avail. **Amenities:** A/C, cable TV w/movies, dataport. **Services:** Twice-daily maid svce. Buffet breakfast served daily in Cafe, also lunch, and dinner. **Facilities:** 1 restaurant, 1 bar, sauna, whirlpool. **Rates (BB):** $160–$300 S. Extra person $20. Children under age 18 stay free. Parking: Outdoor, free. AE, CB, DC, DISC, JCB, MC, V.

RESTAURANTS

♥ Gaddi's Restaurant
In Marriott Schaumburg, 50 N Martingale Rd; tel 847/240-0100. **American.** The decor at this award-winning eatery—beautiful Japanese figurines, oil paintings, and subdued lighting—makes a great setting for a special meal. The chef takes advantage of the freshest ingredients available each week; wild game is often among them. **FYI:** Reservations recommended. **Open:** Mon–Sat 5:30–9:30pm. **Prices:** Main courses $21–$25. AE, CB, DC, DISC, ER, MC, V.

Garfields Cafe
In Woodfield Mall, 1700 E Woodfield Rd; tel 847/517-1700. **American.** Casual dining in the Woodfield Mall area. Fresh fish, burgers, salads. Takeout available. **FYI:** Reservations accepted. Children's menu. **Open:** Mon–Thurs 11am–10pm, Fri–Sat 11am–11pm, Sun 10am–9pm. **Prices:** Main courses $9–$13. AE, CB, DC, DISC, MC, V.

Skokie

This northern suburb of Chicago has long been an agricultural center, although it is now diversifying into high-tech industries. The town's main street (now known as Lincoln Avenue) grew from trails carved by farm wagons on their way to market. **Information:** Skokie Chamber of Commerce, 8322 N Lincoln Ave, PO Box 53, Skokie, 60077-0053 (tel 847/673-0240).

MOTELS

Holiday Inn
5300 W Touhy Ave, 60077; tel 847/679-8900 or toll free 800/HOLIDAY; fax 847/679-7447. Off I-94. Clean appearance. Lobby and many guest rooms located around large indoor sports area; the cheerful, games-oriented ambience may not appeal to everyone—quieter seating areas in the lobby are available. Located at a busy intersection, fronted by a parking lot. **Rooms:** 224 rms. Executive level. CI 3pm/CO noon. Nonsmoking rms avail. **Amenities:** A/C, cable TV w/movies, refrig. Some units w/minibars. Hair dryers available on request. **Services:** Facilities: 1 restaurant, 1 bar, games rm, sauna, whirlpool, washer/dryer. Shuffleboard, badminton courts, Ping-Pong table, pool table. **Rates:** $98–$125 S; $115–$137 D. Extra person $12. Children under age 19 stay free. Parking: Outdoor, free. Discounts for senior citizens and government and airline employees. AE, CB, DC, DISC, JCB, MC, V.

Howard Johnson Hotel
9333 Skokie Blvd, 60077; tel 847/679-4200 or toll free 800/654-2000 in IL; fax 847/679-4218. 1 mi S of Old Orchard Shopping Ctr. Located in a busy commercial area and fronted by a parking lot. Entire facility is spotless. Sports facility across the street. **Rooms:** 133 rms and stes. Executive level. CI 3pm/CO 1pm. Nonsmoking rms avail. Attractively and tastefully furnished. **Amenities:** A/C, satel TV w/movies, VCR. All units w/terraces, some w/whirlpools. **Services:** Car-rental desk, babysitting. Free transportation to airport, but no pick-up service. Staff is pleasant and very helpful. **Facilities:** 2 restaurants, 1 bar, sauna, whirlpool. The pool and deck areas are spacious and eye-catching. **Rates (BB):** $74–$104 S; $74–$114 D; $150–$200 ste. Children under age 18 stay free. Parking: Outdoor, free. Discounts for senior citizens. AE, CB, DC, DISC, MC, V.

RESTAURANT

★ Don's Fishmarket & Tavern
9335 Skokie Blvd; tel 847/677-3424. 1 mi S of Old Orchard Shopping Ctr. **Seafood.** Owned and operated by Howard Johnson's, this eatery is well known for seafood, although other standard dishes available. Favorites include little neck clams, whole Maine lobster, and soft-shelled crab. Nautical decor with solid, glossy hardwood tables. Before 6pm diners receive $2 discount. Don's Tavern, located in same building, serves traditional American and Mexican dishes and has sandwich menu; design is eclectic but tasteful, with comfortable and roomy booths and tables. **FYI:** Reservations accepted. **Open:** Mon–Sun 11:30am–10pm, Sun 4–10pm. **Prices:** Main courses $8–$23. AE, DC, DISC, MC, V.

Springfield

Seat of Sangamon County. The capital of Illinois, Springfield is also in the geographically center of the state. Of all the cities that claim Abraham Lincoln as their own, Springfield probably has the most justification for doing so. Lincoln lived here for nearly 25 years (until he took office as president) and his body was interred here after his assassination in 1865. **Information:** Springfield Convention & Visitors Bureau, 109 N 7th, Springfield, 62701 (tel 217/789-2360).

HOTELS

≣≣≣ Renaissance Springfield Hotel

701 E Adams, 62701 (Downtown); tel 217/544-8800 or toll free 800/HOTELS-1; fax 217/544-8079. At 7th St. Elegant 12-story upscale hotel just two blocks from major Lincoln sites. Tasteful understated decor in public and private areas. Excellent reputation and service. Great for midsize conventions and meetings, business travelers, and honeymooners. **Rooms:** 316 rms and stes. Executive level. CI 4pm/CO noon. Nonsmoking rms avail. Elegant furnishings and decor. Club Level rooms have ornate mirrors and antique furnishings. **Amenities:** 🛅 👜 📺 A/C, cable TV w/movies. All units w/minibars, some w/whirlpools. Bath and Body Works brand toiletries in all rooms. Club Level rooms have plush bathrobes and bars. **Services:** ✕ ☞ VP 🚗 🛏 ↩ Twice-daily maid svce, babysitting. VCRs available. Club Level includes lounge with free breakfast and afternoon hors d'oeuvres. **Facilities:** 🔥 🛄 720 🖥 ఈ 3 restaurants (*see* "Restaurants" below), 2 bars, games rm, sauna, steam rm, whirlpool. **Rates:** Peak (Feb 15–Nov) $96–$116 S; $108–$128 D; $136–$148 ste. Extra person $12. Children under age 18 stay free. Lower rates off-season. Parking: Indoor, $5/day. Weekend packages avail. AE, CB, DC, DISC, MC, V.

≣≣≣ Springfield Hilton

700 E Adams, 62701 (Downtown); tel 217/789-1530 or toll free 800/HILTONS; fax 217/789-0709. At 7th St. This 30-floor Springfield landmark has the best (and only) views of the city. Just blocks from major Lincoln sites. Excellent meeting/conference facilities. Great for children. Good value. **Rooms:** 368 rms and stes. Executive level. CI 3pm/CO 1pm. Nonsmoking rms avail. Rooms have either one king-size or two queen-size beds. Lovely decor and furnishings. Almost all rooms have views. Executive level on 28th floor has spacious suites. **Amenities:** 🛅 👜 📺 🍷 A/C, cable TV w/movies, voice mail. Some units w/whirlpools. Executive level suites have bathrobes. **Services:** ✕ ☞ VP 🚗 🛏 ↩ 🍴 Twice-daily maid svce, children's program, babysitting. VCRs available. Turn-down service available. Executive level offers complimentary breakfast and afternoon hors d'oeuvres. Summertime "Vacation Station" offers children use of hand-held video games, board games, coloring books, and toys. Excellent management and staff. **Facilities:** 🔥 🛄 1500 ఈ 2 restaurants (*see* "Restaurants" below), 2 bars (w/entertainment), sauna, beauty salon. Restaurant/lounge on top floor has good views. Fitness Center offers twice-daily aerobics, tanning bed, and full range of weight equipment. First floor area includes men's clothing store, women's boutique, art gallery, and espresso bar. **Rates:** $79–$129 S; $89–$139 D; $135–$300 ste. Extra person $10. Children under age 21 stay free. Parking: Indoor, $5/day. AE, CB, DC, DISC, MC, V.

MOTELS

≣ Courtyard by Marriott

3462 Freedom Dr, 62702; tel 217/793-5300 or toll free 800/321-2211; fax 217/793-5300. Nice but generic motel near major shopping area. Caters to families, weddings, and reunions. Very congested location—there can be traffic problems entering and exiting major thoroughfare from road leading to motel. **Rooms:** 78 rms and stes. CI 3pm/CO 1pm. Nonsmoking rms avail. **Amenities:** 🛅 👜 🍷 A/C, cable TV w/movies, dataport. Some units w/terraces. **Services:** 🛏 ↩ Breakfast buffet in lobby. Linens changed every other day for multi-night stays. **Facilities:** 🔥 🛄 60 ఈ 1 restaurant (bkfst only), 1 bar, whirlpool, washer/dryer. **Rates:** Peak (Apr–Sept) $68–$75 S; $75 D; $119 ste. Min stay special events. Lower rates off-season. Parking: Outdoor, free. AE, CB, DC, DISC, JCB, MC, V.

≣≣ Days Inn

3000 Stevenson Dr, 62703; tel 217/529-0171 or toll free 800/329-7466; fax 217/529-9431. Exit 94 off I-55. Just off main highway in commercial district surrounded by other motels, movie theaters, restaurants, and strip mall. Lincoln sites 10 minutes away. Lake Springfield (with fishing, swimming beach, golf course, parks, and playgrounds) 1 mile away. Good summertime stop for families. **Rooms:** 210 rms. CI 3pm/CO noon. Nonsmoking rms avail. All rooms have outside entrances and parking available near room. **Amenities:** 🛅 A/C, cable TV w/movies, refrig, voice mail. **Services:** 🚗 🛏 ↩ 🍴 Fax and copy machines available at minimal charge. VCRs and toiletries available at front desk. Catering available for meetings. **Facilities:** 🔥 🛄 65 ఈ Complimentary passes to Club Fitness Center, two miles away. **Rates (CP):** Peak (June–Aug) $42–$47 S; $49–$54 D. Extra person $5. Children under age 12 stay free. Min stay special events. Lower rates off-season. Parking: Outdoor, free. AE, CB, DC, DISC, JCB, MC, V.

≣≣ Hampton Inn

3185 S Dirksen Pkwy, 62703; tel 217/529-1100 or toll free 800/426-7866; fax 217/529-1105. East Lake Dr/Stevenson exit 94 off I-55. Well-run establishment just off main highway in commercial district surrounded by motels, movie theaters, strip mall, and restaurants. Lincoln sites 10 minutes away. Lake Springfield (fishing, beach, playgrounds, parks, golf course) one mile away. **Rooms:** 123 rms. CI 2pm/CO noon. Nonsmoking rms avail. **Amenities:** 🛅 👜 A/C, cable TV, dataport, VCR. All rooms for guests with disabilities connect with standard doubles. **Services:** 🛏 ↩ 🍴 Babysitting. Small pets only. Excellent staff. **Facilities:** 🔥 🛄 40 ఈ Whirlpool. Large screen TV in lobby. **Rates (CP):** Peak (Apr–Oct) $52–$57 S; $57–$63 D. Extra person $5. Children under age 18 stay free. Lower rates off-season. Parking: Outdoor, free. AE, CB, DC, DISC, MC, V.

Holiday Inn East Holidome
3100 S Dirksen Pkwy, 62703; tel 217/529-7171 or toll free 800/HOLIDAY; fax 217/529-5063. Exit 96B off I-55. One of the largest Holidome facilities in the Midwest. Caters to large conventions, meetings, groups, and business travelers. Also perfect for year-round weekend getaways for families. Climate-controlled walkway between buildings. Full service. Received award from state Coalition for Citizens with Disabilities. Near restaurants, movie theater, and small shopping mall. **Rooms:** 378 rms and stes. CI 3pm/CO noon. Nonsmoking rms avail. **Amenities:** A/C, cable TV w/movies, dataport, voice mail. Some units w/whirlpools. **Services:** Babysitting. Roving security guards 24 hours. Top-notch sales and front desk staff. **Facilities:** 3 restaurants, 2 bars (1 w/entertainment), games rm, sauna, whirlpool, playground, washer/dryer. Holidome offers shuffleboard, pool table, putting green, Ping-Pong, and extra large whirlpool. **Rates:** $58–$83 S; $63–$83 D; $110–$175 ste. Children under age 18 stay free. Min stay special events. Parking: Outdoor, free. Corporate rate avail. AE, CB, DC, DISC, JCB, MC, V.

Holiday Inn South
625 E St Joseph St, 62703; tel 217/529-7131 or toll free 800/HOLIDAY; fax 217/529-7160. Well-run establishment serves families and small meetings/conventions with good value. **Rooms:** 119 rms and stes. CI 3pm/CO noon. Nonsmoking rms avail. **Amenities:** A/C, cable TV w/movies. 1 unit w/whirlpool. Nice assortment of toiletries in basket, including razors, shaving cream, and toothpaste. Suites have microrefrigerator and microwave; many have whirlpools surrounded by mirrors in living area. **Services:** Children's program, babysitting. Turndown service on request. During summer, special parties for children available, plus toys and board games. Will arrange special business center setup for meetings. Excellent service. **Facilities:** 1 restaurant, 1 bar, washer/dryer. Complimentary passes to Club Fitness Center three blocks away. **Rates (CP):** Peak (Apr–Sept) $59–$65 S or D; $100–$150 ste. Children under age 18 stay free. Lower rates off-season. Parking: Outdoor, free. AE, CB, DC, DISC, MC, V.

Mansion View Inn and Suites
529 S 4th St, 62701; tel 217/544-7411 or toll free 800/252-1083; fax 217/544-6211. Across from Governor's Mansion. Newly renovated motel is a step up from the usual. Unique location across from Governor's Mansion. Richly upholstered cherry Queen Anne furniture graces lobby and guest rooms. Close to government and historic sites. **Rooms:** 93 rms and stes. Executive level. CI 2pm/CO noon. Nonsmoking rms avail. **Amenities:** A/C, cable TV w/movies, dataport. Some units w/whirlpools. **Services:** Babysitting. VCRs and videos available at front desk. Small pets only, with cats to be kept in carriers. Room service available from more than 20 local restaurants daily to 10pm. Abundant tourism materials available. **Facilities:**

Games rm, spa, washer/dryer. Lovely health spa—whirlpool with TV seats 15. **Rates (CP):** $56 S or D; $65–$145 ste. Extra person $6. Children under age 16 stay free. Min stay special events. Parking: Outdoor, free. Special packages avail for wedding parties. AE, CB, DC, DISC, MC, V.

Ramada Limited
3281 Northfield Dr, 62702; tel 217/523-4000 or toll free 800/272-6232; fax 217/523-4080. Exit 100B off I-55. Lovely new hotel on city's north side near State Fairgrounds and minutes from Rail golf course. Sits between woods and open prairie; however, view from one side looks onto commercial property. Peaceful and fairly quiet. Outside lighted patio overlooks midsize lake with ducks. Restaurants nearby. **Rooms:** 97 rms and stes. CI 2pm/CO noon. Nonsmoking rms avail. **Amenities:** A/C, cable TV w/movies, refrig, dataport. Some units w/whirlpools. **Services:** Babysitting. VCRs available for small charge. **Facilities:** Games rm, washer/dryer. Jogging path is ⅓-mile long. Meeting rooms overlook pool and lake. **Rates (CP):** $51 S; $57 D; $100–$125 ste. Extra person $6. Children under age 18 stay free. Min stay special events. Parking: Outdoor, free. Special "Baseball Weekend" packages avail in summer. AE, CB, DC, DISC, ER, JCB, MC, V.

Super 8 Lodge
3675 S 6th St, 62703; tel 217/529-8898 or toll free 800/800-8000; fax 217/529-4354. Worn Swiss chalet exterior. Good value for quick overnight stop. **Rooms:** 122 rms and stes. CI 11am/CO 11am. Nonsmoking rms avail. **Amenities:** A/C, cable TV w/movies. Some units w/terraces. Microwave/refrigerator units available for small charge. **Services:** 24-hour coffee bar. Fax and copy service available. **Facilities:** Washer/dryer. **Rates:** Peak (Apr–Sept) $39–$45 S; $42–$55 D; $65–$75 ste. Children under age 12 stay free. Min stay special events. Lower rates off-season. Parking: Outdoor, free. AE, CB, DC, DISC, MC, V.

RESTAURANTS

Cancun
2849 S 6th St; tel 217/753-0088. Near Stevenson Dr. **Mexican.** Bright, fun place with very friendly service. Specialities include Enchiladas Supremas (four corn tortillas—each filled with beef, chicken, cheese, or beans—topped with sauce, cheese, lettuce, tomato, and sour cream), and a combination platter with chalupa, taco, chile relleno, tamale, and enchilada. Vegetarian dinners and à la carte items also available. Expect a wait on Friday and Saturday nights. **FYI:** Reservations not accepted. Children's menu. **Open:** Mon–Sat 11am–10pm. **Prices:** Main courses $5–$20. AE, DISC, MC, V.

Floreale
In Renaissance Springfield Hotel, 701 E Adams St (Downtown); tel 217/544-8800. At 7th St. **New American.** Both the menu and the decor here are extraordinarily elegant, especially for this part of the country. The art nouveau color scheme in the dining room is accented by exquisite pale-

mauve lighting fixtures. Menu specialties focus on lighter dishes, such as pasta and vegetarian entrees, although steak and seafood are also available. Superb service. **FYI:** Reservations recommended. Jacket required. **Open:** Tues–Sat 5:30–10pm. **Prices:** Main courses $13–$30. AE, CB, DC, DISC, MC, V. 💗 🔽 VP 🔁

Gumbo Ya Yas
In Springfield Hilton Hotel, 700 E Adams St (Downtown); tel 217/789-1530 ext 3030. **Cajun.** Fun and fast-paced restaurant decorated with vivid folk art paintings by local artist Mike Manning. Cajun-style caesar salad; "bronzed" or blackened fish, chicken, and pork. **FYI:** Reservations recommended. Guitar/jazz/piano. Children's menu. Dress code. **Open:** Dinner Tues–Thurs 5–9pm, Fri–Sat 5–10pm; brunch Sun 10am–2pm. **Prices:** Main courses $11–$20; prix fixe $17–$19. AE, CB, DC, DISC, MC, V. 🏞️ 👥 🔁

Ⓢ ✦ Maldaner's Restaurant
222 S 6th St (Downtown); tel 217/522-4313. At Monroe St. **Eclectic.** One of Springfield's most famous eating establishments. Chef Higgins grows his own herbs and vegetables, and he prides himself on using only the freshest ingredients. Summer favorites on the seasonally changing menu include fresh chanterelle mushrooms with pasta and chives; pork confit with corn, new red potatoes, and Italian flat beans in a rosemary sauce; and chilled rock shrimp and cucumber soup. Year-round offerings include warm goat cheese with roasted peppers and rocket lettuce, beef Wellington, and salmon crusted with pistachio nuts. **FYI:** Reservations recommended. **Open:** Lunch Mon–Fri 11am–2:30pm; dinner Tues–Thurs 5–9pm, Fri–Sat 5–10pm. Closed Sept 1–14. **Prices:** Main courses $5–$15. AE, MC, V. 🍷

Robbie's
4 S Old Capitol Plaza (Downtown); tel 217/528-1901. **American.** This lunchtime favorite, situated directly across from the Old State Capitol, is a great place to grab a quick but filling bite between historic site tours. The Weird Sarah sandwich features piles of roast beef covered with lettuce and ranch dressing. Cheese-broccoli soup is popular, and there's a variety of salads. Homemade cream pies daily. **FYI:** Reservations accepted. Blues/jazz. **Open:** Mon–Fri 11am–7pm, Sat 11am–3pm. Closed Dec 24–Jan 1. **Prices:** Lunch main courses $4–$7. AE, MC, V. 🔁

ATTRACTIONS 🏛️
Old State Capitol State Historic Site
5th and Adams Sts; tel 217/785-7960. This Greek Revival style building served as the Illinois statehouse from 1839 to 1876. Today, guests may tour the rooms that served as the offices of Abraham Lincoln. On Fridays and Saturdays, actors dressed in 1850s period clothing lead guided tours through Lincoln's rooms. **Open:** Peak (May–Oct) daily 9am–5pm. Reduced hours off-season. **$**

State Capitol
2nd St and Capitol Ave; tel 217/782-2099. Built in 1868–1888, the Capitol is still one of the largest buildings in central Illinois. The dome is more than 360 feet high and can be seen from miles away. The interior features murals depicting events in the state's history and a bas-relief frieze within the dome. On the grounds are statues of Abraham Lincoln and Stephen A Douglas. Guided tours leave from the information desk on the first floor. **Open:** Mon–Fri 8am–5pm, Sat–Sun 9am–4pm. **Free**

Lincoln Home National Historic Site
413 S 8th St; tel 217/491-4150. The historic site encompasses four city blocks and includes the only home that Abraham Lincoln ever owned. Start your visit at the Lincoln Home Visitors Center, where you can obtain free tickets for the Lincoln Home tour. (Tickets are required and are distributed on a first-come, first-served basis.) The tour examines Lincoln's formative years, his marriage to Mary Todd, the growth of his family as reflected in the expansion of his home, and his early political career. **Open:** Daily 8:30am–5pm. **Free**

The Lincoln Tomb
Oak Ridge Cemetery; tel 217/782-2717. The 117-foot-tall crypt contains the remains of the 16th president, his wife, and three of his sons. The exterior features a bronze bust of Lincoln as well as a plaque featuring the US coat of arms. Inside are statues by Daniel Chester French, Leonard Crunelle, Lorado Taft, and Augustus Saint-Gaudens, all of which commemorate important periods in Lincoln's career. **Open:** Peak (Mar–Oct) daily 9am–5pm. Reduced hours off-season. **Free**

Lincoln Memorial Garden
2301 E Lake Dr; tel 217/529-1111. Located along the southern shore of Lake Springfield, the gardens were designed by landscape architect Jens Jensen and cover 77 acres. Five miles of nature trails traverse the grounds filled with maple trees, dogwoods, and wildflowers, and benches along the paths are inscribed with inspirational sayings by Abraham Lincoln. **Open:** Garden, daily sunrise–sunset; nature center, Tues–Sat 10am–4pm, Sun 1–4pm. **Free**

Lincoln Depot
10th and Monroe Sts; tel 217/544-8695. Also known as the Great Western Depot, this is where Abraham Lincoln boarded a train to Washington on February 11, 1861, for his inauguration as the 16th president. A visitors center features a slide show recreating his 12-day journey as well as historical pictures and graphics depicting Lincoln's life in Springfield. **Open:** Apr–Aug, daily 10am–4pm. **Free**

Sycamore

See De Kalb

Union

This tiny northern Illinois town features outdoor displays of historic and antique railroad cars and steam engines.

ATTRACTION 🏛

Illinois Railway Museum
7000 Olson Rd; tel 815/923-4000. Visitors can learn about rail transportation and rail safety while getting a close up look at more than 300 railroad cars and engines. Many pieces of equipment in the collection have been restored to run on the museum's five mile demonstration railroad and the one mile trolley loop, including an antique steam locomotive, a 1920s interurban train, a 1950s diesel commuter train, and a Chicago streetcar. **Open:** Peak (Mem Day–Labor Day) Mon–Fri 10am–4pm. Reduced hours off-season. **$$$**

Utica

See also Ottawa, Peru

LODGE 🏨

UNRATED **Starved Rock Lodge & Conference Center**
Starved Rock State Park, PO Box 570, 61373; tel 815/667-4211; fax 815/667-4455. Nestled in some of the state's most magnificent natural beauty, this low-rise lodge is a real find. The cozy lobby and great room have many windows, fireplaces, and highly polished log furniture. The lodge is in the center of the state park, which has many fun and educational activities for children, as well as for families and adults. Just 10 minutes from a local country club, where lodge guests are extended golf privileges. For all the extras available through the lodge and the surrounding state park, the rates are an exceptional value. A very popular property—busy seasons are booked way in advance (as much as two years for Oct stays). **Rooms:** 72 rms and stes; 11 cottages/villas. CI 3pm/CO 11am. Nonsmoking rms avail. Junior (one room) suites available in lodge. Some cabins recently renovated. Pioneer cabins have showers only (no bathtubs). **Amenities:** 🛏 👗 A/C, cable TV w/movies. Only a few cabins have fireplaces. **Services:** 🔑 🍴 **Facilities:** 🏊 🎱 🎿 220 👗 2 restaurants, 1 bar, games rm, sauna, whirlpool, playground. Indoor pool has plenty of comfortable deck space and is right next to veranda. Miles of hiking trails run along waterways, through thick woods, and up and down canyons. Entertainment may include live jazz programs, vocalists, classical music, guitarists, karaoke singers, and/or storytellers. Sometimes theme nights for menu and entertainment in summer. **Rates:** $60–$77 S; $66–$77 D; $47–$77 cottage/villa. Extra person $9. Children under age 12 stay free. Min stay wknds. Parking: Outdoor, free. Many group rates avail. AE, DC, DISC, MC, V.

Vandalia

Seat of Fayette County, in south-central part of state. A statue known as *Madonna of the Trail,* in front of the old State House, marks the end of the National Road, a 591-mile-long road linking Vandalia with Cumberland, MD. Vandalia was state capital from 1819–1839, until Abraham Lincoln led a successful campaign to move the capital to Springfield. **Information:** Vandalia Chamber of Commerce, 1408 N 5th St, PO Box 238, Vandalia, 62471 (tel 618/283-2728).

MOTELS 🏨

🏨🏨 **Days Inn**
US 51 and I-70, PO Box 316, 62471; tel 618/283-4400 or toll free 800/325-2525; fax 618/283-4240. Exit 63 off I-70, N on US 51 to entrance. A bright turquoise awning marks the entrance to this recently renovated, well-maintained facility. Easy access to highway. Golf and tennis nearby. **Rooms:** 95 rms. CI open/CO noon. Nonsmoking rms avail. Even-numbered rooms face pool. **Amenities:** 🛏 A/C, cable TV, dataport. Mini-suite has whirlpool. **Services:** ✕ 🚐 🍴 🐾 Deposit required for pets. **Facilities:** 🏊 400 1 restaurant, playground. Cafe 51 restaurant on premises. **Rates:** $32–$42 S; $38–$52 D. Extra person $7. Children under age 12 stay free. Parking: Outdoor, free. AE, DC, DISC, MC, V.

🏨 **Jay's Motel**
I-70 and US 51, 62471; tel 618/283-1200; fax 618/283-2363. Exit 63 off I-70, S on US 51 to IL 185, W to Frontage Rd entrance. Basic accommodations with easy access to highway. Fine for overnight, but not much longer. Near several fast food restaurants. **Rooms:** 30 rms. CI open/CO noon. Nonsmoking rms avail. Rooms in rear wing are smaller and older, with showers only. **Amenities:** 🛏 📺 A/C, cable TV w/movies. **Services:** 🐾 **Facilities:** 15 Shares pool facilities with motel next door. **Rates:** Peak (May–Oct) $23–$32 S; $28–$39 D. Children under age 12 stay free. Lower rates off-season. Parking: Outdoor, free. AE, DISC, MC, V.

🏨🏨🏨 **Ramada Limited**
US 40 W, PO Box 316, 62471; tel 618/283-1400 or toll free 800/2-RAMADA; fax 618/283-3465. Exit 61 off I-70, US 40 E to entrance. Just outside Vandalia, this newer facility offers business travelers comfortable accommodations in an elegant atmosphere. Bowling alley and skating rink nearby. **Rooms:** 61 rms and stes. CI 2pm/CO noon. Nonsmoking rms avail. **Amenities:** 🛏 👗 A/C, cable TV w/movies, dataport. **Services:** 🖼 🍴 🐾 VCR rentals available at desk. Express checkout available to Ramada Business Cardholders. Pets permitted in smoking rooms only. Ponderosa Steakhouse next door delivers meals to rooms. Next day laundry/dry cleaning available Mon–Thurs; Fri and Sat drops returned on Mon. **Facilities:** 🏊 50 👗 **Rates:** Peak (May–Sept) $45 S; $53 D; $69–$77 ste. Extra person $8. Children under age 13 stay free. Lower rates off-season. Parking: Outdoor, free. AE, DC, DISC, MC, V.

Travelodge

1500 N Sixth St, 62471; tel 618/283-2363 or toll free 800/255-3050; fax 618/283-2363. Exit 63 off I-70, S on US 51 to IL 185, W to Frontage Rd entrance. Comfortable motel with lobby fireplace. Several restaurants nearby. **Rooms:** 48 rms. CI open/CO noon. Nonsmoking rms avail. **Amenities:** A/C, cable TV w/movies. **Services:** Complimentary toiletries at front desk. **Facilities:** Playground. **Rates:** Peak (May–Oct) $37 S; $47 D. Children under age 12 stay free. Lower rates off-season. Parking: Outdoor, free. AE, DISC, MC, V.

ATTRACTION

Vandalia Statehouse State Historic Site

315 W Gallatin St; tel 618/283-1161. The third capitol building to stand in Vandalia before the capital of Illinois was moved to Springfield in 1839. Abraham Lincoln served his second term in the state legislature in 1836 in this building. Today, the statehouse has been restored to its 1836 appearance with reconstructed offices and period furnishings. **Open:** Daily 9am–5pm.

Vernon Hills

RESTAURANT

Cafe Pyrenees

In Rivertree Court Shopping Center, 701 N Milwaukee Ave; tel 847/918-8850. SE corner of IL 60 and IL 21. **French.** Don't let its location at the end of a busy strip mall fool you: this is an unassuming, cozy, and tastefully decorated bistro offering a wide spectrum of dishes. The wine list offers over 100 selections. **FYI:** Reservations recommended. No smoking. **Open:** Lunch Tues–Fri 11:30am–2pm; dinner Tues–Thurs 5:30–9pm, Fri 5:30–10pm, Sat 5–10pm. **Prices:** Main courses $14–$19; prix fixe $20. AE, CB, DC, DISC, MC, V.

Waukegan

Seat of Lake County, in northeast corner of state. Waukegan is home to the Great Lakes Naval Training Center and was the birthplace of comedian Jack Benny and science fiction author Ray Bradbury. **Information:** Lake County Chamber of Commerce, 5221 W Grand Ave, Gurnee, 60031-1818 (tel 847/249-3800).

MOTELS

Best Inns of America

31 N Green Bay Rd, 60085; tel 847/336-9000 or toll free 800/237-8466; fax 847/336-9000. A basic, well-maintained motel with friendly management. **Rooms:** 89 rms. CI 2pm/CO 11am. Nonsmoking rms avail. Plain rooms. Small bath- rooms with adjacent dressing rooms. **Amenities:** A/C, cable TV w/movies, dataport. **Services:** Breakfast served in lobby. **Facilities:** Small pool in pleasant private area adjacent to a prairie. **Rates (CP):** Peak (May–Sept) $50–$55 S; $57–$63 D. Extra person $6. Children under age 18 stay free. Lower rates off-season. Parking: Outdoor, free. Special rates for seniors and Best Inns Preferred Guest. AE, CB, DC, DISC, EC, ER, JCB, MC, V.

Courtyard by Marriott

800 Lakehurst Rd, 60085; tel 847/689-8000 or toll free 800/321-2211; fax 847/689-0135. At Jct IL 43 and IL 120. Nicely landscaped inner courtyard with garden, tables, and gazebo; pleasant lounge overlooks the courtyard. Six Flags Great America nearby. **Rooms:** 149 rms and stes. CI 3pm/CO 1pm. Nonsmoking rms avail. Brightly furnished rooms. **Amenities:** A/C, satel TV w/movies, dataport. All units w/terraces. **Services:** Car-rental desk. **Facilities:** 1 restaurant (bkfst only), 1 bar, whirlpool, washer/dryer. Fitness center has weight machine and bicycles. **Rates:** Peak (June–Sept) $85 S; $95 D; $109 ste. Children under age 18 stay free. Lower rates off-season. Parking: Outdoor, free. Special rewards for Courtyard Club members. AE, CB, DC, DISC, MC, V.

Ramada Inn

200 N Green Bay Rd, 60085; tel 847/244-2400 or toll free 800/272-6232; fax 847/249-9716. Off I-132 E exit. A full-service motel. Clientele during the week is corporate, and on the weekends families of servicepeople at Great Lakes Naval Base. **Rooms:** 181 rms and stes. CI 3pm/CO noon. Nonsmoking rms avail. Furnishings plain but adequate, with pleasant watercolors on walls. **Amenities:** A/C, cable TV, dataport. Corporate rooms have coffeemakers; suites have refrigerators. **Services:** Car-rental desk. Sun brunch and Fri and Sat early morning buffet. **Facilities:** 1 restaurant, 1 bar (w/entertainment), games rm, sauna, whirlpool. Indoor pool in separate glass domed building. **Rates:** Peak (June–Aug) $70–$75 S; $80–$85 D; $90–$125 ste. Extra person $5. Children under age 16 stay free. Lower rates off-season. Parking: Outdoor, free. AE, CB, DC, DISC, MC, V.

RESTAURANT

★ Mathon's

In Waukegan Harbor, 6 E Clayton St (Waukegan Harbor); tel 847/662-3610. Off IL 132. **Seafood.** Since 1939, noted for fresh seafood from Great Lakes, fillet of lake perch, Lake Superior whitefish, lake trout, etc. Nautical decor complements its harbor position. Banquets, parties, and takeout available. **FYI:** Reservations recommended. Children's menu. **Open:** Peak (May–Sept) Tues–Thurs 11am–9pm, Fri–Sat 11am–10pm, Sun noon–8:30pm. **Prices:** Main courses $12–$16. AE, CB, DC, DISC, MC, V.

Westmont

MOTEL

〓〓 Best Western Ambassador Inn
669 Pasquinelli Dr, 60559; tel 630/323-1515 or toll free 800/528-1234; fax 630/323-1516. 1 block W of jct IL 83/US 34. Located in a high-tech research and development corridor, this two-story motel offers comfortable accommodations and easy access to shopping, airports, and expressways. **Rooms:** 44 rms. CI noon/CO noon. Nonsmoking rms avail. **Amenities:** A/C, cable TV w/movies. Some rooms have dataports. **Services:** Separate check-in for groups on request. **Facilities:** Sauna, whirlpool. **Rates (CP):** Peak (May–Oct) $60–$70 S; $65–$75 D. Extra person $5. Children under age 18 stay free. Lower rates off-season. Parking: Outdoor, free. AE, CB, DC, DISC, MC, V.

Wheeling

This northern Illinois town was founded in 1833; soon after, a stagecoach route linking Chicago and points north was established through the center of town. **Information:** Wheeling-Prospect Heights Area Chamber of Commerce & Industry, 395 E Dundee Rd, #300, Wheeling, 60090 (tel 847/541-0170).

RESTAURANTS

★ Bob Chinn's Crab House Restaurant
393 S Milwaukee Ave; tel 847/520-3633. On IL 21 just S of IL 68. **Seafood/Steak.** A popular hangout occupying the remnants of a 100-year-old roadhouse. Fresh crab, shrimp, and lobster are flown in daily (as proof, the air freight bills are displayed on the dining room walls). Raw bar, salad bar, and burgers also available. **FYI:** Reservations not accepted. Children's menu. **Open:** Lunch Mon–Sat 11am–2:30pm; dinner Mon–Thurs 4:30–10:30pm, Fri–Sat 4:30–11:30pm, Sun 3–10pm. **Prices:** Main courses $14–$38. AE, CB, DC, DISC, MC, V.

♣ Le Français
269 S Milwaukee Ave; tel 847/541-7470. S of Dundee Rd/IL 68. **French.** Owned and operated by chefs Mary Beth and Roland Liccioni, who prepare their innovative cuisine in this elegantly casual bistro. The building, set back from road, is surrounded by flowers and shrubs for a country-inn feeling. Gourmet creations include snapper and lobster tail with hazelnut oil, and beef tip au jus. Two degustation menus (four- or seven-course) are also available. Mary Beth's gourmet chocolates can be ordered for dessert or to take home. **FYI:** Reservations recommended. No smoking. **Open:** Lunch Tues–Fri 11:30am–2pm; dinner Mon–Thurs 5–9pm, Fri–Sat 6–9:30pm. Closed Jan 1–7. **Prices:** Main courses $29–$32. AE, CB, DC, DISC, MC, V.

94th Aero Squadron
1070 S Milwaukee Ave; tel 847/459-3700. 3 mi S of IL 68 (Dundee Rd) or ½ mi N of Palatine Rd on E side of Palwaukee Airport. **Seafood/Steak.** Aviation is the theme at this unique eatery on the east side of Palwaukee Airport. Vintage aircraft and gun positions add interest and atmosphere to the restaurant grounds, while more World War I memorabilia can be found inside. There are even headphones in each booth to allow diners to listen in on conversations in the airport tower. Exhibition kitchen gives diners a view of the chef preparing steak, pasta, and seafood. **FYI:** Reservations accepted. Children's menu. Dress code. **Open:** Lunch Mon–Sat 11am–2:30pm; dinner Mon–Sat 4–10pm; brunch Sun 9am–2:30pm. **Prices:** Main courses $12–$39. AE, DC, DISC, MC, V.

Weber Grill
920 N Milwaukee Ave; tel 847/215-0996. **American.** Charcoal grilling—of fish, chicken, steak, and ribs—is the name of the game here. Even Irish coffee is prepared tableside on—you guessed it—a charcoal grill. Some windows in the dining room provide a chance to watch the cooks and their giant Weber kettle grills at work. **FYI:** Reservations recommended. Children's menu. **Open:** Lunch Mon–Fri 11:30am–2:30pm, Sat noon–2:30pm; dinner Mon–Thurs 4:30–10pm, Fri–Sat 4:30–11pm, Sun 3–9pm. **Prices:** Main courses $10–$25. AE, CB, DC, DISC, MC, V.

Willowbrook

MOTELS

〓 Budgetel Inn
855 W 79th St, 60521; tel 630/654-0077 or toll free 800/4-BUDGET; fax 630/654-0181. Modest motel, fine for overnight or short-term stays. **Rooms:** 137 rms. CI noon/CO noon. Nonsmoking rms avail. **Amenities:** A/C, satel TV w/movies, dataport. **Services:** Separate check-in for groups on request. **Facilities:** Washer/dryer. **Rates (CP):** $46–$53 S; $49–$60 D. Children under age 18 stay free. Parking: Outdoor, free. AE, CB, DC, DISC, MC, V.

〓〓 Fairfield Inn
820 W 79th St, 60521; tel 630/789-6300 or toll free 800/228-2800; fax 630/789-6300 ext 700. N of I-55 1 block off US 83. This three-story chain motel is bright, clean, and conveniently located near championship golf courses. Guests have full access to the nearby Willowbrook Athletic Club, which boasts eight indoor tennis courts, swimming pool, and track. A good deal compared to other options in the area. **Rooms:** 129 rms. CI 3pm/CO noon. Nonsmoking rms avail. **Amenities:** A/C, cable TV w/movies, dataport. **Services:** **Facilities:** **Rates (CP):** Peak (June–Aug 15) $45–$48 S; $55–$60 D. Extra person $7. Children under age 18 stay free. Lower rates off-season. Parking: Outdoor, free. AE, DC, DISC, MC, V.

🛏 Red Roof Inn
7535 Kingery Hwy, 60521; tel 630/323-8811 or toll free 800/THE-ROOF; fax 630/323-2714. IL 83 N exit off I-55. Modest motel in a suburban location. Fine for overnight or short-term stays. **Rooms:** 109 rms. CI 2pm/CO noon. Nonsmoking rms avail. **Amenities:** 🛁 A/C, satel TV w/movies. Some rooms have refrigerators. **Services:** 🍴 🏊 Free coffee. Guests get 15% off food bill at local Max & Erna's restaurants. **Facilities:** ⅃. **Rates:** Peak (May 15–Oct 15) $42–$53 S; $51–$80 D. Extra person $8. Children under age 18 stay free. Lower rates off-season. Parking: Outdoor, free. AE, CB, DC, DISC, MC, V.

RESTAURANT 🍴

★ Dell Rhea's Chicken Basket
645 Joliet Rd; tel 630/325-0780. **American.** Opened in 1946, this popular stop along famed Route 66 was inducted into the Route 66 Hall of Fame in 1992. The specialty here is fried chicken, and a good bet is the family-style chicken dinner: soup, salad bar, homemade biscuits, platter of fried chicken, baked mostacholli, stuffing, homemade mashed potatoes, fresh butter green beans, and cobbler. Also burgers, steaks, seafood, fresh catfish. **FYI:** Reservations recommended. Blues. Children's menu. **Open:** Sun–Thurs 11am–11pm, Fri–Sat 11am–2am. **Prices:** Main courses $5–$14. AE, DC, DISC, MC, V. 🍺 🖼 👥 ✅ ⅃

Wilmette

A northern suburb of Chicago, on Lake Michigan. Baha'i House of Worship draws visitors from around the world. Also home of Mallinckrodt College and a US coast guard station. **Information:** Wilmette Chamber of Commerce, 1150 Wilmette Ave, Wilmette, 60091 (tel 708/251-3800).

RESTAURANTS 🍴

★ Convito Italiano
In Plaza del Lago, 1515 N Sheridan Rd; tel 847/251-3654. At N end of Wilmette, 1 mi N of Bahai Temple. **Italian.** One of the jewels of Plaza del Lago, an area of town that has been transformed from a chunk of abandoned lakefront property into a graceful, Spanish-inspired shopping area. (Try to build some time in for wandering around before or after your meal.) The grilled herbed chicken breast on julienned vegetables with orange sauce or beef tenderloin medallions with spinach risotto in porcini mushroom sauce will let you in on the secret of why people actually call ahead from New York or Los Angeles to make reservations. An onsite Italian market/deli sells authentic fare to take home. **FYI:** Reservations accepted. Beer and wine only. No smoking. **Open:** Sun–Thurs 11:30am–8:30pm, Fri–Sat 11:30am–9:45pm. **Prices:** Main courses $7–$15. AE, DC, DISC, MC, V. 🍶 👥 ⅃

Kamakura
1116 Central Ave; tel 847/256-6783. Just E of Wilmette Ave. **Japanese.** A modern Japanese restaurant in the heart of downtown Wilmette. Solid black, oblong blocks topped with flower arrangements visually break up the space, lending privacy and beauty to the tables. Large, framed photographs by Sato adorn the walls, and the service is quietly pleasant and efficient. Traditional sushi is offered in addition to main course dishes such as tempura, teriyaki, tonkatsu, and sukiyaki. Fine food, well presented. **FYI:** Reservations recommended. Beer and wine only. **Open:** Lunch Tues–Sat 11:30am–2:30pm; dinner Tues–Thurs 5–9:45pm, Fri–Sat 5–10:30pm, Sun 4–9pm. **Prices:** Main courses $8–$20. AE, CB, DC, DISC, MC, V. ⅃

ATTRACTION 🖼

Baha'i House of Worship
Linden Ave and Sheridan Rd; tel 847/853-2300. The most visited of al the sights in Chicago's northern suburbs, the temple strongly reveals the Eastern influence of the Baha'i faith's native Iran. Designed by the French Canadian Louis Bourgeois, the temple features a lacelike facade and 135-foot dome, and is surrounded by formal gardens. Guided tours; visitors center. **Open:** Peak (May–Sept) daily 10am–10pm. Reduced hours off-season. **Free**

Woodridge

One of Chicago's western suburbs. **Information:** Woodridge Chamber of Commerce, PO Box 8159, Woodridge, 60517 (tel 630/852-9878).

RESTAURANT 🍴

★ Clara's Pasta di Casa
In Hobson Valley Industrial Park Shopping Center, 6740 S IL 53; tel 630/968-8899. **Italian.** A "hole in the wall" restaurant worth every second spent searching for it. Clara herself makes different fresh pastas every day, along with individual pizzas and other personal creations. Heart-healthy entrees available. Clara has built up a loyal clientele, so you can expect a line on most nights. **FYI:** Reservations recommended. Children's menu. **Open:** Tues–Thurs 11am–10pm, Fri–Sat 11am–11pm, Sun 2–9pm. **Prices:** Main courses $6–$17. AE, CB, DC, DISC, MC, V. 👥 ⅃

Woodstock

Seat of McHenry County, in northern Illinois. The town square remains Victorian, with its fancy gazebo, wooded park, and cobblestone streets, and many historic houses and buildings now contain antique shops. **Information:** Woodstock Chamber of Commerce, 136 Cass St, PO Box 725, Woodstock, 60098 (tel 815/338-2436).

RESTAURANT ⅋

ⓢ Joey T's Cafe Italiano

228 Main St; tel 815/337-0015. **American.** A large bar occupies the center of this restaurant situated in a historic building with painted tin ceiling, brick walls, and pine-pegged floors. Noted for generous portions of pasta, yellow fin tuna with garlic sauce, veal piccata. **FYI:** Reservations recommended. Children's menu. **Open:** Lunch Mon–Sat 11am–3pm; dinner Mon–Thurs 5–10pm, Fri–Sat 5–11pm. **Prices:** Main courses $9–$16. AE, MC, V. 🍴 ⅋

ATTRACTION 📷

Woodstock Opera House

121 Van Buren St; tel 815/338-4212. Built in 1889 in what has been described as a "steamboat gothic" style reflecting the cathedral shape of its exterior and the similarities of the auditorium's interior to a riverboat salon. A variety of programming is hosted by the Opera House including community theater, a Woodstock Mozart Festival, and summer band concerts. In addition, art exhibitions feature the work of regional artists. **Open:** Mon–Sat 9:30am–5pm. **$$$$**

INDIANA

Hoosier Hospitality

STATE STATS

CAPITAL
Indianapolis

AREA
36,185 square miles

BORDERS
Michigan, Ohio,
Kentucky, Illinois

POPULATION
5,658,323 (1992)

ENTERED UNION
December 11, 1816
(19th state)

NICKNAME
Hoosier State

STATE FLOWER
Peony

STATE BIRD
Cardinal

FAMOUS NATIVES
Larry Bird, Michael Jackson,
David Letterman,
Kurt Vonnegut, Jimmy Hoffa

There isn't a basketball hoop in *every* yard in Indiana; it just seems that way. When Bobby Knight's Hoosiers play at home in Indiana University's Assembly Hall, the arena is packed. Fans still talk about the 1987 season when IU won the NCAA championship, beating Syracuse by only 1 point. The Purdue Boilermakers, IU's intrastate rival, keep fans in West Lafayette occupied. (IU fans like to joke that "You know it's spring when IU is still playing basketball and Purdue isn't," while Purdue fans like to say they are "Hoosier by birth, Boilermaker by the grace of God.") Fans all over the state are still proud of Milan, the real Indiana town depicted in the 1986 film *Hoosiers*. In 1954, tiny Milan—with a high school enrollment of only 161—beat powerhouse Muncie Central for the state basketball championship. There are also the Pacers, the NBA team that attracts crowds in Market Square Arena in Indianapolis, and the CBA's Fury in Fort Wayne. Yes, the words "Hoosier," "hysteria," and "basketball" often seem to go together.

Basketball is far from the only sport on Hoosiers' minds, however. In recent years Indianapolis, the state capital, has earned the title of Amateur Sports Capital of the World. In the mid-1970s, the city began building sports facilities and executing marketing strategies to attract top sporting events—all as part of a plan to use sports as an economic and community development tool. Today's visitor will find the RCA Dome (formerly the Hoosier Dome), Market Square Arena, Indiana University Track and Field Stadium, Indiana University Natatorium, Indianapolis Tennis Center, Major Taylor Velodrome, National Institute for Fitness and Sport, and the William Kuntz Soccer Center here. In the summer of 1987 the city hosted the Pan American Games, and each year Indiana sponsors the White River Park Games for its state's amateur athletes. All this alongside the Indianapolis 500, the largest one-day sporting event in the world, when the number of spectators in the Speedway exceeds the entire population of Miami.

Hoosier life has a strong spiritual side as well. Groups have come here seeking religious refuge for years, from the Moravians who settled in Hope in 1830 to the utopian experiments in New Harmony to the Quakers, who founded Earlham College in Richmond. Mennonites and Amish are still seen, driving their wagons on the back roads. Bloomington is the site of a 90-acre Tibetan Cultural Center led by the elder brother of the Dalai Lama. And, of course, the University of Notre Dame in South Bend is one of the foremost Catholic institutions in the country.

Politically, Indiana is considered a conservative, Republican state. Even in the 1980s, when the economic recession closed factories and sent unemployment soaring, the Republicans maintained power. Hamilton County, just north of Indianapolis, has long been considered one of the strongest Republican enclaves in the country. Locals say there are two political parties in the county—the Republicans who are in office and the Republicans who are out of office. Former vice president Dan Quayle is a native son.

Farming is still big here, but so is business. Indiana is one of the country's largest producers of corn, soybeans, and popcorn—and of steel, electrical equipment, and vehicle parts. One of history's most successful businesspeople—Michael Jackson —grew up with his brothers in Gary. Indiana has countless small towns (many with colorful names like French Lick, Bean Blossom, and Peru), as well as Indianapolis, the country's 12th largest city, with more than 800,000 residents. Southern Indiana has a strong Southern flavor, while nearby Chicago colors the northern part of the state.

Most Hoosiers have their feet firmly on the ground, and they pride themselves on staying deeply rooted to their past. Traditions are important here; among them is that friendliness called Hoosier hospitality. Perhaps it's simply a continuation of the tradition of the isolated pioneers who, hungry for company, eagerly called out, "Who's here?" when someone approached.

Fun Facts

- The post office at Santa Claus, Indiana, processes more than half a million pieces of mail for remailing, with the Santa Claus postmark, during the Christmas season.
- Johnny Gruelle, a political cartoonist for the *Indianapolis Star,* created the famous Raggedy Ann doll.
- Although it is 38th among US states in land area, the Hoosier Sate ranks 14th in population.
- Elvis Presley gave what would be his last performance at Market Square Arena in Indianapolis on June 27, 1977.

A Brief History

Earliest Residents More than 300 million years ago, much of Indiana was under water. Proof of the state's watery past exists nears Clarksville in southern Indiana, where the world's largest exposed fossil bed, once a coral reef, allows you to walk on and examine what was once a fertile sea.

The first residents left no written record, but they did leave other traces of their culture. The mound-building Adena and Hopewell peoples were among the earliest residents, here between 1000 BC and AD 900. They created giant mounds of earth that are believed to have served as burial grounds. The largest, nearly 1,200 feet around and 9 feet high, can be found in Anderson at Mounds State Park.

Some time between 900 and 1500, the Mississippians built a fortified city and mounds to elevate the houses of their leaders. No one knows why the city disappeared, but 11 of these so-called Angel Mounds have been discovered near Evansville. Other Native Americans passed in and out of the Hoosier region for hundreds of years, never settling down and never leaving much of a mark. The first Europeans to spend time in the area were the French fur traders, who arrived in the 17th century. They cultivated a mutually beneficial relationship with the Native Americans, who were excellent trappers. In 1733 the French built the state's first permanent settlement in Vincennes.

The British, however, paid higher prices for furs than did the French, and in addition sold firearms to the Native Americans. The struggle for the fur trade led to years of battle between the French and the British. The French ultimately lost, and in 1767 France relinquished its claims to the Indiana region to Great Britain.

Settlement & Statehood British troops began to occupy Indiana during the Revolutionary War. Eventually the Americans gained control of the region, and in 1787 Indiana became part of the Northwest Territory.

The new settlers were interested in farming and sought to colonize the land held by Native Americans, many of whom had been pushed into the Indiana territory from farther east. The resulting tensions lasted for decades and eventually put the names of Tecumseh, a Shawnee chief, and William Henry Harrison, a territorial governor who became the ninth US president, into American history books. Harrison's troops defeated the Native Americans in the Battle of Tippecanoe in 1811. And when Native Americans allied themselves with the British during the War of 1812, Harrison defeated the newly combined forces, ending British influence in the territory and halting Native American attacks.

In 1816 Indiana was named a state, with Corydon as its capital. Nine years later, when legislators realized the capital was too far from the developing areas to the north, the capital was moved to Indianapolis. While most of Indiana's settlements grew haphazardly, Indianapolis was a planned city from the start. It was designed by surveyor Alexander Ralston, who had worked with Pierre L'Enfant, the planner of Washington, DC. Four major diagonal streets lead from Monument Circle, in the center of the city. Within the circle stands the massive 1902 Soldiers' and Sailors' Monument, only 15 feet shorter than the Statue of Liberty.

Crossroads of America The state grew through the construction of canals, then railroads, and finally highways. The east–west National Road (US 40) and the north–south Michigan Road, both laid in the early 19th century, crossed in Indianapolis. Today, more major highways intersect in Indiana than in any other state, and Indianapolis is within a 12-hour drive from half the population of the United States.

As the Civil War approached, political opinion about slavery threatened to split the state. Newcomers in the northern part of the state were pro-Union and antislavery; the southern portion of the state defended the right of Southerners to own slaves.

Despite a state constitution that made it illegal to assist an escaped slave, many Hoosiers did just that. Fountain City near Richmond in east-central Indiana became known as the "Grand Central Station of the Underground Railroad."

When the war began, however, the great majority of Indiana residents supported President Abraham Lincoln, who was a former Hoosier himself. More than 200,000 Indianans joined the Union ranks, and more of them gave their lives than in any other conflict in the nation's history, including World War II. Only New York contributed more men to the Union cause.

Industrial Boom Years The post–Civil War years marked the beginnings of industrialization, which brought fortune to many Indiana entrepreneurs and inventors. James Oliver of South Bend developed a hardened steel plow more efficient than older models; Sylvanus Bowser of Fort Wayne designed the world's first practical gasoline pump; Gilbert Van Camp of Indianapolis opened a canning company to market his family recipe for pork and beans; and the Ball family of Muncie became famous for its jars and other glass products. Madame C J Walker of Indianapolis peddled her own brand of beauty products and became the nation's first self-made black woman millionaire.

Until it was eclipsed by Detroit, Indiana showed great strength in the infant auto industry. In 1894 Elwood Haynes of Kokomo designed one of the first successful gasoline-powered automobiles. In 1902 the Studebaker brothers' company in South Bend made its first electric-powered vehicles, and in 1904 it began manufacturing gasoline-powered cars. From 1900 to 1920 more than 200 different makes of cars were produced in Indiana, among them Duesenbergs, Auburns, Stutzes, and Maxwells.

World War I increased factory output and crop prices. With peace came plummeting farm prices,

DRIVING DISTANCES

Indianapolis
51 mi N of Bloomington
63 mi SE of Lafayette
110 mi NW of Cincinnati
110 mi N of Louisville
118 mi SW of Fort Wayne
162 mi NE of Evansville
175 mi SE of Chicago

Fort Wayne
82 mi SE of South Bend
91 mi N of Richmond
155 NW of Cincinnati
160 mi E of Chicago
160 mi NW of Columbus, OH
165 mi SW of Detroit
188 mi NE of Terre Haute

Evansville
110 mi W of Louisville
116 mi SW of Bloomington
162 mi SW of Indianapolis
210 mi SW of Cincinnati
231 mi SW of Richmond
290 mi S of Chicago
320 mi SW of Columbus, OH

however, and many farmers faced bankruptcy. For the first time, the number of urban dwellers outnumbered rural residents. In addition to Indiana farmers, blacks from the South and immigrants from Europe arrived in Indiana's cities for factory jobs. However, the Depression of the 1930s brought many of these factories to a standstill.

World War II & Beyond   It was World War II that brought prosperity once again, and Indiana's factories were a major part of the war effort. Early in the war, for example, so many Studebaker trucks were sent from South Bend to the Soviet Front that the Soviets believed "Studebaker" was the American word for "truck."

Many Hoosier cities continued to grow throughout the post–World War II years, despite the closing of the Studebaker plant in South Bend in the 1960s, the decline of the steel industry in northern Indiana in the 1970s, and the loss of jobs at International Harvester plants in Fort Wayne in the 1980s. During the recession of the early 1980s, Indiana's unemployment rate was one of the worst in the nation, but economic diversification in the late 1980s and throughout the 1990s has led to a new period of growth. Today, Indiana is once again looking at a bright future.

AVG MONTHLY TEMPS (°F) & RAINFALL (IN)		
	South Bend	**Indianapolis**
Jan	22/1.8	24/2.1
Feb	26/1.7	28/2.1
Mar	37/2.8	39/3.4
Apr	49/3.6	51/3.9
May	60/3.7	61/4.2
June	69/3.9	70/3.8
July	73/3.8	74/4.3
Aug	71/3.6	71/3.8
Sept	64/3.5	65/3.0
Oct	53/2.7	53/2.7
Nov	41/3.1	42/3.3
Dec	28/2.9	30/3.1

A Closer Look

GEOGRAPHY

Although the state is usually thought of as being uniformly flat, Indiana actually has three main land regions: the Great Lakes Plains in the north, the Till Plains in the middle of the state, and the Southern Hills and Lowlands. The northernmost region lies along the Great Lakes shoreline and has many small lakes and low hills. A highlight is the Indiana sand dune area. More than 400 lakes, including the state's largest, Lake Wawasee, are found here, as are major cities like Fort Wayne, South Bend, Gary, and Hammond.

The Till Plains in the state's midsection are part of the Midwestern Corn Belt, where the rich soil is very favorable for growing crops and raising livestock.

Indianapolis lies here, just about in the center of the state. Lafayette is a little more than an hour northwest of Indianapolis, Richmond about an hour east along the Ohio border.

The Southern Hills and Lowlands is the hilliest and most scenic in the state. The region has several steep hills with stretches of lowlands in between. The Ohio River forms the state's southern boundary. You'll find Bloomington and Columbus in south central Indiana; Evansville is in the southwestern corner along the Ohio. Floyd's Knobs, a range of low-lying mountains, crisscross the south-central region.

CLIMATE

The entire state shares pretty much the same Midwestern climate, with four distinctive seasons. Summers are often hot and humid; winters are cold and snowy, especially around Lake Michigan. (Hoosiers expect, and often get, a snowstorm about the time of the high school boys' basketball finals in March.) With no mountains to act as a buffer, strong winds and tornadoes sometimes twist across the state in the spring and summer.

WHAT TO PACK

Most residents consider air conditioning a necessity rather than a luxury during the humid and often hot summers, and most public places are air conditioned. Cool, cotton clothing is fine for this time of year. The winter months, on the other hand, can be cold and often snowy. Warm winter clothes with hats, gloves, and boots are desired. Spring and fall, those in-between seasons, can be warm and sunny or chilly and wet. A light jacket and an umbrella are especially welcome in April.

TOURIST INFORMATION

Free state maps and tourist information may be obtained by calling 800/289-6646. Additional information is available from the State Department of Tourism, One North Capitol, Suite 700, Indianapolis 46204. The Access Indiana Information Network maintains a World Wide Web page (http://www.state.in.us) with links to general information about the state. Contact information for local tourist bureaus is listed under specific cities in the listings section of this book.

DRIVING RULES AND REGULATIONS

The legal age for drivers in Indiana is 16; all licenses are probationary for drivers under 18. The speed limit on interstates is 65 mph unless otherwise posted; 55 mph on highways. A right turn on red is permitted after a complete stop unless otherwise posted. Seat belts are mandatory for the driver and all front seat passengers; the fine for noncompliance is $5 to $25. Child restraints are mandatory for children 5 years of age and younger, and helmets are required for those under 18 on a motorcycle.

RENTING A CAR

The following car rental firms have offices throughout the state:

- **Alamo** (tel 800/327-9633)
- **Avis** (tel 800/831-2847)
- **Budget** (tel 800/527-0700)
- **Dollar** (tel 800/800-4000)
- **Hertz** (tel 800/654-3131)
- **National** (tel 800/227-7368)

ESSENTIALS

Area Codes: Indiana has three area codes. Northern Indiana (including South Bend, Gary, and Fort Wayne) lies in the **219** area code. Central Indiana (including the Indianapolis area) lies in the **317** area code, while southern Indiana (including Evansville, Bloomington, Columbus, and Terre Haute) lies in the **812** area code.

Emergencies: Most—but not all—emergency police, fire, and ambulance services can be reached by dialing 911.

Gambling: Hoosier Park in Anderson is the state's first horse racing and pari-mutuel racetrack. It features live harness and thoroughbred racing April–October. Off-track betting is available in downtown Indianapolis, Merrillville, Fort Wayne, and Anderson. Riverboat gambling began in Evansville in 1995 and will be available in other parts of the state starting in 1996.

Liquor Laws: The legal drinking age for beer, wine, and alcohol is 21. There is no retail sale of alcoholic beverages on Sunday, except in licensed restaurants for on-site consumption. Many grocery stores sell beer and wine. Those under 21 are not permitted in bars; they may, however, go into establishments that sell both food and liquor.

Road Info: Call the Indiana State Police at 800/261-7623 for the latest road updates.

Smoking: Indiana is increasingly anti-smoking. Many public buildings are smoke-free, and many eating establishments have separate smoking and non-smoking sections.

Taxes: The statewide retail sales tax is 5%. Many counties have a local innkeeper's tax and several counties have special food and liquor taxes.

Time Zone: Indiana is one of only five states which does not uniformly switch to daylight saving time. Consequently, most of the state is always on Eastern Standard Time. Six counties along the Ohio River (Clark, Dearborn, Floyd, Harrison, Ohio, and Switzerland) are the exception, switching to daylight savings time in conformance with their closest major metropolitan center (Cincinnati or Louisville). Eleven counties in the northwest (Lake, Porter, LaPorte, Newton, Jasper, and Starke) and southwest (Posey, Vanderburgh, Gibson, Warrick, and Spencer) are in the Central time zone, and observe central daylight time in summer.

Best of the State

WHAT TO SEE AND DO

Below is a general overview of some of the top sights and attractions in Indiana. To find out more detailed information, look under "Attractions" for individual cities in the listings portion of this book.

National Parks & Forests Indiana Dunes National Lakeshore offers dune climbing, swimming, biking, camping, fishing, boating, picnicking, horseback riding, winter activities, and environmental education on more than 12,000 acres along the southern shoreline of Lake Michigan.

Hoosier National Forest covers more than 189,000 acres in south-central Indiana. Hiking, camping, fishing, and rock climbing are a few of the recreational activities that bring summer visitors; in fall, carloads of people come to view the glorious fall foliage. The 1,200-acre **Hardin Ride Recreation Area,** located in the forest near Lake Monroe, features boat launches, nature walks, and interpretive programs and displays.

State Parks Among the most notable of Indiana's state parks are **Brown County State Park,** offering miles of hiking trails and the state's only horseback campground; **Clifty Falls State Park** in southern Indiana, with waterfalls and a deep bouldered canyon; and **Lincoln State Park,** where the future president spent his youth.

Museums The **Lincoln Museum,** located in the corporate headquarters of Lincoln National Corp in Fort Wayne, houses the world's largest private collection of Abraham Lincoln memorabilia in 11 galleries, combining historic artifacts with computerized multimedia presentations. Among the artifacts are family photos, artwork inspired by Lincoln, and Mary Todd Lincoln's ''insanity files.''

The **Children's Museum** in Indianapolis bills itself as the largest children's museum in the world. It has five stories of ever-changing interactive displays as well as a revitalized antique carousel, a cave, the world's largest water clock, and the world's largest public display of toy trains. There's even an archeological dig for kids to get involved in.

The **Eiteljorg Museum of American Indian and Western Art** in Indianapolis, which opened in 1989, has one of the best collections of American Western and Native American artifacts in the country. The Native American Collection comprises art and artifacts from throughout North America, including pottery, basketry, and clothing; the American Western Culture Collection, spanning the early 19th century to the present, displays paintings, drawings, graphics, and sculptures.

The **Indiana State Museum,** housed in what was once the Indianapolis City Hall, is a showplace for the state's cultural and natural history. Among its permanent exhibits are a 450-million-year-old fossil, the state's first television camera (which was used to telecast the 1949 Indianapolis 500), the landscape works of Indiana artist T C Steele, and an examina-

tion of the phenomenon that is Indiana basketball.

The **Indianapolis Museum of Art** has a sculpture garden, botanical gardens, greenhouses, wildlife refuge, and restaurant located on the grounds, along with the main exhibition buildings that include the country's largest collection of JMW Turner watercolors and prints.

Three museums pay tribute to Indiana's role in the development of the automobile. The **Indianapolis Motor Speedway Hall of Fame Museum** has more than 30 Indianapolis 500 winning cars on display, including the Marmon Wasp driven by Ray Harroun in 1911 during the first 500-mile race. (Visitors can take a narrated bus ride around the 2½-mile racetrack.) The **Studebaker National Museum** in South Bend has a collection of 80 vehicles spanning the history of Studebaker from 1852 (when the Studebaker brothers started out supplying wagons for the Union Army) to 1966. The collection includes the first and last automobiles built by the former Studebaker Company, as well as four presidential carriages. The **Auburn-Cord-Duesenberg Museum** in Auburn has 140 vintage, antique, classic, and special-interest automobiles in the original 1930 art deco showroom. The luxurious Duesenberg, which sold for up to $20,000 even during the Depression, was the automaker's most famous product. Only 481 were produced, each custom-made for its owner.

Family Favorites The **Indianapolis Zoo,** opened in 1988, features more than 2,000 animals in a ''cageless'' setting. It has one of the world's largest, totally enclosed whale and dolphin pavilions, which can be viewed from above or below the water.

Indiana has an abundance of amusement parks offering something for everyone in the family. **Indiana Beach,** near Monticello, offers a 100-foot drop on the Hoosier Hurricane Roller Coaster, along with camping, lodging, and a water park. **Splash Down Dunes** in Porter offers free falling, twisting, curving water thrill rides, and the largest wave pool in the Midwest, while **Holiday World Theme Park and Splashin' Safari** in Santa Claus has more than 60 rides, shows, games, water slides, an action river, and a wave pool. Holiday World also has the largest wooden roller coaster in the state.

The **Squire Boone Caverns** in Corydon were discovered by the famous Boone brothers—Daniel and Squire—in 1790. (Folk legend says they were hiding out from Indians at the time.) Today, cavern tours with underground waterfalls, stalactites, and stalagmites are offered, while above ground an 1800s pioneer village, petting zoo, grist mill and hay rides, a fossil dig, and sluicing for "gold" are available.

Historic Sites & Towns Several sites pay tribute to Indiana's more famous residents. **The Lincoln Boyhood National Memorial and Living Historical Farm** near Lincoln City covers 80 acres of the Lincoln family's original homestead and is where Abe lived from age 7 to 21, when he went off to Illinois. **The George Rogers Clark National Historical Park** near Vincennes honors Clark's Revolutionary War victories.

Amish Acres in Nappanee is an 80-acre historic farm with 18 restored buildings dedicated to interpreting the ways of the Amish to the outside world. The "plain people's" past is visually portrayed by interpreters and domestic craftsmen at work on the century-old farm, which is listed on the National Register of Historic Places. The Mennonites and the Amish continue to live in the area; horse-drawn buggies driven by black-clad Amish men and women are a common sight throughout the area.

Billie Creek Village in Rockville is a re-created turn-of-the-century village with 38 authentic buildings and three covered bridges. The staff dresses is period costumes; the village features craft demonstrations, horse-pulled wagon rides, and an antique carousel. Parke County features 32 authentic, wooden covered bridges dating from 1856 to 1920; each is listed on the National Register of Historic Places.

New Harmony in western Indiana is the site of two of America's earliest and most important utopian communities. A group of Germans called Harmonists tried to establish a utopian community here between 1814 and 1824. Later Robert Owen, a British social reformer, attempted to create his own utopian society here. The heritage of both communities has been preserved and interpreted at several sites, including the Roofless Church, the Harmonist Labyrinth, and Tillich Park.

The city of **Columbus** is ranked sixth in the nation by the American Institute of Architects for architectural quality and innovation. It began in the 1950s when Cummins, the city's largest employer, financed the architectural fees for 25 buildings. The idea snowballed with other institutions offering to pay for the design of additional buildings. Architects including I M Pei, Eero and Eliel Saarinen, Robert Trent Jones, and Harry Weese have designed projects ranging from banks, churches, and schools to storefronts and golf courses.

EVENTS AND FESTIVALS

- **Little 500,** Bloomington. The Bill Armstrong Stadium on the IU campus hosts a 500-lap bicycle race, with proceeds going to the IU Scholarship Fund. (This is the race memorialized in the Oscar-winning film *Breaking Away*.) Late April. Call 812/855-8311.
- **The Spirit of Vincennes Rendezvous,** near Vincennes. Historical and educational event featuring 18th- and 19th-century crafts, early American foods, period music, and battle re-enactments commemorating George Rogers Clark's capture of Fort Sackville in 1779. May. Call 812/882-7079.
- **Indianapolis 500.** Many race-related activities throughout the month—including queen coronation, mini-marathon, mayor's breakfast, celebrity softball game, ball, parade, hot air balloon race—all leading up to the auto race. Late May.
- **Madison River Days.** This festival highlights Madison's history, with Civil War encampment, historic demonstrations, river boats. June. Call 812/265-2956.
- **Riverfest,** Terre Haute. Homemade raft race on the Wabash, plus crafts, baby contest, Jonah fish fry. June. Call 812/299-1121.
- **Germanfest,** Fort Wayne. A celebration of the state's German heritage, with music, dancing, food, genealogy workshops. June. Call 800/767-7752.
- **Bluegrass Festival,** at the Bill Monroe Bluegrass Hall of Fame and Museum in Bean Blossom. Longest-running bluegrass festival in the country. June. Call 615/868-3333.
- **Thunder on the Ohio,** Evansville. Sanctioned hydroplane race on the Ohio River. June. Call 812/422-1072.
- **Indiana Black Expo Summer Celebration,** Indianapolis. National art competition, health fair, job fair, more than 1,000 exhibit booths. Indiana Convention Center and RCA Dome. July. Call 317/925-2702.
- **International Festival,** Indianapolis. Dozens of ethnic cultural booths, food, entertainment. Indiana State Fairgrounds. October. Call 317/577-8841.

- **Feast of the Hunter's Moon,** Lafayette. Re-creation of a gathering of French and Native Americans in the mid-1700s; voyageurs arrive by canoe on the Wabash River. Authentic crafts, period clothing. Fort Quiatenon Historic Park. October. Call 317/742-8411.
- **Parke County Covered Bridge Festival,** near Rockville. Ten-day countywide festival with covered bridges, historic reenactments, arts and crafts. October. Call 317/569-5226.

SPECTATOR SPORTS

Auto Racing Indianapolis in May means the Indianapolis 500, and the city is known as the World Capital of Motorsports. The main event is the Indianapolis 500 (the largest one-day sporting event in the world) on Memorial Day weekend, but the entire month of May is filled with race-related events from the mini-marathon and the mayor's breakfast to Carburetion Day and the hot-air balloon classic. For years the Indy 500 was the only race held at the Indianapolis Motor Speedway (tel 317/484-6700), on the west side of the city. In 1994 the Brickyard 400, held in early August, joined its schedule. On days when the Speedway is not in use for racing, practice, or testing, tourists can take a mini-ride around the famous 2.5-mile oval.

The Speedway is not the only auto racing spot around, however. Indianapolis Raceway Park (tel 317/291-4090) is the site for ESPN's Thursday Night Thunder shows. One of the finest racing facilities in the country, it has three tracks: an oval, a road course, and the drag strip that hosts the National Hot Rod Association US Nationals on Labor Day weekend. Thanks to the Real Sports Club of America, you can drive a spec racer at the raceway in one of three courses: a three-hour introduction-to-racing class; a three-day competition driving school; or a five-day competition driving school.

Baseball The AAA Indianapolis Indians are the farm team of the Cincinnati Reds. The Indians moved into their new downtown ballpark, Victory Field, in 1996 (tel 317/269-3545). The Fort Wayne Wizards, a Class A farm team of the Minnesota Twins, play at Memorial Stadium in Fort Wayne (tel 219/482-6400).

College Basketball The Hoosiers of Indiana University, led by legendary coach Bobby Knight, play at Assembly Hall in Bloomington (tel 812/555-4006). Their Big Ten rivals, the Boilermakers of Purdue University, play at Mackey Arena in West Lafayette (tel 317/494-3194 or 800/497-7678).

Professional Basketball The Indiana Pacers of the NBA play at Market Square Arena in Indianapo-

---

SELECTED PARKS & RECREATION AREAS

- **Bass Lake State Beach,** 5838 S IN 10, Knox 46534 (tel 219/772-3382 in summer; 219/946-3213 in winter)
- **Brown County State Park,** Box 608, Nashville 47448 (tel 812/988-6406)
- **Chain O'Lakes State Park,** 2355 E 75 S, Albion 46701 (tel 219/636-2654)
- **Clifty Falls State Park,** 1501 Green Rd, Madison 47250 (tel 812/265-1331)
- **Falls of the Ohio State Park,** 201 W Riverside Dr, Clarksville 47129 (tel 812/280-9970)
- **Harmonie State Park,** Rte 1, Box 5A, New Harmony 47631 (tel 812/682-4821)
- **Indiana Dunes State Park,** 1600 N 25 E, Chesterton 46304 (tel 219/926-1952)
- **Lincoln State Park,** Box 216, Lincoln City 47552 (tel 812/937-4710)
- **McCormick's Creek State Park,** Rte 5, Box 282, Spencer (tel 812/829-2235)
- **Mounds State Park,** 4306 Mounds Rd, Anderson 46017 (tel 317/642-6627)
- **Ouabache State Park,** 6720 E 100 S, Bluffton 46714 (tel 219/824-0926)
- **Pokagon State Park,** 450 Lane 100 Lake James, Angola 46703 (tel 219/833-2012)
- **Potato Creek State Park,** 25601 IN 4, N Liberty 46554 (tel 219/656-8186)
- **Shades State Park,** Rte 1, Box 72, Waveland 47989 (tel 317/435-2810)
- **Shakamak State Park,** Rte 2, Box 120, Jasonville 47438 (tel 812/665-2158)
- **Spring Mill State Park,** Box 376, Mitchell 47446 (tel 812/849-4129)
- **Summit Lake State Park,** 5993 N Messick Rd, New Castle 47362-9309 (tel 317/766-5873)
- **Tippecanoe River State Park,** Rte 4, Box 95A, Winamac 46996 (tel 219/946-3213)
- **Turkey Run State Park,** Rte 1, Box 164, Marshall 47859 (tel 317/597-2635)
- **Versailles State Park,** Box 205, US 50, Versailles 47042 (tel 812/689-6424)
- **Whitewater Memorial State Park,** 1418 S IN 101, Liberty 47353 (tel 317/458-5565)

lis (tel 317/263-2100). The Fort Wayne Fury of the CBA play at Memorial Coliseum in Fort Wayne (tel 219/424-6233).

College Football The Fighting Irish of Notre Dame are perhaps *the* quintessential college football team. Catch a game at Notre Dame Stadium (tel 219/631-5000), designed by the legendary player and coach Knute Rockne in 1930.

Professional Football The Indianapolis Colts of the NFL play at the RCA Dome in Indianapolis (tel 317/297-7000).

Hockey The Indianapolis Ice, affiliate of the Chicago Blackhawks and member of the IHL, play at Market Square Arena in Indianapolis (tel 317/266-1234). The Fort Wayne Komets, an independent team in the KHL, play at Memorial Coliseum in Fort Wayne (tel 219/483-0011).

ACTIVITIES A TO Z

Bicycling The Hoosier Bikeway System is made up of six separate but connected bicycle touring routes covering nearly 800 miles of Indiana's countryside. The routes connect cities, parks, and historic sites throughout 31 of the state's 92 counties. The routes are marked and 11 different guidebooks are available by calling the **Indiana Department of Natural Resources** (tel 317/232-4070).

Boating With 550 square miles of water, Indiana offers much for boating enthusiasts. Contact the **Indiana Department of Natural Resources** (tel 317/232-4070) for information.

Camping Hundreds of campsites are available through the state and national park systems as well as at private campgrounds. Contact the Indiana Department of Natural Resources (tel 317/232-4070) or the National Association of RV Parks and Campgrounds (tel 703/734-3000).

Canoeing Copies of the *Indiana Canoeing Guide*, featuring 26 canoe trails on nearly 1,600 miles of rivers, are available from the **Indiana Department of Natural Resources** (tel 317/232-4070). The department can also provide information on the state's canoe liveries.

Fishing Available throughout the state. Contact the Indiana Department of Natural Resources (tel 317/232-4070).

Golfing Courses are located throughout the state. The 36-hole course at **Purdue University** (tel 317/494-3139) is especially well kept; while travelers in the Indianapolis area might want to try the Pete Dye–designed course at the **Indianapolis Motor Speedway** (tel 317/2341-2500).

Hiking Four distinct seasons provide a variety of hiking opportunities. A brochure, trail maps, and a list of hiking organizations are available from the **Indiana Department of Natural Resources** (tel 317/232-4070).

Skiing Even relatively flat Indiana has several options for schussers. Snow skiing is available at Paoli Peaks (tel 812/723-4696) in Paoli and at Ski World (tel 812/968-6638), near Nashville in Brown County. Both parks use snowmaking machines and are very beginner-friendly.

Tobogganing The state's only chilled toboggan run (toboggans provided) is at Angola's **Pokagon State Park** (tel 219/833-2012), in the northern part of the state.

Driving the State

Start	Columbus
Finish	Oliver Winery, north of Bloomington
Distance	Approximately 110 miles
Time	1–2 days
Highlights	Architectural tour, Nashville shops, winter skiing/summer water sliding, Indiana's largest state park, Indiana University, the state's largest winery

Brown County, in the wooded ridges and deep valleys of south central Indiana, has long attracted visitors because of its spectacular scenery. That rural beauty still calls—especially when the arrival of fall turns the leaves into a bright palette of red, gold, and orange—but a new array of recreational activities, shopping opportunities, and world-class entertainment adds to the visitor's choice of things to see and do.

It was in the dawn of this century that the area's beauty began attracting artists like T C Steele and Adolph Shulz, and soon an artists' colony was formed. Brown County continues to thrive as an artistic community today; more than 50 artists call it home. IN 46, the major highway in Brown County, is a two-lane road that twists and turns with the terrain. Smaller roads such as IN 135 are narrow and even more winding and mandate a slower pace as you travel the "hills and hollers" of Brown County.

Overnight stays are available at several locations. Try the rustic **Abe Martin Lodge** at Brown County State Park (tel 812/988-4418), the modest but comfortable **Green Valley Motor Lodge** in Nashville (tel 812/988-0231), or the full-service **Holiday Inn Conference Center** in Columbus (tel 812/372-1541).

For additional information on accommodations, restaurants, and attractions in the region covered by the tour, look under specific cities in the listings portion of this chapter.

We begin our tour just east of Brown County, in the Bartholomew County seat of:

1. **Columbus,** at exit 68 off I-65. Members of the American Institute of Architects have ranked Columbus sixth in the nation for architectural quality and innovation, right behind Chicago, New York, San Francisco, Boston, and Washington. The architectural innovations started with the First Christian Church, designed by Eliel Saarinen, in 1942, and have gone on to include such famous luminaries as Pei, Pelli, Barnes, and Roche.

The first stoplight after exiting the interstate is at a T-road with the junction of IN 11. Turn left, go across the bridge and follow the S curve, staying in the left-hand lane. Turn left onto Washington, drive to 5th St, turn 1 block right to Franklin. The **Columbus Area Visitors Center** (tel 812/379-4457), in the historic Storey House at 506 Fifth St, offers a free multimedia presentation highlighting the community's architecture and its history. They also provide maps for self-guided walking or driving tours, and recorders and tape cassettes outlining architectural highlights may be rented for a small price. Two-hour narrated architectural bus tours leave the center at 10am Monday–Friday, at 10am and 2pm Saturday, at 11am Sunday (advance reservations required). Included in the tour are some buildings not open to the public on a consistent basis, such as St Peter's Lutheran Church.

Take a Break

Be sure to include **Zaharako's Ice Cream Parlor** downtown at 329 Washington St (tel 812/379-9329) in your Columbus itinerary. This old-fashioned soda fountain—opened in 1900 and decorated with Mexican onyx soda fountains, a marble counter, a mahogany-and-marble backbar with Tiffany-style lamps, and stained glass and mirrors—has been operated by the same Greek family for three generations. Sandwiches (try the Sloppy Joe cheeseburger for $1.95) are offered along with homemade ice cream and fountain drinks such as the Green River phosphate. Entrees range from $2 to $6.

Backtrack about 3 miles on IN 46 to I-65. Drive north 8 miles on I-65 to exit 76B. Get off at US 31 and head for outlet shopping at the new:

2. **Horizon Outlet Center** (tel 812/526-9764) in Edinburgh. More than 65 outlets offer savings on brand-name apparel, shoes, gifts, home furnishings, luggage, children's wear, jewelry, cosmetics, and more. Famous names include Tommy Hilfiger, Ann Taylor, Van Heusen, Levi's, Bugle Boy, and Eddie Bauer. Mall hours are 9am–8pm Monday-Saturday, 11am–6pm Sunday.

Stash your packages in the trunk of your car and leave the hustle and bustle of mall shopping; drive

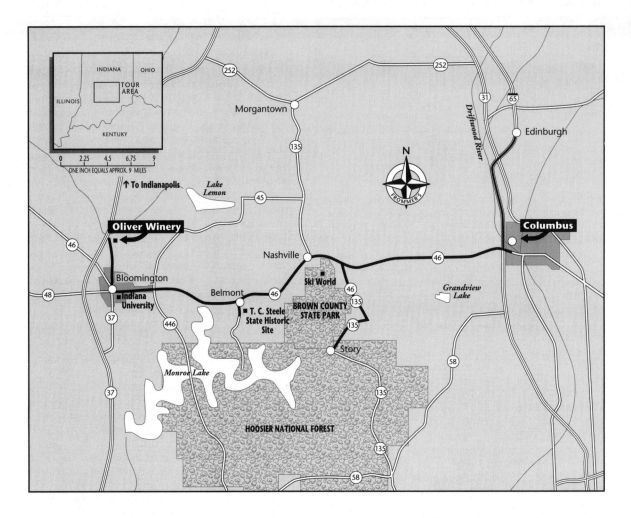

south on I-65 and return to exit 68. This time turn west and head toward Nashville on IN 46, driving a little more than 14 miles to the north entrance of:

3. **Brown County State Park** (tel 812/988-6406), the state's largest park. Its 16,000 acres encompass a lodge, campgrounds, cabins, and the state's largest campground for horseback riders. A swimming pool, tennis courts, and a playground will keep the kids happy, and there's an on-site country store selling picnic supplies in case you didn't bring your own. The park's nature center has a snake exhibit, bird-watching room, and other displays; naturalist services are available year-round. About 70 miles of bridle trails and more than 12 miles of hiking trails lead through the steep forested hills.

Backtrack and leave the park through the north entrance and continue west not quite 2 miles on combined IN 46 and IN 135 to the intersection of IN 46 and IN 135. Turn north on IN 135 to the village of:

4. **Nashville.** This small village of fewer than 900 residents showcases close to 300 antique, craft, and specialty shops, so be prepared for plenty of people and limited parking spaces, especially in the peak autumn season. (Many small lots, as well as the high school parking lot, charge $3 per day for parking space. Take advantage of these spaces, since you won't need a car to get from store to store; the entire shopping district covers only a few blocks.)

You can begin your tour of Nashville with a "train" tour. The **Nashville Express,** a truck disguised as an old locomotive, will take you on a guided tour of the village. It will also stop at some of the hotels; if you're staying at The Seasons or the Brown County Inn, leave your car in the hotel parking lot and take the train downtown. The 20-minute tour is $3 per person. Catch the train at Fearrin's Depot downtown at Franklin and Van Buren Sts or at one of the aforementioned hotels. Tours run April–November, daily 10am–5pm.

The **Brown County Historical Museum** (tel 812/988-6422), one block east of the county courthouse, includes an 1826 blacksmith shop, 1844 cabin, 1879 jail, and 1898 doctor's office. Museum volunteers offer tours from 1–5pm Saturday, Sunday, and holidays May through October for a donation of $1.50.

Stroll leisurely along the main streets and alleys of Nashville for any number of interesting shops where craftspeople work their trade then sell the results. You'll find dulcimers at **Mountain Made Music** on W Main, rugs and clothing at the **Brown County Weavery** on W Franklin, primitive collectibles at **Bear Paw Acres** on Old Schoolhouse Way, clocks and lace doilies at the **Alley Shop** on Molly's Lane, hand-carved candles at **Distinctive Creations** on N Van Buren, and blown glass at the **Lawrence Family Glassblowers** in Franklin Square on Van Buren.

Pay attention to the architecture of the village, too. Many of the homes are more than a century old. While many continue to serve as homes and are not open to the public, their architecture and restoration are visible from the streets and sidewalks. The **Banner Brummet cabin,** two blocks west and one block north of the courthouse at Johnson and Gould Sts, was built in 1830 by Brummet, who laid out the town. The **Judge Hester House,** on Jefferson St near Mound, was built in 1855 by Judge James S Hester, first circuit judge for Brown, Bartholomew and Monroe Counties. The **Bartley House,** at Van Buren and Franklin Sts, built in 1886, was for years the home of photographer Frank Hohenberger, known for his richly detailed black-and-white portraits of turn-of-the-century Brown County residents.

Top country-music performers appear regularly at the **Little Nashville Opry,** 1 mile west of the village on IN 46. Entertainment is also available at the **Pine Box Theater** at 168 Jefferson St or the **Melchoir Marionette Theatre** on S Van Buren St. And there's the **John Dillinger Museum** at 90 W Washington St.

Autumn colors the hills of Brown County more

Take a Break

To many, Brown County means fried biscuits and apple butter, both of which are staples at **The Nashville House** (tel 812/988-4554) at Main and Van Buren Sts. Country fried chicken ($13.75) and fried ham steak with red gravy ($15.75) are the most popular entrees in this rustic eatery, where dinner entrees cost $11 to $17.

---

brightly than just about any other spot in the state, and October is its busiest month. Expect up to 12,000 fall visitors daily in Nashville.

Add your shopping items to the trunk of the car and backtrack on IN 46, driving east on combined IN 46 and IN 135 for 3 miles. When the two roads split, take IN 135 south for a little more than 9 miles to:

5. **Story.** Today, tiny Story is basically a one-owner town, but at the end of the 19th century it was the largest town in the county. It wasn't until the state began to buy up land to create Brown County State Park that the population of Story dwindled and Nashville became the area's business center.

There are now just a few buildings in Story, most of them owned by Bob and Gretchen Haddix. The general store has become a restaurant and four-room B&B.

Take a Break

The gourmet menu at **The Story Inn** (tel 812/988-2273), 6404 S IN 135, changes seasonally to make use of the freshest local ingredients. Popular entrees include herbed chicken and dumplings; filet of beef with pepper sauce served atop a sweet-potato pancake and accompanied by black beans; and orange roughy and julienne vegetables steamed in parchment, served with jasmine white rice and spicy black beans. The restaurant has won awards for its artichoke romano dip and turtle cheesecake. Entrees cost $14–$21.

Retrace your path along IN 135 back to IN 46. Drive west on combined IN 46 and IN 135 3 miles to their junction; turn west onto IN 46 where the two split and drive about 5 miles to:

6. **Ski World,** with downhill and cross-country skiing in the winter months; water slides, dry toboggan rides, go-carts, and bumper cars in the summer. **Country Time Music Hall** at Ski World attracts a regional crowd with featured performer Lloyd Wood and his band.

Continue along IN 46 another 3 miles to Belmont. Watch for signs and turn south onto T C Steele Road and drive 1½ miles to the:

7. **T C Steele State Historic Site,** on the National Register of Historic Places. Theodore Clement Steele was a noted Indiana artist and member of the Hoosier Group of American regional painters. In 1907 he bought 211 acres in Brown County and began construction of the home he named "The

House of the Singing Winds." Steele built a large studio to accommodate his work, and his wife created several acres of gardens.

Steele died in 1926, and the site was bequeathed to the state after his wife's death in 1945. The Indiana State Museum and Historic Sites Division of the Department of Natural Resources provides free guided tours through the house and studio. Self-guided hiking trails and the 90-acre Selma Steele Nature Preserve are also open to the public.

Backtrack to IN 46 and once again turn west. In about 8 miles you'll reach Bloomington. Continue west on IN 46 (3rd St) for a little more than 1 mile. Continue straight west on 3rd St when IN 46 splits from it. In less than 1 mile you will be on the campus of:

8. **Indiana University,** One of the oldest state universities west of the Alleghenies. Founded in 1820, it began as the Indiana State Seminary and graduated its first class ten years later. The campus was rated as one of the five most beautiful in the United States by Thomas A Gaines in his book, *The Campus as a Work of Art.*

Each August, 35,000 IU students descend upon this sleepy midwestern town. And while the city is in many ways typically southern Indiana, the influence of the university is evident in the scholarly bookstores, the ethnic restaurants, and the myriad of languages spoken on the local streets. Locals and students alike follow Big Ten football in the fall, basketball at Assembly Hall in the winter, and the famous Little 500 bicycle race in April.

Highlights on campus include the extensive collection of rare books and manuscripts at the Lilly Library (with a Gutenberg Bible, letters of Ernest Hemingway and George Washington, and an original copy of the Declaration of Independence). Across from the Lilly Library on 7th St is the I M Pei–designed Indiana University Art Museum; in the middle of 7th St is the **Showalter Fountain,** a popular rallying point after IU basketball victories. The **Indiana Memorial Union** is the largest student union in the world, complete with a bowling alley, a hotel, a post office, and several restaurants.

Take a Break

From campus, head downtown to **The Irish Lion** (tel 812/336-9076), 212 W 5th St at Kirkwood Ave. Located in an 1882 tavern, this pub is filled with authentic late–19th-century furnishings like a tin ceiling, a well-worn bar, gas lights, and stained glass windows. Pub-keeper Larry McConnaughy serves authentic Irish dishes such as mutton pie, coddle, and craibheachain as well as seafood flown in fresh from the East Coast. And of course you'll find soda bread and corned beef and cabbage. Local students are especially fond of the yard-long glasses of Guinness. Entrees range from $5 to $9.

From downtown Bloomington, drive north on Walnut for 5 miles to IN 37. Continue north on IN 37 about 3 more miles to the:

9. **Oliver Winery** (tel 812/876-5800), the oldest and largest winery in Indiana. Oliver has produced more than 18 award-winning wines. Each year a different Indiana artist designs the label for that year's vintage. Daily tastings and weekend cellar tours are offered at no charge. Picnic tables surround a small lake next to the winery, and cheese, sausage, crackers, and other picnic foods are available year-round. Free concerts are held on the grounds every Saturday in June and July.

The wine shop is open, with free wine tasting, 10am to 6pm Monday through Saturday, noon to 6pm Sunday. In June and July the wine shop is open until 8pm on Friday and Saturday. Free cellar tours are available on the half hour, noon to 4:30pm Saturday, 1 to 4:30pm Sunday.

From the Oliver Winery, Indianapolis is 35 miles to the north on IN 37. Interstates connect Indianapolis to most other points in the state.

Indiana Listings

Anderson

Seat of Madison County, in central part of state. Site of a Delaware village along the White River, the city is today a center of automobile manufacturing, agriculture, and livestock. Historic Gaslight District downtown contains many restored Victorian homes. **Information:** Anderson/Madison County Visitors & Convention Bureau, 6335 Scatterfield Rd, Anderson, 46013-9603 (tel 317/643-5633).

MOTELS 🏨

≣≣ Best Inns of America

5706 Scatterfield Rd, 46013 (Applewood); tel 317/644-2000 or toll free 800/237-8466; fax 317/644-2000. Exit 26, I-69 to IN 9. Opened in 1991, it's one of the newest in the group of motels located one-half mile from Hoosier Park, 35 miles northwest of Indianapolis. Two-story, red brick structure. **Rooms:** 93 rms. CI 6am/CO 1pm. Nonsmoking rms avail. **Amenities:** 🏨 ⚱ A/C, cable TV w/movies. **Services:** 🛏 🖇 **Facilities:** ⚱ Games rm, washer/dryer. **Rates (CP):** $40 S; $48 D. Extra person $6. Children under age 18 stay free. Min stay special events. Parking: Outdoor, free. AE, CB, DC, DISC, MC, V.

≣≣ Comfort Inn

2205 E 59th St, 46013 (Applewood); tel 317/644-4422 or toll free 800/221-2222; fax 317/644-4422. Exit 26, I-69 to IN 9. Two-story, basic motel one block from interstate. Good for small families. Close to inexpensive restaurants. **Rooms:** 56 rms and stes. CI 2pm/CO 11am. Nonsmoking rms avail. **Amenities:** 🏨 ⚱ A/C, cable TV w/movies. **Services:** 🛏 **Facilities:** ⚱ & Whirlpool. **Rates (CP):** $44 S; $50 D; $53–$58 ste. Extra person $5. Children under age 18 stay free. Min stay special events. Parking: Outdoor, free. AE, CB, DC, DISC, MC, V.

≣≣≣ Holiday Inn

5920 Scatterfield Rd, 46013 (Applewood); tel 317/644-2581 or toll free 800/HOLIDAY; fax 317/642-4585. Exit 26, I-69 to IN 9. Renovated in 1995, this motel with accompanying Holidome has a clean and sparkling appearance inside and out. Located right off the interstate, it's in what local residents call "Motel Alley." Indiana's first pari-mutuel horse-racing track, Hoosier Park, is only half a mile away. **Rooms:** 158 rms and stes. CI 3pm/CO 11am. Nonsmoking rms avail. A little more upscale than the ordinary Holiday Inn. Furniture is slightly higher quality, too. **Amenities:** 🏨 ⚱ 🖥 A/C, cable TV, dataport. Some units w/minibars. **Services:** ✗ 🖇 🛏 **Facilities:** ⚱ ▢400 & 1 restaurant, 1 bar, basketball, games rm, lawn games, whirlpool, washer/dryer. **Rates:** $71 S; $78 D; $157–$200 ste. Extra person $7. Children under age 18 stay free. Min stay special events. Parking: Outdoor, free. AE, CB, DC, DISC, MC, V.

≣≣ Lees Inn

2114 E 59th St, 46013 (Applewood); tel 317/649-2500 or toll free 800/733-5337; fax 317/643-0349. Exit 26, I-69 to IN 9. Located in cluster of motels one block from interstate. Two-story, red brick building with well-maintained areas surrounding parking lots. **Rooms:** 72 rms. CI 2pm/CO noon. Nonsmoking rms avail. Basic rooms. **Amenities:** 🏨 ⚱ A/C, cable TV w/movies. **Services:** 🖙 🖇 🛏 Guests enjoy continental breakfast in unusually attractive room off lobby. **Facilities:** ▢60 ⬜ & **Rates (CP):** $59–$135 S; $67–$143 D. Extra person $8. Children under age 12 stay free. Min stay special events. Parking: Outdoor, free. AE, DC, DISC, MC, V.

≣ Motel 6

5810 Scatterfield Rd, 46013 (Applewood); tel 317/642-9023 or toll free 800/440-6000; fax 317/642-9023. Exit 26, I-69 to IN 9. Usual economy motel, located in congested area just off interstate. Many restaurants and a shopping center nearby. **Rooms:** 125 rms. CI 2pm/CO noon. Nonsmoking rms avail. Standard rooms. **Amenities:** 🏨 ⚱ A/C, cable TV. Free coffee anytime. **Services:** 🛏 🖇 **Facilities:** ⚱ & **Rates:** $29 S; $35 D. Extra person $3. Children under age 17 stay free. Min stay wknds and special events. Parking: Outdoor, free. AE, CB, DC, DISC, MC, V.

ATTRACTIONS 🏛

Mounds State Park

IN 232; tel 317/642-6627. Located atop limestone bluffs overlooking White River, this 259-acre park contains a number of prehistoric tumuli believed to have been constructed by the Adena and Hopewell cultures circa 160 BC. (The largest is an earthwork mound that is 9 feet tall and 1,280 feet in circumference). A naturalist provides historical tours, and excavations are open to viewing. Swimming pool, hiking, cross-country ski trails, campgrounds, and picnic areas offered. Canoe and ski rentals available. **Open:** Daily sunrise–sunset. **$**

Historical Military Armor Museum
2330 Crystal St; tel 317/649-TANK. Collection of military vehicles including half-tracks, trucks, tanks (World War I through Vietnam), and commander's cars. Other items include President Truman's 1947 Cadillac limousine and a Howe fire truck. **Open:** Tues, Thurs, and Sat 1–4pm. **$**

Anderson Fine Arts Center
226 W 8th St; tel 317/649-1248. Located in the Alford House, a restored late 19th-century home. Several galleries display series of changing art exhibits showcasing local, regional, and national artists. **Open:** Tues–Sat 10am–5pm, Sun 2–5pm. **Free**

Angola

Seat of Steuben County. Wooded hills surround this town in the heart of northeastern Indiana's resort area. **Information:** Steuben County Tourism Bureau, 207 S Wayne St, Angola, 46703 (tel 219/665-5386).

MOTEL

Holiday Inn of Angola
3855 N IN 127, 46703; tel 219/665-9471 or toll free 800/HOLIDAY; fax 219/665-5899. Exit 144 off I-80/90. This well-kept, older facility with a new canopy in front is located on a hill with a broad view of nearby Lake James. **Rooms:** 149 rms and stes. CI 2pm/CO noon. Nonsmoking rms avail. **Amenities:** A/C, satel TV w/movies. **Services:** X **Facilities:** 1 restaurant, 1 bar, games rm, whirlpool. Attractive, three-level wooden sun deck and barbecue grills for guest use. View from glass-walled restaurant is especially pretty in fall. Children under age 12 eat free in restaurant. **Rates:** Peak (June 30–Labor Day) $79 S or D; $125–$195 ste. Children under age 19 stay free. Lower rates off-season. Parking: Outdoor, free. Holiday Inn, AARP, and other discounts accepted. AE, CB, DC, DISC, MC, V.

RESORT

Potawatomi Inn and Conference Center
6 Lane 100A, Lake James, 46703; tel 219/833-1077; fax 219/833-4087. 1,200 acres. Named for the Native American tribe that once inhabited this region, this attractive facility sits on the shore of Lake James within state park property. Built in 1927 on rolling land formed by Ice Age glaciers, the structure was modernized in the 1960s; the last renovation, completed in late 1995, added guest rooms but left unchanged the building's original rustic appeal. Many recrea-

tional activities available. **Rooms:** 142 rms and stes; 4 cottages/villas. CI 4pm/CO noon. Nonsmoking rms avail. Patio rooms, located on ground floor with lake view and direct outside access, are studio-style with double bed, sleeper sofa, and extra amenities. Cabins have two double beds but no kitchen facilities. Rooms in oldest section are dated in decor, but comfortable. Ask for a lake view. **Amenities:** A/C, TV w/movies. Some units w/terraces, some w/whirlpools. **Services:** Social director. VCRs available. **Facilities:** 2 restaurants, 2 beaches (lake shore), lifeguard, games rm, lawn games, sauna, whirlpool, playground, washer/dryer. Library, checkers table for children. Recreational opportunities through inn or park office also include nature center, pony rides, hay rides, refrigerated toboggan slide. Gift shop. **Rates:** $50–$56 S or D; $129 ste; $56 cottage/villa. Children under age 18 stay free. Parking: Outdoor, free. Rates listed by number of beds in room, not number of guests. Weekday rates are cheaper; two-for-one rates available Sun–Thurs. Specials offered Thanksgiving–Feb. Reservations may be made up to two years in advance. AE, DISC, MC, V.

RESTAURANT

The Hatchery
118 S Elizabeth St; tel 219/665-9957. 1 block from Soldier's Monument. **Seafood/Steak.** This award-winning restaurant earns its reputation for fine dining with maximum privacy in an upscale atmosphere. The nightly menu features fresh fish flown in daily, as well as entrees like rack of lamb baked with herb crust and served with cabernet-mint sauce, and grilled medallions of beef with blue crabmeat and béarnaise sauce. Extensive wine list, occasional wine-tasting events. The dark bar area (where there are two TVs) serves a fairly good, separate menu. **FYI:** Reservations recommended. Piano. Dress code. **Open:** Lunch Tues–Fri 11am–1:30pm; dinner Mon–Thurs 5–9pm, Fri–Sat 5–10pm. **Prices:** Main courses $17–$21. AE, CB, DC, DISC, MC, V. ♥

ATTRACTION

Fun Spot Amusement Park
2365 N 200 W; tel 219/833-2972. Features more than 20 rides, including two roller coasters, a dual water flume, a 50-foot Ferris wheel, and numerous kiddie rides. Other highlights include beach volleyball courts, a miniature-golf course, go-cart track, picnic facilities, and live entertainment. **Open:** Mid-May–mid-Sept, Tues–Fri 11am, Sat–Sun 10am. **$$$**

Auburn

Seat of DeKalb County, in northeast part of state. Today, the town is a busy farm trading center; in the early part of this century, the now-defunct Auburn Automobile Company was one of the foremost car manufacturers in the country. **Information:** Auburn Chamber of Commerce, 136 W 7th St, PO Box 168, Auburn, 46706 (tel 219/925-2100).

ATTRACTION 📷

Auburn Cord Duesenberg Museum
1600 S Wayne St; tel 219/925-1444. On display in the art deco–style showrooms of the now-defunct Auburn Automobile Company are more than 100 vintage, antique, and classic automobiles from horseless carriages to the sports cars of today. Among the types of cars on display are Duesenberg, Packard, Cord, Cadillac, Auburn, and Rolls Royce. **Open:** Daily 9am–5pm. $$$

Batesville

Neat, compact southeast Indiana town founded by German artisans. Nearby, a restored 14-mile section of the Whitewater Canal offers horse-drawn boat cruises and a gristmill. **Information:** Batesville Area Chamber of Commerce, 132 S Main St, Batesville, 47006 (tel 812/934-3101).

HOTEL 📷

≣≣≣ The Sherman House Inn
35 S Main St, 47006; tel 812/934-2407 or toll free 800/445-4939; fax 812/934-1230. Exit 149 off I-74, 6 blocks S on IN 229. Old World charm in one of the area's oldest buildings, opened as a coaching tavern in 1852. Exceptional value. Batesville, halfway between Indianapolis and Cincinnati, is known for fine furniture. **Rooms:** 23 rms, stes, and effic. CI 1pm/CO 11am. Nonsmoking rms avail. Quaint rooms, like those usually found in better bed-and-breakfasts. **Amenities:** 📷 🍷 A/C, cable TV. 1 unit w/minibar, 1 w/whirlpool. **Services:** ✗ 🍽 **Facilities:** 🔲 250 🔲 ♿ 1 restaurant (see "Restaurants" below), 1 bar. **Rates:** $35–$45 S; $40–$49 D; $49–$59 ste; $50–$59 effic. Children under age 12 stay free. Parking: Outdoor, free. AE, CB, DC, MC, V.

RESTAURANT 🍴

⑤ ✹ Sherman House
35 S Main St; tel 812/934-2407. Exit 149 off I-74, 6 blocks S on IN 229. **American/German.** Originally an 1852 coaching tavern, it features old-world charm with a Bavarian influence. With continued modernization, the inn shows no signs of age or neglect. Chef/general manager Joseph Shook offers popular standards like Wiener schnitzel, sauerbraten with red cabbage, sausage and kraut. Smaller portions available at reduced price. **FYI:** Reservations recommended. Children's menu. **Open:** Mon–Thurs 6:30am–9pm, Fri–Sat 6:30am–10pm, Sun 6:30am–8pm. **Prices:** Main courses $9–$16. AE, CB, DC, MC, V. ♥ 🏛 👪 🔲 ♿

Bedford

Seat of Lawrence County. This southern Indiana town is the center of the state's limestone quarrying industry. The Hoosier National Forest is both north and south of town, spreading through nine counties. **Information:** Bedford Area Chamber of Commerce, 1116 16th St, PO Box 68, Beford, 47421-0068 (tel 812/275-4493).

MOTELS 📷

≣ Mark III Motel
1711 M St, 47421; tel 812/275-5935. Family-owned and -operated, comfortable, standard motel in town. Some long-term guests, such as construction crews. It's a bus stop for American Trailways. Mama's restaurant is next door. **Rooms:** 21 rms. CI open/CO 11am. Nonsmoking rms avail. **Amenities:** 📷 🍷 🔲 A/C, cable TV w/movies, dataport. **Services:** 🍽 🍽 Small pets only. **Facilities:** ♿ **Rates:** $30 S; $34 D. Extra person $3. Children under age 18 stay free. Parking: Outdoor, free. AE, DC, DISC, MC, V.

≣ Plaza Motel
US 50 E, 47421; tel 812/834-5522. 10 mi E of IN 37. Family-owned and -operated. Close to Lake Monroe, Hidden Falls Salvation Army Camp, and Spring Mill State Park. Often takes the spillover during the busiest seasons in Brown County and Bloomington. **Rooms:** 19 rms and effic. CI noon/CO 11am. Standard rooms. **Amenities:** A/C, satel TV, refrig. No phone. **Services:** 🍽 **Facilities:** 🔲 Basketball, games rm, playground, washer/dryer. **Rates:** Peak (Apr–Sept) $25–$40 S or D. Children under age 18 stay free. Lower rates off-season. Parking: Outdoor, free. Efficiencies rented to long-term guests only for $110 per person per week. DISC, MC, V.

ATTRACTIONS 📷

Bluespring Caverns
US 50; tel 812/279-9471. From within lighted boats, visitors can see rare blind fish and crayfish and the intricately weathered limestone walls of this extensive underground cave system. Temperature is a constant 52°; a light jacket is recommended. **Open:** Apr, Sat–Sun 9am–5pm; May–Oct, daily 9am–5pm. $$$

Hoosier National Forest
Forest Headquarters, 811 Constitution Ave; tel 812/275-5987. Approximately 189,000 acres of scenic wonders—including huge rock bluffs, woods, waterfalls, streams, and box canyons—are part of this huge park. Activities include swimming, fishing, hunting, hiking, and boating. Campsites (available on a first-come basis) are available at the recreation areas of Hardin Ridge in Monroe County; German Ridge, Saddle Lake, Celina Lake in Perry County; and Springs Valley in Orange County. The National Forest also encompasses the

88-acre Pioneer Mothers Memorial Forest (located south of Bedford) with its stand of huge white oak and black walnut trees. **Open:** Daily 24 hours. **Free**

Bloomington

Seat of Monroe County, in the central part of the state. The main campus of Indiana University, with its notable library and museums and its world-class music school, is located here, as is a small but flourishing winemaking industry. Lake Monroe, McCormick Creek, and Brown County State Park are all nearby. **Information:** Bloomington County Convention & Visitors Bureau, 2855 N Walnut St, Bloomington, 47404 (tel 812/334-8900).

HOTEL 🏨

▤▤▤ Holiday Inn

1710 Kinser Pike, 47404; tel 812/334-3252 or toll free 800/HOLIDAY; fax 812/333-1702. Bloomington's largest full-service hotel. Tastefully decorated throughout. Close to Indiana University, Lake Monroe, and Brown County. **Rooms:** 187 rms and stes. CI 3pm/CO noon. Nonsmoking rms avail. **Amenities:** 🛁 🍷 📺 A/C, cable TV w/movies. **Services:** ✕ 🚐 🗄 🛎 Complimentary shuttle service to and from Indiana University and Monroe County Airport. **Facilities:** 🏋 🎱 🏊 ⚫ 1 restaurant, 1 bar (w/entertainment), games rm, sauna, whirlpool. Complimentary YMCA privileges. **Rates (BB):** $83–$135 S or D; $99–$135 ste. Extra person $6. Children under age 18 stay free. Parking: Outdoor, free. AE, CB, DC, DISC, MC, V.

MOTELS

▤▤ Comfort Inn

1722 N Walnut, 47401; tel 812/339-1919 or toll free 800/222-2121; fax 812/339-2052. Good for business travelers and families. Close to Indiana University (within walking distance of stadium) and Brown County State Park. **Rooms:** 89 rms and stes. Executive level. CI 3pm/CO noon. Nonsmoking rms avail. Every room has indoor and outdoor entrances. **Amenities:** 🛁 A/C, cable TV, dataport. Some units w/whirlpools. Some rooms have two phones, coffeemakers, microwaves, and refrigerators. Executive suite has six-person whirlpool. **Services:** 🗄 🛎 Continental breakfast with cereal offered in a dining room setting. **Facilities:** 🏋 🏊 **Rates (CP):** $52–$62 S or D; $125 ste. Extra person $5. Children under age 18 stay free. Min stay special events. Parking: Outdoor, free. AE, DC, DISC, MC, V.

▤ Courtyard Inn

4501 E 3rd St, 47401; tel 812/332-2141; fax 812/332-8441. 2½ mi E of College Mall. On Bloomington's east side, convenient to Indiana University, College Mall, Lake Monroe, and Brown County. Adjacent to Fisherman's Dock restaurant. **Rooms:** 99 rms. CI 3pm/CO noon. Nonsmoking rms avail. Recently refurbished rooms. Bathroom counter space is exceptionally large. **Amenities:** 🛁 A/C, cable TV. **Services:** 🗄 🛎 🐾 **Facilities:** 🏋 ⚫ **Rates (CP):** $40–$46 S or D. Extra person $6. Parking: Outdoor, free. AE, DC, DISC, MC, V.

▤ Days Inn Bloomington

200 Matlock Rd, PO Box 2475, 47402; tel 812/336-0905 or toll free 800/DAYS-INN; fax 812/336-0905 ext 153. Standard budget motel near Indiana University (within walking distance of football and basketball stadiums). Close to Lake Monroe, Brown County. Close to 24-hour restaurants. **Rooms:** 49 rms, stes, and effic. CI 3pm/CO noon. Nonsmoking rms avail. **Amenities:** 🛁 A/C, cable TV. 1 unit w/whirlpool. **Services:** 🆚 🗄 🛎 🐾 **Facilities:** 🏃 🏊 📺 ⚫ **Rates (CP):** Peak (Apr–Oct) $49–$54 S or D; $125 ste; $54–$85 effic. Extra person $5. Children under age 18 stay free. Lower rates off-season. Parking: Outdoor, free. Discounts avail, including military discount. AE, CB, DC, DISC, MC, V.

INN

▤▤▤ Grant Street Inn

310 N Grant St, 47408; tel 812/334-2353 or toll free 800/328-4350; fax 812/331-8673. At 7th St, 2 blocks from Indiana University. Charming Victorian-style bed-and-breakfast created by moving the 1883 Ziegler House and connecting it to the Gilstrap House via the breakfast room. Large porch and terrace areas. Walking distance to downtown Bloomington and Indiana University. Unsuitable for children under 13. **Rooms:** 14 rms and stes. CI 3pm/CO noon. Nonsmoking rms avail. Each room has several windows and is individually decorated, some with antiques. Some rooms have outside entrances. **Amenities:** 🛁 🍷 A/C, cable TV. Some units w/terraces, some w/fireplaces, some w/whirlpools. **Services:** 🗄 Afternoon tea served. **Facilities:** Washer/dryer, guest lounge. **Rates (BB):** $75–$95 S; $80–$100 D; $95–$125 ste. Extra person $5. Higher rates for special events/hols. Parking: Outdoor, free. AE, DISC, MC, V.

RESTAURANTS 🍴

Grisanti's

850 Auto Mall Rd; tel 812/339-9391. S of College Mall off Cadillac Buick Blvd. **Italian.** A casual Italian bistro popular for Friday night dates and weekend visits with the parents. Special menu options include cheese lasagna (with layers of provolone, Romano, mozzarella, Parmesan, and ricotta) served with fresh marinara and bolognese meat sauces; lightly fried eggplant topped with ricotta, Parmesan, mozzarella, and fresh marinara; and grilled chicken breast marinated in a light lemon-basil sauce and served with angel-hair pasta and sautéed vegetables. Unlimited Tuscan-style bread, salad, and beverage. Carryout available. **FYI:** Reservations accepted. Children's menu. **Open:** Mon–Thurs 11am–10pm, Fri–Sat 11am–11pm, Sun 11am–9pm. **Prices:** Main courses $7–$13. AE, DC, DISC, MC, V. 🍷 ⚫

★ **Irish Lion**
212 W 5th St (Downtown); tel 812/336-9076. **Irish.** Located in an 1882 tavern and filled with the sort of items—tin ceiling, well-worn bar, gas lights, stained-glass windows, and mounted animals—one might expect to see in Dublin. Pubkeeper Larry McConnaughy serves authentic Irish pub grub and some fancier meals, including mutton pie, Celtic stew, cabbage soup, coddle, and New England oysters flown in fresh. Blarney puffballs are the most-requested appetizer, Irish apple walnut cake and whiskey pie are favorite desserts. Soda bread and corned beef and cabbage are always available. Irish, English, and German beers on tap. **FYI:** Reservations accepted. **Open:** Mon–Sat 11am–2am, Sun 4pm–12:30am. Closed Dec 25–Jan 4. **Prices:** Main courses $9–$16. AE, DC, DISC, MC, V. ▮

Norbu Cafe
415 E 4th St; tel 812/335-1297. Near Indiana University. **Himalayan.** Upscale Himalayan cuisine in the middle of Indiana. Each of the 50 tables in the intimate dining room are decorated with delicate flowers. Featured are *tsei thukpa dhangma* (cold noodles with vegetables), vegetarian curry, and the house stew of curried beef or chicken with potatoes, vegetables, mushrooms, and bean thread. *Tenmo* (homemade steamed rolls) and *momo* (steamed dumplings filled with beef and vegetables) are good to start, while green tea ice cream makes a nice finish. **FYI:** Reservations accepted. No liquor license. No smoking. **Open:** Lunch Mon–Fri 11:30am–2:30pm; dinner Mon–Thurs 5:30–9pm, Fri–Sun 5–9:30pm. **Prices:** Main courses $7–$9. MC, V.

Runcible Spoon
1412 E 6th St; tel 812/334-3997. 1 block off Kirkwood between Dunn and Grant; near Indiana University. **Cafe.** A casual coffeehouse popular with students from nearby Indiana University. The bohemian atmosphere features well-worn wooden booths, artwork on the walls, and a front porch and patio for summertime dining. The menu includes sandwiches—such as tofu Reuben or ham and swiss on rye—but the Runcible is best known for its desserts (like carrot cake or fruit pies), handrolled bagels, and gourmet coffee made from freshly roasted beans. The funkiness even extends to the unisex bathroom, where a school of goldfish swim in the bathtub. Monthly poetry readings. **FYI:** Reservations not accepted. No liquor license. No smoking. **Open:** Sun–Thurs 8am–11pm, Fri–Sat 8:30am–12:30am, Sun 8am–2pm. **Prices:** Lunch main courses $3–$6. CB, DC, MC, V.

Snow Lion
113 S Grant; tel 812/336-0835. Near Indiana University. **Tibetan.** Owned and operated by a nephew of the 14th Dalai Lama, this was the second Tibetan restaurant to open in the United States. Although classic Tibetan dishes are available, the menu draws heavily on Indian, Chinese, Japanese, and even Cajun influences as well. (The chef will accommodate those who prefer milder flavors.) Popular picks: *thukpa ngopa* (fried egg noodles with beef strips and vegetables), *pinsha*

(bean thread sautéed with strips of beef and vegetables), and Seafood Delight (lobster, scallops, shrimp, and vegetables). *Dey see* (Tibetan rice pudding) served for dessert. **FYI:** Reservations accepted. No liquor license. Additional location: 2825 Middle Rd, Columbus (tel 376-7674). **Open:** Lunch Mon–Fri 11:30am–2pm; dinner daily 5–10pm. **Prices:** Main courses $7–$11. MC, V. &

ATTRACTIONS 🏛

Indiana University
Tel 812/855-9053. Basketball is what many people think of when Indiana University is mentioned, although there's much more to the school than that. Founded in 1820, IU is one of the nation's leading state universities and is currently enrolling approximately 35,000 students. The **Lilly Library of Rare Books and Manuscripts** houses over 400,000 books and six million manuscripts, and boasts a Gutenberg Bible, four Shakespeare folios, and Thomas Jefferson's copy of the Bill of Rights. The **Glenn A Black Lab of Archaeology** features a diverse collection, including artifacts of Indiana's first inhabitants as well as those of more recent tribal cultures. The IU School of Music is world renowned, and the **Hoagy Carmichael Room** in the Student Union Building showcases memorabilia from the famous songwriter and IU alumnus. Another attraction on the campus is the **Indiana University Cyclotron**, housing a variable-energy light-ion cyclotron, which can be toured. Also of interest are the Thomas Hart Benton murals featured in the auditorium of Woodburn Hall, and the University Theater. **Free**

Indiana University Art Museum
Fine Arts Plaza at E 7th St; tel 812/855-5445. Postmodern building designed by renowned architect I M Pei. Inside is a permanent collection of over 30,000 works, with representative pieces by Matisse, Monet, Picasso, Rodin, and Warhol, as well as sculpture, jewelry, woodcarvings, and other works from early Japanese and Greek cultures. The African, Oceanic, and Art of the Americas collections are especially impressive. **Open:** Wed–Thurs 10am–5pm, Fri 10am–8pm, Sat–Sun noon–5pm. **Free**

Jordan Hall Greenhouse
E 3rd St; tel 812/855-7717. Located on the Indiana University campus, this large collection of flora is maintained by the Department of Biology and includes exotic, tropical, and desert plants. **Open:** Mon–Fri 8am–4pm, Sat–Sun 9am–3pm. **Free**

Musical Arts Center
Indiana University School of Music; tel 812/855-9846. Headquarters of the world-renowned IU School of Music. (Alumni include violin prodigy Joshua Bell, and the faculty includes retired ballerina Patricia McBride.) Year-round schedule of student performances includes the opera department (recent productions have included *Così Fan Tutte*, *Rigoletto*, *Hansel and Gretel*, and *The Tales of Hoffman*) and the ballet department. In addition, the School of Music presents an Orchestra

Concert Series, Band Concert Series, Jazz Concert Series, and Choral Concert Series, with visiting artists. **Open:** Box office, Mon–Fri noon–4:45pm $$$$

Monroe County Historical Society Museum
202 E 6th St; tel 812/332-2517. Located in an early 20th-century Classical-style structure that once served as a library, this local history museum houses exhibits on early settlers, Native Americans, and the limestone industry. Clothing, farm and household implements, and a log cabin are some of the main displays. **Open:** Tues–Fri 10am–5pm, Sat 10am–4pm, Sun 1–4pm. **Free**

Butler Winery
1022 N College Ave; tel 812/339-7233. Although the actual vineyard is located 9 mi NE of Bloomington, the entire wine-making process (from crushing the grapes to bottling the finished product) is conducted in this 80-year-old house right in the heart of town. Free tours and tastings; garden with outdoor seating. **Open:** Tues–Sat 11am–6pm, Sun noon–7pm. **Free**

Oliver Winery
8024 N IN 37; tel 812/876-5800. Produces wines from vinifera grapes such as merlot, sauvignon blanc, and gewürztraminer. Free wine tastings, weekend cellar tours, outdoor picnic area. Gift shop also sells grape preserves and other gift items. **Open:** Mon–Thurs 10am–6pm, Fri–Sat 10am–8pm, Sun noon–6pm. **Free**

Clarksville

Founded in 1784 by George Rogers Clark. The land overlooked Corn Island, on which Clark had established a military post. Today, Clarksville is a northern suburb of Louisville, KY, on the opposite side of the Ohio River. **Information:** Clark-Floyd County Convention & Visitors Bureau, 540 Marriott Dr, #7, Clarksville, 47129 (tel 812/282-6654).

RESTAURANT 🍴

Major McCulloch Steakhouse
318 W IN 131; tel 812/945-0611. Exit 4 off I-65; 1½ mi W. **American/Steak.** Built in 1870, this Italianate-style farmhouse is the last remaining structure associated with the McCullough family, who were among the early settlers of Clarksville. The family operated a farm on the site for nearly 100 years, until the house was sold in the 1940s. Today, McCulloch family photos line the walls. The kitchen staff specializes in steak, prime rib, rack of ribs, and smothered chicken breast. Entrees are served with fried biscuits and apple butter. Casual dining is downstairs; the upstairs room is more formal. Carryout available. **FYI:** Reservations accepted. Guitar. Children's menu. **Open:** Mon–Thurs 11am–10pm, Fri–Sat 11am–midnight, Sun 11am–9pm. **Prices:** Main courses $8–$16. AE, CB, DISC, MC, V. 🅿 🏠 ♿

ATTRACTIONS 📷

RiverFair Family Fun Park, in the River Falls Mall
951 E IN 131; tel 812/284-FAIR. Located on the second level of the River Falls Mall, this indoor amusement park features bumper cars, a carousel, a miniature-golf course, and games of skill. **Open:** Mon–Thurs 11am–9pm, Fri–Sat 10am–10pm, Sun noon–6pm. $$

Wave Tek Water Park
Stanifer Ave exit off I-65; tel 812/282-8509. Named for its Olympic-size pool (which generates three-foot waves every few minutes), Wave-Tek also boasts a giant water roller coaster and other splashy rides. **Open:** Mem Day–Labor Day, daily 10am–6pm. $$$

Columbus

Seat of Bartholomew County, in south-central part of state. Columbus was founded in 1820 and served as a Union depot during the Civil War. In recent years, this attractive city has won international acclaim for its array of masterpieces by 20th-century architects including Eliel Saarinen, I M Pei, and Eliot Noyes. **Information:** Columbus Area Visitors Center, PO Box 1589, Columbus, 47201 (tel 812/378-2622 or toll free 800/468-6564).

HOTEL 🏨

☰☰☰ Holiday Inn Conference Center
2480 Jonathan Moore Pike, 47201; tel 812/372-1541 or toll free 800/HOLIDAY; fax 812/378-9049. Exit 68 off I-65. Charming turn-of-the-century decor in part of the hotel with furnishings from historic buildings, including stained and etched glass, marble and bronze sculptures, intricate wood carvings, and an antique register. Exteriors of rooms facing Holidome look like turn-of-the-century storefronts. **Rooms:** 253 rms and stes. CI 4pm/CO noon. Nonsmoking rms avail. Some suites have an international decor. **Amenities:** 📺 ♨ A/C, satel TV w/movies, dataport, voice mail. Some units w/terraces. Many rooms have two telephones. Some have hair dryers, refrigerators, and microwaves. Fax capabilities available in every room. Voice mail available. **Services:** ✕ 📠 ↻ Tours of hotel, with emphasis on historic furnishings, available. **Facilities:** 🏌 👥 ▢1000▢ 1 restaurant, 2 bars (1 w/entertainment), games rm, sauna, whirlpool, beauty salon. In-house bakery offers wide selection of homemade breads and pastries. First Holidome in Indiana has nine-hole putting green, heated pool, table tennis, billiards, tanning beds. Audio-visual equipment available for meetings. Complimentary passes to local athletic club. **Rates:** $69–$109 S; $79–$119 D; $125–$150 ste. Extra person $10. Children under age 18 stay free. Parking: Outdoor, free. AE, CB, DC, DISC, JCB, MC, V.

MOTEL

≡≡≡ Ramada Inn

2485 Jonathan Moore Pike, 47201; tel 812/376-3051 or toll free 800/272-6232; fax 812/376-0949. Exit 68 off I-65. Sunken area with fireplace in lobby. Close to Brown County. **Rooms:** 115 rms, stes. CI 3pm/CO noon. Nonsmoking rms avail. **Amenities:** 📶 🛁 📺 🍴 A/C, cable TV. All units w/terraces. Most rooms have refrigerators, suites have hot tubs. **Services:** ✗ 🚐 🛋 🍴 Free expanded continental breakfast Sun–Thurs. **Facilities:** 🏋 ⛺ 🛥 🏊 🍴 🥤 ⛳ 1 restaurant, 2 bars (1 w/entertainment), volleyball, whirlpool. Stocked lake offers free fishing. **Rates (BB):** Peak (mid-Sept–mid-Nov) $62–$96 S; $70–$106 D; $165 ste. Extra person $8. Children under age 18 stay free. Lower rates off-season. Parking: Outdoor, free. AE, CB, DC, DISC, JCB, MC, V.

RESTAURANT 🍽

Weinantz Food & Spirits

3450 Jonathan Moore Pike; tel 812/379-2323. Exit 68 off I-65; ¼ mi W on IN 46. **American.** The casual atmosphere at this family-owned and -operated eatery is accompanied by local artwork (mostly sculptures, oils, and water colors). The prime rib and chicken breast Romanoff (stuffed with broccoli, herbed rice, pecans, and cheddar cheese, and served with béarnaise sauce) are notable, as well as the pork chops, ribs, and orange roughy. Desserts range from fruit cobblers to turtle sundaes and hot fudge balls. Two of owner Robert Weinantz's sons grow popcorn locally; it's sold alone or in gift packages at the restaurant. Small selection of carryout liquor available. **FYI:** Reservations accepted. Piano. Children's menu. **Open:** Mon–Thurs 11am–9:30pm, Fri 11am–10pm, Sat 5–10pm. **Prices:** Main courses $9–$17. AE, CB, DC, DISC, MC, V. 👥 ♿

REFRESHMENT STOP 🍵

★ Zaharako's Ice Cream Parlor

329 Washington St (Downtown); tel 812/379-9329. **Ice cream.** An old-fashioned soda fountain originally opened in 1900 that features Mexican onyx soda fountains bought from the St Louis World Exposition and a German player piano-type pipe organ with 185 pipes. The ambience in the dining room is pure 1950s, with gray, marbled formica kitchen tables, mirrored walls, and child-size round table and ice cream parlor chairs. The most popular items at this local favorite are the cheeseburger and the homemade ice creams. **Open:** Mon–Sat 10am–4pm. No CC. ■ 👥

Corydon

Seat of Harrison County, in southern Indiana. Scene of the only Civil War battle fought on Indiana soil, Corydon was the seat of the Indiana Territorial government from 1813 to 1816. Squire Boone (brother of Daniel) discovered nearby Squire Boone Caverns. **Information:** Chamber of Commerce of Harrison County, 310 N Elm St, Corydon, 47112 (tel 812/738-2137).

MOTELS 🏨

≡ Best Western Old Capitol Inn

I-64 and IN 135, PO Box 124, 47112; tel 812/738-4192 or toll free 800/528-1234; fax 812/738-4192. Exit 105 off I-64. An older motel, with a white Colonial appearance. It's a boarding station for the 1883 scenic railroad, which offers a 16-mile excursion with special events, such as train robberies on Sat and Sun, Mem Day–Labor Day. **Rooms:** 77 rms. CI 3pm/CO noon. Nonsmoking rms avail. **Amenities:** 📶 A/C, cable TV w/movies, dataport. **Services:** 🛋 🍴 🐾 **Facilities:** 🏋 🍴 ♿ Washer/dryer. **Rates:** $48–$66 S or D. Extra person $4. Children under age 12 stay free. Parking: Outdoor, free. AE, CB, DC, DISC, JCB, MC, V.

≡≡ Budgetel Inn

2495 Landmark Ave, PO Box 370, 47112; tel 812/738-1500 or toll free 800/428-3438; fax 812/738-1503. Exit 105 off I-64; S on IN 135. Well maintained. **Rooms:** 80 rms, stes, and effic. CI open/CO noon. Nonsmoking rms avail. Larger-than-average rooms. **Amenities:** 📶 📺 A/C, cable TV, dataport. **Services:** 🍴 **Facilities:** 🍴 ♿ Washer/dryer. **Rates (CP):** $45 S; $52 D; $51–$58 ste; $45–$52 effic. Extra person $7. Children under age 18 stay free. Parking: Outdoor, free. Guests stay free on 13th night. AE, CB, DC, DISC, MC, V.

INN

≡≡≡ Kintner House Inn

101 N Capitol St, 47112; tel 812/738-2020; fax 812/738-7430. Exit 105 off I-64; at Chestnut St. Elegant 1873 bed-and-breakfast, restored in 1986, on National Register of Historic Places. Original wood floors, antique furniture, rocking chairs on porch. Called a "hideaway for romantics," it was featured in two 1991 Hallmark Christmas cards. Located in historic downtown Corydon, Indiana's first state capital. **Rooms:** 15 rms and effic. CI 1pm/CO 11am. No smoking. Victorian theme on first and second floors, country ambience on third. **Amenities:** 📶 A/C, cable TV. Some units w/fireplaces. Five rooms have fireplaces, seven have VCRs. **Services:** 🛋 🍴 Afternoon tea served. Breakfast may include ham and cheese puffs, or sausage and cheese grits. Apple cider or lemonade and cookies available daily until 10pm. Free gift for honeymooners. Pet boarding available nearby. **Facilities:** 🍴 ♿ Games rm, guest lounge w/TV. **Rates (BB):** $39–$89 D; $59–$79 effic. Extra person $5. Children under age 18 stay free. Higher rates for special events/hols. Parking: Outdoor, free. AE, CB, DC, DISC, MC, V.

ATTRACTIONS

Squire Boone Caverns and Village
Squire Boone Caverns Rd; tel 812/732-4381. 10 mi S of Corydon on IN 135, then 3 mi E. In 1790, Daniel Boone's brother came upon these caverns while he was hiding from hostile natives. The caverns themselves feature an unusual variety of underground formations: travertine and twisted helictite formations, stalactites, stalagmites, and rimstone dams, as well as underground streams and waterfalls. Above ground, the village re-creates the feel of Daniel Boone's era and includes a restored water-powered gristmill, a petting zoo, log cabin craft shops with demonstrations, hayrides, and a 110-acre forest featuring trails and picnic areas. A 73-step spiral staircase must be climbed on the 1-hour tour of the caverns. **Open:** Mem Day–Labor Day, daily 10am–6pm. **$$$$**

Marengo Cave National Landmark
Marengo Cave Rd, off I-64, Marengo; tel 812/365-2705. Visitors can take one of two guided tours through this underground cave. The Crystal Palace tour winds its way through rooms filled with stalagmites and flowstone deposits to the Crystal Palace cave room. The Dripstone Trail tour leads visitors past a profusion of soda-straw formations, helictites, and stalagmites. Aboveground recreation area offers hiking, fishing, horseback riding, canoeing, and picnicking. **Open:** Daily 9am–5pm. **$$$**

Corydon 1883 Scenic Railroad
Walnut and Water Sts; tel 812/738-3171. The Louisville, New Albany & Corydon Railroad, established in 1883 to haul freight from Corydon to Corydon Junction, is one of the shortest railroads in the nation at just under 8 miles in length. Each weekend during the spring-to-fall season, the railroad offers 1½-hour round-trip tours through Southern Indiana hill country. The depot exhibits antique railroad equipment. **Open:** Apr–Sept, Sat–Sun, call for schedule. **$$$$**

Crawfordsville

Seat of Montgomery County, in west-central part of state. Home of Wabash Collage, this small city is a center of agriculture and dairy production in the state. **Information:** Montgomery County Convention & Visitors Bureau, 412 E Main St, Crawfordsville, 47933 (tel 317/362-5200).

MOTELS

Holiday Inn
2500 N Lafayette Rd, 47933; tel 317/362-8700 or toll free 800/465-4329. Exit 34 off I-74. Tastefully decorated with nice landscaping. Canoeing available on nearby Sugar Creek. **Rooms:** 150 rms. CI 3pm/CO noon. Nonsmoking rms avail. **Amenities:** A/C, cable TV w/movies, dataport. **Services:** Babysitting. **Facilities:** 1 restaurant, 1 bar (w/entertainment), games rm, washer/dryer. **Rates:** $56–

$80 S or D. Children under age 19 stay free. Parking: Outdoor, free. Special food and lodging packages sometimes avail. AE, CB, DC, DISC, JCB, MC, V.

Super 8 Motel
1025 Corey Blvd, 47933; tel 317/364-9999 or toll free 800/800-8000. Exit 34 off I-74. More than just a budget chain motel. Canoeing available on scenic Sugar Creek. **Rooms:** 58 rms and stes. CI 11am/CO 11am. Nonsmoking rms avail. All rooms have recliners. Some rooms have waterbeds. A triple room is available. **Amenities:** A/C, cable TV w/movies. Some units w/whirlpools. **Services:** **Facilities:** Whirlpool, washer/dryer. **Rates (CP):** Peak (May–Oct) $40–$57 S or D; $99 ste. Extra person $5. Children under age 12 stay free. Lower rates off-season. Parking: Outdoor, free. AE, CB, DC, DISC, MC, V.

RESTAURANTS

The Bungalow
210 E Pike St (Downtown); tel 317/362-2596. **American/Steak.** Dining in a cozy, quaint house with old-fashioned charm: lace curtains, hatboxes, waiters in tuxedo shirts and cummerbunds. Customers can request specific bone china cups and saucers to use from the collection on display at the entrance. Photos of movie stars cover the walls, and the collection of old hats in the lounge includes one from *This is Your Life*'s Ralph Edwards. The specialty is steak grilled outdoors, available year-round. **FYI:** Reservations recommended. Guitar/piano. Children's menu. **Open:** Lunch Mon–Fri 11am–2pm; dinner Mon 4:30pm–midnight, Wed–Sat 4:30pm–midnight. **Prices:** Main courses $8–$17. MC, V.

Joe's Bar & Grill
127 S Green St (Downtown); tel 317/362-5637. **American.** Don't let the name or the exterior fool you: This is no ordinary place. It's upscale casual, with a somewhat later-than-normal dinner rush. Joe's favorite is penne ziti regate (pasta with chicken, broccoli, and prosciutto in a tarragon sauce). If you try every one of Joe's 37 beers, you'll get your own personalized mug. **FYI:** Reservations recommended. Blues. **Open:** Mon 5–10pm, Tues–Sat 11am–10pm. **Prices:** Main courses $9–$25. AE, DC, MC, V.

The Redwood Inn
1570 US 231S; tel 317/362-6507. 1 mi S of town. **American.** Old-fashioned meals in a country setting. Favorites are Swiss steak, chicken and dumplings (served every Sun), and sugar cream pie. Breads and desserts are available for retail sales; ask for the bakery carryout menu. **FYI:** Reservations accepted. Children's menu. Beer and wine only. **Open:** Sun 11am–4pm, Mon–Thurs 11am–8pm, Fri–Sat 11am–9pm. **Prices:** Main courses $7–$11. AE, DC, MC, V.

ATTRACTIONS

Gen Lew Wallace Study
E Pike St and Wallace Ave; tel 317/362-5769. Housed a 1896 building, this Turkish-style study is where Gen Lew Wallace wrote the famed novel *Ben Hur*. Now a museum, it contains memorabilia ranging from war relics and art objects to personal items that chronicles his roles as a lawyer, state senator, Civil War general, scholar, painter, and writer. **Open:** Apr–Oct, Wed–Sat 10am–4:30pm, Tues and Sun 1–4:30pm. **$**

Henry Lane Home
212 S Water St; tel 317/362-3416. The 1845 home of Col Henry S Lane, governor of Indiana, US senator, and early political supporter of Abraham Lincoln. The home's diverse collection of historical artifacts includes Civil War memorabilia; furnishings from the colonial, federal, and Victorian eras; dolls and china; and an authentically appointed log cabin. Guided tours available by reservation. **Open:** Apr–Oct, Tues–Sun 1–4pm. **$**

Old Jail Museum
225 N Washington St; tel 317/362-5222. Built in 1882, the unique feature of this jail was its two-story cell block that rotated within the three story jail building. The rotating cells had only one access point, thus limiting contact between prisoners and jailers. (The system ended in the 1930s.) Native American and pioneer artifacts, period costumes, works by local artists, and items relating to the jail itself are also on display. **Open:** Peak (June–Aug) Tues and Sun 1–4:30pm, Wed–Sat 10am–4:30pm. Reduced hours off-season. **Free**

Decatur

See Fort Wayne

Elkhart

Founded in 1824 at the confluence of the St Joseph and Elkhart Rivers in northern Indiana. For over a century, Elkhart has been the chief producer of band instruments in the country, with over a dozen companies manufacturing over half the nation's band instruments. **Information:** Elkhart Chamber of Commerce, 418 S Main St, Elkhart, 46516 (tel 219/293-1531).

HOTEL

Quality Inn City Centre
300 S Main St, 46516; tel 219/295-0280 or toll free 800/221-2222; fax 219/522-6868. Downtown; behind Civic Plaza. Centrally located in downtown Elkhart, this four-story hotel is undergoing major renovation. Central location for the annual downtown Elkhart Jazz Festival. **Rooms:** 137 rms and stes. CI 3pm/CO noon. Nonsmoking rms avail. Many rooms on second and third floors overlook central indoor pool area. **Amenities:** A/C, cable TV w/movies. **Services:** Late checkout available. **Facilities:** 2 restaurants, 2 bars (w/entertainment), whirlpool. Regular entertainment featured in Golden Dragon with lively piano music Tues and Thurs, and in Paradise with live bands or DJ Fri–Sat. **Rates:** $49–$64 S; $59–$74 D; $80–$89 ste. Extra person $10. Children under age 18 stay free. Min stay special events. Parking: Outdoor, free. Minimum stays and price increases during the Elkhart Jazz Festival the third weekend in June, the Elkhart Grand Prix (go-cart races) the second weekend in July, and Notre Dame home football games in the fall. AE, DC, DISC, MC, V.

MOTELS

Comfort Inn
52137 Plaza Court, 46514; tel 219/264-0404 or toll free 800/221-2222; fax 219/264-0404. Small, clean motel offering basic services and direct entrance to rooms. Wheelchair-accessible entrance on north side. Next door to D'Antini's restaurant, a local favorite. Other restaurants nearby, but car is needed. **Rooms:** 54 rms. CI 2pm/CO 11am. Nonsmoking rms avail. All queen-size and king-size beds. **Amenities:** A/C, cable TV w/movies. Rooms with king-size beds have Jacuzzis. **Services:** Limited continental breakfast. **Facilities:** Pool is small, but clean and suitable for young children. **Rates:** Peak (Mar 15–Nov) $61 S; $65 D. Extra person $8. Children under age 18 stay free. Lower rates off-season. Parking: Outdoor, free. Rates on Jacuzzi rooms increase by $10 on holiday weekends. AE, DC, DISC, MC, V.

Ramada Inn
3011 Belvedere Rd, 46514; tel 219/262-1581 or toll free 800/2-RAMADA; fax 219/262-1590. Located on busy road adjacent to interstate, 17 miles from Notre Dame University, this older facility maintains stable reputation. Popular locally for business travelers, meetings, and receptions. Chain restaurants nearby, but heavy traffic makes car necessary. **Rooms:** 145 rms and stes. CI 2pm/CO noon. Nonsmoking rms avail. Some rooms dark, dated-looking although renovated in early 1990s. **Amenities:** A/C, cable TV w/movies. **Services:** **Facilities:** 1 restaurant, 2 bars (1 w/entertainment), games rm, whirlpool. Indoor pool very attractive with live trees and plants. **Rates:** $65–$88 S; $73–$95 D; $95–$115 ste. Extra person $8. Children under age 16 stay free. Min stay special events. Parking: Outdoor, free. Two-night minimum and increased room rates for special weekends, such as Notre Dame home football games. AE, CB, DC, DISC, EC, JCB, MC, V.

Red Roof Inn
2902 Cassopolis St, 46514; tel 219/262-3691 or toll free 800/843-7663; fax 219/262-3695. Immaculate facility located off busy commercial street. Tastefully landscaped with pine trees and perennial flowers and plants. Frequented by K-9 officers and dogs who come to Elkhart for training.

Rooms: 80 rms. CI open/CO noon. Nonsmoking rms avail. No drawers, but generous storage space. **Amenities:** 🏠 A/C, cable TV w/movies. **Services:** 🍴 🛎 **Facilities:** ⛄ **Rates:** Peak (May–Oct) $44–$53 S; $52–$59 D. Extra person $8. Children under age 19 stay free. Lower rates off-season. Parking: Outdoor, free. AE, CB, DC, DISC, MC, V.

≣≣ Signature Inn
3010 Brittany Court, 46514; tel 219/264-7222 or toll free 800/822-5252; fax 219/264-7222. Turn left onto IN 19S (Cassopolis St) off I-80/90, exit 92. Lobby redone in 1993 with wood-lined, vaulted ceiling and lots of glass. Set back from nearby commercial IN 19 in a woody, shady setting. Caters to business travelers, with large in-room desk areas. Restaurants within walking distance. **Rooms:** 125 rms. Executive level. CI 3pm/CO noon. Nonsmoking rms avail. Queens are rooms furnished with 12′ desk area and recliner chair. **Amenities:** 🏠 ⚿ A/C, cable TV w/movies. All rooms have modem and 25′ telephone cord. **Services:** 📠 🍴 Offices with calculator, typewriter, phone, and modem available to guests at no extra charge. **Facilities:** 👥 💯 🖥 ⛄ **Rates (CP):** Peak (June–Aug) $61 S; $65 D. Children under age 18 stay free. Lower rates off-season. Parking: Outdoor, free. Double rates increase on weekends with Notre Dame home football games. AE, DC, DISC, MC, V.

≣≣ Weston Plaza Hotel and Conference Center
2725 Cassopolis St, 46514; tel 219/264-7502 or toll free 800/521-8400; fax 219/264-0042. Turn left onto IN 19 S (Cassopolis St) off I-80/90, exit 92. Built in the mid-1960s as a Holiday Inn, the Weston has retained the Holidome's central indoor pool/recreation area; guests preferring quieter accommodations should request non-poolside rooms. Building is somewhat dated. Families will appreciate fast food and family restaurants next door, across the street, within walking distance, and a short drive away. **Rooms:** 200 rms and stes. CI 3pm/CO noon. Nonsmoking rms avail. Drab guest rooms currently being renovated with new bedspreads, drapes, and carpeting. **Amenities:** 🏠 A/C, cable TV w/movies. **Services:** ✗ 📠 🍴 Twice-daily maid service available on request. **Facilities:** 👥 💯 ⛄ 1 restaurant (bkfst and lunch only), 1 bar, games rm, sauna, whirlpool, washer/dryer. Dinner served Fri–Sat only. Bar/lounge area features live bands Fri–Sat, karaoke Thurs and Sun; it can be noisy. **Rates:** Peak (Apr–Nov) $52–$55 S; $59–$65 D; $95–$225 ste. Extra person $10. Children under age 18 stay free. Lower rates off-season. Parking: Outdoor, free. AE, CB, DC, MC, V.

RESTAURANTS 🍽

★ Casey's
411 S Main St; tel 219/293-5741. Across from Elco Performing Arts Center. **American.** Decorated with Indiana University sports logos, posters, and photographs, this busy downtown restaurant has been popular for business lunches and weekend dinners for over 40 years. Known for its Sterling Silver–certified choice beef, especially the Texas cut of roast

prime rib. The menu also features Italian dishes and Australian cold-water lobster tail and other seafood. **FYI:** Reservations recommended. **Open:** Lunch Mon–Sat 11am–2pm; dinner Mon–Sat 5–11pm. **Prices:** Main courses $8–$29. AE, DISC, MC, V.

$ ★ Exchange Bakery
109 W Lexington Ave; tel 219/293-5175. ½ block W of S Main St. **New American/Coffeehouse.** Locals flock to this delightful meeting spot, with its white walls, natural woodwork, colorful tablecloths, and ever-changing exhibits of artwork by local artists. Situated in a charming old two-story building in the heart of the city, the Exchange specializes in fresh, healthy, made-from-scratch selections. The hand-drawn menu changes daily but favorites include tomato-basil soup, spinach-and-feta-cheese–stuffed encroûtes, and shrimp and avocado salad. Seasonal fresh fruit compotes, carrot cake, and chocolate-raspberry torte are among the desserts. **FYI:** Reservations accepted. No liquor license. **Open:** Mon–Fri 6:30am–2pm. Closed week after Christmas/week after July 4. **Prices:** Lunch main courses $4–$6. No CC. 🍺

♣ Flytraps Main Street Bar & Grill
505 S Main St (Downtown); tel 219/522-9328. **New American.** One of the best restaurants in town, Flytraps is known for its fresh and inventive cuisine. Typical entrees might include grilled portobello mushrooms with black bean chili salsa; or a salad of mixed greens, sliced d'anjou pears, gorgonzola cheese, toasted walnuts, and raspberry vinaigrette. Fresh seafood is flown in twice weekly; ask for day's best catch. Herb crusted sea bass served with fresh warmed spinach, and Santa Fe filet with blackened tomato and oregano sauce are popular with locals. The wine cellar contains more than a hundred California labels as well as several French champagnes. Special desserts made daily. **FYI:** Reservations recommended. Blues. Dress code. **Open:** Lunch Mon–Fri 11am–2pm; dinner Mon–Sat 5–10pm. **Prices:** Main courses $15–$22. AE, MC, V.

Lucchese's Italian Ristorante and Deli
205 E Jackson Blvd (Downtown); tel 219/522-4137. 1 block E of Main St. **Deli/Italian.** This casual family-run restaurant specializes in traditional Italian: veal Marsala, pork chops Italian-style, shrimp scampi, pizzas, and tiramisù. Pastas and crusty bread are made on premises. Deli items are available for take-out. **FYI:** Reservations recommended. **Open:** Mon–Thurs 11am–9pm, Fri–Sat 11am–10pm. **Prices:** Main courses $7–$12. AE, DISC, MC, V. 👥

Matterhorn Restaurant
2041 Cassopolis St; tel 219/262-1500. On the N side of Elkhart on IN 19; 2 mi S of I-80/90, exit 92. **Continental.** A solid eatery catering to big appetites. Popular menu offerings include prime rib, rib eye, filet mignon, trout, orange roughy, grilled shrimp with linguine, Hawaiian chicken, and whole lobster. Children's portions available on any item. **FYI:** Reservations recommended. Dress code. **Open:** Lunch Mon–

Fri 11am–2pm; dinner Mon–Sat 5–10pm; brunch Sun 10am–2pm. **Prices:** Main courses $9–$17. AE, CB, DC, DISC, MC, V. 🅥 📷 &

ATTRACTIONS 📷

Midwest Museum of American Art

429 S Main St; tel 219/293-6660. Housed in a renovated neoclassical-style bank building, this 7,500-square-foot museum places special emphasis on movements in 19th- and 20th-century American art, including impressionism, abstract expressionism, pop art, and regionalism. The permanent collection boasts paintings, prints, drawings, and photographs by Grant Wood, Robert Henri, Alfred Stieglitz, Grandma Moses, and Norman Rockwell. Guided tours, lectures, and gallery talks; Thursday night film series. Admission free on Sundays. **Open:** Tues–Fri 11am–5pm, Sat–Sun 1–4pm. **$**

National New York Central Railroad

721 S Main St; tel 219/294-3001. Located in an 1880s freight house, this museum specializes in memorabilia from the old New York Central railroad. Authentically restored trains (including the E-8 diesel locomotive, the GG-1 electric locomotive, and a 3001 L-3a Mohawk steam locomotive) are featured, along with entire railroad stations and a video presentation of the history of the NYC. Donation suggested. **Open:** Tues–Fri 10am–2pm, Sat–Sun 10am–3pm. **Free**

Evansville

Seat of Vanderburgh County. Evansville is the major shipping and manufacturing center in southwestern Indiana, with one of the best harbors on inland waterways. **Information:** Evansville Convention & Visitors Bureau, 623 Walnut St, Evansville, 47708 (tel 812/425-5402 or toll free 800/433-3025).

HOTELS 📷

≣≣≣ Evansville Airport Marriott

7101 US 41 N, 47711; tel 812/867-7999 or toll free 800/228-9290; fax 812/867-0241. Exit 25 off I-64, S 10 mi. ½ mi W of Dress Regional Airport. Large garden-style atrium right past the lobby has a pool, indoor playground, games, and several seating areas. Glass-enclosed elevator and abundance of plants. **Rooms:** 201 rms and stes. Executive level. CI 4pm/CO 11am. Nonsmoking rms avail. Many rooms face atrium. **Amenities:** 🛏 ⚲ A/C, cable TV w/movies. Some units w/terraces. Iron and ironing board in every room. **Services:** ✕ 🚐 📷 🖐 Babysitting. Courtesy phone to Thrifty car rental. **Facilities:** 🏊 🏋 🛝 & 1 restaurant, 1 bar (w/entertainment), games rm, spa, whirlpool, playground. **Rates:** $129 S or D; $250–$350 ste. Extra person $10. Children under age 18 stay free. Parking: Outdoor, free. AE, CB, DC, DISC, ER, JCB, MC, V.

≣≣≣ Holiday Inn Airport

4101 US 41 N, 47711; tel 812/424-6400 or toll free 800/HOLIDAY; fax 812/424-6409. Exit 25 off I-64; S 12 mi on US 41. Full-service hotel located 1½ miles from airport. Fully renovated in 1994–95. **Rooms:** 198 rms and stes. CI 3pm/CO noon. Nonsmoking rms avail. **Amenities:** 🛏 ⚲ 📞 A/C, satel TV w/movies, dataport. **Services:** ✕ 🚐 📷 🖐 Nintendo available. **Facilities:** 🏊 🏋 🛝 3000 & 1 restaurant, 1 bar, basketball, spa, sauna, whirlpool, playground, washer/dryer. Holidome has the largest hotel pool in the state. **Rates:** $69–$76 S or D; $79–$86 ste. Extra person $7. Children under age 18 stay free. Parking: Outdoor, free. AE, DC, DISC, MC, V.

MOTELS

≣≣ Comfort Inn

5006 E Morgan Ave, 47715; tel 812/477-2211 or toll free 800/221-2222; fax 812/477-2211. Exit 9B off I-164; W 1 mi. Well-maintained, three-story facility near shopping and entertainment. **Rooms:** 52 rms and stes. CI 3pm/CO 11am. Nonsmoking rms avail. Chair and ottoman in singles. **Amenities:** 🛏 ⚲ A/C, cable TV. **Services:** 📷 🖐 🛎 Specials with adjacent Appleby's restaurant. **Facilities:** 🏊 & Games rm, whirlpool. **Rates (CP):** $53–$60 S or D; $58–$64 ste. Extra person $7. Children under age 18 stay free. Parking: Outdoor, free. 13th night free. AE, DC, DISC, ER, JCB, MC, V.

≣≣ Days Inn

5701 US 41 N, 47711; tel 812/464-1010 or toll free 800/329-7466; fax 812/464-2742. Exit 25 off I-64; S 11 mi. Three-story facility near the airport. **Rooms:** 120 rms and stes. CI 3pm/CO noon. Nonsmoking rms avail. **Amenities:** 🛏 A/C, cable TV. **Services:** ✕ 🚐 📷 🖐 **Facilities:** 🏊 350 & 1 restaurant, 1 bar (w/entertainment), sauna, whirlpool. Rock-n-Roll Heaven Lounge offers music from the 1950s and 1960s. **Rates (CP):** $45–$48 S or D; $75 ste. Extra person $3. Children under age 18 stay free. Parking: Outdoor, free. AE, CB, DC, DISC, MC, V.

≣≣ Drury Inn Evansville

3901 US 41 N, 47711; tel 812/423-5818 or toll free 800/325-8300; fax 812/423-5818. US 41 exit off I-64; 12 mi S. 2 mi S of Dress Regional Airport. Large skylight brightens lobby area. Adjacent to 24-hour restaurant. **Rooms:** 151 rms. CI 3pm/CO noon. Nonsmoking rms avail. Rooms updated in late 1995. **Amenities:** 🛏 ⚲ A/C, cable TV w/movies, dataport. Some rooms have microwaves and refrigerators. **Services:** 📷 🖐 🛎 Fax services available. **Facilities:** 🏊 75 & Whirlpool. Free passes to nearby fitness center. **Rates (CP):** $56 S; $64–$69 D. Extra person $8. Children under age 18 stay free. Parking: Outdoor, free. 11th night free at all Drury Inns. AE, CB, DC, DISC, MC, V.

≣≣≣ Hampton Inn

8000 Eagle Crest Blvd, 47715; tel 812/473-5000 or toll free 800/426-7866; fax 812/473-5000. At exit 7B off I-164. Five-story facility that's exceptionally clean and modern looking. Close to shopping and restaurants. **Rooms:** 143 rms. CI 2pm/CO noon. Nonsmoking rms avail. Rooms refurbished in 1995. **Amenities:** 📞 🚰 A/C, cable TV, dataport. **Services:** 📠 🍴 **Facilities:** 🏊 ⛳ 🎾 30 ♿ Outdoor sun deck by pool. Guest passes to nearby athletic club. **Rates (CP):** $53–$70 S or D. Children under age 18 stay free. **Parking:** Outdoor, free. AE, DC, DISC, MC, V.

🏨 Holiday Inn East
100 S Green River Rd, 47715; tel 812/473-0171 or toll free 800/HOLIDAY; fax 812/473-5021. Quiet motel in heart of east-side business and shopping district, convenient to Roberts Stadium, cinemas, and restaurants. Great for business travelers. Nice grounds. **Rooms:** 109 rms. CI 2pm/CO noon. Nonsmoking rms avail. All bathrooms have extra tall gooseneck showers. **Amenities:** 📞 🚰 A/C, satel TV w/movies, dataport. **Services:** ✕ 📠 🍴 **Facilities:** 🏊 150 ♿ 1 restaurant, 1 bar. Outdoor pool is covered. Privileges (for a minimal fee) at athletic club within walking distance. **Rates:** $59–$75 S; $66–$82 D. Extra person $7. Children under age 18 stay free. **Parking:** Outdoor, free. AE, CB, DC, DISC, JCB, MC, V.

🏨 Lees Inn
5538 E Indiana St, 47715; tel 812/477-6663 or toll free 800/733-5337; fax 812/477-1471. Exit 7B off I-164; W 1 mi. Bright entrance and lobby area with large chandelier above stairs leading to second floor. Near shopping and restaurants. **Rooms:** 75 rms and stes. CI 2pm/CO noon. Nonsmoking rms avail. **Amenities:** 📞 🚰 A/C, cable TV. Some units w/whirlpools. **Services:** 🚐 📠 🍴 🛎️ **Facilities:** 80 🖥️ ♿ Free passes to nearby health club. **Rates (CP):** $56 S; $64 D; $71–$79 ste. Extra person $7. Children under age 15 stay free. **Parking:** Outdoor, free. AE, DC, DISC, MC, V.

🏨 Super 8 Motel
4600 Morgan Ave, 47715; tel 812/476-4008 or toll free 800/800-8000; fax 812/476-4008. Exit 9B off I-164; W 1½ mi. Standard budget motel near restaurants. **Rooms:** 62 rms. CI 3pm/CO 11am. Nonsmoking rms avail. **Amenities:** 📞 A/C, cable TV w/movies. **Services:** 🍴 🛎️ Babysitting. **Facilities:** ♿ Reduced rates at nearby fitness center. **Rates:** $43–$49 S; $47–$49 D. Extra person $3. Children under age 18 stay free. **Parking:** Outdoor, free. 13th night free. AE, CB, DC, DISC, ER, JCB, MC, V.

RESTAURANTS 🍴

★ Elliott's Steakhouse
4701E Powell Ave; tel 812/473-3378. E on Washington Ave off US 41; S on Green River Rd; left at first light. **Steak.** Diners are invited to cook their own steak in one of the two huge indoor charcoal pits. Inside, the rustic atmosphere showcases wood beams, elaborately detailed woodwork and carvings, and stained-glass windows. The *Evansville Sunday Courier and Press* says Elliott's has the best steak in the tristate

area. **FYI:** Reservations accepted. Children's menu. **Open:** Mon–Sat 4–10pm, Sun 11am–10pm. **Prices:** Main courses $9–$20. AE, DC, DISC, MC, V. ♥ 💟

Jungle Mornings Coffee House and Restaurant
415 Main (Downtown); tel 812/425-JAVA. On the Walkway. **American/Coffeehouse.** Listed on the National Register of Historic Places, this beautifully renovated 1875 building has what the owners call a "fun Victorian" ambience. Embossed tin walls and ceiling, mosaic-tiled iron staircase, and a "jungle room" with animal-print furniture set the eclectic and wonderfully inviting mood. The dining room is filled with sculptures and lithographs, most with an animal theme. (A portion of restaurant profits goes to animal conservation and environmental groups.) A wide variety of coffees is roasted inhouse and served at the turn-of-the-century bar as well as at comfortable tables. Nightly specials often include seafood. Live entertainment on the second floor is telecast to all three floors of the restaurant. **FYI:** Reservations recommended. Blues/jazz. Children's menu. Beer and wine only. **Open:** Mon 7:30am–3pm, Tues–Thurs 7:30am–10pm, Fri 7:30am–midnight, Sat 4:30am–midnight. **Prices:** Main courses $9–$17. MC, V. 🍺 ♿

★ Mattingly's 23
1700 Morgan Center Dr; tel 812/473-4323. Morgan Ave exit off I-164; W 1 mi. **American.** Owned by Don Mattingly, the former New York Yankee (No 23, hence the restaurant's name), and formerly a graduate of Evansville's Memorial High School. Sports memorabilia fills the place: Items from baseball greats dominate the Legends Room, while Indiana sports memorabilia is the focus in the Hoosier Room. The lounge, with several big-screen and regular TVs, has a floor marked like a baseball diamond. Yankee games are always telecast, but the lounge is busiest during IU basketball games. Strawberry butter on homemade bread goes well with the traditional American fare. **FYI:** Reservations recommended. Children's menu. **Open:** Mon–Thurs 11am–10pm, Fri–Sat 11am–10:30pm. **Prices:** Main courses $8–$25. AE, DISC, MC, V. 👥 💟 ♿

My Brother's Place
4614 Vogel Rd; tel 812/479-6794. Just W of Green River Rd; across from Eastland Mall. **American.** Prime rib is the specialty in this restaurant/lounge that's a favorite with the locals. People *do* talk about the jackass soup, but don't let the name fool you—the meat in this homemade soup is really prime rib. Daily specials are offered. **FYI:** Reservations accepted. Children's menu. **Open:** Lunch Mon–Fri 11am–2pm; dinner Mon–Thurs 4:30–9pm, Fri–Sat 5–10pm. **Prices:** Main courses $7–$13. AE, DISC, MC, V. 👥 💟 ♿

ATTRACTIONS 🖼️

Evansville Museum of Arts and Sciences
411 SE Riverside Dr; tel 812/425-2406. Wide-ranging exhibits cover the worlds of art, science, technology, and anthropology. The art collection ranges from the 16th century up to

the present; the anthropology gallery emphasizes the cultures of the native inhabitants of the Americas; the Koch Science Center and Planetarium focus on science and technology. Rivertown USA re-creates a late 19th-century American river town; an antique steam locomotive, tavern car, and caboose make up the railroad display. Guided tours available. **Open:** Tues–Sat 10am–5pm, Sun noon–5pm. **Free**

Reitz Home Museum

224 SE 1st St; tel 812/426-1871. Built by lumber baron John Augustus Reitz in 1871, this Second Empire–style mansion features parquet floors, stained-glass windows, ornate chandeliers, hand-painted ceilings, silk damask–covered walls, and molded plaster friezes. Nearly 20 rooms (including bedrooms, dining room, parlor, and drawing room) are decorated with original period furnishings and open to the public. **Open:** Tues–Sat 11am–4pm, Sun 1–4pm. **$**

Evansville Dance Theatre

333-E North Plaza East Blvd; tel 812/473-8937. This highly acclaimed regional company presents a full season of performances with orchestral accompaniment by the Evansville Philharmonic Orchestra. Recent pieces have included *The Nutcracker, Sleeping Beauty,* and *Giselle.* **Open:** Office, Mon–Fri 8:30am–5pm. Call for performance schedule. **$$$$**

Mesker Park Zoo

2421 Bement Ave; tel 812/428-0715. More than 700 animals are housed at this 70-acre wooded zoo. The most popular highlights include a petting zoo, an aviary, a lake with paddleboats, and a sidewalk tram. **Open:** Peak (Mem Day–Labor Day) Mon–Fri 9am–4pm, Sat–Sun 9am–7pm. Reduced hours off-season. **$$**

Fishers

INN 🏨

≣≣≣ Frederick-Talbot Inn

13805 Allisonville Rd, 46038; tel 317/578-3600 or toll free 800/566-2337. 2½ acres. This English country bed-and-breakfast occupies two buildings and opened in 1994. Part of one house dates back to 1870 and was bought with Irish sweepstakes winnings. Lace curtains and charming window treatments on long windows throughout. Both buildings abound with old photos, hats, clothing items, antique furniture. Hardwood floors in one parlor and in breakfast area. Good for executive retreat meetings. **Rooms:** 11 rms. CI 4pm/CO 11am. Nonsmoking rms avail. **Amenities:** 🛁 🔺 A/C, cable TV. Some units w/terraces, 1 w/fireplace, some w/whirlpools. **Services:** 🚗 🛎 📞 VCRs and toiletries available. Buffet breakfast served in sunny enclosed porch and sitting room with fireplace. Specialties include chocolate raspberry strata, sherried egg casserole, stuffed French toast, and strawberry tea. Small pets accepted with advance notice. **Facilities:** 🏬 ♿ Washer/dryer. Two meeting rooms. **Rates**

(BB): $89–$169 S; $135 D. Children under age 18 stay free. Higher rates for special events/hols. Parking: Outdoor, free. Packages avail with Conner Prairie pioneer museum and the Eller House restaurant during Conner Prairie's season. AE, DISC, MC, V.

RESTAURANT 🍽

The Eller House

7050 E 116th St; tel 317/849-2299. Exit 35 off I-465; N on Allisonville Rd; W on 116th St. **American.** Built in 1877, this two-story brick farmhouse features the original entrance doors and some original wood trim. There are several different dining rooms; the enclosed front porch has a nice, homey atmosphere. Roast pork with dressing is its chef's signature entree; other popular items are chicken Florentine and Dijon-crusted salmon. Homemade side dishes include sweet-and-sour salad with red cabbage and chunky applesauce with raisins, cinnamon, and nutmeg. The house dessert is bourbon bread pudding. **FYI:** Reservations recommended. Jazz. Children's menu. **Open:** Mon–Thurs 10:30am–10pm, Fri–Sat 10:30am–11pm, Sun 9am–9pm. **Prices:** Main courses $11–$18. AE, CB, DC, DISC, MC, V. 🍴 ♿

ATTRACTION 🏛

Conner Prarie Pioneer Settlement

13400 Allisonville Rd, Noblesville; tel 317/776-6000. 10 mi NW of Fishers. Village from the 19th century faithfully reproduces pioneer life between 1820 and 1840 with the help of 36 minutely restored buildings, including a blacksmith's forge, a cobbler's workshop, and a Federal style home. Visitors can experience authentic frontier activities, including a camp meeting, a wedding celebration, a town meeting, and the preservation of a whole hog. Handcraft demonstrations by craftsmen in period costume. **Open:** Peak (May–Oct) Tues–Sat 10am–5pm, Sun noon–5pm. Reduced hours off-season. **$$$**

Fort Wayne

See also Auburn, Decatur, Huntington

Seat of Allen County, in northeast part of state. The Miami tribe headquartered here, where the St Joseph and St Mary's Rivers meet to form the Maumee. In the 17th century, Fort Wayne was a French, then an English, trading center; today it is the state's second-largest city. **Information:** Fort Wayne Convention & Visitors Bureau, 1021 S Calhoun St, Fort Wayne, 46802 (tel 219/424-3700).

HOTELS 🏨

≣≣≣ Courtyard by Marriott Fort Wayne

1619 W Washington Center Rd, 46818; tel 219/489-1500 or toll free 800/321-2211; fax 219/489-1500. Exit 111B off I-69. Colorful outdoor plantings at large canopy entrance are matched with beautiful flowers and shrubs in courtyard. Handsome wooden stairway dominates dramatic two-story lobby, which has large fieldstone fireplace. Two charming gazebos in courtyard. A favorite with business travelers and weekending families. **Rooms:** 142 rms and stes. CI 3pm/CO noon. Nonsmoking rms avail. King-bedded rooms have sleeper sofas. **Amenities:** 🛍 🗑 📺 🎧 A/C, cable TV, dataport. Some units w/whirlpools. Irons and ironing boards in rooms. Executive suites feature especially long phone cords, additional phone jacks, and whirlpools. **Services:** 🖼 🧺 **Facilities:** 🏋 🏌 🏊 ⚓ 1 restaurant (bkfst only), 1 bar, games rm, whirlpool. **Rates:** $74 S; $84 D; $100–$229 ste. Extra person $10. Children under age 18 stay free. Min stay special events. Parking: Outdoor, free. Charge for extra person applies to weekend only. AE, CB, DC, DISC, JCB, MC, V.

≣≣≣ Don Hall's Guesthouse
1313 W Washington Center Rd, 46825; tel 219/489-2524 or toll free 800/348-1999; fax 219/489-7067. Exit 111B off I-69. Gracious, beautifully furnished lobby with large fieldstone fireplace, handsome traditional furniture, and a number of special imported pieces. One phone booth is a former cashier's stall from a butcher shop in London; another is the "lift" from a private residence in London. Personal touches add warmth to all public areas. There's also a lavishly landscaped center courtyard. **Rooms:** 130 rms. CI 3pm/CO noon. Nonsmoking rms avail. A small foyer separates each pair of rooms. Tiled floors in bathrooms are heated. **Amenities:** 🛍 🗑 📺 A/C, cable TV. **Services:** 🖼 🚗 🧺 🧺 **Facilities:** 🏋 🏌 🏊 ⚓ 2 restaurants, 1 bar (w/entertainment), games rm, whirlpool. **Rates (CP):** $59 S; $66 D. Extra person $10. Children under age 18 stay free. Parking: Outdoor, free. AE, CB, DC, DISC, MC, V.

≣≣≣ Fort Wayne Hilton
1020 S Calhoun St, 46802; tel 219/420-1100 or toll free 800/HILTONS; fax 219/424-7775. At the Convention Center. This favorite downtown location for business travelers is connected to all Convention Complex facilities and is across the street from the Foellinger-Freimann Botanical Conservatory. Near all museums. Generous plantings in corridors of public areas. **Rooms:** 249 rms and stes. CI 3pm/CO 11am. Nonsmoking rms avail. **Amenities:** 🛍 🗑 📺 🎧 A/C, cable TV, dataport, voice mail. **Services:** 🖼 🚗 🧺 🧺 Babysitting. **Facilities:** 🏋 🏌 🏊 ⚓ 2 restaurants, 2 bars (1 w/entertainment), whirlpool. **Rates:** $99–$149 S; $109–$159 D; $200–$350 ste. Extra person $10. Children under age 18 stay free. Parking: Indoor, $2.50/day. AE, CB, DC, DISC, MC, V.

≣≣≣ Fort Wayne Marriott
305 E Washington Center Rd, 46802; tel 219/484-0411 or toll free 800/228-9290; fax 219/483-2892. Exit 112B off I-69. Be sure to get into far right lane as you exit I-69 so you can make right turn into hotel driveway. Beautiful floral plantings in center of courtyard earned this hotel an award from the city of Fort Wayne for the best-landscaped facility. **Rooms:** 224 rms and stes. CI 3pm/CO noon. Nonsmoking

rms avail. **Amenities:** 🛍 🗑 📺 🎧 A/C, cable TV, voice mail. **Services:** 🖼 🧺 🧺 ⚓ **Facilities:** 🏋 🏌 🏊 ⚓ 1 restaurant (bkfst and dinner only), 1 bar, games rm, lawn games, whirlpool. Miniature golf. Boardroom-sized meeting area with private garden. **Rates:** $94 S or D; $119–$170 ste. Extra person $10. Children under age 18 stay free. Parking: Outdoor, free. Weekend package includes breakfast for two in restaurant. AE, MC, V.

≣≣ Holiday Inn Airport
3939 Ferguson Rd, 46809 (Fort Wayne Int'l Airport); tel 219/747-9171 or toll free 800/HOLIDAY; fax 219/747-1848. Small lobby, new upholstered pieces, giant planters, and greenery in lobby and corridors. **Rooms:** 146 rms. CI 3pm/CO noon. Nonsmoking rms avail. Complete refurbishing of all rooms in progress. **Amenities:** 🛍 🗑 🎧 A/C, cable TV. **Services:** 🖼 🚗 🧺 🧺 ⚓ **Facilities:** 🏋 🏌 🏊 ⚓ 1 restaurant, 1 bar, sauna. **Rates:** $74 S; $82 D. Extra person $8. Children under age 18 stay free. Parking: Outdoor, free. AE, CB, DC, DISC, MC, V.

≣≣≣ Holiday Inn Hotel and Suites
300 E Washington Blvd, 46802 (Downtown); tel 219/422-5511 or toll free 800/HOLIDAY; fax 219/424-1511. Complete refurbishing is in process. Close to downtown attractions and convention center complex. **Rooms:** 224 rms and stes. Executive level. CI 2pm/CO noon. Nonsmoking rms avail. Some suites on executive level feature two-person whirlpools. King-bedded rooms have sleeper sofas. A number of smaller rooms are being converted to suites. **Amenities:** 🛍 🗑 📺 A/C, cable TV, dataport. Some units w/whirlpools. **Services:** 🖼 🚗 🧺 🧺 ⚓ **Facilities:** 🏋 🏌 🏊 ⚓ 2 restaurants, 1 bar, spa, sauna, whirlpool, washer/dryer. **Rates:** $89 S; $90 D; $109–$125 ste. Extra person $8. Children under age 18 stay free. Parking: Outdoor, free. AE, DC, DISC, MC, V.

≣≣≣ Holiday Inn Northwest
3330 W Coliseum Blvd, 46808; tel 219/484-7711 or toll free 800/HOLIDAY; fax 219/482-7429. Exit 109A off I-69. A favorite with business travelers, but filled with families on weekends. Tropical landscaping in Holidome, complete with live lovebirds. Closest Holiday Inn to Fort Wayne Zoo. **Rooms:** 260 rms. CI 4pm/CO noon. Nonsmoking rms avail. **Amenities:** 🛍 🗑 A/C, cable TV. **Services:** 🖼 🧺 🧺 **Facilities:** 🏋 🏌 🏊 1 restaurant, 1 bar, games rm, sauna, whirlpool, playground, washer/dryer. **Rates:** $84 S or D. Extra person $6. Children under age 18 stay free. Parking: Outdoor, free. AE, CB, DC, DISC, MC, V.

≣≣ Ramada Inn
1212 Magnavox Way, 46804; tel 219/436-8600 or toll free 800/272-6232; fax 219/432-9764. Exit 105A off I-69. Glamorous entry with dramatic staircase curving to each side of two-story lobby. Minimal landscaping. **Rooms:** 148 rms. CI 3pm/CO 11am. Nonsmoking rms avail. New furnishings, bedspreads, and floor coverings. **Amenities:** 🛍 A/C, cable

TV. **Services:** ✗ 🖼 ⤵ Friendly front desk staff. **Facilities:** 🗗 🏊 ⑤ ₫ 1 restaurant, 1 bar (w/entertainment), games rm, washer/dryer. Guests may use nearby health spa at reduced rates. **Rates:** $65 S; $70 D. Extra person $5. Children under age 18 stay free. Parking: Outdoor, free. Special weekend packages. AE, CB, DC, DISC, MC, V.

MOTELS

⩶⩶ Best Inns of America
3017 W Coliseum Blvd, 46808; tel 219/483-0091 or toll free 800/237-8466; fax 219/483-0091. Exit 109B off I-69. Convenient to Fort Wayne's world-famous zoo and 1 mile to Glenbrook Square, Indiana's largest enclosed mall—it has its own indoor skating rink. Good value. **Rooms:** 105 rms. CI noon/CO 1pm. Nonsmoking rms avail. Comfortable rooms with exceptionally quiet room air conditioners. **Amenities:** 🖥 A/C, cable TV. **Services:** ⤵ ⤸ **Rates (CP):** $36 S; $44–$47 D. Extra person $6. Children under age 18 stay free. Parking: Outdoor, free. AE, CB, DC, DISC, MC, V.

⩶⩶ Comfort Inn
2908 Goshen Rd, 46808; tel 219/484-6262 or toll free 800/221-2222; fax 219/482-8463. Exit 109A off I-69; E to Goshen Rd. This older, well-maintained facility is an economical lodging for a short stay. Very convenient to Fort Wayne Zoo; 1 mile to Glenbrook Square. **Rooms:** 52 rms. CI 1pm/CO 11am. Nonsmoking rms avail. **Amenities:** 🖥 🗄 A/C, cable TV. **Services:** ⤵ ⤸ $25 refundable deposit for pets. **Facilities:** 🗗 ₫ Small pool in front area. **Rates (CP):** $36–$38 S; $43 D. Extra person $5. Children under age 18 stay free. Parking: Outdoor, free. Prices increase over Labor Day weekend. AARP discount. AE, CB, DC, DISC, MC, V.

⩶⩶ Days Inn
5250 Distribution Dr, 46825; tel 219/484-9681 or toll free 800/329-7466; fax 219/483-2217. Exit 111A off I-69. This large facility is in the process of complete renovation, so some areas are still showing signs of past neglect. **Rooms:** 160 rms and stes. CI 3pm/CO noon. Nonsmoking rms avail. Rooms are spacious, well mirrored, and are being refurbished in warm, dark woods and floral bedspreads and wall treatments. **Amenities:** 🖥 A/C, cable TV. 1 unit w/whirlpool. **Services:** ✗ ⤵ ⤸ **Facilities:** 🗗 ⑤ ₫ 1 restaurant (bkfst and dinner only), 1 bar (w/entertainment), games rm, sauna, whirlpool. Indoor and outdoor pools are a long walk from some rooms. Lounge is popular local gathering place. **Rates (CP):** $32–$44 S; $38–$50 D; $50–$125 ste. Extra person $6. Children under age 12 stay free. Parking: Outdoor, free. Special golf packages. AE, DC, MC, V.

⩶⩶ Days Inn Downtown
3730 E Washington Blvd, 46803; tel 219/424-1980 or toll free 800/329-7466. Exit 102A off I-69; E on US 24. Confusing name—downtown is some distance away. Easy access to Memorial Coliseum and Stadium. Very modest exterior and lobby, but attractive center courtyard surrounding the pool. Good lodging value and central location. **Rooms:** 122 rms. CI

noon/CO 11am. No smoking. Rooms open to courtyard. **Amenities:** 🖥 🗄 A/C, cable TV. **Services:** ⤵ ⤸ Pets $4/day. **Facilities:** 🗗 1 restaurant, 2 bars (1 w/entertainment). **Rates:** Peak (May–Sept) $30 S; $35 D. Extra person $4. Children under age 12 stay free. Lower rates off-season. Parking: Outdoor, free. AE, CB, DC, DISC, MC, V.

RESTAURANTS 🍴

Back Forty Junction
1011 N 13th St, Decatur; tel 219/724-3355. **American/Swedish.** Just a short ride from Fort Wayne, this restaurant is worth a visit just to see the amazing array of antiques and collectibles that fill every wall and corner of the dining room and bar. They run the gamut from original posters of the Barnum & Bailey Circus to the chandelier from the home of movie actress Carole Lombard—with mementoes of Abraham Lincoln and Victorian toys side by side with the ticket seller's window from an old railroad station. The Swedish-style buffet table is piled high with homemade soups and breads plus Swedish meatballs and other foods. **FYI:** Reservations recommended. Children's menu. **Open:** Mon–Sat 11am–9pm, Sun 11am–7pm. **Prices:** Main courses $8–$19. AE, CB, DC, DISC, MC, V. 🍷 👥 ₫

♥ Cafe Johnell
2529 S Calhoun St; tel 219/456-1939. At Woodland Ave; 2 mi S of downtown. **Mediterranean.** Currently under the direction of master chef Nike Spillson, daughter of the original owners and a graduate of the Cordon Bleu in Paris, this landmark restaurant with one of the finest wine cellars in the Midwest sits inconspicuously in a modest neighborhood south of downtown. But when you step inside, you are faced with European elegance—from the grand paintings on the walls to the sparkling white linen and fine china and stemware. The menu reflects the chef's ingenuity in such treats as braided salmon and whitefish in a light salsa sauce, and fresh sweetbreads in house sauce. The avgolemono (egg lemon) soup, sausage en brioche moutarde, and oysters Johnell can start your special dining experience. **FYI:** Reservations recommended. **Open:** Peak (May–Aug) lunch Mon–Thurs 11:30am–2pm; dinner Mon–Thurs 5–9pm, Fri 5–10pm, Sat 6–11pm. **Prices:** Main courses $18–$30; prix fixe $18. AE, DC, MC. ♥ 🍷 📹 ₫

⑤ The Elegant Farmer
1820 N Coliseum Blvd; tel 219/482-1976. 2 mi N of Coliseum. **Seafood/Steak.** You can't tell this is a special place as you approach the building, but once inside there are many treats to delight the eye: the owner's fine antiques in the circular foyer, the handsome wooden gazebo in the center of the dining room. Prime rib is the specialty of the house, but the 10-oz rib eye steak, yellowfin tuna with Cajun glaze, and honey-mustard chicken are also a good bet. Personalized service. **FYI:** Reservations accepted. Children's menu. **Open:**

Lunch Mon–Fri 11am–2pm; dinner Mon–Sat 5–9pm; brunch Sun 10am–2pm. **Prices:** Main courses $6–$9. AE, MC, V. 🍽 👨‍👩‍👧

Flanagan's

6525 Covington Rd; tel 219/432-6666. **Eclectic.** A feeling of good spirit prevails in the gaily decorated dining room, filled with antique knickknacks and brightly colored banners. The very eclectic menu lists everything from Mexican munchies and entrees to Italian pastas and pizza. The chicken New Orleans is a special treat; the baby back ribs and New York strip steak are also favorites. **FYI:** Reservations accepted. Children's menu. **Open:** Daily 11am–midnight. **Prices:** Main courses $7–$10. AE, DISC, MC, V. 🍽 👨‍👩‍👧 ♿

★ Old Gas House Restaurant

305 E Superior; tel 219/426-3411. ½ mi W of Downtown. **Seafood/Steak.** A sumptuous salad bar in the bed of an antique farm wagon? It goes perfectly with the exposed brick walls and casual decor of the warm, pleasant dining room. Good, simple fare—chicken Kiev, prime rib, blackened whitefish, and Lake Michigan perch—is enjoyed by an after-work crowd as well as families. **FYI:** Reservations recommended. Children's menu. **Open:** Mon–Thurs 11am–10:30pm, Fri–Sat 11am–11:30pm, Sun 11:30am–9pm. **Prices:** Main courses $9–$28. AE, DC, MC, V. 🍽 👨‍👩‍👧 💳 ♿

ATTRACTIONS 🏛

Fort Wayne Children's Zoo

3411 Sherman Blvd; tel 219/427-6800. Located on 10 acres, the zoo features an Indonesian Rain Forest complete with tropical birds, butterflies, and a rare Komodo dragon. The Australian Adventure area recreates the Great Barrier Reef in a 20,000-gallon aquarium, and is also home to Tasmanian devils, kangaroos, and dingoes. On Safari covers 22 acres of African grassland where animals such as giraffes, cheetahs, and zebras roam free while visitors traverse the area by car. Also children's petting zoo, miniature train, and new orangutan habitat. **Open:** Apr–Oct, Mon–Sat 9am–5pm, Sun 9am–6pm. $$

Allen County-Fort Wayne Historical Society

302 E Berry St; tel 219/426-2882. Located in an 1894 Richardsonian-style city hall, this museum's exhibits focus on six themes and/or periods in local history: prehistoric times to the Civil War; 19th-century industrialization; culture and society from 1894-1920; 20th-century technology and industry; old city jail and law enforcement (1820–1970); and ethnic heritage. Temporary exhibits also presented. **Open:** Tues–Fri 9am–5pm, Sat–Sun noon–5pm. $

Fort Wayne Museum of Art

311 E Main St; tel 219/422-6467. Works by such significant artists as Pablo Picasso, Henri Matisse, Edouard Manet, Henri de Toulouse-Lautrec, Auguste Renoir, Edward Hopper, Andy Warhol, Jasper Johns, and Willem de Kooning make up the bulk of this 1,300-piece permanent collection.

There are also small collections of Japanese prints; Native American works; pre-Columbian art; and Egyptian, Greek, and Roman statuary. **Open:** Tues–Sat 10am–5pm, Sun noon–5pm. $

Cathedral of the Immaculate Conception

Bounded by Calhoun, Jefferson, Clinton, and Lewis Sts; tel 219/424-1485. Located in the center of Fort Wayne, this Gothic-style church is notable for its Bavarian stained-glass windows and hand-carved wooden altar. Numerous statues and furnishings are also of interest. Maps available for self-guided tours. A museum in the MacDougal Memorial Chapel, adjacent to the church, displays books, vestments, and religious artifacts. **Open:** Daily 8am–5pm. **Free**

Foellinger-Freimann Botanical Conservatory

1100 S Calhoun St; tel 219/427-6440. One of the Midwest's largest solar conservatories is divided into three distinct areas. The Showcase houses seasonal displays (chrysanthemums in the fall, poinsettias at Christmas, tulips in the spring). The Tropical House is home to towering palms, birds-of-paradise, and cascading waterfalls, while the Arid House is filled with desert flora native to the Sonora Desert (such as the Saguaro cactus, acacias, and paloverde). **Open:** Mon–Sat 10am–5pm, Sun noon–4pm. $

Embassy Theater

121 W Jefferson St; tel 219/424-6287. Built in 1928, this lavish, 2,700-seat art deco theater still hosts big name entertainers (such as Barry Manilow, Yanni, and the Statler Brothers) as well as the Fort Wayne Philharmonic and traveling theater productions. **Open:** Tours Mon–Fri 9am–5pm, by appointment. $

Fremont

MOTEL 🏨

�� Holiday Inn Express

6245 N Old 27, 46737; tel 219/833-6464 or toll free 800/HOLIDAY; fax 219/833-6464. Located in a pleasant, woodsy setting, in a building noted for its natural wood siding and stone-trimmed pillars. Brick, flower-edged patio in back has picnic tables. Near upscale outlet mall. **Rooms:** 61 rms and stes. CI 3pm/CO noon. Nonsmoking rms avail. **Amenities:** 📺 🔥 A/C, cable TV w/movies. Some units w/whirlpools. **Services:** ⬭ Free local calls. **Facilities:** 🏋 🏃 🅿 ♿ **Rates (CP):** Peak (Mem Day–Labor Day) $79 S; $87 D; $135–$160 ste. Extra person $8. Children under age 19 stay free. Lower rates off-season. Parking: Outdoor, free. AE, CB, DC, DISC, JCB, MC, V.

French Lick

Named for a French trading post and a nearby salt lick, this small town is famous as a health and vacation resort, thanks to its mineral-rich springs. **Information:** French Lick-West Baden Chamber of Commerce, PO Box 347, French Lick, 47432 (tel 812/936-2405).

LODGE

≣≣ The Pines at Patoka Lake Village

Lake Village Dr, 47432; tel 812/936-9854. 10 mi S of French Lick on IN 145. 150 acres. Luxury log cabins in the heart of the Patoka Lake state recreational area. The Pines has 150 acres of its own; Patoka's land area encompasses 16,920 acres. Patoka Lake is 8,880 acres, which makes it Indiana's second largest body of water. Boat ramps, beach, nature trails, interpretive center are nearby. Guests need bring only food, soap, towels, personal belongings. **Rooms:** 13 cottages/ villas. CI 3pm/CO 11am. Each two-bedroom cabin sleeps six and has sleeper sofa, covered deck, picnic table, and outdoor closet for fishing and skiing gear. One A-frame cabin sleeps eight or more in a loft. **Amenities:** ☕ ☎ A/C, TV, refrig. No phone. All units w/terraces, 1 w/fireplace. Full kitchens with both microwave and conventional ovens, barbecue grill. **Services:** ⛴ 🐕 Books available in each cabin—if you haven't finished reading one when you leave, you may take it with you and "return it or send one of your own." Discounts for golf and horseback riding at French Lick Springs Resort. **Facilities:** 🛥 🐎 50 ৬ Volleyball, games rm, playground, washer/dryer. Boat parking, fish and game cleaning facilities. **Rates:** Peak (May–Oct) $60–$75 cottage/villa. Extra person $10. Children under age 5 stay free. Lower rates off-season. Parking: Outdoor, free. AE, DISC, MC, V.

RESORT

≣≣≣ French Lick Springs Resort

8670 W State Rd, 47432; tel 812/936-9300 or toll free 800/ 936-9300; fax 812/936-2100. 2,600 acres. The French were attracted to the area by the water, and their livestock benefited by licking the mineral deposits found at the springs—thus, French Lick's name. The area was touted for its mineral waters, and a hotel was built in 1834. It burned in 1897, and the present facility, known for both luxury and relaxation, opened in the early 1900s and became a mecca for the rich, famous, and politically influential. A major restoration of guest rooms, public areas, and grounds was begun in 1991 and is just being completed. The French Lick Scenic Railway, adjacent to the resort, takes riders through 20 miles of southern Indiana on Sat, Sun and major holidays Apr–Nov. Tours of the nearby West Baden Hotel, called the eighth wonder of the world, also available. **Rooms:** 525 rms and stes. CI 4pm/CO noon. Nonsmoking rms avail. Kimball furniture, wallpaper, and elegant drapes in newly restored guest rooms. **Amenities:** 📺 ♨ A/C, cable TV w/movies, dataport. Some units w/terraces, some w/fireplaces. **Services:** ✗ ☎ 🚗 ⛴ 🐕 Twice-daily maid svce, social director, masseur, children's program, babysitting. Health spa services include reflexology, aromatherapy, salt rub, and mineral bath. Chuck Wagon

cookouts, surrey rides, picnic lunches, bowling available. Day-care center for ages 5–12 available in summer. Cabaret shows twice a week during high season. Pets under 15 lbs only. **Facilities:** 🏊 ▶36 🏌 🎿 🚴 🏓 🎳18 🐎 4000 💻 ৬ 6 restaurants, 3 bars (1 w/entertainment), basketball, volley-ball, games rm, lawn games, racquetball, spa, sauna, steam rm, whirlpool, beauty salon, playground. One outdoor pool has retractable dome. Country Club Hill Course designed by Donald Ross Shops. **Rates:** $79 S or D; $129 ste. Extra person $10. Children under age 18 stay free. MAP rates avail. Parking: Outdoor, free. Packages include holiday, golf, ten-nis, spa, ranch, and romantic. AE, DC, DISC, MC, V.

Goshen

Seat of Elkhart County, in northern Indiana. This small city is home to Goshen College, as well as several Amish and Mennonite colonies. **Information:** Goshen Chamber of Com-merce, 109 E Clinton St, Goshen, 46526 (tel 219/533-2102).

MOTELS

≣≣ Courtyard by Marriott

1930 Lincolnway E, 46526; tel 219/534-3133 or toll free 800/321-2211; fax 219/534-3133. 1½ mi SE of downtown Goshen on US 33 S. A sleeper, with small-town ambience. Located off fairly busy state highway, near fast food restau-rants and discount stores. **Rooms:** 91 rms and stes. CI 3pm/ CO noon. Nonsmoking rms avail. Larger rooms/suites avail-able. **Amenities:** 🛏 ♨ A/C, cable TV w/movies. Some rooms have whirlpools and wet bars. **Services:** 🛎 ⛴ 🐕 $50 pet deposit required. In-room Super Nintendo and videos avail-able. Accommodating personnel. **Facilities:** 🏊 100 ৬ 1 restaurant (bkfst only). 24-hour exercise room. **Rates:** Peak (mid-May–Nov) $79 S or D; $119–$254 ste. Extra person $7. Children under age 18 stay free. Lower rates off-season. Parking: Outdoor, free. AE, CB, DC, DISC, MC, V.

≣≣ Holiday Inn

1375 Lincolnway E, 46526; tel 219/533-9551 or toll free 800/HOLIDAY; fax 219/533-2840. 1 mi S of downtown Goshen on US 3 SE. Oriented towards business travelers. Recently renovated. Spotlessly clean. **Rooms:** 211 rms. CI 3pm/CO 11am. Nonsmoking rms avail. **Amenities:** 🛏 ♨ A/C, cable TV w/movies. All rooms have computer hook-ups/ modems available on telephones. **Services:** ✗ 🛎 ⛴ Conti-nental breakfast offered in summer months; Mon–Fri $6 credit on full weekday breakfasts during low season. VCRs and videos available to rent. **Facilities:** 🏊 🐎 250 ৬ 1 restaurant, 1 bar (w/entertainment), games rm, sauna, whirl-pool, washer/dryer. Holidome/recreation facility on prem-ises with exercise equipment—can be warm in humid sum-mer months. **Rates:** Peak (mid-May–mid-Oct) $76 S or D. Children under age 18 stay free. Min stay special events. Lower rates off-season. Parking: Outdoor, free. Two-night minimum during Notre Dame home football game weekends. Packages avail with breakfast buffet. AE, CB, DC, DISC, JCB, MC, V.

INN

≣≣≣ The Checkerberry Inn

62644 CR 37, 46526; tel 219/642-4445; fax 219/642-4445. S of I-80/90; take IN 4 E from Goshen, turning S on CR 37. 100 acres. Reminiscent of a gracious European country inn, the Checkerberry is situated off a sparsely traveled road in the seclusion of Amish farmland. The entire inn may be reserved for special occasions. Unsuitable for children under 12. **Rooms:** 13 rms and stes. CI 1pm/CO 11am. No smoking. Lovely rooms and suites are individually decorated and look out on unspoiled rolling countryside. **Amenities:** 🛅 📞 📺 A/C, TV. Some units w/whirlpools. **Services:** Breakfast served 8–10am and includes fresh nut and fruit breads, muffins with strawberry butter, homemade granola, fresh fruit, hard-boiled eggs, juices, coffee, and tea. **Facilities:** 🛋 🏃 🌳 1 restaurant (*see* "Restaurants" below), lawn games, guest lounge w/TV. 100 private acres include 20 acres of virgin woods, paths for walking/jogging/biking, and croquet court that doubles as chipping green for golfers. **Rates (CP):** $80–$100 S; $112–$140 D; $120–$325 ste. Extra person $30. Parking: Outdoor, free. Closed Jan. AE, MC, V.

RESTAURANTS 🍽

The Brick House Restaurant

16820 CR 38; tel 219/534-4949. 1000 feet W of US 33 S. **Regional American.** Situated in a century-old country home with a white frame porch, 10-foot-high ceilings, and original tin roof, the Brick House offers dining in nine rooms on two floors. While the atmosphere is somewhat formal, children and family celebrations are welcomed. Specialties of the house include a baked, one-pound pork chop and smoked baby back ribs, both served with exclusive-recipe red sauce. A variety of fish, steaks, veal, and pasta are also on the menu, as well as a changing selection of homemade desserts. **FYI:** Reservations recommended. Children's menu. No smoking. **Open:** Lunch Tues–Fri 11am–2:30pm; dinner Tues–Sat 5–9pm; brunch Sun 11am–2pm. Closed week of July 4. **Prices:** Main courses $10–$18. AE, DISC, MC, V. 💗 🍴 👨‍👩‍👧 &

♣ The Checkerberry Restaurant

In the Checkerberry Inn, 62644 CR 37; tel 219/642-4445. S of I-80/90. Take IN 4 E from Goshen, turning S on CR 37. **Eclectic.** Providing a sunlit, cheerful atmosphere for lunch and a quiet, candlelit, romantic ambience for dinner, this small and tastefully decorated bistro offers consistently gracious service. The four course dinner begins with a variety of mixed greens tossed with house vinaigrette. An intermezzo of sorbet precedes the entree. Entrees change seasonally but might include pan-roasted duck breast served with organic wild rice, mango-rhubarb chutney, and sauce of three berries; tandoori pork tenderloin grilled with Indian spice, accompa-

nied by saffron rice and sweet-and-sour red onion glaze; or free-range Rocky Mountain lamb marinated in olive oil, rosemary and garlic, served with wilted greens. Wide array of desserts. **FYI:** Reservations recommended. Dress code. Beer and wine only. No smoking. **Open:** Peak (June–Sept) lunch Wed 11:30am–1pm; dinner Tues–Sat 6–9pm. Closed Jan. **Prices:** Main courses $26–$40. AE, MC, V. 💗 🍴 🏞 💟 &

★ South Side Soda Shop & Diner

1122 S Main St; tel 219/534-3790. 1 mi S of downtown. **Diner.** A soda shop since the 1940s, with a strong local following. Known for its chili, this popular spot also features a wide variety of sandwiches, Philly cheese steaks and subs, salads, and homemade soups. Ice cream and fountain specialties include tin roofs, turtle sundaes, malts, cones, and ice cream sodas. Fresh whole pies and other baked goods to go. Children's portions are half-price **FYI:** Reservations accepted. No liquor license. No smoking. **Open:** Tues–Sat 11am–8pm. **Prices:** Main courses $6–$7. No CC. 🍴

REFRESHMENT STOP 🍦

★ Olympia Candy Kitchen

136 N Main St; tel 219/533-5040. Across from the courthouse. **Burgers/Sandwiches.** The tempting aroma of homemade chocolate candies and fudge wafts from the kitchen at this authentic, old-fashioned ice cream parlor owned by the same family since the 1920s. Recommended are the vegetable soup, olive-nut sandwich, and ice cream specialties, as well as the famous chocolate-covered cashews, available to take home. A supplier of chocolates to US presidents as well as Valentine sweethearts, the Olympia lives up to its reputation as "the sweetest little place in town." No public rest rooms. **Open:** Mon–Tues 7am–5pm, Thurs–Fri 7am–5pm, Sat 7am–3:30pm, Sun 7am–12:30pm. No CC. 🍴

Greenfield

Seat of Hancock County, in central part of state. Boyhood home of "the Hoosier poet," James Whitcomb Riley. The James Whitcomb Riley Festival is held on the weekend closest to his birthday (October 7). **Information:** Greater Greenfield Chamber of Commerce, 110 S State St, Greenfield, 46140 (tel 317/462-4188).

MOTELS 🏨

≣ Howard Hughes Motor Lodge

1310 W Main St, 46140; tel 317/462-4493. Exit 104 off I-70, S on IN 9, W on US 40. US 40 location convenient to Indianapolis. Good for business travelers. **Rooms:** 23 rms. CI noon/CO noon. Nonsmoking rms avail. **Amenities:** 🛅 📞 📺 A/C, cable TV. **Services:** 🛎 **Rates:** $32–$37 S; $39 D. Extra person $4. Parking: Outdoor, free. Higher rates for Indianapolis 500 in May and Brickyard 400 in Aug. AE, CB, DC, DISC, MC, V.

≣≣ Super 8 Motel

2100 N State St, 46140; tel 317/462-8899 or toll free 800/800-8000; fax 317/462-8899. Exit 104 off I-70. Guests enjoy the comfortable, decorated lobby with fireplace. **Rooms:** 80 rms and stes. CI noon/CO 11am. Nonsmoking rms avail. **Amenities:** 🛅 A/C, cable TV. **Services:** 🗑 VCRs available. **Facilities:** 🖼 🔲35 🔥 Games rm, whirlpool. Adult-only pool hours: 11pm–midnight. **Rates:** $40–$42 S; $42–$49 D; $45–$53 ste. Extra person $2. Children under age 12 stay free. Parking: Outdoor, free. Three-day packages avail for Indianapolis 500 in May and Brickyard 400 in Aug. AE, CB, DC, DISC, MC, V.

Hammond

A highly industrialized town on the south shore of Lake Michigan. Chief products include railroad equipment, petrochemicals, and surgical supplies. **Information:** Hammond Chamber of Commerce, 200 Russell St, #125, Hammond, 46320 (tel 219/931-1000).

HOTEL 🖼

≣≣ Holiday Inn

3830 179th St, 46323; tel 219/844-2140 or toll free 800/HOLIDAY; fax 219/845-7760. Exit 5A off I-80/94. Large porte cochere, shrubs and floral plantings, plus two inviting benches at pleasing entry. **Rooms:** 152 rms and stes. Executive level. CI 3pm/CO noon. Nonsmoking rms avail. **Amenities:** 🛅 🅿 A/C, satel TV, dataport, in-rm safe. **Services:** ✕ 🗑 🗑 🗑 Continental breakfast for executive level only. Pets $10 a day. **Facilities:** 🖼 🍴 🔲110 🔥 1 restaurant, 1 bar, sauna, steam rm, whirlpool. **Rates:** Peak (May–Sept) $79–$85 S or D; $200 ste. Extra person $8. Children under age 18 stay free. Lower rates off-season. Parking: Outdoor, free. Up to five persons per room at no extra charge. AE, CB, DC, DISC, MC, V.

Huntington

Seat of Huntington County, in northeastern part of state. Named for Samuel Huntington, a member of the Continental Congress. **Information:** Huntington County Visitor & Convention Bureau, 305 Warren St, PO Box 212, Huntington, 46750 (tel 219/359-TOUR or toll free 800/848-4282).

MOTEL 🖼

≣≣ Days Inn

2996 W Park Dr, 46750; tel 219/359-8989 or toll free 800/329-7466; fax 219/356-8989. Jct US 24 W/IN 9. Set well back in large service plaza at junction of two highways, this recently renovated motel is bright and attractive with pastel-tinted trim on doorways and lobby entrance. Large restaurant adjacent. Modest but well-kept facility for an economical

short stay. **Rooms:** 66 rms and stes. CI 1:30pm/CO noon. Nonsmoking rms avail. New addition has two-room suites. All other rooms being refurbished. **Amenities:** 🛅 🅿 A/C, cable TV. Some units w/whirlpools. **Services:** 🗑 🗑 🗑 Pets $7/day. **Facilities:** 🖼 🔲30 **Rates:** $40–$44 S; $43–$48 D; $56–$62 ste. Extra person $5. Parking: Outdoor, free. Rates increase over Labor Day weekend. AE, CB, DC, DISC, MC, V.

Indiana Dunes National Lakeshore

"The Dunes," Carl Sandburg wrote, "are to the Midwest what the Grand Canyon is to Arizona and Yosemite is to California. They constitute a signature of time and eternity." The 13,000-acre site consists of dunes which rise 180 feet above Lake Michigan's southern shore, as well as stretches of uncrowded beaches, prairie, bird-filled marshes, oak and maple forests, and bogs. Hiking, swimming, fishing, boating, biking, camping, and cross-country skiing, and picnicking are popular recreational activities. Rangers lead bog, wildflower and bird walks, dune hikes, wildlife talks, and many other programs.

Within the National Lakeshore area is the 2,182-acre **Indiana Dunes State Park** which features the lakeshore's highest sand dune, the 192-foot-tall Mount Tom. The 1,500-acre **Dunes State Nature Preserve** boasts more species of trees than any other similarly sized area in the Midwest. Cowles Bog, immediately south of Dune Acres, and Pinhook Bog, six miles south of Michigan City, are of special interest for their variety of plants and animals. This habitat includes the northern range of many birds and plants as well as bogs representative of cooler climates. It is a haven for at least 223 species of birds. The Paul H Douglas Center for Environmental Education is located in Miller Woods, a combination of open beach, dunes, and oak forest.

For more information contact Superintendent, Indiana Dunes National Seashore, 1100 N Mineral Springs Rd, Porter, IN 46304 (tel 219/926-7561).

Indianapolis

See also Fishers, Greenfield

Once derided as "Naptown," the largest city and capital of Indiana has become a modern, clean, and very attractive city. Its athletic facilities are unprecedented for a city of its size: the downtown Hoosierdome hosts the NFL Colts and the NBA Pacers, the Indianapolis Velodrome is one of the only facilities of its kind in the country, and the Indianapolis Motor Speedway is home to the world-famous Indianapolis 500. "Indy" is also home to Butler University and a number of world-class museums. **Information:** Indianapolis Convention & Visitors Bureau, One Hoosier Dome, #100, Indianapolis, 46225 (tel 317/639-4282).

PUBLIC TRANSPORTATION

City **bus service** is provided by Metro Transit. Fare during morning and evening rush hours is $1 (50¢ for seniors), and 75¢ (35¢ for seniors) during all other times. Exact change or monthly pass (purchased at the Metro Transit office at 936 N Delaware) required. For information call 317/635-3344.

HOTELS 🏨

≡≡ Best Western Waterfront Plaza Hotel

2930 Waterfront Pkwy W Dr, 46214; tel 317/299-8400 or toll free 800/528-1234; fax 317/299-9257. Exit 16A off I-465; W on US 136 ¼ mi. Three-story facility on a picturesque man-made lake on the west side of Indianapolis. Near Indianapolis Motor Speedway and Raceway Park, 15 minutes to downtown and the new Circle Centre Mall, 10 minutes to airport. **Rooms:** 144 rms and stes. Executive level. CI 3pm/CO 11am. Nonsmoking rms avail. **Amenities:** 🛆 🐱 🎧 A/C, cable TV, voice mail. Some units w/minibars. Steamers, instead of irons, available. **Services:** ✕ 🚗 🛆 🛎 **Facilities:** 🔥 💺 500 🖥 & 1 restaurant, 1 bar, sauna, whirlpool. Free passes to nearby health club. **Rates:** Peak (Apr–Oct) $64–$70 S; $70–$76 D; $119–$125 ste. Extra person $6. Children under age 18 stay free. Lower rates off-season. Parking: Outdoor, free. Gold Crown Club International memberships available. AE, CB, DC, DISC, MC, V.

≡≡≡≡ Canterbury

123 S Illinois St, 46225; tel 317/634-3000 or toll free 800/538-8186; fax 317/685-2519. At the S end of Circle Centre Mall, just N of Union Station. The management boasts that if you want to enjoy "a bit of England," stay at the Canterbury. The small European-style hotel has plenty of ambience. There is an entrance from the hotel to the new Circle Centre Mall. Member of Preferred Hotels and Resorts. **Rooms:** 99 rms and stes. CI 3pm/CO noon. Nonsmoking rms avail. Large rooms with quality furniture, including four-posters and huge armoires. **Amenities:** 🛆 🐱 🎧 A/C, cable TV w/movies, refrig, dataport, VCR, bathrobes. Bathrooms have telephones. **Services:** 🍽 🔑 VP 🚗 🛆 🛎 ⚙ Twice-daily maid svce, car-rental desk, masseur, babysitting. Tea served daily at 4pm in lovely atrium as pianist entertains. **Facilities:** 150 & 1 restaurant (*see* "Restaurants" below), 1 bar. Guests may use health club across the street. **Rates (CP):** $165–$195 S; $190–$220 D; $225–$1,100 ste. Extra person $25. Children under age 12 stay free. Min stay special events. Parking: Indoor, $5–$9/day. AE, CB, DC, DISC, EC, JCB, MC, V.

≡≡≡ Courtyard by Marriott

501 W Washington St, 46204 (Downtown); tel 317/635-4443 or toll free 800/321-2211; fax 317/687-0029. At West St. Great location, on edge of White River State Park, which is under development. Across the street from the Eiteljorg Museum of Western American and Indian Art. A minor

league baseball field is under construction just behind the hotel. **Rooms:** 233 rms. CI 3pm/CO noon. Nonsmoking rms avail. Unusually clean and well-maintained rooms are surprisingly bright and cheerful. **Amenities:** 🛆 🐱 🎧 🍽 A/C, cable TV w/movies, in-rm safe. 1 unit w/minibar, some w/terraces. **Services:** ✕ 🚗 🛆 🛎 Babysitting. **Facilities:** 🔥 300 & 2 restaurants, 1 bar. TGI Friday's, recently named best franchise restaurant of the year, on the premises. **Rates:** $89–$99 S; $99–$109 D. Extra person $10. Children under age 18 stay free. Min stay special events. Parking: Outdoor, free. AE, CB, DC, DISC, MC, V.

≡≡≡ Courtyard by Marriott Indianapolis North

10290 N Meridian St, 46290; tel 317/571-1110 or toll free 800/321-2211; fax 317/571-0416. Exit 31 off I-465, N on US 31 ½ mi. Elegance in large welcoming lobby and sunken lounge area with fireplace that overlooks courtyard gazebo and pool. Adjacent to Thompson Consumer Electronics, on northwest side of Indianapolis. **Rooms:** 149 rms and stes. CI 3pm/CO 1pm. Nonsmoking rms avail. **Amenities:** 🛆 🐱 🎧 A/C, cable TV w/movies, dataport. All units w/terraces. **Services:** ✕ 🚗 🛆 🛎 Twice-daily maid svce, car-rental desk. Complimentary newspapers, and hors d'oeuvres in early evening. **Facilities:** 🔥 💺 45 & 1 restaurant (bkfst only), 1 bar, whirlpool, washer/dryer. **Rates:** $76–$86 S; $86 D; $89–$99 ste. Extra person $10. Children under age 12 stay free. Parking: Outdoor, free. Courtyard Club memberships avail. AE, DC, DISC, JCB, MC, V.

≡≡≡ Embassy Suites Downtown

110 W Washington St, 46204; tel 317/236-1800 or toll free 800/362-2779; fax 317/236-1816. Downtown. Above Claypool Courts, connected by skybridge to new Circle Centre Mall and other downtown sites. Glass elevators overlook atrium with lush greenery and fountains. Recently renovated. **Rooms:** 360 stes. Executive level. CI 4pm/CO noon. Nonsmoking rms avail. **Amenities:** 🛆 🐱 🎧 🍽 A/C, cable TV w/movies, refrig, voice mail. Some units w/terraces, some w/whirlpools. All suites have two TVs, wet bars with refrigerators, microwaves, irons, and full-size ironing boards. **Services:** ✕ 🛆 🛎 Car-rental desk, babysitting. VCRs available. Two hours of complimentary beverages each evening. **Facilities:** 🔥 💺 250 & 2 restaurants (lunch and dinner only), 1 bar, whirlpool, washer/dryer. **Rates (BB):** $129–$189 ste. Extra person $20. Children under age 12 stay free. AE, CB, DC, DISC, MC, V.

≡≡≡ Embassy Suites North

3912 Vincennes Rd, 46268; tel 317/872-7700 or toll free 800/EMBASSY. S of I-465 on Michigan Rd. Beautiful motel inside and out. Exterior looks like rose-and-beige Moorish castle. Large brick-paved entryway highlighted with three-tiered fountain. Paintings in pastels adorn walls. On ground level of eight-story atrium, water falls into small lagoons amid green foliage. Hotel is standout in area saturated with hotels, motels, restaurants, service stations, and bars. **Rooms:** 250 stes. CI 3pm/CO 11am. Nonsmoking rms avail. Large and well-furnished rooms. **Amenities:** 🖥 🛁 📺 📶 A/C, satel TV w/movies, refrig, dataport. Some units w/terraces. Two TVs in suites. **Services:** ✗ 🍴 📠 🛎 ⚡ Twice-daily maid svce, social director. Two hours of complimentary cocktails each evening. **Facilities:** 🏊 🏌 600 ⚡ 1 restaurant, 2 bars, basketball, games rm, sauna, whirlpool. **Rates (BB):** $115–$179 ste. Children under age 18 stay free. Min stay special events. Parking: Outdoor, free. AE, DC, DISC, MC, V.

≡≡≡ Holiday Inn
2501 S High School Rd, 46241 (Indianapolis Int'l Airport); tel 317/244-6861 or toll free 800/317/465-4329; fax 317/243-1059. A Holiday Inn Select facility on grounds of Indianapolis Int'l Airport, 10 minutes from downtown. Glass elevators overlook atrium. A place of both comfort and quality. Good for business travelers. **Rooms:** 274 rms and stes. Executive level. CI 3pm/CO noon. Nonsmoking rms avail. **Amenities:** 🖥 🛁 📺 📶 A/C, satel TV w/movies, dataport, voice mail. Some units w/terraces, some w/whirlpools. Nintendo hookups, irons, and ironing boards in each room. **Services:** ✗ 🍴 📠 ⚡ Car-rental desk. VCRs available. **Facilities:** 🏊 🏌 600 ⚡ 2 restaurants (see "Restaurants" below), 2 bars (1 w/entertainment), games rm, sauna, whirlpool. Largest number of small meeting rooms in city, with amphitheater and 20 meeting rooms. Award-winning French restaurant. Two saunas. **Rates:** $109–$189 S or D; $189 ste. Children under age 18 stay free. Parking: Outdoor, free. Kids Eat Free program. AE, CB, DC, DISC, JCB, MC, V.

≡≡≡ Hyatt Regency Indianapolis
1 S Capitol Ave, 46204 (Downtown); tel 317/632-1234 or toll free 800/233-1234; fax 317/231-7569. A 20-story atrium with a 20′ lobby waterfall and glass elevator in the National City Center. Recently renovated. Connected by skywalk to Circle Centre Mall, Convention Center/RCA Dome. Walking distance to Union Station, Capitol, shopping, and restaurants. **Rooms:** 497 rms and stes. Executive level. CI 3pm/CO noon. Nonsmoking rms avail. **Amenities:** 🖥 🛁 A/C, satel TV w/movies, dataport, voice mail. **Services:** ✗ 🔑 VP 📠 ⚡ Car-rental desk, masseur, babysitting. **Facilities:** 🏊 🏌 🏌 900 💻 ⚡ 2 restaurants, 2 bars (1 w/entertainment), spa, sauna, steam rm, whirlpool, beauty salon. Largest health and fitness facility of any downtown hotel. Twelve retail shops (including jewelry store, florist, bookstore, Hallmark, McDonald's, two airline offices). Revolving rooftop Eagle's Nest restaurant. **Rates:** $85–$150 S; $110–$175 D; $300–$1,000 ste. Extra person $25. Children under age 18 stay free. Parking: Indoor, $9/day. AE, CB, DC, DISC, EC, ER, JCB, MC, V.

≡≡≡ Indianapolis Marriott
7202 E 21st St, 46219; tel 317/352-1231 or toll free 800/228-9290; fax 317/352-9775. Exit 89 (Shadeland Ave) off I-70. Full-service hotel on east side of Indianapolis with fireplace in lobby. Near Washington Square shopping mall and restaurants. **Rooms:** 252 rms and stes. Executive level. CI 4pm/CO noon. Nonsmoking rms avail. **Amenities:** 🖥 🛁

A/C, cable TV w/movies, dataport, voice mail. Some units w/terraces, some w/whirlpools. **Services:** ✗ 🔑 📠 🛎 ⚡ ⚡ Babysitting. Satellite available for teleconferencing. **Facilities:** 🏊 🏌 1100 💻 ⚡ 1 restaurant, 1 bar (w/entertainment), games rm, spa, whirlpool, washer/dryer. Indoor/outdoor pool. **Rates:** Peak (Apr–Oct) $104–$114 S or D; $300 ste. Extra person $10. Children under age 18 stay free. Lower rates off-season. Parking: Outdoor, free. AE, CB, DC, DISC, JCB, MC, V.

≡≡≡ Omni Indianapolis North Hotel
8181 N Shadeland Ave, 46250; tel 317/849-6668 or toll free 800/THE-OMNI; fax 317/849-4936. Exit 1 off I-69. This high-rise hotel and conference center with an English ambience is the only full-service facility in the city's northeast corner, close to Castleton Square Mall shopping and restaurants, Deer Creek Music Center, and Conner Prairie pioneer museum. **Rooms:** 215 rms and stes. Executive level. CI 3pm/CO noon. Nonsmoking rms avail. **Amenities:** 🖥 🛁 📺 A/C, cable TV w/movies, dataport. Some units w/whirlpools. Refrigerators available. Robes in suites. **Services:** ✗ VP 🚐 📠 ⚡ Car-rental desk, social director, children's program, babysitting. VCRs available. Select guests have twice-daily maid service. **Facilities:** 🏊 🏌 🏌 500 💻 ⚡ 2 restaurants, 1 bar, games rm, sauna, washer/dryer. **Rates:** Peak (Apr–Oct) $99–$126 S or D; $175–$250 ste. Children under age 18 stay free. Lower rates off-season. Parking: Outdoor, free. AE, CB, DC, DISC, MC, V.

≡≡≡ Omni Severin Hotel
40 W Jackson Place, 46225; tel 317/634-6664 or toll free 800/THE-OMNI; fax 317/767-0003. This beautifully restored hotel has a new lobby with marble floors, brass trimming, and lovely chandeliers. A circular drive and new canopy mark the main entrance directly across from Union Station. **Rooms:** 423 rms and stes. Executive level. CI 3pm/CO noon. Nonsmoking rms avail. Rooms were recently redone. **Amenities:** 🖥 🛁 A/C, cable TV w/movies. Some units w/terraces. **Services:** ✗ 🔑 VP 🚐 📠 ⚡ Car-rental desk. **Facilities:** 🏊 🏌 400 ⚡ 2 restaurants, 1 bar. **Rates:** $99–$170 S or D; $225–$280 ste. Extra person $20. Children under age 18 stay free. Min stay special events. AE, CB, DC, DISC, MC, V.

≡≡≡ Radisson Plaza and Suite Hotel
8787 Keystone Crossing, 46240; tel 317/846-2700 or toll free 800/333-3333; fax 317/846-2700. The largest major hotel in the city outside the downtown area, situated in the middle of an upscale fashion mall and office building complex. **Rooms:** 552 rms and stes. CI 3pm/CO noon. Nonsmoking rms avail. Rooms are larger than customary, with beautiful cherry furniture and an attractive decor. Plenty of drawer space and a sizable desk. **Amenities:** 🖥 🛁 📺 📶 A/C, cable TV w/movies, refrig, dataport, voice mail. Some units w/terraces, some w/whirlpools. Ironing board and iron in each closet. **Services:** ✗ 🔑 VP 📠 ⚡ ⚡ Babysitting. **Facilities:** 🏊 🏌 ⚡3 🏌 400 💻 ⚡ 2 restaurants, 1 bar (w/entertainment),

games rm, spa, sauna, steam rm, whirlpool, washer/dryer. Fitness center just a few steps from the hotel. **Rates:** Peak (during Indy 500 and Brickyard 400 auto races) $120–$140 S; $140–$160 D; $140–$160 ste. Extra person $10. Children under age 12 stay free. Min stay special events. Lower rates off-season. Parking: Indoor/outdoor, free. AE, CB, DC, DISC, ER, JCB, MC, V.

≣≣ Ramada Plaza Hotel

31 W Ohio St, 46204 (Downtown); tel 317/635-2000 or toll free 800/228-2828; fax 317/236-2534. 1 block from Circle Centre Mall. A 12-story building in the heart of the city. Especially patronized by business travelers, airline attendants, and sales personnel. Lobby needs better maintenance. **Rooms:** 371 rms and stes. CI 3pm/CO noon. Nonsmoking rms avail. Rooms are worn. **Amenities:** 🛅 🐚 A/C, cable TV w/movies. **Services:** ✗ 🚗 🛆 🤝 Car-rental desk. **Facilities:** 🔥 🔲750 🛆 2 restaurants, 1 bar. Sun deck. Indoor parking garage. **Rates:** $110 S or D; $95–$150 ste. Extra person $10. Children under age 18 stay free. Min stay special events. Parking: Indoor, $6/day. AE, CB, DC, DISC, MC, V.

≣≣ Renaissance Tower Historic Inn

230 E 9th St, 46204; tel 317/261-1652 or toll free 800/676-7786; fax 317/262-8648. Exit 113 off I-65; N to 9th St; E 2 blocks. Located in the historic St Joseph District on the north side of downtown. Listed in the National Register of Historic Places. **Rooms:** 81 stes. Executive level. CI 3pm/CO noon. Nonsmoking rms avail. **Amenities:** 🛅 🐚 🖳 A/C, cable TV, refrig, voice mail. Suites have fully equipped kitchens with eating and cooking utensils. **Services:** 🔑 Car-rental desk. VCRs and movies available. **Facilities:** 🛆 Washer/dryer. **Rates:** Peak (Jan–Sept) $75–$105 ste. Children under age 18 stay free. Lower rates off-season. Parking: Outdoor, free. Weekend specials. Long-term stays avail. AE, MC, V.

≣≣≣ University Place Conference Center and Hotel

850 W Michigan St, 46202; tel 317/269-9000 or toll free 800/626-2700; fax 317/231-5168. On campus of Indiana and Perdue Universities at Indianapolis. A much needed facility for the rapidly growing campus of the state's two largest universities. Well equipped to handle large groups. Rates a little on the high side considering the location. **Rooms:** 276 rms and stes. CI 3pm/CO noon. Nonsmoking rms avail. Rooms are well furnished and functional. **Amenities:** 🛅 🐚 A/C, cable TV, refrig, dataport, voice mail. **Services:** ✗ 🔑 🛆 🤝 Car-rental desk, babysitting. **Facilities:** 🔲1000 🛆 2 restaurants, 1 bar, basketball, beauty salon, day-care ctr. Guests can use campus facilities, including $25-million world-class natatorium, fitness center, and track-and-field stadium. Two main restaurants, plus food court with eight fast food outlets. Indoor parking garage. **Rates:** $115 S; $130 D; $300–$600 ste. Extra person $15. Children under age 18 stay free. Min stay special events. Parking: Indoor, $4.75/day. AE, DISC, MC, V.

≣≣≣ The Westin Hotel Indianapolis

50 S Capitol Ave, 46204; tel 317/262-8100 or toll free 800/228-3000; fax 317/231-3928. Downtown. Luxury hotel with sky bridge to Circle Centre Mall and Convention Center/RCA Dome. Walking distance to Union Station and downtown attractions, restaurants, and shops. **Rooms:** 573 rms and stes. Executive level. CI 3pm/CO noon. Nonsmoking rms avail. **Amenities:** 🛅 🐚 🖳 A/C, cable TV w/movies, dataport, voice mail. Some units w/minibars, 1 w/whirlpool. Refrigerators available. **Services:** 🍽 🔑 VP 🚗 🛆 🤝 Car-rental desk, children's program, babysitting. VCRs available. Special kids club with age-related welcoming gifts (tippy cup, night light, crayons and coloring books, baseball hat, etc). Beverage containers are refilled at no charge throughout the stay. **Facilities:** 🔥 🏋 🔲2500 🖳 🛆 2 restaurants, 1 bar, whirlpool. **Rates:** $160 S; $185 D; $195–$1,000 ste. Extra person $25. Children under age 18 stay free. Parking: Indoor, $6.50/day. Premier frequent travel program. AE, CB, DC, DISC, JCB, MC, V.

MOTELS

≣≣ The Brickyard Resort & Inn

4400 W 16th St, 46222; tel 317/241-2500 or toll free 800/926-8276; fax 317/241-2133. Indianapolis Motor Speedway. 600 acres. A conventional two-story motel with a first-class 18-hole golf course. Registration, lobby, restaurant, bar, and golf pro shop in separate building across from entrance. Location is unique, right outside turn two on speedway track—it can be noisy when events are taking place, but approximately 11 months out of the year the motel is rather quiet. Rates are reasonable considering the location. **Rooms:** 108 rms. CI 3pm/CO noon. No smoking. Nonsmoking rms avail. Rooms are ordinary. **Amenities:** 🛅 🐚 🖳 A/C, cable TV, refrig. Some units w/terraces. **Services:** ✗ 🚗 🛆 🤝 🔔 Babysitting. **Facilities:** 🔥 ▶18 🔲400 1 restaurant, 1 bar (w/entertainment). **Rates:** $52–$58 S; $58–$63 D. Extra person $6. Children under age 15 stay free. Parking: Outdoor, free. AE, CB, DC, DISC, MC, V.

≣≣ Comfort Inn North

3880 W 92nd St, 46268; tel 317/872-3100 or toll free 800/221-2222; fax 317/872-3100. Exit 27 off I-465, S ½ mi, W on 92nd St. Standard budget motel with three floors. Close to Beef & Boards dinner theater. **Rooms:** 58 rms and stes. CI 1pm/CO 11am. Nonsmoking rms avail. **Amenities:** 🛅 🐚 A/C, cable TV. Irons and boards available. **Services:** 🛆 🤝 🔔 **Facilities:** 🔥 🔲10 🛆 Games rm, whirlpool. **Rates (CP):** Peak (May–Oct) $45–$52 S or D; $61–$75 ste. Extra person $7. Children under age 17 stay free. Lower rates off-season. Parking: Outdoor, free. 13th night free. AE, DC, DISC, MC, V.

≣≣≣ Crowne Plaza at Union Station

123 W Louisiana St, 46206; tel 317/631-2221 or toll free 800/2-CROWNE; fax 317/236-7474. Between Illinois St and Capitol Ave. When the abandoned Union Station was turned

into a festival marketplace, this motel was built in what had been adjoining railroad warehouses; 26 rooms are on real Pullman cars on the lobby level. Pedestrian corridor runs from motel to the station. Excellent location: RCA Dome and Convention Center only three blocks away. **Rooms:** 276 rms and stes. Executive level. CI 4pm/CO noon. Nonsmoking rms avail. Typical Holiday Inn rooms. **Amenities:** 🚪🕐📺📞 A/C, cable TV w/movies, dataport, voice mail. **Services:** ✕🛏️ⓋⓅ 🚐⬛️🪄 **Facilities:** 🏊‍♂️🏌️200 ♿ 2 restaurants, 1 bar, games rm, spa, whirlpool, beauty salon, playground. **Rates:** $118–$147 S; $133–$162 D; $177–$207 ste. Extra person $15. Children under age 18 stay free. Min stay special events. Parking: Indoor/outdoor, $2.50–$8/day. AE, CB, DC, DISC, MC, V.

≣≣ Days Inn

5151 Elmwood Dr, 46230 (Beech Grove); tel 317/783-5555 or toll free 800/DAYS-INN; fax 317/786-4297. I-465 S and Emerson Ave. Lobby and registration in separate building. No hallways—rooms open to outdoors and surrounding parking area. One of the early properties in this chain. **Rooms:** 119 rms. Executive level. CI 2pm/CO 11am. Nonsmoking rms avail. Neat, but rather Spartan. **Amenities:** 🚪🕐 A/C, cable TV. **Services:** 🪄 Car-rental desk. **Facilities:** ♿ **Rates (CP):** $50–$65 S or D. Children under age 12 stay free. Min stay special events. Parking: Outdoor, free. AE, CB, DC, DISC, MC, V.

≣ Days Inn Airport

5860 Fortune Circle W, 46241 (Indianapolis Int'l Airport); tel 317/248-0621 or toll free 800/DAYS-INN; fax 317/247-6737. Standard budget motel near the airport. **Rooms:** 238 rms and stes. CI 2pm/CO noon. Nonsmoking rms avail. **Amenities:** 🚪📺 A/C, cable TV w/movies. **Services:** ✕🚐🛏️ 🪄 **Facilities:** 🏊‍♂️🏌️400 ♿ 1 restaurant, 1 bar, volleyball. **Rates:** $49–$54 S or D; $85 ste. Extra person $5. Children under age 18 stay free. Parking: Outdoor, free. Special park-and-fly program. AE, DC, DISC, MC, V.

≣≣ Economy Inn

602 E Thompson Rd, 46227 (Southside); tel 317/788-0331; fax 317/787-9805. 1 block S of I-465 at US 31 S and Thompson Rd. This motel, sandwiched in between competitors with higher rates, attracts the more frugal traveler. Fairly large. **Rooms:** 140 rms. CI 2pm/CO 11am. Nonsmoking rms avail. Rooms are small and devoid of extras. Some have waterbeds at no extra charge. **Amenities:** 🚪🕐 A/C, cable TV. 1 unit w/whirlpool. **Facilities:** ♿ **Rates:** $30–$33 S; $37–$40 D. Children under age 18 stay free. Min stay special events. Parking: Outdoor, free. AE, CB, DC, DISC, MC, V.

≣≣ Fairfield Inn College Park

9251 Wesleyan Rd, 46268; tel 317/879-9100 or toll free 800/228-2800; fax 317/879-9100. Exit 27 off I-465. New facility, at College Park in northwest corner of Indianapolis. Close to Beef & Boards dinner theater. Many restaurants within walking distance. **Rooms:** 131 rms. CI 3pm/CO noon.

Nonsmoking rms avail. **Amenities:** 🚪🕐 A/C, satel TV w/movies, dataport. **Services:** 🚐🛏️🪄 Car-rental desk. Complimentary dessert at nearby Mountain Jack's restaurant. **Facilities:** 🏊‍♂️8 ♿ Complimentary passes to nearby health club. **Rates (CP):** $45–$70 S or D. Extra person $8. Children under age 18 stay free. Parking: Outdoor, free. INNsiders Club memberships avail. AE, CB, DC, DISC, MC, V.

≣≣≣ Hampton Inn South

7045 McFarland Blvd, 46237 (McFarland Farms); tel 317/889-0722 or toll free 800/HAMPTON; fax 317/889-0722. At I-465 S and Southport Rd. Located across the street from a lovely residential development, this four-story Hampton Inn has the appearance of being in a park-like setting. Spacious grounds are well manicured and spotless. Parking areas are well maintained, too. **Rooms:** 113 rms. CI 3pm/CO noon. No smoking. Rooms are large enough for families. The furniture, while not expensive, is becoming. **Amenities:** 🚪🕐 A/C, cable TV. **Services:** 🛏️🪄 **Facilities:** 🏊‍♂️♿ **Rates (CP):** $48–$54 S; $52–$58 D. Extra person $6. Children under age 18 stay free. Min stay special events. Parking: Outdoor, free. AE, CB, DC, DISC, MC, V.

≣ Howard Johnson East

7050 E 21st St, 46219 (East Side); tel 317/352-0481 or toll free 800/447-9961; fax 317/353-0914. Average motel with no outstanding features. **Rooms:** 125 rms. CI 2pm/CO noon. Nonsmoking rms avail. Adequate but no frills. **Amenities:** 🚪 A/C, cable TV, refrig. 1 unit w/whirlpool. **Services:** 🪄 **Facilities:** 🏊‍♂️300 ♿ Washer/dryer. **Rates (CP):** $48 S or D. Extra person $4. Children under age 13 stay free. Min stay special events. Parking: Outdoor, free. AE, DISC, MC, V.

≣≣ Quality Inn East

3525 N Shadeland Ave, 46226; tel 317/549-2222 or toll free 800/221-2222; fax 317/549-2222. Exit 89 (Shadeland Ave) off I-70. A motel serving both families and business travelers. Close to wide variety of restaurants and regional shopping centers, 3 miles to state fairgrounds, 7 miles to Children's Museum, 8 miles to downtown and Circle Centre Mall. **Rooms:** 123 rms and stes. Executive level. CI 3pm/CO 11am. Nonsmoking rms avail. **Amenities:** 🚪🕐 A/C, satel TV w/movies. Some units w/terraces, all w/whirlpools. **Services:** ✕🛏️🪄 Car-rental desk. Nintendo available in every room. **Facilities:** 🏊‍♂️🏌️500 🖥️ 1 restaurant, 1 bar (w/entertainment), games rm, whirlpool, washer/dryer. **Rates:** Peak (Mar–Oct 15) $49–$95 S; $54–$115 D; $95–$169 ste. Extra person $5. Children under age 18 stay free. Lower rates off-season. Parking: Outdoor, free. AE, CB, DC, DISC, ER, JCB, MC, V.

≣≣≣ Ramada Inn East

7701 E 42nd St, 46226; tel 317/897-4000 or toll free 800/272-6232; fax 317/897-8120. Exit 42 off I-465. Standard motel close to Fort Harrison, US Army Finance Center, two regional shopping centers; 15–20 minutes away from anything in Indianapolis. **Rooms:** 192 rms and stes. CI 3pm/CO noon. Nonsmoking rms avail. **Amenities:** 🕾 A/C, cable TV. Some units w/whirlpools. Coffeemakers and dataports in some rooms. **Services:** ✗ 🖎 ⌔ **Facilities:** 🖼 🔟⁵⁰ 🖈 1 restaurant, 1 bar, games rm, washer/dryer. **Rates:** Peak (Feb–Sept) $53–$66 S or D; $110–$150 ste. Extra person $10. Children under age 18 stay free. Lower rates off-season. Parking: Outdoor, free. AE, CB, DC, DISC, ER, JCB, MC, V.

🛏 Red Roof Inn North
9520 Valparaiso Court, 46268; tel 317/872-3030 or toll free 800/THE-ROOF; fax 317/872-3476. Exit 27 off I-465; N on Michigan Rd. Two separate buildings with outside entrances on the city's northwest side. Close to Beef & Boards dinner theater, and restaurants. **Rooms:** 108 rms. CI 3pm/CO noon. Nonsmoking rms avail. **Amenities:** 🕾 A/C. **Services:** 🚐 ⌔ ⇗ Car-rental desk, babysitting. **Facilities:** 🖈 **Rates:** Peak (Apr–Oct) $38–$46 S; $52–$60 D. Extra person $8. Children under age 16 stay free. Lower rates off-season. Parking: Outdoor, free. RediCard memberships avail. AE, CB, DC, DISC, MC, V.

🛏 Red Roof Inn Speedway
6415 Debonair Lane, 46224; tel 317/293-6881 or toll free 800/THE-ROOF; fax 317/293-9892. Located on small, dead-end street, motel is difficult to find. Benefits from being on direct route to Indianapolis Motor Speedway two miles away and from chain's centralized reservation system. **Rooms:** 108 rms. CI 3pm/CO noon. Nonsmoking rms avail. **Amenities:** 🕾 A/C, cable TV. **Services:** ⇗ Free coffee in lobby anytime. **Facilities:** 🖈 **Rates:** $38 S; $46–$70 D. Children under age 18 stay free. Min stay special events. Parking: Outdoor, free. AE, DC, DISC, V.

🛏🛏 Signature Inn Castleton
8380 Kelly Lane, 46250 (Commercial); tel 317/849-8555 or toll free 800/822-5252. At I-465 and Allisonville Rd. Both the grounds and motel are neat and clean. Establishment borders an interstate ramp. Attracts business travelers. Restaurants nearby. **Rooms:** 125 rms. CI 3pm/CO noon. Nonsmoking rms avail. Rooms are comfortable, but not luxurious. Desks are large and well lighted. **Amenities:** 🕾 🖲 A/C, cable TV, dataport. 1 unit w/whirlpool. **Services:** 🖎 ⌔ Laundry. **Facilities:** 🖼 🔟⁸⁰ 🖈 Adequate outdoor swimming pool. Two small meeting rooms. **Rates (CP):** Peak (May–Sept) $65–$72 S; $62–$69 D. Children under age 17 stay free. Min stay special events. Lower rates off-season. Parking: Outdoor, free. AE, CB, DC, DISC, MC, V.

🛏🛏🛏 Signature Inn West
3850 Eagle View Dr, 46254; tel 317/299-6165 or toll free 800/822-5252; fax 317/299-6165 ext 500. Exit 17 (38th St) off I-465. Good for business travelers. Close to Indianapolis Motor Speedway and Indianapolis Raceway Park, 5 minutes to regional shopping center, 15 minutes to downtown and Circle Centre Mall. **Rooms:** 101 rms. CI 2pm/CO noon. Nonsmoking rms avail. **Amenities:** 🕾 🖲 A/C, cable TV, dataport. 1 unit w/whirlpool. Hair dryers, irons, and ironing boards available at desk. **Services:** 🚐 🖎 ⌔ Car-rental desk. VCRs and movies available. **Facilities:** 🖼 🏃 🔟⁸⁵ 🖳 🖈 Free pass to nearby spa. **Rates (CP):** $65–$72 S or D. Children under age 18 stay free. Parking: Outdoor, free. Signature Club memberships avail. AE, DC, DISC, MC, V.

RESTAURANTS 🍴

★ The Aristocrat Pub & Restaurant
5212 N College Ave (Broad Ripple); tel 317/283-7388. **American.** A warm and comfortable ambience is created by the stained-glass and beveled-glass fixtures, old-fashioned train engines, and mounted animal heads in the dining room. Fun, inventive dishes include shrimp Vesuvius (tiger shrimp, basil, tomatoes, rosemary, peppers, mushrooms, red peppers, jalapeños, and onions in a garlicky oil and white wine sauce ladled over chili fettuccine noodles and topped with Parmesan cheese); fresh tomato, basil, and brie tortellini; and chicken with rosemary, garlic, capers, and tomatoes. **FYI:** Reservations not accepted. Folk/Irish. Children's menu. **Open:** Mon–Thurs 11am–11pm, Fri–Sat 11am–midnight, Sun 10am–11pm. **Prices:** Main courses $8–$15. AE, DC, DISC, MC, V. ♥ 🍴

Bangkok Restaurant
In Norgate Plaza Shopping Center, 7269 N Keystone Ave; tel 317/255-7799. 1 mi S of I-465. **Thai.** Hot and spicy Thai dishes served in a room tastefully decorated with Southeast Asian artifacts. Luncheon buffets daily plus dinner buffet Mon. **FYI:** Reservations not accepted. Beer and wine only. **Open:** Lunch daily 11:30am–3pm; dinner Sun–Thurs 5–9pm, Fri–Sat 5–10pm. **Prices:** Main courses $7–$9. AE, DC, DISC, MC, V. 🖾 🖈

Battery Park Saloon
In Capital Center Office Building, 201 N Illinois (Downtown); tel 317/237-3388. 2 blocks E of state capitol. **American/Pub.** Popular with office workers from this twin-tower structure and nearby government facilities. A trendy publike atmosphere prevails. The menu lists an unusually large number of appetizers, such as buffalo shrimp and crab cakes. Sandwiches, salads, pasta, and a few entrees available. **FYI:** Reservations accepted. Dress code. **Open:** Mon–Fri 11am–7:30pm. **Prices:** Main courses $7–$12. AE, DC, MC, V. 🖈

♥ Chanteclair
In Holiday Inn, 2501 S High School Rd (Indianapolis Int'l Airport); tel 317/244-6861. At I-465 S. **French.** This gourmet French occupies the top floor of the hotel, located across the street from the main airport entrance. Expertly prepared cuisine is served in an exquisite setting enhanced by a strolling violinist who serenades diners nightly. More than 200 wines in city's largest wine cellar. **FYI:** Reservations recommended. Violin. Jacket required. **Open:** Mon–Thurs 6–10pm, Fri–Sat 6–11pm. **Prices:** Main courses $25–$50. AE, CB, DC, DISC, MC, V. ♥ 🖈

GT South's Rib House

5711 E 71st St; tel 317/849-6997. 1 block W of IN 37. **Barbecue/Burgers.** "Cook it low and smoke it low" is the motto at this joint, where pulled pork is the house specialty. The delicious sauce that accompanies it—mild or hot—has diners asking for more. Also deli sandwiches, white bean soup, and Brunswick stew. Located in a small strip mall. **FYI:** Reservations accepted. Blues. Dress code. **Open:** Mon–Thurs 10am–9pm, Fri–Sat 10am–10pm. **Prices:** Main courses $6–$14. DC, DISC, MC, V. 🏞

★ Hollyhock Hill

8110 N College Ave (Williams Creek); tel 317/251-2294. 6 blocks E of Meridian St; 5 blocks S of 86th St. **Regional American.** A unique eatery known for its country setting and family-style dining. Fried chicken—the most popular dinner—includes appetizer and relishes, followed by a platter of chicken "hand-fried like mother used to do," potatoes, gravy, two vegetables, salad, hot bread, and dessert. **FYI:** Reservations recommended. Children's menu. **Open:** Tues–Sat 5–8pm, Sun noon–7:30pm. **Prices:** Main courses $13–$18. AE, MC, V. 🏞 &

Iron Skillet

2489 W 30th St and Cold Spring Rd (Riverside); tel 317/923-6353. 6 mi NW of downtown. **American.** Since 1953, this city landmark has been serving family-style meals in a white brick mansion built in the 1870s. The building sits on a hill overlooking one of the city's busiest public golf courses. Hostesses in quaint colonial costumes greet patrons and escort them to the attractive dining rooms. Menu is limited to chicken, shrimp, fish, and steak. **FYI:** Reservations recommended. Children's menu. Dress code. **Open:** Wed–Sat 5–8:30pm, Sun noon–7:30pm. **Prices:** Main courses $12–$16. AE, DC, MC, V. 🏞 🏞 &

The Jazz Cooker

In Broad Ripple Village, 925 E Westfield Blvd; tel 317/253-2883. **Regional American/Cajun.** Fair-weather diners enjoy the large, shady terrace of this trendy restaurant in the heart of young, artsy Broad Ripple Village. Jambalaya is one of the favorite Cajun dishes. **FYI:** Reservations accepted. Jazz. Children's menu. **Open:** Daily 5–10pm. **Prices:** Main courses $9–$16. AE, DC, DISC, MC, V. ❤ 🍴 🏞

♀ Keystone Grill

8650 Keystone at the Crossing; tel 317/848-5202. **Seafood/Steak.** Upscale but comfortable describes the atmosphere here, from the glass-and-brass doors to the wrought-iron chandelier to the carousel-type brass canopy in the center of the lounge area. Fresh seafood is the Grill's trademark, but certified Angus beef, pork, veal, and poultry are also available. The chef uses an Aztec wood grill (burning a blend of mesquite, oak, and cherry woods) to bring out the full flavor of the meat. Wine list features over 50 American labels. **FYI:** Reservations recommended. Jazz. **Open:** Lunch Mon–Sat 11am–3pm; dinner Mon–Thurs 5–11pm, Fri–Sat 5pm–mid-night, Sun 3–10pm; brunch Sun 10am–1:30pm. **Prices:** Main courses $15–$60; prix fixe $17. AE, CB, DC, DISC, MC, V. &

Key West Shrimp House

In Union Station marketplace, 59 Jackson Place (Union Station); tel 317/635-5353. 1 block S of Circle Centre Mall. **Seafood/Steak.** One of the city's most popular restaurants, it was located on the south side for many years before relocating. Hopes to regain its past glory with its familiar shrimp dishes and steak. **FYI:** Reservations recommended. Dress code. **Open:** Mon–Sat 11am–10pm, Sun 4–8pm. **Prices:** Main courses $8–$36. AE, CB, DC, DISC, MC, V. 🏞 &

Malibu Grill

4503 E 82nd St; tel 317/845-4334. 1 mi W of Allisonville Rd and I-465. **New American.** Very popular, award-winning eatery with a casual and contemporary atmosphere. Diners can watch orders being prepared in the glass-enclosed kitchen. Features wood-grilled steaks, fresh fish, and wood-fired pizza. **FYI:** Reservations not accepted. Children's menu. Dress code. **Open:** Lunch Mon–Thurs 11am–2pm, Fri–Sat 11am–11pm; dinner Mon–Thurs 5–10pm, Fri–Sat 11am–11pm, Sun noon–9pm. **Prices:** Main courses $9–$19. AE, CB, DC, DISC, MC, V. ❤ 🏞 &

Marker

In Adam's Mark Hotel, 2544 Executive Dr; tel 317/381-6146. 2 blocks E of Indianapolis Int'l Airport, just off Airport Expwy. **Eclectic.** Splendid cuisine expertly served, with piano accompaniment in an attractive French country setting. Dishes from the Americas include Black Angus filet mignon with wild mushrooms and sherry demiglacé; rack of lamb; grilled Atlantic salmon with cucumber salad; and grilled swordfish with tortilla sauce, black bean chili, and salsa. **FYI:** Reservations recommended. Jazz. Dress code. **Open:** Lunch Mon–Fri 11am–2pm; dinner Mon–Sat 5:30–10pm, Sun 5:30–9pm; brunch Sun 10:30am–2pm. **Prices:** Main courses $16–$24. AE, CB, DC, DISC, MC, V. ❤ 🛎 🏞 &

The Restaurant

In Canterbury Hotel, 123 S Illinois St (Union Station); tel 317/634-3000. At S edge of Circle Centre Mall; N of Union Station. **American/Continental.** The only thing simple about this restaurant is its name. A small, elegant dining room, with mahogany-paneled walls and gorgeous table settings, is the setting for delicious continental cuisine. Sample dishes: grilled Muscovy duck breast with dried cherry and basil sauce; broiled New York steak with cracked peppercorn sauce and sweet onion; and pocket of salmon stuffed with lobster, spinach, and pine nuts and flavored with lemon grass and star anise. **FYI:** Reservations recommended. **Open:** Breakfast daily 7–10am; lunch daily 11:30am–2pm; dinner daily 5–10pm. **Prices:** Main courses $18–$26. AE, CB, DC, DISC, ER, MC, V. ❤ VP &

★ **St Elmo Steak House**
127 S Illinois (Union Station); tel 317/637-1811. At S edge of new Circle Centre Mall. **American/Steak.** For more than 90 years at the same location, this has been the city's premier steak house—it's even on the National Register of Historic Sites. The original bar and back bar are still in operation, and waiters wear tuxedos as they always have. With the capitol just blocks away, the eatery is popular with legislators and lobbyists with big expense accounts. **FYI:** Reservations recommended. Dress code. **Open:** Mon–Fri 4–10pm, Sun 5–9:30pm. **Prices:** Main courses $23–$33. AE, CB, DC, DISC, MC, V. 🍷 &.

The Teller's Cage
In National Bank of Detroit Tower, 1 Indiana Square (Downtown); tel 317/266-5211. In midst of financial section 2 blocks from Circle Centre Mall. **American.** One of the best views of the city can be enjoyed from this eatery on the 35th floor. The food is just as good as the panorama, with a highly diversified menu ranging from Jamaican chicken salad to chimichangas. **FYI:** Reservations accepted. Dress code. **Open:** Lunch Mon–Fri 11am–2pm; dinner Mon–Fri 5–8:30pm. **Prices:** Main courses $9–$14. AE, CB, DC, DISC, MC, V. 🏞 &.

ATTRACTIONS 🏛

Indianapolis Motor Speedway
4790 W 16th St; tel 317/248-6747. Built in 1909, this is one of the most celebrated auto raceways in the world. Each May, nearly 400,000 spectators throng to the 2.5-mile oval course to watch the Indianapolis 500. This race has resulted in numerous automotive advancements, including the rearview mirror, balloon tires, and ethyl gasoline. The **Indianapolis Motor Speedway Hall of Fame Museum** (fee) is situated within the track's oval, and houses a vast collection of racing, classic, and antique passenger cars; racing trophies; films of classic races; and more than 30 winning Indy 500 cars. The 433-acre speedway also features a PGA course (4 holes inside the track and 14 outside). Guided bus tours of the oval are available when the track is not in use. No fee to tour Speedway grounds. **Open:** Daily 9am–5pm.

Indianapolis Museum of Art
1200 W 38th St; tel 317/923-1331. Three theme pavilions make up this museum: the Clowes Pavilion features medieval and Renaissance art; the Krannert Pavilion houses a collection of Oriental and primitive art; and the Lily Pavilion of Decorative Arts contains European and American paintings (including Turner watercolors and works by El Greco, Claude Lorrain, Rembrandt, and Van Dyck). The sculpture garden includes Robert Indiana's famed *LOVE*. Guided tours available. **Open:** Tues–Wed and Fri–Sat 10am–5pm, Thurs 10am–8:30pm, Sun noon–5pm. **Free**

The Children's Museum of Indianapolis
3000 N Meridian St; tel 317/924-5431. One of the world's largest children's museums with 110,000 artifacts, 10 galleries connected by a skylit open core, and 356,000 feet of interactive displays. Highlights include an Egyptian tomb complete with mummies, dinosaur area with mastodon skeleton, SpaceQuest Planetarium, a turn-of-the-century carousel, and a miniature railroad network. **Open:** Peak (Mem Day–Labor Day) Mon–Sat 10am–5pm, Sun noon–5pm. Reduced hours off-season. **$$$**

Indiana State Museum
202 N Alabama St; tel 317/232-1637. Located in the former city hall, the museum documents the history of Indiana since the pioneer era. Of special interest are the Indiana Museum of Sports and a gallery of works by Indiana artists. **Open:** Mon–Sat 9am–4:45pm, Sun noon–4:45pm. **Free**

Eiteljorg Museum of American Indian and Western Art
500 W Washington St, White River State Park; tel 317/636-9378. Impressive $14 million building houses one of the country's most noted collections of Native American and western art including works by Frederic Remington and Georgia O'Keeffe. Included in the displays are 240 paintings, 150 bronzes, and more than a thousand examples of old Native American handcrafts such as wickerwork, pottery, and masks. **Open:** Peak (June–Aug) Mon–Sat 10 am–5pm, Sun noon–5pm. Reduced hours off-season. **$**

Indiana Medical History Museum
3045 W Vermont St; tel 317/635-7329. Housed in the state's first medical center, this museum holds some 15,000 medical artifacts. Of special interest is the collection of "quack" devices used in the 19th and early 20th century. **Open:** Wed–Sat 10am–4pm. **$**

Morris-Butler House
1204 N Park Ave; tel 317/636-5409. Housed in a mid-Victorian mansion dating from 1862, this museum focuses on Victorian decorative arts such as fine silver, tapestries, and Belter & Meeks furniture. **Open:** Tues–Sat 10am–4pm, Sun 1–4pm. **$**

National Art Museum of Sport
111 Monument Circle; tel 317/687-1715. Collection of sports-related works of art throughout the ages, including drawings, paintings, sculptures, and prints. A Greek bronze from the fifth-century BC depicts an Olympic athlete. **Open:** Mon–Fri 9am–5pm, Sat 10am–4pm. **Free**

Indiana University/Purdue University
East bank of the White River; tel 317/274-2323. The Indianapolis campuses of the state's two largest universities were merged in 1969 into the present educational complex. IUPUI is home to more than 28,000 students at 19 schools, including the famed Indiana University Medical Center, one of the country's premier centers for research in sports medicine, heart surgery, cancer treatment, and organ transplants. IUPUI is also famous for its high-caliber sports teams, particularly basketball, and the Indianapolis Sports Center is the site of national and international athletic events, includ-

ing the US Men's Hard Court Tennis Championships; the Track and Field Stadium holds world-class meets. Guided tours leave from the Union Building at 620 Union Dr. **Open:** Visitors Center, Mon–Fri 8am–5pm. **Free**

Indianapolis Zoo
1200 W Washington St; tel 317/630-2001. The nation's first major totally new zoo in decades, this $64-million, 64-acre facility houses 2,000 animals roaming through simulated environments. Rare birds and the world's largest totally enclosed Whale and Dolphin Pavilion are among the highlights. Miniature train rides take visitors around to the various exhibits. **Open:** Peak (Mem Day–Labor Day) daily 9am–5pm. Reduced hours off-season. **$$$**

Garfield Park Conservatory
2450 S Shelby St; tel 317/784-3044. The main attraction of this 128-acre park is a greenhouse planted with flora from around the world. More than 500 tropical plant varieties—including orchids, palms, succulents, and cacti—are set among a series of pools filled with tropical fish and fed by a 15-foot waterfall. The presence of brightly colored parrots and macaws heightens the tropical atmosphere. The conservatory holds a bulb show in the spring, a chrysanthemum show in late November; and a poinsettia show in December. The sunken garden outside the conservatory features a colorful array of blooms from May through October. The park also houses a restored pagoda, and an amphitheater that presents live musical performances. Picnic area, swimming pool, tennis and horseshoe courts. Guided tours available. **Open:** Tues–Sat 10am–5pm, Sun noon–5pm. **Free**

Clowes Memorial Hall
4600 Sunset Ave at Butler University; tel 317/940-6444 or 940-9696 or toll free 800/732-0804. Considered Indiana's premier entertainment facility, this performing arts center on the campus of Butler University is home to the Indianapolis Opera, Indianapolis Ballet Theater, and the Indiana Chamber Orchestra. Other performances at CMH range from Judy Collins to the National Theater of the Deaf. **Open:** Box office, Mon–Sat 10am–6pm. **$$$$**

Indiana Repertory Theatre
140 W Washington St (Downtown); tel 317/635-5277. Presents classical and modern theater performances September–May. Call for schedule. **$$$$**

Indianapolis Raceway Park
10267 E US 136; tel 317/291-4090. Owned and operated by the National Hot Rod Association, the IRP's three courses host more than 60 events a year. Highlights include drag racing, car shows, and the NHRA US Nationals (held during Labor Day weekend). **Open:** Apr–Sept, call for schedule.

RCA/Hoosier Dome
100 S Capitol Ave; tel 317/635-7329. This 61,000-seat stadium with an air-supported dome is the home of the NFL's Indianapolis Colts, in addition to many conventions, concerts, and trade shows. Guided one-hour tours available. **Open:** Call for schedule. **$$$$**

Jasper

See also Santa Claus

Seat of Dubois County, in southwestern part of state. Founded by German Catholic immigrants in 1838. During Prohibition, the locality became noted for the excellence of its moonshine whiskey, called "Jasper corn." **Information:** Jasper Chamber of Commerce, 302 W 6th St, PO Box 307, Jasper, 47547-0307 (tel 812/482-6866 or 482-7716).

MOTELS

Holiday Inn
US 231 S, 47546; tel 812/482-5555 or toll free 800/872-3176; fax 812/482-7908. Exit 57 off I-74; 12 mi N. It's the largest area motel, close to Holiday World, Splashin' Safari water park, Paoli Peaks ski resort, Patoka Lake Reservoir, Indiana Baseball Hall of Fame. **Rooms:** 200 rms and stes. CI 5pm/CO noon. Nonsmoking rms avail. Furniture is locally made. Extra-tall shower heads in most rooms. **Amenities:** A/C, cable TV w/movies, dataport. Some units w/minibars. Irons and ironing boards. **Services:** Babysitting. **Facilities:** 1 restaurant, 1 bar (w/entertainment), games rm, sauna, whirlpool, washer/dryer. Holidome includes indoor putting green. **Rates:** Peak (July–Aug) $57–$69 S or D; $75 ste. Children under age 12 stay free. Lower rates off-season. Parking: Outdoor, free. Packages avail for four nearby championship golf courses: Sultan's Run, Jasper Municipal, Ruxer Municipal, Christmas Lake. AE, CB, DC, DISC, MC, V.

Sleep Inn
75 Indiana, 47546; tel 812/481-2008 or toll free 800/221-2222; fax 812/634-2338. Exit 57 off I-74; 17 mi N on US 231. New facility, clean and comfortable. Close to Holiday World, Splashin' Safari water park, Paoli Peaks ski resort, Patoka Lake Reservoir, Indiana Baseball Hall of Fame. **Rooms:** 56 rms and stes. CI 3pm/CO noon. Nonsmoking rms avail. **Amenities:** A/C, cable TV w/movies, dataport. **Services:** **Facilities:** **Rates (CP):** Peak (May–Oct) $59–$79 S or D; $62 ste. Extra person $5. Children under age 18 stay free. Lower rates off-season. Parking: Outdoor, free. AE, CB, DC, DISC, ER, JCB, MC, V.

RESTAURANT

★ Schnitzelbank
393 3rd Ave; tel 812/482-2640. On IN 162. **American/German.** The original Schnitzelbank was a beer hall built in 1903 to serve the liquid and culinary needs of Jasper. Three generations of the Hanselman family now carry on the tradition of serving German and traditional American fare in

this predominantly German city. The original Schnitzelbank song can be heard on the hour before and after lunch and dinner on the musical glockenspiel. Among the dinner favorites are the German sampler platter and wurst platter, as well as roast prime rib and New York strip steak. Desserts are hot apple strudel or German chocolate pie. The Schnitz's own white wine, a Gerwurztraminer, and German wheat beer called Schnitzelbank Weiss are sold at the bar and in the gift shop. **FYI:** Reservations accepted. Children's menu. **Open:** Mon–Sat 8am–10pm. **Prices:** Main courses $7–$19. DISC, MC, V. 🖼 💟 ⚕

Kokomo

Seat of Howard County, in north-central part of state. Elwood Haynes invented the first clutch-driven automobile here in 1894; today, Kokomo's manufacturing base lies in rubber, high technology, and auto parts. **Information:** Kokomo/Howard County Convention & Visitors Bureau, 112 N Washington St, Kokomo, 46901 (tel 317/457-6802).

MOTELS 🏨

🏩🏩 Comfort Inn

522 Essex Dr, 46901; tel 317/452-5050 or toll free 800/221-2222; fax 317/452-5050. Two-story motel surrounded by parking lot with well-maintained grounds. Located on access road from US 31 Bypass. A notch above the economy establishments. **Rooms:** 63 rms. CI 2pm/CO 11am. Nonsmoking rms avail. Attractive rooms. **Amenities:** 🛎 ⚕ A/C, cable TV w/movies. **Services:** ⚙ ⚙ **Facilities:** ⚐ ⚕ Whirlpool. Passes available for nearby health and fitness spa. **Rates (CP):** $48 S; $54 D. Extra person $5. Children under age 18 stay free. Min stay special events. Parking: Outdoor, free. AE, DC, DISC, JCB, MC, V.

🏩🏩 Econo Lodge

2040 S Reed Rd, 46902; tel 317/457-7561 or toll free 800/55-ECONO; fax 317/868-1123. Typical two-story motel with large parking area and landscaping around the edges. Small lobby. Renovation in the works. **Rooms:** 103 rms. CI 2pm/CO 11am. Nonsmoking rms avail. Standard rooms. **Amenities:** 🛎 ⚕ A/C, cable TV w/movies. **Services:** ⚙ ⚙ Free continental breakfast Mon–Fri. **Facilities:** ⚐ ⚕ Whirlpool. **Rates:** $32–$37 S; $42–$47 D. Extra person $10. Children under age 12 stay free. Parking: Outdoor, free. AE, DISC, MC, V.

🏩 Motel 6

2808 S Reed Rd, 46902; tel 317/457-8211; fax 317/454-9774. Typical motel for economy-minded travelers. Very plain, with small lobby area. Many restaurants in the area. **Rooms:** 92 rms. CI 2pm/CO noon. Nonsmoking rms avail. Standard. **Amenities:** 🛎 ⚕ A/C, cable TV. **Services:** ⚙ Free

coffee anytime. **Facilities:** ⚕ **Rates:** $33 S; $38 D. Extra person $3. Children under age 17 stay free. Min stay special events. Parking: Outdoor, free. AE, CB, DISC, MC, V.

🏩 Ramada Inn

1709 E Lincoln Rd, 46902; tel 317/459-8001 or toll free 800/843-6264; fax 317/459-8001. On US 31 Bypass. This two-story motel is scheduled for full renovation, and it isn't any too soon. Located five miles from downtown, on the US 31 bypass, one of the most congested stretches of highway in the state, with automobile plants, shopping centers, filling stations, and restaurants. **Rooms:** 132 rms and stes. CI 3pm/CO noon. Nonsmoking rms avail. Standard rooms. **Amenities:** 🛎 ⚕ A/C, cable TV w/movies. 1 unit w/whirlpool. **Services:** ✕ ⚙ ⚙ **Facilities:** ⚐ 🏊 ⚕ 1 restaurant, 1 bar (w/entertainment), whirlpool. Use of facilities of nearby health and fitness spa. **Rates (BB):** $59–$65 S; $69–$75 D; $99–$135 ste. Extra person $10. Children under age 18 stay free. Parking: Outdoor, free. AE, CB, DC, DISC, MC, V.

RESTAURANTS 🍴

Colorado Steak House

3201 S LaFountain St; tel 317/455-1280. **American.** Western-style eatery housed in a large log cabin. Porterhouse steak, prime rib, seafood, fish, chicken. **FYI:** Reservations accepted. Children's menu. Dress code. **Open:** Mon–Thurs 11am–10pm, Fri–Sat 11am–11pm, Sun 11am–9pm. **Prices:** Main courses $10–$16. AE, CB, DC, DISC, MC, V. 💟 ⚕

Wheatfield

2900 S Washington St; tel 317/453-1200. **American/Greek.** Located across the street from Maple Crest Plaza, one of Kokomo's biggest shopping center, is this large restaurant with a menu to match (more than 100 selections plus approximately 25 daily lunch and dinner specials). Particularly popular are charbroiled T-bone and sirloin steaks, and roast chicken with gravy. **FYI:** Reservations not accepted. Children's menu. Dress code. Beer and wine only. **Open:** Daily 6:30am–10:30pm. **Prices:** Main courses $6–$18. AE, DISC, MC, V. 🖼 ⚕

ATTRACTIONS 🏛

Elwood Haynes Museum

1915 S Webster St; tel 317/452-3471. Exhibits cover the life and career of the inventor of the first commercially built gasoline-powered automobile. Housed in Haynes' former residence, the collection contains personal memorabilia and Haynes automobiles from 1905, 1923, and 1924, as well as other Haynes inventions (including the Haynes Stellite, an alloy used in spacecraft jet engines, dental instruments, and nuclear power plants). Turn-of-the-century furnishings, audiovisual presentation; guided tours available. **Open:** Tues–Sat 1–4pm, Sun 1–5pm. **Free**

Howard County Historical Museum
1200 W Sycamore St; tel 317/452-4314. Housed in the former Seiberling Mansion (built in 1891), which features hand-carved interior woodwork, brass hardware, and art nouveau stained glass. Several rooms offer period furnishings, while others depict a range of cultures throughout Indiana history. The museum offers exhibits on county history; manufacturing artifacts also featured. **Open:** Tues–Sun 1–4pm. **Free**

Lafayette

Seat of Tippecanoe County, in the west-central part of the state. Located on the east bank of the Wabash River, this midsized city was named for Revolutionary War hero Marquis de LaFayette. Purdue University is located in West Lafayette, on the other side of the Wabash. **Information:** Greater Lafayette Convention & Visitors Bureau, 301 Frontage Rd, PO Box 5547, Lafayette, 47905-4564 (tel 317/447-9999 or toll free 800/872-6648).

HOTEL 🏨

≣≣≣ **Ramada Inn**
4221 IN 26 E, 47905; tel 317/447-9460 or toll free 800/2-RAMADA; fax 317/447-4905. Exit 172 off I-65. Four-story, full-service hotel located seven miles from Purdue University. **Rooms:** 146 rms and stes. Executive level. CI 3pm/CO noon. Nonsmoking rms avail. **Amenities:** 🛁 🐾 A/C, cable TV w/movies, dataport, in-rm safe. Some units w/terraces, some w/whirlpools. **Services:** ✗ 🖎 🗗 🐾 Babysitting. Board games available. Special amenities to members of Ramada business class. Three car rental agencies will provide cars within 30 minutes. **Facilities:** 🗗 🏃 🖼 🔟 ⅙ 1 restaurant, 1 bar, washer/dryer. Complimentary business center. **Rates:** Peak (Apr–Oct) $60–$65 S; $67–$72 D; $90–$130 ste. Extra person $7. Children under age 18 stay free. Lower rates off-season. Parking: Outdoor, free. Bed-and-breakfast package avail. AE, CB, DC, DISC, JCB, MC, V.

MOTELS

≣ **Days Inn**
400 Sagamore Pkwy S, 47905; tel 317/447-4131 or toll free 800/DAYS-INN; fax 317/447-7423. Standard motel on main thoroughfare, within walking distance of several restaurants. **Rooms:** 189 rms and stes. CI 3pm/CO 11am. Nonsmoking rms avail. **Amenities:** 🛁 A/C, cable TV w/movies, dataport. Refrigerators, irons, and ironing boards available. **Services:** 🖎 🗗 🐾 **Facilities:** 🗗 🏃 🔟 ⅙ 1 restaurant (bkfst only), 1 bar (w/entertainment), games rm. **Rates (BB):** $49–$64 S; $44–$64 D; $75–$105 ste. Extra person $5. Children under age 18 stay free. Parking: Outdoor, free. AE, CB, DC, DISC, JCB, MC, V.

≣≣ **Fairfield Inn by Marriott**
4000 IN 26 E, 47905; tel 317/449-0083 or toll free 800/228-2800; fax 317/449-0083. Exit 172 off I-65. New budget motel within walking distance to several restaurants and seven miles from Purdue University. **Rooms:** 79 rms and stes. CI 2pm/CO 11am. Nonsmoking rms avail. **Amenities:** 🛁 🐾 A/C, cable TV w/movies. **Services:** 🖎 🗗 🐾 Board games and fax service available. **Facilities:** 🗗 🏃 🔟 ⅙ Games rm, whirlpool. **Rates (CP):** Peak (May–Sept) $64–$90 S or D; $70–$90 ste. Children under age 19 stay free. Lower rates off-season. Parking: Outdoor, free. 13th night free. AE, DC, DISC, ER, JCB, MC, V.

≣ **Family Inns of America**
1920 Northwestern Ave, 47906; tel 317/463-9511 or toll free 800/932-8383; fax 317/463-3891. Exit 175 off I-65. Older budget motel, ½ mile from Purdue University. Golf course across the street. **Rooms:** 100 rms and effic. CI 11am/CO 11am. Nonsmoking rms avail. **Amenities:** 🛁 A/C, cable TV. Some units w/terraces. Many rooms have refrigerators and microwaves. **Services:** ✗ 🚐 🗗 Babysitting. **Facilities:** 🗗 🏃 🔟 ⅙ 1 restaurant, 1 bar, beauty salon. **Rates (CP):** $27–$45 S or D; $35 effic. Extra person $5. Children under age 12 stay free. Parking: Outdoor, free. AE, CB, DC, DISC, MC, V.

≣ **Knights Inn**
4110 IN 26 E, 47905; tel 317/447-5611 or toll free 800/843-5644; fax 317/449-4996. Exit 172 off I-65. Average motel. Close to Fort Quiatenon, site of the Feast of the Hunters' Moon festival each Oct. Many restaurants within walking distance. **Rooms:** 112 rms and effic. CI 3pm/CO noon. Nonsmoking rms avail. **Amenities:** 🛁 A/C, cable TV. **Services:** 🖎 🗗 🐾 VCRs and movies can be rented. **Facilities:** 🗗 🔟 ⅙ **Rates:** Peak (Apr–Nov) $34–$55 S or D; $34–$55 effic. Extra person $5. Children under age 18 stay free. Lower rates off-season. Parking: Outdoor, free. AE, CB, DC, DISC, MC, V.

≣≣ **Red Roof Inn**
4201 IN 26 E, 47905; tel 317/448-4671 or toll free 800/843-7663; fax 317/448-9796. Exit 172 off I-65. Motel facility close to many restaurants and seven miles from Purdue University. **Rooms:** 80 rms. CI noon/CO noon. Nonsmoking rms avail. **Amenities:** 🛁 A/C, cable TV. Hair dryer available. **Services:** 🗗 🐾 Coffee bar in morning. Free newspaper. **Facilities:** ⅙ **Rates:** Peak (Mar–Oct) $36–$46 S or D. Extra person $9. Children under age 18 stay free. Lower rates off-season. Parking: Outdoor, free. AE, CB, DC, DISC, MC, V.

≣≣≣ **University Inn and Conference Center**
3001 Northwestern Ave, West Lafayette, 47906; tel 317/463-5511 or toll free 800/777-9808; fax 317/497-3850. Exit 175 off I-65. Newly renovated, with large central garden atrium. Located two miles north of Purdue University. Golf available at adjacent golf course. **Rooms:** 149 rms and stes. CI 2pm/CO 11am. Nonsmoking rms avail. **Amenities:** 🛁 🐾 A/C, cable TV w/movies, dataport, voice mail. **Services:** ✗

Babysitting. VCRs available. Free shuttle service to Purdue University and airport. Complimentary social hour 5–7pm Mon–Fri. **Facilities:** 1 restaurant, 1 bar, games rm, whirlpool, washer/dryer. Garden Cafe has extensive Sun champagne brunch. Reduced fee at nearby fitness center. **Rates:** $63–$78 S or D; $105–$135 ste. Extra person $5. Children under age 12 stay free. **Parking:** Outdoor, free. AE, DC, DISC, MC, V.

RESTAURANTS

Mountain Jack's
4211 IN 26 E; tel 317/448-1521. Exit 172 off I-65; ¼ mi W on IN 26. **American/Steak.** Award-winning prime rib, plus sirloin with whiskey-peppercorn sauce and mushroom-stuffed filet mignon, top the list of favorites in this upscale yet casual bistro. Each table is equipped with a salad wheel filled with vegetables, dressings, and other salad essentials. Mountain-High Mud Pie or Irish cream mousse complete the meal. Three fireplaces add warmth. **FYI:** Reservations recommended. Children's menu. **Open:** Mon–Thurs 5–10pm, Fri–Sat 4–10pm, Sun noon–9pm. **Prices:** Main courses $14–$20. AE, CB, DC, MC, V.

Sorrento Restaurant
601 Sagamore Pkwy W, West Lafayette; tel 317/463-5537. Exit 175 off I-65; W on IN 25 to US 52 (Sagamore Pkwy); 3 mi N. **Continental.** Casual dining in an elegant atmosphere surrounded by stained glass in the ceiling, crystal chandeliers, and fountains. Sorrento's own crabmeat Remick is a great start to any meal. Entrees include lasagna, breast of chicken Donal (boneless breast of chicken, shrimp, dry chablis, herbs, butter, fresh bread crumbs, and Parmesan cheese, broiled), veal piccata, filet mignon and barbecued baby back ribs. **FYI:** Reservations accepted. Children's menu. **Open:** Mon–Wed 11am–10pm, Thurs–Sat 11am–11pm, Sun 4–9pm. **Prices:** Main courses $10–$16. AE, CB, DC, DISC.

ATTRACTIONS

Greater Lafayette Museum of Art
101 S 9th St; tel 317/742-1128. The permanent collection focuses on 19th- and 20th-century American art, national and regional arts and crafts, and works by current Indiana artists. There are four art studios and a rental gallery; classes, lectures, library, and gift shop also available. **Open:** Tues–Sun 1–5pm. **Free**

Tippecanoe Battlefield
IN 43 exit off I-65; tel 317/567-2147. On November 7, 1811, William Henry Harrison (then the governor of the Indiana Territory) defeated a band of Native American warriors on this site. The 90-acre park is now home to a 85-foot-tall memorial and a museum, which provides a comprehensive account of the battle. A scenic trail winds through the battle site (musket balls are still to be found in the older trees); numerous picnic areas dot the grounds. **Open:** Peak (Mar–Nov) daily 10am–5pm. Reduced hours off-season. **$**

La Porte

Manufacturing center whose products include radiators and farm machinery. **Information:** Greater La Porte Chamber of Commerce, 414 Lincolnway, PO Box 486, La Porte, 46352 (tel 219/362-3178).

HOTEL

Holiday Inn and Holidome
444 Pine Lake Rd, 46350; tel 219/362-4585 or toll free 800/HOLIDAY; fax 219/324-6993. Exit 40A off I-94; US 35 S to Pine Lake Rd. Simple brick exterior and understated decor in lobby contrast with the Holidome, which has a southwestern flavor. Nooks and crannies of simulated adobe. **Rooms:** 147 rms and stes. CI 4pm/CO noon. Nonsmoking rms avail. **Amenities:** A/C. Some units w/terraces. Rooms that encircle the Holidome have small private patios. Some rooms are set aside for business meetings and have coffeemakers and other amenities. **Services:** **Facilities:** 1 restaurant, 1 bar (w/entertainment), games rm, spa, sauna, steam rm, whirlpool, beauty salon. The Timbers Restaurant features Mexican food. **Rates:** Peak (May–Aug) $80–$100 S; $90–$110 D; $119 ste. Extra person $8. Children under age 18 stay free. Lower rates off-season. **Parking:** Outdoor, free. Weekend getaway packages. AE, CB, DC, DISC, JCB, MC, V.

RESTAURANT

Tangerine
601 Michigan Ave (Downtown); tel 219/326-8000. **Continental/Steak.** Twenty years ago it was an old boarding house; now it is an elegant art deco jewel, with a background of pink and soft mauve, tiny lights outlining the dining areas, and jet-black napkins set against white linen tablecloths. Menu highlights include baby-back ribs, beef Wellington, and roast duck, all complemented by herb seasonings and accompanied by a special house rice. **FYI:** Reservations accepted. **Open:** **Prices:** Main courses $13–$19. AE, CB, DC, MC, V.

Logansport

Seat of Cass County, in north-central part of state. Founded in 1828 at the confluence of the Wabash and Eel Rivers, this agricultural town was an active Native American trading post. Cole Porter was born in nearby Peru in 1891. **Information:** Logansport/Cass County Chamber of Commerce, 300 E Broadway, Suite 103, Logansport, 46947-3108 (tel 219/753-6388).

ATTRACTIONS

Riverside City Park
Riverside Dr, between 11th and 15th Sts; tel 219/753-6388. This park contains one of only two all-wood, hand-carved

merry-go-rounds still operating in Indiana. Produced by Gustav A Dentzel (one of the premier carousel makers of the early 20th-century), the carousel consists of 31 horses, three goats, three reindeer, three giraffes, a lion, and a tiger. The park also has a playground, a miniature golf course, basketball and tennis courts, and picnic areas. **Open:** Daily sunrise–sunset. **Free**

Cass County Society Museum

1004 E Market St; tel 219/753-3866. Housed in the restored Jerolaman-Long House (circa 1853), this living-history museum contains period rooms (such as a kitchen and a parlor), Native American artifacts, Civil War memorabilia, and other items depicting the history of Cass County. **Open:** Tues–Sat 1–5pm. **Free**

Madison

Seat of Jefferson County, in southeast part of state. Elegant antebellum homes and Hanover College give charm to this Ohio River town named for President James Madison. **Information:** Madison Area Chamber of Commerce, 301 E Main St, Madison, 47250 (tel 812/265-3135 or 265-5143).

MOTEL 🏨

≣≣ Best Western of Madison

700 Clifty Dr, 47250; tel 812/273-5151 or toll free 800/528-1234; fax 812/273-4300. On US 62; 3 mi E of the N entrance to Clifty Falls State Park. Exceptionally clean standard motel, halfway between Louisville and Cincinnati. More rooms than any other motel in Madison. **Rooms:** 69 rms. CI 2pm/CO noon. Nonsmoking rms avail. **Amenities:** 🛇 A/C, cable TV w/movies. Some units w/terraces. **Services:** ✕ 🖾 ⟲ ⟳ **Facilities:** 🔲 🍴 120 🔳 1 restaurant (lunch and dinner only), 1 bar. **Rates (CP):** $46 S; $59 D. Extra person $4. Children under age 12 stay free. Parking: Outdoor, free. AE, DC, DISC, MC, V.

RESORT

≣≣ Clifty Inn and Motor Lodge

IN 56, PO Box 387, 47250; tel 812/265-4135; fax 812/273-5720. On a 400′ bluff overlooking historic Madison in the 1,360 acres of Clifty Falls State Park. Waterfalls, hiking trails, bicycle trails, nature center with naturalist in the summer, wildlife. Skiing at nearby Gen Butler State Park in Kentucky, public golf course five miles away. **Rooms:** 71 rms. CI 4pm/CO noon. Nonsmoking rms avail. Half of the rooms overlook the Ohio River. **Amenities:** 🛇 🔲 A/C, TV w/movies. Some units w/terraces. **Services:** ⟳ Social director, children's program. **Facilities:** 🔲 🏓 🔳 🔳 200 🔳 1 restaurant, volleyball, games rm, lawn games, playground. Dining room overlooks the Ohio River. **Rates:** $42–$45 S; $46–$49 D. Children under age 18 stay free. Parking:

Outdoor, free. Guests must pay the state park fee ($2 for Indiana residents, $5 for nonresidents) to get into the park Mar–Oct. AE, DISC, MC, V.

ATTRACTION 🏛

Clifty Falls State Park

IN 56; tel 812/265-1331. This 1,360 acre park contains several waterfalls including the impressive 60 foot drop of Big Clifty Falls. Also within the park is Clifty Canyon State Nature Preserve, accessible only by foot. Swimming pool, hiking trails. **Open:** Daily sunrise–sunset. **$**

Marion

Seat of Grant County, in north-central part of state. This industrial and agricultural town is just north of Fairmount, hometown of actor James Dean and *Garfield* cartoonist Jim Davis. **Information:** Grant County Convention & Visitors Bureau, 215 S Adams St, Marion, 46952 (tel 317/668-5435 or toll free 800/662-9474).

MOTELS 🏨

≣ Broadmoor Motel

1323 N Baldwin Ave, 46952; tel 317/664-0501; fax 317/664-0501. One-story tan brick motel. Basic, no-frills. Nicely landscaped. Many restaurants nearby. **Rooms:** 61 rms. CI 9:30am/CO 11am. Nonsmoking rms avail. Conventional rooms with doors opening onto parking area. **Amenities:** 🛇 🛇 A/C, cable TV. **Services:** 🖾 ⟲ **Facilities:** 🔲 🔳 Whirlpool. **Rates:** $32–$38 S; $38–$45 D. Extra person $3. Children under age 12 stay free. Min stay special events. Parking: Outdoor, free. AE, DC, MC, V.

≣≣ Days Inn

1615 N Baldwin Ave, 46952; tel 317/664-9021 or toll free 800/DAYS-INN; fax 317/662-7451. W on IN 15 to IN 9. Two-story brick motel located three blocks from downtown area. Location makes it well suited for business travelers. **Rooms:** 106 rms, stes. CI 2pm/CO 11am. Nonsmoking rms avail. Some rooms recently redone. **Amenities:** 🛇 🛇 A/C, cable TV. 1 unit w/whirlpool. **Services:** ✕ 🖾 ⟲ **Facilities:** 🔲 🔳 1 restaurant, 1 bar, whirlpool. **Rates:** $45–$47 S; $51–$55 D; $65–$81 ste. Extra person $10. Children under age 12 stay free. Min stay special events. Parking: Outdoor, free. AE, DC, DISC, MC, V.

≣≣ Holiday Inn

501 E 4th St, 46952; tel 317/668-8801 or toll free 800/HOLIDAY; fax 317/662-6827. Exit 64 off I-69. Five-story motel renovated in 1995, with a fresh, clean look. Large parking area surrounds motel. Best suited for small families. **Rooms:** 120 rms. CI 2pm/CO noon. Nonsmoking rms avail. Bright and airy standard rooms refurbished during renovation. **Amenities:** 🛇 🛇 🔲 A/C, cable TV w/movies, dataport. **Services:** ✕ 🖾 ⟲ **Facilities:** 🔲 500 🔳 1 restaurant, 1 bar.

Rates: $62 S; $64 D. Extra person $5. Children under age 13 stay free. Min stay special events. Parking: Outdoor, free. AE, DC, DISC, MC, V.

Marshall

RESORT 🏨

≣≣ Turkey Run Inn

IN 47, RR 1, Box 444, 47859; tel 317/597-2211; fax 317/597-2660. Surrounded by the 2,182 acres of "primitive America" in Turkey Run State Park, Indiana's second state park, with a large veranda on the second floor. More than 14 miles of hiking trails reveal sandstone gorges formed more than 300 million years ago. Sugar Creek runs through the park; Billie Creek Village is nearby. Parke County has 32 covered bridges with an annual festival in Oct. Canoe trips nearby. **Rooms:** 61 rms and stes; 21 cottages/villas. CI 4pm/CO noon. Nonsmoking rms avail. **Amenities:** 🛆 🐾 A/C, TV w/movies. **Services:** 🛎 Social director, children's program, babysitting. VCRs and movies available. Nature center features star-projection system, wildlife observation room, children's corner, library, and interactive displays. **Facilities:** 🛆 🚲 🏊 ⛵ 🎣 🛶 ⏰ 500 🛆 1 restaurant, volleyball, games rm, lawn games, playground. **Rates:** $47–$51 S; $52–$57 D; $63–$68 ste; $58–$68 cottage/villa. Children under age 18 stay free. Lower rates off-season. Parking: Outdoor, free. Rates are per room, not per person. Guests must pay state park fee ($2 for Indiana residents, $5 for nonresidents) to get into the park Mar–Oct. Two nights for price of one Dec–Feb. AE, DISC, MC, V.

Merrillville

This bustling city in northwest Indiana was once a stopover point for westward wagon trains, as well as the starting point of the Old Sauk Trail. **Information:** Lake County Convention & Visitors Bureau, 5800 Broadway, #S, Merrillville, 46410 (tel 219/980-1617 or toll free 800/ALL-LAKE).

HOTELS 🏨

≣≣≣ Merrillville Courtyard

7850 Rhode Island Ave, 46410; tel 219/756-1600 or toll free 800/321-2211; fax 219/756-2080. Exit 253 off I-65. Beautifully landscaped approach. Rustic, lodge-like fieldstone building. Spacious lobby has two-story fieldstone fireplace, open balcony, traditional decor. Good use of wood throughout. **Rooms:** 112 rms and stes. CI 3pm/CO noon. Nonsmoking rms avail. Queen-bedded rooms have sofa sleeper and living room area. **Amenities:** 🛆 🐾 A/C, satel TV, voice mail. Some units w/whirlpools. Deluxe suite has unstocked wet bar and entertainment center. **Services:** 🛆 🛎 **Facilities:** 🛆 🍴 100 🖥 🛆 1 restaurant (bkfst only), 1 bar, playground. **Rates:**

Peak (May–Sept) $75–$99 S or D; $80–$225 ste. Extra person $10. Children under age 12 stay free. Lower rates off-season. Parking: Outdoor, free. AE, CB, DC, DISC, MC, V.

≣≣≣ Radisson Hotel at Star Plaza

800 E 81st Ave, 46410; tel 219/769-6311 or toll free 800/333-3333; fax 219/769-1462. Exit 253 off I-65. Spacious building and separate convention center entrance. Jungle decor. Direct connection via walkway to Star Theatre. **Rooms:** 347 rms and stes. CI 4pm/CO 11am. Nonsmoking rms avail. King-bedded room has loveseat sleeper. A few rooms have dataport connection. **Amenities:** 🛆 🐾 🛢 📺 A/C, voice mail. Some units w/terraces, some w/whirlpools. **Services:** ✗ VP 🚗 🛆 🛎 🕯 Car-rental desk. Special TV channel displays all hotel activities and facilities, and information on private party locations and convention programs. **Facilities:** 🛆 🍴 2000 🛆 2 restaurants (see "Restaurants" below), 3 bars (w/entertainment), games rm, sauna, steam rm, whirlpool, playground, washer/dryer. Indoor pool and sand-filled children's playground in jungle area—with real rocks, not plastic. Bar in lobby area also has jungle theme. Some bi-level suites can accommodate business conferences. **Rates:** $79–$135 S or D; $185–$400 ste. Extra person $10. Children under age 12 stay free. Parking: Outdoor, free. AE, CB, DC, DISC, MC, V.

MOTELS

≣≣ Fairfield Inn

8275 Georgia St, 46410; tel 219/736-0500 or toll free 800/228-2800; fax 219/736-0500. Exit 253 off I-65. Attractive blue accents on white building. Access across US 30 to Star Theatre. Adjacent to Celebration Station, a children's game and activity complex with miniature golf, workout track, batting cages, arcade games. **Rooms:** 132 rms. CI 3pm/CO noon. Nonsmoking rms avail. **Amenities:** 🛆 🐾 A/C, satel TV. **Services:** 🚗 🛆 🛎 **Facilities:** 🛆 16 🛆 Washer/dryer. **Rates (CP):** $55–$69 S; $65–$69 D. Extra person $10. Children under age 16 stay free. Parking: Outdoor, free. AE, CB, DC, DISC, MC, V.

≣≣ La Quinta Inn

8210 Louisiana Ave, 46410; tel 219/738-2870 or toll free 800/531-5900; fax 219/738-2870. Exit 253 off I-65. One mile from Star Theatre, ¼-mile from Southlake shopping mall. Little landscaping. Standard La Quinta architecture. Husband-and-wife managers live on premises. **Rooms:** 120 rms. CI 3pm/CO noon. Nonsmoking rms avail. **Amenities:** 🛆 🐾 A/C, cable TV. **Services:** 🛆 🛎 🕯 **Facilities:** 🛆 30 🛆 **Rates (CP):** $55–$61 S or D. Extra person $6. Children under age 18 stay free. Parking: Outdoor, free. AE, CB, DC, MC, V.

≣ Motel 6

8290 Louisiana St, 46410; tel 219/738-2701; fax 219/793-9237. Exit 253 off I-65. Short distance from Southlake shopping mall, one mile from Star Theatre. No grounds. Plain, utilitarian building. **Rooms:** 125 rms. CI 2pm/CO noon. Nonsmoking rms avail. Basic furnishings. All rooms equipped with special new locks for extra security. **Amenities:** A/C, satel TV. **Services:** **Facilities:** **Rates:** Peak (May–Sept) $38–$44 S; $44–$50 D. Extra person $3. Children under age 17 stay free. Lower rates off-season. Parking: Outdoor, free. AE, CB, DC, DISC, MC, V.

Red Roof Inn

8290 Georgia St, 46410; tel 219/738-2430 or toll free 800/THE-ROOF; fax 219/738-2436. Exit 253 off I-65. Older facility. Satisfactory maintenance, but very basic appearance. Short walk to Celebration Station, a children's game and play complex. Across US 30 from Star Theatre. **Rooms:** 108 rms. CI 2pm/CO noon. Nonsmoking rms avail. Basic furnishings. **Amenities:** A/C, cable TV. **Services:** Pets allowed, but must not be left alone in room. **Facilities:** **Rates:** Peak (May–Oct) $38–$71 S or D. Extra person $7. Children under age 18 stay free. Lower rates off-season. Parking: Outdoor, free. AE, CB, DC, DISC, MC, V.

RESTAURANT

Jolly Ginger's

In Radisson Hotel at Star Plaza, 800 E 81st Ave; tel 219/769-6311. **American.** Attractive nautical decor, quiet ambience. Particular favorites are chargrilled Alaskan salmon accented with a caper, cayenne, and chunky tomato sauce. Gulf shrimp are sautéed with fresh vegetables, simmered in Alfredo sauce, and tossed with fettucine. All dinners come with house salad prepared tableside. **FYI:** Reservations recommended. Children's menu. **Open:** Dinner Mon–Thurs 5–10pm, Fri–Sat 5–11pm; brunch Sun 9am–2pm. **Prices:** Main courses $15–$25. AE, CB, DC, DISC, MC, V.

ATTRACTION

Star Theatre

Jct I-65 and US 30; tel 219/769-6600. The 3,400-seat theater is attached to the Radisson Hotel. An eclectic array of performers such as BB King, Bill Cosby, Willie Nelson, Donna Summer, and Travis Tritt have been featured here, in addition to Broadway-style musicals and special children's entertainment such as Sesame Street Live. **Open:** Call for schedule. $$$$

Michigan City

Founded in 1832 as the northern terminus of the old Michigan Road. This industrial city is the chief gateway to the Indiana Dunes region, with its many miles of fine beaches. Mount Baldy, the largest dune in the National Lakeshore, is nearby on US 12. **Information:** La Porte County Convention & Visitors Bureau, 1503 S Meer Rd, Michigan City, 46360 (tel 219/872-5055 or toll free 800/634-2650).

HOTEL

Holiday Inn Executive Conference Center

5820 S Franklin St, 46360; tel 219/879-0311 or toll free 800/HOLIDAY; fax 219/879-2536. Exit 34B off I-94. Handsome brick exterior and flower plantings make an inviting entry. Entrance to convention facilities is well separated, and generous lobbies outside meeting rooms provide ample space for relaxation and discussion. **Rooms:** 165 rms and stes. CI 3pm/CO 11am. Nonsmoking rms avail. **Amenities:** A/C, cable TV. Some units w/terraces, some w/whirlpools. Poolside rooms have individual patios with table and chairs. **Services:** **Facilities:** 1 restaurant, 1 bar, games rm, sauna, steam rm, whirlpool. **Rates:** Peak (May–Oct) $77–$130 S or D; $130 ste. Children under age 18 stay free. Lower rates off-season. Parking: Outdoor, free. Bed-and-breakfast packages avail. AE, CB, DC, DISC, MC, V.

MOTELS

Hampton Inn

4128 S Franklin St, 46360; tel 219/879-9994 or toll free 800/HAMPTON; fax 219/874-9640. Exit 34B off I-94, US 421 N 1 mi. Recent change in management has brought renovation and refurbishing of grounds, lobby, and all of the rooms. New plantings enhance the large, canopied entry. Small patio outside lobby. Close to major shopping centers and convenient to municipal beach at Lake Michigan. **Rooms:** 107 rms. CI 4pm/CO noon. Nonsmoking rms avail. **Amenities:** A/C, satel TV. **Services:** Continental breakfast served in spacious lobby. **Facilities:** Pool grounds are landscaped. **Rates (CP):** Peak (May–Sept) $64–$72 S or D. Children under age 18 stay free. Lower rates off-season. Parking: Outdoor, free. AE, CB, DC, DISC, MC, V.

Knights Inn

201 W Kieffer Rd, 46360; tel 219/874-9500 or toll free 800/KNIGHTS; fax 219/874-5122. Exit 34B off I-94. Units extend deep into the property, providing privacy. Large shade trees and shrub plantings make grounds attractive. **Rooms:** 103 rms. CI 2pm/CO noon. Nonsmoking rms avail. **Amenities:** A/C, satel TV. **Services:** **Facilities:** **Rates:** Peak (May–Oct) $58 S; $68 D. Extra person $8. Children under age 18 stay free. Lower rates off-season. Parking: Outdoor, free. AARP discounts. AE, MC, V.

Red Roof Inn

110 W Kieffer Rd, 46360; tel 219/874-5251 or toll free 800/THE-ROOF; fax 219/874-5287. Exit 32B (US 42 IN) off I-94. Short distance from antique mall and other large shopping centers, this motel caters to business travelers and families looking for well-maintained, economical lodgings. Fieldstone pillars, attractive plantings, and bright lobby area. **Rooms:** 79 rms. CI 2pm/CO noon. Nonsmoking rms avail. Business king rooms have large desks. **Amenities:** A/C, satel TV. **Services:** Desk staff and congenial manager

make extra effort to guarantee satisfactory stay. **Facilities:** Rates: Peak (May–Sept) $30–$40 S; $37–$44 D. Extra person $7. Children under age 18 stay free. Lower rates off-season. Parking: Outdoor, free. AE, CB, DC, DISC, MC, V.

INN

≡≡≡ Creekwood Inn

US 20/35, 46360; tel 219/872-8357. Exit 40B off I-94. 33 acres. The original English cottage house, built in 1930s, has been renovated, and added wing blends nicely. Wooded acres give complete privacy and serenity. New Conservatory—two-story lounge and parlor—suitable for business meetings. Unsuitable for children under 12. **Rooms:** 13 rms and stes. CI 4pm/CO noon. Nonsmoking rms avail. **Amenities:** A/C, cable TV, refrig, bathrobes. Some units w/minibars, some w/terraces, some w/fireplaces. **Services:** Babysitting, afternoon tea and wine/sherry served. Appointments can be made with local masseur. **Facilities:** 1 restaurant (bkfst and dinner only), 1 bar, games rm, whirlpool, guest lounge w/TV. Dinner available Fri and Sat evenings, with noted Chicago chef in charge. **Rates (CP):** Peak (May–Oct) $98–$122 S; $105–$129 D; $150 ste. Min stay peak and wknds. Lower rates off-season. Higher rates for special events/hols. Parking: Outdoor, free. Special corporate midweek rates. Gourmet getaway weekends. AE, DC, MC, V.

RESTAURANT

★ Oriental Pearl Restaurant

Franklin St and 9th St; tel 219/874-1411. Off US 421 N. **Chinese.** Not just your ordinary chop suey here—the chef trained in some of Hong Kong's finest restaurants, and the sauces and seasonings are very special. A weekly trip is made to Chicago for authentic Chinese ingredients that yield crispy crab meat dumplings with cream cheese, pot stickers, sour and hot soup, curry beef with onions, sesame chicken, shrimp with walnuts, and Singapore-style rice noodles. **FYI:** Reservations accepted. No liquor license. **Open:** Tues–Thurs 11:30am–9:30pm, Fri 11:30am–10:30pm, Sat noon–10:30pm, Sun noon–9pm. **Prices:** Main courses $7–$9. MC, V.

ATTRACTION

Barker Mansion

631 Washington; tel 219/873-1520. John H Barker made millions of dollars in the manufacture of freight cars; he spent a great deal of that fortune on the 1905 renovation of this English manor-style mansion. All of the furnishings, tapestries, and objets d'art in the house's 38 rooms belonged to the Barker family. Decorative highlights include hand-carved marble fireplaces, walnut and mahogany woodwork, and an Italian sunken garden. **Open:** Peak (June–Oct) Mon–Fri 10am–1pm, Sat–Sun noon–2pm. Reduced hours off-season. **$**

Middlebury

HOTEL

≡≡≡ Essenhaus Country Inn

240 US 20, PO Box 2608, 46540; tel 219/825-9447; fax 219/825-9447. Tucked off the highway in Indiana's Amish country, the inn is part of the Miller family's Das Dutchmen Essenhaus complex of two inns, a restaurant, shops, and a bakery. The staff prides itself on its warm, friendly Amish hospitality. Amish buggy rides on carriage trails and through a covered bridge are offered in season. Individual or bus tours of Amish Country available with antique, fabric, furniture, clothing, and craft shops nearby. **Rooms:** 40 rms and stes. CI 3pm/CO 11am. Nonsmoking rms avail. Efficiently laid out and spotless, rooms are charmingly decorated with handmade hardwood furniture and colorful, handcrafted quilts. **Amenities:** A/C, cable TV w/movies. 1 unit w/whirlpool. **Services:** Complimentary continental breakfast offered Sun. **Facilities:** 1 restaurant, playground. Be sure to visit the Amish Country Kitchen. **Rates:** Peak (Apr–Nov 18) $53–$63 S; $73–$83 D; $99–$129 ste. Extra person $10. Children under age 12 stay free. Lower rates off-season. Parking: Outdoor, free. Special packages avail. AE, DISC, MC, V.

Mishawaka

This northern industrial city is divided in half by the St Joseph River. The southwestern quarter of the city was more or less taken over by Belgians in the years following World War I.

RESTAURANT

★ Doc Pierce's

120 N Main St; tel 219/255-7737. ½ block N of US 33 on Main St. **American.** A nostalgic saloon-type atmosphere is established via dark-wood paneling and ceilings accented with over 60 Tiffany-style lamps. The menu features an original seafood chowder, hand-cut aged beef, fresh boned chicken ambrosia in Polynesian marinade or Mornay sauce, and an array of sandwiches and salads for lighter appetites. Celebrated its 20th anniversary in 1996. **FYI:** Reservations accepted. Dress code. **Open:** Lunch Mon–Sat 11am–2pm; dinner Mon–Thurs 5–10pm, Fri–Sat 5–11pm. **Prices:** Main courses $5–$14. AE, CB, DC, DISC, MC, V.

Muncie

Seat of Delaware County, in east-central part of state. Founded in 1818 on a bend of the White River, Muncie was named after the Munsee tribe, whose settlement it marked. Today, this midsized city is the site of the international headquarters of the famous Ball food preserving jars and the home of Ball

State University. **Information:** Muncie Visitors Bureau, 425 N High St, Muncie 47305-1642 (tel 317/284-2700 or toll free 800/568-6862).

MOTEL

≡≡ Comfort Inn
4011 W Bethel, 47304; tel 317/282-6666 or toll free 800/221-2222; fax 317/282-6666. Exit 41 off I-69. Two-story motel located in commercial area near Ball State University campus. **Rooms:** 66 rms. CI 3pm/CO 11am. Nonsmoking rms avail. Standard rooms. **Amenities:** 🛏 ♨ A/C, cable TV w/movies, refrig. **Services:** ⛵ 🍴 **Facilities:** 🛗 ♿ Whirlpool. **Rates (CP):** $65 S; $65 D. Extra person $5. Children under age 14 stay free. Min stay special events. Parking: Outdoor, free. AE, DC, DISC, MC, V.

RESTAURANT

Foxfire's
3300 Chadam Lane; tel 317/284-5235. IN 332 NW exit off I-69. **American/Seafood.** Owned by Muncie native Jim Davis, the creator of Garfield the Cat. The eatery is divided into two distinct sections—gourmet and casual—and both rooms have atriums, cathedral ceilings, and neutral colors. Menu specialties such as wild game can be accompanied by a selection from the huge wine cellar, which contains more than 500 labels. **FYI:** Reservations recommended. Dress code. **Open:** Lunch Mon–Sat 11am–2pm; dinner Mon–Sat 5–10pm. **Prices:** Main courses $17–$24. AE, CB, DC, DISC, MC, V. ♥ ♿

ATTRACTIONS

Ball State University Museum of Art
Riverside and University Aves; tel 317/285-5242. The museum, located in the Fine Arts Building on the campus, features collections of Italian Renaissance and 19th-century American art, contemporary prints and drawings, and decorative arts. **Open:** Tues–Fri 9am–4:30pm, Sat–Sun 1:30–4:30pm. **Free**

Minnetrista Cultural Center
1200 N Minnetrista Pkwy; tel 317/282-4848. The four galleries in this 70,000-square-foot museum house changing exhibits on Native American history, local art, and science and technology. The center's 20 landscaped acres also include floral gardens and an apple orchard; free concerts are held on the outdoor pavilion during the summer months. **Open:** Tues–Sat 10am–5pm, Sun 1–5pm. **$**

Nappanee

In the center of northeast Indiana Amish country, between Goshen and Warsaw. Horse and buggy combinations are a common sight on the roads, and neat Amish farms dot the surrounding countryside. An Amish Arts and Crafts Festival is held at nearby Amish Acres every August. **Information:** Nappanee Area Chamber of Commerce, 215 W Market St, Nappanee, 46550 (tel 219/773-7812).

MOTELS

≡≡ The Inn at Amish Acres
1234 W Market St, 46550; tel 219/773-2011 or toll free 800/800-4942; fax 219/773-2078. On US 6/Market St; 1 mi W of downtown. Built in the white clapboard Germanic architecture typical of most Amish farmsteads, this inn, on a historic, 80-acre restored Amish farm, welcomes its guests with oak rocking chairs on the front porches, a lobby adorned with handmade quilts, and a tin roof designed to sing when it rains. True country feeling is compromised, however, by its location too close to the highway. Quaint shops on the property; more within driving distance. **Rooms:** 64 rms and stes. CI 2pm/CO noon. Nonsmoking rms avail. Rooms furnished with plain pine furniture, wrought iron lamps, highback rockers, and replicas of Amish quilts. **Amenities:** 🛏 ♨ A/C, cable TV w/movies. Some units w/whirlpools. **Services:** 🍴 Offers guided tours of the complex and countryside, craft demonstrations, and a documentary movie. Local vet will board pets. **Facilities:** 🛗 🅿 ♿ 1 restaurant (see "Restaurants" below), playground. 400-seat Round Barn Theater features live productions of *Plain & Fancy*, the 1955 Broadway play about Amish life and love. Horse-and-buggy rides. **Rates (CP):** Peak (June–Oct) $84 S; $89 D; $190 ste. Extra person $10. Children under age 18 stay free. Min stay wknds. Lower rates off-season. Parking: Outdoor, free. Special Amish Acres and dinner theater packages avail. AE, DC, DISC, MC, V.

UNRATED Nappanee Inn
2004 W Market St, 46550; tel 219/773-5999 or toll free 800/800-4942; fax 219/773-5988. ¼ mi W of Amish Acres on US 6/Market St; 1¼ mi from downtown. Simple, attractive facility celebrating lifestyle of Old Order Amish and run by same company that owns Amish Acres. Pictures of local farm animals displayed on walls in public spaces and guest rooms. Too close to busy state highway, but near scenic family farmsteads. **Rooms:** 66 rms. CI 2pm/CO noon. Nonsmoking rms avail. Hand-carved red oak furniture crafted in Indiana, including extra long double beds in every room. **Amenities:** 🛏 ♨ A/C, cable TV w/movies. Some units w/whirlpools. **Services:** 🍴 **Facilities:** 🛗 ♿ **Rates (CP):** Peak (June–Oct) $74 S; $79 D. Extra person $10. Children under age 17 stay free. Min stay wknds. Lower rates off-season. Parking: Outdoor, free. Special Amish Acres and dinner theater packages avail. AE, DC, DISC, MC, V.

RESTAURANT

Amish Acres Barn Restaurant
1600 W Market St; tel 219/773-4188. **Regional American.** Family-style dining in a large room under the hand-hewn beams of a barn, originally built in 1870 and reconstructed

on this property in 1977. The award-winning Thresher's Dinner features an iron kettle of thick bean soup; seasonal relishes, beef and noodles, mashed potatoes, sage dressing, and giblet gravy; shoofly pie or other dessert, and a beverage. Also choice of roasted turkey or beef, broasted country chicken, or cider-baked, hickory-smoked ham. **FYI:** Reservations not accepted. No liquor license. No smoking. **Open:** Peak (May–Oct) Mon–Sat 11am–7:30pm, Sun 11am–6pm. Closed Dec 30–Feb 28. **Prices:** Prix fixe $14. DISC, MC, V. 🔲 👪 &

Nashville

Seat of Brown County, in south-central part of state. This tiny tourist town in the heart of Indiana's loveliest scenery is a mecca for artists, photographers, and antiques shoppers, especially during autumn. Brown County State Park (the largest in Indiana) is two miles south of town on IN 46. **Information:** Brown County Convention & Visitors Bureau, PO Box 840, Nashville, 47448 (tel 812/988-7303).

HOTELS 📷

🏳🏳🏳 Brown County Inn
IN 46 and IN 135, PO Box 128, 47448; tel 812/988-2291 or toll free 800/772-5249. Rustic-looking with modern amenities and exceptional resortlike grounds. Not quite as businesslike as its sister hotel, the Seasons. Within walking distance of more than 300 shops in Nashville. Near Brown County State Park, Ski World, Little Nashville Opry. **Rooms:** 99 rms. CI 4pm/CO noon. Nonsmoking rms avail. Every room has two rocking chairs. **Amenities:** 🛁 👜 A/C, cable TV. Irons, ironing boards, and hair dryers available. **Services:** VP 🚐 🍴 Free coffee in lobby; free popcorn in lounge. Old-fashioned pig roast on patio every Sat June–Aug. Shuttle "train" through Nashville available. **Facilities:** 🏋 🎱 ²𝅘 300 & 1 restaurant, 1 bar (w/entertainment), basketball, volleyball, games rm, lawn games, playground, washer/dryer. The Corncrib Lounge has an old corncrib in it; the Harvest Dining Room resembles an old barn. Miniature golf, shuffleboard. **Rates:** Peak (June–Sept) $95 S or D. Extra person $6. Children under age 18 stay free. Min stay wknds. Lower rates off-season. Parking: Outdoor, free. Golf packages to nearby Salt Creek Golf Club avail. AE, CB, DC, DISC, MC, V.

🏳🏳🏳🏳 Hotel Nashville Resort
245 N Jefferson St, 47448; tel 812/988-0740 or toll free 800/848-6274; fax 812/988-1235. Upscale country look within walking distance to more than 300 shops in Nashville. Beautiful grounds. Designated parking spaces. **Rooms:** 44 stes. CI 4pm/CO 11am. All rooms are suites with living room, dining room, kitchen facilities, master bedroom, two baths, and balcony view. **Amenities:** 🛁 👜 🎦 A/C, cable TV, refrig. All units w/terraces, some w/whirlpools. Washer/dryer in one suite. **Services:** 🍴 **Facilities:** 🏋 🎱 50 & 1 restaurant (lunch only), 1 bar, sauna, whirlpool. Outdoor gazebo

with gas grills. **Rates:** Peak (Sept–Oct) $99–$119 ste. Extra person $10. Children under age 13 stay free. Min stay wknds. Lower rates off-season. Parking: Outdoor, free. Golf, ski, Little Nashville Opry packages avail. AE, DISC, MC, V.

🏳🏳🏳 The Seasons Lodge & Conference Center
560 IN 46 E, PO Box 187, 47448; tel 812/988-2284 or toll free 800/365-7327; fax 812/988-2284. Rustic-looking with modern amenities, on a small hill on the edge of town. Good for both business travelers and families. Close to more than 300 shops in Nashville, Brown County State Park, Ski World, Little Nashville Opry. **Rooms:** 80 rms. CI 4pm/CO noon. Nonsmoking rms avail. **Amenities:** 🛁 👜 A/C, satel TV w/movies. All units w/terraces, some w/fireplaces. **Services:** ✕ 🚐 🍴 Shuttle "train" through Nashville available. **Facilities:** 🏋 🎱 1100 & 1 restaurant, 1 bar (w/entertainment), basketball, volleyball, games rm, playground. Saloon lounge has Tex-Mex night on Wed. All meals in Accent include Brown County's famous hot fried biscuits and apple butter. Canvas bubble covers pool in cold months. Horseshoes. **Rates:** Peak (June–Sept) $95 S or D. Extra person $5. Children under age 18 stay free. Min stay wknds. Lower rates off-season. Parking: Outdoor, free. Golf packages avail at nearby Salt Creek Golf Club. AE, CB, DC, DISC, MC, V.

MOTEL

🏳🏳 Green Valley Motor Lodge
692 IN 46 W, 47448; tel 812/988-0231. Exceptionally clean, owner-operated motel in a very quiet, country setting on a highway outside of town. A notch above the average. Walking distance to the Little Nashville Opry. **Rooms:** 32 rms. CI open/CO 11am. Nonsmoking rms avail. A few rooms are standard motel fare, but most are individually decorated in a homey, country style, with quilts, gingham curtains, and rocking chairs. Some antique furniture. Two rooms have canopied beds—one solid oak and the other solid cherry. Sheets are line-dried outdoors. **Amenities:** 👜 A/C, cable TV. No phone. Some units w/terraces. **Services:** 🍴 Babysitting. **Facilities:** 🏋 🎱 **Rates:** Peak (Mar–Nov) $50–$115 S or D. Extra person $5. Min stay wknds. Lower rates off-season. Parking: Outdoor, free. DISC, MC, V.

RESORT

🏳🏳 Abe Martin Lodge
IN 46E, PO Box 547, 47448; tel 812/988-4418; fax 812/988-7334. Named after a 1905–1930 cartoon character in the *Indianapolis News*. Lodge is surrounded by 16,000 acres of Brown County State Park, largest state park in Indiana. Cultural arts, nature programs. Two lobbies with two fireplaces each. Near more than 300 quaint specialty shops in Nashville, Little Nashville Opry, TC Steele State Memorial, Yellowwood State Forest. Brown County is best known for its fall colors; Oct is the county's busiest month. **Rooms:** 84 rms; 74 cottages/villas. CI 4pm/CO noon. Nonsmoking rms avail. **Amenities:** 🛁 👜 A/C, TV, dataport, in-rm safe. Some units

w/terraces, some w/fireplaces. **Services:** Social director, children's program. VCRs and movies available. **Facilities:** 1 restaurant, basketball, volleyball, games rm, lawn games, playground. **Rates:** $47–$52 D; $43–$78 cottage/villa. Children under age 18 stay free. Parking: Outdoor, free. Guests must pay one gate admission charge ($2 for Indiana residents, $5 for nonresidents) Mar–Oct. Older cabins closed Dec–Mar. AE, DISC, MC, V.

RESTAURANTS

The Nashville House
Main and Van Buren Sts (Downtown); tel 812/988-4554. **Southern.** Country-fried chicken and fried ham steak with red gravy are a couple of the Southern classics offered at this rustic eatery with checked tablecloths and country furnishings. Fried biscuits and apple butter are included with each meal, and coconut cream pie is the signature dessert. A gift shop/country store sells pottery, "penny" candy, apple butter, jams, and honey. **FYI:** Reservations recommended. Children's menu. No liquor license. **Open:** Peak (Oct) Sun–Mon 11:30am–8pm, Wed–Thurs 11:30am–8pm, Fri–Sat 11:30am–9pm. **Prices:** Main courses $11–$17. AE, DISC, MC, V.

The Ordinary
Van Buren St (Downtown); tel 812/988-6166. **American.** The rustic interior of this down-home eatery includes a huge rock fireplace, various farm implements, and an old pump organ. The hearty fare includes wild game (usually pheasant and turkey), barbecued ribs, and smoked pork chops; several vegetarian sandwiches also available. Free snacks are always waiting in the lounge. The restaurant's private-label wine is made by Brown County Winery. **FYI:** Reservations accepted. Piano. Children's menu. **Open:** Peak (Oct) Tues–Thurs 11:30am–8pm, Fri–Sat 11:30am–10pm, Sun 11:30am–8pm. **Prices:** Main courses $10–$15. AE, DISC, MC, V.

The Story Inn
6404 S IN 135, Story; tel 812/988-2273. 13 mi S of Nashville. **New American.** Gourmet dining in a turn-of-the-century general store atmosphere that features a pot-bellied stove, cracker barrel, and liars' bench. Menu changes frequently to showcase seasonal items grown nearby. Entrees include herbed chicken and dumplings; peppered shrimp with sweet potatoes and mandarin oranges; and orange roughy and julienne vegetables steamed in parchment, served with jasmine white rice and spicy black beans. **FYI:** Reservations recommended. Children's menu. No smoking. **Open:** Tues–Fri 9am–8pm, Sat–Sun 8am–8pm. **Prices:** Main courses $15–$20. CB, DC, DISC, MC, V.

ATTRACTIONS

Brown County Art Guild
Van Buren and Main Sts; tel 812/988-6185. Brown County's serene beauty and accommodating pace have attracted artists for years. Located in the historic Minor House, the guild presents changing exhibits of the work of local and regional artists. **Open:** Mon–Sat 10am–5pm, Sun 11am–5pm. **Free**

Ski World Recreation Complex
2887 IN 46 W; tel 812/988-6638. A year-round recreational complex with skiing and snow boarding in winter on eight slopes and trails with a vertical drop of 250 feet. Fair weather activities include an alpine slide, water slides, batting cages, and go-cart and bumper-boat rides. **Open:** Call for schedule. $$$$

Brown County State Park
IN 46; tel 812/988-6406. The largest park in Indiana, the 27-square-mile recreation area offers fishing, hiking and riding trails, a nature center, picnic areas, a playground, an Olympic-size swimming pool, and tennis courts. **Open:** Daily sunrise–sunset. **Free**

New Castle

Seat of Henry County, in east-central part of state. There are numerous manufacturing plants in this productive city, and the Indiana Basketball Hall of Fame pays tribute to the state's favorite sport. **Information:** New Castle-Henry County Chamber of Commerce, 100 S Main St, #108, PO Box 485, New Castle, 47362-0485 (tel 317/529-5210).

MOTEL

Best Western Raintree Inn
2836 State Rd 3, 47362; tel 317/521-0100 or toll free 800/528-1234; fax 317/521-0100. Exit 123 off I-70, N 2 mi. Set amid farmland and open fields, this convenient motel offers a rural atmosphere. Indiana Basketball Hall of Fame is in New Castle; Aviator Wilbur Wright Memorial is in nearby Milville. **Rooms:** 105 rms and stes. CI noon/CO noon. Nonsmoking rms avail. Some rooms have views of open land, cornfields. **Amenities:** A/C, cable TV w/movies. Some units w/minibars, some w/terraces, some w/whirlpools. **Services:** Free coffee in lobby. Free VCRs; movies available. **Facilities:** 1 restaurant, 1 bar, games rm, whirlpool, washer/dryer. Restaurant off lobby offers straight-forward Midwestern cuisine seven days a week. Sun brunch and Fri evening buffet. Art deco bar, also off lobby. **Rates:** $42–$47 S; $46–$60 D; $80–$120 ste. Extra person $4. Children under age 16 stay free. Parking: Outdoor, free. Corporate and senior citizen rates. Higher rates for Indianapolis 500 in May and Brickyard 400 in Aug. AE, DC, DISC, MC, V.

ATTRACTIONS

Indiana Basketball Hall of Fame
4 Trojan Lane; tel 317/529-1891. Baseball may be the national pastime, but it is basketball that really makes Hoosier hearts beat fast with excitement. This 14,000-square-foot

museum pays tribute to "Hoosier Hysteria" with multimedia presentations, computerized data banks filled with basketball facts and figures, and an exhibit that allow guests to play against a mechanical opponent. Research library, video collection, and memorabilia also available. **Open:** Tues–Sat 10am–5pm, Sun 1–5pm. **$**

Henry County Historical Society Museum
606 S 14th St; tel 317/529-4028. Located in the restored 1870 home of Civil War Gen William Grose. In addition to period rooms, the museum includes Victorian-era antiques, clothing, and artwork, as well as Native American artifacts. **Open:** Mon–Sat 1–4:30pm. **Free**

Henry County Memorial Park
2221 N Memorial; tel 317/529-1004. Built in 1920 in honor of veterans of World War II. The 312 acre park features picnic shelters, volleyball and basketball courts, a golf course, nature trails, and playgrounds. Fishing and boating are popular during the summer, while winter brings out the ice skaters and ice fishers. **Open:** Daily sunrise–sunset. **Free**

New Harmony

Second home of the Harmony Society, a religious group led by German religious leader George Rapp that prospered in Harmony, PA, before moving to Indiana in 1814-1815 to found New Harmony. This new city flourished, but in 1825 the founders sold the land to Robert Owen and returned to PA to found a third town. Under Owen's leadership, a communistic community was established that became renowned as a center of learning, attracting well-known intellectuals. The society dissolved in 1828, unable to survive internal dissent. The town remained an intellectual center, however, and claims the nation's first kindergarten, first free public school, first free library, and first school offering equal education to boys and girls.

HOTEL 🏨

≣≣≣ The New Harmony Inn
504 North St, PO Box 581, 47631; tel 812/682-4491. 2 blocks N of town's only stoplight. Adjacent to New Harmony, a community founded in 1814 as an experimental Utopian colony and known historically as an intellectual and cultural center. The inn, built in 1974, combines Harmonist simplicity with contemporary comforts in two dorms. People visit for relaxation and a spiritual renewal as well as for the town's historic significance. On the well-manicured, estate-like grounds are the roofless church, Paul Tillich Park, Red Geranium Bookstore, Carol Owen Coleman Memorial Garden, and artwork ranging from sculptures to oils to water colors. **Rooms:** 90 rms and effic; 4 cottages/villas. CI 3pm/CO noon. Nonsmoking rms avail. Simplicity is the keynote in the rooms, each different from another, Shaker-style wood furniture, hardwood floors, scatter rugs. Four units have

sleeping lofts. **Amenities:** 🛏 🐕 A/C, cable TV, dataport. Some units w/terraces, some w/fireplaces. Three units have kitchenettes. **Services:** 🚐 🛎 Babysitting. The inn works closely with Historic New Harmony to provide tours for its guests. **Facilities:** 🔥 🚲 🏊 🏀2 🎳 🅿300 🐕 2 restaurants (*see* "Restaurants" below), 1 bar, volleyball, games rm, spa, sauna, whirlpool. Enclosed greenhouse swimming pool used year-round. **Rates:** Peak (Apr–Oct) $65 S; $75 D; $75 effic; $195–$600 cottage/villa. Extra person $10. Children under age 12 stay free. Lower rates off-season. Parking: Outdoor, free. Seasonal packages avail. AE, DISC, MC, V.

RESTAURANTS 🍴

Bayou Grill
In the New Harmony Inn complex, 504 North St; tel 812/682-4491. 2 blocks N of town's only stoplight. **American.** Contemporary, casual dining. Diverse selections range from omelettes to hearty sandwiches to fried chicken and daily specials. The Sunday brunch offers a wide variety of breakfast and lunch entrees highlighted by displays of fresh fruit and cheeses, ice carvings, and homemade desserts. **FYI:** Reservations recommended. Children's menu. **Open:** Peak (June–Aug) daily 7am–9pm. **Prices:** Main courses $6–$12. AE, DISC, MC, V. &

🏆 Red Geranium
In the New Harmony Inn complex, 504 North St; tel 812/682-4431. 2 blocks N of town's only stoplight. **American.** Diners in the Tillich Refectory look out over estatelike grounds, while those in the main dining room enjoy a gracious 19th-century atmosphere. Traditional American fare includes regional favorites such as chateaubriand bouquetière, rack of lamb persille, pork tenderloin, and pork chops. Shaker lemon pie is the signature dessert. The on-site bakery is open early in the morning with fresh breads, doughnuts, pastries. **FYI:** Reservations recommended. Children's menu. **Open:** Tues–Thurs 11am–10pm, Fri–Sat 11am–11pm, Sun 11am–8pm. **Prices:** Main courses $15–$35. AE, DISC, MC, V. 🍷 &

ATTRACTIONS 🏛

Atheneum
North and Arthur Sts; tel 812/682-4474. Designed by renowned architect Richard Meier, this compelling structure is a monument to the spirit and accomplishments of the two Utopian communal societies that settled here in the first half of the 19th century. The building is also functional, serving as a visitors center with exhibits, a film on the history of New Harmony, and an observation deck. Tickets to view the historic sites of the community must be purchased here. **Open:** Peak (Apr–Oct) daily 9am–5pm. Reduced hours off-season. **$$**

New Harmony Gallery of Contemporary Art
506 Main St; tel 812/682-3156. Paintings, sculpture, prints, and modern furniture by contemporary Midwestern artists are exhibited on a changing basis. **Open:** Tues–Sat 9am–5pm, Sun 1–5pm. **Free**

Plymouth

Seat of Marshall County. This small northern Indiana town was the site of the last Potawatomi village in the area before the tribe's tragic evacuation to Kansas in 1838. **Information:** Plymouth Area Chamber of Commerce, 120 N Michigan St, Plymouth, 46563 (tel 219/936-2323).

HOTEL 🏨

≣≣ Holiday Inn
2550 N Michigan St, 46563; tel 219/936-4013 or toll free 800/HOLIDAY; fax 219/936-4553. Exit IN 17 off US 30, 1 block N. An older hotel with catwalk access to rooms. Beautiful flowers and shrubs, and two small wooden gazebos. Tile floor in lobby complements the brick. **Rooms:** 108 rms. CI 2pm/CO noon. Nonsmoking rms avail. All units face central courtyard. **Amenities:** 🛋 ⚂ A/C. **Services:** ✕ 🖼 ⤶ ⟨⟩ **Facilities:** 🛋 & 1 restaurant, 1 bar, washer/dryer. Access to nearby health spa for $5. **Rates:** $60 S or D. Extra person $5. Children under age 18 stay free. Parking: Outdoor, free. Rates increase during Notre Dame football games. Special packages for New Year's Eve and Valentine's Day. AE, CB, DC, DISC, MC, V.

MOTEL

≣ Days Inn
2229 N Michigan St, 46563; tel 219/935-4276 or toll free 800/325-2525. Exit US 30 to IN 17 N. Set well back from IN 17. Recently painted exterior, grounds clean and well kept. Functional lodging for one-night stay. **Rooms:** 40 rms. CI 2pm/CO 11am. Nonsmoking rms avail. Rooms newly painted, with some new floor coverings and furnishings. **Amenities:** 🛋 A/C, cable TV. **Services:** ⤶ ⟨⟩ Small pets allowed. **Rates:** $44 S; $48 D. Children under age 13 stay free. Parking: Outdoor, free. AE, DISC, MC, V.

ATTRACTION 🏛

Chief Menominee Monument
Twin Lakes. Statue of the chief forms part of the granite memorial at the site of the last Potawatomi village in this area. (The tribe was forcibly removed in 1838 under order from the governor of Indiana.) **Open:** Daily 24 hours. **Free**

Richmond

Seat of Wayne County, in the east-central part of the state. Founded in 1806 by Quaker settlers from North Carolina.

Earlham College, one of the foremost Quaker colleges in the country, is located here. **Information:** Wayne County Convention & Tourism Bureau, 5701 National Rd E, Richmond, 47374 (tel 317/935-8687 or toll free 800/828-8414).

HOTEL 🏨

≣≣≣ Holiday Inn
5501 National Rd E, 47374; tel 317/966-7511 or toll free 800/548-2473; fax 317/966-4612. Exit 156A off I-70; 1 mi W on US 40. Newly renovated and tastefully decorated. **Rooms:** 132 rms, stes, and effic. CI 3pm/CO noon. Nonsmoking rms avail. Guests can rent two, three, or four rooms in a suite. **Amenities:** 🛋 ⚂ 🖥 A/C, cable TV w/movies, dataport, voice mail. Some units w/minibars, some w/whirlpools. **Services:** ✕ 🖼 ⤶ ⟨⟩ Babysitting. **Facilities:** 🛋 🎳 🎱 & 1 restaurant, 1 bar (w/entertainment), games rm, sauna, whirlpool. **Rates (CP):** $72 S or D; $90–$200 ste; $300 effic. Extra person $7. Children under age 19 stay free. Parking: Outdoor, free. AE, CB, DC, DISC, JCB, MC, V.

MOTELS

≣≣ Best Western Inn
3020 E Main St, 47374; tel 317/966-1505 or toll free 800/528-1234; fax 317/935-1426. Older building that is exceptionally well maintained. Good for business travelers. **Rooms:** 45 rms and effic. CI open/CO 11am. Nonsmoking rms avail. Standard motel rooms. **Amenities:** 🛋 ⚂ A/C, cable TV w/movies. Some rooms have microwaves and refrigerators. **Services:** 🖼 ⤶ ⟨⟩ Free coffee in lobby. **Facilities:** 🛋 & **Rates (CP):** $30–$40 S; $40–$50 D; $45–$55 effic. Extra person $2. Children under age 12 stay free. Parking: Outdoor, free. AE, CB, DC, DISC, MC, V.

≣≣ Comfort Inn
912 Mendelson Dr, 47374; tel 317/935-4766 or toll free 800/221-2222; fax 317/935-4766. Exit 151A off I-70. Clean, standard motel well suited to business travelers and families. **Rooms:** 52 rms and stes. CI 1pm/CO 11am. Nonsmoking rms avail. Typical motel rooms. **Amenities:** 🛋 A/C, cable TV w/movies. **Services:** 🖼 ⤶ ⟨⟩ **Facilities:** 🛋 & Games rm, whirlpool. **Rates (CP):** $53–$58 S or D; $60–$65 ste. Extra person $5. Children under age 18 stay free. Parking: Outdoor, free. Guests of any motel in this chain stay free on 13th night. AE, CB, DC, DISC, ER, JCB, MC, V.

≣ Days Inn
540 W Eaton Pike, 47374; tel 317/966-7591 or toll free 800/DAYS-INN; fax 317/962-8565. Exit 156A off I-70. Older building. **Rooms:** 95 rms. CI 2pm/CO 11am. Nonsmoking rms avail. Some rooms are being renovated. **Amenities:** 🛋 A/C, cable TV. **Services:** ⤶ ⟨⟩ **Facilities:** 🛋 & Washer/dryer. Large truck parking area. **Rates (CP):** $40–$70 S or D. Extra person $5. Children under age 12 stay free. Parking: Outdoor, free. AE, CB, DC, DISC, JCB, MC, V.

≋≋ Ramada Inn

4700 National Rd E, ; tel 317/962-5551 or toll free 800/917-2011; fax 317/966-6250. Exit 156A off I-70, then 1 mi W on US 40. Plantings add color and life to this older, recently refurbished building. **Rooms:** 158 rms and stes. CI 3pm/CO noon. Nonsmoking rms avail. More rooms than any other motel in the city. **Amenities:** ☎ ⓦ A/C, cable TV w/movies. **Services:** ✗ ⌷ ⌵ ⌇ **Facilities:** ⌷ ⌷₂₀₀ ⌷ 1 restaurant, 1 bar, games rm. **Rates:** $39–$68 S; $48–$78 D; $136–$142 ste. Extra person $10. Children under age 18 stay free. Parking: Outdoor, free. AE, CB, DC, DISC, MC, V.

RESTAURANTS ☯

★ Bud King's "Taste of the Town"

1616 E Main St; tel 317/935-5464. Exit 156A off I-70, then 3.2 mi W on US 40. **American.** Bud King is the drawing card here, and he's almost always here to welcome guests to dine in his comfortable, casual eatery. Favorites are steak and prime rib. Garlic toast is served as soon as you're seated. **FYI:** Reservations accepted. Piano. Children's menu. **Open:** Mon–Fri 11am–10pm, Sat 4–10pm. **Prices:** Main courses $8–$15. AE, DISC, MC, V. 🎞 ⓦ

The Olde Richmond Inn

138 S 5th St; tel 317/962-2247. 1 block S of courthouse. **American/Seafood.** Don't let the numerous one-way streets deter you: dining in the 1892 Grothaus residence with hand-carved wood paneling and lace curtains is well worthwhile. Owner/chef Galo Molina specializes in seafood flown in from Boston and prime meats. Tour groups with reservations welcome. **FYI:** Reservations recommended. Children's menu. **Open:** Mon–Thurs 11am–9pm, Fri–Sat 11am–10pm, Sun 11am–8pm. **Prices:** Main courses $9–$18. MC, V. ⓦ 🍴 ⓦ

ATTRACTIONS ☷

Art Association of Richmond

350 Hub Etchison Pkwy; tel 317/966-0256. Extensive permanent collection containing works by local and nationally known artists. **Open:** Sept–May, Mon–Fri 9am–4pm, Sun 1–4pm. **Free**

Hays Regional Arboretum

801 Elks Rd; tel 317/962-3745. This 355-acre nature preserve features a variety of indigenous flora and fauna. Highlights include a solar-heated greenhouse (Indiana's first), a 40-acre beech-maple forest, a fern garden, a 10-acre collection of native woody plants, a wild bird sanctuary, and a nature center housed in a 180-year-old barn. There's a 3½-mile auto tour, two self-guided nature trails, and 10 miles of hiking trails. **Open:** Tues–Sat 9am–5pm, Sun 1–5pm. **Free**

Indiana Football Hall of Fame

315 N A St; tel 317/966-2235. Displays and exhibits illustrate the history of football from the 1890s to the present, with a special emphasis on Hoosier players and teams. Individuals honored in the Hall of Inductees include Weeb Ewbank,

Knute Rockne, Ara Perseghian, and Billy Hillenbrand. **Open:** Peak (May–Oct) Mon–Fri 10am–4pm. Reduced hours off-season. **$**

Rockville

RESTAURANT ☯

The Herb Garden

114 S Market (Downtown); tel 317/569-6055. W side of courthouse square. **American.** A profusion of trees, flowers, waterfalls, stuffed animals, potpourri, and—of course—herbs reflect the theme of this quaint eatery. Both decor and menu change with the seasons and the wait staff are referred to as "gardeners." Menu highlights include homemade soups, light entrees, freshly baked pies, and a wide selection of teas. Country Grapevine gift shop on site. **FYI:** Reservations recommended. No liquor license. No smoking. **Open:** Tues–Sat 11am–3pm. **Prices:** Lunch main courses $4–$6. No CC. ⓦ

Santa Claus

ATTRACTION ☷

Holiday World & Splashin' Safari

Jct IN 162/245; tel 812/937-4401 or toll free 800/GO-SANTA. Holiday World has more than 60 rides, shows, and attractions, many with holiday themes. One of the most popular activities is a visit with Santa. Splashin' Safari is a hot weather haven with water slides, a wave pool, and action river. The fee includes admission to both parks. **Open:** Peak (mid-May–mid-Aug) daily at 10am. Call for closing times. **$$$$**

South Bend

See also Elkhart, Mishawaka

Seat of St Joseph County, in northern Indiana. The French explorer La Salle met with chiefs of the Miami and Illinois confederations beneath the Council Oak here in 1681. Football fans think of South Bend as the home of the University of Notre Dame; the Studebaker Company was founded here in 1852. **Information:** Convention & Visitors Bureau of South Bend-Mishawaka, 401 E Colfax, #310, PO Box 1677, South Bend, 46634-1677 (tel 219/234-0051 or 234-0079).

HOTELS ☷

≋≋ Best Inns of America

425 Dixie Hwy, 46637; tel 219/277-7700 or toll free 800/BEST-INN; fax 219/277-7700. Exit 77 off I-80/90. Attrac-

tive stone construction. Very well maintained, with clean, well-kept grounds. Designed for business traveler, good value for mature travelers. **Rooms:** 93 rms. CI open/CO 1pm. Nonsmoking rms avail. **Amenities:** 📞 A/C, cable TV. **Services:** 🍴 🍽 Bright, clean seating area in lobby for continental breakfast. **Facilities:** 🛗12 ⚓ **Rates (CP):** Peak (May–Sept) $44–$55 S; $50–$52 D. Extra person $6. Children under age 18 stay free. Min stay special events. Lower rates off-season. Parking: Outdoor, free. AE, CB, DC, DISC, MC, V.

📧📧 Holiday Inn University Area
515 Dixie Hwy, 46637; tel 219/272-6600 or toll free 800/HOLIDAY; fax 219/272-5553. Exit 77 off I-80/90. Well set back from highway. Natural brick construction, rustic appearance. **Rooms:** 228 rms. CI 3pm/CO noon. Nonsmoking rms avail. **Amenities:** 📞 🛏 🍹 A/C, cable TV. **Services:** ✗ 🆅🅿 🚐 🛄 🍴 🍽 Children's program, babysitting. "Guest of the day," chosen from frequent traveler program, receives large basket of fresh fruit. **Facilities:** 🎣 🏌 🛗185 💻 ⚓ 1 restaurant (bkfst and dinner only), 1 bar (w/entertainment), games rm, spa, sauna, whirlpool, playground, washer/dryer. Holidome area has pool tables, Ping-Pong, arcade games, miniature golf course, and heated pool. **Rates:** Peak (May–Oct) $72 S; $82 D. Extra person $10. Children under age 12 stay free. Lower rates off-season. Parking: Outdoor, free. AE, CB, DC, DISC, MC, V.

📧📧📧 The Inn At Saint Mary's
53993 Hwy 31, 46637; tel 219/232-4000; fax 219/289-0986. Exit 77 off I-80/90. Dark brown, brick building has look of utilitarian dormitory building, but lobby is breathtaking: three-story, all glass, with central stairway to all floors, wrought-iron trim throughout, and art deco fixtures. Magnificent flowers and plantings. **Rooms:** 120 rms and stes. CI 3pm/CO noon. Rooms with king-size beds have additional sofa sleepers. Partial partition separates sitting area from sleeping area. **Amenities:** 📞 🛏 🖥 A/C, cable TV, dataport, voice mail. Some units w/whirlpools. **Services:** 🗝 🚐 🛄 🍽 **Facilities:** 🛗50 💻 ⚓ 1 bar, washer/dryer. **Rates (CP):** $74 S; $84 D; $94–$124 ste. Extra person $10. Children under age 12 stay free. Min stay special events. Parking: Outdoor, free. AE, CB, DC, DISC, JCB, MC, V.

📧📧📧 Marriott Hotel South Bend
123 St Joseph St, 46601; tel 219/234-2000 or toll free 800/228-9290; fax 219/234-0077. Dramatic glass-enclosed lobby and seven-story atrium restaurant and bar area; atrium also connects to major bank building. Attracts families on weekends. **Rooms:** 299 rms and stes. Executive level. CI 3pm/CO noon. Nonsmoking rms avail. **Amenities:** 📞 🛏 A/C, cable TV, dataport, voice mail. **Services:** ✗ 🗝 🛄 🍽 Social director, babysitting. **Facilities:** 🎣 🏌 🛗400 💻 ⚓ 1 restaurant, 1 bar, spa, sauna, whirlpool. **Rates:** $94–$100 S; $112 D; $150–$375 ste. Extra person $8–$10. Children under age 12 stay free. Parking: Indoor, $4/day. Rates increase during Notre Dame football weekends. AE, CB, DC, DISC, JCB, MC, V.

📧📧📧 Ramada Inn
52890 Hwy 31 N, 46637; tel 219/272-5220 or toll free 800/2-RAMADA; fax 219/272-3956. Exit 77 off I-80/90. Architecture of exterior is Southern, with a large porte cochere with attractive white columns. **Rooms:** 201 rms and stes. CI 3pm/CO noon. Nonsmoking rms avail. King-bedded rooms have recliner chairs. New carpeting and wall coverings. Limited availability of suites and efficiencies. **Amenities:** 📞 🛏 A/C, cable TV. Some units w/minibars. Business suites have coffeemakers and refrigerators. **Services:** ✗ 🚐 🛄 🍽 Car-rental desk. Video rentals and VCRs available. Business suites get full breakfast and free fax services. **Facilities:** 🎣 🛗350 ⚓ 1 restaurant, 1 bar (w/entertainment), basketball, games rm, whirlpool, washer/dryer. Miniature golf. **Rates (CP):** $63 S; $68–$78 D; $115 ste. Extra person $8. Children under age 18 stay free. Parking: Outdoor, free. Super-saver weekend rates, special business rates for suites. Closed . AE, CB, DC, DISC, MC, V.

📧📧 Signature Inn
215 Dixie Way S, 46637; tel 219/277-3211 or toll free 800/822-5252; fax 219/277-3211. Exit 77 off I-80/90. Simple brown brick exterior. Good use of natural wood and stonework. **Rooms:** 123 rms. CI 3pm/CO noon. Nonsmoking rms avail. **Amenities:** 📞 🛏 A/C, cable TV w/movies. **Services:** 🛄 🍽 **Facilities:** 🎣 🏌 🛗85 ⚓ Spa, sauna, whirlpool. Large pool area with extensive plantings, tables, chairs, and attractive wall murals. **Rates (CP):** Peak (Mar–Oct) $68 S; $75 D. Extra person $7. Children under age 17 stay free. Min stay special events. Lower rates off-season. Parking: Outdoor, free. Special rates and benefits for those who stay 12 nights during one year. Frequent traveler program; Signature Club. AE, DC, DISC, MC, V.

MOTELS

📧📧 Days Inn
52747 Hwy 31 N, 46637; tel 219/277-0510 or toll free 800/DAYS-INN; fax 219/277-9316. Exit 77 off I-80/90. Older facility, well maintained. Property extends deep into wooded area. Building undergoing gradual updating. **Rooms:** 180 rms. CI 3pm/CO noon. Nonsmoking rms avail. Rooms with king-size beds have recliner chairs. Carpeting in process of replacement throughout. **Amenities:** 📞 A/C. **Services:** 🚐 🛄 🍽 🍴 Car-rental desk, babysitting. **Facilities:** 🎣 🛗35 ⚓ **Rates (CP):** Peak (May–Sept) $55–$60 S; $61–$66 D. Children under age 18 stay free. Min stay special events. Lower rates off-season. Parking: Outdoor, free. All rates increase during Notre Dame football season. AE, CB, DC, DISC, JCB, MC, V.

📧 Knights Inn
236 Dixie Hwy, 46637; tel 219/277-2960 or toll free 800/KNIGHTS; fax 219/277-0203. Exit 77 off I-80/90. Property runs deep into lot, next to farm area in rear. Very quiet. **Rooms:** 107 rms, stes, and effic. CI noon/CO noon. Nonsmoking rms avail. **Amenities:** 📞 A/C, cable TV. Some units

w/whirlpools. **Services:** 🖼️ 🛎️ 📺 VCRs available; movie tape rental machine in lobby. Pets $5 per day. **Facilities:** 🏠 ♿ **Rates (CP):** $40–$65 S; $46–$71 D; $69–$109 ste; $55–$65 effic. Extra person $8. Children under age 18 stay free. Min stay peak. Parking: Outdoor, free. Higher rates for football weekends at Notre Dame. AE, CB, DC, MC, V.

RESTAURANTS 🍽️

🏆 The Carriage House

24460 Adams Rd; tel 219/272-9220. Bus 31 (Brick Rd) to Orange Rd, right 3 mi. **Eclectic.** This jewel of a restaurant was created from an abandoned Brethren Church built in 1851. The impeccable interior of the main dining room features the original beamed ceiling, and throughout are splendid floral arrangements and luxurious appointments, wall coverings, and artwork. Sample dishes include rabbit sausage appetizer, beef Wellington, venison, and rack of lamb. All desserts made on premises. **FYI:** Reservations recommended. **Open:** Tues–Sat 5–9:30pm. Closed Jan 2–16. **Prices:** Main courses $16–$28. AE, CB, DC, DISC, MC, V. 🍴 🍰 🏞️

Hans Haus

2803 S Michigan St; tel 219/291-5522. **American/German.** White walls crisscrossed with dark-wood paneling, sturdy wooden chairs and tables, wrought-iron light fixtures, and paintings of the Bavarian Alps provide a perfect setting for classic Central European fare. Favorite menu items include a variety of schnitzels, the *schlact platte* (bratwurst, knackwurst, and rippchen), *kasseler rippchen* (grilled smoked pork loin), sauerkraut soup, and a wide variety of spaetzle side dishes. The exhaustive beer list includes selections from Europe, Japan, Australia, and the Philippines, along with several American microbrews. **FYI:** Reservations accepted. Children's menu. **Open:** Lunch Mon–Sat 11am–2pm; dinner Mon–Sat 4–9pm. **Prices:** Main courses $7–$11. AE, DC, MC, V. 🍴 👨‍👩‍👧 ♿

LaSalle Grill

115 W Colfax Ave; tel 219/288-1155. Next to Morris Civic Center. **International.** Frank Lloyd Wright's Prairie style is evident throughout this American bistro, originally a hotel in the 1920s. Works by local artists (for sale) are exhibited, as are the busy workings of the kitchen staff in the exhibition kitchen window in front. Produce from local farmers is used, plus Amish-grown chickens. Specialties are rack of New Zealand lamb and Canadian back pork loin. Appetizers include peppered beef tartare, sautéed fresh squid, and roasted tomato soup. Menu recommends wine selection for each entree. **FYI:** Reservations recommended. Jazz/piano. No smoking. **Open:** Mon–Thurs 5–10pm, Fri–Sat 5–11pm. **Prices:** Main courses $15–$29. AE, CB, DC, MC, V. 💚 ♿

★ Tippecanoe Place

620 W Washington St; tel 219/234-9077. 6 blocks W of downtown. **American.** A historic treasure that dates from 1888, this mansion comprises separate dining rooms for maximum intimacy, all furnished with excellent reproductions of Victorian tables and chairs. The entrance opens to a large lobby and a grand staircase leading to the second floor. Menu specialties are baked Brie, crab-stuffed mushrooms, Indiana duckling, charbroiled swordfish, brandy-Dijon tenderloin, and prime rib. **FYI:** Reservations recommended. Piano. Children's menu. Dress code. **Open:** Lunch Mon–Fri 11:30am–2pm; dinner Mon–Thurs 5–10pm, Fri 5–11pm, Sat 4:30–11pm, Sun 4–9pm; brunch Sun 9am–2pm. **Prices:** Main courses $13–$18. AE, CB, DC, MC, V. 🍴 👨‍👩‍👧 ♿

ATTRACTIONS 🏛️

University of Notre Dame

US 31/33; tel 219/631-7367. Founded in 1842, this is one of the premier universities in the country. Buildings of special interest include the **Grotto of Our Lady of Lourdes** (a replica of the Grotto of Lourdes in France) and the 1871 **Basilica of the Sacred Heart** (which features stained-glass windows, an exquisite baroque altar, and one of the oldest carillons in North America). The campus's **Main Building** (1879) is marked by its prominent golden dome surmounted by a statue of the Virgin Mary, and has murals illustrating Columbus's life executed by Vatican artist Luigi Gregori. The two million-volume **Theodore M Hesburgh Library** boasts an 11-story granite mural on an outer wall, while the **Snite Museum of Art** houses over 19,000 works of art including masterpieces by Picasso, Chagall, and Rodin. The university is also known for its sports programs, particularly its football and basketball teams. Student-led guided tours available. **Free**

The Snite Museum of Art

Dorr Rd; tel 219/631-5466. Located on the University of Notre Dame campus, this museum's 20,000-piece permanent collection boasts important works by Frederick Remington, Georgia O'Keeffe, and Jim Dine, as well as drawings and etchings by Degas and Rembrandt. Impressive displays of Greek and Roman antiquities. **Open:** Tues–Sat 10am–4pm, Sun 1–4pm; Thurs 10am–8pm when classes in session. **Free**

Northern Indiana Center for History

808 W Washington; tel 219/235-9664. A complex of historical sites including **Copshaholm,** (see below); **Dom Robotnika,** a worker's home (built 1870) which celebrates the ethnic, working class heritage of the community; and the **History Center,** which features an interactive children's museum and nine permanent galleries with exhibits that explore the history of the St Joseph River Valley. **Open:** Tues–Sat 10am–5pm, Sun noon–5pm. **$**

Capshaholm, the Oliver Mansion

808 W Washington; tel 219/235-9664. Part of the Northern Indiana Center for History, this 38 room stone house was built in 1895 for local businessman Joseph Doty Oliver. The interior is of oak, cherry, and mahogany, with patterned parquet floors and leaded-glass windows. All furnishings in the mansion are the original possessions of the Olivers.

Copshaholm is surrounded by 2½ acres of landscaped grounds, with a formal Italianate garden, rose garden, tea house, fountain, and tennis court. Guided tours required, reservations recommended. **Open:** Tues–Sat 10am–5pm, Sun noon–5pm. **$$**

Studebaker National Museum

525 S Main St; tel 219/235-9714. The world's most extensive collection of vehicles produced by the Studebaker company, from wagons build by founder Clement Studebaker for the Union Army to the last car to roll off the assembly line at the South Bend Studebaker plant in 1966. Items of special interest include the Studebaker in which Abraham Lincoln rode to Ford's Theater the night of his assassination, carriages belonging to Presidents Grant and McKinley, World War I horse-drawn wagons, and an amphibious Weasel from World War II. Other exhibits document the history of the corporation and the economic development of South Bend. **Open:** Mon–Sat 9am–5pm, Sun noon–5pm. **$$**

Potawatomi Zoo

Greenlawn Ave; tel 219/235-9800. This 22-acre zoo, set among flowers and tropical plants in 64-acre Potawatomi Park, features animals from five continents. Petting zoo and learning center for the kids. **Open:** Daily 10am–5pm. **$**

Story

See Nashville

Terre Haute

Seat of Vigo County, in western Indiana. The commercial and cultural hub of the fertile Wabash Valley, Terre Haute (French for "high ground") is home to Indiana State University and St Mary-of-the-Woods College. Author Theodore Dreiser (*Sister Carrie, An American Tragedy*) was born here in 1871. **Information:** Terre Haute Convention & Visitors Bureau of Vigo County, 643 Wabash Ave, Terre Haute, 47807 (tel 812/234-5555 or toll free 800/366-3043).

HOTELS 🏨

≣≣≣ Best Western the Linden

3325 US 41 S, 47802; tel 812/234-7781 or toll free 800/528-1234; fax 812/232-6618. Glass elevator gives guests a dynamic view of the Terre Haute and Indiana State University skyline. Next to Terre Haute regional mall, close to city parks. **Rooms:** 97 rms and stes. CI 2pm/CO noon. Nonsmoking rms avail. **Amenities:** 🛏 A/C, cable TV, dataport, VCR. All units w/terraces, 1 w/fireplace. **Services:** ✕ 🖂 ↻ ⬦ **Facilities:** 🛆 ⌷₁₅₀ ₺ 1 bar (w/entertainment), games rm, sauna, whirlpool. BeBop Night Club features the Top 40s on Fri–Sat nights. Guest privileges at two nearby fitness centers.

Rates (CP): $50–$77 S; $53–$80 D; $125–$175 ste. Extra person $8. Children under age 18 stay free. **Parking:** Outdoor, free. AE, DC, DISC, MC, V.

≣≣≣ Holiday Inn

3300 US 41 S, 47802; tel 812/232-6081 or toll free 800/465-4329; fax 812/238-9934. Exit 7 off I-70. More amenities than many lodgings in the area. Holidome with plants. **Rooms:** 230 rms. CI 3pm/CO 1pm. Nonsmoking rms avail. **Amenities:** 🛏 ₺ ⊡ A/C, cable TV, voice mail. **Services:** ✕ 🖂 ↻ ⬦ Babysitting. **Facilities:** 🛆 ⌶ ⌷₃₀₀ ₺ 1 restaurant, 1 bar (w/entertainment), basketball, games rm, sauna, whirlpool, washer/dryer. **Rates:** $83–$87 S or D. Extra person $8. Children under age 12 stay free. **Parking:** Outdoor, free. AE, CB, DC, DISC, MC, V.

MOTELS

≣ Knights Inn

401 Margaret Ave, 47802; tel 812/234-9931 or toll free 800/843-5644; fax 812/234-0890. Exit 7 off I-70. Newly remodeled budget motel, close to Cracker Barrel. **Rooms:** 125 rms and effic. CI 3pm/CO 11am. Nonsmoking rms avail. **Amenities:** 🛏 A/C, cable TV w/movies, voice mail. **Services:** ⓋⓅ 🖂 ↻ ⬦ 24-hour coffee in lobby. **Facilities:** 🛆 ₺ **Rates (CP):** $43–$57 S or D; $169 effic. Extra person $4. Children under age 17 stay free. **Parking:** Outdoor, free. Weekly rates avail. AE, DC, DISC, MC, V.

≣ Pick Motor Inn

4800 US 41 S, 47802; tel 812/299-1181. Exit 7 off I-70; S 1½ mi. Inexpensive lodging. Many guests are working persons, such as construction crews, who need long-term lodging. **Rooms:** 210 rms and effic. CI 2pm/CO noon. Nonsmoking rms avail. **Amenities:** 🛏 A/C, cable TV w/movies. **Services:** ↻ **Facilities:** 🛆 ⌷₄₀ ₺ 1 restaurant, 1 bar (w/entertainment), playground, washer/dryer. **Rates:** $27–$32 S; $32–$45 D; $150–$175 effic. Extra person $4. Children under age 10 stay free. **Parking:** Outdoor, free. Long-term stays avail. Efficiencies rented on a weekly basis. AE, MC, V.

≣≣ Signature Inn

3053 US 41 S, 47802; tel 812/238-1461 or toll free 800/522-8282; fax 812/238-1461. At exit 7. Comfortable facility with inviting lounge. Accessible to Indiana State University and downtown Terre Haute. **Rooms:** 157 rms. Executive level. CI 3pm/CO noon. Nonsmoking rms avail. **Amenities:** 🛏 ₺ A/C, cable TV w/movies, dataport. 1 unit w/whirlpool. **Services:** 🖂 ↻ ⬦ Social director, babysitting. Complimentary newspaper. **Facilities:** 🛆 ⌶ ⌷₁₀₀ ▯ ₺ Spa, whirlpool. **Rates (CP):** $61 S; $58 D. Extra person $7. Children under age 17 stay free. **Parking:** Outdoor, free. AE, DC, DISC, MC, V.

RESTAURANTS 🍴

Farrington House Restaurant
1000 S 6th St; tel 812/232-2150. Farrington St exit off IN 41; 3 blocks E. **American.** Located in an elegant Italianate mansion built in 1873 and now listed on the National Register of Historic Homes. Attention to details shows throughout the beautifully maintained interior: oak woodwork retains its original coat of varnish, tall oak doors have heavy brass hinges and doorknobs, original shutters cover the windows, and six rooms have their original metal fireplaces. Private rooms are available for intimate dinners. The kitchen is known for its one-pound pork chop. On-site gift shop. **FYI:** Reservations recommended. **Open:** Mon–Sat 5–10pm. **Prices:** Main courses $13–$21. AE, CB, DC, DISC, MC, V. ❤ 🍴🏊♿

Western Rib-Eye
100 S Fruitridge; tel 812/232-5591. Exit 11 off I-70; N to US 40; ¾ mi to Fruitridge; S to restaurant. **Seafood/Steak.** The casual country atmosphere matches the down-home cooking available here. Charbroiled steak, prime rib, and fish are the most-requested entrees. All dinners come with hot whole-wheat molasses bread and herbal butter. **FYI:** Reservations recommended. Children's menu. **Open:** Sun–Thurs 11am–9pm, Fri 11am–10pm, Sat 4–10pm. **Prices:** Main courses $9–$16. AE, DC, MC, V. 👥

ATTRACTIONS 🏛

Sheldon Swope Art Museum
25 S 7th St; tel 812/238-1676. The permanent collection features works by Ansel Adams, Edward Hopper, Andy Warhol, Thomas Hart Benton, Grant Wood, and other 19th- and 20th-century American artists. Film, lectures, special exhibits, and performing arts events offered. **Open:** Tues–Fri 10am–5pm, Sat–Sun noon–5pm. **Free**

Historical Museum of the Wabash Valley
1411 S 6th St; tel 812/235-9717. Antiques and local memorabilia fill 15 rooms of this 1868 house. Also on the grounds are re-creations of a late 19th-century schoolroom, a general store and post office, and a dressmaker's shop. **Open:** Tues–Sun 1–4pm. **Free**

Children's Science and Technology Museum of Terre Haute
523 Wabash Ave; tel 812/235-5548. Changing interactive exhibits include a hologram room and fossil exhibit. **Open:** Tues–Sat 9am–4pm. **$**

Valparaiso

Seat of Porter County, in the northwestern part of the state. The Sauk passed through here yearly on the Old Sauk Trail, on their way to Detroit to collect annuities from the British for services in the War of 1812. A Popcorn Festival takes place every September at Valparaiso University. **Information:** Greater Valparaiso Chamber of Commerce, 150 W Lincoln Sq, #1005, PO Box 330, Valparaiso, 46384-0330 (tel 219/462-1105).

MOTEL 🏨

≣≣ Holiday Inn Express
760 Morthland Dr, 46383; tel 219/464-8555 or toll free 800/HOLIDAY; fax 219/464-8555. 2 mi W of jct US 49/30. An unusual octagon-shaped canopy highlights the entryway, and bright blue trim and matching small blue canopies give the building a neat, nautical look. Large facility for children's activities directly across the street, including go-cart track, batting cages, miniature golf, and rides; busy traffic is a hazard, so adult supervision is essential. **Rooms:** 55 rms. CI 3pm/CO noon. Nonsmoking rms avail. **Amenities:** 📺♨A/C, cable TV. **Services:** 🛗🍴 **Facilities:** 🏊♿ **Rates (CP):** Peak (May–Oct) $65 S; $73 D. Extra person $8. Children under age 18 stay free. Lower rates off-season. Parking: Outdoor, free. AE, CB, DC, DISC, MC, V.

RESTAURANT 🍴

★ Strongbow Inn
2405 US 30E; tel 219/462-5121. At Jct US 49 and US 30. **American.** Opened as a family restaurant by Bess Thrun in 1940, the Strongbow has been expanded many times on its way to becoming a local institution. Memorabilia throughout recalls early Indiana days, but the star attraction here is turkey—prepared most any way. (The turkey farm operated by Bess and her partner provided the birds for the first meals.) Individual turkey pie is the particular favorite. Chicken, steak, and seafood are also available; freshly baked breads and pastries are for sale in the bakery. Airplane buffs will love the model planes hanging from the ceiling in Blue Yonder Lounge. **FYI:** Reservations accepted. Piano. Children's menu. **Open:** Mon–Sun 11am–9pm, Fri–Sat 11am–9:30pm. **Prices:** Main courses $9–$18. AE, CB, DC, DISC, MC, V. 🍴🏊👥🚗♿

ATTRACTION 🏛

Chapel of the Resurrection
IN 49 and US 30; tel 219/464-5093. Located on the campus of Valparaiso University, this 3,000-seat auditorium is the largest collegiate chapel in the nation. The chancel's limestone piers ascend 98 feet and culminate in a roof shaped like a nine-pointed star, and the exterior walls are lined with stained-glass windows. A separate 140-foot-tall campanile plays morning and evening hymns. **Open:** Peak (Sept–May) daily 8am–10:30pm. Reduced hours off-season. **Free**

Vincennes

Seat of Knox County, in southwestern part of state. As early as 1683, French fur traders were camping on this site along the Wabash River. During the American Revolution, Gen George Rogers Clark's capture of Vincennes was a key victory for the colonists and opened up the Northwest territory for settlement. Today, the city is a center of tourism and recreation. **Information:** Vincennes Area Chamber of Commerce, 27 N Third St, PO Box 553, Vincennes, 47591-0553 (tel 812/882-6440 or toll free 800/886-6443).

ATTRACTIONS 📷

George Rogers Clark National Historical Park
US 50 and US 41; tel 812/882-1776. A granite-and-marble memorial stands in the midst of this 25-acre park built on the site where George Rogers Clark and his troops captured Fort Sackville from the British. Seven murals within the structure depict his feats, and exhibits and a film (shown every half-hour) at the visitors center tell the story of the campaign. The annual Spirit of Vincennes Rendezvous Memorial Day weekend features historic re-enactments. **Open:** Daily 9am–5pm. **$**

Indiana Territory State Historic Site
1st and Harrison Sts; tel 812/882-7472. This two-story white frame building (now located on the Vincennes University campus) was capital of Indiana Territory from 1811 to 1813. Nearby is the reconstructed print shop that issued the *Western Sun* (initially the *Indiana Gazette*), the territory's first newspaper, and the 1842 home of Maurice Thompson, author of *Alice of Old Vincennes*. Donations accepted. **Open:** Wed–Sat 9am–5pm, Sun 1–5pm. **Free**

Old State Bank Historic Site
112 N 2nd St; tel 812/882-7422. This Greek Revival building functioned as the State Bank of Indiana until 1877. Now it houses permanent and changing exhibits of paintings, sculpture, and crafts by local and regional artists. **Open:** Mar–Nov, Wed–Sun 1–4pm. **Free**

Wabash

Seat of Wabash County, in northern Indiana. Native Americans called the town *Oubache* (meaning "water over white stones"). **Information:** Wabash County Convention & Visitors Bureau, 67 S Wabash St, PO Box 746, Wabash, 46992 (tel 219/563-1168).

ATTRACTION 📷

Wabash County Historical Museum
Memorial Hall, 79 W Hill St; tel 219/563-0661. Located in Memorial Hall (built circa 1899), the museum displays a wide range of area artifacts including fossils and mastodon bones, period clothing, Civil War records, and maps and photographs. **Open:** Tues–Sat 9am–1pm. **Free**

MICHIGAN
The Great Lake State

STATE STATS

CAPITAL
Lansing

AREA
58,527 square miles

BORDERS
Lakes Erie, Huron, Michigan, and Superior; Ohio, Indiana, Wisconsin

POPULATION
9,496,000 (1994)

ENTERED UNION
January 26, 1837 (26th state)

NICKNAMES
Wolverine State, Auto State, Great Lake State

STATE FLOWER
Apple blossom

STATE BIRD
Robin

FAMOUS NATIVES
Madonna, Henry Ford, Charles A Lindbergh, Bob Seger, Thomas Dewey

Michigan's "handprint" on the earth makes it one of the few states distinguishable from space—and the only one that appears to be wearing a mitten. It is also the only state divided into two peninsulas: the "mittened" Lower Peninsula, and the Upper Peninsula (commonly known as the "UP," although no one refers to the bottom half as the "LP"). The two parts have been physically linked only since 1957, when a five-mile-long suspension bridge over the Straits of Mackinac was completed.

The state motto is, appropriately, "If you seek a pleasant peninsula, look about you." Surrounded by the big lakes—Erie, Huron, Michigan, and Superior—there is a sense of isolation from the rest of the nation. To be sure, there are brushes with Ohio and Indiana to the south, and Wisconsin knocks at the Upper Peninsula's western door. Mostly, though, Michiganians—particularly those in the upper parts of the state—are not confined by boundaries of land but relish a sense of independence and unlimited possibility. The lakes, which have also been sources of industry and recreation, give Michigan its magic—even its name, which was derived from *michigama,* a Chippewa word meaning "great lake."

Recreational possibilities flourish. Boating, fishing, waterskiing, swimming, and canoeing enthusiasts have been joined on the waters by jet skiers, underwater divers exploring preserved shipwrecks, and sailboarders. Though the only regularly scheduled Great Lakes cruise is the car and passenger ferry between Ludington, Michigan and Manitowoc, Wisconsin, many communities offer dinner and tour boat cruises off the Great Lakes shores and on inland lakes and rivers. Come winter, trails crisscrossing the state are ready for snowmobilers, and ski resorts have made room for snowboarders. Snowshoes, which are enjoying a revival in Michigan, are welcome on most cross-country ski trails. There are even places where you can experience the thrill of a luge ride, or rent a sled and dogs and be a musher for a day. All this in addition to ice skating, sledding, ice fishing, and snowball fights.

Michigan isn't all woods and water. Turn-of-the-century resort towns—with grand hotels and Victorian summer homes once accessible only by Great Lakes steamship or railroad—still have the welcome mat out today. Golf resorts—some quite deluxe—dot the state, and their scenic surroundings compete for your attention on the green. Casinos owned and operated by Native Americans are popping up seemingly everywhere but in metropolitan Detroit, though there is an effort to introduce them there too. In addition to the Motor City, urban pleasure-seekers will find fine museums, cultural experiences, historic attractions, entertainment, and events in several mid-size cities in the lower half of the Lower Peninsula.

More than three-quarters of Michigan's residents live in urban areas located in the southern tier of the Lower Peninsula, with about half of the state's population concentrated in metropolitan Detroit alone. Perhaps that's why so many residents have such a curious relationship with the land known as "Up North." Although there it will probably never be resolved, most "Downstaters" can agree that Up North is anyplace above an imaginary line running from Lake Huron to Lake Michigan, through Saginaw. Above that line, the population becomes sparser, the fields and forests more numerous, and the recreational opportunities (including the number of resort golf courses) multiply. Those who take Up North very seriously and cross the Mackinac Bridge to venture into the Upper Peninsula are known as "trolls" (people who live below the bridge) to the "Yoopers" (UP-ers) who live there. In Michigan, your peninsular location is everything.

A Brief History

Land Between the Lakes In 1701, Frenchman Antoine de la Mothe Cadillac established a fur trading post on the banks of the strait (*détroit*) that links Lake Huron and Lake Erie. But Cadillac wasn't the first explorer to park his canoe in Michigan. Around 1618, a young adventurer named Etienne

Fun Facts

• Michigan's 3,200-mile shoreline—created by Lakes Erie, Huron, Michigan, and Superior—is longer than that of the entire Atlantic coast of the eastern United States.
• The Michigan State Fair is the oldest in the nation.
• With more than 10,000 inland lakes and 36,000 miles of streams and rivers, you're never farther than 6 miles from water at any point in Michigan.
• At Detroit, Canada is actually south of the United States.
• Detroit installed the nation's first mile of paved road, and the first freeway.

Brulé found the Upper Peninsula instead of the hoped-for passageway to the Pacific Ocean and China. He is the first known European to see Michigan, and was followed by French explorer Jean Nicolet, who realized the riches in the furs. France claimed the land, although they had been preceded by Native Americans some 12,000 years earlier.

Missionaries followed, and in 1668 Father Jacques Marquette and a group of fellow Jesuits founded a mission at Sault Ste Marie. Marquette became one of the best loved missionaries in the state; in addition to the Upper Peninsula city named in his honor there are two memorial parks in St Ignace, where he established a mission in 1671.

Though the fur trade flourished in Michigan, in the 1750s only about 1,000 French had settled here. By 1760, in the midst of British expansion efforts against the French and Native resistance, England's Rogers' Rangers took Detroit from France without a fight. The change was not popular with Michigan's native population, who, led by an Ottawa chief named Pontiac, commenced a six-month siege of Detroit in 1763. Inspired by Pontiac, Native Americans throughout the region followed suit; in May of 1763 warriors at the Straits of Mackinac cleverly seized Fort Michilimackinac. Without support from the French, however, Pontiac was unable to seize Detroit and gave up the fight later that year.

Detroit was ideally positioned to benefit from the riches of the territory to its north and west, and although it was the center of the region's fur trade, by the late 1770s Michigan had only about 2,000 settlers. Even following the Revolutionary War and the slow surrender by the British of its forts, the Michigan territory's vast resources were virtually untapped. It wasn't until the arrival of the first steamship in 1818 that any number of people bothered to venture into Michigan.

A building boom in the 1820s saw Ann Arbor, Kalamazoo, Grand Rapids, and Saginaw added to the map. Michigan's first railroad was built in the 1830s, and by 1837 the territory gained statehood. But first there was a little matter that had to be settled with neighboring Ohio over a piece of land known as the Toledo Strip. In 1836 the US government awarded the disputed area to Ohio; all Michigan received was the Upper Peninsula. That was the scene of America's first great mining boom, the copper rush of the 1840s. Prospectors and accompanying parties had soon constructed boom towns all over Copper Country, and in 1845 iron ore was also discovered nearby.

Meanwhile, Michigan had become a top lumber-producing state, and its cities were booming with other industries as well. By the late 1800s Grand Rapids' Furniture City's reputation was growing, and in Battle Creek the brothers Kellogg had developed health regimes that included cereal. Flint was manufacturing carriages, and Detroit's riverfront was evolving into an industrial wonderland. By the end of the 19th century the city was a leader in shipbuilding and metal bending, and the production of brass fittings, steam engines, railroad cars, and stoves for heating and cooking.

Cult of the Car In 1896 Charles King drove the first "horseless carriage" on the streets of Detroit, and his accomplishment was quickly followed by Henry Ford as well as Ransom E Olds in Lansing. The automobile era was born, and Michigan was at the forefront of design, development, and production. Olds was the first to open a plant for manufacturing large numbers of cars, though the vehicles were really a novelty for the wealthy. Dozens of car companies sprang up and most failed, until Ford's assembly-line concept made it possible to produce cars quickly and cheaply enough for the average American.

Thousands of immigrants flocked to the cities in search of auto industry work and brought with them their diverse cultures, threads of which are alive in pockets of the cities today. During the World Wars Detroit turned its attention to manufacturing airplanes, engines, tanks, and trucks, earning it the title "Arsenal of Democracy."

A post–World War II building boom dispersed urban populations to the wide-open suburbs. The automobile meant freedom, and it affected Michigan in terms of industry, population shifts, housing construction, retail habits, and recreation. The nation's first sprawling suburban mall opened in a suburb of Detroit in 1954. The completion of the Mackinac Bridge in 1957 made it possible to drive between the two peninsulas. As housing developments began to ring the old city neighborhoods, office buildings, services, and retail outlets followed in hot pursuit. None of this was happy news for the central cities and those "left behind." The notorious Detroit riots of 1967 were partially a result of this urban economic decline.

Sound of Young America At the same time another uniquely Detroit industry was growing in the heart of the city. Against all odds, songwriter Berry Gordy Jr founded a record company in 1959 to showcase young black musicians whose talent, intensity, drive, and ambition matched his own. The Motown Sound could be heard in the work of Diana Ross and the Supremes, Stevie Wonder, the Temptations, Four Tops, and so many others, many of them from the Detroit projects.

Michigan claims many famous and talented people as its own: actors Tom Selleck and Julie Harris, comedians Robin Williams and Lily Tomlin, novelists Joyce Carol Oates and Elmore "Dutch" Leonard, athletes Joe Louis and Al Kaline, Charles Lindbergh, Malcolm X, and President Gerald R Ford.

A Closer Look

GEOGRAPHY

When the last glaciers retreated from Michigan some 10,000 years ago they left a fairly flat land rippled with hills that rise to mountains in the northwestern reaches of the state. We also have the Ice Age to thank for leaving behind the largest bodies of fresh water on earth, four of which give shape to the two peninsulas known as Michigan.

Michigan's coastline is varied: rock strewn beach

DRIVING DISTANCES

Detroit

85 mi SE of Lansing
150 mi SE of Grand Rapids
167 mi NW of Cleveland
267 mi SE of Traverse City
266 mi E of Chicago

Traverse City

102 mi SW of Mackinaw City
139 mi N of Grand Rapids
193 mi NW of Lansing
267 mi NW of Detroit
308 mi N of Chicago

Marquette

165 mi W of Sault Ste Marie
316 mi NW of Traverse City
377 mi NE of Minneapolis
369 mi N of Chicago
503 mi NW of Detroit

in some areas; others that are wide sugar sand sometimes rising to bluffs and dunes; elsewhere it's rugged cliff against pounding waves. It is a diverse land, as well, with inland lakes, rivers, streams, wetlands, swamps, meadows, forests, mountains, and islands—even an archipelago. Michigan's lowest point, at just 572 feet above sea level, is in the very southeast corner of the state along Lake Erie. Its highest peak, Mount Arvon at 1,979 feet above sea level, is in the western UP. In the vast distance between, the land juts and jags and rolls gently and lies flat. Human beings have engineered methods of connecting the two peninsulas (Mackinac Bridge), adjusting for differences in lake depths to accommodate shipping traffic (Soo Locks at Sault Ste Marie), and extracting its treasures. Among its natural resources are a variety of minerals including copper and iron ore, sand, gravel, salt, oil, and gas.

The renewable resource— trees—covers about half of the land, and contributes significantly to the state's economy; forestry management programs are intended to keep it that way. Unlike the lumbering industry of the 1800s which destroyed virtually all of the virgin pines and hardwoods that covered the state, commercial logging operations today plant more trees each year than they cut.

Farmers grow everything from asparagus to zucchini in the Lower Peninsula, particularly along the Lake Michigan shore. This is the state's fruit belt, where blueberries, asparagus, and grapes for juice and wine take advantage of the "lake effect" and sandy soil. Sugar beets and beans are big in the Lake Huron "Thumb" region, and the "Little Finger" of the state is the nation's top producer of tart cherries. Cattle and dairy farms populate the central Lower Peninsula and the UP on land cleared from forests and rocky fields.

With more than 10,000 inland lakes and 36,000 miles of rivers and streams, fishing is very important to Michigan both commercially and recreationally. Count whitefish, salmon, walleye, perch, and a variety of trout among the population of the waters in and around the state, which is one of the top issuers of fishing licenses in the country. The water and woods provide habitat for waterfowl and small and large game, and licensed hunting of waterfowl, turkey, elk, bear, and deer is permitted.

The coasts of both peninsulas are sprinkled with islands, from Detroit's 1,000-acre Belle Isle Park with its museums and herd of tame deer, to rugged and wild Isle Royale National Park in Lake Superior. Between the peninsulas Mackinac Island's elaborate Victorian "cottages" for summertime visitors contrast sharply with the easy-going air of the archipelago to the east, Les Cheneaux (referred to as The Snow), that has also been a popular summertime resort area since the late 19th century.

Narrow waterways are all that separate Michigan from Canada at three points: the International Bridge connects Sault Ste Marie in the Upper Peninsula with the city of the same name in Canada; in the Thumb the Blue Water Bridge takes travelers between Port Huron and Sarnia, Ontario; and at Detroit, which also has a vehicular tunnel under the Detroit River, the Ambassador Bridge is a convenient link to Windsor, Ontario.

AVG MONTHLY TEMPS (°F) & RAINFALL (IN)		
	Sault Ste Marie	Detroit
Jan	13/2.4	23/1.8
Feb	14/1.7	25/1.7
Mar	24/2.3	36/2.5
Apr	38/2.3	47/2.9
May	51/2.7	58/2.9
June	58/3.1	68/3.6
July	64/2.7	72/3.2
Aug	63/3.6	70/3.4
Sept	55/3.7	63/2.9
Oct	45/3.2	51/2.1
Nov	33/3.4	40/2.7
Dec	19/2.9	28/2.9

CLIMATE

Locals exaggerate a bit when they say, "If you don't like Michigan's weather, wait 10 minutes—it'll change." Likewise those in the Upper Peninsula claim two seasons—winter and August. Truth is, Michigan's Great Lakes location gives it a moderate climate with mild summers and winters, particularly in the Lower Peninsula. The distance is great from the Ohio border to the tip of the Keweenaw Peninsula however, and differences in the two peninsulas can be extreme, even within the same day.

The surrounding Great Lakes tend to protect the Lower Peninsula from Arctic chills: summertime warming of their waters and their tendency to cool slowly takes the bite out of the winter winds. It is this lake effect that gives Michigan's west coast its ideal "fruit belt" growing conditions, second only to California in some crops. Summer days are warm enough statewide to encourage a wide range of outdoor activity in and around the water, and the warm weather usually extends well into autumn in the southern Lower Peninsula. As the cool air rolls in from the north, Michigan's extended and spectacular fall foliage season unfolds in tiers, from the tip of the UP in early September to the southern border of the state in mid-to-late October.

The Great Lakes don't freeze completely, but channels such as the Straits of Mackinac do, and piles of ice pushed to the shores of the Great Lakes make a spectacular sight. Spring is usually well established before the snow and ice are completely melted in the UP. The northern Lower Peninsula gets its share of snow, but bleak, gray winter days are more common than heavy snowfall in the lower portions of the state.

WHAT TO PACK

Think in terms of two peninsulas and four seasons when you pack. If you'll be traveling from Detroit in the south to Keweenaw in the northern reaches, be prepared for hot sun, rain showers, cool breezes, high humidity, and chilly evenings even in the height of summer. Many "Downstate" travelers who left home in 90°F weather have enriched the UP economy with purchases of sweatshirts and long pants to cover-up their shorts and T-shirts. Winter is dependably cold in every corner of the state.

If you're planning to visit Canada, don't forget to bring identification (passport, birth certificate, or US voter registration card will do).

TOURIST INFORMATION

For a free state highway map and a copy of *Michigan Travel Ideas* magazine, as well as personal itinerary-planning assistance, contact the **Michigan Travel Bureau** at PO Box 3393, Livonia 48151-3393 (tel 800/543-2YES). The Bureau also maintains a page on the World Wide Web (http://www.travel-michigan.state.mi.us), with links to travel information. To find out how to obtain tourist information for individual cities and parks in Michigan, look under specific cities in the listings section of this book.

DRIVING RULES AND REGULATIONS

Minimum driving age is 16. Seat belts are required for front-seat passengers of any age, and rear-seat passengers to age 16. Infants anywhere in the vehicle, and children under four riding in the front seat, must be in an approved safety seat.

The speed limit on Michigan highways is 55 mph; on interstates the maximum is 55 mph or 65 mph, as posted. Helmets are required for motorcyclists. Radar detectors are permitted, as is right turn on red after full stop (unless posted otherwise). Michigan has been getting tougher on drunk drivers in recent years.

RENTING A CAR

All major car rental firms are represented at Detroit Metropolitan Airport. Some are found throughout the state at airports in Grand Rapids, Traverse City, Marquette, and elsewhere.

- **Alamo** (tel 800/327-9633)
- **Avis** (tel 800/831-2847)
- **Budget** (tel 800/527-0700)
- **Discount** (tel 800/231-7368)
- **Dollar** (tel 800/365-5276)
- **Enterprise** (tel 800/325-8007)
- **Hertz** (tel 800/654-3131)
- **National** (tel 800/227-7368)
- **Sears** (tel 800/527-0770)
- **Thrifty** (tel 800/367-2277)

ESSENTIALS

Area Codes: Michigan has five area codes. Detroit and its immediate suburbs are in the **313** area code. North of Detroit and up through the "Thumb" are **810.** To the west and north of metropolitan Detroit on the east side of the Lower Peninsula, the area code is **517,** while the western half of the Lower Peninsula is in the **616** area. All of the Upper Peninsula is area code **906.**

Emergencies: In most communities in the state you can now access emergency police, fire, and medical assistance by dialing **911.**

Liquor Laws: You must be 21 to purchase or consume alcoholic beverages in Michigan. Bars may serve until 2am. No alcohol may be sold or served before noon on Sundays.

Road Info: Volunteers at the Michigan Emergency Patrol can assist with road

Smoking: emergencies as well as road condition information (tel 800/332-0233). Restaurants that permit smoking are required to provide nonsmoking areas. Most hotels now prohibit smoking in a large percentage of their rooms. Shopping malls and an increasing number of public areas no longer permit smoking or severely limit it.

Taxes: Michigan's state sales tax is 6%. Many areas also add an assessment or tax on lodging; the percentage varies by region.

Time Zone: Most of Michigan is in the Eastern time zone, except for four counties along the Wisconsin border which are in the Central time zone. The entire state observes daylight saving time.

Best of the State
WHAT TO SEE AND DO

Below is a general overview of some of the top sights and attractions in Michigan. To find out more detailed information, look under "Attractions" for individual cities in the listings portion of this book.

National Parks & Refuges **Sleeping Bear Dunes National Lakeshore** consists of a 31½-mile stretch of Lake Michigan coast line. The area offers breathtaking views and a variety of activities including dune climbing, picnicking, hiking, camping, and boat trips to South Manitou Island.

Seney National Wildlife Refuge in the east-central UP is the largest such area east of the Mississippi River. The area is best explored by foot, canoe, or mountain bike, although there's also an auto tour route through portions of the 96,000-acre wilderness.

Pack your imagination and take a boat cruise out of Munising to see the best views of Lake Superior's **Pictured Rocks National Lakeshore.** These colorful sandstone cliffs rise for 200 feet in some places. The Lakeshore Trail runs the entire 15-mile length of the park, from Munising to Grand Marais.

If wilderness beckons, make the boat ride across 50 miles of Lake Superior to **Isle Royale National Park,** northwest of the Keweenaw Peninsula. Hiking, camping, fishing, canoeing, and nature walks are the order of the day. There is also a lodge for noncampers. The island is the habitat for one of the few surviving wolf packs in the Midwest.

State Parks Landlubbers may prefer the Porkies, the affectionate name for Michigan's mountain range on the western edge of the Upper Peninsula. **Porcupine Mountains Wilderness State Park,** the largest and most remote in the system, is bordered by Lake Superior and counts the lovely Lake of the Clouds in its inventory of natural wonders. The Upper Peninsula boasts more than 150 waterfalls, from small, unnamed ones to the mighty **Upper and Lower Tahquamenon Falls** in the state park of the same name.

Historic Buildings Peek into the private pasts of automobile dynasties and those who tapped the state's natural resources for their fortunes on tours of the mansions of some of Michigan's wealthiest and most influential residents: **Fairlane,** the home of Henry Ford I and his wife Clara; the lakeshore Cotswolds-style home of his son Edsel and wife Eleanor Ford; the ornate Detroit Riverfront mansion of the Fisher Brothers; and **Meadow Brook Hall,** the estate of Matilda Dodge Wilson, widow of Horace Dodge.

Lansing's Victorian Capitol building has been splendidly restored and offers free tours. Also of that period is the preserved **Voight House** in Grand Rapids, left almost completely intact by the family who occupied it for nearly 80 years.

The **Laurium Manor,** built in 1908 by a wealthy copper mine owner in the Upper Peninsula's Keweenaw, features elephant-hide wall covering and a 1,300-sq-ft ballroom. It now operates as a museum and bed-and-breakfast.

Museums Many people have collections, but few can compare to Henry Ford. Among other things, the automobile giant collected buildings he felt were significant to American history—such as Thomas Edison's **Menlo Park Laboratory** and the bicycle shop in which the Wright Brothers tinkered with the airplane. Ford had these and dozens of other homes, workshops, stores, and industrial buildings relocated to an 80-acre site at **Greenfield Village** in Dearborn, a suburb west of Detroit. With the adjacent 14-acre **Henry Ford Museum** collections of transportation, communication, farming, household, and other items, this indoor/outdoor complex aims to tell the entire story of America's progression from a rural to an industrial nation. The village's costumed interpreters demonstrate and describe the activities appropriate to the day, and there is a full schedule of themed events.

Michigan's story is told in dynamic displays at the **Michigan Historical Museum** in Lansing. There are exhibits on the fur trapping, lumber, and mining eras, a scene from a classic Detroit auto show, and more.

The town of **Fayette** serves as a living-history museum depicting life in a typical 1860s industrial community. Homes, town buildings, and charcoal pig-iron kilns and furnace survive from the original town.

Restored red barns house an outstanding collection of antique and classic vehicles at the **Gilmore Classic Car Club of America Museum** near Kalamazoo, where a summerlong schedule of themed events highlights special marques or car collections.

Family Favorites The **Detroit Zoological Park** is the largest in the state. Detroit's was one of the first zoos in the nation to introduce naturalized settings for the animals. The Penguinarium and chimp exhibits are highlights.

Crossroads Village near Flint is a kind of historical theme park, with a collection of working industrial buildings, the Huckleberry Railroad (a narrow-gauge steam engine train), and the *Genesee Belle* paddle-wheel riverboat. Costumed workers and special events add to the flurry of activity.

Families can combine history with fun in the Straits of Mackinac. Tying the LP and the UP together is the magnificent **Mackinac Bridge,** a five-mile-long suspension bridge and awesome engineering feat. On the west side of Mackinaw City, **Colonial Michilimackinac State Park** re-creates the fort built by the French in the early 1700s and occupied by the British before they moved their military post to Mackinac Island. A few miles to the southeast, **Mill Creek State Park** depicts the water-powered sawmill constructed in the 1780s to support and supply the new fort on Mackinac Island.

Located in the Straits between the Upper and Lower Peninsulas, Mackinac Island is a novelty few kids could resist: Most people take a ferry to reach it; no motorized (except emergency) vehicles are allowed; there are fudge shops seemingly every few feet on the main street; and the 200-year-old fort invites exploring.

EVENTS AND FESTIVALS

LOWER PENINSULA

- **North American International Auto Show,** Cobo Center in Detroit. This dazzling display of new and concept cars showcase Detroit's reputation as Motor City USA. Mid-January. Call 810/643-0250.
- **Ice Sculpture Spectacular,** Plymouth. Blocks of ice are transformed into sparkling figures and objects by artists and chefs from the United States and elsewhere. Mid-January. Call 313/459-6969.
- **Irish Festival,** Clare. Parade, arts and crafts, and dancing honor the founder of this town, who named it after his native County Clare. Week before St Patrick's Day. Call 517/386-2442.
- **Vermontville Maple Syrup Festival,** Vermontville. It's a sweet salute to Michigan's maple syrup, maple cream, and other maple sweets. Late April. Call 517/726-0394.
- **Tulip Time Festival,** Holland. Millions of tulips herald spring in this Dutch city on Michigan's west coast. Three parades and entertainment add to the colorful spectacle. May. Call 800/822-2770.
- **Cereal Festival,** Battle Creek. The Cereal City, home of Kellogg's, attempts to hold onto its Guinness Record for world's longest breakfast table. Early June. Call 616/962-2240.
- **Detroit Grand Prix,** Belle Isle Park. Indy cars race around the 1,000-acre downtown island park. Early June. Call 313/259-7749.
- **International Freedom Festival,** Detroit and Windsor, Ontario. Neighboring cities celebrate Independence Day and Canada Day in this annual series of special events, highlighted by North America's largest fireworks display, over the Detroit River. Week leading up to July 4. Call 313/923-7400.
- **National Cherry Festival,** Traverse City. The Cherry Capital of the World promotes its product and offers family fun, from concerts to midway to golf and fireworks. Early July. Call 616/947-4230.
- **Au Sable River Canoe Marathon,** Oscoda. Challenging canoe race from Grayling to Oscoda with festive accompaniments. Late July. Call 800/235-4625.
- **Michigan Festival,** East Lansing. Arts and crafts, children's programs, parades, food, fun and big-

name concerts make this an event for the entire family. Early August. Call 517/351-6620.

- **Montreux-Detroit Jazz Festival.** The Detroit Riverfront Hart Plaza is the heart of this free event, with performances by all types of jazz represented. Labor Day weekend. Call 313/963-7622.
- **Michigan Wine and Harvest Festival,** Kalamazoo and Paw Paw. Sample Michigan wines at tastings and wineries. Early September. Call 616/381-4003.
- **Oktoberfest,** Frankenmuth. This Bavarian-themed town celebrates its roots with music, dancing, foods, and the local brew. Mid-September. Call 800/FUN-FEST.
- **Fall Harvest Days,** Greenfield Village, Dearborn. Spend a day on historic farms of the 18th, 19th, and early 20th centuries. Early October. Call 313/271-1620.
- **Victorian Sleighbell Parade and Olde Christmas Weekend,** Manistee. Horse drawn units, period costumes, and Jolly Old Saint Nick highlight this holiday event in Michigan's Victorian port city. Early December. Call 616/723-2575.

UPPER PENINSULA

- **UP 200 Sled-Dog Championship,** Marquette and Escanaba. It should take about 36 hours for the first of 30 teams of mushers and canines to race across the Upper Peninsula from Marquette on Lake Superior to Escanaba on Lake Michigan and back. In the meantime there are parties in both cities. Mid-February. Call 800/544-4321.
- **Lilac Festival,** Mackinac Island. Lovely lilacs fill the island with a sweetly scented welcome for the summer season. Mid-June. Call 906/847-6418.
- **UP Championship Rodeo,** Iron County Fairgrounds. Professional cowboys compete in the Upper Peninsula's only rodeo. Late July. Call 906/265-3822.
- **Antique Wooden Boat Show and Festival of Arts,** Hessel. Beautifully preserved or refinished runabouts star at this one-day show of classic boats in this picturesque part of the Upper Peninsula. Early August. Call 906/484-3935.
- **Labor Day Mackinac Bridge Walk,** St Ignace–Mackinaw City. Some 70,000 people take advantage of the only day that pedestrians are allowed to walk the five-mile span of the "Mighty Mac."

SPECTATOR SPORTS

Auto Racing Michigan International Speedway (tel 800/354-1010) is the state's largest, and hosts professional auto racing including NASCAR and Indy cars in the Michigan 500 in June, July, and August in Brooklyn, southeast of Jackson.

Baseball American League action lives at historic Tiger Stadium, home of the **Detroit Tigers** (tel 800/730-4386). Three of the state's mid-sized cities have caught on to minor league ball: the **West Michigan Whitecaps** play in Grand Rapids (tel 616/784-4131); the **Lansing Lugnuts** play in the Capital City (tel 517/485-4500); and the **Battle Creek Battle Cats** keep the Cereal City popping (tel 800/324-4428).

Basketball Michigan roundball fans, holding dear the memory of repeat NBA championships in 1989 and 1990, still flock to see the **Detroit Pistons** play at the Palace of Auburn Hills (tel 810/377-0100). There's college basketball excitement around the **University of Michigan Wolverines** (tel 313/764-0247), who play in Ann Arbor, and **Michigan State University Spartans** (tel 517/355-1610), who hold court in East Lansing.

Football NFL fans religiously file into the Pontiac Silverdome's 80,000 seats to watch the **Detroit Lions** (tel 810/335-4151). The **Wolverines** of the University of Michigan take the football field at Ann Arbor (tel 313/764-0247) and the **Spartans** of MSU play in East Lansing (tel 517/355-1610).

Hockey Fans of the **Detroit Red Wings** had their sights set on the team's first Stanley Cup since 1955, but were disappointed again in 1996. Still, it's nearly impossible to get tickets at the Joe Louis Arena in this hockey town (tel 810/645-6666). Several collegiate teams consistently perform well in tournament play: **Lake Superior State University** in Sault Ste Marie (tel 906/635-2602); **Northern Michigan University,** Marquette (tel 906/227-1032); **Michigan Technological University,** Houghton (tel 906/487-2073); **University of Michigan,** Ann Arbor (tel 313/764-0247); and **Michigan State University,** East Lansing (tel 517/355-1610).

Horse Racing The major horse action is in the Detroit area. Thoroughbreds run at **Detroit Race Course** in Livonia from March through November (tel 313/525-7300), and there's harness racing October through April at **Northville Downs** (tel 810/349-1000) and at Hazel Park Harness Raceway (tel 810/398-1000).

ACTIVITIES A TO Z

Ballooning   Visitors can drift over rolling country-side, farms, and streams with Capt Phogg of **Balloon Quest** (tel 810/634-3095), one of several companies that offer ballooning packages. For more information, call the **Michigan Travel Bureau** (tel 800/543-2YES).

Bicycling   Plenty of two-lane highways welcome two-wheelers to cruise through scenic countryside. Rails to Trails options include the 35-mile Kal-Haven, from Kalamazoo to South Haven on Lake Michigan, and the Hart-Montague Trail to the north. **Michigan Bicycle Touring** (tel 616/263-5885) has packages that include country inns and bed-and-breakfasts throughout the state. For a calendar of biking events contact the **League of Michigan Bicyclists** (tel 616/452-BIKE).

Boating   It's only natural that in a state surrounded by water and populated by 10,000 inland lakes there should be a sizable number (600,000) of registered boaters. Get your copy of the *Michigan Public Boat Launch Directory* from the Michigan Department of Natural Resources, PO Box 30257, Lansing 48909 (tel 517/373-9900).

Camping   Rustic or fully equipped, campgrounds at state parks and private facilities cater to a wide range of campers. The Department of Natural Resources offers Rent-A-Tent and Rent-A-Tipi programs in selected state parks, for those who are without their own equipment. You can reserve campsites, tents, and cabins at public facilities by calling the Michigan Travel Bureau (tel 800/543-2YES). For a directory of private campgrounds, send $3 (to cover shipping and handling) to the Michigan Association of Private Campground Owners, 9700 MI 37 S, Buckley 49620.

Canoeing   The state's lakes, Great and small, as well as rushing rivers and silent streams, await canoe enthusiasts. Contact the **Recreational Canoeing Association** (tel 616/745-1554) for a free listing of canoe liveries.

Dune Riding   Off-Road Vehicles (four-wheelers, dirt bikes, dune buggies) can drive right on the Lake Michigan sand dunes at **Silver Lake State Park** (tel 616/873-3083), the only place this is allowed in the state. An ORV permit is required and may be purchased at the park. Those without an ORV can enjoy the spectacular scenery on a ride in the open-air vehicles of a local concessionaire.

SELECTED PARKS & RECREATION AREAS

- **Huron-Manistee National Forest,** c/o Supervisor, 421 S Mitchell St, Cadillac 49601 (tel 800/821-6263)
- **Sleeping Bear Dunes National Lakeshore,** PO Box 277, Empire 49630 (tel 616/326-5134)
- **P J Hoffmaster State Park,** 6585 Lake Harbor Rd, Muskegon 49441 (tel 616/798-3711)
- **Holland State Park,** 2215 Ottawa Beach Rd, Holland 48424 (tel 616/399-9390)
- **Holly State Recreation Area,** 8100 Grange Hall Rd, Holly 48442 (tel 313/634-8811)
- **Leelanau State Park,** PO Box 49, Rte 1, Northport 49670 (tel 616/386-5422)
- **Petoskey State Park,** 2475 Harbor-Petoskey Rd, Petoskey 49770 (tel 616/347-2311)
- **Rifle River State Recreation Area,** 2550 E Rose City Rd, Lupton 48653 (tel 517/473-2258)
- **Silver Lake State Park,** PO Box 187, Rte 1, Mears 49436 (tel 616/873-3083)
- **Albert E Sleeper State Park,** 6573 State Park Rd, Caseville 48725 (tel 517/856-4411)
- **Sterling State Park,** 2800 State Park Rd, Rte 5, Monroe 48161 (tel 313/289-2715)
- **Tawas Point State Park,** 686 Tawas Beach Rd, East Tawas 48730 (tel 517/362-5041)
- **Warren Dunes State Park,** Red Arrow Hwy, Sawyer 49125 (tel 616/426-4013)
- **Waterloo State Recreation Area,** 16345 McClure Road, Chelsea 48118 (tel 313/475-8307)

UPPER PENINSULA

- **Isle Royale National Park,** 87 N Ripley St, Houghton 49931 (tel 906/482-0984)
- **Hiawatha National Forest,** c/o Supervisor, 2727 N Lincoln Rd, Escanaba 49829 (tel 906/786-4062)
- **Ottawa National Forest,** c/o Supervisor, 2100 E Cloverland Dr, Ironwood 49938 (tel 906/932-1330)
- **Pictured Rocks National Lakeshore,** PO Box 40, Munising 49862 (tel 906/387-3700 or 387-2607)
- **Fayette State Park,** 13700 13.25 Lane, Garden 49835 (tel 906/644-2603)
- **Mackinac Island State Park,** PO Box 370, Mackinac Island 49757 (tel 906/847-3328)
- **Porcupine Mountains Wilderness State Park,** 599 MI 107, Ontonagon 49953 (tel 906/885-5275)
- **Tahquamenon Falls State Park,** PO Box 225, Star Rte 48, Paradise 49768 (tel 906/492-3415)
- **Wilderness State Park,** Carp Lake 49718 (tel 616/436-5381)

Fishing   Whether you prefer salmon fishing on the Great Lakes or angling for trout in one of the rivers, Michigan is a fishing paradise. Get a free directory of boat charters from the **Michigan Charter Boat Association** (tel 800/MCBA-971). Licenses are required and can be purchased at bait-and-tackle shops, food stores, and taverns near good fishing sites. For specifics on fishing licenses contact the Michigan Department of Natural Resources, License Control Division, PO Box 30028, Lansing 48909 (tel 517/373-1204).

Fruit Picking   Michigan's agricultural bounty includes fruits ripe for the picking at berry farms and orchards in every part of the state. Pick-your-own with the help of the **Southwest Michigan Tourism Council** (tel 616/925-6301) and the **Michigan Travel Bureau** (tel 800-MI-4-FALL).

Golf   Michigan's reputation for good golf has grown beyond the region. The Grand Traverse area in the northwest corner of the Lower Peninsula calls itself "Michigan's Golf Coast," and with the Gaylord region lead the state with designer resort courses and well-regarded public courses. Contact the **Traverse City Convention and Visitors Bureau**, 415 Munson Ave, Ste 200, Traverse City 49684 (tel 616/947-1120 or 800/TRAVERS); or **Discover Golf on Michigan's Sunrise Side**, 1361 Fletcher St, National City 48748 (tel 800/729-9373).

Hang Gliding   **Warren Dunes State Park** (tel 616/426-4014), in the southwestern corner of the Lower Peninsula, welcomes certified gliders. Permits, which are required, are available at the park headquarters in Sawyer.

Hunting   Duck, bear, deer: Michigan's forest yield a variety of game. For information on hunting seasons and hunting licenses contact the Michigan Department of Natural Resources, License Control Division, PO Box 30028, Lansing 48909 (tel 517/373-1204).

Kite Flying   Parks and beaches on both peninsulas offer ample opportunity for kite flying; Oval Beach in Saugatuck is especially popular for that purpose. For an organized effort, check out the Kalamazoo Kitefest at **River Oaks Park** (tel 616/383-8778), held the last weekend in April.

Luge   At **Muskegon State Park** (tel 616/744-9629 in winter or 616/744-3480 year-round), you can learn the basics of this fast-moving wintertime sport. Special luge packages include instruction and rental equipment.

Rock Hounding   Lake Superior's shore is an agate-hunter's paradise. The state stone, the Petoskey, can be found on Lake Michigan near the city of the same name.

Scuba Diving   The Great Lakes hold the remains of many shipwrecks, some of which are popular with scuba divers. Contact the **Michigan Underwater Preserves Council**, 11 S State St, St Ignace 49781 (tel 800/338-6660) for a free directory of the preserves and area dive shops.

Snow Sports   Michigan's winter generally means great skiing at nearly four dozen downhill facilities and on 2,000 miles of cross-country trails. Snow shoeing, snow boarding, and snowmobiling are other recreational favorites at Michigan state parks in winter. Consult the *Michigan Travel Ideas* brochure, available from the **Michigan Travel Bureau** (tel 800/543-2YES).

Driving the State

Start	Mackinaw City
Finish	Sault Ste Marie
Distance	180 miles round trip
Time	2–3 days
Highlights	Views of three of the Great Lakes, a historic island where no cars are allowed, waterfalls, forests full of brilliant foliage in autumn, forts, a lighthouse, a shipwreck museum, and a short visit to Paradise.

This tour takes you from a bridge that joins Michigan's Lower and Upper Peninsulas to another bridge that connects Michigan with Ontario, Canada. The first bridge goes across the Straits of Mackinac, a passage between two great lakes—Huron and Michigan. The second crosses the "Soo," at the head of St Mary's River, where a system of locks makes it possible for ships to navigate between Lake Huron and Lake Superior. You can make the trip in less than an hour on the fast I-75, but the flavor, beauty, and history of this small area deserves a closer and more lingering look.

The tour begins at Mackinaw City, at the south end of the Straits. And before you start talking to the natives, be sure you understand that whether the word is spelled "Mackinac" (as in Island) or "Mackinaw" (as in City or Bridge), it is always properly pronounced *mackinaw*.

For additional information on lodgings, dining, and attractions in the region covered by the tour, look under specific cities in the listings portion of this chapter.

Your first stop is right beneath the southern end of the Mackinaw Bridge:

1. **Colonial Michilimackinac** is a reconstruction of a walled village and fort constructed by French fur traders and soldiers in 1715. This spot was a gathering place for Native Americans long before the Europeans arrived, and it was later used as a center for trade between the French and the natives. During summer months interpretive programs are presented by costumed guides, many of whom are students and scholars in history or archeology. They present a detailed picture of life in this once-thriving commercial village. Visitors can also see work going on at the longest ongoing archeological dig in the United States. And you can get a good view of the bridge from the water's edge, just outside the walls.

Colonial Michilimackinac is one of three sections of the **Mackinac State Historic Parks** (tel 616/436-5563). A second one is **Historic Mill Creek,** four miles southeast of Mackinaw City on US 23. Mill Creek is a water-powered sawmill, where workers use only tools that were available at the time of the American Revolution to produce lumber as it was made in the original mill on this site. This unit of the park also offers nature trails, a picnic area, a maple sugar shack, and a working beaver colony. (The third unit of the state park is on Mackinac Island.) Combination admission to all three units is $12.50 for adults, and there are special family rates and season passes.

Return to I-75 N and proceed across the

2. **Mackinac Bridge.** A marvel of engineering, and truly beautiful as well, this five-mile total suspension bridge is the world's longest. "Big Mac" takes on a fairylike aura at night, when thousands of lights outline it. A popular annual event on Labor Day is the Bridge Walk, when vehicles are restricted to two lanes and thousands of people cross the bridge from north to south on foot.

At the north end of the bridge, take the US 2 exit. Stretching along the east side of I-75 is **Straights State Park,** with modern campground facilities and an observation deck for viewing and photographing the bridge. Along the west side of the highway is the **Father Marquette National Memorial and Museum.** Father Jacques Marquette, a young Jesuit priest from France, founded a small mission in this vicinity in 1617, a couple of years before he set out with Louis Joliet to explore the Mississippi River. The museum exhibits and programs interpret the early meeting of the European and North American cultures.

You are now in the resort city of:

3. **St Ignace** (tourist info at tel toll free 800/338-6660). US 2 E connects with State St, which runs parallel to the shore of Lake Huron. There are about 40 motels and hotels strung along both sides of State St, the main drag in St Ignace. The winter population of fewer than 3,000 swells by many thousands during the tourist seasons, mainly by people taking day trips to Mackinac Island. If you plan to spend a little extra time in St Ignace, perhaps you'd like to visit the **Kewadin Casino** at the north edge of town.

Before catching the ferry, visit **Marquette Mission Park and Museum of Ojibwa Culture,** 500 N

are scattered across Michigan, Wisconsin, Minnesota, and Ontario today.

Three ferry lines have regular service from both Mackinaw City and St Ignace to Mackinac Island. Since no automobiles are permitted on the island, the ferry lines provide free all-day parking in large lots beside the docks. Advance reservations are a very good idea. The **Arnold Line** (tel toll free 800/542-8528) has both catamarans and historic ferry boats; the **Star Line** (tel toll free 800/638-9892) operates hydrojets; **Shepler's** (tel 616/436-5023) has a hydroplane fleet.

If you have time before leaving for the island, take a walk along the **Huron Boardwalk,** a gray, weathered, wooden walk close to the shore. The boardwalk offers several displays relating to the history of the town, as well as seating areas with views of the lake and Mackinac Island. The walk ends across the street from the Museum of Ojibwa Culture. Cross over and walk back along the strip of souvenir shops, then board the ferry for

4. **Mackinac Island.** This is one of the most popular tourist destinations in all of the Midwest. There are only two ways to get here—by boat or by small airplane. In winter many of the businesses close up shop and the town grows quiet. There are some year-round residents on the island, however, and when the lake freezes over and boats can no longer make the passage, another means of transportation comes into play. Once the ice gets thick enough to be safe, people make the crossing on snowmobiles, on an ice road marked by Christmas trees. (Visitors to the area are *strongly* advised not to try this on their own, without the services of a local guide who can keep them clear of weak spots.)

Mackinac Island has been important to several successive peoples. Native Americans used it as a spiritual refuge, the French used it as a fur trading post, and the British built **Fort Mackinac** on the east bluff of the island during the 1770s. A century later the Americans closed the fort and the State of Michigan designated the island as its first state park.

The restored **Fort Mackinac** is the third unit of the Mackinac State Historic Parks. Fourteen origi-

State St. The small museum has excellent exhibits about the Native Americans who lived here when the French traders arrived, and whose descendants

nal buildings surround spacious parade grounds. Guided tours and daily programs (during summer only) re-enact the lives of the soldiers who were quartered here. Authentic uniforms, period music, and antique rifle and cannon firings bring the past alive.

For an overview of this historic and beautiful island, take a **Carriage Tour.** The ticket office is close to the ferry docks. Enjoy the clop-clop of the horses as guides point out historic landmarks such as the **Astor Warehouse,** where fur pelts were graded and cleaned for shipment to market, and natural wonders like **Arch Rock.** If you prefer, you can explore the island on foot or rented bicycle. Dedicated shoppers have a fine time wandering the 19th-century island's streets. You can buy everything from tacky souvenirs and T-shirts to good sports clothing and fine gifts—plus lots and lots of fudge. A sugary smell fills the air and most tourists succumb to it, which is why some natives call the tourists "fudgies."

There are two dozen hotels, bed-and-breakfasts, and inns on the island, but the most famous and venerable lodging is the **Grand Hotel** (tel 906/847-3331 in summer; 517/349-4600 in winter). Opened in 1887, this four-story (six if you count the Cupola Bar) white building fronted by a 700-foot long pillored veranda is not just a hotel, it's a historic landmark and a major attraction in and of itself. Everyone who comes to the island wants to see it. In fact, touring the hotel has become so popular that nonguests entering the hotel before 6pm are charged an admission fee; however, the fee can be credited toward the buffet luncheon served in the main dining room.

In the tradition of grand, historic hotels, the Grand is fairly expensive. But many a Michigan family vacationing on a budget has spent at least one night here, even if they camp out the rest of the time. The experience is worth it.

Return to St Ignace and drive north on I-75 about 5 miles to MI 123. Via this rural and scenic route, especially glorious during the autumn foliage season, it is only 55 miles to

5. **Paradise.** A small but popular year-round resort village on the shore of Whitefish Bay, Paradise began as a lumber town. Today it attracts fishers and scuba divers in summer, snowmobilers and cross-country skiers in winter. Stay on MI 123 when it makes a sharp left in Paradise and drive ten miles to **Lower Tahquamenon Falls,** where the Tahquamenon River plunges down a 22-foot drop around an island and a number of boulders. There is a lookout on a high bluff, and paddleboats to take guests to a scenic island with a series of lower falls.

Four miles farther on are the even more spectacular **Upper Tahquamenon Falls,** the second-largest waterfall east of the Mississippi River. Each season brings its own beauty to this wilderness area. In spring the water flow is heavy from snow runoff and the woods are full of wildflowers. Summer brings lush growth to the forest, and autumn turns the leaves to brilliant reds and yellows accented by the dark green of the pine growth. And in winter, huge icicles reflect rainbow colors above the tea-brown waters of the falls.

From the falls, return to Paradise and continue north along the shore of Whitefish Bay to the next stop:

6. **Whitefish Point.** This expanse of Lake Superior has been called the Graveyard of the Great Lakes, because so many ships have met disaster here. The **Whitefish Point Light Station,** site of the first light tower on Lake Superior and no longer used by the Coast Guard, is now home to the **Great Lakes Shipwreck Historical Museum.** Exhibits include underwater films of shipwreck discoveries in these 600-foot deep waters, considered one of the most dangerous marine sites in the world. The shipping lanes were congested during the mining boom days of the 19th century, and more than 300 ships went down in the 80-mile stretch west from Whitefish Point. Models of some of them are on display, along with artifacts recovered from the deep and a huge lighthouse lens with 344 crystal prisms. This museum is small, but exceptionally well done. The museum shop carries books and souvenirs of the area.

Walk outside to the sandy point and look across to Canada. This is a good spot to do a little rock hunting for banded agates and other attractive colored stones. In spring, migrating hawks take off from this point for their flight across the water. The Michigan Audubon Society's **Whitefish Point Bird Observatory** is next door to the museum grounds, and avid birdwatchers flock to the area to see some 300 species of birds.

Ten miles south of Paradise, turn east (left) on a local road called the

7. **Curly Lewis Highway.** This road, much of it within **Hiawatha National Forest,** is a little shorter and considerably more scenic than the more prominent highways marked MI 123 and MI 28. The US Forest Service has designated 27 miles of this highway as the **Whitefish Bay Scenic Byway.** It's worth a leisurely drive and a couple of brief stops if you are so inclined. There are several picnic areas and campgrounds along the way. The **Pendills Creek National Fish Hatchery** breeds millions of lake trout to be released into the Great Lakes. The **Point**

Iroquois Light Station and Museum features a 65-foot tower with an excellent vantage point for watching freighters entering the St Marys River. Beachcombers are apt to find collectible colored rocks and pieces of driftwood along the shore, and the lightkeepers' house contains a small museum.

Close by is **Mission Hill,** overlooking some of the best panoramas in the Upper Peninsula, including two lakes, Sault Ste Marie, and the Laurentian hills in Ontario. **Brimley** is a small resort town with a beach park.

From here go south to MI 28 east, then take I-75 north to

8. **Sault Ste Marie** (tel toll free 800/MI-SAULT). The Soo, as it is affectionately known, refers to the area that includes the two sister cities on either side of the US/Canadian border as well as the 21-foot white-water drop in the St Mary River. **The Soo Locks** are a National Historic Site and an outstanding engineering wonder. The first locks began operating in 1855, making it possible for ships to navigate the mighty rapids between Lake Huron and Lake Superior. Since the St Lawrence Seaway opened in 1959, ships from many parts of the world have come through the locks.

Your visit to the Soo should start at the **Locks Information Center,** on Portage Ave in the middle of town, where a short film shows how the locks were built. There's also a large working model of the locks, a relief map of the Great Lakes, and a sign on the wall showing the time the next freighters are due to be coming through. Inside the center you can see ships going through the locks on a live TV screen, but for a much better look, go outside to the elevated viewing platform. Watch huge cargo ships, many of them loaded with grain or iron ore, being lowered for an eastbound voyage to Lake Huron or raised to go west into Lake Superior. The center is set in a lovely, restful park with benches and a fountain.

Portage Ave is full of nondescript souvenir shops, but there are also a few places where you can purchase shipwreck artifacts and works by local artists.

Soo Locks Boat Tours (tel toll free 800/432-6301) are operated seven days a week from mid-May to mid-October. They embark from two docks,

at 515 and 1157 E Portage Ave. Ten-mile, two-hour narrated cruises take passengers through the locks, sometimes right next to big freighters. Sunset dinner cruises, lasting for 2 hours and 45 minutes, include a bountiful buffet.

Take a Break

A place to have some wild and crazy fun and enjoy good steaks, fish, and other regional foods is **The Antlers,** 804 E Portage Ave (tel 906/632-3571). The collection of "stuff" hanging from the ceiling and covering the walls of this publike restaurant has to be seen to be believed.

If you want to spend the night here, the 1928 **Ojibway Hotel** (tel 906/632-4100), at 240 W Portage St, is a landmark well worth visiting. Public rooms and guest rooms have warm, comfortable period furnishings. Its Freighters Restaurant has fine views of the river and the locks, and musical entertainment and dancing are offered on weekend nights. Prices are higher than at some of the motels in town, but the Ojibway is well worth it for location and atmosphere. If your taste runs more to a Las Vegas kind of vacation, you might enjoy staying at the **Clarion Kewadin Hotel and Casino** (tel 906/635-1400) run by the Sault Ste Marie tribe of Chippewas.

The *Valley Camp,* a 1917 steam-powered freighter, is docked at 501 E Water St. Visitors can explore the interior of the ship and see where the crew lived, slept, and worked. The steam engine, pilot house, and other areas are open for viewing, and a large array of exhibits bring Great Lakes maritime history to life. Especially interesting is the *Edmund Fitzgerald* Memorial, containing two lifeboats recovered from that tragic shipwreck.

A couple of blocks west of the ship is the **International Bridge** to Canada. Most visitors who come this far north want to spend a little time in another country. You can drive across the bridge in your own vehicle or take one of the guided **Twin Soo Tours** (tel 906/635-5912).

To return to Mackinaw City from Sault Ste Marie, just take I-75 south for 58 miles.

Michigan Listings

Ada

See Grand Rapids

Allen Park

A suburb of Detroit. Products manufactured here include automobiles, tires, liquor, bread, and potato chips. **Information:** Allen Park Chamber of Commerce, 6720 Park Ave, Allen Park, 48101 (tel 313/382-7303).

HOTEL 🏨

≣ ≣ ≣ Best Western Greenfield Inn
3000 Enterprise Dr, 48101; tel 313/271-1600 or toll free 800/528-1234; fax 313/271-1600. I-94 at Oakwood Blvd, exit 206A. Step into this pink Victorian mansion alongside busy I-94, between the airport and downtown Detroit, and step back in time. The gardens with gazebos invite lounging. **Rooms:** 210 rms. CI open/CO noon. Nonsmoking rms avail. The rooms are furnished in either colonial or Victorian decor; some have courtyard views. **Amenities:** 🛁 🔥 🌐 A/C, cable TV w/movies, refrig, VCR, in-rm safe. Some units w/whirlpools. Exercise bikes in some rooms. **Services:** ✗ 🚐 📠 🍴 ⟲ Free transportation between airport, train station, Greenfield Village. **Facilities:** 🏋 🏊50 🔥 1 restaurant, 1 bar, spa, sauna, whirlpool, washer/dryer. **Rates:** $70–$150 S or D. Extra person $6. Children under age 18 stay free. Parking: Outdoor, free. AE, CB, DC, DISC, MC, V.

Alma

Small central Michigan town located 10 miles south of the Isabella Indian Reservation. The Frank Knox Memorial Room on the campus of Alma College contains mementos of the former Navy secretary. Highland Festival and Games take place here every Memorial Day weekend. **Information:** Gratiot Area Chamber of Commerce, 110 W Superior St, PO Box 516, Alma, 48801-0516 (tel 517/463-5525).

MOTELS 🏨

≣ ≣ Comfort Inn
3110 W Monroe Rd, 48801; tel 517/463-4400 or toll free 800/221-2222; fax 517/463-2970. A decent motel with extensive, well-landscaped grounds. **Rooms:** 82 rms. CI 3pm/CO 11am. Nonsmoking rms avail. **Amenities:** 🛁 📺 🌐 A/C, cable TV w/movies, refrig. Some units w/terraces, some w/whirlpools. **Services:** ✗ 🚐 🍴 ⟲ **Facilities:** 🏋 📠 300 💻 🔥 Washer/dryer. **Rates:** $46–$135 S or D. Extra person $5. Parking: Outdoor, free. AE, MC, V.

≣ ≣ Travel Inn
7996 N Alger, 48801; tel 517/463-6131. Provides a comfortable stay and a heated indoor pool and sauna. **Rooms:** 51 rms. CI 3pm/CO 11am. No smoking. **Amenities:** 🛁 🔥 📺 🌐 A/C, cable TV w/movies. **Services:** 🍴 **Facilities:** 🏋 🏊 📠40 🔥 Sauna. **Rates:** $43–$47 S; $49–$57 D. Extra person $5. Children under age 12 stay free. Parking: Outdoor, free. AE, DISC, MC, V.

Alpena

Seat of Alpena County, in northeast part of state. This recreation center at the head of Thunder Bay offers excellent diving, wildlife viewing, and fishing. Brown Trout Festival takes place every July. **Information:** Convention & Visitors Bureau of Thunder Bay Region, 133 Johnson St, PO Box 65, Alpena, 49707-0065 (tel 517/354-4181 or toll free 800/4-ALPENA).

MOTELS 🏨

≣ ≣ Best Western of Alpena
1286 MI 32 W, 49707; tel 517/356-9087 or toll free 800/528-1234. 2 mi W of US 23. Located one mile from local public beach. **Rooms:** 38 rms. CI 3pm/CO 11am. Nonsmoking rms avail. **Amenities:** 🛁 🔥 A/C, cable TV w/movies. Some units w/whirlpools. **Services:** 🍴 **Facilities:** 🏊 🔥 1 restaurant, 1 bar, games rm, playground, washer/dryer. **Rates:** Peak (May 22–Oct 3) $44–$50 S or D. Extra person $6. Children under age 12 stay free. Lower rates off-season. Parking: Outdoor, free. AE, DISC, MC, V.

≝ Fletcher Motel
1001 US 23 N, 49707; tel 517/354-4191 or toll free 800/
334-5920. On US 23 1 mi N of downtown. Standard lodgings. **Rooms:** 96 rms, stes, and effic. CI 2pm/CO 11am.
Nonsmoking rms avail. **Amenities:** ▦ ☉ ▣ A/C, cable TV
w/movies, refrig. Some units w/terraces, some w/whirlpools.
Services: ⊿ ⌂ ⬟ Babysitting. **Facilities:** ⌂ ⚓ ▭ ⚐ 1
restaurant (*see* "Restaurants" below), 1 bar (w/entertain-
ment), volleyball, sauna, whirlpool, washer/dryer. **Rates:**
Peak (June–Oct) $61 D; $100 ste; $75 effic. Extra person $6.
Children under age 12 stay free. Lower rates off-season.
Parking: Outdoor, free. AE, DC, DISC, ER, MC, V.

≝≝ Holiday Inn
1000 US 23 N, 49707; tel 517/356-2151. Offers many
amenities and facilities, including Holidome indoor recreation center. **Rooms:** 147 rms. CI 1pm/CO noon. Nonsmoking rms avail. **Amenities:** ▦ ☉ A/C, cable TV w/movies. Some
units w/whirlpools. **Services:** ✕ ⊿ ⌂ ⬟ **Facilities:** ⌂ ⚓
▦ ▭ ⚐ 1 restaurant, 1 bar (w/entertainment), volleyball,
games rm, spa, sauna, whirlpool. **Rates:** Peak (June–Aug)
$80–$95 D. Extra person $10. Children under age 19 stay
free. Lower rates off-season. Parking: Outdoor, free. AE, CB,
DISC, MC, V.

RESTAURANT 🍴

The Grove
In Fletcher Motel, 1001 US 23 N; tel 517/354-4191. **Sea-
food/Steak.** The hearty, simple menu at this roadside diner
features prime rib, burgers, and the freshest local whitefish.
FYI: Reservations accepted. Karaoke. **Open:** Daily 6am–
11pm. **Prices:** Main courses $7–$16. AE, DISC, MC, V.

ATTRACTION 🏛

Old Presque Isle Lighthouse and Museum
US 23, Presque Isle; tel 517/595-2787. Located 23 mi N of
Alpena, on Presque Isle Harbor. This picturesque 1840
lighthouse now houses a museum with nautical instruments,
marine artifacts, and other antiques. **Open:** May–Oct, daily
9am–5pm. $

Ann Arbor

Seat of Washtenaw County, in southeast part of state. Home
of the main campus of the University of Michigan, the Gerald
R Ford Presidential Library, and an ever-growing number of
high-technology companies. Two glacial moraines intersect
nearby; the city is hilly and full of trees. **Information:** Ann
Arbor Convention & Visitors Bureau, 120 W Huron St, Ann
Arbor, 48104-1318 (tel 313/995-7281).

HOTELS 🏨

≝≝≝ Bell Tower Hotel
300 S Thayer St, 48104 (University of Michigan); tel 313/
769-3010 or toll free 800/999-8693; fax 313/369-4339.
Across from Hill Auditorium. This 1945 hotel, winner of an
award for outstanding historic preservation, combines Old
World elegance with gracious service. Intimate lobby with
fireplace. **Rooms:** 66 rms and stes. CI 4pm/CO noon.
Nonsmoking rms avail. **Amenities:** ▦ ☉ A/C, cable TV. Some
units w/minibars, some w/terraces. **Services:** ✕ ▣P ⬟ ⊿ ⌂
Twice-daily maid svce, social director, babysitting. **Facilities:**
⚓ ▭ 1 bar. Guests have access to U of Michigan recreation
arena and Campus Inn fitness center. **Rates (CP):** $101–
$113 S or D; $129–$210 ste. Extra person $12. Children
under age 6 stay free. Parking: Indoor, free. AE, CB, DC,
MC, V.

≝≝≝ Campus Inn
615 E Huron St, 48104; tel 313/769-2200 or toll free 800/
666-8693; fax 313/769-6222. At State St. Slick, modern
tower has newly remodeled interior with old-fashioned elegance. Great views of the city and campus from every
window. **Rooms:** 208 rms and stes. Executive level. CI 4pm/
CO noon. Nonsmoking rms avail. **Amenities:** ▦ ☉ A/C, cable
TV, dataport. Some units w/minibars. **Services:** ✕ ⊿ ⌂
Babysitting. **Facilities:** ⌂ ⚓ ▦ ▭ 1 restaurant, 1 bar,
sauna, steam rm. Guests have access to U of Michigan campus
recreation building. **Rates:** $103–$113 S; $115–$125 D;
$147–$265 ste. Extra person $12. Children under age 7 stay
free. Min stay special events. Parking: Outdoor, free. AE, DC,
DISC, JCB, MC, V.

≝≝≝ Clarion Atrium & Conference Center
2900 Jackson Rd, 48103; tel 313/665-4444 or toll free 800/
221-2222; fax 313/665-5558. Exit 172 off I-94; W on
Jackson Rd to entrance. Newly renovated, with easy access to
highway, shopping, and restaurants. Plenty of on-site activities make it ideal for families; convenient location makes it a
good business choice too. **Rooms:** 221 rms and stes. Executive level. CI 3pm/CO noon. Nonsmoking rms avail.
Amenities: ▦ ☉ ▣ A/C, cable TV w/movies, dataport. Some
units w/whirlpools. **Services:** ✕ ⊿ ⌂ Car-rental desk, babysitting. **Facilities:** ⌂ ▦ ▭ ⚐ 1 restaurant, 1 bar (w/enter-
tainment), games rm, sauna, whirlpool, washer/dryer. **Rates:**
$79–$119 S or D; $150–$275 ste. Children under age 18 stay
free. Min stay special events. AP and MAP rates avail.
Parking: Outdoor, free. AE, CB, DC, DISC, MC, V.

≝≝≝ Crowne Plaza Hotel
610 Hilton Blvd, 48108; tel 313/761-7800 or toll free 800/2-
CROWNE; fax 313/995-1085. Adjacent to the Briarwood
Shopping Center, this elegant hotel has a European atmo-
sphere, with green and white marble, Austrian lace curtains,
and a large fireplace in the lobby. **Rooms:** 198 rms and stes.
CI 3pm/CO 11am. Nonsmoking rms avail. **Amenities:** ▦ ☉
▣ ⚑ A/C, satel TV w/movies. **Services:** ✕ ⊿ ⌂ Car rental

across street. **Facilities:** 🖼 🏃 🛴 🅿 ♿ 1 restaurant, 1 bar, games rm, spa, sauna, whirlpool. New ballroom under construction. Private meeting room in lobby available for guest use. **Rates:** $95–$119 S or D; $225 ste. Children under age 18 stay free. Min stay special events. Parking: Outdoor, free. $10 for roll-away in room. AE, CB, DC, DISC, JCB, MC, V.

⬛⬛⬛ Marriott Residence Inn

800 Victors Way, 48108; tel 313/996-5666 or toll free 800/331-3131. Exit 177 off I-94; N to Victors Way; E to entrance. Condominium-type units designed for stays of 30 days or more. Ideal for relocating families or those on temporary business assignments. **Rooms:** 72 stes. CI 3pm/CO 11am. Nonsmoking rms avail. Single suites are oversized studios; penthouses have two bedrooms and two baths. **Amenities:** 📺 🍷 🖥 A/C, cable TV w/movies, refrig, dataport. Some units w/terraces, some w/fireplaces. **Services:** 🚐 🖼 🧺 🛎 Car-rental desk, babysitting. Grocery shopping and food delivery services available. Children's program in summer. Guest social Mon–Thurs evenings. Emphasis on personal service. **Facilities:** 🖼 🏃 🎾 🅿 ♿ Basketball, volleyball, whirlpool, washer/dryer. Guest have access to local fitness center. **Rates (CP):** Peak (Apr–Sept) $79–$175 ste. Children under age 18 stay free. Min stay. Lower rates off-season. Parking: Outdoor, free. AE, CB, DC, DISC, JCB, MC, V.

MOTELS

⬛⬛ Ann Arbor Hampton Inn North

2300 Green Rd, 48105; tel 313/996-4444 or toll free 800/HAMPTON; fax 313/996-0196. Easy access to highway from this clean, comfortable inn located in business park. **Rooms:** 130 rms and stes. CI 3pm/CO noon. Nonsmoking rms avail. **Amenities:** 📺 🍷 A/C, satel TV w/movies, dataport. **Services:** ✕ 🚐 🖼 🧺 🛎 **Facilities:** 🖼 🏃 🛴 🅿 ♿ Whirlpool, washer/dryer. Table tennis and sun deck adjoin pool. **Rates (CP):** $59–$66 S or D; $65 ste. Children under age 18 stay free. Min stay special events. Parking: Outdoor, free. AE, CB, DC, DISC, JCB, MC, V.

⬛⬛ Ann Arbor Hampton Inn South

925 Victors Way, 48108; or toll free 800/722-7220; fax 313/665-8452. Exit 177 off I-94; N on State to Victors Way; E to entrance. Clean, comfortable accommodations without lots of frills. Fine for short-term stays. **Rooms:** 150 rms. CI 3pm/CO noon. Nonsmoking rms avail. **Amenities:** 📺 🍷 A/C, satel TV w/movies. **Services:** 🚐 🖼 🧺 **Facilities:** 🖼 🛴 🅿 ♿ Whirlpool, washer/dryer. **Rates (CP):** Peak (June–Nov) $59–$65 S; $65–$75 D. Children under age 18 stay free. Lower rates off-season. Parking: Outdoor, free. AE, CB, DC, DISC, JCB, MC, V.

⬛⬛ Comfort Inn and Business Center

2455 Carpenter Rd, 48108; tel 313/973-6100 or toll free 800/973-6101; fax 313/973-6142. Exit 37A off US 23 to Carpenter Rd; S to entrance. Easy access to highway. Several restaurants nearby. **Rooms:** 126 rms and stes. CI 3pm/CO noon. Nonsmoking rms avail. Clean, comfortable accommo-

dations. **Amenities:** 📺 🍷 A/C, cable TV w/movies. Some units w/whirlpools. Phones and TVs can be adapted for deaf and hard of hearing. **Services:** 🖼 🧺 🛎 Public fax machine in lobby. **Facilities:** 🖼 🅿 🖥 ♿ Games rm, whirlpool, washer/dryer. **Rates (CP):** $58–$75 S or D; $80–$120 ste. Extra person $7. Children under age 18 stay free. Min stay special events. Parking: Outdoor, free. AE, CB, DC, DISC, JCB, MC, V.

⬛⬛⬛ Courtyard by Marriott

3205 Boardwalk, 48108; tel 313/995-5900 or toll free 800/321-2211; fax 313/995-2937. Exit 177 off I-94. Easy access to highways and shopping from this clean, polished establishment. Near golf. **Rooms:** 159 rms and stes. CI 3pm/CO noon. Nonsmoking rms avail. **Amenities:** 📺 🍷 🖥 A/C, cable TV w/movies, dataport. **Services:** ✕ 🖼 🧺 Room service available through local restaurants in "Take Out Taxi" program. **Facilities:** 🖼 🛴 🅿 ♿ 1 restaurant (bkfst and lunch only), 1 bar, games rm, whirlpool, washer/dryer. Guests have access to local athletic center. **Rates:** $83–$93 S or D; $103 ste. Children under age 18 stay free. Min stay special events. Parking: Outdoor, free. Two for breakfast weekend package includes complimentary breakfast. AE, CB, DC, DISC, MC, V.

⬛⬛ Days Inn Ann Arbor

2380 Carpenter Rd, 48104; tel 313/971-0700 or toll free 800/DAYS-INN; fax 313/971-1492. Exit 37A off US 23; E to Carpenter Rd, S to entrance. Easy access to highway. **Rooms:** 127 rms. CI 3pm/CO noon. Nonsmoking rms avail. Clean and comfortable rooms. **Amenities:** 📺 🍷 A/C, cable TV, in-rm safe. All units w/terraces, 1 w/whirlpool. **Services:** 🚐 🖼 🧺 Free local phone calls. **Facilities:** 🖼 🏃 🅿 🖥 ♿ 1 restaurant, volleyball, games rm, sauna, whirlpool, washer/dryer. Large, indoor heated pool. **Rates (CP):** Peak (June–Sept) $56–$89 S or D. Extra person $5. Children under age 18 stay free. Lower rates off-season. Parking: Outdoor, free. AE, CB, DC, DISC, ER, JCB, MC, V.

⬛⬛ Fairfield Inn

3285 Boardwalk, 48108; tel 313/995-5200 or toll free 800/228-2800; fax 313/995-5394. Exit 177 off I-94; N on State to Victors Way; E to Boardwalk; N to entry. Attractive facility. Golf nearby. **Rooms:** 110 rms. CI 3pm/CO noon. Nonsmoking rms avail. **Amenities:** 📺 🍷 A/C, satel TV w/movies, dataport. **Services:** 🚐 🖼 🧺 Car-rental desk. Nintendo setup available on request. Friendly staff. **Facilities:** 🖼 ♿ Whirlpool. Full-service gym nearby. **Rates (CP):** Peak (June–Aug) $53–$69 S; $59–$69 D. Extra person $6. Children under age 18 stay free. Lower rates off-season. Parking: Outdoor, free. AE, CB, DC, DISC, MC, V.

⬛⬛⬛ Holiday Inn North Campus

3600 Plymouth Rd, 48105; tel 313/769-9800 or toll free 800/800-5560; fax 313/761-1290. Exit 41 off US 23; W on Plymouth Rd to entrance. Relaxing accommodations, conveniently located, with a sporty theme. **Rooms:** 222 rms. CI

3pm/CO 11am. Nonsmoking rms avail. **Amenities:** ⬛⬛⬛⬛ A/C, satel TV w/movies. Some units w/terraces. Poolside rooms have patios. **Services:** ✗⬛⬛⬛ Babysitting. Free shuttle service available during business hours. **Facilities:** ⬛ ⬛2 ⬛ ⬛375 ⬛ 1 restaurant, 1 bar (w/entertainment), basketball, volleyball, games rm, sauna, whirlpool. Pool table located poolside. **Rates:** $61–$110 S or D. Extra person $10. Children under age 18 stay free. Parking: Outdoor, free. AE, CB, DC, DISC, JCB, MC, V.

RESTAURANTS ⬛

Bella Ciao
118 W Liberty (Downtown); tel 313/995-2107. Just E of Ashley. **Italian.** An intimate, casual bistro with green-marble tabletops and high-backed booths. The nouvelle Italian specialties include cannelloni stuffed with veal and spinach, linguini with fresh herbs, and pasta with caramelized sea scallops. **FYI:** Reservations accepted. No smoking. **Open:** Mon–Sat 5:30–10pm. **Prices:** Main courses $10–$21; prix fixe $21. AE, DC, DISC, MC, V. ⬛

Don Carlos Mexican Restaurante
4890 Washtenaw Ave; tel 313/572-0050. Exit 37A off US 23; E 1 mi. **Mexican.** Brightly colored bricks set the festive mood at this casual eatery. Sixteen different kinds of burritos, fajitas, enchiladas, chimichangas, tostados, and tacos are available. For the gringos, there are burgers and steaks, with or without a touch of salsa. **FYI:** Reservations accepted. Children's menu. Dress code. **Open:** Daily 11am–9pm. **Prices:** Main courses $5–$13. AE, DISC, MC, V. ⬛

★ The Earle
121 W Washington (Downtown); tel 313/994-0211. Just E of Ashley. **Continental.** A cellar bistro and wine bar with cool brick and tile, warm upholstered armchairs, and a cabaret atmosphere. The menu changes regularly, but may include sautéed beef tenderloin with fresh herbs; or vegetable ragout with eggplant, peppers, tomatoes, zucchini, onion, garlic, and goat cheese. Wine bar serves lighter fare. The wine cellar has over 800 bottles, and about a dozen labels are available by the glass. **FYI:** Reservations recommended. Piano. **Open:** Sun–Fri 5:30–9pm, Sat 6–9pm. **Prices:** Main courses $12–$21. AE, CB, DC, DISC, MC, V. ⬛⬛

Ⓢ Gandy Dancer
401 Depot St; tel 313/769-0592. Next to Amtrak station. **New American/Seafood.** Housed in a restored 1886 railroad station, where a windowed platform allows diners to watch the daily Amtrak run speed by. The stone walls, slate roof, stained-glass windows, red oak ceilings, and fireplace are original, although the station has been broken into several dining areas for a greater sense of intimacy. The menu changes daily to allow the chef to take advantage of the freshest catch of the day, but typical entrees include shrimp fettuccine, chargrilled sea scallops, and Charley's bucket (whole Maine lobster served with steamer clams, redskin potatoes, mussels, and corn on the cob). **FYI:** Reservations

recommended. Children's menu. **Open:** Lunch Mon–Sat 11:30am–3:30pm; dinner Mon–Thurs 4:30–10pm, Fri–Sat 4:30–11pm, Sun 3:30–9pm; brunch Sun 10am–2pm. **Prices:** Main courses $6–$28. AE, CB, DC, DISC, MC, V. ⬛⬛⬛

Metzger's German Restaurant
203 E Washington St (Downtown); tel 313/668-8987. At 4th Ave. **American/German.** Ann Arbor's oldest restaurant, this historic landmark is watched over by the third generation of Metzgers. Family photos and elaborately carved cuckoo clocks line the walls. Along with daily specials, there are plenty of Old World favorites such as cabbage rolls, bratwurst, and sauerbraten. **FYI:** Reservations accepted. Children's menu. **Open:** Mon–Thurs 11am–9pm, Fri–Sat 11am–10pm, Sun 11:30am–8pm. **Prices:** Main courses $5–$8. AE, CB, DC, DISC, MC, V. ⬛⬛⬛

Mountain Jack's
300 S Maple Rd; tel 313/665-1133. Exit 172 off I-94. **Seafood/Steak.** Popular, medium-priced chain restaurant famous for its slow roasted prime rib. Traditional steak and seafood dishes, such as mushroom steak and smoked salmon, are also offered. The setting is comfortable and relaxed. **FYI:** Reservations accepted. Children's menu. **Open:** Lunch Mon–Fri 11:30am–2pm; dinner Mon–Thurs 5–10pm, Fri 5–11pm, Sat 4–11pm, Sun noon–9pm. **Prices:** Main courses $12–$19. AE, CB, DC, MC, V. ⬛⬛

♣ Moveable Feast
326 W Liberty; tel 313/663-3278. At 2nd Ave; W of downtown. **New American/French.** Located in an 1870 Victorian mansion and garnished with original art and a hand-painted frieze, this intimate dining room delivers attentive but unhurried service and meals that make you want to linger. For those with lighter appetites, the "Menage a Trois" prix fixe dinner includes choice of appetizer, soup or salad, and dessert. Entrees available á la carte include spicy grilled swordfish, beef tenderloin with Madeira wine sauce, and quick-roasted duckling breast with apple-ginger sauce. There's also a serious bakery, so leave room for dessert. Voted one of "America's Top 250 Places to Eat" by *Condé Nast Traveler* magazine. **FYI:** Reservations recommended. No smoking. **Open:** Lunch Tues–Fri 11:30am–2pm; dinner Mon–Sat 6–9pm. **Prices:** Main courses $14–$25; prix fixe $16–$37. AE, DC, DISC, MC, V. ⬛

Paesano's Restaurant
3411 Washtenaw Ave; tel 313/971-0484. Exit 37B off US 23; W to 2nd light. **Italian.** Bright and airy dining room is the perfect atmosphere in which to enjoy fine Italian pastas, wines, and oils. The kitchen shows off its skills with dishes like lemon basil fettuccine with salmon, and chicken with artichoke, asparagus, and crabmeat. Nutrition information available for all dishes. **FYI:** Reservations recommended. Children's menu. **Open:** Mon–Thurs 11am–11pm, Fri 11am–midnight, Sat noon–midnight, Sun 10am–10pm. **Prices:** Main courses $9–$19. AE, CB, DC, DISC, MC, V. ⬛

ATTRACTIONS 🏛

University of Michigan
University Ave; tel 313/764-1817. One of the largest (35,000 students) and oldest (founded in 1817) universities in the Midwest. (The school was actually founded in Detroit, and moved here in 1837.) The 1,300-acre campus boasts many classic Gothic buildings; other highlights include libraries, botanical gardens, museums of art, archeology, and natural history. The U of M is also home to the Gerald R Ford Presidential Library. **Free**

Kelsey Museum of Archeology
434 S State St; tel 313/764-9304. Situated on the central campus of the University of Michigan, this museum houses a permanent collection of nearly 100,000 artifacts from the ancient and early medieval cultures of Egypt, the Middle East, Greece, and Rome. Highlights include textiles, glass, pottery, sculptures, coins, and an array of relics of daily life from Roman Egypt. Lectures, gallery tours, workshops, and films also offered. **Open:** Mon–Fri 9am–4pm, Sat–Sun 1–4pm. **Free**

University of Michigan Matthaei Botanical Gradens
1800 N Dixboro Rd; tel 313/998-7061. Situated along Fleming Creek, these 600-acre gardens include a conservatory (with a diverse collection of over 2,000 plants) nestled amid nature trails, woodlands, wetlands, and ponds. Hour-long conservatory trail tours offered on most weekends. **Open:** Daily 8am–sunset. **$**

National Center for the Study of Frank Lloyd Wright
30 Frank Lloyd Wright Dr; tel 313/995-4258. This $30 million repository contains manuscripts, videotapes, and oral histories about the great architect's work—all set among furniture, lamps, metalwork, and ceramics designed by him. **Open:** Mon–Fri 10am–6pm, Sat–Sun noon–5pm. **$**

Classic Car Museum
44 Frank Lloyd Wright Dr; tel 313/668-7319. Vintage Corvettes, T-Birds, Duesenbergs, and a 1931 Bugatti Royale worth over $8 million are among the 250 classics housed here. Gift shop. **Open:** Mon–Thurs 10am–6pm, Fri–Sat 11am–9pm, Sun noon–5pm. **$$**

Kempf House
312 S Division; tel 313/994-4898. Antique Victorian furnishings and local historical artifacts are displayed in this restored Greek Revival–style Victorian house. Call for tour schedule. **$**

Battle Creek

See also Marshall

Located in south-central Michigan, about 20 miles east of Kalamazoo. This midsized city was built by W K Kellogg and C W Post, and the cereal plants they established still have a major impact on the local economy. Anti-slavery crusader Sojourner Truth is buried here. **Information:** Greater Battle Creek/Calhoun County Visitors & Convention Bureau, 34 W Jackson, Suite 4B, Battle Creek, 49017-3505 (tel 616/962-2240)

HOTEL 🏨

▤▤▤ McCamly Plaza Hotel
50 Capital Ave SW, 49017; tel 616/963-7050 or toll free 800/468-3571; fax 616/963-3880. Exit 98B (MI 66) off I-94. Elegant, full-service, 16-story downtown hotel, adjoining McCamly Place Shopping Center and Kellogg Arena. Bike rentals, golf, and tennis nearby. **Rooms:** 244 rms and stes. Executive level. CI 3pm/CO 1pm. Nonsmoking rms avail. Spacious rooms with excellent views of the city. **Amenities:** 🛗 ⓐ 🖥 🍷 A/C, satel TV w/movies, refrig, dataport. All units w/minibars. **Services:** 🍽 🔑 VP 🛍 ☒ ⌧ Twice-daily maid svce, babysitting. Attentive staff with emphasis on personal service. **Facilities:** 🔸 🏋 🏊 💻 ⚓ 2 restaurants (see "Restaurants" below), 2 bars (1 w/entertainment), spa, sauna, whirlpool, beauty salon. City Lights lounge also located rooftop. **Rates:** Peak (May–Sept) $123 S; $143 D; $150 ste. Children under age 18 stay free. Lower rates off-season. Parking: Indoor/outdoor, $1/day. Golf packages avail. AE, CB, DC, DISC, ER, JCB, MC, V.

MOTELS

▤▤▤ The Apple Tree Inn
4786 Beckley Rd, 49017; tel 616/979-3561 or toll free 800/388-7829; fax 616/979-1400. Exit 97 off I-94 E. Comfortable and clean single-story motel with easy access to highways, restaurants, and shops. Near several golf courses. **Rooms:** 87 rms and effic; 1 cottage/villa. CI 3pm/CO noon. Nonsmoking rms avail. **Amenities:** 🛗 ⓐ 🖥 A/C, satel TV w/movies, dataport. Some units w/whirlpools. **Services:** ☒ ⌧ ⚓ 10% discount at area restaurants; free passes to comedy club. **Facilities:** 🏊 ⚓ Privileges at local health club. **Rates (CP):** $41–$45 S; $42–$53 D; $47–$63 effic; $50 cottage/villa. Extra person $4–$6. Children under age 18 stay free. Parking: Outdoor, free. AE, DC, DISC, ER, MC, V.

▤▤▤ Battle Creek Inn
5050 Beckley Rd, 49015; tel 616/979-1100 or toll free 800/232-3405; fax 616/979-1899. Exit 97 off I-94. Well-maintained facility with easy access to major highways, shopping, and golf. **Rooms:** 211 rms. CI 3pm/CO noon. Nonsmoking rms avail. All rooms open onto interior courtyard; many have sofa beds in addition to standard sleeping area. **Amenities:** 🛗 ⓐ 🖥 A/C, satel TV w/movies, dataport. Some units w/whirlpools. **Services:** ✗ ☒ ⌧ ⚓ Twice-daily maid svce, car-rental desk, babysitting. **Facilities:** 🔸 🏋 🏊 ⚓ 1 restaurant, 1 bar (w/entertainment), games rm. Bring own putter to use natural grass putting green on property. Privileges at local health club. **Rates:** $55 S; $60–$73 D.

Extra person $8. Children under age 18 stay free. Parking: Outdoor, free. Golf packages avail. AE, CB, DC, DISC, JCB, MC, V.

🛏 Comfort Inn
165 Capital Ave SW, 49015; tel 616/965-3976 or toll free 800/221-2222; fax 616/965-7580. Exit 98B (MI 66) off I-94. Basic, tidy downtown motel near convention and federal centers. Nearby shops, restaurants, and fitness trail. **Rooms:** 54 rms and effic. CI 3pm/CO noon. Nonsmoking rms avail. **Amenities:** 🛏 🗜 A/C, cable TV w/movies, in-rm safe. **Services:** 🚗 🖂 ⌇ **Facilities:** 🔒 1 bar (w/entertainment). **Rates (CP):** Peak (May–Sept) $37–$49 S; $47–$66 D; $64 effic. Extra person $7. Children under age 18 stay free. Lower rates off-season. Parking: Outdoor, free. Golf packages avail. AE, DC, DISC, JCB, MC, V.

🛏 Knights Inn
2595 Capital Ave SW, 49015; tel 616/964-2600 or toll free 800/843-5644; fax 616/964-1682. 1 mi N of exit 97 off I-94. Clean single-story motel off interstate. Fine for overnight stay. **Rooms:** 95 rms and effic. CI 3pm/CO noon. Nonsmoking rms avail. **Amenities:** 🛏 A/C, satel TV w/movies. **Services:** 🖂 ⌇ 🍴 **Facilities:** 🔒 🚗 & **Rates:** $35–$40 S; $41–$48 D; $45–$56 effic. Extra person $3. Children under age 18 stay free. Parking: Outdoor, free. AE, CB, DC, DISC, MC, V.

🛏🛏 Super 8 Motel
5395 Beckley Rd, 49015; tel 616/979-1828 or toll free 800/800-8000; fax 616/979-1828. ½ mi E of exit 97 off I-94. Clean three-story motel with easy access to highway. No frills. **Rooms:** 62 rms and stes. CI 1pm/CO 11am. Nonsmoking rms avail. First-floor rooms recently renovated. **Amenities:** 🛏 A/C, cable TV, dataport. **Services:** ⌇ 🍴 **Facilities:** 🔒 & **Rates:** Peak (Apr–Sept) $39–$42 S; $44 D; $59–$74 ste. Extra person $5. Children under age 12 stay free. Lower rates off-season. Parking: Outdoor, free. AE, CB, DC, DISC, MC, V.

RESTAURANTS 🍴

Clara's on the River Restaurant
44 N McCamly; tel 616/963-0966. **American.** An award-winning eatery in a restored 1880s train station listed on the National Register of Historic Places. Outdoor patio overlooks landscaped riverfront; antique furnishings and prints decorate the five indoor dining areas. Sixteen-page menu includes pocket-stuffed pizzas, fajitas, pastas, chicken Hawaiian, burgers, and steaks. **FYI:** Reservations accepted. Guitar. Children's menu. Additional location: 637 E Michigan Ave, Lansing (tel 517/372-7120). **Open:** Sun 10am–11pm, Fri–Sat 11am–2am, Mon–Thurs 11am–12am. **Prices:** Main courses $5–$16. AE, DC, DISC, MC, V. ♿ &

♣ McCamly's Roof
In McCamly Plaza Hotel, 50 Capital Ave SW; tel 616/963-7050. **American.** A top-notch view and elegant cuisine are what's in store at this roof-top restaurant. The menu changes regularly but maintains an emphasis on fresh foods accented with sauces, such as grilled salmon with saffron and chive cream sauce, oven-roasted veal chop in morel cream sauce, or grilled filet of beef with béarnaise sauce. Mostly domestic wines. **FYI:** Reservations recommended. Children's menu. **Open:** Breakfast Mon–Sat 6:30–11:30am; lunch Mon–Fri 11am–5:30pm; dinner Mon–Thurs 5:30–10pm, Fri–Sat 5:30–11pm; brunch Sun 11am–2pm. **Prices:** Main courses $8–$22. AE, CB, DC, DISC, ER, MC, V. 🏔 VP &

ATTRACTIONS 🏛

Kimball House Museum
196 Capital Ave NE; tel 616/966-2496. Restored 1886 Victorian house pays tribute to the town's medical heritage, with exhibits of old appliances, tools, and medical instruments. Herb garden and country store also on grounds. **Open:** Tues–Sat 12:30–4:30pm. $

Oak Hill Cemetery
South Ave and Oak Hill Dr; tel 616/964-7321. Best known as the burial place of antislavery crusader Sojourner Truth. Her gravesite is marked by a plain-looking square monument. **Open:** Daily sunrise–sunset. **Free**

Binder Park Zoo
7400 Division St; tel 616/979-1351. Exotic and domestic animal exhibits can be seen in a natural setting. A miniature train ride and nature trails take guests from area to area; there's also a restaurant and gift shop. **Open:** Apr–Oct, Mon–Fri 9am–5pm, Sat 9am–6pm, Sun 11am–6pm. $$

Kingman Museum of Natural History/Leila Arboretum
W Michigan Ave at 20th St; tel 616/965-5117. The museum includes permanent exhibits such as "Walk in the Footsteps of the Dinosaurs" and "Mammals of the Ice Age," as well as a planetarium and an interactive Discovery Room. Surrounding the building is a 72-acre park filled with native trees and shrubs. **Open:** Peak (July–Aug) Mon–Sat 9am–5pm, Sun 1–5pm. Reduced hours off-season. $

Bay City

Seat of Bay County, in eastern Michigan. Many gracious Victorian and Georgian mansions grace this port city on Saginaw Bay. **Information:** Bay Area Convention & Visitors Bureau, 901 Saginaw St, Bay City, 48708-5672 (tel 517/893-1222 or toll free 800/424-5114).

HOTEL 🏨

🛏🛏 Best Western Inn
6285 Westside Saginaw Rd, 48706; tel 517/686-0840. Located right in downtown Saginaw, adjacent to a restaurant. **Rooms:** 71 rms. CI 2pm/CO 11am. Nonsmoking rms avail. **Amenities:** 🛏 🗜 A/C, cable TV w/movies, refrig. 1 unit

w/whirlpool. **Services:** 🛏 ⤴ ⬳ **Facilities:** 🎣 🏃 ᴴⱽᴴ 🎱50 ⚿ Games rm, spa, sauna, whirlpool. **Rates:** Peak (June–Aug) $50–$60 S or D. Extra person $5. Children under age 12 stay free. Lower rates off-season. Parking: Outdoor, free. AE, MC, V.

MOTELS

⧱ Euclid Motel
809 N Elucid Ave, 48706; tel 517/684-9455. Comfortable, basic motel. **Rooms:** 36 rms. CI noon/CO 11am. No smoking. **Amenities:** 🛁 ⚲ A/C, cable TV w/movies. Some rooms have refrigerators. **Services:** ⤴ **Facilities:** 🎣 🏃 Playground. **Rates:** Peak (June–Aug) $40–$55 D. Extra person $4. Lower rates off-season. Parking: Outdoor, free. AE, DISC, MC, V.

⧱⧱ Holiday Inn
501 Saginaw St, 48708; tel 517/892-3501 or toll free 800/HOLIDAY; fax 517/892-9342. Hotel with full facilities, near restaurants, Veterans Park, boating, and marina. **Rooms:** 100 rms. CI 1pm/CO noon. Nonsmoking rms avail. **Amenities:** 🛁 ⚲ 📺 A/C, cable TV. **Services:** 🛏 ⤴ ⬳ **Facilities:** 🎣 🏃 🎱150 ⚿ 1 restaurant, 1 bar, games rm, sauna, whirlpool. **Rates:** Peak (June–Aug) $73–$79 D. Children under age 12 stay free. Lower rates off-season. Parking: Outdoor, free. MC, V.

RESORT

⧱⧱⧱ Bay Valley Hotel and Resort
2470 Old Bridge Rd, 48706; tel 517/686-3500 or toll free 800/292-5028; fax 517/686-6931. Exit 160 off I-75. 400 acres. First-class, four-season hotel and resort with nice grounds. The lobby in the main lodge is furnished with antiques. Fishing charters in nearby bay. **Rooms:** 150 rms, stes, and effic. CI 3pm/CO noon. Nonsmoking rms avail. **Amenities:** 🛁 ⚲ 📺 🍽 A/C, cable TV w/movies, refrig, dataport, VCR. Some units w/terraces. **Services:** ✕ 🚐 🛏 ⤴ ⬳ Car-rental desk, babysitting. **Facilities:** 🎣 🚵 ⛺ ▶18 🏌 🎣6 🎣6 ᴴⱽᴴ 🎱200 1 restaurant, 1 bar (w/entertainment), volleyball, games rm, lawn games, whirlpool, playground. Championship Jack Nicklaus golf course; SUPTS-certified pro, indoor/outdoor spa with fully equipped fitness room. **Rates:** Peak (May–Sept) $79–$100 D; $125 ste; $125 effic. Extra person $10. Lower rates off-season. Parking: Outdoor, free. Golf packages avail. AE, MC, V.

RESTAURANTS ᵼᵼᵼ

Brass Lantern
1019 N Water St; tel 517/894-0772. At 3rd St. **American.** Located on the waterfront close to "Antique Row," the Brass Lantern offers a hot buffet every night as well as a number of steak and seafood entrees. There are large booths for seating and handcrafted brass artwork on the walls. The downstairs bar has a three-tier deck and serves special "Bay City Boat" cocktails and appetizers. **FYI:** Reservations accepted. **Open:** Mon–Thurs 11am–9pm, Fri–Sat 11am–10pm, Sun 10am–8pm. **Prices:** Main courses $6–$13. AE, MC, V. ♥ ⬱ 🖼

Terry & Jerry's O Sole Mio Restaurante
1005 Saginaw St; tel 517/893-3496. **Italian.** Owners Terry and Jerry originally came to town as entertainers; a stage and antique piano in the dining room recall the old days. Italian menu specialties include seafood, veal, and the usual variety of pastas. Guests are invited into the wine cellar to select their favorite vino. **FYI:** Reservations recommended. Guitar/piano/singer. Children's menu. **Open:** Peak (June–Aug) Tues–Sat 5–10pm. **Prices:** Main courses $9–$25. AE, DC, MC, V. ♥

ATTRACTIONS 🏛

City Hall and Bell Tower
301 Washington Ave; tel 517/894-8200. This restored Romanesque structure features a 31-foot-long woven tapestry depicting the history of Bay City. **Open:** Mon–Fri 8am–5pm. **Free**

Historical Museum of Bay County
321 Washington Ave; tel 517/893-5733. Changing gallery exhibits are put together from a permanent collection of more than 60,000 local historical artifacts—photographs, documents, tools, original materials used in fur trading, coal mining, shipbuilding, and agriculture industries. The museum also organizes a biannual tour of historic homes, a quilt show, and the annual "River of Time" living history encampment. Research library, gift shop. **Open:** Mon–Fri 10am–5pm, Sun 1–5pm. **Free**

Bay City State Park
3582 State Park Dr; tel 517/684-3020. Located 5 mi N of Bay City. This 200-acre park boasts a campground with modern sites and full hookups, a swimming beach, and a newly remodeled nature center. Recreational facilities include a playground, basketball and volleyball courts, miniature golf course, batting cages, bumper boats, and a picnic area with five rental shelters equipped with electricity and a large grill. **Open:** Daily 8am–10pm. **$$**

Bellaire

Seat of Antrim County, in northwest part of state. A resort town popular with skiers. **Information:** Bellaire Area Chamber of Commerce, PO Box 205, Bellaire, 49615 (tel 616/533-6023).

RESORT 🏛

⧱⧱⧱ Shanty Creek Resort
MI 88 E, 49615; tel 616/533-8621 or toll free 800/678-4111. 2 mi E of Bellaire. A first-class resort on 2,000 acres. Breathtaking views of ski lifts from summit. **Rooms:** 200 rms, stes, and effic; 400 cottages/villas. CI 6pm/CO noon. Nonsmoking rms avail. Deluxe villa or golf-side condominiums, as well as standard rooms. **Amenities:** 🛁 ⚲ 📺 A/C, cable TV w/movies, refrig, VCR. Some units w/terraces,

some w/fireplaces, some w/whirlpools. **Services:** X 🛎 🚐 🛌 🧺 Social director, masseur, children's program, babysitting. Transportation to Traverse City airport for $25. **Facilities:** 🏊 🚲 ⛳54 🎿 🛶 🎣 🏊4 ⛳4 🎾 🏇900 👤 2 restaurants, 2 bars (w/entertainment), basketball, volleyball, games rm, lawn games, spa, beauty salon, day-care ctr, playground. Range of sports activities available, plus Arnold Palmer "Legend" golf course. **Rates:** Peak (mid-June–Aug) $129–$134 S or D; $165–$175 ste; $175 effic; $260–$330 cottage/villa. Extra person $10. Children under age 17 stay free. Lower rates off-season. Parking: Outdoor, free. AE, DC, DISC, MC, V.

Benton Harbor

See also St Joseph

Located in southwest part of state, on the shore of Lake Michigan and near the St Joseph River. Nearby Warren Dunes State Park draws visitors here. **Information:** Lake Michigan Convention & Visitors Bureau, 185 E Main St, PO Box 428, Benton Harbor, 49023-0428 (tel 616/925-6100).

HOTEL 🏨

≡≡≡ **Courtyard by Marriott**
1592 Mall Dr, 49022; tel 616/925-3000 or toll free 800/321-2211; fax 616/925-3000. Exit 29 off I-94. Large, two-story lobby features dramatic curved wood stairway to second level and rugged fieldstone fireplace. Generous plantings add color to public areas. **Rooms:** 98 rms and stes. CI 3pm/CO noon. Nonsmoking rms avail. **Amenities:** 🛜 🍴 📺 A/C, cable TV. Some units w/whirlpools. Iron and ironing board in each room. **Services:** 🚐 🛌 🧺 🍴 Small pets accepted with $50 security deposit. **Facilities:** 🏊 🎾 🏊100 👤 1 restaurant (bkfst only), 1 bar. Indoor/outdoor pool just off lobby. **Rates:** Peak (June–Sept) $90–$100 S or D; $109–$249 ste. Extra person $10. Children under age 18 stay free. Lower rates off-season. Parking: Outdoor, free. AARP discounts and special corporate rates avail. AE, CB, DC, DISC, JCB, MC, V.

MOTEL

≡≡ **Comfort Inn of Benton Harbor**
1598 Mall Dr, 49022; tel 616/925-1880 or toll free 800/228-5150; fax 616/925-1880. Exit 29 off I-94. Recently renovated motel has upgraded furnishings and floor and wall coverings. Convenient to restaurants and shopping. **Rooms:** 52 rms. CI 2pm/CO 11am. Nonsmoking rms avail. **Amenities:** 🛜 🍴 A/C, cable TV. **Services:** 🚐 🛌 🧺 🍴 **Facilities:** 🏊 Games rm, whirlpool. **Rates (CP):** Peak (June–Sept) $50–$65 S; $55–$70 D. Extra person $5. Children under age 18 stay free. Lower rates off-season. Parking: Outdoor, free. AARP discounts and special corporate rates avail. AE, CB, DC, DISC, MC, V.

Big Rapids

Seat of Mecosta County, in central Michigan. This small town was founded in 1854 on the shores of the Muskegon River. Today, it is best-known as a gateway to Manistee National Forest. **Information:** Mecosta County Convention & Visitors Bureau, 246 N State St, Big Rapids, 49307-1445 (tel 616/796-7640).

HOTEL 🏨

≡≡≡ **Holiday Inn**
1005 Perry St, 49307; tel 616/796-4400 or toll free 800/999-9069; fax 616/796-0220. Opened in 1990, this first-class hotel providing exceptional service is a prime choice for families and business travelers alike. **Rooms:** 118 rms and stes. CI 4pm/CO noon. Nonsmoking rms avail. **Amenities:** 🛜 🍴 📺 A/C, cable TV w/movies, refrig, dataport. Some units w/whirlpools. **Services:** X 🚐 🛌 🧺 Car-rental desk. **Facilities:** 🏊 🛶 🏊2 🏇700 👤 2 restaurants, 2 bars, racquetball, sauna, whirlpool. Access to nearby tennis and workout facility. **Rates:** $68 S; $78–$87 D; $150 ste. Extra person $10. Children under age 19 stay free. Parking: Outdoor, free. Corporate rates, meeting and golf packages avail. AE, DISC, MC, V.

Birmingham

This northwest suburb of Detroit has a small-town feel. **Information:** Birmingham-Bloomfield Chamber of Commerce, 124 W Maple Rd, Birmingham, 48009-3382 (tel 810/644-1700).

HOTEL 🏨

≡≡≡≡ **The Townsend Hotel**
100 Townsend St, 48009 (Downtown); tel 810/642-7900; fax 810/645-9061. 2 blocks S of Maple, 2 blocks W of Woodward. European elegance is everywhere in this small but beautifully appointed downtown hotel, from the hand-painted murals on the lobby walls to the Waterford crystal chandelier and the Italian marble floors. Celebrities from Madonna to Margaret Thatcher have enjoyed these luxurious accommodations. **Rooms:** 87 rms and stes. CI 4pm/CO noon. Nonsmoking rms avail. Marble and brass fixtures throughout; beveled glass; individually designed floral displays in all rooms. Baths have scales. Mylar lock system can identify who entered any room and when. **Amenities:** 🛜 🍴 🍷 A/C, cable TV w/movies, dataport, VCR, voice mail, in-rm safe, bathrobes. All units w/minibars, some w/terraces, some w/whirlpools. **Services:** 🍽 🛎 VP 🚐 🛌 🧺 🍴 Twice-daily maid svce, car-rental desk, babysitting. Turndown service provides ice and fresh baked sweets. Massages can be arranged. Permission required for pets. **Facilities:** 🛶 🏇200 1 restaurant (see "Restaurants" below), 1 bar. Access to local

healthcare facilities can be arranged. **Rates:** $189–$199 S or D; $215–$235 ste. Extra person $10. Children under age 15 stay free. Parking: Indoor, free. AE, CB, DC, DISC, MC, V.

RESTAURANT

Rugby Grille

In the Townsend Hotel, 100 Townsend St; tel 810/642-7900. **Continental.** This elegant eatery presents two faces to the world. The dining room is dark and masculine, like an English club, with fireplace, sporting pictures, and upholstered club chairs. The gallery, set up in the hall outside, is bright and airy, with floral and linen tablecloths, a couch, and wing-back chairs. Spa menu items (tasty low-fat selections) change daily. Dinner selections include chargrilled chicken breast with citrus barbeque sauce, seafood fettucine, and hand-cut Angus steaks. Pastries and breads freshly baked at the Townsend Bakery. **FYI:** Reservations recommended. Piano. **Open:** Sun–Thurs 6:30am–midnight, Fri–Sat 6:30am–1am. **Prices:** Main courses $27–$33. AE, CB, DC, DISC, MC, V. VP &

Bloomfield Hills

A small, prestigious residential community nestled between Detroit and a band of glacial lakes. Many automobile industry CEOs call this posh suburb home. Site of the Cranbrook Educational Community.

HOTEL

Kingsley Hotel

1475 N Woodward Ave, 48304; tel 810/644-1400 or toll free 800/KI-HOTEL; fax 810/644-5449. Exit 75 off I-75. This Bloomfield Hills landmark is situated in a quiet suburban location near major business, shopping, and entertainment centers. Golf and year-round ice skating rink nearby. **Rooms:** 160 rms, stes, and effic. CI 3pm/CO noon. Nonsmoking rms avail. Comfortable, carefully appointed rooms. **Amenities:** A/C, cable TV w/movies, dataport, voice mail. Some units w/terraces. **Services:** X VP On-site limo service available. **Facilities:** 2 restaurants, 1 bar (w/entertainment), whirlpool, beauty salon, washer/dryer. **Rates (CP):** $94 S or D; $109–$359 ste; $119–$149 effic. Extra person $10. Children under age 18 stay free. Parking: Outdoor, free. AE, CB, DC, DISC, JCB, MC, V.

MOTEL

Holiday Inn

1801 Telegraph Rd, 48302; tel 810/334-2444 or toll free 800/465-4329; fax 810/334-4937. Exit 75 off I-75, 4 mi W to Telegraph Rd. Modern two-story motel in tree-lined courtyard setting. Fishing, golfing, Lakeland Ice Rink nearby. **Rooms:** 143 rms. CI 1pm/CO noon. Nonsmoking rms avail. Clean, comfortable rooms. **Amenities:** A/C, satel TV w/movies, dataport. Some units w/whirlpools. **Services:** X

Twice-daily maid svce. **Facilities:** 1 restaurant, 1 bar, washer/dryer. **Rates:** Peak (May–Oct) $62–$123 S; $69–$123 D. Extra person $4. Children under age 18 stay free. Lower rates off-season. AP and MAP rates avail. Parking: Outdoor, free. Ski packages avail. AE, CB, DC, DISC, JCB, MC, V.

RESTAURANTS

The Lark

6430 Farmington Rd, West Bloomfield; tel 810/661-4466. **Continental.** This intimate room, reminiscent of a Portuguese inn, seats only 50 and is booked three to four weeks in advance. Pewabic-tile wall murals decorate the foyer and cafe area, while a massive fireplace dominates the main dining room. The four-course prix fixe menu includes crispy, honey-glazed roast duckling, rack of lamb, Atlantic salmon with salmon caviar, or, weather permitting, an outdoor wood-grilled special. **FYI:** Reservations recommended. Jacket required. **Open:** Tues–Thurs 6–9pm, Fri–Sat 6–11pm. **Prices:** Prix fixe $50–$58. AE, DC, MC, V. &

Mountain Jack's Bloomfield Hills

2262 Telegraph Rd; tel 810/334-4694. **Seafood/Steak.** Popular, medium-priced chain restaurant that specializes in slow-roasted prime rib and offers other traditional steak and seafood dishes. Comfortable and relaxed setting is very popular with families. **FYI:** Reservations recommended. Children's menu. **Open:** Lunch Mon–Fri 11:30am–2pm; dinner Mon–Thurs 5–10pm, Fri 5–11pm, Sat 4–11pm, Sun noon–9pm. **Prices:** Main courses $12–$19. AE, CB, DC, MC, V. &

ATTRACTIONS

Cranbrook Art Museum

1221 N Woodward; tel 810/645-3312. Part of the Cranbrook Academy of Art (founded in 1920), the museum offers temporary exhibitions focusing on contemporary trends in the visual arts. One-person exhibitions have focused on the work of such diverse artists as Terry Allen, Keith Haring, Yoko Ono, Toshiko Takaezu, and Peter Voulkos. The museum also displays works by some of the academy's most notable graduates, including Finnish architect Eliel Saarinen and Swedish sculptor Carl Milles. **Open:** Wed, Fri–Sun 1–5pm, Thurs 10am–9pm. $$

Cranbrook Institute of Science

1221 N Woodward Ave; tel 810/645-3200. An observatory, a physics hall, and a planetarium with laser-light shows are among the most popular displays here. Prearranged group tours available; national touring exhibits come to the museum during the summer. **Open:** Mon–Thurs 10am–5pm, Fri–Sat 10am–10pm, Sun 1–5pm. $$

Cranbrook House and Gardens Auxiliary

380 Lone Pine Rd; tel 810/645-3149. This renowned center of education and culture was endowed early in this century by

Detroit News publisher George G Booth. The 288-acre estate is home to an academy of fine arts, a scientific institute with an observatory and planetarium, the picturesque Neo-Gothic Christ Church, and an impressive 1908 Tudor-style manor house (designed by Albert Kahn), all standing amid beautiful landscaped gardens with groves and fountains. House tours conducted June–Sept (Sun at 1:30 and 3pm, Thurs at 11am and 1:15pm). **Open:** Gardens, May–Aug, Mon–Sat 10am–5pm, Sun 11am–5pm. Reduced hours Sept–Oct. **$**

Holocaust Memorial Center
6602 W Maple Rd, West Bloomfield; tel 810/661-0840. The first of its kind in the United States, this center uses state-of-the-art technology to portray the Holocaust and the events leading up to it. Photographs, video testimony from survivors, artifacts depicting daily life in Nazi Germany, and a memorial flame for the six million Jewish victims of the Holocaust are among the displays. There is also a video theater and an extensive research library with books, oral histories, and microfilmed documents. **Open:** Sept–May, Sun–Thurs 10am–3:30pm, Fri 9am–12:30pm. **Free**

Boyne City

Near the northern tip of the Lower Peninsula, just south of Lake Charlevoix. Alpine-style Boyne Mountain, at nearby Boyne Falls, is a ski resort in winter, with golf and tennis in the summer. **Information:** Boyne City Chamber of Commerce, 28 S Lake St, Boyne City, 49712 (tel 616/582-6222).

HOTEL 🏨

📧📧📧 Water Street Inn
200 Front St, 49712; tel 616/582-3000 or toll free 800/456-4313. On the lakeshore with a private beach. **Rooms:** 27 stes. CI 3pm/CO 11am. Nonsmoking rms avail. Condominium suites are individually decorated to reflect a turn-of-the-century waterfront resort. **Amenities:** 🎯 🅑 🔟 A/C, cable TV w/movies, refrig, VCR. Some units w/terraces, some w/fireplaces, some w/whirlpools. **Services:** Babysitting. **Facilities:** 🅖 1 beach (lake shore). **Rates:** Peak (June–Aug) $139–$159 ste. Extra person $10. Children under age 13 stay free. Min stay special events. Lower rates off-season. Parking: Outdoor, free. Ski and golf packages avail. MC, V.

RESORT

📧📧📧 Boyne Mountain Resort
US 131, Boyne Falls, 49713; tel 616/549-6000 or toll free 800/GO-BOYNE. 6,000 acres. A year-round resort built in 1948 and rated in America's top five for snowmaking. More than 40 ski runs, with the longest being more than 5,200′. Summer guests enjoy six championship golf courses. **Rooms:** 160 rms, stes, and effic. CI 5pm/CO 1pm. Nonsmoking rms avail. **Amenities:** 🎯 🅑 A/C, cable TV w/movies, refrig. Some units w/terraces, some w/fireplaces, some w/whirlpools.

Services: ✕ 🛎 Social director, masseur, children's program, babysitting. **Facilities:** 🅖 🚲 ▶36 🛶 🖼 🎱12 🔟1000 🅖 4 restaurants, 3 bars (1 w/entertainment), 1 beach (lake shore), volleyball, lawn games, sauna. **Rates (CP):** Peak (June 16–Aug 20) $69 S or D; $96 ste; $126–$216 effic. Children under age 12 stay free. Min stay wknds. Lower rates off-season. Parking: Outdoor, free. AE, DISC, MC, V.

RESTAURANT 🍴

Stafford's One Water Street
1 Water St; tel 616/582-3434. **Regional American.** Waterfront cafe with views of Lake Charlevoix, a gazebo, and lots of greenery. The "American Heartland" menu focuses on wild game and fresh local seafood: whitefish dusted in spices and "blackened" in an iron skillet, chicken Dennison, grilled Norwegian salmon. **FYI:** Reservations accepted. Children's menu. **Open:** Mon–Sat 11:30am–11pm, Sun noon–10pm. **Prices:** Main courses $17–$25. AE, DISC, MC, V. ♥ 🏔 📷 🅖

Boyne Falls

See Boyne City

Cadillac

Seat of Wexford County, in northwest part of state. This former lumbering town was founded in 1871 on the shores of Lakes Cadillac and Mitchell. Nearby William Mitchell State Park has about 260 acres between the two lakes. **Information:** Cadillac Area Visitors Bureau, 222 Lake St, Cadillac, 49601 (tel 616/775-9776).

HOTELS 🏨

📧📧📧 Best Western Bill Oliver's Resort and Conference Center
865 S Lake Mitchell Dr, 49601; tel 616/775-2458 or toll free 800/OLIVER-5; fax 616/775-8383. On MI 55, W of MI 115. A four-season hotel with conference and banquet facilities for up to 500 people. **Rooms:** 66 rms. CI 3pm/CO 11am. No smoking. **Amenities:** 🎯 🅑 A/C, cable TV w/movies, VCR. Some units w/terraces, some w/fireplaces. **Services:** ✕ 🆅🅿 🛎 🛎 Babysitting. **Facilities:** 🅖 🛶 🖼 🔟500 🅖 1 restaurant, 2 bars (w/entertainment), basketball, volleyball, lawn games, spa, sauna, whirlpool. Many sports available, including bowling. **Rates (CP):** Peak (July–Aug/Dec–Feb) $56–$72 S or D. Extra person $5. Children under age 16 stay free. Lower rates off-season. Parking: Outdoor, free. Weekend, corporate, and golf packages. AE, MC, V.

📧📧 Days Inn Cadillac
6001 MI 115, 49601; tel 616/775-4414 or toll free 800/325-2525; fax 616/779-0370. An especially nice Days Inn located downtown. **Rooms:** 60 rms and stes. CI 3pm/CO 11am. Nonsmoking rms avail. **Amenities:** 🎯 🅑 A/C, cable TV

w/movies, refrig, in-rm safe. Some units w/whirlpools. **Services:** ⬡⬡⬡ Nice staff and friendly service. **Facilities:** ⬡⬡⬡⬡⬡⬡ Whirlpool. **Rates (CP):** Peak (Feb–Mar/July–Aug/Dec) $45–$70 S; $50–$100 D; $95–$120 ste. Extra person $5. Children under age 12 stay free. Lower rates off-season. Parking: Outdoor, free. AE, MC, V.

MOTEL

⬭⬭ Sun and Snow Motel
301 S Lake Mitchell, 49601; tel 616/775-9961 or toll free 800/477-9961; fax 616/775-3846. Jct MI 115/55; on Lake Mitchell. Alpine appearance, with three acres and many trees. Swimming, fishing, paddleboating, bicycling, tennis, skiing, and snowmobiling nearby. Close to popular restaurant. A four-season motel. **Rooms:** 29 rms and stes. CI 3pm/CO 11am. Nonsmoking rms avail. The rooms have a rustic feel with knotty pine walls. **Amenities:** ⬡⬡ A/C, cable TV w/movies, refrig, VCR. **Services:** ⬡⬡ **Facilities:** ⬡⬡ 1 beach (lake shore). **Rates:** Peak (June–Oct) $48–$69 S or D; $110 ste. Extra person $5. Children under age 12 stay free. Lower rates off-season. Parking: Outdoor, free. DISC, MC, V.

RESORTS

⬭⬭ Cadillac Sands Resort
6319 MI 115, 49601; tel 616/775-2407 or toll free 800/647-2637. Jct MI 115/55. A 1960s hotel. **Rooms:** 53 rms and stes. Executive level. CI 3pm/CO 11am. No smoking. **Amenities:** ⬡⬡ A/C, cable TV w/movies, refrig. Some units w/terraces, some w/whirlpools. Theme rooms (Art Deco, Elvis, Jungle, etc) available with whirlpools. **Services:** ⬡⬡ **Facilities:** ⬡⬡⬡⬡⬡⬡⬡⬡ 1 restaurant (dinner only), 2 bars (1 w/entertainment), 1 beach (lake shore), volleyball. Large night club. Boat and snowmobile rentals, bicycles, and jet skis. **Rates (CP):** Peak (June–Sept) $69–$125 S or D; $185 ste. Extra person $5. Children under age 12 stay free. Lower rates off-season. Parking: Outdoor, free. Special corporate rates avail. AE, DC, DISC, MC, V.

UNRATED McGuire's Resort
7880 Mackinaw Trail, 49601; tel 616/775-9947 or toll free 800/632-7302; fax 616/775-9621. 320 acres. A four-season recreational resort with a panoramic 27-hole golf course and exercise trails. Close to other ski areas, ice skating, fishing, sailing, canoeing, waterskiing, sailboarding. **Rooms:** 123 rms and stes. CI 4pm/CO 11am. Nonsmoking rms avail. **Amenities:** ⬡⬡⬡ ⬡ A/C, cable TV, refrig, dataport. Some units w/terraces, some w/whirlpools. **Services:** ✕⬡⬡ **Facilities:** ⬡⬡⬡⬡⬡⬡⬡⬡⬡⬡ 1 restaurant, 2 bars (1 w/entertainment), basketball, volleyball, games rm, lawn games, sauna, whirlpool, washer/dryer. Nordic cross country ski trails on golf course in winter. **Rates:** Peak (June–Aug) $65–$99 S; $89–$99 D; $99–$179 ste. Lower rates off-

season. Parking: Outdoor, free. Golf academy package offered in May. Golf and tennis packages and holiday packages also avail. AE, MC, V.

RESTAURANTS ⏚

★ Burke's Waterfront Restaurant
2501 Sunnyside Dr; tel 616/775-7555. **American.** A friendly spot with booths, patio dining, and a lovely view of Lake Cadillac. The menu focuses on sandwiches and seafood entrees. Dinner buffet offered Friday to Sunday. **FYI:** Reservations accepted. Children's menu. **Open:** Peak (June–Sept) daily 6am–11pm. **Prices:** Main courses $8–$15. AE, DISC, MC, V. ⬡⬡⬡

⬯★ Hermann's European Cafe & Inn
214 N Mitchell St; tel 616/775-9536. **International.** International specialties—including Weiner schnitzel, chicken breast piccata, shrimp tempura, Swedish-style wild boar, and various pastas, salads, and cold plates—served in a romantic, European atmosphere. Chef/owner Hermann is originally from Austria but he says he has cooked his way around the world. Chef's Deli next door offers carryout wine, beer, and food. **FYI:** Reservations accepted. **Open:** Mon–Sat 11am–10pm. **Prices:** Main courses $8–$20. MC, V. ⬡⬡

ATTRACTION ⬯

Huron-Manistee National Forests
Forest Supervisor, 421 S Mitchell; tel toll free 800/821-6263. These two forests, on opposite shores of the Lower Peninsula, cover nearly 1 million acres of land. The Huron National Forest (on the shore of Lake Huron) is traversed by the Au Sable River and the 22-mile River Road Scenic Byway, which runs parallel to the river. Also in the Huron section is the Lumberman's Monument, a bronze statue commemorating the early loggers of the area. Today, the Au Sable is a haven for canoeing and trout fishing.

The highlight of the Manistee section is the Lake Michigan Recreation Area, which provides opportunities for hiking, biking, camping and picnicking along the western coast of the Lower Peninsula. Both forests also offer cross-country skiing and horseback riding. **Open:** Daily 24 hours. **Free**

Calumet

See also Hancock, Houghton

Small Upper Peninsula town perched on the Keweenaw Peninsula, which juts into Lake Superior. The elaborate 1899 Calumet Theatre, built with boom town wealth, hosted the likes of Lillian Russell, Sarah Bernhardt, Lon Cheney, Otis Skinner, Douglas Fairbanks, and John Philip Sousa. **Information:** Keweenaw Tourism Council, 1197 Calumet, Calumet, 49913 (tel 906/337-4579).

MOTEL 🏨

≣ Whispering Pine Motel
Rt 41, PO Box 85, 49913; tel 906/482-5887; fax 906/482-6173. Traditional motel nestled in a shady pine forest. Convenient to downtown Houghton shopping and rural skiing. Close to the Quincy Mine Tour. **Rooms:** 16 rms. CI 11am/CO 11am. Nonsmoking rms avail. **Amenities:** 🛁 TV. No A/C or phone. **Services:** 🚗 ➔ **Facilities:** 🏃 🎦 **Rates:** $30 S; $36 D. Parking: Outdoor, free. AE, CB, DC, DISC, MC, V.

ATTRACTION 🏛

Calumet Theatre
340 6th St; tel 906/337-2610. Stars like Lillian Russell, Sarah Bernhardt, Lon Chaney, Douglas Fairbanks, and John Philip Sousa appeared at this ornate turn-of-the-century theater. It has been restored in recent years and now presents live performances. **Open:** Tours, Mon–Thurs 10am–4pm, Fri 10am–1pm, Sat–Sun noon–4pm. Call for theater schedule. $

Cascade

See Grand Rapids

Cedar

See Traverse City

Charlevoix

Seat of Charlevoix County in the northwest part of state. A ferry steamer makes the two-hour trip to Beaver Island in Lake Michigan. **Information:** Charlevoix Area Convention & Visitors Bureau, 408 Bridge St, Charlevoix, 49720 (tel 616/547-2101).

HOTELS 🏨

≣≣ Sleep Inn
801 Petoskey Ave, 49720; tel 616/547-0300 or toll free 800/221-2222. On MI 31. A new hotel (opened in 1995) at the edge of town. **Rooms:** 59 rms. CI 3pm/CO 11am. Nonsmoking rms avail. **Amenities:** 🛁 🛁 A/C, cable TV w/movies. **Services:** ➔ 🛎 Friendly staff. **Facilities:** 🎦 🏃 🎦 🏊 ⅓ Whirlpool. Nice indoor pool. **Rates:** Peak (June–Aug) $78–$116 S or D. Extra person $5. Children under age 12 stay free. Lower rates off-season. Parking: Outdoor, free. AE, MC, V.

≣≣≣ Weathervane Terrace Hotel
111 Pine River Lane, 49720; tel 616/547-9955 or toll free 800/552-0025; fax 616/547-9955. Well-known hotel located on channel and convenient to downtown and public beach.

Rooms: 68 rms, stes, and effic. CI 3pm/CO 11am. Nonsmoking rms avail. **Amenities:** 🛁 🛁 📺 🍴 A/C, cable TV w/movies, refrig, VCR. Some units w/terraces, some w/fireplaces, some w/whirlpools. **Services:** 🛥 🛎 **Facilities:** 🎦 🏃 🎦 🏊 Spa. **Rates (CP):** Peak (June 23–Sept 3) $95–$115 S or D; $160–$170 ste; $115 effic. Extra person $5. Children under age 13 stay free. Min stay special events. Lower rates off-season. Parking: Outdoor, free. AE, DISC, MC, V.

MOTELS

≣ Archway Motel
1440 S Bridge St, 49720; tel 616/547-2096. Just N of MI 66 on US 31. Nice, functional motel, located at the edge of town. **Rooms:** 14 rms. CI noon/CO 10am. Nonsmoking rms avail. **Amenities:** 🛁 🛁 A/C, cable TV w/movies. **Services:** 🚗 ➔ 🛎 Transportation to and from Charlevoix Airport and Round Lake available for guests arriving by plane or boat. **Facilities:** 🎦 **Rates:** Peak (July 1–Aug 15) $80–$99 S; $89–$99 D. Extra person $5. Children under age 12 stay free. Min stay peak. Lower rates off-season. Parking: Outdoor, free. DISC, MC, V.

≣ Capri Motel
1445 S Bridge St, 49720; tel 616/547-2545. Jct US 31/MI 66. Basic motel at edge of town; offers reasonable rates for the area. **Rooms:** 17 rms. CI 11am/CO 11am. Nonsmoking rms avail. **Amenities:** 🛁 🛁 A/C, cable TV. **Rates:** Peak (June–Aug) $65 S or D. Extra person $6. Children under age 12 stay free. Lower rates off-season. Parking: Outdoor, free. AE, MC, V.

UNRATED The Lodge of Charlevoix
US 31 N, 49720 (Downtown); tel 616/547-6565. In business for a long time, motel overlooks Pine River Channel and Round Lake Harbor. Walking distance to everything downtown. **Rooms:** 40 rms, stes, and effic. CI 1:30pm/CO 11am. Nonsmoking rms avail. **Amenities:** 🛁 🛁 A/C, cable TV w/movies, refrig. Some units w/terraces. **Services:** 🛎 Pets $12. **Facilities:** 🎦 ⅓ **Rates:** Peak (June–Aug) $95–$105 S or D; $155 ste; $165 effic. Extra person $5. Children under age 12 stay free. Lower rates off-season. Parking: Outdoor, free. AE, DC, MC, V.

RESTAURANTS 🍴

★ Alexander's
557 Petoskey Ave (US 31N); tel 616/547-2550. **Seafood/Steak.** Located five minutes north of downtown Charlevoix, Alexander's is known locally for good breakfasts and casual dining in a cozy atmosphere. The menu offers a range of items including chicken, steak, shrimp, and vegetable stir fry. **FYI:** Reservations accepted. Children's menu. **Open:** Mon–Sat 6:30am–10pm, Sun 6:30am–1pm. **Prices:** Main courses $8–$14. AE, MC, V. 👥 ⅓

Stafford's Weathervane Restaurant
106 Pine River Lane; tel 616/547-4311. **American.** A well-known local spot in a historic stone building at the Pine River Bridge. Most tables have good views of the drawbridge on the Pine River Channel. A good place for lunch or dinner, Stafford's serves premium steaks, fresh local whitefish, and other seafood. **FYI:** Reservations recommended. **Open:** Lunch Mon–Fri 11:30am–4pm, Sat 11:30am–4pm, Sun noon–4pm; dinner Mon–Thurs 5–10pm, Fri–Sat 5–11pm, Sun 5–10pm. **Prices:** Main courses $16–$23. AE, MC, V. ♥ 🖼️ ⛰️ ♿

Whitneys of Charlevoix
305 Bridge St; tel 616/526-7800. **Eclectic.** Reminiscent of a turn-of-the-century New England oyster house, Whitney's offers a casual atmosphere and a wide variety of dishes to suit every taste. Over 70 beers from around the world are available, as well as wine by the bottle or glass. The menu consists of sandwiches, steaks, seafood, and other simple fare. **FYI:** Reservations accepted. Jazz/piano. **Open:** Lunch daily 11:30am–3pm; dinner Sun–Thurs 5–10pm, Fri–Sat 5–10:30pm. **Prices:** Main courses $7–$22. MC, V. ♥

Cheboygan

Seat of Cheboygan County. This northern Michigan town is surrounded by Douglas, Burt, and Mullet Lakes—not to mention Lake Michigan, Lake Huron, and the Cheboygan River. The icebreaker *Mackinaw* and the ferry to Mackinac Island both dock here. **Information:** Cheboygan Area Chamber of Commerce, 124 N Main St, PO Box 69, Cheboygan, 49721 (tel 616/627-7183 or toll free 800/968-3302).

HOTELS 🏨

Best Western River Terrace
847 Main St, 49721; tel 616/627-5688 or toll free 800/528-1234. An especially nice Best Western located on the Cheboygan River, the famous 40-mile inland waterway. Guests can walk along the river boardwalk. Close to Cheboygan State Parks and snowmobiling or cross-country skiing. 15 miles to Mackinaw Bridge. **Rooms:** 53 rms. CI 1pm/CO 11am. Nonsmoking rms avail. **Amenities:** 🛏️ 👤 📶 A/C, cable TV w/movies, refrig. Some units w/terraces, some w/whirlpools. **Services:** 🛎️ **Facilities:** 🏋️ 🏊 🚲 ♿ Spa, whirlpool. 700′ of boat dockage. Nice indoor pool area with an outside view. **Rates:** Peak (July–Aug) $77–$107 S or D. Extra person $10. Lower rates off-season. Parking: Outdoor, free. AE, MC, V.

Days Inn
889 S Main St, 49721; tel 616/627-3126 or toll free 800/DAYS-INN. Located on Cheboygan River. **Rooms:** 28 rms and stes. CI 3pm/CO 11am. Nonsmoking rms avail. All rooms have river view. **Amenities:** 🛏️ 👤 A/C, cable TV w/movies, refrig. Some units w/terraces. **Services:** 🧺 🛎️ 🛎️

Facilities: 🏊 **Rates:** Peak (June–Aug) $78–$90 S or D; $125–$150 ste. Children under age 12 stay free. Lower rates off-season. Parking: Outdoor, free. AE, DISC, MC, V.

RESTAURANT 🍴

The Boathouse
106 Pine St; tel 616/627-4316. **American.** Originally built over the Cheboygan River in 1940, this boathouse-turned-cafe is a great place for casual dining in an elegant atmosphere. The menu includes burgers and sandwiches, and entrees such as chargrilled salmon Santiago, New Zealand rack of lamb, and seafood ravioli. Blue-plate specials available. **FYI:** Reservations accepted. Children's menu. **Open:** Sun–Thurs 11am–9pm, Fri–Sat 11am–10pm. **Prices:** Main courses $8–$20; prix fixe $12. AE, MC, V. ♥ ⛰️ ♿

ATTRACTION 🏛️

The Opera House
403 N Huron St; tel 616/627-5432 or toll free 800/357-9408. Originally constructed in 1877 but ravaged by fires in 1888 and 1903, this reconstructed gem of a building now houses its original combination of City Hall, Police Department, Fire Department, and the historic Opera House itself. Since reopening in 1984, the 582-seat Opera House has seen performances by the Detroit Symphony Orchestra, the Grand Rapids Symphony, the Michigan Opera Theater, Donny and Marie Osmond, the Indianapolis Ballet Theater, and other well-known productions. Guided tours are offered during the summer months between the hours of 1–4pm; winter tours available by appointment. **Open:** Office: Tues–Fri 9:30am–4:30pm. Call for performance schedule. $$$$

Clare

Central Michigan town just north of the Isabella Indian Reservation. Settled by Irish immigrants, the town celebrates its heritage with an Irish Festival every March. **Information:** Clare Area Chamber of Commerce, 609 McEwan St, Clare, 48617 (tel 517/386-2442).

MOTEL 🏨

Budget Host Clare Motel
1110 N McEwan, 48617; tel 517/386-7201 or toll free 800/825-2738; fax 517/386-2362. Average motel located eight miles from Mott and Snowshoe Mountains. **Rooms:** 43 rms. CI 3pm/CO 11am. Nonsmoking rms avail. **Amenities:** 🛏️ 👤 📶 A/C, cable TV w/movies, refrig. Some units w/whirlpools. **Services:** 🛎️ 🛎️ **Facilities:** 🏋️ 🏊 **Rates:** $38–$44 S; $52–$100 D. Extra person $7. Children under age 12 stay free. Parking: Outdoor, free. AE, DISC, MC, V.

RESTAURANT 🍽

★ **Town and Country**
1395 N McEwan; tel 517/386-7567. **American.** Sicilian steak, 18-oz New York strip steak, and fresh lake perch are among the highlights at this large, family-friendly place. There's a salad bar for lighter appetites, and homemade pies for dessert. Smaller entree portions are available. **FYI:** Reservations accepted. Children's menu. **Open:** Peak (May–Oct) Mon–Sat 4–10pm, Sun noon–6pm. **Prices:** Main courses $6–$15. AE, DISC, MC, V. 🅿️ &

Coldwater

Seat of Branch County, in southern Michigan. This handsome city is handy to Coldwater Lake, a destination loved by boaters. The beautifully renovated Tibbits Opera House (built in 1882) is home to a professional summer theater series. **Information:** Branch County Tourism Bureau, 20 Division St, Coldwater, 49036 (tel 517/278-5985 or toll free 800/968-9333).

HOTEL 🏨

🏳🏳🏳 **Quality Inn and Convention Center**
1000 Orleans Blvd, 49036; tel 517/278-2017 or toll free 800/638-2657; fax 517/279-7214. Exit 13 off I-69; W to first light; N to entrance. Arched windows give the exterior a southwestern look, but inside, everything is geared to a New Orleans theme. Easy access to highway. Washer/dryer for guests' use located at adjoining hotel. **Rooms:** 122 rms, stes, and effic. CI 3pm/CO 11am. Nonsmoking rms avail. **Amenities:** 🛋 Ⓐ A/C, cable TV, dataport. Some units w/terraces, 1 w/whirlpool. **Services:** ✕ 🖼 🛎 🛜 Local airport transportation. Small pets only, with permission. **Facilities:** 🏊 🏋 📺 & 1 restaurant, 1 bar (w/entertainment), games rm, whirlpool. **Rates (CP):** $56–$61 S or D; $85–$125 ste; $60–$80 effic. Extra person $5. Children under age 18 stay free. Min stay special events. Parking: Outdoor, free. AE, DC, DISC, JCB, MC, V.

MOTEL

🏳 **Little King Motel**
847 E Chicago Rd, 49036; tel 517/278-6660 or toll free 800/341-8000. Exit 13 (US 12) off I-69; E ½ mi to entrance. The old-time comic strip character "Little King" marks the entrance to this single-story motel. **Rooms:** 18 rms. CI noon/CO 11am. **Amenities:** 🛋 A/C, cable TV w/movies. **Services:** 🛎 🛜 **Facilities:** 🏊 Picnic area and grills. **Rates:** Peak (May–Oct) $34–$38 S; $38–$46 D. Extra person $4. Children under age 3 stay free. Min stay special events. Lower rates off-season. Parking: Outdoor, free. AE, DISC, MC, V.

ATTRACTIONS 🏛

Wing House Museum
27 S Jefferson St; tel 517/278-2871. Now open to the public, this beautifully renovated Empire-style home (built circa 1875) has more than three-quarters of its original furniture, china, and crystal still in place. Displays include a well-preserved collection of period art and family photographs. **Open:** Daily 1–5pm. **$**

Tibbits Opera House
14 S Hanchett St; tel 517/278-6029. Built in 1881, this renovated Victorian-style opera house is home to professional summer theater performances and year-round concerts in classical music, jazz, and folk. **Open:** Box office, Mon–Fri 9am–5pm. **$$$**

Copper Harbor

Michigan's northernmost village (at the tip of the Keweenaw Peninsula) is a small but lovely resort with summer ferry service to Isle Royale National Park. Many nearby streams and inland lakes provide fishing opportunities. Nearby Fort Wilkins, built in 1844, has been restored to its frontier post atmosphere.

MOTELS 🏨

🏳 **Astor House**
560 Gratiot, PO Box 31, 49918; tel 906/289-4448. Overlooks Copper Harbor and near downtown shops and restaurants. Its appearance is somewhat marred by a tacky gift shop on the property. Private saunas available across the street for $5. **Rooms:** 13 rms; 12 cottages/villas. CI 2pm/CO 10:30am. Cottages sleep up to 10 guests. **Amenities:** Ⓐ Cable TV, refrig. No A/C or phone. **Services:** 🛎 🛜 Babysitting. **Facilities:** 🏛 Small antique and Native American artifact museum on premises. **Rates:** $45 S or D; $45–$85 cottage/villa. Parking: Outdoor, free. Closed Oct–May. DISC, MC, V.

🏳🏳 **Bella Vista Motel**
160 6th St, 49918; tel 906/289-4213. Casual family atmosphere, with a gorgeous view of Copper Harbor. Within walking distance of enchanting shops, restaurants, and ferry to Isle Royale. **Rooms:** 22 rms; 8 cottages/villas. CI 3pm/CO 11am. Standard motel rooms. **Amenities:** Cable TV, refrig. No A/C or phone. Some units w/terraces, some w/fireplaces. Rooms have lovely lakeside balconies. **Services:** 🛎 Babysitting. The host is likely to lend you cooking utensils for your cottage. Freshly baked cookies often lure guests to the office. Friendly, personal service. **Facilities:** 🏖 🅿️ 🏛 1 beach (lake shore), snorkeling, playground. **Rates:** $38–$45 S; $42–$50 D; $234–$360 cottage/villa. Extra person $3. Parking: Outdoor, free. Closed Oct–May. MC, V.

RESORT

≡≡≡ Keweenaw Mountain Lodge

US 41, 49918; tel 906/289-4403. 167 acres. Gorgeous wooded resort originally built by the WPA in the 1930s featuring furnished log cabins. Good spot for hiking. Though situated high in the hills, there is a constant cooling breeze from Lake Superior. **Rooms:** 8 rms; 36 cottages/villas. CI 1pm/CO 10am. **Amenities:** Cable TV w/movies, bathrobes. No A/C. Some units w/fireplaces. **Services:** **Facilities:** 1 restaurant, 1 bar, lawn games. **Rates:** $55 S; $74 D; $74 cottage/villa. Extra person $5. Parking: Outdoor, free. Closed Oct–May. MC, V.

Dearborn

One of the oldest Detroit suburbs (founded in 1763), and home of the world headquarters of Ford Motor Company. Henry Ford was born here in 1863; in 1929, he established the Henry Ford Museum and Greenfield Village. Called "Henry Ford's attic," the museum stands as a tribute to American resourcefulness and technology. **Information:** Dearborn Chamber of Commerce, 15544 Michigan Ave, Dearborn, 48126 (tel 313/584-6100).

HOTELS

≡≡≡ The Dearborn Inn—A Marriott Hotel

20301 Oakwood Blvd, 48124 (Greenfield Village); tel 313/271-2700 or toll free 800/321-2049; fax 313/271-7464. MI 39 to Oakwood; W 2 mi. Opened as the world's first airport hotel in 1931, this Georgian-style inn on 23 acres was another of Henry Ford's ideas. The onetime airport across the street is now a Ford test track, but the hotel's location, about three blocks from Greenfield Village and halfway between Detroit Metro Airport and downtown Detroit, is still convenient for business and pleasure travelers. Colonial decor throughout hotel, two adjacent lodges, and five replica historic homes, including those of Edgar Allan Poe and Patrick Henry. **Rooms:** 222 rms and stes; 5 cottages/villas. Executive level. CI 4pm/CO noon. Nonsmoking rms avail. **Amenities:** A/C, cable TV w/movies, dataport, voice mail. Some units w/terraces. **Services:** Car-rental desk, babysitting. **Facilities:** 3 restaurants, 1 bar (w/entertainment), volleyball. **Rates:** Peak (May–Nov) $149 S; $155 D; $175 ste; $175 cottage/villa. Extra person $15. Children under age 12 stay free. Min stay special events. Lower rates off-season. Parking: Outdoor, free. AE, CB, DC, DISC, MC, V.

≡≡ Hampton Inn Dearborn

20061 Michigan Ave, 48124 (Greenfield Village); tel 313/436-9600 or toll free 800/HAMPTON; fax 313/436-8345. ¼ mi W of MI 39. Henry Ford Museum and Greenfield Village are backyard neighbors of this well-kept property. **Rooms:** 119 rms and stes. CI 3pm/CO noon. Nonsmoking

rms avail. Rooms on back side of hotel overlook historic buildings of Greenfield Village. **Amenities:** A/C, cable TV w/movies, dataport, voice mail. **Services:** Babysitting. Extended continental breakfast buffet. **Facilities:** Washer/dryer. **Rates (CP):** Peak (May–Sept) $69 S; $79 D; $83–$93 ste. Children under age 18 stay free. Lower rates off-season. Parking: Outdoor, free. AE, CB, DC, DISC, MC, V.

≡≡≡ Hyatt Regency Dearborn

Fairlane Town Center, 48126; tel 313/593-1234 or toll free 800/233-1234; fax 313/593-3366. W of MI 39; N of Michigan Ave. Crescent-shaped with bronze reflective glass exterior, this convention hotel caters to business travelers and tour groups. Within walking distance of sprawling Fairlane Mall. **Rooms:** 771 rms and stes. Executive level. CI 3pm/CO noon. Nonsmoking rms avail. Spacious rooms with wide views of metro area. **Amenities:** A/C, satel TV w/movies. Coffeemakers, hair dryers, irons at additional cost. **Services:** Car-rental desk, masseur, babysitting. **Facilities:** 2 restaurants, 2 bars, games rm, spa, sauna, whirlpool. **Rates:** $155 S; $180 D; $350–$750 ste. Extra person $15. Children under age 18 stay free. Min stay special events. Parking: Outdoor, free. AE, CB, DC, DISC, MC, V.

≡≡≡≡ The Ritz-Carlton Dearborn

300 Town Center Dr, 48126 (Fairlane Town Center); tel 313/441-2000 or toll free 800/241-3333; fax 313/441-2051. Just W of MI 39 S off Hubbard Dr. Quiet luxury, with fine art and antiques in lobby and adjacent public areas. A favorite of visiting celebrities. **Rooms:** 308 rms and stes. Executive level. CI 3pm/CO noon. Nonsmoking rms avail. Well-appointed rooms with views of Ford Motor country. **Amenities:** A/C, cable TV w/movies, in-rm safe, bathrobes. All units w/minibars. **Services:** Twice-daily maid svce, car-rental desk, masseur, babysitting. Visit the tea room for afternoon refreshments. The cordial staff prides itself on its dedication to service. Covered valet parking $12/day. **Facilities:** 1 restaurant, 1 bar (w/entertainment), spa, sauna, whirlpool. Guests may use athletic facilities at nearby Fairlane Club for nominal fee. **Rates:** $135–$195 S or D; $375–$425 ste. Extra person $15. Children under age 18 stay free. Parking: Outdoor, free. Special rates for family connecting rooms. AE, CB, DC, DISC, ER, JCB, MC, V.

MOTELS

≡≡ Courtyard by Marriott Dearborn

5200 Mercury Dr, 48126; tel 313/271-1400 or toll free 800/321-2211; fax 313/271-1184. E of MI 39; between Ford Rd and Michigan Ave. Courtyard reliability in location convenient to Henry Ford Museum and Greenfield Village, Ford World Headquarters. **Rooms:** 147 rms and stes. CI 3pm/CO noon. Nonsmoking rms avail. **Amenities:** A/C, cable TV w/movies, dataport, voice mail. Some units w/terraces. **Services:** Breakfast buffet available. **Facilities:** 1 restaurant (bkfst only), 1 bar, washer/dryer.

Rates: Peak (June–Aug) $69–$85 S or D; $95 ste. Children under age 18 stay free. Min stay special events. Lower rates off-season. Parking: Outdoor, free. AE, CB, DC, DISC, MC, V.

▤ Knights Inn
23730 Michigan Ave, 48124; tel 313/565-7250 or toll free 800/843-5644; fax 313/565-0708. I-94 to Telegraph Rd N. On busy Michigan Ave, convenient for budget-minded Greenfield Village visitors who can overlook the motel's shabby exterior. **Rooms:** 80 rms. CI 2pm/CO noon. Nonsmoking rms avail. Very well-kept rooms needing minor maintenance. **Amenities:** 🛏 🕹 📺 🍷 A/C, cable TV, refrig. Some units w/whirlpools. **Services:** ✕ **Facilities:** 🖼 ᕒ 1 restaurant. **Rates:** Peak (Apr–Sept) $49–$80 S or D. Extra person $5. Children under age 12 stay free. Lower rates off-season. Parking: Outdoor, free. AE, CB, DC, DISC, MC, V.

▤▤ Quality Inn Dearborn
21430 Michigan Ave, 48124; tel 313/565-0800 or toll free 800/228-5151; fax 313/565-2813. Off US 39. Surprisingly quiet for its location on Dearborn's six-lane main street. **Rooms:** 100 rms. CI 3pm/CO noon. Nonsmoking rms avail. Unremarkable, tidy rooms. **Amenities:** 🛏 🕹 A/C, cable TV w/movies, refrig, VCR. Some units w/whirlpools. **Services:** 🚗 ⌹ ⌂ **Facilities:** 🖼 ⌷ ᕒ **Rates (CP):** $79–$119 S or D. Extra person $5. Children under age 18 stay free. Parking: Outdoor, free. Greenfield Village packages avail. AE, CB, DC, DISC, MC, V.

▤ Red Roof Inn Dearborn
24130 Michigan Ave, 48124; tel 313/278-9732 or toll free 800/843-7663; fax 313/278-9741. At Telegraph Rd. Tucked away and relatively quiet, despite location near busy interchange. **Rooms:** 112 rms. CI 2pm/CO noon. Nonsmoking rms avail. Tidy rooms. **Amenities:** 🛏 A/C, satel TV w/movies, dataport. **Services:** ⌂ ⟨⟩ **Facilities:** ᕒ **Rates:** Peak (May–Sept) $39–$54 S; $49–$64 D. Extra person $10. Children under age 18 stay free. Lower rates off-season. Parking: Outdoor, free. AE, DC, DISC, MC, V.

RESTAURANTS 🍽

Big Fish
700 Town Center Dr (Fairlane Town Center); tel 313/336-6350. N of Michigan Ave; W of US 39. **Seafood.** No need to guess about the menu here: From the name to the photos, sculpture, and place mats, this dining room's emphasis on seafood couldn't be plainer. In addition to great fresh fish, the menu lists pasta, lamb shank, and strip steak. **FYI:** Reservations accepted. Jazz/piano. Children's menu. Additional location: 111 W 14 Mile, Madison Heights (tel 810/585-9533). **Open:** Mon–Thurs 11am–10pm, Fri 11am–11pm, Sat 11:30am–11pm. **Prices:** Main courses $11–$27. AE, DISC, MC, V. 🖼 ᕒ

Kiernan's Steak House
21931 Michigan Ave; tel 313/565-8975. 1½ mi W of US 39. **American.** A family-owned institution, started in 1965, with a dark and clubby barroom. Silk-fringed lamps over each table lend a red glow to the leather chairs, banquettes, and booths in the dining room. If you don't want steak, try the 16-oz lobster tails. **FYI:** Reservations recommended. **Open:** Mon–Fri 11am–midnight, Sat 5pm–midnight, Sun 4–9pm. **Prices:** Main courses $7–$27. AE, MC, V. 🅥🅟 ᕒ

The Mad Hatter Cafe
1024 Monroe; tel 313/274-0000. 1 block S of Michigan Ave, 1½ mi W of US 39. **Cafe/Coffeehouse.** Alice would feel at home in this storefront cafe and coffeehouse featuring scenes from Wonderland as well as a teapot collection. Special marinated chicken breasts are featured on a menu with a Middle Eastern twist. Vegetarian entrees, too. **FYI:** Reservations accepted. Blues/folk/jazz/classical. No liquor license. **Open:** Sun–Thurs 10:30am–midnight, Fri–Sat 10:30am–2am. **Prices:** Main courses $8–$12. AE, MC, V.

ATTRACTIONS 🏛

Henry Ford Museum and Greenfield Village
Village Rd and Oakwood Blvd; tel 313/271-1620 or toll free 800/835-2246. Established in 1929 by Henry Ford, the museum is intended as a tribute to the dynamism and inventiveness of the American people. It presents a complete panorama of the country's technological and cultural development, with a very rich collection of art and handcrafts; an aircraft and automobile museum (including the first car built by Henry Ford, a great 600-ton Allegheny locomotive, and the Fokker aircraft in which Admiral Byrd first flew over the North Pole in 1926); and a vintage merry-go-round.

The adjacent Greenfield Village comprises 100 or so 17th-, 18th-, and 19th-century buildings drawn from all parts of the country and restored with scrupulous care. Among them are Henry Ford's birthplace, Edison's laboratory, and the courthouse in which Abraham Lincoln appeared as an attorney. **Open:** Daily 9am–5pm. **$$$$**

Henry Ford Estate—Fair Lane
4901 Evergreen Rd; tel 313/593-5590. On the University of Michigan–Dearborn campus. This pseudo-Scottish castle was built by Henry Ford in 1915 at the then-exorbitant cost of $2 million. The rough-stone main house has 56 rooms and—suitably enough—a garage for 12 cars. The 72-acre property also encompasses gardens, grottos, a children's playhouse, and miles of hiking paths. **Open:** Mon–Sat 10am–2:30pm, Sun 12:30–4pm. **$$**

Detroit

See also Allen Park, Birmingham, Bloomfield Hills, Dearborn, Farmington Hills, Madison Heights, Novi, Northville, Plymouth, Romulus, Southfield, Southgate, Sterling Heights, Troy, Warren

Founded by the French in 1701 as a fort and fur-trading settlement, Detroit is one of the oldest US cities west of the original 13 colonies. Long known as Motor City due to its prominence in the automotive industry, the city's new maturity is seen in the marble-white buildings of the civic center, the four towers of the Renaissance Center, the remarkable architecture of Wayne State University, and the city's abundance of museums, art galleries, and libraries. Detroit is the largest city in Michigan, and one of the few cities in the United States where you can look due south into Canada. **Information:** Metropolitan Detroit Convention & Visitors Bureau, 100 Renaissance Center, #1900, Detroit, 48243-1056 (tel 313/259-4333).

PUBLIC TRANSPORTATION

The **People Mover** (313/224-2160), an elevated, automated rail system, circles downtown and stops at major hotels and attractions; fare is 50¢ (exact change or tokens accepted). For city **bus service** information, call 313/933-1300.

HOTELS 🏨

☰☰☰ Atheneum Suite Hotel and Conference Center

1000 Brush Ave, 48226 (Greektown); tel 313/962-2323 or toll free 800/772-2323; fax 313/962-2424. At Lafayette, 4 blocks N of Renaissance Center. It's all Greek—from floors of imported marble to the imposing 25-foot tall mural—but the translation is simple: luxurious lodging. A popular Cajun restaurant, Fishbones, is adjacent, and Greektown nightlife and dining is one block away. **Rooms:** 174 stes. CI 3pm/CO noon. Nonsmoking rms avail. Suites range from studios (one room, two levels) to a spacious Presidential Apartment, housed in the former Ferry Morse Seed Company warehouse. **Amenities:** 🛁 ⚡ 🗑 A/C, satel TV w/movies, dataport, voice mail, in-rm safe. All units w/minibars, some w/whirlpools. **Services:** 🍽 🗝 VP 🚐 🛏 Twice-daily maid svce, masseur, babysitting. **Facilities:** 🛗 📺 1000 🛗 1 bar, beauty salon. **Rates:** $125–$525 ste. Extra person $20. Children under age 18 stay free. Parking: Indoor, $5/day. AE, CB, DC, DISC, MC, V.

☰☰☰ Crowne Plaza Pontchartrain Hotel

2 Washington Blvd, 48226 (Downtown); tel 313/965-0200 or toll free 800/2-CROWNE; fax 313/965-9464. Adjacent to Cobo Conference Center. The lobby of this newly renovated property is adorned with a portrait of Count Pontchartrain and scenic murals that commemorate Detroit's original settlement, Fort Pontchartrain, which stood at this site. **Rooms:** 415 rms and stes. Executive level. CI 3pm/CO noon. Nonsmoking rms avail. Distinctive architecture features saw-tooth window design that affords Detroit River views from many rooms. **Amenities:** 🛁 ⚡ 🗑 A/C, cable TV w/movies, dataport, voice mail. Executive club floors have in-room fax machines. **Services:** ✕ 🗝 VP 🚐 🛏 🛏 Car-rental desk, babysitting. **Facilities:** 🛗 📺 400 🖥 🛗 1 restaurant, 1 bar, games rm, spa, sauna, steam rm. **Rates:** $145–$165 S or D; $250–$550 ste. Extra person $10. Children under age 17 stay free. Min stay special events. Parking: Indoor, $10/day. AE, CB, DC, DISC, JCB, MC, V.

UNRATED Detroit Airport Marriott

Detroit Metropolitan Airport, 48242; tel 313/941-9400 or toll free 800/228-9290; fax 313/941-2522. Between the two main airport terminals. **Rooms:** 160 rms. CI 3pm/CO noon. Nonsmoking rms avail. **Amenities:** 🛁 ⚡ 🗑 A/C, cable TV w/movies, dataport, voice mail. **Services:** 🗝 🚐 🛏 Complimentary evening hors d'oeuvres and nighttime dessert station. **Facilities:** 🛗 **Rates (CP):** $129–$150 S or D. Children under age 18 stay free. Parking: Indoor/outdoor, free. AE, CB, DC, DISC, ER, JCB, MC, V.

☰☰☰ DoubleTree Hotel Detroit

333 E Jefferson Ave, 48226; tel 313/222-7700 or toll free 800/THE-OMNI; fax 313/222-8517. In the Millender Center. Connected by elevated skywalks and People Mover to Renaissance Center and other downtown attractions and buildings. **Rooms:** 254 rms and stes. CI 3pm/CO 1pm. Nonsmoking rms avail. Larger-than-average rooms, some with Detroit River views. **Amenities:** 🛁 ⚡ 🗑 A/C, cable TV w/movies, dataport. Some units w/terraces. **Services:** ✕ VP 🚐 🛏 🛏 Car-rental desk, masseur, babysitting. **Facilities:** 🛗 📺 2 🛗 300 🛗 1 restaurant, 1 bar, racquetball, spa, sauna, steam rm, whirlpool, washer/dryer. Well-equipped Health Club includes free weights and machines, plus rooftop tennis courts and jogging track. **Rates:** $170 S; $185 D; $250–$1,000 ste. Extra person $20. Children under age 18 stay free. Min stay special events. Parking: Indoor, $9/day. AE, CB, DC, DISC, MC, V.

☰☰ Holiday Inn Fairlane–Dearborn

5801 Southfield Service Dr, 48228; tel 313/336-3340 or toll free 800/HOLIDAY; fax 313/336-7037. NW corner of Ford Rd and US 39. Busy with meeting attendees on weekdays and families and visitors to nearby Henry Ford Museum and Greenfield Village on weekends. **Rooms:** 347 rms and stes. CI 3pm/CO noon. Nonsmoking rms avail. Some rooms have sofa sleepers. **Amenities:** 🛁 ⚡ 🗑 A/C, satel TV w/movies. Some units w/whirlpools. **Services:** ✕ 🚐 🛏 🛏 🍳 **Facilities:** 🛗 📺 600 🛗 1 restaurant, 1 bar, games rm, sauna, whirlpool. **Rates:** Peak (Mar–Dec) $94 S or D; $175 ste. Children under age 12 stay free. Min stay special events. Lower rates off-season. Parking: Outdoor, free. AE, CB, DC, DISC, ER, MC, V.

☰☰☰ Hotel St Regis

3071 W Grand Blvd, 48202 (New Center Area); tel 313/873-3000 or toll free 800/848-4810; fax 313/873-2574.

Across from General Motors Headquarters. Elegantly furnished public areas. Connected by covered walkways to shopping and the Fisher Building. **Rooms:** 223 rms and stes. CI 1pm/CO noon. Nonsmoking rms avail. Rooms are strictly traditional. **Amenities:** 🛏 🅰 🍸 A/C, cable TV w/movies, dataport. Some units w/whirlpools. **Services:** ✕ VP 🚐 🖨 🕁 Twice-daily maid svce, babysitting. **Facilities:** 🍴 300 🕭 1 restaurant, 1 bar (w/entertainment). **Rates:** $79–$115 S; $94–$130 D; $115–$200 ste. Children under age 18 stay free. Parking: Outdoor, $7/day. Fisher Theatre packages in season. AE, CB, DC, DISC, EC, ER, JCB, MC, V.

🏳🏳🏳 The River Place, A Grand Heritage Hotel

1000 River Place, 48207 (Riverfront); tel 313/259-9500 or toll free 800/890-9505; fax 313/259-3744. Off Jefferson Ave, 1 mi E of downtown. Elegant lodging carved from the former offices and laboratory of Parke-Davis Pharmaceuticals. Tranquil Detroit Riverfront setting with view of Canada. **Rooms:** 108 rms and stes. Executive level. CI 3pm/CO noon. Nonsmoking rms avail. Individual layouts and decor. River views from corner rooms are special. **Amenities:** 🛏 🅰 🍸 A/C, cable TV w/movies, dataport, voice mail, in-rm safe. Some units w/whirlpools. Some rooms and suites accessible for guests with disabilities. **Services:** ✕ ⌨ VP 🚐 🖨 🕁 🐕 Twice-daily maid svce, masseur, children's program, babysitting. Complimentary transportation to downtown Detroit. **Facilities:** 🍴 🅿2 🍴 100 💻 🕭 1 restaurant, 1 bar (w/entertainment), spa, sauna, steam rm, whirlpool. Croquet lawn sanctioned by USCA. Patio dining along river. **Rates:** $125–$165 S; $145–$185 D; $159–$510 ste. Extra person $20. Children under age 18 stay free. Parking: Outdoor, $6/day. AE, CB, DC, DISC, JCB, MC, V.

🏳🏳🏳 The Westin Hotel Renaissance

Renaissance Center, 48243; tel 313/568-8000 or toll free 800/228-3000; fax 313/568-8118. On Jefferson Ave at the Detroit Riverfront. A bustling convention hotel, the 73-story centerpiece of a seven-tower office/retail/entertainment center dominates Detroit's skyline. **Rooms:** 1,400 rms and stes. Executive level. CI 3pm/CO 1pm. Nonsmoking rms avail. Floor-to-ceiling windows reveal downtown, the sprawling Metro Detroit area, Detroit River, and Canada. For best views, ask for rooms above the 39th floor. **Amenities:** 🛏 🅰 🍸 A/C, cable TV w/movies, dataport, voice mail, in-rm safe. Some units w/minibars. **Services:** 🍽 VP 🚐 🖨 🕁 Masseur, children's program, babysitting. **Facilities:** 🍴 🍴 2200 🕭 3 restaurants, 3 bars, spa, sauna, steam rm. **Rates:** $125–$175 S or D; $280–$1,200 ste. Extra person $20. Children under age 18 stay free. Parking: Indoor/outdoor, $7–$10/day. AE, CB, DC, DISC, ER, JCB, MC, V.

MOTELS

🏳🏳 Residence Inn by Marriott Dearborn

5777 Southfield Service Dr, 48228; tel 313/441-1700 or toll free 800/331-3131; fax 313/441-4144. At NW corner of Ford Rd and US 39. Convenience to several corporate offices makes it a favorite for business travelers; amenities and nearby attractions appeal to families. **Rooms:** 128 stes. CI 3pm/CO noon. Nonsmoking rms avail. Some two-bedroom, two-level suites. **Amenities:** 🛏 🅰 🍸 A/C, satel TV w/movies, refrig, dataport, voice mail. Some units w/fireplaces, 1 w/whirlpool. **Services:** 🚐 🖨 🕁 🐕 Babysitting. Complimentary continental breakfast, snacks, light dinners weeknights. **Facilities:** 🍴 🅿1 25 🕭 Whirlpool, playground, washer/dryer. Patio, grill for guest use. **Rates (CP):** $120–$200 ste. Children under age 18 stay free. Min stay special events. Parking: Outdoor, free. AE, CB, DC, DISC, JCB, MC, V.

🏳 Shorecrest Motor Inn

1316 E Jefferson Ave, 48207 (Downtown); tel 313/568-3000 or toll free 800/992-9616; fax 313/568-3002. 2 blocks E of Renaissance Center. A no-frills, family-run operation since 1965. Good downtown location. **Rooms:** 54 rms and stes. CI open/CO noon. Tidy rooms meet basic needs. Suites are larger rooms with sofa beds. **Amenities:** 🛏 🅰 A/C, refrig. **Services:** ✕ 🚐 🖨 🕁 🐕 **Facilities:** 1 restaurant. **Rates:** $48–$60 S; $54–$66 D; $80–$135 ste. Children under age 18 stay free. Parking: Outdoor, free. AE, CB, DC, DISC, MC, V.

RESTAURANTS 🍴

★ American Coney Island

114 W Lafayette (Downtown); tel 313/961-7758. At Michigan Ave and Griswold. **American.** Everyone, from bridal parties to sports fans, comes here for Detroit's "original" Coney Island hot dogs, served with or without the chili. **FYI:** Reservations not accepted. Beer and wine only. **Open:** Daily 24 hrs. **Prices:** Main courses $2–$4. No CC. 🕐24

The Caucus Club

150 W Congress (Downtown); tel 313/965-4970. **Continental.** A fine dining tradition in Detroit since 1949. Dark and intimate even at lunchtime, with wood paneling, banquettes, and an eclectic decor. Dover sole leads the fresh seafood list, and the baby back ribs have a dedicated following. Barbra Streisand sang here before hitting it big. **FYI:** Reservations recommended. Piano. **Open:** Mon–Fri 11:30am–8pm. **Prices:** Main courses $16–$22. AE, CB, DC, DISC, MC, V. 🕭

Fishbone's Rhythm Kitchen Cafe

In International Marketplace, 400 Monroe St (Greektown); tel 313/965-4600. At Brush. **New American/Creole.** Located at the edge of Greektown, this lively, bustling place is the setting for fresh Gulf Coast seafood prepared with a Creole touch. **FYI:** Reservations accepted. Children's menu. **Open:** Breakfast Mon–Sat 6:30–10am, Sun 6:30–10:30am; lunch Mon–Sat 11am–4pm; dinner Sun–Thurs 4pm–midnight, Fri–Sat 4pm–2am; brunch Sun 10:30am–2pm. **Prices:** Main courses $10–$19. AE, CB, DC, DISC, MC, V. 🕭

Jacoby's Since 1904
624 Brush St (Bricktown); tel 313/962-3334. 3 blocks N of Renaissance Center. **American/German.** The grandson of the original owners recently turned the keys over to an enthusiastic young entrepreneur who intends no major changes to the lively, narrow dining/barroom or its menu of fresh perch dinners and German specialties, but he has added a coffeehouse on the second floor to capture the late night crowd from nearby Greektown. **FYI:** Reservations accepted. **Open:** Mon–Thurs 10:30am–11pm, Fri 10:30am–11pm, Sat 11am–11pm. **Prices:** Main courses $8–$15. AE, CB, DC, DISC, MC, V. ▆

★ New Hellas Cafe
583 Monroe (Greektown); tel 313/961-5544. **Greek.** Anchoring a corner of Greektown, this family operation has been a favorite place for lamb, moussaka, and grape leaves since 1901. Parking in nearby structure. **FYI:** Reservations accepted. Beer and wine only. **Open:** Tues–Thurs 11am–midnight, Fri–Sat 11am–2am, Sun 11am–midnight. **Prices:** Main courses $6–$17. AE, CB, DC, MC, V. ▦

♣ Opus One
565 E Larned; tel 313/961-7766. At St Antoine, a few blocks N of Renaissance Center. **American/French.** Picture broiled fingers of Norwegian salmon fillet nested between latticed pastry fences and fresh spinach cakes—and imagine it tasting as good as it looks. One of the city's finest dining rooms offers lunchtime business crowds and evening intimates an inventive approach to cuisine, from hot and cold appetizers to too-pretty-to-eat pastries. Award-winning wine list. Bistro Bar menu served daily 2:30–5:30pm. **FYI:** Reservations recommended. Piano. **Open:** Mon–Thurs 11:30am–10pm, Fri 11:30am–11pm, Sat 5–11pm. **Prices:** Main courses $20–$35; prix fixe $32–$47. AE, CB, DC, DISC, MC, V. ◉ VP &

Pegasus in the Fisher
In the Fisher Building, 3011 W Grand Blvd; tel 313/875-7400. **Continental.** Wine stored in the lower level vault gives it away: The attractive art deco dining room with soaring ceilings was once a bank. But exchanging currency has been replaced with serving fresh fish, lamb chops, veal, and steak. Special Greek desserts. **FYI:** Reservations recommended. Dancing/jazz. **Open:** Mon–Thurs 11am–9pm, Fri 11am–midnight, Sat 4pm–midnight. **Prices:** Main courses $9–$18. AE, CB, DC, DISC, MC, V. VP &

♣ The Rattlesnake Club
In River Place, 300 River Place (Rivertown); tel 313/567-4400. 1½ mi E of Renaissance Center, on Joseph Campau. **New American.** It's hard to go wrong at any of chef/restaurateur Jimmy Schmidt's several Detroit-area restaurants, but this one is the star. An attractive bar, views of the Detroit River, contemporary art in the dining rooms, and specially designed china vie for attention with rack of lamb and innovative creations like WAM, a dessert of homemade white chocolate ice cream with roasted macadamia nuts on purees of passion fruit and raspberry. Choice wine list. **FYI:**

Reservations recommended. Blues/jazz. **Open:** Lunch Mon–Fri 11:30am–5:30pm; dinner Mon–Thurs 5:30–10pm, Fri–Sat 5:30pm–midnight. **Prices:** Main courses $13–$30. AE, CB, DC, DISC, MC, V. VP &

♣ The Whitney
4421 Woodward Ave; tel 313/832-5700. At Canfield. **American.** Tiffany stained-glass windows, Victorian-era antiques, and crystal chandeliers grace the dining room in this restored 1894 mansion. The lengthy menu lists many creative variations on classic American cuisine: Fresh seafood, rack of lamb, veal, and beef are among the dining options. Inventive desserts. The top floor's Winter Garden bar provides a cozy retreat. **FYI:** Reservations recommended. Cabaret. **Open:** Lunch Fri 11am–2pm; dinner Mon–Tues 6–9pm, Wed–Sat 5pm–midnight, Sun 5–8pm; brunch Sun 11am–2:30pm. **Prices:** Main courses $19–$38. AE, DC, MC, V. ◉ ▆ ▼ VP &

ATTRACTIONS 🖼

MUSEUMS

The Detroit Institute of Arts
5200 Woodward Ave; tel 313/833-7900. One of the largest fine arts museums in the country, the DIA's holdings are especially strong in French Impressionist, German Expressionist, American and Flemish paintings. Among the most famous works here are Diego Rivera's acclaimed fresco *Detroit Industry*, Caravaggio's *Conversion of Mary Magdalene*, Titian's *Man with a Flute*, and Cézanne's *Mme Cézanne*. There are also works by contemporary American painters such as Mark Rothko and Andy Warhol, in addition to works from Italy, Africa, and Asia. A reconstructed 18th-century American country house contains period furnishings, European sculpture and decorative arts, and a collection of medieval armor. **Open:** Wed–Fri 11am–4pm, Sat–Sun 11am–5pm. **$$**

Motown Historical Museum
2648 W Grand Blvd; tel 313/875-2264. Housed at Hitsville USA—the original home of Motown Record Corporation—this humble museum documents the history of Motown and its impact on 20th-century culture. Displays chronicle the rise of Motown and its artists via vintage performance costumes, manuscript sheet music, photographs, promotional materials, business records, and other artifacts. Guests may tour the sound studio where the Jackson Five, Smokey Robinson, Diana Ross, and other Berry Gordy discoveries made their first recordings. There's even a special Michael Jackson Room. **Open:** Tues–Sat 10am–5pm, Sun–Mon noon–5pm. **$$$**

Detroit Science Center
5020 John R St at Warren St; tel 313/577-8400. High-tech museum housing a wide variety of push-button and interactive exhibits on diverse scientific subjects. Spherical cinema

with 360° projection of science films is one of the main attractions. **Open:** Tues–Fri 9am–4pm, Sat 10am–7pm, Sun noon–7pm. **$$**

Museum of African-American History
315 E Warren; tel 313/833-9800. One of the largest museums of its kind in the world. Permanent exhibits depict African village life, slave passage to the Americas, and life under slavery. Changing exhibits cover modern culture and arts. Annual African World Festival celebrates the people of various African cultures and their descendants through art and music. **Open:** Wed–Sat 9:30am–5pm, Sun 1–5pm. **$**

Children's Museum
67 E Kirby at Cultural Center; tel 313/494-1210. A joint venture between the Detroit Board of Education and the Museum of Art. Highlights include arts and crafts displays, an international array of dolls and toys, and a planetarium. **Open:** Mon–Fri 1–4pm, Sat 9am–4pm. **Free**

International Institute of Metropolitan Detroit
111 E Kirby St; tel 313/871-8600. Hosts cultural programs and exhibits from five continents. A variety of ethnic festivals are held here throughout the year; call for schedule. **Open:** Mon–Fri 8:30am–5pm. **Free**

Detroit Historical Museum
5401 Woodward Ave; tel 313/833-1805. Permanent exhibits include "Streets of Old Detroit" (which features replicas of 19th century street scenes), "Toys on Parade" (a collection of toys from the past 100 years); and "Furs to Factories: Detroit at Work 1701–1901." The Booth-Wilkinson Costume Gallery contains over 50,000 woman's garments and accessories. Guided tours available. **Open:** Wed–Fri 9:30am–5pm, Sat–Sun 10am–5pm. **$**

Engine No 18 Detroit Fire Dept
3812 Mount Elliott; tel 313/922-8811. Built in 1892, this is the oldest active fire station in Michigan. Today, it also houses the Detroit Fire Museum, which contains photographs and displays of apparatus and equipment used by previous generations of firefighters. **Open:** Daily 9am–5pm. **Free**

SPORTS VENUES

Tiger Stadium
Michigan Ave and Trumbull; tel 313/963-9944. This 52,000-seat stadium is home to baseball's Detroit Tigers plus concerts and other special events. **Open:** Call for schedule. **$$$$**

Joe Louis Arena
600 Civic Center Dr; tel 313/567-6000. Indoor 15,000-seat stadium; home to the Detroit Red Wings of the National Hockey League and other special events. **Open:** Call for schedule. **$$$$**

Palace of Auburn Hills
3777 Lapeer Rd, Auburn Hills; tel 810/377-0100. Home of the National Basketball Association's Detroit Pistons, who play from October to April. The stadium seats up to 22,000 fans. **$$$$**

OTHER ATTRACTIONS

Rennaissance Center
Jefferson Ave at Beaubien; tel 313/568-5600. This spectacular grove of skyscrapers was built on the edge of the Detroit River in 1977. The exceptional modern design bears the stamp of John Portman. Giant hotel, stores, restaurants, movie theaters, and indoor gardens are housed in seven buildings ranging from 20 to 73 floors in height. **Open:** Daily 24 hours. **Free**

Fisher Building
W Grand and 2nd Blvds; tel 313/874-4444. A 28-story masterpiece (with two 11-story wings) of 1930s art deco designed by renowned architect Albert Kahn. Today, the beautifully renovated structure houses restaurants, boutiques, theaters, and art galleries. **Open:** Daily 24 hours. **Free**

Detroit Symphony Orchestra
3711 Woodward Ave; tel 313/833-3700. Recently renovated 2,000-seat concert hall dating from 1920. This "acoustic miracle" (in the words of the great cellist Pablo Casals) is home to the Detroit Symphony Orchestra (Sept–May). Call for schedule. **$$$$**

Detroit Garden Center
1460 E Jefferson Ave; tel 313/259-6363. Walled-in formal gardens located at the Moross House, the oldest existing brick home in the city. **Open:** Tues–Thurs 9am–3:30pm. **Free**

Historic Trinity Lutheran Church
1345 Gratiot Ave; tel 313/567-3100. Built in 1931, this small neo-Gothic cathedral is adorned with more than 400 religious statues and much stained glass. The Luther Tower is modeled after one from a 16th-century monastery in Erfurt, Germany. **Open:** Mon–Fri 9am–4pm. **Free**

Trappers Alley
508 Monroe (Greektown); tel 313/963-5445. Originally one of the largest fur- and pelt-processing complexes in the world, Trapper's Alley has been beautifully restored and renovated. The five-story building in the heart of Greektown is now home to an eclectic mix of multicultural shops, restaurants, galleries, and entertainment. **Open:** Mon–Thurs 10am–9pm, Fri–Sat 10am–11pm, Sun noon–7pm. **Free**

Boblo Island
In Detroit River; tel 313/284-2288. Amusement park located on a 272-acre island in the Detroit River with more than 75 rides, shows, and restaurants. The rotating observation deck atop the 314-foot Sky Tower offers a 20-mile view of Canada, Michigan, and Ohio. Ferries from Gibraltar, Detroit, and Amherstburg (in Ontario) provide transportation to the park. **Open:** Mem Day–Labor Day, daily, call for schedule. **$$$$**

Belle Isle
Royal Oak; tel 810/398-0900. On a 3-mile-long island in the Detroit River stands this 1,000-acre park. In addition to swimming, hiking, and picnicking, the park features a 13-acre

zoo, an aquarium, and a conservatory with palms, cacti, ferns, seasonal flowers, and tropical plants. From Detroit, the park is accessible via MacArthur Bridge. **Open:** Daily 24 hours. **$**

Detroit Zoo

8450 W Ten Mile Rd, Royal Oak; tel 810/398-0900. Located 10 mi N of Detroit. One of the first zoos in the country to use barless exhibits, there are now more 1,200 animals here (representing 400 species), all living in careful reconstructions of their natural habitats. Popular stops include the reptiles, penguins, and marine mammals. A miniature train takes visitors from exhibit to exhibit. **Open:** Daily 10am, closing times vary. **$$$**

Empire

MOTEL 🏨

≣≣ Lakeshore Inn

Jct MI 22/72, 49630; tel 616/326-5145. The only motel in historic Empire. Walking distance to Lake Michigan and South Bar beaches and everything in Empire. **Rooms:** 12 rms. CI 2pm/CO 11am. Nonsmoking rms avail. **Amenities:** 🛁 🍸 A/C, cable TV, refrig. All units w/terraces. **Services:** Friendly local staff. **Facilities:** 👤 **Rates:** Peak (May–Nov) $60–$65 S or D. Children under age 12 stay free. Lower rates off-season. Parking: Outdoor, free. MC, V.

RESTAURANT 🍴

Joe's Friendly Tavern

10233 Front St; tel 616/326-5506. **American/Burgers.** A simple, family-friendly eatery with a menu large enough so that everyone can find something they like. Mexican food, steak, and seafood platters complement a variety of burgers prepared to order. **FYI:** Reservations not accepted. Children's menu. **Open:** Peak (June–Aug) daily 7am–11pm. **Prices:** Main courses $7–$12. No CC. 🍴

Escanaba

Seat of Delta County, on the Upper Peninsula. Escanaba is the only ore-shipping port on Lake Michigan. Nearby Hiawatha National Forest borders three Great Lakes (Huron, Michigan, and Superior). The Upper Peninsula State Fair takes place here every August. **Information:** Delta County Tourism & Convention Bureau, 230 Ludington St, Escanaba, 49829 (tel 906/786-2192 or toll free 800/437-7496).

HOTEL 🏨

≣≣ Budget Host Terrace Bay Inn & Resort

7146 P Rd Box 453, 49829; tel 906/786-7554 or toll free 800/BUD-HOST; fax 906/786-7554. Two facilities—motel and resort—offer a wealth of recreational opportunities. Close to cross-country ski and snowmobile trails, as well as

beaches. **Rooms:** 71 rms. CI 2pm/CO 11am. No smoking. Nice views of Little Bay De Noc from restaurant and some rooms. **Amenities:** 🛁 🍸 A/C, cable TV w/movies, VCR. Some units w/terraces. **Services:** 🍽 Continental breakfast Oct–Apr. **Facilities:** 👤 🛶 1 restaurant (bkfst and dinner only), 1 bar (w/entertainment), games rm, spa, sauna. **Rates:** Peak (June 15–Aug 31) $48–$72 S or D. Extra person $5. Lower rates off-season. Parking: Outdoor, free. 10% senior discount Sept–June. AE, CB, DISC, MC, V.

MOTELS

≣≣ Best Western Inn

2635 Ludington St, 49829; tel 906/786-0602 or toll free 800/528-1234. Typical Best Western. Convenient to local attractions. **Rooms:** 40 rms. CI noon/CO 11am. Nonsmoking rms avail. **Amenities:** 🛁 🍸 📻 A/C, cable TV w/movies, refrig. Some units w/terraces, some w/whirlpools. **Services:** 🚐 🍽 **Facilities:** 👤 👤 1 beach (lake shore). **Rates:** Peak (July 1–Aug 19) $59–$99 S; $79–$149 D. Extra person $5. Children under age 12 stay free. Lower rates off-season. Parking: Outdoor, free. AE, DISC, MC, V.

≣≣ Super 8 Motel

2415 N Lincoln Rd, 49829; tel 906/786-1000 or toll free 800/800-8000. Very nice motel—a good overnight stop. At the northern city limits. **Rooms:** 90 rms. CI 2pm/CO 11am. Nonsmoking rms avail. **Amenities:** 🛁 🍸 A/C, cable TV w/movies. Some units w/whirlpools. **Services:** 🍽 **Facilities:** 👤 👤 📷 👤 Sauna, whirlpool, washer/dryer. **Rates:** Peak (June–Sept) $44 S; $49–$53 D. Extra person $6. Children under age 12 stay free. Lower rates off-season. Parking: Outdoor, free. AE, MC, V.

≣ Value Host Motor Inn

921 N Lincoln Rd, 49829; tel 906/789-1066. Basic. Convenient to downtown. **Rooms:** 51 rms and effic. CI open/CO 11am. Nonsmoking rms avail. All rooms have one or two queen-size beds. **Amenities:** 🛁 🍸 A/C, cable TV w/movies. **Services:** 🍽 **Facilities:** 👤 📷 👤 **Rates (CP):** Peak (June 15–Oct 1) $35–$39 S or D; $57–$61 effic. Extra person $4. Children under age 12 stay free. Lower rates off-season. Parking: Outdoor, free. DISC, MC, V.

RESTAURANTS 🍴

★ Log Cabin Supper Club

7831 US 2; tel 906/786-5621. **American.** Serving the area since 1930, this charming restaurant offers fine beef, fresh local fish, and views of picturesque Little Bay de Noc. Specialties include Whitefish de Noc, Kabin Kabob, raspberry chicken, and vegetables Mornay. Lighter Side menu available. **FYI:** Reservations accepted. **Open:** Peak (June–Aug) Mon–Sat 4:30–10pm, Sun 4–9pm. **Prices:** Main courses $11–$16. AE, MC, V. ♥

★ **The Stonehouse and Carport Lounge**
2223 Ludington Ave; tel 906/786-5003. **American.** The rugged stone exterior and antique-car theme in the bar and dining room are the trademarks of this locally popular restaurant. Hot spinach salad and frog legs are among the unique appetizers; Alaskan walleye and Black Angus New York strip are available as main courses. **FYI:** Reservations accepted. Children's menu. **Open:** Peak (June–Aug) lunch Mon–Fri 11am–2pm; dinner Mon–Sat 5–10pm, Sun 5–9pm. **Prices:** Main courses $12–$18. AE, DC, DISC, MC, V. ♥

ATTRACTION 🏛

Hiawatha National Forest
Forest Supervisor, 2727 N Lincoln Rd; tel 906/786-4062. Located in the Upper Peninsula, this 893,000-acre forest offers its guests opportunities for lake and stream fishing, hunting, swimming, sailing, motorboating, canoeing, camping, picnicking, hiking, cross-country skiing, snowmobiling, and horseback riding. Both modern and primitive campsites available. A series of scenic drives connects the different areas and provides views of three different Great Lakes: Superior, Huron, and Michigan. **Open:** Daily 24 hours. **Free**

Farmington Hills

Northwest suburb of Detroit, with many recreational facilities nearby. Farmington Founders Festival takes place in mid-July. **Information:** Farmington/Farmington Hills Chamber of Commerce, 33000 Thomas, #101, Farmington, 48336-2347 (tel 810/474-3440).

HOTELS 🏨

Best Western Executive Hotel and Suites
31525 12 Mile Rd, 48334; tel 810/553-0000 or toll free 800/221-2222; fax 810/553-7630. Two double-helix chandeliers light the atrium lobby in this recently renovated facility. Extra safety measures make it a favorite with women travelers. Golf nearby. **Rooms:** 204 rms and stes. CI 3pm/CO noon. Nonsmoking rms avail. **Amenities:** A/C, cable TV w/movies. Some units w/whirlpools. Two-bedroom suites with refrigerators available. Complimentary amenities available at front desk. **Services:** X ☒ ⊖ Local van transportation provided. **Facilities:** 🏋 ♨ □ 🖥 ♿ 1 restaurant, 1 bar, whirlpool, washer/dryer. **Rates (CP):** $69–$79 S or D; $99–$119 ste. Extra person $6. Children under age 16 stay free. Parking: Outdoor, free. AE, CB, DC, DISC, JCB, MC, V.

Botsford Inn
28000 Grand River Ave, 48336; tel 810/474-4800. Just N of Eight Mile Rd. On the National Register of Historic Places, this 1836 home is Michigan's oldest operating inn. Once owned by Henry Ford, the inn has been restored and is a showcase of Americana, with its massive fireplaces, Hitchcock chairs, unique collection of antiques, and a double porch that extends the full length of the building. Dry cleaning available across the street. **Rooms:** 65 rms. CI 3pm/CO 1pm. Nonsmoking rms avail. Historic Wing rooms individually furnished with antiques, and showers only. East Wing rooms are most modern. Several rooms available as residential units on monthly basis. **Amenities:** A/C, cable TV. **Services:** 🚐 ⊖ **Facilities:** ♨ 1 🔲 ♿ 1 restaurant (see "Restaurants" below), 1 bar (w/entertainment), washer/dryer. **Rates (BB):** $65–$70 S; $75–$85 D. Extra person $5. Children under age 12 stay free. Parking: Outdoor, free. AE, DC, DISC, MC, V.

Holiday Inn
38123 W 10 Mile Rd, 48335; tel 810/477-4000 or toll free 800/465-4329; fax 810/476-4570. At Grand River Ave. Clean, comfortable hotel shares an entry with Brandys Restaurant. Fishing, golf, boating, volleyball, racquetball, and tennis nearby. **Rooms:** 258 rms and stes. Executive level. CI 3pm/CO 11am. Nonsmoking rms avail. **Amenities:** A/C, satel TV w/movies. Some units w/terraces, 1 w/whirlpool. Microwave available for rental. **Services:** X 🚐 ☒ ⊖ ⊗ Weekend children's program. **Facilities:** 🏋 ♨ 🔲 ♿ 1 restaurant, 1 bar (w/entertainment), games rm, sauna, whirlpool, washer/dryer. Outdoor pool attended on weekends. Holidome has pool table, table tennis, and putting greens. **Rates (CP):** $74–$88 S; $149–$199 ste. Children under age 18 stay free. Parking: Outdoor, free. AE, CB, DC, DISC, JCB, MC, V.

Radisson Suite Hotel
37529 Grand River Ave, 48335; tel 810/477-7800 or toll free 800/333-3333; fax 810/477-6512. Easy access to major highways. Fine for overnight or an extended stay. **Rooms:** 137 stes. CI 3pm/CO noon. Nonsmoking rms avail. Each unit is a two-room suite. Comfortable. **Amenities:** A/C, cable TV w/movies, refrig, dataport. Some units w/whirlpools. **Services:** X ☒ ⊖ Twice-daily maid svce, babysitting. **Facilities:** 🏋 ♨ 🔲 ♿ 1 restaurant, 1 bar, games rm, sauna, steam rm, whirlpool. **Rates (BB):** $89–$119 ste. Extra person $5. Children under age 16 stay free. Parking: Outdoor, free. AE, CB, DC, DISC, ER, JCB, MC, V.

MOTEL

Knights Inn
37527 Grand River Ave, 48335; tel 810/477-3200 or toll free 800/843-5644; fax 810/477-2370. Off MI 102. Fine for overnight travelers. Easy access to highway. **Rooms:** 105 rms, stes, and effic. CI 4pm/CO noon. Nonsmoking rms avail. Clean, comfortable lodgings with traditional decor. Efficiencies available on weekly basis. **Amenities:** A/C, cable TV w/movies. Some units w/whirlpools. Complimentary toiletries available at front desk. Microwave rentals available. **Services:** ⊖ ⊗ **Facilities:** 🏋 🔲 ♿ **Rates (CP):** $35–$47 S; $53–$65 D; $82–$109 ste; $245–$268 effic. Extra person $5. Children under age 12 stay free. Parking: Outdoor, free. Efficiency rates are weekly. AE, DISC, MC, V.

RESTAURANT 🍽

The Coach Room

In Botsford Inn, 28000 Grand River Ave; tel 810/474-4800. **American.** Located in a landmark building, the dining room retains the look of a Victorian tavern, its original incarnation. Each of the smaller rooms has its own unique characteristics, such as the original fireplace, foot-wide floor boards, or an extensive antique bottle collection. The chicken pot pie is from an 1860s recipe, but the tri-color cheese tortellini with sun-dried tomatoes and garlic cream sauce couldn't be more modern. Service is friendly and meticulous. **FYI:** Reservations recommended. Jazz. **Open:** Mon 9am–8pm, Tues–Sat 7am–8pm, Sun 10am–8pm. **Prices:** Main courses $8–$19. AE, DISC, MC, V. 🔲 🏵 ♿

Flint

Seat of Genesee County, in southeast part of state. This former fur-trading post is now an important automobile manufacturing center. Flint College and Cultural Center is a complex of several colleges, planetarium, and museum of antique autos. **Information:** Flint Area Convention & Visitors Bureau, 400 N Saginaw St, #101A, Flint, 48502 (tel 810/232-8900 or toll free 800/288-8040).

HOTEL 🏨

UNRATED Holiday Inn Express

1150 T Robert Longway Blvd, 48503; tel 810/238-7744 or toll free 800/278-1810; fax 810/233-7444. Attractive motel close to Cultural Center and Crossroad Village. **Rooms:** 124 rms. CI 1pm/CO noon. No smoking. Nonsmoking rms avail. **Amenities:** 🛏 🏵 A/C, cable TV w/movies, refrig. **Services:** 🚐 ☒ 🖂 Free local calls. Business center open 24 hours. **Facilities:** 🏋 🔲 Free guest passes to university health club. **Rates (CP):** $65 S or D. Children under age 18 stay free. Parking: Outdoor, free. MC, V.

Frankenmuth

This town in the eastern part of the Lower Peninsula was founded by German immigrants in 1845, and it still holds onto its heritage. Bavarian architecture (often with glockenspiels and bell carillons) and German food abound; the Bavarian Festival takes place here in mid-June. **Information:** Frankenmuth Convention & Visitors Bureau, 635 S Main St, Frankenmuth, 48734 (tel 517/652-6106 or toll free 800/386-8696).

HOTEL 🏨

≣ ≣ ≣ Bavarian Inn

1 Covered Bridge Lane, 48734; tel 517/652-2651; fax 517/652-6711. Cross the wooden bridge to get to the inn, and you're in Bavaria. The exceptional lodge has a spacious lobby, decorated seasonally. A first-class Bavarian-style hotel, good for families or couples. **Rooms:** 356 rms and stes. CI 3pm/CO 11am. Nonsmoking rms avail. Rooms are named for German settlers and have their familiy histories on wall. **Amenities:** 🛏 🏵 A/C, cable TV w/movies, refrig. Some units w/terraces, some w/whirlpools. **Services:** ✕ 🚐 🖂 Car-rental desk. Shuttles to downtown restaurants and shops. **Facilities:** 🔲 🏊 4 🏋 🍴 300 💻 ♿ 1 restaurant (see "Restaurants" below), 2 bars (w/entertainment), games rm, sauna, whirlpool, beauty salon. Miniature 18-hole golf course, childrens' play village, family fun center, gift shops. **Rates:** Peak (June–Aug) $99–$119 S or D; $119–$269 ste. Extra person $10. Lower rates off-season. Parking: Outdoor, free. "Queen of Hearts" package offered in Feb for Valentine getaways. AE, MC, V.

RESTAURANTS 🍽

★ Bavarian Inn Restaurant

713 S Main St; tel 517/652-9941. **American/German.** Established in 1888, this complex consists of seven German-themed dining rooms with a total of 1,200 seats. Family-style German specialties like Weiner schnitzel and sauerbraten with homemade sauces are served up by waitresses in Bavarian dress. The lower level houses a gift shop, bake shop, wine shop, and toy factory. **FYI:** Reservations accepted. **Open:** Daily 11am–9:30pm. **Prices:** Main courses $10–$17. AE, MC, V. ♥ 🖼

Big John's Lamplighter

565 S Main St; tel 517/652-3809. **American.** A casual downtown restaurant with booths and tables. The menu offers Mexican food, gourmet burgers, steak, veal, Greek salad, and many other items. The steak-and-onion sub is a hit with the regulars. **FYI:** Reservations not accepted. No liquor license. **Open:** Daily 7am–9pm. **Prices:** Main courses $6–$10. MC, V. 🖼

Edelweiss Restaurant

1118 Weiss St; tel 517/652-6811. **American.** Good for takeout pizza as well as steak, seafood, and sandwiches. A limited number of booths and tables are scattered around the small dining room. **FYI:** Reservations not accepted. Children's menu. No liquor license. **Open:** Mon–Fri 6am–9:30pm, Sat–Sun 7am–9:30pm. **Prices:** Main courses $6–$8. MC, V. 🖼

Horn's Dead Creek Eatery & Saloon

S Main St; tel 517/652-8382. **Burgers/Sandwiches.** At the edge of Frankenmuth, this popular local bar has a western saloon feeling. The menu is basic sandwiches and burgers, supplemented by a changing array of specials (Monday night spaghetti buffet, Friday night grilled whitefish). The honky-tonk decor—complete with pool table, arcade machines, and a juke box—is quite a change from the prevailing Bavarian atmosphere in town. **FYI:** Reservations not accepted. Children's menu. **Open:** Peak (June–Aug) daily 10am–10pm. **Prices:** Main courses $5–$8. MC, V. 🖼

Tiffany's

656 S Main St; tel 517/652-6881. **American.** The name of this well-liked bar and eatery comes from the collection of Tiffany lamps that decorates the place. Outside seating in the summer allows for even more socializing while waiting for steaks, salmon, pasta, pizza, and sandwiches. **FYI:** Reservations accepted. **Open:** Daily 11am–11pm. **Prices:** Main courses $8–$14. AE, MC, V. 🖼

★ Zehnder's of Frankenmuth

730 S Main St; tel 517/652-9925. **American/German.** A Frankenmuth institution since 1927, this family-owned and-operated rathskeller is located in a beautiful vintage building right downtown. Traditional German fare, fried chicken, steaks, seafood, and many other choices are listed on the varied menu. Zehnder's is especially famous for their pastries. **FYI:** Reservations accepted. Children's menu. **Open:** Daily 11am–9:30pm. **Prices:** Main courses $10–$18. MC, V. 🍴🖼 ♿

ATTRACTIONS 🖼

Michigan's Own Military and Space Museum

1250 Weiss St; tel 517/652-8844. The museum honors Michigan's military veterans. Uniforms, decorations, photos, as well as displays on Medal of Honor recipients, astronauts, and former governors who were in the military. **Open:** Mar–Dec, Mon–Sat 10am–5pm, Sun noon–5pm. **$**

Frankenmuth Historical Museum

613 S Main St; tel 517/652-9701. Exhibits of local folk art, period rooms, and other artifacts document the history of this Bavarian-inspired town. A video is shown hourly; gift shop on the premises. **Open:** Daily 9am–5pm. **Free**

Bronner's Christmas Wonderland

25 Christmas Lane; tel 517/652-9931. Bronner's, which advertises itself as the world's largest Christmas store, offers over 50,000 Christmas decorations and accessories. Each year, over two million visitors roam the 27 acres of landscaped grounds, which are peppered with life-size figurines and thousands of Christmas lights. **Open:** Peak (June–Dec) Mon–Sat 9am–9pm, Sun noon–7pm. Reduced hours off-season. **Free**

Frankfort

A popular resort area and important harbor on the shore of Lake Michigan, and burial site of Father Marquette. Nearby is Sleeping Bear Dunes National Lakeshore, where a dune climb takes visitors up to a panoramic view of Glen Lake and the surrounding countryside.

HOTEL 🏨

🏨🏨 Hotel Frankfort

Main St, 49638; tel 616/882-7271. Victorian-style hotel built in 1902. Antiques in lobby and halls. Walking distance to downtown and harbor. **Rooms:** 16 rms and stes. Executive level. CI 3pm/CO 11am. Each room has unique personality, including Knight, Teddy Bear, and Victorian themes. **Amenities:** 🛁 🍷A/C, cable TV. Some units w/terraces, some w/whirlpools. **Services:** ✕ ◁ Dinner packages offered at restaurant. **Facilities:** 🍽 1 restaurant (see "Restaurants" below), 1 bar (w/entertainment). **Rates (MAP):** $185–$240 S or D; $185–$240 ste. Extra person $18. Parking: Outdoor, free. AE, DISC, MC, V.

MOTEL

🏨🏨 Harbor Lights Motel and Condominiums

15 2nd St, 49635; tel 616/352-9614 or toll free 800/346-9614; fax 616/352-6580. A large, year-round motel complex located right on the beach. Close to many sports activities and parks. **Rooms:** 130 rms, stes, and effic. CI open/CO 11am. No smoking. All rooms have Lake Michigan view. Condominiums available. **Amenities:** 🛁🔧📺 A/C, cable TV w/movies, refrig, VCR. All units w/terraces. **Services:** ◁ Babysitting. **Facilities:** 🔧 🌊 💻 ♿ 1 beach (lake shore), games rm, whirlpool, washer/dryer. The beach is a highlight. **Rates:** Peak (June–Aug) $80–$90 S or D; $100–$150 ste; $120–$200 effic. Extra person $20. Children under age 12 stay free. Lower rates off-season. Parking: Outdoor, free. Daily or weekly rentals avail. AE, DISC, MC, V.

RESORT

🏨🏨 Chimney Corners

1602 Crystal Dr, 49635; tel 616/352-7522. 7 mi N of Frankfort on MI 22. A tucked-away, first-class resort on Lake Crystal, outside of Frankfort, with 300 acres and a private beach. Lodge is rustic with stone fireplaces. Family owned for 80 years. **Rooms:** 28 rms; 13 cottages/villas. CI 2pm/CO 10am. Nonsmoking rms avail. Cottages on beach and hillside; apartments near beach; lodge rooms. **Amenities:** Refrig. No A/C, phone, or TV. Some units w/terraces, some w/fireplaces. **Services:** ◁ ◁ Babysitting. **Facilities:** ⚓ 🌊 🍽 1 restaurant (bkfst and lunch only), 1 beach (lake shore), volleyball, lawn games. Boats can be docked on the premises. **Rates:** Peak (Aug) $40–$45 D; $760–$795 effic; $1,100–$1,195 cottage/villa. Extra person $7. Children under age 18 stay free. Lower rates off-season. Parking: Outdoor, free. Efficiency and cottage rates are weekly. Closed May–Oct. No CC.

RESTAURANT 🍴

★ Frankfort Hotel Restaurant

Main St; tel 616/882-7271. At 3rd St. **Seafood/Steak.** A traditional and understated mood reigns at this restaurant located in the historic Hotel Frankfort. The spacious dining room, filled with antiques, is a wonderful setting for the classic cuisine, featuring prime rib, fresh seafood, and homemade desserts. **FYI:** Reservations recommended. Jazz/

Dixieland. Children's menu. **Open:** Peak (June–Aug) daily 8am–10pm. **Prices:** Main courses $10–$17. AE, MC, V. 💟🎦 &

Gaylord

Seat of Otsego County, in the northern part of the Lower Peninsula. Call of the Wild Museum displays more than 150 life-size animals in natural surroundings. The area is popular for both downhill and cross-country skiing; Alpenfest is celebrated in late July. **Information:** Gaylord Area Convention & Tourism Bureau, 101 W Main St, PO Box 3069, Gaylord, 49735 (tel 517/732-6333 or toll free 800/345-8621).

HOTELS 🏨

🗮🗮 Best Western Royal Crest
803 S Otsego, 49735; tel 517/732-6451 or toll free 800/876-9252. On old 27 N at edge of town. Convenient to town and popular with skiers and golfers. **Rooms:** 44 rms. CI 3pm/CO 11am. Nonsmoking rms avail. **Amenities:** 🎁 🕭 📺 A/C, cable TV. Some units w/whirlpools. **Services:** 🖐️ 🍽️ Babysitting. **Facilities:** 🏃 🎣 & Spa. **Rates (CP):** Peak (June 16–Sept 4) $68–$79 S or D. Children under age 16 stay free. Lower rates off-season. Parking: Outdoor, free. Ski and golf packages avail. AE, DISC, MC, V.

🗮🗮 Comfort Inn of Gaylord
137 West St, 49735; tel 517/732-7541 or toll free 800/221-2222. Recently renovated, convenient to town and I-75. **Rooms:** 117 rms, stes, and effic. CI 3pm/CO 11am. Nonsmoking rms avail. **Amenities:** 🎁 🕭 A/C, cable TV. Some units w/whirlpools. **Services:** ✕ 🖐️ **Facilities:** 🗊 🏃 🎣 70 & 1 restaurant, 1 bar, whirlpool. **Rates (CP):** Peak (June 15–Oct 21) $69–$91 S or D; $125–$165 ste; $155 effic. Extra person $5. Children under age 12 stay free. Lower rates off-season. Parking: Outdoor, free. Golf packages avail in summer. AE, DISC, MC, V.

MOTEL

🗮🗮 Super 8 Motel
1042 Main St, PO Box 601, 49735; tel 517/732-5193 or toll free 800/800-8000; fax 517/732-5194. Pleasant, convenient to town and highway. Golfing, skiing, and snowmobiling are nearby. **Rooms:** 82 rms and stes. CI 3pm/CO 11am. Nonsmoking rms avail. **Amenities:** 🎁 🕭 A/C, cable TV w/movies, refrig. Some units w/terraces, some w/whirlpools. **Services:** 🖐️ 🍽️ **Facilities:** 🗊 🏃 🎣 🛁 200 & Games rm, sauna, whirlpool. **Rates (CP):** Peak (Jan–Mar/May–Oct) $74–$89 S or D; $89–$150 ste. Extra person $5. Children under age 12 stay free. Lower rates off-season. Parking: Outdoor, free. AE, MC, V.

RESORTS

🗮🗮 El Rancho Stevens
2332 E Dixon Lake Rd, PO Box 495, 49735; tel 517/732-5090. 40 acres. A true ranch and resort, perfect for horse lovers and those who like a quiet, rural atmosphere. Great for families. Lakefront access to Lake Dixon is lovely. **Rooms:** 29 rms. CI 3pm/CO 11am. Nonsmoking rms avail. Lodge rooms, suites, cottages/town houses available. Rooms are rustic. **Amenities:** 🕭 A/C, refrig. No phone or TV. Some units w/terraces. **Services:** 🖐️ Social director, children's program. Very friendly staff. **Facilities:** 🗊 ⛺ 🛶 🏃 🐎 🎣 🐕¹ 1 restaurant (lunch and dinner only), 1 bar (w/entertainment), 1 beach (lake shore), basketball, volleyball, games rm, lawn games. Recreation room with bar. Refreshments offered by the pool. **Rates (CP):** Peak (June 18–Aug 19) $95–$113 S; $142–$176 D. Extra person $71. Children under age 12 stay free. Min stay peak. Lower rates off-season. MAP rates avail. Parking: Outdoor, free. Closed Oct–May. MC, V.

🗮🗮🗮 Marsh Ridge Golf and Nordic Ski Resort
4815 Historic US 27 S, 49735; tel 517/732-6794 or toll free 800/743-PLAY. A luxury resort with plush, spacious grounds. A golfer's paradise in summer. **Rooms:** 54 rms, stes, and effic; 5 cottages/villas. CI 4pm/CO 11am. Nonsmoking rms avail. Four two-bedroom log town houses. **Amenities:** 🎁 🕭 🍴 A/C, cable TV w/movies, refrig. Some units w/terraces, some w/whirlpools. Jacuzzi suites. **Services:** 🖐️ **Facilities:** ▶18 🏃 🎣 330 & 20K of groomed and tracked ski trails for snowmobiling or cross-country skiing. **Rates (CP):** $95–$125 S or D; $95–$150 ste; $160–$225 effic; $325–$390 cottage/villa. Extra person $10. Children under age 16 stay free. Parking: Outdoor, free. Special packages include "Me Week" with cardiovascular training and spa cuisine, and weekend packages. AE, DC, MC, V.

RESTAURANTS 🍴

Big Buck Brewery & Steakhouse
550 S Wisconsin; tel 517/732-5781. **American.** A realtively new microbrewery that is branching out into the restaurant business. The spacious dining area is furnished with four big-screen TVs for sports lovers. Sandwiches, burgers, steak, and seafood dominate the menu, with big appetites going for the 28-oz "Big Buck" sirloin. The local brew can be bought to go. **FYI:** Reservations accepted. Children's menu. **Open:** Mon–Sat 11:30am–10pm, Sun noon–10pm. **Prices:** Main courses $10–$19. MC, V. 🖼️ &

★ Busia's of Gaylord
2782 Old 27S; tel 517/732-2790. At I-75. **Polish.** Lace curtains, wooden chairs, Polish music, and Busia's family photo album at the entrance add up to old-world atmosphere. True Polish specialties include homemade kielbasa and Busia's sampler (pierogi, sauerkraut and sausage, chicken, *kluski* and gravy, and sweet-and-sour *kapusta*). Dinner

buffet. **FYI:** Reservations accepted. Children's menu. **Open:** Peak (Apr–Oct) Mon–Fri 11am–9pm, Sat–Sun 8am–9pm. **Prices:** Main courses $9–$14. MC, V.

★ Sugar Bowl
216 W Main St; tel 517/732-5524. **American.** Opened in 1919, this cozy Greek restaurant has been run by the same family for three generations. Lake Superior whitefish, scampi, Athenian chicken, and other menu specialties are prepared on an open hearth. Very friendly service. **FYI:** Reservations accepted. Children's menu. **Open:** Peak (June–Aug) daily 7am–11pm. Closed late Mar–early Apr. **Prices:** Main courses $10–$20. AE, DISC, MC, V.

ATTRACTION

Call of the Wild
850 S Wisconsin Ave; tel 517/732-4336 or toll free 800/835-4347. An adventure park with a wide range of attractions, including a wildlife museum (with over 150 animals in naturalistic environments), the Bavarian Falls 18-hole miniature-golf course, a ¼-mile Grand Prix–style go-cart track; and a shop selling cowboy-style gear. **Open:** Peak (June 15–Labor Day) daily 8:30am–9pm. Reduced hours off-season. $$

Glen Arbor

On Lake Michigan, just north of Sleeping Bear Dunes National Lakeshore. A nearby maritime museum, located in a restored US Coast Guard Station, documents the shipping history of the region.

RESTAURANT

Boone Docks
Jct MI 22/109; tel 616/334-6444. **American.** The menu here offers an array of steaks and seafood; fresh lake perch is a house specialty. The wait staff is very accommodating and there's an extensive wine list. The outdoor deck is a very popular spot during the summer, when musical acts appear on the nearby dock. **FYI:** Reservations recommended. **Open:** Mon–Thurs 11am–10pm, Fri 11am–10:30pm, Sat 11am–11pm, Sun noon–10pm. **Prices:** Main courses $13–$30. AE, MC, V.

REFRESHMENT STOP

★ Glen Arbor Farm Market & Bakery
PO Box 459; tel 616/334-3466. **American.** Nestled under pine trees, this shop offers gourmet foods, sandwiches, bakery goods, and other specialties. Homemade breads, gourmet vinegars, and northern Michigan jams are among the many items sold. **Open:** Peak (June–Aug) Mon–Wed 7:30am–8pm, Thurs–Sat 7:30am–9pm, Sun 7:30am–8pm. Closed Nov–May. DISC, MC, V.

Grand Haven

Seat of Ottawa County, in western part of state. This Lake Michigan port city is a center of commercial and recreational fishing, tourism, and retail. Local Coast Guard base is celebrated with National Coast Guard Festival every July. **Information:** Grand Haven-Spring Lake Convention & Visitors Bureau, One S Harbor Dr, Grand Haven, 49417 (tel 616/842-4499 or toll free 800/303-4096).

MOTEL

Fountain Inn
1010 S Beacon Blvd, 49417; tel 616/846-1800 or toll free 800/745-8660. Simple, clean facility located just outside downtown. Large grassy area, shade trees, and picnic tables out front. **Rooms:** 47 rms. CI 4pm/CO 11am. Nonsmoking rms avail. **Amenities:** A/C, cable TV w/movies. **Services:** **Facilities:** Small hospitality room. **Rates (CP):** Peak (Mem Day–Labor Day) $75 S; $80 D. Extra person $5. Children under age 12 stay free. Lower rates off-season. Parking: Outdoor, free. AE, DISC, MC, V.

RESTAURANTS

♣ Arboreal Inn
18191 174th Ave (Old Grand Haven Rd), Spring Lake; tel 616/842-3800. **New American/Continental.** Like a magical cottage hidden among the trees, this surprise of a restaurant seems to appear out of nowhere. Belying its rather unremarkable exterior, the small Arboreal has three separate dining areas, each with a distinct decor that ranges from rustic to formal. Regular evening menu includes New York strip, filet mignon, whitefish, shrimp in the shell (boiled in beer and spices), and Alaskan king crab legs. Call 24 hours ahead for entrees like rack of lamb or chateaubriand for two. Over 200 wines. **FYI:** Reservations recommended. Dress code. **Open:** Lunch Mon–Fri 11am–2pm; dinner Mon–Sat 5–10pm. **Prices:** Main courses $12–$27. AE, DISC, MC, V.

Kirby Grill
2 Washington St (Downtown); tel 616/846-3299. At Harbor Ave. **American/Steak.** Built as the Gildner Hotel in 1876, this historic building now houses a lively eatery. A checkerboard linoleum floor, brick walls, ceiling fans, and a long bar with two TVs help create an easy, casual atmosphere. Menu entrees include medallions of pork tenderloin served with pear, apple, and cherry chutney; and sautéed chicken breast with fresh strawberries, capers, and garlic. Also pasta, quiche, burgers, and sandwiches. Attractive outdoor deck for summer dining. **FYI:** Reservations accepted. Children's menu. **Open:** Peak (June–Aug) Mon–Thurs 11am–11pm, Fri–Sat 11am–2am, Sun 11am–10pm. **Prices:** Main courses $6–$12. AE, MC, V.

Porto Bello

In Harborfront Place, 41 Washington St (Downtown); tel 616/846-1380. **Italian.** A friendly, sometimes noisy eatery with an outdoor patio and glass-enclosed area overlooking it. A small electric train circles the top of the bar. Standard fare includes pizza, pastas, and steaks, plus veal pizzaiola and roasted chicken Porto Bello with garlic and fresh dill. More upscale, non-Italian specials offered on weekends **FYI:** Reservations not accepted. Jazz/singer. Children's menu. **Open:** Peak (May–Oct) Mon–Thurs 11am–10pm, Fri–Sat 11am–11pm, Sun noon–10pm. **Prices:** Main courses $8–$15. AE, MC, V. 🍺 👪 👤 ♿

Twenty-Two Harbor

22 Harbor Ave (Downtown); tel 616/842-5555. Across from Grand River channel. **New American.** During summer months, you can eat outdoors under the shade of maple trees while watching boats glide along the Grand River channel. Indoors are two gracious dining areas and a small, librarylike bar. Small courses on the attractive menu include salmon loaf with red pepper puree and a tomato tart puff pastry with basil pesto and Roma tomatoes. Light entrees range from large salads with grilled tuna or chicken to marinated flank steak quesadilla. Some options for full entrees are leek and basil stuffed swordfish, beef tenderloin with sun-dried tomato butter; and grilled teriyaki pork chop with pineapple-papaya relish. Delicious fresh pastries and desserts **FYI:** Reservations recommended. Piano. Children's menu. **Open:** Peak (Mem Day–Labor Day) lunch Mon–Sat 11am–3pm; dinner Mon–Thurs 5–10pm, Fri–Sat 5–11pm, Sun 5–8:30pm; brunch Sun 11am–2:30pm. **Prices:** Main courses $12–$20. AE, MC, V. ♥ 🍺 🖼 🔽 ♿

REFRESHMENT STOP ☕

The Coffee Grounds

In Harbourfront Place, 41 Washington St (Downtown); tel 616/844-3078. At 1st St. **Coffeehouse.** This small, bright and cheery new spot is perfect for a quick, hot cup of caffe latte, cappuccino, or hot chocolate to go or to stay. Quick bites include muffins, fresh bagels, caramel or cinnamon rolls, cookies, turtle brownies, raspberry wheels, and strawberry cream cheese croissants. In addition to coffees, the shop sells coffeemakers, pitchers, grinders, flavorings, and souvenir T-shirts **Open:** Daily 7am–11pm. MC, V. ♿

Grand Marais

Located on the shore of Lake Superior, on the Upper Peninsula. This tiny village is surrounded by clear lakes, trout streams, and agate beaches. Pictured Rocks National Lakeshore begins at the western edge of town and continues almost 50 miles to Munising.

MOTELS 🏨

📗📗 Budget Host Welker's Resort

Canal St, PO Box 277, 49839; tel 906/494-2361 or toll free 800/BUD-HOST; fax 906/494-2371. A friendly and congenial cozy resort motel. Recommended for families. Close to a historical lighthouse; maritime museum next door. **Rooms:** 51 rms, stes, and effic. CI 2pm/CO 11am. Nonsmoking rms avail. One- and two-bedroom efficiencies available. **Amenities:** 🍺 🐕 📺 Cable TV w/movies, refrig. No A/C. 1 unit w/terrace. Some rooms don't have phones. **Services:** 🚗 🐾 Babysitting. **Facilities:** 🏌 🛥 1 🏊 1 restaurant, 1 bar, 2 beaches (lake shore), sauna, whirlpool, playground, washer/dryer. Popular restaurant with harbor view and home cooking. **Rates:** Peak (July–Sept) $34–$44 S; $40–$55 D; $55–$70 ste; $230–$300 effic. Extra person $5. Lower rates off-season. Parking: Outdoor, free. Weekly rates and family rates avail. AE, DISC, MC, V.

📗📗 Voyageurs Motel

E Wilson St, 49839 (Downtown); tel 906/494-2389. Good motel located in quiet spot downtown with harbor views. **Rooms:** 10 rms. CI 2pm/CO 11am. Nonsmoking rms avail. **Amenities:** 🍺 🐕 A/C, cable TV w/movies. **Services:** 🚗 🐾 **Facilities:** 🛥 Whirlpool with waterfront view. **Rates:** Peak (June–Aug/Christmas week) $42–$50 S or D. Extra person $5. Children under age 12 stay free. Lower rates off-season. Parking: Outdoor, free. DISC, MC, V.

RESTAURANT 🍴

★ Sportsman's

204 Lake St; tel 906/494-2671. **American/Steak.** A cozy and popular hangout where the cooking and the decor are very down-home. There are booths and a counter, and antique farm tools are hung on the wall. The menu includes house specialties such as teriyaki tenderloin and maple-cured ham steak. Seafood and steaks are also available. Friendly staff. **FYI:** Reservations accepted. **Open:** Mon–Fri 11am–11pm, Sat–Sun 8am–11pm. **Prices:** Main courses $6–$12. MC, V. 👪

Grand Rapids

Seat of Kent County, in western Michigan. This furniture manufacturing center gets its name from the rapids in the Grand River that flows through the heart of the city. Gerald R Ford, the 38th president, grew up here. **Information:** Grand Rapids Area Visitor & Convention Bureau, One NW 3rd St, Grand Rapids, 55744 (tel 218/326-9607).

HOTEL 🏨

📗📗📗 Amway Grand Plaza Hotel

187 Monroe St NW, 49503 (Downtown); tel 616/774-2000 or toll free 800/253-3590; fax 616/776-6489. On E bank of Grand River at Pearl St. West Michigan's largest and most

complete hotel/convention complex lavishly blends two hotels into one in a two-block area. The 12-story Grand Plaza East, originally the Pantlind Hotel, was built in 1913 and fashioned in English Adams architectural style by the designers of New York's Grand Central Station and Biltmore Hotel. Purchased by Amway in 1978, it underwent a three-year, $24 million restoration. The Grand Plaza West, completed in 1983, is a 29-story glass tower with lush furnishings in an eclectic mix of traditional and contemporary design. A two-story concourse joins the two. High-caliber amenities, facilities, and service. **Rooms:** 682 rms and stes. Executive level. CI 3pm/CO noon. Nonsmoking rms avail. Rooms in Grand Plaza East feature finely crafted furniture and rich fabrics. Many tower rooms offer sweeping views of river and downtown area. Specify whether you want a more designer contemporary room or a lovely, old restored room. Luxurious, multi-room suites also available. **Amenities:** 🛗 ⌕ A/C, cable TV w/movies, voice mail. Some units w/minibars, some w/whirlpools. **Services:** 🍴 🗝 VP 🚗 🛆 ↵ Masseur. Tower Club has own concierge, library, and lounge with cocktail hours. **Facilities:** ⛱ 🏋 📺 📞 🏧 💻 ⚕ 7 restaurants (*see* "Restaurants" below), 2 bars (w/entertainment), racquetball, squash, sauna, whirlpool, beauty salon. Eating choices include extensive, gourmet takeout deli; old-time saloon; streetfront cafe; casual dining; and elegant, innovative cuisine. Different types of live music and dancing available. Fitness center includes 30′ by 50′ pool in large, glassed-in area overlooking outdoor tennis courts. Sun deck. Art, clothing, gift, and service shops in hotel. **Rates:** $130 S; $145 D; $215–$1,500 ste. Extra person $15. Children under age 12 stay free. Parking: Indoor, $4/day. AE, CB, DC, DISC, MC, V.

MOTELS

▤▤ Best Western Midway Hotel
4101 28th St SE, 49512 (Kent County Airport); tel 616/942-2550 or toll free 800/528-1234; fax 616/942-2446. Older facility near airport whose greatest asset is its large, atrium-style pool area with live trees and plants. **Rooms:** 146 rms. Executive level. CI 3pm/CO 1pm. Nonsmoking rms avail. **Amenities:** 🛗 ⌕ 📺 A/C, cable TV w/movies, dataport. **Services:** 🍴 🚗 🛆 ↵ Friendly, helpful staff. **Facilities:** ⛱ 🏋 📞 ⚕ 1 restaurant (*see* "Restaurants" below), 1 bar (w/entertainment), games rm, sauna, whirlpool. Billiards, table games. Play equipment for tots. **Rates (CP):** Peak (Jan–Apr) $75–$86 S; $80–$96 D. Extra person $10. Children under age 18 stay free. Lower rates off-season. Parking: Outdoor, free. AE, DC, DISC, MC, V.

UNRATED Days Inn
310 Pearl St NW, 49504 (Downtown); tel 616/235-7611 or toll free 800/325-2525; fax 616/235-1995. Well-maintained facility, centrally located. Caters to weekday business travelers, but usually fills up on weekends with families because of new museum across the street. Advance reservations recommended. **Rooms:** 175 rms. Executive level. CI 3pm/CO 11am. Nonsmoking rms avail. **Amenities:** 🛗 ⌕ A/C, cable TV w/movies. Some units w/minibars. **Services:** 🍴 🛆 ↵ ⚕ **Facilities:** ⛱ 🏋 📞 ⚕ 1 restaurant, 1 bar, whirlpool, washer/dryer. **Rates:** $72 S; $79 D. Extra person $7. Children under age 17 stay free. Min stay special events. Parking: Outdoor, free. Winter, ski, shopping, and honeymoon weekend packages avail. AE, CB, DC, DISC, MC, V.

▤ Exel Inn
4855 28th St SE, 49512; tel 616/957-3000 or toll free 800/356-8013; fax 616/957-0194. Exit 43A off I-96. Simple, bare-bones facility is economical alternative to more pricey area motels. Numerous chain restaurants nearby. **Rooms:** 110 rms. CI 3pm/CO noon. Nonsmoking rms avail. Rooms being renovated. **Amenities:** 🛗 ⌕ A/C, satel TV w/movies. **Services:** 🛆 ↵ ⚕ Friendly, accommodating front desk staff. **Facilities:** 🏋 ⚕ Games rm, washer/dryer. **Rates (CP):** $36 S; $44 D. Extra person $4. Children under age 18 stay free. Parking: Outdoor, free. AE, CB, DC, DISC, MC, V.

UNRATED Grand Rapids Airport Hilton Inn
4747 28th St SE, 49512 (Kent County Airport); tel 616/957-0100 or toll free 800/HILTONS; fax 616/957-2977. At Patterson St. Attractive facility with tastefully decorated lobby, including marble floors, full-length draperies, recessed meeting area with chess table, and artwork. Caters to business community on weekdays, families on weekends. Minutes from downtown. Golf, tennis, and other outdoor recreational activities nearby. **Rooms:** 226 rms and stes. CI 2pm/CO noon. Nonsmoking rms avail. Oversized desks. **Amenities:** 🛗 ⌕ A/C, satel TV w/movies, dataport. **Services:** 🍴 🚗 🛆 ↵ **Facilities:** ⛱ 🏋 📞 ⚕ 1 restaurant (*see* "Restaurants" below), 1 bar, sauna, whirlpool. Fitness center has exercise bikes, six-station weight machine, rowing machine, and treadmill. Outdoor sun deck adjoins pool area. **Rates:** $82 S; $91 D; $150–$235 ste. Extra person $9. Children under age 12 stay free. Parking: Outdoor, free. AE, CB, DC, DISC, MC, V.

▤▤▤ Harley Hotel of Grand Rapids
4041 Cascade Rd SE, 49546; tel 616/949-8800 or toll free 800/321-2323; fax 616/949-4303. Exit 40A (Cascade Rd) off I-96. Older facility set back in quiet location. Caters to weekday business and weekend travelers. **Rooms:** 149 rms and stes. CI 3pm/CO 11am. Nonsmoking rms avail. **Amenities:** 🛗 ⌕ A/C, cable TV w/movies. Some units w/terraces. **Services:** 🍴 🚗 🛆 ↵ **Facilities:** ⛱ 🏋 📺 📞 ⚕ 1 restaurant, 1 bar (w/entertainment), games rm, sauna. Sigee's restaurant features contemporary jazz Fri and Sat nights. **Rates:** $69–$89 S; $74–$106 D; $175 ste. Extra person $10. Children under age 18 stay free. Parking: Outdoor, free. One-night Fri, Sat, and Sun packages avail. AE, CB, DC, DISC, MC, V.

▤▤ Lexington Hotel Suites
5401 28th St Court SE, 49546 (Kent County Airport); tel 616/940-8100 or toll free 800/441-9628; fax 616/940-0914.

At Patterson St. Efficiency suites in locally owned property dating from 1989. **Rooms:** 121 effic. CI 4pm/CO noon. Nonsmoking rms avail. Very clean. **Amenities:** 🎙 🛎 📺 A/C, cable TV w/movies, refrig, dataport. **Services:** 🛍 🍴 No shuttle from airport but will pay cab fare. Corporate hospitality hour (no alcohol) 5:30–6:30pm Mon–Thurs. Extended continental breakfast Mon–Thurs. Helpful, congenial staff. **Facilities:** 🏊 🏋 🈁 💻 ♿ Games rm, whirlpool, washer/dryer. **Rates (CP):** Peak (mid-May–Labor Day) $79–$118 effic. Extra person $8. Children under age 17 stay free. Min stay special events. Lower rates off-season. Parking: Outdoor, free. Children stay free at standard rate; extra charge at corporate rate. Special winter weekend packages avail. AE, CB, DC, DISC, MC, V.

RESTAURANTS 🍴

★ Cascade Roadhouse

6817 Cascade Rd; tel 616/949-1540. 1 block N of 28th St. **American.** Tucked away in the gently rolling hills of the Cascade area southeast of the city, this casual hangout is popular with locals for its cozy, friendly atmosphere. Recommended choices include mariner's jumbo shrimp and sea scallops, simmered in chunky tomato sauce with artichoke hearts, olives, and pepperoncini; and roasted half duckling with fruit and nut dressing and black cherry sauce. Steaks, burgers (including vegetarian), and stuffed potatoes, too. Warm, freshly baked popovers with honey butter are served with all entrees **FYI:** Reservations accepted. Children's menu. **Open:** Mon–Thurs 11:30am–10pm, Fri–Sat 11:30am–11pm. **Prices:** Main courses $9–$15. AE, DISC, MC, V. �ⓐ ♿

Charley's Crab

63 Market St SW (Downtown); tel 616/459-2500. **Seafood.** Fresh seafood—broiled, grilled, poached, sautéed, blackened—is the specialty of this nautically accented restaurant, a pleasant blend of sophisticated, asymmetrical architecture and relaxed ambience. An outdoor dining area overlooks the Grand River. Menu changes seasonally with the availability of different varieties of fresh fish and produce; the catch of the day may be Lake Superior whitefish, Louisiana catfish, Wyoming coho salmon, Florida mahimahi, Atlantic salmon, swordfish, or yellowfin tuna. **FYI:** Reservations recommended. Jazz/piano. Children's menu. **Open:** Lunch Mon–Sat 11:30am–4:30pm; dinner Mon–Thurs 4:30–10pm, Fri–Sat 4:30–11pm, Sun 4:30–9pm; brunch Sun 10am–2pm. **Prices:** Main courses $12–$30. AE, CB, DC, DISC, MC, V. 🅿 🚗 📷 👪 ⓥ VP ♿

🍸 Cygnus

In Amway Grand Plaza Hotel, 187 Monroe St NW (Downtown); tel 616/776-6425. **American/Mediterranean.** One of the finest restaurants in the area operates in an elegant top-of-the-tower setting that allows for stunning night views of the river and city below. Named for the swan-shaped constellation visible through the glass ceiling, it's reached by a glass-walled express elevator. The menu showcases the region's

freshest ingredients in dishes like veal chop with lobster brioche; seared rack of baby boar in red currant sauce; and roasted free-range chicken breast with rillettes, Swiss chard, black-eyed peas, and roasted garlic juice. Heart Healthy cuisine also available. Lounge and a small dance floor, surrounded by lush foliage **FYI:** Reservations recommended. Jazz. Jacket required. **Open:** Tues–Thurs 5:30–10:30pm, Fri–Sat 5:30–11pm. **Prices:** Main courses $16–$32. AE, CB, DC, DISC, MC, V. 🅿 📷 VP ♿

★ Duba's

420 E Beltline NE; tel 616/949-1011. Exit 38 off I-96. **Seafood/Steak.** A tradition since 1949, this fine restaurant offers a stylish, yet warm and friendly, setting for its upscale following. Guests are greeted by an array of colorful flowers outside the front entrance in warm weather. Sample entrees include broiled Lake Michigan whitefish fillet, charbroiled Alaskan halibut served with citrus butter, roast prime rib, and sautéed veal liver with bacon and onions. Nightly specials; lobster and king crab in season. Children's portions available **FYI:** Reservations recommended. **Open:** Mon–Thurs 11am–10pm, Fri–Sat 11am–11pm. **Prices:** Main courses $14–$22. AE, MC, V. 🅿 ⓥ ♿

Gibson's

In the Clark/Wurzburg Mansion, 1033 Lake Dr SE; tel 616/774-8535. Fuller St exit off I-96. **Continental.** Built in 1874 in Italianate design by Augustus Paddock, a silver miner turned lumber baron, this old structure housed a number of interesting and successful Grand Rapids families before being sold to the St Bernadette Order of the Franciscan Friars in the 1940s. Now listed on the National Register of Historic Places and restored to its original beauty, Paddock Place is home to this unique restaurant, named after a turn-of-the-century resident who epitomized that era's Gibson girl. The lovely main dining rooms feature more formal dining, while the Grapevine has a casual, come-as-you-are atmosphere and separate menu. Entrees include twin medallions of filet mignon sautéed with shallots and wild mushrooms in a three-mustard sherry-cream sauce; sole en croûte stuffed with mousse of sea scallops and fine herb butter with sauce verte. Trout, steaks, lamb, and fowl also on menu. Over 100 wines with many selections by the glass. Outdoor dining and a game of croquet when weather permits. **FYI:** Reservations recommended. Piano. Jacket required. **Open:** Lunch Mon–Fri 11:30am–2pm; dinner Mon–Thurs 5:30–10pm, Fri 5:30–11pm, Sat 5–11pm. **Prices:** Main courses $14–$25. AE, DC, DISC, MC, V. 🅿 ▪ 🚗 VP ♿

The Great Lakes Shipping Company Restaurant

2455 Burton St SE; tel 616/949-9440. At Breton St; adjacent to Breton Village Mall. **Seafood/Steak.** Great Lakes–themed establishment, with life preservers, pictures of lighthouses, and other nautical memorabilia displayed in the dimly lit dining room. Meals include aged beef and fresh seafood, plus dishes like boneless chicken served with shallots, mushrooms, lemon, and chardonnay, and London Caesar salad topped with choice of lemon-peppered sirloin, shrimp, or chicken. Happy hour Mon–Fri. **FYI:** Reservations recommended. Children's menu. **Open:** Lunch Mon–Fri 11:30am–2pm; dinner Mon–Thurs 5–10pm, Fri–Sat 5–11pm. **Prices:** Main courses $10–$21. AE, DISC, MC, V. 💗 ☎

Hoffman House

In Best Western Midway Hotel, 4101 28th St SE; tel 616/949-3880. **American.** Small hotel-style dining facility with an airy atmosphere. House specialties come with salad bar and dessert buffet. Offerings include stuffed pork chop with homemade sage dressing, simmered in rosemary sauce; chicken roasted in citrus juices and herbs; and Virginia-style baked ham with molasses-baked beans. Create-your-own pasta dishes and sandwiches, too. **FYI:** Reservations accepted. Children's menu. **Open:** Breakfast Mon–Fri 6:30–11am, Sat–Sun 7–11am; lunch daily 11am–2pm; dinner daily 5–10pm. **Prices:** Main courses $10–$18. AE, DC, DISC, MC, V. 📷 ♿

The 1913 Room

In Amway Grand Plaza Hotel, 187 Monroe St NW (Downtown); tel 616/774-2000. **American.** Named for the year ground was broken for the Pantlind Hotel—the Grand Plaza East's original structure—this award-winning restaurant was designed to echo the opulence of the region's lumber baron period. Deep, rich woods and furnishings are reminiscent of the Victorian era. Creatively prepared dishes include fillet of beef tenderloin; lobster-stuffed shrimp with piquante sauce; herb-roasted pheasant breast with mushroom whipped potatoes and savoy cabbage; and a vegetarian potpourri of grilled, roasted and steamed vegetables, grains, pasta, and tempeh with a sweet carrot, cucumber, and chili relish. **FYI:** Reservations recommended. **Open:** Mon–Thurs 5:30–10:30pm, Fri–Sat 5:30–11pm. **Prices:** Main courses $15–$30. AE, CB, DC, DISC, MC, V. 🔲 VP ♿

★ Rose's

550 Lakeside Dr, East Grand Rapids (Gaslight Village); tel 616/458-1122. **Mediterranean.** A landmark since 1901, when it was known for its ice cream sodas and popcorn, Rose's has been brought back to life as a casual, lakeside dining spot. The popular outdoor deck has an extended season, courtesy of the large heaters. Inside, a wood-fired oven produces imaginative pizzas. In addition to intriguing pastas and seasonal specialties, entrees include an anchovy-rubbed, grilled New York strip steak with pancetta polenta and fresh corn salsa, and wood-roasted Norwegian salmon Vesuvio with potatoes, olive oil, and white wine. **FYI:** Reservations not accepted. Children's menu. No smoking. **Open:** Mon–Sat 11am–11pm, Sun 9am–2pm. **Prices:** Main courses $10–$19. MC, V. 🔲 ☎ 🏔

⑤ San Chez

38 W Fulton St (Downtown); tel 616/774-8272. Across from City Centre at Commerce St. **Spanish.** This lively, fun restaurant, easy to identify by its burgundy awnings, draws an eclectic crowd to its open main dining room with original tin ceiling, dark woodwork, colorful columns, and Spanish-inspired artwork. The menu features delicious hot and cold tapas choices in addition to Spanish pasta and paella and such entrees as raspberry-guava lamb ribs with anchiote chili sauce, grilled chicken mole with five-onion relish, and vegetable saffron rice with scallions and habañero coulis. **FYI:** Reservations not accepted. Blues/jazz. Children's menu. **Open:** Peak (Oct–May) Mon–Wed 11am–10pm, Thurs 11am–11pm, Fri 11am–midnight, Sat noon–midnight, Sun 4–10pm. **Prices:** Main courses $4–$15. AE, DC, MC, V. 🔲 ♿

★ The Schnitzelbank

342 Jefferson Ave SE; tel 616/459-9527. 1 block S of St Mary's Hospital. **German.** Wooden shutters and painted scenes of life in old Germany decorate the exterior of this local landmark, owned and run by the same family for over 60 years. Inside, old-world warmth is reflected in Bavarian details, dark wood tables and chairs, cuckoo clocks, and a collection of mugs and steins (many for sale). Friendly service is provided by waitresses wearing traditional garb; several staff members are German-speaking. Generous portions of Wiener schnitzel, sauerbraten, beef rouladen, braised lamb shanks, and boiled pork hocks; pan-fried rainbow trout and Lake Superior whitefish also available. Extensive selection of lunch sandwiches. **FYI:** Reservations recommended. Children's menu. **Open:** Lunch Mon–Sat 11:30am–2:30pm; dinner Mon–Thurs 5–8pm, Fri 5–9pm, Sat 4–9pm. **Prices:** Main courses $8–$16. AE, MC, V. 🔲 📷 💗 ♿

★ Spinnaker Seafood Restaurant

In Grand Rapids Airport Hilton, 4747 28th St SE (Kent County Airport); tel 616/957-1111. At Patterson St. **Seafood.** A local favorite for well-prepared fresh seafood, featuring a wide variety from the Great Lakes. Rows of shelved books and polished wood floors with wide carpeted aisles lend a library atmosphere. Beef, chicken, and vegetable selections, plus burgers and sandwiches, also served. Attractive brass-accented lounge with raised, curtained booths has small dance floor. **FYI:** Reservations recommended. **Open:** Mon–Fri 6:30am–11pm, Sat 7am–11pm, Sun 7am–10pm. **Prices:** Main courses $12–$25. AE, CB, DC, DISC, MC, V. 💗 ♿

Thornapple Village Inn

445 Thornapple Village Dr SE, Ada; tel 616/676-1233. Lowell/Flint exit off I-96. **New American.** Worth the short drive from East Grand Rapids, this delightful surprise is hidden at the back of the Thornapple shopping center in a dark brown building with green and white awnings. Menu choices include seared Digby scallops with corn-bacon relish and smoked tomato-basil coulis; sautéed scallop of veal with glaze, fine herbs, and cognac; and roasted rack of South Dakota lamb with rosemary–pine nut crust and natural juices. Also pastas, sandwiches, and salads. Impressive collection of 160 wines, one dating back to 1916; wine tastings and private parties held in the wine cellar. The Tap Room serves a smaller, more limited menu, while a flower-trimmed deck has

pleasant dining in season. **FYI:** Reservations recommended. Big band/jazz. Children's menu. No smoking. **Open:** Mon–Thurs 11:30am–10pm, Fri–Sat 11:30am–11pm. **Prices:** Main courses $11–$23. AE, CB, DC, DISC, MC, V. ♥⚓✓♿

⑤ Tuscan Express
6450 28th St SE, Cascade; tel 616/956-5522. **Italian.** This relatively new restaurant has already attracted a loyal following for its authentic cuisine and ultra-modern look. The two young chef-owners often stop by tables to welcome and chat with their guests. All dishes on the simple but clever menu are à la carte, from the variety of imaginative pastas to spit-roasted chicken to creative pizzas baked in the wood-fired oven in the open kitchen. **FYI:** Reservations not accepted. Beer and wine only. No smoking. **Open:** Mon–Thurs 11am–10pm, Fri–Sat 11am–11pm. **Prices:** Main courses $4–$10. AE, CB, DC, DISC, MC, V. 📷♿

ATTRACTIONS 📎

Gerald R Ford Museum
303 Pearl St NW; tel 616/451-9263. The life and presidency of Gerald R Ford (the 38th president and a Grand Rapids native) are the focus of this complex. One of the most popular exhibits is the full-scale reproduction of the Oval Office, decorated as it was during Ford's presidency. Gifts to Ford from other world leaders are also on display, and a film on the Ford presidency is shown every hour. **Open:** Daily 9am–4:45pm. $

The Grand Rapids Art Museum
155 Division N; tel 616/459-4677. Highlights of the permanent collection include Renaissance, German Expressionist, French, and American paintings; there's also a children's gallery and special traveling installations. **Open:** Tues and Sun noon–4pm, Wed, Fri and Sat 10am–4pm, Thurs 10am–9pm. $

Van Andel Museum Center of the Public Museum of Grand Rapids
272 Pearl St NW; tel 616/456-3966. A wide range of exhibits dealing with the natural and social history of West Michigan are featured here. Highlights include "Gaslight Village," a re-creation of downtown Grand Rapids in the 1890s; the Roger B Chaffee Planetarium (see below); a turn-of-the-century furniture factory; dioramas depicting Michigan's wildlife habitats and environments; and a 76-foot whale skeleton suspended above the three-story Galleria. **Open:** Daily 9am–5pm. $$

Roger B Chaffee Planetarium
233 Washington SE; tel 616/456-3985. Presentations at this 86-seat domed theater (located in the Public Museum) include laser-light and sky shows. Special *Star Trek* theme programming and Hall of the Universe (with exhibits on astronomy and space science) also offered. **Open:** Shows, Thurs–Fri 8pm, Sat 11:30am, 1:30, and 8pm. $

John Ball Zoological Gardens
Fulton and Valley SW; tel 616/776-2590. Home to over 500 animals, representing 145 species. Aquarium, conservatory, South American exhibits, penguin exhibit, herpetarium, nocturnal animal exhibits, and garden. Children's zoo features a 60-foot waterfall and petting zoo. Picnic area. **Open:** Daily 10am–4pm. $

Grayling

Seat of Crawford County, in north-central part of state. Many local outfitters offer canoe trips on the Manistee and Au Sable Rivers. Hartwick Pines State Park, seven miles northeast, has cross-country ski trails and a lumberman's museum. **Information:** Grayling Regional Chamber of Commerce, 213 N James St, PO Box 406, Grayling, 49738 (tel 517/348-2921 or toll free 800/937-8837).

HOTELS 📷

≣≣ Holiday Inn
2650 I-75 Business Loop, PO Box 473, 49738; tel 517/348-7611 or toll free 800/292-9055. Family-oriented motel/convention center. **Rooms:** 151 rms and stes. CI open/CO 11am. Nonsmoking rms avail. **Amenities:** 🛁 ⚷ 📺 A/C, satel TV w/movies, refrig. 1 unit w/whirlpool. **Services:** ✕ 🚙 ⊠ 🛎 🧳 Car-rental desk, babysitting. Very cordial staff. **Facilities:** 🏋 🦺 🏊 600 ♿ 1 restaurant, 1 bar (w/entertainment), basketball, volleyball, games rm, sauna, whirlpool, playground. Indoor children's pool and play area. Speakeasy Saloon with live entertainment. Ski shop and ski/snowmobile trails from the door. **Rates:** Peak (July–Aug) $80–$90 S or D; $150–$175 ste. Extra person $6. Children under age 19 stay free. Lower rates off-season. Parking: Outdoor, free. Packages Sept–June and group rates. AE, MC, V.

UNRATED Hospitality House
1232 I-75 Business Loop, 49738; tel 517/348-8900 or toll free 800/722-4151; fax 517/348-6509. Exit 254 or 256 off I-75. Family owned and operated on 10 wooded acres. Close to Hartwick Pines State Park for cross-country skiing and hiking and other points of interest. Hanson Park and Lake Margarethe offer family fun, swimming, and fishing. **Rooms:** 64 rms and stes. CI 2pm/CO 11am. Nonsmoking rms avail. Honeymoon suites and family whirlpool suite available. **Amenities:** 🛁 ⚷ A/C, cable TV w/movies, refrig. Some units w/minibars, some w/fireplaces, some w/whirlpools. Nation's largest in-room movie system. Specialty and whirlpool suites with heart-shaped tubs. Waterbeds available. **Services:** 🛎 **Facilities:** 🏋 🦺 🏊 1 bar, games rm, whirlpool, washer/dryer. Picnic area and barbecue. **Rates:** Peak (June–Oct) $53–$80 S or D; $99–$165 ste. Extra person $5. Children under age 16 stay free. Lower rates off-season. Parking: Outdoor, free. AE, DC, DISC, MC, V.

MOTEL

≣≣ Aquarama Motor Lodge

2307 I-75 Business Loop, 49738; tel 517/348-5405. Adjacent to exit 254. Convenient to downtown. Easy access to restaurants, golf, skiing, snowmobiling, and fishing. Quality lodging at a reasonable rate. **Rooms:** 43 rms and stes. CI 2pm/CO 11am. **Amenities:** 🛏 ⚬ A/C, cable TV w/movies. **Facilities:** 🏊 🐟 🍴15 **Rates (CP):** Peak (June–Aug) $45–$70 D; $95 ste. Extra person $5. Lower rates off-season. Parking: Outdoor, free. AE, DC, MC, V.

RESTAURANT 🍴

Bear's Country Inn

608 McClellan; tel 517-348-5516. **Seafood/Steak.** A cozy family-style eatery with lace curtain and ample seating. Breakfast specialties include the Grizzly (homemade sausages and gravy served over biscuits, with two eggs on the side), while dinner items include chicken, batter-dipped cod, and prime rib at an 8- or 16-oz cut. The service is good. **FYI:** Reservations accepted. Children's menu. No liquor license. **Open:** Mon–Thurs 6am–9pm, Fri–Sat 6am–10pm, Sat 7am–7pm. Closed Nov–May. **Prices:** Main courses $8–$14. CB, MC, V. 👥 ♿

Hancock

See also Calumet, Houghton

This Upper Peninsula village is the site of Suomi College, the only Finnish college in the country. Street signs in town are in both English and Finnish. The area was once studded with copper mines, but the local economy now relies on tourism.

MOTEL 🏨

≣≣ Best Western Copper Crown Motel

235 Hancock Ave, PO Box 217, 49930; tel 906/482-6111 or toll free 800/528-1234; fax 906/482-0185. Off US 41. Standard motel notable primarily for its location. Hancock (across the river from Houghton) averages over 200 inches of snow per year, making it a skiing and snowmobiling paradise. Two blocks from groomed snowmobile trails and within a mile of downhill and cross-country skiing. Close to Suomi College and Michigan Tech. **Rooms:** 47 rms. CI 2pm/CO 11am. Nonsmoking rms avail. **Amenities:** 🛏 A/C, cable TV w/movies. **Services:** 🍴 **Facilities:** 🏊 🐟 60 ♿ Sauna, whirlpool. **Rates:** $46–$54 S; $48–$61 D. Extra person $3. Children under age 15 stay free. Parking: Indoor/outdoor, free. AE, CB, DC, DISC, MC, V.

Harbor Springs

Located on Little Traverse Bay in northern Michigan. The small town is the starting point of Shore Drive (MI 119),

known as one of the state's most scenic routes. The area is home to several ski resorts. **Information:** Harbor Springs Chamber of Commerce, PO Box 37, Harbor Springs, 49740 (tel 616/347-0200 or 526-7999).

HOTELS 🏨

≣≣ Birchwood Inn

7077 Lake Shore Dr, 49740; tel 616/562-2151 or toll free 800/530-9951. 40 acres. Off the beaten path and in a quiet area three miles from downtown Harbor Springs. Five buildings with main lodge that has nice fireplace and sitting room. Bike riders might like the long back road. Appropriate for vacationers, weddings, and small conferences. Close to Thornswift Nature Preserve and a beachfront with hiking. Golf facilities also nearby. **Rooms:** 47 rms, stes, and effic. CI 2pm/CO 11am. Nonsmoking rms avail. **Amenities:** 🛏 ⚬ 📺 A/C, cable TV, refrig. Some units w/terraces. **Services:** 🍴 One of the owners offers craft seminars on china painting and water color painting in summer and fall. Bicycling class weekend two times per year. Cordial staff at front desk. **Facilities:** 🏊 🏊 🐟 2 75 Lawn games, playground. **Rates:** Peak (July–Aug) $55 S; $99 D; $109–$215 ste; $105 effic. Extra person $10. Children under age 16 stay free. Lower rates off-season. Parking: Outdoor, free. MC, V.

≣≣≣ Colonial Inn

210 Artesian Ave, 49740; tel 616/526-2111. Offers spacious accommodations in three buildings and personalized service. The lobby with fireplace in the main building takes you back in time. Nice front porch for cocktails or relaxing. Many guests return year after year. **Rooms:** 44 rms, stes, and effic. Executive level. CI open/CO Open. Nonsmoking rms avail. Unique rooms. All have two double beds or double bed and king-size bed. **Amenities:** 🛏 ⚬ 📺 A/C, cable TV, refrig. Some units w/terraces, some w/fireplaces. **Services:** 🍴 **Facilities:** 🏊 🏊 🐟 1 restaurant (dinner only), 1 bar. Private dock. **Rates:** Peak (July–Aug) $138–$158 S or D; $188 ste; $138–$158 effic. Lower rates off-season. Parking: Outdoor, free. Rates are for up to four persons per room. Extra $10 for fireplace, kitchenette, corner view, or rollaway bed. Rates vary depending on length of stay and season. Spring and fall weekend packages avail. No credit cards for deposits. Closed Sept–Apr. MC, V.

≣≣≣ Harborside Inn

266 E Main St, PO Box 666, 49740; tel 616/526-6238 or toll free 800/526-6238; fax 616/526-6248. A contemporary Victorian inn that features fully equipped luxury suites. Walking distance from downtown shops. **Rooms:** 24 rms. CI 3pm/CO 11am. Nonsmoking rms avail. Suites can accommodate up to four guests. All beds are "Murphy" style and fold easily into the wall to leave a nicely furnished suite. **Amenities:** 🛏 ⚬ 📺 A/C, cable TV, refrig. All units w/terraces, all w/whirlpools. The Bayside Suites have balconies with views of harbor. **Services:** 🅅🅿 📠 🍴 **Facilities:** 🏊 🐟

[200] Spacious sun deck with good view of harbor. **Rates (CP):** Peak (June 14–Sept 4) $125–$175 S or D. Lower rates off-season. Parking: Outdoor, free. AE, MC, V.

INN

≡≡ Harbor Springs Cottage Inn

145 Zoll St, 49740; tel 616/526-5431. A unique one-story inn featuring antiques. Golf and other sports facilities nearby. Guests can walk to downtown shops and restaurants. **Rooms:** 21 rms and stes; 1 cottage/villa. CI 3pm/CO 11am. Nonsmoking rms avail. Some rooms individually decorated with brass beds, wicker furniture, and antiques. Cozy ambience. **Amenities:** 🛁 🍴 🏠 A/C, cable TV, refrig. 1 unit w/fireplace. **Services:** 🚗 🍸 🛎 Owners are exceptionally friendly and offer personalized hospitality—will even take guests out on 24-foot sailboat for no charge. **Facilities:** 🚲 🏃 🦢 **Rates (CP):** Peak (June 16–Sept 9/Dec 17–Jan 2) $130 cottage/villa. Extra person $5. Children under age 14 stay free. Lower rates off-season. Parking: Outdoor, free. Honeymoon and restaurant packages avail. AE, DISC, MC, V.

RESTAURANTS 🍽

Arboretum

Lakeshore Dr (MI 119); tel 616/526-6291. 10 minutes from downtown. **American.** Far off the beaten track, this quiet oasis stands out because of the white wooden lattice on the front of the building. The Atlantic salmon and whitefish served with dressing of crabmeat, proscuitto, green onions, and mushrooms with shallot butter is particularly appealing. Cognacs, brandies, eau-de-vies, and delectable desserts make a great finish to any meal. **FYI:** Reservations accepted. **Open:** Daily 5:30–10pm. **Prices:** AE, MC, V. ♥

The New York

101 State St; tel 616/526-6285. **American.** Housed in a vintage former hotel, this classy downtown dining room features brass appointments and lace curtains. Lunches feature salads, vegetarian sandwiches, burgers, pasta, and a "heart smart" dish of the day, while dinner entrees include chicken Tuscany, pasta, fish, seafood, and vegetarian lasagna. Wine list with over 200 labels plus a wide selection of beers and spirits. **FYI:** Reservations recommended. **Open:** Mon–Fri 11am–9pm, Sat–Sun 10am–9pm. Closed Apr. **Prices:** Main courses $9–$15. AE, MC, V. 🍴 &

Stafford's Pier Restaurant

102 Bay St; tel 616/526-6201. **American.** Offering some of the best views in town, this waterfront cafe serves up fresh, inventive cuisine amid views of the nearby yacht basin. Traditional dinners are served in the Chart Room, lighter offerings in the Pointer Room. Lake perch, chicken Dijon and buffalo steak are menu standouts. **FYI:** Reservations recommended. Children's menu. **Open:** Lunch daily 11:30am–4pm; dinner daily 4:30–11pm; brunch Sun 11:30am–2pm. **Prices:** Main courses $18–$29. AE, MC, V. ♥ 🏞 🔽

Holland

Located at the mouth of the Black River, across Lake Michigan from Racine, WI, this village was founded in 1847 by Dutch settlers seeking religious freedom in the New World. Windmill Island is home to *De Zwaan* ("the swan"), a 225-year-old working windmill. Area heritage is celebrated at the Tulip Time Festival in May. **Information:** Holland Area Convention & Visitors Bureau, 100 E 8th St, #120, Holland, 49423 (tel 616/394-0000).

HOTELS 🏨

≡≡≡ Country Inn

12260 James St, 49424; tel 616/396-6677 or toll free 800/456-4000; fax 616/396-1197. A spacious white veranda with wicker furniture, and the lobby's rustic pine furniture and floral touches create a country mood. Delft tiles around the fireplace remind you you're in Michigan's Holland. Adjacent to the Outlet Mall, Dutch Village, Star Theatre. **Rooms:** 116 rms. CI 3pm/CO noon. Nonsmoking rms avail. **Amenities:** 🛁 🍴 A/C, cable TV, dataport. Some units w/whirlpools. **Services:** 🧳 🍸 "Did you forget?" service at front desk offers toiletries you didn't pack at no charge. **Facilities:** [80] **Rates (CP):** Peak (May–Sept) $74–$88 S; $81–$95 D. Extra person $5. Children under age 18 stay free. Lower rates off-season. Parking: Outdoor, free. Prices increase during Tulip Time Festival. Special weekend escape packages avail mid-Nov–Mar. AE, CB, DC, DISC, MC, V.

≡≡≡ Holiday Inn Conference Center

650 E 24th St, 49423; tel 616/394-0111 or toll free 800/HOLIDAY; fax 616/394-4832. 24th St exit off US 31. The austere exterior is deceiving: The atrium lobby is filled with light and bright color, with a winding staircase and lavish plantings. Short ride to Dutch Village, Outlet Mall, and Wooden Shoe Factory. **Rooms:** 168 rms. CI 4pm/CO noon. Nonsmoking rms avail. Angled windows overlook pool and Holidome. **Amenities:** 🛁 🍴 🍷 A/C, cable TV, dataport. Some units w/terraces. Irons and ironing boards in each room. **Services:** ✗ 🧳 🍸 Car-rental desk, children's program, babysitting. Calypso nightclub adjacent to restaurant provides complimentary buffet 4–7pm on weekdays. **Facilities:** 🏋 🎱 [500] & 1 bar (w/entertainment), games rm, sauna, whirlpool, washer/dryer. Ping-Pong, pool tables, arcade games in Holidome. **Rates:** Peak (May–Sept) $82–$93 S; $92–$103 D. Extra person $5. Children under age 18 stay free. Lower rates off-season. Parking: Outdoor, free. Rates increase for Tulip Time Festival. AE, CB, DC, DISC, JCB, MC, V.

MOTELS

≡≡ Best Western Holland Inn

482 E 32nd St, 49423; tel 616/396-1424 or toll free 800/428-7666; fax 616/396-1428. Exit 52 off I-196 N; exit 49 off I-196 S. Floral plantings brighten entryway and parking lot;

large lawn in rear shaded by several clusters of large, old trees. **Rooms:** 114 rms. CI 1pm/CO 11am. Nonsmoking rms avail. **Amenities:** 🛏 A/C, cable TV. **Services:** 🖺 🖐 **Facilities:** 🖼 🏊 ⑦⓪ ♿ 1 restaurant (lunch and dinner only), 1 bar, washer/dryer. Free access to nearby fitness center. **Rates (CP):** Peak (May–Oct) $60–$72 S; $70–$90 D. Extra person $5. Children under age 12 stay free. Lower rates off-season. Parking: Outdoor, free. Corporate and AARP discounts. AE, CB, DC, DISC, MC, V.

🏨🏨 The Blue Mill Inn
409 US 31, 49423; tel 616/392-7073; fax 616/392-7339. 16th St exit off US 31. Long-established motel adjacent to Wooden Shoe Factory provides good economical lodging for families and business travelers. Short distance to Dutch Village and Outlet Mall; easy access to Windmill Island. **Rooms:** 81 rms. CI 3pm/CO noon. Nonsmoking rms avail. **Amenities:** 🛏 A/C, cable TV. **Services:** 🖐 🐾 Pets allowed in smoking rooms only. **Facilities:** ♿ **Rates:** Peak (July–Sept) $52 S; $64 D. Extra person $5. Children under age 12 stay free. Lower rates off-season. Parking: Outdoor, free. Rates increase for Tulip Time Festival. AE, DISC, MC, V.

🏨🏨 Days Inn
717 Hastings St, 49423; tel 616/392-7001 or toll free 800/DAYS-INN; fax 616/396-5151. 3rd St exit off US 31. Standard brick exterior and minimal lobby area, but well-kept grounds and rooms. Dutch Village and Outlet Mall a short ride away. **Rooms:.** CI 2pm/CO noon. Nonsmoking rms avail. **Amenities:** 🛏 A/C, cable TV. **Services:** 🖺 🖐 🐾 Efficient service at front desk. **Facilities:** 🖼 ♿ Washer/dryer. **Rates:** Peak (May–Sept) $50–$56 S; $62–$70 D. Extra person $6. Children under age 18 stay free. Lower rates off-season. Parking: Outdoor, free. Rates increase at Tulip Time Festival. AE, DISC, MC, V.

🏨🏨 Fairfield Inn
2854 W Shore Dr, 49424; tel 616/228-9700 or toll free 800/228-2800; fax 616/786-9700. Felch St exit off US 31. Newly built, economy-priced Marriott motel. Bright blue trim on white exterior, generous plantings in front and around pool areas. Across the street from West Shore Shopping Mall. **Rooms:** 64 rms. CI 3pm/CO 11am. Nonsmoking rms avail. **Amenities:** 🛏 🗄 A/C, cable TV. **Services:** 🖺 🖐 🐾 Pets in smoking rooms only. **Facilities:** 🖼 ⑥⓪ ♿ Whirlpool. **Rates (CP):** Peak (May–Sept) $62–$90 S or D. Children under age 12 stay free. Lower rates off-season. Parking: Outdoor, free. Rates increase for Tulip Time Festival. AARP, military, and corporate discounts. AE, CB, DC, DISC, MC, V.

RESTAURANTS 🍴

Alpenrose
4 E 8th St; tel 616/393-2111. At Central St. **Coffeehouse/German.** A coffee shop at the front of the establishment serves up light lunches and refreshments; with freshly baked pastries available for carry out. In the back is a large dining room and several smaller dining areas. Everywhere is the work of master German woodworkers, from the beautifully carved ceilings to the paneling and moldings. Well-prepared seafood, lamb, and duck; traditional German dishes. **FYI:** Reservations accepted. Children's menu. **Open:** Mon–Thurs 9am–9pm, Fri–Sat 9am–10pm, Sun 10:30am–2pm. **Prices:** Main courses $13–$18. AE, DISC, MC, V. ♥ 👥 ♿

🍴 Sandpiper
2225 S Shore Dr; tel 616/335-5866. 32nd St exit off US 31; 6 mi W to shore of Lake Macatawa. **Eclectic.** Housed in a gray batten-board structure on the shore of Lake Macatawa, with an entire wall of windows facing the harbor. Grilled veal chop stuffed with mozzarella and wild-mushroom ragout is a special treat, as is the roast duckling with peach-macadamia glaze and quinoa timbale. The fresh local seafood is prepared with unusual herbs and sauces, and the rack of lamb comes with a fennel relish and coconut-plantain flan. Rum vanilla custard is a must for dessert. The loft above the dining room has a wonderful open view of the lake. **FYI:** Reservations recommended. **Open:** Lunch Mon–Fri 11:30am–2pm, Sat noon–3pm; dinner Mon–Sat 5–9:30pm, Sun 5–8:30pm; brunch Sun 10am–2pm. **Prices:** Main courses $13–$22. AE, DISC, MC, V. ♥ 🍷 🏞 👥

ATTRACTIONS 📷

Cappon House Museum
228 W 9th St; tel 616/392-6740. Built in 1874, this was the residence of the town's first mayor. The Victorian interior features original handcrafted woodwork, bronze hardware, and Cappon family furnishings. Special summer events celebrating Victoriana are held here. Group tours by appointment. **Open:** May–Sept, Fri–Sat 1–4pm. **$**

The Holland Museum
31 W 10th St; tel 616/392-9084. Located in a Classical Revival building on Centennial Park, this museum presents permanent and changing exhibits that reflect the history of the area. Highlights include the Netherlands Collection of decorative arts (with Delftware, pewter, paintings, and furniture); the Volendam Room, a fisherman's cottage in the style of "old" Holland; exhibits from the Netherlands Pavilion of the 1939 New York World's Fair; and a marquetry mural from the Great Lakes steamship *Alabama.* **Open:** Mon, Wed, Fri–Sat 10am–5pm, Thurs 10am–8pm, Sun 2–5pm. **$**

Poll Museum of Transportation
US 31; tel 616/399-1955. More than 40 gas, steam, and electric cars from all eras, including several fire trucks dating back to 1902. A military display includes uniforms, vehicles, and other memorabilia. **Open:** May–Sept, Mon–Sat 9am–4:30pm. **$**

Windmill Island
7th and Lincoln Aves; tel 616/396-5433. Located on an island in the Black River, this park features one of the only authentic operating windmills in the United States. The 225-year-old *De Zwaan* towers more than 120 feet above tulip

gardens, canals, and Little Netherlands, a miniature reproduction of Old Holland. The park also offers costumed guides, free rides on a Dutch-style carousel, and a slide presentation on Dutch history. **Open:** Peak (May/July–Aug) Mon–Sat 9am–6pm, Sun 11:30am–6pm. Reduced hours off-season. $

Dutch Village

US 31 and James St; tel 616/396-1475. This 20-acre theme park—complete with windmills, formal gardens, and canals—recreates a 19th-century village in the Netherlands. Popular attractions include a giant "wooden shoe" slide for children, a restored antique carousel, and the *Hexenwaag*, a 200-year-old witches' scale. The village also has a museum of Dutch culture, gift shops, and a restaurant serving Dutch and American fare. **Open:** Daily 9am–5pm. $$

Houghton

See also Calumet, Hancock

Seat of Houghton County, on the shore of Portage Lake in the Upper Peninsula. America's first mineral strike took place here in 1843, and the surrounding hills are still rich in copper and iron. Most of the mines have closed and the area now depends on tourism, especially skiing, for its economic survival. **Information:** Keweenaw Tourism Council, 326 Shelden Ave, PO Box 336, Houghton, 49931 (tel 906/482-2388 or toll free 800/338-7982).

HOTEL

Best Western Franklin Square Inn

820 Shelden Ave, 49931; tel 906/487-1700 or toll free 800/528-1234; fax 906/487-9432. Overlooks the canal. Convenient to downtown, skiing, and colleges. **Rooms:** 77 rms and stes. CI 2pm/CO 11am. Nonsmoking rms avail. Many rooms have a breathtaking view of the canal and the mountain beyond. **Amenities:** A/C, cable TV w/movies. Some units w/whirlpools. **Services:** **Facilities:** 1 restaurant, 1 bar (w/entertainment), sauna, whirlpool. **Rates:** Peak (June–Aug) $65–$75 S; $73–$79 D; $100 ste. Extra person $6. Children under age 18 stay free. Lower rates off-season. Parking: Outdoor, free. AE, DC, DISC, MC, V.

MOTEL

Best Western King's Inn

215 Shelden Ave, 49931; tel 906/482-5000 or toll free 800/528-1234; fax 906/482-9795. 1 block E of lift bridge over canal. In the heart of downtown Houghton, a short walk from dining and shops. Close to Michigan Tech and Suomi College. Excellent skiing and snowmobiling nearby. **Rooms:** 70 rms and stes. CI 1pm/CO 11am. Nonsmoking rms avail. **Amenities:** A/C, cable TV w/movies. **Services:** Upbeat, professional staff. **Facilities:** Sauna,

whirlpool. **Rates (CP):** Peak (July–Sept) $57–$64 S; $63–$70 D; $88–$108 ste. Extra person $6. Children under age 17 stay free. Min stay special events. Lower rates off-season. Parking: Outdoor, free. AE, CB, DC, DISC, EC, MC, V.

RESTAURANTS

Hunan Garden

301 Shelden Ave; tel 906/482-8588. Off US 41, 2 blocks E of Houghton Bridge. **Chinese.** A good choice for lunch, known locally for its Szechuan cooking. Hundreds of egg rolls and crab meat Rangoon appetizers are served daily. Wide variety of stir-fries to choose from—beef, pork, seafood, vegetarian. **FYI:** Reservations recommended. **Open:** Peak (July–Sept) Sun noon–10pm, Mon–Thurs 11:30am–10pm, Fri–Sat 11:30am–11pm. **Prices:** Main courses $7–$13. MC, V.

Los Dos Amigos

52 N Huron St; tel 906/482-1991. Off US 41. **Mexican.** This wacky, not-too-authentic Mexican restaurant doesn't take itself seriously, yet serves up large, delicious meals at very reasonable prices. Much of its decor, from Mexican piñatas to business card tables, has been donated by customers over the years. It can be crowded, especially on the weekends, so reservations are strongly advised for parties of five or more. A fun night out. **FYI:** Reservations recommended. Blues/folk/bluegrass. Dress code. **Open:** **Prices:** Main courses $3–$10. DC, DISC, MC, V.

ATTRACTION

Isle Royale National Park

Park Headquarters, 800 E Lake Shore Dr; tel 906/482-0984. Actually closer to Ontario than to Michigan, this 45-mile-long island is located in northwestern Lake Superior. The island's remote location has helped to preserve the beauty of its unspoiled stretches of forest, shorelines, lakes, and seascapes. Cars are not allowed on Isle Royale, but there are miles of hiking trails for visitors curious to see the native moose, wolves, and foxes. Boat and canoe rentals, fishing charters, and lodging are available at Rock Harbor and at Windigo on the island's southwest end. Rock Harbor also has a full-service marina, gift shop, snack bar, and camper store. Windigo's facilities include a store which sells sandwiches and marine gasoline. Passenger boats (originating at Grand Portage, MN, and Houghton and Copper Harbor, MI) and seaplane (from Houghton) are the only means of transportation to the island. Official National Park Service craft the *Ranger III* makes the 70-mile trip from Houghton twice a week; call ahead for reservations. **Open:** Daily 24 hours. **Free**

Houghton Lake

HOTEL 🏨

≣≣ Holiday Inn

9285 MI 55, 48629; tel 517/422-5175 or toll free 800/HOLIDAY; fax 517/422-3071. Jct US 55/27. Full services and complete banquet and meeting facilities. **Rooms:** 100 rms. CI 3pm/CO noon. No smoking. **Amenities:** �� 🛢 🖵 A/C, cable TV w/movies. **Services:** ✗ ⤵ ⟁ **Facilities:** 🛋 🚣 🏊 ⅄ 1 restaurant, 1 bar (w/entertainment), games rm, sauna, whirlpool, playground, washer/dryer. **Rates:** Peak (June–Sept) $71–$81 S or D. Extra person $6. Children under age 19 stay free. Lower rates off-season. Parking: Outdoor, free. AE, CB, DC, DISC, JCB, MC, V.

MOTEL

≣≣ The Big Oak Motel

4990 W Houghton Lake Dr, 48629; tel 517/366-9126. An especially nice motel for lakeside leisure and fun. A great place to watch the sunset. Close to shops and restaurants. **Rooms:** 16 rms. CI 2pm/CO 10am. Nonsmoking rms avail. **Amenities:** 🛢 🖵 Cable TV w/movies, refrig, CD/tape player. No A/C or phone. **Services:** ⟁ In-room movies available. Very friendly owners. **Facilities:** △ ⅄ 🏊 1 beach (lake shore), volleyball, lawn games. Three acres of picnic and playground area, with picnic tables, lawn furniture, and barbecue grills. 210′ private beach, 160′ boat dock. Motor boats and pontoon boats for daily rental. **Rates:** Peak (June–Aug) $39–$45 D. Extra person $5. Children under age 12 stay free. Lower rates off-season. Parking: Outdoor, free. Weekly rate on efficiency unit. Special weekly rates. AE, DISC, MC, V.

LODGE

UNRATED Woodbine Villa

12122 W Shore Dr, 48629; tel 517/422-5349. Modern rustic log cottages close to fishing, hunting, snowmobiling, ice fishing, and skiing. A four-season getaway, and a great family place. Nearby sights include Lumbermen's Monument, Ogemaw Game Reserve, Call of the Wild Museum, and 176,000 acres of state land for hiking and exploring. **Rooms:** 9 cottages/villas. CI 4pm/CO 10am. Comfortable two-bedroom cottages accommodate up to six guests. **Amenities:** 🖵 Cable TV w/movies, refrig. No A/C or phone. Fully equipped kitchens. **Services:** ⤵ **Facilities:** △ 🛢 🏊 1 beach (lake shore), lawn games, playground. 120′ pier, 300′ sandy beach, outside grills, picnic tables. **Rates:** Peak (June–Aug) $525 cottage/villa. Extra person $50. Children under age 6 stay free. Min stay peak. Lower rates off-season. Parking: Outdoor, free. Cottage rates are per week for four persons. MC, V.

RESTAURANTS 🍽

Brass Lantern

729 Houghton Lake Dr, Prudenville; tel 517/366-8312. **American.** Romantic lakefront restaurant with lace curtains, plants, and a cozy bar. The menu includes Filet Marquis (charbroiled with cheese, wine, and herbs, then wrapped in bacon and topped with mushrooms); New York strip, seafood platters, sandwiches, and lighter fare. **FYI:** Reservations accepted. Children's menu. **Open:** Peak (June–Aug) lunch Sun noon–5pm; dinner daily 4–10pm. **Prices:** Main courses $10–$20. DISC, MC, V. ♥ ⅁

Coyles

9074 Old US 27; tel 517/422-3812. At MI 55. **American.** A large salad buffet and an array of steaks, chicken and seafood entrees are the highlights at this large, family-friendly eatery. Small gift shop on site. **FYI:** Reservations accepted. **Open:** Peak (June–Aug) Sun–Thurs 8am–10pm, Fri–Sat 8am–11pm. **Prices:** Main courses $7–$19. MC, V. 👪

Holiday on the Lake

100 Clearview; tel 517/422-5195. **American.** A well-liked sports bar with a stone fireplace, an outside patio, a 300-foot dock, and a nice view of the lake. And of course, there are six TVs if you insist on catching the big game. Crab cakes, seafood Alfredo, northern Michigan whitefish, and a 16-oz Cattleman's Sizzler Steak are among the dinner options. **FYI:** Reservations accepted. Karaoke. **Open:** Mon–Sat 11am–10pm, Sun 9am–10pm. **Prices:** Main courses $10–$17; prix fixe $15. DISC, V. 🗹

★ Rebecca's

2919 W Houghton Lake Dr; tel 517/366-4715. **Eclectic.** Recommended by locals, Rebecca's is a small place with a cozy, pleasant atmosphere. Service is good and the cuisine is exceptionally inventive: Santa Fe chicken, plum chops (basted in plum sauce), seafood stir fry, and fajita salad are among the typical offerings. Homemade soups and daily specials also available. **FYI:** Reservations accepted. Children's menu. Beer and wine only. **Open:** Peak (June–Sept) Mon–Sat 11am–9pm, Sun noon–8pm. **Prices:** Main courses $8–$11. DISC, MC, V. 👪

ATTRACTIONS 🏛

Higgins Lake

US 27. This 9,600-acre lake—with more than 50 miles of shoreline—is a favorite with fishing enthusiasts. **Open:** Daily sunrise–sunset. **Free**

Houghton Lake

US 27. The largest inland lake in Michigan boasts a 70-mile shoreline, countless boat launches, and many resorts. **Open:** Daily sunrise–sunset. **Free**

St Helen Lake

MI 76. Nestled in the midst of a pine forest, this relatively small lake has 18 miles of beaches and is a popular spot for fishing. **Open:** Daily sunrise–sunset. **Free**

Indian River

A small northern Michigan city offering many opportunities for fishing, boating, camping, and other outdoor recreation. Area liveries rent canoes, kayaks and tubes for use on the nearby Pigeon and Sturgeon Rivers. **Information:** Indian River Resort Region Chamber of Commerce, 3435 Straits Hwy, PO Box 57, Indian River, 49749 (tel 616/238-9325).

MOTEL 🏨

☰ NorGate Motel
4846 Straits Hwy S, 49749; tel 616/238-7788. Off Old US 27; 1¼ mi S of town. A rustic motel, good for families. Popular with snowmobilers in winter and those passing through town. **Rooms:** 14 rms and effic; 1 cottage/villa. CI noon/CO 11am. Nonsmoking rms avail. One- and two-bedroom units. Also a cabin and a trailer for rent. **Amenities:** 🛗 ⚗ A/C, cable TV w/movies, refrig. **Services:** ⌂ Friendly owner. **Facilities:** ⚑ ⛾ **Rates:** Peak (June–Aug/Christmas week) $40–$46 S or D; $40–$68 effic; $50–$65 cottage/villa. Children under age 1 stay free. Lower rates off-season. Parking: Outdoor, free. DISC, MC, V.

ATTRACTION 🏛

Cross in the Woods
7078 MI 68; tel 616/238-8973. This 55-foot redwood cross, fronted by a seven-ton image of the crucified Jesus, was inspired by the memory of Kateri Tekakwitha, a 17th-century Mohawk who converted to Christianity. A gift shop offers a large selection of religious artifacts, including rosaries, medals, and pictures; there's also a doll museum and an outdoor shrine. **Open:** Daily 8am–8pm. **Free**

Iron Mountain

Seat of Dickinson County, on the Upper Peninsula near the Menominee River. Local high-grade iron shafts are now closed, but several local disused mines may be toured by mine train. Pine Mountain Lodge, three miles north of town, hosts a ski jumping tournament every February. **Information:** Upper Peninsula Travel & Recreation Association, 618 S Stephenson Ave, PO Box 400, Iron Mountain, 49801 (tel 906/774-5480 or toll free 800/562-7134).

MOTELS 🏨

UNRATED Comfort Inn
1555 N Stephenson Ave, 49801; tel 906/744-5505 or toll free 800/228-5150; fax 906/774-2631. Off US 2. Near downtown. Caters to business travelers. Bowling alley with games room and bar just across the parking lot. **Rooms:** 48 rms. CI 3pm/CO 11am. Nonsmoking rms avail. Quiet, clean rooms. **Amenities:** 🛗 ⚗ A/C, cable TV w/movies, dataport. **Services:** 🖨 ⌂ Copy and fax machines available at desk.

Facilities: ⚑ ⛾ 🏊 🚼 ⛾ Whirlpool, washer/dryer. **Rates (CP):** $50–$80 S or D. Extra person $6. Children under age 18 stay free. Parking: Outdoor, free. AE, CB, DC, DISC, ER, JCB, MC, V.

☰☰ Park Inn International of Iron Mountain
1609 S Stephenson, 49801; tel 906/774-6220 or toll free 800/437-PARK; fax 906/774-6618. On US 2. Newly renovated with striking lobby and atrium area that overlooks the outdoor heated pool. Management has local reputation for efficiency. Convenient to downtown Iron Mountain. **Rooms:** 64 rms. CI 3pm/CO noon. Nonsmoking rms avail. **Amenities:** 🛗 ⚗ A/C, cable TV w/movies, voice mail. **Services:** 🖨 ⌂ ⇄ Social director, babysitting. **Facilities:** 🏛 ⚑ ⛾ 🏊 ⛾ Whirlpool. **Rates (CP):** $35–$52 S or D. Extra person $6. Children under age 17 stay free. Parking: Outdoor, free. AE, DC, DISC, EC, MC, V.

☰☰ Timbers Motor Lodge
200 S Stephenson Ave, 49801; tel 906/774-7600. Centrally located on US 2. **Rooms:** 50 rms. CI 3pm/CO noon. Nonsmoking rms avail. Basic rooms. **Amenities:** 🛗 ⚗ A/C, cable TV w/movies. 1 unit w/whirlpool. **Services:** ⌂ **Facilities:** 🏛 ⚑ ⛾ 🏊 ⛾ Sauna, whirlpool. **Rates (CP):** $38–$44 S or D. Extra person $5. Parking: Outdoor, free. AE, DC, DISC, MC, V.

ATTRACTIONS 🏛

Cornish Pumping Engine and Mining Museum
300 Kent St; tel 906/774-1086. The Cornish pumping engine, designed in 1890 by Edwin Reynolds, is the focal point of this small local museum. Exhibits of mining equipment, geological specimens, historic mining photographs and artifacts tell the story of iron mining on the Eastern Menominee Range. **Open:** May–Oct, Mon–Sat 9am–5pm, Sun noon–4pm. **$$**

Menominee Range Historical Foundation Museum
300 E Ludington St; tel 906/774-1086. A repository for artifacts, library materials, manuscripts, photographs, and other items documenting the history and development of the Dickinson County area and the rest of the Menominee Range. Exhibits include a replica of a Victorian parlor, a typical turn-of-the-century general store, and a bustling kitchen, along with items such as children's toys and period clothing. **Open:** Apr–Nov, Mon–Sat 10am–4pm. **$$**

Iron County Museum
Brady St, Iron River; tel 906/265-2617 or 265-3942. 35 mi NE of Iron Mountain. Eight-acre complex with over 100 major exhibits reflecting the logging, pioneering, mining, and transportation history of the region. Highlights include iron mining artifacts; a logger's homestead, logging camp, and one-room schoolhouse from 1896; the oldest steel headframe in the Midwest, standing 108 feet tall; and a wildlife art gallery. **Open:** Peak (June–Aug) Mon–Sat 9am–5pm, Sun 1–5pm. Reduced hours off-season. **$$**

Iron Mountain Iron Mine

US 2; tel 906/563-8077. Visitors board trains for guided tours through 2,600 feet of underground drifts and tunnels. Experienced miners operate modern mining machinery as guides recount tales of mining lore and history in upper Michigan's iron mines. A lighted cavern offers views of unique geological formations. Gift shop specializes in rocks and minerals, souvenirs, and antique ironware. **Open:** June–Oct, daily 9am–5pm. **$$$**

Ironwood

A summer and winter recreation center on the Upper Peninsula, near the Montreal River. This former fur trading and mining town on the Menominee Range is now a major ski destination, with three resorts nearby. **Information:** Gogebic Area Visitors & Convention Bureau, 137 E Cloverland Dr, PO Box 706, Ironwood, 49938-0706 (tel 906/932-4850).

MOTELS 🏨

≡≡ Comfort Inn

210 E Cloverland Dr, 49938; tel 906/932-2224 or toll free 800/572-9412; fax 903/932-9929. On US 2, in the midst of commercial Ironwood. Near extensive downhill and cross-country skiing and snowmobiling. Suited to a wide range of travelers. **Rooms:** 63 rms and effic. CI 1pm/CO 11am. Nonsmoking rms avail. **Amenities:** 🛁 🍴 A/C, cable TV w/movies. 1 unit w/minibar, some w/whirlpools. **Services:** 🛎 **Facilities:** 🛗 🏃 🍴 🏊 🔥 Whirlpool. **Rates (CP):** Peak (Dec 20–Jan 5) $38–$60 S; $50–$80 D; $50–$100 effic. Extra person $6. Children under age 20 stay free. Lower rates off-season. Parking: Outdoor, free. AE, CB, DC, DISC, EC, ER, JCB, MC, V.

≡≡≡ Sandpiper Motel

1200 Cloverland Dr, 49938; tel 906/932-2000; fax 906/932-2000. A quaint motel located on US 2, near restaurants and shopping. Convenient to downhill and cross-country skiing. **Rooms:** 28 rms. CI 2pm/CO 10am. Nonsmoking rms avail. Rooms are individually decorated. **Amenities:** 🛁 🍴 A/C, cable TV. **Services:** 🚐 🛎 Copy machine available in lobby. Motel owners live on property and are friendly, efficient, and accessible. **Facilities:** 🏃 🍴 Sauna. **Rates:** Peak (Dec–Mar/July–Aug) $30–$40 S; $35–$50 D. Extra person $6. Lower rates off-season. Parking: Outdoor, free. Closed Oct, Apr. DISC, MC, V.

≡≡ Super 8 Motel

160 E Cloverland Dr, 49938; tel 906/932-3395 or toll free 800/800-8000; fax 906/932-2507. On US 2, near restaurants and downhill skiing. **Rooms:** 42 rms. CI open/CO 11am. Nonsmoking rms avail. **Amenities:** 🛁 A/C, satel TV. **Services:** 🛎 🚐 **Facilities:** 🏃 🍴 🔥 Sauna, whirlpool. **Rates:**

Peak (Nov–Apr) $37–$57 S; $43–$64 D. Extra person $5. Children under age 13 stay free. Lower rates off-season. Parking: Outdoor, free. AE, CB, DC, DISC, MC, V.

≡ Towne House Motor Lodge

215 S Suffolk St, 49938; tel 906/932-2101. Off Business US 2. Known locally for the attached supper club and for hosting wedding receptions. Decorated in dark wood with dim lighting. Located in the business district. **Rooms:** 20 rms. CI noon/CO 11am. Nonsmoking rms avail. Uneven quality of cleanliness. Decor varies. **Amenities:** 🛁 🍴 A/C, cable TV. **Services:** 🍴 🛎 🚐 Deposit required for pets. **Facilities:** 🏃 🍴 🔢225 1 restaurant (lunch and dinner only), 1 bar, games rm. **Rates:** Peak (Dec 15–Mar 15) $29–$40 S; $39–$50 D. Extra person $6–$10. Children under age 12 stay free. Min stay peak. Lower rates off-season. Parking: Outdoor, free. AE, CB, DISC, MC, V.

LODGE

≡≡≡ The Black River Lodge

N 12390 Black River Rd, 49938; tel 906/932-3857 or toll free 800/666-9916. Off US 2, 2 mi N of Airport Rd. 150 acres. Extensive property borders the Black River and includes hiking/cross-country skiing trails. Downhill skiing and ski jumping facilities are just minutes away. A bargain for families and groups regardless of season. **Rooms:** 30 rms, stes, and effic. CI 3pm/CO 11am. Each room has unique size, decor, and layout. Many rooms feature cathedral ceilings. **Amenities:** 🛁 🍴 Satel TV w/movies, refrig, VCR. No A/C. Some units w/terraces, some w/fireplaces, some w/whirlpools. **Services:** 🔑 🚗 🛎 🚐 Babysitting. Pickup from county airport. Shuttle to Bessemer shops and restaurants and ski areas during peak season. **Facilities:** 🏃 🍴 🔢100 1 restaurant (bkfst and dinner only), 1 bar, volleyball, games rm, whirlpool. **Rates:** Peak (Dec 26–Mar 15) $25–$87 S or D; $55–$98 ste; $30–$98 effic. Min stay peak. Lower rates off-season. Parking: Outdoor, free. DISC, MC, V.

ATTRACTIONS 📷

Copper Peak

CR 513; tel 906/932-3500. This peak in "Big Snow Country" offers the only ski flying facility in North America. (A lift takes intrepid skiers up to a 470-foot slide towering above the summit of Copper Peak.) The complex also features snowshoeing, dog sledding, and over 60 miles of groomed cross-country skiing trails. Gift shop on the grounds. **Open:** Mem Day–Labor Day, daily 9am–5pm. **$$$**

Hiawatha—World's Tallest Indian

Houk St. This 52-foot-high, 8-ton statue of the legendary Iroquois looks north to the waters of Lake Superior. **Free**

Big Powderhorn Mountain Ski Resort

N11375 Powderhorn Rd, Bessemer; tel 906/932-4838. 5 mi E of Ironwood. Located 15 minutes from Lake Superior, this resort offers a variety of winter sports activities and scenic beauty in Michigan's "Big Snow Country." Big Powderhorn provides 24 trails (split evenly among black diamond, intermediate, and beginner) over 215 acres—the longest run is 1 mile—as well as nine double lifts. The vertical drop is 600 feet. Snowboarding, NASTAR, night skiing, ski school, and rentals also available. For the latest information on snow conditions, call toll free 800/272-7000. **Open:** Dec–Mar, daily 8am–4pm. $$$$

Ishpeming

The name of this Upper Peninsula town means "high ground." Nearby Mount Arvon (at nearly 2,000 feet tall) is the tallest point in the state. Suicide Bowl, at east end of city, includes five jumping hills and four cross-country trails. **Information:** Ishpeming-Negaunee Area Chamber of Commerce, 661 Palms Ave, Ishpeming, 49849 (tel 906/486-4841).

HOTEL 🏨

🗏🗏 Best Western Country Inn
850 US 41 W, 49849; tel 906/485-6345 or toll free 800/528-1234. Off US 41. Offers all services, including a conference facility. Convenient to highway. Located 15 minutes from snowmobile and cross-country ski trails and the US National Ski Hall of Fame and Museum. **Rooms:** 60 rms and stes. CI 3pm/CO noon. Nonsmoking rms avail. **Amenities:** 🗏 🖥 A/C, cable TV w/movies. 1 unit w/whirlpool. **Services:** ✗ 🗏 🖘 **Facilities:** 🗂 🏊 🗔 🖢 1 bar (w/entertainment), games rm, whirlpool. **Rates:** Peak (June–Oct) $61–$71 S or D; $90 ste. Extra person $5. Children under age 18 stay free. Lower rates off-season. Parking: Outdoor, free. AE, MC, V.

ATTRACTIONS 🏛

Suicide Bowl
Cliffs Dr; tel 906/485-4242. A small ski facility, popular with locals. Facilities are not plush or extensive, but they do include the basics: five ski-jumping hills and four cross-country trails (with one trail lit for night skiing). **Open:** Nov–Mar, call for hours. $$$$

US National Ski Hall of Fame and Museum
US 41 and 3rd St; tel 906/485-6323. Sponsored by the US Ski Association, this museum houses US National ski trophies, a replica of a 4,000-year-old ski and ski pole, exhibits on Olympic skiing, and plaques with photos and biographical sketches of great skiers. An 18-minute orientation film covers the history of skiing in America. **Open:** Peak (June–Sept) daily 10am–8pm. Reduced hours off-season. $

Jackson

Seat of Jackson County, in southern Michigan. This industrial town is perched at the crossroads of four major highways and is surrounded by more than 600 lakes. The Republican Party was officially born here in 1854. The Hot-Air Balloon Jubilee takes place in mid-July. **Information:** Jackson Convention & Tourist Bureau, 6007 Ann Arbor Rd, Jackson, 49201-8884 (tel 517/764-4440 or toll free 800/245-5282).

MOTELS 🏨

🗏 Budgetel Inn
2035 Service Dr, 49202; tel 517/789-6000 or toll free 800/4-BUDGET; fax 517/782-6836. Exit 138 off I-94; N on US 127 to Springport Rd; W to entrance. No frills, with easy access to highway. **Rooms:** 67 rms and stes. CI 3pm/CO noon. Nonsmoking rms avail. Clean, comfortable rooms. **Amenities:** 🗏 🖥 🖫 A/C, satel TV w/movies. **Services:** 🗏 🖘 🖘 Friendly service. **Facilities:** 🏊 🗔 🖢 **Rates (CP):** $40–$53 S; $47–$60 D; $53–$60 ste. Extra person $7. Children under age 18 stay free. Min stay special events. Parking: Outdoor, free. Charge for extra person is for second guest; third and fourth guests are free. AE, CB, DC, DISC, MC, V.

🗏🗏 Country Hearth Inn
1111 Boardman Rd, 49202; tel 517/783-6404 or toll free 800/848-5767. Exit 138 off I-94; S to Boardwalk; W to entrance. Convenient location and homey atmosphere. Not many frills, but those available are nicely done. Shopping, restaurants, and theaters within walking distance. **Rooms:** 73 rms. CI 1pm/CO noon. Nonsmoking rms avail. Recliner in each room; parlor suites have privacy curtain between sitting and sleeping area. **Amenities:** 🗏 A/C, cable TV, dataport. 1 unit w/whirlpool. **Services:** 🖭 🗏 🖘 Midweek manager's receptions Tues–Thurs evenings. **Facilities:** 🖳 🖢 Free passes to local fitness center. **Rates (CP):** $53–$67 S or D. Extra person $6. Children under age 18 stay free. Min stay special events. Parking: Outdoor, free. Golf packages avail. AE, CB, DC, DISC, MC, V.

🗏🗏🗏 Holiday Inn
2000 Holiday Inn Dr, 49202; tel 517/738-2681 or toll free 800/HOLIDAY; fax 517/783-5744. Exit 138 off I-94; N on US 127 to Springport Rd; W to entrance. A Holidome entertainment complex makes this an excellent choice for families. Easy-to-follow signs lead from highway to entrance. **Rooms:** 180 rms. CI 4pm/CO 11am. Nonsmoking rms avail. **Amenities:** 🗏 🖥 A/C, satel TV w/movies, voice mail. Some units w/terraces. Rooms adjoining Holidome have small patio area. **Services:** ✗ 🗏 🖘 🖘 **Facilities:** 🗂 🏊 🖙 🗔 🖢 1 restaurant, 2 bars, games rm, sauna, whirlpool, playground, washer/dryer. Nine-hole miniature golf, putting green, table tennis, and a variety of other options available in Holidome. Whirligig Bar & Restaurant on premises. **Rates (BB):** Peak (June–Aug) $70–$112 S or D. Children under age 18 stay free. Min stay wknds. Lower rates off-season. Parking: Outdoor, free. AE, CB, DC, DISC, JCB, MC, V.

🗏 Super 8 Motel
2001 Shirley Dr, 49202; tel 517/788-8780 or toll free 800/800-8000; fax 517/788-8780. Exit 138 off I-94; to Spring-

port Rd exit; E to Shirley Dr. Easy access to highway. Fine for business travelers; acceptable for overnight for families. **Rooms:** 54 rms and stes. CI 2pm/CO 11am. Nonsmoking rms avail. Clean, comfortable rooms. **Amenities:** 🖭 A/C, cable TV w/movies. **Services:** 🛌 🗘 🖉 Permission and deposit required for pets. Friendly staff. **Facilities:** 🔲20 🔲 🖕 **Rates (CP):** Peak (May–Sept) $42–$47 S or D; $48–$51 ste. Extra person $5. Children under age 12 stay free. Lower rates off-season. Parking: Outdoor, free. AE, CB, DC, DISC, JCB, MC, V.

RESTAURANTS 🍽

Brandywine Restaurant

2125 Horton Rd; tel 517/783-2777. **Seafood/Steak.** A massive fireplace dominates the lounge area; the greenhouse room is filled with plants, and antique Tiffany lamps illuminate the tables. Gilded elephant heads and seated lions, once legs for ornate pool tables, grace the entrances to the various dining rooms. The menu changes quarterly, but always includes selections for those with a "lighter appetite." Among the choices: Lady Godiva chicken, broiled and skinless breast covered with steamed vegetables; battered Icelandic haddock, and a 12-oz New York strip steak. **FYI:** Reservations recommended. Children's menu. Dress code. **Open:** Mon–Thurs 4–10pm, Fri–Sat 4–11pm. **Prices:** Main courses $7–$18. AE, MC, V. ❤ 🍷 🖻 🖤 🖕

★ Gilbert's Steak House

2323 Shirley Dr; tel 517/782-7135. Exit 138 (US 127) off I-94; N to Springport Rd exit; E to Shirley Dr. **Seafood/Steak.** Since 1946, this popular steak house has been known for its friendly service and reliable cuisine. Tiffany lamps and carved bars decorate each of the several dining rooms. Roast prime rib of beef (served au jus) is the best seller, but other steak choices are available. Other entree options include sweet-and-sour pork chops, chicken and pasta modena, and broiled seafood tarragon. All entrees come with house cheese spread and vegetable dip appetizer. **FYI:** Reservations recommended. Children's menu. **Open:** Mon–Thurs 11am–10pm, Fri–Sat 11am–11pm, Sun noon–7pm. **Prices:** Main courses $7–$19. AE, CB, DC, DISC, MC, V. 🍷 🖕

ATTRACTIONS 🏛

Michigan Space and Science Center

2111 Emmons Rd; tel 517/787-4425. Located in a futuristic geodesic-domed structure on the campus of Jackson Community College, this $30 million museum houses space artifacts provided by NASA and the Smithsonian Institute. Exhibits include the *Mercury Redstone* rocket; the *Apollo 9* command module, a piece of moon rock, spacecraft from the Mercury and Gemini programs, and a Lunar Rover moon vehicle. Interactive exhibits allow visitors to sit in a space capsule, look inside a black hole, or examine a three-dimensional

recreation of the moon's surface. Films and special presentations; gift shop. **Open:** Peak (May–Labor Day) Tues–Sat 10am–5pm, Sun noon–5pm. Reduced hours off-season. **$$**

Cascades Falls Park

Exit 138 off I-94; tel 517/788-4320. Park centered around 15 man-made 500-foot waterfalls; at night, six fountains are illuminated and set to music. The park itself spans 450 acres and features picnicking; a miniature-golf course; a driving range; basketball, tennis, and horseshoe courts; fishing pond and pier; and a restaurant. **Open:** Mem Day–Labor Day, daily 11am–11pm. **Free**

Ella Sharp Park

4th St; tel 517/788-4066. A 530-acre park with tennis courts, ballfields, 18-hole golf course, swimming pool, gardens, and picnic facilities. Houses the Ella Sharp Museum, a complex of historic buildings including a Victorian schoolhouse and log cabin. **Open:** Daily 24 hours. **Free**

Dahlem Environmental Education Center

7117 S Jackson Rd; tel 517/782-3453. Each year, more than 25,000 visitors roam the five miles of nature trails through forest land, marshes, and fields of wildflowers. Naturalist programs, workshops, expeditions, and special events are offered throughout the year. The Center hosts the nationally known Bluebird Festival and Wildlife Art Show (held annually on the first weekend in March). **Open:** Tues–Fri 8am–5pm, Sat–Sun noon–5pm. **Free**

Kalamazoo

Seat of Kalamazoo County, in southwest part of state. This midsized industrial city with plenty of culture and recreation in the outlying areas. Kalamazoo College, founded in 1833, hosts an annual Bach festival. **Information:** Kalamazoo County Convention & Visitors Bureau, 128 N Kalamazoo Mall, PO Box 1169, Kalamazoo, 49007 (tel 616/381-4003).

HOTELS 🏨

≡≡≡ Holiday Inn Airport

3522 Sprinkle Rd, 49002; tel 616/381-7070 or toll free 800/HOLIDAY; fax 616/381-4341. Exit 80 S off I-94. Unusual, attractive brickwork at entrance to lobby continues in interior areas. Generous use of plants and art throughout. Inner courtyard with large shade trees can be viewed from corridors and restaurant windows. **Rooms:** 146 rms. CI 3pm/CO noon. Nonsmoking rms avail. **Amenities:** 🖭 🖵 A/C, cable TV. **Services:** ✕ 🚗 🛌 🗘 🖉 Babysitting. **Facilities:** 🔲 🔲200 🖕 1 restaurant, 1 bar, games rm, sauna, whirlpool, washer/dryer. **Rates (CP):** Peak (May–Sept) $75 S; $83 D. Extra person $8. Children under age 18 stay free. Lower rates off-season. Parking: Outdoor, free. Special rates for golf weekends and New Year's Eve holiday weekend. AE, CB, DC, DISC, MC, V.

☰☰☰ Lees Inn

2615 Fairfield Rd, 49002; tel 616/382-6100 or toll free 800/733-5337; fax 616/382-2136. Exit 78 off I-94. New facility of a growing independent hotel chain in Michigan and Indiana. Simple brick exterior hides elaborate, two-story lobby with lavish crystal chandelier, winding stairway of handsome natural wood, and large lounge area set aside for generous continental breakfast. The motto here is "affordable luxury," and it is reflected in the special touches throughout. **Rooms:** 75 rms and stes. CI 2pm/CO noon. Nonsmoking rms avail. **Amenities:** 🛁 🖧 A/C, cable TV. Some units w/whirlpools. **Services:** 🚐 ⚟ 🖓 **Facilities:** 🔢 🖳 🖧 **Rates (CP):** Peak (May–Oct) $58–$80 S; $64–$88 D; $72–$95 ste. Extra person $8. Children under age 18 stay free. Lower rates off-season. Parking: Outdoor, free. Discounts for AARP, government employees, military personnel, and corporations. AE, DC, DISC, MC, V.

☰☰☰ Radisson Plaza Hotel

100 W Michigan Ave, 49007; tel 616/343-3333 or toll free 800/333-3333; fax 616/381-1560. Plain, almost severe entryway opens to spacious lobby and arcade of lovely shops. Beautifully appointed atrium lounge area on second level. Generous greenery throughout and even small courtyard on lower level. **Rooms:** 281 rms and stes. Executive level. CI 3pm/CO noon. Nonsmoking rms avail. **Amenities:** 🛁 🖧 A/C, cable TV, dataport. **Services:** ✕ 🗝 🆅🅿 🚐 ⚟ 🖓 Masseur, babysitting. **Facilities:** 🔢 🖼 🔢 🖧 3 restaurants (see "Restaurants" below), 2 bars (1 w/entertainment), spa, sauna, steam rm, whirlpool, beauty salon. Business facilities available at concierge level. Complete locker rooms for women and men in health club. **Rates:** $90–$135 S; $100–$145 D; $150–$275 ste. Extra person $10. Children under age 18 stay free. Parking: Indoor, $3.50/day. AE, CB, DC, DISC, JCB, MC, V.

MOTELS

☰☰ Days Inn

1912 E Kilgore Rd, 49002; tel 616/382-2303 or toll free 800/329-7466; fax 616/381-0032. Exit 78A off I-94 S; exit 78B off I-94 N. Clean, economical lodging for a short stay. Easy access to I-94 and close to airport. **Rooms:** 68 rms. CI 3pm/CO noon. Nonsmoking rms avail. **Amenities:** 🛁 A/C, cable TV. **Services:** 🚐 ⚟ 🖓 🍴 **Facilities:** 🔢 🔢 🖧 1 restaurant, 1 bar. **Rates:** Peak (May–Sept) $40–$60 S; $53–$65 D. Extra person $6. Children under age 12 stay free. Lower rates off-season. Parking: Outdoor, free. Participant in Days Inn "September Days Club," with special rates and benefits for senior travelers. AE, CB, DC, DISC, MC, V.

☰☰ La Quinta Inn

3750 Easy St, 49002; tel 616/388-3551 or toll free 800/531-5900; fax 616/342-9132. Exit 80 S off I-94. Attractive southwest decor, typical of this motel chain. **Rooms:** 120 rms. CI 3pm/CO noon. Nonsmoking rms avail. **Amenities:** 🛁 🖧 A/C. **Services:** 🚐 ⚟ 🖓 🍴 Bright, comfortable lounge adjacent to lobby for early continental breakfast. **Facilities:**

🔢 🔢 🖧 Washer/dryer. **Rates (CP):** $48–$55 S; $54–$61 D. Extra person $6. Children under age 18 stay free. Parking: Outdoor, free. AE, CB, DC, MC, V.

☰☰ Quality Inn

5300 S Westnedge Ave, 49008; tel 616/382-1000 or toll free 800/228-5151; fax 616/382-1000. Exit 76B off I-94. Easy access from interstate and on direct route to downtown area. **Rooms:** 102 rms. CI 3pm/CO noon. Nonsmoking rms avail. **Amenities:** 🛁 🖧 A/C, cable TV. Some units w/whirlpools. **Services:** 🚐 ⚟ 🖓 **Facilities:** 🔢 🔢 🖧 1 bar (w/entertainment). Free admission to nearby fitness center. **Rates (CP):** Peak (June–Sept) $62–$115 S or D. Extra person $8. Children under age 18 stay free. Lower rates off-season. Parking: Outdoor, free. AE, DC, DISC, MC, V.

☰ Red Roof Inn West

5425 W Michigan Ave, 49009; tel 616/375-7400 or toll free 800/THE-ROOF; fax 616/375-7533. Set on a winding road off busy US 131, the two buildings of the motel are separated by a wide lawn, beautiful floral plantings, and clusters of ornamental crab apple trees. Residential surroundings. **Rooms:** 108 rms. CI 2pm/CO noon. Nonsmoking rms avail. **Amenities:** 🛁 A/C, cable TV. **Services:** 🖓 🍴 **Facilities:** Guests have use of fitness center across the street for $2. **Rates:** Peak (May–Sept) $35 S; $47 D. Extra person $5. Children under age 19 stay free. Lower rates off-season. Parking: Outdoor, free. AE, DC, DISC, MC, V.

INN

☰☰☰ Stuart Avenue Inn

237 Stuart Ave, 49007; tel 616/342-0230; fax 616/385-3442. The Bartlett-Upjohn House, built in the 1880s, is the centerpiece of the inn's cluster of houses, and it is a treasure trove of magnificent antiques, many from the private collection of the innkeepers. The other two houses are also filled with furniture and accessories from the past. On the grounds is an acre of flowers, shrubs, and trees, with paths that wind between the plantings and lead to a small lily pond and a charming gazebo. Unsuitable for children under 15. **Rooms:** 17 rms and stes. CI 4pm/CO noon. No smoking. **Amenities:** 🛁 🖧 A/C, cable TV, refrig. Some units w/fireplaces, some w/whirlpools. **Services:** 🆅🅿 Breakfast served in two main dining parlors. **Facilities:** 🧍 🔢 Guest lounge. **Rates (CP):** Peak (Apr–Oct) $49 S; $59–$75 D; $100–$130 ste. Extra person $10. Min stay wknds. Lower rates off-season. Parking: Outdoor, free. AE, CB, DC, DISC, JCB, MC, V.

RESTAURANTS 🍴

Black Swan

In Parkview Hills Condominium Complex, 3501 Greenleaf Blvd; tel 616/375-2105. Exit 36A off I-131. **Eclectic.** Part of a condominium complex a short drive from the city, this large, airy restaurant overlooks the greenery of the surrounding area, as well as an attractive pond and fountain. Unique specialties include Amish duck, served with Michigan chutney; venison and morels in black currant sauce; mushroom and asparagus soup; and coconut shrimp. **FYI:** Reservations recommended. Children's menu. **Open:** Lunch Mon–Sat 11:30am–2pm; dinner Mon–Thurs 5:30–9pm, Fri–Sat 5–9:30pm, Sun 5–8:30pm; brunch Sun 11am–2pm. **Prices:** Main courses $15–$20. AE, CB, DC, DISC, MC, V. ♥ 🖼 ▲▲ VP &

⑤ ★ Carlos Murphy's
5650 W Main St; tel 616/343-0330. Exit 38A off I-131 N. **American.** A fun experience for the family, in a setting filled with crazy memorabilia and unusual relics from the travels of the restaurant's mysterious namesake. The menu is eclectic as well: quesadillas and Irish chili nachos, black bean and rice soup, grilled shark, specialty tacos and burritos. Also Mexican combos, burgers, sandwiches. **FYI:** Reservations accepted. Children's menu. **Open:** Mon–Thurs 11:30am–10pm, Fri–Sat 11:30am–11:30pm, Sun 11:30am–11pm. **Prices:** Main courses $6–$14. AE, CB, DC, DISC, MC, V. ▮ 🖼 &

Webster's
In Radisson Plaza Hotel, 100 W Michigan Ave; tel 616/343-4444. **American.** Noah Webster's library offers erudite dining, with a backdrop of pages from his original dictionary, warm walnut paneling, and soft leather chairs. Classy fare includes herb-roasted quail and seafood-stuffed corn crepes, and blackened Atlantic salmon, breasts of duckling and pheasant, and rack of lamb. The adjoining bar area, with attractive fireplace and comfortable seating, is a welcome spot to relax. **FYI:** Reservations accepted. Piano. Jacket required. No smoking. **Open:** Lunch Mon–Fri 11:30am–2pm; dinner Mon–Fri 5:30–9:30pm, Sat 5:30–10:30pm. **Prices:** Main courses $15–$20; prix fixe $27–$30. AE, DC, DISC, MC, V. ♥ ▮ VP &

ATTRACTIONS 📷

Kalamazoo Air Zoo
3101 E Milham Rd; tel 616/382-6555. Aviation history museum with more than 40 examples of World War II and Cold War–era aircraft, a flight simulator and cockpit mock-ups, and a large collection of aviation and military art. During summer months, the museum flies its classic 1929 Ford Tri-Motor as well as offering a "flight of the day" at 2pm in one of the antique planes that are on display. **Open:** Peak (June–Aug) Mon–Sat 9am–6pm, Sun noon–6pm. Reduced hours off-season. **$$**

Kalamazoo Institute of Arts
314 S Park St; tel 616/349-7775 or 349-3959. Twentieth-century American art—including works by Alexander Calder, Ed Pashke, and Helen Frankenthaler—is the primary focus of the permanent collection. Library and auditorium host educational programs; there's also a gift shop. **Open:** Tues–Sat 10am–5pm, Sun 1–5pm. **Free**

State Theater
404 S Burdick St; tel 616/344-9670. Originally built in 1927, this beautifully restored Spanish-style theater now hosts concerts and stage productions. **Open:** Call for schedule. **$$$$**

Echo Valley
8495 E "H" Ave; tel 616/349-3291. A winter sports park offering tobogganing, tubing, and ice skating. Visitors are charged solely for the attractions they use, with unlimited usage on the day of purchase. **Open:** Mid-Dec–Feb, Fri 6–9pm, Sat 10am–10pm, Sun noon–7pm. **$$$**

Kalamazoo Nature Center
7000 N Westnedge; tel 616/381-1574. This 600-acre nature center includes 11 miles of hiking trails, a herb garden and arboretum, and the restored 1858 DeLano Homestead (housing crafts and artifacts of local history). A re-created 1830s settlers farm is also featured. **Open:** Mon–Sat 9am–6pm, Sun 1–6pm. **$**

Lake Leelanau

REFRESHMENT STOP ☕

Manitou Farm Market
40 N Manitou Trail; tel 616/256-9165. **American/Deli.** Good for a roadside stop or light lunch, this is a true market and store that features a deli and a bakery stocking home-made foods and local area produce. Cherries are popular, as well as other fresh fruit and local jams. A variety of wines can be bought here, including local Michigan varieties. Winery in back. **Open:** Peak (May–Aug) daily 7am–7pm. Closed Nov–Apr. No CC. 🖼

Lakeside

See New Buffalo

Lansing

The State Capitol building, completed in 1879, emulates the architectural style of the National Capitol in Washington. In the early 20th century, Lansing was the home of the Oldsmobile; later, General Motors and other industrial employers moved here. Michigan State University, in neighboring East Lansing, was founded in 1855 as one of the country's first land-grant universities. **Information:** Greater Lansing Convention & Visitors Bureau, 119 Pere Marquette, PO Box 15066, Lansing, 48901-5066 (tel 517/487-6800).

HOTEL 🏨

⊟⊟⊟ Sheraton Lansing Hotel

925 S Creyts Rd, 48917; tel 517/323-7100 or toll free 800/325-3535; fax 517/523-2180. Off I-496. Attractive and comfortable with easy access to shopping and downtown. Sheraton's 1994 Hotel of the Year. Bike rentals, horseback riding, golf, and tennis nearby. **Rooms:** 219 rms and stes. Executive level. CI 3pm/CO noon. Nonsmoking rms avail. **Amenities:** 🛋 🕭 ☎ 🖥 A/C, cable TV w/movies, dataport. **Services:** ✕ 🚗 🗂 🛏 🛎 Twice-daily maid svce, babysitting. **Facilities:** 🛢 🏋 🗔 ₁₀₀₀ ⅙ 1 restaurant, 1 bar, racquetball, spa, sauna, whirlpool. Nautilus and weight room on pool level. **Rates:** $97–$115 S or D; $225 ste. Extra person $12. Children under age 18 stay free. AP and MAP rates avail. Parking: Outdoor, free. Golf packages avail. AE, CB, DC, DISC, ER, JCB, MC, V.

MOTELS

⊟⊟ Best Western Governor's Inn & Conference Center

6133 S Pennsylvania, 48911; tel 517/393-5500 or toll free 800/528-1234; fax 517/393-5500. At exit 104 off I-94. Comfortable, basic motel with easy access to highway. **Rooms:** 131 rms and stes. CI 3pm/CO noon. Nonsmoking rms avail. **Amenities:** 🛋 🕭 A/C, cable TV w/movies. Some units w/whirlpools. **Services:** ✕ 🗂 🛏 🛎 Car-rental desk. **Facilities:** 🛢 ₂₀₀ ⅙ 1 restaurant, 1 bar, games rm, sauna, whirlpool, playground. Brewster's American Grill and Lounge on premises. **Rates:** $49–$69 S or D; $69–$119 ste. Children under age 18 stay free. Parking: Outdoor, free. AE, CB, DC, DISC, MC, V.

⊟⊟⊟ ClubHouse Inn

2701 Lake Lansing Rd, 48912; tel 517/482-0500 or toll free 800/258-2466; fax 517/482-0557. At Lake Lansing exit off US 127. A home-away-from-home atmosphere for the business traveler. Near golf, tennis, and horseback riding. **Rooms:** 129 rms and stes. CI 3pm/CO noon. Nonsmoking rms avail. **Amenities:** 🛋 🕭 A/C, cable TV w/movies, dataport. Some units w/terraces, some w/whirlpools. **Services:** 🛏 🗂 🛎 Social director. Manager's reception with cocktails, soda, and snacks every evening 5–7pm. Emphasis on service. **Facilities:** 🛢 ₃₅ 🖥 ⅙ Whirlpool, washer/dryer. Passes to health club and racquet court available. **Rates (BB):** $62–$79 S; $79–$89 D; $78–$95 ste. Extra person $8. Children under age 16 stay free. AP and MAP rates avail. Parking: Outdoor, free. AE, CB, DC, DISC, MC, V.

⊟⊟⊟ East Lansing Marriott at University Place

300 MAC Ave, East Lansing, 48823; tel 517/337-4440 or toll free 800/646-4678; fax 517/337-5001. 1 block N of MSU campus. Centrally located lodgings, adjacent to MSU campus. Within walking distance of downtown stores and restaurants. Close to sports center, golf, tennis, bike and canoe rentals, jogging path. **Rooms:** 179 rms and stes. CI 3pm/CO noon. Nonsmoking rms avail. **Amenities:** 🛋 🕭 A/C, cable TV w/movies, dataport. Some units w/terraces. **Services:** ✕ 🚗 🗂 🛏 Babysitting. Express breakfast service provided. Fax and copy services available at front desk. On-command video service. **Facilities:** 🛢 🏋 ₆₀₀ ⅙ 1 restaurant, 1 bar, sauna, whirlpool, washer/dryer. Outdoor sundeck; Chesapeake Crab House seafood restaurant. **Rates:** Peak (Feb 15–June/Aug–Nov 15) $99–$129 S or D; $350 ste. Extra person $10. Children under age 18 stay free. Min stay special events. Lower rates off-season. AP and MAP rates avail. Parking: Indoor, free. Golf packages avail. AE, CB, DC, DISC, ER, JCB, MC, V.

⊟⊟ Hampton Inn

525 N Canal Rd, 48917; tel 517/627-8381 or toll free 800/426-7866; fax 517/627-5502. Exit 93B off I-96 to Saginaw. Comfortable, attractive lodging. No frills. Fine for business travelers. **Rooms:** 109 rms and stes. CI 3pm/CO noon. Nonsmoking rms avail. **Amenities:** 🛋 🕭 A/C, cable TV w/movies, refrig, dataport. Some units w/terraces. **Services:** ✕ 🗂 🛏 🛎 Babysitting. **Facilities:** ₇₅ ⅙ **Rates (CP):** Peak (May–Sept) $54–$59 S; $60–$65 D; $79 ste. Extra person $6. Children under age 18 stay free. Lower rates off-season. Parking: Outdoor, free. AE, CB, DC, DISC, MC, V.

⊟⊟⊟ Holiday Inn South/Convention Center

6820 S Cedar St, 48911; tel 517/694-8123 or toll free 800/333-8123; fax 517/699-3753. Exit 104 (Bus 96) off I-94. Attractive, comfortable lodgings near highway. Good for business and family travelers. Beautifully landscaped courtyards. **Rooms:** 300 rms and stes. Executive level. CI 3pm/CO noon. Nonsmoking rms avail. **Amenities:** 🛋 🕭 🖥 A/C, cable TV w/movies, refrig. Some units w/minibars, some w/whirlpools. **Services:** ✕ 🍽 🚗 🗂 🛏 Babysitting. Extended continental breakfast and complimentary cocktail hour for Executive Club members. **Facilities:** 🛢 🏋 ₅₀₀ 🖥 ⅙ 1 restaurant, 1 bar, games rm, sauna, whirlpool. Guests eligible for $5 daily membership at local health club. **Rates (CP):** $90–$115 S or D; $160 ste. Children under age 18 stay free. Parking: Outdoor, free. AE, CB, DC, DISC, MC, V.

⊟⊟ Park Inn International

1100 Trowbridge Rd, East Lansing, 48823; tel 517/351-5500 or toll free 800/437-PARK; fax 517/351-5509. Trowbridge Rd exit off I-496 and US 127. Serviceable accommodations for business travelers, students, and groups. Near MSU Stadium and ice arena. Golf nearby. **Rooms:** 172 rms, stes, and effic. CI 3pm/CO noon. Nonsmoking rms avail. **Amenities:** 🛋 🕭 🖞 A/C, cable TV w/movies. Some units w/whirlpools. **Services:** 🚗 🗂 🛏 🛎 Babysitting. **Facilities:** 🛢 ₂₀₀ ⅙ 1 restaurant, 1 bar, whirlpool, washer/dryer. **Rates:** $42–$55 S; $44–$68 D; $69–$109 ste; $69–$109 effic. Extra person $3. Children under age 18 stay free. Min stay special events. Parking: Outdoor, free. Golf and history tour packages avail. AE, CB, DC, DISC, ER, JCB, MC, V.

≣≣ Quality Inn

3121 E Grand River Rd, 48912; tel 517/351-1440 or toll free 800/221-2222; fax 517/351-6220. Grand River/Saginaw exit off US 127. Clean, comfortable, city motel. Golf nearby. **Rooms:** 100 rms and stes. CI 3pm/CO noon. Nonsmoking rms avail. **Amenities:** 🛁 A/C, cable TV w/movies. Some units w/whirlpools. **Services:** 🛏 🗘 **Facilities:** 🖈 💯 🖥 🕭 1 restaurant (bkfst and lunch only), 1 bar, whirlpool. Pool table, game arcade, exercise bikes. Health club across the street. **Rates (CP):** $52–$62 S; $59–$69 D; $90–$100 ste. Extra person $7. Children under age 18 stay free. Parking: Outdoor, free. AE, CB, DC, DISC, ER, JCB, MC, V.

≣≣≣ Quality Suites

901 Delta Commerce Dr, 48917; tel 517/886-0600 or toll free 800/228-5151; fax 517/886-0103. Saginaw exit off I-96. Gardenlike public areas and atrium courtyard with gazebo bring the outdoors inside at this attractive motel. Ideal for long-term guests. Golf and horseback riding nearby. **Rooms:** 117 stes. Executive level. CI 3pm/CO 11am. Nonsmoking rms avail. **Amenities:** 🛁 🕭 A/C, cable TV w/movies, refrig. Some units w/terraces, 1 w/whirlpool. TVs in both living and bedroom areas, wet bars, and microwaves. **Services:** 🚐 🛏 🗘 🖘 Babysitting. Complimentary cocktail hour in atrium every evening. **Facilities:** 🖈 🏊 🖥 🕭 Spa, sauna. **Rates (BB):** $56–$90 ste. Extra person $10. Children under age 18 stay free. Min stay special events. Parking: Outdoor, free. AARP discount and extended stay rates avail. AE, DC, DISC, JCB, MC, V.

≣≣≣ Residence Inn

1600 E Grand River Ave, East Lansing, 48823; tel 517/332-7711 or toll free 800/331-3131; fax 517/332-7711. On MI 43 E, ½ block E of Hagadorn Rd. Secluded suites, ideal for long-term stays. Resembles a town-house development. Nearby fishing, golf, and bike rentals. **Rooms:** 60 effic. CI 3pm/CO noon. Nonsmoking rms avail. Condominium-like units with complete kitchens. Two-story penthouses have full-size Murphy bed downstairs; sleeping area upstairs. **Amenities:** 🛁 🕭 📺 A/C, cable TV w/movies, refrig. Some units w/terraces, some w/fireplaces. **Services:** 🛏 🗘 🖘 Afternoon reception with soft drinks and snacks Mon–Thurs. Free grocery shopping service. VCR and movie rentals. **Facilities:** 🖈 🕭 Basketball, volleyball, whirlpool, washer/dryer. Guests have access to local health center. **Rates (CP):** $69–$129 effic. Extra person $10. Children under age 14 stay free. Parking: Outdoor, free. Rate discounts based on length of stay. AE, CB, DC, DISC, MC, V.

RESTAURANTS 🍴

Begger's Banquet

218 Abbott Rd, East Lansing; tel 517/351-4540. **American.** Popular eatery decorated with original artworks from local sculptors, painters, and photographers. Homemade patchwork quilt tablecloths. Dinners range from the "vegomatic" sandwich to braised short ribs and salmon chardonnay. **FYI:** Reservations recommended. Blues/string quartet. **Open:** Mon–Fri 11am–11:30pm, Sat 10am–12:30am, Sun 10am–10:30pm. **Prices:** Main courses $4–$19. DISC, MC, V. 🍷

Clara's Train Station

637 E Michigan Ave; tel 517/372-7120. 6 blocks E of capitol building. **American.** Located in a restored train station, this charming eatery is filled with crystal chandeliers, antique furnishings, friendly service, and good food. Sixteen-page menu includes Hawaiian chicken salad, light pork chop, and fillet and shrimp combination. **FYI:** Reservations accepted. Children's menu. **Open:** Mon–Thurs 11am–11pm, Fri–Sat 11am–midnight, Sun 10am–10pm. **Prices:** Main courses $5–$16. AE, MC, V. 🍽 🕭

Parthenon

227 S Washington Sq; tel 517/484-0573. 1 block S, 2 blocks E of capitol. **Greek.** Step into a Greek temple with a glass-enclosed sidewalk cafe in the middle of a downtown shopping area. You can get a lunch or dessert to go from the deli or stay for an early dinner. Traditional Greek specialties: moussaka, spanakotiropita, and souvlakia and scorpios (beef kabobs and shrimp) with rice pilaf. **FYI:** Reservations accepted. **Open:** **Prices:** Main courses $7–$14. AE, CB, DC, DISC, MC, V. 🕭

Sneekers

600 N Homer; tel 517/337-9201. US 127. **American.** A bright hot-air balloon marks the site of this popular sports bar and eatery with a spacious interior. Meals range from burgers to chicken à la king and from fried gizzards to fresh fruit plates. Rolls are served in individual "flower pots." Award-winning ribs. **FYI:** Reservations accepted. Children's menu. **Open:** Sun–Thurs 11am–9pm, Fri–Sat 11am–10pm. **Prices:** Main courses $5–$14. DISC, MC, V. 🕭

ATTRACTIONS 🏛

Michigan State University

East Lansing; tel 517/355-4458. Established in 1855, MSU is one of the oldest and most distinguished research institutions in the Midwest. Regularly scheduled walking tours of the parklike campus are conducted by student guides; special tours can be arranged for groups of 10 or more. **Open:** Daily 24 hours. **Free**

Abrams Planetarium

Shaw Lane, East Lansing; tel 517/355-4672. Sky theater presenting fantastic star shows produced by the newly installed state-of-the-art computer graphics star projector. The planetarium also serves as an astronomy and space science education resource center. **Open:** Daily 8:30am–4:30pm. **$**

State Capitol

Capitol and Michigan Aves; tel 517/373-2353. Victorian-era building designed by Elijah E Myers, one of the foremost architects of public buildings during Michigan's Gilded Age.

Tours of the public areas and the House and Senate galleries are available. **Open:** Mon–Fri 9am–4pm, Sat 10am–5pm, Sun noon–4pm. **Free**

Impression 5 Science Museum
200 Museum Dr; tel 517/485-8116. Housed in a 100-year-old building on the banks of the Grand River, this sophisticated hands-on museum introduces kids of all ages to the physical and natural sciences. An excellent selection of interactive science-related toys is offered at the museum store. **Open:** Mon–Sat 10am–5pm, Sun noon–5pm. **$$**

Michigan Historical Museum
208 N Capitol Ave; tel 517/373-3559. Major exhibits in this four-level museum include a three-story relief map of Michigan, a walk-through Upper Peninsula copper mine, a one-room schoolhouse, a re-created street scene from the 1920s, and a lakes-and-lands diorama complete with a rustic cabin and lighthouse. The State Archives of Michigan and Library of Michigan are also located in the Michigan Library and Historical Center complex. **Open:** Mon–Fri 9:30am–4:30pm, Sat noon–4:30pm. **Free**

R E Olds Transportation Museum
240 Museum Dr; tel 517/372-0422. Named in honor of automobile pioneer and local resident Ransom Eli Olds, the founder of Oldsmobile. In addition to housing an impressive collection of Oldsmobiles (including the first model, built in 1897), the museum also displays other Lansing-built transportation vehicles: trucks, bicycles, and even an airplane. Photographs of Olds's Victorian home, auto memorabilia, and period clothing also showcased. Gift shop. **Open:** Mon–Sat 10am–5pm, Sun noon–5pm. **$**

Fenner Nature Center
2020 E Mount Hope; tel 517/483-4224. Five miles of self-guided nature trails wind through 120 acres of various habitats, including maple forests, oak uplands, marshy thickets, fence rows, ponds, old fields, pine plantations, and swampland. Visitors center offers various educational programs. **Open:** Tues–Fri 9am–4pm, Sat 10am–5pm, Sun 11am–5pm. **Free**

Potter Park Zoo
1301 S Pennsylvania Ave; tel 517/483-4222. Beautiful 100-acre park, gardens, and zoo, located in the midst of a mature oak forest alongside the Red Cedar River. More than 400 species of wildlife are housed here, including rare Eastern black rhinoceroses, red pandas, Siberian tigers, snow leopards, mandrills, bongos, lemus, penguins, and kangaroos. New exhibits include the Encounters Farmyard and the Trappers Cabin–Wolf Exhibit. Large picnic pavilions. Camel rides, pony rides, and canoe rentals available seasonally. **Open:** Daily 8am–dusk. **Free**

Fitzgerald Park
133 Fitzgerald Park Dr, Grand Ledge; tel 517/627-7351. 10 mi W of Lansing. Located on top of the ancient sedimentary rocks that line the shores of the Grand River, this 78-acre park provides excellent opportunities for geological exploration. It offers approximately three miles of nature trails, two miles of cross-country ski trails, and recreational facilities including volleyball and basketball courts, a playground, several picnic sites, a disc golf course, two horseshoe pits, and a Nature Center. Skis and canoes can be rented. Naturalist presentations are available for groups. **Open:** Daily 8am–dusk. **Free**

Leland

LODGE 🏨

≡≡≡ **Leland Lodge**
565 Pearl St, PO Box 344, 49654; tel 616/256-9848; fax 616/256-8812. A handsome lodge appropriate for conferences, weddings, group seminars, or vacationers. Close to public golf courses and charter fishing from the Port of Leland. Walking distance from downtown shops and restaurants. **Rooms:** 25 rms and effic. CI 3pm/CO 11am. **Amenities:** 🛏 🔥 A/C, cable TV. Some units w/terraces. **Services:** 🍴 Babysitting. **Facilities:** 🎣 ⛴ ⅃ 1 restaurant (lunch and dinner only), 1 bar. Visitors can watch golfers on range next door from restaurant or deck outside. **Rates (CP):** Peak (July–Aug) $99–$139 S or D; $129–$179 effic. Extra person $10. Children under age 18 stay free. Lower rates off-season. Parking: Outdoor, free. AE, DISC, MC, V.

RESTAURANTS 🍽

Bluebird of Leland
102 River St; tel 616/256-9081. **American.** Located downtown on the river and within walking distance of shops and the harbor. Fresh Lake Michigan whitefish is the house specialty; the menu also lists grilled steaks, seafood, homemade soups, desserts, and the locally famous Bluebird cinnamon rolls. Nice atmosphere, good wine list. **FYI:** Reservations recommended. **Open:** Peak (June–Aug) lunch Tues–Sun 11:30am–3pm; dinner Mon–Sat 5–10pm, Sun 4–9pm; brunch Sun 10am–2pm. **Prices:** Main courses $9–$18. MC, V. 🅿

The Cove
111 River St; tel 616/256-9834. **Eclectic.** Located downtown near the harbor, the Cove offers outdoor dining on a wonderful deck with views of Lake Michigan. Service is uniformly excellent, from the wait staff to the cordial owner. As one might expect, the menu emphasizes seafood, including five preparations for whitefish. **FYI:** Reservations accepted. Children's menu. **Open:** Peak (June–Aug) daily 11am–10pm. Closed mid-Oct–mid-May. **Prices:** Main courses $11–$20. AE, MC, V. ♥ 🏞 ♿

Ludington

Seat of Mason County, in western Michigan. This Lake Michigan port city is surrounded by miles of forests, lakes, streams, and dunes. Auto ferry service to Manitowoc, WI during the warm months. **Information:** Ludington Area Convention & Visitors Bureau, 5827 W US 10, Ludington, 49431 (tel 616/845-0324 or toll free 800/542-4600).

HOTEL

Ramada Inn and Convention Center

4079 W US 10, 49431; tel 616/845-7311 or toll free 800/228-2828; fax 616/843-8551. Jct US 10/31. Fully equipped for conventions, seminars, meetings, weddings, parties, and conferences with seating and food service for 500. **Rooms:** 115 rms. CI 3pm/CO 11am. Nonsmoking rms avail. **Amenities:** A/C, cable TV, VCR. **Services:** Social director, babysitting. **Facilities:** 2 restaurants, 1 bar (w/entertainment), spa, sauna, whirlpool. Convention center, recreation room with Ping-Pong, game room. Pleasant, casual Main Sail Restaurant and First Cabin Restaurant for fine dining. Locals go to bar for karaoke entertainment. **Rates:** Peak (June 15–Labor Day) $84 S; $94 D. Extra person $10. Children under age 18 stay free. Lower rates off-season. Parking: Outdoor, free. Special dinner and theater packages avail. AE, DC, DISC, MC, V.

MOTELS

Four Seasons Motel

717 E Ludington Ave, 49431; tel 616/843-3448 or toll free 800/968-0180. Conveniently located with cordial husband and wife owners. Offers a good range of rates for the average traveler. **Rooms:** 33 rms. CI open/CO 11am. Nonsmoking rms avail. **Amenities:** A/C, cable TV. Some units w/minibars, some w/whirlpools. **Services:** **Facilities:** **Rates (CP):** Peak (July–Aug) $49–$86 S; $59–$96 D. Extra person $8. Children under age 12 stay free. Lower rates off-season. Parking: Outdoor, free. MC, V.

Pier House

801 W Ludington Ave, PO Box 667, 49431; tel 616/845-7346 or toll free 800/968-3677; fax 616/843-4441. Located by the beach, this basic motel offers a good location and fine rooms. Walking distance to the car ferry, marina, restaurants, shops, and local park. Good rates for the beach area. **Rooms:** 28 rms. CI open/CO 11am. Nonsmoking rms avail. **Amenities:** A/C, cable TV, VCR. Some units w/terraces. **Services:** **Facilities:** Spa. **Rates (CP):** Peak (June 19–Labor Day) $69 S; $79 D. Extra person $10. Children under age 1 stay free. Lower rates off-season. Parking: Outdoor, free. Off-season packages avail. Closed Nov–Apr. DISC, MC, V.

Snyder's Shoreline Inn

903 W Ludington Ave, PO Box 667, 49431; tel 616/845-1261; fax 616/843-4441. 4 mi from jct US 10/31. A unique family-owned country inn located at the beach, with a half-mile "Harbor Walk" along the channel between Lake Michigan and Pere Marquette Lake. A few miles from Ludington State Park. Tennis courts and golf courses nearby. Local shopping at antique shops, craft stores, gift shops, the local woolen outlet, and candy makers. There is also berry picking at a local blueberry patch. Book by May for summer and June for the fall colors. **Rooms:** 44 rms and stes. CI 3pm/CO 11am. Nonsmoking rms avail. Mostly luxury rooms that are individually decorated with antiques and/or handmade reproductions. Some have lace canopy beds. Visitors may opt for a cozy cabin or a Victorian bedchamber. Bridal suites available. **Amenities:** A/C, cable TV w/movies, refrig, VCR. Some units w/terraces, some w/whirlpools. Most rooms have individual patios or private balconies with a view of Lake Michigan or the pool. **Services:** Lending library. Personalized service. **Facilities:** 1 beach (lake shore), whirlpool. **Rates (CP):** Peak (June 15–Labor Day) $89–$199 S; $99–$199 D; $169–$209 ste. Extra person $10. Min stay special events. Lower rates off-season. Parking: Outdoor, free. AE, DC, MC, V.

The Viking Arms Inn

930 E Ludington Ave, 49431; tel 616/843-3441; fax 616/845-7703. A very cozy inn/motel. Nice grounds with gazebo and outside lawn chairs. Very hospitable owners. Known for exceptional quality. Close to all the attractions in Ludington, including the state park. **Rooms:** 45 rms. CI 2pm/CO 11am. Nonsmoking rms avail. Some rooms have an "inn" decor and are exceptionally decorated. **Amenities:** A/C, cable TV w/movies, VCR, CD/tape player. Some units w/minibars, some w/fireplaces, some w/whirlpools. **Services:** Twice-daily maid svce. Owners will arrange favorite flowers, wine, champagne, or fruit baskets in rooms on request. Movie library. **Facilities:** Whirlpool. **Rates:** Peak (May–Sept) $80–$120 S or D. Extra person $5. Lower rates off-season. Parking: Outdoor, free. Children stay free off-season. MC, V.

RESTAURANTS

Gibbs Country House Restaurant

3951 W US 10; tel 616/845-0311. **American.** Established in 1947, Gibbs serves home-style cooking in all three of its bustling dining rooms. Menus change seasonally and are usually organized around a theme, such as the springtime Asparagus Festival, Christmas in July, Big Fish Story (fish only), and A Taste of Autumn. Salad bar, dessert bar. All baked goods are made onsite, including their trademark sticky buns. **FYI:** Reservations recommended. Children's menu. **Open:** Peak (July–Aug) daily 8am–10pm. Closed Jan. **Prices:** Main courses $5–$25. MC, V.

★ PM Steamers

502 W Loomis; tel 616/843-9555. On the harbor. **Steak.** Known throughout Michigan as a place for fine dining. PM Steamers is tucked away at the waterfront with a beautiful

view of the harbor and car ferries. The restaurant has a tradition of ringing the Captain's bell each time a car ferry arrives or departs from the city marina. Stir-fry dishes, a vegetarian delight, homemade soups, and homemade desserts are among the menu options. **FYI:** Reservations recommended. **Open:** Lunch Tues–Fri 11:30am–2pm; dinner Tues–Thurs 5–9pm, Fri–Sat 5–10pm; brunch Sun 10:30am–2pm. Closed Jan. **Prices:** Main courses $9–$18. AE, MC, V. 🌑 🏔 ₺

★ Scotty's

5910 E Ludington; tel 616/843-4033. **Seafood/Steak.** Wooden lattices and plants give an outdoor air to this long-time Ludington favorite. Dinners include prime rib of beef (cut to 16- 10-, or 8-oz portions), Italian specialties, seafood, and pork chops. **FYI:** Reservations accepted. Children's menu. **Open:** Breakfast Sun 9am–1pm; lunch Mon–Fri 11:30am–2pm; dinner Mon–Thurs 5–10pm, Fri–Sat 5–10pm. Closed mid-Mar–mid-Apr. **Prices:** Main courses $9–$17. AE, MC, V. 🌑 🎮 ♡ ₺

Mackinac Island

See also Mackinaw City, St Ignace

This tiny resort island (pronounced "Mack-i-naw") allows no motorized traffic. Horse-drawn carriages meet the ferry from Mackinaw City; bicycles are also a popular mode of transportation. Mackinac Island State Park comprises about 80% of the island, and includes Fort Mackinac and the house of Dr William Beaumont. **Information:** Mackinac Island Chamber of Commerce, Main St, PO Box 451, Mackinac Island, 49757 (tel 906/847-6418 or 847-3783).

HOTELS 🏨

⊨⊨⊨ The Island House

PO Box 1410, 49757; tel 906/847-3347 or toll free 800/626-6304; fax 906/847-3819. Established in 1852, it was the first summer hotel on Mackinac Island. A long porch wraps around the front of the building. Large hotel. **Rooms:** 97 rms and stes. CI 3pm/CO 11am. Nonsmoking rms avail. Rooms, either standard or deluxe, have views of marina and Mackinac Harbor. **Amenities:** 🎴 ₺ 🖩 A/C, satel TV, refrig. Some units w/whirlpools. **Services:** 🛎 Babysitting. **Facilities:** 🍴 🔲50 1 restaurant (bkfst and dinner only; see "Restaurants" below), 1 bar (w/entertainment), games rm, whirlpool. **Rates:** $115–$155 S or D; $400 ste. Extra person $20. Children under age 13 stay free. AP and MAP rates avail. Islander getaway, classic weekend, and romantic retreat packages avail. Closed Nov–Apr. MC, V.

⊨⊨⊨ Lake View Hotel

1 Huron St, PO Box 190, 49757; tel 906/847-3384. Built in 1858, this is the oldest continuously operating hotel on Mackinac Island. **Rooms:** 85 rms. CI 3pm/CO 11am. Nonsmoking rms avail. Rooms have lake views, and third and

fourth floors have nice balconies. **Amenities:** 🎴 ₺ A/C, cable TV. Some units w/whirlpools. **Services:** 🛎 Babysitting. Friendly staff. **Facilities:** 🍴 🔲100 ₺ 1 restaurant, 1 bar, sauna, whirlpool. **Rates:** $119–$245 S; $149–$275 D. Children under age 16 stay free. Parking: Outdoor, free. Good deals offered on packages for special holidays and general getaways. Closed Oct 14–May 3. MC, V.

⊨⊨⊨ Madame La Framboise Harbor View Inn

Huron and Church Sts, PO Box 1207, 49757; tel 906/847-0101. Elegant hotel in large, restored, Victorian-style mansion built in 1820. Originally the home of a respected and renowned Midwest fur trader and granddaughter of Returning Cloud, chief of the Ottawa Indian Nation. Couples have been married on the balconies with views of the water. **Rooms:** 39 rms and stes. CI 3pm/CO 11am. Nonsmoking rms avail. Period furniture; garden and harbor views. **Amenities:** 🎴 ₺ 🖩 A/C, cable TV, refrig. Some units w/terraces, some w/whirlpools. **Services:** 🛎 **Facilities:** 🔲50 **Rates (CP):** $165–$235 D; $225 ste. Children under age 12 stay free. Closed Nov–May. AE, MC, V.

INN

⊨⊨⊨ Metivier Inn

Market St, PO Box 285, 49757; tel 906/847-6234. A quiet, Victorian-style inn off the main street. **Rooms:** 22 rms, stes, and effic. CI 3pm/CO 11am. No smoking. **Amenities:** 🎴 ₺ 🖩 A/C, cable TV, refrig. **Services:** 🛎 Wine/sherry served. **Facilities:** 🍴 ₺ **Rates (CP):** $145 D; $245 ste; $180 effic. Extra person $20. Rates are by the accommodation, not the number of people. DISC, MC, V.

RESORTS

⊨⊨⊨⊨ Grand Hotel

Mackinac Island, 49757; tel 906/847-3331 or toll free 800/334-7263; fax 906/847-3259. One of America's classics, this National Historic Monument is now in remarkably fine fettle for a centenarian following a top-to-bottom renovation in 1993. Its five-story, white-pillared facade rises above its famed 660-foot-long veranda trimmed with 2,000 potted geraniums and lined with white wicker rockers overlooking rolling acres of lawns and flower gardens. Being a landmark, the family-owned hotel overflows at times with curious visitors seeking a look around—but that lasts only until 6pm. **Rooms:** 320 rms and stes. CI 3pm/CO noon. Nonsmoking rms avail. Guestrooms come in many sizes, shapes, furnishings, colors, each one individually (and rather expensively) decorated in styles that range from Country Inn Sweet to Chateau Chic. Most rooms have freestanding wardrobes rather than closets and bath/shower units of preformed plastic. **Amenities:** 🎴 ₺ No A/C or TV. All units w/minibars, some w/terraces. No frills, including no radio and no TV (although sets are being installed room by room). Only some rooms have air conditioning, but all have portable fans. **Services:** ✗ 🛌 🛎 Twice-daily maid svce, social director, masseur, children's program, babysitting. Staff of 550 (including gardeners, greenskeepers, and squads of sweepers to follow the horses around) is jolly and helpful despite fact that tipping is forbidden. The hotel and ferryboat company move luggage from mainland directly to guestrooms—worth the $5 fee, but as a result corridors are often cluttered with bags waiting to be collected for the return journey. **Facilities:** ⛳ 🚴 ▶18 ⚓ 🏖 🍴4 🎿 [600] ♿ 8 restaurants, 4 bars (2 w/entertainment), volleyball, games rm, lawn games, sauna, whirlpool, beauty salon, day-care ctr. Sinuous free-form pool named for Esther Williams (who made a movie there with Jimmy Durante) is surrounded by lawns and loungers. Miles of hiking and jogging trails. Garden tours available. Buffet spread of 60-plus dishes in main dining room (a bargain at $19, even if you have to line up with non-hotel guests); also two-level Cupola Bar for wraparound views and dancing every evening, and nightly five-course dinners (jackets and ties for men) in Salle a Manger. **Rates (MAP):** Peak (mid-June–early Sept) $255–$435 S; $320–$500 D; $1,350 ste. Extra person $95. Children under age 4 stay free. Lower rates off-season. Because of variations within room categories, guests should preview a few rooms before unpacking to make sure they're getting the best value. Rates do not include 18% service charge (calculated *before* state tax is added to bill). Special package rates for theme weekends available. Overall, a good value, especially in spring and fall. Closed Oct–mid-May. MC, V.

≣≣≣ Mission Point Resort
Lake Shore Dr, PO Box 430, 49757; tel 906/847-3312 or toll free 800/833-7711. A 10 minute walk from the ferry dock. 18 acres. Spacious, first-class, luxury resort that has an enormous main lodge with three fireplaces. **Rooms:** 236 rms and stes. CI 11am/CO 3pm. Nonsmoking rms avail. **Amenities:** 🛏 🍴 A/C, cable TV w/movies, refrig, VCR. Some units w/terraces, 1 w/fireplace, some w/whirlpools. **Services:** ✗ 🔌 🛎 Social director, masseur, children's program, babysitting. Valet bike parking. Kids Klub for ages 12 and under. Very good service. **Facilities:** ⛳ 🍴3 🎿 [400] ♿ 2 restaurants, 1 bar (w/entertainment), 1 beach (lake shore), volleyball, sauna, whirlpool. Skate rentals, hay rides, singing wait staff, theater in-season. Kids eat free. **Rates:** Peak (June 16–Aug 26) $155–$205 S or D; $195–$695 ste. Extra person $20. Children under age 18 stay free. Lower rates off-season. Closed Nov–Apr. MC, V.

RESTAURANTS 🍴

Carriage House Restaurant
In Iroquois Hotel, Main St; tel 906/847-3321. **American.** A beautiful dining room with a garden atmosphere and views of the Straits of Mackinac. Steak, seafood, and vegetarian dishes are featured, and there's an extensive wine list. **FYI:** Reservations recommended. Piano. Children's menu. **Open:** Break-fast daily 8–11am; lunch daily 11:30am–3pm; dinner daily 5–10pm. Closed mid-Oct–mid-May. **Prices:** Main courses $18–$25. DISC, MC, V. ♥ ♿

♥ Governor's Dining Room
In the Island House, Main St; tel 906/847-3347. **American.** One of the top fine dining places on the island. The decor has a casual yet elegant ambience and the menu consists of traditional seafood, steak, and other fine dishes. Sesame seared tuna, pan-roasted salmon, and Grecian lamb chops are among the house specialties. **FYI:** Reservations accepted. Piano. Children's menu. **Open:** Breakfast daily 7:30–10:30am; dinner daily 5:30–10pm. Closed Oct 23–May 12. **Prices:** Main courses $19–$26. MC, V. ♥ ▮

Horns Gaslight Bar & Restaurant
Main St; tel 906/847-6154. **Eclectic.** Established in 1933, Horn's claims to have been one of the first bars to open after the repeal of Prohibition. There's a nicely carved wooden bar as well as table seating. The menu is somewhat eclectic, but relies heavily on burgers and traditional American food. **FYI:** Reservations not accepted. Children's menu. **Open:** Peak (mid-Apr–mid-Nov) daily 11am–2am. Closed Nov–May. **Prices:** Main courses $8–$9. MC, V. ▮ 📷

ATTRACTION 🏛

Mackinac Island State Park
MI 185; tel 906/847-3328. Michigan's first state park was established here, on the site of an important 18th-century British military outpost. (The park encompasses almost 80 percent of the three-mile-long island.) Shoreline and inland hiking trails offer exceptional vistas of the Straits of Mackinac and several surrounding geological formations such as the Sugarloaf (75-foot limestone pinnacle at the island's center) and Arch Rock (a massive natural bridge capping a lakeside cliff). Historic buildings on the island include Fort Mackinac (used as a British and American military outpost from 1780 through 1895), an Indian Dormitory dating from 1838, an 1830 Mission Church, and the 1780 Biddle House.

Cars are not allowed on Mackinac; transportation on the island is limited to horse-drawn carriages and bicycles. (Bicycle rentals are available.). Ferry service to the island is available from St Ignace and Mackinaw City; by air from St Ignace, Pellston, and Detroit. **Open:** Peak (June–Aug) daily 9am–6pm. Reduced hours off-season. **Free**

Mackinaw City

See also Mackinac Island, St Ignace

This tiny northern Michigan town lies in the shadow of Mackinac Bridge, a five-mile-long suspension bridge over the Straits of Mackinac. Fort Michilimackinac, located at the foot of the bridge, commemorates the town's founding as a fur-trading village. **Information:** Mackinaw Area Tourist Bureau, 708 S Huron, PO Box 160, Mackinaw City, 49701 (tel 616/436-5664 or toll free 800/666-0160).

HOTELS

≣ ≣ Best Western of Mackinaw City
112 Old US 31, PO Box 777, 49701; tel 616/436-5544 or toll free 800/647-8286; fax 616/436-7180. Exit 337 off I-75 N; exit 338 off I-75 S. Hotel has the largest pool in Mackinaw City. **Rooms:** 73 rms. CI 1pm/CO 11am. Nonsmoking rms avail. All rooms recently renovated, some with skylights. **Amenities:** ☎ ⚏ A/C, cable TV w/movies, refrig. **Services:** ⊲⊳ Full breakfast served in breakfast room outside near pool. **Facilities:** Games rm, whirlpool, washer/dryer. **Rates (CP):** Peak (June–Aug) $89–$110 S or D. Children under age 12 stay free. Lower rates off-season. Parking: Outdoor, free. Closed Nov–May. AE, MC, V.

≣ ≣ Quality Inn
917 S Huron Dr, 49701; tel 616/436-5051. A basic hotel at the edge of town. Convenient for travelers: 1 mile to golfing on Belvedere's golf course, 3 miles to nature trails at Fisherman's Island State Park, and 10 miles south on US 31 to Antrim Dells. **Rooms:** 60 rms. CI 3pm/CO 10am. Nonsmoking rms avail. **Amenities:** ☎ ⚏ A/C, cable TV w/movies. Some units w/terraces, some w/whirlpools. **Services:** ⊲⊳ Babysitting. **Facilities:** ⚏ 1 beach (lake shore), steam rm, whirlpool. **Rates:** Peak (June 20–Aug 21) $70–$145 S or D. Extra person $8. Children under age 18 stay free. Lower rates off-season. Parking: Outdoor, free. 10% discount for seniors 60 and over. Closed Oct 21–Apr. AE, DC, DISC, MC, V.

≣ ≣ Ramada Inn Convention Center
450 S Nicolet St, 49701; tel 616/436-5535; fax 616/436-5849. Off I-75; near exit 337. A new Ramada Inn and the only full-service hotel in the area. **Rooms:** 162 rms and stes. CI 3pm/CO 11am. Nonsmoking rms avail. **Amenities:** ☎ ⚏ A/C, cable TV w/movies, refrig. Some units w/whirlpools. **Services:** ⊲⊳ **Facilities:** 500 1 restaurant, 1 bar, games rm, sauna, whirlpool, washer/dryer. **Rates:** Peak (June–Aug) $59–$150 S or D; $95–$185 ste. Extra person $8. Children under age 12 stay free. Lower rates off-season. Parking: Outdoor, free. Discounts on holidays and for special events. AE, DC, DISC, MC, V.

MOTELS

≣ Affordable Inns
206 Nicolet St, PO Box 334, 49701; tel 616/436-8961 or toll free 800/388-9508. Centrally located, convenient to parks and ferries. Reasonable rates for area. **Rooms:** 56 rms. CI 1pm/CO 11am. Nonsmoking rms avail. **Amenities:** ☎ ⚏ A/C, cable TV w/movies. 1 unit w/whirlpool. **Services:** ⊲⊳ **Facilities:** Whirlpool. **Rates:** Peak (June–Aug) $46–$76 S or D. Children under age 12 stay free. Lower rates off-season. Parking: Outdoor, free. AE, DISC, MC, V.

≣ The Beachcomber Motel
1011 S Huron St, PO Box 159, 49701; tel 616/436-8451. Located on the water with its own sandy beach. Jet-ski rentals nearby. **Rooms:** 18 rms; 1 cottage/villa. CI 2pm/CO 11am. Nonsmoking rms avail. Some beachfront units. Housekeeping cottage for rent on weekly basis. **Amenities:** ☎ ⚏ A/C, cable TV w/movies. Some units w/terraces, some w/whirlpools. **Services:** ⊲⊳ **Facilities:** ⚏ 1 beach (lake shore). **Rates:** Peak (July–Aug) $52–$69 S or D. Extra person $3. Lower rates off-season. Parking: Outdoor, free. Closed Nov–May. DISC, MC, V.

≣ ≣ Best Western Dockside
5050 S Huron St, PO Box 722, 49701; tel 616/436-5001 or toll free 800/528-1234. Located on lakefront, with nice sun deck and all the amenities. Adjacent to Mackinac Island ferries, shops, and restaurants. **Rooms:** 88 rms and stes. CI 2pm/CO 11am. Nonsmoking rms avail. Lakefront rooms. **Amenities:** ☎ ⚏ ⚏ A/C, cable TV w/movies. Some units w/terraces, some w/whirlpools. **Services:** ⊲⊳ **Facilities:** ⚏ ⚏ 1 beach (lake shore), whirlpool. 300′ private sandy beach. **Rates:** Peak (June–Aug) $38–$195 S or D; $98–$385 ste. Children under age 12 stay free. Lower rates off-season. Parking: Outdoor, free. Casino package avail. Closed Nov–May. AE, CB, DC, DISC, MC, V.

≣ ≣ Econo Lodge Lakeside
519 S Huron, 49701; tel 616/436-7111 or toll free 800/55-ECONO. Off US 23. Nice hotel on the water. Walking distance to shops, restaurants, and ferries to Mackinac Island. **Rooms:** 59 rms. CI 2pm/CO 11am. Nonsmoking rms avail. Lakefront rooms. **Amenities:** ☎ ⚏ ⚏ A/C, cable TV w/movies, refrig. Some units w/terraces, some w/whirlpools. **Services:** ⊲⊳ **Facilities:** ⚏ ⚏ 1 beach (lake shore), sauna, whirlpool. Private beach and picnic tables. **Rates:** Peak (July–Aug) $58–$140 S or D. Extra person $6. Children under age 18 stay free. Lower rates off-season. Parking: Outdoor, free. Discounts for seniors. Closed Oct 25–Apr 15. AE, DISC, MC, V.

≣ ≣ ≣ Friendship Inn
712 S Huron, PO Box 282, 49701; tel 616/436-5777 or toll free 800/253-7216. Nestled within seven acres of northern pines, directly across from Mackinac Island ferry docks, this motel offers privacy. Good for families. **Rooms:** 40 rms; 22 cottages/villas. CI 2pm/CO 10am. Nonsmoking rms avail. Standard motel units and one- to three-bedroom chalets. **Amenities:** ☎ ⚏ A/C, cable TV, refrig. Some units w/terraces, 1 w/whirlpool. **Services:** ⊲⊳ **Facilities:** ⚏ ⚏ Lawn games, sauna, whirlpool, playground. Extensive family play area, including free miniature golf, basketball, and shuffleboard. **Rates:** Peak (July–Aug) $70–$95 S or D; $70–$135 cottage/villa. Extra person $5. Children under age 18 stay free. Lower rates off-season. Parking: Outdoor, free. Closed Nov–Mar. AE, CB, DISC, MC, V.

≣≣ Rainbow Motel

602 S Huron St, 49701; tel 616/436-5518 or toll free 800/888-6077. Off US 23 at the edge of town. Cozy atmosphere, one block from Mackinac Island ferry dock, restaurants, and shops. Recently renovated. **Rooms:** 29 rms. CI 3pm/CO 11am. Nonsmoking rms avail. Quiet first-floor units. **Amenities:** 🛏️⚟🖥️ A/C, cable TV w/movies, CD/tape player. Some units w/whirlpools. **Services:** 🍽️ **Facilities:** 🛗 Small yard or play area with outside seating and gazebo. Two whirlpools, one indoors and one outdoors. **Rates:** Peak (July–Aug) $52–$109 S or D. Extra person $5. Children under age 4 stay free. Lower rates off-season. Parking: Outdoor, free. Some off-season discounts. Closed Oct 21–Apr. DC, DISC, MC, V.

≣ Riviera Motel

520 N Huron St, PO Box 96, 49701; tel 616/436-5577. Exit 339 off I-75. Fantastic view of Mackinaw Bridge from grounds and outside pool. Reasonable rates. **Rooms:** 24 rms. CI 3pm/CO 11am. Nonsmoking rms avail. **Amenities:** 🛏️⚟ A/C, cable TV w/movies. Some units w/terraces, 1 w/whirlpool. **Services:** 🍽️ Friendly owners. **Facilities:** 🛗 **Rates:** Peak (June–Aug) $80–$100 S or D. Extra person $5. Min stay special events. Lower rates off-season. Parking: Outdoor, free. Closed Nov–Apr. MC, V.

≣≣ Super 8 Motel

601 N Huron Ave, 49701; tel 616/436-5252 or toll free 800/800-8000; fax 616/436-7004. Near the Mackinac Bridge. Relatively new, near Mackinac Bridge. **Rooms:** 50 rms. CI 3pm/CO 11am. Nonsmoking rms avail. **Amenities:** 🛏️⚟ A/C, cable TV. Some units w/terraces, some w/whirlpools. **Services:** 🍽️ 🍹 **Facilities:** 🛗 🎮 ♿ Games rm, sauna, whirlpool, washer/dryer. **Rates:** Peak (mid-June–Aug) $78 S; $78–$83 D. Extra person $4. Lower rates off-season. Parking: Outdoor, free. AE, DISC, MC, V.

≣≣ Surf Motel

907 S Huron, PO Box 58, 49701; tel 616/436-8831 or toll free 800/822-8314. Good for families. Located close to ferries, within walking distance of Arnold Ferry to Mackinac Island. **Rooms:** 40 rms and stes. CI 2pm/CO 11am. Nonsmoking rms avail. Beachfront rooms and two-bedroom family suites available. **Amenities:** 🛏️⚟ A/C, cable TV, dataport. Some units w/terraces. **Services:** 🍽️ 🍹 **Facilities:** 🛗 ♿ 1 beach (lake shore), volleyball, whirlpool, playground. Nice beach with rentals for adventure water sports, wave runners, paddleboats, wet suits, sun cats, and sailboats. **Rates:** Peak (July–Aug) $99–$119 S or D; $99–$119 ste. Extra person $5. Children under age 12 stay free. Lower rates off-season. Parking: Outdoor, free. Off-season specials; vacation and casino packages avail. Closed Oct–Apr. DISC, MC, V.

RESTAURANTS 🍴

Admiral's Table

502 S Huron St; tel 616/436-5687. Across from the Arnold Ferry Line. **American.** A nautical theme dominates the decor at this friendly and casual eatery. Fish (much of it caught in local waters) is delivered fresh daily; steaks, chicken, and a variety of salads round out the full menu. **FYI:** Reservations accepted. Children's menu. **Open:** Peak (June–Sept) breakfast daily 7–10am; lunch daily 11am–5pm; dinner daily 5–10pm. Closed Oct–May. **Prices:** Main courses $9–$15. DISC, MC, V. 💳♿

★ Audie's

314 Nicolet St; tel 616/436-5744. Near the bridge. **American.** Audie's is a well-known spot for a first-class meal. The Family Room is just that—a casual place to eat burgers, sandwiches, and hearty, family-style entrees. The more elegant Chippewa Room offers fine dining and Native American decor, with an emphasis on whitefish, steaks, seafood, and pasta. **FYI:** Reservations accepted. Children's menu. **Open:** Peak (June–Aug) breakfast Mon–Fri 7:30–10am, Sat–Sun 7–10am; lunch Mon–Sat 10:30am–2pm, Sun 11am–2pm; dinner daily 5–10pm. **Prices:** Main courses $12–$28. MC, V. 🌑

Ⓢ Crossroads Restaurant & Lounge

314 E Central Ave; tel 616/436-5788. **American.** A casual dining place, good for families and lighter meals. Diners can choose between the front dining room or the booths in the bar. Sandwiches, Mexican food, and pizza are all big hits here, as is the homemade Krazy Bread (made of pizza crust and melted cheese). **FYI:** Reservations not accepted. **Open:** Mon–Fri 11am–10pm, Sat–Sun 8am–10pm. Closed mid-Oct–mid-Mar. **Prices:** Main courses $5–$9. MC, V. 💳♿

The Embers

810 S Huron St; tel 616/436-5773. Across from the Arnold Ferry Dock. **American.** Located across from the Arnold Line Dock. A smorgasbord is available three meals a day, with many inventive uses of seafood including conch chowder and stuffed cod. A small on-site gift shop sells dolls and teddy bears. **FYI:** Reservations accepted. **Open:** Peak (June–Aug) daily 7am–10pm. Closed Nov–May. **Prices:** Main courses $9–$23. MC, V. 💳

Pancake Chef

327 Central Ave; tel 616/436-5578. **American.** Pancake Chef is a 30-year tradition in downtown in Mackinaw City. Good for families or a casual meal, the menu features a wide variety of pancakes and other breakfast specials as well as lunch items and dinner entrees. Salad bar and daily buffet available. **FYI:** Reservations not accepted. No liquor license. **Open:** Daily 7am–9pm. Closed Oct 15–May 15. **Prices:** Main courses $9–$11. DC, DISC, MC, V. 💳♿

ATTRACTIONS 🏛

Wilderness State Park
US 31; tel 616/436-5381. Located on Lake Michigan and the Straits of Mackinac, this 8,200-acre park features activities for all seasons, including beaches, waterskiing, boating, fishing, hunting, cross-country skiing, and snowmobiling. Camping sites available. **Open:** Daily sunrise–sunset. **$**

Colonial Michilimackinac
Southern end of Mackinac Bridge; tel 616/436-5563. Built in 1715 by the French as a military outpost and fur-trading center, Michilimackinac was taken over by the British in 1761 and by the Americans in 1781. Other restored buildings on the 27-acre site include a priest's house, blockhouses, barracks, a storehouse, St Anne's Church, a guardhouse, stockades, and a blacksmith shop. Costumed guides provide historical re-enactments and cooking and blacksmithing demonstrations. Outside the fort's walls, members of the Ojibwa tribe re-create an 18th-century Native American encampment. "Treasures from the Sand" (late June–Labor Day) allows visitors to view an archeological excavation. Visitors center presents dioramas, a video orientation, and other exhibits on Michilimackinac's history. **Open:** Peak (June–Sept) daily 9am–6pm. Reduced hours off-season. **$$$**

Madison Heights

Northern Detroit suburb. The Detroit Zoo is located in nearby Royal Oak. **Information:** Greater Madison Heights Chamber of Commerce, 26345 John R, Madison Heights, 48071 (tel 810/542-5010).

MOTELS 🏨

🎏🎏 Fairfield Inn
32800 Stephenson Hwy, 48071; tel 810/588-3388 or toll free 800/228-2800; fax 810/588-3388. S of 14 Mile Rd, W of I-75. Economy and comfort. Choice of restaurants nearby. **Rooms:** 134 rms. CI 3pm/CO noon. Nonsmoking rms avail. **Amenities:** 🛁 ⚙ A/C, cable TV w/movies, dataport. **Services:** 🛌 🍴 **Facilities:** 🔧 ⚫ **Rates (CP):** Peak (May–Oct) $47–$60 S or D. Extra person $4. Children under age 18 stay free. Lower rates off-season. Parking: Outdoor, free. AE, DC, DISC, MC, V.

🎏🎏 Residence Inn by Marriott Troy Southeast
Stephenson Hwy, 48071; tel 810/583-4322 or toll free 800/331-3131; fax 810/583-9092. Apartmentlike accommodations appeal to extended-stay business travelers. **Rooms:** 96 effic. CI 3pm/CO noon. Nonsmoking rms avail. **Amenities:** 🛁 ⚙ 📺 A/C, cable TV w/movies, refrig, dataport. Some units w/terraces, some w/fireplaces. **Services:** 🚐 🛌 🍴 🐕 Mon–Thurs evening social; Wed dinner. **Facilities:** 🔧 ⚽ 📺 ⚫ Basketball, volleyball, whirlpool, playground, washer/dryer. **Rates (CP):** $119–$159 effic. Children under age 18 stay free. Parking: Outdoor, free. AE, CB, DC, DISC, MC, V.

Manistee

Seat of Manistee County, in northwest part of state. This small, tourist-friendly town is one of the country's foremost producers of salt. Its position between Lake Michigan and Manistee Lake makes it a top vacation destination, with nearby Huron-Manistee National Forest and the Lake Michigan Recreation Area among the top draws. National Forest Festival takes place the week of July 4. **Information:** Manistee Area Chamber of Commerce, 11 Cypress St, Manistee, 49660 (tel 616/723-2575).

HOTELS 🏨

🎏🎏 Days Inn of Manistee
1462 US 31, 49660; tel 616/723-8385 or toll free 800/805-8385. 3 mi S of Manistee. Conveniently located with the usual Days Inn amenities. **Rooms:** 89 rms. CI open/CO 11am. Nonsmoking rms avail. **Amenities:** 🛁 ⚙ 🍴 A/C, cable TV w/movies, VCR. Some units w/whirlpools. **Services:** 🍴 **Facilities:** 🔧 📺 Whirlpool. **Rates:** Peak (July–Aug 10) $89 S or D. Extra person $6. Children under age 12 stay free. Lower rates off-season. Parking: Outdoor, free. AE, DC, DISC, MC, V.

🎏🎏 Manistee Inn & Marina
378 River St, 49660; tel 616/723-4000 or toll free 800/968-6277. A new hotel located on the river in downtown Manistee with private docks. Great for boaters. **Rooms:** 25 rms and effic. CI 2pm/CO 11am. Nonsmoking rms avail. **Amenities:** 🛁 ⚙ A/C, cable TV, refrig, VCR. Some units w/whirlpools. **Services:** 🍴 **Facilities:** 📺 15 docks available for $5 per night, and fish cleaning facilities. **Rates (CP):** Peak (June–mid-Sept) $61–$68 D; $61–$68 effic. Extra person $8. Children under age 12 stay free. Lower rates off-season. Parking: Outdoor, free. AE, DC, DISC, MC, V.

MOTELS

🎏 Lakeshore Motel
101 S Lakeshore Dr, 49660; tel 616/723-2667. A rustic motel located at the beach in Manistee. Walking distance from the "river walk" and Douglas Park. **Rooms:** 20 rms. CI open/CO 11am. Rooms have doors that open to beach. **Amenities:** 🛁 ⚙ 📺 A/C, cable TV. **Services:** 🐕 **Facilities:** 1 beach (lake shore). Beach has a playground. **Rates:** Peak (June–Aug) $60 S; $65 D. Extra person $3. Lower rates off-season. Parking: Outdoor, free. AE, DC, DISC, MC, V.

🎏🎏 Riverside Motel and Marina
520 Water St, 49660; tel 616/723-3554. On the Riverwalk. Great location on the "river walk" and close to historic downtown Manistee. **Rooms:** 21 rms; 1 cottage/villa. CI 3pm/CO 11am. **Amenities:** 🛁 📺 A/C, cable TV. **Services:** 🍴 🐕 Twice-daily maid svce. On special nights the owner offers pontoon boat rides for up to 12 guests. **Facilities:** 🔧 🎣 ⚫ **Rates:** Peak (June–Aug) $40–$70 S or D; $100 cottage/villa.

Extra person $5. Children under age 12 stay free. Lower rates off-season. Parking: Outdoor, free. Offers charter fishing packages. AE, DISC, MC, V.

RESTAURANTS 🍽

Dockside
445 River St; tel 616/723-3046. **American.** A casual diner in downtown Manistee offering booths by the bar as well as a separate dining area. Pizzas, sandwiches, and salads offer something for everyone. **FYI:** Reservations accepted. Children's menu. **Open:** Mon–Thurs 11am–10pm, Fri–Sat 11am–11pm. **Prices:** Main courses $7–$13. MC, V. 👪

Four Forty West
440 River St; tel 616/723-7902. **American.** Good food and friendly service amid breathtaking views of the Manistee River. Light fare such as chicken, seafood, and salads is the focus of the menu. Extensive wine list. **FYI:** Reservations accepted. **Open:** Mon–Thurs 11am–10pm, Fri–Sat 11am–10pm, Sun 10am–10pm. **Prices:** Main courses $9–$22. MC, V. ❤ 🏞 👪

ATTRACTION 🏛

Manistee County Historical Museum
425 River St; tel 616/723-5531. Housed in a drugstore from the 1870s, this museum relates the history of 19th-century Manistee, when it was an important lumber town and the third-busiest port on Lake Michigan. Exhibits include a replica of an early drugstore complete with apothecary scales, pill makers, and medicine jars; a re-created country store; and various antiques. **Open:** Tues–Sat 10am–5pm. $

Manistique

Seat of Schoolcraft County, on the Upper Peninsula. The area is well known for its coho salmon fishing, and a floating bridge with a roadway that is four feet below water level. Gateway for Manistee National Forest. **Information:** Schoolcraft County Chamber of Commerce, US 2, PO Box 72, Manistique, 49854 (tel 906/341-5010).

MOTELS 🏨

⬔ Budget Host Manistique Motor Inn
Rt 1, Box 1505, 49854; tel 906/341-2552 or toll free 800/283-4678. Nice motel with friendly owners and basic amenities. Popular with snowmobilers. **Rooms:** 24 rms and stes. CI 2pm/CO 11am. Nonsmoking rms avail. **Amenities:** 🛁🍴 A/C, cable TV w/movies, refrig. 1 unit w/whirlpool. **Services:** 🛏 🏳 **Facilities:** 🏕 🎿 🔥 Lawn games. **Rates:** Peak (June–Aug) $35–$40 S; $45–$53 D; $75 ste. Extra person $4. Children under age 12 stay free. Lower rates off-season. Parking: Outdoor, free. AE, CB, DC, DISC, MC, V.

⬔⬔ Ramada Inn
East Lakeshore Dr, 49854; tel 906/341-6911 or toll free 800/2-RAMADA; fax 906/341-6471. Motel with campground and full RV facilities adjacent. Near Big Springs. **Rooms:** 40 rms. CI noon/CO noon. Nonsmoking rms avail. **Amenities:** 🛁🍴 A/C, cable TV w/movies. **Services:** ✕ 🏳 **Facilities:** 🏕 🎿 ⬚250 🔥 1 bar (w/entertainment), sauna, whirlpool. **Rates:** Peak (June 16–Aug 31) $69–$79 S or D. Extra person $6. Children under age 12 stay free. Lower rates off-season. Parking: Outdoor, free. Snowmobile packages avail. AE, CB, DC, DISC, MC, V.

Marquette

See also Ishpeming

The largest city on the Upper Peninsula, Marquette is surrounded by miles of beaches, forests, and fruit orchards. The city has long been a center of iron and granite shipping; the loading of ore freighters may be viewed from Presque Isle Park. **Information:** Marquette County Tourism Council, 2552 US 41, #300, Marquette, 49855 (tel 906/228-7749 or toll free 800/544-4321).

HOTEL 🏨

⬔⬔⬔ Holiday Inn
1951 US 41 W, 49855; tel 906/225-1351 or toll free 800/HOLIDAY; fax 906/228-4329. Beautiful, high-ceiling lobby with stone fireplace. Convenient to downtown. Caters to families with children under 12. **Rooms:** 203 rms. CI 2pm/CO noon. Nonsmoking rms avail. **Amenities:** 🛁🍴 A/C, satel TV w/movies, dataport. **Services:** ✕ 🚐 🏳 🔑 Babysitting. Board games available at desk. Friendly, professional staff. **Facilities:** 🏕 🎿 🏊 ⬚400 🔥 1 restaurant, 1 bar (w/entertainment), games rm, sauna, whirlpool, washer/dryer. Gym available nearby. **Rates:** $45–$79 S or D. Extra person $4. Children under age 19 stay free. Parking: Outdoor, free. Ski packages avail. AE, CB, DC, DISC, EC, ER, JCB, MC, V.

MOTELS

⬔⬔⬔ Comfort Suites of Marquette
2463 US 41 W, 49855; tel 906/228-0028 or toll free 800/228-5151; fax 906/228-0028. Conveniently located, elegantly designed and decorated. Particularly well suited to families and business travelers. **Rooms:** 60 stes. CI 3pm/CO 11am. Nonsmoking rms avail. **Amenities:** 🛁🍴🍽 A/C, cable TV w/movies, refrig. Some units w/whirlpools. **Services:** 🍴 🔑 🚐 🏊 🏳 **Facilities:** 🏕 🎿 🏊 🌊 ⬚100 🔥 1 bar, games rm, spa, sauna, steam rm, whirlpool, washer/dryer. **Rates (CP):** Peak (June–Aug) $62–$125 ste. Extra person $6. Children under age 18 stay free. Lower rates off-season. Parking: Outdoor, free. AE, DC, DISC, MC, V.

Days Inn
2403 US 41 W, 49855; tel 906/225-1393 or toll free 800/ DAYS-INN; fax 906/225-1393. Comfortable, basic motel. **Rooms:** 65 rms and stes. CI 2pm/CO 11am. No smoking. **Amenities:** 🗄 🖭 A/C, cable TV w/movies. **Services:** 🚐 🕼 Friendly, helpful staff. **Facilities:** 🗄 🏃 🖭 🔟 ᴕ Sauna, whirlpool. **Rates (CP):** Peak (July–Aug) $50 S; $68–$95 D; $75–$90 ste. Extra person $5. Children under age 18 stay free. Lower rates off-season. Parking: Outdoor, free. AE, DC, DISC, MC, V.

Super 8 Motel
1275 US 41 W, 49855; tel 906/228-8100 or toll free 800/ 800-8000; fax 906/228-8100. A clean, efficient, basic motel. Located close to skiing and other winter sports. Convenient to downtown Marquette. **Rooms:** 80 rms. CI 2pm/CO noon. Nonsmoking rms avail. **Amenities:** 🗄 🖭 A/C, cable TV w/movies. **Services:** 🕼 Helpful staff. **Facilities:** 🗄 🏃 🖭 🔟 ᴕ Games rm, sauna, whirlpool, washer/dryer. **Rates (CP):** $46 S; $57 D. Extra person $5. Children under age 18 stay free. Parking: Outdoor, free. AE, DC, DISC, MC, V.

Tiroler Hof Motel
1880 US 41 S, 49855; tel 906/226-7516 or toll free 800/ 892-9376. Built into the side of a hill, featuring authentic Austrian architecture. Private ski hill and house chapel on grounds. Public access beach near the hotel, but not attached to it. **Rooms:** 45 rms and stes. CI open/CO 11am. Decor of the rooms is somewhat dated, but the beautiful view of Lake Superior from every window makes up for it. **Amenities:** 🗄 Satel TV. No A/C. Some units w/terraces. **Services:** 🕼 **Facilities:** 🗄 🏃 🖭 1 restaurant, games rm, sauna. **Rates:** Peak (mid-May–mid-Oct) $46–$50 D; $64–$68 ste. Extra person $6. Lower rates off-season. Parking: Outdoor, free. DISC, MC, V.

Value Host Motor Inn
1101 US 41 W, 49855; tel 906/225-5000 or toll free 800/ 929-5996. On US 41. Basic, inexpensive, clean motel. No frills. Close to hiking and downtown Marquette. **Rooms:** 50 rms and effic. CI 3pm/CO 11am. Nonsmoking rms avail. **Amenities:** 🗄 A/C, cable TV w/movies. **Services:** 🆅🅿 Friendly staff. **Facilities:** 🏃 🖭 🔟 ᴕ Sauna, whirlpool. **Rates (CP):** $35–$38 S; $37–$42 D; $50–$55 effic. Extra person $4. Children under age 12 stay free. Parking: Outdoor, free. DISC, MC, V.

RESTAURANTS 🍴

Northwoods Supper Club
260 Northwoods Rd; tel 906/228-4343. ½ mi off US 41. **American.** Don't let the name fool you: lunch and a colossal Sun brunch are also served. Owned and run by the Klumb family since 1934, when Fred Klumb began selling chicken dinners out of his cabin. The cabin has since been integrated into a much larger building, which includes the dining room, banquet rooms, and Freddy's Lounge. Lounge offers sandwiches and hosts live music Sun and Wed nights. Alice, the

gardener/botanist, leads tours through the extensive blooming garden Tues, Wed, and Fri at 10am—the tour culminates with lunch and costs $8. **FYI:** Reservations recommended. Cabaret/folk. Children's menu. **Open:** Mon–Thurs 11am–10pm, Fri–Sat 11am–11pm, Sun 10am–10pm. **Prices:** Main courses $7–$30. AE, DISC, MC, V. 🍱 🏞 ᴕ

★ Vierling Saloon & Sample Room
119 S Front St; tel 906/228-3533. **American.** A gathering place for locals since 1883. Its current incarnation is a restored, beautifully decorated brick building. The restaurant specializes in Lake Superior whitefish (offering five daily selections) and a sample platter of six different domestic and imported beers. Also served is an excellent selection of hamburgers, chicken entrees, and steaks; raspberry shortcake is a stand-out dessert. The basement level houses a microbrewery. **FYI:** Reservations recommended. **Open:** Mon–Sat 11am–midnight. **Prices:** Main courses $4–$13. AE, DC, DISC, MC, V. 🍱 🏞 ᴕ

ATTRACTIONS 💼

Marquette County Historical Museum
213 N Front St; tel 906/226-3571. Exhibits include a Native American diorama and a re-creation of a fur trading post. Gift shop sells books on Upper Peninsula history. **Open:** Mon–Fri 10am–4:30pm. **$**

Presque Isle Park
Lake Shore Blvd; tel 906/228-0460. A suburban park offering a wide range of recreational activities. During summer months, visitors may choose to picnic, swim, play tennis, or go boating on Lake Superior. During the winter, the park is a magnet for winter sports, including cross-country skiing, sledding, snowshoeing, and ice fishing. **Open:** Mid-May–Nov, daily 7am–11pm. **Free**

Marshall

Seat of Calhoun County. This southern Michigan town lost its bid to become state capital in 1847, but many of the substantial homes built during its mid-19th-century period of influence still remain and are open for tours. **Information:** Marshall Area Chamber of Commerce, 109 E Michigan Ave, Marshall, 49068 (tel 616/781-5163 or toll free 800/ 877-5163).

MOTEL 🏨

Arbor Inn
15435 W Michigan Ave, 49068; tel 616/781-7772 or toll free 800/424-0807; fax 616/781-2660. Two single-story buildings just off highway outside of town. Lake behind, but no beach. **Rooms:** 48 rms and effic. CI 4pm/CO noon. Nonsmoking rms avail. **Amenities:** 🗄 A/C, cable TV w/movies. Microwaves available for rental. **Services:** 🕼 🐾 Babysitting. Free coffee 24 hours/day. Pets allowed in smoking rooms

only. **Facilities:** 🏕 🎣 🚐 ♿ Volleyball, playground. Horseshoe pits, picnic tables, grills. Tent available for party use. Free access to local fitness center. **Rates:** $46–$67 S; $49–$70 D; $55–$76 effic. Extra person $3. Children under age 12 stay free. Parking: Outdoor, free. AE, CB, DC, DISC, MC, V.

INNS

☰☰☰ McCarthy's Bear Creek Inn

15230 C Drive N, 49068; tel 616/781-8383. At Michigan Ave. Surrounded by hand-built fieldstone fences, this handsome house and barn, once part of a working farm, now house 14 unique rooms, seven in each building. Business travelers will appreciate the quiet; couples will relish the romantic surroundings; families will enjoy the location. **Rooms:** 14 rms. CI 3pm/CO noon. Nonsmoking rms avail. Most furniture handcrafted by owners. House rooms are generally large, and all have private baths: some with shower only, some with tub only, some with both. Rooms in barn are more modern, with full baths. Views overlook Bear Creek or meadow and farmlands. **Amenities:** ⛱ A/C. No phone or TV. Some units w/terraces. TV available on request. Rooms in barn have private balconies. **Services:** ⫝ **Facilities:** 🚐 Guest lounge. **Rates (BB):** $65–$98 S or D. Extra person $10. Children under age 18 stay free. Parking: Outdoor, free. Deposit of 50% required when reservations are made; cancellation notice required 10 days in advance for full refund. AE, MC, V.

☰☰☰ The National House Inn

102 S Parkview, 49068; tel 616/781-7374. Built as a stagecoach stop in 1835, this distinctive lodging in the heart of downtown Marshall is characterized by its massive beam-and-brick open hearth fireplace and freshly popped popcorn. **Rooms:** 16 rms and stes (2 w/shared bath). CI 3pm/CO noon. No smoking. Each room individually decorated and handsomely appointed with antiques, reproductions, and modern conveniences. **Amenities:** ☎ ⛱ A/C, cable TV. **Services:** ⫝ Babysitting, afternoon tea served. Popcorn always available. **Facilities:** 🚐 ♿ Guest lounge w/TV. Access to health club; racquetball and tennis courts can be arranged. **Rates (CP):** $66–$68 S or D w/shared bath, $85–$95 S or D w/private bath; $125–$130 ste. Extra person $10. Children under age 7 stay free. Min stay special events. Parking: Outdoor, free. 50% deposit required to hold rooms; one-week cancellation notice required for full refund. Packages include candlelight, home tour, and mystery weekends. AE, MC, V.

RESTAURANT 🍴

Schuler's

115 S Eagle St; tel 616/781-0600. Exit 110 off I-94 or exit 36 off I-69. **American.** Distinctive dining in a bowling alley–livery stable–hotel turned restaurant, presided over by four generations of Schulers. Cheery checked cloths cover tables

and famous sayings dot the walls and rafters. Entrees emphasize local products, such as Michigan rainbow trout, Allegan County wood-grilled pork steaks, farm-raised duck, and garden cannelloni Palermo. **FYI:** Reservations recommended. Children's menu. **Open:** Mon–Fri 11am–10pm, Sat 11am–11pm, Sun 10am–9pm. **Prices:** Main courses $11–$20. AE, DC, DISC, MC, V. 🍴 ♿

ATTRACTION 🏛

Honolulu House Museum

107 N Kalamazoo Ave; tel toll free 800/877-5163. A bit of Hawaii in the Midwest. This 1860 Victorian house mixes classic Italianate architecture with tropical decorative motifs. Among its unique features are a pagoda-capped tower, intricately painted 15-foot ceilings, and a raised veranda. **Open:** May–Oct, daily noon–5pm. **$**

Marysville

See Port Huron

Midland

Seat of Midland County. This small central Michigan city is the site where Herbert Henry Dow founded (in 1897) the chemical company that bears his name; Dow Chemical Company's world headquarters is still based here. Dow's son Alden, an architect who studied under Frank Lloyd Wright, designed nearly 50 buildings in town. **Information:** Midland County Convention & Visitors Bureau, 300 Rodd St, Midland, 48640 (tel 517/839-9901 or toll free 800/678-1961).

HOTEL 🏨

☰☰ Holiday Inn

1500 W Wackerly Rd, 48640; tel 517/631-4220 or toll free 800/622-4220; fax 517/631-3776. Typical Holiday Inn with all the amenities, close to local area attractions. **Rooms:** 235 rms and stes. Executive level. CI 4pm/CO 1pm. Nonsmoking rms avail. **Amenities:** ☎ ⛱ 🗎 A/C, cable TV w/movies, refrig, bathrobes. **Services:** ✕ 🔑 🖙 ⫝ 🛎 Babysitting. **Facilities:** 🏊 🏋 🎱 🍸 400 🖥 ♿ 1 restaurant, 1 bar (w/entertainment), games rm, racquetball, sauna, whirlpool. **Rates:** $71–$74 S; $71–$84 D; $150 ste. Extra person $10. Children under age 12 stay free. Parking: Outdoor, free. AARP discount and corporate rates avail. AE, DISC, MC, V.

RESTAURANT 🍴

Bamboo Garden

2600 N Saginaw Rd; tel 517/832-7966. **Chinese.** A classy Chinese restaurant with very nice decor and a relaxing atmosphere. House specialties include sizzling steak, almond chicken, mu shu pork with mandarin pancakes, and Buddha duck. **FYI:** Reservations accepted. **Open:** Peak (June–Aug)

Mon–Thurs 11:30am–9pm, Fri 11:30am–10pm, Sat 5–10pm, Sun noon–8pm. **Prices:** Main courses $9–$16. MC, V. ♥

ATTRACTIONS 📷

Midland Center for the Arts
1801 W St Andrews; tel 517/631-5930. Housed in a building designed by Alden Dow, son of Herbert Dow and protégé of Frank Lloyd Wright. The center's highlight is the Hall of Ideas, an interactive museum with exhibits on science and technology as well as the arts and humanities. Live music, theater, and dance performances are held here throughout the year. **Open:** Daily 10am–6pm. **$**

Herbert H Dow Historical Museum
3100 Cook Rd; tel 517/832-5319. This museum documents the life and contributions of Herbert H Dow, founder of Dow Chemical Company and a pioneering figure in industry, science, and philanthropy. Exhibits include a laboratory, a drillhouse, and the renovated workshop of Joseph Dow (Herbert's father). Tours are available by appointment. **Open:** Wed–Sat 10am–4pm, Sun 1–5pm. **$**

The Dow Gardens
Eastman Rd and W St Andrews St; tel 517/631-2677. Started in 1899 by Dow Chemical founder Herbert H Dow, this 96-acre garden features a wide variety of trees, evergreens, and flowers, along with waterfalls and streams. Educational programs offered. **Open:** Daily 10am–sunset. **$**

Chippewa Nature Center
Jct Pine River and Badour Rds; tel 517/631-0830. More than 900 acres of woods, fields, ponds, rivers, and wetlands are traversed by 12 miles of hiking and cross-country skiing trails. Also on the grounds are a log schoolhouse (built circa 1880) and a homestead farm (built circa 1870); costumed interpreters are on hand to answer visitors' questions. **Open:** Visitors center, Mon–Fri 8am–5pm, Sat 9am–5pm, 1–5pm. **Free**

Monroe

Seat of Monroe County, in the southeastern corner of the state. Named in honor of President James Monroe. This former industrial city sits on the banks of the River Raisin, so named because of the grapes that grow in the region. Old French Town Days is held here every August. **Information:** Monroe County Convention & Tourism Bureau, 111 E 1st St, PO Box 1094, Monroe, 48161 (tel 313/457-1030 or toll free 800/252-3011).

MOTELS 🛏

🏨🏨 Holiday Inn
1225 N Dixie Hwy, 48161; tel 313/242-6000 or toll free 800/242-6008; fax 313/242-0555. Exit 15 off I-75, W to entrance. Rustic timbers and antique western photos capitalize on Monroe's history as the birthplace of General Custer.

For business or family travelers. Golf nearby; state park with lake beach nearby. **Rooms:** 127 rms. CI 2pm/CO noon. Nonsmoking rms avail. Clean, comfortable accommodations. **Amenities:** 🛏 ⚬ A/C, satel TV w/movies, dataport. **Services:** ✕ 🖼 ↩ 🍴 **Facilities:** 🏊 🏢 ⅙ 1 restaurant, 1 bar (w/entertainment), games rm, spa, sauna, whirlpool. **Rates:** $60–$68 S or D. Extra person $8. Children under age 18 stay free. Parking: Outdoor, free. Weekend golf packages avail. AE, CB, DC, DISC, MC, V.

🏨🏨 Monroe Lodge
1440 N Dixie Hwy, 48161; tel 313/289-4000; fax 313/289-4262. Exit 15 (MI 50) off I-75; E to entrance. Conveniently located near 38-hole golf course and outlet mall, motel offers comfortable lodgings and pleasant facilities. **Rooms:** 115 rms. CI 1:30pm/CO noon. Nonsmoking rms avail. All rooms have entry from interior hall. **Amenities:** 🛏 ⚬ 🔳 A/C, cable TV, dataport. Some units w/terraces. Second-story rooms have separate balconies. **Services:** ✕ 🖼 ↩ 🍴 **Facilities:** 🏊 🏢 1 restaurant, 1 bar, games rm, sauna, whirlpool. **Rates:** Peak (June–Aug) $43 S or D. Extra person $6. Children under age 18 stay free. Lower rates off-season. Parking: Outdoor, free. AE, CB, DC, DISC, MC, V.

ATTRACTION 📷

Monroe County Historical Museum
126 S Monroe St; tel 313/243-7137. Home of one of the largest collections of 18th- and 19th-century artifacts relating to southeastern Michigan. Main exhibits include items from the region's French Canadian settlers; relics and trophies from the life of Gen George Custer (he lived in Monroe for a brief time); and Victorian furniture, decorative arts, and clothing. **Open:** Peak (June–Aug) daily 10am–5pm. Reduced hours off-season. **$**

Mount Pleasant

Seat of Isabella County, in central Michigan. A center of oil production since the 1920s, the area also produces maple syrup, apples, and other fruits. Home of Central Michigan University. **Information:** Mount Pleasant Area Convention & Visitors Bureau, 114 E Broadway, Mount Pleasant, 48858-1698 (tel 517/772-4433).

RESTAURANT 🍴

Embers
1217 S Mission St; tel 517/773-5007. **American.** Pasta, steak, and seafood, served in a casual yet elegant atmosphere. The kitchen is well known for its 16-oz pork chop and Embers-style caesar salad. **FYI:** Reservations accepted. **Open:** Dinner Mon–Thurs 5–9pm, Fri–Sat 5–10pm, Sun noon–7pm; brunch Sun 10am–2pm. **Prices:** Main courses $16–$26. MC, V. ♥

Munising

Seat of Alger County, on the Upper Peninsula. Multicolored sandstone cliffs rise as high as 200 feet at nearby Pictured Rocks National Lakeshore. Erosive action of waves, rain and ice has carved the cliffs into caves, arches, columns, and promontories. **Information:** Munising Visitors Bureau, PO Box 405, Munising, 49862 (tel 906/387-2138).

HOTELS

Best Western of Munising

MI 28 E, PO Box 310, 49862; tel 906/387-4864 or toll free 800/528-1234. 3 mi E of town. Groomed snowmobile trails adjacent to motel. **Rooms:** 80 rms and stes. CI 1pm/CO 11am. Nonsmoking rms avail. **Amenities:** A/C, cable TV, refrig. **Services:** **Facilities:** 1 restaurant, 1 bar (w/entertainment), sauna, whirlpool. Largest indoor pool complex in the area. **Rates:** Peak (June 23–Sept 4) $60–$85 S; $65–$90 D; $80–$100 ste. Extra person $5. Children under age 12 stay free. Lower rates off-season. Parking: Outdoor, free. DISC, MC, V.

Days Inn

Bay St, 49862; tel 906/387-2493 or toll free 800/DAYS-INN; fax 906/387-5214. Comfortable. Pictured Rocks Cruises are five blocks away; downtown is three blocks away. **Rooms:** 66 rms and stes. CI 3pm/CO 11am. Nonsmoking rms avail. Lakefront rooms available. **Amenities:** A/C, cable TV w/movies, refrig. 1 unit w/fireplace, 1 w/whirlpool. Kitchenettes available. **Services:** **Facilities:** Sauna, whirlpool. Snowmobile trails start at the door. **Rates:** Peak (June–Aug) $80 S or D; $125 ste. Children under age 18 stay free. Lower rates off-season. Parking: Outdoor, free. DISC, MC, V.

Mirage

MI 28 E, PO Box 276, 49862; tel 906/387-5292. Located close to Munising, opposite Mackinac Bridge. **Rooms:** 61 rms. CI 1pm/CO 11am. Nonsmoking rms avail. Large family units and two-bedroom suites. **Amenities:** A/C, cable TV. Some units w/whirlpools. **Services:** **Facilities:** Games rm, whirlpool, washer/dryer. Nice sun deck. **Rates (CP):** Peak (June–Aug) $60–$85 S or D. Extra person $6. Children under age 18 stay free. Lower rates off-season. Parking: Outdoor, free. Senior discounts. AE, DC, DISC, MC, V.

MOTELS

Alger Falls Motel

Rte 1 Box 967, 49862; tel 906/387-3536. 2 mi E of town. Basic motel convenient to town. **Rooms:** 17 rms; 1 cottage/villa. CI noon/CO 11am. Nonsmoking rms avail. **Amenities:** A/C, cable TV. **Services:** **Facilities:** **Rates:** Peak (June–Sept/Dec–Apr) $45–$58 S or D; $65 cottage/villa. Extra person $4. Children under age 5 stay free. Lower rates off-season. Parking: Outdoor, free. DISC, MC, V.

Sunset Resort Motel

1315 Bay St, 49862; tel 906/387-4574. Off MI 58; 1 mi from town on Lake Superior. Rustic resort on the water. **Rooms:** 16 rms, stes, and effic. CI 3pm/CO 11am. All knotty pine rooms, with view of Lake Superior. **Amenities:** Cable TV, refrig, dataport. No A/C or phone. **Services:** **Facilities:** 1 beach (lake shore), playground. Dock, picnic tables, and places to barbecue. **Rates:** Peak (mid-June–Labor Day) $42–$46 S or D; $51 ste; $51 effic. Extra person $3. Children under age 5 stay free. Lower rates off-season. Parking: Outdoor, free. Weekly rates available. Closed Nov–Apr. MC, V.

RESTAURANT

Dogpatch

820 E Superior St; tel 906/387-9948. **American.** The emphasis here is on good, simple food—and lots of it. Local and traveling Abners and Daisy Maes especially enjoy the Friday night seafood buffet, the Saturday night steak fry and prime rib special, and the Sunday brunch. **FYI:** Reservations accepted. Children's menu. **Open:** Peak (June–Aug) daily 7am–10pm. **Prices:** Main courses $9–$15. MC, V.

ATTRACTION

Pictured Rocks National Lakeshore

Tel 906/387-3700. Named for the multicolored sandstone cliffs that rise as high as 200 feet above the southern shore of Lake Superior, this park is one of the scenic highlights of the Upper Peninsula. The park stretches alongside the lakeshore for more than 40 miles, and includes cliffs, beaches, sand dunes, waterfalls, and forest. Boat tours allow for better views of the rocks themselves; some are so distinctive that they have been named. Elsewhere in the park, a series of small lakes, ponds, and streams offer opportunities for fishing and boating. The 40-mile Lakeshore Trail is just that, linking the cities of Munising and Grand Marais at opposite ends of the park. At the Grand Marais end are the Grand Sable Dunes and Twelvemile Beach, the site of summertime hiking and picnicking and wintertime cross-country skiing. Three modern campgrounds and numerous primitive campsites are available. **Open:** Daily sunrise–sunset. **Free**

Muskegon

Seat of Muskegon County, in western Michigan. More than three million tons of cargo pass through Muskegon Channel each year. A freshwater reef off Père Marquette Park attracts a variety of fish, including trout, perch, and several varieties of salmon. **Information:** Muskegon Economic Growth Alliance, 230 Terrace Plaza, 2nd Floor, PO Box 1087, Muskegon, 49440-1087 (tel 616/722-3751 or toll free 800/235-3866).

HOTEL 🏨

≣≣≣ Holiday Inn Muskegon Harbor

939 3rd St, 49440; tel 616/722-0100 or toll free 800/ HOLIDAY; fax 616/722-5118. 1 block from Walker Auditorium. The largest facility in the downtown area, with easy access to theaters, the sports auditorium, and the nearby community college. Recently renovated, the atrium lobby has a handsome chandelier, and generous plantings brighten public areas. **Rooms:** 193 rms. CI 3pm/CO noon. Nonsmoking rms avail. **Amenities:** 🏠 🔱 📺 A/C, cable TV. **Services:** ✕ 🚐 🛆 🕹️ **Facilities:** 🔄 🏊 🛁 ⌐750⌐ 🔱 1 restaurant, 1 bar, spa, sauna, steam rm, whirlpool. Pool is on second level with attractive open deck beyond it. **Rates:** Peak (May–Sept) $80 S or D. Children under age 12 stay free. Lower rates off-season. Parking: Indoor, free. Package rates avail for use of Pleasure Island facilities. Theater packages avail. AE, CB, DC, DISC, MC, V.

MOTELS

≣ Bel Aire Motel

4240 Airline Rd, 49444; tel 616/733-2196. An older-style motel, with parking at each doorway—a favorite with fishers and boaters who can keep their equipment right at their entranceways. **Rooms:** 16 rms. CI 4pm/CO 11am. Nonsmoking rms avail. **Amenities:** 🏠 A/C, cable TV. **Services:** 🕹️ 🖐️ **Facilities:** 🏊 **Rates (CP):** $48 S; $56 D. Extra person $5. Parking: Outdoor, free. AE, MC, V.

≣≣ Best Western Park Plaza

2967 Henry, 49441; tel 616/733-2651 or toll free 800/ 727-5752; fax 616/733-5202. An elaborate mirrored stairway to the second level highlights the spacious lobby, and a large patio beyond the outside pool adds a welcoming note to an otherwise standard exterior. **Rooms:** 108 rms and stes. CI 3pm/CO noon. Nonsmoking rms avail. **Amenities:** 🏠 A/C, cable TV. **Services:** ✕ 🛆 🕹️ 🖐️ **Facilities:** 🔄 🏊 ⌐150⌐ 🔱 1 restaurant, 2 bars (1 w/entertainment), games rm, sauna, whirlpool. **Rates:** Peak (May–Sept) $56 S; $64 D; $90–$160 ste. Extra person $6. Children under age 17 stay free. Lower rates off-season. Parking: Outdoor, free. AARP discount. AE, CB, DC, DISC, MC, V.

≣≣ Comfort Inn

1675 E Sherman Rd, 49444; tel 616/739-9092 or toll free 800/221-2222; fax 616/739-2264. Simple brick exterior highlighted with board-and-batten trim. Inner court area beyond pool is handsomely planted, and umbrella tables add splash of color. **Rooms:** 117 rms and stes. CI 3pm/CO 11am. Nonsmoking rms avail. **Amenities:** 🏠 🔱 A/C, cable TV. Some units w/whirlpools. **Services:** 🛆 🕹️ **Facilities:** 🔄 🏊 🛁 ⌐150⌐ 🔱 1 bar, games rm, sauna, steam rm, whirlpool, washer/ dryer. **Rates (CP):** Peak (May–Sept) $71–$75 S; $76–$80 D; $91 ste. Extra person $5. Children under age 18 stay free. Lower rates off-season. Parking: Outdoor, free. AE, CB, DC, DISC, MC, V.

≣≣ Days Inn

150 E Seaway Dr, 49444; tel 616/739-9429 or toll free 800/ 329-7466; fax 616/733-1930. The indoor pool, just off the lobby, brings bright light into the entryway. Closest facility to the Portolum Rd exit to Michigan's Adventure Amusement Park and its neighboring Wild Water Adventure Park. **Rooms:** 152 rms. CI 3pm/CO 11am. Nonsmoking rms avail. **Amenities:** 🏠 A/C, cable TV. **Services:** ✕ 🛆 🕹️ **Facilities:** 🔄 🏊 ⌐40⌐ 🔱 1 restaurant, whirlpool, washer/dryer. **Rates:** Peak (May–Sept) $58 S; $58–$72 D. Extra person $6. Children under age 18 stay free. Lower rates off-season. Parking: Outdoor, free. Weekend rates are lower. 10% discount for members of Days Inn ICC (Incredible Card Club). AE, CB, DC, DISC, MC, V.

≣ Seaway Motel

631 Norton Ave, 49444; tel 616/733-1220; fax 616/ 733-1220. **Rooms:** 29 rms. CI 1pm/CO 11am. Nonsmoking rms avail. **Amenities:** 🏠 A/C, cable TV, refrig. **Services:** 🕹️ 🖐️ Babysitting. **Facilities:** 🔄 🏊 **Rates:** Peak (June–Sept) $32–$45 S; $35–$60 D. Extra person $5. Children under age 18 stay free. Lower rates off-season. Parking: Outdoor, free. AE, DC, DISC, MC, V.

RESTAURANTS 🍽️

★ Doo Drop Inn

2410 Henry St; tel 616/755-3791. **Seafood/Steak.** A neighborhood standby known for more than 60 years as a place for good, solid food. Baby back ribs, 22-oz porterhouse, beef kabobs, and the cabbage roll dinner are popular. Perch, pan-fried to a tender crispness, is brought in from Lake Erie. **FYI:** Reservations accepted. Karaoke/piano. Children's menu. **Open:** Peak (June–Sept) Mon–Thurs 11am–9pm, Fri–Sat 11am–midnight, Sun 11am–9pm. **Prices:** Main courses $6– $19. AE, CB, DC, DISC, MC, V. 🖐️ 🚗 🗂️ 🔱

Ⓢ The Hearthstone

In the Cornerstone Motor Inn, 3350 Glade St; tel 616/ 733-1056. **American.** An intimate restaurant decorated in dark wood and leather, with a small hearthstone fireplace near the entryway. Soup, made fresh every day and served with a wonderful french bread, is the specialty. A favorite sandwich features corned beef, ham, Swiss or Havarti cheese, spicy mustard, and house dressing on rye bread. Other popular entrees are shrimp and snow peas in a cream sauce and spinach linguine with marinated tomatoes. **FYI:** Reservations accepted. Children's menu. **Open:** Peak (June–Labor Day) Mon–Thurs 11am–11pm, Fri–Sat 11am–midnight, Sun 5–10pm. **Prices:** Main courses $6–$12. AE, DC, MC, V. 🗂️ 🖐️ 🚗 🔱

House of Chan

375 Gin Chan Ave; tel 616/733-9624. **Chinese.** On its own personally named street, this rather imposing restaurant offers seating at booths enclosed in miniature pagodas. Menu options include seafood Wo Buy (shrimp, scallops, and lobster stir-fried with bok choy) and Hong Kong breaded

chicken breast in oyster sauce. A special Chinese-American lunch buffet is available Tues, Thurs, and Sun. **FYI:** Reservations recommended. Children's menu. **Open:** Tues–Thurs 11:30am–10pm, Sat 4–11pm, Sun noon–10pm. **Prices:** Main courses $6–$18. AE, MC, V.

Rafferty's

601 Terrace Point Blvd; tel 616/722-4461. **New American.** Diners enjoy casual waterfront dining with panoramic views of Muskegon's harbor area. Seafood is the best bet here: pan-fried Canadian walleye is made with a pretzel crumb crust and served with whole grain mustard, and there are crispy crab cakes pan-fried and served with red-pepper cream. Ready for a 16-oz pork chop? It's here—accented with smokey apple chutney, chargrilled, and accompanied with caramelized onions and homemade mashed potatoes. **FYI:** Reservations recommended. Children's menu. **Open:** Lunch Mon–Fri 11:30am–5pm; dinner Mon–Thurs 5–10pm, Fri–Sat 5–11pm; brunch Sun 10am–2pm. **Prices:** Main courses $14–$22. AE, MC, V.

★ Tony's Club

785 W Broadway; tel 616/739-7196. At Henry St. **Greek.** It's the best Greek food in this part of Michigan, and a weekly trip to Chicago's Greektown means the freshest and most authentic ingredients. *Psari plaki* (Greek-style whitefish) is very popular, as are the Greek-style pork chops and lamb chops. Tony's is the original home of Sam's Famous Bar Cheese, an appetizer now sold throughout the area. **FYI:** Reservations recommended. Children's menu. Jacket required. **Open:** Mon 11:30am–9pm, Tues–Thurs 11:30am–10pm, Fri 11am–11pm, Sat 5–11pm. **Prices:** Main courses $10–$18. AE, CB, DC, DISC, MC, V.

ATTRACTIONS

Muskegon Museum of Art

296 W Webster Ave; tel 616/722-2600. The impressive permanent collection includes paintings, prints, photography, sculpture, and glassworks by American and European masters of the 19th and 20th centuries. Pissarro, Degas, Homer, Hopper, Rembrandt, Remington, and Whistler are among the artists represented. **Open:** Tues–Fri 10am–5pm, Sat–Sun noon–5pm. **Free**

USS *Silversides*

1346 Bluff; tel 616/755-1230. Legendary World War II submarine restored to look as it did when it served with the Pacific Fleet. Guided tours available. **Open:** Peak (June–Aug) daily 10am–5:30pm. Reduced hours off-season. **$$**

Pleasure Island Water Fun Park

Pontaluna Rd; tel 616/798-7857. Amusement park featuring a variety of slides, tube rides, swimming areas, bumper and pedal boats, and water cannons. There's an arcade and a miniature-golf course if you'd rather not get wet. Picnic area and concessions also on grounds. **Open:** Mem Day–Labor Day, daily 10am–9pm. **$$$$**

Michigan's Adventure

4750 Whitehall Rd; tel 616/766-3377. Family-friendly amusement park with more than 30 rides and attractions, including three roller coasters and a giant gondola Ferris wheel. The park is also home to Wild Water Adventure, a water park with slides, a wave pool, and a 613-foot man-made river. **Open:** Mem Day–Labor Day, daily, call for hours. **$$$$**

Newberry

Seat of Luce County, on the Upper Peninsula. This former lumber mill town celebrates its heritage at the Lumberjack Days Festival, held every August. **Information:** Newberry Area Tourism Association, MI 28 and MI 123, PO Box 308, Newberry, 49868 (tel 906/293-5562 or toll free 800/831-7292).

HOTELS

≡≡ Best Western Zellar's Village Inn

S Newberry Ave, PO Box 474, 49868; tel 906/293-5114 or toll free 800/528-1234; fax 906/293-5116. 2½ mi N of MI 28 on MI 123. In the center of state and federal parks with 350 miles of groomed snowmobile trails. **Rooms:** 20 rms. CI open/CO 11am. Nonsmoking rms avail. **Amenities:** A/C, cable TV. **Services:** **Facilities:** 1 restaurant, 1 bar (w/entertainment), games rm. Attractive restaurant offers homemade food and baking **Rates:** Peak (June 16–Oct 15) $38–$42 S; $60–$64 D. Extra person $6. Children under age 12 stay free. Lower rates off-season. Parking: Outdoor, free. AE, MC, V.

≡≡ Comfort Inn

Jct MI 28/123, 49868; tel 906/293-4000. Close to snowmobile trails and Manistique Lake. **Rooms:** 54 rms and stes. CI 1pm/CO 10am. Nonsmoking rms avail. **Amenities:** A/C, cable TV w/movies. Some units w/whirlpools. **Services:** **Facilities:** Games rm, spa, washer/dryer. Large whirlpool and sauna. **Rates (CP):** Peak (June–Aug) $42–$80 S or D; $84 ste. Extra person $6. Children under age 18 stay free. Lower rates off-season. Parking: Outdoor, free. AE, DC, MC, V.

MOTEL

≡ Manor Motel

S Newberry Ave, 49868; tel 906/293-5000. Quiet, small, local motel, located 25 miles from scenic falls. Good rates for the area. **Rooms:** 12 rms. CI 3pm/CO 11am. Nonsmoking rms avail. **Amenities:** A/C, cable TV w/movies. No phone. **Services:** **Facilities:** **Rates:** Peak (July–Sept) $52–$66 S or D. Children under age 18 stay free. Lower rates off-season. Parking: Outdoor, free. Closed Oct 20–May 20. DISC, MC, V.

ATTRACTION 🏛

Luce County Historical Museum

411 W Harrie St; tel 906/293-5946. Formerly a sheriff's residence and jail, this Queen Anne–style structure is now a museum housing local historical artifacts and records. The jail cells are still intact and are open to visitors. **Open:** July 4–Aug, Tues–Wed and Sat 2–4pm. **Free**

New Buffalo

Small town on Lake Michigan, close to Indiana. A summer mall is open in the old roundhouse, and there is a public marina. Nearby Warren Dunes State Park draws many visitors. **Information:** Harbor Country Chamber of Commerce, 3 W Buffalo St, New Buffalo, 49117 (tel 616/469-5409 or toll free 800/362-7251).

HOTELS 🏨

🎗🎗 Gordon Beach Inn

16220 Lakeshore Rd, Union Pier, 49129; tel 616/469-0800. A favorite resort hotel in the 1920s, this has undergone a thorough renovation, yet retains the charm of an earlier time. A large fireplace in the lobby is ringed with comfortable chairs. Hallways are brightened with lovely hand-stenciled borders of Native American patterns and botanical themes of the area. Local artists exhibit weekends in the Gallery downstairs. Three blocks from beach. **Rooms:** 20 rms and stes. CI 3pm/CO noon. Nonsmoking rms avail. Modest furnishings, but a bentwood rocker is a pleasant addition to each room. **Amenities:** 🛋 🕯 TV. No A/C. Some units w/terraces, some w/whirlpools. **Services:** 🛎 Babysitting. **Facilities:** 🏋 🛒20🛒 1 restaurant (dinner only). **Rates (CP):** Peak (May–Oct) $75–$125 S or D; $125 ste. Children under age 18 stay free. Lower rates off-season. Parking: Outdoor, free. DISC, MC, V.

🎗🎗🎗 Lakeside Inn

15281 Lakeshore Rd, Lakeside, 49116; tel 616/469-0600; fax 616/469-1914. Exit 6 off I-94. Set high on a bluff overlooking Lake Michigan, this was a favorite resort in the 1920s and 1930s and is being restored to its original charm. Complete renovation is underway, with loving attention to detail. The 100′-long front porch is a favorite spot for watching sunsets over Lake Michigan. Beach is across the street. **Rooms:** 30 rms. CI 3pm/CO noon. No smoking. **Amenities:** 🛋🕯A/C, TV. Some units w/whirlpools. **Services:** 🛎 **Facilities:** 🚲 🏋 🛒30🛒 🕹 1 beach (lake shore). **Rates (BB):** Peak (May–Sept) $75–$90 S; $100–$150 D. Children under age 18 stay free. Lower rates off-season. Parking: Outdoor, free. Rates slightly higher for lakeside rooms. DISC, MC, V.

MOTEL

🎗🎗 Comfort Inn

11529 O'Brien Court, 49117; tel 616/469-4440; fax 616/469-5972. Exit 1 off I-94. Set well back from the busy traffic into Plaza One, a popular truck stop on the interstate, this well-kept motel provides good accommodations. Spacious central courtyard with bird feeders and benches. **Rooms:** 96 rms and stes. CI 3pm/CO 11am. Nonsmoking rms avail. **Amenities:** 🛋 A/C, TV. Some units w/whirlpools. **Services:** 🛋🖰🐾 **Facilities:** 🏊🛒18🛒🏋 🛒50🛒🕹 **Rates (CP):** Peak (June–Sept) $60–$70 S; $66–$76 D; $76–$99 ste. Extra person $6. Children under age 18 stay free. Lower rates off-season. Parking: Outdoor, free. AE, CB, DC, DISC, MC, V.

INN

🎗🎗🎗 The Inn at Union Pier

9708 Berrien St, Union Pier, 49129; tel 616/469-4700; fax 616/469-4720. Exit 6 off I-94. A family resort of the 1920s has been converted into a beautiful inn for the 1990s, with a complex of three buildings, each with its own group of charming rooms. The inn boasts the largest private collection of antique Swedish fireplaces—these "kakelugns" were imported and installed by Swedish craftspeople. Sandy Lake Michigan beach across the street. Unsuitable for children under 12. **Rooms:** 16 rms and stes. CI 4pm/CO noon. No smoking. Furnishings are wonderful blend of antiques and modern pieces. Details of rooms based on ceramic decorations on fireplaces. Each room is a delight of light and color. **Amenities:** 🛋 🕯 🎵A/C. No TV. Some units w/terraces, some w/fireplaces, some w/whirlpools. **Services:** 🛋 Afternoon tea served. Refreshments always on hand in large lounge area, and sunny breakfast room is filled each morning with aroma of freshly baked muffins and breads. Fax and copier services available. **Facilities:** 🚲 🏋 🛒25🛒 🕹 Lawn games, guest lounge w/TV. A/V equipment and 46″ TV with VCR available for meetings. **Rates (BB):** Peak (May–Oct) $105–$130 D; $150–$175 ste. Extra person $20. Children under age 18 stay free. Min stay wknds. Lower rates off-season. Parking: Outdoor, free. Discounts on Sun–Thurs lodging. Corporate rates avail. DISC, MC, V.

RESTAURANTS 🍴

Brewster's

11 W Merchant St (Downtown); tel 616/469-3005. 1 block N of US 12. **Deli/Italian.** The name doesn't convey it, but this restaurant is akin to a Tuscan villa in its food and atmosphere. A huge wood-burning oven is the star attraction in the open kitchen; a grand array of cheeses, salamis, prosciutto, and other items waits in the deli display case. The menu, which changes daily, includes unusual pasta and pizza specials. Many types of muffins available for breakfast. **FYI:** Reservations accepted. **Open:** Peak (June–Labor Day) Mon–Thurs 9am–9pm, Fri–Sat 9am–10pm, Sun 9am–9pm. **Prices:** Main courses $6–$9. AE, CB, DC, DISC, MC, V. 🍽 🖰 🏋 🕹

Dakota's

203 W Buffalo (US 12); tel 616/469-6255. **Seafood/Steak.** The owner's special interest in the Old West inspires the decor at this popular place, with its sand-colored walls, cowhide and rope accents, and fine collection of Remington prints and cowboy sculptures. Great steak, plus pasta and seafood. **FYI:** Reservations accepted. **Open:** Peak (May–Sept) Mon–Fri 5:30–10pm, Sat–Sun 9am–11pm. **Prices:** Main courses $13–$20. AE, CB, DC, MC, V. &

Miller's Country House

16409 Red Arrow Hwy, Union Pier; tel 616/469-5950. Exit 6 off I-94. **New American.** The owner's private collection of antiques adds a rustic note to this very appealing dining room, and there's a small exhibition kitchen for those who want to see their food being prepared. A wall of windows in the main dining room allows visitors a glimpse of the on-site herb garden, where fresh seasonings are grown for use in the rack of New Zealand lamb, tournedos of tuna, and prime aged steaks. Menu changes weekly. **FYI:** Reservations accepted. **Open:** Mon–Thurs noon–10pm, Fri–Sat noon–11pm, Sun noon–10:30pm. **Prices:** Main courses $12–$20. AE, DC, MC, V. 🖼 🖼 &

⑤ Redamak's

616 E Buffalo St (US 12); tel 616/469-4522. Exit 4 off I-94. **Burgers.** Large, airy dining rooms characterize the interior of this well-known Harbor Country restaurant that has been around for more than 20 years. Hamburgers are prepared to satisfy most every taste—you can build your own if you wish. Also perch, hot dogs, chicken sandwiches, and frogs' legs (on Friday nights). **FYI:** Reservations accepted. Children's menu. **Open:** Mon–Thurs 11am–9:30pm, Fri–Sat 11am–11pm, Sun 11am–10pm. Closed Nov 19–Mar 1. **Prices:** Main courses $7–$8. No CC. 🚢 🖼 &

Northville

MOTEL 🏨

🚩🚩 Detroit-Novi Travelodge

21100 Haggerty Rd, 48167; tel 810/349-7400 or toll free 800/578-7878; fax 810/349-7454. From I-275, exit 8 Mile Rd, W to Haggerty, N to entrance. Comfortable lodgings adjacent to restaurants with easy access to highway. Jogging path located behind property. **Rooms:** 125 rms. Executive level. CI 3pm/CO noon. Nonsmoking rms avail. **Amenities:** 🛏 🖵 A/C, cable TV w/movies, voice mail. **Services:** ✕ 🖼 🖵 Audio-visual equipment available on premises. Room service available through local restaurants noon–midnight. **Facilities:** 🏃 🖼 🄬 & **Rates (CP):** $48–$55 S; $55–$65 D. Extra person $6. Children under age 17 stay free. Parking: Outdoor, free. AE, CB, DC, DISC, MC, V.

ATTRACTION 🖼

Northville Downs

301 S Center St; tel 810/349-1000. Pari-mutuel harness racetrack offering both grandstand and clubhouse admission. Daily doubles, perfectas, trifectas, and super trifectas offered daily. **Open:** Mid-Oct–Mar, call for schedule. $$

Novi

An upscale suburb of Detroit, just west of Farmington Hills. **Information:** Novi Convention & Visitors Bureau, 43700 Expo Center Dr, #100, Novi, 48375 (tel 810/349-7940 or 349-3743).

HOTELS 🏨

🚩🚩🚩 Hilton Novi

21111 Haggerty Rd, 48050; tel 810/349-4000 or toll free 800/HILTONS; fax 810/349-4066. Exit 167 off I-96/275, W to Haggerty Rd, N to entrance. Easy access to highway from this sleek, modern facility, designed to serve both business and family travelers. Spacious, comfortable lobby with large-screen TV overlooks indoor pool. Nearby 18-hole golf course. **Rooms:** 239 rms, stes, and effic. Executive level. CI 2pm/CO noon. Nonsmoking rms avail. **Amenities:** 🛏 🖵 🖵 A/C, cable TV w/movies, dataport, voice mail, in-rm safe. Concierge level rooms have coffeemakers. **Services:** 🍴 🚗 🖼 🖵 🖐 ATM machine and guest services desk located in lobby. Public fax available. **Facilities:** 🄬 🖼 🔳 & 1 restaurant, 1 bar (w/entertainment), games rm, spa, sauna, whirlpool. Lobby bar has entertainment on weekends. **Rates:** $70–$145 S or D; $150–$500 ste. Extra person $15. Children under age 18 stay free. Parking: Outdoor, free. AE, CB, DC, DISC, ER, JCB, MC, V.

🚩🚩🚩 Wyndham Garden Hotel

42100 Crescent Blvd, 48375; tel 810/344-8800 or toll free 800/WYNDHAM; fax 810/344-8535. Exit 162 off I-96; S to Novi Town Center entrance (Crescent Blvd); left to entrance. Oversized guest rooms encircle a lush garden setting at this attractive hotel. **Rooms:** 148 rms and stes. CI 3pm/CO noon. Nonsmoking rms avail. **Amenities:** 🛏 🖵 🖵 A/C, cable TV w/movies, voice mail. Voice mail in four languages. **Services:** ✕ 🚗 🖼 🖵 Babysitting. VCR available. **Facilities:** 🄬 🏃 🖼 🔳 & 1 restaurant, 1 bar, sauna, whirlpool. Off-site, full-service fitness center adjoins hotel. **Rates (BB):** $79–$139 S or D; $79–$139 ste. Children under age 18 stay free. Parking: Outdoor, free. AE, CB, DC, DISC, JCB, MC, V.

RESTAURANTS 🍴

Ah Wok

In Novi Plaza, 41563 10 Mile Rd; tel 810/349-9260. Just W of Meadowbrook. **Chinese.** A cut above the standard shopping mall Chinese restaurant. Szechuan specialties complement standard Cantonese fare. Besides chow mein and fried rice, you can sample Szechuan shrimp sautéed with pea pods, water chestnuts, bamboo shoots, and mushrooms, or sizzling steak served over mushrooms with a rich sauce. **FYI:** Reservations recommended. **Open:** Mon–Thurs 11am–9:30pm, Fri 11am–11:30pm, Sat 4–11:30pm, Sun 4–9:30pm. **Prices:** Main courses $6–$19. AE, DC, MC, V. 🚗 ♿

Novi Mansion
43180 W 9 Mile Rd; tel 810/347-0095. 1 mi E of Novi Rd. **New American.** Two-story white colonial pillars border the entrance to this 1929 mansion. Two small dining rooms, both with fireplaces, on the first floor, and a grand staircase leads to additional rooms on the second floor. In addition to formal entrees such as plank-roasted salmon and fillet of beef Wellington, traditional favorites like chicken and dumplings, beef pot pie, and stuffed cabbage are also available. **FYI:** Reservations recommended. Guitar/violin. **Open:** Daily 4–10pm. **Prices:** Main courses $9–$20. AE, CB, DC, DISC, MC, V. 🍖 ♿

Too Chez
27155 Sheraton Dr; tel 810/348-5555. Exit 162 off I-96. **Eclectic.** A wildly painted entrance welcomes diners to this innovative eatery. The glass-walled wine cellar is a focal point, as is the enclosed patio area. Spicy linguine with shrimp, roast pork loin, and vegetable-stuffed whitefish are standouts on the regular menu. For the adventurous, there's roast leg of ostrich and a dish called *brugel* (elk with braised duck leg served with cherries, potatoes, corn, cabbage, and green beans). **FYI:** Reservations accepted. Cabaret. **Open:** Mon–Thurs 11:30am–10pm, Fri–Sat 11:30am–11pm. **Prices:** Main courses $6–$29. AE, CB, DC, DISC, MC, V. 🆅🅿 ♿

Onekama

MOTEL 🏨

▐ Portage Lake Motel
4714 Main St, PO Box 414, 49675; tel 616/889-4921 or toll free 800/890-4921. This basic motel is a fisher's dream. Small beach and dock are great places to watch sunset. Good rates for the average traveler. Public lake access nearby and small park. Onekama is an undiscovered special place on Portage Lake. **Rooms:** 15 rms and effic. CI open/CO 11am. Nonsmoking rms avail. Motel rooms and two rustic kitchen units. **Amenities:** 🕹 📺 A/C, cable TV, refrig. No phone. **Services:** 🆅🅿 Owners are especially nice. **Facilities:** 🏖 1 beach (lake shore). **Rates:** Peak (June–Aug) $40–$65 S or D; $280–$370 effic. Children under age 12 stay free. Lower rates off-season. Parking: Outdoor, free. MC, V.

RESORT

▐▐ Portage Point Inn
8513 S Portage Point Dr, PO Box 596, 49675; tel 616/889-4222 or toll free 800/878-7248. Off US 31 N. 18 acres.

A historic inn originally built on 18 acres in 1902, when vacationers arrived by steamship. Year-round inn. **Rooms:** 75 rms and stes; 10 cottages/villas. Executive level. CI 3pm/CO 11am. No smoking. Cottages and eclectic rooms and suites in main building. Only 12 units in winter in separate building. **Amenities:** 🏨 🕹 📺 Cable TV w/movies, refrig, VCR. No A/C. Some units w/terraces, some w/fireplaces. **Services:** 🛎 Social director, children's program, babysitting. **Facilities:** 🚴 ⚠ 🎱1 🏌450 ♿ 2 restaurants (see "Restaurants" below), 2 bars (1 w/entertainment), 1 beach (lake shore), volleyball, games rm, lawn games, playground. The restaurant offers fine dining and music. Casino recreation/multi-function building. **Rates:** Peak (June–Aug) $50–$75 S or D; $110–$150 ste; $75–$250 cottage/villa. Children under age 12 stay free. Lower rates off-season. MAP rates avail. Parking: Outdoor, free. AE, MC, V.

RESTAURANTS 🍽

Glenwood Restaurant
4604 Main St; tel 616/889-3734. **Eclectic.** This new eatery is quickly developing a reputation for fine dining. The dining room itself is housed in part of an old 1920s resort, with an inviting front porch to remind visitors of the grand old days. Beef Wellington and twin lobster tails are featured on the menu, along with homemade salad dressings and desserts. **FYI:** Reservations accepted. Children's menu. **Open:** Daily 5–10pm. **Prices:** Main courses $8–$17. MC, V. ♥ ♿

Portage Point Inn Restaurant
8513 S Portage Point Dr; tel 616/889-4222. **American.** Fine dining in a historic inn. The spacious dining room offers views of the lake. Seafood and steak; extensive wine list. **FYI:** Reservations accepted. Jazz. **Open:** Peak (June–Aug) breakfast daily 8am–11pm; dinner daily 6–10pm. **Prices:** Main courses $12–$19. MC, V. 🍖

Ontonagon

Seat of Ontonagon County, on the Upper Peninsula. This town on the shore of Lake Superior is a popular destination for skiers. **Information:** Ontonagon County Chamber of Commerce, PO Box 266, Ontonagon, 49953 (tel 906/884-4735).

MOTELS 🏨

▐▐▐ Best Western Porcupine Mountain Lodge
120 Lincoln St, 49953; tel 906/885-5311 or toll free 800/528-1234; fax 906/885-5847. Excellent location just a few miles from Porcupine Mountain State Park, which offers some of the best hiking in the Midwest. **Rooms:** 49 rms, stes, and effic. CI 3pm/CO 11am. Nonsmoking rms avail. Very well kept up. Many rooms face Lake Superior. **Amenities:** 🏨 🕹 A/C, cable TV w/movies, dataport. Some units w/whirlpools. **Services:** ✗ 🚐 🛎 🐾 Babysitting. $10 fee for

pets. **Facilities:** 🔥 🚶 🐕 300 ♿ 1 restaurant, 1 bar, 1 beach (lake shore), sauna, whirlpool. Large sandy beach with picnic tables. **Rates:** Peak (June–Oct; Dec–Mar) $65–$75 S; $68–$78 D; $85–$95 ste; $100 effic. Extra person $5. Children under age 13 stay free. Min stay peak. Lower rates off-season. Parking: Outdoor, free. AE, CB, DC, DISC, MC, V.

🏠🏠 Lambert's Cottages

287 Lakeshore Rd, 49953; tel 906/884-4230. Off US 64. Cottages on the shore of Lake Superior within several miles of hiking and skiing at Porcupine Mountain State Park. **Rooms:** 16 cottages/villas. CI 4pm/CO 11am. Nonsmoking rms avail. **Amenities:** 🛗 ♿ 🍴 Cable TV w/movies, refrig. No A/C. Some units w/terraces, some w/fireplaces, some w/whirlpools. **Services:** 🚗 🍴 **Facilities:** ⚠ 🚶 🐕 1 beach (lake shore). Beautiful beach. Canoes, paddleboats, lawn chairs, grills, and snowshoes. **Rates:** $48–$215 cottage/villa. Extra person $10. Min stay peak. Parking: Outdoor, free. AE, DISC, MC, V.

ATTRACTION 🏛

Porcupine Mountain Wilderness State Park

412 S Boundary Rd; tel 906/885-5275. This 60,000-acre park is one of the few remaining large wilderness areas in the Midwest. The "Porkies" feature towering virgin timber, secluded lakes, and miles of wild rivers and streams. There are over 90 miles of foot trails and 16 rustic trailside cabins; skiing opportunities include 14 alpine ski runs (four black diamond, seven intermediate, three beginner) covering 11 miles of slopes and over 25 miles of cross-country ski trails. There are four lifts (one triple, one double, two surface) and a vertical drop of 600 feet. Ski school, rentals available. The Visitor Center provides displays, maps, park products, and information. For the latest information on snow conditions, call toll free 800/272-7000. **Open:** Daily sunrise–sunset.

Oscoda

The Au Sable River empties into Lake Huron in this resort community near Huron National Forest. The river offers excellent trout fishing. Each July, the Au Sable River Canoe Marathon begins in Grayling and runs 140 miles to Oscoda. **Information:** Oscoda-Au Sable Chamber of Commerce, 4440 N US 23, Oscoda, 48750 (tel 517/739-7322 or toll free 800/235-4625).

MOTELS 🏨

🏠🏠 Lake Trail Motel

5400 US 23 N, 48750; tel 517/739-2096 or toll free 800/843-6007. Friendly motel on Lake Huron with attractive grounds. **Rooms:** 44 rms, stes, and effic; 2 cottages/villas. CI 2pm/CO 11am. Nonsmoking rms avail. Lakeside cottages, rooms, suites. **Amenities:** 🛗 ♿ A/C, cable TV w/movies. Some units w/terraces, some w/whirlpools. **Services:** 🚗

Facilities: 🚶 🐟1 1 beach (lake shore), basketball, volleyball, games rm, lawn games. 300′ sugar-fine sand beach with picnic tables and grills. Golf practice area. **Rates:** Peak (June–July) $40–$60 S or D; $70–$120 ste; $60–$70 effic; $85 cottage/villa. Extra person $5. Children under age 12 stay free. Lower rates off-season. Parking: Outdoor, free. Cottages can be rented by the week. DISC, MC, V.

🏠🏠 Redwood Motor Lodge

3111 US 23 N, 48750; tel 517/739-2021. Motor lodge located in scenic, quiet area. **Rooms:** 37 rms; 9 cottages/villas. CI 2pm/CO 11am. **Amenities:** 🛗 ♿ 🍴 A/C, cable TV w/movies, refrig. 1 unit w/fireplace, some w/whirlpools. **Services:** 🚗 🍴 **Facilities:** 🔥 🚶 100 ♿ 1 bar, 1 beach (lake shore), games rm, sauna, whirlpool, playground. Indoor pool area in lodge has pool table and games. **Rates:** Peak (June–Aug) $50–$71 S or D; $85–$125 cottage/villa. Extra person $5. Children under age 12 stay free. Lower rates off-season. Parking: Outdoor, free. Cottages rent by the week only in summer for $425–$580. DISC, MC, V.

🏠🏠 Rest-All Inn

4270 US 23 N, 48750; tel 517/739-8822 or toll free 800/866-4322; fax 517/739-0160. A highway motel with a waterfront, within walking distance of Au Sable River boat launch and pier. Nearby cross-country ski trails. **Rooms:** 76 rms, stes, and effic. CI 2pm/CO 11am. Nonsmoking rms avail. **Amenities:** 🛗 ♿ 🍴 A/C, cable TV, refrig. Some units w/whirlpools. **Services:** 🍴 **Facilities:** 🚶 ♿ 1 beach (lake shore), games rm, playground, washer/dryer. **Rates:** Peak (May 25–Dec 30) $50–$55 D; $66–$70 ste; $76–$85 effic. Extra person $3. Children under age 12 stay free. Lower rates off-season. Parking: Outdoor, free. Group rates avail. DISC, MC, V.

🏠🏠 Surfside Motel & Condos

6504 N US 23, 48750; tel 517/739-5363. A nice getaway place, this motel and condo lodging is on ample grounds with a beautiful 840-foot beach. **Rooms:** 28 rms, stes, and effic. CI 3pm/CO 10am. Rustic motel rooms. One- and two-bedroom condo units also available. **Amenities:** 🛗 ♿ 🍴 A/C, cable TV w/movies, refrig. Some units w/terraces, some w/fireplaces, some w/whirlpools. **Services:** 🍴 🚗 **Facilities:** 🐟1 1 beach (lake shore), basketball, volleyball, lawn games, playground, washer/dryer. **Rates:** Peak (June–Aug) $56–$165 S or D; $85 ste; $66 effic. Children under age 12 stay free. Lower rates off-season. Parking: Outdoor, free. AE, MC, V.

RESTAURANT 🍴

The Pack House

5014 N US 23; tel 517/739-0454. **Seafood/Steak.** Located in an 1878 mansion built by lumber baron Greene Pack, this is a good place for a step back in time and a pleasant lunch or dinner. The decor includes many family heirlooms and other Victorian antiques. Items on the menu include burgers, seafood, chicken (the charbroiled herb chicken is a winner), steaks, and a vegetable en pappilote (vegetables topped with feta cheese and dill sauce, then baked in parchment). **FYI:** Reservations accepted. Children's menu. **Open:** Mon–Thurs 11am–9pm, Fri–Sat 11am–10pm. Closed Dec–Apr. **Prices:** Main courses $9–$18. AE, MC, V. ⬛ &

Paw Paw

Seat of Van Buren County, in southwest part of state. Center of an important grape-growing area, the town is named for the Paw Paw River, which in turn was named by Native Americans for the papaw trees that grew along its banks. **Information:** Paw Paw Chamber of Commerce, PO Box 105, Paw Paw, 49079 (tel 616/657-5395).

ATTRACTIONS 🏛

Warner Vineyards

706 S Kalamazoo St; tel 616/657-3165 or toll free 800/756-5357. After enjoying a tour of the champagne cellar and an explanation of the traditional French *methode champenoise*, guests are invited to indulge in a free tasting of Warner's wines and sparkling juices. **Open:** Mon–Sat 10am–5pm, Sun noon–5pm. **Free**

St Julian Wine Company

716 S Kalamazoo St; tel 616/657-5568. The state's oldest and largest winery, located in a region known for vineyards. Tours (followed by a complimentary tasting) depart every half-hour. **Open:** Mon–Sat 9am–5pm, Sun noon–5pm. **Free**

Petoskey

See also Harbor Springs

Seat of Emmet County, in northern Michigan on the shore of Little Traverse Bay. A quaint Historic Shopping District draws many visitors. Annual Art in the Park festival takes place in July. **Information:** Petoskey/Harbor Springs/Boyne Country Visitors Bureau, 401 E Mitchell St, PO Box 694, Petoskey, 49770-0694 (tel 616/348-2755 or toll free 800/845-2828).

HOTELS 🏨

🏴🏴🏴 Bay Winds Inn of Petoskey

909 Spring St (US 31), 49770; tel 616/347-4193; fax 616/347-5927. Off US 131 S. Cozy inn/motel with personal touch. Award winner in renovation in 1994. Lobby has fireplace and antiques. Large front porch. **Rooms:** 48 rms. CI 3pm/CO 11am. Nonsmoking rms avail. **Amenities:** 🗄 ⚗ A/C, cable TV. Some units w/terraces, some w/whirlpools. **Services:** VP ⚲ Free local calls. **Facilities:** 🗄 ⚓ 🏊 ᴴᵒᵗ & Games rm, whirlpool. Largest indoor pool in the area. **Rates (CP):** Peak (July–Sept) $88–$96 S or D. Extra person $5. Children under age 5 stay free. Lower rates off-season. Parking: Outdoor, free. AE, DISC, MC, V.

🏴🏴 Best Western Inn

US 131, 49770; tel 616/347-3925 or toll free 800/528-1234. Pleasant accommodations located on the edge of town. **Rooms:** 85 rms and stes. CI 3pm/CO 11am. Nonsmoking rms avail. **Amenities:** 🗄 ⚗ 🍴 A/C, cable TV, refrig. Some units w/whirlpools. **Services:** VP ⚲ **Facilities:** 🗄 ⚓ 🏊 ᴴᵒᵗ & Games rm, sauna, whirlpool, beauty salon. **Rates:** Peak (Apr–Labor Day) $60–$99 S; $70–$100 D; $110–$120 ste. Extra person $5. Children under age 12 stay free. Min stay special events. Lower rates off-season. Parking: Outdoor, free. Special group rates avail. AE, MC, V.

🏴🏴 Days Inn

630 Mitchell St, 49770; tel 616/347-8717 or toll free 800/329-7466. Jct US 31/131. Located at edge of town. **Rooms:** 95 rms and stes. CI 4pm/CO 11am. Nonsmoking rms avail. **Amenities:** 🗄 ⚗ A/C, cable TV w/movies. **Services:** ⚲ 🐾 **Facilities:** 🗄 🚲 ⚓ 🏊 ⁵⁰ Spa, whirlpool, washer/dryer. Pleasant indoor pool with small outside deck. **Rates (CP):** Peak (June–Sept) $67–$76 S or D; $125–$135 ste. Extra person $5. Children under age 13 stay free. Lower rates off-season. Parking: Outdoor, free. Golf packages avail at new Chestnut Valley Golf Course nearby. AE, DC, MC, V.

🏴🏴🏴 Holiday Inn

1444 US 131 S, 49770; tel 616/347-6041; fax 616/347-6041. A full-service Holiday Inn. **Rooms:** 144 rms and stes. Executive level. CI 3pm/CO noon. Nonsmoking rms avail. Some suites recently remodeled. **Amenities:** 🗄 ⚗ 📺 🍴 A/C, refrig. Some units w/terraces. **Services:** ✕ ⚲ **Facilities:** 🗄 ⚓ 🏊 ²²⁰ & 1 restaurant, 1 bar (w/entertainment), lawn games, whirlpool. **Rates:** Peak (June–Aug/Jan–Mar) $79–$105 S or D; $120–$140 ste. Children under age 19 stay free. Lower rates off-season. Parking: Outdoor, free. AE, MC, V.

🏴🏴🏴 Stafford's Perry Hotel

Bay and Lewis Sts, 49770 (Downtown); tel 616/347-4000 or toll free 800/456-1917. Built in 1899, this first-class hotel is located in center of town in Gas Light Shopping District, overlooking Traverse Bay. Wonderful front porch for dining or just sitting. Lobby and rooms are fabulous, with antiques and very nice decor. Walk to shops. A very special hotel. **Rooms:** 81 rms and stes. CI 3pm/CO 11am. No smoking. Rooms are individually decorated with views of bay and town. Some rooms have handpainted country-style furnishings. **Amenities:** 🗄 ⚗ A/C, cable TV, refrig. Some units w/terraces. **Services:** ✕ 🚐 🖼 ⚲ Car-rental desk, babysitting. Warm hospitality and excellent service. **Facilities:** ⚓ ᴴᵒᵗ ⁷² & 2 restaurants (*see* "Restaurants" below), 2 bars (1 w/entertainment), spa. **Rates:** Peak (June 15–Oct) $69–$165 S or D; $185 ste. Extra person $5. Children under age 10 stay free. Lower rates off-season. Parking: Outdoor, free. AE, DC, MC, V.

MOTEL

⊨⊨ Econo Lodge

1858 US 131 S, 49770; tel 616/348-3324. On the outskirts of town. Very nice Econo Lodge. **Rooms:** 59 rms and stes. CI open/CO 11am. Nonsmoking rms avail. Nicely decorated rooms. **Amenities:** 🛅 ⏶ A/C, cable TV w/movies. Some rooms have refrigerators. **Services:** 🖚 🖘 **Facilities:** 🖾 🏃 ⛾ ⅙ Whirlpool. **Rates:** Peak (Jan–Mar/June–Aug) $38–$85 S or D; $110 ste. Extra person $6. Children under age 18 stay free. Lower rates off-season. Parking: Outdoor, free. Ski packages avail in winter. AE, DC, DISC, MC, V.

INN

⊨⊨⊨ Stafford's Bayview Inn

613 Woodland Ave, PO Box 3, 49770; tel 616/347-2771 or toll free 800/456-1917. 15 minutes from downtown. First-class centennial country inn located on shore of Little Traverse Bay. Exceptional rooms and fine dining restaurant. Antiques in lobby; wonderful sun room. Front porch offers view of bay. **Rooms:** 31 rms and stes. CI 3pm/CO 11am. Nonsmoking rms avail. Remarkable rooms that are individually decorated with quilts, nice linens, and fabulous decor. **Amenities:** ⏶ 🖳 A/C, cable TV. No phone. Some units w/terraces, some w/fireplaces, some w/whirlpools. **Services:** ✗ 🖘 Babysitting, afternoon tea served. Guests receive welcome bottle of wine. Very personalized hospitality. **Facilities:** 🖧 🏃 ⛾ 🔲 ⅙ 1 restaurant (see "Restaurants" below), 1 beach (lake shore), washer/dryer, guest lounge w/TV. Floor phones available. Library/sitting room with television, books, chess, fireplace, and coffee. Guests have access to private beach, and to Bayview Country Club and Tennis Courts for a fee. **Rates (CP):** $108–$185 D; $108–$195 ste. Extra person $18. Higher rates for special events/hols. Parking: Outdoor, free. Closed Apr. AE, MC, V.

RESTAURANTS 🍴

♥ HO Rose Room

In Stafford's Perry Hotel, Bay and Lewis Sts; tel 616/348-6014. **Seafood/Steak.** A very classy dining room located in the historic Perry Hotel, which was built in 1899. Guests can dine on the spacious front porch or enjoy the waterfront view from an indoor table. The kitchen likes to make the most of local ingredients, which leads to such exotic specilaties as cold cherry soup (offered during the summer cherry season). Food is exceptional across the board, and so is the service. **FYI:** Reservations accepted. **Open:** Breakfast Mon–Sat 7am–10:30pm; lunch Mon–Sat 11:30am–3pm; dinner daily 5:30–10pm; brunch Sun 10am–2pm. **Prices:** Main courses $9–$22. AE, DISC, MC, V. ♥ 🍺 🖼 ⅙

La Señorita

1285 US 31 N; tel 616/347-7750. **Mexican.** An attractive and colorful local hangout offering all the popular Mexican dishes. Drinks available include sangria and 15 flavors of margaritas. **FYI:** Reservations accepted. Children's menu. Jacket required. **Open:** Mon–Thurs 11am–11pm, Fri–Sat 11am–midnight, Sun noon–10pm. **Prices:** Main courses $5–$10. AE, DISC, MC, V. 🖼 ⅙

♥ Stafford's Bayview Inn

613 Woodland Ave; tel 616/347-2771. **American.** Enjoy wonderful hospitality and service in the historic centennial Bay View Inn on the shores of Little Traverse Bay. The restaurant has a view of the hotel grounds and a lovely front porch. Pecan chicken, grilled rack of lamb, whitefish, and salads are part of the menu. **FYI:** Reservations recommended. No liquor license. **Open:** Mon–Sat 5–9pm, Sun 10am–2pm. Closed Apr. **Prices:** Main courses $16–$24. MC, V. ♥ 🍺

★ Villa Ristorante Italiano

887 Spring St; tel 616/347-1440. **Italian.** Locals cherish the romantic atmosphere of this cozy little trattoria, complete with checkered tablecloths, straw-covered wine bottles and baskets hanging from the ceiling. Pasta, chicken, and steak are among the most-requested main courses. **FYI:** Reservations accepted. Children's menu. **Open:** Daily 4–11pm. **Prices:** Main courses $13–$18. MC, V. ♥

Plymouth

Once a stage stop between Detroit and Ann Arbor, this small town has many beautifully maintained colonial-style buildings. Every January, chefs carve hundreds of ice sculptures in the Ice Sculpture Spectacular. Their works line the streets and are lit at night. **Information:** Plymouth Community Chamber of Commerce, 386 S Main, Plymouth, 48170 (tel 313/453-1540).

HOTEL 🏨

⊨⊨⊨ The Mayflower Bed & Breakfast Hotel

827 W Ann Arbor Trail, 48170; tel 313/453-1620; fax 313/453-0193. Exit 28 off I-275; W to Main St; N to Ann Arbor Trail. Located in the heart of downtown Plymouth, this Michigan landmark features elegant but comfortable surroundings, and is well known for its fine food—particularly its re-creation of the First Thanksgiving Dinner with recipes that date back to 1620. A good getaway for couples. Golf and racquetball available nearby. Within walking distance of 150 specialty shops. **Rooms:** 18 rms and stes. CI 3pm/CO 11am. Nonsmoking rms avail. Rooms furnished with antiques. **Amenities:** 🛅 ⏶ A/C, TV, refrig. Some units w/terraces, some w/whirlpools. **Services:** ✗ 🖂 🖘 Babysitting. **Facilities:** 🔲 ⅙ 2 restaurants, 1 bar (w/entertainment). On-premises fitness center under construction. **Rates (BB):** Peak (Nov–Mar) $65–$85 S or D; $148–$175 ste. Extra person $10. Children under age 8 stay free. Lower rates off-season. Parking: Outdoor, free. AE, CB, DC, DISC, MC, V.

MOTEL

▤▤ Quality Inn

40455 Ann Arbor Rd, 48170; tel 313/455-8100 or toll free 800/4-CHOICE; fax 313/455-5711. Exit 28 off I-275/96, W to first road on left (Don Massey Dr), left to entrance. Central spiral staircase gives spacious lobby an elegant feel. Convenient to highway. **Rooms:** 123 rms. CI 3pm/CO noon. Nonsmoking rms avail. Clean, comfortable rooms, many with large working area. **Amenities:** ☎ ♨ A/C, cable TV w/movies. **Services:** ✕ ⊠ ⊲ Room service available through several local restaurants. **Facilities:** ⓕ ▣ ⬜ ♿ Free use of interview center for overnight guests. Free passes to two local fitness facilities. **Rates (CP):** Peak (Apr–Sept) $64–$74 S or D. Extra person $7. Children under age 18 stay free. Lower rates off-season. Parking: Outdoor, free. AE, CB, DC, DISC, JCB, MC, V.

RESTAURANTS ⑪

Cafe Bon Homme

844 Penniman; tel 313/453-6260. **New American/Continental.** At this cool, sleek bistro, the food looks as good as it tastes. A variety of daily specials complements menu standbys like roulade of chicken stuffed with boursin cheese, spinach, and roasted red pepper; poached Norwegian salmon; and English mixed grill of lamb, veal, and beef. The experience is enhanced by attentive service, although the tables are a bit on the small side. **FYI:** Reservations recommended. No smoking. **Open:** Mon–Fri 11:30am–10pm, Sat noon–11pm. **Prices:** Main courses $20–$28. AE, CB, DC, MC, V. ⬤

Ernesto's

41661 Plymouth Rd; tel 313/453-2002. ¼ mi W of Haggerty Rd. **Italian.** This restaurant bills itself as an "Italian country inn," and, in fact, truly resembles one. Each room has its own fireplace, and there is dining outdoors. Main specialties include penne with tomatoes, basil, and spices; breast of chicken with mushroom and artichoke hearts simmered in white wine sauce; and medallions of beef tenderloin with Chianti gravy. **FYI:** Reservations recommended. Piano. Dress code. **Open:** Lunch Mon–Sat 11am–3pm; dinner Mon–Thurs 5–10pm, Fri–Sat 5–11pm, Sun noon–9pm. **Prices:** Main courses $10–$21. AE, DC, DISC, MC, V. 📷

Pontiac

Seat of Oakland County, in southeast part of state. Named for Chief Pontiac of the Ottawa tribe, who lived here for part of the year and is said to be buried nearby. Pontiac is now home to the Pontiac Division of General Motors. The NFL's Detroit Lions play their home games at the Pontiac Silverdome. **Information:** Oakland County Chamber of Commerce, 1760 S Telegraph, #207, Bloomfield Township, 48302-0182 (tel 810/456-8600).

ATTRACTIONS ⬚

Meadow Brook Hall

Oakland University, Adams Rd, Rochester; tel 810/370-3140. 12 mi E of Pontiac. Located on the campus of Oakland University. This enormous Tudor-style manor house was built in 1926 by the widow of automobile tycoon John Dodge, and contains around 100 richly furnished and decorated rooms. Guided tours available; annual summer music festival. **Open:** Peak (July–Aug) Mon–Sat 10:30am–5pm. Reduced hours off-season. $$$

Pontiac Lake

MI 59; tel 810/666-1020. Activities for all seasons are offered at this 3,700-acre recreation area: swimming, fishing, waterskiing, boating, horseback riding, hunting, snowshoeing, cross-country skiing. Facilities include archery and rifle ranges, picnicking areas, concessions, and camping. **Open:** Daily sunrise–sunset. $

Pontiac Silverdome

1200 Featherstone; tel 810/335-4151. The world's largest inflatable dome hosts the home games of Detroit's professional football team, the Lions. **Open:** Call for schedule. $$$$

Port Huron

Seat of St Clair County, in southeast part of state. Thomas Edison lived and went to school here as a boy in the 1850s. Gratiot Lighthouse, the oldest on the Great Lakes, guards the St Clair Straits, and an international bridge connects the city to Sarnia, Ontario. **Information:** Blue Water Convention & Tourist Bureau, 520 Thomas Edison Pkwy, Port Huron, 48060 (tel 810/987-8687 or toll free 800/852-4242).

MOTELS ⬚

▤ Days Inn

70 Gratiot Blvd, Marysville, 48040; tel 810/364-8400 or toll free 800/DAYS-INN; fax 810/364-8401. Off Business Route I-69/94. At the edge of Port Huron in a quiet area. **Rooms:** 26 rms. CI noon/CO 11am. Nonsmoking rms avail. **Amenities:** ☎ ♨ ⬚ A/C, cable TV w/movies, refrig. **Services:** ⊲ **Facilities:** ⓕ **Rates (CP):** Peak (May–Sept) $48–$58 S; $53–$72 D. Extra person $5. Children under age 12 stay free. Lower rates off-season. Parking: Outdoor, free. AE, DC, DISC, JCB, MC, V.

▤ Main Street Lodge

514 Huron Ave, 48060; tel 810/984-3166. A downtown motel within walking distance to shops and waterfront. Good rates for the area. **Rooms:** 40 rms. CI open/CO 11am. Nonsmoking rms avail. **Amenities:** ☎ ♨ A/C, cable TV w/movies, refrig. **Services:** ⊲ **Rates:** Peak (June–Aug) $47–$50 S; $51–$56 D. Extra person $5. Children under age 12 stay free. Lower rates off-season. Parking: Outdoor, free. AE, DISC, MC, V.

RESTAURANTS 🍴

Fogcutter
511 Fort St; tel 810/987-3300. **American.** A romantic and classy setting for fine dining and gorgeous views of the water. The menu includes classic favorites such as duckling with orange sauce, Hawaiian chicken, various cuts of steak, and lobster. Fresh local seafood is available as well. **FYI:** Reservations accepted. Piano. **Open:** Mon–Fri 11am–4:30pm, Sat noon–10pm, Sun noon–7pm. **Prices:** Main courses $10–$19. MC, V. ♥

Pilot House
3136 Military St; tel 810/982-7221. **Seafood/Steak.** Brass lanterns and other seaworthy objects line the walls of this well-liked hangout. The maritime theme is continues in the menu, which features walleye, yellowfin tuna, and coconut shrimp in addition to a variety of steaks. There's a fine view of the St Clair River. **FYI:** Reservations accepted. Children's menu. **Open:** Mon–Sat 11am–9pm, Sun noon–8pm. **Prices:** Main courses $12–$20. MC, V. ♥ 🏔

ATTRACTION 🏛

Museum of Arts and History
1115 6th St; tel 810/982-0891. Displays documenting over 300 years of local and regional history, including a pioneer log home, Native American artifacts, memorabilia from Thomas Edison's boyhood home, 19th-century period furnishings, and marine-related items. **Open:** Wed–Sun 1–4:30pm. **Free**

Prudenville

See Houghton Lake

Romulus

HOTELS 🏨

🎗🎗 Courtyard by Marriott Detroit Metro Airport
30653 Flynn Dr, 48174; tel 313/721-3200 or toll free 800/321-2211; fax 313/721-1304. Exit 198 off I-94. Pleasantly landscaped courtyard with gazebo and comfortable lobby. **Rooms:** 147 rms and stes. CI 3pm/CO noon. Nonsmoking rms avail. **Amenities:** 📺 ⊘ A/C, cable TV w/movies, voice mail. Some units w/terraces. **Services:** ✗ 🚐 🖨 🛎 **Facilities:** 🏊 🏋 🎱40 ♿ 1 restaurant, 1 bar, whirlpool, washer/dryer. **Rates:** $59–$88 S or D; $90–$103 ste. Children under age 18 stay free. Parking: Outdoor, free. AE, DC, DISC, MC, V.

🎗🎗🎗 Crowne Plaza Detroit Metro Airport
8000 Merriman Rd, 48174; tel 313/729-2600 or toll free 800/HOLIDAY; fax 313/729-9414. Exit 198 N off I-94, E of I-275. Striking 11-story hotel with sunny atrium. **Rooms:** 364 rms and stes. Executive level. CI 3pm/CO noon. Nonsmoking rms avail. Balcony rooms overlook atrium. **Amenities:** 📺 ⊘ 🖥 🍳 A/C, cable TV w/movies, dataport, voice mail. Some units w/minibars, some w/terraces. **Services:** 🍴 ⓋⓅ 🚐 🖨 🛎 🐕 Car-rental desk. **Facilities:** 🏊 🏋 🍴650 ♿ 1 restaurant, 2 bars, games rm, whirlpool. **Rates:** $110–$125 S or D; $179–$249 ste. Extra person $10. Children under age 18 stay free. Parking: Outdoor, free. AE, CB, DC, DISC, ER, JCB, MC, V.

UNRATED Detroit Metro Airport Hilton Suites
8600 Wickham Rd, 48174; tel 313/728-9200 or toll free 800/HILTONS; fax 313/728-9278. Plush lobby welcomes travelers to the airport's only all-suite hotel. **Rooms:** 151 stes. CI 3pm/CO noon. Nonsmoking rms avail. Some three-room conference suites available. **Amenities:** 📺 ⊘ 🖥 🍳 A/C, satel TV w/movies, refrig, dataport, VCR. Some units w/terraces. **Services:** ✗ 🚐 🖨 🐕 Twice-daily maid svce. Extended breakfast buffet. Nightly social hour. Services cater to business travelers. **Facilities:** 🏊 🏋 🍴80 🖥 ♿ 1 restaurant, 1 bar (w/entertainment), whirlpool, washer/dryer. **Rates (BB):** $119–$139 ste. Extra person $10. Children under age 18 stay free. Parking: Outdoor, free. AE, CB, DC, DISC, ER, MC, V.

🎗🎗 Hampton Inn Detroit Metro Airport
30847 Flynn Dr, 48174; tel 313/721-1100 or toll free 800/HAMPTON; fax 313/721-9915. I-94 exit 198, first street on right. Air traffic overhead can't be missed in the atrium lobby, but good soundproofing in the guest rooms eliminates much of the noise. **Rooms:** 136 rms. CI 3pm/CO noon. Nonsmoking rms avail. **Amenities:** 📺 ⊘ A/C, cable TV w/movies. **Services:** 🚐 🖨 🐕 **Facilities:** 🏊 🏋 🍴100 ♿ **Rates (CP):** $65 S; $75 D. Children under age 18 stay free. Parking: Outdoor, free. AE, CB, DC, DISC, ER, MC, V.

🎗🎗 Quality Inn Metro Airport Suites
31800 Wick Rd, 48174; tel 313/326-2100 or toll free 800/228-5151; fax 313/326-9020. Exit 198 off I-94. Functional and friendly. **Rooms:** 123 rms. CI 3pm/CO noon. Nonsmoking rms avail. **Amenities:** 📺 ⊘ 🍳 A/C, satel TV, dataport. Some units w/whirlpools. **Services:** 🚐 🖨 🐕 **Facilities:** 🍴80 ♿ 1 restaurant (dinner only). **Rates (CP):** $55–$97 S or D. Children under age 18 stay free. Parking: Outdoor, free. AE, DISC, JCB, MC, V.

🎗🎗🎗 Romulus Marriott at Detroit Airport
30559 Flynn Dr, 48174; tel 313/729-7555 or toll free 800/321-2049; fax 313/729-8634. I-94 to Merriman Rd exit, W on Flynn Dr. Overstuffed sofas, marble floor, and view of courtyard greet guests. Location near end of road provides some seclusion despite proximity to airport. **Rooms:** 246 rms and stes. Executive level. CI 3pm/CO noon. Nonsmoking rms avail. **Amenities:** 📺 ⊘ 🍳 A/C, cable TV w/movies, dataport, voice mail. **Services:** ✗ 🔑 🚐 🖨 🐕 🐾 **Facilities:** 🏊 🏋 🍴500 ♿ 1 restaurant, 1 bar, spa, whirlpool. **Rates:** $107–$129 S or D; $250–$375 ste. Children under age 18 stay free. Parking: Outdoor, free. AE, CB, DC, DISC, EC, JCB, MC, V.

≣≣≣ Wyndham Garden Hotel Detroit Airport

8600 Merriman Rd, 48174; tel 313/728-7900 or toll free 800/822-4200 in the US, 800/631-4200 in Canada; fax 313/728-6518. Exit 198 off I-94. Newly renovated public areas. Cozy reading area off lobby entrance. No elevator to second floor. **Rooms:** 153 rms. CI 3pm/CO noon. Nonsmoking rms avail. Recently renovated. **Amenities:** 📞 🅰 📺 🍷 A/C, cable TV w/movies, dataport. **Services:** ✕ 🚗 🛄 🗘 Babysitting. **Facilities:** 🛝 🔟 💻 🅰 1 restaurant, 1 bar. **Rates (BB):** $89 S; $99 D. Extra person $10. Children under age 18 stay free. Min stay special events. Parking: Outdoor, free. AE, CB, DC, DISC, MC, V.

Saginaw

South of Saginaw Bay, off Lake Huron. Originally inhabited by the Sauk tribe, the area was taken over by the logging industry early in the 19th century. Today, manufacturing and agriculture are the mainstays of the local economy. **Information:** Saginaw County Convention & Visitors Bureau, 901 S Washington Ave, Saginaw, 48601 (tel 517/752-7164 or toll free 800/444-9979).

HOTELS 🏨

≣≣ Best Western Inn

3325 Davenport Ave, 48602; tel 517/793-2080 or toll free 800/528-1234; fax 517/793-5791. Nice, in downtown Saginaw, close to shopping. **Rooms:** 117 rms. CI 3pm/CO 11am. Nonsmoking rms avail. **Amenities:** 📞 🅰 A/C, cable TV w/movies, refrig. **Services:** 🛄 🗘 🗘 **Facilities:** 🛝 🔟 🅰 1 restaurant, 1 bar, washer/dryer. Pleasant outdoor pool area. **Rates:** Peak (June 11–Sept 12) $41–$51 S; $43–$60 D. Extra person $4. Children under age 12 stay free. Lower rates off-season. Parking: Outdoor, free. AE, DC, DISC, MC, V.

≣≣≣ Four Points Hotel by Sheraton

4960 Towne Centre Rd, 48604; tel 517/790-5050 or toll free 800/428-1470; fax 517/790-1466. Award-winning Sheraton, located at Fashion Square Mall. Golf and tennis 15 minutes away. **Rooms:** 156 rms. CI 3pm/CO noon. Nonsmoking rms avail. **Amenities:** 📞 🅰 🍷 A/C, cable TV w/movies, refrig, dataport. **Services:** ✕ 🚗 🛄 🗘 🗘 Car-rental desk. **Facilities:** 🛝 🔟 🅰 1 restaurant, 1 bar (w/entertainment), games rm, sauna, whirlpool. **Rates:** Peak (June–Aug) $78–$88 S or D. Extra person $10. Children under age 18 stay free. Lower rates off-season. Parking: Outdoor, free. AE, DISC, V.

≣≣ Hampton Inn

2222 Tittabawassee Rd, 48604; tel 517/792-7666 or toll free 800/HAMPTON. Off I-75. The location, at Fashion Square Mall, makes it convenient to shopping and restaurants, as well as local attractions. **Rooms:** 120 rms. CI 3pm/CO noon. Nonsmoking rms avail. **Amenities:** 📞 🅰 A/C, cable TV w/movies. **Services:** 🛄 🗘 🗘 **Facilities:** 🛝 🅰 🔟 🅰 **Rates (CP):** Peak (June–Aug) $61–$65 D; $54–$65 S or D. Extra person $7. Children under age 18 stay free. Lower rates off-season. Parking: Outdoor, free. Special rates for guests 50 and older. AE, DISC, MC, V.

≣ Super 8 Motel

4848 Towne Centre Rd, 48603; tel 517/791-3003 or toll free 800/800-8000; fax 517/791-3003. Tittabawassee Rd exit off I-675. Comfortable, right by Fashion Square Mall. **Rooms:** 62 rms. CI 1pm/CO 11am. Nonsmoking rms avail. **Amenities:** 📞 🅰 A/C, cable TV w/movies, refrig. **Services:** 🗘 **Facilities:** 🅰 🅰 **Rates:** Peak (Apr–Sept) $38–$48 S or D. Extra person $5. Children under age 12 stay free. Lower rates off-season. Parking: Outdoor, free. AE, MC, V.

RESTAURANT 🍽

★ Applebee's Grill and Bar

2260 Tittabawassee Rd; tel 517/793-0119. Off I-675. **American.** A colorful and popular neighborhood bar and grill with Tiffany lamps and a sports theme. Salads, pizza, sandwiches, low-fat dishes, and burgers offer something for everyone. **FYI:** Reservations not accepted. Children's menu. Beer and wine only. **Open:** Mon–Thurs 11am–11pm, Fri–Sat 11am–1pm, Sun 11am–10pm. **Prices:** Main courses $9–$12. AE, MC, V. 👶 🅰

ATTRACTIONS 🏛

Saginaw Art Museum

1126 N Michigan Ave; tel 517/754-2491. Located in a 1904 Georgian-Revival mansion, this museum houses permanent and changing exhibits of 19th- and 20th-century American art, Asian art, contemporary prints, plaster sculpture by John Rogers, and textiles. Gardens are populated with bronze and stone sculptures. **Open:** Tues–Sat 10am–5pm, Sun 1–5pm. **Free**

Castle Museum of Saginaw County History

500 Federal Ave; tel 517/752-2861. In 1898, this post office was designed and built in the style of a French castle in homage to the area's founding by French voyageurs and fur traders. (The building's chateâuesque turrets and gargoyles are complemented by carvings of the pinnacles and finials reflecting the flora and fauna of Michigan.) Today, the museum's exhibits include Native American artifacts (including an entire model village), an 1826 fur trading post, and clothing from 1890 to the present. **Open:** Mon–Fri 10am–4:30pm, Sun 1–4:30pm. **$**

Japanese Cultural Center and Tea House

527 Ezra Rust Dr; tel 517/579-1648. An unique example of multiculturalism, sponsored by Saginaw and its sister city in Japan, Tokushima. Visitors can tour several authentic Japanese buildings, learn about the culture and rituals of Japan, and participate in a traditional tea ceremony. **Open:** Tues–Sat 9am–6pm, Sun noon–6pm. **$**

Children's Zoo
Jct MI 46/13; tel 517/759-1657. More than 20 different species housed on 8½ acres, including timber wolves and red tail hawks. Tour on the zoo train, or take a pony ride. Educational programs and lectures available. **Open:** Mon–Sat 10am–5pm, Sun 11am–6pm. **$**

Saginaw Rose Garden
423 Rust Ave; tel toll free 800/444-9979. Beautifully landscaped circular garden features more than 1,000 rose bushes representing 60 varieties. Fountain in the center of the garden is illuminated at night. **Open:** Daily 10am–5pm. **Free**

Anderson Water Park and Wave Pool
MI 46; tel 517/759-1386. Highlights of this water amusement park include a pool with 3-foot waves and a 350-foot double water slide; a kiddie wading pool is available for the youngsters. **Open:** Mem Day–Labor Day, daily 10am–5pm. **$$$**

St Ignace

See also Mackinac Island, Mackinaw City

Seat of Mackinac County, on the Upper Peninsula. In 1671, Father Marquette established a mission at this site on the Straits of Mackinac. Marquette is buried here, in Marquette Mission Park. **Information:** St Ignace Area Tourist Association, 11 S State St, St Ignace, 49781 (tel 906/643-8717 or toll free 800/338-6660).

HOTELS

Days Inn
1074 N State St, 49781; tel 906/643-8008 or toll free 800/732-9746; fax 906/643-9400. Off I-75. Views of Lake Huron and Mackinac Island. Half-mile to ferries to Mackinac Island and three miles to Kewadin Shores Casino. **Rooms:** 123 rms and stes. CI 2pm/CO 10am. Nonsmoking rms avail. Many lakefront rooms. **Amenities:** A/C, cable TV w/movies. Some units w/terraces, some w/whirlpools. **Services:** **Facilities:** Games rm, sauna, whirlpool, washer/dryer. Sun deck. **Rates (CP):** Peak (June 9–Sept 3) $59–$139 S or D; $99–$179 ste. Extra person $6. Children under age 12 stay free. Lower rates off-season. Parking: Outdoor, free. AE, DISC, MC, V.

Econo Lodge
1030 N State St, PO Box 651, 49781; tel 906/643-8060 or toll free 800/424-4777. Exit 344A off I-75. Half-mile to Mackinac Bridge and ferry. One mile to shops downtown. **Rooms:** 50 rms. CI 1pm/CO 10am. Nonsmoking rms avail. **Amenities:** A/C, cable TV w/movies, refrig. 1 unit w/whirlpool. **Services:** **Facilities:** Whirlpool. Pool area out front and deck with outside tables. **Rates:** Peak (June 22–Aug 26) $71–$107 S or D. Extra person $6. Children under age 12 stay free. Lower rates off-season. Parking: Outdoor, free. DISC, MC, V.

Kewadin Inn of St Ignace
1140 N State St, 49781; tel 906/643-9141 or toll free 800/345-9457. Good hotel close to Vegas-style gaming, dining, and entertainment at Kewadin Shores Casino. **Rooms:** 72 rms. CI 3pm/CO 11am. Nonsmoking rms avail. Family suites available. **Amenities:** A/C, cable TV w/movies. **Services:** 24-hour shuttle service to casino. **Facilities:** Volleyball, playground. **Rates (CP):** Peak (June–Aug) $50–$71 S or D. Extra person $11. Lower rates off-season. Parking: Outdoor, free. Casino packages avail. AE, DISC, MC, V.

Quality Inn Lakefront
1021 N State St, 49781; tel 906/643-7581 or toll free 800/221-2222. 2 mi N of Mackinac Bridge. An all new, lakefront, colonial-style building and spacious landscaped grounds. **Rooms:** 77 rms. CI noon/CO 10am. Nonsmoking rms avail. **Amenities:** A/C, cable TV w/movies. Some units w/fireplaces. Private balconies. **Services:** **Facilities:** Games rm. **Rates (CP):** Peak (July–Aug) $88–$160 S or D. Children under age 12 stay free. Lower rates off-season. Parking: Outdoor, free. Closed Nov–Mar. AE, MC, V.

MOTELS

Aurora Borealis Motor Inn
635 US 2 W, 49781; tel 906/643-7488. Convenient to downtown shops and ferry docks. **Rooms:** 56 rms. CI 3:30pm/CO 10am. Nonsmoking rms avail. **Amenities:** A/C, cable TV w/movies, refrig. Some units w/fireplaces. **Services:** **Facilities:** **Rates:** Peak (June–Aug) $70–$74 S or D. Lower rates off-season. Parking: Outdoor, free. 20% discount for seniors 50 and over. DISC, MC, V.

Bay View Motel
1133 N State St, 49781; tel 906/643-9444. 1 mi from downtown. Cozy motel on the water with a small garden and a nice view of Lake Huron. Close to downtown shops and restaurants. **Rooms:** 19 rms. CI noon/CO 10am. Nonsmoking rms avail. Rustic rooms with the essentials. **Amenities:** A/C, cable TV. No phone. **Services:** **Facilities:** **Rates:** Peak (June–Aug) $53–$58 S or D. Extra person $4. Children under age 12 stay free. Lower rates off-season. Parking: Outdoor, free. Closed end of Oct–May. Winter phone is 413/339-5321. Closed Nov–Apr. DISC, MC, V.

Budget Host Golden Anchor Motel
700 N State St, 49781; tel 906/643-9666 or toll free 800/BUD-HOST. Well-managed motel close to Mackinac Island ferry docks and 3½ miles from the casino. Recipient of Budget Host's Inn of the Year award 1993–94. **Rooms:** 56 rms and stes. CI 3pm/CO 11am. Nonsmoking rms avail. **Amenities:** A/C, cable TV, refrig. Some units w/terraces, some w/whirlpools. All suites have microwaves. **Services:** **Facilities:** Games rm, whirlpool, playground, washer/dryer. **Rates (CP):** Peak (mid-June–Aug)

$55–$59 S or D; $92–$120 ste. Lower rates off-season. Parking: Outdoor, free. Casino packages avail. AE, DISC, MC, V.

☰☰☰ Harbour Pointe Motor Inn

797 N State St, 49781; tel 906/643-9882 or toll free 800/642-3318. 11 acres. An especially nice resort/motor inn with nice grounds and an 800-foot beach. Good for couples, seniors, and families. Minutes from Mackinac Island boat docks and attractions. **Rooms:** 20 rms. CI 3pm/CO 11am. Nonsmoking rms avail. Two-bedroom family units available. Most rooms offer beautiful lake views. **Amenities:** 📷 🛁 A/C, cable TV w/movies. Some units w/terraces, some w/whirlpools. **Services:** 🍽 Nightly beachfront bonfire. **Facilities:** 🏖 🏊 🍽 🛎 1 beach (lake shore), volleyball, games rm, lawn games, whirlpool, playground. Sun deck. **Rates (CP):** Peak (July–Aug) $69–$135 S or D. Children under age 18 stay free. Lower rates off-season. Parking: Outdoor, free. Casino and getaway packages avail. AE, DISC, MC, V.

RESTAURANTS 🍴

Dockside

1101 N State St; tel 906/643-7911. **American.** Planked whitefish cooked on a maplewood board and served with Dutchess potatoes and vegetable medley is only one of the fine dinners served here. The wait staff is friendly and there are nice views of the harbor from every table. **FYI:** Reservations accepted. Children's menu. **Open:** Daily 7am–10pm. Closed Oct–May. **Prices:** Main courses $14–$20. DISC, MC, V. ⛰

★ The Galley

241 N State St; tel 906/643-7960. **American.** A downtown fixture for more than 50 years. Popular dishes include the Galley steak, chicken Parmesan, Cajun whitefish, and catfish. **FYI:** Reservations accepted. Children's menu. **Open:** Daily 24 hrs. Closed Oct–Apr. **Prices:** Main courses $8–$16. DISC, MC, V. ▊ ⛰ ♿

The Huron Landing Restaurant

441 N State St; tel 906/643-9613. **American.** An informal setting with views of Lake Huron and Mackinac Island. Specials include whitefish, prime rib, and honey-Dijon pork chops. **FYI:** Reservations accepted. Children's menu. **Open:** Mon–Sat 7am–10pm, Sun 9am–1pm. **Prices:** Main courses $8–$11. AE, MC, V. ⛰ 👫 ♿

ATTRACTION 🏛

Marquette Mission Park and Museum of Ojibwa Culture

500 N State St; tel 906/643-9161. Located in downtown St Ignace across from the ferry docks, with exhibits documenting the history of the Ojibwa tribe and the area's early French settlers. The fur trade, the Ojibwa migration, the conflict between technology and nature, and Ojibwa family life are illustrated in various displays. A Longhouse Theatre hosts ongoing video showings; a non-commercial gift shop sells native crafts and history books. **Open:** Peak (Mem Day–Labor Day) daily 10am–8pm. Reduced hours off-season. $

St Joseph

See also Benton Harbor

Seat of Berrien County, in southwest corner of state. This small town at the mouth of the St Joseph River is known for its mineral springs and its quaint downtown area (complete with benches, flowers, and sculpture). Lake Bluff Art Fair—one of the state's major art shows—is held here every July.

HOTELS 🏨

☰☰☰ The Boulevard

521 Lake Blvd, 49085 (Downtown); tel 616/983-6600 or toll free 800/875-6600; fax 616/983-0520. An all-suite hotel, across the street from the lakefront and adjacent to the Curious Kids Museum. Generous floral arrangements and plantings complement fine furniture and wall coverings of attractive lobby. **Rooms:** 84 stes. CI 4pm/CO noon. Nonsmoking rms avail. **Amenities:** 📷 🛁 📺 A/C, cable TV, refrig, voice mail. **Services:** ✕ 🅥🅟 🛎 🍽 Car-rental desk. **Facilities:** 🛎 ♿ 1 restaurant. Guests have use of fitness center at nearby YWCA. **Rates (CP):** Peak (May–Sept) $84–$114 ste. Extra person $10. Children under age 17 stay free. Min stay special events. Lower rates off-season. Parking: Outdoor, free. Higher rates for rooms with lake view. Executive boardroom suites available at higher rate. AE, MC, V.

☰☰☰ Holiday Inn

100 Main St, 49085 (Downtown); tel 616/983-7341 or toll free 800/HOLIDAY; fax 616/983-0650. Good central location, one block from river, near park and beach areas, adjacent to attractive pedestrian shopping mall. Sparsely furnished lobby. **Rooms:** 155 rms and stes. Executive level. CI 4pm/CO noon. Some rooms have views of Lake Michigan and nearby park. **Amenities:** 📷 🛁 A/C, cable TV. Some units w/minibars. **Services:** ✕ 🖨 🛎 🍽 **Facilities:** 🏊 🛎 ♿ 1 restaurant, sauna, steam rm, whirlpool, washer/dryer. **Rates:** Peak (May–Oct) $65–$82 S; $70–$89 D; $89–$125 ste. Children under age 19 stay free. Lower rates off-season. Parking: Outdoor, free. AE, CB, DC, DISC, MC, V.

MOTELS

☰☰ Best Western Golden Link

2723 Niles Ave, 49085; tel 616/983-6321 or toll free 800/528-1234; fax 616/983-7630. Exit 27 off I-94; 2½ mi N. Having the manager in residence means careful attention to detail and the needs of guests. Well-maintained facilities offer good value. **Rooms:** 36 rms and effic. CI 2pm/CO noon. Nonsmoking rms avail. Rooms all open to parking area. Larger rooms can sleep six. Bathrooms have double vanities. **Amenities:** 📷 🛁 A/C, cable TV. Some units w/whirlpools.

Services: ⊠ ⊐ ⊲ Grounds patrolled throughout the night for extra security. **Facilities:** ⛨ **Rates (CP):** Peak (May–Oct) $31–$44 S; $44–$55 D; $52 effic. Extra person $4. Children under age 12 stay free. Lower rates off-season. Parking: Outdoor, free. AE, CB, DC, DISC, MC, V.

≡≡ Days Inn

2699 MI 139, 49085; tel 616/925-7021; fax 616/925-7115. Exit 28 off I-94. A-frame structure adds bright sunshine to small lobby of this older, well-maintained facility. **Rooms:** 121 rms. CI 2pm/CO noon. Nonsmoking rms avail. **Amenities:** ⛨ ⚴ A/C, cable TV. Refrigerators on request. Microwaves in larger rooms. **Services:** ✗ ⊠ ⊐ ⊲ Restaurant next door will deliver meals. Cheerful welcome at registration desk. **Facilities:** ⛨ 🍺 🏊50 ⛾ Games rm, sauna, whirlpool. **Rates:** Peak (June–Aug) $45–$54 S; $60–$66 D. Extra person $5. Children under age 18 stay free. Lower rates off-season. Parking: Outdoor, free. AE, DC, MC, V.

RESTAURANTS 🍴

★ Grand Mere Inn

5800 Red Arrow Hwy, Stevensville; tel 616/429-3591. Exit 22 off I-94. **American.** The charming, antique-filled dining room overlooks a beautiful garden, a wide lawn, and the waters of Lake Michigan. (If you've come for dinner, you may be treated to a magnificent lake sunset.) Michigan memorabilia in the foyer shows you what this area was like at the turn of the century. Lake perch is still a special feature on the menu, and the barbecued back ribs are a local favorite. **FYI:** Reservations recommended. Jacket required. **Open:** Tues–Fri 4:30–10pm, Sat 4:30–11pm. **Prices:** Main courses $10–$19. AE, CB, DC, MC, V. 🍽 🖼 🏞 👥 ⛾

★ Schuler's

5000 Red Arrow Hwy, Stevensville; tel 616/429-3273. Exit 23 off I-94. **American.** A favorite with generations of Michigan families, Schuler's has been offering quality food since 1908. Repeat customers keep coming back for the classic roast prime rib of beef and rib eye of roast pork, and the special appetizer of barbecued meatballs is a Schuler tradition. Also Great Lakes whitefish, roasted herb chicken. **FYI:** Reservations accepted. Children's menu. **Open:** Mon–Thurs 11am–10pm, Fri–Sat 11am–11pm, Sun 10am–10pm. **Prices:** Main courses $14–$18. AE, CB, DC, DISC, MC, V. 🍽 🖼 👥 ⛾

Saugatuck

Located at the mouth of the Kalamazoo River, this posh Lake Michigan resort and major Midwest art colony hosts many summer arts and craft shows. There's a prehistoric Native American burial mound on the northern edge of town. **Information:** Saugatuck/Douglas Convention & Visitors Bureau, 303 Culver St, PO Box 28, Saugatuck, 49453 (tel 616/857-1701).

HOTEL 🏨

≡≡≡ Beachway Resort

106 Perryman, 49453; tel 616/857-3331; fax 616/857-3912. Exit 36 off I-196 N. Closest hotel to Oval Beach, Saugatuck's finest beach on Lake Michigan. Faces Kalamazoo Harbor and is only steps from hand-cranked chain ferry that crosses harbor. Well maintained, relaxed, and comfortable. **Rooms:** 25 rms, stes, and effic. CI 2pm/CO 11am. Nonsmoking rms avail. Efficiencies and two- and three-bedroom apartments face pool. Antique furnishings in many rooms. **Amenities:** ⛨ ⚴ A/C, cable TV. **Facilities:** ⛨ 🏋 ⛾ Basketball, games rm. **Rates (CP):** Peak (July–Sept) $75 S; $75–$165 D; $110–$165 ste; $110 effic. Extra person $10. Children under age 4 stay free. Min stay peak. Lower rates off-season. Parking: Outdoor, free. AE, DISC, MC, V.

MOTELS

≡≡≡ Lake Shore Resort

2885 Lake Shore Dr, 49453; tel 616/857-7121. Exit 36 off I-196 N; exit 41 off I-196 S. Wide, open grounds on a bluff overlooking Lake Michigan. Constant updating keeps all facilities in excellent condition, and owner/manager is in residence to guarantee good service. **Rooms:** 30 rms. CI 3pm/CO 11am. Nonsmoking rms avail. Units are set far back on lawn for quiet and privacy; lake views from every window. **Amenities:** ⛨ ⚴ A/C, cable TV, refrig. All units w/terraces. **Services:** ⊐ **Facilities:** ⛨ 🏋 🏋 ⛾ 1 beach (lake shore). Four-story walk down to beach, with several decks for convenient resting places. Beach chairs at water's edge and free rafts. Miles of hiking trails in woods beyond property. **Rates (CP):** Peak (July–Aug) $90–$130 S or D. Extra person $30. Min stay wknds. Lower rates off-season. Parking: Outdoor, free. Discount packages avail. MC, V.

≡≡ Timberline Motel

Blue Star Hwy, 49453; tel 616/857-2147 or toll free 800/257-2147; fax 616/857-2147. Exit 36 off I-196 N; exit 41 off I-196 S. An older facility that is very well maintained, though furnishings are somewhat sparse. Luxuriant evergreens line front of grounds, screening off busy highway. **Rooms:** 28 rms. CI noon/CO 11am. Nonsmoking rms avail. **Amenities:** ⛨ A/C, cable TV. **Services:** ⊐ Attention paid to guests' needs. **Facilities:** ⛨ 🏋 Lawn games, whirlpool, washer/dryer. Large pool attractive to families. **Rates:** Peak (June–Aug) $65–$85 S; $70–$95 D. Children under age 2 stay free. Min stay special events. Lower rates off-season. Parking: Outdoor, free. $10 per day for rollaway bed. AE, DISC, MC, V.

INNS

≡≡≡ Maplewood Hotel

428 Butler, 49453; tel 616/857-1771; fax 616/857-1773. 2 blocks from city center. Built in 1860, this has undergone a complete renovation and combines the finest in traditional

furnishings with handsome antiques. The architecture is pure Greek Revival, with the dark green trim and canopy contrasting nicely with the white exterior. There's a screened porch for meal service or relaxation. Public park and playground immediately adjacent; harbor and all attractions a few blocks away. Unsuitable for children under 8. **Rooms:** 15 rms. CI 3pm/CO noon. No smoking. **Amenities:** 🕿 📺 A/C, cable TV. Some units w/fireplaces. **Services:** 🖘 Fax and copy service available. **Facilities:** 🛗 🏊 🔲 ♿ Guest lounge w/TV. **Rates (BB):** Peak (May–Oct) $90 S; $90–$155 D. Extra person $15. Children under age 8 stay free. Min stay wknds. Lower rates off-season. Higher rates for special events/hols. Parking: Outdoor, free. Corporate rates, golf packages, boat cruise packages avail. Entire inn can be reserved for meetings. AE, MC, V.

≡≡≡ Rosemont Inn

83 Lake Shore Dr, 49453; tel 616/857-2637 or toll free 800/721-2637. 1 acre. Built in the 1880s, this inn retains its Victorian charm, with a delightful gazebo on the front lawn and a long veranda. Unsuitable for children under 18. **Rooms:** 14 rms. CI 3pm/CO noon. No smoking. Rooms furnished with fine antiques. **Amenities:** 🕿 📺 A/C. No TV. Some units w/fireplaces, some w/whirlpools. **Services:** Breakfasts of fresh rolls, pastries, and quiches served in two-story great room. **Facilities:** 🛗 🏊 1 beach (lake shore), sauna, whirlpool, washer/dryer, guest lounge w/TV. **Rates (BB):** Peak (July–Aug) $125–$165 D. Extra person $25. Min stay peak. Lower rates off-season. Higher rates for special events/hols. Parking: Outdoor, free. Rates increase during Tulip Time Festival in Holland, MI. Golf packages avail. AE, CB, DC, DISC, MC, V.

≡≡ Twin Gables Country Inn

900 E Lake St, 49453; tel 616/857-4346. Exit 36 off I-196 N. Old-time country charm, with large, inviting common gathering room with stone fireplace just off entryway. Short drive to city center. On 1½ acres of land, overlooks Kalamazoo River, with beautiful sunset views. Unsuitable for children under 4. **Rooms:** 14 rms. CI 3pm/CO 11am. No smoking. Names of rooms describe the decor. Antiques and hand-painted borders in rooms and hallways. **Amenities:** 🕿 📺 A/C. No TV. **Services:** Afternoon tea served. **Facilities:** 🛗 🏊 Whirlpool, guest lounge w/TV. **Rates (CP):** Peak (May–Sept) $78–$89 S; $78–$108 D. Extra person $10. Lower rates off-season. Parking: Outdoor, free. Special weekend packages. AE, CB, DISC, MC, V.

RESTAURANTS 🍽

Chequers

220 Culver St (Downtown); tel 616/857-1868. **British/Pub.** A bit of London in western Michigan. Relaxed, clublike atmosphere, dark paneled walls, stained glass, and leather accents. Grub includes fish and chips, shepherd's pie, ploughman's platter, and bangers and mash (a very spicy beer-duck sausage with buttered mashed potatoes). Good English cheese and a wide variety of ales and beers on hand. **FYI:** Reservations not accepted. **Open:** Mon–Thurs 11:30am–10pm, Fri–Sat 11:30am–11pm, Sun noon–10pm. **Prices:** Main courses $9–$16. AE, CB, DC, DISC, MC, V. 🍺 🖼 ♿

⑤ Loaf & Mug

236 Culver St (Downtown); tel 616/857-2974. **New American.** This charming spot features an enclosed garden area in the rear and an intimate inside dining room. Here you can have your meal and eat the dish it came in: wonderful soups and pastas are served in special bread bowls that absorb the flavors of their contents. Creamed chicken and creamed shrimp soups, chili, crab fettuccine, and some salads are served this way. A variety of croissant sandwiches make a light lunch. Take-out counter for breads, pastries, deli meats, cheeses, fresh-ground coffees. **FYI:** Reservations not accepted. Children's menu. Wine only. **Open:** Peak (Apr 1–Sept 3) Mon–Thurs 8am–4pm, Fri–Sat 8am–8pm, Sun 8am–3pm. Closed Jan. **Prices:** Main courses $8–$12. AE, CB, MC, V. 🍺 🖼 👥

ATTRACTIONS 🏛

SS *Keewatin* Marine Museum

South of Saugatuck-Douglas Bridge; tel 616/857-2151. Turn-of-the-century passenger steamship that sailed the Great Lakes for the Canadian Pacific Railroad until 1965. Guided tours include carefully restored cabins with original furnishings, woodwork, and brass fixtures. Engine room also open to the public. **Open:** Mem Day–Labor Day, daily 10am–4:30pm. **$**

Fenn Valley Vineyards

6130 122nd Ave, Fennville; tel 616/561-2396. 7 mi SE of Saugatuck. A small family-owned vineyard and wine cellar located in the rolling hills of western Michigan. Wine tastings are offered; visitors can view the cellar on self-guided tours and learn about the winemaking process. Wine-related gift items and supplies sold. Picnic area. **Open:** Mon–Sat 10am–5pm, Sun 1–5pm. **Free**

Sault Ste Marie

Seat of Chippewa County, on the Upper Peninsula. The locks on the St Mary's River are a vital shipping link between Lake Huron and Lake Superior. An international bridge connects this town to its Canadian namesake. **Information:** Sault Ste Marie Tourist Bureau, 2581 I-75 Business Spur, Sault Ste Marie, 49783 (tel 906/632-3301 or toll free 800/MI-SAULT).

HOTELS 🏨

≡≡≡ Clarion Kewadin Hotel and Casino

2150 Shunk Rd, 15781; tel 906/635-1400 or toll free 800/KEWADIN. Off I-75. Hotel and casino owned and operated by Sault Ste Marie Tribe of Chippewa Indians. Over 118,000 feet of Vegas-style gaming, dining, lodging, and entertainment. **Rooms:** 52 rms. CI open/CO 11am. Nonsmoking rms avail. Some rooms have canopy beds. **Amenities:** 🔒 💧 📺 🍴 A/C, cable TV w/movies, refrig, VCR. Some units w/whirlpools. **Services:** 🍽️ 🆅🅿️ 📐 🛎️ **Facilities:** ♿ 1 restaurant, 1 bar. 24-hour casino. **Rates:** Peak (June–Aug) $90–$171 S; $98–$179 D. Extra person $10. Children under age 18 stay free. Lower rates off-season. Parking: Outdoor, free. AE, DC, DISC, MC, V.

📧📧📧 Ojibway Hotel

240 W Portage St, 49783; tel 906/632-4100 or toll free 800/654-2929. Exit 394 off I-75. The finest hotel in town, built in 1928. **Rooms:** 71 rms and stes. CI 3pm/CO 11am. Nonsmoking rms avail. Suites are decorated with period-style furnishings. **Amenities:** 🔒 💧 A/C, cable TV w/movies, refrig, dataport. Some units w/whirlpools. **Services:** 📐 🛎️ **Facilities:** 🍴 [200] ♿ 1 restaurant (*see* "Restaurants" below), 1 bar (w/entertainment), sauna, whirlpool. Restaurant has view of Soo Locks and is highly rated. **Rates:** Peak (June 15–Oct 15) $114 S or D; $195 ste. Children under age 18 stay free. Lower rates off-season. Parking: Outdoor, free. AE, DC, MC, V.

📧📧 Ramada Inn

I-75 Business Spur, 49783; tel 906/635-1523 or toll free 800/228-2828; fax 906/635-2941. Appropriate for families and equipped for conferences. **Rooms:** 131 rms and stes. CI 2pm/CO noon. Nonsmoking rms avail. **Amenities:** 🔒 💧 🍴 A/C, cable TV w/movies, refrig. Some units w/terraces, some w/whirlpools. **Services:** ✗ 📐 🛎️ **Facilities:** 🍴 🎳 [400] ♿ 1 restaurant, 1 bar (w/entertainment), games rm, sauna, whirlpool. Karaoke Thurs–Sat. **Rates:** Peak (June–Oct) $72–$93 S or D; $110–$150 ste. Extra person $10. Children under age 17 stay free. Lower rates off-season. Parking: Outdoor, free. AE, MC, V.

MOTELS

📧 Bavarian Lodge Budget Host

2006 Ashmun St, 49783; tel 906/632-6864 or toll free 800/BUD-HOST. On I-75 Business Spur. A convenient Budget Host close to Soo Area attractions. **Rooms:** 18 rms, stes, and effic. CI 2pm/CO 11am. Nonsmoking rms avail. Family rooms available. **Amenities:** 🔒 💧 📺 A/C, cable TV w/movies, refrig. **Services:** 🛎️ **Rates:** Peak (June 15–Oct 15) $49–$74 D; $85 ste; $95 effic. Extra person $8. Children under age 18 stay free. Lower rates off-season. Parking: Outdoor, free. DISC, MC, V.

📧📧 Crestview Thrifty Inn

1200 Ashmun St, 49783; tel 906/635-5213 or toll free 800/955-5213; fax 906/635-9672. Exit 392 on I-75 Business Spur. Convenient, close to restaurants, shopping, and attractions. **Rooms:** 44 rms. CI open/CO 11am. No smoking. **Amenities:** 🔒 💧 A/C, cable TV w/movies, refrig. **Services:** 🔑 🛎️ 📠 Dataport, fax machine, and copy machine available. **Rates:** Peak (mid-June–mid-Oct) $54–$80 S or D.

Children under age 18 stay free. Lower rates off-season. Parking: Outdoor, free. Agawa Canyon and snow train packages avail. AE, CB, DC, DISC, MC, V.

📧📧 Days Inn

3651 I-75 Business Spur, 49783; tel 906/635-5200 or toll free 800/325-2525. Good for business or vacation travelers. Close to the Soo Locks and Lake Superior State University. **Rooms:** 85 rms. CI 3pm/CO 11am. Nonsmoking rms avail. **Amenities:** 🔒 💧 A/C, cable TV w/movies. Some units w/whirlpools. **Services:** 🛎️ **Facilities:** 🍴 ♿ Games rm, whirlpool, washer/dryer. **Rates:** Peak (June 1–Oct 15) $93–$125 S or D. Extra person $6. Children under age 12 stay free. Lower rates off-season. Parking: Outdoor, free. AE, DC, DISC, MC, V.

📧 Laker Inn

1712 Ashmun St, 49783; tel 906/632-3581 or toll free 800/551-6126. Motel close to Soo area attractions with all ground-floor units. **Rooms:** 12 rms. CI noon/CO 10am. Nonsmoking rms avail. **Amenities:** 🔒 💧 📺 A/C, cable TV. **Services:** 🛎️ **Rates:** Peak (June–Aug) $58 S or D. Extra person $4. Lower rates off-season. Parking: Outdoor, free. Kewadin Casino package avail. MC, V.

📧📧 Super 8 Motel

3826 I-75 Business Spur, 49783; tel 906/632-8882 or toll free 800/800-8000; fax 906/632-3766. A convenient Super 8 that is relatively new. **Rooms:** 61 rms and stes. CI 2pm/CO 11am. Nonsmoking rms avail. **Amenities:** 🔒 💧 A/C, cable TV, dataport. Some units w/whirlpools. **Services:** 🛎️ 🐾 Pets allowed, with $50 deposit. **Facilities:** [50] ♿ Washer/dryer. **Rates (CP):** Peak (July) $55 S; $61–$63 D; $73 ste. Extra person $3. Children under age 12 stay free. Lower rates off-season. Parking: Outdoor, free. AE, DC, DISC, MC, V.

RESTAURANTS 🍴

★ The Antlers

804 E Portage Ave; tel 906/632-3571. **American.** The walls and ceilings of this very popular eatery are hung with dozens of stuffed wild animals (including a full-size polar bear), antlers, tools, and other outdoorsy decor. The staff salutes special occasions by blowing a loud ship's whistle, ringing bells, and generally encouraging a noisy, enthusiastic friendliness. Known for their Paul Bunyan Burger, Antlers also offers up great Mexican food, homemade bread, and extraordinary desserts. **FYI:** Reservations not accepted. Children's menu. **Open:** Peak (June–Aug) daily 11am–11pm. **Prices:** Main courses $9–$16. MC, V.

Freighter's Restaurant

In Ojibway Hotel, 240 W Portage St; tel 906/632-4211. **American.** A classy spot to have dinner while watching the boats go through the Soo Locks. White tablecloths and flower arrangements hanging from the ceiling add to the dining room's romantic atmosphere. Lake Superior whitefish, Alaskan crab, mesquite-smoked breast of pheasant, and sesame-fried lemon chicken are among the main courses. Extensive wine list. **FYI:** Reservations accepted. Children's menu. **Open:** Peak (Feb–Nov) daily 6–10pm. **Prices:** Main courses $15–$37. AE, MC, V. ♥ ▣ ⛰ ♥ ⚹

Robin's Nest
3520 I-75 Business Spur; tel 906/632-3200. **American.** A casual, family-friendly eatery offering a full buffet at breakfast. Later in the day, seafood dominates the menu, with fresh local whitefish and lake trout among the catch available. Steaks, chicken, burgers also available. **FYI:** Reservations accepted. Children's menu. **Open:** Peak (June–Aug) daily 7am–10pm. **Prices:** Main courses $10–$26. AE, MC, V. ▦ ⚹

Studebaker's Restaurant and Lounge
3585 I-75 Business Spur; tel 906/632-4262. **American.** A real Studebaker stands outside this beloved local eatery, and the car theme is continued in the dining room. There's a breakfast buffet daily and a dinner buffet on weekends, with Mexican specialties galore. **FYI:** Reservations accepted. Children's menu. **Open:** Peak (June 15–Oct 15) daily 6am–10pm. **Prices:** Main courses $9–$25. AE, MC, V.

ATTRACTIONS ▣

Museum Ship *Valley Camp*
East of Soo Locks; tel 906/632-3658. Launched in 1917, the 11½-ton steamer *Valley Camp* was finally taken out of service in 1966 and is now the only vessel of its type preserved as a maritime museum. Highlights include an exhibit on the wreck of the *Edmund Fitzgerald* (including lifeboats); a 32-foot model of the *Belle River*; navigational artifacts; maritime paintings, a Marine Hall of Fame, and six 1,200-gallon aquariums. Guided tours of the steam engine, galley, dining rooms, crew's quarters, and pilot house also available. **Open:** Peak (July–Aug) daily 9am–9pm. Reduced hours off-season. **$$$**

Soo Locks
St Marys Falls Canal, Portage Ave; tel 906/635-3484. The world-famous Soo Locks provide deep-draft ships with passage around the rapids in the St Mary River, where the water falls about 21 feet from the level of Lake Superior to the level of the lower lakes. The Visitors Center was renovated in 1995, and contains a working model of a lock which illustrates its entire operation, a viewing room which shows movies every hour, and other artifacts of interest including a fountain with colored lights and synchronized music. **Open:** Peak (mid-June–Labor Day) daily 7am–11pm. Reduced hours off-season. **Free**

Tower of History
326 E Portage Ave; tel 906/632-3658. A 21-story observation tower offering a spectacular 20-mile view. The lobby houses educational exhibit with a multimedia show on the history of the Great Lakes and Sault Ste Marie. **Open:** May–Oct, daily 10am–6pm. **$**

Sleeping Bear Dunes National Lakeshore

For lodgings and dining, see Empire, Frankfort, Glen Arbor, Leland, Traverse City

Sand dunes, sphagnum moss bogs, cedar swamps, and hardwood forests make up this 75,000-acre park that stretches along the Lake Michigan shoreline. Porcupines, deer, bobcats, and more than 120 species of birds are among the many kinds of animals inhabiting the area. Sand dunes rise to nearly 500 feet. There are 35 miles of hiking trails and a 7.6-mile scenic drive by the lake. The park headquarters and visitors center houses exhibits on the geological history of the park and of the region.

Southfield

This northwestern suburb of Detroit is a business center, as well as the home of Lawrence Institute of Technology and a branch campus of Wayne State University. **Information:** Southfield Chamber of Commerce, 16250 Northland Dr, #130, Southfield, 48075 (tel 810/557-6400).

HOTELS ▥

▤▤▤ DoubleTree Guest Suites
28100 Franklin Rd, 48034; tel 810/350-2000 or toll free 800/222-TREE; fax 810/350-1185. Sleek, luxury hotel for business and vacation travelers. Dining, shopping, and theater nearby. **Rooms:** 230 stes. Executive level. CI 3pm/CO 11am. Nonsmoking rms avail. **Amenities:** ▤ ⚹ ▯ ♦ A/C, cable TV w/movies, refrig, voice mail. 1 unit w/whirlpool. **Services:** ✕ ▨ ♨ **Facilities:** ▨ ⛋ 200 ▯ ⚹ 1 restaurant, 1 bar, spa, sauna, whirlpool, washer/dryer. Guests have access to nearby Franklin Racquet Club. **Rates:** $109–$139 ste. Extra person $20. Children under age 12 stay free. AP and MAP rates avail. Parking: Outdoor, free. AE, CB, DC, DISC, MC, V.

▤▤▤ Hilton Garden Inn
26000 American Dr, 48034; tel 810/357-1100 or toll free 800/HILTONS; fax 810/799-7030. Casual, friendly atmosphere with easy access to major expressways. Ideal for business travelers during the week; families on weekends. **Rooms:** 195 rms and stes. CI 3pm/CO 1pm. Nonsmoking rms avail. Clean, comfortable rooms. **Amenities:** ▤ ⚹ ▯ A/C, cable TV w/movies, dataport, voice mail. **Services:** ✕ ▨ ♨ ♦ Twice-daily maid svce, children's program, babysitting. Complimentary hors d'oeuvres daily; manager's reception with cocktails every Wed. Complimentary transportation within 7 mile radius. Book and magazine library in lobby. **Facilities:** ▨ ⛋ 100 ⚹ 1 restaurant, 1 bar, spa, sauna, whirlpool. Complimentary use of small meeting room. Patio with grills. Access to Franklin Racquet Club can be arranged.

Rates: $65 S or D; $175 ste. Extra person $10. Children under age 18 stay free. Parking: Outdoor, free. Adult children staying with their parents stay free. Weekend packages avail with complimentary extended continental breakfast. AE, CB, DC, DISC, MC, V.

≣≣≣ Marriott Hotel

27033 Northwestern Hwy, 48034; tel 810/356-7400 or toll free 800/228-9290; fax 810/356-4627. Located next to Southfield's corporate business park, this provides business travelers with services and facilities designed to make work easier. **Rooms:** 222 rms and stes. Executive level. CI 3pm/CO noon. Nonsmoking rms avail. Comfortable accommodations. **Amenities:** 🖀 ⓑ ⓠ A/C, cable TV w/movies, dataport. Some units w/terraces. **Services:** ✕ ⬤ 🚗 ⬛ ⬑ ⬤ Car-rental desk, babysitting. **Facilities:** ⬛ 🔑 [200] ⬜ ⬥ 1 restaurant, 1 bar, spa, sauna, steam rm, whirlpool. **Rates:** $49–$139 S or D; $250 ste. Extra person $10. Children under age 18 stay free. Parking: Outdoor, free. Weekend packages with complimentary breakfast avail. AE, CB, DC, DISC, MC, V.

≣≣≣ The Plaza Hotel

16400 JL Hudson Dr, 48075; tel 810/559-6500 or toll free 800/800-5112; fax 810/559-3625. Adjacent to Northland Mall. An older hotel, carefully maintained to preserve its European ambience while continuing to provide the services contemporary travelers value. Near major expressways and adjacent to one of Michigan's largest shopping centers. Jogging path adjacent to hotel. **Rooms:** 252 rms and stes. Executive level. CI 3pm/CO noon. Nonsmoking rms avail. **Amenities:** 🖀 ⓑ A/C, cable TV w/movies. Some units w/whirlpools. All rooms have phones with two lines. **Services:** ✕ [VP] 🚗 ⬛ ⬑ ⬤ Car-rental desk. Limo service desk in lobby. **Facilities:** ⬛ ⬤1 🔫 [1500] ⬥ 1 restaurant, 1 bar (w/entertainment), basketball, sauna. Putting green. **Rates:** $79–$109 S or D; $250–$450 ste. Extra person $15. Parking: Outdoor, free. Corporate rates, weekend and holiday packages, custom group packages avail. AE, CB, DC, DISC, MC, V.

≣≣≣≣ Radisson Plaza Hotel at Town Center

1500 Town Center, 48075; or toll free 800/333-3333; fax 810/827-1364. Northwestern Service Dr at Evergreen and Ten Mile Rd. Located in the Prudential Town Center Complex, this modern building has a copper-colored, mirrored exterior, and handsomely appointed atrium lobby. Great choice for business meetings or personal getaways. Beauty salon, Southfield pavilion health and fitness area, and horseback riding nearby. **Rooms:** 385 rms and stes. Executive level. CI 3pm/CO noon. Nonsmoking rms avail. Spacious guest rooms. **Amenities:** 🖀 ⓑ ⓠ A/C, cable TV w/movies, dataport. Some units w/whirlpools. **Services:** ⏸ ⬤ [VP] 🚗 ⬛ ⬑ ⬤ Car-rental desk, babysitting. Prior permission required for pets. Plaza Club floor has complimentary breakfast, hors d'oeuvres, and late-night snacks. **Facilities:** ⬛ ⓧ 🐟 🔫 [600] ⬜ ⬥ 2 restaurants (see "Restaurants" below), 1 bar (w/entertainment), games rm, spa, sauna, steam rm,

whirlpool, day-care ctr, playground, washer/dryer. **Rates:** $129–$149 S or D; $225–$525 ste. Extra person $20. Children under age 16 stay free. AP and MAP rates avail. Parking: Indoor/outdoor, free. Special packages avail, such as gourmet adventures and children's slumber party. AE, CB, DC, DISC, ER, JCB, MC, V.

MOTELS

≣≣≣ Courtyard by Marriott

27027 Northwestern Hwy, 48034; tel 810/358-1222 or toll free 800/228-9290; fax 810/354-3820. Low stucco cluster arranged around an interior courtyard, artfully landscaped, adjacent to highway. Car rental desk at next door full-service Marriott. **Rooms:** 147 rms and stes. CI 3pm/CO noon. Nonsmoking rms avail. Large and comfortable rooms. **Amenities:** 🖀 ⓑ A/C, cable TV w/movies, dataport, voice mail. Some units w/terraces. **Services:** 🚗 ⬛ ⬑ Social director. **Facilities:** ⬛ 🔫 [25] ⬥ 1 restaurant (bkfst only), 1 bar, whirlpool, washer/dryer. **Rates:** $89 S or D; $88–$99 ste. Children under age 18 stay free. Parking: Outdoor, free. AE, CB, DC, DISC, MC, V.

≣≣ Hampton Inn

27500 Northwestern Hwy, 48075; tel 810/585-8881 or toll free 800/HAMPTON; fax 810/356-2083. Lobby fireplace gives warm, homey feel to this sleek, modern facility. **Rooms:** 154 rms. CI 3pm/CO noon. Nonsmoking rms avail. Poolside rooms available. **Amenities:** 🖀 ⓑ A/C, cable TV w/movies, dataport. **Services:** ✕ ⬛ ⬑ ⬤ Babysitting. Safety deposit box at front desk. Local deli provides limited room service. Prior permission and deposit required for pets. **Facilities:** ⬛ 🔫 [25] ⬥ Whirlpool, washer/dryer. **Rates (CP):** Peak (May–Sept 5) $65–$85 S or D. Extra person $10. Children under age 18 stay free. Min stay special events. Lower rates off-season. Parking: Outdoor, free. AE, CB, DC, DISC, MC, V.

≣≣ Holiday Inn

26555 Telegraph Rd, 48034; tel 810/353-7700 or toll free 800/465-4329. At Swanson. Sixteen-floor tower with Holidome attached. Easy access to major highway. **Rooms:** 417 rms and stes. CI 3pm/CO noon. Nonsmoking rms avail. Comfortable accommodations. **Amenities:** 🖀 ⓑ A/C, satel TV w/movies, dataport. **Services:** ✕ 🚗 ⬛ ⬑ ⬤ Car-rental desk. Guests eligible for discount fees at nearby 18-hole golf course. **Facilities:** ⬛ 🔫 [250] ⬥ 1 restaurant, 1 bar (w/entertainment), games rm, whirlpool. **Rates:** $79–$90 S or D; $175–$250 ste. Children under age 18 stay free. Parking: Outdoor, free. AE, CB, DC, DISC, ER, JCB, MC, V.

≣≣ Travelodge

27650 Northwestern Hwy, 48034; tel 810/353-6777 or toll free 800/225-3050; fax 810/353-2944. Off US 24 S, just S of 12 Mile Rd. Conveniently located in town's corporate area. Particularly attentive to needs of business travelers, but well suited to families, too. **Rooms:** 110 rms. CI 2pm/CO noon. Nonsmoking rms avail. **Amenities:** 🖀 ⓑ ⓠ A/C, satel TV w/movies. Some units w/whirlpools. **Services:** ⬛ Coffee bar and free popcorn. Room service available through local restaurants; meals at selected area restaurants can be charged to room. **Facilities:** **Rates (CP):** $45–$55 S; $50–$60 D. Extra person $6. Children under age 13 stay free. Parking: Outdoor, free. Senior discounts and special packages avail. AE, CB, DC, DISC, MC, V.

RESTAURANTS

Chianti Villa Italia

28565 Northwestern Hwy; tel 810/350-0055. On W side of MI 10, just S of 12 Mile Rd. **Italian.** Trompe l'oeil painting makes this family-style Italian look like an entire village street from the outside. The interior is dark and cozy; and the large space is broken into several smaller rooms. Pastas such as fettucine alla bolognese and lasagna al Chianti share the menu with veal scaloppine with wild mushroom sauce and baked whitefish with roasted garlic and white wine sauce. **FYI:** Reservations recommended. Children's menu. **Open:** Mon–Thurs 11:30am–10pm, Fri 11:30am–11pm, Sat 5–11pm, Sun 4–9pm. **Prices:** Main courses $12–$18. AE, CB, DC, DISC, MC, V.

Golden Mushroom

18100 W 10 Mile Rd; tel 810/559-4230. **Continental.** This award-winning restaurant is noted for its extensive wine list, famous chefs, and exquisite cuisine. Health dishes prepared without butter, cream, or sugar include poached Norwegian salmon and simmered chicken. Menu also features tournedos with foie gras, Madeira sauce, and fettucine with truffles; roast rack of lamb; and broiled lobster with a truffle-stuffed baked potato. Downstairs is the more casual Mushroom Cellar, which has similar specials at slightly reduced prices, plus burgers, pizza, and pasta dishes. **FYI:** Reservations recommended. Dress code. **Open:** Lunch Mon–Fri 11:30am–4pm; dinner Mon–Thurs 5–11pm, Fri 5pm–midnight, Sat 5:30pm–midnight. **Prices:** Main courses $16–$32. AE, CB, DC, DISC, MC.

Le Metro

In Applegate Square Shopping Center, 29855 Northwestern Hwy; tel 810/353-2757. **Regional American.** The staff won't hurry you at this cozy little bistro, so you can linger over specials like spicy shrimp with vegetables over long-grain brown rice, or a mixed grill of veal medallion, beef tenderloin, and lamb chops. Reservations or not, expect a wait later in the evening. **FYI:** Reservations recommended. **Open:** Lunch Mon–Sat 11:30am–4:30pm; dinner Mon–Thurs 5:30–10pm, Fri–Sat 5:30–11pm. **Prices:** Main courses $7–$22. AE, CB, DC, DISC, MC, V.

Sweet Lorraine's Cafe

29101 Greenfield Rd; tel 810/559-5985. ¼ block N of 12 Mile Rd. **New American.** Trendy, colorful restaurant offering tasty fare. Pecan chicken is a favorite; also choose from Mediterranean pasta salad, Lake Superior whitefish, and shrimp Creole. A different vegetarian entree is offered every day. **FYI:** Reservations accepted. Jazz. Children's menu.

Open: Mon–Thurs 11am–10:30pm, Fri–Sat 11am–midnight, Sun 11am–9pm. **Prices:** Main courses $6–$16. AE, DC, DISC, MC, V.

TC Linguini's

In Radisson Plaza Hotel at Town Center, 1500 Town Center; tel 810/827-4000. **Italian.** Irresistible Italian restaurant broken up into several small dining areas. Menu changes quarterly and includes items such as tortellini alla fini (with prosciutto, snow peas, and garlic parmesan sauce); sautéed chicken tosca with tomato basil sauce; and an Adriatic salad of linguine, crabmeat, shrimp, cucumber, and plum tomatoes. **FYI:** Reservations accepted. Piano. No smoking. **Open:** Lunch Mon–Fri 11:30am–2pm; dinner Mon–Sat 5:30–10pm. **Prices:** Main courses $9–$16. AE, CB, DC, DISC, ER, MC, V.

Southgate

HOTEL

Ramada Hotel Heritage Center 3

17201 Northline Rd, 48195; tel 313/283-4400 or toll free 800/2-RAMADA; fax 313/283-6855. Exit 37 off I-75; E on Northline Rd to entrance. Attractive accommodations with plenty of activities for every family member. Services to accommodate business travelers as well. Golf and tennis nearby. **Rooms:** 160 rms and stes. Executive level. CI 3pm/CO noon. Nonsmoking rms avail. Relocation apartments available. **Amenities:** A/C, satel TV w/movies, dataport. Some units w/whirlpools. **Services:** **Facilities:** 1 restaurant, 1 bar (w/entertainment), whirlpool, washer/dryer. Dinner theater on-site, with performances Fri and Sat evenings. Peak (June–Sept) $89–$96 S or D; $190 ste. Extra person $6. Children under age 18 stay free. Lower rates off-season. Parking: Outdoor, free. Weekend, theater, and family packages avail. AE, CB, DC, DISC, MC, V.

South Haven

The lion's share of the state's blueberries are grown in this area of southwest Michigan, and South Haven is the site of the National Blueberry Festival (held every July or August). **Information:** Lakeshore Convention & Visitors Bureau, 415 Phoenix St, South Haven, 49090 (tel 616/637-5252 or toll free 800/SO-HAVEN).

MOTELS

Econo Lodge

09817 MI 140, 49090; tel 616/637-5141 or toll free 800/955-1831; fax 616/637-1109. Exit 18 off I-196, W to MI 140. Bright red trim is fresh contrast to white buildings. Standard motel units, plus newly built suite building. **Rooms:** 60 rms and stes. CI 3pm/CO 11am. Nonsmoking rms avail.

Amenities: 🛏 🕯 ☎ A/C, cable TV. Some units w/terraces, some w/whirlpools. **Services:** ✗ ⌨ 🛏 🍽 **Facilities:** 🏠 🛐 🚰 ♿ 1 restaurant, basketball, volleyball, games rm, racquetball, spa, sauna, whirlpool, playground, washer/dryer. Large fitness center with pool and workout equipment on grounds is free to guests. **Rates:** Peak (June–Sept) $60–$70 S; $75–$85 D; $100–$115 ste. Extra person $5. Children under age 18 stay free. Min stay wknds. Lower rates off-season. Parking: Outdoor, free. Golf packages avail. AE, CB, DC, DISC, MC, V.

≣ Lake Bluff Motel

76648 11th Ave, 49090; tel 616/637-8531 or toll free 800/686-1305; fax 616/637-8532. Exit 18 off I-196. A distance from town center, but perched high above Lake Michigan for wonderful view of sunsets over lake. Extra wide expanse of lawn with plenty of running space for children. A popular choice for families. **Rooms:** 46 rms and effic. CI 4pm/CO 11am. Nonsmoking rms avail. Room furnishings are very modest. **Amenities:** 🛏 ☎ A/C, cable TV. Some units w/fireplaces, some w/whirlpools. **Services:** 🚗 🍽 **Facilities:** 🏠 🛐 Lawn games, whirlpool, playground. **Rates:** Peak (May–Sept) $59–$69 S; $78–$130 D; $66–$69 effic. Children under age 18 stay free. Min stay wknds. Lower rates off-season. Parking: Outdoor, free. AE, CB, DC, DISC, MC, V.

INN

≣ ≣ ≣ Yelton Manor Bed and Breakfast

140 North Shore Dr, 49090; tel 616/637-5220; fax 616/637-4957. The two Victorian houses that make up the inn are so special that tours of the rooms are conducted twice a week. Sunny porch room and friendly parlor are accented with antique pieces from owner's collection. Yard area is not large, but is filled with roses and other flowers. Lake Michigan beach directly across the street. Unsuitable for children under 12. **Rooms:** 17 rms and stes. CI 3pm/CO 11am. No smoking. Each of the upstairs rooms shows a flair for innovative decoration. Six gigantic white pillows are at the head of each bed. Lavish bathroom appointments in several rooms. **Amenities:** 🛏 🍷 A/C, cable TV. Some units w/terraces, some w/fireplaces, some w/whirlpools. Each suite in Manor House, across the yard, has balcony, fireplace, whirlpool, and VCR. **Services:** Hors d'oeuvres offered every afternoon. **Facilities:** 🛐 Guest lounge w/TV. **Rates (BB):** Peak (May–Oct) $95–$170 D; $170–$205 ste. Min stay wknds. Lower rates off-season. Parking: Outdoor, free. AE, MC, V.

RESTAURANTS 🍴

Ⓢ ✸ Clementine's

Phoenix & Center Sts (Downtown); tel 616/637-4755. **American.** Originally a bank, this historic setting for good family dining features exposed brick walls and the original tin ceiling, bank safe, and teller windows. Wonderful old pictures of Lake Michigan steamers and their captains and crews hang on the walls; the magnificently carved bar is from one of the steamboats that served the city long ago. Highlights of the extensive menu are Claim Jumper (spinach, mushrooms, and crab on sautéed chicken breast, served on a croissant and topped with Alfredo sauce) and Phoenix Street Special (charbroiled prime rib with grilled mushrooms, onions and roasted red peppers). **FYI:** Reservations not accepted. Children's menu. **Open:** Peak (Mem Day–Labor Day) Mon–Thurs 11am–10:30pm, Fri–Sat 11am–11:30pm, Sun noon–10:30pm. **Prices:** Main courses $7–$17. AE, DISC, MC, V. 🍴 👪 ♿

Magnolia Grille

In the Idler Riverboat in Old Harbor Village, 515 Williams St; tel 616/637-8435. **American/Cajun/Creole.** Built as a private steamer at the turn of the century and now home to an elegant yet modestly priced restaurant. The kitchen is in the bow and each of the staterooms is a private dining room. Seating in open areas offers views of the Black River harbor and marina. Beautiful oak and cherry wood paneling contrasts nicely with the bright white linen cloths. Menu specialties are blackened chicken and Louisiana steak salads, Great Lakes perch, and the Maui-Wowie sandwich (grilled teriyaki chicken breast). The Calypso Bar on the top deck stays open late and offers a light bar menu. **FYI:** Reservations accepted. Children's menu. **Open:** Lunch daily 11am–2pm; dinner daily 5–10pm. Closed Oct–Apr. **Prices:** Main courses $15–$20. AE, DC, DISC, MC, V. ♥ 🍴 ⛰ 👪

The Sea Wolf

176 Blue Star Hwy; tel 616/637-2007. Exit 22 off I-196. **American.** Worth the short ride out of the city to enjoy elegant dining in these lovely surroundings. Owner Wolf's grandparents had a family resort here in the 1920s, and he has returned to create an upscale, gracious room with prices that won't strain most budgets. Whitefish, walleye pike, lake perch, shrimp, and catfish head the menu. **FYI:** Reservations recommended. Children's menu. **Open:** Mon–Sat 5–9:30pm, Sun 3:30–8:30pm. Closed May 1–Oct 15. **Prices:** Main courses $14–$18. DISC, MC, V. 🍴 👪 ♿

ATTRACTIONS 🏛

Michigan Maritime Museum

260 Dyckman Ave; tel 616/637-8078. Highlighting the maritime heritage of Michigan's Great Lakes, this museum includes exhibits on historic schooners and steamers, maps made by Great Lakes explorers, presentations on Native Americans and settlers of the region, and marine art. Public lectures, research library, guided tours. **Open:** Wed–Sun 10am–5pm. $

Van Buren State Park

I-196; tel 616/637-2788. Beautiful wooded sand dunes fill this 326-acre park. Swimming, hunting, and camping are available, as are picnic areas and concessions. **Open:** Daily sunrise–sunset. $

Spring Lake

See Grand Haven

Sterling Heights

A northern suburb of Detroit, located on the Clinton River. **Information:** Sterling Heights Area Chamber of Commerce, 12900 Hall Rd, #110, Sterling Heights, 48313 (tel 810/731-5400)

MOTEL 🏨

▤▤▤ Best Western Sterling Inn & Conference Center

34911 Van Dyke Ave, 48312; tel 810/979-1400 or toll free 800/953-1400; fax 810/979-0430. MI 53 at 15 Mile Rd. Enclosed second-story walkway above parking lot connects conference center and room wings. Golf nearby. **Rooms:** 158 rms and stes. CI 2pm/CO noon. Nonsmoking rms avail. **Amenities:** 🏨 🕭 A/C, cable TV w/movies, refrig, dataport. **Services:** ✕ 🚐 🖄 ⤶ Twice-daily maid service on request. **Facilities:** 🛋 🏐 600 🖥 ❧ 1 restaurant (see "Restaurants" below), 1 bar, basketball, sauna, whirlpool. **Rates (BB):** $75–$85 S; $80–$90 D; $150–$275 ste. Extra person $5. Children under age 15 stay free. Parking: Outdoor, free. Senior citizen discounts, corporate and group rates, weekend and honeymoon packages avail. AE, CB, DC, DISC, MC, V.

RESTAURANT 🍴

Loon River Cafe

In Best Western Sterling Inn, 34911 Van Dyke Ave; tel 810/979-1420. At 15 Mile Rd. **Regional American.** This charming dining room, with its huge fireplace, wildlife prints, wooden floors, and large windows, will make you think you're eating in a North Woods lodge. Select a live trout from the tank next to the salad bar, or enjoy dishes like stewed capon with redskin potatoes, celery, and carrots; smoked pork chops, or hunter's goulash of beef tips, tomatoes, onions, mushrooms, and peppers over spaetzle. Regularly scheduled "wild game" nights may include elk, bear, or quail. Patrons over 60 get 20% discount Sun–Thurs. **FYI:** Reservations accepted. Children's menu. **Open:** Breakfast Mon–Fri 6–10am, Sat–Sun 7–11am; lunch daily noon–5pm; dinner Mon–Fri 5–11pm, Sat 5pm–midnight, Sun 5–10pm; brunch Sun 10am–2pm. **Prices:** Main courses $4–$13. AE, CB, DC, DISC, MC, V. 🛋 ♥ ♿

Stevensville

See St Joseph

Tawas City

Seat of Iosco County, in northeast part of state. The somewhat sheltered Tawas Bay is often teeming with perch and other fish. A shore-to-shore hiking/biking/riding trail connects Lake Huron to Lake Michigan at Tawas City. **Information:** Tawas Bay Tourist & Convention Bureau, 402 E Lake St, PO Box 10, Tawas City, 48764-0608 (tel 517/362-8643 or toll free 800/55-TAWAS).

MOTELS 🏨

▤▤▤ Holiday Inn

300 E Bay St, 48730; tel 517/362-5111 or toll free 800/336-8601. On N US 23. Located on Lake Huron. Close to hiking, snowmobiling, and cross-country skiing areas. **Rooms:** 103 rms. CI 4pm/CO noon. Nonsmoking rms avail. **Amenities:** 🏨 🕭 🖵 A/C, cable TV w/movies. Some units w/whirlpools. **Services:** 🖄 ⤶ Social director, children's program. Children's program in summer. Sometimes evening bonfires. Friendly staff. **Facilities:** 🛋 🏊 200 ♿ 1 restaurant, 1 bar (w/entertainment), 1 beach (lake shore), volleyball, lawn games, sauna, whirlpool, playground. 900' of sandy beach. Dock available for boaters. Beachfront for paddleboats and wave runners nearby. **Rates:** Peak (June–Aug) $87–$140 D. Extra person $8. Children under age 19 stay free. Min stay special events. Lower rates off-season. Parking: Outdoor, free. DC, DISC, MC, V.

▤ Martin's Motel

706 E Bay St, 48730; tel 517/362-2061 or toll free 800/362-3640. Basic motel with nice seating area beside water. Minutes from main pier in downtown Tawas City. **Rooms:** 20 rms and effic. CI 2pm/CO 11am. Nonsmoking rms avail. **Amenities:** 🏨 A/C, cable TV w/movies, refrig. **Services:** ⤶ **Facilities:** 🏊 **Rates:** Peak (June–Aug) $54–$59 S or D; $75–$85 effic. Extra person $5. Lower rates off-season. Parking: Outdoor, free. AE, DISC, MC, V.

Three Rivers

In southern part of state, midway between Kalamazoo and the Indiana border. Swiss Valley Ski Area is 10 miles west of town. **Information:** Three Rivers Area Chamber of Commerce, 103 S Douglas, Three Rivers, 49093 (tel 616/278-8193).

HOTEL 🏨

▤▤▤ Three Rivers Inn

1200 W Broadway, 49093; tel 616/273-9521 or toll free 800/553-4626; fax 616/278-7205. Bright turquoise blue canopy and soft trim enliven simple brick exterior. Generous plantings. Brick walls and warm, natural woods. **Rooms:** 100 rms. CI 2pm/CO 11am. Nonsmoking rms avail. Rooms surrounding pool have small, individual patios. **Amenities:** 🏨

◊ A/C, cable TV. **Services:** ✕ ▨ ⊖ ⊙ **Facilities:** ▥ ♠ 150 ♿ 1 restaurant, 1 bar (w/entertainment), games rm, whirlpool, washer/dryer. Large pool and terrace complex with arcade games just off lobby. **Rates:** $65 S; $70 D. Extra person $5. Children under age 12 stay free. Parking: Outdoor, free. Ski and golf packages. AE, CB, DC, DISC, MC, V.

MOTEL

▤ Redwood Motel
59389 US 131, 49093; tel 616/278-1945. Jct MI 60. A convenient stop-over from the I-80/90 tollway to Kalamazoo, MI. Older style, simple structure with modest rooms for an economical one-night stay. **Rooms:** 15 rms. CI 2pm/CO 11am. Nonsmoking rms avail. **Amenities:** ▥ A/C, cable TV. **Services:** ⊖ **Facilities:** ▥ ♠ **Rates:** Peak (May–Sept) $28–$35 S; $42–$45 D. Extra person $5. Lower rates off-season. Parking: Outdoor, free. DISC, MC, V.

Traverse City

Seat of Grand Traverse County, in northwest part of state. This year-round resort at the foot of Grand Traverse Bay produces more than 100 million pounds of cherries every year. Seven ski areas are within a half-hour drive. The National Cherry Festival takes place here in early July. **Information:** Grand Traverse Convention & Visitors Bureau, 415 Munson Ave, #200, Traverse City, 49684 (tel 616/947-1120 or toll free 800/872-8377).

HOTELS ▥

▤▤ Days Inn
420 Munson Ave, 49686; tel 616/941-0208; fax 616/941-7521. Off US 31 N. Conveniently located to downtown Traverse City. **Rooms:** 183 rms and stes. CI 3pm/CO 11am. Nonsmoking rms avail. Computer-friendly rooms. **Amenities:** ▥ ◊ A/C, cable TV w/movies, voice mail. Some units w/whirlpools. **Services:** ⊖ Babysitting. Fax and copier machines. **Facilities:** ▥ ♠ ▨ 40 ♿ Whirlpool, washer/dryer. **Rates:** Peak (June 16–Sept 3) $95 S or D; $112–$125 ste. Extra person $5. Children under age 12 stay free. Min stay special events. Lower rates off-season. Parking: Outdoor, free. AE, MC, V.

▤▤ Holiday Inn
615 E Front St, 49686; tel 616/947-3700 or toll free 800/888-8020. On US 31 N. Average for this chain. **Rooms:** 173 rms. Executive level. CI 4pm/CO 11am. Nonsmoking rms avail. **Amenities:** ▥ ◊ A/C, cable TV w/movies. Some units w/whirlpools. **Services:** ✕ ⊶ ⊻ ⊠ ⊖ ⊙ Babysitting. Pets allowed in smoking rooms. **Facilities:** ▥ ♠ ▨ ⊡ 450 1 restaurant, 1 bar (w/entertainment), 1 beach (lake shore), games rm, spa, sauna, whirlpool. **Rates:** Peak (June–Aug)

$82–$135 S or D. Extra person $8. Children under age 12 stay free. Lower rates off-season. Parking: Outdoor, free. Getaway packages avail. AE, MC, V.

▤▤ Main Street Inns USA
618 E Front St, 49686; tel 616/929-0410 or toll free 800/255-7180; fax 616/929-0489. Good location for downtown Traverse City. Low-rise units. Good for bus groups. **Rooms:** 93 rms, stes, and effic. CI 3pm/CO 11am. Nonsmoking rms avail. **Amenities:** ▥ ◊ A/C, cable TV. Some units w/whirlpools. **Services:** ⊶ ⊖ ⊙ Coupons for dinner at Pepper's restaurant nearby. **Facilities:** ▥ ♠ ▨ 25 ♿ **Rates:** Peak (June–Aug) $84–$125 S or D; $200 ste; $94–$99 effic. Extra person $6. Lower rates off-season. Parking: Outdoor, free. Casino packages avail. AE, DISC, MC, V.

▤▤▤ Park Place Hotel
300 E State St, 49684 (Downtown); tel 616/946-5000 or toll free 800/748-0133; fax 616/946-2772. Built in 1930, the hotel offers first-class rooms with traditional feel. Accommodates conventions and meetings. **Rooms:** 140 rms. CI 4pm/CO 11am. Nonsmoking rms avail. Victorian furnishings and views of Grand Traverse Bay. **Amenities:** ▥ ◊ ▤ ⊰ A/C, cable TV w/movies, refrig. Some units w/terraces, some w/whirlpools. **Services:** ✕ ⊶ ⊯ ⊠ ⊖ Babysitting. **Facilities:** ▥ ♠ ▨ ⊡ 700 ♿ 2 restaurants (see "Restaurants" below), 2 bars (1 w/entertainment), spa, sauna, whirlpool. Restaurant and cocktail lounge at top of hotel offer best view of Traverse Bay, with elegant art deco atmosphere that continues 1930s decor of hotel. **Rates:** Peak (July–Aug) $125–$135 S or D. Extra person $15. Children under age 16 stay free. Lower rates off-season. Parking: Outdoor, free. AE, DISC, MC, V.

▤▤▤ Pointes North Inn
2211 US 31 N, 49686; tel 616/938-9191 or toll free 800/968-3422. Luxury hotel/resort/condominium that is appropriate for all seasons. **Rooms:** 52 rms. CI 3pm/CO 11am. Nonsmoking rms avail. **Amenities:** ▥ ◊ ▤ A/C, cable TV w/movies, refrig, VCR. Some units w/whirlpools. **Services:** ⊖ **Facilities:** ▥ ♠ ▨ ♿ 1 beach (bay). 300-foot beach. **Rates:** $135–$144 D. Children under age 12 stay free. Parking: Indoor, free. AE, DISC, MC, V.

▤▤▤ Sugar Beach Resort Hotel
1773 US 31 N, 49686; tel 616/938-0100 or toll free 800/509-1995; fax 616/938-0200. On Traverse Bay. New, very attractive, beachfront hotel that features luxury rooms. **Rooms:** 95 rms and stes. CI 3pm/CO 11am. Nonsmoking rms avail. Rooms are beachfront or courtyard. **Amenities:** ▥ ◊ A/C, cable TV w/movies, refrig, VCR. Some units w/terraces, some w/whirlpools. **Services:** ⊖ Babysitting. **Facilities:** ▥ ♠ ▨ 18 1 beach (bay), whirlpool. **Rates (CP):** Peak (June 16–Sept 3) $138–$154 S or D; $188–$208 ste. Extra person $10. Min stay wknds. Lower rates off-season. Parking: Outdoor, free. Charges for extra people in room: children (16 and under) $5, adults $10. AE, DC, DISC, V.

≡≡≡ **Waterfront Inn and Conference Center**
2061 US 31 N, 49685; tel 616/938-1100 or toll free 800/
551-9283. Full-service resort hotel with 775 feet of beach on
East Traverse Bay with deluxe accommodations. **Rooms:** 128
rms, stes, and effic. CI 2pm/CO 11am. Nonsmoking rms
avail. **Amenities:** 🛅 🕭 A/C, cable TV w/movies, refrig. Some
units w/terraces, some w/whirlpools. **Services:** 🆅🅿 ⌧ ↩
Babysitting. **Facilities:** 🗗 🏌 🐟 🍴 🔢350 💻 🕭 1 restaurant
(*see* "Restaurants" below), 1 bar, 1 beach (bay), games rm,
sauna, whirlpool. Nice deck area in back with gazebo bar and
refreshments, plus upstairs sun deck. Paddleboats,
sailboards, and wave runners available for rent at beach.
Rates: Peak (June–Sept) $118–$148 S or D; $251 ste; $130
effic. Extra person $10. Children under age 18 stay free.
Lower rates off-season. Parking: Outdoor, free. AE, MC, V.

MOTELS

≡≡ **Driftwood Motel**
1861 US 31 N, 49686; tel 616/938-1600. Unassuming motel
with two rustic cabins. Beachfront property located on highway, 1½ miles from downtown. Reasonable rates for the area.
Rooms: 39 rms and effic; 2 cottages/villas. CI 2pm/CO
11am. Nonsmoking rms avail. **Amenities:** 🛅 🕭 🖳 A/C, cable
TV w/movies, refrig. Some units w/minibars, some w/ter-
races, some w/whirlpools. **Facilities:** 🗗 🏌 🐟 1 beach (bay),
games rm, whirlpool, playground. Nice indoor pool. **Rates:**
Peak (June–Sept 3) $75–$105 S or D; $750 cottage/villa.
Extra person $5. Children under age 18 stay free. Lower
rates off-season. Parking: Outdoor, free. Cottage rates are
weekly MC, V.

≡≡ **Super 8 Motel**
1870 US 31 N, 49684; tel 616/938-1887; fax 616/938-2451.
Convenient to downtown Traverse City. **Rooms:** 67 rms and
stes. CI open/CO 11am. Nonsmoking rms avail. **Amenities:**
🛅 🕭 A/C, cable TV w/movies, refrig. Some units w/fire-
places, some w/whirlpools. **Services:** ↩ ⊲⊳ Friendly staff and
manager. **Facilities:** 🏌 🐟 🕭 Spa, sauna, whirlpool, washer/
dryer. **Rates (CP):** Peak (June–Aug) $68 S; $72 D; $115 ste.
Extra person $3. Children under age 12 stay free. Lower
rates off-season. Parking: Outdoor, free. AE, CB, MC, V.

≡≡≡ **Traverse Beach Motel and Condominium**
877 Munson Ave, 49686; tel 616/946-5262 or toll free 800/
634-6113. Waterfront condominiums and motel rooms that
offer a luxury vacation setting. Eight golf courses and a
variety of sports activities and sites within 30 minutes.
Rooms: 87 rms and stes. CI open/CO 11am. Nonsmoking
rms avail. **Amenities:** 🛅 🕭 A/C, cable TV w/movies, refrig.
Some units w/terraces, some w/whirlpools. **Services:** 🖘 🚐
↩ **Facilities:** 🗗 🏌 🐟 🍴 🕭 1 beach (bay). **Rates (CP):** Peak
(June–Aug) $118–$133 S or D; $198 ste. Children under age
12 stay free. Lower rates off-season. Parking: Outdoor, free.
Special packages include Summer Fun Special and Cabin
Fever Special for Two. AE, DC, DISC, MC, V.

≡ **The Waterland Motel**
834 E Front St, 49684; tel 616/947-8349. A basic motel with
low rates and all the necessities. Walking distance to downtown. **Rooms:** 18 rms and effic. CI 1pm/CO 11am. Nonsmoking rms avail. **Amenities:** 🛅 🕭 🖳 A/C, cable TV, refrig.
Services: 🆅🅿 ⊲⊳ **Rates:** Peak (July–Aug) $89–$99 S or D; $99
effic. Extra person $5. Children under age 12 stay free.
Lower rates off-season. Parking: Outdoor, free. AE, DC,
DISC, MC, V.

RESORTS

≡≡≡ **Bayshore Resort**
833 E Front St, 49686; tel 616/935-4400 or toll free 800/
634-4401; fax 616/935-0262. Off US 31 N. Very fine resort
on beach of West Grand Traverse Bay. Nice grounds and
beach access. No sports, but rentals and facilities nearby.
Public tennis courts next door. **Rooms:** 120 rms and stes. CI
4pm/CO 11am. No smoking. **Amenities:** 🛅 🕭 🍴 A/C, cable
TV w/movies, refrig. Some units w/minibars, some w/ter-
races, some w/fireplaces, some w/whirlpools. **Services:** 🚐
⌧ ↩ **Facilities:** 🗗 ⚠ 🏌 🐟 🍴 🔢250 🕭 1 beach (bay), games
rm, spa, whirlpool, washer/dryer. **Rates (CP):** Peak (June 16–
Aug 19) $80–$180 S or D; $225–$290 ste. Extra person $10.
Lower rates off-season. Parking: Outdoor, free. Romance,
golf, and casino packages avail. AE, DISC, MC, V.

≡≡≡ **Grand Beach Resort Hotel**
1683 US 31 N, 49686; tel 616/938-4455 or toll free 800/
968-1992. About 15 minutes from center of town. Along with
its sister facility, the Sugar Beach Resort Hotel, the hotel
boasts the finest sugar sand beaches in the renowned "Mira-
cle Mile" of East Grand Traverse Bay. A large complex
appropriate for business trips, family vacations, or couples'
get-a-ways. **Rooms:** 95 rms and stes. CI 3pm/CO 11am.
Nonsmoking rms avail. Beachfront rooms have views of Old
Mission Peninsula and coastline. **Amenities:** 🛅 🕭 🍴 A/C,
cable TV w/movies, refrig, VCR. Some units w/minibars,
some w/terraces, some w/whirlpools. All beachfront rooms
have full balconies. **Services:** ↩ **Facilities:** 🗗 🏌 🐟 🔢25 🕭 1
beach (lake shore), games rm, spa, whirlpool, washer/dryer.
300-foot sugar sand beach. **Rates (CP):** Peak (July–Aug) $138
D; $188–$208 ste. Extra person $10. Children under age 12
stay free. Min stay wknds and special events. Lower rates off-
season. Parking: Outdoor, free. DISC, MC, V.

≡≡≡ **Pinestead Reef Resort**
1265 US 31 N, 49684; tel 616/947-4010. Offers one- and
two-bedroom time-share condominiums. **Rooms:** 46 cot-
tages/villas. CI 4pm/CO 11am. All rooms face the beach with
a bay view. **Amenities:** 🛅 🕭 🖳 A/C, cable TV w/movies,
refrig. Some units w/terraces. **Services:** ↩ Children's program, babysitting. Organized activities include exercise class,
coffee hour, kid's craft hour on beach, weekly cookout on
deck, and co-ed volleyball tournament on beach. **Facilities:**
🗗 🏌 🐟 🍴 🔢60 🕭 1 beach (bay), volleyball, games rm, spa,
sauna, whirlpool, washer/dryer. Beach access. Parasailing

available. **Rates:** Peak (June 16–Sept 3) $139–$169 cottage/villa. Extra person $10. Lower rates off-season. Parking: Indoor, free. AE, DISC, MC, V.

≣≣≣ Sugar Loaf Resort

4500 Sugar Loaf Mountain Rd, Cedar, 49621; tel 616/228-5461 or toll free 800/968-0576. Four-season resort with tradition. **Rooms:** 150 rms. CI 4pm/CO noon. Nonsmoking rms avail. **Amenities:** 🛁 ⚷ A/C, cable TV. Some units w/fireplaces, some w/whirlpools. **Services:** ⌑ Car-rental desk, social director, children's program, babysitting. Summer Kids' Kamp. **Facilities:** 🏊 ⚲ 🅿36 🎿 🎣 🎣3 🌐 🎾2 ⛳ 500 🚹 1 restaurant (*see* "Restaurants" below), 1 bar, volleyball, lawn games, whirlpool, day-care ctr, playground, washer/dryer. New Arnold Palmer Golf Course nearing completion. **Rates:** Peak (Dec–Jan) $125 S or D. Extra person $10. Children under age 18 stay free. Lower rates off-season. Parking: Outdoor, free. Golf, family, and holiday packages avail. Closed Apr–Nov. AE, MC, V.

RESTAURANTS 🍴

Bay Winds

1265 US 31 N; tel 616/929-1044. **American.** Casual waterfront dining with a lodge decor and nice views. The full-range menu includes local fish (prepared in a variety of ways), 20-oz New York strip steak, and veal and chicken dishes. In nice weather, an outside deck is also available for dining. **FYI:** Reservations accepted. Singer. Children's menu. **Open:** Breakfast Sat 8–11am; lunch Mon–Sat 11am–4pm; dinner Sun–Thurs 4–10pm, Fri–Sat 4–11pm; brunch Sun 10am–2pm. **Prices:** Main courses $11–$15. AE, DISC, MC, V. ❤ 🍴 🏔 ⅋

The Boathouse Restaurant

14039 Peninsula Dr; tel 616/223-4030. **American/Seafood.** Located on the beautiful Old Mission Peninsula, this cottagelike dining room enjoys a lovely ambience and wonderful views of a small harbor and boats. Noteworthy items include salmon, scallops, Gulf shrimp, chicken Wellington, tournedos morel, linguine, and Greek salad. The owner and staff are very cordial. **FYI:** Reservations accepted. Children's menu. **Open:** Breakfast daily 8–11am; lunch daily 11:30am–3pm; dinner Mon–Wed 5–10pm, Thurs–Sat 5–11pm, Sun 5–9pm. **Prices:** Main courses $10–$18. AE, MC, V. ❤ 🏔 ⅋

DJ Kelley's

120 Park St; tel 616/941-4550. **International.** Nice downtown cafe known for its steak and seafood. There are also vegetarian dishes, pastas, and such specialties as chicken tarragon with spinach fettuccine, Gruyère fondue, Cajun barbecue shrimp, and tournedos of pork. Large selection of specialty beers. **FYI:** Reservations accepted. **Open:** Lunch Mon–Sat 11am–3pm; dinner Mon–Thurs 5–10pm, Fri–Sat 5–11pm. **Prices:** Main courses $7–$17. AE, MC, V. ❤ 🖼

Four Seasons Restaurant

In Sugar Loaf Resort, 4500 Sugar Loaf Mountain Rd, Cedar; tel 616/228-1820. **American.** A spacious, mountainside eatery overlooking the Leelanau Peninsula and Lake Michigan. The atmosphere in the dining room is relaxed yet elegant. The regular dinner menu emphasizes steak and seafood, while the all-you-can-eat Sunday brunch includes over 60 items such as roast prime rib, turkey, a salad bar and special desserts. The Friday fish fry is very popular. **FYI:** Reservations recommended. Children's menu. **Open:** Dinner Sun–Thurs 5:30–9pm, Fri–Sat 5:30–10pm; brunch Sun 10:30am–2pm. **Prices:** Main courses $9–$18. MC, V. 🖼

La Señorita

1245 S Garfield St; tel 616/947-8820. **Mexican.** *Comida Mexicana tradicional* is the motto at this humble taqueria. The Mexican ambience is enhanced by colorful murals and a large stone fireplace in the bar. Fajitas, burritos, and tacos are expertly prepared with the freshest ingredients. Very friendly staff. **FYI:** Reservations accepted. Children's menu. **Open:** Peak (June–Aug) Mon–Thurs 11am–11pm, Fri–Sat 11am–midnight, Sun noon–10pm. **Prices:** Main courses $7–$11. AE, DC, DISC, V. ❤ 🖼 ⅋

Reflections

In Waterfront Inn Hotel, 2061 US 31 N; tel 616/938-2321. **American.** Window seats at this rooftop dining room have gorgeous views of the East Bay and Old Mission Peninsula. As one might expect, the menu leans heavily toward fish (from the Atlantic as well as from the Great Lakes). Salmon and Southwestern rainbow trout are particularly well prepared. Lamb, veal, pork loin marsala, and a variety of pasta dishes and salads round out the menu. The bar offers a cafe menu with salads and hors d'oeuvres. **FYI:** Reservations accepted. Singer. Children's menu. **Open:** Breakfast Mon–Fri 7–11am, Sat 8am–noon, Sun 8–11am; lunch Mon–Fri 11am–3pm, Sat noon–3pm; dinner daily 5–10pm. **Prices:** Main courses $13–$35. AE, MC, V. ❤ 🏔 ⅋

Schelde's

714 Munson Ave; tel 616/946-0981. **Steak/Ribs.** A busy but cozy little place that serves a range of steak and chicken entrees plus soups, salads, and specialty desserts. Teriyaki and stir-fry dishes are available. **FYI:** Reservations recommended. Children's menu. **Open:** Daily 8am–midnight. **Prices:** Main courses $11–$20. MC, V. 🖼 ⅋

★ Sleder's Family Tavern

717 Randolph St; tel 616/947-9213. Off US 31/37 (Division St) Downtown Traverse. **American.** Established in 1882, Sleder's has an old-time tavern feeling. It's a place where people come to "eat, drink, tell lies, and kiss the moose," or so the locals say. The menu lists a wide variety of options: everything from burgers to Mexican food to whitefish to steak. **FYI:** Reservations not accepted. **Open:** Peak (June–Aug) Sun–Thurs 11am–11pm, Fri–Sat 11am–midnight. **Prices:** Main courses $7–$13. MC, V. ▮

Sweitzer's

13890 W Bay Shore Dr; tel 616/947-0493. On US 31, ¼ mi from Tall Ship Malabar. **American.** Located near the Tall Ship Malabar, this popular spot has nice views of Traverse Bay. Chicken Charlie and stir-fried salmon (served with a medley of fresh vegetables on a bed of rice pilaf) are two of the kitchen's specialties. **FYI:** Reservations recommended. Children's menu. **Open: Prices:** Main courses $8–$12. AE, MC, V. ♥ ▲ 👥 ♿

♟ Top of the Park

In Park Place Hotel, 300 E State St; tel 616/946-5000. **American.** Lovely art deco dining room, with perhaps the best bay view in Traverse City. Offers wide range of steak, seafood, and pasta selections. Smooth, efficient service. **FYI:** Reservations accepted. Piano. Children's menu. No smoking. **Open:** Sun–Thurs 5–10pm, Fri–Sat 5–11pm. **Prices:** Main courses $23–$26. AE, DC, DISC, MC, V. ♥ 🖳 ▲ ♿

ATTRACTIONS 🔲

Interlochen State Park

MI 137; tel 616/276-9511. Located near the Interlochen Center for the Arts, this 187-acre park features lakes with sand beaches. Swimming, boating, and fishing are popular activities. Picnicking areas, playground, concessions, and campsites also available. **Open:** Daily sunrise–sunset. **$**

Sugar Loaf Resort

4500 Sugar Loaf Mountain Rd, Cedar; tel 616/228-5461. Located on the Leelanau Peninsula, this resort offers some of the best skiing in the Midwest. During the December—March ski season, Sugar Loaf provides 23 trails (split evenly among black diamond, intermediate, and beginner) that stretch out over 80 acres (the longest run is 1 mile), seven lifts (one triple, five doubles, one surface), and a vertical drop of 500 feet. Snowboarding, NASTAR, and night skiing also available, as well as a rental shop and ski school. The resort also features two 18-hole golf courses staffed with professional instructors, organized day-trip excursions, a free shuttle to the nearby Leelanau Sands Casino, and special programs for children. For the latest information on snow conditions, call 616/228-5461. **Open:** Daily, call for schedule. **$$$$**

Interlochen Center for the Arts

MI 137, Interlochen; tel 616/276-7200. 10 mi SW of Traverse City. More than 1,400 students—ages 8 through 18—study music, theater arts, dance, and visual art here during the school year. Some 750 concerts, visual art exhibits, and theater and dance productions are presented annually. In summer, the school hosts one of the largest and best-known arts-oriented summer programs in the world. The 5,000-seat Interlochen Bowl has featured concerts by famous musicians ranging from Percy Grainger to John Philip Sousa; recent guests have included Itzhak Perlman, Bill Cosby, Yo-Yo Ma, Marvin Hamlisch, and the Detroit Symphony Orchestra. **Open:** Call for schedule. **Free**

Troy

Established by a series of early-19th-century land grants, Troy is now a northern suburb of Detroit. Many large corporations have migrated here in recent years. **Information:** Troy Chamber of Commerce, 4555 Corporate Dr, #300, Troy, 48098-6338 (tel 810/641-0545).

HOTELS 🏨

🚩🚩 Courtyard by Marriott Troy

1525 E Maple Rd, 48083; tel 810/528-2800 or toll free 800/321-2211; fax 810/528-0963. Pleasant accommodations convenient to both Detroit and its northern suburbs. **Rooms:** 147 rms and stes. CI 3pm/CO 1pm. Nonsmoking rms avail. **Amenities:** 📺 🕎 📞 A/C, cable TV w/movies, dataport, voice mail. Some units w/terraces. **Services:** 🚐 🖨 🔧 Babysitting. **Facilities:** 🏋 🏊 🏐 25 ♿ 1 restaurant (bkfst only), 1 bar, whirlpool, washer/dryer. Evening lounge Mon–Fri. **Rates:** $94 S or D; $110 ste. Extra person $10. Children under age 18 stay free. Parking: Outdoor, free. AE, CB, DC, DISC, MC, V.

🚩🚩🚩 DoubleTree Guest Suites Troy

850 Tower Dr, 48098; tel 810/879-7500 or toll free 800/222-TREE; fax 810/879-9139. Exit 72 (Crooks Rd) off I-75; in Northfield office park. All-suite hotel with steely glass exterior sits comfortably in office park. **Rooms:** 251 stes. CI 3pm/CO 11am. Nonsmoking rms avail. **Amenities:** 📺 🕎 📞 A/C, cable TV w/movies, refrig, dataport. Some units w/minibars, 1 w/whirlpool. All suites have microwaves. **Services:** ✕ 🚐 🖨 🔧 Car-rental desk. **Facilities:** 🏋 🏊 🏐 200 🖳 ♿ 1 restaurant, 1 bar (w/entertainment), sauna, whirlpool, washer/dryer. **Rates:** $79–$144 ste. Extra person $20. Children under age 18 stay free. Parking: Outdoor, free. Rates higher for larger corner suites and Presidential Suite. AE, CB, DC, DISC, MC, V.

🚩 Drury Inn Troy

575 W Big Beaver Rd, 48084; tel 810/528-3330 or toll free 800/325-8300; fax 810/528-3330. At I-75 E exit. Good accommodations in prime location at economy price. Hershel's deli-style restaurant is adjacent. **Rooms:** 153 rms. CI 3pm/CO noon. Nonsmoking rms avail. **Amenities:** 📺 🕎 A/C, cable TV w/movies, dataport. **Services:** 🚐 🖨 🔧 🐾 Quikstart breakfast bar included in price. **Facilities:** 🏋 15 ♿ Guests may use nearby Power House Gym at nominal cost. **Rates (CP):** $69–$79 S; $75–$85 D. Extra person $6. Children under age 12 stay free. Parking: Outdoor, free. AE, CB, DC, DISC, MC, V.

🚩🚩 Holiday Inn Troy

2537 Rochester Court, 48083; tel 810/689-7500 or toll free 800/HOLIDAY; fax 810/689-9015. A bit out of the way from the city's business activities and industrial parks—which some view as an advantage. Basic accommodations. **Rooms:** 153 rms. CI 3pm/CO noon. Nonsmoking rms avail. **Amenities:** 📺 🕎 A/C, cable TV w/movies, dataport. Some units w/terraces, some w/whirlpools. **Services:** ✗ 🚐 ⊠ ↵ ⇔ **Facilities:** 🎣 📺 300 ♿ 1 restaurant, 1 bar, basketball, sauna, washer/dryer. **Rates:** $89–$102 S or D. Children under age 18 stay free. Parking: Outdoor, free. AE, CB, DC, DISC, JCB, MC, V.

☰☰☰ Northfield Hilton

5500 Crooks Rd, 48098; tel 313/879-2100 or toll free 800/ HILTONS; fax 810/879-6054. Exit 72 (Crooks Rd) off I-75. Contemporary sculpture dominates grounds of this long and low, gently curved structure. **Rooms:** 191 rms and stes. CI 3pm/CO noon. Nonsmoking rms avail. Spacious rooms. **Amenities:** 🛁 🅿 📺 ⬥ A/C, satel TV w/movies, dataport. Some units w/terraces. **Services:** ✗ 🚐 ⊠ ↵ ⇔ Masseur, babysitting. **Facilities:** 🎣 📺 1000 ♿ 1 restaurant, 1 bar, sauna, washer/dryer. **Rates (CP):** $109–$119 S or D; $250–$300 ste. Children under age 18 stay free. Parking: Outdoor, free. AE, CB, DC, DISC, MC, V.

☰☰☰ Somerset Inn

2601 W Big Beaver Rd, 48084; tel 810/643-7800 or toll free 800/228-TROY, 800/227-TROY in MI; fax 810/643-2220. W of I-75. Classic contemporary, with marble and rich woods in lobby. Wonderful location next to exclusive shops at Somerset Collection as well as several corporate office centers. **Rooms:** 250 rms and stes. CI 2pm/CO noon. Nonsmoking rms avail. Newly decorated rooms. **Amenities:** 🛁 🅿 A/C, satel TV w/movies, dataport, voice mail. Some units w/terraces. Interior courtyard rooms on first floor have small, outdoor patios, poolside. **Services:** ✗ 🚐 ⊠ ↵ Babysitting. **Facilities:** 🎣 600 💻 ♿ 1 restaurant, 1 bar. Guests may use Vic Tanny athletic facilities next door. **Rates:** $110–$130 S; $125–$145 D; $235–$325 ste. Extra person $15. Children under age 18 stay free. Min stay special events. Parking: Outdoor, free. AE, CB, DC, DISC, MC, V.

☰☰☰ Troy Marriott

200 W Big Beaver Rd, 48084; tel 810/680-9797 or toll free 800/777-4096; fax 810/680-9774. E of I-75. Soaring atrium lobby welcomes business travelers, convention guests, and visiting NBA and NFL teams. Guests may use tennis courts and jogging track at former school yard next door. **Rooms:** 350 rms and stes. Executive level. CI 3pm/CO noon. Nonsmoking rms avail. Recently redecorated rooms. **Amenities:** 🛁 🅿 ⬥ A/C, cable TV w/movies, dataport, voice mail. **Services:** ✗ 🔑 VP 🚐 ⊠ ↵ ⇔ Twice-daily maid svce, car-rental desk, masseur, babysitting. Shoe-shine stand off lobby. **Facilities:** 🎣 🏊 ⚲4 📺 1000 ♿ 1 restaurant, 2 bars (1 w/entertainment), spa, sauna, steam rm, whirlpool. **Rates:** $154 S; $184 D; $300–$750 ste. Extra person $20. Children under age 18 stay free. Min stay special events. Parking: Indoor/outdoor, free. AE, CB, DC, DISC, JCB, MC, V.

MOTELS

☰☰ Red Roof Inn Troy

2350 Rochester Rd, 48083; tel 810/689-4391 or toll free 800/THE-ROOF; fax 810/689-4397. At I-75. Good econ-omy lodging in pricey area. **Rooms:** 109 rms. CI noon/CO noon. Nonsmoking rms avail. **Amenities:** 🛁 A/C, satel TV w/movies. **Services:** ↵ ⇔ Airport shuttle offers drop-off service only. **Facilities:** ♿ **Rates:** $36–$54 S; $45–$63 D. Extra person $9. Children under age 18 stay free. Parking: Outdoor, free. AE, CB, DC, DISC, MC, V.

☰☰ Residence Inn by Marriott Troy Central

2600 Livernois Rd, 48083; tel 810/689-6856 or toll free 800/331-3131; fax 810/689-3788. S of Big Beaver Rd off I-75. Home-away-from-home for those attending to business in Troy. **Rooms:** 152 stes and effic. CI 3pm/CO noon. Nonsmoking rms avail. **Amenities:** 🛁 🅿 📺 A/C, cable TV w/movies, refrig, dataport. Some units w/terraces, some w/fireplaces. **Services:** 🚐 ⊠ ↵ ⇔ Babysitting. Breakfast buffet and evening refreshments. Enthusiastic staff. **Facilities:** 🎣 ⚲1 30 ♿ Basketball, whirlpool, playground, washer/dryer. Guests may use fitness facilities at nearby Troy Marriott Hotel and Powerhouse Gym. **Rates (CP):** Peak (June–Nov 15) $179 ste; $129–$179 effic. Extra person $10. Children under age 16 stay free. Min stay peak. Lower rates off-season. Parking: Outdoor, free. AE, CB, DC, DISC, EC, JCB, MC, V.

RESTAURANTS 🍴

★ Charley's Crab

5498 Crooks Rd; tel 810/879-2060. Exit 72 (Crooks Rd) off I-75. **Seafood.** After studying the extensive menu, diners can read about the amazing collection that decorates this Detroit-area institution, including several artifacts from an 1878 square-rigged whaling ship, an anchor that traveled from Maine to hang over the piano bar, and the entire living room of a 1929 Grosse Pointe mansion. Charley's Mediterranean-style fish chowder and Charley's bucket (20-oz Maine lobster, Dungeness crab, shellfish, redskin potatoes, and fresh corn-on-the-cob) are favorites; landlubbers like the rack of lamb. **FYI:** Reservations recommended. Piano. Children's menu. **Open:** Mon–Thurs 11:30am–10pm, Fri 11:30am–11pm, Sat 5–11pm, Sun 2–9pm. **Prices:** Main courses $14–$30. AE, DC, DISC, MC, V. ▮ VP ♿

Mon Jin Lau

1515 E Maple Rd; tel 810/689-2332. At Stephenson Hwy. **Chinese.** The nouveau Asian menu is matched by contemporary touches in the richly colored Far East decor. Appetizers such as ginger-garlic stuffed eggplant and Chinese ravioli are followed by Mandarin filet mignon with shiitake mushrooms, and Asiatic shellfish stew. The lively crowd at the twisting, green marble bar has a good view of local girl Madonna's red bustier, displayed as art. **FYI:** Reservations recommended. Dress code. **Open:** Mon–Fri 11am–4pm, Sat 4pm–1am, Sun 3pm–midnight. **Prices:** Main courses $9–$19. AE, DC, MC, V. ♥ ♿

Sebastian's Grill

In the Somerset Collection, 2745 W Big Beaver Rd (Somerset); tel 810/649-6625. W of I-75. **American Bistro.** This upscale mall diner employs cosmopolitan decor and a varied menu appropriate to its tony address. Fresh fish, pasta, pizza, and fresh sourdough bread and desserts to please hungry shoppers. Friendly service, too. **FYI:** Reservations recommended. Children's menu. **Open:** Mon–Thurs 11am–10pm, Fri–Sat 11am–11pm, Sun noon–5pm. **Prices:** Main courses $10–$17. AE, CB, DC, MC, V. 🆅🅿 &

ATTRACTION 🏛

Troy Museum and Historic Village
60 W Wattles Rd; tel 810/524-3570. Highlights include a log cabin built in the 1820s, the Greek Revival–style Caswell House (built in 1832), and the Poppleton School (1877). These are all fully restored and house artifacts from their respective periods. **Open:** Tues–Sat 9am–5:30pm, Sun 1–5pm. **Free**

Union Pier

See New Buffalo

Warren

A small farmland community until the 1930s, this northern Detroit suburb burgeoned with the establishment of General Electric's Carboloy Division. Eero Saarinen (son of Eliel) designed the General Motors Technical Center. **Information:** Warren-Center Line-Sterling Heights, 30500 Van Dyke Ave, #118, Warren, 48093-2178 (tel 810/751-3939).

HOTELS 🏨

🚇 Budgetel Inn Detroit (Warren Tech Center)
30900 Van Dyke Rd, 48093; tel 810/574-0550 or toll free 800/4-BUDGET; fax 810/574-0750. S of 13 Mile Rd. Extra touches in lobby and public areas indicate why these basic, well-cared for accommodations welcome back so many business travelers. **Rooms:** 102 rms. CI open/CO noon. Nonsmoking rms avail. **Amenities:** 📺 ⚙ 🖥 A/C, satel TV w/movies, dataport. **Services:** ⬛ 🧺 ⬦ **Facilities:** 🔲 & Washer/dryer. **Rates (CP):** $37 S; $57 D. Children under age 18 stay free. Parking: Outdoor, free. AE, CB, DC, DISC, MC, V.

🚇🚇 Courtyard by Marriott Warren
30190 Van Dyke Ave, 48093; tel 810/751-5777 or toll free 800/321-2211; fax 810/751-4463. S of 13 Mile Rd. Pleasant retreat for those on business to surrounding office buildings and General Motors Tech Center. **Rooms:** 197 rms and stes. CI 3pm/CO 1pm. Nonsmoking rms avail. **Amenities:** 📺 ⚙ 🖥 A/C, satel TV w/movies, dataport, voice mail. Some units w/terraces. **Services:** 🚐 ⬛ 🧺 Babysitting. **Facilities:** 🔲 🛏 🔲 & 1 restaurant (bkfst only), 1 bar, whirlpool, washer/

dryer. Lounge Mon–Thurs evenings. **Rates:** $82–$92 S; $92–$102 D; $92–$109 ste. Children under age 18 stay free. Parking: Outdoor, free. AE, CB, DC, DISC, MC, V.

🚇🚇 Hampton Inn Warren
7447 Convention Blvd, 48092; tel 810/977-7270 or toll free 800/HAMPTON; fax 810/977-3889. 2½ mi N of I-696. Very clean and pleasant basic accommodations. **Rooms:** 124 rms and stes. CI 3pm/CO noon. Nonsmoking rms avail. **Amenities:** 📺 ⚙ A/C, satel TV w/movies, dataport. Some units w/terraces. **Services:** ⬛ 🧺 **Facilities:** 🔲 & Free use of local health club. **Rates (CP):** $62–$68 S or D; $85 ste. Children under age 18 stay free. Parking: Outdoor, free. AE, CB, DC, DISC, ER, JCB, MC, V.

🚇🚇 Van Dyke Park Suite Hotel
31800 Van Dyke Ave, 48093; tel 810/939-2860; fax 810/268-4880. 3 mi N of I-696. Park and garden theme carried throughout, from names of extensive meeting facilities to prints and posters decorating halls. **Rooms:** 240 rms and stes. CI 3pm/CO 1pm. Nonsmoking rms avail. **Amenities:** 📺 ⚙ 🍽 A/C, cable TV, voice mail. Some units w/terraces, some w/whirlpools. **Services:** ✗ 🚐 ⬛ 🧺 Masseur, children's program, babysitting. **Facilities:** 🔲 🛏 🔲 🖥 & 1 restaurant (dinner only; *see* "Restaurants" below), 1 bar (w/entertainment), games rm, spa, sauna, whirlpool, beauty salon, day-care ctr, washer/dryer. **Rates (CP):** $67–$79 S or D; $89–$300 ste. Extra person $15. Children under age 12 stay free. Parking: Outdoor, free. AE, CB, DC, DISC, MC, V.

MOTELS

🚇 Cross Country Inn
25800 Dequindre Rd, 48093; tel 810/754-5527 or toll free 800/621-1429. At I-696. Basics at a budget price. **Rooms:** 120 rms. CI open/CO noon. Nonsmoking rms avail. **Amenities:** 📺 A/C, cable TV w/movies. **Services:** 🚐 🧺 ⬦ **Facilities:** 🔲 & **Rates:** $33–$45 S; $41–$57 D. Children under age 18 stay free. Parking: Outdoor, free. 25% discount for senior citizens. AE, CB, DC, DISC, MC, V.

🚇🚇 Fairfield Inn Detroit—Warren
7454 Convention Blvd, 48092; tel 810/939-1700 or toll free 800/228-2800; fax 810/939-1700. 2½ mi N of I-696. Pleasant accommodations with restaurants nearby. **Rooms:** 132 rms. CI 3pm/CO noon. Nonsmoking rms avail. **Amenities:** 📺 ⚙ A/C, cable TV w/movies, dataport. **Services:** 🚐 ⬛ 🧺 Babysitting. **Facilities:** 🔲 & **Rates (CP):** Peak (June–Sept) $55–$65 S or D. Extra person $7. Children under age 16 stay free. Lower rates off-season. Parking: Outdoor, free. AE, CB, DC, DISC, MC, V.

🚇🚇 Homewood Suites
30180 N Civic Center Blvd, 48093; tel 810/558-7870 or toll free 800/CALL-HOME; fax 810/558-8072. 2 mi N of I-696. Welcoming "lodge" open 24-hours for guest use. **Rooms:** 76 stes and effic. CI 2pm/CO noon. Nonsmoking rms avail. Comfortable, spacious suites. **Amenities:** 📺 ⚙ 🖥 A/C, cable

TV w/movies, refrig, dataport, VCR, voice mail. Some units w/fireplaces. **Services:** 🚐 ⬙ 🍴 🛎 Babysitting. Continental breakfast buffet and Mon–Thurs refreshments. Free fax and copy services. Complimentary local transportation. **Facilities:** 🏋 🏌 ⌷25 💻 Basketball, whirlpool, washer/dryer. **Rates (CP):** $89–$139 ste; $89–$139 effic. Children under age 18 stay free. Parking: Outdoor, free. AE, CB, DC, DISC, MC, V.

▦ Red Roof Inn
26300 Dequindre Rd, 48091; tel 810/573-4300 or toll free 800/THE-ROOF; fax 810/573-6157. Just N of I-696. Very tidy accommodations. **Rooms:** 136 rms. CI 1pm/CO noon. Nonsmoking rms avail. **Amenities:** 🛗 A/C, satel TV w/movies. **Services:** ⬙ 🍴 🛎 **Facilities:** ᵹ **Rates:** Peak (Mar–Oct) $35–$60 S or D. Extra person $7. Children under age 18 stay free. Lower rates off-season. Parking: Outdoor, free. AE, CB, DC, DISC, MC, V.

▦▦ Residence Inn Warren
30120 Civic Center Blvd, 48093; tel 810/558-8050 or toll free 800/331-3131; fax 810/558-8214. 2 mi N of I-696, E of Van Dyke Ave. Comfortable, apartmentlike one-room and two-bedroom suites. **Rooms:.** CI 2pm/CO noon. Nonsmoking rms avail. **Amenities:** 🛗 ☕ 🖥 A/C, cable TV w/movies, refrig, dataport, voice mail. All units w/terraces, some w/fireplaces. **Services:** 🚐 ⬙ 🍴 🛎 Breakfast buffet, evening refreshments. **Facilities:** 🏋 🎾 🏌 ᵹ Basketball, whirlpool, playground, washer/dryer. **Rates (CP):** $79–$109 ste; $104–$129 effic. Children under age 18 stay free. Min stay special events. Parking: Outdoor, free. AE, DC, DISC, MC, V.

RESTAURANTS 🍽

★ Buddy's Pizza
8100 Old 13 Mile Rd; tel 810/574-9200. Just E of Van Dyke Ave. **Pizza.** The basement room decor is a salute to the original Buddy's, which has been a Detroit landmark since 1936. Buddy's square deep-dish pizza is consistently voted the best pizza in the area; the menu also carries pastas, sandwiches, and burgers. Sander's Hot Fudge Cream Puffs are a delight. **FYI:** Reservations not accepted. Children's menu. Additional locations: 17125 Conant, Detroit (tel 313/892-9001); 22148 Michigan Ave, Dearborn (tel 313/562-5900). **Open:** Mon–Thurs 11am–11pm, Fri–Sat 11am–midnight, Sun noon–10pm. **Prices:** Main courses $4–$15. AE, CB, DC, DISC, MC, V. 📷 ᵹ

Lilli's in the Park
In Van Dyke Park Suite Hotel, 31800 Van Dyke Ave; tel 810/939-2990. 3 mi N of I-696. **American.** A serviceable hotel dining room that is locally popular for its traditional American food. Barbecued ribs, steaks, chicken, and seafood are all good choices. **FYI:** Reservations accepted. Children's menu. **Open:** Mon–Sat 4:30–11pm. **Prices:** Main courses $8–$20. AE, CB, DC, DISC, MC, V. ᵹ

West Bloomfield
See Bloomfield Hills

Whitehall
Located on an inlet of Lake Michigan, this small central Michigan town is the site of a circa 1875 lighthouse. Just north of town, in Montague, is the world's largest weather vane—48 feet tall and weighing 3,500 pounds, and topped with a lumber schooner model. **Information:** White Lake Area Chamber of Commerce, 124 W Hanson St, Whitehall, 49461 (tel 616/893-4585 or toll free 800/879-9702).

HOTEL 🏨

▦▦▦ Ramada Inn
2865 Colby Rd, 49461; tel 616/893-3030; fax 616/893-0030. Right off US 31. Large grounds in front of hotel. Good for a family or business person. Muskegon State Park and cross-country skiing 10 miles away. **Rooms:** 66 rms and stes. CI open/CO 11am. Nonsmoking rms avail. **Amenities:** 🛗 ☕ 🖥 A/C, cable TV w/movies, VCR. Some units w/whirlpools. **Services:** 🍴 Fax machine, copy machine, modem-ready phones available. **Facilities:** 🏋 🎾 🏌 ⌷400 💻 ᵹ 1 restaurant, 1 bar, volleyball, games rm, lawn games, spa, sauna, whirlpool, playground, washer/dryer. Picnic tables, grills, and kids play gym. **Rates:** Peak (July–Aug) $82–$92 S or D; $107 ste. Children under age 12 stay free. Lower rates off-season. Parking: Outdoor, free. Discounts for AARP, military, government, Professional Drivers, and Ramada Business Card Holders. Group rates avail. AE, MC, V.

MOTEL

▦ Super 8 Motel
3080 Colby Rd, 49461; tel 616/894-4848 or toll free 800/800-8000; fax 616/893-1705. Convenient to US 31 and main road through Ludington. Standard motel. **Rooms:** 54 rms. CI open/CO 11am. Nonsmoking rms avail. **Amenities:** 🛗 ☕ 🖥 A/C, cable TV w/movies, VCR. Some units w/whirlpools. **Services:** 🍴 **Facilities:** ᵹ **Rates:** $56–$61 S or D. Extra person $3. Children under age 12 stay free. Parking: Outdoor, free. DISC, MC, V.

ATTRACTIONS 🛍

Montague City Museum
Church and Main Sts; tel 616/894-6813. Local history museum with exhibits illustrating the history of the lumbering industry and its importance to the area. **Open:** June–Sept, Sat–Sun 10am–5pm. **Free**

White River Light Station Museum
White Lake Channel; tel 616/894-8265. The museum focuses on maritime life in the Great Lakes region during the 19th century, a time when the Muskegon–White Lake area was

known as "The Lumber Queen of the World." Exhibits encompass a wide range of nautical and navigational devices including binnacles, compasses, and chronographs. Visitors can climb the spiral stairs of the tower and see the original Fresnel reflecting lens. Guided tours available by arrangement. **Open:** Peak (May–Aug) Tues–Fri 11am–5pm, Sat–Sun noon–6pm. Reduced hours off-season. **$**

World's Largest Weather Vane

US 31; tel 616/893-4585. This 48-foot tall weather vane (weighing nearly two tons) is topped with a model of the *Ellenwood,* a well-known lumber schooner of the nineteenth century. The vane was built and donated to the community by Whitehall Metal Studios, Inc. **Free**

Ypsilanti

Located southwest of Detroit. Named for Greek patriot Demetrius Ypsilanti, the city has many fine examples of Greek Revival architecture. The Frog Island Jazz Festival takes place here every June. **Information:** Ypsilanti Area Visitors & Convention Bureau, 301 W Michigan Ave, #101, Ypsilanti, 48197 (tel 313/483-4444 or 930-6300).

MOTELS 🛏

🏳 Harmony House Motel

615 E Michigan Ave, 48198; tel 313/485-4200. Jct US 12/MI 17. Two-story old-fashioned motel. Fine for overnight, but no longer. Several fast food restaurants nearby. **Rooms:** 27 rms. CI noon/CO 11am. Clean rooms with no frills. **Amenities:** 🛁 A/C, cable TV w/movies. **Rates:** Peak (Apr–Dec) $32–$36 S; $36–$40 D. Extra person $5. Children under age 12 stay free. Lower rates off-season. Parking: Outdoor, free. AE, DISC, MC, V.

🏳 Mayflower Motel

5610 Carpenter Rd, 48197; tel 313/434-2200. Exit 34 off US 23; W to Carpenter Rd. No frills, nothing fancy. **Rooms:** 21 rms and stes. CI noon/CO 11am. Nonsmoking rms avail. **Amenities:** 🛁 ⚊ A/C, cable TV. 1 unit w/whirlpool. **Services:** ⚑ **Facilities:** 🏃 🔲 1 restaurant, 1 bar. **Rates:** $38–$45 S; $46–$55 D; $76–$97 ste. Extra person $6. Children under age 11 stay free. Parking: Outdoor, free. AE, MC, V.

RESTAURANTS 🍴

★ Haab's

18 W Michigan Ave; tel 313/483-8200. At Huron. **American.** Established in 1934, this Ypsilanti landmark continues to serve the freshest ingredients in a simple, straightforward manner. Generous servings of homemade bread are a perfect complement to hearty entrees such as chicken in the rough (pan-fried chicken), prime rib, and smoked pork chops. The three dining rooms have dark-wood wainscotting, Tiffany-style lamps, pressed tin ceilings, and floral wallpaper. Each year on the third Monday in October, three items from the

original menu are served at 1934 prices. **FYI:** Reservations recommended. Children's menu. **Open:** Sun–Thurs 11am–9pm, Fri–Sat 11am–10pm. **Prices:** Main courses $6–$17. AE, CB, DC, DISC, MC, V. 🍴

Main Street Restaurant

11 W Michigan Ave; tel 313/484-1200. On Business US 12. **Barbecue.** Ribs are the mainstay of this local favorite housed in a converted granary on the banks of the Huron River. Blackened chicken, broiled or blackened yellowfin tuna, and the Tex-Mex combo (ribs, beans, and a beef tostada) are among the other specialties. Pool table and game room are behind dining room. **FYI:** Reservations accepted. **Open:** Mon–Thurs 4–10pm, Fri–Sat 4–11pm. **Prices:** Main courses $5–$12. AE, MC, V.

ATTRACTIONS 🏛

Ypsilanti Historical Museum

220 N Huron St; tel 313/482-4990. Provides a glimpse of life as it was in 19th-century Ypsilanti. The museum is located in a Victorian brick mansion built by Asa Dow in 1860; several rooms have been furnished to reflect the period while the rest of the building is devoted to local historical displays, special exhibitions and the storage of collections. The museum also houses local historical archives. **Open:** Thurs, Sat–Sun 2–4pm. **Free**

Ford Lake Park

S Huron River Dr; tel 313/483-0774. A wide range of activities offered, including fishing, boating, volleyball, tennis and handball courts, horseshoes, softball field, and four picnic shelters. **Open:** Daily sunrise–sunset. **$**

MINNESOTA

More Than Just Wilderness

Minnesota is synonymous with fresh air, sky-blue waters, and open spaces. But while there are timber wolves (both in the wilds and on the basketball court) and trees (one-third of the state is forested), the state is not as backwoods in mind or spirit as one might think. Listening to Garrison Keillor's homespun broadcasts of *Prairie Home Companion* or reading Minnesota author Sinclair Lewis's satirical novels on small-town conformity, it is easy to picture a quiet folk huddled around quaint potbellied stoves. Long-suffering Minnesotans smile at those images—though sometimes while gritting their teeth. But they good-naturedly make jokes about themselves on their way to the magnificent Ordway Music Theater in St Paul to hear Ladysmith Black Mambazo or to the New York Mills Regional Cultural Center for the Great American Think-Off philosophy debates. Of course, many Minnesotans *do* have fishing poles or ice skates in their back hallways—but the poles and blades are often next to the golf clubs.

A guest to Minnesota can stay at a four-star resort or bunk in a sod hut. On the evening before a backwoods camping trip, you can go highbrow with the Minnesota Orchestra or hip hop with music musclemen Jimmy Jam and Terry Lewis. Combine all that cultural diversity with the wonderfully complex spices in Minnesota's stew. More Southeast Asian Hmong emigres live here than in any other northern state. And, of course, there are more Swedes, Norwegians, and Finns than almost anywhere else on the globe. You should also count the Native Americans, African Americans, Irish Americans, Polish Americans, German Americans, Slovak Americans, and a host of others who have added their respective heritages to the state's cultural complexion. Foods, festivals, music, art shows, and historical attractions reflect comfortably on all that mixing.

STATE STATS

CAPITAL
St Paul

AREA
84,068 square miles

BORDERS
Wisconsin, North Dakota, South Dakota, Iowa; Manitoba and Ontario, Canada

POPULATION
4,375,099 (1990)

ENTERED UNION
May 11, 1858 (32nd state)

NICKNAMES
North Star State, Gopher State

STATE FLOWER
Pink and white lady slipper

STATE BIRD
Loon

FAMOUS NATIVES
Charles Shultz, Judy Garland, F Scott Fitzgerald, Sinclair Lewis, Walter Mondale

This combination of people and heritages—plus plenty of pine trees and lakes to give an icing on the cake—gives Minnesota its multiple personality. This rich diversity is an eye-opener to the uninitiated, and it's appreciated by the familiar. Minnesota is always a place for discovery.

A Brief History

Glacial Lakebed to Fur Trading Minnesota was once the bed of the Lake Agassiz, a shallow glacial lake that covered most of the upper Midwest and lower Canada. The ice eventually retreated, leaving rich soil, a generally "pancaked" landscape, and the Great Lakes. As the last ice receded from the North Country barely 10,000 years ago, prehistoric hunters and gatherers were already roaming what would be Minnesota. The state's thick forests and abundant wildlife and water provided everything they needed, from building materials to lunch. Subsequent Native American nations followed over the centuries, with the Ojibwe (Chippewa) and the Sioux eventually marking out their territories.

The first Europeans to arrive were French explorers Pierre Radisson and the sieur des Groseilliers. In 1654 and 1660, they led expeditions into Minnesota's interior. Their trailblazing opened the way for more voyageurs and entrepreneurs, rugged men who built missions, trading posts, and forts across the region. Among them were the sieur Du Lhut (Duluth) and Father Louis Hennepin. As history is wont to do, their now-famous names have subsequently been attached to all manner of streets, hotels, cities, restaurants, parks, galleries, and office complexes.

When the Seven Years' War between France and England ended in 1763, resource-rich northern and eastern Minnesota became British territory. Aggressive English traders took the place of the French, eventually edging most of them out of the lucrative fur trade. Jonathan Carver, Peter Bond, and David Thompson were among this new breed of adventur-ers. Thompson was the first to detail the topography of the state, following his extended travels in 1797 and 1798.

After the American Revolution, the territory of eastern Minnesota was handed over to the new government. But the United States was too weak in 1783 to exercise much control over its new holdings. The British, through the North West Company, continued to trade in the area until well after the War of 1812. When the upstart Yanks finally chased the English out of the region, the American Fur Company became predominant.

The Louisiana Purchase gave western Minnesota to the United States. Zebulon Pike, sent in to explore the region, concluded a treaty with the Sioux by which Fort Snelling was eventually established. That historic site at the junction of the Minnesota and Mississippi Rivers is now the site of the city of St Paul. Under the fort's protective umbrella, the Minnesota frontier sprang open, as settlers poured in via steamboat, ox cart, mule train, and by foot. Churches were established and schools were opened. By 1848, the region was populated enough to gain status as a territory. A land boom brought in tens of thousands of settlers, many of them from Scandinavia and Germany. Alexander Ramsey, a self-made tycoon with multifaceted business interests, became the first territorial governor.

Statehood & War Minnesota was admitted as the 32nd state on May 11, 1858, just in time to gear up for the Civil War. With new-found fervor, Minnesota was the first Union state to offer troops to the Northern cause. Eventually, 22,000 men enlisted to serve in President Lincoln's army. But as the men marched off to defend the Union, a more serious problem for the home folks broke out. In 1862, starving Sioux rebelled against government strictures and broken promises of aid. They swept across the lower portion of Minnesota and scoured it clean of settlers. By the time the army regained control, almost a thousand white settlers and untold numbers of Native Americans had been killed.

Fun Facts

• At one time, Minnesota was the only place in the world where you could get real wild rice. Today, it is harvested in the traditional way by Ojibwe in canoes.

• The "Land of 10,000 Lakes" actually has more than 14,000 lakes.

• International Falls, Minnesota is the northernmost city of the contiguous 48 states.

• The Ice Palace built in St Paul for the city's 1888 winter festival was one of the biggest buildings in the world—until the weather warmed up and it melted.

• The Kensington Runestone, a 200-pound slab of stone discovered in 1898 on a farm near Kensington, Minnesota, is carved with runes describing a Norse expedition to the area in 1362. Authenticity has been hotly disputed.

Rich Natural Resources The lumbering industry brought pluses and minuses to Minnesota. Men grew rich and communities prospered from the harvesting of this "green gold." At one time, 60% of the state was forested. But when vast tracts of land were first opened, timber companies went through the forest with ax and saw, and hardly anything that grew more than three inches in diameter was left across thousands of acres. This wholesale devastation of the forests profoundly changed the natural face of Minnesota.

Today, where once there were virgin stands of towering white pine, are now second- and third-generation stands of jack pine, maple, oak, and basswood. These days, the state has better management practices with which to develop the timber. Millions of board feet of lumber are still harvested annually, but with environmental concerns in mind. Today, about one-third of the state is again forestland. The lumber industry remains one of the primary industries in the state, with products ranging from Christmas trees to pulpwood.

Iron ore was discovered in the northeastern part of the state in the late 19th century. For a time, 80% of all the ore in the United States was mined in Minnesota. The Mesabi, Cuyani, and Vermilion ranges were the "buckles" on the Iron Range. Two-fisted towns such as Hibbing, Ely, and Chisholm drew thousands of immigrants to live and work both underground and in the monster pits. More than two billion tons of ore have since been mined from the region since 1892. The Hull-Rust-Mahoning Mine near Hibbing was the largest open pit mine in the world during its heyday, encompassing 1,275 acres of earth ripped open to the air.

The open plains and timber-cleared land gave rise to rich farms, and Minnesota has been among the top states in production of butter, eggs, and milk. Tourism has gained strength as another primary industry in Minnesota, with attractions ranging from resorts, campgrounds, casinos, and major league baseball and football to dance companies, canoeing, bike riding, downhill skiing, and theater.

Into the Future The Twin Cities are the cultural gems of the upper Midwest with their broad array of museums, festivals, and fairs. The region is also a financial hub, with insurance, feed/grain, and high-tech industries filling in the Oz-like skyline of Minneapolis. St Paul, even though it is the state capital, is more laid-back than its sibling city. Tree-lined boulevards, lakes, and parkland provide an out-of-doors feel to both cities, even amid the 20th-century glitter and glass.

There are more notable universities and colleges per inch in the state than one can imagine, many of which are tributes to early pioneer love of learning. The world-renowned University of Minnesota, which straddles Minneapolis/St Paul, is the flagship of a public system that reaches from Duluth to St Cloud. Private colleges such as St Catherine's, St Thomas, and Macalester in St Paul; St Mary's in Winona; Carleton, St Olaf, and St John's in Northfield; and many others lend their research, cultural, and academic muscle to the life of the state.

A Closer Look
GEOGRAPHY

While much of the state is gently rolling prairie land, other sections are more rockbound and rough edged. Whether flying over or driving through Minnesota, a visitor immediately understands why the state's license plates proudly proclaim that it is the Land of 10,000 Lakes. From the air, it appears as if giant mirrors had been shattered, with the shards tumbling to earth. There are some four million acres of water in this, the 12th largest state in the country. In fact, the name "Minnesota" was taken from two Native American words translated as "sky-tinted water."

The state is the basin for three major drainage systems in North America. Water flows north to Hudson Bay, south to the Gulf of Mexico, and east to the Atlantic. No water flows into the state.

DRIVING DISTANCES

Minneapolis/St Paul
77 mi N of Rochester
147 mi SW of Duluth
212 mi NE of Luverne
241 mi SE of Moorehead
289 mi S of International Falls
300 mi SW of Grand Portage

Duluth
147 mi NE of Minneapolis/St Paul
153 mi SW of Grand Portage
163 mi SE of International Falls
224 mi NE of Rochester
244 mi E of Moorehead
342 mi NE of Luverne

International Falls
163 mi NW of Duluth
246 mi NE of Moorehead
272 mi W of Grand Portage
289 mi N of Minneapolis/St Paul
366 mi N of Rochester
433 mi NE of Luverne

A small tip of Minnesota, known as the North West Angle, lies north of the 49th Parallel. It is the hunk of the continental United States closest to Arctic country. This spit of land is almost surrounded by the Lake of the Woods with 65,000 miles of shoreline and 14,000 islands.

The south and west central sections, and the Red River Valley of the far northwest, are fertile prairie, the *Coteau des Prairies* of the French trapper era. You can still see wave-carved ridges and shorelines where today's rivers have exposed that ancient geology. Peas, green beans, wheat, and corn grow easily in this rich soil.

Next is the rugged northeast, commonly known as Arrowhead Country because of its pointed shape. Washed by the cold waters of Lake Superior, the northeast's highlands provide breeze-in-your-hair adventure. The ancient Sawtooth mountain range, extending inland from the lake for about five miles, offers ski slopes in the winter and rugged hiking in the summer. Other trekking opportunities are along the Gunflint and North Country trails which meander for miles through the pine-lined and rock-ribbed landscape. For water enthusiasts, the Boundary Waters Canoe Area Wilderness along the Canadian border is accessible only by canoe.

Moose, bear, and wolves rumble through the backcountry. But don't worry, there are civilized resorts and bed and breakfasts, as well as campsites and canoeing. Hilly Duluth is a major port city on the lake. Here also is Iron Range country, where millionaires were made of iron ore rather than gold.

The glaciated region of southeastern Minnesota butts its granite head against the Mississippi River. Commonly called Bluff Country, this is the best place to be in autumn, when the maples and oaks explode with crimson and gold. Hiking, biking, canoeing, fishing, and hunting draw many visitors. This is also Amish country, especially around Harmony, so expect to see roadside signs warning of horse-drawn buggy traffic. Often youngsters in their plain black and gray clothing perch along the roads selling freshly baked cookies, pies and breads. The closest major city is Rochester, home of the world-famous Mayo Clinic.

The center of the state was once were carpeted by hundreds of thousands of acres of timber. Now only the Big Woods State Park and isolated woodlots remain of a vast sea of trees that greeted those pioneers more than a century ago. This region runs up to the doorstep of the Twin Cities: Minneapolis and St Paul. The cities straddle the mighty gorge of the Mississippi River, born in northern Minnesota and fed by numerous smaller navigable rivers and stream. Once frontier boom towns at the edge of the prairie, the cities retain their New World vibrancy.

AVG MONTHLY TEMPS (°F) & RAINFALL (IN)		
	Minneapolis/ St Paul	International Falls
Jan	5/12.5	-8/13.1
Feb	13/9.2	6/9.1
Mar	34/11.6	29/9.3
Apr	46/3.6	38/5.4
May	61/0.1	54/0.5
June	70/0.0	64/0.0
July	70/0.0	65/0.0
Aug	67/0.0	62/0.0
Sept	64/0.0	57/0.1
Oct	52/0.4	47/1.9
Nov	38/7.3	31/11.2
Dec	24/11.3	19/12.8

CLIMATE

Don't believe everything you hear concerning Minnesota's weather, despite the average monthly temperature. The state is not permanently in the Ice Age. International Falls on the Canadian border is seemingly always making the night-time news for its winter weather, and the North West Angle is the northernmost part of the continental United States Although Minnesota does have some bone-crunching cold in the dead of winter, the temperatures are generally temperate: warm in the summer, cool in the fall.

WHAT TO PACK

The Twin Cities, and many other larger communities in Minnesota, have extensive skywalks or underground passages between buildings for winter walking. As such, you often don't even notice the outside frostiness. The layered look is best regardless of the season. Simply shed the appropriate sweatshirt or sweater when it warms up. Add on when it chills. If you plan on trucking around in a real outdoor winter, thermal underwear, caps, mittens, and coats are de rigueur. Restaurants, as a rule, are casual, especially in vacation country. There are some top-of-the-line city nightspots that recommend a jacket and tie for men. Naturally, for a fancy night out at the theater or the opera, dress the part.

TOURIST INFORMATION

The Minnesota Office of Tourism has numerous publications on what to see and do around the state.

Contact the office at 100 Metro Square, 121 7th Place E, St Paul 55101-2112 (tel 612/296-5028 or 800/657-3638; fax: 612/296-7095). They'll be happy to send you material and answer any specific questions. North Star Minnesota Government Information and Services maintains a World Wide Web page (http://www.state.mn.us) with links to general information about the state. Contact information for local tourist bureaus is listed under specific cities in the listings section of this book.

DRIVING RULES AND REGULATIONS

Minimum age for drivers is 16 years. Unless otherwise noted, the speed limit on Minnesota highways is 65 mph during daylight hours and 55 mph at night. (In urban areas, the speed limit is always 30 mph.) Drivers, front seat passengers, and all children between 3 and 11 are required to wear seat belts; younger children must be in a child safety seat. Motorcyclists under age 18 must wear helmets.

RENTING A CAR

Major rental car companies have offices in Minnesota. Minimum age requirements range from 21 to 25. With some companies, a surcharge of up to $10 a day extra is levied if a driver is under 25; a credit card in the driver's name is also required for those younger drivers. A collision damage waiver (CDW) is available separately. Confirm with your own credit card or insurance company to see if you are covered. You can also rent cars at some local dealerships.

- **Alamo** (tel 800/327-9633)
- **Avis** (tel 800/831-2847)
- **Budget** (tel 800/527-0700)
- **Dollar** (tel 800/800-4000)
- **Hertz** (tel 800/654-3131)
- **National** (tel 800/328-4567)
- **Thrifty** (tel 800/367-2277)

ESSENTIALS

Area Codes: There are four area codes for all of Minnesota. For Rochester and the southern region, the code is **507**. The code is **612** for the mid-section and the Twin Cities, except for the western suburbs of the Twin Cities, which have moved to the new **320** area code. For the north, focusing on Duluth, the area code is **218**.

Emergencies: For police, ambulances and the fire department, dial 911.

Liquor Laws: To purchase or consume alcoholic beverages, you must be 21 years old and have proper identification.

Road Info: Call 800/542-0220; for the Twin Cities metro area, call 612/552-7539.

Smoking: All state buildings, a majority of hospitals, and many restaurants are smokefree. Some eateries still offer smoking areas or separate smokefree rooms, and patrons can usually smoke in bars and taverns.

Taxes: Minnesota's state sales tax is 6.5%. Local taxes apply in some areas. For instance, Minneapolis has an entertainment tax of 0.5% in the downtown area. Hotel taxes around the state are generally 3%. There is also a car rental tax of 6.2% for rentals of 29 days or less.

Time Zone: Minnesota is in the Central time zone and switches to daylight savings time from April to October.

Best of the State

WHAT TO SEE AND DO

Below is a general overview of some of the top sights and attractions in Minnesota. To find out more detailed information, look under "Attractions" for individual cities in the listings portion of this book.

State Parks **Mille Lacs Kathio State Park** is tucked along the shores of Ogechie Lake and the banks of the rolling Rum River. A 100-foot observation tower provides a panoramic view of the countryside. Glacial meltwater created Lake Bemidji, but the water at **Lake Bemidji State Park** is now perfect for swimming and angling for bass. **Crow Wing State Park,** nine miles south of Brainerd; **Camden State Park,** near Marshall; and **Gooseberry Falls State Park** north of Two Harbors showcase the timberland, prairie, and mountains that make up the state.

Natural Wonders For centuries, the sacred quarries at the **Pipestone National Monument** have been utilized by Native American nations for making pipes and other artifacts. The reddish quartzite is soft enough to be shaped by skilled artisans. **Lake**

Pepin, the widest part of the Mississippi River, is about 28 miles long and three miles wide. It is a center for boating, fishing, and sailing. **North Shore Drive** stretches 150 miles from Duluth to the Canadian border, with views of the rocky shore of Lake Superior on one side and the wooded ridges of the **Sawtooth Mountain Range** on the other side.

Family Favorites The **End-O-The-Line Railroad Park and Museum** in Currie has a turn-of-the-century depot and train cars to explore, plus the only hand-operated train turntable remaining in the state. In the Dinosaurs and Fossils Hall of the **Science Museum of Minnesota** in St Paul, kids can get a *Jurassic Park* thrill. In the Experiment Gallery, they can even touch a mini-tornado. Traveling shows, such as one featuring movie special effects, are regularly booked. At the **Como Park Zoo and Conservatory** in Minneapolis, the great ape and big cat exhibits always draw "oohs" and "aahs." The conservatory has permanent and seasonal plant and flower exhibits, and storyteller programs and concerts are regularly held amid the flora.

The **Jeffers Petroglyphs** at Bingham Lake can make anyone feel young in comparison. The rock wall pictures are several thousand years old, dating from prehistoric people who lived in southwest Minnesota. The **Mall of America** in Bloomington is the place to shop until the kids really drop. Bloomingdale's, Nordstrom, and Sears are among the anchor retail tenants, surrounded by dozens of shoe stores, trendy clothing outlets, video arcades, and even several comedy clubs. When the youngsters are tired, take them past the LEGO Showcase or to a break at Camp Snoopy, a fullblown theme park within the megacomplex. There's a roller coaster, Ferris wheel, and other thrill rides for the young at heart. The **Paul Bunyan Amusement Center** in Brainerd includes a talking Paul Bunyan along with its own roller coasters and Ferris wheels.

Historic Buildings Minnesota is dotted with historically significant structures, from houses to frontier forts. The **Split Rock Lighthouse,** built on a Lake Superior cliff in 1910, is now the focal point of a state park. The small, two-story frame **W W Mayo House** in Le Sueur is the early home of the founders of the world-renowned Mayo Clinic. William James Mayo, one of the two Mayo brothers, was born in the house in 1861. The building has been restored to how it looked at that time. The elder Mayo, William W, along with his sons William (Will) and James Charles (Charlie), founded the internationally known clinic in Rochester after the family left Le Sueur in 1864. In addition to the Mayos, three presidents of the Green Giant canning company also lived in the home. The house is now a state historic site.

Architecture & Notable Structures The 27-story **Dain Tower** in Minneapolis was built in 1929 in true art deco style with zigzag floors and a magnificent relief frieze on the facade. The **Pillsbury Center,** also in Minneapolis, shows off more contemporary design. Built in 1981, the twin towers are of white travertine marble. One tower is 22 stories and the other is 40. The blue glass, pink design elements, and stepped-back curves of the **Opus Building** in Minneapolis is another skyline standout. Add the Minneapolis' **Norwest Center** (built in 1988), with its stone and glass facade, and St Paul's **Minnesota History Center** (which opened in 1992) and you can see how the Twin Cities skyline glitters. A Norwest Bank building designed by Louis Sullivan in 1907 still stands in downtown Owatonna. Considered one of his premier works, the building's construction pulled him out of a slump and helped him regain his place in architectural history. Architectural students come from around the country to look at the marble, the stained glass windows and terra cotta decorations. With the interplay of light on the stone, Sullivan called his bank a "color symphony."

Blue Earth, in southwestern Minnesota, is where the **Jolly Green Giant** holds court. A statue of the Big Fella stands supreme in a park at I-90 exit 119. A firm believer in eating his veggies, J G G weighs in 8,000 pounds. Of course, Minnesota has to have an oversize statue of folklore hero **Paul Bunyan** and his blue ox, Babe. The two (at 18 feet tall) can be seen in Bemidji. In Akeley, there is another statue of Bunyan. Here the giant lumberjack (30 feet tall) is kneeling at the entrance to the Akeley City Museum.

Flowers & Gardens Minnesota's integrated roadside resource management program has marked out wildflower routes through the state. These routes have patches of native flowers, trees and grasses growing along the roadways. Saved from the rush of cultivation and development, these stands have plants ranging from orchids to oaks. Some of the best sights in the colorful spring are along trunk highways 56, 212, 10, 11, 218 and 9. The **Noerenberg Gardens** on Lake Minnetonka are on the estate of 19th-century brewing magnate Frederick Noerenberg, now managed by Hennepin Parks. The grounds, which are open from early spring through mid-October, feature ornamental grasses, daylilies, azaleas, and numerous other varieties. **Farmamerica,** Minnesota's agricultural interpretive center in Waseca, has a complex of old farm buildings. Its large plots show off historic gardening techniques and plants.

Wildlife There is hardly anything more exciting than the cry of a wolf in the wilds. A pack of timber wolves at the **International Wolf Center** in Ely provides a fascinating up-close study of this rare species. Visitors can even go howling out in the woods (with the help of a guide, of course) and hope that a wolf responds. Interpreters explain wolf behavior. Moose provide a memorable image of Minnesota's wild remoteness, and there are many places where the lumbering creatures can be readily seen. The sloughs and streams of the **Superior** and **Chippewa National Forests,** in far northern Minnesota, are prime sites for moose watching.

Buffalo, officially called American bison, are often seen within sniffing range at **Blue Mounds State Park,** five miles south of Luverne. The largest prairie park in Minnesota is home to a herd of the big beasts, which once covered the landscape from horizon to horizon.

EVENTS AND FESTIVALS

- **Winter Sports Festival,** Duluth. Everything you could want in outdoors winter excitement, from skiing to snowmobiling. January. Call 218/722-4011.
- **St Paul Winter Carnival,** St Paul. The country's oldest winter carnival, complete with royal court and ice palaces. Late January to early February. Call 612/297-6953.
- **Mora Vasaloppet,** Mora. Minnesota's largest cross-country ski race attracts thousands of racers from around the Midwest. February. For race information, call 800/291-5792.
- **Grumpy Old Men Festival,** Wabasha. The city was the site of the hit film *Grumpy Old Men* and celebrates with a lookalike contest, snowmobile rodeo, pig roast and dance. Late February. Call 612/565-4158.
- **Winona Eagle Watch,** Winona. Spend a weekend learning about eagle nesting habitats, with field trips and lectures by wildlife experts. Early March. Call 800/657-4972,

- **Governor's Fishing Opener,** Brainerd. The fishing season traditionally opens when the governor casts his first lure. Early May. Call 218/829-2838.
- **Scandinavian Heritage Festival,** Fergus Falls. Norwegians and Swedes celebrate their ethnic roots. June. Call 218/736-6979 for details.
- **Moose Mountain Mountain Bike Classic.** This is a real test for calf muscles as racers crunch up and down the Lutsen Mountains. June. Call 218/663-7804
- **Laura Ingalls Wilder Pageant,** Walnut Grove. This outdoor pageant depicts the life and times of author Wilder, whose writings provided the basis for the television series *Little House on the Prairie.* Weekend in late June/early July. Call 800/657-7070.
- **Annual Threshing Show,** Little Log House, Hastings. See how old-time harvesting is done. July. Call 612/437-2693.
- **Ugly Truck Contest,** Pelican Rapids. Junkers, hot shots, and monster trucks vie for the title. Mid-July. For entry details and other info, call 800/545-3711.
- **Catfish Derby Days,** Franklin. Fishing contest, softball tournament, flea market, and street dance spark the weekend in Minnesota's self-proclaimed "Catfish Capital." Fourth weekend in July. Call 507/557-2259.
- **Song of Hiawatha Pageant,** Pipestone. The tale of Hiawatha is retold by community theater players. Late July and early August. Call 507/825-4126 for ticket information.
- **State Chili Cookoff,** Nevis. Top chili makers gather from around the state to strut their hot stuff. August. For information, call 218/652-3474.
- **Defeat of Jesse James Days Celebration,** Northfield. The bad guys are routed out of town in a re-enactment of their historic small town raid. Weekend after Labor Day. Call 800/658-2548.
- **1827 Fur Trade Weekend,** Minneapolis. Recreate the frontier days at historic Fort Snelling with trappers, Native Americans, and soldiers in period uniforms. September. Call 612/725-2413.
- **Tri-State Band Festival,** Luverne. Flashy marching bands from Minnesota, Iowa, and South Dakota polish their brass for tough competition. Call 507/283-4061. Late September.
- **Minnesota Irish Heritage Fair,** St Paul. This Gathering of the Gaels is better than a St Pat's Day party. October. Call 612/690-3888.

- **Holiday at Pioneer Village,** Montevideo. Learn about holiday customs from the Minnesota frontier era. Early December. Call 800/269-5527.

SPECTATOR SPORTS

Auto Racing   Fans of auto racing have numerous opportunities throughout the state to indulge their passion. Dirt-track racing is a feature at many of the county fairgrounds, with private tracks also dotting the state. Several of the biggest venues are **Raceway Park** in Shakopee (tel 612/445-2257) for drag racing and stock; **Elko Speedway** (tel 612/461-7223); **Brainerd International Raceway** (tel 218/829-9836); and the **Jackson Speedway** (tel 507/847-2084). Racing season officially runs during the summer months, but some brave speedsters take to frozen lakes in the winter for drag racing on ice.

Baseball   The Hubert H Humphrey Metrodome is home to the **Minnesota Twins** of the American League. For tickets, call 800/33-TWINS or 612/375-1116. For the pro minors, the **St Paul Saints** (tel 612/644-6659) play at Municipal Stadium. Many small towns feature farm clubs or semi-pro leagues doing their sporting thing on hot summer weekends. Watching the Pipestone A's play the Renner Monarchs makes for the perfect evening.

Basketball   The NBA's **Minnesota Timberwolves** rattle the rims at the Target Center (tel 612/337-3865). The **University of Minnesota Golden Gophers** (tel 612/624-8080) play at Williams Area on campus.

Football   Again at the HHH Metrodome, the **Minnesota Vikings** lock horns with their NFL rivals. The covered stadium protects the fans and players from the cold weather outside. Call 612/989-5151 for ticket details. On the college scene, the **University of Minnesota Golden Gophers** shakes the Big Ten with their hard knuckle formations and speed. Games are played at the Metrodrome. For tickets, call 612/624-8080.

Hockey   Everywhere you turn in Minnesota is a hockey rink for kids' leagues through high school, college, and pros. The **Golden Gophers** (tel 612/624-8080) show their skills at Mariucci Arena on the University of Minnesota campus.

Horse Racing   Thoroughbred racing at **Canterbury Park** in Shakopee runs from mid-May to mid-August. Races are held Thursday through Sunday. Post time is 4pm Thursday and Friday and 2pm weekends and holidays. Call 800/340-6361 for more information.

ACTIVITIES A TO Z

Antiquing   Scrounging for antiques is a passion in Minnesota. There are probably more quality shops dealing in great-grandma stuff than anywhere else in the upper Midwest. Among the hot spots is the Heart of the Lake district in west central Minnesota, around Ottertail Lake and its environs. The Cuckoo's Nest in Pelican Rapids; F&F Antiques in Underwood; Earl's in Dent; Collector's Corner in Fergus Falls; Old Clitherall Granary in Clitherall; Lost Arrow Antiques in Detroit Lakes; and East Main Antiques in Perham offer pottery, furniture, quilts, glassware, farm items, horse-drawn equipment, books, and other goodies. The Shady Hollow Flea Market in Detroit Lakes brings together more than 100 vendors on weekends during the summer. This is a good place for wicker lovers to find just that right piece.

Biking   Minnesota is a leader in developing bike trails along old railroad right-of-ways around the state. Among them are the Cannon Valley, Douglas, Gateway Heartland, Luce Line, Root River, Sakatah Singing Hills Trails, and two segments of the Willard Munger Trail. The systems are gentle and easy on the legs, since they have less than a three-percent grade. Several require $2/day trail passes, secured at the trailhead. For tougher mountain biking, try the tracks through the Superior or Chippewa National Forests or Giants Ridge Recreation Area north of Duluth. These take riders over rugged terrain and through thick woods, often over logging roads. In the Twin Cities area, the 38 miles of the Grand Rounds Parkway in Minneapolis takes riders around lakes, past Minnehaha Falls, and along the Mississippi River. In St Paul, five miles of Mississippi River bottomland pedaling eventually hook into the Boulevard Parkway, for a combination of nature and cityscape settings. "Explore Minnesota Bikeways" maps can be secured from the **Minnesota Department of Transportation** (tel 612/296-6911), 395 John Ireland Blvd, MS 260, St Paul 55155.

Birdwatching   For bird watchers, there are eagles fishing along the Mississippi River and bluebirds in Afton State Park near the lower St Croix National Scenic Riverway. Hundreds of waterfowl species can be seen along the 36-mile Minnesota Valley Trail between Jordan and Belle Plaine, southwest of Minneapolis. The rare piping plover can sometimes be spotted at Zippel Bay State Park, 10 miles north of Baudette. The small bird loves the beaches along the shores of the 950,000-acre Lake of the Woods. Up to 150,000 Canada geese can be counted at one time in the wetlands at Lac qui Parle Wildlife Management Area near Montevideo. The 35,000 acres of shallow waters and small islands annually hosts on one of the greatest concentrations of migrating birds in the Midwest.

Camping The proximity of woods, hills, and lakes to Minnesota's urban centers makes a camping getaway real breeze. The outdoors lover doesn't need to travel for hours and hours to enjoy fresh open spaces. The Minnesota state park system has an extensive array of facilities, many of them with historical connections that augment the outdoors experience. The 316-acre Father Hennepin State Park, in central Minnesota's Mille Lacs County, was named after the famed explorer-priest. Hennepin traveled through this region in 1679 as one of the first European adventurers. The heart of Southeastern Minnesota's Forestville State Park is a turn-of-the-century village not far from a 73-site campground. Forestville also is rich with natural wonders, as well. The park's Mystery Cave has 12 miles of underground passages. The Charles A Lindbergh State Park, in central Minnesota, contains the home where the famed aviator grew up. An interpretive center, the Lindbergh House and Weyerhauser Museum are less than a mile from the camping grounds. Blue Mounds State Park, the largest prairie park in Minnesota, come complete with buffalo. The herd, of course, is well distanced from the facility's 73 campsites.

Camping fees range from $8 to $12 per night and $2.50 for electrical hookups. Permits can be secured at each park or from the Department of Natural Resources, Division of Parks and Recreation, 612/296-6157.

Canoeing Minnesota's many waterways have a wide range of canoeing options, from the easy Class I to dangerous Class VI flowages. Among the best is a route along the Mississippi River from Itasca to Bemidji, a novice run of 536 miles. The St Croix River above William O'Brien State Park offers 140 miles of fine water through fantastic scenery. Put in almost anywhere along the 145 mile stretch of the Rum River between Mille Lacs Lake and Anoka. For 90 miles, the Root River from Chatfield to the Mississippi River takes canoeists through high bluffs and past extensive woods. Outfitters throughout the state can help with equipment and drop off/pick ups.

Dog Sledding January's John Beargrease Sled Dog race follows the mail delivery route of an early postal carrier who served the North Shore along

---

SELECTED PARKS & RECREATION AREAS

- **Voyageurs National Park,** Rte 9, Box 600, International Falls 56649 (tel 218/283-9821)
- **Chippewa National Forest,** Cass Lake 56633 (tel 218/335-8600)
- **Superior National Forest and Boundary Waters Canoe Area Wilderness,** Box 338, Duluth 55801 (tel 218/720-5324; 218/720-5440 for reservations only)
- **Minnesota Valley National Wildlife Refuge,** 3815 E 80th St, Bloomington 55425-1600 (tel 612/854-5900)
- **St Croix National Scenic Riverway,** Box 708, St Croix Falls, WI 54024 (tel 715/483-3284)
- **Cannon Valley Regional Trail,** 306 W Mill St, Cannon Falls 55009 (tel 507/263-5843)
- **Charles A Lindbergh State Park,** Rte 3, Box 246, Little Falls 56345 (tel 612/632-9050)
- **George Crosby Manitou State Park,** c/o Tettegouche State Park, 1233 MN 61E, Silver Bay 55614 (tel 218/226-3539)
- **Judge C R Magney State Park,** Grand Marais 55604 (tel 218/387-2929)
- **Lake Bronson State Park,** Box 9, Lake Bronson 56734 (tel 218/754-2200)
- **Lake Louise State Park,** Rte 1, Box 184, LeRoy 55951 (tel 507/324-5249)
- **Moose Lake Recreation Area,** 1000 Cty Rd 127, Rte 2, Moose Lake 55767 (tel 218/485-4059)
- **O L Kipp State Park,** Rte 4, Winona 55987 (tel 507/643-6849)
- **Paul Bunyan State Forest,** c/o Park Rapids Area Forest Supervisor, Box 113, 607 W First St, Park Rapids 56470 (tel 218/732-3309)
- **Rum River State Forest,** Department of Natural Resources, Area Forest Supervisor, 915 MN 65, Cambridge 55008 (tel 612/689-2832)
- **St Croix State Park,** Rte 3, Box 450, Hinckley 55037 (tel 612/384-6591)
- **Zippel Bay State Park,** HC2 Box 25, Williams 56686 (tel 218/783-6252)

Lake Superior. The annual race attracts thousands of spectators and dozens of international participants for the 500-mile round-trip run from Duluth to Grand Portage. The race often takes up to five days to complete, so there is plenty of opportunity to watch the tail-wagging, fast-paw action.

Fishing In the land of 10,000 lakes, nibbles are assured almost anywhere a fisher-fan drops a line. The state has more angling licenses sold per capita than anywhere else in the country. Bass, muskies, panfish, trout, lake salmon—you name it and Minnesota's got it. The governor's fishing opener has been hosted in International Falls, the entry to Voyageurs National Park and its hundreds of square miles of clear, cool water. Visitors can secure guides, boats, and gear in the Falls if necessary. Excellent fishing is also available on the historic voyageur route along Crane, Sand Point, Namakan, Kebetogama, Little Vermilion, Loon, and Lac La Croix Lakes of north central Minnesota. The waterways around Mankato, St Peter, Northfield, Austin, and Albert Lea (in southern Minnesota) are also popular.

Skiing Minnesotans can often step off their porches and schuss. There are thousands of miles of cross-country trails, many groomed both for traditional Nordic as well as the fast-growing skate-ski technique. A Minnesota ski pass is required for most trails ($5 individual adult for one year, $14 for three years). To order by phone call the **Department of Natural Resources** (tel 612/296-6157). Here's a variety of trails that are guaranteed great: Grand Portage Ski Trail at Grand Portage; Flathorn-Gegoka Trail near Isabella; Lester-Amity Trail in Duluth; Carleton College Arboretum in Northfield; and the Spidahl Ski Gard Trail in Erhard.

Downhillers should check out the Detroit Mountain fishing along the Mississippi River and bluebirds in Afton State Park near the lower St Croix National Scenic Riverway. Hundreds of waterfowl species can Ski Area in Detroit Lakes; Spirit Mountain in Duluth; Mount Frontenac Ski Area in Frontenac; and Wild Mountain near Taylors Falls. While it isn't the Rockies, Minnesota's slopes have drops of up to 800 feet, with runs up to 6,000 feet.

Snowmobiling Sure, there's winter in Minnesota, so take advantage of interlocking snowmobile trails that meander across the state. Some of the top trails include the 170-mile run along the Taconite Trail System in north central Minnesota, which weaves its way through the Iron Range. Also in the north, the Arrowhead State Corridor Trail takes snowmobilers along a 120-mile on an old voyageur route. The 154-mile North Shore Trail takes in some of the state's most rugged country, running between Duluth and Grand Marais. Typical of the grid system, spurs to the south from the North Shore Trail move to the Two Harbors, Red Dot, Sawtooth, and Tettegouche trails along Lake Superior. Some 875 miles of trails loop through the Minnesota River Valley in the Southern Harmony system. More than 100 miles of the Paul Bunyan Trail system extend through Brainerd to Lake Bemidji. The trails originate in Fort Ridgely State Park and consist of numerous branches in southwestern Minnesota. More than 2,150 miles of trails whip through southeastern Minnesota's bluff country. Even the Twin Cities metro area has snowmobile trails. For information on where to go, order a copy of *Destinations*, a publication put out by the Minnesota Sports Publishing Network, 19285 Highway 7, Suite 4, Excelsior 55331 (tel 612/470-0600).

Driving the State

Start	Duluth
Finish	Grand Portage
Distance	Approximately 142 miles
Time	1–2 days
Highlights	Short hikes that let you see some of the most beautiful mountains, rivers, and picturesque views of Lake Superior in all of Minnesota; visits to Glensheen Mansion and Split Rock Lighthouse; shopping in Grand Marais; tea at the Naniboujou Lodge; living history at the Grand Portage National Monument

As you travel north along the Minnesota shore of Lake Superior, you can't help but be amazed that each new bend in the road somehow offers an even better view of the lake to your right, the mountains to your left, and the rivers surging over rocks and down to the beach. The route is dotted with small and not-so-small parks and scenic turnouts that seldom disappoint. You are often past them by the time you notice them, though, so don't be afraid to turn around and go back.

Be prepared to share the road with logging trucks. Usually it is only a couple of miles between truck passing lanes. Though this is definitely a route to be driven in daylight, don't let bad weather deter you. Lake Superior storms are a magnificent sight, and the rain or fog can add a haunting look to the bays and inlets.

For additional information on accommodations, restaurants, and attractions in the region covered by the tour, look under specific cities in the listings portion of this chapter.

Duluth is located about 160 miles north of Minneapolis/St Paul. If starting in the Twin Cities, take I-35 north to Duluth. The interstate ends by turning into MN 61 just a few blocks west of our first stop:

1. **Glensheen Mansion,** 3300 London Rd (tel 218/724-8863). Chester Adgate Congdon, a Duluth attorney, politician, and philanthropist, had the house built on his 22-acre estate in 1908, at a cost of just under a million dollars. The manor was built to resemble a 17th-century English manor house. Today, guests can stroll through the rooms and admire the hand carving on the woodwork and the beautiful leaded art glass windows. Antique collectors will also admire Glensheen's authentic furnishings.

   Tours are offered daily April–December, on weekends only January–March. Budget travelers might consider buying a $4 Grounds Pass, which allows you to stroll along the lake, get a good look at the exterior of the building, and check out the carriage house, bowling green, boat house, clay tennis court, formal gardens, and gardener's cottage.

   From Glensheen, drive north on MN 61. As you move out of the city of Duluth and further along the coast, you'll begin to notice the terrain growing more mountainous. Keep an eye out for freighters out on Lake Superior, on their way to or from Duluth. And on your left, watch for enchanting streams bubbling down the rocks. Continue on MN 61 for 46 miles to:

2. **Split Rock Lighthouse State Park,** MN 61 in Two Harbors, (tel 218/226-3065). The lighthouse itself is the main attraction here. Built in 1910 on top of a 200-foot-high cliff after a storm destroyed 29 vessels in the area, the 50-foot-high lighthouse warned ore boats away from the rocks during heavy fog. The original beacon was visible from 72 miles away.

   The visitors center offers several exhibits on the area and the history of the lighthouse. After viewing the 20-minute interpretive movie there, you can tour the lighthouse itself. The park also sports six miles of foot trails (offering excellent views of the lake and the lighthouse), campsites, and a picnic area. Visitors with disabilities can tour the lighthouse area by means of a paved pathway. The center is open daily during the summer and on weekends during the rest of the year.

   From here, drive north on MN 61 about 35 miles to:

3. **Temperance River State Park,** MN 61 near Schroeder (tel 218/663-7476). Park in the parking areas on either side of the road just past the bridge. (There's another lot at the entrance to the campground, but parking there will only give you a longer walk.)

   One of the most wonderful things about the parks in Minnesota is that they render the beauty and the wonder of the place available for you to experience. Helpful maps make it easy to use the trail systems, but guard rails and warning signs are kept to a minimum, forcing you to rely on common sense.

   Follow the trail from the parking area west (upstream) and you'll soon find yourself looking down at an intricate series of rocky rapids. Though

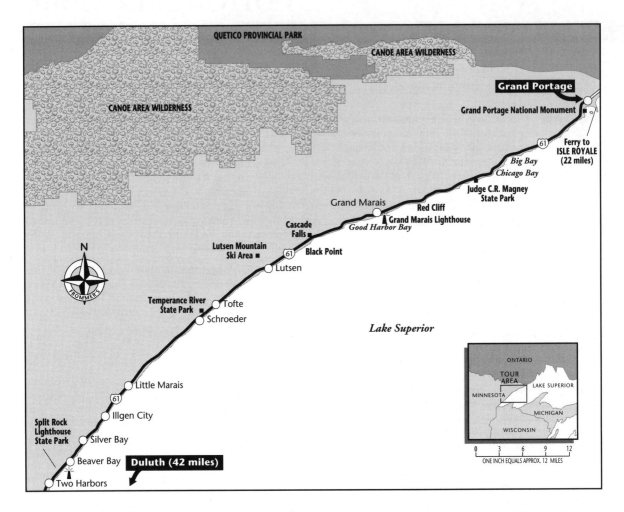

it is hard to believe, local legend attributes the Temperance River's unusual name to a bad pun—it has no "bar" where it flows out into Lake Superior. The river cascades down an inactive fault line, creating breathtaking rapids. In some places, the water scours the rock with small pebbles and carves out perfectly round, bowl-shaped holes, some of which are so deep that a person can stand inside them. Keep your eyes open for deer, moose, and other animals coming here to drink the cool, clear water.

Once back in your car, drive north 8½ miles to the entrance to:

The Lutsen Mountain Ski Area, MN 61 in Lutsen (tel 218/663-7281). Follow the road back to the ski lodge and walk a short distance to the gift shop, where you can purchase tickets for the gondola ride to the top of Moose Mountain, the highest point on the North Shore. The two-mile-long ride, in a four-person cable car, will carry you over a remote stretch of woods and up a sheer cliff. Get off at the summit and walk through the woods to the observation deck. From there you can see miles up and down the Superior coast.

Tickets for the sky ride vary in cost depending on the time of year and the ticket package you purchase. Tickets can also be used for the nearby alpine slide, a wheeled luge run down a concrete pathway.

From the ski area, turn left onto MN 61 and drive northeast 20 miles to Grand Marais. Continue through town to the traffic light, then turn right, drive about a block, and park. You are now at the intersection of the Gunflint Trail (Rte 12) and MN 61, in the waterfront shopping district of:

5. **Grand Marais.** Although it has been both a logging town and a mining town in its day, Grand Marais now serves mainly as a jumping-off point for canoeists and campers in the Boundary Waters Canoe Area. The waterfront area offers specialty shops, outfitters (where you can pick up anything from

bug spray to a beautiful wood canoe), and a nice walk along the lake and harbor area. Although Lake Superior water is usually too cold for all but the heartiest to swim in, Grand Marais does have a municipal pool that is open to the public.

A short drive up the Gunflint Trail (about 3 miles) is an overlook that gives you an excellent view of the entire Grand Marais area. This is a lovely spot for a picnic; bring a blanket, though, because there are no tables.

If you plan to stay overnight, Grand Marais gives you several good lodging choices. The Naniboujou Lodge (tel 218/387-2688), located 14 miles northeast of Grand Marais on MN 61 in Ely, offers excellent dining, charming rooms, and a beautiful view of Lake Superior. Rooms are moderately priced. Nelson's Traveler's Rest, on MN 61 in Grand Marais (tel 800/249-1285), is a more affordable alternative with housekeeping cabins and a play area perfect for the traveling family.

Take a Break

One of Grand Marais's most charming restaurants is the **Blue Water Cafe** (tel 218/387-2633). The Blue Water specializes in typical American fare, serving up specialties like pancakes, french toast, eggs, sausage, and corned-beef hash for breakfast, and burgers and sandwiches for lunch and dinner. Find a seat upstairs for an excellent view of the harbor area. On your way out, have a look at the faded photos on the wall, which show scenes from Grand Marais's pioneer days.

Turn your car north on MN 61 once again and drive about 14 miles to:

6. **Justice C R Magney State Park** (tel 218/387-2929). By far the most interesting attraction in the park is the Devil's Kettle, a mysterious cavelike opening into which half of the raging Brule River disappears. Despite the best efforts of scientists, divers, and other experts, no one has yet found the river's outlet after it enters the cave. To get to the Devil's Kettle, follow the signs from any of the parking lots to the path on the eastern side of the Brule. This scenic 1½-mile walk will give you several stunning views of the Brule, and the cliffs that surround it. You'll go past the lower and upper falls, and along the ridge to the Devil's Kettle. Should you choose, you can continue to walk to Brule Lake, a popular spot for anglers. Scan the far bank for wildlife: wolves, black bear, deer, moose, raccoon, and porcupine all live within the park's boundaries. Fall

visitors will enjoy the stunning colors along the trail, while those who stop by during the winter can take advantage of the excellent cross-country skiing and snowshoeing.

Take a Break

After all that hiking, you'll have worked up an appetite for the home-baked goods available at the **Naniboujou Lodge and Restaurant** (tel 218/387-2688). Located on MN 61 across the road from the Magney State Park, the Naniboujou began as an exclusive private club back in the 1920s, when it included Babe Ruth, Jack Dempsey, and Ring Lardner among its members. The beautiful dining room, patterned after the inside of a Cree lodge, features Minnesota's largest native-rock fireplace. For a scrumptious lunch, order a Trapper (focaccia with pesto, sauces, fresh tomatoes, pepperoni, and three kinds of cheese). High tea is served from 3 to 5pm in the Arrowhead Room overlooking Lake Superior. Excellent dinner entrees include medallions of pork with apricot sauce, Paddlers' Pasta Alfredo, and several fresh fish selections. The restaurant is open mid-May to mid-October, and dinner entrees cost $8 to $15.

From the park, turn left (north) and continue 21 miles to:

7. **Grand Portage National Monument** (tel 218/387-2788). When you step through the high wooden gates into the fort, you will seem to be moving back in time to the 18th-century days of fur-trappers and voyageurs. Though the height of activity in the monument occurs during the elaborate re-creation of a trade gathering, which takes place in mid-August, visitors at any time of the year will enjoy walking through the fort and talking with the actors in period costume. You can watch bread being baked in a stone oven, visit the dining room formerly reserved for the elite company managers, view a demonstration of how a fur press works, and tour the Native American village and the trader encampment just south of the fort.

During the time period represented here, Grand Portage was the largest settlement for hundreds of miles. It served as the headquarters for the North West Company and was perhaps the most important part of the 2,500-mile fur trade route. The fort stands on Lake Superior at the beginning of an 8½-mile path that the fur traders used to carry their canoes and gear over land before continuing their journey on the upper Pigeon River.

The buildings are open from mid-May to mid-October, dawn to dusk. The fort also offers a self-guided hiking tour of the portage path itself. The trail is a tough one though, with some steep inclines and slippery conditions. Visitors should also come armed with a good bug repellent, as the mosquitoes and black flies can become an annoyance.

From here, overnight visitors might consider taking the ferry to Isle Royale, a rocky, forested, undeveloped state park where backpackers can count on seeing untamed country and a wide variety of animal life. In addition to being a jumping-off point for Isle Royale, the town of Grand Portage also has its own international border crossing to Thunder Bay, Ontario.

Minnesota Listings

Albert Lea

Seat of Freeborn County, in southern Minnesota. Settled by Scandinavian and German farmers in 1855 and named for one of the area's surveyors, Albert Lea features four downtown buildings which are listed on the National Register of Historic Places. **Information:** Albert Lea Convention & Visitors Bureau, 202 N Broadway, Albert Lea, 56007 (tel 507/373-3938 or toll free 800/345-8414).

MOTELS 🏨

▤▤▤ Best Western Albert Lea
2301 E Main St, 56007; tel 507/373-8291 or toll free 800/528-1234; fax 507/373-4043. Fireplace in lobby; children's play area outside with swings. **Rooms:** 124 rms and stes. CI 2pm/CO 11am. Nonsmoking rms avail. Tables instead of desks. **Amenities:** 🛏 🖥 A/C, cable TV w/movies, refrig, dataport, VCR. Some units w/minibars. **Services:** ✕ 🖼 🛎 🐾 Social director. Breakfast Mon–Fri 6:30–11am in the Country Peddler. Social director makes arrangements for community tours and dinner reservations at area restaurants. $5 for pets. **Facilities:** 🏗 🛝 🎱 450 🖥 ♿ 1 restaurant, 1 bar (w/entertainment), games rm, sauna, whirlpool, playground, washer/dryer. Pool is clean and opens onto a party area. **Rates:** Peak (June–Aug) $42–$48 S; $50–$59 D; $115–$197 ste. Extra person $5. Children under age 18 stay free. Lower rates off-season. Parking: Outdoor, free. AE, CB, DC, DISC, EC, ER, JCB, MC, V.

▤▤ Countryside Inn
2102 E Main St, PO Box 782, 56007; tel 507/373-2446 or toll free 800/341-8000; fax 507/373-3530. Exit 11 off I-35 N exit 12 off I-35 S. Family-owned and -operated place consisting of older and newer buildings. Living room–like lobby with bear rugs in front of fireplace. Close to parks with walking, biking, and skiing paths and public golf course. **Rooms:** 50 rms. CI 2pm/CO 11am. Nonsmoking rms avail. **Amenities:** 🛏 🍴 A/C, cable TV w/movies. **Services:** 🛎 🐾 Twice-daily maid svce. **Facilities:** 🛝 ♿ **Rates (CP):** Peak (June–Sept) $34–$42 S; $46–$52 D. Extra person $3. Chil-

dren under age 12 stay free. Lower rates off-season. Parking: Outdoor, free. Senior discount avail. AE, CB, DC, DISC, MC, V.

▤▤▤ Days Inn
2306 E Main St, 56007; tel 507/373-6471 or toll free 800/DAYS-INN; fax 507/373-7517. On US 35. Interior courtyard is landscaped with benches and walkway. **Rooms:** 129 rms. CI 2pm/CO 11am. Nonsmoking rms avail. Table instead of desk, with two chairs. **Amenities:** 🍴 🖥 A/C, cable TV w/movies. No phone. **Services:** ✕ 🖼 🛎 🐾 Babysitting. **Facilities:** 🏗 🛝 350 1 restaurant, 1 bar (w/entertainment), games rm, washer/dryer. **Rates:** Peak (June–Sept) $43–$65 S; $51–$75 D. Extra person $5. Children under age 18 stay free. Lower rates off-season. Parking: Outdoor, free. AE, CB, DC, DISC, EC, ER, JCB, MC, V.

▤▤ Super 8 Motel
2019 E Main St, 56007; tel 507/377-0591 or toll free 800/800-8000; fax 507/377-0591. Exit 11 off I-35 N, exit 12 off I-35 S. Used by many business travelers. Close to parks with walking, biking, and skiing paths and public golf course. **Rooms:** 60 rms. CI noon/CO 11am. Nonsmoking rms avail. **Amenities:** 🛏 A/C, cable TV w/movies. **Services:** 🚐 🛎 🐾 Pets allowed with prior notice. Management very efficient, attempts to meet special requests. **Facilities:** 🛝 10 ♿ Can arrange use of YMCA/YWCA. **Rates:** $37–$46 S; $40–$47 D. Extra person $5. Children under age 12 stay free. Parking: Outdoor, free. AARP, corporate, government discounts avail. AE, CB, DC, DISC, MC, V.

RESTAURANT 🍴

Krystal's
In Albert Lea Golf Club, 1701 Country Club Rd; tel 507/377-1683. **American.** Located at the Albert Lea golf course, this casual, pleasantly decorated restaurant has windows on three sides that offer a view of the golf course. The dining room is open and light, and there is a fireplace in the bar. Peppered pork chops are a specialty. **FYI:** Reservations recommended. Children's menu. **Open:** Peak (Mar–Sept) lunch Tues–Fri 11:30am–2pm; dinner Tues–Sat 5:30–9pm. **Prices:** Main courses $8–$15. MC, V.

ATTRACTION 🏛️

Freeborn County Historical Museum and Pioneer Village
1031 Bridge Ave; tel 507/373-8003. The 14 restored buildings that make up the pioneer village include a log cabin, a general store, a switchboard office, a blacksmith shop, and a train depot. On-site museum has displays from kitchens and living rooms of pioneer times including musical instruments, toys, and dolls. **Open:** Peak (May–Sept) Tues–Fri 10am–5pm, Sat–Sun 1–5pm. Reduced hours off-season. **$**

Alexandria

Seat of Douglas County, in west-central part of state. Alex, as the locals call their town, is surrounded by 200 lakes. An alleged Viking rune stone was found on a nearby farm in 1898. (If the stone is genuine, Alexandria was explored over a century before the arrival of Columbus.) **Information:** Alexandria Convention & Visitors Bureau, 206 Broadway, Alexandria, 56308 (tel 320/763-3161 or toll free 800/245-ALEX).

MOTELS 🏨

≣≣ AmericInn
4520 MN 29 S, 56308; tel 320/763-6808 or toll free 800/634-3444; fax 320/763-6808. Exit 103 off I-94. Relatively new building with gray, weather-beaten, rustic exterior. It has kind of a country kitsch feel to it. Lobby has fireplace. **Rooms:** 53 rms and stes. CI 3pm/CO 11am. Nonsmoking rms avail. Bright and airy atmosphere. **Amenities:** 🛁 🕹️ A/C, cable TV w/movies. Some units w/whirlpools. **Services:** 🛎️ **Facilities:** 🚗 🏃 🔳 🛗 Sauna, whirlpool, washer/dryer. Video games in pool area. **Rates (CP):** Peak (Mem Day–Labor Day) $40–$60 S; $43–$61 D; $47–$99 ste. Extra person $6. Children under age 12 stay free. Lower rates off-season. Parking: Outdoor, free. AE, DC, DISC, MC, V.

≣≣ Comfort Inn
507 50th Ave W, 56308; tel 320/762-5161 or toll free 800/228-5150. Located on a main street with groceries, fast food outlets, and other stores. **Rooms:** 48 rms. CI 3pm/CO 11am. Nonsmoking rms avail. **Amenities:** 🛁 🕹️ A/C, cable TV w/movies. **Services:** 🛎️ **Facilities:** 🚗 🏃 🔳 🛗 🛗 Games rm, whirlpool. **Rates (CP):** Peak (May–Sept) $49–$57 S; $57–$63 D. Extra person $6. Children under age 18 stay free. Lower rates off-season. Parking: Outdoor, free. AE, DC, DISC, JCB, MC, V.

≣ Days Inn
4810 MN 29 S, 56308; tel 320/762-1171 or toll free 800/DAYS-INN. Exit 103 off I-94. Simple, nice-looking building located right on the main drag of Alexandria. **Rooms:** 60 rms. CI 2pm/CO noon. Nonsmoking rms avail. **Amenities:** 🛁 🕹️ A/C, cable TV w/movies, VCR. **Services:** 🛎️ Pets ($5) in smoking rooms only. VCR/movie rentals. **Facilities:** 🏃 🔳 🛗 Games rm, washer/dryer. **Rates (CP):** Peak (May 16–Sept 15) $43–$47 S or D. Extra person $6. Children under age 17 stay free. Lower rates off-season. Parking: Outdoor, free. AE, CB, DC, DISC, JCB, MC, V.

≣ Super 8 Motel
4620 MN 29 S, 56308; tel 320/763-6552 or toll free 800/800-8000; fax 320/763-6552. At exit 343. Very clean building along a commercial strip. **Rooms:** 57 rms. CI 2pm/CO 11am. Nonsmoking rms avail. **Amenities:** 🛁 A/C, cable TV w/movies. **Services:** 🛎️ 🛎️ Pets allowed by permission only. **Facilities:** 🏃 🔳 🛗 Games rm. **Rates (CP):** Peak (Mem Day–Labor Day) $43–$53 S or D. Extra person $4. Children under age 12 stay free. Lower rates off-season. Parking: Outdoor, free. AE, CB, DC, DISC, MC, V.

RESORT

≣≣≣ Arrowwood, A Radisson Resort
2100 Arrowwood Lane, 56308; tel 320/762-1124 or toll free 800/333-3333; fax 320/762-0133. 450 acres. This 25-year-old family resort is only a few minutes outside of town. The main building, of gray weather-beaten wood, is built into the side of a hill on very extensive grounds. Many common areas for socializing. **Rooms:** 200 rms, stes. CI 4pm/CO noon. Nonsmoking rms avail. Most rooms have view of Lake Darling. Decor varies throughout resort. **Amenities:** 🛁 🕹️ A/C, cable TV w/movies. Some units w/terraces, some w/fireplaces, some w/whirlpools. **Services:** ✕ 🆅🅿 🚗 🖼️ 🛎️ 🛎️ Car-rental desk, children's program, babysitting. Lapdogs allowed. Children's program, Camp Arrowood, runs daily 9am–3pm during peak season. Aqua aerobics, beach bonfires, sunset cruises are just some activities. **Facilities:** 🏌️ 🚲 🔺 🏐 ▶️18 ⛳ 🎿 🏃 ⛴️4 ⛷️ 🛶 🏊 500 🛗 3 restaurants, 2 bars (1 w/entertainment), 1 beach (lake shore), basketball, volleyball, games rm, lawn games, squash, sauna, whirlpool, playground, washer/dryer. 14,400-square-foot indoor tennis facility. Two sand volleyball courts are lit for night games. Great gift shop off lobby. **Rates:** Peak (Mem Day–Labor Day) $85–$169 S or D; $124–$234 ste. Extra person $15. Children under age 18 stay free. Lower rates off-season. Parking: Outdoor, free. AE, CB, DC, DISC, MC, V.

ATTRACTION 🏛️

Runestone Museum
206 Broadway; tel 320/763-3160. The main attraction here is a 202-pound native graywacke stone believed to have been etched by Vikings in 1362. The runic engravings tell the story of the exploration party and how they came to America. **Open:** Mon–Sat 9am–5pm, Sun noon–5pm. **$$**

Anoka

Located north of Minneapolis on the Mississippi River. Originally a trading post and lumber town, Anoka prospered as a farm trade center. **Information:** Anoka Area Chamber of Commerce, 222 E Main St, Anoka, 55303 (tel 612/421-7130).

MOTEL 🏨

≝≝ Super 8 Motel

1129 W US 10, 55303; tel 612/422-8000 or toll free 800/800-8000. At Thurston Ave. Two blocks from Anoka-Hennepin Technical College and five miles from Anoka Ramsey College, so parents, teachers and students use facility. **Rooms:** 56 rms and stes. CI 2pm/CO 11am. Nonsmoking rms avail. **Amenities:** 🛏 A/C, satel TV w/movies, refrig, dataport. Some units w/whirlpools. **Services:** 🖨 🛎 **Facilities:** 🏋 📺 24 ♿ Washer/dryer. **Rates:** $41 S; $63 D; $85 ste. Extra person $6. Children under age 12 stay free. Parking: Outdoor, free. AE, DC, DISC, EC, MC, V.

Austin

Seat of Mower County. This southeastern Minnesota city is famous as the home of Hormel, makers of Spam and other canned meat products. Austin is surrounded by acres of corn and soybeans and has more than 20 parks within its city limits. **Information:** Austin Convention & Visitors Bureau, 300 N Main St, PO Box 613, Austin, 55912 (tel 507/437-4563 or toll free 800/444-5713).

RESTAURANT 🍴

★ The Old Mill

County Road 25; tel 507/437-2076. **American.** Built in 1884 as a mill along the Cedar River and transformed into a restaurant in 1950. Offers a great view of the dam. Specialties are prime rib (with the bone left in) and seafood in season. Popular with business groups in evenings. The adjacent bar has a cozy fireplace and features Minnesota beers (New Ulm, Minnesota Brewing Company, Grain Belt). **FYI:** Reservations recommended. Children's menu. **Open:** Lunch Mon–Fri 11:30am–2pm; dinner Mon–Sat 5:30am–10pm. **Prices:** Main courses $5–$20. CB, DC, DISC, MC, V. ❤ 🍴 📷 🏞 👥

Babbitt

LODGE 🏨

≝≝ Bear Island Resort

2624 Bear Island Resort Rd, PO Box 149, 55731; tel 218/827-3396 or toll free 800/345-BEAR; fax 218/827-3374. 88 acres. Large, wooded property on peninsula with 2,000 feet of beach property. Miles of hiking and cross country skiing trails. Lodge-to-lodge dogsledding available, weather permitting, Dec–Mar. **Rooms:** 14 cottages/villas. CI 3pm/CO 9am. Each cabin is different; all are comfortably furnished. **Amenities:** 📺 TV, refrig, voice mail. No A/C or phone. Some

units w/terraces, some w/fireplaces. **Services:** 🚐 🛎 Babysitting. **Facilities:** 🏊 ⛺ 📺 🏌 🏋 15 1 beach (lake shore), lawn games, sauna, whirlpool, playground. Badminton, shuffleboard, canoes, and boats available. **Rates:** Peak (mid-June–mid-Sept/Dec–Feb) $540–$1,230 cottage/villa. Extra person $15. Children under age 3 stay free. Min stay. Lower rates off-season. Parking: Outdoor, free. Children 12 and under are charged half the adult rate. Two-night minimum stay required during off-season. One-week minimum stay required July–Aug. DISC, MC, V.

Baudette

Seat of Lake of the Woods County, in northern Minnesota. Baudette is a gateway to the Lake of the Woods, the most northerly lake in the country.

MOTEL 🏨

≝ Walleye Inn Motel

MN 11, 56623; tel 218/634-1550; fax 218/634-1550. Newer motel of wood frame and stained siding construction located in the heart of the "Walleye Capital of the World," Baudette. **Rooms:** 39 rms and stes. CI open/CO 11am. Nonsmoking rms avail. Simple and clean rooms. Rooms in newer addition are especially comfortable. **Amenities:** 🛏 A/C, cable TV w/movies. 1 unit w/whirlpool. **Services:** 📠 🛎 Desk personnel make pizzas for guests. **Facilities:** ♿ **Rates (CP):** $37 S; $48 D; $67–$79 ste. Extra person $5. Parking: Outdoor, free. AE, DISC, MC, V.

LODGE 🏨

≝≝≝ Sportsman's Lodge

MN 172 (Wheeler's Point Rd), 56623; tel 218/634-1342 or toll free 800/862-8602; fax 218/634-1342. Large resort on Lake of the Woods specializes in summer and some winter activities. **Rooms:** 30 rms; 20 cottages/villas. CI 2pm/CO 11am. Hotel rooms and one- to four-bedroom cabins available. **Amenities:** 🛏 📺 A/C, cable TV w/movies, refrig. 1 unit w/minibar. Rooms have freezers for storing fish. **Services:** 🍽 🚐 🛎 🛎 Social director, babysitting. Owns two large buses, outfitted with wetbar and card tables, for group pickup and expeditions. **Facilities:** 🏊 ⛺ 📺 9 🏌 🏋 🎣 75 2 restaurants, 2 bars (1 w/entertainment), 1 beach (lake shore), basketball, volleyball, games rm, lawn games, whirlpool, playground. Canoeing, fishing, hunting; winter ice-fishing, snowmobiling. **Rates:** Peak (May–Nov) $30–$45 S; $40–$65 D; $66–$199 cottage/villa. Extra person $5. Children under age 13 stay free. Lower rates off-season. AP and MAP rates avail. Parking: Outdoor, free. DISC, MC, V.

ATTRACTION 🖼️

Lake of the Woods

MN 172; tel 218/783-6252. Approximately 14,000 islands are contained within this 2,000-square-mile lake which straddles the international border between Minnesota and the Canadian provinces of Manitoba and Ontario. The area is famed for its unspoiled natural beauty, excellent fishing (particularly for walleyed pike), canoeing, sandy beaches, and camping. The lake is ringed on the north by Northwest Angle State Forest, and on the south by the 3,000-acre Zipple Bay State Park, which offers hiking, fishing, swimming, boating, picnicking, snowmobiling, and camping. **Open:** Daily sunrise–sunset. **Free**

Bemidji

Seat of Beltrami County, in northern Minnesota near the source of the Mississippi. An 18-foot-tall statue of Paul Bunyan stands next to an information center that relates the story of how Paul and Babe the Blue Ox formed Minnesota's many lakes and the Mississippi. **Information:** Bemidji Visitors & Convention Bureau, PO Box 66, Bemidji, 56601 (tel 218/759-0164 or toll free 800/458-2223).

HOTEL 🏨

≡≡≡ Northern Inn

3600 Moberg Dr (US 2 W), 56601; tel 218/751-9500 or toll free 800/NORTH-85; fax 218/751-8122. Large hotel of fieldstone and brick construction is ideally suited for large group gatherings. **Rooms:** 123 rms and stes. CI 3pm/CO noon. Nonsmoking rms avail. Clean rooms. **Amenities:** 🛏️ ⚙️ ⁑ A/C, cable TV w/movies, dataport. Some units w/whirlpools. **Services:** ✕ 🚗 🛅 ⌓ ⌯ Babysitting. Good service. **Facilities:** 🎱 🏊 📺 🍴 📞 ₺ 1 restaurant, 1 bar (w/entertainment), games rm, sauna, whirlpool, beauty salon, washer/dryer. **Rates:** Peak (May–Sept/Dec–Feb) $38–$69 S; $48–$79 D; $130 ste. Extra person $10. Children under age 19 stay free. Lower rates off-season. Parking: Outdoor, free. AE, CB, DC, DISC, MC, V.

MOTELS

≡≡ AmericInn of Bemidji

1200 Paul Bunyan Dr NW, 56601; tel 218/751-3000 or toll free 800/634-3444; fax 218/751-3000. Comfortable, recently built chain hotel on Bemidji's main street. **Rooms:** 62 rms. CI 3pm/CO 11am. Nonsmoking rms avail. **Amenities:** 🛏️ ⚙️ A/C, cable TV w/movies. Some units w/whirlpools. **Services:** ⌓ Nintendo and children's board games available at desk. Extremely friendly and helpful staff. **Facilities:** 🎱 🏊 📺 ₺ Games rm, sauna, whirlpool, washer/dryer. **Rates (CP):** $46–$52 S or D. Extra person $6. Children under age 12 stay free. Parking: Outdoor, free. AE, CB, DC, DISC, MC, V.

≡≡≡ Best Western Bemidji Inn

2420 Paul Bunyan Dr NW, 56601; tel 218/751-0390 or toll free 800/528-1234; fax 218/751-2887. Jct MN 71/US 2 N. Located at intersection of two Bemidji highways. Brick and shingle, two-story building. **Rooms:** 60 rms and effic. CI 1pm/CO noon. Nonsmoking rms avail. Newly renovated rooms. **Amenities:** 🛏️ ⚙️ A/C, cable TV w/movies, dataport. **Services:** ⌓ ⌯ **Facilities:** 🎱 🏊 📺 🍴 ₺ 2 restaurants, 1 bar, games rm, sauna, whirlpool, washer/dryer. Large indoor pool. **Rates (CP):** Peak (May–Sept/Nov–Feb) $37–$49 S; $42–$57 D; $80–$105 effic. Extra person $6–$10. Children under age 17 stay free. Lower rates off-season. Parking: Outdoor, free. AE, CB, DC, DISC, JCB, MC, V.

≡≡ Edgewater Motel

1015 Paul Bunyan Dr NE, 56601; tel 218/751-3600 or toll free 800/776-3343; fax 218/751-3600 ext 292. Located on shore of Lake Bemidji, motel features a few extras and is close to a variety of summer and winter activities, including snowmobile and ski trails. **Rooms:** 73 rms, stes, and effic. CI 2pm/CO 11am. Nonsmoking rms avail. Basic rooms. **Amenities:** 🛏️ ⚙️ ⁑ A/C, cable TV. Some units w/terraces, 1 w/fireplace. **Services:** ✕ 🚗 🛅 ⌓ ⌯ Babysitting. **Facilities:** 🔺 🏊 📺 🕕 1 restaurant, 1 beach (lake shore), lifeguard, sauna, steam rm, whirlpool, playground. Guests' boats are welcome. **Rates:** Peak (June 15–Sept 15) $28–$48 S; $48–$75 D; $120–$180 ste; $60–$70 effic. Extra person $5. Children under age 12 stay free. Lower rates off-season. AP and MAP rates avail. Parking: Outdoor, free. AE, DC, DISC, JCB, MC, V.

≡≡ Super 8 Motel

1815 Paul Bunyan Dr NW, 55601; tel 218/751-8481 or toll free 800/800-8000; fax 218/751-8870. Two-story hotel convenient to many Bemidji locations and activities. **Rooms:** 100 rms and stes. CI 2pm/CO 11am. Nonsmoking rms avail. Basic rooms are very comfortable and clean. **Amenities:** 🛏️ ⚙️ A/C, cable TV, dataport. 1 unit w/fireplace. **Services:** 🛅 ⌓ **Facilities:** 🏊 📺 🕕 ₺ 1 restaurant (lunch and dinner only), 1 bar, sauna, whirlpool. **Rates (CP):** Peak (June–Aug) $35–$39 S; $45–$55 D; $69 ste. Extra person $5. Children under age 12 stay free. Lower rates off-season. Parking: Outdoor, free. AE, DC, DISC, MC, V.

RESORT

≡≡≡ Ruttger's Birchmont Lodge

530 Birchmont Beach Rd NE, 56601; tel 218/751-1630 or toll free 800/726-3866; fax 218/751-9519. 8 acres. Lovely large resort on Lake Bemidji. Easy access to summer fun—rental boats, beach, and golf within 1 mile. Winter recreation includes snowmobile trail from front door, cross country skiing, snowshoeing, etc. **Rooms:** 30 rms and stes; 38 cottages/villas. CI 4:30pm/CO 11:30am. Tastefully decorated lodge rooms, plus more elaborately furnished log cabins and town homes. **Amenities:** 🛏️ ⚙️ Cable TV w/movies. No A/C. Some units w/terraces, some w/fireplaces. **Services:** ✕ 🚗 🛅

🏊 🏄 Social director, children's program, babysitting. Extensive children's program offers six options daily. Airport transportation for $8. Accommodating staff. **Facilities:** 🛗 🚲 ⛰ 🏠 👤 📷 📞2 ⛴ 💺 🔲200 ♿ 1 restaurant, 1 bar, 1 beach (lake shore), basketball, volleyball, board surfing, games rm, lawn games, sauna, whirlpool, playground, washer/dryer. **Rates:** Peak (July–Aug) $48–$148 S; $66–$84 D; $128–$148 ste; $108–$244 cottage/villa. Extra person $5–$10. Children under age 4 stay free. Min stay peak. Lower rates off-season. AP rates avail. Parking: Outdoor, free. Weekly rates avail. Cabins and town homes open all winter. AE, DC, DISC, MC, V.

ATTRACTION 🖼

Paul Bunyan House Information Center
Paul Bunyan Dr; tel 218/751-3541. According to legend, Bemidji was the birthplace of logging's greatest personage, the mythic Paul Bunyan. Giant statues of Paul and his faithful companion, Babe the Blue Ox, stand majestically in front of this center, which houses a collection of Bunyan tools and memorabilia accompanied by witty and playful commentary. (The statues are thought to be among the most photographed in America.) Another display of special interest is the Fireplace of the States, with stones representing all the states (except Alaska and Hawaii) and most Canadian provinces. There is also the Historical & Wildlife Museum, which exhibits mounted animals set against a painted backdrop of regional wildlife, and Native American and pioneer artifacts. **Open:** Peak (June–Sept) daily 9am–6pm. Reduced hours off-season. **Free**

Bloomington

This attractive southern suburb of Minneapolis has recently become famous for its Mall of America. The largest complex of its kind in the country, the Mall contains more than 4 million square feet of shops, entertainment, and recreational facilities. **Information:** Bloomington Convention & Visitors Bureau, 1550 E 79th St, #450, Bloomington, 55425-3104 (tel 612/858-8500 or toll free 800/346-4289).

HOTELS 🏨

📶📶📶 Best Western Thunderbird Hotel and Convention Center
2201 E 78th St, 55425; tel 612/854-3411 or toll free 800/328-1931; fax 612/854-1183. Across from Mall of America. Native American–themed hotel complete with old paintings and designed curtains in both lobby and rooms. Large convention area. **Rooms:** 263 rms and stes. CI 3pm/CO 11am. Nonsmoking rms avail. Native American relics and furnishings. **Amenities:** 🛗 👁 🍴 A/C, satel TV w/movies. Some units w/whirlpools. **Services:** ✕ 🚗 🖨 🏊 🏄 Babysitting. **Facilities:** 🛗 👤 📷 💺 🔲1000 ♿ 1 restaurant, 1 bar, games rm, sauna, whirlpool. **Rates:** $82–$90 S; $88–$96 D;

$125–$360 ste. Extra person $6. Children under age 11 stay free. Parking: Outdoor, free. AE, CB, DC, DISC, ER, JCB, MC, V.

📶📶 Comfort Inn
1321 E 78th St, 55425; tel 612/854-3400 or toll free 800/221-2222; fax 612/854-2234. Comfortable, basic hotel without a lot of exterior frills. Functional, easily accessible. **Rooms:** 269 rms and stes. CI 3pm/CO 11am. Nonsmoking rms avail. Well-appointed rooms with quality furniture. **Amenities:** 🛗 👁 🍴 A/C, cable TV w/movies. **Services:** 🚗 🖨 🏊 Babysitting. **Facilities:** 🛗 👤 📷 💺 🔲250 ♿ 1 restaurant, 1 bar, games rm. **Rates:** Peak (June–Sept) $85 S or D; $115 ste. Extra person $7. Children under age 18 stay free. Lower rates off-season. Parking: Outdoor, free. AE, CB, DC, DISC, MC, V.

📶📶📶 Country Inn & Suites By Carlson
2221 Killebrew Dr, 55425; tel 612/854-5555 or toll free 800/456-4000; fax 612/854-5564. Across from Mall of America. Homey atmosphere, with hardwood floors and fireplace in lobby. **Rooms:** 140 rms and stes. CI 3pm/CO noon. Nonsmoking rms avail. Country-style furnished rooms. **Amenities:** 🛗 👁 🍴 🏺 A/C, cable TV w/movies, refrig, dataport. Some units w/whirlpools. Each suite has two telephones, hair dryer, and refrigerator. **Services:** ✕ 🚗 🖨 🏊 Free transportation to Mall of America. Complimentary cookies and mints at front door. Reduced prices available for all-day unlimited use ticket to Camp Snoopy Amusement Park. **Facilities:** 🛗 👤 📷 🔲45 ♿ 1 restaurant (lunch and dinner only), 1 bar, whirlpool, washer/dryer. **Rates (CP):** Peak (June–Sept) $95–$125 S or D; $115–$155 ste. Extra person $10. Children under age 18 stay free. Min stay peak and special events. Lower rates off-season. Parking: Outdoor, free. AE, CB, DC, DISC, EC, ER, JCB, MC, V.

📶📶📶 Crown Sterling Suites Airport
7901 34th Ave S, 55425; tel 612/854-1000 or toll free 800/433-4600; fax 612/854-6557. I-494 to 34th Ave exit, turn right. Serves corporate travelers during the week and mostly families on weekends. Atrium is alive with plants—so many that hotel has full-time horticulturalist on staff. **Rooms:** 310 stes. CI 3pm/CO 1pm. Nonsmoking rms avail. Bathrooms have two vanities with two sinks. Executive rooms have small conference areas with table and chairs. **Amenities:** 🛗 👁 🍴 🏺 A/C, cable TV w/movies, refrig, dataport, voice mail. All rooms have microwaves and wet bars. **Services:** ✕ 🚗 🖨 🏊 Free *USA Today* daily. Free shuttle service to airport and Mall of America. **Facilities:** 🛗 🔲300 ♿ 1 restaurant (lunch and dinner only), 1 bar (w/entertainment), games rm, sauna, whirlpool, washer/dryer. Pool has time allotted for adult swimming only. Atrium houses restaurant, gazebo, and bar. **Rates (BB):** $149–$159 ste. Extra person $10. Children under age 12 stay free. Parking: Outdoor, free. AE, CB, DC, DISC, EC.

≣≣≣ Embassy Suites Hotel

2800 W 80th St, 55431; tel 612/884-4811 or toll free 800/362-2779; fax 612/884-8137. Clean establishment with airy lobby. **Rooms:** 219 stes. Executive level. CI 4pm/CO noon. Nonsmoking rms avail. Some room balconies overlook center atrium area. **Amenities:** 🛏 🗄 🖵 📺 A/C, satel TV w/movies, refrig, dataport, voice mail. Some units w/terraces, some w/whirlpools. Rooms equipped with stoves, ovens, and sinks. **Services:** ✕ 📻 🖼 🖵 Babysitting. Complimentary two hours of cocktails (alcoholic and non-alchoholic) and popcorn daily. **Facilities:** 🖼 🏃 🖼 🖼 700 🖼 1 restaurant (lunch and dinner only), 1 bar, games rm, sauna, steam rm, whirlpool, washer/dryer. **Rates (BB):** Peak (Mem Day–Labor Day) $99–$159 ste. Extra person $10. Children under age 12 stay free. Lower rates off-season. Parking: Outdoor, free. AE, CB, DC, DISC, JCB, MC, V.

≣≣≣ The Grand Hotel

7901 24th Ave S, 55424; tel 612/854-2244 or toll free 800/222-8733; fax 612/854-7183. 24th Ave exit off I-494. Family-oriented hotel with large, comfortable lobby. **Rooms:** 321 rms and stes. Executive level. CI 3pm/CO noon. Nonsmoking rms avail. **Amenities:** 🛏 🗄 A/C, satel TV w/movies, voice mail. Some units w/terraces. **Services:** ✕ 📻 🖼 🖵 Car-rental desk, babysitting. Quick front desk service. **Facilities:** 🖼 🏃 🖼 🖼 800 🖵 🖼 1 restaurant, 1 bar, games rm, sauna, steam rm, whirlpool. **Rates (CP):** $99–$149 S or D; $250–$450 ste. Extra person $20. Children under age 18 stay free. Parking: Outdoor, free. AE, CB, DC, DISC, EC, ER, JCB, MC, V.

≣≣≣ Marriott Hotel Airport

2020 E 79th St, 55429; tel 612/854-7441 or toll free 800/228-9290; fax 612/854-7671. Across the street from the Mall of America, it's a very clean establishment easily accessible for shoppers. **Rooms:** 475 rms and stes. Executive level. CI 4pm/CO noon. No smoking. **Amenities:** 🛏 🗄 📺 A/C, cable TV w/movies, dataport, voice mail. Some units w/terraces. **Services:** ✕ 📻 📻 🖼 🖵 🖼 Social director, babysitting. Free shuttle service to mall. **Facilities:** 🖼 🏃 🖼 🖼 800 🖼 1 restaurant, 1 bar, games rm, sauna, whirlpool, washer/dryer. **Rates:** $75–$120 S or D; $138 ste. Children under age 18 stay free. Parking: Outdoor, free. Special packages with breakfast avail. AE, DC, DISC, MC, V.

≣≣≣ Radisson Hotel South and Plaza Tower

7800 Normandale Blvd, 55439; tel 612/835-7800 or toll free 800/333-3333; fax 612/893-8419. Close to Mall of America and variety of restaurants. Caters to leisure travelers and conventioneers. **Rooms:** 581 rms and stes. Executive level. CI 3pm/CO noon. Nonsmoking rms avail. **Amenities:** 🛏 🗄 🖵 📺 A/C, cable TV w/movies, dataport, voice mail. Some units w/terraces, some w/whirlpools. **Services:** ✕ 📻 📻 🖼 🖵 🖼 Car-rental desk, babysitting. **Facilities:** 🖼 🖼 2400 🖵 🖼 2 restaurants, 2 bars, games rm, spa, sauna, whirlpool, washer/dryer. ATM machine in lobby. **Rates:** $109–$159 S; $109–

$159 D; $275–$400 ste. Extra person $10. Children under age 18 stay free. AP and MAP rates avail. Parking: Outdoor, free. AE, CB, DC, DISC, MC, V.

≣≣≣ Sheraton Airport Hotel

2500 E 79th St, 55425; tel 612/854-1771 or toll free 800/847-6255; fax 612/854-5898. Clean, large establishment. **Rooms:** 250 rms and stes. CI 3pm/CO noon. Nonsmoking rms avail. **Amenities:** 🛏 🗄 🖵 A/C, satel TV w/movies, dataport. **Services:** ✕ 📻 🖼 🖵 **Facilities:** 🖼 🏃 🖼 🖼 400 🖼 1 restaurant, 1 bar, whirlpool. **Rates:** Peak (June–Aug) $94–$125 S; $104–$135 D; $135–$155 ste. Extra person $10. Children under age 12 stay free. Lower rates off-season. Parking: Outdoor, free. Special weekend rates Thurs–Sun with breakfast included. AE, DISC, MC, V.

≣≣≣ Sofitel Hotel

5601 W 78th St, 55420; tel 612/835-1900 or toll free 800/876-6303; fax 612/835-2696. This modernistic, spacious, and airy hotel is the most international of the Bloomington hotels. Near many top-rated restaurants and home to its own gourmet facility. **Rooms:** 282 rms and stes. Executive level. CI 3pm/CO noon. Nonsmoking rms avail. **Amenities:** 🛏 🗄 🖵 📺 A/C, satel TV w/movies, refrig, dataport, voice mail. Some units w/minibars, some w/terraces, some w/whirlpools. **Services:** ✕ 📻 VP 📻 🖼 🖵 Twice-daily maid svce, babysitting. Bilingual English/French staff. **Facilities:** 🏃 🖼 🖼 500 🖵 🖼 3 restaurants, games rm. **Rates:** Peak (June–Sept) $127–$164 S or D; $145–$190 ste. Extra person $15. Children under age 18 stay free. Lower rates off-season. Parking: Outdoor, free. AE, CB, DC, EC, ER, JCB, MC, V.

≣≣≣ Wyndham Garden Hotel

4460 W 78th St Circle, 55435; tel 612/831-3131 or toll free 800/WYNDHAM; fax 612/831-6372. Clean establishment in a commercial area. **Rooms:** 209 rms and stes. CI 3pm/CO noon. Nonsmoking rms avail. **Amenities:** 🛏 🗄 🖵 📺 A/C, satel TV w/movies, dataport, voice mail. Refrigerators in some rooms. **Services:** ✕ 📻 🖼 🖵 Car-rental desk, babysitting. Shuttle service to Mall of America and Mystic Lake Casino. **Facilities:** 🖼 🏃 🖼 🖼 500 🖵 🖼 1 restaurant, 1 bar, whirlpool, washer/dryer. **Rates:** Peak (June–Nov) $69–$139 S; $79–$149 D; $89–$159 ste. Extra person $10. Children under age 12 stay free. Lower rates off-season. Parking: Outdoor, free. On weekends, extra person stays free. Weekly or corporate guests can arrange package that includes breakfast. AE, DC, DISC, MC, V.

MOTELS

≣≣≣ Days Inn Airport

1900 Killebrew Dr, 55425; tel 612/854-8400 or toll free 800/329-7466; fax 612/854-3331. Across from Mall of America. Decent facility. **Rooms:** 207 rms. CI 3pm/CO 11am. Nonsmoking rms avail. **Amenities:** 🛏 🗄 A/C, cable TV w/movies, dataport, in-rm safe. Some units w/terraces. **Services:** 📻 🖼 🖵 Babysitting. Friendly employees. **Facilities:** 🖼 🏃 🖼 600 🖼 1 restaurant, 1 bar (w/entertainment), games rm, sauna, whirlpool, washer/dryer. **Rates:** Peak (June–Aug) $75–$95 S; $85–$115 D. Extra person $10. Children under age 12 stay free. Lower rates off-season. Parking: Outdoor, free. Corporate and AARP discounts. AE, DC, DISC, JCB, MC, V.

≡≡ Exel Inn
2701 E 78th St, 55425; tel 612/854-7200 or toll free 800/ 356-8013; fax 612/854-8652. Sparkling establishment, ideal for business travelers on a budget. **Rooms:** 204 rms. CI 2pm/ CO noon. Nonsmoking rms avail. **Amenities:** 🛁 ⚲ A/C, satel TV w/movies, dataport. Some units w/whirlpools. **Services:** 🚐 🖃 🕹 🔑 **Facilities:** 🏄 🏊 🚺 Washer/dryer. **Rates (CP):** Peak (June 1–Sept 15) $52–$62 S; $61–$69 D. Extra person $5. Children under age 17 stay free. Lower rates off-season. Parking: Outdoor, free. Corporate and AARP discounts. Full-week discounts. AE, CB, DISC, MC, V.

≡≡ Friendly Host Inn
1225 E 78th St, 55425; tel 612/854-3322 or toll free 800/ 341-8000; fax 612/854-0245. Friendly, clean motel. Understated lobby. **Rooms:** 47 rms. CI 2pm/CO 11am. Nonsmoking rms avail. **Amenities:** 🛁 A/C, TV w/movies. **Services:** 🚐 🔑 Motel pays for taxi to and from airport. **Facilities:** 🛗 🏄 🏊 🚺 Whirlpool. **Rates:** $39–$44 S; $49–$54 D. Extra person $5. Children under age 18 stay free. Parking: Outdoor, free. Park and Fly rates avail. AE, DC, DISC, MC, V.

≡≡≡ Holiday Inn Airport
5401 Green Valley Dr, 55420; tel 612/831-8000 or toll free 800/HOLIDAY; fax 612/831-8426. Located 15 minutes west of the airport. Elaborately decorated front lobby complete with ferns and flowers. **Rooms:** 258 rms. CI 3pm/CO noon. Nonsmoking rms avail. **Amenities:** 🛁 ⚲ 🍴 A/C, satel TV w/movies, dataport. **Services:** 🚐 🔑 Free shuttle to nearby Bally's US Swim and Fitness. **Facilities:** 🛗 🏄 🏊 🚺 1 restaurant, 1 bar, games rm, sauna, whirlpool. Free passes to Bally's. **Rates:** Peak (June–Aug) $74–$92 S or D. Children under age 19 stay free. Lower rates off-season. Parking: Outdoor, free. AE, CB, DC, DISC, JCB, MC, V.

≡≡≡ Select Inn
7851 Normandale Blvd, 55435; tel 612/835-7400 or toll free 800/641-1000; fax 612/835-4124. Clean, affordable establishment. **Rooms:** 148 rms and stes. CI 2pm/CO 11am. Nonsmoking rms avail. Fresh-smelling rooms. **Amenities:** 🛁 A/C, satel TV w/movies. Some units w/terraces. **Services:** 🚐 🔑 🕹 **Facilities:** 🛗 🏄 🏊 🔢150 🚺 Games rm, washer/dryer. **Rates (CP):** $40–$45 S; $49–$57 D; $99 ste. Extra person $4. Children under age 12 stay free. Parking: Outdoor, free. AE, CB, DC, DISC, EC, ER, JCB, MC, V.

≡≡ Super 8 Motel
7800 2nd Ave, 55420; tel 612/888-8800 or toll free 800/ 800-8000; fax 612/888-3469. Standard motel rooms. **Rooms:** 147 rms and stes. CI 3pm/CO 11am. Nonsmoking rms avail. **Amenities:** 🛁 A/C, cable TV w/movies. Some units w/whirlpools. **Services:** 🚐 🖃 🔑 🕹 **Facilities:** 🏄 🏊 🚻

🔢15 🚺 Games rm, sauna, whirlpool, washer/dryer. **Rates:** Peak (June–Sept) $53–$63 S; $61–$73 D; $96–$103 ste. Extra person $5. Children under age 18 stay free. Lower rates off-season. Parking: Outdoor, free. Corporate and AARP discounts. AE, CB, DC, DISC, JCB, MC, V.

RESTAURANTS 🍴

California Cafe
In Mall of America, 368 South Blvd; tel 612/854-2233. **International.** Very bright and airy place that provides a pleasant refuge from the hubbub of the mall. There are several dining levels, some overlooking the amusement park, and the kitchen area is open to view. The menu contains some interesting surprises, such as roasted garlic appetizer and zesty wild rice and mushroom soup. Extensive wine list. **FYI:** Reservations recommended. Children's menu. **Open:** Lunch Mon–Sat 11am–4pm; dinner Mon–Thurs 5–10pm, Fri–Sat 5–10:30pm. **Prices:** Main courses $9–$22. AE, CB, MC, V. 🚺

da Afghan
In Industrial Park, 929 W 80 St; tel 612/888-5824. **Afghani.** Comfortable, exotically decorated restaurant, owned by the Gharwal family from southern Afghanistan, with service that makes guests feel at home. Traditional offerings include the Afghani Sampler, five entrees served on an ornate tray; meat stews; vegetarian dishes; and homemade flat bread. There are also many low-calorie and low-fat entrees. Extensive beer and wine list. **FYI:** Reservations accepted. Jacket required. Beer and wine only. **Open:** Lunch Thurs–Fri 11am–2pm; dinner Mon–Wed 3:30–10pm, Thurs–Sat 3:30–11pm, Sun 5–10pm. **Prices:** Main courses $8–$17. AE, MC, V. 🟢 ◼ 🚺

Healthy Express
In Mall of America, 126 South Blvd; tel 612/854-1400. **Health/Spa.** A health food nut's paradise, selling everything from yogurt, fruit smoothies, and other healthy treats to cookbooks and utensils. While you're enjoying your food, you can also watch health food videos shown on an oversized TV screen. **FYI:** Reservations not accepted. No liquor license. No smoking. **Open:** Mon–Sat 8am–9:30pm, Sun 9am–7pm. **Prices:** Main courses $4–$10. AE, DC, DISC, MC, V. 👥 🚺

★ Johnny Rockets
In Mall of America, 370 South Blvd; tel 612/858-8158. **American.** This 1950s-themed burger joint has plenty of old-time feel, with counter seating and jukeboxes placed every couple of seats. The singing and dancing staff provides the entertainment. **FYI:** Reservations not accepted. Children's menu. No liquor license. No smoking. **Open:** Mon–Fri 10am–9:30pm, Sat 10am–10pm, Sun 11am–7:30pm. **Prices:** Main courses $3–$5. DISC, MC, V. ◼ ⛰ 👥

Kincaid's Steak Chop and Fish House
In Normandale Towers, 8400 Normandale Lake Blvd; tel 612/921-2255. **Seafood/Steak.** Located on the ground level of an office building. Features trendy, modern decor and a beautiful wooden bar. Large, airy dining room, with plants

separating the tables. As for the menu, the name says it all. **FYI:** Reservations recommended. Children's menu. No smoking. **Open:** Lunch Mon–Fri 11am–2:30pm; dinner Mon–Thurs 5–10pm, Fri–Sat 5–11pm, Sun 5–9pm; brunch Sun 10am–2pm. **Prices:** Main courses $16–$27. AE, DC, DISC, MC, V. 🅿️ ♿

Napa Valley Grille
In Mall of America, 220 W Market; tel 612/858-9934. **Californian.** A sophisticated setting for fine dining with a wine theme: Recommended vintages are linked to menu items. California fare includes the ahi club sandwich and fennel-crusted walleye for lunch, grilled Caribbean salmon and grilled sesame-crusted swordfish for dinner. **FYI:** Reservations recommended. Children's menu. No smoking. **Open:** Lunch daily 11am–4pm; dinner Mon–Thurs 5–10pm, Fri–Sat 5–10:30pm, Sun 4:30–8:30pm; brunch Sun 11am–3:30pm. **Prices:** Main courses $16–$25. AE, DC, DISC, MC, V. ♿

★ Planet Hollywood
In Mall of America, 402 South Blvd; tel 612/854-7827. **Californian.** Colorful movie-themed restaurant, part of a worldwide chain, featuring a great collection of memorabilia, pictures, costumes, and props sure to delight kids and movie buffs. A large model of the Demolition Man character hangs above unsuspecting diners; the car from *Ferris Bueller's Day Off* can also be viewed. The second floor has a science fiction theme. Full-service bar is fashioned like a swimming pool, complete with diving board overhead. Some specialties are the chicken crunch and Arnold Schwarzenegger's mother's apple strudel. **FYI:** Reservations not accepted. **Open:** Peak (June–Aug) Sun–Fri 11am–1am, Sat 10:30am–1am. **Prices:** Main courses $8–$18. AE, DISC, MC, V. 🅿️ ♿

Rainforest Cafe
In Mall of America, 102 South Blvd; tel 612/854-7500. **American/Caribbean.** Located on the first floor of the mall, this is a great place to bring the kids. The cafe encompasses a large area designed around faux-rock formations and waterfalls that holds a restaurant, bar, and retail store. Five sound systems play the sounds of the jungle. Traditional American fare is presented with a Caribbean flair. Favorites include Rasta pasta (bow-tie pasta, pesto, chicken, and broccoli) and Castaway pizza (green sauce, cheese, and bacon). The Amazon burger is extra large. **FYI:** Reservations not accepted. Children's menu. No smoking. **Open:** Mon–Thurs 10:30am–10pm, Fri 10:30am–11pm, Sat 10am–11pm, Sun 10:30am–9pm. **Prices:** Main courses $9–$15. AE, CB, DC, DISC, ER, MC, V. 🅿️ ♿

Tucci Benucch
In Mall of America, 114 W Market; tel 612/853-0200. **Italian.** Owned by two sisters, Tucci and Benucch, this restaurant is designed to look like an Italian country home, with dining areas in different rooms. The menu is illustrated with family snapshots and features lots of hearty dishes, including baked spaghetti. **FYI:** Reservations accepted. Accordian. Children's menu. No smoking. **Open:** Mon–Fri 11:15am–10pm, Sat 11:15am–11pm, Sun noon–9pm. **Prices:** Main courses $8–$14. AE, CB, DC, DISC, ER, MC, V. 🅿️ ♿

ATTRACTIONS 📷

Mall of America
60 E Broadway; tel 612/851-3500. The country's largest shopping-and-entertainment complex is a city of its own. Within the four-level, 4.2-million-square-foot mall there is a chapel, a school, a medical clinic, a dental center, 400 specialty stores, a 7-acre enclosed theme park (see Camp Snoopy, below), a giant walk-through aquarium, 18 movie theaters, nine nightclubs, and dozens of restaurants and bars. Shopping opportunities consist of four famous department stores—Macy's, Bloomingdale's, Nordstrom, and Sears—and hundreds of carefully selected specialty shops, carts, stalls, and tiny boutiques. Wolfgang Puck's Pizzeria and Planet Hollywood are among the many restaurants. You can get in touch with any mall tenant by calling 612/883-8800. **Open:** Mon–Sat 10am–9:30pm, Sun 11am–7pm.

Knott's Camp Snoopy
5000 Center Court; tel 612/883-8600. The centerpiece of the gigantic Mall of America, this seven-acre indoor amusement park offers something for all ages. Particularly popular among the youngest visitors to the mall is the **Snoopy Bounce,** which takes place within the spacious stomach of the world's most famous beagle. For older visitors there are thrills aplenty on the **Log Chute,** a splashy ride in a hollowed-out log ending in a 40-foot drop over a gushing waterfall. (All rides are priced individually.)

More entertainment awaits at Camp Snoopy's four separate theaters including the **Ford Playhouse Theatre,** which offers live shows and 3-D films. Peanuts characters are on hand throughout Camp Snoopy to meet, greet, and be photographed with visitors. **Open:** Daily, call for hours.

Minnesota Zoo
13000 Zoo Blvd, Apple Valley; tel 612/432-9000. Five themed "trails" are the focus at this 500-acre zoo. The Tropics Trail boasts a coral reef with tropical fish, while the Minnesota Trail houses animals native to the area (such as beavers, otters, lynx, and weasels). The Discovery Trail features bird shows, elephant rides, and a petting zoo; on the Northern Trail, you'll be surrounded by Siberian tigers, Asian lions, camels, and moose. A monorail links the various parts of the zoo and provides a bird's-eye view of the animals. **Open:** Open daily at 9am, closing hours vary. **$$$**

Valleyfair
1 Valleyfair Dr, Shakopee; tel 612/445-7600. This 68-acre amusement park offers rides and attractions for fun seekers of all ages. Small children have a petting zoo plus games and rides appropriate to their age and size. Children can also dig for fossils in the **Dinosaur Pit,** climb **Spooky Old Tree,** and

even test their computer skills in **Actual Factual's Museum.** For those who enjoy more hair-raising entertainment, there's river-raft ride, a large Ferris wheel, a water-log flume, and four different roller coasters, among them Excalibur, which has convoluted curves and a 60° drop. There are some 50 rides and attractions in all. Also on site is an IMAX theater whose six-story screen displays entertaining as well as educational films. **Open:** Mid-May–mid-Sept, call for schedule. **$$$$**

Minnesota Valley National Wildlife Refuge

3815 E 80th St; tel 612/854-5900. Located barely 10 miles from downtown Minneapolis, this is one of only a few urban wildlife refuges in the nation. The refuge extends 34 miles along the Minnesota River, and is home to hundreds of species of wild plants and animals (wild coyotes, bald eagles, badgers, and beavers, to name a few). It encompasses marshes, lakes, bottomland hardwoods, wetlands, floodplain forests, and oak savanna. There are miles of hiking, biking, horseback-riding and skiing trails, and there's a visitors center with four levels of interactive exhibits on the refuge's various ecosystems. **Open:** Tues–Sun 9am–5pm. **Free**

Normandale Japanese Garden

France Ave and 98th St W; tel 612/832-6269. Located on the campus of Normandale Community College, this sanctuary contains the essential elements of a Japanese strolling garden: a traditional entrance gate, a waterfall, two small islands, several bridges, a stream, and other authentic objects. Of special interest is the Bentendo, an impressive structure donated by Japanese Americans stationed in Minnesota during World War II. **Open:** June–Sept, daily sunrise–sunset. **Free**

Brainerd

Seat of Crow Wing County, in central Minnesota. The 464 lakes surrounding Brainerd are said to be a result of a wrestling match between Paul Bunyan and his ox, Babe. (Wherever they landed, the spot filled with water.) **Information:** Brainerd Lakes Area Convention & Visitors Bureau, 124 N 6th St, Brainerd, 56401 (tel 218/829-2838 or toll free 800/450-2838).

MOTELS 🖼

▤ Econo Lodge

2655 MN 371 S, 56401; tel 218/828-0027 or toll free 800/553-2666; fax 218/828-0807. At Andrews St. Small motel also houses a bus station. Clean, but unremarkable. **Rooms:** 34 rms. Executive level. CI 1pm/CO noon. Nonsmoking rms avail. **Amenities:** 🛋 A/C, cable TV w/movies. **Services:** ⦿ ⤸ 🐾 **Facilities:** 🏃 🐟 ᴋ **Rates (CP):** Peak (May–Aug) $47 S; $54 D. Children under age 12 stay free. Lower rates off-season. Parking: Outdoor, free. AE, DC, DISC, MC, V.

▤▤ Paul Bunyan Motel

1800 Fairview, 56401; tel 218/829-3571 or toll free 800/553-3609; fax 218/829-3571. Located next door to Paul Bunyan Land, this one-story motel appeals to families. **Rooms:** 34 rms and stes. CI 2pm/CO noon. Nonsmoking rms avail. **Amenities:** 🛋 A/C, cable TV w/movies. Some units w/whirlpools. **Services:** ⤸ **Facilities:** 🏃 🐟 ᴋ Games rm, sauna, whirlpool. **Rates (CP):** Peak (June–Labor Day) $55 S; $60 D; $85 ste. Lower rates off-season. Parking: Outdoor, free. AE, CB, DC, DISC, ER, JCB, MC, V.

▤▤ Super 8 Motel

MN 210 and MN 371 N, 56401; tel 218/828-4288 or toll free 800/800-8000; fax 218/828-4288. Very clean, well-maintained motel located on main road to big resort areas of Nisswa and Pequot Lakes, across the way from Paul Bunyan Land. **Rooms:** 64 rms. CI 1pm/CO 11am. Nonsmoking rms avail. Rooms are good size. **Amenities:** 🛋 ⦿ A/C, cable TV w/movies. **Services:** 🚐 ⤸ **Facilities:** 🏃 🐟 🔲 ᴋ Games rm. **Rates (CP):** Peak (May–Sept) $46 S; $54 D. Children under age 12 stay free. Lower rates off-season. Parking: Outdoor, free. AE, DC, DISC, MC, V.

RESORTS

▤▤▤ Breezy Point Resort

Big Pelican Lake, Breezy Point, 56472; tel 218/562-7811 or toll free 800/432-3777. 18 mi N of Brainerd, 5 mi E on CR 11. 3,000 acres. Located 140 miles north of the twin cities metropolitan area, this resort is basically its own little town. Built in the 1920s, the Breezy Point—which has one building left from its original structure—offers resort, time-share, and rental options. Buildings are log wood with orange trim. **Rooms:** 250 rms, stes, and effic; 4 cottages/villas. CI 5pm/CO noon. Nonsmoking rms avail. Rooms have nice view of lake or of beautiful woods. Because of variety of ownerships (time-share, for example), interior decors vary. **Amenities:** 🛋 ⦿ 🔲 A/C, cable TV w/movies. Some units w/terraces, some w/fireplaces, some w/whirlpools. **Services:** 🚐 ⛵ ⤸ Car-rental desk, social director, children's program, babysitting. Linens changed every other day for multi-night stays. **Facilities:** 🏌 🚴 △ 🎣 ▶36 🏃 🐟 🏃 ⚓4 ≛ ⛳ 🔲700 ᴋ 1 restaurant, 2 bars (w/entertainment), 2 beaches (lake shore), basketball, volleyball, games rm, lawn games, sauna, whirlpool, beauty salon, playground, washer/dryer. **Rates (MAP):** Peak (June–Labor Day) $88–$109 S or D; $109–$136 ste; $109–$136 effic; $100–$125 cottage/villa. Children under age 18 stay free. Min stay special events. Lower rates off-season. Parking: Indoor/outdoor, free. AE, CB, DC, DISC, MC, V.

▤▤ Cragun's

2001 Pine Beach Rd W, 56401; tel 218/829-3591 or toll free 800/272-4867. 39 acres. This family-run, rustic resort dating from 1940 offers plenty of amenities and is located in woods on east side of beautiful Gull Lake. Buildings are dark log with blue trim. Main lodge houses lobby and check-in area and has big beautiful fireplace and lots of seating. Well suited for families, couples, and business groups. Access to eight golf courses and horseback riding up the road. Busy seasons are conference seasons (Mar–May and Sept–Oct) and snow season (Jan–Mar). **Rooms:** 300 rms and stes; 38 cottages/villas. CI 5pm/CO noon. Nonsmoking rms avail. Good-sized rooms with pleasant decor. All rooms except poolside rooms have views of lake. **Amenities:** 🛎 📷 📺 A/C, cable TV w/movies, refrig, voice mail, bathrobes. Some units w/terraces, some w/fireplaces, some w/whirlpools. **Services:** 🚐 ⇩ Masseur, children's program, babysitting. Winter plug-ins for car. Arrangements can be made for tee times at Pine Meadows Golf Course through direct computer link. **Facilities:** 🏌 🚴 ⛺ 🛏 🏞 🎿 🎾 🏐 ⛵ 🎯 🐴 500 ♿ 2 restaurants, 2 bars, 2 beaches (lake shore), basketball, volleyball, games rm, lawn games, spa, sauna, whirlpool, playground, washer/dryer. Outdoor and indoor tennis. One pool inside lodge and one with children's pool by south beach. **Rates:** Peak (July–Aug) $100–$157 S or D; $160–$185 ste; $148–$225 cottage/villa. Extra person $9. Children under age 11 stay free. Min stay wknds. Lower rates off-season. MAP rates avail. Parking: Outdoor, free. AE, DISC, MC, V.

≣≣≣ Grand View Lodge

S 134 Nokomis, Nisswa, 56468; tel 218/963-2234 or toll free 800/432-3788; fax 218/963-2269. 660 acres. Located on beautiful Gull Lake. Built in 1918, the lodge has been owned by one family since 1935. Immaculate grounds, beautiful gardens, very quiet and private. **Rooms:** 214 rms; 130 cottages/villas. CI 4:30pm/CO 12:30pm. Nonsmoking rms avail. All rooms have spectacular views and are uniquely decorated. Varied accommodations available, including cottage/villas that can sleep up to eight. **Amenities:** 🛎 📷 📺 A/C, cable TV, refrig. All units w/terraces, some w/fireplaces, some w/whirlpools. **Services:** ✗ 🚐 ⇩ Car-rental desk, social director, children's program, babysitting. Kids Club with varied activities for children ages 3–12; those with disabilities are welcome. On Kid's Night Out (Mon–Sat), children are served a big, delicious dinner while they watch a surprise feature film. **Facilities:** 🏌 🚴 ⛺ 🛏 36 🏞 🏞 🐴 🎿 🎯 11 🛶 500 🖥 ♿ 4 restaurants, 4 bars (1 w/entertainment), 1 beach (lake shore), lifeguard, basketball, volleyball, games rm, lawn games, whirlpool, day-care ctr, playground, washer/dryer. Two highly rated championship golf courses; golf tee times fill up far in advance. Peak (July–Labor Day) $240–$280 D; $140–$435 cottage/villa. Lower rates off-season. Parking: Outdoor, free. Rates are complicated, with many different packages and rates, including weekend specials and off-season discounts; call ahead. AE, DISC, MC, V.

RESTAURANT 🍴

★ Iven's on the Bay

5195 N MN 371; tel 218/829-9872. **American.** Located on the north end of Gull Lake, this great little place offering lovely views of the bay is highly recommended by the locals.

While the menu focuses mainly on seafood, it does offer some pasta and vegetarian, chicken, and beef entrees as well. **FYI:** Reservations recommended. Children's menu. **Open:** Dinner daily 5–9:30pm; brunch Sun 10am–1pm. **Prices:** Main courses $10–$20; prix fixe $28–$30. AE, CB, DC, MC, V. ❤ 🏔 ☑ ♿

ATTRACTION 📷

Paul Bunyan Amusement Center

Jct MN 210/371; tel 218/829-6342. Home to more than 29 rides and attractions and a miniature golf course, as well as a talking statue of the gentle giant. Gift shop. **Open:** Mem Day–Labor Day, daily 10am–6pm. $$$

Breezy Point

See Brainerd

Cloquet

Just west of Duluth, Cloquet is built on the ashes of a sawmill town at the rapids of the St Louis River. Here is the only gas station designed by Frank Lloyd Wright. No posts support the 32-foot copper canopy over the gas pumps. **Information:** Cloquet Area Chamber of Commerce, 411 Sunnyside Dr, PO Box 426, Cloquet, 55720-1149 (tel 218/879-1551 or toll free 800/554-4350).

HOTEL 📷

≣≣ AmericInn

111 Big Lake Rd, 55720; tel 218/879-1231 or toll free 800/634-3444; fax 218/879-2237. Exit 237 off I-35; MN 33 N 2 mi, turn left at light to hotel. Newer hotel, convenient to hiking, cross country skiing, and a casino. **Rooms:** 51 rms and stes. CI 2pm/CO 11am. Nonsmoking rms avail. Clean, comfortable rooms. **Amenities:** 🛎 📷 A/C, cable TV w/movies, dataport. **Services:** 🛎 ⇩ 🍽 **Facilities:** 🏌 🐴 30 ♿ Games rm, sauna, whirlpool. **Rates (CP):** $43–$64 S; $49–$64 D; $61–$78 ste. Extra person $6. Children under age 12 stay free. Parking: Outdoor, free. Snowmobiling and casino packages avail. AE, CB, DC, DISC, MC, V.

MOTEL 📷

≣ Super 8 Motel

121 Big Lake Rd, 55720; tel 218/879-1250 or toll free 800/800-8000; fax 218/879-1250. Exit 237 (MN 33) off US 35. Quiet, comfortable motel close to hiking and a casino. **Rooms:** 47 rms, stes, and effic. CI 2pm/CO 11am. Nonsmoking rms avail. **Amenities:** 🛎 A/C, cable TV w/movies, voice mail. Some units w/whirlpools. **Services:** ⇩ 🍽 $3 pet fee. **Facilities:** 🐴 10 ♿ **Rates (CP):** Peak (June–Sept) $40–$42 S; $45–$49 D; $65–$95 ste; $96 effic. Extra person $5.

Children under age 14 stay free. Lower rates off-season. Parking: Outdoor, free. VIP Club takes 10% off rates. AE, DC, DISC, MC, V.

Cook

This central Minnesota town lies in the fertile valley of the Little Fork River. Spruce and balsam trees from the surrounding forests are cut and shipped to all parts of the country for use as Christmas trees

LODGE 🏨

▆▆▆ Ludlow's Island Lodge

8166 Ludlow Dr, PO Box 1146B, 55723; tel 218/666-5407; fax 218/666-2488. 8 acres. Located on an island in Vermillion Lake, accessible only by boat. When you arrive at the main-land dock, you call on the courtesy phone and someone from the island will come over in a motor launch and pick you up. Guests enjoy extensive water recreation and an isolated environment. The gourmet grocery store carries useful basics and other items, such as pasta, plus the best ice cream selection in Northern Minnesota outside of Duluth. **Rooms:** 18 cottages/villas. CI open/CO open. Nonsmoking rms avail. Cabins are unique and sleep anywhere from 4 to 10 people. Cabins with more than one bedroom have at least two baths. **Amenities:** 🛏 Refrig. No A/C, phone, or TV. All units w/terraces, all w/fireplaces, some w/whirlpools. Kitchens are completely stocked with cooking utensils, from popcorn poppers to wine glasses. **Services:** 🔑 🚐 🛎 Social director, children's program, babysitting. Kids' activities include pontoon boat rides, tree planting, and Ojibway crafts. Business center includes e-mail and faxing capability. Library and reading area. Fish cleaning and packaging service. Extremely friendly and helpful staff ready to accommodate special requests. **Facilities:** ⚓ 🛶 🎱² 💻 1 beach (lake shore), basketball, games rm, lawn games, racquetball, sauna, playground, washer/dryer. Beautiful two-level dock and sun deck combination offers excellent view of lake swimming area. **Rates:** $150–$180 cottage/villa. Extra person $25. Min stay. Parking: Outdoor, free. Reserve in fall for following summer if possible. Closed Oct–early May. AE, MC, V.

Crookston

Seat of Polk County, in northwest part of state. This Old West town just across the border from North Dakota has dozens of turn-of-the-century commercial buildings listed on the National Register of Historic Places. A designated canoe route along the Red Lake River passes through town. **Information:** Crookston Area Chamber of Commerce, 1915 University Ave, #2, Crookston, 56716-2810 (tel 218/281-4320 or toll free 800/809-5997).

HOTEL 🏨

▆▆ Northland Inn

2200 University Ave, PO Box 117, 56716; tel 218/281-5210 or toll free 800/423-7541; fax 218/281-1019. Newer hotel very close to University of Minnesota Crookston, and golf, ice skating, bowling, and tennis facilities. **Rooms:** 74 rms. CI 2pm/CO noon. Nonsmoking rms avail. Standard rooms are clean and comfortable with firm bed, small table and chairs. **Amenities:** 🛏 🍴 A/C, cable TV. **Services:** 🛎 🛎 $3 pet fee. **Facilities:** 🍴 🏃 400 💻 🍴 1 restaurant, 1 bar (w/entertainment), games rm, whirlpool. **Rates:** $46–$50 S; $45–$50 D. Extra person $6. Children under age 13 stay free. Parking: Outdoor, free. AE, DC, DISC, MC, V.

Detroit Lakes

Seat of Becker County, in northwest part of state. The town's main street sits on the highest point between Winnipeg and New Orleans, so that waters to the west of the street flow ultimately to Hudson Bay; those to the east go to the Gulf of Mexico. Hundreds of lakes in the area are teeming with walleye. **Information:** Detroit Lakes Regional Chamber of Commerce, 700 Washington Ave, PO Box 348, Detroit Lakes, 56502-0348 (tel 218/847-9202 or toll free 800/542-3992).

HOTEL 🏨

UNRATED Holiday Inn

US 10 E, 56501; tel 218/847-2121 or toll free 800/HOLIDAY; fax 218/847-2121. Large hotel located next to public boat landing. **Rooms:** 103 rms. CI 3pm/CO noon. Nonsmoking rms avail. **Amenities:** 🛏 🍴 🛏 A/C, cable TV. Some units w/terraces. **Services:** ✗ 🛏 🛎 🛎 **Facilities:** 🍴 🚲 ⚓ 🛶 🏃 🦞 🏊 450 🍴 1 restaurant, 1 bar (w/entertainment), 1 beach (lake shore), basketball, volleyball, games rm, sauna, whirlpool, washer/dryer. 500 feet of beach access. Paddleboats $8/hour. **Rates (CP):** Peak (May–Aug) $50–$100 S or D. Min stay wknds. Lower rates off-season. AP rates avail. Parking: Outdoor, free. AE, CB, DC, DISC, MC, V.

MOTELS

▆▆ Budget Host Inn

895 US 10 E, 56501; tel 218/847-4454 or toll free 800/888-2124. Newly renovated motel serves as Detroit Lakes Greyhound bus stop and is one mile from public beach. Cross country ski trails across the road. **Rooms:** 23 rms; 1 cottage/villa. CI 1pm/CO 11am. Nonsmoking rms avail. Clean. **Amenities:** 🛏 🍴 🛏 A/C, cable TV w/movies. 1 unit w/terrace. **Services:** 🛎 🛎 Free winter auto plug-ins and car starting service. Friendly service. **Facilities:** 🏃 🦞 **Rates:** Peak (June 20–Labor Day) $30–$55 S; $36–$62 D; $50–$80

cottage/villa. Extra person $4. Children under age 12 stay free. Lower rates off-season. Parking: Outdoor, free. AE, DISC, MC, V.

UNRATED Super 8 Motel

400 Morrow Ave, 56501; tel 218/847-1651 or toll free 800/800-8000. Jct US 59/10. Standard Super 8 convenient to casinos and fishing provides predictably clean lodging. **Rooms:** 39 rms. CI noon/CO 11am. Nonsmoking rms avail. **Amenities:** 🛏 A/C, cable TV w/movies. **Services:** 🍽 🐾 Pets free, but must be on a leash. **Facilities:** 💻 ⚓ **Rates (CP):** Peak (May–Aug) $38–$45 S; $50–$56 D. Extra person $4. Children under age 12 stay free. Lower rates off-season. Parking: Outdoor, free. AE, DC, DISC, MC, V.

RESTAURANT 🍴

★ Zorbaz Pizza & Mexican Restaurant

402 W Lake Dr; tel 218/847-5305. At Summit Ave. **Mexican/Pizza.** Zorbaz Restaurant's motto says it all, "The world's only Italian-Mexican restaurant run by two Swedes—you figure it out!" This wacky lakeside bar and restaurant is always up to something (hosting a local log roll, giving away tickets to shows) in addition to serving up a huge beer selection, pizzas, and Mexican food. Drop by after a day at the beach or on your way through town and give a Zorbaz Zuper Pizza or a Geno'z Pregnant Burrito a try. **FYI:** Reservations accepted. Beer and wine only. **Open:** Peak (Apr–Sept) Mon–Fri 3pm–1am, Sat–Sun 11am–1am. Closed mid-Nov–late Jan. **Prices:** Main courses $2–$6. AE, DC, DISC, MC, V. 🍰

ATTRACTION 🏛

Tamarac National Wildlife Refuge

Jct MN 26/29; tel 218/847-2641. Trumpeter swans, grouse, and bald eagles are among the countless migratory waterfowl at this 43,000-acre refuge, which is also home to deer and beaver. Its 21 lakes provide fishing opportunities. Picnic areas; visitors center. **Open:** Peak (Mem Day–Labor Day) Mon–Fri 7:30am–4pm, Sat–Sun noon–5pm. Reduced hours off-season. **Free**

Duluth

See also Cloquet

Seat of St Louis County, in northeast part of state. This former fur-trading post (and third-largest city in Minnesota) now relies on shipping for its economic livelihood, as everything from molasses to iron ore passes through Duluth Harbor on its way to the West. A skyway system connects downtown shopping and office centers. A lakewalk stretches for several miles along the shore of Lake Superior, with plenty of park benches and a separate bike path. Duluth Aerial Lift Bridge connects the city to Minnesota Point, while the 1½-mile-long Duluth-Superior High Bridge links the city

to Wisconsin. **Information:** Duluth Convention & Visitors Bureau, 100 Lake Place Dr, Duluth, 55802 (tel 218/722-4011 or toll free 800/4-DULUTH).

HOTELS 🏨

▤▤▤ Best Western Edgewater

2400 London Rd, 55812; tel 218/728-3601 or toll free 800/777-7925; fax 218/728-3727. Exit 258 off I-35. Actually two large modern hotels across the street from each other. Activities available make it a good choice for families. **Rooms:** 283 rms and stes. CI 3pm/CO noon. Nonsmoking rms avail. **Amenities:** 🛏 🔥 🖥 A/C, cable TV w/movies, refrig, dataport. Some units w/terraces, some w/whirlpools. **Services:** 🚗 🖼 🍽 🐾 **Facilities:** 🏊 🏋 🎿 🎱 🔲220 ⚓ Basketball, games rm, lawn games, sauna, whirlpool, beauty salon, playground, washer/dryer. Mini-golf, shuffleboard. **Rates (CP):** Peak (mid-June–Labor Day) $46–$75 S; $59–$99 D; $91–$122 ste. Extra person $6. Children under age 18 stay free. Lower rates off-season. Parking: Outdoor, free. AE, CB, DC, DISC, ER, JCB, MC, V.

▤ Days Inn Duluth

909 Cottonwood St, 55811; tel 218/727-3110 or toll free 800/DAYS-INN; fax 218/727-3110. Inexpensive hotel on outskirts of Duluth, 10 minutes from airport. Miller Hill Mall, with restaurants and shopping, across the street. **Rooms:** 86 rms. CI 3pm/CO noon. Nonsmoking rms avail. **Amenities:** 🛏 A/C, cable TV w/movies. **Services:** 🍽 🐾 **Facilities:** 🏋 🎿 🔲20 ⚓ **Rates (CP):** Peak (June–Aug) $39–$59 S; $46–$79 D. Extra person $6. Children under age 16 stay free. Min stay special events. Lower rates off-season. Parking: Outdoor, free. AE, CB, DC, DISC, JCB, MC, V.

▤▤ Duluth Comfort Suites

408 Canal Park Dr, 55802; tel 218/727-1378 or toll free 800/228-5150; fax 218/727-1947. Large, newer hotel in convenient lake view location—six blocks from downtown, two blocks from convention center, lake view walk just outside the door. Huge veranda wraps around the building. **Rooms:** 82 stes. CI 2pm/CO 11am. Nonsmoking rms avail. **Amenities:** 🛏 🔥 A/C, cable TV w/movies, refrig, dataport. Some units w/whirlpools. **Services:** 🖼 🍽 **Facilities:** 🏊 🏋 🎿 🔲50 ⚓ Whirlpool, washer/dryer. **Rates (CP):** Peak (May–Sept) $69–$109 ste. Extra person $8. Children under age 18 stay free. Min stay special events. Lower rates off-season. Parking: Outdoor, free. AE, CB, DC, DISC, ER, JCB, MC, V.

▤▤▤ Fitger's Inn

600 E Superior St, 55802; tel 218/722-8826 or toll free 800/726-2982; fax 218/722-8826. Lake St exit off I-35. Hotel is part of the elegant 1885 Fitger's Brewery Complex in downtown Duluth. Once 11 separate buildings, properties have been renovated, unified, and now include restaurants, bars, and specialty shops. Rather pricey, but worth the splurge. **Rooms:** 60 rms and stes. CI 3pm/CO noon. Nonsmoking rms avail. Each room is artfully decorated. **Amenities:** 🛏 🔥 A/C, cable TV w/movies. Some units w/minibars, some w/terraces,

some w/fireplaces, some w/whirlpools. **Services:** ✕ VP ⌧ ⌂ Very professional staff works hard to please. **Facilities:** 🎣 ⛵ ⌷ ⅙ 2 restaurants, 2 bars (1 w/entertainment), games rm, beauty salon. Lake boardwalk right outside the door. **Rates (CP):** Peak (May–Oct) $85–$110 S or D; $140–$295 ste. Children under age 16 stay free. Lower rates off-season. Parking: Indoor/outdoor, free. AE, CB, DC, DISC, EC, MC, V.

≣≣≣ Radisson Hotel Duluth

505 W Superior St, 55802; tel 218/727-8981 or toll free 800/333-3333; fax 218/727-0162. Circular high rise design in great downtown location overlooking harbor. Across the street from library; two blocks to convention center; walking distance to Arts Center, casino, and waterfront attractions. **Rooms:** 268 rms and stes. Executive level. CI 3pm/CO noon. Nonsmoking rms avail. **Amenities:** 📺 ⚗ A/C, satel TV w/movies, dataport. **Services:** ✕ ⌧ ⌂ ⌷ Babysitting. **Facilities:** 🎣 🏊 ⛵ 🏋 ⌷ 🖥 ⅙ 2 restaurants, 2 bars (1 w/entertainment), games rm, sauna, whirlpool. **Rates (CP):** Peak (June–mid-Oct) $49–$100 S; $59–$120 D; $135 ste. Extra person $10. Children under age 18 stay free. Min stay special events. Lower rates off-season. Parking: Outdoor, free. AE, CB, DC, DISC, JCB, MC, V.

≣ Select Inn

200 S 27th Ave W, 55806; tel 218/723-1123 or toll free 800/641-1000; fax 218/723-1123. Exit 254 off I-35. Located right off I-35, yet in a quiet setting. Newer chain hotel with few extras. Very reasonable rates. **Rooms:** 100 rms and stes. CI 2pm/CO 11am. Nonsmoking rms avail. Clean, comfortable rooms. **Amenities:** 📺 ⚗ A/C, cable TV w/movies. **Services:** ⌷ ⌂ $25 refundable pet deposit. **Facilities:** 🏊 ⛵ ⅙ Washer/dryer. **Rates:** Peak (May–Oct) $35–$45 S; $55–$65 D; $75–$100 ste. Extra person $5. Children under age 12 stay free. Lower rates off-season. Parking: Outdoor, free. AE, DC, DISC, MC, V.

MOTELS

≣ Allyndale Motel

510 N 66th Ave W, 55807; tel 218/628-1061 or toll free 800/341-8000. Cody St exit off I-35 S; Central Ave exit off I-35 N. Relaxing, four-acre grassy spot in Western Duluth. Close to Spirit Mountain downhill skiing. Very economical for a clean, quiet spot. **Rooms:** 21 rms, stes, and effic. CI 2pm/CO 11am. Nonsmoking rms avail. **Amenities:** 📺 ⚗ A/C, cable TV, refrig. 1 unit w/terrace. **Services:** ⌷ ⌂ **Facilities:** 🏊 ⛵ Playground. **Rates:** Peak (mid-June–mid-Aug) $31–$38 S; $41–$48 D; $60 ste; $80 effic. Extra person $5. Min stay special events. Lower rates off-season. Parking: Outdoor, free. AE, DISC, MC, V.

≣ Best Western Downtown

131 W 2nd St, 55802; tel 218/727-6851 or toll free 800/528-1234; fax 218/727-6779. Mesaba exit off I-35. Steel and concrete motel in very convenient location in downtown Duluth. Basic accommodations at a reasonable price. No

frills. **Rooms:** 45 rms. CI 2:30pm/CO noon. Nonsmoking rms avail. **Amenities:** 📺 ⚗ A/C, cable TV w/movies. **Services:** ⌧ ⌂ ⌷ **Facilities:** 🏊 ⛵ ⅙ **Rates (CP):** Peak (June–Aug) $40–$77 S or D. Extra person $5. Children under age 18 stay free. Lower rates off-season. Parking: Outdoor, free. AE, CB, DC, DISC, ER, JCB, MC, V.

≣≣ Park Inn International

250 Canal Park Dr, 55802; tel 218/727-8821 or toll free 800/777-8560; fax 218/727-8821. Lake Ave exit off I-35. Standard hotel with excellent location—near lake boardwalk and center city. **Rooms:** 145 rms and stes. CI 4pm/CO 11am. Nonsmoking rms avail. Some rooms have view of lake. **Amenities:** 📺 ⚗ A/C, cable TV w/movies, voice mail. 1 unit w/minibar, 1 w/whirlpool. **Services:** ✕ 🚐 ⌧ ⌂ ⌷ **Facilities:** 🏋 🏊 ⛵ ⌷ ⅙ 1 restaurant, 1 bar (w/entertainment), games rm, sauna, whirlpool, washer/dryer. **Rates (BB):** Peak (June–mid-Sept) $43–$89 S or D; $150 ste. Extra person $5. Children under age 18 stay free. Lower rates off-season. Parking: Outdoor, free. AE, CB, DC, DISC, EC, JCB, MC, V.

RESTAURANTS 🍽

Grandma's Saloon and Deli

522 Lake Ave; tel 218/727-4192. **American.** This boisterous restaurant is divided into a saloon and grill. The grill menu focuses on pasta while the saloon serves more pub grub, but both sections give generous portions of traditional fare. Huge onion rings and mouth-watering ribs are a big hit, so expect a wait. **FYI:** Reservations accepted. Children's menu. **Open:** Peak (Mem Day–Labor Day) Mon–Fri 11:30am–10:30pm, Sat–Sun 11am–10:30pm. **Prices:** Main courses $7–$19. AE, DISC, MC, V. ⅙

Pickwick

508 E Superior St; tel 218/727-8901. Next to Fitger Brewery complex. **International.** Step through the front door and back in time to old-world days at this special family-run institution, originally opened in 1888. Dark oak paneling provides the backdrop for fine German, English, and Dutch food. Specialties include walleye pike (fresh from the Lake of the Woods), grilled pork chops, and the house burger. **FYI:** Reservations recommended. Children's menu. **Open:** Mon–Sat 10:30am–1am. **Prices:** Main courses $6–$21. AE, CB, DC, DISC, MC, V. 🍺 ⅙

ATTRACTIONS 🏛

Superior National Forest

PO Box 338; tel 218/720-5324. Of the three million acres which make up this forest, one million have been set aside as the Boundary Waters Canoe Area (BWCA), an area stretching 150 miles along the Minnesota-Ontario border that comprises several thousand lakes linked by overland trails, deep pine forests, and rugged outcroppings of billion-year-old volcanic rock. There are no roads or stores here and motor boats are banned; however, there are resorts, campgrounds, and other accommodations on the periphery of the wilderness area, near Ely, Crane Lake, and Lake Vermilion to the west, and along the Gunflint Trail out of Grand Marais. Superior National Forest operates dozens of primitive campgrounds, most of which are drive-in sites on lakes with no boat motor restrictions. **Open:** Daily 24 hours. **Free**

Lake Superior Zoological Garden

7210 Fremont St; tel 218/723-3748. Vietnamese pigs, Australian emus and kangaroos, crocodiles, Siberian tigers, cougars, snow leopards, and polar bears are just some of the over 500 animals from around the world (including several endangered species) that are featured at this zoo. There's a nocturnal exhibit with flying squirrels, owl monkeys, tree porcupines, and a wide-eyed slow loris. Children's zoo and petting area keeps the young ones entertained. Group tours, picnic area, playground, gift shop. **Open:** Peak (Apr–Oct) daily 9am–6pm. Reduced hours off-season. **$$**

The Depot (St Louis County Heritage and Arts Center)

506 W Michigan St; tel 218/727-8025. A series of exhibits and museums leads visitors through two centuries of local history. Highlights include the Immigrants' Waiting Room; the two-story walk-through Habitat Tree; a mid-19th-century collection of Ojibwa portraits by Eastman Johnson; and an assortment of antique trains, glassware, and period furnishings. **Open:** Peak (May–Sept) daily 10am–5pm. Reduced hours off-season. **$$**

SS *William A Irvin*

Museum, 350 Harbor Dr; tel 218/722-5573. For more than 40 years, the SS *William A Irvin* was the flagship of US Steel's Great Lakes Fleet. It carried iron ore and coal to Great Lakes ports, and occasionally housed dignitaries and other guests in elegance and comfort. Hour-long guided tours go from bow to stern of this 610-foot ship. **Open:** May–mid-Oct. Call for schedule. **$$$**

Corps of Engineers Canal Dark Museum

600 Lake Ave S; tel 218/727-2497. Exhibits highlight the history of commercial navigation in the area, with scaled-down ship models, a replicated ship pilothouse and cabins, full-size steam engines, and other ship machinery. **Open:** June–Aug, daily 10am–9pm. **Free**

Elk River

Seat of Sherburne County. This central Minnesota town is located just north of Minneapolis on the Mississippi River. Gateway for Sherburne National Wildlife Refuge. **Information:** Elk River Area Chamber of Commerce, 509 US 10, Elk River, 55330-1415 (tel 612/441-3110).

MOTELS 🏨

≣≣ AmericInn Motel

17432 US 10, 55330; tel 612/441-8554 or toll free 800/634-3444. Cozy lobby has fireplace, several aquariums, crafts, chairs, couches, and two overhead fans. Outside decor is classy gray, weathered-wood finish. **Rooms:** 42 rms and stes. CI 3pm/CO 11am. Nonsmoking rms avail. **Amenities:** 🛎 A/C, cable TV w/movies, refrig. 1 unit w/minibar, 1 w/fireplace, some w/whirlpools. **Services:** ⟲ ⟳ Twice-daily maid svce. Snacks, such as nachos and popcorn, available on weekdays 4–7pm. Small pets allowed for $5. **Facilities:** 🛶 🏃 ✴ ⅙ Sauna, whirlpool. **Rates (CP):** Peak (May–Oct) $48–$53 S; $59–$64 D; $85–$96 ste. Extra person $5. Children under age 12 stay free. Lower rates off-season. Parking: Outdoor, free. AE, CB, DC, DISC, EC, MC, V.

≣≣ Red Carpet Inn

17291 US 10, 55330; tel 612/441-2424 or toll free 800/251-1962. Although it's in an industrial area, on busy US 10 with lots of traffic, it's set back from road and quiet. **Rooms:** 50 rms, stes, and effic. CI 1pm/CO 11am. Nonsmoking rms avail. Rooms are fresh and new looking—regular remodeling and redecorating has been going on since 1993. All rooms open to parking lot. **Amenities:** 🛎 ⅙ A/C, satel TV w/movies, refrig. Some units w/terraces, 1 w/whirlpool. **Services:** 🅥🅟 ⟲ ⟳ **Facilities:** 🛶 🏃 ✴ 🔲 1 restaurant (lunch and dinner only). **Rates: Rates (CP):** $30–$49 S; $35–$65 D; $65–$80 ste; $42–$59 effic. Extra person $4. Children under age 12 stay free. Parking: Outdoor, free. AE, CB, DC, DISC, EC, MC, V.

Ely

Located 20 miles south of the US/Canada border, in the heart of Superior National Forest. Ely is a world-class center for wilderness outfitters, wolf and black bear research, and cross-country skiing. In mid-January, the Ely All-American Sled Dog Races take place. **Information:** Ely Chamber of Commerce, 1600 E Sheridan St, Ely, 55731 (tel 218/365-6123).

LODGE 🏨

≣≣ Silver Rapids Lodge

CR 58/16, 55731; tel 218/365-4877 or toll free 800/950-9425; fax 218/365-3540. 60 acres. Large resort offers cabins and rooms and a variety of summer and winter activities. 38 RV sites also available. **Rooms:** 11 effic; 14 cottages/villas. CI 2pm/CO 10am. Log cabins and rooms built into hillside, overlooking beautiful, wooded lake. **Amenities:** 🛎 📺 A/C, TV, refrig. Some units w/terraces, some w/fireplaces, some w/whirlpools. **Services:** ✕ 🚐 ⟲ Social director, children's program, babysitting. **Facilities:** 🚴 ⛵ 🛶 ✴ 🏃 🔲 1 restaurant, 1 bar (w/entertainment), 1 beach (lake shore), basketball, volleyball, games rm, lawn games, whirlpool, playground, washer/dryer. Winter options include ski, snowshoe, and snowmobile rental; ice skating on lake; and free toboggan run. **Rates:** Peak (May–mid-Aug/Dec–Mar) $45–$90 effic; $95–$325 cottage/villa. Extra person $10–30. Children under age 2 stay free. Lower rates off-season. AP and MAP rates avail. Parking: Outdoor, free. AE, MC, V.

ATTRACTIONS 🏛

Tower-Soudan Historical Society Museum
W Main St at Train Depot, Soudan; tel 218/753-3041. Historical museum located in old (1912) steam train. Features exhibits on mining, logging, and pioneer and Native American artifacts. Also, collection of photographs documenting the area from the 1880s to present. **Open:** Mem Day–Labor Day, daily 10am–4pm. $

Soudan Underground Mine State Park
MN 169, Soudan; tel 218/753-2245. The Soudan Iron Mine—the first underground mine in Minnesota—closed down in 1962 after 80 years of commercial production. Today, visitors may descend 2,400 feet to the obsolete workings, which can be toured via electric train. (The temperature in the mine is a constant 52°F, so dress accordingly.) **Open:** Daily 9am–5pm. $$

Eveleth

This northern iron-mining town is considered the birthplace of hockey in North America. **Information:** Iron Trail Convention & Visitors Bureau, 551 Hat Trick Ave, PO Box 559, Eveleth, 55734-0559 (tel 218/744-2441 or toll free 800/777-8497).

HOTELS 🏛

⊫⊫⊫ Holiday Inn Eveleth Virginia
US 53, PO Box 708, 55734; tel 218/744-2703 or toll free 800/HOLIDAY; fax 218/744-5865. Large, modern building right next door to Hockey Hall of Fame. **Rooms:** 145 rms. CI 2pm/CO noon. Nonsmoking rms avail. **Amenities:** 🛏 👜 A/C, cable TV, dataport. Some units w/terraces. **Services:** ✕ 🚐 🖼 🍴 🍹 Car-rental desk. **Facilities:** 🛶 🚗 👜 1 restaurant, 1 bar (w/entertainment), volleyball, games rm, sauna, whirlpool, washer/dryer. Beautiful, large, indoor pool area features volleyball court, mini golf, and Ping-Pong. **Rates:** Peak (Jan–Mar/June–Aug) $39–$89 S; $56–$89 D. Children under age 18 stay free. Min stay special events. Lower rates off-season. Parking: Outdoor, free. AE, CB, DC, DISC, MC, V.

⊫⊫ Super 8 Motel Eveleth
US 53, PO Box 555, 55734; tel 218/744-1661 or toll free 800/800-8000; fax 218/744-4343. On US 53, yet set back from the road and quiet. Across the road from Hockey Hall of Fame. **Rooms:** 52 rms. CI 2pm/CO 11am. Nonsmoking rms avail. Very clean and secure rooms. **Amenities:** 🛏 👜 A/C,

cable TV w/movies, dataport. **Services:** 🍴 🍹 **Facilities:** 🛶 🚗 [25] 👜 Sauna, whirlpool, washer/dryer. **Rates (CP):** Peak (Nov–Mar/June–Aug) $46–$51 S; $50–$55 D. Extra person $4. Children under age 12 stay free. Lower rates off-season. Parking: Outdoor, free. Lots of golf, dinner, casino, and skiing packages avail. AE, CB, DC, DISC, MC, V.

Fairmont

Seat of Martin County, in southern Minnesota. This city near the Iowa border is in the vicinity of several small lakes. **Information:** Fairmont Convention & Visitors Bureau, PO Box 976, Fairmont, 56031-0976 (tel 507/235-8585 or toll free 800/657-3280).

HOTEL 🏛

⊫⊫⊫ Holiday Inn
I-90 at MN 15, PO Box 922, 56031; tel 507/281-4771 or toll free 800/HOLIDAY; fax 507/238-9371. Exit 102 off I-90. One of three motels (Super 8 and Comfort Inn are the other two) that seem to work as one. Of the three, this one provides the most services. **Rooms:** 105 rms and stes. CI 2pm/CO noon. Nonsmoking rms avail. Rooms are spacious and nicely decorated. **Amenities:** 🛏 👜 A/C, cable TV. Some units w/whirlpools. **Services:** ✕ 🚐 🖼 🍴 🍹 Dry cleaning/laundry service Mon–Fri. **Facilities:** 🛶 🚗 👜 [500] 🍴 1 restaurant, 1 bar, games rm, sauna, whirlpool, washer/dryer. Kids under 18 eat free. **Rates:** $58–$67 S; $68–$77 D; $90–$163 ste. Extra person $10. Children under age 18 stay free. Parking: Outdoor, free. AE, CB, DC, DISC, JCB, MC, V.

MOTEL

⊫⊫ Super 8 Motel
MN 15 at I-90, 56031; tel 507/238-9444 or toll free 800/800-8000. Exit 102 off I-90. Three motels at this central location (Super 8, Holiday Inn, and Comfort Inn) are under the same management. **Rooms:** 47 rms. CI 2pm/CO noon. Nonsmoking rms avail. **Amenities:** 🛏 👜 A/C, cable TV. **Services:** 🚐 🖼 🍴 🍹 **Facilities:** 👜 Washer/dryer. **Rates (CP):** $42–$45 S; $51–$54 D. Extra person $5. Children under age 12 stay free. Parking: Outdoor, free. AE, CB, DC, DISC, JCB, MC, V.

Faribault

Seat of Rice County. Settled in 1826 by French fur trader Alexander Faribault, this southern Minnesota town is now the headquarters of Faribault Woolen Mill. Many of the buildings here are listed on the National Register of Historic Places. **Information:** Faribault Area Chamber of Commerce, 530 Wilson Ave, PO Box 434, Faribault, 55021 (tel 507/334-4381).

MOTELS

≋≋ Select Inn

State Rd 60 W, 55021; tel 507/334-2051 or toll free 800/641-1000; fax 507/334-2051. Exit MN 60 off I-35. Popular stopover for truckers that's located next to head of Sakatah Singing Hills Trail, a 50-mile trail that follows MN 60 on the old Chicago-Great Western railroad bed. Nice outdoor deck faces wooded area. **Rooms:** 67 rms. CI 3pm/CO 11am. Nonsmoking rms avail. Rooms in back of facility face area where parked semitrailers idle all night. **Amenities:** 🛅 A/C, satel TV w/movies. **Services:** 🛏️ 🐕 Deposit of $25 required for pets. **Facilities:** 🚗 🏃 🎱 ⛹️ Games rm. Pool table. **Rates (CP):** $33–$38 S; $38–$53 D. Children under age 13 stay free. Parking: Outdoor, free. AARP and corporate discounts. AE, DISC, MC, V.

≋≋ Super 8 Motel

2509 N Lyndale Ave, 55021; tel 507/334-1634 or toll free 800/800-8000. US 60. Comfortable, clean. Pool table off lobby. Located near National Guard Armory. **Rooms:** 34 rms and stes. CI open/CO 11am. Nonsmoking rms avail. **Amenities:** 🛅 A/C, satel TV w/movies, VCR. 1 unit w/minibar. **Services:** 🛏️ **Facilities:** 🏃 **Rates:** Peak (May–Sept) $35–$38 S; $47–$50 D; $49–$69 ste. Children under age 12 stay free. Lower rates off-season. Parking: Outdoor, free. AE, CB, DC, DISC, EC, ER, JCB, MC, V.

RESTAURANTS

Lavender Inn

2424 Lyndale Ave; tel 507/334-3500. **American.** Each of the three dining rooms at this steak and seafood place seats about 100. Heads of stuffed animals protrude from the walls. Monthly fish specials (like walleye) offered. Large bar area, and art gallery and craft shop attached (with cards, jewelry, wildlife paintings, lamps, clocks). **FYI:** Reservations accepted. Children's menu. **Open:** 11am–10pm. **Prices:** Main courses $11–$20. AE, CB, DC, DISC, MC, V. 💟

Macnamara's Pub

429 Central Ave; tel 507/334-0074. **Burgers/Pub.** Mainly pub fare: fish fry, some Mexican-style standards, daily specials. **FYI:** Reservations not accepted. Deejay. **Open:** Mon–Sat 4pm–1am. **Prices:** Main courses $5–$8. MC, V. ⛹️

ATTRACTIONS

Rice Co Museum of History

1814 NW 2nd Ave; tel 507/332-2121. The Native American, fur-trading, and pioneer-era history of Rice County is illustrated via historical displays, a genealogical research center, and an audiovisual presentation room. The grounds are also home to an 1856 log cabin, the Holy Innocents Episcopal Church (1869), and a restored one-room schoolhouse. Harvest Hall and Heritage Hall contain agricultural displays. **Open:** Mon–Fri 9am–4pm, Sat–Sun 1–4pm. $

Alexander Faribault House

Tel 507/334-7913. Built in 1853 for the town's founder and namesake. The Fairbault mansion is one of the oldest existing buildings in the state, and now includes period furnishings and a museum of Native American artifacts. **Open:** May–Oct, daily 1–5pm. $

Fergus Falls

Seat of Otter Tail County, in west-central part of state. Founded in 1856, this quaint town on the banks of the Otter Tail River has five lakes within its city limits. Riverwalk, five shady blocks of stores, is located downtown. **Information:** Fergus Falls Area Chamber of Commerce, 202 S Court St, Fergus Falls, 56537 (tel 218/736-6951).

MOTELS

≋≋ Comfort Inn

425 Western Ave, 56537; tel 800/221-2222 or toll free 800/228-5150. Opened in 1993, motel is just off interstate but set far back—away from traffic noise. **Rooms:** 35 rms and stes. CI 2pm/CO 11am. Nonsmoking rms avail. Rooms feel very homey, yet are modern. **Amenities:** 🛅 🌀 A/C, cable TV w/movies. Some units w/whirlpools. **Services:** 🚐 🛏️ **Facilities:** ⛹️ Whirlpool, washer/dryer. **Rates (CP):** Peak (May–Sept) $39–$59 S; $49–$69 D; $69–$99 ste. Children under age 18 stay free. Lower rates off-season. Parking: Outdoor, free. AE, CB, DC, DISC, ER, JCB, MC, V.

≋≋ Days Inn

610 Western Ave, 56537; tel 218/739-3311 or toll free 800/329-7466. Exit 54 off I-94. Exterior and interior in good shape, but not special. **Rooms:** 57 rms and stes. CI 2pm/CO 11am. Nonsmoking rms avail. **Amenities:** 🛅 A/C, cable TV w/movies, voice mail. 1 unit w/whirlpool. **Services:** 🚐 🛏️ **Facilities:** 🚗 🎱 ⛹️ Games rm, whirlpool, washer/dryer. **Rates (CP):** Peak (May–Oct) $37–$41 S; $47 D; $55–$75 ste. Extra person $3. Children under age 12 stay free. Lower rates off-season. Parking: Outdoor, free. AE, CB, DC, DISC, JCB, MC, V.

≋ Super 8 Motel

2454 College Way, 56537; tel 218/739-3261 or toll free 800/800-8000. This older building is in decent condition, but rooms need a face-lift. **Rooms:** 32 rms. CI 1pm/CO 11am. Nonsmoking rms avail. **Amenities:** 🛅 A/C, cable TV w/movies. **Services:** 🛏️ **Facilities:** ⛹️ **Rates (CP):** Peak (Apr–Sept) $37 S; $46 D. Extra person $2. Children under age 12 stay free. Lower rates off-season. Parking: Outdoor, free. AE, CB, DC, DISC, MC, V.

Glenwood

This town on Lake Minnewaska is the center for Pope County's summer activities. Fish in various stages of growth may be seen at DNR Fisheries, where stock is grown for a four-county area. **Information:** Glenwood Area Chamber of Commerce, 137 E Minnesota Ave, Glenwood, 56334 (tel 320/634-3636 or toll free 800/782-9937).

MOTEL

≣≣ Hi-View Motel
255 MN 55 N, 56334; tel 320/634-4541. 1 mi NE on MN 55. Small, plain, one-story building on top of a hill, about five minutes from downtown. Minimally adequate. **Rooms:** 12 rms. CI 5pm/CO 11am. Rooms are small and dark; there is no separation for smoking and nonsmoking areas. All rooms look out on a lake. **Amenities:** A/C, cable TV w/movies. **Services:** No regular airport service but will provide rides if needed. **Facilities:** Washer/dryer. **Rates:** $26–$36 S; $36–$46 D. Extra person $7. Parking: Outdoor, free. DISC, MC, V.

Grand Marais

Seat of Cook County in northeast corner of state. Located 110 miles northeast of Duluth on the north shore of Lake Superior, the tiny town is a final destination as well as a gateway to Superior National Forest and Boundary Waters Canoe Area Wilderness. The famous Gunflint Trail begins right in the middle of town. **Information:** Grand Marais Chamber of Commerce, 15 N Broadway, PO Box 1048, Grand Marais, 55604 (tel 218/387-2524 or toll free 800/622-4014).

HOTELS

≣≣ Best Western Superior Inn & Suites
MN 61, 55604; tel 218/387-2240 or toll free 800/842-8439; fax 218/387-2244. Located right on the harbor, near the Superior Hiking Trail, golf, skiing, and downtown shops. **Rooms:** 50 rms and stes. Executive level. CI 2pm/CO 11am. Nonsmoking rms avail. Rooms are spacious and have lots of seating. All have lakefront views. **Amenities:** Cable TV w/movies, refrig. No A/C. Some units w/terraces, some w/fireplaces, some w/whirlpools. About half of the rooms have air conditioning. **Services:** **Facilities:** 1 beach (lake shore), whirlpool, washer/dryer. **Rates (CP):** Peak (June 16–Oct 22) $35–$99 S; $45–$99 D; $59–$119 ste. Extra person $10. Children under age 2 stay free. Min stay wknds. Lower rates off-season. Parking: Outdoor, free. AE, CB, DC, DISC, ER, MC, V.

≣≣ Econo Lodge
MN 61, PO Box 667, 55604; tel 218/387-2547 or toll free 800/247-6020. Convenient to downtown Grand Marais shops and restaurants. Ideal for business travelers. **Rooms:** 51 rms and stes. CI 3pm/CO 11am. Nonsmoking rms avail. Some rooms have lake view. **Amenities:** A/C, cable TV w/movies, refrig, dataport. Some units w/whirlpools.

Services: **Facilities:** Sauna, whirlpool. **Rates:** Peak (late Apr–Oct) $42–$79 S; $42–$89 D; $74–$138 ste. Extra person $8. Children under age 12 stay free. Min stay special events. Lower rates off-season. Parking: Outdoor, free. AE, DC, DISC, MC, V.

MOTELS

≣≣ Nelson's Traveler's Rest Cabins & Motel
MN 61, 55604; tel 218/387-1464 or toll free 800/249-1285. Family-run establishment close to Grand Marais, yet secluded in the woods with a view of Lake Superior. Indoor municipal pool nearby. Very economical for the amount of space provided—great for families. **Rooms:** 2 rms; 9 cottages/villas. CI 2:30pm/CO 10am. Lakeside cabins and motel rooms. **Amenities:** Cable TV w/movies, refrig. No A/C or phone. Some units w/terraces, some w/fireplaces. **Services:** **Facilities:** 1 beach (lake shore), basketball, volleyball, playground. Nice playground and sand play area. **Rates:** $42–$50 S or D; $42–$69 cottage/villa. Extra person $9. Parking: Outdoor, free. Closed Nov–Apr. DISC, MC, V.

≣ Sandgren Motel
MN 61, PO Box 1056, 55604; tel 218/387-2975 or toll free 800/796-2975. Small, family-owned motel. Reasonable rates. **Rooms:** 9 rms; 1 cottage/villa. CI 2pm/CO 10:30am. No smoking. Rooms are fairly small, but clean. Decor and layout are slightly different in each room. **Amenities:** Cable TV. No A/C or phone. **Services:** **Facilities:** **Rates:** $44–$52 S; $50–$75 D; $65–$75 cottage/villa. Extra person $5. Min stay special events. Parking: Outdoor, free. DISC, MC, V.

≣≣ Shoreline
20 S Broadway, 55604; tel 218/387-2633 or toll free 800/247-6020; fax 218/387-2633. 1 block S of US 61. This restored, 40-year-old building has a lovely beachside deck overlooking Lake Superior. Located in downtown Grand Marais. **Rooms:** 30 rms. CI 2pm/CO 11am. Nonsmoking rms avail. **Amenities:** Cable TV w/movies, refrig. No A/C. **Services:** Children's program. **Facilities:** 1 beach (lake shore). **Rates (CP):** Peak (July–Aug) $48–$95 S; $52–$95 D. Extra person $8. Children under age 12 stay free. Min stay special events. Lower rates off-season. Parking: Outdoor, free. AE, CB, DC, DISC, EC, MC, V.

≣≣ Super 8 Motel
MN 61, 55604; tel 218/387-2448 or toll free 800/800-8000; fax 218/387-2448. Clean, reasonable hotel for family travelers. Hotel consists of older and newer buildings. **Rooms:** 35 rms. Executive level. CI 2pm/CO 11am. Nonsmoking rms avail. Newer rooms are more spacious; however, both are clean and quiet. **Amenities:** A/C, cable TV w/movies, refrig, dataport. **Services:** **Facilities:** Sauna, whirlpool. **Rates (CP):** Peak (July–Oct) $43–$90 S; $50–$90 D. Extra person $8. Children under age 12 stay free. Min stay special events. Lower rates off-season. Parking: Outdoor, free. AE, DISC, MC, V.

≣≣ Tomteboda Motel

1800 W MN 61, 55604; tel 218/387-1585 or toll free 800/622-2622. Economical motel offers easy access to Superior Hiking Trail and both cross-country and downhill skiing. Good for families on a budget. **Rooms:** 17 rms; 2 cottages/villas. CI open/CO 10am. Nonsmoking rms avail. **Amenities:** ⬛ ⬛ A/C, cable TV w/movies, refrig. All units w/fireplaces, all w/whirlpools. **Services:** ⬛ ⬛ **Facilities:** ⬛ ⬛ ⬛ Playground. **Rates:** Peak (June–Sept) $30–$55 S or D; $75 cottage/villa. Min stay peak. Lower rates off-season. Parking: Outdoor, free. AE, DC, DISC, MC, V.

LODGES

UNRATED Bearskin Lodge

275 Gunflint Trail, 55604; tel 218/388-2292 or toll free 800/388-4170; fax 218/388-4410. Log and wood lodge, with series of wood cabins, located on beautiful, quiet Bearskin Lake. **Rooms:** 11 cottages/villas. CI 4pm/CO 10am. Nonsmoking rms avail. **Amenities:** ⬛ Refrig. No A/C, phone, or TV. All units w/terraces, all w/fireplaces, 1 w/whirlpool. **Services:** ⬛ ⬛ Children's program. **Facilities:** ⬛ ⬛ ⬛ ⬛ ⬛ ⬛ ⬛ 1 restaurant (dinner only), 1 beach (lake shore), volleyball, games rm, snorkeling, sauna, whirlpool, washer/dryer. Groomed trails for cross-country skiing and snowshoeing; some lighted for night skiing. In summer, have lunch on the patio overlooking the lake. **Rates:** Peak (June–Aug/Christmas–Mar) $100–$140 effic; $83–$198 cottage/villa. Children under age 3 stay free. Min stay peak. Lower rates off-season. Parking: Outdoor, free. DISC, MC, V.

≣≣≣ Gunflint Lodge

750 Gunflint Trail, 55604; tel 218/388-2294 or toll free 800/328-3325; fax 218/388-9429. 10 acres. Gorgeous north woods property on Bearskin Lake, just across from Canadian border. **Rooms:** 23 cottages/villas. CI 2pm/CO 11am. Comfortable, one- to four-bedroom cabins. **Amenities:** ⬛ Refrig, VCR, CD/tape player. No A/C, phone, or TV. Some units w/terraces, all w/fireplaces, some w/whirlpools. Many cabins have saunas. **Services:** ⬛ ⬛ ⬛ ⬛ Social director, masseur, children's program, babysitting. Extensive nature programs for children and adults. **Facilities:** ⬛ ⬛ ⬛ ⬛ ⬛ 1 restaurant, 1 beach (lake shore), snorkeling, playground. **Rates:** Peak (mid-June–mid-Oct/Christmas–late Mar) $199–$239 cottage/villa. Children under age 4 stay free. Min stay. Lower rates off-season. Parking: Outdoor, free. AE, DC, DISC, MC, V.

≣≣ Hungry Jack Lodge & Campground

Gunflint Trail Box 475, 55604; tel 218/388-2265 or toll free 800/338-1566. Secluded property on Hungry Jack Lake with rustic cabins and an owner/innkeeper who loves to tell stories. Great spot for lake canoeing, boating, and fishing. **Rooms:** 12 cottages/villas. CI 3pm/CO 10am. Nonsmoking rms avail. Simple cabins. **Amenities:** Refrig. No A/C, phone, or TV. All units w/terraces, some w/fireplaces. Cabins have cooking facilities, plus decks, grills, and picnic tables outside.

Services: ⬛ ⬛ ⬛ ⬛ Babysitting. **Facilities:** ⬛ ⬛ ⬛ ⬛ ⬛ ⬛ ⬛ ⬛ ⬛ 1 restaurant, 1 bar, 1 beach (lake shore), games rm, lawn games, snorkeling, sauna, playground. **Rates:** Peak (May–Oct) $630 cottage/villa. Min stay. Lower rates off-season. Parking: Outdoor, free. Rates are weekly. AE, DISC, MC, V.

≣≣≣ Naniboujou Lodge

HC80, Box 505, 55604; tel 218/387-2688; fax 218/387-2688. This beautifully restored lodge with a large Lake Superior beach was built in the 1920s as an exclusive club, whose members included Babe Ruth and Jack Dempsey. Great hiking and fishing in CR Magney State Park across the street. **Rooms:** 24 rms. Executive level. CI 2pm/CO 10:30am. No smoking. Small, lovely rooms. **Amenities:** No A/C, phone, or TV. Some units w/fireplaces. **Services:** ⬛ Babysitting. June–Oct, high tea 3–5pm. **Facilities:** ⬛ ⬛ 1 restaurant, 1 beach (lake shore), basketball, volleyball, lawn games. Excellent restaurant with massive native stone fireplace open to public. Extensive Sun brunch. **Rates:** $50–$85 S; $65–$85 D. Extra person $10. Children under age 3 stay free. AP rates avail. Parking: Outdoor, free. Closed mid-Oct–Dec 26/mid-Mar–May 17. DISC, MC, V.

≣≣ NorWester Lodge

550 Gunflint Trail, 55604; tel 218/388-2252 or toll free 800/992-4386. 55 acres. Located on shore of Poplar Lake, offering lots of good fishing and boating. Owned by same family since 1930s. **Rooms:** 10 cottages/villas. CI 2pm/CO 10am. No smoking. Rustic cabins. **Amenities:** ⬛ Refrig. No A/C, phone, or TV. All units w/terraces, all w/fireplaces. **Services:** ⬛ ⬛ ⬛ Babysitting. VCRs available for rent. **Facilities:** ⬛ ⬛ ⬛ ⬛ ⬛ ⬛ 1 restaurant (lunch and dinner only), 1 beach (lake shore), basketball, volleyball, games rm, lawn games, snorkeling, whirlpool, playground, washer/dryer. **Rates:** Peak (July–Aug/Christmas–mid-Feb) $65–$165 cottage/villa. Extra person $10–$25. Min stay. Lower rates off-season. AP and MAP rates avail. Parking: Outdoor, free. No charge for child if family brings own crib. Five-night stay required during high season; two-night stay required during regular season. DISC, MC, V.

RESTAURANT 𝍢

Blue Water Cafe

Wisconsin St and 1st Ave W; tel 218/387-1597. **American.** Convenient to several hiking trails and ski runs, this typical American diner cheerfully serves up omelettes, burgers, sandwiches, and broasted chicken to locals and tourists alike. The upstairs dining room has a lovely view of Lake Superior. **FYI:** Reservations not accepted. Children's menu. No liquor license. **Open:** Peak (June–Aug) daily 6am–8pm. **Prices:** Main courses $4–$11. MC, V. ⬛ ⬛ ⬛

Grand Portage National Monument

This heavily wooded area in northern Minnesota was named for the nine-mile "portage road" along Lake Superior. Native Americans—and later, French fur trappers—would carry their canoes along this trail as they went from Lake Superior to the inland lakes along the US/Canadian border. (Today, hikers and off-road bikers make their way along the moss-covered rocks of the trail.) The area was long a center of trading between the voyageurs and the natives, with goods from all over North America trading hands here. At Grand Portage, a 1788 fur-trading post has been reconstructed to its original form and is open for tours. On the grounds of the fort, artisans create authentic crafts ranging from clothing to Chippewa-style canoes. A Great Hall houses exhibits and an audiovisual program. Entrance to the monument is from US 61, which also offers a panoramic drive along Lake Superior. Picnic area, primitive camping. Grand Portage is also a departure point for passenger ferry service to **Isle Royale National Park** in Michigan. For more information contact Grand Portage National Monument, Box 668, Grand Marais, MN 55604 (tel 218/387-2788).

Grand Rapids

Seat of Itasca County, in northern Minnesota. Named for a stretch of rapids that blocked further traffic up the Mississippi, this town was once a center of mining and logging but now tourism is taking over as the prime industry. Judy Garland was born here in 1922, and the town holds a Judy Garland Festival every June. **Information:** Grand Rapids Area Convention & Visitors Bureau, 1 NW 3rd St, Grand Rapids, 55744 (tel 218/326-9607).

HOTELS 🏨

≡≡ Best Western Rainbow Inn

1300 US 169, 55744; tel 218/326-9655 or toll free 800/528-1234; fax 218/326-9651. Older though well-maintained hotel is not particularly attractive from the outside, but interior furnishings are clean and modern. Near airport, shopping, Taconite Trail, and skiing. **Rooms:** 80 rms and stes. CI 1pm/CO noon. Nonsmoking rms avail. **Amenities:** 🛆 A/C, cable TV w/movies. **Services:** ✗ 🚗 🖼 ⌂ ⌣ **Facilities:** 🛆 🏊 🖼 🖳 1 restaurant, 1 bar (w/entertainment), spa, sauna, steam rm, whirlpool. **Rates:** $68 S or D; $75 ste. Children under age 12 stay free. Parking: Outdoor, free. AE, CB, DC, DISC, EC, MC, V.

≡≡≡ Sawmill Inn

2301 Pokegama Ave S, 55744; tel 218/326-8501 or toll free 800/235-6455; fax 218/326-1039. Large hotel serves families and businesses. Decor is patterned after north woods log construction. Great meeting rooms with lots of wood offer excellent space for wedding receptions, reunions, conventions, and parties. **Rooms:** 124 rms and stes. CI 2pm/CO noon. Nonsmoking rms avail. **Amenities:** 🛆 🖳 A/C, cable TV w/movies. **Services:** ✗ 🚗 🖼 ⌂ ⌣ Babysitting. **Facilities:** 🛆 🖼 🏊 🖳 1 restaurant, 1 bar (w/entertainment), games rm, sauna, whirlpool. Beautiful indoor pool area. **Rates:** $51–$63 S or D; $84–$94 ste. Extra person $4. Children under age 13 stay free. AP and MAP rates avail. Parking: Outdoor, free. AE, DC, DISC, MC, V.

MOTELS

≡≡≡ Country Inn by Carlson

2601 US 169, 55744; tel 218/327-4960 or toll free 800/456-4000; fax 218/327-4964. Newer chain motel. Very clean. Next door to Judy Garland birthplace and close to cross-country skiing and Forest History Center. **Rooms:** 46 rms. CI 2pm/CO noon. Nonsmoking rms avail. **Amenities:** 🛆 🖳 A/C, cable TV w/movies. **Services:** 🚗 🖼 ⌂ ⌣ Babysitting. Very guest-conscious. **Facilities:** 🛆 🏊 🖳 Whirlpool, washer/dryer. **Rates (CP):** Peak (June–Sept) $59–$69 S or D. Extra person $5. Children under age 18 stay free. Lower rates off-season. Parking: Outdoor, free. AE, CB, DC, DISC, MC, V.

≡ Days Inn

311 E US 2, 55744; tel 218/326-3457 or toll free 800/DAYS-INN; fax 218/326-3795. Privately owned for 18 years, less than a mile from Grand Rapids's central business district. **Rooms:** 34 rms. CI 2pm/CO 11am. Nonsmoking rms avail. **Amenities:** 🛆 A/C, cable TV w/movies. **Services:** 🚗 🖼 ⌂ ⌣ Babysitting. Auto plug-ins and snowmobile rentals in winter. Pets allowed in smoking rooms only. **Facilities:** 🏊 🖼 🖳 Playground. **Rates:** Peak (May–Oct) $45–$60 S; $68–$74 D. Extra person $4. Children under age 12 stay free. Lower rates off-season. Parking: Outdoor, free. AE, CB, DC, DISC, MC, V.

≡ Pine Grove Motel

1420 NW 4th St, 55744; tel 218/326-9674. Clean, inexpensive motel in midst of downtown Grand Rapids. Minimal decor and not a lot of extra facilities. **Rooms:** 40 rms and effic. CI 3pm/CO 11am. Cozy, comfortable rooms. **Amenities:** 🛆 A/C, cable TV w/movies. **Services:** ⌂ ⌣ **Rates (CP):** $40–$45 S or D; $45–$50 effic. Extra person $10. Children under age 10 stay free. Parking: Outdoor, free. AE, DISC, MC, V.

≡≡ Super 8 Motel

MN 169 S, PO Box 335, 55744; tel 218/327-1108 or toll free 800/800-8000; fax 218/327-1108. Clean, comfortable, two-story hotel on main highway of Grand Rapids. **Rooms:** 58 rms. CI 1pm/CO 11am. Nonsmoking rms avail. **Amenities:** 🛆 🖳 A/C, cable TV w/movies. **Services:** ⌂ **Facilities:** 🏊 🖳 Washer/dryer. **Rates (CP):** Peak (June–Sept) $46–$54 S or D. Children under age 12 stay free. Lower rates off-season. Parking: Outdoor, free. AE, CB, DC, DISC, MC, V.

RESTAURANT

Forest Lake Restaurant & Lounge

1201 4th St NW; tel 218/326-3423. On US 2 W. **American.** This establishment actually consists of two restaurants: the upstairs is slightly more casual, with knotty-pine paneling and bearskin rugs on the wall; the downstairs is a slightly more formal steak house. Both offer a variety of entrees from a variety of cuisines, from scrod and ribs to fettuccine and chimichangas. Homemade bread. **FYI:** Reservations recommended. Children's menu. **Open:** Peak (June–Oct) Mon–Sat 6am–9pm, Sun 7am–9pm. **Prices:** Main courses $4–$18. AE, CB, DC, DISC, MC, V. &

ATTRACTION

Central School

Jct MN 2/US 169; tel 218/326-6431. Now home to the Itasca County Historical Society and Museum, this restored 1895 schoolhouse also contains a Judy Garland Exhibit featuring memorabilia relating to the movie star's life. (Garland's parents operated a Grand Rapids vaudeville house, and she lived here as an infant.) Antiques, shops, and a restaurant are also on the premises. **Open:** Peak (Mem Day–Labor Day) Mon–Sat 9am–5pm. Reduced hours off-season. **$**

Granite Falls

ATTRACTIONS

Yellow Medicine County Historical Museum

MN 67; tel 320/564-4479 or 564-2166. Local and state history is narrated through a collection of pioneer and Native American artifacts. Among the exhibits are two log cabins and a bandstand, as well as a four billion year old rock outcropping. **Open:** May–Oct, Tues–Fri 11am–3pm, Sat–Sun noon–4pm. **Free**

Swensson Farm Museum

Cty Rd 6, Montevideo; tel 320/269-7636. Housed on the estate of Olof Swensson, a master builder and designer who settled here in 1869. Structures open for public tours include a large timber-framed 1890s barn, a 22-room wood-frame house, and the remnants of a small grist mill; Another building on the site houses farm artifacts from the period such as a walking plow, a walk-behind cultivator, a fanning mill, a two-seater buggy, and corn picker. Early tractors are also on display. **Open:** Mem Day–Labor Day, Sun 1–5pm. **$**

Hastings

Seat of Dakota County, in southeast part of state. Founded in 1850 at the junction of the St Croix and Vermillion rivers as they flow into the Mississippi, the city's riverfront downtown looks much as it did a century ago. Lock and Dam No 2, just north of town, includes an observation platform for viewing barges as they pass through on their way to St Paul. **Information:** Hastings Area Chamber of Commerce, 119 W 2nd St, #201, Hastings, 55033 (tel 612/437-6775).

MOTELS

AmericInn

2400 Vermillion St, 55033; tel 612/437-8877 or toll free 800/634-3444; fax 612/437-8184. On US 61 on the S side of town. Newer hotel. Large lobby has fireplace, sofas, chairs, and overhead fan. **Rooms:** 27 rms and stes. CI noon/CO 11am. Nonsmoking rms avail. **Amenities:** A/C, cable TV w/movies, dataport. Mini-refrigerators available for rent. Portable grab bar for bath available at front desk. **Services:** Babysitting. **Facilities:** Washer/dryer. **Rates (CP):** Peak (May–Oct) $44 S; $48 D; $70 ste. Extra person $6. Children under age 12 stay free. Lower rates off-season. Parking: Outdoor, free. AE, CB, DC, DISC, EC, JCB, MC, V.

UNRATED Hastings Inn

1520 Vermillion St, 55033; tel 612/437-3155; fax 612/437-3530. At 15th St. All rooms face parking lot. **Rooms:** 44 rms and effic. CI 2pm/CO 11am. Nonsmoking rms avail. **Amenities:** A/C, cable TV w/movies, refrig. **Services:** **Facilities:** Games rm, sauna, whirlpool, washer/dryer. **Rates (CP):** Peak (May–Oct) $34–$44 S; $39–$49 D; $60–$75 effic. Extra person $5–$8. Children under age 12 stay free. Lower rates off-season. Parking: Outdoor, free. Discount of 10% for registering 10 or more rooms. AE, CB, DC, DISC, EC, JCB, MC, V.

Super 8 Motel

2450 Vermillion St, 55033; tel 612/438-8888 or toll free 800/800-8000; fax 612/438-8888. New building with 18 units added in 1992. Clean and well kept. **Rooms:** 50 rms and stes. CI 3pm/CO 11am. Nonsmoking rms avail. **Amenities:** A/C, satel TV w/movies. 1 unit w/whirlpool. **Services:** **Facilities:** Whirlpool, washer/dryer. Free use of Supreme Gym & Fitness Club, a five-minute drive away. Locked spa area accessible only by separate key at front desk—you need to reserve ahead of time. **Rates: Rates (CP):** Peak (May–mid-Oct) $43–$46 S; $53–$56 D; $73–$91 ste. Extra person $6. Children under age 12 stay free. Lower rates off-season. Parking: Outdoor, free. AE, CB, DC, DISC, EC, JCB, MC, V.

RESTAURANT

Mississippi Belle

101 E 2nd St; tel 612/437-4814. **Seafood/Steak.** Built in 1850 as a trading post by Henry G Bailly, this setting had such varied incarnations as the city's first hotel, a church, a tavern, and a courthouse before becoming a restaurant. New chef-owner Erich Schummacher, Swiss-born, has introduced tableside cooking, seasonal beers from regional breweries, and wine promotions. Steak, lobster, frogs' legs, and rib eye steak are among the specialties. **FYI:** Reservations recom-

mended. Children's menu. **Open:** Peak (Sept–Oct) lunch Mon–Sat 11am–2:30pm, Sun 11:30am–2:30pm; dinner Mon–Sat 4:30–10pm, Sun 2:30–9pm. **Prices:** Main courses $10–$29. AE, DISC, MC, V. ♥ ■ ▨ ⅊

Hibbing

Located in the heart of the Mesabi Iron Range. Hibbing was the site of the world's largest open pit iron ore mine; more than three miles long, two miles wide, and 535 feet deep, it produced more than a quarter of the nation's iron ore during World War II. Childhood home of singer Bob Dylan and birthplace of baseball great Roger Maris. **Information:** Hibbing Area Chamber of Commerce, 211 E Howard St, PO Box 727, Hibbing, 55746-1763 (tel 218/262-3895 or toll free 800/4-HIBBING).

ATTRACTION 📷

Ironworld Discovery Center
Hwy 169, Chisholm; tel 218/254-3321 or toll free 800/372-6437. Located 5 mi N of Hibbing. Costumed guides lead tours through a variety of regional historical settings, including an Ojibwe camp, a French voyageur's fur post, and a ride on a vintage electric trolley past the historic Glen Godffrey Open Pit Mine. A hands-on interpretive center presents exhibits on the history of iron mining and the ethnic heritage of the region. Outdoor amphitheater features top performers during the summer. **Open:** June–Aug, Wed–Sun 10am–7pm, Mon–Tues 10am–5pm. **$$$**

Hinckley

Halfway point between the Twin Cities and Duluth. More than 400 people died when the entire town was destroyed by the Great Hinckley Fire of 1894.

MOTELS 🏨

▤▤ **Days Inn**
104 Grindstone Court, 55037; tel 320/384-7751 or toll free 800/559-8951; fax 320/384-6403. New, well-kept, attractive establishment, close to Grand Casino. **Rooms:** 69 rms, stes, and effic. CI 3pm/CO 11am. Nonsmoking rms avail. **Amenities:** 🛁 ⚙ A/C, cable TV. Some units w/whirlpools. **Services:** ✕ ⤸ **Facilities:** 🏋 👤 ⅊ Washer/dryer. **Rates (CP):** Peak (June–Aug) $50–$65 S or D; $125–$135 ste; $55–$65 effic. Extra person $5. Children under age 17 stay free. Lower rates off-season. Parking: Outdoor, free. AE, DISC, MC, V.

▤▤ **Holiday Inn Express**
604 Weber Ave, 55037; tel 320/384-7171 or toll free 800/558-0612. Clean, neat, new facility, with minimal space outside. **Rooms:** 102 rms. CI 3pm/CO noon. Nonsmoking rms avail. **Amenities:** 🛁 ⚙ 📺 A/C, cable TV w/movies, refrig.

Some units w/whirlpools. **Services:** ✕ ⤸ Free shuttle service to Hinckley Grand Casino. **Facilities:** 🏋 👤 ⅊ Sauna, whirlpool, washer/dryer. **Rates (CP):** Peak (May–Sept) $47–$129 S or D. Extra person $10. Children under age 19 stay free. Min stay special events. Lower rates off-season. Parking: Outdoor, free. AE, CB, DC, DISC, MC, V.

RESTAURANTS 🍽

$ ★ **Cassidy's Gold Pine Restaurant**
I-35 and MN 48; tel 320/384-6129. **Regional American.** Rustic establishment with plenty of woodwork, well known to locals as a great bargain for the past 30 years. The popular salad bar features local produce and homemade dressings; other attractions are the soups and fresh breads and pastries. The restaurant caters to traveling families; breakfast served all day. **FYI:** Reservations accepted. Children's menu. Beer and wine only. **Open:** Daily 7am–10:30pm. **Prices:** Main courses $5–$14. AE, DC, DISC, MC, V. 👶 ⅊

★ **Marge's Cafe**
305 Old MN 61 S; tel 320/384-6209. **American.** Local hangout for the coffee-klatsch crowd, and a great place for breakfast: eggs, bacon, and pancakes. Burgers, fries, and chicken for lunch; specialties are hot pork and beef sandwiches with homemade gravy. Homemade soups include cream of chicken with wild rice. Less than a mile from Grand Casino, the cafe is a convenient stop after winning or losing. **FYI:** Reservations not accepted. Children's menu. No liquor license. **Open:** Mon–Fri 6am–4pm, Sat 6am–3pm. **Prices:** Lunch main courses $3–$5. No CC. 👶

ATTRACTION 📷

Hinckley Fire Museum
106 Old MN 61; tel 320/384-7338. In 1894 a massive fire destroyed six towns, including Hinckley. The local railroad depot was destroyed in the fire, but has since been rebuilt and now houses this museum. Logging and agricultural exhibits, period rooms, and local historical artifacts—as well as displays on the fire and its consequences—are shown. **Open:** May–Oct, daily 10am–5pm. **$**

International Falls

Seat of Koochiching County, in northern Minnesota. The falls that once rushed down the Rainy River have been harnessed to generate hydroelectric power for the region; the other main industry is paper production. Since 1903, the International Bridge has connected the Falls with Fort Francis, Ontario. **Information:** International Falls Area Chamber of Commerce, 200 4th St, PO Box 169, International Falls, 56649 (tel 218/283-9400 or toll free 800/FALLS-MN).

HOTEL

UNRATED Holiday Inn

1500 US 71, 56649; tel 218/283-4451 or toll free 800/331-4443; fax 218/283-3774. Large, chain hotel convenient to downtown International Falls and close to snowmobiling and fishing. **Rooms:** 126 rms and stes. CI 2pm/CO noon. Nonsmoking rms avail. **Amenities:** 🛏 🐧 A/C, cable TV w/movies, dataport. Some units w/whirlpools. **Services:** ✗ 🚐 ⛱ 🍴 🍷 Babysitting. **Facilities:** 🏂 💿 💻 ⅙ 1 restaurant, 1 bar (w/entertainment), games rm, sauna, whirlpool, washer/dryer. **Rates:** Peak (Dec–Mar/mid-May–mid-Sept) $55–$85 S or D; $95–$100 ste. Children under age 16 stay free. Lower rates off-season. Parking: Outdoor, free. Snowmobiling packages avail. AE, CB, DC, DISC, JCB, MC, V.

MOTEL

≣≣ Super 8 Motel

2326 US 53 Frontage Rd, 56649; tel 218/283-8811 or toll free 800/800-8000; fax 218/283-8880. Basic chain hotel located right off US 53. Near snowmobile trail and airport, five miles from Rainy Lake. Very reasonable rates for a restful night's sleep. **Rooms:** 53 rms. CI 1pm/CO 11am. Nonsmoking rms avail. Clean, comfortable rooms. **Amenities:** 🛏 A/C, cable TV w/movies. Some units w/whirlpools. **Services:** 🍷 🍴 **Facilities:** 🏂 💿 ⅙ Washer/dryer. **Rates:** Peak (May–Aug) $34–$39 S; $43–$47 D. Extra person $6. Children under age 12 stay free. Lower rates off-season. Parking: Outdoor, free. AE, CB, DC, DISC, MC, V.

LODGES

≣≣ Island View Lodge & Motel

Rte 8, PO Box 11, 55350; tel 218/286-3511 or toll free 800/777-7856; fax 218/286-5036. Rustic lodge on Rainy Lake popular with fishing families, cross-country skiers, and snowmobilers. **Rooms:** 9 rms; 12 cottages/villas. CI 3pm/CO 11am. Basic rooms and cabins. **Amenities:** 🛏 A/C, TV. Some units w/terraces, 1 w/fireplace. **Services:** 🚐 🍷 🍴 Babysitting. **Facilities:** ⚠ 💿 🏂 🖼 🏊 1 restaurant, 1 bar, 1 beach (lake shore), games rm, lawn games, playground, washer/dryer. Fishing boats available for rent. **Rates:** Peak (May–Oct) $47–$65 S or D; $95–$195 cottage/villa. Extra person $10. Children under age 12 stay free. Lower rates off-season. AP and MAP rates avail. Parking: Outdoor, free. AE, DISC, MC, V.

≣≣ Thunderbird Lodge and Motor Inn

MN 11 E, 55649; tel 218/286-3151 or toll free 800/351-5133; fax 218/286-3004. Wooden hotel and modern cabins situated on calm, huge Rainy Lake bordering Canada. **Rooms:** 15 rms; 10 cottages/villas. CI 3pm/CO 10am. **Amenities:** 🛏 A/C, cable TV w/movies. All units w/terraces. **Services:** ✗ 🚐 🍷 🍴 Babysitting. Pets allowed in cabins only. **Facilities:** ⚠ 💿 🏂 🍴² 🖼 💻 1 restaurant, 1 bar (w/entertainment). Houseboats, fishing boats, canoes, and

guide available for hire. **Rates:** $50–$75 S or D; $100–$165 cottage/villa. Extra person $6. Children under age 11 stay free. AP and MAP rates avail. Parking: Outdoor, free. Weekly rates avail. AE, DISC, MC, V.

RESTAURANT

Barney's

1323 3rd St; tel 218/283-3333. **American.** The decor is made to look like a typical living room, and the menu is equally homey, with lots of soups, salads, pizza, dinner entrees, daily specials, and desserts. **FYI:** Reservations accepted. Children's menu. Beer and wine only. **Open:** Daily 6am–10pm. **Prices:** Main courses $4–$12. MC, V. ⅙

ATTRACTIONS

Grand Mound History Center

MN 11; tel 218/285-3332. Located 17 mi E of International Falls at the junction of the Big Fork and Rainy Rivers, these prehistoric burial grounds are believed to be over 2,000 years old. The on-site History Center features exhibits of Native American artifacts and audiovisual presentations. Surrounding area offers picnic area, nature trails, and cross-country skiing. **Open:** Peak (May–Labor Day) Mon–Sat 10am–5pm, Sun noon–5pm. Reduced hours off-season. **$**

Smokey Bear Statue

3rd St and 6th Ave. A 26-foot-tall statue of the renowned fire fighting bear is the main attraction at this municipal park site. There's also a 22-foot-tall giant thermometer near the entrance. **Open:** Daily sunrise–sunset. **Free**

Jackson

Seat of Jackson County, in southern Minnesota. Founded in 1856 along the tree-lined Des Moines River, Jackson is now a center of farm machinery production and agriculture. **Information:** Jackson Area Chamber of Commerce, 1000 US, 71 N, Jackson, 56143 (tel 507/847-3867).

ATTRACTION

Fort Belmont

Jct Cty Rd 34/US 71; tel 507/847-5840. A re-creation of an 1864 civilian fort built by Norwegian settlers to fend off hostile Sioux. Items on display include a replica of a waterwheel-operated flour mill, the original Belmont Log chapel, and a sod house. A museum (located within the stockade) houses antique cars, pioneer kitchen utensils, and one of the oldest pinball machines in America. **Open:** Mem Day–Labor Day, Mon–Sat 9am–6pm, Sun noon–5pm. **$**

Lake Itasca

LODGE 🛄

≣≣ Douglas Lodge

Park R, 56460; tel 218/266-2122 or toll free 800/246-2267. In Itasca State Park. Use E entrance, go 1¼ mi. This is a beautiful, historic alternative for those who want to spend time in Itasca State Park, but do not want to camp. The lodge itself is a log cabin structure built in 1903; inside it is renovated and quite comfortable. It features meeting rooms and a dining room as well as lodging. **Rooms:** 25 rms and stes; 23 cottages/villas. CI 4pm/CO 11am. No smoking. Individual log cabins available; some have screened-in porches with views of Lake Itasca. The Clubhouse is a large, 10-bedroom facility with central lobby and fireplace that rents as a single unit—perfect for large family gatherings. **Amenities:** No A/C, phone, or TV. Some units w/terraces, some w/fireplaces. **Services:** 🛎 Children's program. **Facilities:** 🚲 🛦 🗂 🎣 🛶 🍴 1 restaurant, 1 beach (lake shore), volleyball, playground. **Rates:** $36–$65 S or D; $65 ste; $65–$115 cottage/villa. Extra person $10. Children under age 12 stay free. AP and MAP rates avail. Parking: Outdoor, free. No charge for meeting rooms for registered guests. Closed mid-Oct–late May. AE, DISC, MC, V.

ATTRACTION 📷

Lake Itasca State Park

MN 200; tel 218/266-2114. Minnesota's oldest state park contains more than a quarter of the old-growth pine in the state. This is also the location of the Mississippi headwaters, where you can wade across the mighty river in just a dozen steps. (The river picks up water from Lake Itasca and many other Minnesota lakes before making its 2,500-mile trip south to the Gulf of Mexico). Popular activities in the park include boating, fishing and swimming in Lake Itasca, and canoeing near the headwaters. There's also an 11-mile wilderness drive, two dozen hiking trails (open in winter for cross-country skiing), and several picnic areas and campgrounds. **Open:** Daily 8am–10pm. $

Lakeville

A small city 20 miles south of Minneapolis, midway between the Minnesota and Mississippi Rivers. **Information:** Lakeville Chamber of Commerce, 8790 207th St, #201, PO Box 12, Lakeville, 55044-0012 (tel 612/469-2020).

MOTELS 🛄

≣≣ Friendly Host Inn At Lakeville

17296 I-35, 55046; tel 612/435-7191 or toll free 800/341-8000. Exit 85 off MN 50. Petunia box in front of entryway, by canopy. **Rooms:** 48 rms and effic. CI 2pm/CO 11am. Nonsmoking rms avail. Beautiful heavy quilts in some rooms. **Amenities:** 🛏 A/C, cable TV w/movies, refrig. All units w/terraces. **Services:** 🛎 🐕 **Facilities:** 🗂 🛦 🎣 🕹 Games rm, whirlpool, playground. Sun deck and wading pool outside interior game room/pool area. Table tennis, pool table. **Rates:** Peak (May–Oct) $35–$55 S; $45–$65 D; $55–$65 effic. Extra person $5. Children under age 18 stay free. Lower rates off-season. Parking: Outdoor, free. AE, DC, DISC, EC, MC, V.

≣ Motel 6

11274 210th St, 55044; tel 612/469-1900. Exit 81 off I-35. Located at entrance to small shopping mall with barber, chiropractor, sandwich shop, laundromat, and bank. McStop (McDonald's) truck stop is across parking lot, which makes for loud noise outside; however, interior of facility is quiet. **Rooms:** 84 rms. CI 2pm/CO noon. Nonsmoking rms avail. **Amenities:** 🛏 A/C, cable TV w/movies. **Services:** 🛎 🐕 Twice-daily maid svce. **Facilities:** 🛦 🎣 🕹 **Rates:** Peak (May–mid-Dec) $32–$40 S or D. Extra person $6. Children under age 17 stay free. Lower rates off-season. Parking: Outdoor, free. AE, CB, DC, DISC, MC, V.

≣≣ Super 8 Motel

20800 Kenrick Ave, 55044; tel 612/469-1134 or toll free 800/800-8000. Lobby has open, airy atmosphere with chairs and sofas; newspaper kiosks in entryway. **Rooms:** 133 rms and stes. CI 3pm/CO 11am. No smoking. Nonsmoking rms avail. **Amenities:** 🛏 A/C, cable TV w/movies, refrig. Some units w/minibars. **Services:** ✗ 🛎 🐕 Twice-daily maid svce. **Facilities:** 🗂 🛦 🎣 🍴 🕹 1 restaurant, 1 bar (w/entertainment), whirlpool. **Rates:** $46 S; $56 D; $76 ste. Extra person $6. Children under age 17 stay free. Parking: Outdoor, free. AE, DC, DISC, EC, MC, V.

Little Falls

Seat of Morrison County, in central Minnesota. In 1805, Zebulon Pike built Fort Pike, now under the waters of the Blanchard dam and reservoir. Aviator Charles Lindbergh lived here as a child. **Information:** Little Falls Tourism & Convention Bureau, 200 NW 1st St, Little Falls, 56345 (tel 320/632-5642 or toll free 800/325-5916).

ATTRACTION 📷

Charles A Lindbergh House

1200 Lindbergh Dr S; tel 320/632-3154. The famous aviator's childhood summer home, located near the rapids of the Mississippi River. A history center on the premises tells the story of the younger Lindbergh's exploits as well as covering the career of his father, Congressman Charles Lindbergh Sr. **Open:** Peak (May–Labor Day) Mon–Sat 10am–5pm, Sun noon–5pm. Reduced hours off-season. $$

Lutsen

On Lake Superior's north shore, Lutsen provides some of the best downhill skiing in the Midwest. In summer, the alpine slide and ski lifts are open to sightseers.

MOTELS 🏨

≣≣≣ Best Western Cliff Dweller

MP 86, MN 61, 55612; tel 218/663-7273 or toll free 800/223-2048; fax 218/663-7273. On MN 61 between Tofte and Lutsen, moments away from hiking, golfing, and skiing. **Rooms:** 22 rms. CI 3pm/CO 11am. Nonsmoking rms avail. **Amenities:** 🏠 Satel TV w/movies. No A/C. All units w/terraces. Some Lake Superior-view balconies. **Services:** ✗ 🛎 🐶 Twice-daily maid svce, babysitting. **Facilities:** 🚲 🏋 🏊 ⚕ 2 restaurants. Two dining rooms (one smoking, one nonsmoking) offer some of the best ribs around. **Rates:** Peak (June–Sept) $44–$69 S; $49–$79 D. Extra person $6. Children under age 12 stay free. Lower rates off-season. Parking: Outdoor, free. AE, CB, DC, DISC, MC, V.

≣≣≣ Bluefin Bay Motel

US 61, 55612; tel 218/663-7296 or toll free 800/BLUE-FIN. Located on shore of Lake Superior, offering easy access to all sorts of year-round activities. **Rooms:** 72 rms, stes, and effic. CI 4pm/CO noon. Nonsmoking rms avail. Majority of units are fully stocked modern condominiums rented as motel rooms. Many have vaulted ceilings and overlook Lake Superior. **Amenities:** 🏠 TV, VCR, CD/tape player. No A/C. Some units w/terraces, some w/fireplaces, some w/whirlpools. **Services:** 🗝 🛎 🐶 Social director. Free shuttle to skiing, canoeing, and hiking. **Facilities:** 🏠 🚲 △ 🏊 🏋 🍴 🏊 50 ⚕ 2 restaurants, 1 bar (w/entertainment), 1 beach (lake shore), volleyball, games rm, sauna, whirlpool, playground, washer/dryer. **Rates:** Peak (June 30–Oct 22/Dec 25–31/Feb 26–Mar 31) $49–$69 S or D; $169–$179 ste; $219–$345 effic. Extra person $10. Children under age 12 stay free. Min stay wknds and special events. Lower rates off-season. Parking: Outdoor, free. DISC, MC, V.

≣≣ The Mountain Inn at Lutsen

Ski Hill Rd, PO Box 58, 55612; tel 218/663-7244 or toll free 800/686-4669; fax 218/663-7248. Nestled among birch trees, this friendly, modern motel is close to downhill and cross-country skiing, mountain biking, and fine dining. **Rooms:** 30 rms. CI 4pm/CO noon. Nonsmoking rms avail. **Amenities:** 🏠 ⚙ A/C, cable TV w/movies. **Services:** 🛎 🐶 **Facilities:** 🏊 🏋 10 ⚕ **Rates (CP):** Peak (Aug 1–Sept 3) $54–$94 S or D. Extra person $8. Children under age 18 stay free. Min stay wknds. Lower rates off-season. Parking: Outdoor, free. AE, DISC, MC, V.

≣≣ Thomsonite Beach

MP 103, MN 61, 55612; tel 218/387-1532; fax 218/387-1532. Owner Tani Feigal's lifetime love of the gem thomsonite led her and her husband to purchase a thomsonite-rich beach 35 years ago. Lovely property on Lake Superior. **Rooms:** 4 rms and stes; 6 cottages/villas. CI noon/CO 10am. Simple, clean rooms. **Amenities:** 🏠 ⚙ Satel TV w/movies, refrig. No A/C. Some units w/terraces, some w/fireplaces. **Services:** 🛎 🐶 Babysitting. **Facilities:** 🏊 🏋 1 beach (lake shore), playground. Gemstone museum on premises. **Rates:** Peak (July–Oct) $52–$66 S or D; $67–$81 ste; $111–$139 cottage/villa. Extra person $6–$9. Children under age 2 stay free. Min stay peak. Lower rates off-season. Parking: Outdoor, free. Rates vary widely depending on size of unit and time of year. AE, DISC, MC, V.

ATTRACTION 🏛

Lutsen Mountains Ski Area

MN 61; tel 218/663-7281. During the November–April ski season, Lutsen provides 30 trails (split evenly among black diamond, intermediate, and beginner), 7 lifts (1 gondola, 5 doubles, 1 surface), and a vertical drop of 1,008 feet (the highest in the region). Moose Mountain features wide boulevards with impressive vistas of Lake Superior. Other activities include snowboarding and NASTAR. Condos, cafeteria, and bar. For the latest information on snow conditions, call 218/663-7281. **Open:** Nov–Apr, call for schedule. $$$$

Mankato

Seat of Blue Earth County. South central Minnesota's leading metropolis, Mankato is a major trade, medical, and educational center. Home of Mankato State University and the Mankato Symphony Orchestra. **Information:** Mankato Area Convention & Visitors Bureau, PO Box 999, Mankato, 56001 (tel 507/345-4519 or toll free 800/657-4733).

MOTELS 🏨

≣≣ Budgetel Inn

111 W Lind Court, 56001; tel 507/345-8800 or toll free 800/428-3438; fax 507/345-8921. Nestled in front of woods, motel has a rural look. **Rooms:** 66 rms. CI open/CO noon. Nonsmoking rms avail. **Amenities:** 🏠 ⚙ A/C, cable TV w/movies, dataport. 1 unit w/whirlpool. **Services:** 🛗 🛎 🐶 Breakfast (juice and roll) is hung in bag on outside door knob. **Facilities:** 🏊 ⚕ Sauna, whirlpool, washer/dryer. **Rates:** Peak (May–Oct) $32–$46 S; $34–$79 D. Extra person $7. Children under age 18 stay free. Lower rates off-season. Parking: Outdoor, free. AE, CB, DC, DISC, EC, ER, JCB, MC, V.

≣≣ Days Inn

1285 Range St, 56001; tel 507/387-3332 or toll free 800/329-7466; fax 507/387-3332. Just S of US 14 on MN 169. Situated on Hinicker Pond with swimming beach and grassy areas for children to play. **Rooms:** 50 rms, stes, and effic. CI 3pm/CO 11am. Nonsmoking rms avail. Cramped bathrooms. **Amenities:** 🏠 ⚙ A/C, cable TV w/movies. Some units w/whirlpools. **Services:** 🛗 🛎 🐶 Service extremely friendly. **Facilities:** 🏠 🏋 30 ⚕ Games rm, whirlpool. **Rates (CP):**

Peak (June–Aug) $42–$66 S or D; $52–$130 ste; $60–$130 effic. Extra person $5. Children under age 18 stay free. Lower rates off-season. Parking: Outdoor, free. AARP and senior discounts. Discounts on some holidays. AE, DC, DISC, MC, V.

≣≣≣ Holiday Inn

101 E Main St, PO Box 3386, 56001 (Downtown); tel 507/345-1234 or toll free 800/465-4329; fax 507/345-1248. Large, well-maintained convention property. **Rooms:** 150 rms. Executive level. CI 3pm/CO noon. Nonsmoking rms avail. Noticeable smell of smoke in the rooms. **Amenities:** 🛏 🅰 🗣 A/C, cable TV w/movies, refrig, dataport. Some units w/minibars, some w/terraces. **Services:** ✗ 🚐 🖼 🛎 🖐 **Facilities:** 🅕 🏋 🖼 [500] ♿ 1 restaurant, 1 bar (w/entertainment), games rm, sauna, whirlpool, washer/dryer. Blazer Lounge with jazz open daily 3pm–1am. 101 Main (restaurant) open weekdays 6am–10pm, and weekends 7am–10pm. **Rates:** $58–$70 S or D. Extra person $5. Children under age 12 stay free. Parking: Indoor/outdoor, free. AE, CB, DC, DISC, EC, ER, JCB, MC, V.

≣≣ Super 8 Motel

US 169 N, 56001; tel 507/387-4041 or toll free 800/800-8000; fax 507/387-4107. Adjacent to a restaurant. **Rooms:** 61 rms. CI noon/CO 11am. Nonsmoking rms avail. **Amenities:** 🛏 A/C, cable TV w/movies. 1 unit w/whirlpool. **Services:** 🛎 🖐 Popcorn machine in lobby. **Facilities:** 🏋 ♿ Sauna, whirlpool. **Rates:** $36 S; $42 D. Extra person $3. Parking: Outdoor, free. AE, CB, DC, DISC, JCB, MC, V.

RESTAURANT 🍴

★ Adrian's Eatery & Saloon

1812 S Riverfront Dr; tel 507/625-6776. S on MN 169 and 60. **American/Steak.** This family-owned and -operated local favorite started out serving breakfast only, then steadily expanded its facility and services to meet popular demand. Hearty fare includes barbecue ribs, pasta, and sirloin steak. Burgers named for local historic streets. An owner always on hand to assure quality dining and bright, friendly atmosphere. **FYI:** Reservations recommended. Children's menu. **Open:** Mon–Sat 11am–11pm. **Prices:** Main courses $7–$13. AE, CB, DISC, MC, V. ♿

ATTRACTION 📷

Hubbard House

606 S Broad St; tel 507/345-4154. The Victorian era comes alive in this restored 1871 home, which contains features such as cherry woodwork, silk wall coverings, marble fireplaces and Tiffany lampshades. Tours available. Gift shop. **Open:** Peak (May–Sept) Tues–Sun 1–4pm. Reduced hours off-season. $

Marshall

Seat of Lyon County, in southwest part of state. This agricultural community rests on a bend of the Redwood River, and is home to Southwest State University. The hot, dry winds that constantly sweep the area are harvested for electrical power. **Information:** Marshall Convention & Visitors Bureau, 501 W Main St, Marshall, 56258 (tel 507/537-1865).

MOTELS 🏨

≣≣≣ Best Western Marshall Inn

1500 E College Dr, 56258; tel 507/532-3221 or toll free 800/528-1234. Located right at edge of town. Huge doors lead into very large lobby with sweeping grand staircase. Overall, building has been well taken care of. **Rooms:** 100 rms and stes. CI 3pm/CO noon. Nonsmoking rms avail. Some rooms are larger than average. **Amenities:** 🛏 🅰 A/C, cable TV w/movies. **Services:** ✗ 🚐 🛎 🖐 Babysitting. Small pets allowed. **Facilities:** 🅕 🖼 [250] ♿ 1 restaurant, 1 bar, sauna, whirlpool, washer/dryer. **Rates:** $51–$59 S; $56–$64 ste. Extra person $5. Children under age 17 stay free. Parking: Outdoor, free. AE, DC, DISC, JCB, MC, V.

≣≣≣ Comfort Inn

1511 E College Dr, 56258; tel 507/532-3070 or toll free 800/221-2222. Jct MN 23/19. Opened in 1989, with new section added in 1994. Very clean and up-to-date. **Rooms:** 49 rms and stes. CI 3pm/CO 11am. Nonsmoking rms avail. Rooms are clean, bright, and cheery. **Amenities:** 🛏 🅰 A/C, cable TV w/movies. Some units w/whirlpools. **Services:** 🖼 🛎 🖐 VCRs for rent. **Facilities:** [25] ♿ Whirlpool, washer/dryer. **Rates (CP):** $48 S; $54 D; $95–$105 ste. Extra person $6. Children under age 18 stay free. Parking: Outdoor, free. AE, CB, DC, DISC, MC, V.

Minneapolis

See also Bloomington, St Paul

Seat of Hinnepin County. Minneapolis is the larger and more cosmopolitan half of Minnesota's Twin Cities. When the first white explorers came up the Mississippi, they found the huge river roaring over an 18-foot precipice. Today, the Falls of St Anthony is tamed and bypassed by lock and dam. First settled by New Englanders in 1847, waves of immigrants from Scandinavia, Germany, and Britain followed in the latter half of the 19th century. Today, Minneapolis is the state's foremost center of business, education, and culture. **Information:** Minneapolis Convention & Visitors Bureau, 4000 Multifoods Tower, 33 S 6th St, Minneapolis, 55402 (tel 612/661-4700).

PUBLIC TRANSPORTATION

The Metropolitan Transit Commission (MTC) provides **bus service.** Fares range from $1 to $1.25, depending on the time of day and distance traveled, and are payable with exact change, token, or commuter ticket. With the MTC's "Quarter Zone," 25¢ will take you to most places in the downtown area. For longer MTC expeditions, you can get maps, pocket schedules, and tokens at the MTC Transit Store, 719 Marquette Ave. For MTC information, call 612/349-7000.

HOTELS 🏨

≣≣≣ Crowne Plaza Northstar Hotel

618 2nd Ave S, 55402; tel 612/338-2288 or toll free 800/556-STAR; fax 612/338-2288. 2 blocks S of Nicollet Ave. The actual entrance on the street level is somewhat small, but a bellhop directs you to the lobby. **Rooms:** 226 rms and stes. Executive level. CI 3pm/CO noon. Nonsmoking rms avail. Average-size rooms; views of other skyscrapers. **Amenities:** 🛗 🛁 📺 🍴 A/C, cable TV w/movies, dataport, VCR, voice mail, bathrobes. Some units w/minibars, 1 w/terrace. **Services:** ✗ 🛏 🚗 🗚 🗝 Twice-daily maid svce, babysitting. On route of Airport Express, which leaves every 15 minutes until midnight—$10 one-way or $16 round-trip. **Facilities:** 🏋 🗂200 🛗 2 restaurants (see "Restaurants" below), 1 bar, washer/dryer. **Rates:** $97–$130 S; $97–$160 D; $175–$500 ste. Extra person $15. Children under age 16 stay free. Parking: Indoor, $10/day. AE, CB, DC, DISC, EC, MC, V.

≣≣ Days Inn University

2407 University Ave SE, 55414; tel 612/623-3999 or toll free 800/375-3990; fax 612/331-2152. I-94 to 35 W, then N to University Ave. Located three blocks from University of Minnesota. Caters to business and university people, as well as visitors to university hospital. **Rooms:** 131 rms. CI 1pm/CO 11am. Nonsmoking rms avail. **Amenities:** 🛗 🛁 A/C, cable TV w/movies, dataport, in-rm safe. **Services:** ✗ 🗚 🗝 Car-rental desk. Free shuttle service to hospital and university. **Facilities:** 🏋 🗂52 🛗 1 restaurant, washer/dryer. **Rates (CP):** Peak (May–Oct) $59–$89 S or D. Extra person $6. Children under age 17 stay free. Lower rates off-season. Parking: Outdoor, free. AE, CB, DC, DISC, EC, ER, JCB, MC, V.

≣≣ Hampton Inn

10420 Wayzata Blvd, 55305; tel 612/541-1094 or toll free 800/426-7866; fax 612/541-1905. W of downtown. North side of hotel looks out on residential section with grass and trees. Caters mostly to corporate and senior travelers. **Rooms:** 127 rms and stes. CI 3pm/CO noon. Nonsmoking rms avail. **Amenities:** 🛗 🛁 A/C, satel TV, dataport. **Services:** 🗚 🗝 **Facilities:** 🗂50 🛗 **Rates (CP):** Peak (June–Oct) $68–$76 S or D; $79–$85 ste. Extra person $8. Children under age 18 stay free. Lower rates off-season. Parking: Outdoor, free. AE, CB, DC, DISC, MC, V.

≣≣≣ Holiday Inn Metrodome

1500 Washington Ave S, 55454; tel 612/333-4646 or toll free 800/HIT-DOME; fax 612/333-7910. S of downtown. Located close to Metrodome, central downtown, and University of Minnesota. **Rooms:** 265 rms and stes. CI 3pm/CO noon. Nonsmoking rms avail. **Amenities:** 🛗 🛁 A/C, satel TV w/movies, dataport, voice mail. Some units w/whirlpools.

Services: ✗ 🚗 🗚 🗝 🗝 **Facilities:** 🏋 🗂600 🛗 1 restaurant, 1 bar, spa, sauna, whirlpool. **Rates:** Peak (May–Nov) $79–$120 S; $89–$130 D; $129–$159 ste. Extra person $10. Children under age 18 stay free. Lower rates off-season. AP and MAP rates avail. AE, CB, DC, DISC, EC, MC, V.

≣≣≣ Hotel Luxeford

1101 La Salle Ave, 55403; tel 612/332-6800 or toll free 800/662-3232; fax 612/332-8246. At 11th St. Very convenient to convention center and other downtown locations. **Rooms:** 230 stes. Executive level. CI 3pm/CO 11am. Nonsmoking rms avail. All rooms are suites with pull-out queen-size sofa, and are well furnished. Apartmentlike suites offer a little more space and comfort. Views of downtown area. **Amenities:** 🛗 🛁 📺 🍴 A/C, cable TV w/movies, refrig, CD/tape player, voice mail. Some units w/minibars, some w/whirlpools. All rooms have wet bars; microwaves; and TVs in both sitting and sleeping areas. **Services:** ✗ 🚗 🗚 🗝 Babysitting. **Facilities:** 🏋 🗂75 🛗 1 restaurant, 1 bar (w/entertainment), sauna, whirlpool, washer/dryer. Restaurant and bar boasts some of the best jazz in town, seven nights a week. Guests pay reduced fee for YMCA, located nearby. **Rates:** $160–$170 ste. Extra person $10. Children under age 18 stay free. AP and MAP rates avail. Parking: Indoor/outdoor, $8/day. AE, CB, DC, DISC, MC, V.

≣≣≣ Hyatt Regency Minneapolis

1300 Nicollet Mall, 55403; tel 612/370-1234 or toll free 800/233-1234; fax 612/370-1333. Located at the end of Nicollet Mall, this elegant hotel is also close to uptown. Lobby area is spacious and bright with many plants and plenty of seating. Caters to corporate and convention travelers. **Rooms:** 533 rms and stes. Executive level. CI 3pm/CO noon. Nonsmoking rms avail. Rooms beautifully furnished. **Amenities:** 🛗 🛁 📺 🍴 A/C, cable TV w/movies, dataport, voice mail. All units w/minibars, some w/terraces. **Services:** ✗ 🛏 📼 🚗 🗚 🗝 Twice-daily maid svce, masseur, babysitting. **Facilities:** 🏋 🗂 🗂1500 💻 🛗 5 restaurants (see "Restaurants" below), 1 bar, basketball, racquetball, spa, sauna, steam rm, whirlpool, beauty salon. Small retail area with a few shops and boutiques. **Rates:** Peak (Apr–Aug) $160–$185 S; $175–$210 D; $290–$500 ste. Extra person $25. Children under age 18 stay free. Lower rates off-season. Parking: Indoor, $9.50/day. AE, CB, DC, DISC, EC, MC, V.

≣≣≣ Marquette Hotel

710 Marquette Ave, 55402; tel 612/333-4545 or toll free 800/32-VISTA; fax 612/376-7419. Elegant hotel in IDS Tower in heart of downtown. **Rooms:** 278 rms and stes. Executive level. CI 3pm/CO noon. Nonsmoking rms avail. **Amenities:** 🛗 🛁 📺 🍴 A/C, cable TV w/movies, dataport, voice mail. All units w/minibars, some w/whirlpools. **Services:** ✗ 🛏 🚗 🗚 🗝 🗝 Babysitting. **Facilities:** 🗂 🗂2000 💻 🛗 1 restaurant, 1 bar (w/entertainment), sauna. **Rates:** $79–$180 S; $79–$200 D; $250–$330 ste. Children under

age 18 stay free. MAP rates avail. Parking: Indoor, $13/day. Children stay free with parents. AE, CB, DC, DISC, EC, JCB, MC, V.

Minneapolis Hilton and Towers

1001 Marquette Ave S, 55403 (Downtown); tel 612/376-1000 or toll free 800/HILTONS; fax 612/397-4875. At 10th. In heart of downtown, connected to Convention Center, Orchestra Hall, and many other downtown facilities via skyway. Enormous lobby, and a few retail shops upstairs. **Rooms:** 814 rms and stes. Executive level. CI 3pm/CO noon. Nonsmoking rms avail. **Amenities:** A/C, cable TV w/movies, dataport, voice mail. **Services:** Twice-daily maid svce, car-rental desk. **Facilities:** 2 restaurants, 2 bars (1 w/entertainment), spa, sauna, whirlpool. **Rates:** Peak (May–Oct) $170–$195 S; $190–$215 D; $700–$1,200 ste. Extra person $20. Children under age 17 stay free. Lower rates off-season. Parking: Indoor, $9.50/day. AE, CB, DC, DISC, EC, JCB, MC, V.

Minneapolis Marriott City Center

30 S 7th St, 55402; tel 612/349-4000 or toll free 800/228-9290; fax 612/332-7165. Between Hennepin and Nicollet. Within walking distance of Target Center and much nightlife, this facility caters mostly to conventioneers. **Rooms:** 583 rms and stes. Executive level. CI 3pm/CO noon. Nonsmoking rms avail. Unremarkable, functional layout and furnishings. **Amenities:** A/C, cable TV w/movies, dataport, voice mail. Some units w/minibars, some w/whirlpools. **Services:** Social director, masseur, babysitting. **Facilities:** 2 restaurants (see "Restaurants" below), 1 bar, spa, sauna, steam rm, whirlpool. **Rates:** Peak (May–Oct) $124–$154 S; $144–$174 D; $199–$229 ste. Extra person $15. Children under age 18 stay free. Lower rates off-season. Parking: Indoor, $3–11/day. "Two for Breakfast" package avail. AE, CB.

Minneapolis-St Paul Airport Hilton

3200 E 80th St, 55425; tel 612/854-2100 or toll free 800/637-7453; fax 612/854-8002. I-494 W to 34th Ave, left to 80th St. Undergoing $5 million renovation. Within walking distance of Minnesota Valley National Wildlife Refuge. **Rooms:** 300 rms and stes. Executive level. CI 3pm/CO noon. Nonsmoking rms avail. **Amenities:** A/C, satel TV w/movies, dataport. Some units w/terraces, some w/fireplaces, some w/whirlpools. **Services:** Car-rental desk. Complimentary appetizers in Flamingo Bar 5–7pm weekdays. Free shuttle service to Mall of America and other locations within mile radius. **Facilities:** 2 restaurants, 2 bars (1 w/entertainment), games rm, spa, sauna, whirlpool. Pool area is in atrium and has two whirlpools. **Rates:** $79–$135 S; $89–$145 D; $155–$695 ste. Extra person $10. Children under age 17 stay free. AP and MAP rates avail. Parking: Outdoor, free. AE, CB, DC, DISC, MC, V.

Nicollet Island Inn

95 Merriam St, 55401; tel 612/331-1800; fax 612/331-6528. This lovely inn, which began operating in 1988, used to be a window shade and blind company back in 1893. Country-style furniture and fireplaces in the lobby. Close to Riverplace shopping, dining, and business facility. **Rooms:** 24 rms. CI 3pm/CO noon. Nonsmoking rms avail. Each room is furnished differently. Beds have air mattresses and down comforters. **Amenities:** A/C, cable TV w/movies, VCR. Some units w/whirlpools. Cookies and mineral water in every room. **Services:** Babysitting. **Facilities:** 1 restaurant (see "Restaurants" below), 1 bar. **Rates:** $110–$145 S or D. Extra person $15. Children under age 10 stay free. AP and MAP rates avail. Parking: Outdoor, free. AE, CB, DC, DISC, EC, JCB, MC, V.

UNRATED Normandy Inn

405 S 8th St, 55404; tel 612/370-1400 or toll free 800/372-3131; fax 612/370-0351. The exterior resembles an old European chalet—a bit out of place in downtown Minneapolis—but the inside is very tastefully done, and the inviting lobby features very tasteful, living room–like furniture. **Rooms:** 159 rms and stes. Executive level. CI 4pm/CO noon. Nonsmoking rms avail. Standard rooms with unusually nice furniture. **Amenities:** A/C, cable TV w/movies. Some units w/terraces. **Services:** Twice-daily maid svce. **Facilities:** 1 restaurant, 1 bar, sauna, whirlpool. **Rates:** Peak (Apr–Nov) $85 S or D; $95 ste. Extra person $10. Children under age 12 stay free. Lower rates off-season. AP and MAP rates avail. Parking: Outdoor, free. AE, CB, DC, DISC, EC, MC, V.

Radisson Plaza Hotel Minneapolis

35 S 7th St, 55402 (Downtown); tel 612/339-4900 or toll free 800/333-3333; fax 612/337-9798. Just off Hennepin Ave. This gracious hotel directly across from City Center is a welcome respite from the downtown scene. Its mahogany-paneled lobby, with marble floors, opens into a 17-story atrium the centerpiece of which is a 2,000-pound marble ball that rotates on water pressure. **Rooms:** 357 rms and stes. Executive level. CI 3pm/CO noon. Nonsmoking rms avail. Rooms, very comfortable though not particularly spacious, are decorated with elegant yet homelike furniture. **Amenities:** A/C, cable TV w/movies, dataport, bathrobes. Some units w/minibars, some w/terraces, some w/whirlpools. **Services:** Twice-daily maid svce, masseur, babysitting. Executive lounge has a mini-library. **Facilities:** 2 restaurants, 2 bars (1 w/entertainment), spa, sauna, whirlpool, beauty salon. **Rates:** $87–$160 S or D; $255–$450 ste. Extra person $15. Children under age 16 stay free. AP and MAP rates avail. Parking: Indoor, $10/day. AE, CB, DC, DISC, EC, ER, JCB, MC, V.

Radisson University Hotel

615 Washington Ave SE, 55414; tel 612/379-8888 or toll free 800/822-MPLS; fax 612/379-8682. On University of Minnesota campus. The hotel's architecture blends in so well

with that of the university's that it can be hard to find. Most guests are here for university-related conferences. **Rooms:** 304 rms and stes. CI 3pm/CO noon. Nonsmoking rms avail. **Amenities:** 🛅 🕹 🖥 📺 A/C, cable TV w/movies, dataport. Some units w/whirlpools. **Services:** ✗ VP 🛄 ↩ 🔄 Babysitting. Carlson Travel Agency has office in lobby. **Facilities:** 🖥 750 🚭 2 restaurants, 2 bars, games rm, beauty salon, washer/dryer. For $5, guests can use University Health Club, a $30-million complex otherwise restricted to students and staff. **Rates:** $102–$114 S; $112–$124 D; $135–$325 ste. Extra person $10. Children under age 18 stay free. AP and MAP rates avail. Parking: Outdoor, $6.80/day. AE, CB, DC, DISC, ER, JCB, MC, V.

☰☰☰ Regal Minneapolis Hotel

1313 Nicollet Ave, 55403 (Downtown); tel 612/332-0371 or toll free 800/222-8888; fax 612/359-2160. Between 13th and Grant. Built in 1962 and updated through the years, this comfortable, reliable hotel stands at one end of the Nicollet Mall. **Rooms:** 330 rms and stes. CI 3pm/CO noon. Nonsmoking rms avail. The older rooms feature exposed brick; new rooms have impressive furnishings. **Amenities:** 🛅 🕹 🖥 📺 A/C, cable TV w/movies, dataport, voice mail, in-rm safe, bathrobes. **Services:** ✗ 🔑 🚗 🛄 ↩ 🔄 Car-rental desk, babysitting. **Facilities:** 🖥 🛗 700 🚭 1 restaurant, 1 bar, sauna, whirlpool, washer/dryer. **Rates:** Peak (Apr 15–Nov 15) $89–$189 S; $99–$199 D; $199–$250 ste. Extra person $10. Children under age 17 stay free. Lower rates off-season. AP and MAP rates avail. Parking: Indoor, $8/day. AE, CB, DC, DISC, EC, MC, V.

☰☰☰ Regency Plaza Best Western

41 N 10th St, 55403 (Downtown); tel 612/339-9311 or toll free 800/423-4100; fax 612/339-4765. At Hawthorne St. The exterior of this hotel, located next to a downtown bus station, is not the most elegant, but the reasonably comfortable rooms and low rates help make up for it. **Rooms:** 187 rms and stes. CI 3pm/CO noon. Nonsmoking rms avail. **Amenities:** 🛅 A/C, cable TV w/movies, in-rm safe. **Services:** ✗ 🔑 🚗 🛄 ↩ **Facilities:** 🖥 300 🚭 1 restaurant, 2 bars (1 w/entertainment), games rm, whirlpool, washer/dryer. Large indoor area. Small, quaint bar has live piano music Thurs–Sat. **Rates:** $66–$70 S; $72–$84 D; $85–$125 ste. Extra person $6. Children under age 18 stay free. Parking: Outdoor, free. AE, CB, DC, DISC, MC, V.

☰☰☰ Sheraton Minneapolis Metrodome

1330 Industrial Blvd NE, 55413; tel 612/331-1900 or toll free 800/777-3277; fax 612/331-6827. North of downtown and a bit out of the congestion, this hotel has a small, attractive courtyard area. Celebrities (Dolly Parton, Alan Jackson) have stayed here. **Rooms:** 252 rms and stes. Executive level. CI 4pm/CO 11am. Nonsmoking rms avail. **Amenities:** 🛅 🕹 🖥 A/C, cable TV w/movies, dataport. **Services:** ✗ 🔑 🚗 🛄 ↩ 🔄 Social director, masseur, babysitting. Shuttle service operates within 5-mile radius; destinations include airport, Mall of America, downtown,

local malls and restaurants. **Facilities:** 🖥 🛗 500 🚭 1 restaurant (see "Restaurants" below), 1 bar (w/entertainment), games rm, spa, sauna, whirlpool. **Rates:** Peak (Aug–Nov) $79–$129 S; $89–$139 D; $150 ste. Extra person $10. Children under age 18 stay free. Lower rates off-season. Parking: Outdoor, free. AE, CB, DC, DISC, EC, MC, V.

☰☰☰ Sheraton Park Place

1500 Park Place Blvd, 55416; tel 612/542-8600 or toll free 800/542-5566; fax 612/542-8068. Located 3½ mi west of downtown, close to business and commercial facilities. Small, attractive pond area in back. **Rooms:** 297 rms and stes. Executive level. CI 3pm/CO 11am. Nonsmoking rms avail. **Amenities:** 🛅 🕹 🖥 A/C, cable TV w/movies, dataport. Some units w/terraces, some w/whirlpools. **Services:** 🍽 🔑 🚗 🛄 ↩ 🔄 Complimentary van service shuttles guests within 3-mile radius. **Facilities:** 🖥 🛗 750 🖥 🚭 1 restaurant, 1 bar (w/entertainment), games rm, sauna, whirlpool, washer/dryer. Pool area is in a spacious atrium. **Rates:** Peak (June 9–Nov 14) $99–$119 S or D; $124–$144 ste. Extra person $15. Children under age 18 stay free. Lower rates off-season. AP and MAP rates avail. Parking: Outdoor, free. AE, CB, DC, DISC, EC, ER, JCB, MC, V.

☰☰☰ The Whitney Hotel

150 Portland Ave, 55401; tel 612/339-9300 or toll free 800/248-1879; fax 612/339-1333. This 18th-century European-style hotel, located three blocks from the Metrodome on the banks of the Mississippi River, was once actually a 19th-century flour mill; it has been a hotel since 1987. A patio sits next to the river with a fountain and outdoor seating. **Rooms:** 97 rms, stes, and effic. Executive level. CI 3pm/CO noon. Nonsmoking rms avail. Each room is shaped differently and is of average to small size; many standard rooms have high ceilings. All are very comfortable and feature nice wood furniture. South-facing rooms have views of river and outdoor patio and fountain. **Amenities:** 🛅 🕹 🖥 A/C, cable TV w/movies, refrig, dataport, voice mail, bathrobes. All units w/minibars, 1 w/terrace, 1 w/fireplace, 1 w/whirlpool. **Services:** 🍽 🔑 VP 🚗 🛄 ↩ 🔄 Twice-daily maid svce, babysitting. **Facilities:** 150 🚭 1 restaurant (see "Restaurants" below), 1 bar (w/entertainment). **Rates:** $145–$160 S; $165–$200 ste; $1,500 effic. Extra person $10. Children under age 18 stay free. AP and MAP rates avail. Parking: Outdoor, $6/day. Penthouse costs $1,500/night. AE, CB, DC, DISC, EC, MC, V.

RESTAURANTS 🍴

Anchorage Restaurant

In Sheraton Minneapolis Metrodome, 1330 Industrial Blvd NE; tel 612/379-4444. **Seafood.** Relaxed, comfortable setting, with a librarylike bar area. Offers a variety of traditional American cuisine but specializes in seafood. **FYI:** Reservations recommended. Country music. Children's menu. **Open:** Mon–Fri 6am–10:30pm, Sat–Sun 7am–10:30pm. **Prices:** Main courses $14–$26. AE, CB, DC, DISC, ER, MC, V. 🚭

Black Forest Inn

1 E 26th St; tel 612/872-0812. **German.** The building's exterior resembles an old German house, down to the flower boxes below the windows. Dark wood, stained-glass windows, hand-painted walls and ceilings, and a rustic bar area distinguish the interior, while the patio charms with its vines and tiny fountain. Authentic sauerbraten, Wiener schnitzel, bratwurst, and other German specialties await. **FYI:** Reservations not accepted. **Open:** Mon–Sat 11am–1am, Sun noon–midnight. **Prices:** Main courses $7–$14. AE, DC, DISC, MC, V. 🚢 ♿

Brit's Pub & Eating Establishment

1110 Nicollet Mall (Downtown); tel 612/332-3908. **British.** This downtown bar offers a more commercialized version of an English pub, complete with a gift shop selling familiar British products and T-shirts. Serves great shepherd's pie, authentic fish-and-chips, and British beers. Pool tables upstairs. **FYI:** Reservations not accepted. **Open:** Mon–Sat 11am–1am, Sun 10am–midnight. **Prices:** Main courses $6–$12. AE, CB, DC, DISC, ER, MC, V. 🍽 🚢 📷 ♿

⭐ Buca

1204 Harmon Place; tel 612/638-2225. At 12th St. **Italian.** Located on the garden level of a downtown building, this popular, casual restaurant prepares Italian family-style meals. Garlic mashed potatoes and chicken marsala are recommended. **FYI:** Reservations not accepted. Additional location: 2728 Gannon Rd, St Paul (tel 772-4388). **Open:** Mon–Thurs 5–10pm, Fri 5–11pm, Sat 4:30–11pm, Sun 4:30–10pm. **Prices:** Main courses $7–$20. AE, CB, DC, MC, V. ♿

D'Amico Cucina

In Butler Square, 100 N 6th St; tel 612/338-2401. **Italian.** Beautifully decorated restaurant with a distinctive atmosphere, tile floors, exposed whitewashed wood beams, and French doors leading to the dining room. Creative Italian dishes include pollo in tegame con gnocchi e taleggio (chicken with a potato dumpling and parsley sauce). Over 150 Italian wines. **FYI:** Reservations recommended. Piano. **Open:** Mon–Thurs 5:30–10pm, Fri–Sat 5:30–11pm, Sun 5–9pm. **Prices:** Main courses $20–$26. AE, CB, DC, MC, V. VP

du Jours

89 S 10th St; tel 612/333-1855. Between Nicollet and Marquette. **American.** Very solid food is available at this easygoing breakfast-and-lunch establishment. The menu includes open-faced sandwiches, soups (French onion, black bean), and traditional American meals. Egg substitutes are offered at breakfast for the cholesterol-conscious. **FYI:** Reservations not accepted. No liquor license. **Open:** Mon–Fri 6:30am–2:30pm, Sat–Sun 7am–2:30pm. **Prices:** Lunch main courses $4–$8. AE, MC, V. ♿

Edwardo's Natural Pizza Restaurant

1125 Marquette Ave (Downtown); tel 612/339-9700. At S 12th St. **Pizza.** Part of a chain known for its stuffed pizza. A good choice for family dining. **FYI:** Reservations accepted. Children's menu. Beer and wine only. No smoking. Additional locations: 533 Hennepin Ave (tel 339-9700); 2633 Southtown Dr, Bloomington (tel 884-8400). **Open:** Mon–Thurs 11am–10pm, Fri–Sat 11am–11pm. **Prices:** Main courses $6–$15. AE, MC, V. 👥 ♿

The Egg and I Restaurant

2828 Lyndale Ave; tel 612/872-7282. At 28th St. **American.** This local favorite for 18 years serves home-cooked, breakfast-type meals at a good price in a comfortable atmosphere. Every month the walls of the restaurant display a different local artist's work, which is available for purchase. Friendly waitstaff. **FYI:** Reservations accepted. No liquor license. Additional location: 2550 University Ave, St Paul (tel 647-1292). **Open:** Mon–Fri 6am–3pm, Sat–Sun 8am–3pm. **Prices:** Lunch main courses $4–$6. No CC. 🚢 ♿

510 Restaurant

510 Groveland Ave (Loring Park); tel 612/874-6440. **New American.** In a 1920s-era building close to Loring Park, this restaurant has classically decorated rooms with big chandeliers, but still feels homey. American food is presented with a French flair, with such savory entrees as roasted rack of lamb roasted finished in a Dijon mustard sauce. Reasonably priced, frequently changing wine list. **FYI:** Reservations recommended. No smoking. **Open:** Mon–Sat 5:30–10pm. **Prices:** Main courses $15–$20; prix fixe $19–$29. AE, CB, DC, DISC, ER, MC, V. VP ♿

Gasthof Zur Gemütlichkeit

2300 NE University Ave; tel 612/781-3860. At 23rd. **German.** The interior walls of this German restaurant located in the northeast part of the city are painted to replicate an old German cottage. The menu offers large portions (you receive a certificate if you're able to finish your meal) of authentic German fare such as rouladen and bratwurst with sauerkraut and potato salad. **FYI:** Reservations recommended. Polka. Children's menu. **Open:** Lunch Mon–Fri 11am–2pm; dinner Mon–Sat 4–10pm, Sun 2–9:30pm; brunch Sun 10:30am–2pm. **Prices:** Main courses $10–$21; prix fixe $13–$17. AE, CB, DC, DISC, MC, V. ♿

Goodfellow's

In the Conservatory, 800 Nicollet Mall (Downtown); tel 612/332-4800. At 8th St. **Regional American.** This comfortably elegant restaurant serves an American menu which changes seasonally. Polished ambience with very impressive table settings. All pastas, breads, stocks, and pastries are made from scratch. The extensive wine list highlights American vintages. Bar open throughout hours. **FYI:** Reservations recommended. **Open:** Lunch Mon–Fri 11:30am–2pm; dinner Mon–Thurs 5:30–9pm, Fri–Sat 5:30–10pm. **Prices:** Main courses $19–$30. AE, CB, DC, DISC, MC, V. ●

Gustino's

In Minneapolis Marriott City Center, 30 S 7th St; tel 612/349-4075. Between Nicollet Mall and Hennepin Ave. **Italian.** Specializing in northern Italian food, this relaxed yet sophisticated restaurant offers a sixth-floor view of Minneapolis. A waitstaff of professional singers entertains with Italian opera and show tunes while you wait for your food. Popular choices include scampi sautéed in olive oil, garlic, lemon, and white wine; and chicken breast with prosciutto, fontina cheese, and sautéed green beans. **FYI:** Reservations recommended. Singer. **Open:** Mon–Thurs 6–10pm, Fri–Sat 6–11pm. **Prices:** Main courses $12–$24; prix fixe $25. AE, CB, DC, DISC, MC, V. VP &

★ Jax Cafe

1928 University Ave NE; tel 612/789-7297. At 20th. **American.** This elegant spot, which has been around since 1933, offers five private dining rooms, each decorated differently (and some with their own bar), which can serve anywhere from 20 to 325 people. Outdoor dining looks out at beautiful flower gardens, a waterfall, and a mill wheel. Standard American fare. Pick your own rainbow trout from the pond. **FYI:** Reservations recommended. Piano. **Open:** Lunch Mon–Sat 11am–3pm; dinner Mon–Sat 4–11pm, Sun 3:30–10pm; brunch Sun 10am–3pm. **Prices:** Main courses $15–$28. AE, CB, DC, DISC, MC, V. 🍴 🖼 &

Jerusalem's Restaurant

1518 Nicollet Ave; tel 612/871-8883. Just N of Franklin Ave; just S of Nicollet Mall. **Middle Eastern.** A tiny restaurant in a domed building popular for its classic Middle Eastern food and atmosphere. The interior features animal skins and rugs, maroon-colored fabric, and small, metallic hanging lamps. Menu choices include marinated lamb grilled on vertical spits, hummus, tabbouleh, and other favorites, all served with pita bread. A belly dancer entertains guests Thurs–Sat. **FYI:** Reservations accepted. Beer and wine only. **Open:** Mon–Thurs 11am–10pm, Fri 11am–11pm, Sat noon–11pm, Sun noon–10pm. **Prices:** Main courses $8–$16. CB, DC, MC, V. 🍴

Kikugawa

45 Main St SE (Riverplace); tel 612/378-3006. **Japanese.** Tastefully decorated and featuring views of beautiful Nicollet Island Park and the Mississippi River, this is considered by many to be the best Japanese restaurant in the city. The dining area offers both Japanese- and Western-style seating, a sushi bar, and a karaoke bar. Aside from the ever-popular tempura, teriyaki, and sushi, there are unique dishes that combine the cooking styles of both Japan and Minnesota—as in walleye kasuzuke, marinated in rice wine (kasu) and then broiled. **FYI:** Reservations recommended. Karaoke. **Open:** Lunch daily 11:30am–2pm; dinner daily 5–10pm. **Prices:** Main courses $8–$18; prix fixe $25. AE, DISC, MC, V. VP &

Little Szechuan

2800 27th Ave S; tel 612/724-6666. At 28th St. **Chinese.** This tiny restaurant situated in a residential area offers a lunch buffet for $4.75 with over 10 items to choose from.

FYI: Reservations accepted. No liquor license. **Open:** Daily 11am–9pm. **Prices:** Main courses $5–$9; prix fixe $7–$13. No CC.

Loon Cafe

500 1st Ave N (Warehouse District); tel 612/332-8342. At 5th St. **American.** This casual restaurant, close to the Target Center, is popular with a young professional crowd. The primarily American menu includes some Mexican dishes and various types of chili. An atmosphere of fun is reflected in whimsically named menu offerings like the tasty Loon Addict, a lightly breaded chicken breast sandwich served with mayonnaise and lettuce. The popular bar area comes alive at night. **FYI:** Reservations accepted. **Open:** Mon–Sat 11am–1am, Sun 11:30am–midnight. **Prices:** Main courses $6–$11. AE, CB, DC, DISC, MC, V.

The Malt Shop

809 W 50th St; tel 612/824-1352. At Bryant. **American.** This old-style malt shop, with a jukebox, an old piano, and wooden booths, lies just a few blocks from Lake Harriet. Menu ranges from vegetarian (ratatouille, pita stuffed with vegetables sautéed in peanut sauce) to gourmet burgers. Also malts, shakes, and sundaes. **FYI:** Reservations not accepted. Folk/guitar/piano. No liquor license. **Open:** Daily 11am–10:30pm. **Prices:** Main courses $4–$7. AE, CB, DC, DISC, MC, V. 📺 &

Manny's

In Hyatt Regency Minneapolis, 1300 Nicollet Mall (Downtown); tel 612/339-9900. **Steak.** Nationally regarded steak house, with a somewhat bright interior and simple decor, and a bar area plastered with photographs of happy patrons. Nice wine display. **FYI:** Reservations recommended. **Open:** Mon–Thurs 5:30–10pm, Fri–Sat 5:30–11pm, Sun 5:30–9pm. **Prices:** Main courses $15–$25. AE, CB, DC, DISC, MC, V. &

★ Monte Carlo Bar & Grill

219 3rd Ave N (Warehouse District); tel 612/333-5900. **American.** Located in the warehouse district of downtown, this favorite old-timer has been around since 1906. Textured ceilings, low lighting, and booths give the place a very comfortable ambience and a touch of elegance. Offerings include a variety of specialty sandwiches (crab salad sandwich, turkey Reuben), classic pasta dishes, steaks, pork, and seafood. **FYI:** Reservations recommended. **Open:** Daily 11am–1am. **Prices:** Main courses $7–$17. AE, CB, DC, DISC, MC, V. 🍴 VP

Morton's of Chicago

555 Nicollet Mall; tel 612/673-9700. **Steak.** Located off the Nicollet Mall, this well-known steakhouse with dark wood furniture and booths offers a comfortable setting for elegant, intimate dining. Some of the kitchen can be seen from the dining area. Specialties include double filet mignon in béarnaise sauce and tenderloin brochette with diablo sauce. **FYI:** Reservations recommended. Dress code. **Open:** Lunch

Mon–Fri 11:30am–2:30pm; dinner Mon–Sat 5:30–11pm, Sun 5–10pm. **Prices:** Main courses $17–$30. AE, CB, DC, MC, V. [VP] &

Mud Pie Vegetarian Restaurant

2549 Lyndale Ave S; tel 612/872-9435. At 26th St. **Vegetarian.** Very casual, highly regarded eatery offering veggie burgers, a reuben made with a tempeh burger instead of corned beef, and Mexican dishes. Takeout available. **FYI:** Reservations accepted. Beer and wine only. No smoking. **Open:** Mon–Thurs 11am–10pm, Fri 11am–11pm, Sat 8am–11pm, Sun 8am–10pm. **Prices:** Main courses $9–$13. AE, CB, DC, DISC, MC, V. 🍴 &

Murray's

26 S 6th St (Downtown); tel 612/339-0909. **American.** Located in the heart of downtown, this family-owned establishment recently celebrated its 50th anniversary in Minneapolis. Recommended are its special Silver Butter Knife steaks and garlic toast. Award-winning wine list with over 500 wines. Afternoon tea in a very relaxed setting. **FYI:** Reservations recommended. Piano/violin. Children's menu. Dress code. **Open:** Mon–Thurs 11am–10:30pm, Fri 11am–11pm, Sat 4–11pm, Sun 4–10pm. **Prices:** Main courses $10–$34. AE, CB, DC, DISC, MC, V. ♥ &

The New French Cafe

128 N 4th St (Warehouse District); tel 612/338-3790. Between 1st and 2nd Aves N. **French.** A very comfortable setting for French country cuisine, with the quaint bar and kitchen visible from the dining area. Satisfying entrees include Black Angus beef fillet with a ragoût of Roma tomato, mushrooms, and thyme served with shallot-roasted new potatoes. Bakery with fresh breads, pastries, and desserts; separate tables are available. **FYI:** Reservations accepted. **Open:** Breakfast Mon–Fri 7–11am; lunch Mon–Fri 12:30–2:30pm; dinner Mon–Thurs 5:30–10pm, Fri–Sat 5:30–11pm; brunch Sat–Sun 8am–2pm. **Prices:** Main courses $17–$21; prix fixe $18. AE, DC, MC, V. [VP] &

The Nicollet Island Inn Restaurant

95 Merriam St; tel 612/331-1800. **Regional American.** This beautiful restaurant offers a lovely view of the Mississippi River and a seasonal American menu with a Minnesota touch. Walleye amandine with asparagus, poached salmon with citrus vinaigrette and basmati rice, and wild rice soup are just a few treats you might find. Everything is made from scratch—even the ketchup. On weekends, the bar serves food after the dining area closes. **FYI:** Reservations recommended. **Open:** Breakfast Mon–Fri 7–10am, Sat 8–11am; lunch Mon–Sat 11:30am–2pm; dinner Mon–Fri 5:30–10pm, Sat 5:30–10:30pm, Sun 5:30–9pm; brunch Sun 9:30am–2pm. **Prices:** Main courses $14–$29; prix fixe $24. AE, CB, DC, DISC, MC, V. [VP] &

Nora's

3118 W Lake St; tel 612/927-5781. At Excelsior. **American.** This family-style restaurant, located just a few blocks from Lake Calhoun, features a casual dining room with flowered wallpaper and old photos for a distinctly homey quality. Food is as basic as it gets: macaroni and cheese, turkey and potatoes, soup and salad bar, breakfast buffet. A putt-putt golf course is located just behind the building. **FYI:** Reservations accepted. Children's menu. **Open:** Mon–Fri 11am–10pm, Sat–Sun 7am–10pm. **Prices:** Main courses $6–$13. DISC, MC, V. 🚼 &

Ping's

1401 Nicollet Ave; tel 612/874-9404. At 14th St. **Chinese.** Excellent food in a classy setting, decorated in a style more upscale American than Chinese. Special Szechuan dishes include chicken with a spicy black bean and pepper sauce. There is wine list of about 50 wines, with suggested accompaniments for each entree. Weekday lunch and Sunday dinner buffets are available. **FYI:** Reservations recommended. **Open:** Mon–Thurs 11am–10pm, Fri 11am–midnight, Sat noon–midnight, Sun noon–9pm. **Prices:** Main courses $7–$15. AE, CB, DC, DISC, MC, V. 🚗 [VP] &

Rosewood Room

In Crowne Plaza Northstar Hotel, 618 2nd Ave S (Downtown); tel 612/338-2288. **Mediterranean.** An elegant setting with touches of the Mediterranean. As you walk in, there is a table decorated with olive oils and a beautiful bread basket. Specialties include veal marsala (sautéed scallops of veal with mushrooms and onions, simmered in marsala, served over fettuccine) and a rolled breast of chicken stuffed with spinach and served with parmesan risotto. Separate, lively bar area. **FYI:** Reservations accepted. Children's menu. **Open:** Breakfast Mon–Sat 6–11am; lunch Mon–Fri 11:30am–2pm; dinner Tues–Sun 5:30–9:30pm; brunch Sun 8am–1pm. **Prices:** Main courses $10–$25. AE, CB, DC, DISC, MC, V. ♥ &

Rudolph's Bar-B-Que

1933 Lyndale Ave S; tel 612/871-8969. At Franklin. **Barbecue.** Decorated with pictures of Rudolph Valentino and other early film stars, this popular barbeque joint is famous for its sauces and spices, which can also be purchased. The atmosphere is very comfortable, and the bowl placed on each table for disposing bones is a nice convenience. **FYI:** Reservations recommended. Children's menu. **Open:** Daily 11am–midnight. **Prices:** Main courses $6–$30. AE, CB, DC, MC, V. 🚼 ♥

Ⓢ Sidney's

2120 Hennepin Ave; tel 612/870-7000. At 22nd St. **Californian.** This uptown locale serves truly exceptional California cuisine, with especially fine individual gourmet pizzas. Inside the comfortable, cedar-cabinlike interior with gas-burning stone fireplace you'll find guests come dressed in everything from evening gowns to athletic wear. One of the many specialties is marinated rotisserie chicken Provençal (lemon, garlic, herbs) served with roasted potatoes and vegetables. **FYI:** Reservations not accepted. Beer and wine only. No smoking. Additional locations: Galleria Shopping Center,

Edina (tel 925-2002); 156000 W MN 7, Minnetonka (tel 933-1000). **Open:** Mon–Thurs 7am–11pm, Fri 7am–midnight, Sat 10am–midnight, Sun 10am–11pm. **Prices:** Main courses $6–$10. AE, CB, DC, DISC, MC, V. 📠 &

The Whitney Grill
In the Whitney Hotel, 150 Portland Ave; tel 612/339-9300. On bank of Mississippi River. **American.** This elegant restaurant offers a seasonal American menu highlighted by various meat and fish dishes with creative sauces. One unique offering is roasted sesame breast of Minnesota pheasant, filled with lobster, spinach, and shiitake mushrooms and finished with a maple butter sauce. The new back room, called Richard's, features a formal setting and a $60 prix fixe weekly menu. **FYI:** Reservations recommended. Blues/jazz. No smoking. **Open:** Breakfast Mon–Fri 6:30–11:30am, Sat 7–11:30am, Sun 7–9am; lunch Mon–Sat 11:30am–2pm; dinner daily 5–10pm; brunch Sun 9am–2pm. **Prices:** Main courses $14–$29. AE, CB, DC, DISC, MC, V. 🔲 VP &

ATTRACTIONS 🖼️

MUSEUMS

The Minneapolis Institute of Arts
2400 3rd Ave; tel 612/870-3000. The MIA's permanent collection of over 80,000 objects of fine and decorative art represents more than 25,000 years of history. Highlights include a 2,000-year-old mummy, a first-century BC Roman sculpture, and a Paul Revere silver tea service. There are re-created period rooms; African, Oceanic, and New World galleries; collections of photographs, textiles, and prints; and paintings by such European masters as Rembrandt and Monet. **Open:** Tues–Sat 10am–5pm, Thurs 10am–9pm, Sun noon–5pm. **Free**

Frederick R Weisman Art Museum
333 E River Rd; tel 612/625-9464. Standing high on a bluff overlooking the Mississippi River and the downtown Minneapolis landscape, this uniquely designed building located on the University of Minnesota campus houses what one major art critic calls "five of the most gorgeous galleries on earth." With its irregular shape and brushed steel and terra-cotta brick facade, this Frank Gehry–designed building is the most immediately recognizable structure on campus. The museum houses over 13,000 objects, and the emphasis is on American art; it has the world's largest collection of work by Marsden Hartley, Alfred H Maurer, and BJO Bordfeldt. Other highlights include an extensive collection of Asian, American, European, and Native American ceramics. Group tours available. **Open:** Tues–Wed 10am–5pm, Thurs 10am–8pm, Fri 10am–5pm, Sat–Sun 11am–5pm. **Free**

James Ford Bell Museum of Natural History
University and 17th Aves, 612/624-7083; tel 612/624-7083. Located on the Minneapolis campus of the University of Minnesota, this museum is famous for its three-dimensional scenes of Minnesota wildlife. Among the stuffed specimens on hand are moose, elk, and caribou. In the popular "Touch and See" room, children can examine the skins, bones, and skulls of a wide variety of animals, including mammoths and dinosaurs. **Open:** Tues–Fri 9am–5pm, Sat 10am–5pm, Sun noon–5pm. **$**

Walker Art Center/Minneapolis Sculpture Garden
Vineplace Place; tel 612/375-7622. The Walker Art Center is famous for its permanent collection of contemporary art ranging from painting and sculpture to drawings, photographs, and multimedia installations. It is also known for the popular presentations it offers through its Departments of Film and Video, Performing Arts, and Education. Museum admission is free every Thursday and on the first Saturday of each month.

Across Vineland Place is the **Minneapolis Sculpture Garden**, the most extensive garden of its kind in the United States. The wide variety of 20th-century sculpture on display here includes work by Henry Moore, Isamu Noguchi, and George Segal, as well as the spectacular Claes Oldenburg–Coosje van Bruggen fountain-sculpture *Spoonbridge and Cherry*. **Open:** Museum: Tues–Sat 10am–8pm, Sun 11am–5pm. Sculpture garden: daily 6am–midnight. **$$**

Flanders Contemporary Art Gallery
400 1st Ave N; tel 612/344-1700. The works owned by this art gallery span all media: paintings, sculpture, drawings, photographs, and prints. Works are drawn from the 18th, 19th, and 20th centuries, with special emphases on French and American impressionism. Masters from the 19th century (Van Gogh, Gauguin, Monet, Cassatt) are presented alongside modern masters like Henry Moore, Georgia O'Keeffe, Helen Frankenthaler, and Robert Motherwell. **Open:** Tues–Sat 11am–4pm. **Free**

Kramer Gallery
1012 Nicollet Mall; tel 612/338-2911. This distinguished gallery specializes in local, national, and European artworks of the 19th and early 20th centuries; also featured is an extensive collection of Native American art and artifacts. **Open:** Mon–Fri 10am–6pm, Sat 10am–4pm. **Free**

Minnesota Air Guard Museum
Minnesota Air National Guard Base; tel 612/725-5609. Located at the Minneapolis/St Paul International Airport. Vintage and current aircraft, artifacts, memorabilia, and photographs tell the story of the Minnesota Air Guard from 1921 to present. The most popular exhibit is the A-12 Blackbird, a spy plane used during the Cold War. **Open:** Mid-Apr–mid-Sept, Sat–Sun 11am–4pm. **$**

Baseball Museum
406 Chicago Ave S; tel 612/375-0428. Old uniforms, autographed bats and balls, photographs, and record books are among the numerous items dealing with the national pastime. Located just steps away from the Metrodome. **Open:** Mon–Fri 9am–4pm, Sat 11am–3pm. **$**

PARKS & GARDENS

Minnehaha Park

Minnehaha Pkwy; tel 612/348-2143. This park on the Mississippi River is the site of the famed Minnehaha Falls, the "laughing water" Longfellow celebrated in his poem *Song of Hiawatha*. A statue of Hiawatha and Minnehaha is situated above the waterfall. Other attractions include 15 miles of jogging and biking trails along the Minnehaha Parkway; Stevens House, a historic frame house that was the first to be built west of the Mississippi; and several picnic areas. **Open:** Daily sunrise–sunset. **Free**

Eloise Butler Wildflower Garden and Bird Sanctuary

Theodore Wirth Pkwy; tel 612/348-5702. A 20-acre natural wildflower habitat offering natural bogs and swamp areas, with hiking and bicycle trails winding through so you can get a closer look. Guided tours available. **Open:** Apr–Oct, daily 7:30am–sunset. **Free**

SPORTS & ENTERTAINMENT VENUES

Orchestra Hall

1111 Nicolet Mall; tel 612/371-5656. For more than 20 years, this 2,400-seat hall has been home to the internationally acclaimed Minnesota Orchestra. It has offered diverse programs featuring a wide range of artists, from Isaac Stern and Itzhak Perlman to Andy Williams and the late Pearl Bailey. Since 1980, the annual Viennese Sommerfest has drawn very large audiences for programs including everything from light classics to orchestral masterworks. **Open:** Call for schedule. **$$$$**

The Guthrie Theater

725 Vineland Place; tel 612/377-2224. In 1964, the Tyrone Guthrie Theater gained worldwide fame as the home of a new classical repertory company. Since then, the theater has housed award-winning productions of Greek tragedies by Euripides, Aeschylus, and Sophocles, and other classics of Western theater. Before entering the auditorium, audiences are surrounded by a tempting array of dining, drinking, and shopping choices. The Guthrie shares an entry lobby with the adjacent Walker Art Center and is just steps away from the Walker's extensive, and often expensive, selection of gifts and souvenirs. The Guthrie's own smaller gift shop carries a variety of gifts and theater-related items.

Performances begin at 7:30pm Tues–Thurs, 8pm Fri–Sat, and 7pm on Sun. Matinees are usually presented at 1pm Wed and Sat. Call for performance schedule. **Open:** Box office, Mon–Sat 9am–8pm, Sun 11am–7pm. **$$$$**

Hubert H Humphrey Metrodome

900 S 5th St; tel 612/332-0386. One of the most recognized structures in downtown Minneapolis, this indoor stadium is home to professional football (Vikings) and baseball (Twins) games. For the Twins, it seats up to 55,000; for the Vikings, the dome holds up to 62,000. **Open:** Call for schedule. **$$$$**

OTHER ATTRACTIONS

Fort Snelling

MN 55; tel 612/725-2413. Located 1 mi E of Minneapolis–St Paul International Airport. In 1819, Col Josiah Snelling and his troops began construction of a fort here, establishing an official presence in the wilderness that had recently been won from Great Britain. Families arrived, and after a treaty opened up additional lands 20 years later, some of the homesteaders moved across the river to form the city later known as St Paul. Today, Fort Snelling is a living museum, where costumed guides re-create the activities of everyday army life during the 1820s. Handcrafted Native American jewelry is on sale in the gift shop. **Open:** Peak (May–Oct) daily sunrise–sunset. Reduced hours off-season. Closed Dec–Mar. **$$**

University of Minnesota

Between Mississippi and University Aves and 10th Ave and Oak St SE; tel 612/625-5000 or toll free 800/752-1000. One of the Midwest's oldest (1851) and most important universities, with 41,000 students. The campus has three significant museums—James Ford Bell Museum of Natural History (see above), the University Art Gallery, and the Frederick R Weisman Art Museum (see above). The 4,800-seat Northrop Auditorium has been a home for distinguished performances since 1929; the University Theatre has four separate stages. Guided tours leave from the Admissions Office, 240 Williamson Hall, Mon–Fri at 10am and 1pm. **Free**

Minneapolis City Hall

5th St and 3rd Ave; tel 612/673-2491. The imposing 1891 City Hall, with its Big Ben–style clock tower, is a surprising contrast to its next-door neighbor, the ultramodern Hennepin County Government Center. Here you will find the *The Father of Waters*, billed as the largest statue ever carved from a single block of Carrara marble. **Open:** Mon–Fri 9am–5pm. **Free**

Minneapolis Planetarium

300 Nicollet Mall; tel 612/372-6644. Located in the downtown branch of the Minneapolis Public Library. More than a dozen public programs are offered here, including the immensely popular Skywatch (a "guided tour" of the night sky with film projected overhead on the 40-foot-high domed ceiling). **Open:** Call for schedule. **$$**

Moorhead

Seat of Clay County, in western Minnesota. Across the Red River from Fargo, ND, Moorhead enjoys the advantages of a small town along with the culture and sophistication of a larger metropolitan area. Concordia Lutheran College's conservatory of music is world renowned. **Information:** Moorhead Area Chamber of Commerce, 725 Center Ave, PO Box 719, Moorhead, 56561-0719 (tel 218/236-6200).

HOTEL 🛅

≣≣≣ The Madison Hotel

600 30th Ave, 56560; tel 218/233-6171 or toll free 800/328-6174; fax 218/233-0945. Larger, independent hotel. A good place for large meetings and receptions. **Rooms:** 174 rms. CI 3pm/CO noon. Nonsmoking rms avail. Nicely furnished rooms with newer fabrics and wood furniture. **Amenities:** 🛁 A/C. Some units w/terraces. **Services:** 🍽️ 🚐 ⚞ ⟲ ⟳ Large, professional staff. **Facilities:** ⚞ 🏊 ⚞ 500 ⛴ 1 restaurant, 1 bar (w/entertainment), games rm, sauna. **Rates:** $39–$49 S; $45–$55 D. Children under age 18 stay free. Parking: Outdoor, free. AE, DISC, MC, V.

MOTEL

≣≣ Super 8 Motel

3621 S 8th St, 56560; tel 218/233-8880 or toll free 800/800-8000; fax 218/233-8880. Off US 75 S. Located near Concordia College and Moorhead State University. **Rooms:** 61 rms. CI 3pm/CO noon. Nonsmoking rms avail. Clean, comfortable rooms. **Amenities:** 🛁 A/C, cable TV w/movies. **Services:** ⚞ ⟲ Winter auto plug-ins. Friendly staff. **Facilities:** ⚞ Games rm, washer/dryer. **Rates:** $31–$38 S or D. Extra person $4. Children under age 13 stay free. Parking: Outdoor, free. AE, CB, DC, DISC, MC, V.

RESTAURANT 🍽️

♣ Tree Top Restaurant

In the FM Building, 403 Center Ave; tel 218/233-1393. **Continental.** The terrific river view from this seventh-floor restaurant adds to diners' enjoyment, but this restaurant's reputation hinges on its excellent food. Try herb-crusted salmon, chateaubriand, or tournedos Colleen. All entrees are beautifully presented and are accompanied by Tree Top's famous popovers, served with honey butter. Save room for coffee and dessert—perhaps Death by Chocolate, or strawberries flambée prepared tableside. **FYI:** Reservations recommended. Piano. **Open:** Lunch Mon–Fri 11am–2pm; dinner Mon–Sat 5–10pm. **Prices:** Main courses $14–$26. AE, CB, DC, DISC, MC, V. ♥ 🏔️

ATTRACTIONS 🏛️

Plains Art Museum

521 Main Ave; tel 218/236-7383. This museum, located in a 1913 building, contains a permanent collection of Native American, West African, and contemporary American art. Changing exhibits include works by prominent local and regional artists in a variety of media. The museum offers lectures, films, musical performances, and workshops; tours available. **Open:** Tues–Sat 10am–5pm, Sun noon–5pm. **Free**

Heritage Hjemkomst Interpretive Center

202 1st Ave N; tel 218/233-5604. Home to the *Hjemkomst*, a 76-foot replica of a Viking ship. Visitors center houses an interpretive video and exhibits on the making of the ship. The

Clay County Museum, also on site, details the history of the area through exhibits on frontier settlement, baseball, and railroads. **Open:** Mon–Wed, Fri–Sat 9am–5pm, Thurs 9am–9pm, Sun noon–5pm. **$$**

Comstock Historic House

506 8th St S; tel 218/233-0848. Built in 1882 for Solomon Comstock (the founder of Moorhead State College), this stately and impressive Victorian mansion has been completely restored and is now open to the public. It contains the Comstock family's furnishings (including ornate, colorful Queen Anne and Eastlake furniture and tapestries) set amid varnished-oak and butternut trim. Open year-round for groups with reservations. **Open:** Sat–Sun 1–4:15pm. **$**

Morris

Seat of Stevens County. On the Pomme de Terre River, this western town is home to the University of Minnesota at Morris. **Information:** Morris Area Chamber of Commerce & Agriculture, 511 Oregon Ave, Morris, 56267 (tel 320/589-1242).

HOTEL 🛅

UNRATED Prairie Inn

MN 28, PO Box 348, 56267; tel 320/589-3030 or toll free 800/535-3035. 2 mi N of town. An older building which recently changed ownership. Fast food outlets nearby. **Rooms:** 95 rms, stes, and effic. CI 2pm/CO noon. Nonsmoking rms avail. **Amenities:** 🛁 A/C, cable TV w/movies. 1 unit w/whirlpool. **Services:** ⚞ ⟲ **Facilities:** ⚞ 🏊 175 ⛴ 1 restaurant (dinner only), 1 bar, games rm, whirlpool. **Rates:** $22–$32 S; $33–$52 D; $40–$62 ste; $35–$62 effic. Extra person $6. Children under age 16 stay free. Parking: Outdoor, free. AE, CB, DC, DISC, MC, V.

New Ulm

Seat of Brown County, in southern Minnesota. German settlers withstood Sioux attacks to build this town at the confluence of the Cottonwood and Minnesota rivers. Downtown, a 45-foot-tall glockenspiel chimes the time of day. **Information:** New Ulm Area Chamber of Commerce, 1 N Minnesota St, PO Box 384, New Ulm, 56073 (tel 507/354-4217).

MOTELS 🛅

≣ Budget Holiday Hotel

1316 N Broadway, 56073; tel 507/354-4145. One-story building with parking at doors to rooms, located just north of town on main drag, near stores and food outlets. Okay for brief stay only. **Rooms:** 45 rms. CI 3pm/CO noon. Nonsmoking rms avail. Some rooms are nicer than others, but all are pretty drab and in need of some change. **Amenities:** 🛁 A/C, cable TV. **Services:** 🦮 Babysitting. **Facilities:** ⅄ **Rates:** $25–$50 S; $32–$60 D. Extra person $5. Children under age 15 stay free. Parking: Outdoor, free. AE, DC, DISC, MC, V.

≣≣≣ Holiday Inn
2101 S Broadway, 56073; tel 507/359-2941 or toll free 800/HOLIDAY. In keeping with German heritage of New Ulm, hotel resembles German chalet, with lots of dark wood trim. Signs are carved in wood. Huge picture of Bavarian castle on stair landing, and front desk staff members wear Bavarian costumes. **Rooms:** 126 rms and stes. CI 2pm/CO noon. Nonsmoking rms avail. **Amenities:** 🛖 🔊 🎞 A/C, cable TV w/movies. Some units w/terraces, 1 w/fireplace. **Services:** ✕ 🦮 Babysitting. **Facilities:** 🔋 ⅄ 🦺 🦺 ⅃ 300 🦽 1 restaurant, 1 bar (w/entertainment), games rm, sauna, whirlpool, washer/dryer. **Rates:** $59–$86 S or D; $107–$122 ste. Extra person $10. Children under age 18 stay free. Min stay special events. Parking: Outdoor, free. AE, CB, DC, DISC, JCB, MC, V.

≣≣ Super 8 Motel
1901 S Broadway, 56073; tel 507/359-2400 or toll free 800/800-8000; fax 507/359-1751. Fairly new motel located at south end of town, near fast food eateries. **Rooms:** 62 rms and stes. CI 3pm/CO 11am. Nonsmoking rms avail. Some rooms have full-length mirrors. **Amenities:** 🛖 A/C, cable TV w/movies. 1 unit w/whirlpool. **Services:** 🛏 🦮 Pets allowed with permission. **Facilities:** ⅄ 🦽 **Rates:** $35–$44 S; $38–$47 D; $99–$120 ste. Extra person $5. Children under age 12 stay free. Parking: Outdoor, free. AE, CB, DC, DISC, MC, V.

ATTRACTIONS 🏛

Hermann Monument
Center and Monument Sts; tel 507/354-4910. Erected in 1897 in honor of ancient Teutonic hero Hermann of Cherusci, the father of Germanic independence. The 102-foot-tall monument provides an excellent vantage points for views of New Ulm and the entire Minnesota River Valley. Hermann Heights Park, which surrounds the monument, is a popular site for picnics. **Open:** Mem Day–Labor Day, daily noon–4pm. **$**

Brown County Historical Museum
2 N Broadway; tel 507/354-2016. This former local post office (built in 1910 and now listed on the National Register of Historical Places) houses permanent exhibits depicting the history of the Native Americans and early settlers to this area. Other exhibits have dealt with World War II, the heritage and development of New Ulm, and the struggle for women's suffrage. An interactive children's area provides hands-on experiences. Gift shop. **Open:** Mon–Fri 10am–5pm, Sat–Sun 1–5pm. **$**

Schell Brewing Company
Schell's Park; tel 507/354-5528. Founded in 1860, this award-winning brewery is New Ulm's oldest industry. The brewery itself, which is housed in its original brick buildings, is open for tours during the summer and during New Ulm's major festivals. The grounds also include gardens, a deer park, and the August Schell Museum of Brewing. **Open:** Mem Day–Labor Day, daily call for schedule. **$**

Nisswa
See Brainerd

Northfield
This southeastern Minnesota town is home to Carleton College and the Norwegian St Olaf College. St Olaf's world-famous a capella choir carries on the tradition of F Melius Christiansen, its founder. The James-Younger gang was badly mauled when it tried to rob the First National Bank here on September 7, 1867. **Information:** Northfield Area Chamber of Commerce, 500 Water St S, PO Box 198, Northfield, 55057-0198 (tel 507/645-5604 or toll free 800/658-2548).

MOTELS 🏨

≣ College City Motel
875 MN 3 N, 55057; tel 507/645-4426 or toll free 800/775-0455. Good value for budget travelers. **Rooms:** 24 rms. CI noon/CO 11am. Nonsmoking rms avail. All rooms open to parking area. **Amenities:** 🛖 🔊 A/C, cable TV w/movies. **Services:** 🛏 🦮 Complimentary coffee in lobby. **Facilities:** ⅄ **Rates:** $24–$27 S; $35–$39 D. Parking: Outdoor, free. AE, DISC, MC, V.

≣ Super 8 Motel
1420 Riverview Dr, 55057; tel 507/663-0371 or toll free 800/800-8000; fax 507/663-0185. Off MN 3. Recently renovated. **Rooms:** 40 rms and stes. CI 2pm/CO 11am. Nonsmoking rms avail. **Amenities:** 🛖 🔊 A/C, cable TV. **Services:** 🛏 **Facilities:** ⅄ 🦽 Washer/dryer. **Rates:** $43–$45 S; $53 D; $56–$85 ste. Extra person $3. Parking: Outdoor, free. AARP, corporate, government, and Super 8 VIP discounts. AE, CB, DC, DISC, MC, V.

RESTAURANT 🍴

★ The Tavern of Northfield
In The Archer House Hotel, 212 Division St (Historic Riverfront); tel 507/663-0342. **American/Southwestern.** This pleasant eatery with a relaxed atmosphere is in the historic Archer House Hotel (built 1877) on the banks of the Cannon River in downtown. Roast duck, braised walleye, and lamb in pita bread are features, along with a wide selection of sandwiches. All breads and desserts made on premises. **FYI:** Reservations accepted. Children's menu. **Open:** Sun–Thurs 6:30am–10pm, Fri–Sat 6:30am–11pm. **Prices:** Main courses $5–$12. AE, MC, V. ∎

Owatonna

Seat of Steele County, in southern Minnesota. One of the wealthiest cities in the state, Owatonna offers a variety of recreational and cultural venues. In 1893, Casey Jones shuttled Old Engine 201, at the restored Union Depot, to Chicago's World Columbian Exposition. **Information:** Owatonna Convention & Visitors Bureau, 320 Hoffman Dr, PO Box 331, Owatonna, 55060 (tel 507/451-7970 or toll free 800/423-6466).

MOTELS 🏨

≣≣≣ AmericInn

245 Florence Ave, 55060; tel 507/455-1142 or toll free 800/634-3444; fax 507/444-0545. Exit 41 off I-35. Delightful stenciling in lobby adds nice touch to roomy sitting area with sofas and fireplace. **Rooms:** 69 rms and stes. CI 3pm/CO 11am. Nonsmoking rms avail. **Amenities:** 🛏 🔥 🖭 A/C, cable TV w/movies. Some units w/fireplaces, some w/whirlpools. Nordic Trak can be wheeled into room. **Services:** 🖼 📳 Babysitting. Winter car plug-ins. **Facilities:** 🔟 🏋 🏊 🚗25 🔥 Games rm, spa, sauna, whirlpool, washer/dryer. Very large pool area with lots of windows and pool table. **Rates (CP):** $52–$89 S; $58–$95 D; $65–$105 ste. Extra person $6. Children under age 12 stay free. Parking: Outdoor, free. Senior and corporate discounts avail. AE, CB, DC, DISC, MC, V.

≣ Oakdale Motel

1418 S Oak St, 55060; tel 507/451-5480; fax 507/451-5481. Near the fairgrounds. Small, but good for budget travelers. One block from fairgrounds. **Rooms:** 25 rms and effic. CI 11am/CO 11am. Nonsmoking rms avail. Neat, clean rooms with well-used furniture. All rooms face parking lot. **Amenities:** 🛏 🔥 A/C, cable TV. 1 unit w/whirlpool. VCRs can be rented; films available from grocery store one block from motel. **Services:** 📳 🖐 Twice-daily maid svce. **Facilities:** 🏋 **Rates:** Peak (May–Oct) $22–$35 S; $30–$45 D; $35–$45 effic. Extra person $3. Lower rates off-season. Parking: Outdoor, free. AE, DC, DISC, MC.

≣≣≣ Ramada Inn

1212 I-35, PO Box 609, 55060; tel 507/455-0606; fax 507/455-3737. Lobby has pleasant seating area. **Rooms:** 119 rms and stes. CI 2pm/CO noon. Nonsmoking rms avail. Tables instead of desks. **Amenities:** 🛏 🔥 🖭 A/C, cable TV w/movies, refrig, VCR. 1 unit w/minibar, some w/whirlpools. **Services:** ✗ 🚗 🖼 📳 🖐 $10 pet fee. **Facilities:** 🔟 🏋 🗔200 🔥 1 restaurant, 1 bar, games rm, sauna, whirlpool, washer/dryer. **Rates:** $45–$55 S; $55–$65 D; $120 ste. Extra person $5. Children under age 12 stay free. Parking: Outdoor, free. AE, CB, DISC, MC, V.

RESTAURANT 🍴

⑤ ✹ Jerry's Supper Club Owatonna

203 N Cedar St; tel 507/451-6894. **American.** One block from the main park downtown, this has a great collection of mugs and whiskey decanters in shapes of cars, movie stars, etc, located around the bar area. Specialties are steaks and prime rib. Comfortable padded seats. TV and eight tables in lounge. **FYI:** Reservations recommended. Children's menu. **Open:** Lunch Mon–Sat 11am–2:30pm; dinner Mon–Thurs 5–10pm, Fri–Sat 5–11pm. **Prices:** Main courses $8–$23. AE, DISC, MC, V. 🎗 🍴 📷

ATTRACTIONS 🏛

Village of Yesteryear

1448 Austin Rd; tel 507/451-1420. Eleven historic buildings restored with period furnishings and memorabilia provide a re-creation of 19th-century life. The complex features log cabins, schoolhouse, church, railroad depot, fire station, blacksmith shop, country store, family home, farm machinery building, and a museum. **Open:** May–Oct, daily 1–5pm. $$

Owatonna Arts Center

435 Dunnell Dr; tel 507/451-0533. Old Romanesque structure is home to a sculpture garden, a performing arts hall marked by 14-foot stained-glass panels, studios, and a main gallery. The permanent collection features garments from all over the world. The sculpture garden houses works by Minnesota artists Paul Grandlund, Charles Gagnon, John Rood, and Richard and Donald Hammel. **Open:** Tues–Sun 1–5pm. **Free**

Park Rapids

Seat of Hubbard County, in north-central Minnesota. The headwaters of the mighty Mississippi are a half-hour's drive north of town. At one point, you can actually cross the nascent river from stone to stone. **Information:** Park Rapids Area Chamber of Commerce, 71 S, PO Box 249, Park Rapids, 56470-0249 (tel 218/732-4111 or toll free 800/247-0054).

HOTEL 🏨

≣≣ C'mon Inn

MN 34 E, PO Box 189, 56470; tel 218/732-1471 or toll free 800/258-6891; fax 218/732-9304. Natural wood and stone structure built around enclosed courtyard pool area. Heartland Trail is five blocks away. Near Itasca State Park (headwaters of the Mississippi); 18 holes of golf just 1½ miles away. Also close to hunting, fishing, good dining, and shopping. **Rooms:** 44 rms and stes. CI 3pm/CO noon. Nonsmoking rms avail. Many rooms on both floors overlook pool area. **Amenities:** 🛏 A/C, cable TV w/movies. Some units w/terraces, some w/whirlpools. **Services:** 🚗 🖼 📳 Babysitting. **Facilities:** 🔟 🏋 📺 🗔40 🔥 Games rm, whirlpool. Lovely, large, indoor pool area. **Rates (CP):** $44–$54 S; $50–$60 D; $73 ste. Extra person $6. Children under age 12 stay free. Parking: Outdoor, free. AE, DISC, MC, V.

MOTELS

🏨🏨 Super 8 Motel
MN 34 E, PO Box 388, 56470; tel 218/732-9704 or toll free 800/800-8000; fax 218/732-9704. Located near the Heartland Trail, which starts in Park Rapids, runs over 30 miles in length, and is ideal for biking in summer and snowmobiling in winter. **Rooms:** 38 rms. CI 1pm/CO 11am. Nonsmoking rms avail. **Amenities:** 🕿 🛁 A/C, cable TV w/movies. **Services:** 🗘 **Facilities:** 🏊 🛌 Games rm, sauna, whirlpool, washer/dryer. Game room includes Ping-Pong, pinball, and pool table. **Rates (CP):** Peak (June–Labor Day) $38–$53 S; $45–$53 D. Extra person $5. Children under age 12 stay free. Lower rates off-season. Parking: Outdoor, free. AE, CB, DC, DISC, JCB, MC, V.

🏨🏨 Terrace View Motor Lodge
716 N Park, 56470; tel 218/732-1213 or toll free 800/731-1213. Basic motel overlooking the Fish Hook River. **Rooms:** 20 rms; 4 cottages/villas. CI 2pm/CO 11am. A variety of single and double motel rooms as well as cabins. Newer double rooms have bath and shower. **Amenities:** 🕿 🛁 A/C, cable TV. 1 unit w/terrace. Newer double rooms have small refrigerators. **Services:** ✗ 🚐 🗘 ⬧ **Facilities:** ⛁ ▢ 🏊 30 1 restaurant (lunch and dinner only), 1 bar, 1 beach (lake shore), playground. **Rates:** Peak (Mem Day–Labor Day) $27–$30 S; $38–$43 D; $45–$66 cottage/villa. Extra person $6. Children under age 12 stay free. Lower rates off-season. Parking: Outdoor, free. AE, DISC, MC, V.

RESTAURANT 🍴

The Pines Resort and Supper Club
HC 06, Box 133A; tel 218/732-0164. US 71 N to Northern Pine Rd; turn right and go 1½ mi to stop sign; turn left and go 1 mi to restaurant. **American.** Don't let the 2½-mile gravel road leading up to the Pines deter you—the dinner will be worth the trip. You might wish to start off with some broiled mushroom caps stuffed with crabmeat and cheeses while you decide on a main course—maybe the mesquite sampler (pork chop and chicken breast served in olive oil and mesquite seasonings), chicken Veronique (sautéed in white wine with shallots, green grapes, garlic, and heavy cream), or roast duck. Window tables have great views of serene Potato Lake. **FYI:** Reservations accepted. Piano. Children's menu. **Open:** Peak (Mem Day–Labor Day) Wed–Thurs 5–9pm, Fri–Sat 5–10pm, Sun 5–9pm. **Prices:** Main courses $9–$19. AE, DISC, MC, V. ♿

ATTRACTION 🏛

Lake Itasca Tours
Itasca State Park; tel 218/732-5318 or 266-2101. These 1½-hour narrated tours explore the history, geology, and wildlife of Lake Itasca and the headwaters of the Mississippi River. **Open:** Mid-May–mid-Oct, daily 11am–3pm. $$$

Pine River

Located 20 miles south of Chippewa National Forest, this tiny town in central Minnesota lies amidst many lakes.

MOTEL 🏨

🏨🏨 Trailside Inn
MN 371 S, PO Box 466, 56474; tel 218/587-4499 or toll free 800/450-4499. Across the street from the 100-mile Brainerd-to-Bemidji Paul Bunyan Trail, which is ideal for hiking, jogging, biking, and snowmobiling. **Rooms:** 30 rms. CI 2pm/CO 11am. Nonsmoking rms avail. **Amenities:** 🕿 🛁 A/C, cable TV w/movies. **Services:** 🗘 ⬧ Very professional staff. **Facilities:** 🚴 ▣ 🏊 🎿 🛌 Sauna, whirlpool, washer/dryer. Complete fitness center with showers. **Rates (CP):** Peak (Mem Day–Labor Day) $35–$65 S or D. Extra person $5. Children under age 12 stay free. Lower rates off-season. Parking: Outdoor, free. AE, DISC, MC, V.

Pipestone

Seat of Pipestone County, in southwest part of state. The town is named for the red-colored quartzite used in Native Americans' peace pipes. Pipestone National Monument was established in 1937 in order to preserve this precious resource for future generations of Native Americans. **Information:** Pipestone Convention & Visitors Bureau, 117 8th Ave SE, PO Box 8, Pipestone, 56164 (tel 507/825-3316 or toll free 800/336-6125).

MOTELS 🏨

🏨🏨 Arrow Motel
600 8th Ave NE, 56164; tel 507/825-3331. On US 75. One-story motel where you park your car at your door. Very clean operation, frequented by regulars who stay for extended time. Laundry facility four blocks away. **Rooms:** 17 rms. CI 2pm/CO 11am. Nonsmoking rms avail. Rooms are small but clean. **Amenities:** 🕿 A/C, cable TV. **Services:** 🗘 ⬧ **Facilities:** ⛁ 12 **Rates (CP):** $24–$31 S; $36–$57 D. Extra person $5. Children under age 12 stay free. Parking: Outdoor, free. DISC, MC, V.

🏨🏨🏨 The Historic Calumet
104 W Main St, 56164; tel 507/825-5871 or toll free 800/535-7610. This inn has a long history. It was opened in 1888 and enlarged in 1913, and in 1979 the hotel's new owners

began a $3 million renovation. Much of the building was returned to its original look, but with modern conveniences added. In 1993, the current owners took over, and they have so far maintained the high standards that are the inn's hallmark. A favorite for retreats and tour groups. **Rooms:** 38 rms and stes. CI 2pm/CO 11am. Nonsmoking rms avail. All rooms individually decorated and imbued with turn-of-the-century feel; many have antiques. Bathrooms have old-fashioned tubs and toilets. **Amenities:** ☎ ⚲ A/C, cable TV. 1 unit w/whirlpool. **Services:** ✕ ⤴ VCRs available for rent. **Facilities:** ⌸75 ⅁ 1 restaurant (lunch and dinner only), 2 bars, washer/dryer. Gift shop features Native American works. Lounge occupies what was once a bank, and vault serves as wine room. **Rates (CP):** Peak (mid-July–mid-Aug) $46–$70 S; $53–$90 D; $65 ste. Extra person $4. Children under age 12 stay free. Lower rates off-season. AP rates avail. Parking: Outdoor, free. AE, DC, DISC, MC, V.

☰ Super 8 Motel
605 8th Ave SE, 56164; tel 507/825-4217 or toll free 800/800-8000. Corner of US 75, MN 23, and MN 30. Typical Super 8, next door to Gannon's Restaurant. **Rooms:** 39 rms. CI 2pm/CO 11am. Nonsmoking rms avail. **Amenities:** ☎ ⚲ A/C, cable TV w/movies. 1 unit w/whirlpool. **Services:** ⤴ ⤵ Pets allowed with permission and deposit. **Facilities:** ⅁ Washer/dryer. **Rates:** Peak (June–Labor Day) $39–$69 S; $48 D. Extra person $4. Children under age 12 stay free. Lower rates off-season. Parking: Outdoor, free. AE, CB, DC, DISC, MC, V.

RESTAURANT ⑆

Gannon's
Jct MN 30/US 75/MN23; tel 507/825-3114. **American.** Located right next door to the Super 8, this place offers the option of eating in the coffeeshop or in the steakhouse. There is also a lounge in the building, which is very dark with blue lighting. **FYI:** Reservations recommended. Reservations accepted. Children's menu. **Open:** Daily 6am–1am. **Prices:** Main courses $5–$10; prix fixe $6. AE, DISC, MC, V. ⛐

ATTRACTION ⛫

Pipestone National Monument
Jct US 75/MN 30/MN 23; tel 507/825-5464. Pipestone is a soft stone that ranges in color from mottled pink to brick red. It was highly prized by Native Americans in the 17th century for making ceremonial pipes, and by all accounts this location came to be the preferred source for pipestone among the Plains tribes. By about 1700, the Yankton Sioux controlled the quarries and distributed the stone only through trade. In 1928 the Yanktons, now resettled on a reservation 150 miles away, sold their claim to the federal government. Pipestone National Monument was signed into existence in 1937 and opened to the public with quarrying limited to Native Americans.

The 283-acre monument provides visitors with the opportunity to watch demonstrations of pipe making by native artisans, explore interpretive exhibits, and take a ¾-mile self-guiding tour of the monument. Keep in mind that the grounds are still used by Native Americans for a variety of activities and that it is unlawful to remove the pipestone. **Open:** Peak (Mem Day–Labor Day) Mon–Thurs 8am–6pm, Fri–Sun 8am–8pm. Reduced hours off-season. $

Red Wing

Seat of Goodhue County. Located on the Mississippi bluffs in southeastern Minnesota, Red Wing is best known for Red Wing Shoes and Red Wing Pottery. **Information:** Red Wing Area Chamber of Commerce, 420 Levee St, Red Wing, 55066 (tel 612/388-4719).

HOTEL ⍜

☰☰☰ St James Hotel
406 Main St, 55066; tel 612/388-2846 or toll free 800/252-1875; fax 612/388-5226. At Bush St. Historic Victorian hotel built in 1875 and listed on National Register of Historic Places. Many antiques and old pictures of Mississippi River days hang on walls throughout the hotel. **Rooms:** 60 rms. CI 3pm/CO noon. Nonsmoking rms avail. Rooms named after historic riverboats. **Amenities:** ☎ ⚲ A/C, cable TV w/movies, bathrobes. Some units w/whirlpools. **Services:** ✕ ⬛ ⊠ ⤴ Twice-daily maid svce, social director, babysitting. **Facilities:** ⚐ ⛾ ⌸250 ⅁ 2 restaurants (see "Restaurants" below), 2 bars (1 w/entertainment), beauty salon. Full book store, barber shop, clothing stores in hotel. Vouchers ($5) for local YMCA, one-half block from hotel (if guest is Y member elsewhere, admission is free). **Rates:** $75–$155 S or D. Extra person $10. Children under age 18 stay free. Parking: Indoor/outdoor, free. AE, CB, DC, DISC, EC, MC, V.

MOTELS

☰☰ AmericInn
1819 Old W Main St, 55066; tel 612/385-9060 or toll free 800/634-3444; fax 612/385-8139. Opened in 1994. Large comfortable lobby with fresh flowers and plants. **Rooms:** 43 rms and stes. CI 3pm/CO 11am. Nonsmoking rms avail. **Amenities:** ☎ ⚲ A/C, cable TV. Some units w/whirlpools. **Services:** ⊠ ⤴ ⤵ Dogs under 14 inches the only pets allowed. **Facilities:** ⛊ ⚐ ⛾ ⌸20 ⅁ Sauna, whirlpool, washer/dryer. Video games in pool area. **Rates (CP):** Peak (May–Oct) $70 S; $76 D; $86–$96 ste. Extra person $6. Children under age 12 stay free. Lower rates off-season. Parking: Outdoor, free. AE, CB, DISC, EC, MC, V.

☰☰☰ Best Western Quiet House Suites
752 Withers Harbor Dr, 55066; tel 612/388-1577 or toll free 800/528-1234; fax 612/388-1150. All-suite facility. Lobby has fireplace, benches, chairs, tables, and dried flower ar-

rangements. Adjacent to Perkins Restaurant. **Rooms:** 51 stes. CI 2pm/CO 11am. Nonsmoking rms avail. **Amenities:** 🛏 🛁 A/C, satel TV w/movies, dataport. Some units w/whirlpools. **Services:** 🛌 ⟶ **Facilities:** 🏋 🏊 🦮 🎾 ⚽ Whirlpool. Two video games in vending machine room. Pool open in winter. **Rates:** Peak (May–Oct) $67–$150 ste. Extra person $10. Children under age 5 stay free. Lower rates off-season. Parking: Outdoor, free. AE, CB, DC, DISC, EC, MC, V.

▤▤ Days Inn
955 E 7th St, 55066; tel 612/388-3568 or toll free 800/329-7466; fax 612/385-1901. US 61/63, 1½ mi S of downtown. Ranch-style building with pleasant entrance. Lots of grass, shrubs, and flowers. **Rooms:** 48 rms. CI 3pm/CO 11am. Nonsmoking rms avail. All rooms face parking lot. **Amenities:** 🛏 🛁 📺 A/C, cable TV w/movies. **Services:** ⟶ ⟶ Pet deposit $7. **Facilities:** 🏋 🏊 🦮 ⚽ Whirlpool. **Rates (CP):** Peak (May–Oct) $44–$62 S; $44–$72 D. Extra person $5. Children under age 12 stay free. Lower rates off-season. Parking: Outdoor, free. Ski packages avail. AE, CB, DC, DISC, JCB, MC, V.

▤▤ Red Carpet Inn
235 Withers Harbor Dr, 55066; tel 612/388-1502 or toll free 800/251-1962; fax 612/388-1501. Enclosed front entrance with no canopy. **Rooms:** 39 rms and stes. CI 2pm/CO 11am. Nonsmoking rms avail. **Amenities:** 🛏 🛁 A/C, cable TV w/movies, refrig. 1 unit w/whirlpool. **Services:** 🛌 ⟶ **Facilities:** 🏋 🏊 🦮 ⚽ Whirlpool. Three video games in back lobby. Separate whirlpool with key at desk—use by reservation only. **Rates:** Peak (May–Oct) $44–$54 S; $49–$64 D; $69–$120 ste. Extra person $5. Children under age 2 stay free. Lower rates off-season. Parking: Outdoor, free. AE, CB, DC, DISC, EC, MC, V.

▤▤ Super 8 Motel
232 Withers Harbor Dr, 55066; tel 612/388-0491 or toll free 800/800-8000; fax 612/388-1066. Standard, predictable motel accommodations. **Rooms:** 60 rms. CI 2pm/CO 11am. Nonsmoking rms avail. **Amenities:** 🛏 🛁 A/C, cable TV w/movies. Some units w/whirlpools. **Services:** 🛌 ⟶ **Facilities:** 🏋 🏊 🦮 🛐 ⚽ Whirlpool. **Rates:** Peak (May–Sept) $43 S; $53 D. Extra person $5. Children under age 2 stay free. Lower rates off-season. Parking: Outdoor, free. AE, CB, DC, DISC, EC, MC, V.

RESTAURANTS 🍴

★ Nybo's Landing
233 Withers Harbor Dr; tel 612/388-3597. **American.** One block from the Mississippi River, this facility opened in 1946 as a bowling alley (still in operation) with a little restaurant in the same building. It's a local favorite for baked chicken and barbecue ribs, plus pizza, and burgers. **FYI:** Reservations accepted. Children's menu. Beer and wine only. **Open:** Daily 7am–10pm. **Prices:** Main courses $5–$12. AE, CB, DC, DISC, MC, V. ▪️ 👥 ♥ ♿

♣ Port of Red Wing
In St James Hotel, 406 Main St (Downtown); tel 612/388-2846. **American/French.** A romantic, dimly lit downstairs dining room, with lots of space between tables. The menu offers ribs, steaks, fish, potatoes, and vegetables, with some light French-style dishes such as poached salmon with mustard hollandaise. Other recommendations are medallions of pork with Wisconsin cranberry cream sauce; New York strip steak with burgundy–green peppercorn sauce; and vegetable strudel with provolone and mozzarella, wrapped in phyllo dough, baked, and served with basil cream sauce. **FYI:** Reservations recommended. Piano. Beer and wine only. **Open:** Peak (Sept–Oct/mid-Dec–Jan) lunch Mon–Sat 11am–3pm; dinner daily 5–9:30pm; brunch Sun 11am–2:30pm. **Prices:** Main courses $19–$22. AE, CB, DC, DISC, ER, MC, V. ▪️ 🛁 👥 ♥

Rochester

Seat of Olmsted County, in southeast part of state. Home of the famed Mayo Clinic, which evolved from the private practice of local doctor Dr William Worall Mayo. **Information:** Rochester Convention & Visitors Bureau, 150 S Broadway, #A, Rochester, 55904 (tel 507/288-4331 or toll free 800/634-8277).

HOTELS 🏨

▤▤▤ Clinic View Inn
9 3rd Ave NW, 55902; tel 507/289-8646 or toll free 800/533-1655; fax 507/282-4478. Located in heart of hospital area of downtown Rochester. **Rooms:** 266 rms, stes, and effic. CI 3pm/CO 3pm. Nonsmoking rms avail. **Amenities:** 🛏 📺 A/C, cable TV w/movies. Some units w/terraces. **Services:** ✗ 🚗 🛌 ⟶ ⟶ Babysitting. Grocery store and travel agent on premises. Translation services available through Mayo Clinic. **Facilities:** 🏋 🏊 💯 ⚽ 1 restaurant, 1 bar, sauna, whirlpool, beauty salon, washer/dryer. Yankee Peddler bar open 3–9pm Mon–Fri. **Rates:** $68 S; $78 D; $93–$108 ste; $103–$118 effic. Extra person $10. Children under age 18 stay free. Parking: Indoor/outdoor, free. AE, CB, DC, DISC, EC, ER, JCB, MC, V.

UNRATED Days Inn
6 1st Ave NW, 55902; tel 507/282-3801 or toll free 800/329-7466. Older downtown property in good shape, adjacent to hospital district. **Rooms:** 71 rms and effic. CI 1pm/CO noon. Nonsmoking rms avail. "Mini-suites" have a kitchenette area. **Amenities:** 🛏 A/C, satel TV. Some units w/whirlpools. **Services:** 🛌 ⟶ ⟶ **Facilities:** 🏊 1 restaurant. **Rates:** $43–$65 S; $49–$65 D; $65 effic. Children under age 16 stay free. Parking: Outdoor, free. AE, CB, DC, DISC, EC, ER, JCB, MC, V.

Kahler Hotel
20 2nd Ave SW, 55902; tel 507/282-2581 or toll free 800/533-1655; fax 507/285-2701. Downtown Rochester kitty-corner from Mayo Clinic. Gracious property operating as hotel for over 70 years, offering deluxe accommodations in heart of city center. Up-to-date decor throughout. Connected by skyway-subway to Mayo Clinic and Galleria Mall. **Rooms:** 695 rms and stes. Executive level. CI 2pm/CO 2pm. Nonsmoking rms avail. **Amenities:** A/C, satel TV w/movies. Some units w/minibars, 1 w/fireplace. **Services:** Car-rental desk, masseur. Day care next door, courtesy shuttle to hospitals, nursing service available. **Facilities:** 1000 5 restaurants (*see* "Restaurants" below), 2 bars, games rm, sauna, whirlpool, beauty salon, washer/dryer. Five restaurants provide some of the area's finest dining. Large pool and whirlpool in 11th-floor domed rooftop recreation area, which has view of city on three sides. Sun deck on roof. **Rates:** $55–$135 S; $55–$145 D; $300–$1500 ste. Extra person $10. Children under age 18 stay free. Parking: Indoor, $3/day. AE, DC, DISC, MC, V.

Kahler Plaza Hotel
101 1st Ave SW, 55902; tel 507/280-6000 or toll free 800/533-1655; fax 507/280-8531. Jazz in lobby Friday afternoons. Connected to medical buildings via underground passage; connected to Kahler Hotel via skyway. **Rooms:** 194 rms and stes. Executive level. CI open/CO 2pm. Nonsmoking rms avail. **Amenities:** A/C, cable TV w/movies, dataport. All units w/minibars, some w/terraces, some w/whirlpools. **Services:** VP Social director, babysitting. Translations through Mayo Clinic. **Facilities:** 468 1 restaurant, 1 bar (w/entertainment), games rm, sauna, whirlpool, beauty salon, washer/dryer. Exercise room. Off premises health club one mile away. **Rates:** Peak (May–Sept) $125 S or D; $160–$1,750 ste. Children under age 18 stay free. Lower rates off-season. Parking: Indoor, $3/day. AE, CB, DC, DISC, EC, ER, JCB, MC, V.

Radisson Plaza Hotel
150 S Broadway, 55904; tel 507/281-8000 or toll free 800/333-3333; fax 507/281-4280. Received 1992 President's Award from Radisson Corp. **Rooms:** 212 rms and stes. Executive level. CI 3pm/CO noon. Nonsmoking rms avail. **Amenities:** A/C, satel TV w/movies, dataport, bathrobes. Some units w/minibars, some w/whirlpools. **Services:** VP Social director, children's program, babysitting. Masseur available through front desk; VCR rentals from gift shop ($8); international satellite television hookups for Middle East and Europe. Staff speaks Spanish, French, Arabic, and English. Free kids' program (no set times, but on demand with notice) takes youngsters to area attractions, with supervisors from area colleges. Concierge level offers complimentary continental breakfast (6:30–9:30am), and cocktail time (5:30–8pm). **Facilities:** 600 2 restaurants (*see* "Restaurants" below), 2 bars, games rm, spa, steam rm, whirlpool, beauty salon, washer/dryer. **Rates (CP):** Peak (May–Sept) $72–$139 S; $82–$159 D; $99–$650 ste. Children under age 18 stay free. Lower rates off-season. Parking: Indoor/outdoor, $3/day. AE, CB, DC, DISC, EC, ER, JCB, MC, V.

MOTELS

Comfort Inn
111 SE 28th St, 55904; tel 507/286-1001 or toll free 800/221-2222; fax 507/286-1001 ext 115. Off US 63. Lobby has writing tables and fireplace. Set back from highway. **Rooms:** 130 rms, stes, and effic. CI 1pm/CO noon. Nonsmoking rms avail. **Amenities:** A/C, cable TV w/movies. **Services:** Pets allowed in smoking rooms. Complimentary airport van available Mon–Fri 8am–5pm. **Facilities:** John Barleycorn Restaurant/Bar at entrance of property drive. **Rates (CP):** Peak (May–Sept) $54 S; $59 D; $65 ste; $57–$62 effic. Children under age 18 stay free. Lower rates off-season. Parking: Outdoor, free. Trucker rate, $29. AE, CB, DC, DISC, EC, ER, JCB, MC, V.

Days Inn
106 SE 21st St, 55904; tel 507/282-1756 or toll free 800/325-2525. Off US 63. Sitting room in comfortable lobby. **Rooms:** 80 rms. CI 2pm/CO noon. Nonsmoking rms avail. Several rooms have rocking chairs and hassocks. **Amenities:** A/C, satel TV w/movies. **Services:** **Facilities:** **Rates:** $39–$44 S; $44–$48 D; $45–$50 ste. Children under age 17 stay free. Parking: Outdoor, free. AE, CB, DC, DISC, EC, MC, V.

Days Inn/Daystop Inn
11 17th Ave SW, 55902; tel 507/282-2733 or toll free 800/533-2226; fax 507/282-2737. Off US 52. All rooms front outside; outdoor walkway carpeted and covered. Row of four-unit cottage/villas behind main building. **Rooms:** 49 rms and effic; 24 cottages/villas. CI noon/CO noon. Nonsmoking rms avail. **Amenities:** A/C, cable TV w/movies, refrig. Some units w/terraces. Cottage/villas have microwaves. **Services:** Complimentary shuttle van to Mayo Clinic and St Mary's and Methodist Hospitals. **Facilities:** **Rates (CP):** Peak (May–Sept) $42 S; $46 D; $38–$47 effic; $42–$46 cottage/villa. Extra person $5. Children under age 16 stay free. Lower rates off-season. Parking: Outdoor, free. Group rates avail. AE, CB, DC, DISC, EC, ER, JCB, MC, V.

Econo Lodge Downtown
519 3rd Ave SW, 55902; tel 507/288-1855 or toll free 800/533-2226; fax 507/288-1855. An older property spread out in three buildings. Located away from busy streets, but close to clinics, municipal park, and YMCA. **Rooms:** 62 rms. CI 2pm/CO noon. Nonsmoking rms avail. Rooms are accessed directly from outside and face parking area. **Amenities:** A/C, cable TV. Some units w/terraces. **Services:** Courtesy van service to and from Mayo Clinic and hospitals. **Facilities:** Washer/dryer. **Rates (CP):** $43–$50

S; $49–$55 D. Extra person $5. Children under age 18 stay free. Parking: Outdoor, free. Senior, AARP, corporate, and government discounts. AE, CB, DC, DISC, MC, V.

Friendship Inn Centre Towne

116 5th St SW, 55902; tel 507/289-1628 or toll free 800/533-2226; fax 507/289-1628. Older property with quiet atmosphere. Located away from busy steet traffic, pleasantly surrounded by mature trees. Close to Soldiers Field Park. **Rooms:** 59 rms and stes. CI 2pm/CO noon. Nonsmoking rms avail. Some rooms have concrete block construction. **Amenities:** A/C, cable TV. **Services:** Courtesy van to Mayo Clinic and hospitals. Winter car plug-ins. Advance notice required for pets. Friendly, accommodating service. **Facilities:** Games rm, sauna, washer/dryer. **Rates (CP):** Peak (May–July) $39–$44 S; $44–$49 D; $65 ste. Extra person $5. Children under age 18 stay free. Lower rates off-season. Parking: Outdoor, free. AARP, government, corporate, and military discounts. Mayo Clinic package includes 10% discount. Senior ''prime time'' package includes 30% discount upon availability. AE, CB, DC, DISC, MC, V.

Holiday Inn Downtown

220 S Broadway, 55904; tel 507/288-3231 or toll free 800/HOLIDAY; fax 507/288-6602. Lobby connects to parking ramp and is on second floor, accessed by escalators and elevators. Offices on first floor include National Car Rental and Rochester Chamber of Commerce. **Rooms:** 170 rms and stes. Executive level. CI 2pm/CO noon. Nonsmoking rms avail. 60% are nonsmoking, with more expected over next year. **Amenities:** A/C, cable TV w/movies, dataport. **Services:** Car-rental desk, social director, babysitting. Complimentary parking available for convention guests. Courtesy shuttle to hospitals. **Facilities:** 1 restaurant, 1 bar, washer/dryer. Complimentary pass available at front desk for nearby Kahler Health Center. **Rates:** $72–$102 S; $82–$102 D; $154–$174 ste. Children under age 19 stay free. Parking: Indoor, $3/day. AE, CB, DC, DISC, EC, JCB, MC, V.

Holiday Inn South

1630 S Broadway, 55904; tel 507/288-1844 or toll free 800/465-4329; fax 507/288-1844. Rambling facility with a pleasant, contemporary exterior. Skywalk connects buildings. Approximately one mile south of downtown and Mayo Clinic. **Rooms:** 196 rms, stes, and effic. CI 2pm/CO noon. Nonsmoking rms avail. Rooms accessed directly from outside, from hallway, or from poolside. Comfortable, updated interiors. **Amenities:** A/C, cable TV w/movies, dataport, voice mail. Some units w/terraces. **Services:** Social director, children's program, babysitting. Free shuttle to Mayo Clinic, hospitals. Advance notice required for pets. **Facilities:** 1 restaurant, 1 bar (w/entertainment), games rm, sauna, whirlpool, washer/dryer. **Rates:** $45–$109 S; $49–$109 D; $59–$79 effic; $69–$109 cottage/villa. Extra person $5. Children under age 18

stay free. Parking: Outdoor, free. Children eat free. AARP, Mayo Clinic, Great Rates, corporate, and government discounts. Weekend packages. AE, CB, DC, DISC, JCB, MC, V.

Motel 6

2107 W Frontage Rd, 55901; tel 507/282-6625; fax 507/280-7987. Off US 52. Balcony around second floor. No parking of trailers. **Rooms:** 107 rms. CI 2pm/CO noon. Nonsmoking rms avail. Bright bedspreads liven up rooms. All rooms open to outside—no hallways. **Amenities:** A/C, satel TV w/movies. All units w/terraces. **Services:** Complimentary courtesy van to hospitals. **Facilities:** **Rates:** Peak (May–Oct) $28 S; $34 D. Children under age 17 stay free. Lower rates off-season. Parking: Outdoor, free. $3 per person added to flat room rates. AE, CB, DC, DISC, EC, ER, JCB, MC, V.

Ramada Inn

1625 S Broadway, 55904; tel 507/281-2211 or toll free 800/533-2226; fax 507/288-8979. Located two blocks south of Olmstead County Fairgrounds, near restaurants. **Rooms:** 165 rms and stes. Executive level. CI 1pm/CO noon. Nonsmoking rms avail. **Amenities:** A/C, cable TV w/movies. **Services:** Social director. Full complimentary breakfast buffet Mon–Fri 7–11am in the Cobblestone Restaurant; cost for breakfast on Sat is $4, and brunch on Sun is $8. Complimentary van to area hospitals. Translators available through Mayo Clinic. **Facilities:** 1 restaurant, 1 bar, games rm, sauna, whirlpool, washer/dryer. **Rates (CP):** Peak (May–Sept) $49–$63 S; $53–$69 D; $75 ste. Extra person $5. Children under age 17 stay free. Lower rates off-season. Parking: Outdoor, free. AE, CB, DC, DISC, EC, MC, V.

Red Carpet Inn

2214 S Broadway, 55904; tel 507/282-7448 or toll free 800/658-7048. Off MN 53. Older motel located approximately three miles from Mayo Clinic. **Rooms:** 47 rms, stes, and effic. CI 5pm/CO noon. Nonsmoking rms avail. Back rooms in one building face car wash, which is noisy during daytime hours. Some housekeeping units available. **Amenities:** A/C, cable TV w/movies. **Services:** Free shuttle to Mayo Clinic and hospitals. Small pets with advance notice. Friendly and helpful service. **Facilities:** Washer/dryer. **Rates (CP):** $36 S; $40–$42 D; $50 ste; $37–$43 effic. Extra person $5. Children under age 12 stay free. Parking: Outdoor, free. Discounts for Clinic visitors, AARP, seniors, and commercial rates. AE, DISC, MC, V.

Super 8 Motel South #1

1230 S Broadway, 55904; tel 507/288-8288 or toll free 800/800-8000; fax 507/288-0288 ext 350. Adjacent to Olmstead County Fairgrounds (Graham Park) to the south. The closest restaurant is a five-minute drive away. **Rooms:** 79 rms. CI 3pm/CO noon. Nonsmoking rms avail. Some beds squeak. **Amenities:** A/C, cable TV w/movies. Some units w/whirlpools. **Services:** **Facilities:** Whirlpool, washer/dryer. **Rates:** $48–$62 S; $54–$72 D. Extra person $5. Children under age 18 stay free. Parking: Outdoor, free. AE, CB, DC, DISC, EC, MC, V.

≡≡ Super 8 Motel South #2

1850 S Broadway, 55904; tel 507/282-9905 or toll free 800/ 800-8000; fax 507/282-9905 ext 252. Off US 63. Two blocks south of Olmstead County Fairgrounds. **Rooms:** 63 rms and effic. CI open/CO noon. Nonsmoking rms avail. **Amenities:** A/C, cable TV w/movies. **Services:** Courtesy van takes guests to area hospitals. **Facilities:** **Rates (CP):** $40–$46 S; $45–$50 D; $45–$50 effic. Children under age 16 stay free. Parking: Outdoor, free. AE, CB, DC, DISC, EC, MC, V.

≡≡ Super 8 Motel West

1608 2nd St, 55902; tel 507/281-5100 or toll free 800/ 533-2226; fax 507/281-5100. Off MN 53. Older property facing quiet residential street on one side. **Rooms:** 65 rms and effic. CI 1pm/CO noon. Nonsmoking rms avail. **Amenities:** A/C, cable TV. Some units w/terraces. **Services:** Courtesy van to and from Mayo Clinic and hospitals. Pets require advance notice. Friendly, helpful staff. **Facilities:** Washer/dryer. **Rates (CP):** $33–$48 S; $36–$54 D; $36–$58 effic. Extra person $5. Children under age 18 stay free. Parking: Outdoor, free. AARP, corporate, and government discounts. AE, CB, DC, DISC, JCB, MC, V.

≡ Thrift Lodge

1837 S Broadway, 55904; tel 507/288-2031 or toll free 800/ 533-2226; fax 507/289-3981. Off US 63. Small grassy area separates rooms from parking area. **Rooms:** 27 rms. CI noon/CO noon. All rooms face parking lot. **Amenities:** A/C, cable TV w/movies. **Facilities:** **Rates:** $33–$35 S; $40–$45 D. Children under age 10 stay free. Parking: Outdoor, free. AE, CB, DC, DISC, EC, MC, V.

≡≡ Travelodge

426 Second St S, 55902; tel 507/289-4095 or toll free 800/ 533-2226; fax 507/289-5197. An older property. Lobby and porch area with chairs above street level, away from noise. Adjacent to Mayo Clinic and close to hospitals, shopping, and restaurants. **Rooms:** 65 rms, stes, and effic. CI 2pm/CO noon. Nonsmoking rms avail. **Amenities:** A/C, cable TV. Some units w/terraces, some w/whirlpools. Refrigerators available. **Services:** Free courtesy van to clinics and hospitals. Advance notice required for pets. **Facilities:** Whirlpool, washer/dryer. **Rates (CP):** Peak (June–Sept) $39–$64 S or D; $49–$64 ste; $39–$59 effic. Extra person $5. Children under age 16 stay free. Lower rates off-season. Parking: Outdoor, free. AARP, Clinic, corporate, Boy Scout discounts. AE.

RESTAURANTS

♣ Chardonnay

723 2nd St SW; tel 507/252-1310. Just W of Mayo Clinic. **New American/French.** Leaded glass windows and original woodwork decorate this 105-year-old Victorian house. Everything is freshly made and prepared: from pan-seared salmon with mango vinaigrette and almond butter, to grilled eggplant with sun-dried tomato relish, to fudge brownie with chocolate sauce. Menu changes seasonally. The chef "guarantees" that a correct match will be made between a diner's entree and one of the 300 wine labels on the wine list. **FYI:** Reservations recommended. Beer and wine only. No smoking. **Open:** Lunch Mon–Fri 11am–2pm; dinner Mon–Sat 5:30–9:30pm. Closed July 1–4. **Prices:** Main courses $16–$21. AE, CB, DC, DISC, MC, V.

♣ Elizabethan Room

In Kahler Hotel, 20 2nd Ave SW; tel 507/282-2581. **American.** This elegant, plush old room with deep brocaded chairs is a very special setting for some very special dishes. The international clientele dines on such entrees as filet mignon stuffed with crabmeat and roasted in garlic sauce, and veal sweetbreads poached in court bouillon, sautéed with wild mushrooms, and flamed in brandy. For a dramatic touch, try the roast duckling flamed in cognac at tableside. **FYI:** Reservations recommended. Piano/violin. Dress code. **Open:** Lunch Mon–Fri 11:30am–2pm; dinner Mon–Thurs 5:30–9pm, Fri–Sat 5:30–10pm; brunch Sun 10am–2pm. **Prices:** Main courses $6–$52. AE, DC, DISC, MC, V.

McCormick's

In Radisson Plaza Hotel, 150 S Broadway; tel 507/281-8000. **American.** The large menu here can suit many tastes. Fare includes tortellini carbonara, New York strip steak, walleye pike, and burgers. The Mermaid Bar offers appetizers in bar until midnight. **FYI:** Reservations recommended. Children's menu. **Open:** Daily 6:30am–midnight. **Prices:** Main courses $5–$14. AE, CB, DC, DISC, MC, V.

★ Michael's Restaurant

15 S Broadway; tel 507/288-2020. **American.** Opened in 1951 and long a favorite in Rochester. Pictures of famous personalities who have dined here cover walls. A broad menu of American favorites includes broiled Cape Cod scallops and vegetable stir-fry, porterhouse pork chop with honey-dijon glaze, and grilled chicken with apple-maple glaze. **FYI:** Reservations recommended. Children's menu. **Open:** Mon–Thurs 11am–10pm, Fri–Sat 11–11pm. **Prices:** Main courses $11–$25. AE, CB, DC, DISC, MC, V.

★ Smiling Moose

1829 MN 52 N; tel 507/288-1689. Exit 19th St NW. **American.** Even though this popular eatery can be very busy, the atmosphere is relaxed in the rustic interior. Grilled fajitas, Canadian chicken melt, and Mount St Clair nachos are favorites. All desserts and dressings made on premises. Features over 25 beers on tap including seasonal and specialty beers, microbrews, imports, and some regional beers. **FYI:** Reservations not accepted. Children's menu. **Open: Prices:** Main courses $10–$12. AE, DC, DISC, MC, V.

$ ★ Wong's Cafe
4 3rd St SW; tel 507/282-7545. **Chinese.** Wong's has been in this location, a former bank, since 1983, but the family has been in the Rochester restaurant business for 52 years. Basic Cantonese and spicy Szechuan specialties, as well as some curry dishes, are on hand. **FYI:** Reservations recommended. Children's menu. Beer and wine only. **Open:** Mon–Sat 11am–9:30pm, Sun 11am–9pm. **Prices:** Main courses $5–$10. DC, DISC, MC, V. 🍴 ♥

ATTRACTIONS 🖼

Mayo Clinic
200 1st St SW; tel 507/284-2450. Founded in 1914 by Dr William Worral Mayo and his two sons, the Mayo Clinic is the largest and one of the most prestigious group medical practices in the world. It maintains a staff of more than 800 physicians, surgeons, and medical scientists, in addition to 1,500 medical trainees and more than 5,000 paramedical personnel. The Mayo Medical Museum offers a variety of films, videotapes, and exhibits dealing with the human body, illness, and current approaches to medical treatment. Guided tours Mon–Fri at 10am and 2pm. **Free**

Mayowood
1195 County Rd 22 SW; tel 507/282-9447. The splendid home of two generations of the Mayo family, built in 1911 by Dr Charles H Mayo. Perched on 3,000 acres overlooking the Zumbro River Valley, Mayowood has welcomed such famous figures as Helen Keller, Franklin D Roosevelt, and Adlai Stevenson. Over 38 rooms are furnished in American, English, French, Spanish, and Italian antiques. The only way to get to Mayowood is via an Olmstead County Historical Society shuttle bus. **Open:** Apr–Oct, Tues–Sat 11am–2pm. $$$

St Cloud

Seat of Stearns County, in central Minnesota. Founded in 1856 by German settlers, St Cloud is a center of granite quarries, dairy processing, and paper companies. Somewhere nearby is Garrison Keillor's mythical community of Lake Wobegon. **Information:** St Cloud Area Convention & Visitors Bureau, PO Box 487, St Cloud, 56302 (tel 320/251-2940 or toll free 800/264-2940).

HOTEL 🛏

☰☰☰ Best Western Americanna Inn
520 S US 10, 56304; tel 320/252-8700 or toll free 800/950-8701; fax 320/252-8700. A fairly new building, very clean and well kept. Best suited to business travelers. **Rooms:** 63 rms and stes. CI 3pm/CO 11am. Nonsmoking rms avail. **Amenities:** 🛅 ⚙ 🖨 ☎ A/C, cable TV w/movies, dataport. Some units w/whirlpools. **Services:** ✕ 🚐 🖨 ⏚ 🔔 Car-rental desk. Free service to St Cloud airport; service to Minneapolis/St Paul airport for fee. **Facilities:** 🏊 🛎 ⅃ 1

restaurant (lunch and dinner only), 1 bar, games rm, sauna, whirlpool, washer/dryer. **Rates:** $40–$99 S; $55–$99 D; $94–$100 ste. Extra person $5. Children under age 19 stay free. Parking: Outdoor, free. AE, DC, DISC, JCB, MC, V.

MOTELS

☰☰ Fairfield Inn by Marriott
4120 S 2nd St, 56301 (Waite Park); tel 320/654-1881 or toll free 800/228-2800. Relatively new building in Waite Park, a neighborhood five minutes from downtown. **Rooms:** 57 rms and stes. CI 3pm/CO 11am. Nonsmoking rms avail. **Amenities:** 🛅 ⚙ A/C, cable TV w/movies. **Services:** 🚐 🖨 ⏚ 🔔 **Facilities:** 🏊 🛎 16 🛎 Games rm, whirlpool. **Rates (CP):** $38–$63 S; $43–$86 D; $59–$91 ste. Extra person $5. Children under age 18 stay free. Parking: Outdoor, free. AE, DC, DISC, MC, V.

☰ Motel 6
815 1st St S, 56387 (Waite Park); tel 320/253-7070; fax 320/253-0436. Exit 164 off I-94 S; exit 167 off I-94 W. Two-story building. Clean, average rooms. **Rooms:** 94 rms. CI open/CO noon. Nonsmoking rms avail. **Amenities:** 🛅 A/C, satel TV. **Services:** ⏚ 🔔 **Facilities:** 🛎 **Rates:** $29–$41 S; $35–$70 D. Extra person $6. Children under age 17 stay free. Parking: Outdoor, free. AE, CB, DC, DISC, MC, V.

☰ Super 8 Motel
50 Park Ave S, 56301 (Waite Park); tel 320/253-5530 or toll free 800/800-8000. Exit 15N off I-94. Two-story, plain, brick structure. **Rooms:** 68 rms. CI 2pm/CO 11am. Nonsmoking rms avail. **Amenities:** 🛅 ⚙ A/C, cable TV w/movies. **Services:** ⏚ 🔔 **Facilities:** 🛎 **Rates (CP):** $35–$46 S; $37–$59 D. Extra person $5. Children under age 12 stay free. Parking: Outdoor, free. AE, CB, DC, DISC, MC, V.

ATTRACTIONS 🖼

Riverside Park
1515 Riverside Dr SE; tel 320/255-7256. Situated on the east bank of the Mississippi River, this park features flower gardens, picnic areas, tennis courts, and a wading pool, as well as a lighted, half-mile trail for cross-country skiing. Winter skating and sledding are also popular in the winter. Maps available at park's main office and at a shelter located on the ski trail. **Open:** Daily sunrise–sunset. **Free**

Stearns County Heritage Center
235 33rd Ave S; tel 320/253-8424. Features life-size replicas of a granite quarry, a 100-year-old dairy barn, and a wilderness area as it would have appeared in the 1850s. Other exhibits include a 1919 Pan Motor Car, and photographs and maps detailing the history of central Minnesota. **Open:** Peak (June–Aug) Mon–Sat 10am–4pm, Sun noon–4pm. Reduced hours off-season. $

St Paul

See also Hastings, Minneapolis, Stillwater

Seat of Ramsey County, capital of Minnesota, and sister city of Minneapolis, St Paul excels in culture, strong neighborhoods, and architectural beauty. Although smaller than Minneapolis, it still has such world-class cultural institutions as the St Paul Chamber Orchestra and a large number of colleges and universities. Its skyway system is nearly five miles long. **Information:** St Paul Convention & Visitors Bureau, 102 Norwest Center, 55 E 5th St, St Paul, 55101-1713 (tel 612/297-6985).

HOTELS 🏨

🈁🈁 Best Western Kelly Inn

161 St Anthony Ave, 55103; tel 612/227-8711 or toll free 800/528-1234. The building is fairly old and pretty plain, but the accommodations are serviceable for the traveler on the go. Located minutes from downtown. **Rooms:** 126 rms and stes. CI 2pm/CO noon. Nonsmoking rms avail. Views of downtown area in some rooms and of Sears in others. **Amenities:** 🛁 ⚲ A/C, cable TV w/movies. Some units w/whirlpools. **Services:** ✕ 🚗 🖨 ⟲ ⬦ **Facilities:** 🔥 200 1 restaurant, 1 bar (w/entertainment), games rm, sauna, whirlpool. Lots of tables and chairs for lounging by the large, heated pool. **Rates:** Peak (June 15–Sept 15) $74–$84 S; $79–$89 D; $110–$180 ste. Extra person $8. Children under age 16 stay free. Lower rates off-season. Parking: Outdoor, free. Many special packages avail. AE, CB, DC, DISC, MC, V.

🈁🈁 Days Inn Civic Center

175 7th St W, 55102; tel 612/292-8929 or toll free 800/DAYS-INN; fax 612/292-1149. Tall, plain building in heart of downtown St Paul, right across the street from civic center; skyway now under construction connecting hotel to civic center. Best suited for people who are in town for special events and for groups. **Rooms:** 203 rms, stes, and effic. CI 3pm/CO noon. Nonsmoking rms avail. Some views of downtown or cathedral available. **Amenities:** 🛁 ⚲ A/C, cable TV w/movies, voice mail, in-rm safe. **Services:** ✕ 🚗 🖨 ⬦ **Facilities:** 90 ⚤ 1 restaurant, 1 bar. Connected with expo center, good for conferences, banquets. **Rates (CP):** Peak (June–Sept) $57 S; $63 D; $75 ste; $100 effic. Extra person $8. Children under age 12 stay free. Lower rates off-season. Parking: Outdoor, free. AE, DC, DISC, MC, V.

🈁🈁🈁 Radisson Hotel St Paul

11 E Kellogg Blvd, 55101; tel 612/292-1900 or toll free 800/333-3333; fax 612/224-8999. Downtown St Paul, overlooking Mississippi River. Practically on the edge of the Mississippi River; large patio on second floor has nice view. **Rooms:** 475 rms and stes. Executive level. CI 3pm/CO noon. Nonsmoking rms avail. Majority of rooms have views of the river. Some rooms have sliding glass doors leading to pool area. **Amenities:** 🛁 ⚲ 🍽 A/C, cable TV w/movies, dataport, voice mail. Some units w/whirlpools. **Services:** ✕ 🔑 🚗 🖨 ⟲ Twice-daily maid svce, car-rental desk, babysitting. **Facilities:** 🔥 🛳 1800 ⚤ 1 restaurant (see "Restaurants" below), 1 bar, games rm, whirlpool. Live piano music in lobby/bar area. **Rates:** Peak (July–Oct) $79–$140 S or D; $170–$500 ste. Extra person $10. Children under age 12 stay free. Lower rates off-season. AP and MAP rates avail. Parking: Indoor, $9/day. AE, CB, DC, DISC, MC, V.

🈁🈁🈁 Ramada Hotel

1870 Old Hudson Rd, 55119; tel 612/735-2330 or toll free 800/RAMADA; fax 612/735-1953. White Bear exit off I-94. 5 acres. Two buildings have been joined into one hotel, connected by one long corridor. Located in a busy commercial area dotted with fast food restaurants. Just 10 minutes from downtown, and 10–15 minutes from Afton Alps Ski Area. **Rooms:** 201 rms and stes. Executive level. CI 3pm/CO noon. Nonsmoking rms avail. **Amenities:** 🛁 A/C, cable TV w/movies, voice mail. Some units w/terraces. **Services:** ✕ 🔑 🚗 🖨 ⬦ Social director. **Facilities:** 🔥 300 🖥 ⚤ 1 restaurant, 1 bar, games rm, sauna, whirlpool, washer/dryer. Children under age 12 eat free. **Rates (BB):** $83 S; $94 D; $107 ste. Extra person $10. Children under age 18 stay free. Parking: Outdoor, free. AE, DC, DISC, JCB, MC, V.

🈁🈁🈁🈁 The Saint Paul Hotel

350 Market St, 55102 (Downtown); tel 612/292-9292 or toll free 800/292-9292; fax 612/228-9506. At 5th St. This beautiful, sophisticated hotel housed in a 1910 building is a welcome addition to Rice Park. Well suited to business travelers. **Rooms:** 254 rms and stes. CI 4pm/CO noon. Nonsmoking rms avail. Exquisite rooms are decorated in European style, with lots of bright yellows and dark greens. Fine views. **Amenities:** 🛁 ⚲ A/C, cable TV w/movies. Some units w/minibars. Nintendo games in all rooms. Voice mail in Japanese or English. **Services:** ✕ 🔑 VP 🚗 🖨 ⬦ Twice-daily maid svce, car-rental desk. Concierge can arrange for most things, including tailoring (done across the street). Afternoon tea offered each Thurs and Fri at beginning of month—more often during holiday season. Electronic check-out available; separate check-in and check-out for groups. Concierge will arrange to have a treadmill, stair machine, stationary bike, or workout tapes delivered to room (for about an hour or so) at no extra charge. Multilingual staff. **Facilities:** 350 🖥 ⚤ 2 restaurants (see "Restaurants" below), 1 bar. **Rates:** $145 S; $160 D; $175–$675 ste. Extra person $15. Children under age 17 stay free. Parking: Indoor, $10/day. AE, CB, DC, DISC, ER, JCB, MC, V.

MOTELS

🈁🈁🈁 Best Western Maplewood Inn

1780 E County Rd D, 55109; tel 612/770-2811 or toll free 800/528-1234; fax 612/770-2811. At I-694 and White Bear Ave (exit 50). Located just behind Maplewood Mall. Courtyard area with patio furniture in middle of motel. Attracts corporate clients during the week and leisure travelers on weekends. **Rooms:** 118 rms and stes. CI 3pm/CO noon. Nonsmoking rms avail. **Amenities:** 🛏 🍴 📺 🈁 A/C, satel TV w/movies, dataport. Some units w/terraces. **Services:** ✕ 🚐 🧖 🍽 🍴 Car-rental desk, babysitting. **Facilities:** 🏊 300 💻 🚺 1 restaurant, 1 bar (w/entertainment), games rm, sauna, whirlpool, washer/dryer. **Rates:** $58–$90 S; $62–$90 D; $90–$110 ste. Extra person $4. Children under age 18 stay free. AP and MAP rates avail. Parking: Outdoor, free. AE, CB, DC, DISC, JCB, MC, V.

≣≣ Excel Inn of St Paul
1739 Old Hudson Rd, 55106; tel 612/771-5566 or toll free 800/356-8013; fax 612/771-1262. Plain, three-story, brick motel situated 10–15 minutes from Afton Alps ski area. **Rooms:** 100 rms and stes. CI noon/CO noon. Nonsmoking rms avail. **Amenities:** 🛏 🍴 A/C, cable TV w/movies, dataport. 1 unit w/whirlpool. **Services:** 🆅🅿 🧖 🍽 🍴 **Facilities:** 🚺 Games rm, washer/dryer. **Rates (CP):** Peak (June–Aug) $52 S; $59 D; $75–$125 ste. Extra person $4. Children under age 18 stay free. Lower rates off-season. Parking: Outdoor, free. AE, CB, DC, DISC, MC, V.

RESTAURANTS 🍴

Acropol Inn
748 Grand Ave (Summit Hill); tel 612/298-0151. **Greek.** Decorated with paintings of Greek islands and frosted-glass pictures of Greek figures. The menu features the popular lamb shank and a combination plate of four Greek delicacies—perhaps pasticcio, tiropita (feta cheese and spices wrapped in phyllo), spanakopita (spinach and cheese baked in phyllo), and dolmathes (ground meat and rice wrapped in grapes leaves). **FYI:** Reservations recommended. Children's menu. Beer and wine only. **Open:** Mon–Thurs 11am–9pm, Fri–Sat 11am–10pm. **Prices:** Main courses $11–$20. MC, V. 🚺

★ Bread & Chocolate
In Victoria Crossing, 867 Grand Ave; tel 612/228-1017. At Victoria. **Sandwiches/Bakery.** A wonderful sandwich shop in Victoria Crossing West where you can get rolls, cookies, pies, and cakes as well as a good selection of sandwiches with interesting spreads, like vegetable and crab and artichoke. **FYI:** Reservations not accepted. No liquor license. No smoking. **Open:** Mon–Fri 6:30am–5pm, Sat–Sun 7am–5pm. **Prices:** Lunch main courses $3–$6. No CC. 🎦 🚺

♣ The Cafe
In Saint Paul Hotel, 350 Market St (Downtown); tel 612/292-9292. **Regional American.** Set in an elegant but casual room downstairs from the The Grill, this restaurant is quiet and relaxed and offers the same exceptional fare as its upstairs neighbor. The strawberry spinach salad is delicious, and the fish specials are often outstanding. **FYI:** Reservations recommended. **Open:** Breakfast daily 6:30–11am; lunch Mon 11am–2pm, Tues–Sat 11am–1pm, Sun 11am–1:30pm; dinner Tues–Fri 1–9pm, Sat 4:30–10pm. **Prices:** Main courses $8–$22. AE, DC, DISC, MC, V. 🆅🅿 🚺

★ Cafe Latte
850 Grand Ave (Crocus Hill); tel 612/224-5687. At Victoria. **American/Cafeteria.** The owner of Bread and Chocolate, just a few doors away, operates this cafe. The food is the same high quality, but there are more choices. Homemade soups and breads, variety of salads, and excellent desserts (turtle cake is a specialty). **FYI:** Reservations not accepted. Beer and wine only. No smoking. **Open:** Mon–Thurs 9am–11pm, Fri–Sat 9am–midnight, Sun 9am–9pm. **Prices:** Main courses $5–$7. AE, MC, V. 🎦 🚺

Cafe Minnesota by Bon Appetit
In Minnesota History Center, 345 Kellogg Blvd W (Downtown); tel 612/297-4859. Just off I-94 at Marion St exit. **New American/Cafe.** This museum cafeteria serves fine fare which is definitely not typical cafeteria food. The casual, very bright eating area has a nice view. The menu, which changes daily, offers creative soups, salads, panini sandwiches, grilled and carved meats, and main courses, prepared at different stations in the cafeteria. Sample items might include garden vegetable soup, a grilled tuna steak sandwich, lavender-roasted pork loin, and Cajun fried catfish with hush puppies. **FYI:** Reservations not accepted. Children's menu. Beer and wine only. No smoking. **Open:** Mon–Fri 11:30am–2pm, Sat–Sun 11:30am–3pm. **Prices:** Lunch main courses $2–$6. No CC. 🍴 🎦 🚺

Caravan Serai
2175 Ford Pkwy (Highland); tel 612/690-1935. **Afghani.** This Afghan restaurant claims to be the first of its kind in the United States. The Afghan dining room is decorated with pillowed ceilings and beautiful Afghan treasures; seating is American (booths and tables) or Afghan-style (low tables and pillows on the floor). Most dishes are cooked in a special clay pot, such as the half-chicken marinated in 16 spices. Deli area offers take-out. **FYI:** Reservations recommended. Guitar/belly dancer. Children's menu. Beer and wine only. **Open:** Lunch Tues–Fri 11am–2pm; dinner Mon–Thurs 5–9:30pm, Fri–Sat 5–10:30pm, Sun 4:30–9:30pm. **Prices:** Main courses $9–$16. AE, DC, MC, V. 🚺

Carmelo's
238 Snelling Ave S (Groveland/MacAlester); tel 612/699-2448. At St Claire. **Italian.** Intimate, quiet place, with tables draped in green floral cloths and decorated with flowers, and soft music playing in the background. The menu offers many choices, from individual-size pizzas to 15 pastas to outstanding daily specials. Good bets are salmon steak served with lemon and rosemary butter on angel hair pasta and shrimp and chicken kebab. Friendly, efficient staff. **FYI:** Reservations accepted. Beer and wine only. No smoking. **Open:** Lunch Mon–Fri 11am–2pm; dinner Mon–Thurs 5–9pm, Fri–Sat 5–10pm. **Prices:** Main courses $7–$13. MC, V. 🚺

Carousel
In Radisson Hotel, 11 E Kellogg Blvd; tel 612/292-1900. **New American.** The only revolving restaurant in the Twin

Cities provides beautiful views of the bluffs, the Mississippi, and, on a clear day, the skyline of downtown Minneapolis, all from its 22nd-floor perch. The New American dishes include chicken Oscar, a boneless breast of chicken topped with crabmeat and béarnaise sauce with Minnesota wild rice; and pecan walleye pike, walleye dipped in egg and pecan flour and served with toasted pecan maple butter. You can get your favorite cut of steak here as well. **FYI:** Reservations accepted. Children's menu. **Open:** Mon–Thurs 6:30am–10:30pm, Fri 6:30am–11pm, Sat 7am–11pm, Sun 1–10:30pm. **Prices:** Main courses $14–$22; prix fixe $22. AE, CB, DC, DISC, ER, MC, V. 🏔 📧 ⅙

Ciatti's

850 Grand Ave (Summit Hill); tel 612/292-9942. At Victoria. **Italian.** Part of a chain located throughout the Twin Cities area. The mainly Italian menu includes such standards as fettucine ciatti, eggplant Parmesan, and cappellini Florentine, thin pasta tossed in fresh spinach and sun-dried tomatoes. **FYI:** Reservations accepted. Children's menu. **Open:** Lunch Mon–Sat 11am–2pm; dinner Mon–Thurs 2–10pm, Fri–Sat 2–11pm, Sun 2–10pm; brunch Sun 10am–2pm. **Prices:** Main courses $8–$13. AE, DC, DISC, MC, V. ⅙

Cognac McCarthy's Grill

162 N Dale St (Cathedral Hill); tel 612/224-4617. ½ mi W of the cathedral. **American.** Awnings and plants surround an inviting brick exterior, and the interior features large windows, lots of wood, and well-spaced tables. Home-style cooking is the specialty (there is a grill, but no deep-fryer), with one of the favorite items being garlicky French-Cuban rotisserie chicken, served with seasoned small grilled red potatoes. All breads are homemade. Sunday brunch is particularly good. **FYI:** Reservations not accepted. **Open:** Mon–Sat 7am–1am, Sun 9am–9pm. **Prices:** Main courses $8–$10. AE, DC, MC, V. 🍽 📧 ⅙

Cossetta's Italian Market & Pizzeria

211 W 7th St; tel 612/222-3476. 1 block W of Civic Center between Kellogg Blvd and Chestnut. **Italian.** This enterprise began in 1911 as an Italian market; it was not until later that it was expanded to include this simple, fun restaurant. Historic pictures on the walls and an open view of the kitchen area provide charm. The menu features prize-winning pizzas and fine mostaccioli. **FYI:** Reservations not accepted. Beer and wine only. No smoking. **Open:** Mon–Sat 11am–10pm, Sun 11am–8pm. **Prices:** Main courses $5–$10. No CC. 🍽 👥 ⅙

Dakota Bar and Grill

1021 E Bandana Blvd (Energy Park); tel 612/642-1442. Between Lexington and Snelling. **Regional American.** All of the tables are decorated with flowers and offer a good view of the stage where live entertainment is regularly scheduled. Menu has a midwestern theme and features all-local produce, meats, fish, and game (including farm-raised guinea hen, partridge, and duck). The caesar salad and pork chops with cinnamon rhubarb sauce are standouts. **FYI:** Reservations recommended. Jazz. Children's menu. **Open:** Dinner Mon–Thurs 5–10:30pm, Fri–Sat 5–11:30pm, Sun 5–9pm; brunch Sun 10am–2pm. **Prices:** Main courses $12–$21; prix fixe $20. AE, DC, DISC, MC, V. ⅙

★ Dixie's

695 Grand Ave (Summit Hill); tel 612/222-7345. **Cajun.** The menu offers burgers, sandwiches, and other items, all with a Cajun/Southern flair. Favorite items are fried salad, ribs, chili, and red beans and rice. Comfortable, large bar area with lots of seating. **FYI:** Reservations accepted. **Open:** Mon–Sat 11am–midnight, Sun 10am–11pm. **Prices:** Main courses $6–$16. AE, DC, DISC, MC, V. ⅙

Fabulous Ferns

400 Selby Ave (Cathedral Hill); tel 612/225-9414. At Western, 3 blocks W of the Cathedral. **American.** Well-lighted with a fun upbeat ambience, as well as very tasty modern American fare. Offered are a wonderful chicken and dried-cranberry salad, as well as great pasta primavera. Friendly service. **FYI:** Reservations accepted. Children's menu. **Open:** Mon–Thurs 11am–10pm, Fri–Sat 11am–11pm, Sun 10am–10pm. **Prices:** Main courses $9–$12. AE, DC, DISC, MC, V. ⅙

Forepaugh's Restaurant

276 Exchange St; tel 612/224-5606. 3 blocks W of Civic Center. **French.** At this historic mansion, built in 1870 and adjacent to Irvine Park, the grace and grandeur of the architecture is matched only by the gracious French cuisine prepared by chef/owner Eric Schlenker. The formal, Victorian setting encompasses three floors and nine separate dining areas. All baked goods are made on premises. Complimentary shuttle to nearby Ordway Music Theater provided nightly. **FYI:** Reservations recommended. **Open:** Lunch Mon–Fri 11:30am–2pm; dinner Mon–Sat 5:30–9:30pm, Sun 5:30–8:30pm; brunch Sun 10:30am–1:30pm. **Prices:** Main courses $4–$18. AE, DC, MC, V. 🍷 🏛 VP ⅙

Grandview Grill

1818 Grand Ave (Highland); tel 612/698-2346. **American.** Excellent food in a diner-style setting. The sister restaurant to Louisiana Cafe, you can expect the same great breakfasts—such as the elaborate Tex-Mex and Cajun plates—with a touch less spice. Well-executed traditional American dishes for lunch. **FYI:** Reservations not accepted. Children's menu. No liquor license. **Open:** Mon–Sat 6am–3pm, Sun 8am–3pm. **Prices:** Lunch main courses $5–$8. No CC. ⅙

Green Mill

57 S Hamlen Ave (Macalester); tel 612/690-0539. At Grand Ave. **Pizza.** Rich, dark woodwork, hanging plants, and comfortable seating, and great, simple food make this a most inviting place. The pescara pizza is outstanding, and you can order extra ingredients (like spicy chicken and sun-dried tomatoes) on any pizza. There are also burgers and sandwiches. A brewery attached to the restaurant produces its own

distinctive beer. **FYI:** Reservations accepted. Children's menu. **Open:** Mon–Thurs 11am–11pm, Fri–Sat 11am–midnight, Sun 10am–11pm. **Prices:** Main courses $8–$13. AE, DC, DISC, MC, V. 🍷 &

Highland Grill

771 Cleveland Ave S (Highland); tel 612/690-1173. At Ford Pkwy. **Eclectic.** An interesting variation on the traditional diner. While there are booths and a counter, the decor is stylish and features some interesting artwork, which can be purchased. And the food differs from typical greasy diner fare as well. One of the owners is Australian, and it shows in meals like fish-and-chips and Peter's-by-the-Sea burger, topped with a fried egg. Also many innovative specials and organic and vegetarian dishes. Definitely worth the trip. **FYI:** Reservations accepted. Children's menu. Beer and wine only. **Open:** Breakfast Mon–Fri 7–11am, Sat–Sun 8–11am; lunch daily 11am–3pm; dinner Mon–Wed 5:30–9pm, Thurs–Sat 5:30–10pm. **Prices:** Main courses $8–$12. No CC. 🍷

Khyber Pass Cafe

1399 St Clair Ave (Highland); tel 612/698-5403. At Albert. **Afghani.** A small, quaint neighborhood cafe offering authentic Afghani food. Family-run, with a light and casual, relaxed atmosphere, the cafe attracts the locals with simple, hearty dishes like stewed chicken over rice. **FYI:** Reservations accepted. Beer and wine only. No smoking. **Open:** Lunch Tues–Sat 11am–1pm; dinner Tues–Sat 5–9pm. **Prices:** Main courses $6–$12. No CC. 👪 &

La Cucaracha

318 Dale St S (Summit Hill); tel 612/221-9682. At Grand Ave. **Mexican.** Tucked away in a well-hidden spot on the block since 1961, this family-owned restaurant is definitely well worth the search. The menu offers authentic Mexican fare, including enchiladas, burritos, and tostadas, as well as other Mexican standbys. Black-bean burrito and fajitas are favorites. **FYI:** Reservations accepted. Children's menu. Beer and wine only. **Open:** Mon–Thurs 11am–11pm, Fri–Sat 11am–midnight. **Prices:** Main courses $6–$10. AE, DC, MC, V.

Landmark Cafe

410 St Peter St; tel 612/292-1980. ¼ block from 6th St, across from the Landmark Center. **Burgers.** All the tables in this small, simple breakfast-and-lunch place offer a nice view of the Landmark Center right across the street. The Tex-Mex and Cajun breakfast plates are great. Daily lunch specials change, but Thursday walleye pike basket and the Landmark burger served on sourdough bread with bacon and cheese are both treats. **FYI:** Reservations not accepted. Children's menu. No liquor license. **Open:** Mon–Fri 7am–2:30pm, Sat 8am–2pm. **Prices:** Main courses $2–$7. No CC. 🍷 ❤ &

The Lexington

1096 Grand Ave; tel 612/222-5878. At Lexington. **American.** A local favorite that has been around for many years. Lovely main dining area decorated mostly in pink, and tables have candles. Favorites include fresh walleye or salmon, bone-in steer tenderloin, and filet mignon béarnaise. Food also served in the bar. **FYI:** Reservations recommended. **Open:** Lunch Mon–Sat 11am–2pm; dinner Mon–Thurs 2–10pm, Fri–Sat 2–11pm, Sun 4–9pm; brunch Sun 10am–3pm. **Prices:** Main courses $8–$25. AE, DC, DISC, MC, V. ❤ 👪 &

Louisiana Cafe

518 Selby Ave (Ramsey Hill); tel 612/221-9140. At Dale. **American.** Housed in a brick building with attractive awnings and flowers, this bright and clean place is best known for its bountiful breakfast plates, including the Tex-Mex variation—hash browns, onion, sausages, and cheese, all wrapped in a flour tortilla and served with two scrambled eggs. The Cajun breakfast is another favorite. A good find. **FYI:** Reservations not accepted. Children's menu. No liquor license. **Open:** Mon–Sat 7am–2pm, Sun 8am–2pm. **Prices:** Lunch main courses $3–$7. No CC. &

Old City Cafe

1571 Grand Ave; tel 612/699-5347. Near Macalester College. **Jewish/Kosher.** Kosher deli restaurant located in an old building with huge windows, wood trim, and shutters. Everything is vegetarian, except for a few tuna fish items. Falafel Parmesa (baked with vegetables and melted cheese), and Yemenite rice (with vegetables and spicy tomato sauce) are popular items. **FYI:** Reservations not accepted. Beer and wine only. **Open:** Mon–Thurs 11am–9pm, Fri 11am–2pm, Sun 11am–9pm. **Prices:** Main courses $4–$7. No CC.

Patrick McGovern's

225 W 7th St; tel 612/224-5821. **American.** Green is the signature color for both the interior and brick exterior of this popular bar and restaurant—a fun spot for large groups or families. Offers big portions of basic fare like roast turkey with mashed potatoes and gravy. **FYI:** Reservations accepted. Children's menu. **Open:** Mon–Fri 11am–midnight, Sat 8am–midnight. **Prices:** Main courses $5–$14. AE, DISC, MC, V. &

Ristorante Luci

470 Cleveland Ave S (Highland); tel 612/699-8258. **Italian.** Small and intimate, this family-run restaurant offers homemade pastas and breads along with dishes representing different regions in Italy. The saltimbocca is highly recommended: medallions of veal tenderloin layered with prosciutto and fontina cheese, topped with tomato and fresh sage. Over 200 wines. **FYI:** Reservations recommended. Beer and wine only. No smoking. **Open:** Mon–Thurs 5–9:30pm, Fri–Sat 5–10:30pm, Sun 4:30–9pm. **Prices:** Main courses $6–$20; prix fixe $20. MC, V. ❤

River Room

In Dayton's, 411 Cedar St (Downtown); tel 612/292-5174. **New American.** Very pleasant, elegant restaurant, located just off the first floor. The interior is very open and bright, and during the lunch hours it's not too noisy. Variety of wonderful entrees—the open-faced chicken sandwich on focaccia and grilled salmon over a bed of mashed potatoes are recommended. **FYI:** Reservations recommended. **Open:** Mon–Fri 11am–7pm, Sat–Sun 11am–3pm. **Prices:** Main courses $6–$10. AE, CB, DISC, MC, V. 📧 ♿

♦ The St Paul Grill
In Saint Paul Hotel, 350 Market St (Downtown); tel 612/224-7455. **American Grill.** Grilled meats and fish and excellent pastas are prepared here under the supervision of the hotel's executive chef, Robert Bach. The interior is enhanced by fresh flowers and immaculate table settings and features views of the lovely English garden as well as Rice Park. Wine dinners, offered occasionally, are prepared with a specific label of wine. The Grill also carries its own wine label, sauces, and dressings. The restaurant's Scotch bar, famous for its single-malt scotches, is a nice after-theater stop. **FYI:** Reservations recommended. **Open:** Mon 11:30am–midnight, Tues–Sat 11:30am–midnight, Sun 11am–midnight. **Prices:** Main courses $10–$25. AE, CB, DC, DISC, ER, MC, V. ♥ VP ♿

Saji-ya
695 Grand Ave (Summit Hill); tel 612/292-0444. **Japanese.** A traditional Japanese restaurant in decor and cuisine. Patrons enter across a bridge and are given a traditional Japanese greeting by the staff. The dining area offers a view of the kitchen. Separate teppanyaki room. **FYI:** Reservations recommended. **Open:** Lunch Mon–Fri 11am–2pm; dinner Sun–Thurs 5–10pm, Fri–Sat 5–11pm. **Prices:** Main courses $11–$16. AE, DC, DISC, MC, V. ♿

★ Table of Contents
1648 Grand Ave (Macalester/Groveland); tel 612/699-6595. 1 block W of Snelling Ave. **New American.** A great restaurant with a relaxed atmosphere, in the hub of the Macalester College area, connected to the Hungry Mind bookstore. A sure approach to new American cuisine, with creative use of herbs; recommended are the beef tenderloin, garlic-mashed potatoes, and olive tapenade, as well as the original pizzas. All breads and pastas are homemade **FYI:** Reservations recommended. Beer and wine only. No smoking. Additional location: 1310 Hen, Minneapolis (tel 339-1133). **Open:** Mon–Thurs 11:30am–9:30pm, Fri–Sat 11:30am–11:30pm, Sun 10am–9pm. **Prices:** Main courses $5–$20. DC, DISC, MC, V. ♿

Tulips
452 Selby Ave (Cathedral Hill); tel 612/221-1061. Just W of the cathedral; between Dale St and Western Ave. **French Country.** This small, comfortable establishment, in an otherwise unoccupied old brick building, presents the French country cooking of part-owners David Wernz and Andy Klevn. Fine linens and tableware, but an informal atmosphere. Recommended entree: sautéed scallops with béarnaise sauce, served with rice, mushrooms in sherry, and vegetables. A pre-theater menu is available for Ordway patrons **FYI:** Reservations accepted. Beer and wine only.

Open: Lunch Mon–Fri 11:30am–2pm; dinner daily 5–9pm. **Prices:** Main courses $9–$18; prix fixe $24–$29. AE, MC, V. ♥ 📧 ♿

W A Frost and Company
374 Selby Ave (Cathedral Hill); tel 612/224-5715. At Western. **American.** This Victorian setting, in a historic red stone building, has a formal, dimly lit ambience and dark, solid furnishings. The bar area boasts a large outdoor patio shaded by big, beautiful trees. One popular dish is broiled lemon chicken with red peppers, served with pasta salad. **FYI:** Reservations recommended. No smoking. **Open:** Daily 11am–midnight. **Prices:** Main courses $6–$20. AE, DC, DISC, MC, V. ♥ 🍴 ♿

White Lily
758 Grand Ave; tel 612/293-9124. Between Dale and Avon. **Vietnamese.** Satisfying Vietnamese restaurant. The large room with high wooden ceiling, windows the length of one wall, red-tile floor, and many plants has an airy, international feel. The very popular Vietnamese salad has a base of chilled bean sprouts, rice noodles, and lettuce and is topped with hot, wok-cooked chicken and onions and sprinkled with carrots and peanuts; light anchovy dressing is served on the side. Other favorites are chicken with water chestnuts and chicken amandine. **FYI:** Reservations accepted. Beer and wine only. **Open:** Sun–Thurs 11am–9:30pm, Fri–Sat 11am–10:30pm. **Prices:** Main courses $5–$7. MC, V. ♿

ATTRACTIONS 🏛

HISTORIC BUILDINGS AND HOMES

Minnesota State Capitol
700 Wabasha St; tel 612/296-2881. Built in 1905 on a hill overlooking downtown St Paul, this structure was the design of Cass Gilbert, a young St Paul architect whose later work included the Woolworth Building in New York City. The capitol is crowned by the world's largest unsupported marble dome (modeled after the one Michelangelo created for St Peter's Basilica in Rome), at the base of which is a dramatic grouping of gilded figures titled *The Progress of the State*. The interior of the capitol is equally impressive, with its marble stairways, chambers, and halls, and its oil paintings depicting important events in Minnesota history. No fewer than 21 kinds of marble and 25 different kinds of stone were used for this building. **Open:** Mon–Fri 9am–4pm, Sat 10am–3pm, Sun 1–3pm. **Free**

Landmark Center
75 W 5th St; tel 612/292-3225. A fine 1902 example of the Roman Revival style, this restored Federal Court Building is capped by a tall belfry reminiscent of Trinity Church in Boston. You can still visit the courtrooms in which some of this country's most notorious gangsters came to trial. Today, the Landmark is an active cultural center with an auditorium, exhibition galleries, and the Schubert Piano Museum. **Open:** Mon–Fri 8am–5pm, Sat 10am–5pm, Sun 1–5pm. **Free**

Alexander Ramsey House

265 S Exchange St; tel 612/296-8760. The restored 1872 Victorian home of Minnesota's first Territorial Governor has been renovated and outfitted with period furnishings, black walnut woodwork, marble fireplaces, china and silver collections, and crystal chandeliers. Costumed guides lead guests through the mansion's 15 rooms; tours begin on the hour and are preceded by a video on Ramsey's career. **Open:** Apr–Dec, Tues–Sat 11am–2pm. **$**

James J Hill House

240 Summit Ave; tel 612/297-2555. Situated on historic Summit Avenue, this was the house of the Great Northern Railway builder James J Hill. Completed in 1891, the 36,000-square-foot red sandstone residence has five floors, 13 bathrooms, 16 crystal chandeliers, and 22 fireplaces, and features elaborately carved woodwork, stained glass, and a two-story skylit art gallery. Special events held regularly; guided tours offered Wednesday through Saturday. **Open:** Wed–Sat 10am–3:30pm. **$$**

Cathedral of St Paul

239 Selby Ave; tel 612/228-1766. Built in 1915 on the highest point in the city, this replica of St Peter's in Rome boasts a 175-foot-high dome, a west-facing rose window, and massive granite-and-travertine construction. **Open:** Daily 8am–6pm. **Free**

MUSEUMS

Minnesota Museum of American Art

75 W 5th St; tel 612/292/4380. Founded in 1927, this museum presents exhibitions and a full range of art classes designed for young people and adults. Permanent collection includes more than 10,000 objects. The museum's galleries are located on the second floor of the Landmark Center; the art school is on the fifth floor. **Open:** Tues–Fri 10:30am–4:30pm, Sat–Sun 1–4:30pm. **Free**

Minnesota History Center

345 W Kellogg Blvd; tel 612/296-9131. This three-story museum houses an impressive array of artifacts, books, photographs, maps, writings, videos, and interactive displays celebrating the history of Minnesota. An ongoing exhibit called "Minnesota A to Z" pairs each letter of the alphabet with a feature in Minnesota life. (Z stands for "zero," in reference to wintertime temperatures!) **Open:** Tues–Wed and Fri–Sat 10am–5pm, Thurs 10am–9pm, Sun noon–5pm. **Free**

Science Museum of Minnesota

30 E 10th St; tel 612/221-9444. Hands-on exhibits dealing with natural history, science, and technology are the focus at this massive museum. The East Building houses "Our Minnesota," a permanent exhibit featuring a 12-by-14-foot map that permits visitors to "walk" across the state. The Hall of Paleontology features a dinosaur lab. The West Building contains the Hall of Anthropology, the Physics and Technology Gallery, and a succession of traveling exhibits. There's also

an Omnitheater, with a 76-foot domed screen (separate admission charged). **Open:** Mon–Sat 9:30am–9pm, Sun 10am–9pm. **$$$**

Minnesota Children's Museum

7th and Wabasha Sts; tel 612/225-6000. Popular features at this museum include a high-action maze, a historic train, and an outdoor garden. Another top draw is the crane-and-train exhibit, where children can use an electromagnetic crane to pick up and deposit metal disks. The museum also features weekend programming, summer camps, and special group programs. **Open:** Peak (Mem Day–Labor Day) daily 9am–5pm. Reduced hours off-season. **$$$**

ENTERTAINMENT VENUES

Schubert Club

301 Landmark Center; tel 612/292-3267. Founded in 1882 and now one of the oldest musical organizations in the US, the Schubert brings celebrated artists from throughout the world to perform in the Twin Cities. (One of the works it commissioned—*From the Diary of Virginia Woolf* by Dominick Argento—won the Pulitzer Prize for music in 1975.) Other artists that have been brought to the city by the club include Vladimir Horowitz, Isaac Stern, Robert Casadesus, and Beverly Sills. Located in the historic Landmark Center. **Open:** Call for schedule. **$$$$**

The Schubert Club Musical Instrument Museum

75 W 5th St, in Landmark Center; tel 612/292-3267. Collection features 100 historical keyboard instruments spanning 450 years; a vast array of instruments from around the world; and a rotating exhibition of musical manuscripts, letters, and autographs. The International Artists Series, one of the oldest and most distinguished programs of its kind in the country, presents world-renowned artists (Vladimir Horowitz, Leontyne Price, Arthur Rubinstein, Yo-Yo Ma) at the Ordway Music Theatre. **Open:** Mon–Fri 11am–3pm. **Free**

Ordway Music Theater

345 Washington St; tel 612/224-4222. Opera, recitals, pop and classical concerts, and dance performances are presented here. An impressive marble staircase takes you to the second floor, where huge windows provide majestic views of the city. Home of the St Paul Chamber Orchestra. **Open:** Call for schedule. **$$$$**

World Theater

10 E Exchange St; tel 612/290-1221. The home base of Garrison Keillor's famous radio show "Prairie Home Companion." Touring companies also perform at this beautifully restored historic building. **Open:** Call for schedule. **$$$**

OTHER ATTRACTIONS

Como Park

1325 Aida Place; tel 612/489-1740. One of the busiest and most beautiful parks in the Twin Cities, Como Park is best known for its flower conservatory, which includes a formal

Japanese garden, 18-hole golf course, cross-country ski trails, and walking paths. Visitors will also find paddleboats, canoes, bikes, and in-line skates for rent. **Open:** Peak (Apr–Sept) daily 10am–6pm. Reduced hours off-season. **$**

Trains at Bandana

1021 Bandana Blvd E (Bandana Square); tel 612/647-9628. Sponsored by Twin City Model Railroad Club. Club members are assembling a scale-model panorama of railroading in the United States from the 1930s to the 1950s. The 3,000-square-foot O-scale layout features Twin Cities railroad landmarks, artifacts, and displays. Donation requested. **Open:** Mon–Fri 10am–8pm, Sat 10am–6pm, Sun noon–5pm.

Sauk Centre

Located 20 miles northwest of St Cloud. Birthplace of iconoclastic author Sinclair Lewis, who based his scathing novel *Main Street* on the small-town mores of the town and its residents. **Information:** Sauk Centre Area Chamber of Commerce, 1220 S Main St, PO Box 222, Sauk Centre, 56378 (tel 320/352-5201).

MOTELS

Econo Lodge

I-94 and US 71, PO Box 46, 56378; tel 320/352-6581 or toll free 800/553-2666; fax 320/352-6584. Typical Econo Lodge right off the interstate, near gas and food. Building is in good condition. **Rooms:** 38 rms and stes. CI 2pm/CO 11am. Nonsmoking rms avail. **Amenities:** A/C, cable TV w/movies. Some units w/whirlpools. **Services:** Pets allowed only with notification and only in smoking rooms. **Facilities:** 1 restaurant. **Rates (CP):** $38 S; $48 D; $85–$95 ste. Extra person $18. Children under age 18 stay free. Parking: Outdoor, free. AE, DC, DISC, JCB, MC, V.

Gopher Prairie Motel

1222 S Getty St, 56378; tel 320/352-2275 or toll free 800/341-8000; fax 320/352-5120. NW corner I-94 and US 71. A low-rise, barn-red motel, this is an inexpensive place to stay on the edge of town. **Rooms:** 23 rms and effic. CI 11am/CO 11am. Nonsmoking rms avail. **Amenities:** A/C, cable TV w/movies. A few rooms have refrigerators. **Services:** VCRs available for rent. **Facilities:** Games rm. **Rates:** $27–$32 S; $32–$48 D; $32–$48 effic. Extra person $4–$12. Parking: Outdoor, free. AE, CB, DC, DISC, MC, V.

ATTRACTION

Sinclair Lewis Interpretive Center and Museum

1220 S Main; tel 320/352-5201. Nobel Prize–winning author Sinclair Lewis was born and raised in Sauk Centre and based his acclaimed novel *Main Street* on it. Various artifacts from the author's life—including notes, photos, and personal

memorabilia—are housed in his restored birthplace. Picnic area. **Open:** Peak (Mem Day–Labor Day) Mon–Fri 8:30am–5pm, Sat–Sun 9am–5pm. Reduced hours off-season. **Free**

Stillwater

Seat of Washington County, in eastern Minnesota. This popular tourist destination, birthplace of Minnesota Territory in 1849, is on bluffs of the St Croix River. Many of the steep and narrow streets are lined with 19th-century Greek Revival and Victorian mansions. **Information:** Stillwater Area Chamber of Commerce, 423 S Main St, Stillwater, 55082 (tel 612/439-7700).

MOTEL

Best Western Stillwater Inn

1750 Frontage St, 55082; tel 612/430-1300 or toll free 800/647-4039; fax 612/430-0596. Off MN 36. Motel with a homey feeling. Lobby looks like family room in country home, with Scandinavian look and brick fireplace. Hallways stenciled with flowers. **Rooms:** 60 rms and stes. CI 3pm/CO 11am. Nonsmoking rms avail. Each room individually decorated with quality light wood furniture. **Amenities:** A/C, satel TV w/movies, dataport. Some units w/whirlpools. **Services:** Complimentary pastries in lobby. **Facilities:** Spa. **Rates (CP):** Peak (May 19–Oct 19) $52–$68 S; $56–$80 D; $100–$165 ste. Extra person $6. Children under age 14 stay free. Lower rates off-season. Parking: Outdoor, free. AE, DC, DISC, MC, V.

INN

The Lowell Inn

102 N 2nd St, 55082; tel 612/439-1100; fax 612/439-4686. 2 blocks W of Main St. On the site of an inn built in 1848, the current brick building, fronted by 13 pillars that represent the original 13 colonies, was built in 1930. All the furniture is antique, and portraits of the Palmer family are in the lobby. The focus is on couples. Unsuitable for children under 12. **Rooms:** 21 rms and stes. CI 3pm/CO 11am. Each room has distinctive Victorian decor. Some bathroom facilities are in bedroom, separated from rest of room by curtain. **Amenities:** A/C, cable TV. Some units w/whirlpools. Only some rooms have TV. Complimentary wine and bourbon in rooms. **Services:** Twice-daily maid svce, babysitting, wine/sherry served. Fax machine available. **Facilities:** 3 restaurants, 1 bar, guest lounge. **Rates:** Peak (June–Oct) $109–$159 D; $159–$189 ste. Lower rates off-season. AP rates avail. Parking: Outdoor, free. MC, V.

RESTAURANTS

Brine's

219 S Main St; tel 612/439-7556. **American.** This three-story restaurant has been family-run for more than 40 years. The

first floor has a large bar with several tables and dim lighting, while upstairs are two well-lit dining areas; a banquet room is on the third floor. Traditional American breakfasts; hamburgers, deli and chicken sandwiches, soups, and salads for lunch and dinner. All the hamburgers, bacon, and sausages are prepared at the Brine family's meat market; sandwich buns are homemade. Extensive beer selection, local wines. Ribs special on Thurs and Sun nights; Fri night fish special. **FYI:** Reservations accepted. Karaoke/rock. Children's menu. **Open:** Mon–Thurs 8am–9pm, Fri–Sat 8am–10pm, Sun 8am–9pm. **Prices:** Main courses $3–$9. MC, V.

Dock Cafe
425 E Nelson St; tel 612/430-3770. 2 blocks E of Main St. **New American.** A good choice for either casual dining or more sophisticated, romantic ambience. Located on the water's edge of the St Croix River, this restaurant has three separate dining areas plus an outdoor patio, all with great river views. The bright, cheery interior has windows all around, and comfortable couchlike booths complete with throw pillows allow customers to relax while enjoying their food. Steak, chicken, and seafood are typically accompanied with grilled vegetables and seasoned new potatoes. Soups and pastas are made daily on the premises. **FYI:** Reservations accepted. Children's menu. **Open:** Peak (June–Oct) lunch daily 11am–4pm; dinner Mon–Thurs 5–10pm, Fri–Sat 5–11pm, Sun 4–9pm. **Prices:** Main courses $11–$18. AE, MC, V. ❤ ⬤ ▨ ♿

Freight House Restaurant
305 S Water St; tel 612/439-5718. **American.** Inside a historic brick building dating from 1883, this restaurant is a nice place to eat after a day of sightseeing. The dark, rustic interior is simply but tastefully decorated. A large deck looks out on the St Croix River, and the building's loading dock doors are opened during warm weather. Popular dishes include lemon-basil chicken. **FYI:** Reservations not accepted. Jazz/rock. Children's menu. **Open:** Peak (May–Oct) daily 11am–10pm. **Prices:** Main courses $7–$15. AE, DISC, MC, V. ▮ ⬤ ▨ ▦ ♿

Vittorio's
402 S Main St; tel 612/439-3588. **Italian.** A landmark in a historic area. While the outdoor patio looks out onto traffic-congested Main Street, the appealing, distinctive interior brings in a steady stream of people. The most popular dish is cannelloni stuffed with a ricotta, pork, ham, spinach, and spices and covered with a white sauce **FYI:** Reservations accepted. Children's menu. **Open:** Peak (June–Oct) Sun–Thurs 11am–10pm, Fri–Sat 11am–11pm. **Prices:** Main courses $8–$20. AE, DC, DISC, MC, V. ❤ ⬤ ▦ ♿

REFRESHMENT STOP 🗗

Eno's Bakery
826 S 4th St; tel 612/430-0656. At Churchill. **Bakery.** This lovely bakery located in central Stillwater turns out delicious-looking, great-smelling muffins, cookies, cakes, and breads (wild rice and chocolate are two favorites). Wedding cakes—including the rather famous strawberry chantilly one—are also made. **Open:** Mon–Fri 7:30am–6:30pm, Sat 7:30am–2:30pm. No CC.

Thief River Falls

Seat of Pennington County. The area around this northwestern Minnesota city is rife with parks and wildlife sanctuaries, including Agassiz National Wildlife Refuge. **Information:** Thief River Falls Convention & Visitors Bureau, 2017 US 59 SE, Thief River Falls, 56701 (tel 218/681-3720 or toll free 800/827-1629).

HOTELS 🏨

≡≡ Best Western of Thief River Falls
MN 325, 56701; tel 218/681-7555 or toll free 800/569-8123; fax 218/681-7721. This large hotel specializes in weddings and meetings, but also provides clean, comfortable accommodations to any traveler. Near Artco, snowmobiling, and the civic arena for hockey and curling. **Rooms:** 81 rms. CI 2pm/CO noon. Nonsmoking rms avail. **Amenities:** 🛁 📺 A/C, cable TV w/movies. **Services:** ✕ 🍽 ▨ ⤴ 🛎 **Facilities:** 🖼 🏃 🏐 400 ♿ 1 restaurant, 1 bar (w/entertainment), volleyball, games rm, whirlpool. **Rates:** $42–$45 S; $54–$57 D. Extra person $12. Children under age 18 stay free. AP and MAP rates avail. Parking: Outdoor, free. AE, DC, DISC, MC, V.

≡≡ C'mon Inn
1586 US 59 SE, 56701; tel 218/681-3000 or toll free 800/950-8111; fax 218/681-3060. Newer hotel with lots of wood and skylights. Close to casino. **Rooms:** 44 rms and stes. CI 3pm/CO noon. Nonsmoking rms avail. Many rooms look out over airy pool courtyard. **Amenities:** 🛁 A/C, cable TV w/movies. Some units w/terraces, some w/whirlpools. **Services:** 🍽 ▨ ⤴ **Facilities:** 🖼 🏃 50 🖥 ♿ Games rm, whirlpool. **Rates (CP):** $40–$50 S; $56–$63 D; $75–$80 ste. Extra person $7. Children under age 12 stay free. Parking: Outdoor, free. AE, DISC, MC, V.

MOTEL

≡≡ Super 8 Motel
1915 US 59 SE, 56701; tel 218/681-6205 or toll free 800/800-8000; fax 218/681-7519. Clean, quiet, economical rooms located 6 miles and 58 miles from casinos. **Rooms:** 46 rms. CI open/CO 11am. Nonsmoking rms avail. **Amenities:** 🛁 A/C, cable TV. **Services:** ▨ ⤴ 🛎 **Facilities:** 🏃 ♿ **Rates (CP):** $37–$40 S; $46–$48 D. Extra person $4. Children under age 12 stay free. Parking: Outdoor, free. AE, CB, DC, DISC, MC, V.

ATTRACTION 📷

Agassiz National Wildlife Refuge

CR 7; tel 218/449-4115. Dear, moose, elk, timberwolf, and bear are some of the animals that inhabit these 61,000 acres of forest, water, and marshland. There are 280 species of game birds, as well as 41 species of mammals. Observation tower; self-guided auto and walking tours. **Open:** Mon–Fri 7:30am–4pm. **Free**

Virginia

This former mining and logging town in the Mesabi Iron Range is now a center of tourism. The largest taconite mine in the world operates in nearby Mountain Iron. **Information:** Virginia Chamber of Commerce, 1 Vermilion Dr, PO Box 1072, Virginia, 55792 (tel 218/741-2717 or toll free 800/777-7395).

MOTELS 🏨

🏃 Lakeshore Motor Inn

404 N 6th Ave, 55792; tel 218/741-3360 or toll free 800/569-8131. Oder motel located in Virginia's business district, close to walking, ski, and snowmobile trails. It also serves as a bus depot for the area. **Rooms:** 17 rms and stes. CI open/CO 11am. Nonsmoking rms avail. **Amenities:** 🛏 🗔 🖭 A/C, cable TV w/movies. 1 unit w/whirlpool. **Services:** 🍴 📞 **Facilities:** 🏃 **Rates:** Peak (mid-May–mid-Sept) $29–$33 S; $39–$43 D; $69–$89 ste. Extra person $4. Children under age 12 stay free. Lower rates off-season. Parking: Outdoor, free. Snowmobile and ski packages avail. AE, CB, DC, DISC, MC, V.

⊨⊨ Voyageur North Motel

8317 13th St S, 55792; tel 218/741-9235 or toll free 800/235-3524; fax 218/741-9235. Very economical, especially for the traveling family. Decor is basic but cheerful. Next to main highway near restaurant and stores. **Rooms:** 18 rms and stes. CI noon/CO 11am. Nonsmoking rms avail. **Amenities:** 🛏 🗔 A/C, cable TV w/movies, refrig. **Services:** 🍴 📞 **Facilities:** 🏃 🚹 **Rates:** Peak (May–Sept) $25–$32 S; $38–$45 D; $60–$80 ste. Extra person $5. Children under age 12 stay free. Lower rates off-season. Parking: Outdoor, free. AE, DISC, MC, V.

RESTAURANT 🍴

BG's Saloon

910 23rd Ave W; tel 218/741-0512. **American.** Located on the western edge of the city of Virginia, this lively country-western bar serves up lots of drinks, burgers, and sandwiches, including an excellent chicken Parmesan sandwich. **FYI:** Reservations not accepted. Country music. **Open:** Daily 11am–1am. **Prices:** Main courses $2–$6. MC, V.

Walker

Seat of Cass County, in north-central part of state. This tiny town acts as a gateway of the Chippewa National Forest and is a popular destination for snowmobilers and cross-country skiiers. Each February, the International Eelpout Festival is held on frozen Leech Lake. (The eelpout, a bottom feeding coldwater fish, is said to be the ugliest fish in Minnesota waters.) **Information:** Leech Lake Area Chamber of Commerce, PO Box 1089, Walker, 56484 (tel 218/547-1313 or toll free 800/833-1118).

HOTEL 🏨

⊨⊨⊨ AmericInn

MN 371, 56484; tel 218/547-2200 or toll free 800/634-3444. Newer hotel adjacent to the Heartland Trail, perfect for walking or biking in summer, snowmobiling in winter. **Rooms:** 37 rms. CI 3pm/CO 11am. Nonsmoking rms avail. **Amenities:** 🛏 🗔 A/C, TV. Some units w/whirlpools. **Services:** ✕ 🍴 📞 Pets $3. **Facilities:** 🏃 🚹 �30 🚹 1 restaurant, games rm, sauna, whirlpool. Restaurant has piano player nightly. **Rates (CP):** Peak (May–Sept) $43–$53 S; $59–$65 D. Extra person $6. Children under age 12 stay free. Lower rates off-season. Parking: Outdoor, free. AE, DC, DISC, MC, V.

MOTEL

⊨⊨ Lakeview Inn

MN 371, 56484; tel 218/547-1306 or toll free 800/252-5073. Clean, modern building across the street from city park beach access and snowmobile trails. Mini-golf next door. **Rooms:** 13 rms and effic. CI 1pm/CO 10am. **Amenities:** 🛏 🗔 A/C, cable TV w/movies. **Services:** 📞 Winter auto plug-ins. Pets $4. **Facilities:** 🏃 **Rates:** Peak (June–Labor Day) $28–$37 S; $46–$55 D; $56–$65 effic. Extra person $8. Children under age 12 stay free. Lower rates off-season. Parking: Outdoor, free. DISC, MC, V.

RESTAURANT 🍴

Ⓢ The Outdoorsman Cafe

Main St; tel 218/547-3310. **American.** It's nice to know that there are still places where you can eat homemade soup, a good salad, and a tasty, filling entree—all for $5 or less. Choose from BLTs and other sandwiches, chicken tenders, chicken-and-dumpling soup, and daily specials like meat loaf. **FYI:** Reservations not accepted. Children's menu. No liquor license. **Open:** Peak (May–Oct) Mon–Sat 6am–4pm, Sun 6am–noon. **Prices:** Main courses $2–$5. MC, V.

Walnut Grove

ATTRACTION 🏛

Laura Ingalls Wilder Museum
330 8th St; tel 507/859-2358. Laura Ingalls Wilder spent a few years of her childhood in Walnut Grove. The Wilder museum exhibits artifacts from her life, memorabilia relating to the TV show *Little House on the Prairie*, and a doll collection; the Ingalls' Dugout Site is the ruins of the Ingallses' home on the banks of Plum Creek. **Open:** Mem Day–Labor Day, daily 10am–7pm. **$**

Winona

Seat of Winona County, in southeast part of state. Many fine examples of 19th-century American architecture exist in this quiet town on the Mississippi bluffs. Winona's main claim to fame may be as the birthplace of world-famous Gummy Bears candy. **Information:** Winona Convention & Visitors Bureau, 67 Main St, PO Box 870, Winona, 55987-0870 (tel 507/452-2272 or toll free 800/657-4972).

MOTELS 🏨

≡≡≡ Best Western Riverport Inn & Suites
900 Bruski Dr, 55987; tel 507/452-0606 or toll free 800/595-0606; fax 507/452-6489. At jct US 61 and MN 43. Spacious lobby with fireplace surrounded by overstuffed chairs and couches. **Rooms:** 106 rms and stes. Executive level. CI 3pm/CO 11am. Nonsmoking rms avail. Safety bar on first floor windows. **Amenities:** 🛁 🅰 📺 A/C. Some units w/minibars, some w/terraces, some w/whirlpools. **Services:** ✕ 🚐 🖼 🧺 ⚕ Free continental breakfast available in lobby. Shuttle bus service to *Princess Cruises*, a sightseeing-dinner cruise boat that plies the Mississippi River—boat is owned by hotel, so charter and private events can be arranged. Two persons on duty at all times at front desk. Friendly greeting by uniformed clerks. **Facilities:** 🛗 🏃 ♿ 1 restaurant (lunch and dinner only), 1 bar. Two exercise bikes in pool area. Brewskis Pub & Eatery open 11am–1pm. **Rates:** $54–$74 S; $64–$94 D; $65–$85 ste. Extra person $10. Children under age 12 stay free. Parking: Outdoor, free. Four fantasy suites cost $125 Sun–Thurs and $175 Fri–Sat. AE, CB, DC, DISC, EC, ER, JCB, MC, V.

≡≡ Days Inn
420 Cottonwood, 55987; tel 507/454-6930 or toll free 800/DAYS-INN. W of Jct US 14 and US 61. Surrounded by fast food restaurants and discount shopping outlets. Often used by visiting sports teams, youth groups, and others for meetings. Behind property is Gilmore Valley Watershed, a marshy area, and the sluggish waters of Gilmore Creek; easy access to downtown. **Rooms:** 58 rms. CI 3pm/CO noon. Nonsmoking rms avail. **Amenities:** 🅰 📶 A/C, cable TV w/movies. **Services:** 🧺 **Facilities:** 🏃 ⓴ ♿ **Rates:** Peak (May–Oct) $48–

$57 S or D. Children under age 18 stay free. Lower rates off-season. Parking: Outdoor, free. AE, CB, DC, DISC, EC, ER, JCB, MC, V.

≡≡≡ Holiday Inn
956 Mankato Ave, PO Box 336, 55987; tel 507/454-4390 or toll free 800/562-4544; fax 507/452-2187. At Jct US 14/16. Built in 1965, and looks it, although it's clean and tidy. Located along busy US 14/61, which has gas stations and fast food outlets. Nearby Lake Winona has walking paths and is easily reached by guests who want to stroll. View of Sugar Loaf Mountain, local landmark, from front parking lot. **Rooms:** 112 rms and stes. CI 2pm/CO 11am. **Amenities:** 🛁 📶 A/C, cable TV w/movies, VCR. No phone. **Services:** 🍽 🧺 ⚕ Twice-daily maid svce. Friendly staff. **Facilities:** 🛗 🏃 🍽 ♿ 1 restaurant, 1 bar, whirlpool, washer/dryer. Strong chlorine smell from pool area, which was steamy and stuffy. Perkins Restaurant (kids under 12 eat free) and CG's Lounge on premises. **Rates:** Peak (May–Oct) $55–$65 S or D. Extra person $10. Children under age 19 stay free. Lower rates off-season. Parking: Outdoor, free. AE, CB, DC, DISC, EC, ER, JCB, MC, V.

≡ Sterling Motel
1450 Gilmore Ave, 55987; tel 507/454-1120 or toll free 800/452-1235. N of US 61 Jct. Motel was built in 1955 and is showing its age, but is clean and affordable for student travelers and others on a budget. Located along busy US 61, with university playing fields behind property. Numerous fast food outlets and discount shopping stores nearby. **Rooms:** 32 rms. CI 3pm/CO 11am. Nonsmoking rms avail. Furniture well used but clean. **Amenities:** 🅰 A/C, cable TV w/movies. **Services:** ⚕ Small pets $5 extra. Friendly staff. **Facilities:** 🏃 **Rates:** Peak (May–Oct) $21–$31 S; $40–$58 D. Extra person $6. Children under age 17 stay free. Lower rates off-season. Parking: Outdoor, free. AE, CB, DC, DISC, EC, ER, JCB, MC, V.

≡ Sugar Loaf Motel
1066 Homer Rd, 55987; tel 507/452-1491. At Jct US 14/61. From the parking lot, you can see Sugar Loaf Mountain, the remaining hunk of stone left after quarrying operations in the last century. A good value for seniors and travelers on a budget. **Rooms:** 20 rms. CI open/CO noon. Rooms have easy first floor access to parking lot. Some rooms with waterbeds available on request. **Amenities:** 🅰 A/C, cable TV. **Services:** 🧺 ⚕ **Facilities:** 🏃 **Rates:** $30–$56 S or D. Extra person $5. Parking: Outdoor, free. DC, MC, V.

RESTAURANTS 🍽

★ Hot Fish Shop
965 Mankato Ave; tel 507/452-5002. Off US 14/61. **Regional American/Seafood.** Founded in 1931 by the current owner's grandparents, it still specializes in batter-fried fish. Fireplace in lobby, with stuffed fish, seashells, nets, paintings, aquarium with live fish, and historical photos of restaurant and owners. Tartar and cocktail sauces sold in area grocery

stores. Skipper's Bar/Lounge attached to restaurant offers entertainment. **FYI:** Reservations accepted. Country music/dancing/rock. Children's menu. **Open:** Daily 11:30am–10pm. Closed Jan 1–14. **Prices:** Main courses $7–$18. AE, CB, DC, DISC, ER, MC, V. 🎦

Jefferson Pub & Grill

58 Center St; tel 507/452-2718. **American/Burgers.** Located in warehouse district along railroad tracks, but streets are well lit. Families and business clientele during weekdays, and college/young professional crowd in evenings and weekends. Interesting decor features canoe suspended from ceiling and antique signage from gas stations and old stores. Homemade baked goods and soups. Interactive TV can be operated (free) from tables, with monitors over bar. **FYI:** Reservations accepted. Jazz. Children's menu. **Open:** Sun–Thurs 11am–10pm, Fri–Sat 11am–11pm. **Prices:** Main courses $7–$10. AE, CB, DISC, ER, MC, V. 🎦

ATTRACTION 🏛

Winona County Historical Society Museum

160 Johnson St; tel 507/454-2723. Exhibits illustrate the history of Winona and the Mississippi River Valley. They include restored blacksmith and barber shops, country store, and kitchen; early vehicles and fire fighting equipment; displays on the logging and lumbering industries; and Native American artifacts. A new hands-on children's exhibit features a cave, tipi, and a steamboat, and the museum also houses a county time line. **Open:** Mon–Fri 9am–4pm, Sat–Sun 1–4pm. **$**

The Heart of It All

Ohio seems to have it all. The state has abundant natural beauty—such as Hocking Hills with a variety of caves, grottos, and waterfalls—and a diversified industrial climate producing items from plastics and glassware to candy canes and automobile tires, to computers and Jeeps. Ohio has also served as a cornerstone of American history, and is the only state from which eight of its sons were elected to the presidency of the United States.

Each area of Ohio has its own peculiar offerings and settings, from the wanderings of Johnny Appleseed through north-central Ohio to the battlefields of early wars to the modern museums, parks, and sports arenas of today. For example, Cleveland has an unusual grouping of cultural institutions (including the Rock and Roll Hall of Fame and Museum) and professional sports facilities. Just outside Cleveland is Ohio's Amish region, where residents live in much the same way they did 150 years ago. Down along the Ohio River, Cincinnati (known as the Queen City) has a more Southern flavor. (The riverboats *Delta Queen* and *Mississippi Queen* dock there.)

The state is also an outdoor recreational playground. The fishing is almost unparalleled, with walleye, smallmouth bass, crappie, and saugeye being especially plentiful. Visitors can embark on a scenic yet strenuous hike in the Appalachian foothills of western Ohio, take the yacht for a tour of the wineries on the Lake Erie islands, or bicycle along miles of disused canals and railroads.

Today's Ohio is an ideal mix of industrialized cities and shady rural towns, big-city excitement, and outdoors adventure.

A Brief History

First Ohioans The first civilization to be established in the Ohio region was that of the mound builders. These ancient peoples are believed to be the ancestors of the

STATE STATS

CAPITAL
Columbus

AREA
41,222 square miles

BORDERS
Michigan, Indiana, Kentucky, West Virginia, Pennsylvania

POPULATION
10,847,000

ENTERED UNION
March 1, 1803 (17th state)

NICKNAME
Buckeye State

STATE FLOWER
Scarlet carnation

STATE BIRD
Cardinal

FAMOUS NATIVES
Annie Oakley, Thomas Edison, Neil Armstrong, Rutherford B Hayes, Ulysses S Grant

Native Americans later found inhabiting the region of the mounds by European explorers. Five successive cultures of Ohio mound builders have been identified: Adena, Hopewell, Cole, Fort Ancient, and Erie. The Adena people dominated the region at about the same time the Roman Empire ruled the Mediterranean world. Their sometimes massive earthworks were constructed for the burial of their great men or for other ceremonial purposes. From village sites in the Scioto and Miami Valleys, artifacts have been recovered—ornaments of mica and of hammered copper, vessels of pottery, vestiges of circular houses of logs and bark. The Adena were followed by the Hopewell people, who also left their traces in other states. Their mounds were of geometric patterns and their skills were more varied than those of their predecessors. The material used in their tools and ornaments show that they traded with distant tribes, and the Hopewell apparently had an elaborately organized community life. Still later, the Fort Ancient people took over. They were farmers, hunters, and fishermen; makers of baskets and weavers of cloth; and builders of rectangular houses. Before there were any records to describe their culture in detail, it is believed the Fort Ancient people were defeated by or absorbed into tribes from farther east. Finally, the Erie (or Cat Nation) culture inhabited the northeast corner of what is now Ohio for 600 years before Europeans penetrated the region. In 1655 they were completely wiped out by the more warlike Iroquois, neighbors to the east. Hundreds of mounds built by these tribes can still be seen in Ohio, although the contents of many have since been moved to museums.

Early Settlement & Statehood For many years thereafter, Ohio Country was virtually uninhabited, although it was criss-crossed by the warpaths of the Iroquois. Prior to the Revolutionary War, some 15,000 Native Americans lived in the region. Early in the 18th century Ohio became the homeland for

Fun Facts

• Ohio did not officially become a state until March 1953, when Congress tardily passed a law approving Ohio's constitution.

• "Dixie," the rallying song of the Confederacy, was written by Ohio composer Daniel Decatur Emmett for use in a minstrel show.

• Benjamin Goodrich built the world's first rubber plant in Akron in 1870; today, more rubber is made in Akron than in any other city in the world.

• Three of the eight US presidents who have hailed from Ohio served successive terms, from 1868 through 1881.

• The scarlet carnation was chosen Ohio's state flower in honor of Ohio native William McKinley—America's 25th president—who considered the flower good luck.

• Cleveland elected the nation's first black mayor, Carl B Stokes, who served from 1967 to 1971.

four major tribes—the Shawnee, Wyandot, Miami, and Delaware. The Wyandot, a component of the Huron tribe driven out of Ontario, eventually settled in the Maumee and Sandusky Valleys. Their great chief was Tarhe ("The Crane"), who represented all Ohio tribes in the Treaty of Greene Ville, an agreement that was expected to finally settle troubles between the settlers and the Native Americans. Tarhe even led his braves in support of the United States in the War of 1812.

French explorer La Salle came to the Ohio Valley in 1699 and claimed the entire region for France. Missionaries from the Moravian community in Bethlehem, Pennsylvania, would periodically come west to try to Christianize the tribes, but most stayed away. In 1788 two boat loads of pioneers floated down the Ohio to Fort Harmer at the mouth of the Muskingum River, where Brigadier Gen Rufus Putnam established the first organized settlement in the Northwest Territory, at Marietta. Settlements at Gallipolis, Dayton, Chillicothe, Cleveland, and Franklinton (later Columbus) soon followed. Ohio eventually became the 17th state in 1803, with Chillicothe as its first capital.

Canals & Civil War The economic advantages of river travel over land travel gave birth to canal building. In 1807 Sen Thomas Worthington asked Congress to finance a canal for the new state. Ultimately there were two—the Ohio and Erie (1832) from Cleveland to Portsmouth, and the Miami and Erie (1847) from Cincinnati to Dayton (later extended to Toledo). It was a busy and profitable era, with steamboats carrying passengers and cargo from the East to the Ohio River and on to the Mississippi. The canal era was short-lived, however, due to the arrival of the railroads in the 1850s and 1860s.

With the outbreak of the Civil War, Ohio threw its entire weight into the Union cause. Even before the war started, Ohio was a main line for escaping slaves on the Underground Railroad, with a total of 32 stops. The state contributed 320,000 troops to the Union cause—leading all Northern states in proportion to population—and more than 35,000 Ohio soldiers died. The 127th Ohio Volunteer Infantry was composed of 5,000 free blacks, who fought through Virginia and North Carolina from 1863 to 1865. In 1863 Confederate leader John Hunt Morgan and his men invaded the southeastern corner of the state, marking the northernmost skirmish of the Civil War.

Industrial Boom & Bust In the years following the Civil War the economic focus of Ohio shifted from the riverbanks of the south to the coal and oil fields of the north, particularly those around Cleveland. Immigrants flooded into the state in search of factory jobs, adding to the ethnic mix that is the modern population of Ohio. Civil War general Ulysses S Grant became the first of eight US presidents to hail from Ohio, thus adding to the state's pull in national politics.

The Great Depression, coupled with major strikes in the rubber and steel plants during the 1930s, dealt a crushing blow to Ohio's economic base. Although World War II brought some added action back to the plants, the state has needed to shift to a more service- and technology-oriented economy in recent decades.

Toward the Future Today, young people in Ohio are much more likely to be studying the chemical properties of rubber than to be manufacturing rubber goods in a factory. Ohio has long been known for its stellar educational institutions, including the first coeducational college in the country (Oberlin College) and one of the first and largest land-grant schools (Ohio State University). Agriculture and mining still play an important role, however, and tourism is becoming a major industry.

A Closer Look

GEOGRAPHY

Ohio has a varied topography and numerous types of soil between the extremities of its borders. The state's geography can be broken down into three sections. The **Allegheny Plateau** is the unglaciated region that the early explorers and scouts thought of as the last vestige of the forbidding mountain chain stretching across New York, Pennsylvania, and Virginia. The **Lake Plains** are the still visible remnants of a succession of beds, varying in depth from a few miles at the eastern end to 40 miles deep in the west, left behind by a diminishing Lake Erie. The **Central Plains** occupy the rest of the map, gently rolling and eventually flattening out into the interminable prairies characteristic of the states to the west.

The ponderous glaciers that traversed the state carried a vast cargo of rocks and minerals, grinding them up in their progress into the deep, rich, and varied soil that was to make Ohio one of the more fertile agricultural regions. Glaciers made their snake-like invasions at least twice, pushing their monstrous way across the northern and western two-thirds of the state to leave traces, both destructive and creative, along a diagonal line roughly from Cincinnati on the south to Cleveland on the north. To the east of the glacial boundary the land is rocky, less hospitable to the plow, but abounding in iron, clay, coal and its adjuncts, oil and natural gas. About 33 of the state's 88 counties—in southern and eastern Ohio—are wholly or partially unglaciated. All of these factors have had a marked effect on vegetation and account for the wide range of timber species native to Ohio.

CLIMATE

Much of the state enjoys a typical Midwestern climate, with relatively mild summers and winters. To the north, however, Cleveland and the rest of the Lake Erie shore often falls prey to harsh winter winds and so-called "lake effect" snowstorms, in which cold Canadian winds pick up moisture from Lake Erie, dumping snow along the shore. Summers can be hot and humid, especially in the south.

DRIVING DISTANCES

Cincinnati

54 mi S of Dayton
105 mi NE of Louisville, KY
107 mi SW of Columbus
206 mi SW of Toledo
235 mi SW of Akron
249 mi SW of Cleveland

Cleveland

41 mi N of Akron
99 mi W of Erie, PA
112 mi E of Toledo
142 mi NE of Columbus
214 mi NE of Dayton
249 mi NE of Cincinnati

Columbus

72 mi E of Dayton
107 mi NE of Cincinnati
127 mi SW of Akron
129 mi SW of Wheeling, WV
135 mi S of Toledo
142 mi SW of Cleveland

WHAT TO PACK

When and where you go dictates what a visitor packs for a visit to Ohio. Generally, dress is casual, unless one expects to visit the theater, a fancy restaurant, or other more formal event. Lightweight clothes will suffice through much of the late spring, summer, and early fall; however, a warm outfit should be packed just in case, along with a sweater for those brief cold snaps and cool evenings.

Warmer clothes, including sweaters, hat or cap, jacket or parka, gloves, and wool socks, should be packed for most areas during the cold-weather months. It is a good idea to pack thermal underwear, too, if you plan on being outdoors during cooler weather. Rain gear is a must anywhere, anytime. Never forget your sunglasses, because though it may be cloudy, around the many Ohio lakes and rivers the glare from the water can still be irritating.

AVG MONTHLY TEMPS (°F) & RAINFALL (IN)		
	Cleveland	Columbus
Jan	24/2.0	26/2.2
Feb	27/2.2	29/2.2
Mar	37/2.9	41/3.3
Apr	47/3.1	51/3.2
May	58/3.5	61/3.9
June	67/3.7	69/4.0
July	72/3.5	73/4.3
Aug	70/3.4	71/3.7
Sept	64/3.4	65/3.0
Oct	53/2.5	53/2.2
Nov	42/3.2	43/3.2
Dec	30/3.1	39/2.9

TOURIST INFORMATION

The state's tourism information line (tel 800/BUCKEYE) has a database of more than 10,000 attractions, events, hotels, campgrounds, and other tourism-related business. Travel counselors are on hand daily to answer questions and can send you a packet of maps and travel guides tailored to your needs. The **Ohio Division of Travel & Tourism,** 77 S High St, PO Box 1001, Columbus 43266 (tel 800/848-1300 or 614/466-8844) maintains a home page on the World Wide Web (http://www.travel.state.oh.us), and they can send you maps and information.

DRIVING RULES AND REGULATIONS

Minimum age for drivers is 18 years of age, or 16 with driver education. Speed limits are generally 25 to 35 mph in cities and towns; 55 mph on township, county, and state roads; and 55 to 65 mph on expressways and the Ohio Turnpike. The use of restraints is required of drivers and front-seat passengers, and children under 40 pounds or less than 4 years of age must be restrained with a certified child safety restraint. Unless posted otherwise, a right turn on red is permitted after a stop.

RENTING A CAR

All of the major automobile rental firms have offices throughout the state, especially at airports. Minimum age requirement is 21 to 25 years of age. Collision damage waiver (CDW) protection is sold separately (check with your credit card or insurance company to see if you are already covered).

- **Alamo** (tel 800/327-9633)
- **Avis** (tel 800/331-1212)
- **Budget** (tel 800/527-0700)
- **Dollar** (tel 800/421-6868)
- **Hertz** (tel 800/654-3131)
- **National** (tel 800/328-4567)
- **Thrifty** (tel 800/367-2277)

ESSENTIALS

Area Codes: Ohio has four area codes. Northwest Ohio, including Toledo, is **419.** Northeast Ohio, including Cleveland and Akron, is **216.** Central and southeast Ohio, including Columbus, is **614.** Southwest Ohio, including Dayton and Cincinnati, is **513.**

Emergencies: For police, fire, or ambulance dial **911.**

Liquor Laws: To purchase or consume alcoholic beverages, you must be 21 years old and have proper identification.

Road Info: For information on current highway conditions, call the Ohio Highway Patrol (tel 614/466-2660).

Taxes: Ohio's sales tax is 5.5%, with local option for increased increments up to 2%. Local option also permits lodging taxes up to 10%.

Time Zone: Ohio is in the eastern standard time zone and switches to daylight savings time in the summer.

Best of the State

WHAT TO SEE AND DO

Below is a general overview of some of the top sights and attractions in Ohio. To find out more detailed information, look under "Attractions" for individual cities in the listings portion of this chapter.

State Parks Ohio boasts 73 state parks, 19 state forests, more than 100 state-operated wildlife areas, and 77 nature preserves. The jewel in the state parks crown is the new Maumee Bay State Park (tel 419/836-7758), which has a state-of-the-art, $1.1 million Milton Trautman Nature Center filled with $2 million worth of educational exhibits and laboratory equipment. The park has more than 500 campsites, four miles of hiking/cross-country skiing trails, five miles of bridle/snowmobile paths, and a 120-room lodge and restaurant, as well as several cabins, an 18-hole golf course, and a 5,000-foot sand beach for sunning and swimming. Most state parks offer fishing, boating, swimming, camping, picnicking, and hiking, and many have golf courses, boat launching areas, boat and/or canoe rental, summer nature programs, and horseback riding camps.

Eight state park resorts offer lodges with meeting facilities and upgraded guest rooms and amenities. These eight parks are: Burr Oak in Glouster (tel 614/767-3570), Deer Creek in Mount Sterling (tel 614/869-3124), Hueston Woods in College Corner (tel 513/523-6347), Maumee Bay in Oregon (tel 419/836-7758), recently renovated Mohican in Loudonville (tel 419/994-4290), Punderson in Newbury (tel 216/564-2279), Salt Fork in Lore City (tel 614/439-3521), and Shawnee in West Portsmouth (tel 614/858-6652).

Manmade Wonders Prehistoric **tribal mounds** are scattered throughout the state, many of them in good condition and kept up for public visitation. The most interesting of these earthworks are Miamisburg Mound in Miamisburg; Fort Ancient in Lebanon; Fort Hill in Hillsboro; Mound Builders Earthworks and Octagon, both Newark; and Serpent Mound in Locust Grove. Various ruins of the old **Ohio canals and locks** are scattered throughout the state. Some of these ruins have been restored, such as those in Independence Dam State Park in Defiance and Providence Metropark in Grand Rapids.

Family Favorites Ohio boasts three major theme parks. Cedar Point, in Sandusky on Lake Erie, is a rambling entertainment park with 12 roller coasters and is considered the largest ride park in the United States (tel 419/626-0830). Paramount's Kings Island, at Kings Mill north of Cincinnati (tel 513/573-5700), has lots of rides ranging from the scariest roller coasters to kiddie rides for the little ones, and there are musical performances all day long. Sea World, near Aurora, is an aquatic theme park, starring killer whales, sharks, penguins, and seals (tel 800/63-SHAMU).

Smaller amusement parks include Aurora's Geauga Lake (tel 216/562-7131), a combination of wet and dry rides, shows, and exhibits; the Beach Waterpark, across from Paramount's Kings Island (tel 800/886-SWIM), with its white-sand beach and water rides; Wyandot Lake Amusement and Water Park, near Columbus (tel 614/889-9283), a lively collection of amusement rides; and American Amusement Park, near Middleton (tel 513/539-7339).

Any of the state's **scenic railroad lines** can be the focus of a family vacation. Several small lines, restored and carved out of the lines once used by the larger rail companies now carry passengers on short, scenic rides through portions of the state. Each of these trains has a history and most are pulled by vintage steam locomotives. The Cuyahoga Valley Line (tel 800/468-4070) runs through the Cuyahoga Valley Recreation area from Independence to downtown Akron, pulled by a 1918 vintage locomotive. The 26-mile ride follows portions of the Cuyahoga River and the Erie Canal, stops at Hale Farm & Village and at Quaker Square in Akron before its return trip. The Bluebird Special (tel 414/878-2177) crosses the Maumee River on a ¼-mile-long bridge on its trip from Grand Rapids to Whitehouse, and Nelsonville's Hocking Valley Scenic Railway (tel 513/335-0382) runs through the rugged Hocking Valley pulled by a 1916 Baldwin steam locomotive.

Historic Sites The John Brown House in Akron has been remodeled to look the way it did in the 1840s, when the fiery abolitionist lived here. The birthplace of Thomas Alva Edison, the state's most prolific inventor, is in Milan. Malabar Farm, near Lucas, was the home of critic and writer Louis Bromfield but is best known as the site of the wedding of Humphrey Bogart and Lauren Bacall in 1945. (The farm is now owned and operated by the state.) Victorian Mansion Museum, Barberton, is a 26-room house with water tanks in the attic, a copper sink, and a courting fireplace in an alcove. John Johnson House, at the Piqua Historical Area near Piqua, is a working pioneer homestead. Red Brick Tavern, Lafayette, played host to six presidents and cattle drovers of early times. The Golden

Lamb in Lebanon has been putting up guests since 1803, including Mark Twain and Charles Dickens. There's also a museum of Shaker furniture on site. Worthington Inn, Worthington, was founded in 1842 as a station on the Underground Railroad, and was later a stagecoach stop.

Museums Ohio has hundreds of museums, from the tiny village variety to the huge, ornate big-city structures. Must-sees include the **United States Air Force Museum** at Wright Patterson Air Force Base in Dayton, the oldest and largest military air force museum in the world. The flying machines of the Wright Brothers can be seen here alongside World War II bombers, MIG jet fighters, huge transports, and many of today's modern jet planes. The Armstrong Air and Space Museum in Wapakoneta displays a variety of space memorabilia and other items relating to the career of the town's most famous native son, astronaut Neil Armstrong.

Located along the Lake Erie shore in Cleveland, the **Rock and Roll Hall of Fame and Museum** provides an interactive look at rock and roll from its early roots to today's trendsetters. (Pioneering Cleveland deejay Allan Freed was the first to use the term "rock and roll," and many consider the city to be rock's real home.) From the sounds of Motown, Elvis, and rap, visitors learn more about the music through video displays, personal artifacts of the Hall's inductees, and unique exhibits. Hot-pink outfits, jewel-studded jump suits, tie-dyed T-shirts, and grunge wear illustrate rock and roll's unique role in fashion history.

The Center for Science and Industry in Columbus (with a branch in Toledo) has many hands-on exhibits. Exhibits at the Cincinnati Museum of Natural History include a cavern, complete with a 30-foot waterfall, stalactites, and other cave formations. The Taft Museum, also in Cincinnati, has a world-famous art collection housed in an historic 1820s mansion. The **Cleveland Museum of Natural History** is Ohio's largest museum, with displays of mounted dinosaurs and other prehistoric creatures. The state's pioneer trails may be seen in miniature at the National Road–Zane Grey Museum on US 40 near Zanesville.

The College Football Hall of Fame at Kings Mill chronicles college football from its inception; the **Pro Football Hall of Fame** in Canton has films, exhibits, videos, and quizzes to test your professional football IQ. Great Lakes Historical Society Museum, in Vermilion overlooking Vermilion Harbor, chronicles the shipping industry. Stan Hywet Hall in Akron is the former residence of Frank A Seiberling, co-founder of the Goodyear Tire & Rubber Company. The 65-room English country manor is known for its intricate carvings, bold architecture, and furnishings from around the world. The Museum of Art in Toledo has strong collections in American and European paintings as well as a world-class glass collection.

Outdoor Dramas Ohio is home to several popular outdoor dramas, all of them with historical themes. *Tecumseh,* in Chillicothe, portrays the life of the famous Shawnee war chief (tel 614/775-4100; after March 1, 614/775-0700). *Blue Jacket,* in Xenia, depicts the life and battles of the Shanwee in Ohio (tel 513/376-4318). *Trumpet in The Land,* in New Philadelphia, depicts the efforts of Moravian missionaries to convert the local Native Americans to Christianity in the 17th century (tel 216/339-1132).

Historic Villages Ohio has 10 historic villages that preserve and perpetuate earlier lifestyles. Sauder Farm & Craft Village, near Archbold, portrays 19th-century life in the Great Black Swamp area. Hale Farm & Western Reserve Village, outside of Bath, is a complex of restored buildings depicting mid-19th century rural life, including a working farm with livestock. Roscoe Village, Coshocton, is a restored 1830s Ohio & Erie Canal town. Schoenbrunn Village, New Philadelphia, is the reconstructed village abandoned in 1877, and includes Ohio's first schoolhouse. Zoar Village was founded in 1817 by a group of German Separatists seeking religious freedom who joined in community living to survive. A 12-block area of the village has been restored, including extensive gardens.

Wineries Since the 1850s, when Nicholas Longworth planted grapevines in the hills overlooking Cincinnati, Ohio has been a place where many persons are dedicated to the art of winemaking.

The Lake Erie area is the state's best-known wine region, with more than 20 wineries in the coastal towns and on the Lake Erie islands. Popular wineries include Heineman Winery, South Bass Island; Lonz, Middle Bass Island; Kelleys Island Wine Company, Kelleys Island; Grand River Wine Company and Chalet Debonne Vineyards, both in Madison; and Rolling Hills, Conneaut. For information on Ohio wine producers and tours call 800/642-VINE.

EVENTS AND FESTIVALS

NORTHEAST OHIO (INCLUDING CLEVELAND AND AKRON)

- **Craft & Herb Fair,** Quail Hollow State Park, Hartville. Traditional handcraft items; culinary, ornamental, and fragrant herb plants for sale; nature hikes; herb garden tours. Early May. Call 216/877-6652.
- **Frontier Days Festival,** Deersville. Civil War re-enactment, mountain man encampment, food, games, entertainment. Mid-May. Call 614/922-3649.
- **Ohio Scottish Games Weekend,** Oberlin. The arts and traditions of Scotland. Late June. Call 216/442-2147.
- **Olde Canal Days Festival,** Canal Fulton. Canal-boat rides, entertainment, parades. Early July. Call 216/854-2805.
- **Great Mohican Indian Powwow & Rendezvous,** Loudonville. Competition, dancing, music, history, and lore. Mid-July. Call 419/994-3103.
- **Pro Football Hall of Fame Festival,** Canton. A week of entertainment including induction ceremony and a football game between two National Football League teams. Late July through early August. Call 216/456-8207.
- **Ohio Swiss Festival,** Sugarcreek. Late September. Call 216/852-4113.

TOLEDO AND NORTHWEST OHIO

- **Buckeye Farm Antique Club Tractor & Engine Show,** Wapakoneta. Late May. Call 419/738-6615.
- **Walleye Festival,** Port Clinton. Entertainment, parades, food, crafts in Ohio's walleye-fishing capital. Late May. Call 419/732-2864.
- **Rally by the River,** Toledo. Friday nights May through August. Call 419/243-8024.
- **National Threshers Association Reunion,** Wauseon. Oldest organized steam show in the United States. Late June. Call 313/888-1345.
- **German-American Festival,** Oregon. Late August. Call 419/691-4116.

COLUMBUS AND CENTRAL OHIO

- **Native American Powwow,** Columbus. Native American dancing, drumming, music, arts and crafts. Late May. Call 614/443-6120.
- **Ohio Folk Festival,** Dayton. Miami Valley festival with 18th-century crafts, music, games. Mid-May. Call 513/461-4800 ext 527.

- **Campaign of the Pickawillanies,** Piqua. Drills, musters, encampments. Early June. Call 513/773-2522.
- **Lancaster Festival,** Lancaster. A 12-day celebration of the arts, including varieties of dance, music, and visual arts. July. Call 614/687-4808 or 800/526-3378.
- **Ohio State Fair,** Columbus. Competitions, exhibitions, fairway rides, and shows. August. Call 614/644-3247.
- **Circleville Pumpkin Show,** Circleville. Mid-September. Call 614/474-7000.

SOUTHERN OHIO (INCLUDING CINCINNATI AND DAYTON)

- **Wildflower Tour,** Shawnee State Forest, Portsmouth. Guided tours point out diversity of wildflowers. Early May. Call 614/265-6453.
- **Appalachian Festival,** Cincinnati. The best in mountain music, food, handicrafts, and folkways. Mid-May. Call 513/451-3070.
- **Dayton Air Show,** Dayton International Airport, Vandalia. A demonstration of the state's place on the cutting edge of aviation. Mid-July. Call 513/898-3699 or 800/848-3699.
- **Dayton Horse Show,** Dayton. One of the largest multibreed shows in North America. Late July to early August. Call 513/255-5949.
- **Grand American World Trapshooting Tournament,** Vandalia. Mid-August. Call 513/275-7788.
- **Ohio Renaissance Festival,** Waynesville. Re-creation of a 16th-century English county fair. Permanent village is home to 200 master artists. Late August to mid-October. Call 513/897-7000.

SPECTATOR SPORTS

Auto Racing The Mid-Ohio Sports Car Course near Mansfield attracts drivers from every state as well as internationally known drivers of exotic cars. Call 800/MID-OHIO for more information on the May–September season.

Baseball The Cincinnati Reds and the Cleveland Indians are the state's major-league teams. The Reds of the National League (tel 513/421-4510) play at Riverfront Stadium, while the Indians of the American League (tel 216/420-4200) call Jacobs Field home. The Columbus Clippers and Toledo Mud Hens are members of the International League.

Basketball   The NBA's Cleveland Cavaliers play their home games at Gund Arena (tel 216/420-2000).

College Football   Ohio State University is a member of the Big Ten and is generally in the thick of the title chase. Bowling Green State University, Ohio University, and Kent State University compete in the Mid-American Conference.

Professional Football   The home state of the Pro Football Hall of Fame hosts only one NFL team, now that the Cleveland Browns have departed: the Cincinnati Bengals, who roar at Riverfront Stadium (tel 513/621-3550).

Horse Racing   Racing fans have a wide choice of time and place to witness the "sport of kings" in the Buckeye State. Major thoroughbred tracks include Lebanon Raceway at Warren County Fairgrounds in Lebanon (tel 513/932-4936), Raceway Park in Toledo (tel 419/476-7751), Scioto Downs in Columbus (tel 614/491-2515), River Downs in Cincinnati (tel 513/232-8000), and Thistledown in Cleveland (tel 216/662-8600).

ACTIVITIES A TO Z

Bicycling   The Bob Evans Farms Great Ohio Bicycle Adventure (GOBA) is the largest weeklong bicycle tour in the eastern United States. Every June, more than 3,000 riders from all over the world visit a different section of the Buckeye State. For more information, call Columbus Outdoor Pursuits (tel 614/447-1006).

Boating   Thanks to the many natural and man-made lakes and streams—not to mention Lake Erie—boating is a favorite pastime in the Buckeye State. Everything from large, self-contained yachts and cruisers to rowboats and canoes can be found on the state's waterways. The Division of Watercraft of the Ohio Department of Natural Resources (tel 614/265-6480) can provide regulations, licensing information, and maps.

Bird Watching   This is popular in the marshes that border Lake Erie, along several rivers, and in various metropolitan parks, forests, and nature preserves. Ohio lies in the path of the annual spring and fall bird migrations. For more information, contact the Audubon Society of Greater Cleveland (tel 216/861-5093).

Camping   With its abundance of state parks and private campgrounds, Ohio offers a wealth of campsites, ranging from primitive backcountry spots to full-hookup sites. Call 800/BUCKEYE for free brochures and information, or the Division of Parks (tel 614/265-7000).

Fishing   This sport goes hand-in-hand with the abundant rivers and lakes in Ohio. Lake Erie is famous for its walleye, smallmouth bass, and perch fishing. The larger Lake Erie tributaries are popular grounds for walleye and panfish. The Ohio River is prime catfish fishing water. Free maps and regulations can be obtained from the Wildlife Division of the Ohio Department of Natural Resources (tel 614/481-6300).

Golf   Travelers who carry their golf clubs with them will have no problem finding a place to use them, as the state has more than 250 public courses. Many of the courses are of championship caliber, such as the Jack Nicklaus Golf Center at Paramount's Kings Island, and the state annually hosts several top national tournaments. Six state parks feature public 18-hole courses with cart rental and pro shops.

Hiking   Trails traverse most of Ohio's state parks, metroparks, and city parks, and many follow abandoned railroad rights-of-way. The Buckeye Trail circles the entire state. For more information, call 800/BUCKEYE.

Horseback Riding   This is an increasingly popular activity, and there a nearly 300 miles of bridle paths in state and metropolitan parks and state forests. Several riding stables can be found throughout the state.

Hunting   There are nearly a half-million acres of public hunting grounds in the state offering small game, wildfowl, and deer. Laws and maps may be obtained from the Division of Wildlife of the Ohio Department of Natural Resources (tel 614/481-6300).

Pack Trips   Backpackers can travel the Buckeye Trail, which rings the state, as well as make trips in several state parks that have backpacking trails. State Park information may be obtained from the Parks Division of the ODNR (tel 614/265-7000) and the Buckeye Trail Association at PO Box 254, Worthington 43085.

SELECTED PARKS & RECREATION AREAS

- **Cuyahoga Valley National Recreation Area,** 15610 Vaughn Rd, Brecksville 44141 (tel 216/526-5256)
- **Perry's Victory & International Peace Memorial,** PO Box 78, Put-in-Bay 43456 (tel 419/285-2184)
- **Buckeye Lake State Park,** PO Box 488, Millersport 43046 (tel 614/467-2690)
- **Burr Oak State Park,** RD 2, PO Box 286, Glouster 45732 (tel 614/767-3683 (office) or 800/282-7275 (lodge))
- **Cedar Point State Park,** PO Box 759, Sandusky 44870 (tel 419/626-0830)
- **Cleveland Lakefront Park,** 740 E 72nd St, Cleveland 44103 (tel 216/881-8141)
- **Crane Creek State Park,** 13531 W State Rte 2, Oak Harbor 43449 (tel 419/898-2495)
- **Hocking Hills State Park,** 20160 State Rte 664, Logan 43138 (tel 513/523-1060)
- **Hueston Woods State Park,** Rte 1, College Corner 45003 (tel 513/523-6347)
- **John Bryan State Park,** 3790 State Rte 370, Yellow Springs 45387 (tel 513/767-1274)
- **Lake Hope State Park,** Zaleski 45698 (tel 614/596-5253)
- **Maumee Bay State Park,** 6505 Cedar Point Rd, Oregon 43618 (tel 419/836-7758)
- **Portage Lakes State Park,** 5031 Manchester Rd, Akron 44319 (tel 216/644-2220)
- **Punderson State Park,** PO Box 338, 120755 Kinsman Rd, Newbury 44065 (tel 216/564-2279)
- **Pymatuning State Park,** Rte 1, Andover 44003 (tel 216/293-6329)
- **Quail Hollow State Park,** PO Box 823, 13340 Congress Lakes Ave, Hartville 44632 (tel 216/677-6652)
- **Salt Fork State Park,** PO Box 672, Cambridge 43725 (tel 614/439-3521)
- **Shawnee State Forest and Park,** Star Route Box 68, Portsmouth 45662 (tel 614/858-6681)

Sailing Thanks to large Ohio lakes, Lake Erie, and the larger rivers and bays, sailing is very popular, and regattas are given to keen competition among yacht and sailing clubs that line riverfronts and bays from Lake Erie to the Ohio River.

Swimming Depending on where in the state one is, swimming can be a year-round pastime in Ohio. There are thousands of opportunities for swimming in the 500 lakes and 25,000 miles of streams, plus farm ponds, pools, and Lake Erie. The eight state park resorts, scattered throughout Ohio, offer indoor or outdoor swimming pools for lodge or cabin guests, while two state parks provide swimming pools for registered campers. For more information, call 800/BUCKEYE.

OHIO'S NORTHWEST COAST

Start	Cedar Point
Finish	Maumee Bay State Park
Distance	About 130 miles round trip
Time	1–2 days
Highlights	The nation's oldest amusement park, Victorian resort neighborhoods, great boating and fishing waters, some island hopping, panoramic views of Lake Erie, wine tastings, birdwatching, and a resort state park

This tour starts at Cedar Point on Lake Erie's Sandusky Bay, a kidney-shaped portion of western Lake Erie. At the eastern end of the bay, a long and narrow peninsula extends northwest and almost meets another peninsula, also narrow but shorter. On the map they look like two forefingers reaching for, but not quite touching, one another. The bay waters are shallow and warm more quickly in spring than those of the open lake. Fish search out these warmer waters, making fishing for walleye, yellow perch, bullheads, and white bass especially rewarding during the early spring. The tour then crosses the bay to Port Clinton, takes a side trip by boat to one or more islands in the lake, then returns to the mainland and continues north along the shoreline to Maumee Bay, near Toledo.

For additional information on lodgings, dining, and attractions in the region covered by the tour, look under specific cities in the listings portion of this chapter.

Our tour starts at the tip of the southern peninsula of Sandusky Bay, which is about an hour west of Cleveland. From the Ohio Turnpike (I-80), take exit 7 and go north on US 250, or exit 6A and north on OH 4, to Sandusky. Turn right (southeast) on US 6, go 5 miles to Causeway Dr, and turn north (left) to the first stop:

1. **Cedar Point,** One Causeway Dr (tel 419/627-2350). Cedar Point, with the bay on the west and Lake Erie on the east, has been a popular summer resort complex since 1870, when it was a simple bathing beach with a bathhouse. Guests arrived from Sandusky on a steamship ferry to use the lakefront facilities, which were expanded over the years to include diving platforms, bicycle boats, and so on. The park's first roller coaster was built in 1892, a coliseum and hotel were added in 1905, and a midway complete with rides, games, and arcades appeared in 1906.

Cedar Point's popularity grew steadily until the Great Depression. Even then, while the park itself was deteriorating, big bands attracted crowds to Cedar Point to listen and dance. Benny Goodman, Tommy Dorsey, Glenn Miller, and others played in the Coliseum ballroom. Without sacrificing its nostalgic charm, Cedar Point has added high-tech rides to challenge young daredevils. In all there are 10 roller coasters, plus a beach, water rides, miniature golf, go-carts, and shows.

From Cedar Point, drive south along the peninsula, then make a sharp right turn on US 6 to downtown

2. **Sandusky.** This port city has more than 140 buildings listed on the National Register of Historic Places and claims to have the largest number of limestone buildings in Ohio. Coming straight here from the nation's oldest amusement park, it seems appropriate to visit the **Merry-Go-Round Museum,** at the corner of Washington and Jackson Sts, where craftspeople demonstrate the venerable art of carving wooden carousel animals. The nearby 1830s Greek Revival–style **Follett House,** 404 Wayne St, contains a free museum with collections of Civil War and other memorabilia.

Cruises to the Lake Erie Islands are offered by several different lines sailing from Sandusky, Catawba Point, and Port Clinton during good weather. From Sandusky, transportation by small plane is also available year-round (tel 419/734-3149).

Drive west on OH 6 to OH 2, which crosses the Sandusky Bay Bridge to the peninsula that forms the northern shore of the bay, and on to

3. **Port Clinton.** This small city, about 17 miles from Sandusky, faces north toward the main body of Lake Erie. It is the major gateway to the Lake Erie islands and to the resort communities of the **Catawba Island Peninsula** and **Marblehead Peninsula.** Yes, it really is called Catawba Island Peninsula; it once was an island, but over the years land filled in the water that separated it from the mainland. There are beautiful homes, gardens, and orchards on Catawba Island. Exploring the roads in these areas is an enjoyable way to spend an hour or two; you can also take a tour of the region aboard the **Bay Area Trolley,** leaving from 220 W Perry St.

From Madison and Perry Sts in downtown Port Clinton, drive 4 miles east on OH 163 to Lightner

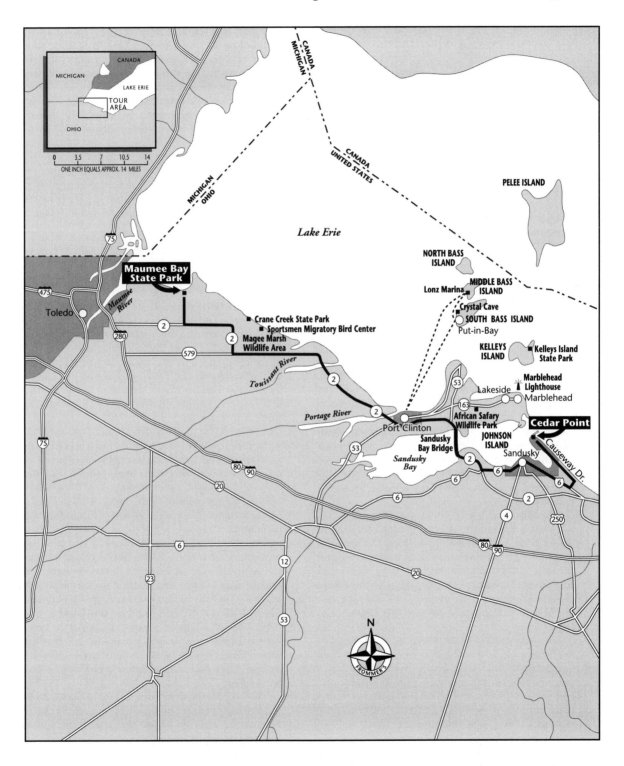

CANADA

MICHIGAN

LAKE ERIE

TOUR AREA

OHIO

0　3.5　7　10.5　14
ONE INCH EQUALS APPROX. 14 MILES

CANADA
MICHIGAN

CANADA
UNITED STATES

MICHIGAN
OHIO

Lake Erie

PELEE ISLAND

NORTH BASS ISLAND

MIDDLE BASS ISLAND

Lonz Marina

Crystal Cave

SOUTH BASS ISLAND

Put-in-Bay

KELLEYS ISLAND

Kelleys Island State Park

75

Maumee Bay State Park

475

Toledo

Maumee River

2

280

579

Crane Creek State Park

Sportsmen Migratory Bird Center

Magee Marsh Wildlife Area

Touissant River

2

Portage River

2

Port Clinton

53

Sandusky Bay Bridge

Sandusky Bay

53

African Safari Wildlife Park

Marblehead Lighthouse

Lakeside

163

Marblehead

Cedar Point

JOHNSON ISLAND

Sandusky

Causeway Dr.

2

6

6

6

6

2

4

250

80　90

20

75

6

12

23

53

80　90

20

N

FROMMER'S

Rd and turn right to the **African Safari Wildlife Park** (tel 419/732-3606), where visitors can drive their own cars through a game preserve to watch exotic animals. Camel rides are offered, too.

Return to OH 163 and take it east to North Shore Blvd, then turn left and drive to the gates of our next stop:

4. **Lakeside,** on Marblehead Peninsula, a community established in 1873 as a Christian camp meeting grounds. It has retained its last-century appearance; most of the buildings are small Victorian family cottages. Nightly entertainment in the Chautauqua tradition—lectures, concerts, ballet—is presented during the summer in the 3,000-seat auditorium. During the summer months a small toll is charged to visitors at the entrance to the gated community.

The village of Marblehead, just south of Lakeside, has a lovely little shopping area called **Main Street Shops.** The buildings look as if they were moved here from a New England coastal town, and the gifts, collectibles, and art objects on sale are of fine quality and taste. You can find everything here from miniature paintings to large oils and watercolors and from handmade jewelry to weavings and pottery.

The **Marblehead Lighthouse,** on the far end of the peninsula, is the oldest continually operating lighthouse on the Great Lakes. Built in 1821, it is one of the most photographed spots in the state, and was the subject of a commemorative stamp issued in 1995. The rocks on the beach below are rich with fossils and other evidence of ancient animal life.

A causeway leads from the peninsula to **Johnson Island,** in Sandusky Bay. Most of the island is covered with private residences, but an interesting bit of history makes the island worth a short stop.

One does not think of northern Ohio as a part of the country in which to find Civil War sites, so it comes as a bit of a surprise to find that Johnson Island was a prison camp for Confederate soldiers during that war. A small US military graveyard contains row after row of small site markers of the 206 young Southern men who died here, not in battle, but from disease and the rigors of a Northern winter.

Back on the mainland, head back south on OH 163 to Port Clinton, where passenger and automobile ferries (such as the Jet Express (tel toll free 800/245-1538), which leaves from the Jefferson St docks) make frequent runs in the summer to the

5. **Lake Erie Islands.** There are five major islands, four of them in Ohio's Ottawa County: Kelleys Island and North, Middle, and South Bass Islands. (The fifth—Pelee Island—is in Canada.) Ferry service connects the US islands.

Millions of years ago, these islands were part of a giant reef. Today they are like rocky walls, or fortresses, thrusting up above the lake's water. Layers of sedimentary rock contain ancient fossils of sea creatures. The soil is thin, but it is sweetened by the limestone and dolomite beneath, making it ideal for growing grapes. According to legend, the first pioneers found wild grapes growing on vines as thick as tree trunks.

The rocks of **Kelleys Island** were carved with giant grooves by a succession of glaciers. Over the years, limestone quarrying has obliterated much of the evidence of this glacial phenomenon, but the area is still a popular getaway spot for Ohioans and visitors. **Kelleys Island State Park** has hiking trails, picnic grounds, campground, and facilities for boat launching.

Vineyards covered much of the acreage of the Bass Islands from the 1860s until Prohibition put the wineries out of business. **Lonz Winery,** on Middle Bass Island, first opened for business during the Civil War as the Golden Eagle Winery and within a decade it had become the largest wine producer in the United States. A Gothic-style structure sits above the original hand-hewn limestone wine cellars. Tours of the winery are conducted several times each day between mid-May and late September.

Guests come to the island and the winery in both public and private boats, dropping in at **Lonz Marina** for a snack, some wine, and some fun as they sit on the terrace and enjoy the lake views. Live entertainment and dancing are offered on weekends.

Put-in-Bay, on South Bass Island, was given that name because it was a good spot for boats to "put in." It has been a popular and low-cost resort town for well over a century, and has all the usual shops and eateries that go with tourism popularity. Ferries to and from the mainland dock right in the center of the action.

At the turn of the century there were 17 wineries on Put-in-Bay. When most of them went out of business during Prohibition, the **Heineman Winery** survived by selling unfermented grape juice. Tours of the winery and of nearby Crystal Cave are offered from early May to late September. Wine tastings are conducted indoors as well as outside in the patio and garden.

While one can take a car on the ferry to Put-in-Bay, many visitors prefer not to, because it is very easy to get around the island on rented bikes, golf carts, or mopeds. There's also the **Put-in-Bay Tour Train** (tel 419/285-4855), which makes hour-long narrated trips around the island.

The most notable landmark on South Bass Island is the **Perry's Victory and International Peace Memorial.** This 352-foot, pink-granite Doric column, topped by an 11-ton bronze urn, was built between 1912 and 1915 to commemorate Commander Oliver Hazard Perry's victory over a British fleet in the War of 1812. There are 37 steps to climb before getting to the elevator, which carries passengers to an observation platform overlooking the lake. On clear days the views of the lake and nearby shores are magnificent.

Ride the ferry back to Port Clinton, take the bypass to OH 2 north and go about 12 miles to:

6. **Magee Marsh Wildlife Area** (tel 419/898-0960). This 2,800-acre wonderland of marsh, meadow, and swamp forest supports a large community of plant and animal life. Waterfowl flight lanes of both the Mississippi and Atlantic flyways pass through Magee Marsh. Large flocks of migrating waterbirds fill the skies in March and April, and again in October and November. One of the most thrilling springtime migrations is that of the whistling swans. More than 300 different species of birds have been identified here: great blue herons, egrets, and many kinds of ducks and geese are common. Spectacular birds of prey—such as bald eagles, pere-

grine falcons, ospreys, hawks, and great horned owls—have also been sighted. Muskrats, minks, raccoons, skunks, opossums, foxes, white-tailed deer, and various aquatic animals live in the grassy marsh.

Crane Creek State Park and Crane Creek Wildlife Research Station, the state center for the study of wetland wildlife, are on this preserve. The research station is located in the **Sportsmen's Migratory Bird Center,** an attractive rustic building on the main entrance road to the park. Visitors can see displays of native wildlife and get information about the area. There is an observation platform overlooking the marsh. A sandy beach lines the shoreline, and there are picnic areas.

If you follow the park road all the way to the end, near the beach, you will find the half-mile-long **Boardwalk Bird Trail,** an area nationally known for its bird-watching opportunities.

Return to OH 2 and drive 17 miles northeast to our last stop:

7. **Maumee Bay State Park.** Maumee Bay, on the shores of both Ohio and Michigan, is the westernmost bay of Lake Erie. The park covers 1,450 acres and is a full-scale resort as well as a magnificent nature preserve. There are 20 deluxe cottages tucked away among the meadows and woods, along with an 18-hole golf course, tennis courts, racquetball courts, saunas, and whirlpools.

Daytime visitors to the park can make use of two swimming beaches, picnic facilities, and 10 miles of hiking and 5 miles of biking and pedestrian trails. A marina welcomes boaters, and boats are also for rent. Winter activities include ice skating, sledding, nature walks, and cross-country skiing. The Trautman Nature Center features a staff of naturalists and a two-mile-long boardwalk trail through the nearby wetlands. Wetlands contain more species of wildlife than any other habitat type, and this park has a wondrous array of creatures. Migrating birds —waterfowl, shorebirds, colorful songbirds, and ring-necked pheasants—are numerous.

From Maumee Bay, it is a short drive east into Toledo, or you can head back east on I-80/I-90 to Cleveland.

Ohio Listings

Akron

Seat of Summit County, in northeast part of state. Akron was once known for its abundance of rubber factories, although the collapse of that industry in the 1980s has led to a new focus on other types of manufacturing. The city also boasts many cultural amenities: the Ohio Ballet, the Akron Symphony, the summer home of the Cleveland Orchestra. **Information:** Akron/Summit Convention & Visitors Bureau, 77 E Mill St, Akron, 44308 (tel 330/374-7560).

HOTELS 🏨

≣≣≣ Akron Hilton Inn at Quaker Square

135 S Broadway, 44308; tel 330/253-5970 or toll free 800/HILTONS; fax 330/253-2574. Unique high-quality hotel built in the silos of the historic Quaker Oats Company. Decor carries original mill memorabilia throughout public areas. Listed in National Register of Historic Places. Near National Inventors Hall of Fame, University of Akron, and John S Knight exhibition hall. **Rooms:** 196 rms. Executive level. CI 3pm/CO 1pm. Nonsmoking rms avail. Round rooms built into massive silos offer modern comforts and views of renovated downtown. **Amenities:** 🛁 🦽 📺 A/C, cable TV w/movies, dataport, voice mail. Some units w/minibars, all w/terraces. **Services:** ✕ 🗝 🚐 🖨 🕭 Twice-daily maid svce, babysitting. **Facilities:** 🏋 🏊 800 💻 ⅙ 3 restaurants (*see* "Restaurants" below), 3 bars (1 w/entertainment), games rm. Connected to Quaker Square shops by enclosed walkway. The Depot, an attractive family restaurant open only on Sat and Sun is in a train car. Tavern in the Square is an elegant dining spot in the stone cellar of the original mill. **Rates (CP):** Peak (May–Sept) $90–$120 S or D. Extra person $10. Children under age 18 stay free. Lower rates off-season. AP and MAP rates avail. Parking: Indoor/outdoor, free. AE, DC, DISC, EC, MC, V.

≣≣≣ Akron West Hilton Inn

3180 W Market St, 44333; tel 330/867-5000 or toll free 800/HILTONS; fax 330/867-1648. Across from Summit Mall. Crisp, elegant lobby and property. **Rooms:** 208 rms, stes, and effic. CI 3pm/CO noon. Nonsmoking rms avail. Clean and comfortable. Newly redecorated rooms. **Amenities:** 🛁 🦽 📺 🗄 A/C, cable TV w/movies. Some units w/whirlpools. **Services:** ✕ 🚐 🏊 🖨 🕭 Twice-daily maid svce, car-rental desk, masseur. **Facilities:** 🏋 🏊 1600 ⅙ 1 restaurant, 1 bar (w/entertainment), spa, sauna, whirlpool, washer/dryer. **Rates (AP):** $75–$110 S; $85–$120 D; $110–$120 ste; $119–$150 effic. Extra person $10. Parking: Outdoor, free. AE, CB, DC, DISC, MC, V.

≣≣ Best Western Executive Inn

2677 Gilchrist Rd, 44305; tel 330/794-1050 or toll free 800/528-1234; fax 330/794-8495. Three-story building off highway. Exterior signs in need of repair. Average lobby. **Rooms:** 120 rms and stes. CI noon/CO noon. Nonsmoking rms avail. **Amenities:** 🛁 🦽 A/C, cable TV w/movies. 1 unit w/whirlpool. **Services:** ✕ 🏊 🖨 Local calls 50¢. **Facilities:** 🏋 🏊 150 ⅙ 1 restaurant, 1 bar (w/entertainment). **Rates:** Peak (May–Sept) $45–$65 S; $50–$70 D; $115–$130 ste. Extra person $6. Children under age 16 stay free. Lower rates off-season. Parking: Outdoor, free. Sea World package avail. AE, CB, DC, DISC, EC, MC, V.

UNRATED Holiday Inn

4073 Medina Rd, 44333; tel 330/666-4131 or toll free 800/HOLIDAY; fax 330/666-7190. Attractive exterior. Efficiently arranged lobby, with restaurant and bar adjacent. **Rooms:** 165 rms and stes. CI 3pm/CO noon. Nonsmoking rms avail. **Amenities:** 🛁 🦽 A/C, cable TV w/movies, dataport. Some units w/terraces. **Services:** ✕ 🚐 🏊 🖨 **Facilities:** 🏋 🏊 800 ⅙ 1 restaurant, 1 bar (w/entertainment), washer/dryer. Meeting facilities in separate wing. **Rates:** $75–$85 S or D; $125–$175 ste. Extra person $8. Children under age 18 stay free. Parking: Outdoor, free. Sea World and Geauga Lake packages avail. AE, CB, DC, DISC, MC, V.

MOTELS

≣≣ Comfort Inn

130 Montrose W Ave, 44321; tel 330/666-5050 or toll free 800/221-2222; fax 330/668-2550. At the Fairlawn Shops. Exterior looks new. Fireplace in lobby. **Rooms:** 132 rms and stes. CI 3pm/CO 11am. Nonsmoking rms avail. **Amenities:** 🛁 🦽 A/C, satel TV w/movies, dataport. Some units w/whirlpools. **Services:** 🏊 🖨 🕭 Hospitality Hour in lobby 5–7pm. **Facilities:** 🏋 50 ⅙ Washer/dryer. Outdoor patio by pool. Passes to Springside Health & Racquet Club available.

Rates (CP): $65–$78 S or D; $78 ste. Extra person $8. Children under age 18 stay free. Parking: Outdoor, free. Sea World and Couples Getaway packages avail. AE, CB, DC, DISC, EC, JCB, MC, V.

UNRATED **Red Roof Inn**

99 Rothrock Rd, 44321; tel 330/666-0566 or toll free 800/843-7663; fax 330/666-6874. New looking property with standard exterior and small lobby. **Rooms:** 108 rms. CI 2pm/CO noon. Nonsmoking rms avail. **Amenities:** 📺 🕹 A/C, cable TV w/movies. **Services:** 🍽 🦮 **Facilities:** 🕹 Use of Springside Health Club for fee. **Rates:** $38–$46 S; $46–$53 D. Extra person $7. Children under age 18 stay free. Parking: Outdoor, free. AE, DC, DISC, MC, V.

UNRATED **Residence Inn by Marriott**

120 Montrose W Ave, 44321; tel 330/666-4811 or toll free 800/331-3131; fax 330/666-8029. Exit 137B off I-77; at the Fairlawn Shops. An apartment/motel concept, catering to long-stay guests. Main building is brick, other units are wood. TVs and fireplace in main lobby. Near shops, businesses, restaurants, and fast food outlets. **Rooms:** 112 effic. CI 3pm/CO noon. Nonsmoking rms avail. **Amenities:** 📺 🕹 📞 A/C, cable TV, refrig. All units w/terraces. **Services:** 🚐 🍽 🦮 Continental breakfast and hospitality hour in lobby. Staff will do grocery shopping for guests. Pets allowed for one-time fee of $75 in regular rooms, $125 in suites. **Facilities:** 🏀 🎣 🕹 Basketball, whirlpool, washer/dryer. **Rates:** $99–$150 effic. Parking: Outdoor, free. AE, DC, DISC, MC, V.

RESTAURANTS 🍴

Diamond Grille

77 W Market St; tel 330/253-0041. Off Main St. **American.** Steaks with all the trimmings and seafood specialties draw the dinner crowds to this restaurant with 1940s decor. **FYI:** Reservations recommended. **Open:** Mon–Fri 11:30am–midnight, Sat 5pm–midnight. **Prices:** Main courses $10–$35. No CC. 👥

House of Hunan

In Fairlawn Town Center, 2717 W Market St; tel 330/864-8215. **Chinese.** Large portions of Hunan and Szechwan dishes are the specialties in this restaurant, once voted the best Asian restaurant in Akron. Special "Eat Hearty" menu offers low-fat and low-sodium options. **FYI:** Reservations recommended. Additional location: 376 E Waterloo (tel 773-1888). **Open:** Lunch Mon–Thurs 11:30am–3pm, Fri 11:30am–3pm, Sat noon–3pm; dinner Mon–Thurs 4–10pm, Fri 4–11pm, Sat 4–11pm, Sun noon–10pm. **Prices:** Main courses $6–$14. AE, DC, DISC, MC, V. 👥 🚗 🗹 🕹

🏆 Ken Stewart's Grille

1970 W Market St; tel 330/867-2555. 5 mi from downtown. **Regional American/Eclectic.** This award-winning restaurant is famous for its steaks, fresh seafood, and fresh-daily lobster, all of which are served with sweet potatoes or vegetables and large salads. Cognac and caramel steak sauces are a specialty.

FYI: Reservations recommended. Children's menu. **Open:** Lunch Mon–Sat 11am–2pm; dinner Mon–Thurs 5–10pm, Fri–Sat 5–11pm. **Prices:** Main courses $14–$24. AE, DC, DISC, MC, V. 👤 🛥 👥 🗹 🕹

Schumachers

In Akron Hilton Inn at Quaker Square, 135 S Broadway; tel 330/253-5970. **American.** Schumachers is popular for its luncheon buffet; selections change daily. Prime rib buffet, served on Fridays and Saturdays, includes sliced stuffed chicken breast and a baked potato bar. Extensive Sunday brunch. **FYI:** Reservations recommended. Children's menu. **Open:** Mon–Thurs 6:30am–9pm, Fri–Sat 6:30am–11pm, Sun 6:30am–9pm. **Prices:** Main courses $8–$30. AE, CB, DC, DISC, MC, V. 🍷 👥 🗹 🕹

🌺 🎭 Tangier Restaurant & Cabaret

532 W Market St; tel 330/376-7171. **American/Middle Eastern.** This exciting restaurant, owned by the same family for over 40 years, is a well-known tourist stop featuring a wide variety of entertainment (including dinner/show packages) and a fountain in the main dining room. Rack of lamb, prepared Middle Eastern style, is the signature entree; interesting side dishes include the Middle Eastern sampler—with kibbee (ground lamb patties), hummus, and other tasty items. Separate menu in Tapas Room. Gift shop sells private-label coffee, wines, and upscale gifts. **FYI:** Reservations recommended. Blues/comedy/country music/jazz/rock. Dress code. **Open:** Fri–Sat 11:30am–2pm, Mon–Thurs 11:30am–midnight, Sun 11:30am–3:30pm. **Prices:** Main courses $14–$22. AE, CB, DC, DISC, MC, V. 👤 🍷 👥 🗹 🕹

The Wine Merchant

1680 Merriman Rd; tel 330/864-6222. **Continental.** Not surprisingly, the menu here focuses on wine-friendly entrees, mostly with French, Italian, and Creole accents. A house favorite is sautéed eggplant stuffed with veal and pork and served on angel-hair pasta. The wine list is reputed to be one of the longest in Ohio, with more than 800 selections from around the world. **FYI:** Reservations recommended. **Open:** Mon–Sat 5:30–10pm, Sun 5–8pm. **Prices:** Main courses $8–$22. AE, MC, V. 👤 👥

ATTRACTIONS 📷

Akron Civic Theatre

182 S Main St; tel 330/535-3179 or 535-3178 (recorded info). Elaborate 1929 theater designed with Moorish motifs (complete with blinking stars and moving clouds) by Viennese architect John Eberson. Hosts live music and dance programs by such groups as the Akron Symphony Orchestra and the Children's Ballet Theater. Guided tours available. $$$

Akron Art Museum

70 E Market St; tel 330/376-9185. Located in an Italian Renaissance Revival structure built in 1899, the museum houses works by Andy Warhol, Frank Stella, William Merritt Chase, Childe Hassam, and Helen Frankenthaler. Other

highlights include an extensive photography collection and an outdoor sculpture gallery. Educational programs offered; group tours available. **Open:** Tues–Fri 11am–5pm, Sat 10am–5pm, Sun noon–5pm. **Free**

Perkins Stone Mansion and John Brown Home

550 Copley Rd; tel 330/535-1120. Furnishings in the Perkins mansion, built in 1837 by Akron founder Simon Perkins Jr, reflect styles of living from the 1830s through 1900. The John Brown House, just across the street, houses a permanent exhibit on the abolitionist's life, as well as a display of the Ohio Canal era which features maps, machine models, and a reconstructed canal-boat captain's cabin. **Open:** Feb–Dec, Tues–Sun 1–5pm. **$**

Akron Zoological Park

500 Edgewood Ave; tel 330/375-2550. The zoo is home to over 300 birds, mammals, and reptiles from around the world. The Ohio Farmyard encounter area and the walk-in aviary allows visitors to enjoy the animals up close. New exhibits feature bald eagles, Chinese alligators, and the Turtle Marsh & Fossil Dig Site. Educational tours offered; gift shop. **Open:** Mid-Apr–mid-Oct, Mon–Sat 10am–5pm, Sun and hols 10am–6pm. **$$**

Alliance

Located northeast of Canton. Established by Quakers in 1805, today it is a modern industrial city on the Mahoning River. **Information:** Alliance Area Chamber of Commerce, 210 E Main St, Alliance, 44601 (tel 330/823-6260).

HOTEL 🏨

≡≡ Comfort Inn

2500 W State St, 44601; tel 330/821-5555 or toll free 800/228-5150; fax 330/821-4919. At Carnation Mall. Large contemporary building at rear of shopping mall. Tiled and mirrored lobby. **Rooms:** 113 rms. CI 2pm/CO noon. Nonsmoking rms avail. **Amenities:** 🛁 ⌂ A/C, cable TV w/movies. Some units w/whirlpools. **Services:** 🚐 ⚫ 🔁 ⚫ Twice-daily maid svce. Fax and copy services available. Pet fee $10. Sea World tickets available. **Facilities:** 🏋 💪 🏊 100 ⚫ Whirlpool, washer/dryer. **Rates (CP):** Peak (June–Aug) $60–$70 S or D. Extra person $8. Children under age 18 stay free. Lower rates off-season. Parking: Outdoor, free. RPM (room, pizza, movie) package avail. AE, CB, DC, DISC, MC, V.

REFRESHMENT STOP 🍹

Heggy's

1306 W State St (Heggy's Plaza); tel 330/821-2051. **American.** An old-fashioned ice cream parlor, complete with jukebox and booths, offers homemade ice cream, sherbet, frozen yogurt, and an array of chocolates. Additional location: 296 E State St, Salem (tel 216/332-5723). **Open:** Mon–Thurs 7am–10pm, Fri–Sat 7am–11pm, Sun 1–10pm. No CC.

Archbold

MOTEL 🏨

≡≡≡ Sauder Heritage Inn

22611 OH 2, PO Box 235, 43502; tel 419/445-6408 or toll free 800/590-9755; fax 419/445-2609. ¼ mi W of OH 66. Located at western edge of Sauder Farm and Craft Village complex, a mid-1800s living history museum. Opened in 1994. Decor uses rich woods and wrought-iron details fashioned by the Craft Village blacksmith. Extensive fine art collection in halls and guest rooms. Heritage Hall, an entertainment center, is nearby. **Rooms:** 33 rms. CI 2pm/CO noon. No smoking. Large, well-lit, comfortable rooms are furnished with rich wooden furniture from the Sauder Woodworking Co. **Amenities:** 🛁 ⌂ 🖥 A/C, cable TV w/movies, refrig, dataport, VCR, voice mail. Some units w/terraces. **Services:** 🔁 Hospitality room is available for guests who must entertain or meet with business clients. **Facilities:** 🏋 💪 200 🖥 💪 Games rm, washer/dryer. **Rates (CP):** Peak (Apr–Oct) $89–$119 S or D. Children under age 18 stay free. Lower rates off-season. Parking: Outdoor, free. Special packages include entry to the farm and village, dinner at the Barn Restaurant, and continental breakfast. Other packages for certain holidays; discounts for seniors and groups. AE, MC, V.

RESTAURANT 🍴

$ ★ The Barn Restaurant

In Sauder Farm Craft Village complex, OH 2; tel 419/445-2231. Off OH 66. **American.** Hearty, country meals served in Amish/Mennonite family style have earned a fabulous local and regional reputation. Diners served by waitresses in 1800s dress sit beneath hand-hewn timbers in the granary, loft, manger, and feedlot of the remodeled 1861 barn. **FYI:** Reservations not accepted. Children's menu. No liquor license. No smoking. **Open:** Mon–Sat 11am–8pm, Sun 11am–2pm. **Prices:** Main courses $6–$15. AE, MC, V. 🍴 💪

Ashtabula

See also Geneva-on-the-Lake

Located at the mouth of the Ashtabula River on the south shore of Lake Erie. According to legend, when Moses Cleaveland's surveying party stopped here in 1796, he offered his cohorts two gallons of wine for the privilege of naming the river. It bore the name "Mary Esther" until the wine was consumed. **Information:** Ashtabula Area Chamber of Commerce, 4366 Main Ave, PO Box 96, Ashtabula, 44004 (tel 216/998-6998).

MOTELS 🏨

≋≋ Budget Luxury Inn
5425 Clarkins Dr, Austintown, 44515; tel 330/793-9806; fax 330/793-7199. Two-story Cape Cod building set back from road and surrounded by trees. Exterior walkways. **Rooms:** 103 rms and effic. CI 2pm/CO noon. No smoking. Clean, fresh rooms. **Amenities:** 🎀 A/C, cable TV. **Services:** 🐾 Pet fee $5. **Facilities:** 🛁 1 bar, games rm, washer/dryer. Two pool tables in lounge off lobby. **Rates (CP):** $38–$44 S; $41–$48 D; $42 effic. Extra person $6. Children under age 18 stay free. Parking: Outdoor, free. AE, CB, DC, DISC, MC, V.

≋≋≋ Holiday Inn
1860 Austinburg Rd, Austinburg, 44010; tel 216/275-2711 or toll free 800/HOLIDAY; fax 216/275-7314. Modest two-story building set back from highway. Lobby is small but light and airy with contemporary furnishings and ceramic tile. **Rooms:** 119 rms. CI 3pm/CO noon. Nonsmoking rms avail. **Amenities:** 🎀 ⚷ A/C, cable TV w/movies. **Services:** ✕ 🖨 🍽 **Facilities:** 🛁 [200] ⚷ 1 restaurant, 1 bar, washer/dryer. Four meeting rooms in separate wing. **Rates:** Peak (June–Aug) $72–$95 S or D. Extra person $8. Children under age 18 stay free. Lower rates off-season. AP and MAP rates avail. Parking: Outdoor, free. AE, DC, DISC, MC, V.

≋≋ Travelodge
2352 OH 45 N, Austinburg, 44010; tel 216/275-2011 or toll free 800/255-3050; fax 216/275-1253. Two-story, two-tone stucco building with colonial columns just off highway. **Rooms:** 48 rms. CI noon/CO noon. Nonsmoking rms avail. **Amenities:** 🎀 📶 A/C, cable TV. **Services:** 🖨 🍽 Twice-daily maid svce, babysitting. **Facilities:** 🛁 [12] ⚷ **Rates (CP):** Peak (May–Sept) $35–$68 S; $45–$78 D. Extra person $5. Children under age 18 stay free. Lower rates off-season. Parking: Outdoor, free. AE, CB, DC, DISC, MC, V.

RESTAURANT 🍴

★ El Grande Steak House
2145 W Prospect St; tel 216/998-2228. **Steak.** This long-time local favorite features a Southwestern decor with wrought-iron railings, steer-horn hat rack, and saddles. The manager has been here for more than 25 years, the chef for over 20. The classic steak house menu lists steak, pasta, and seafood options. **FYI:** Reservations accepted. Children's menu. **Open:** Mon–Thurs 11am–9pm, Fri 11am–10:30pm, Sat 4:30–10:30pm. **Prices:** Main courses $6–$14. MC, V. 👥

ATTRACTION 🏛

Great Lakes Marine and US Coast Guard Memorial Museum
1071 Walnut Blvd; tel 216/964-6847. At Ashtabula Harbor. Housed in an 1898 lighthouse keeper's home, the museum displays marine artifacts, paintings, photos, and models; a scale model of a Hulett ore unloading machine, and a ship's pilot house. Guided tours available by appointment. Picnic area. Donation suggested. **Open:** Mem Day–Oct, Fri–Sun noon–6pm. **Free**

Athens

Seat of Athens County, in southeast part of state. Athens is the home of Ohio University, the first college (founded 1804) in what was once the Northwest Territory. The city itself is surrounded by coal, hills, and hollows. **Information:** Athens Area Chamber of Commerce, PO Box 238, 331 Richland Ave, Athens, 45701 (tel 614/594-2251).

HOTEL 🏨

≋≋≋ Ohio University Inn
331 Richland Ave, 45701; tel 614/593-6661; fax 614/593-6661. ½ mi from Ohio University. Beautiful and spacious hotel with elegant furnishings and decor. **Rooms:** 143 rms. CI 3pm/CO noon. No smoking. Rooms have exquisite views of either the well-tended patio/pool area or of the Ohio University campus. Some bay windows. New addition has rooms with larger bathrooms and counter space. **Amenities:** 🎀 ⚷ A/C, cable TV w/movies, dataport. All units w/terraces. **Services:** ✕ 🖨 🍽 Babysitting. **Facilities:** 🛁 [300] ⚷ 1 restaurant (see "Restaurants" below), 1 bar. Free access to Ohio University health and fitness facilities. **Rates:** $65–$79 S. Children under age 12 stay free. Parking: Outdoor, free. Rates increase for special events at university. AE, CB, DC, DISC, EC, JCB, MC, V.

MOTELS 🏨

≋≋ AmeriHost Inn
20 Home St, 45701; tel 614/594-3000; fax 614/594-5546. At Richland St exit off US 33. Conveniently located, basic, comfortable accommodations. Several restaurants nearby. **Rooms:** 102 rms and stes. CI 3pm/CO noon. Nonsmoking rms avail. **Amenities:** 🎀 ⚷ A/C, cable TV, in-rm safe. Some units w/terraces, some w/whirlpools. **Services:** 🖨 🍽 **Facilities:** 🛁 [40] ⚷ Sauna, whirlpool. **Rates (CP):** Peak (Aug–June) $66–$71 S or D; $105–$110 ste. Extra person $5. Children under age 12 stay free. Lower rates off-season. Parking: Outdoor, free. AE, DISC, MC, V.

≋ Budget Host
US 50 W, 45701; tel 614/594-2294 or toll free 800/283-4678. 2 mi from Ohio University Campus. Basic, simple. Good for overnight stays when cost is a concern. **Rooms:** 29 rms. CI 3pm/CO 11am. Nonsmoking rms avail. **Amenities:** 🎀 A/C, cable TV w/movies. **Services:** 🍽 **Rates:** Peak (May–Oct) $34–$45 S; $41–$65 D. Extra person $4. Children under age 12 stay free. Min stay special events. Lower rates off-season. Parking: Outdoor, free. Rates increase during special events at Ohio University. AE, CB, DC, DISC, MC, V.

Days Inn

330 Columbus Rd, 45701; tel 614/592-4000 or toll free 800/ 329-7466; fax 614/593-7687. Jct OH 13/US 33. Easy access, yet set back off the highway and quiet. Good for overnight stays for families or business travelers, when extras are not important. Next door is a sports complex with miniature golf and batting cages. **Rooms:** 60 rms. CI 3pm/CO noon. Nonsmoking rms avail. **Amenities:** 🛋 🅰 A/C, cable TV w/movies, in-rm safe. **Services:** 🖼 🍴 **Facilities:** 🔥 **Rates (CP):** $46–$60 S; $50–$60 D. Extra person $6. Children under age 13 stay free. Parking: Outdoor, free. AE, CB, DC, DISC, JCB, MC, V.

RESTAURANTS 🍴

Cutler's Restaurant

In Ohio University Inn, 331 Richland Ave; tel 614/593-6661. **American.** Offering a pleasant view of the Ohio University campus, this comfortable eatery gives families and friends a place to dine at reasonable prices. The lunch buffet and evening entree options change daily and are usually built around a specific theme. One of the local favorites is the blue cheese–encrusted filet mignon. The adjoining McGuffy's Pub has a warm friendly atmosphere and features a "hall of fame" wall with photos of prestigious athletes from OU's history. **FYI:** Reservations accepted. Children's menu. No smoking. **Open:** Breakfast Mon–Fri 6:30–11:30am, Sat 7–11am, Sun 8–10am; lunch Mon–Sat 11am–2pm, Sun 10am–2pm; dinner Mon–Sat 5–10pm, Sun 5–9pm. **Prices:** Main courses $8–$16. AE, CB, DC, DISC, MC, V. 🏔 👥 🔥

Seven Sauces

66 N Court St; tel 614/592-5555. 6 blocks N of Ohio University. **International.** A small, cozy place to enjoy a quiet meal. Fresh spices are used abundantly in homemade soups (like gingered creamed carrot soup) and salad dressings (such as onion ranch dressing). Favorite entrees include chicken Parmesan and baked seafood gratin. Not recommended for children. **FYI:** Reservations recommended. Dress code. **Open:** Mon–Thurs 5–9pm, Sat 5–10pm, Sun 5–8:30pm. Closed Christmas week. **Prices:** Main courses $10–$15. AE, CB, DISC, MC, V. ♥

Aurora

Located in the north-central part of the state, midway between Cleveland and Youngstown. This small tourist town is a gateway to the Cuyahoga Valley National Recreation Area. **Information:** Aurora Area Chamber of Commerce, 173 S Chillicothe Rd, Aurora, 44202 (tel 216/562-3355).

HOTEL 🏨

Aurora Inn

30 E Garfield, 44202; tel 216/562-6121 or toll free 800/ 444-6121; fax 216/562-5249. The inn has been in existence since 1927 and was completely rebuilt in 1963. Located in a historic district, it retains a rural charm. **Rooms:** 69 rms. CI 4pm/CO 11am. Nonsmoking rms avail. **Amenities:** 🛋 🅰 A/C, cable TV, dataport. **Services:** 🖼 🚗 🍴 Shuttle to Cleveland airport. **Facilities:** 🔥 🛎 🏊 1 restaurant, 1 bar, sauna, whirlpool. Coach Room Tavern adjoins lobby. The Quilted Cupboard offers family-style dining in a country atmosphere. **Rates:** Peak (May–Sept) $89–$150 S; $99–$175 D. Extra person $10. Children under age 18 stay free. Lower rates off-season. AP and MAP rates avail. Parking: Outdoor, free. AE, CB, DC, DISC, MC, V.

MOTEL

Best Western Aurora Woodlands Inn

800 N Aurora Rd, 44202; tel 216/562-9151 or toll free 800/ 877-7849; fax 216/562-5701. On OH 43, 100 yards from Sea World. Unremarkable exterior. Lobby has grand piano, skylight, and sunken seating area. This is the closest facility to Sea World. **Rooms:** 144 rms and stes. Executive level. CI 4pm/CO 11am. Nonsmoking rms avail. **Amenities:** 🛋 🅰 🎦 A/C, cable TV w/movies, dataport. Some units w/minibars. **Services:** 🖼 🚗 🏊 🍴 Twice-daily maid svce, car-rental desk. Free shuttle to attractions. **Facilities:** 🔥 🛎 🏊 💻 🔥 1 restaurant, 1 bar (w/entertainment), basketball, volleyball, games rm, sauna, whirlpool, washer/dryer. Large atrium pool area. **Rates:** Peak (Mem Day–Labor Day) $78–$145 S or D; $125–$250 ste. Children under age 18 stay free. Lower rates off-season. Parking: Outdoor, free. Packages avail, including Geauga Lake and Sea World. DC, DISC, MC, V.

RESTAURANT 🍴

The Cabin Lounge

In Mario's International Hotel and Spa, 35 E Garfield Rd; tel 216/562-9171. **Northern Italian.** Diners may choose to be seated indoors, amid polished marble, rustic beams, and comfortable upholstery, or on the outdoor patio with its waterfall, marble inlays, and portico. An open pizza oven imported from Italy is situated so that guests can watch some of the meal preparation. Handmade pastas and rack of lamb are especially recommended. **FYI:** Reservations recommended. Piano. **Open:** Mon–Thurs 7am–10pm, Fri–Sat 7am–11pm, Sun 7am–9pm. **Prices:** Main courses $12–$26. AE, DISC, MC, V. ♥ 🍴 👥

ATTRACTIONS 🎪

Geauga Lake

1060 N Aurora Rd; tel 216/562-8303. Highlights among this park's 100-plus rides and attractions include four roller coasters, two water complexes, a two-million-gallon wave pool, an indoor laser show, and a 1926 Marcus Illions carousel with carved-wood horses. **Open:** Mem Day–Labor Day, daily sunrise–sunset. **$$$$**

Sea World of Ohio

1100 Sea World Dr; tel 216/562-8101. Popular 90-acre marine-life park combines entertainment value with wildlife-conservation awareness. A new interactive habitat, **Dolphin Cove,** allows visitors to touch, feed, and observe bottlenose dolphins in a 375,000 gallon naturalistic environment. Other theme areas include **Shark Encounter, Penguin Encounter, Birds of the World Aviaries,** and **Eagle Point,** where visitors can observe rehabilitated bald eagles in a woodlands setting. Entertainment at the park features a killer whale and dolphin show, a *Baywatch*-themed water-skiing show, and evening laser and fireworks shows. **Open:** Peak (Mem Day–Labor Day) daily 10am–sunset. Reduced hours off- season. **$$$$**

Austinburg

See Ashtabula, Geneva-on-the-Lake

Beachwood

An eastern suburb of Cleveland. Nearby Shaker Heights is home to two manmade lakes. **Information:** Beachwood Chamber of Commerce, 25501 Fairmount Blvd, Beachwood, 44122-2257 (tel 216/831-0003).

HOTELS 🏨

≣≣≣ Courtyard by Marriott Cleveland East
3695 Orange Place, 44122; tel 216/765-1900 or toll free 800/321-2211; fax 216/765-1841. I-271 and Chagrin Blvd (US 422). Modern building. New split-level lobby with comfortable seating, two-sided fireplace, bay windows, and atrium walkway. **Rooms:** 113 rms and stes. CI 1pm/CO noon. Nonsmoking rms avail. **Amenities:** 🛏 ⟳ 🖭 A/C, cable TV w/movies, dataport, voice mail. Some units w/terraces. **Services:** ✕ 🚐 🖼 ⌂ Twice-daily maid svce. **Facilities:** 🛎 ⟲ 🍴 🖳 ⧖ 1 restaurant (bkfst only), 1 bar, games rm, sauna, whirlpool, washer/dryer. **Rates:** Peak (May–Sept) $69–$109 S or D; $130–$150 ste. Extra person $10. Children under age 18 stay free. Lower rates off-season. Parking: Outdoor, free. AE, CB, DC, DISC, MC, V.

≣≣≣ Embassy Suites
3775 Park E Dr, 44122; tel 216/765-8066 or toll free 800/EMBASSY; fax 216/765-0930. All-suite hotel with Mediterranean decor, including ceramic tile, lots of greenery, and a pond alive with ducks and turtles. Glass-enclosed elevators lead to open walkways with rooms leading off them. **Rooms:** 216 stes. CI 3pm/CO 1pm. Nonsmoking rms avail. Suites surround atrium courtyard. **Amenities:** 🛏 ⟳ 🖭 🍴 A/C, cable TV w/movies, refrig, dataport, voice mail. Some suites have exercise bikes and workout tapes. **Services:** ✕ 🚐 🖼 ⌂ Car-rental desk, social director, babysitting. Free shuttle to nearby attractions and services. Two-hour manager's hospitality reception in lobby each evening. Fax and copy services available. **Facilities:** 🛎 ⟲ 1 restaurant, 1 bar, games rm,

sauna, whirlpool, washer/dryer. **Rates (BB):** $99–$149 ste. Extra person $15. Children under age 12 stay free. Parking: Outdoor, free. AE, DC, DISC, MC, V.

≣≣≣ Holiday Inn
3750 Orange Place, 44122; tel 216/831-3300 or toll free 800/HOLIDAY; fax 216/831-0486. At the Village Square Shops. Exterior has had a face-lift of paint and stucco. **Rooms:** 169 rms. Executive level. CI 3pm/CO 11am. Nonsmoking rms avail. **Amenities:** 🛏 ⟳ 🖭 A/C, satel TV w/movies. **Services:** ✕ 🚐 🖼 ⌂ Car-rental desk. Fax and copy service available. Pizzeria Uno is connected to lobby and makes room service deliveries. Guest discounts to Sea World and Geauga Lake. **Facilities:** 🛎 [400] ⧖ 1 restaurant, 1 bar, games rm, sauna, washer/dryer. Free use of Bali's Health Spa. **Rates:** $94–$114 S or D. Extra person $10. Children under age 18 stay free. Parking: Outdoor, free. Bed-and-breakfast package avail. AE, DC, DISC, MC, V.

≣≣≣ Marriott Hotel
3663 Park E Dr, 44122; tel 216/464-5950 or toll free 800/334-2118; fax 216/464-8935. Well-landscaped grounds set off this modern, brick, mid-rise building. **Rooms:** 403 rms and stes. Executive level. CI 3pm/CO noon. Nonsmoking rms avail. Major renovation in 1995. **Amenities:** 🛏 ⟳ 🖭 A/C, satel TV w/movies, dataport. **Services:** ✕ 🖘 🚐 ⌂ 🕯 Twice-daily maid svce, car-rental desk, masseur, babysitting. Fax and copy services. Pet fee $50. **Facilities:** 🛎 🏋 [1000] ⧖ 1 restaurant, 1 bar (w/entertainment), games rm, spa, sauna, whirlpool, washer/dryer. Complimentary use of Bally's Health Club. **Rates:** Peak (May 28–Sept 4) $109–$149 S or D; $250–$500 ste. Children under age 18 stay free. Lower rates off-season. AP and MAP rates avail. Parking: Outdoor, free. "Rock Bottom" and "Two for" specials. AE, DC, DISC, EC, ER, MC, V.

≣≣≣ Radisson Hotel Beachwood
25300 Chagrin Blvd, 44122; tel 216/831-5150 or toll free 800/333-3333; fax 216/765-1156. Brick and emerald exterior has clean and cared-for look. Lobby features brass chandelier, fresh flowers, and cherry wood traditional furnishings. **Rooms:** 196 rms and stes. Executive level. CI 3pm/CO noon. Nonsmoking rms avail. **Amenities:** 🛏 ⟳ 🖭 🍴 A/C, cable TV w/movies. Some units w/minibars, some w/whirlpools. **Services:** ✕ 🚐 🖼 ⌂ Twice-daily maid svce, car-rental desk, social director, babysitting. Fax and copy service available at front desk. Pleasant and extremely helpful staff. **Facilities:** 🛎 🏋 [350] ⧖ 1 restaurant, 1 bar, spa, beauty salon, washer/dryer. Charming, cozy cafe off lobby. Six meeting rooms and a ballroom. **Rates:** Peak (May 17–Sept) $92–$125 S or D; $140–$175 ste. Extra person $10. Children under age 18 stay free. Lower rates off-season. AP and MAP rates avail. Parking: Outdoor, free. AE, CB, DC, DISC, MC, V.

MOTEL

⩵⩵ Travelodge Beachwood

3795 Orange Place, 44122; tel 216/831-7200 or toll free 800/578-7878; fax 216/831-0616. Very basic, modest brick exterior, with outside walkways. A good stop for budget travelers. Located at end of Orange Place, near many restaurants and shops. **Rooms:** 128 rms. CI 4pm/CO 11am. Nonsmoking rms avail. **Amenities:** 🛏 🖩 A/C, satel TV, dataport. **Services:** 🚐 🖼 ↴ **Facilities:** 🛏 ₁₅ ⓑ Games rm, washer/dryer. Free use of Scandinavian Health Spa for guests 10 years and older. **Rates (CP):** Peak (June 1–Sept 15) $45–$76 S or D. Extra person $6. Children under age 18 stay free. Lower rates off-season. Parking: Outdoor, free. AE, DC, DISC, MC, V.

RESTAURANTS 🍴

Beverly Hills Cafe

In Beachwood Place, 26300 Cedar Rd (University Heights); tel 216/464-6544. Off I-271. **American.** A very popular and often crowded pit stop for hungry mall shoppers and others. The Cafe is praised for its soups, salads with homemade dressings, vegetarian selections, and other light options. **FYI:** Reservations accepted. Children's menu. **Open:** Mon–Thurs 11am–9pm, Fri–Sat 11am–10pm. **Prices:** Main courses $6–$12. AE, CB, DC, DISC, MC, V. 🖼 ⓑ

Charley's Crab

25765 Chagrin Blvd; tel 216/831-8222. On US 422 W of I-271. **Seafood.** This busy place, with lots of repeat customers, is perfect for a business lunch or a romantic dinner for two. Menus change daily, but selections always include the freshest available fish, as well as pasta and other light options. **FYI:** Reservations recommended. Children's menu. **Open:** Mon–Thurs 11:30am–10pm, Sat 11:30am–11pm, Sun 4–10pm. **Prices:** Main courses $15–$32. AE, DC, DISC, MC, V. ♥ 🖼 ♥ ⓥⓟ

♣ Ristorante Giovanni's

In Chagrin Richmond Plaza, 25550 Chagrin Blvd; tel 216/831-8625. **Italian.** Hand-painted murals and white-paneled walls make a perfect backdrop for the cuisine, as does the efficient and gracious service. All pastas are made freshly daily; other entrees include Canadian halibut served over chipped potatoes and longbone veal chop with potato galette. **FYI:** Reservations recommended. Dress code. **Open:** Lunch Mon–Fri 11:30–2:30; dinner Mon–Fri 5:30–9:30pm, Sat 5:30–10:30pm. **Prices:** Main courses $19–$34. AE, CB, DC, DISC, MC, V. ♥ ⓥⓟ

Samurai Japanese Steak & Seafood

In Chagrin Plaza West, 23611 Chagrin Blvd (Pavillion Mall); tel 216/464-7575. At US 422, OH 87, and Green Rd. **Japanese.** Asian showmen/chefs prepare the steaks and seafood on tableside hibachi tables. Dinners typically start with special Japanese onion soup and Samurai salad with secret ginger dressing; fresh vegetables, rice, and green tea accom-

pany the entrees. Hot sake goes well with this food. **FYI:** Reservations recommended. Children's menu. No smoking. **Open:** Lunch Mon–Thurs 11:30am–2pm; dinner Mon–Thurs 5:30–10pm, Fri 5:30–11pm, Sat 5–11pm, Sun 4:30–9pm. **Prices:** Main courses $12–$24. AE, DC, DISC, MC, V. 🖼 ⓥⓟ

The Tavern

In Eton Collection Shopping Mall, 28699 Chagrin Blvd; tel 216/464-4660. **American.** The indoor dining room is decorated with colonial furniture and upholstered captain's chairs, while an enclosed outdoor dining area has umbrella-topped bistro tables and lots of greenery. Recommended entrees include the pork tenderloin, steaks, and pasta specialties. **FYI:** Reservations recommended. Children's menu. Dress code. **Open:** Lunch Mon–Sat 11:30am–2:30pm; dinner Mon–Sat 5:30–10pm, Fri 5:30–10pm, Sun 5–9pm; brunch Sun 10am–2:30pm. **Prices:** Main courses $10–$20. AE, DC, DISC, ER, MC, V. ♥ ➰ 🖼 🖼 ♥ ⓑ

Bellefontaine

Seat of Logan County, in west part of state. Named "beautiful fountain" by the French for the natural springs. The area also contains several caverns and a ski resort. **Information:** Logan County Convention & Visitors Bureau, 100 S Main St, Bellefontaine, 43311-2083 (tel 513/599-5121).

MOTELS 🖿

⩵⩵ Comfort Inn

260 Northview, 43311; tel 513/599-6666 or toll free 800/221-2222; fax 513/599-2300. Perched atop a hill overlooking the junction of US 33 and US 68 and pastoral scenes. **Rooms:** 73 rms and stes. CI 2pm/CO noon. Nonsmoking rms avail. Rooms have ceiling fans. **Amenities:** 🛏 ⓐ A/C, CD/tape player. Some units w/whirlpools. **Services:** 🖼 ↴ ⟳ $10 for pets. **Facilities:** 🛏 🎿 🖼 🖼 ₇₅ ⓑ 1 bar (w/entertainment), washer/dryer. The Fountain full-service bar has entertainment on the weekends, including bands and DJs. **Rates (CP):** $55–$60 S or D; $79–$84 ste. Children under age 18 stay free. Parking: Outdoor, free. New Year's Eve package avail. AE, CB, DC, DISC, MC, V.

⩵⩵⩵ Holiday Inn

1134 N Main St, 43311; tel 513/593-8515 or toll free 800/HOLIDAY; fax 513/593-4802. Jct US 33 and US 68. A fully renovated, spacious, full-service motel in a good location off the highway. **Rooms:** 102 rms and stes. CI 3pm/CO noon. Nonsmoking rms avail. All rooms have a king-size bed and sofa bed or two double beds. **Amenities:** 🛏 ⓐ A/C, cable TV w/movies, dataport. **Services:** ✕ 🖼 ↴ ⟳ **Facilities:** 🛏 🎿 🖼 🖼 ₂₀₀ ⓑ 1 restaurant, 1 bar (w/entertainment), whirlpool. Bright, clean, and attractive pool area. Large, fully equipped workout room. Mr Roberts Lounge and Restaurant open daily with entertainment in the lounge, including karaoke and live bands. **Rates:** $69 S or D; $75–$120 ste. Children under age 18 stay free. Parking: Outdoor, free. AE, CB, DC, DISC, JCB, MC, V.

ATTRACTIONS 🏛

Zane Caverns

OH 540; tel 513/592-0891. Located 6 mi E of Bellefontaine, these caverns hold fancifully named formations—"the Beehive" and "Niagara Falls"—and extremely rare white "cave pearls" (formed by water dripping through limestone), as well as active stalactites and stalagmites. **Open:** Peak (May–Sept) daily 10am–5pm. Reduced hours off-season. **$$$**

Ohio Caverns

2210 E OH 245, West Liberty; tel 513/465-4017. Ohio's largest cavern system offers exquisite crystal-white stalactite and stalagmite formations with unique colorings. A 35-acre park is located directly above the Caverns and contains a shelter house and picnic tables. Gift shop. **Open:** Peak (Apr–Oct) daily 9am–5pm. Reduced hours off-season. **$$$**

Piatt Castles

OH 245; tel 513/465-2821. Towering over the cornfields around the Mad River area are these two European-style castles. They were completed after the Civil War by Gen Abram Piatt, who called his castle Mac-A-Cheek, and his brother, Col Donn Piatt, who named his castle Mac-O-Chee. The Norman-style Mac-A-Cheek has impressive woodwork and electic furnishings—weapons, first edition books, Native American artifacts, and mastodon teeth; the Flemish Mac-O-Chee features colorful painted ceilings and antiques from America, Europe, and Asia. **Open:** Peak (May–Sept) daily 11am–5pm. Reduced hours off-season. **$$**

Bellevue

Northern town, midway between Cleveland and Toledo. Just south of town, the Old Mist'ry River flows at its lowest level (110 ft). **Information:** Bellevue Area Chamber of Commerce, 110 W Main St, Bellevue, 44811 (tel 419/483-2182).

MOTEL 🏨

≣ ≣ ≣ Best Western Inn

1120 E Main St, 44811; tel 419/483-5740 or toll free 800/528-1234. 1¼ mi W of jct OH 46/20. Appealing, very efficient property. **Rooms:** 89 rms and stes. CI 2pm/CO 11am. Nonsmoking rms avail. Clean and bright rooms with furniture of good quality. **Amenities:** 🕾 🕯 A/C, cable TV. Family rooms have wet bars; some have full kitchens. **Services:** Free morning coffee in bar. **Facilities:** 🎱 🏋 💆 175 🕭 1 restaurant (see "Restaurants" below), 1 bar, games rm, spa, sauna, whirlpool, washer/dryer. Tanning booth. **Rates:** Peak (May 15–Sept 1) $69–$120 S or D; $98–$250 ste. Extra person $4. Children under age 18 stay free. Lower rates off-season. Parking: Outdoor, free. AE, CB, DC, DISC, MC, V.

RESTAURANTS 🍽

Betty's Family Restaurant

In the Best Western Inn, 1120 E Main St; tel 419/483-2238. On US 20 1¼ mi E of OH 4. **American.** Simple, good home-cooked taste, prepared on the broiler and served to hungry patrons under Betty's supervision. Seating at booths and tables. Menu selections are limited during the week; only on special nights are such entrees as prime rib, T-bone steak, and barbecued ribs available. **FYI:** Reservations accepted. Children's menu. Jacket required. No liquor license. **Open:** Daily 6am–10pm. **Prices:** Main courses $5–$10. AE, DISC, MC, V. 🎱🕭

Jenny's Amsden House

116 E Main St (Downtown); tel 419/483-9079. **American.** This is a solid mom-and-pop restaurant, favored by the locals for its basic, tasty, well-prepared meals from the broiler or oven. Breakfast is available at any time of day; the golden french toast, with bacon or sausage, is a popular choice. **FYI:** Reservations not accepted. No liquor license. **Open:** Mon 5:30am–2pm, Tues–Sat 5:30am–8pm, Sun 6am–2pm. **Prices:** Main courses $5–$10. No CC. 🎱 💟 🕭

★ McClain's Restaurant & Old Tyme Saloon

137-139 Main St; tel 419/483-2727. On US 20 at OH 269. **American.** Recognizable by its stained-glass door and green awning, the restaurant—established in 1880 and now in its fourth generation of owner-operators—features a rustic look created by a dark barn wood and brick interior with mounted deer and elk heads. The barbecued ribs, served alone or with barbecued chicken, shrimp, or perch and their special sauce (a secret recipe handed down over generations) are locally famous. Another favorite is broiled steak served with home-fried potatoes, grilled onions, and gravy. **FYI:** Reservations recommended. Karaoke. Children's menu. **Open:** Mon–Sat 11am–10pm. **Prices:** Main courses $7–$26. MC, V. 🍴 🎱

ATTRACTIONS 🏛

Seneca Caverns

15248 TR 178; tel 418/483-6711. Unique underground limestone caverns referred to as "The Caviest Cave in the USA." One-hour guided tour takes visitors through seven levels of electrically lighted caverns; at the lowest level (110 feet below the surface) lies "Ole Mist'ry River." Group tours available upon request. **Open:** Peak (Mem Day–Labor Day) daily 9am–7pm. Reduced hours off-season. Closed mid-Oct–Apr. **$$$**

Mad River and NKP Railroad Museum

233 York St; tel 419/483-2222. Named after a railroad that ran through the area beginning in 1839, this museum features a variety of old railroad cars (the PRR Mailcar, the NKP Dynamometer Car, and the Curtice Depot); original artifacts such as uniforms, timetables, and lanterns; and even china

used in railroad dining cars. Gift shop; group tours by appointment. **Open:** Peak (Mem Day–Labor Day) daily 1–5pm. Reduced hours off-season. **$**

Bellville

See Mansfield

Botkins

See Wapakoneta

Bowling Green

Seat of Wood County, in northwest part of state. In 1886 the town experienced a short-lived oil boom; many of the elaborately turreted houses built at the time still remain. Today, the economy relies mostly upon agriculture and small factories. **Information:** Bowling Green Chamber of Commerce, 163 N Main St, PO Box 31, Bowling Green, 43402-0031 (tel 419/353-7945).

MOTELS

Best Western Falcon Plaza Inn
1450 E Wooster St, 43402 (University); tel 419/352-4671 or toll free 800/528-1234; fax 419/352-5351. ½ mi W of exit 181 off I-75. Located near the interstate and across from a dormitory complex at Bowling Green State University, this facility is a favorite of parents, college students, business persons, and families. The 1½-story lobby is bright and roomy, and has a working fireplace along the outside wall. **Rooms:** 72 rms, stes, and effic. Executive level. CI 3pm/CO noon. Nonsmoking rms avail. **Amenities:** A/C, cable TV w/movies, dataport. **Services:** Continental breakfast is available in a small, bright dining parlor off the lobby. Room-service delivery can be arranged with several nearby restaurants and fast-food facilities. **Facilities:** Rates (CP): $53–$70 S; $58–$75 D; $90–$110 ste; $63–$75 effic. Children under age 12 stay free. Parking: Outdoor, free. AE, CB, DC, DISC, MC, V.

Days Inn Bowling Green
1550 E Wooster St, 43402; tel 419/352-5211 or toll free 800/DAYS-INN; fax 419/354-8030. ½ mi W of exit 181 off I-75. Located across the street from a Bowling Green State University dormitory area, this is a clean and tidy motel. **Rooms:** 100 rms. CI 3pm/CO 11am. Nonsmoking rms avail. **Amenities:** A/C, satel TV w/movies, in-rm safe. **Services:** **Facilities:** Some cabanas available at pool area. **Rates (CP):** $49–$66 S or D. Extra person $6. Children under age 18 stay free. Parking: Outdoor, free. AE, CB, DC, DISC, JCB, MC, V.

Holley Lodge
1630 E Wooster St, 43402; tel 419/352-2521 or toll free 800/553-7829; fax 419/353-5975. ½ mi W of exit 181 off I-75. Full-service, attractive property located across the street from the Bowling Green State University football stadium. **Rooms:** 100 rms. CI 2pm/CO 11am. Nonsmoking rms avail. Poolside rooms are most expensive. Suites are larger rooms, with two double beds and a sofa bed. **Amenities:** A/C, cable TV. Some units w/terraces. **Services:** Babysitting. Coin laundry available. **Facilities:** Games rm, whirlpool, washer/dryer. Games, pool table, and lounge located in atrium off the pool area. **Rates:** $50–$75 S or D. Children under age 18 stay free. Parking: Outdoor, free. Special university weekend packages (graduation, homecoming, and parents' weekend); New Year's Eve package. AE, DC, DISC, MC, V.

RESTAURANT

Ⓢ ★ Kaufman's at the Lodge
1628 E Wooster St; tel 419/354-2535. ½ mi W of I-75. **American.** One of the leading restaurants in this college town, located across the street from the football stadium. Extremely popular with both locals and travelers; without a reservation on weekends, there is little hope of getting seated at a reasonable hour. Ambience is average, decor is subdued, lighting is dim. Fresh pies daily. **FYI:** Reservations accepted. Children's menu. Additional location: 163 S Main St (tel 352-2595). **Open:** Sun–Thurs 6am–10pm, Fri–Sat 6am–11pm. **Prices:** Main courses $6–$11. AE, CB, DC, DISC, MC, V.

Cambridge

Seat of Guernsey County, in eastern Ohio. Founded in 1806, the town took on life with the arrival of the Old National Road (US 40) in 1826. Clay deposits led to pottery production, and in 1901 a large glass factory was established. Cambridge is still a key center for glassmaking. **Information:** Cambridge Area Chamber of Commerce, 918 Wheeling Ave, PO Box 488, Cambridge, 43725-0488 (tel 614/439-6688).

HOTEL

Days Inn
2328 Southgate Pkwy, 43725; tel 614/432-5691 or toll free 800/329-7466; fax 614/432-3526. Exit 178 off I-70; jct I-77. Located at intersection of two major interstates, with easy access off highway. **Rooms:** 103 rms and effic. CI 2pm/CO 11am. Nonsmoking rms avail. King rooms have fold-out sofas. **Amenities:** A/C, cable TV. **Services:** **Facilities:** **Rates (CP):** Peak (May–Oct) $60–$90 S or D; $90 effic. Extra person $5. Children under age 12 stay free. Lower rates off-season. Parking: Outdoor, free. AE, DC, DISC, MC, V.

MOTELS

Best Western Inn
1945 Southgate Pkwy, 43725; tel 614/439-3581 or toll free 800/528-1234; fax 614/439-1824. Exit 178 off I-70. Comfortable, attractive decor. **Rooms:** 95 rms. CI noon/CO 11am. Nonsmoking rms avail. **Amenities:** A/C, cable TV, dataport. All units w/terraces. **Services:** VCR's available at desk. Children of guests eat free at neighboring J & K on the Hill Restaurant. **Facilities:** 1 bar, games rm, playground. **Rates:** Peak (May–Oct) $50–$80 S or D. Children under age 18 stay free. Lower rates off-season. Parking: Outdoor, free. AE, DC, DISC, MC, V.

Holiday Inn
OH 209, 43725; tel 614/432-7313 or toll free 800/465-4329; fax 614/432-2337. Exit 178 off I-70; ¼ mi N. Very nice, comfortable accommodations. **Rooms:** 107 rms. CI 2pm/CO noon. Nonsmoking rms avail. Indoor and outdoor (poolside) entrances in all first-floor rooms. Sliding glass doors to pool/courtyard are very handy, yet pool is far enough away so as not to disturb guests in rooms. **Amenities:** A/C, cable TV w/movies. **Services:** **Facilities:** 150 1 restaurant (*see* "Restaurants" below), 1 bar, games rm, washer/dryer. Passes to nearby YMCA sports and fitness facilities. **Rates:** Peak (May–Sept) $80–$125 S or D. Extra person $8. Children under age 16 stay free. Lower rates off-season. Parking: Outdoor, free. AE, CB, DC, DISC, JCB, MC, V.

Travelodge
OH 209, PO Box 158, 43725; tel 614/432-7375 or toll free 800/578-7878; fax 614/432-5808. Exit 178 off I-70. Lots of extras at a mid-range price. **Rooms:** 48 rms and effic. CI 2pm/CO noon. Nonsmoking rms avail. All rooms have both inside corridor and outside entrances. **Amenities:** A/C, cable TV. Some units w/terraces. **Services:** **Facilities:** Games rm, sauna, whirlpool. Free passes to nearby YMCA. **Rates:** Peak (May–Sept) $50–$65 S or D; $85–$90 effic. Extra person $5. Children under age 18 stay free. Lower rates off-season. Parking: Outdoor, free. AE, DC, DISC, MC, V.

RESORT

Saltfork Lodge
OH 22 E, PO Box 7, 43725; tel 614/439-2751 or toll free 800/282-7275; fax 614/432-6615. In Salt Fork State Park, 6 mi E of US 77. Nestled in the 17,000-plus acres of Salt Fork State Park, the lodge offers lots to do. Ohio's largest inland beach is a short walk away. **Rooms:** 148 rms; 54 cottages/villas. CI 3pm/CO noon. Nonsmoking rms avail. Some rooms have exquisite view of woods, others have spectacular view of lake. Some rooms have fold-out bunks for two extra sleep spots. **Amenities:** A/C, satel TV w/movies. All units w/terraces. Some rooms have dataports, refrigerators, and balconies with seating. **Services:** Social director, children's program. **Facilities:** 18 2 500 2 restaurants, 2 bars (1 w/entertainment), 2 beaches (lake shore), lifeguard, basketball, volleyball, games rm, lawn games, sauna, playground, washer/dryer. Pontoon boats can be rented for the lake. Outdoor pool is Olympic size. Some areas of the lodge are not wheelchair accessible (such as the indoor pool and fitness center). Campsites also available. **Rates:** Peak (Mem Day–Labor Day) $101 D; $525–$625 cottage/villa. Extra person $5. Children under age 18 stay free. Min stay peak. Lower rates off-season. Parking: Outdoor, free. Cabins rented on weekly basis—rates for lakefront cabins are higher. AE, CB, DC, DISC, MC, V.

RESTAURANT

The Landing
In Holiday Inn, OH 209; tel 614/432-7313. Exit 178 off I-70. **American.** An excellent, family-friendly eatery offering solid and unpretentious food such as mushroom chicken with garlic-Parmesan sauce served over linguine. **FYI:** Reservations accepted. Children's menu. **Open:** Breakfast Mon–Fri 6am–2pm, Sat–Sun 7am–noon; dinner daily 5:30–10pm. **Prices:** Main courses $6–$15. AE, CB, DC, DISC, MC, V.

ATTRACTION

Cambridge Glass Museum
812 Jefferson Ave; tel 614/432-3045 or 432-5855. Cambridge has been known for fine glassware since the turn of the century. More than 5,000 pieces of Cambridge glass and 100 pieces of Cambridge art pottery are on display at this museum. **Open:** June–Oct, Mon–Sat 1–4pm. **$**

Canton

Seat of Stark County, in northeast part of state. Native Americans once camped here before traveling over the Old Portage Trail but the city is probably best known as the home of slain President William McKinley, who had a law office here before he ran for office. **Information:** Canton/Stark County Convention & Visitors Bureau, 229 Wells Ave NW, Canton, 44703 (tel 330/454-1439).

HOTELS

Best Suites of America
4914 Everhard Rd, 44718; tel 330/499-1011 or toll free 800/237-8466; fax 330/499-1011. Exit 109 off I-77; at Beldon Village Mall. Arched lobby entrance with skylight. **Rooms:** 102 rms and stes. Executive level. CI 2pm/CO 1pm. Nonsmoking rms avail. **Amenities:** A/C, cable TV w/movies, refrig, VCR. Some units w/whirlpools. **Services:** Free cocktail hour. Helpful staff. **Facilities:** 120 1 bar, games rm, whirlpool, washer/dryer. Snack bar in pool area. **Rates (BB):** $70 S or D; $78–$103 ste. Extra

person $10. Children under age 18 stay free. Parking: Outdoor, free. Golf and Sea World packages avail. AE, DC, DISC, MC, V.

Hampton Inn
5335 Broadmoor Circle NW, 44709; tel 330/492-0151 or toll free 800/HAMPTON; fax 330/492-7523. Exit 109 off I-77. Exterior looks new. Large, efficient, plain lobby. **Rooms:** 107 rms and stes. CI 3pm/CO 1pm. Nonsmoking rms avail. **Amenities:** 🛏 🔥 A/C, cable TV w/movies. **Services:** 🖨 🍴 Fax service available at desk. **Facilities:** 📶 ⚹ Games rm. Free passes to Hall of Fame Fitness Center one block south. **Rates (CP):** $49–$55 S; $51–$57 D; $56–$60 ste. Children under age 18 stay free. Parking: Outdoor, free. "In Crowd" discounts avail. AE, DISC, MC, V.

Hilton Hotel
320 Market Ave S, 44702; tel 330/454-5000 or toll free 800/HILTONS; fax 330/454-5494. At 3rd St. Impressive eight-story hotel in historic courthouse area of downtown Canton. Huge, splendid lobby features marble and polished wood. **Rooms:** 170 rms and stes. CI 3pm/CO noon. Nonsmoking rms avail. **Amenities:** 🛏 🔥 📺 🍽 A/C, cable TV w/movies. **Services:** ✕ 🚗 🖨 🍴 Twice-daily maid svce, car-rental desk. Fax and copy services available. **Facilities:** 📶 🏊 🍽 ⚹ 1 restaurant, 1 bar, games rm, sauna, whirlpool. Clean, large changing rooms at pool. **Rates (CP):** $64–$94 S or D; $199–$245 ste. Children under age 21 stay free. AP and MAP rates avail. Parking: Indoor, $3/day. Bounce Back and Romance packages avail. Weekly and monthly rates avail. AE, DC, DISC, MC, V.

MOTELS

Days Inn Canton
3970 Convenience Circle, North Canton, 44718; tel 330/493-8883; fax 330/493-8801. Exit 109 off I-77, Whipple Ave S. Well-maintained property with huge, attractively furnished lobby. Hook-up spaces for RVs at rear of the property. **Rooms:** 61 rms. CI 3pm/CO 11am. Nonsmoking rms avail. **Amenities:** 🛏 A/C, cable TV w/movies. **Services:** 🍴 🛎 **Facilities:** ⚹ Washer/dryer. Very large, attractive swimming pool and area. **Rates (CP):** Peak (May–Sept) $44–$52 S; $49–$65 D. Extra person $5. Children under age 17 stay free. Lower rates off-season. Parking: Outdoor, free. Weekly rates avail. AE, CB, DC, DISC, MC, V.

Holiday Inn North
4520 Everhard Rd NW, 44718; tel 330/494-2770 or toll free 800/HOLIDAY; fax 330/494-6473. Exit 109 off I-77; at Beldon Village Mall. Neat three-story building. Modern, clean lobby. **Rooms:** 196 rms. CI 2pm/CO noon. Nonsmoking rms avail. **Amenities:** 🛏 🔥 📺 A/C, cable TV w/movies. **Services:** ✕ 🚐 🖨 🍴 🛎 Car-rental desk. Efficient and helpful staff. **Facilities:** 📶 🏊 🍽 ⚹ 1 restaurant, 1 bar (w/entertainment). Local health club privileges. Restaurant adjacent to lobby; children under 12 eat free with adult. **Rates:** Peak (May–Sept) $61–$68 S or D. Children under age

18 stay free. Lower rates off-season. AP and MAP rates avail. Parking: Outdoor, free. Bed-and-breakfast specials. AE, DC, DISC, JCB, MC, V.

Motel 6
6880 Sunset Strip Ave NW, 44720; tel 330/494-7611 or toll free 800/440-6000; fax 330/494-5366. Exit 111 (Portage Rd) off I-77. Basic hotel for budget travelers. **Rooms:** 35 rms and effic. CI 2pm/CO noon. Nonsmoking rms avail. **Amenities:** 🛏 A/C, satel TV. **Services:** 🍴 🛎 Free local calls. Fax available at front desk. **Facilities:** 📶 ⚹ **Rates:** Peak (May–Sept) $36 S or D; $36 effic. Extra person $3. Children under age 17 stay free. Lower rates off-season. Parking: Outdoor, free. AE, DC, DISC, MC, V.

Red Roof Inn
5353 Inn Circle Court NW, 44720; tel 330/499-1970 or toll free 800/843-7663; fax 330/499-1975. Typical for the chain. Good for budget travelers. **Rooms:** 108 rms. CI 2pm/CO noon. Nonsmoking rms avail. **Amenities:** 🛏 A/C, cable TV. **Services:** 🍴 🛎 **Facilities:** ⚹ **Rates:** $37–$46 S; $43–$52 D. Extra person $7. Children under age 18 stay free. Parking: Outdoor, free. AE, DC, DISC, MC, V.

RESTAURANTS 🍴

Bender's Tavern
137 Court Ave SW; tel 330/453-8424. At 2nd. **Seafood.** A turn-of-the-century downtown landmark, Bender's decor features original tin ceilings, stained glass, and murals. The menu is similarly classic, with standard tavern fare such as soups, burgers, steaks, and seafood. Daily specials available. **FYI:** Reservations recommended. Children's menu. Dress code. **Open:** Mon–Thurs 11am–9:30pm, Fri–Sat 11am–10:30pm. Closed July 4 week. **Prices:** Main courses $10–$27. AE, DC, DISC, MC, V. 🛑

⑤ Kapp's
236 Clarendon Ave SW; tel 330/453-1484. Across from Aultman Hospital at 6th and Stanwood Place. **American.** A cozy, old-world style eatery serving up copious quantities of comfort foods. The homemade pies and baklava are a particular favorite with regulars. **FYI:** Reservations accepted. Children's menu. No liquor license. **Open:** Mon–Fri 7am–8pm, Sat 8am–3pm. **Prices:** Main courses $2–$8. MC, V. 🅿

Mulligan's Pub
4118 Belden Village St; tel 330/493-8239. Belden Village Mall off Whipple Rd. **American.** This old-fashioned neighborhood pub has polished wood paneling, Victorian stained-glass ceilings and doors, and historic details salvaged from turn-of-the-century buildings. Hearty pub food, such as steaks and burgers, are the bulk of the menu, although there are a few meatless options for vegetarians. **FYI:** Reservations recommended. **Open:** Mon–Thurs 11am–1am, Fri–Sat 11am–2:30am, Sun 11am–midnight. **Prices:** Main courses $4–$18. AE, MC, V. 🅿

ATTRACTIONS 📖

Pro Football Hall of Fame
2121 George Halas Dr NW; tel 330/456-8207. Opened in 1963, this five-building complex is devoted to honoring the greats of the game through a combination of audiovisual exhibits, interactive presentations, historical displays, memorabilia, and a forthcoming library and research center. During the annual Greatest Weekend celebration (usually in late July or early August), the Hall enshrines new members and holds the AFC-NFC Hall of Fame game in a nearby stadium. The new 100-Yard Universe rotating theater presents NFL action in Cinemascope. Museum store. Group tours available. **Open:** Peak (Labor Day–Mem Day) daily 9am–8pm. Reduced hours off-season. **$$$**

McKinley Museum of History, Science, and Industry
800 McKinley Monument Dr NW; tel 330/455-7043. One division of a comprehensive center that also includes the McKinley National Memorial and Discover World, an interactive children's science center. Scientific, industrial, and historic exhibits at the museum include the Hoover Price Planetarium; History Hall (with four re-created 19th-century rooms); Street of Shops (with guided tours through an 18th-century village); and a presidential and historical research library. Educational programs; museum shop. **Open:** Mon–Sat 9am–5pm, Sun noon–5pm. **$$**

McKinley National Memorial
800 McKinley Monument Dr NW; tel 330/455-7043. Adjacent to the 26-acre McKinley museum complex, this national historic landmark is dedicated to the 25th President of the United States. McKinley was buried here after his assassination in 1901; his tomb consists of a double-domed mausoleum and a statue of McKinley. **Open:** Apr–Nov, Mon–Sat 9am–5pm, Sun noon–5pm. **Free**

Hoover Historical Center
2225 Easton St NW, North Canton; tel 330/499-0287. This Victorian farmhouse—the boyhood home of Hoover Company founder William H Hoover—is now the site of the only known vacuum cleaner museum in the world. An extensive collection of antique and early vacuum cleaners is on display along with memorabilia documenting the growth and development of the Hoover Company and the vacuum cleaner industry as a whole. Group tours available. **Open:** Tues–Sun 1–5pm, or by appointment. **Free**

Canton Garden Center
1615 Stadium Park Dr NW; tel 330/455-6172. The highlight of this information center for gardening enthusiasts is the eclectic garden on the grounds. Garden of the Five Senses for visually impaired guests, free lending library, horticulture lecture programs, and classes. Gift shop. **Open:** Park: sunrise–sunset. Shop: Tues–Fri 10am–4pm. **Free**

Canton Classic Car Museum
555 Market Ave S; tel 330/455-3603. On exhibit are more than 35 beautifully restored antique cars. Visitors may also tour the restoration shop itself, which houses memorabilia, period fashions, and other cultural artifacts. **Open:** Daily 10am–5pm. **$$**

Celina

Seat of Mercer County, in western Ohio. This resort town is on the western shore of Grand Lake, Ohio's largest inland lake. Tourism and dairy production are the prominent industries. **Information:** Celina-Mercer County Chamber of Commerce, 226 N Main St, Celina, 45822-1663 (tel 419/586-2219).

MOTEL 🛏

≡≡ Comfort Inn
1421 OH 703 E, 45822; tel 419/586-4656 or toll free 800/221-2222; fax 419/586-4152. At OH 29. The motel looks out on Grand Lake St Marys, but it does not own any lakefront facilities. **Rooms:** 40 rms, stes, and effic. CI 2pm/CO 11am. Nonsmoking rms avail. Rooms are cozy, clean, and average. **Amenities:** 🛁 ⊘ 🖥 A/C, cable TV w/movies, dataport. Some units w/terraces, 1 w/whirlpool. **Services:** ⊂⊃ ⊲ Room service can be arranged with several of the nearby fast-food establishments. Transportation to the airport can be arranged; however, the airfield is just a feeder to larger airports that provide commercial flights. **Facilities:** 🏋 ⅙ **Rates (CP):** $45–$54 S or D; $70–$85 ste; $50–$58 effic. Extra person $5. Children under age 18 stay free. Parking: Outdoor, free. AE, DC, JCB, MC, V.

Chillicothe

Seat of Ross County, in southern Ohio. First capital of the Northwest Territory (1800) and of Ohio (1803). Many of the Greek revival mansions built by the early settlers still remain. The city is noted for its many paper mills. **Information:** Ross-Chillicothe Convention & Visitors Bureau, 5 W Water, PO Box 353, Chillicothe, 45601 (tel 614/775-0900).

HOTEL 🏨

≡≡≡ Christopher Inn
30 N Plaza Blvd, 45601; tel 614/774-6835 or toll free 800/257-7042; fax 614/774-2001. Jct OH 159/US 35. An elegant hotel, with exquisite, high-quality furnishings at rates comparable to facilities with much less to offer. **Rooms:** 62 rms and stes. Executive level. CI 2pm/CO noon. Nonsmoking rms avail. Spacious rooms have home-like furnishings. Honeymoon suite has king-size bed. **Amenities:** 🛁 ⊘ 🖥 A/C, cable TV, dataport. Some units w/terraces, some w/whirlpools. Phones are programmed to direct dial to local restaurants

that deliver, beauty salons, realtors, and a car rental business. **Services:** ✗ 🚗 🖼 🛏 🐾 Complimentary happy hour Mon–Thurs 5–7pm, with beverages and snacks. **Facilities:** 🏋 🖥 🚻 Sauna, whirlpool, washer/dryer. Passes to local Swim and Racquet Club. **Rates (CP):** Peak (May 16–Nov 14) $70–$80 S or D; $85–$95 ste. Extra person $5. Children under age 18 stay free. Lower rates off-season. Parking: Outdoor, free. AE, CB, DC, DISC, EC, JCB, MC, V.

MOTELS

⧉⧉⧉ Comfort Inn

20 N Plaza Blvd, 45601; tel 614/775-3500 or toll free 800/221-2222; fax 614/775-3588. Jct US 35/OH 159. Exceptional facility for an economical price. **Rooms:** 109 rms and stes. Executive level. CI noon/CO noon. Nonsmoking rms avail. **Amenities:** 🛁 📺 A/C, cable TV, dataport. 1 unit w/minibar, some w/whirlpools. **Services:** ✗ 🖼 🐾 🐾 **Facilities:** 🏋 🍽 🖥 🚻 1 restaurant (lunch and dinner only), 1 bar (w/entertainment), games rm, washer/dryer. Free passes to Chillicothe Swim and Racquet Club. **Rates (CP):** $70 S or D; $75–$80 ste. Extra person $5. Children under age 17 stay free. Parking: Outdoor, free. Corporate, American Express, and AARP discounts avail. New Year's Eve package avail. AE, CB, DC, DISC, JCB, MC, V.

⧉⧉⧉ Days Inn

1250 N Bridge St, 45601; tel 614/775-7000 or toll free 800/DAYS-INN; fax 614/773-1622. ½ mi N of jct US 35/OH 159. Beautifully landscaped, well-maintained facility just 7 miles from the Seven Caves and Tecumseh Outdoor Drama. **Rooms:** 155 rms and stes. CI 4pm/CO 11am. Nonsmoking rms avail. King rooms have fold-out sofas. **Amenities:** 🛁 📺 A/C, cable TV, dataport. Some units w/whirlpools. **Services:** ✗ 🖼 🐾 **Facilities:** 🏋 🍽 🚻 1 restaurant, 1 bar (w/entertainment), washer/dryer. **Rates:** $42–$62 S or D; $90 ste. Extra person $6. Children under age 18 stay free. Parking: Outdoor, free. AE, DC, DISC, MC, V.

RESTAURANT 🍴

★ Harvester Restaurant and Cellar Lounge

9 S Paint St; tel 614/773-4663. In center of town. **American.** Adjacent to several gift and antique shops, this is a good choice for casual dining in a rather rustic atmosphere. Well known for pork loin medallions served with homemade orange-barbecue sauce, and Paint Street Chicken (strips of chicken breast topped with demiglacé, mushrooms, and cheese, and served on toast). **FYI:** Reservations recommended. Children's menu. Dress code. **Open:** Breakfast Mon–Fri 7–10:30am; lunch Mon–Sat 11am–3pm; dinner Mon–Thurs 5–9pm, Fri–Sat 5–10pm. **Prices:** Main courses $7–$16. AE, DISC, MC, V. ⬛

ATTRACTIONS 🏛

Seven Caves

US 50; tel 513/365-1283. Underground, guests may view a wide array of geological formations; above ground, there is a wilderness area with trails that wind through the stunning canyons and cliffs. Picnic area, snack bar; gift shop. **Open:** Daily 9am–sunset. **$$$**

Hopewell Culture National Historical Park

16062 OH 104; tel 614/774-1125. In this 13-acre complex, marked trails lead past geometric earthworks and burial mounds created by the Hopewell, who inhabited the Ohio River Valley between 200 BC and AD 500. "Legacy of the Mound Builders," a 17-minute video shown continuously at the visitors center, explains the Hopewell culture and museum exhibits include pottery, ornaments, and other Hopewell artifacts. Self-guided and ranger-led tours; picnic area. **Open:** Daily 8:30am–5pm. **$**

Ross County Historical Society Museum

45 W 5th St; tel 614/772-1936. Located in a Federal-style home built circa 1838, this impressive small-town archive holds more than 100,000 artifacts, including antiques, furnishings, pioneer crafts, and a choice collection of women's clothing. Theme rooms devoted to the Civil War, Native American experience, and the US Constitution; extensive library containing manuscripts and genealogical materials. **Open:** Peak (Apr–Nov) Tues–Sun 1–5pm. **$**

Franklin House

80 S Paint St; tel 614/772-1936. The heritage of the women of Ross County is preserved at this museum, located in a 1907 Prairie-style house. Items on display include period accessories, clothing, and decorative arts. **Open:** Peak (Apr–Nov) Tues–Sun 1–5pm. Reduced hours off-season. **$**

Cincinnati

See also Hamilton

Seat of Hamilton County, in southwest corner of state. Cincinnati's nickname came from poet Longfellow, who called it the "Queen City of the West." Used as a river crossroads by the Native Americans, it was settled by Europeans in 1788. Today, Cincinnati is home to the University of Cincinnati, Hebrew Union College, and Xavier University, and it has its own symphony, opera, and ballet. Over the past 25 years, the Cincinnati waterfront has been extensively renovated and redeveloped as an entertainment district. The Cincinnati Zoo and Botanical Garden is one of the best in the nation. **Information:** Greater Cincinnati Convention & Visitors Bureau, 300 W 6th St, Cincinnati, 45202 (tel 513/621-2142).

PUBLIC TRANSPORTATION

The **Queen City Metro** provides bus service. Fare is 80¢ during peak hours and 65¢ during off-peak hours; weekend fare is 50¢, and seniors pay 40¢ at all times. Exact change, token, or Metro Monthly Card (available at the Queen City Metro sales office at 122 W 5th St) is required. Call 513/621-4455 for more information.

HOTELS 🏨

≣≣≣ Best Western Mariemont Inn

6880 Wooster Pike, 45227; tel 513/271-2100 or toll free 800/528-1234; fax 513/271-1057. Exit 9 off I-71. A landmark hotel in Cincinnati dating back to 1926. English Tudor style. Wood pegged floors with lovely carpets. Antiques in halls and corridors. Lobby fashioned after English hunting lodge. Fireplace in lounge used during winter season. **Rooms:** 60 rms and stes. CI 3pm/CO noon. Nonsmoking rms avail. Every bedroom different in size, shape, and style. All have antique wooden headboards. **Amenities:** 🖥 ⚲ ⚱ A/C, satel TV. 1 unit w/terrace. **Services:** ✕ ⬓ ⌂ Babysitting. **Facilities:** 🔲 1 restaurant, 2 bars, beauty salon, washer/dryer. **Rates:** $55–$60 S; $62–$68 D; $75–$85 ste. Extra person $5. Children under age 12 stay free. Parking: Outdoor, free. AE, CB, DC, DISC, JCB, MC, V.

≣≣≣≣ The Cincinnatian Hotel Downtown

601 Vine St, 45202 (Downtown); tel 513/381-3000 or toll free 800/942-9000, 800/332-2020 in OH; fax 513/651-0256. At 6th St. This 1882 building was renovated in 1987 for close to 30 million dollars. The grand staircase of walnut and marble still stands—and is just about all that's left from yesteryear. From the elegant lobby to the room furnishings, it's a top-quality hotel. **Rooms:** 148 rms and stes. CI 3pm/CO noon. Nonsmoking rms avail. Decor is in excellent taste. Thick towels and big bathtubs. **Amenities:** 🖥 ⚲ ⚱ A/C, cable TV, dataport, in-rm safe, bathrobes. All units w/minibars, some w/terraces. **Services:** 🍽 ⬓ VP ⬓ ⌂ ⬓ Twice-daily maid svce, car-rental desk, social director, babysitting. Pets allowed with advance notice. Extremely friendly and helpful staff. **Facilities:** 🔲 🔲 ⚲ 2 restaurants (see "Restaurants" below), 1 bar (w/entertainment), sauna, playground. **Rates:** Peak (Apr–July; Sept–Dec) $185–$235 S; $210–$260 D; $450–$750 ste. Extra person $25. Children under age 18 stay free. Min stay special events. Lower rates off-season. AP and MAP rates avail. Parking: Indoor, $12/day. Packages include weekend romance, and art packages. AE, CB, DC, DISC, ER, JCB, MC, V.

≣≣≣ The Cincinnati Marriott

11320 Chester Rd, 45246 (N Cincinnati); tel 513/772-1720 or toll free 800/950-8883; fax 513/772-0117. Exit 15 off I-75 across from Sharonville Convention Center. Property consists of low-rise hotel and tower; elevator service to both sections, but long walk to elevators from lobby. Business-oriented, with large meeting space. **Rooms:** 352 rms and stes. Executive level. CI 3pm/CO noon. Nonsmoking rms avail. **Amenities:** 🖥 ⚲ A/C, cable TV w/movies, VCR, voice mail. Some units w/terraces, some w/whirlpools. **Services:** ✕ ⬓ ⬓ ⌂ ⬓ Car-rental desk, babysitting. **Facilities:** 🔲 🔲 🔲

🖥 ⚲ 2 restaurants, 3 bars, games rm, whirlpool. Guests can swim directly from indoor pool to outdoor pool. Children under 12 eat free when accompanied by adult. **Rates:** Peak (Apr–Oct) $149–$169 S or D; $200–$500 ste. Min stay special events. Lower rates off-season. Parking: Outdoor, free. AE, DISC, MC, V.

≣≣≣ The Garfield House Suite Hotel

2 Garfield Place, 45202 (Downtown); tel 513/421-3355 or toll free 800/367-2155; fax 513/421-3729. At Vine. All-suite hotel offering one and two bedrooms. **Rooms:** 140 stes. CI 3pm/CO noon. Nonsmoking rms avail. **Amenities:** 🖥 ⚲ ⚱ ⚲ A/C, cable TV, refrig, in-rm safe. Some units w/terraces, some w/whirlpools. **Services:** ✕ ⬓ ⬓ ⌂ Pets allowed for additional charge. **Facilities:** 🔲 🔲 ⚲ 1 restaurant, 1 bar, washer/dryer. **Rates (CP):** Peak (Apr–Sept) $150–$165 ste. Lower rates off-season. Parking: Indoor, $4/day. Packages include romantic weekends, and zoo packages. AE, DC, DISC, MC, V.

≣≣≣ The Hampshire House Hotel & Conference Center

30 Tri-County Pkwy, 45246 (Springdale); tel 513/772-5440 or toll free 800/543-4211; fax 513/772-1611. 1 mi S off I-275. A friendly, comfortable hotel in a quiet area near the Tri County Shopping Center area. Fairly busy conference center. Lobby has bookcases with reading material and a fireplace. **Rooms:** 150 rms and stes. Executive level. CI 3pm/CO noon. Nonsmoking rms avail. Rooms and baths are adequate, not outstanding. Limited counter space in bathrooms. **Amenities:** 🖥 ⚲ A/C, cable TV w/movies. 1 unit w/whirlpool. **Services:** ✕ ⬓ ⌂ Social director. Weekly activity for guests at the pool. **Facilities:** 🔲 🔲 🔲 ⚲ 1 restaurant (bkfst and lunch only), 1 bar (w/entertainment), sauna, whirlpool. Bar offers entertainment on Fri and Sat nights. Dome-covered pool is quite attractive. **Rates:** Peak (June–Aug) $75 S or D; $125–$150 ste. Extra person $6. Children under age 18 stay free. Lower rates off-season. Parking: Outdoor, free. AE, DC, DISC, MC, V.

≣≣≣ Harley Hotel

8020 Montgomery Rd, 45236 (Kenwood); tel 513/793-4300 or toll free 800/321-2323; fax 513/793-1413. Exit 12 off I-71. Although there is a sign denoting the hotel, the driveway is easily missed. Extremely small lobby, but functional with enough personnel. **Rooms:** 152 rms and stes. CI 3pm/CO 11am. Nonsmoking rms avail. Rooms are very well maintained and comfortable with upholstered lounge chairs. Separate cosmetic area in bathrooms. **Amenities:** 🖥 ⚲ A/C, cable TV w/movies. All units w/terraces, 1 w/whirlpool. Small, small balconies on upper level rooms. **Services:** ✕ ⬓ ⌂ Babysitting. Complimentary coffee in lobby. Free hors d'oeuvres 5–7pm Mon–Fri. Discount tickets for Cincinnati Zoo, King's Island, The Beach. **Facilities:** 🔲 🔲 🔲 🔲 ⚲ 1 restaurant, 1 bar (w/entertainment), volleyball, games rm, lawn games, sauna, whirlpool. Both indoor and outdoor swimming pools are quite large—one foot shorter than

Olympic size. Entertainment in bar lounge Fri and Sat. **Rates:** $104–$114 S; $114–$124 D; $135–$195 ste. Extra person $10. Children under age 18 stay free. Parking: Outdoor, free. Packages with breakfast for two adults avail. AE, CB, DISC, MC, V.

≡≡≡ Hyatt Regency
151 W 5th St, 45202 (Downtown); tel 513/579-1234 or toll free 800/233-1234; fax 513/579-0107. 1½ block W of Fountain Square. Popular with convention and business people. On the Skywalk connecting sections of downtown Cincinnati. Easy access from I-75 and I-71. Across the street from Cincinnati Convention Center. Nearby shopping. **Rooms:** 485 rms and stes. Executive level. CI 3pm/CO noon. Nonsmoking rms avail. **Amenities:** 🛏 🛁 🍴 A/C, cable TV w/movies. Some units w/minibars. **Services:** ✗ 🗝 📺 🚐 🖼 🖼 Babysitting. **Facilities:** 🏊 2000 🖥 ♿ 2 restaurants, 1 bar, spa, sauna, whirlpool, beauty salon. Elevators are voice activated—great for guests with disabilities. **Rates:** Peak (Apr–Oct) $160 S; $185 D; $400–$500 ste. Children under age 18 stay free. Lower rates off-season. AE, DC, DISC, MC, V.

≡≡ Imperial House Quality Inn West
5510 Rybolt Rd, 45248 (Western Hills); tel 513/574-6000 or toll free 800/543-3018; fax 513/574-6565. Exit 11 off I-74 E and W. Hotel consists of three buildings—two of two stories and one four-story structure; the latter is more hotel-like, while the other two are motel-style. **Rooms:** 197 rms, stes, and effic. CI 2pm/CO noon. Nonsmoking rms avail. **Amenities:** 🛏 A/C, cable TV. Some units w/terraces. **Services:** ✗ 🖼 🖼 🖼 Car-rental desk. One building accepts pets. **Facilities:** 🏊 200 1 restaurant, 1 bar (w/entertainment), sauna, steam rm, washer/dryer. Swimming pool very attractive because of extensive landscaping. Complimentary passes to nearby fitness center. **Rates:** $48–$66 S; $54–$66 D; $110–$140 ste; $48–$66 effic. Extra person $5. Children under age 16 stay free. Parking: Outdoor, free. During some weekends, rates increased. AE, CB, DC, DISC, MC, V.

≡≡≡ Omni Netherland Plaza
35 W 5th St, 45202 (Downtown); tel 513/421-9100 or toll free 800/843-6664; fax 513/421-4291. 1 block W of Fountain Square. Opened in 1931, the hotel is now a National Historic Landmark. Very popular with business travelers. Located in the tall Carew Tower with shopping galore, one block from the Cincinnati Convention Center, near Fountain Square. **Rooms:** 621 rms, stes, and effic. CI 3pm/CO noon. Nonsmoking rms avail. Art deco style carried out in room furnishings. **Amenities:** 🛏 🛁 🖥 🍴 A/C, satel TV w/movies, dataport, voice mail. Some units w/minibars, some w/terraces, some w/whirlpools. **Services:** 🍽 🗝 📺 🚐 🖼 🖼 Car-rental desk. **Facilities:** 🏊 🍴 2700 🖥 ♿ 2 restaurants (see "Restaurants" below), 1 bar (w/entertainment), sauna, steam rm, whirlpool, beauty salon. **Rates:** $145–$195 S; $165–

$205 D; $350–$1,250 ste; $450 effic. Extra person $20. Children under age 18 stay free. Packages avail for Reds or Bengals games, romantic weekends. AE, DC, DISC, MC, V.

≡≡ Quality Inn Central
4747 Montgomery Rd, 45212 (Norwood); tel 513/351-6000 or toll free 800/292-2079; fax 513/351-0215. Exit 7 off I-71 or I-75. Hotel in a heavy commercial area, off Norwood Lateral (OH 562) connecting I-75 and I-71. **Rooms:** 146 rms. Executive level. CI 3pm/CO noon. Nonsmoking rms avail. Color coordinated, attractive, and comfortable. **Amenities:** 🛏 🛁 A/C, satel TV, dataport, voice mail. Some units w/terraces. **Services:** ✗ 🚐 🖼 🖼 🖼 **Facilities:** 🏊 300 ♿ 1 restaurant (lunch and dinner only), 1 bar, beauty salon. **Rates (CP):** $72–$78 S or D. Extra person $5. Children under age 18 stay free. Parking: Outdoor, free. AE, CB, DC, DISC, MC, V.

≡≡≡ Regal Cincinnati Hotel
150 W 5th St, 45202 (Downtown); tel 513/381-3000 or toll free 800/876-2100; fax 513/352-2148. 1½ block W of Fountain Square. Recent renovation gave the hotel a new sparkling look. Across the street from Cincinnati Convention Center and 1½ blocks from Fountain Square—center of downtown. **Rooms:** 887 rms and stes. Executive level. CI 4pm/CO 11am. Nonsmoking rms avail. **Amenities:** 🛏 🛁 A/C, satel TV w/movies. Some units w/minibars. **Services:** ✗ 🗝 📺 🚐 🖼 🖼 Car-rental desk. Free passes to Moore's Nautilus Fitness Center. **Facilities:** 🏊 🍴 1500 🖥 ♿ 2 restaurants (see "Restaurants" below), 2 bars (1 w/entertainment), basketball, racquetball, squash, beauty salon, washer/dryer. **Rates:** Peak (July–Aug/Oct–Nov) $149 S; $159 D; $350–$850 ste. Extra person $10. Children under age 17 stay free. Lower rates off-season. AE, CB, DC, DISC, MC, V.

≡≡ Signature Inn North
11385 Chester Rd, 45246; tel 513/772-7877 or toll free 800/822-5252; fax 513/772-7877. Exit 15 off I-75, next to Sharonville Convention Center. Attractive property, although little landscaping. **Rooms:** 130 rms. CI 3pm/CO noon. Nonsmoking rms avail. Rooms well coordinated in color and fabric. **Amenities:** 🛏 🛁 A/C, satel TV w/movies, dataport. 1 unit w/whirlpool. **Services:** 🖼 🖼 **Facilities:** 🏊 100 ♿ Use of nearby fitness center for small fee. **Rates (CP):** $60–$67 S; $57–$64 D. Extra person $7. Children under age 17 stay free. Parking: Outdoor, free. Rates increase during Jazz Festival in July. AE, DC, DISC, MC, V.

≡≡ Signature Inn Northeast
8870 Governor's Hill Dr, 45249 (Landen); tel 513/683-3086 or toll free 800/822-5252; fax 513/683-3086 ext 500. Exit 19 off I-71. One of three Signature Inns in the Cincinnati area. Minutes away from King's Island, championship golf, and tennis. **Rooms:** 100 rms. CI 2pm/CO noon. Nonsmoking rms avail. Well-coordinated and well-maintained rooms. **Amenities:** 🛏 🛁 A/C, satel TV, dataport. 1 unit w/whirlpool. **Services:** 🖼 🖼 Car-rental desk. Personnel goes out of the

way to be friendly. **Facilities:** ⬚ ⬚ 💻 ♿ Games rm. Pass available to nearby health club for $3/day. **Rates (CP):** Peak (June–Aug) $95 S or D. Extra person $7. Children under age 17 stay free. Lower rates off-season. Parking: Outdoor, free. AE, DC, DISC, MC, V.

UNRATED Vernon Manor

400 Oak St, 45219 (Corryville); tel 513/281-3300 or toll free 800/543-3999; fax 513/281-8933. Taft Rd exit off I-71. A 70-year-old Cincinnati landmark noted for service and spaciousness. Famed guests include John F Kennedy, the Beatles, Nancy Reagan, and George Bush. Extremely popular because of close proximity to hospital and University of Cincinnati. **Rooms:** 173 rms, stes, and effic. Executive level. CI 3pm/CO noon. Nonsmoking rms avail. All suites or studio apartments. **Amenities:** ⬚ ⬚ A/C, satel TV w/movies. **Services:** ✕ ⬚ ⬚ ⬚ Social director, babysitting. Off-duty Cincinnati police provide additional security. **Facilities:** ⬚ ♿ 2 restaurants (*see* "Restaurants" below), 1 bar, washer/dryer. Complimentary passes to Carew Tower Health Club, plus transportation to the club. **Rates:** Peak (Sept–Oct, May–June) $85–$115 S; $125–$145 D; $110–$425 ste; $110–$195 effic. Extra person $10. Children under age 16 stay free. Lower rates off-season. Parking: Outdoor, free. AE, CB, DC, DISC, MC, V.

▰▰▰ The Westin Hotel Cincinnati

21 E 5th St, 45202 (Downtown); tel 513/621-7700 or toll free 800/228-3000; fax 513/852-5690. In center of Fountain Square, the centerpoint of downtown Cincinnati. Located on skywalk, connecting many downtown locations. Shopping nearby. Popular with businesspeople. Motor entrance to hotel is around the corner on Vine St. **Rooms:** 448 rms and stes. Executive level. CI 3pm/CO 1pm. Nonsmoking rms avail. **Amenities:** ⬚ ⬚ ⬚ ⬚ A/C, cable TV w/movies, dataport, voice mail. All units w/minibars. **Services:** ⬚ ⬚ ⬚ ⬚ ⬚ ⬚ ⬚ Babysitting. **Facilities:** ⬚ ⬚ ⬚ 💻 ♿ 2 restaurants, 2 bars, spa, sauna, whirlpool, beauty salon. **Rates:** $80–$165 S; $99–$175 D; $375–$900 ste. Extra person $22. Children under age 18 stay free. Parking: Indoor, $14/day. AE, CB, DC, DISC, ER, JCB, MC, V.

MOTELS

▰ Comfort Inn Northeast

9011 Fields-Ertel Rd, 45249 (Landen); tel 513/683-9200 or toll free 800/221-2222; fax 513/683-1284. Exit 19 off I-71. Typical budget motel with bare necessities for overnight stay. Hallways need cleaning. Located in busy area, but convenient off I-71 N and S. Minutes from King's Island, golf, and tennis. **Rooms:** 115 rms. CI 3pm/CO 11am. Nonsmoking rms avail. **Amenities:** ⬚ ⬚ A/C, satel TV. **Services:** ⬚ ⬚ ⬚ Car-rental desk. **Facilities:** ⬚ ♿ Nearby fitness center allows motel guests to use facilities. **Rates (CP):** Peak (June–Aug) $94 S or D. Extra person $10. Children under age 18 stay free. Lower rates off-season. Parking: Outdoor, free. AE, DC, DISC, MC, V.

▰ Cross Country Inn

4004 Williams Dr, 45255 (Anderson); tel 513/528-7702 or toll free 800/621-1429; fax 513/528-1246. Exit 65 off I-275 E. A typical budget motel. Difficult access—motorist must turn on Williams and beware of almost hidden entrance. **Rooms:** 128 rms. CI 1pm/CO noon. Nonsmoking rms avail. More drawer space than in most motels. **Amenities:** ⬚ A/C, satel TV. **Services:** ⬚ Car-rental desk. Drive-through check-in and checkout. **Facilities:** ⬚ **Rates:** $35 S; $40–$47 D. Extra person $7. Children under age 18 stay free. Parking: Outdoor, free. AE, DC, DISC, MC, V.

▰▰ Days Inn Downtown

2880 Central Pkwy, 45225 (Clifton); tel 513/559-0400 or toll free 800/329-7466; fax 513/559-9662. Exit 3 off I-75. Just off I-75 N and S, 3 miles from downtown Cincinnati, and close to University of Cincinnati. **Rooms:** 103 rms. CI noon/CO 11am. Nonsmoking rms avail. **Amenities:** ⬚ A/C, cable TV. **Services:** ⬚ Coffee in lobby. **Facilities:** ⬚ ⬚ Games rm, washer/dryer. **Rates (CP):** Peak (Mar–Aug) $45–$60 S; $60–$80 D. Children under age 12 stay free. Lower rates off-season. Parking: Outdoor, free. AE, CB, DC, DISC, MC, V.

▰ Howard Johnson North Cincinnati

400 Glensprings Dr, 45246 (Springdale); tel 513/825-3129 or toll free 800/654-2000; fax 513/825-0467. Exit 41 off I-275. A budget motel with some 50% of its occupancy on contract—25% business travelers and 25% seasonal travelers. **Rooms:** 120 rms, stes, and effic. CI 3pm/CO noon. Nonsmoking rms avail. **Amenities:** ⬚ A/C, satel TV, dataport. **Services:** ⬚ ⬚ ⬚ Twice-daily maid svce, car-rental desk. $25 deposit for pets. Only one person at counter during hectic checkout. **Facilities:** ⬚ ⬚ Washer/dryer. Two charcoal grills at small swimming pool. Free pass to nearby fitness center. **Rates (CP):** Peak (June–Aug) $49–$60 S or D; $75–$110 ste; $65–$65 effic. Extra person $7. Children under age 12 stay free. Lower rates off-season. Parking: Outdoor, free. AE, CB, DC, DISC, MC, V.

▰▰ Quality Inn Evendale

1717 Glendale Milford Rd, 45215 (Evendale); tel 513/771-5252 or toll free 800/221-2222; fax 513/771-6569. Exit 14 off I-75, 14 mi N of Cincinnati Center. The lobby, with a vaulted ceiling, has been recently remodeled in a Southwestern decor. **Rooms:** 114 rms. CI 2pm/CO noon. Nonsmoking rms avail. **Amenities:** ⬚ A/C, cable TV. All units w/terraces. **Services:** ✕ ⬚ ⬚ Free local calls. **Facilities:** ⬚ ⬚ ♿ 1 restaurant, 1 bar (w/entertainment), sauna, steam rm, playground. **Rates:** Peak (June–Sept) $79–$83 S; $62–$68 D. Extra person $6. Children under age 18 stay free. Lower rates off-season. Parking: Outdoor, free. AE, DC, DISC, MC, V.

▰ Red Roof Inn Cincinnati East

4035 Mt Carmel-Tobasco Rd, 45255 (Cherrygrove); tel 513/528-2741 or toll free 800/843-7663; fax 513/528-2965. Exit 65 off I-275 E. Typical budget motel. Clean. Located near the interstate. **Rooms:** 109 rms. CI 2pm/CO noon. Nonsmoking rms avail. Rooms are small, but furnishings match. **Amenities:** 📺 A/C, satel TV. **Services:** 🛏 🍽 Car-rental desk. **Facilities:** ⅏ Guests can use nearby fitness center for free. **Rates:** Peak (May–Oct) $35 S; $36–$43 D. Extra person $3–$5. Children under age 18 stay free. Lower rates off-season. Parking: Outdoor, free. AE, CB, DC, DISC, MC, V.

☰ Red Roof Inn North
11345 Chester Rd, 45246 (N Cincinnati); tel 513/771-5141 or toll free 800/843-7663; fax 513/771-0812. Exits N and S off I-75 behind Sharonville Convention Center. Ordinary budget motel with no landscaping. **Rooms:** 108 rms. CI 2pm/CO noon. Nonsmoking rms avail. **Amenities:** 📺 A/C, cable TV. **Services:** 🛏 🍽 **Facilities:** ⅏ **Rates:** Peak (June–Aug) $26–$43 S; $30–$56 D. Extra person $7. Children under age 18 stay free. Lower rates off-season. Parking: Outdoor, free. AE, CB, DC, DISC, MC, V.

☰ Super 8 Motel
11335 Chester Rd, 45246; tel 513/772-3140 or toll free 800/800-8000; fax 513/772-1931. Exit 15 off I-75 next to Sharonville Convention Center. Formerly a La Quinta motel, it still features the typical La Quinta Southwestern architecture. An overnight, inexpensive motel. **Rooms:** 144 rms. CI 3pm/CO noon. Nonsmoking rms avail. **Amenities:** 📺 A/C, cable TV, dataport. **Services:** ⊠ 🛏 🍽 Babysitting. Sandwich vending machine. Pets accepted with prior approval. **Facilities:** 🗚 🈺 ⅏ Washer/dryer. Fitness center off premises available for $5 per day. **Rates (CP):** Peak (June–Aug) $41–$66 S; $35–$59 D. Extra person $6. Children under age 18 stay free. Lower rates off-season. Parking: Outdoor, free. AE, DC, DISC, MC, V.

☰ Travelodge
3244 Central Pkwy, 45225 (Clifton); tel 513/559-1800 or toll free 800/578-7878; fax 513/559-1807. Exit 3 off I-75; 2 lefts to Central Pkwy. Reasonably close to University of Cincinnati. Two-story structure built against a hill, so it's possible to drive to rear to get to second floor without climbing steps. **Rooms:** 71 rms. CI 2pm/CO 11am. Nonsmoking rms avail. **Amenities:** 📺 📶 A/C, cable TV w/movies. **Services:** 🛏 🍽 **Facilities:** 🗚 ⅏ Washer/dryer. Recently renovated swimming pool. **Rates (CP):** Peak (May–Sept) $45–$50 S; $58–$68 D. Extra person $5. Children under age 17 stay free. Lower rates off-season. Parking: Outdoor, free. AE, CB, DC, DISC, MC, V.

RESTAURANTS 🍴

★ Arnold's Bar and Grill
210 E 8th St (Downtown); tel 513/421-6234. Between Main and Sycamore. **American.** The oldest barroom in Cincinnati is alive and well. First floor has the feel of an old pub, with an outdoor dining area in the courtyard. Second floor offers five small dining rooms in what had been living quarters of earlier Arnold owners. Purportedly the bathtub (which is on display) was used to make "gin" during prohibition. Features pasta, plus Greek as well as Italian specialties. Lots of entertainment

weekly, including Celtic, bluegrass, jazz, and swing. Lower floor is not air conditioned; second floor is. Parking across the street. **FYI:** Reservations not accepted. Jazz/bluegrass. **Open:** Mon–Thurs 11am–10pm, Fri–Sat 11am–11pm. **Prices:** Main courses $7–$13. V.

Ban Thai
792 Eastgate South Dr (Clermont); tel 513/752-3200. Exit 63B off I-275 E. **Thai.** Located in a very busy shopping area, this pleasant, inexpensive place offers some of the best (and spiciest) Thai in Cincinnati. The menu does a fine job explaining the many dishes, one of the most popular being the fried noodles with chicken, pork, or shrimp. **FYI:** Reservations recommended. **Open:** Lunch Mon–Fri 11:30am–3pm; dinner Mon–Fri 4–9:30pm, Sat–Sun 4:30–10:30pm. Closed July 4–10. **Prices:** Main courses $6–$13; prix fixe $4–$5. AE, MC, V. ♥ 🏞 ✇ ⅏

Ⓢ Barresi's
4111 Webster Ave (Deer Park); tel 513/793-2540. **Italian.** A magnificent cappuccino and espresso machine greets patrons, who might think they've just arrived in Italy. The menu features favorites of both northern and southern Italian cuisine. The ambience of the two-storied dining is comfortable and elegant. **FYI:** Reservations recommended. **Open:** Mon–Sat 5–10:30pm. **Prices:** Main courses $11–$24. AE, DC, DISC, MC, V. ♥ 🏞 ⅏

Blue Gibbon Chinese Restaurant
1231 Tennessee Ave (Paddock Hills); tel 513/641-4100. Exit 7 off I-75. **Chinese.** Typical Chinese restaurant decor, although more attractive than most. Two dining rooms accommodate up to 200 people; one dining room with a bandstand is often used for private parties. Familiar dishes are prepared well, attracting many locals and even the occasional celebrity. Small, unattractive bar area. **FYI:** Reservations accepted. Children's menu. **Open:** Mon–Thurs 11am–10pm, Fri 11am–11pm, Sat noon–11pm, Sun noon–10pm. **Prices:** Main courses $5–$9. AE, MC, V. 🏞

Cafe at the Palm Court
In the Omni Netherland Plaza, 35 W 5th St (Downtown); tel 513/421-9100. 1 block W of Fountain Square. **New American.** With French art deco style, innovative cuisine, and seamless service, it's no wonder that this is considered a prime downtown spot for any important lunch or dinner. Look for the beautiful high murals of scenes from the reign of Louis XV. **FYI:** Reservations not accepted. Jazz/piano. **Open:** Sun–Thurs 6:30am–10:30pm, Fri–Sat 6:30am–11pm. **Prices:** Main courses $9–$15. AE, DC, DISC, MC, V. ✇ 🆅🅿 ⅏

Celestial Restaurant
1071 Celestial St (Mount Adams); tel 513/241-4455. **American/French.** Beautiful wood-paneled dining areas and a separate barroom afford magnificent views of Cincinnati at this strictly top-notch establishment. Some representative entrees: imported Dover sole poached with lobster and chives en blanc, roasted rack of lamb dressed with fresh thyme

butter, broiled duck breast bathed in ginger barbecue sauce. **FYI:** Reservations recommended. Cabaret/jazz. **Open:** Lunch Mon–Fri 11:30am–2:30pm; dinner Mon–Thurs 5:30–10pm, Fri–Sat 5:30–11pm. **Prices:** Main courses $16–$29. AE, CB, DC, MC, V. 💛 🏔 VP &

★ Charley's Oyster Bar & Grill
9769 Montgomery Rd; tel 513/891-7000. I-71 to Cross County E. **American/Seafood.** Housed in a building almost 150 years old, with a resident ghost named Emily. Dine in one of several rooms—some with fireplaces—all featuring fine table linen, silverware, and china. Fresh seafood and fish, with a raw bar and sushi bar. Excellent wine list. **FYI:** Reservations recommended. Blues/jazz. Children's menu. Dress code. **Open:** Dinner Mon–Thurs 5–10pm, Fri–Sat 5–11pm, Sun 5–9pm. **Prices:** Main courses $17–$23. AE, CB, DC, MC, V. 💛 🍽 ♨ VP

★ Cherrington's
950 Pavilion St (Mount Adams); tel 513/579-0131. **American.** It looks like a tea room, but this restaurant serves three meals a day. There's no printed menu—a large white board lists the day's offerings, whether meat loaf and mashed potatoes, rib eye roast beef with sautéed mushrooms, blackened chicken, or rainbow trout. The small bar area has its own entrance. **FYI:** Reservations recommended. Children's menu. **Open:** Breakfast Tues–Fri 7–10am, Sat 8–11am; lunch Tues–Fri 11am–3pm; dinner Tues–Thurs 5–10pm, Fri–Sat 5–11pm, Sun 4–9pm; brunch Sun 11am–3pm. Closed Aug 7–14. **Prices:** Main courses $10–$23. AE, MC, V. 💛 🍰

★ Chester's Road House
9678 Montgomery Rd (Montgomery); tel 513/793-8700. Off I-71. **American.** The place for romance as well as business, it's a dependable favorite year-in and year-out. Occupying an old historic house beautifully furnished with antiques, Chester's features two private dining rooms on the main floor and one on the second floor with a fireplace. Brick walls and hanging plants and pennants help create a casual, classy ambience for enjoying traditional American dishes and fresh fish. Attentive, personalized service. **FYI:** Reservations recommended. Children's menu. **Open:** Lunch Mon–Fri 11:30am–2:30pm; dinner Mon–Thurs 5–10:30pm, Fri 5:30–10:30pm, Sat 5:30–11pm, Sun 5–9pm. **Prices:** Main courses $15–$30. AE, CB, DC, DISC, MC, V. 💛 ♨ &

China Palace
18 E 7th St (Downtown); tel 513/421-1304. Between Vine and Walnut. **Chinese.** Variety of Chinese fare on menu, from Cantonese-style entrees to dishes from northern China. Family-style dining available. Downtown location is easy to find. **FYI:** Reservations recommended. **Open:** Mon–Fri 11am–9pm, Sat 1–9pm. **Prices:** Main courses $5–$12; prix fixe $11. AE, CB, DC, DISC, MC, V. 👥

Corinthian Restaurant
3253 Jefferson Ave (Clifton); tel 513/961-0013. Mitchell Ave exit off I-75 S. **American/Greek.** Attracts many patrons from nearby hospital complex. The garish decor, peeling wallpaper, and worn carpet may be off-putting, but the Greek-influenced seafood (especially the Fisherman Best) is quite popular. Live Latin music on Fri, live Greek music on Sat. **FYI:** Reservations recommended. **Open:** Mon–Thurs 11am–11pm, Fri–Sat 11am–2am. **Prices:** Main courses $7–$15. AE, CB, DC, DISC, MC, V. 👥

Dante's
5510 Rybolt Rd (Western Hills); tel 513/574-6666. Exit 11 off I-74. **American.** Large, comfortable, and attractive dining room and bar area with flower display; banquette seating is available. Steaks, lobster tails, halibut, chateaubriand; baby back ribs prepared daily in the smokehouse. **FYI:** Reservations accepted. Children's menu. **Open:** Mon–Thurs 6:30am–10pm, Fri 6:30am–11pm, Sat 7am–11pm, Sun 8am–9pm. **Prices:** Main courses $9–$19. AE, CB, DC, DISC, MC, V. ♨ VP &

★ El Coyote
7404 State Rd; tel 513/232-5757. Exit 69 off I-275 E. **Tex-Mex.** Many diners are drawn time and again to this friendly Tex-Mex grill on a hill, housed in an attractive building with lovely landscaping. Large portions of satisfying food can be enjoyed in the two comfortable, spacious dining rooms outfitted with oak tables and booths. The large bar features several unusual stained-glass windows. **FYI:** Reservations not accepted. Children's menu. **Open:** Sun–Thurs 4–10pm, Fri–Sat 4–11pm. **Prices:** Main courses $7–$20. AE, DC, DISC, MC, V. 💛 🍴 👥

♣★ Firehouse On Vine
2701 Vine St (University Village); tel 513/281-3774. At W Charlton St. **American.** This converted firehouse (with memorabilia from the early days on display) features a sometimes-noisy glass-enclosed atrium and an open second floor with iron railings. Popular specialties include cornbread-stuffed trout and double grilled pork chops. **FYI:** Reservations recommended. Children's menu. **Open:** Mon–Tues 11:30–9pm, Wed–Thurs 11:30am–10pm, Fri–Sat 11:30am–11pm. **Prices:** Main courses $10–$17. AE, CB, DC, DISC, MC, V. 💛 🍽 VP &

Forum Room
In Vernon Manor, 400 Oak St (Corryville); tel 513/281-3300. Raft Rd exit off I-71 N; Reading Rd exit off I-71 S. **American.** Attracting business types and older folks, this dining room presents fine food in a pleasing atmosphere. Attractive floral arrangements in the center of the room stand under a large crystal chandelier. Prime rib is the house specialty, but a full menu is available. **FYI:** Reservations recommended. No smoking. **Open:** Lunch Mon–Fri 11am–4:30pm; dinner daily 5–10pm; brunch Sun 10:30am–2:30pm. **Prices:** Main courses $13–$22. AE, CB, DC, DISC, MC, V. 💛 👥 VP &

✭ Graeter's

41 E 4th St (Downtown); tel 513/381-0653. Between Vine and Walnut. **American.** Of the many Graeter's in the Cincinnati area, this downtown location is the only one that serves lunch—a variety of sandwiches, all available on homemade bread. But the chain has built its reputation on its ice cream, proclaimed by locals as the best in the world. Chocolate chip (with huge chunks) is the biggest seller. Graeter's also makes their own pastries and candies. **FYI:** Reservations not accepted. No liquor license. No smoking. Additional locations: 7369 Kenwood Rd (tel 793-5665); 11511 Princeton Pike, Springdale (tel 771-7157). **Open:** Mon–Fri 7am–6pm, Sat 7am–5pm. **Prices:** Lunch main courses $3–$6. No CC. 👥

✭ Izzy's

819 Elm St (Downtown); tel 513/721-4241. Near 9th St. **Deli.** Long known as the place in Cincinnati for a corned beef sandwich (original deli opened in 1901). Frequently raucous, with the personnel yelling at each other or the patrons—an Izzy's trait for decades. Also homemade soups and potato pancakes. No individual tables, but rather long tables seating 8 or 10. **FYI:** Reservations not accepted. Additional location: 612 Main St (tel 241-6246). **Open:** Mon–Fri 8am–7pm, Sat 10am–5pm. **Prices:** Main courses $4–$6. No CC.

La Normandie

118 E 6th St (Downtown); tel 513/721-2761. Between Walnut and Main. **Steak.** Popular in Cincinnati for 60 years, La Normandie is a casual setting, with most seating in large booths or banquettes. Peanut shells dot the floor—it's OK to toss them when munching on the free nuts at the bar. Menu leans to steak, but other entrees also available. **FYI:** Reservations recommended. Children's menu. **Open:** Lunch Mon–Fri 11am–2:30pm; dinner Mon–Fri 5–10:30pm, Sat 5–11pm. Closed 1 week in July. **Prices:** Main courses $14–$28. AE, CB, DC, DISC, MC, V. 🆅🅿

♛ Maisonette

114 E 6th St (Downtown); tel 513/721-2260. Between Walnut and Main. **French.** Unquestionably one of America's premier restaurants, founded in 1949. The decor, including the large collection of paintings by Cincinnati artists, is superb, and table settings are magnificent. Classic French cuisine, plus more modern dishes—like red deer chop with pepper sauce, puree of sweet potatoes, corn flan, and fruit compote, and sautéed red snapper with a coulis fish soup, saffron risotto, and fennel compote with basil. Expensive, but well worth it. **FYI:** Reservations recommended. Jacket required. No smoking. **Open:** Lunch Tues–Fri 11:30am–2:30pm; dinner Mon–Fri 6–10:30pm, Sat 5:30–11pm. Closed 1 week in July. **Prices:** Main courses $20–$33. AE, CB, DC, DISC, MC, V. 🕙 🎫 🆅🅿

Montgomery Inn Boathouse

925 Eastern Ave (Sawers Point); tel 513/721-7427. 1 mi E of Riverfront Stadium. **American/Barbecue.** One of three popular Montgomery Inn restaurants in the area that specialize in barbecued ribs. Two dining levels seat 550 diners. One dining room is dedicated to Bob Hope memorabilia, while the lower level overlooks the Ohio River. Off the huge, comfortable bar lounge area is balcony seating overlooking the river. Popular spot with sports personalities and other celebrities. Menus available in Japanese and in braille. **FYI:** Reservations recommended. Children's menu. Additional locations: 9440 Montgomery Rd (tel 791-3482); Beechmont and I-275 (tel 528-2272). **Open:** Mon–Thurs 11am–10:30pm, Fri 11am–11pm, Sat 3–11pm, Sun 3–10pm. **Prices:** Main courses $10–$20. AE, DC, DISC, MC, V. 🕙 🏔 🆅🅿 ♿

Morton's of Chicago

28 W 4th St (Downtown); tel 513/241-4104. At Race. **Steak.** Dark wood and brick walls create a warm, comfortable ambience at this branch of a national chain noted for consistently top-quality steaks. Portions are huge, but guests may split entrees. All hot entrees are cooked in the open for patrons to see. Three private dining rooms for parties or overflow. Bar area small but cozy. **FYI:** Reservations recommended. **Open:** Dinner daily 5:30–10pm. **Prices:** Main courses $16–$30. AE, CB, DC, MC, V. 🆅🅿 ♿

Mullane's Parkside Cafe

723 Race St (Downtown); tel 513/381-1331. Between 7th and Garfield Place. **Eclectic/Health.** This smallish restaurant offers an eclectic menu. Currently the most popular dish is a spinach sauté with zucchini, yellow squash, tomato, onion, black olives, basil, and feta cheese over rice and pasta. Also features many other health food dishes. Art display is changed each month. Interesting entertainment—a card reader is available each evening, and an acoustical guitarist performs Thurs. **FYI:** Reservations not accepted. Guitar. Children's menu. Beer and wine only. **Open:** Lunch Mon–Fri 11:30am–5pm; dinner Mon–Thurs 5–10pm, Fri–Sat 5–11pm. Closed week before Labor Day. **Prices:** Main courses $6–$13. No CC. ♿

Orchids at Palm Court

35 W 5th St (Downtown); tel 513/421-1772. 1 block W of Fountain Square. **Regional American/Continental.** This famed restaurant is the essence of gourmet dining. Diners here have a great view of the surrounding Palm Court's art deco stylings. Exquisite table settings are topped off with orchids. Dine on grilled veal chop served on a giant marinated portobello mushroom, or blackened salmon fillet served with crab cakes and yogurt-cucumber-dill relish. **FYI:** Reservations recommended. Jazz. Children's menu. **Open:** Lunch Mon–Fri 11am–2pm; dinner Sun–Sat 6–10pm; brunch Sun 10am–2pm. **Prices:** Main courses $16–$32. AE, DC, DISC, MC, V. 🕙 🆅🅿 ♿

♛ The Palace

In the Cincinnatian Hotel Downtown, 601 Vine St (Downtown); tel 513/381-6006. At 6th St. **New American.** Quiet elegance, fine food, and impeccable service are the hallmarks of this superb restaurant whose only drawback is the unfortunate location of the rest rooms (one must leave the restaurant and pass through the lobby area to get to them). A variety of both light and hearty dishes are available: grilled swordfish with sun-dried tomato oil served with balsamic watercress and horseradish whipped potatoes; lamb chops encrusted with walnuts, mint and currants, accompanied by angel hair pasta and vegetables. Lounge serves light luncheon menu. **FYI:** Reservations recommended. Cabaret/piano. **Open:** Breakfast daily 6:30–11:30am; lunch Mon–Sat 11:30am–2:30pm; dinner Mon–Fri 6–10pm, Sat 6–10:30pm, Sun 6–9:30pm; brunch Sun 10:30am–2:30pm. **Prices:** Main courses $24–$30. AE, CB, DC, DISC, MC, V. ♥ ☑ VP ♿

The Phoenix

812 Race St (Downtown); tel 513/721-8901. At 9th St. **American.** Located in a landmark building over a century old with original architecture and features—including the marble and stained-glass windows—still intact. Diners can peer into the kitchen through a window. The reasonably priced menu includes tempura prawns and vegetables with Thai dipping sauce, and fettucine with grilled chorizo sausage, roasted vegetables, garlic, and parmesan. Tasty potatoes gratin Dauphinoise, a specialty side dish, is plenty for two. **FYI:** Reservations recommended. No liquor license. **Open:** Tues–Fri 5–9pm, Sat 5:30–10pm. **Prices:** Main courses $11–$18. AE, CB, DC, DISC, MC, V. VP ♿

The Precinct

311 Delta Ave; tel 513/321-5454. At Columbia Pkwy. **Steak.** This hot spot in a former police station is the place to go for high-energy atmosphere and top-flight steaks. Small tables are packed close together, but who knows—you might rub shoulders with a celebrity. **FYI:** Reservations recommended. No smoking. **Open:** Sun–Thurs 5–11pm, Fri–Sat 5pm–midnight. **Prices:** Main courses $14–$28. AE, CB, DC, DISC, MC, V. VP

The Samurai Steak & Seafood House

126 E 6th St (Downtown); tel 513/421-1688. Between Walnut and Main. **Japanese.** The ambience is that of a restaurant in Tokyo. Customers witness the action as food is prepared in front of them. Menu includes steak, seafood, and a vegetable dinner. Large bar. Free validated parking for dinner at garage across the street. **FYI:** Reservations recommended. Children's menu. **Open:** Lunch Mon–Fri 11:30am–2pm; dinner Mon–Thurs 5:30–10pm, Fri–Sat 5–11pm, Sun 4–9pm. **Prices:** Main courses $12–$24. AE, CB, DC, DISC, MC, V. ☑ ♿

Seafood 32

In Regal Cincinnati Hotel, 150 W 5th St (Downtown); tel 513/352-2160. **Seafood.** This beautiful, top-floor, revolving restaurant offers a 360° view of the city, the Ohio River, and northern Kentucky. Magnificent table settings include beautiful serving plates, lovely crystal and cutlery, and flowers. The bar and lounge are located on floor below; a special elevator whisks guests with disabilities from bar area to dining room. **FYI:** Reservations recommended. Jazz. **Open:** Dinner Tues–

Thurs 5–10pm, Fri–Sat 5–11pm; brunch Sun 10am–2pm. **Prices:** Main courses $15–$26. AE, CB, DC, DISC, MC, V. ♥ ▦ VP

★ Skyline Chili

643 Vine St (Downtown); tel 513/241-2020. At 7th St. **Chili.** Known across the country, Skyline Chili is a Cincinnati tradition. There are several ways to enjoy the uniquely flavored chili, including the "three-way" (spaghetti, chili, cheddar cheese), with diced onions and red beans; and the Cheese Coney, a hot dog covered with chili, onions, and cheese. There are 80 Skyline Chili restaurants in the greater Cincinnati area, with five downtown. **FYI:** Reservations not accepted. Children's menu. No liquor license. Additional locations: 580 Walnut (tel 684-9600); 4th and Sycamore (tel 241-4848). **Open:** Mon–Fri 10:30am–7pm, Sat 11am–3pm. **Prices:** Main courses $1–$5. No CC. ♿

Sweeney's Seafood

8372 Reading Rd; tel 513/821-3654. Exit 10B off I-75. **Seafood.** Reasonably priced fish and shellfish, including salmon and Alaskan halibut, are the draw at this casual, very clean eatery. There's a nice bar in a separate room. **FYI:** Reservations accepted. Children's menu. No smoking. **Open:** Dinner Tues–Thurs 5:30–9:30pm, Fri–Sat 5:30–10:30pm, Sun 5–8:30pm; brunch. **Prices:** Main courses $6–$18. AE, MC, V. ♥ ▦

ATTRACTIONS 🏛

Cincinnati Art Museum

Eden Park, off I-71; tel 513/721-5204. The CAM houses an especially rich collection of European paintings, with emphasis on impressionists and abstract painters. Among the best-known works: El Greco's *Christ on the Cross*, Gainsborough's *Portrait of Mrs Thicknesse*, Cézanne's *Blue Still Life*, Matisse's *The Gray Hat* and Chagall's *The Red Chicken*. The permanent collection also includes sculptures, prints, photographs, costumes, tribal artifacts, and musical instruments. Public tours available; restaurant, gift shop. **Open:** Tues–Sat 10am–5pm, Sun 11am–5pm. **$$**

Cincinnati Zoo & Botanical Garden

3400 Vine St; tel 513/281-4700. The second-oldest zoo in the country and still one of its finest. The park houses 6,000 animals of 800 species in a variety of realistic habitats, and includes a feline collection unmatched in the world. White tigers, 300-pound komodo dragons, gorillas, and a butterfly aviary are other highlights. The adjacent botanical garden boasts an international plant collection. **Open:** Peak (Mem Day–Labor Day) daily 9am–6pm. Reduced hours off-season. **$$$**

Taft Museum

316 Pike St; tel 513/241-0343. Housed in a Federal-style residence dating from 1820 (and once owned by President Taft's half-brother), this fine regional collection focuses on paintings by European masters (Turner, Goya, Rembrandt,

Van Dyck, and Corot are all represented) as well as Chinese and Limoges porcelain. **Open:** Mon–Sat 10am–5pm, Sun noon–5pm. **$**

Cincinnati Museum of Natural History

1301 Western Ave; tel 513/287-7020. The highlight here is the Wilderness Trail area, which features exhibits of local flora and fauna, and a re-created limestone cavern complete with a 32-foot waterfall. The Children's Discovery Center contains exhibits depicting the way the human body works, as well as a time-travel simulator. Planetarium. **Open:** Mon–Sat 9am–5pm, Sun 11am–6pm. **$$**

Museum Center

Cincinnati Union Terminal; tel 513/287-7000. Built in 1931 to serve as a center of travel between the East and the Midwest, Union Station has since been restored to its original Art Deco grandeur. Its huge rotunda is filled with mosaic murals, Verona marble, and terrazzo floors. The **Cincinnati Museum of Natural History,** the **Cincinnati Historical Society Museum and Library,** and the **Robert D Lindner Family Omnimax Theater** are all housed in the 50,000-square-foot complex. **Open:** Mon–Sat 9am–5pm, Sun 11am–6pm. **$$$**

William Howard Taft National Historic Site

2038 Auburn Ave; tel 513/684-3262. This modest three-story brick home, built in 1840, was the birthplace of the 27th president. Now elegantly restored, the house contains four rooms filled with family memorabilia and mementoes from Taft's political and legal career. Guided tours available. **Open:** Daily 10am–4pm. **Free**

Harriet Beecher Stowe House

2950 Gilbert Ave; tel 513/632-5120. From 1832–1836, this simple two-story structure was the home of the author of *Uncle Tom's Cabin.* The fully renovated building now serves as a cultural and educational resource center; some original furnishings are on display. Guided tours and lectures offered. **Open:** Tues–Thurs 10am–4pm. **Free**

Showboat *Majestic*

435 E Mehring Way (Waterfront); tel 513/241-6550. Before movies, malls, and TV, dozens of river towns depended on traveling showboats for their entertainment. First launched in 1923, the *Majestic* continues the tradition by presenting musical revues, comedies, dramas, and classic Broadway musicals. (Productions have included *The Wizard of Oz* and *Carousel.*) Wed–Sat shows at 8pm; Sun shows at 2pm and 7pm. **Open:** Mid-Apr–mid-Oct. **$$$$**

Cleveland

See also Beachwood

Seat of Cuyahoga County, in north part of state. Ohio's second-largest city spreads for 50 miles along the south shore of Lake Erie. It has 39 city parks and is home to many universities, including Case Western Reserve, John Carroll,

and Cleveland State. Terminal Tower, the second-tallest building in Ohio at 52 stories, has recently become the nucleus of a refurbished downtown complex for dining, retail, and entertainment. The city has received much attention lately as the home of the new Rock and Roll Hall of Fame and Museum. **Information:** Greater Cleveland Convention & Visitors Bureau, 3100 Tower City Center, Cleveland, 44113 (tel 216/621-4110).

PUBLIC TRANSPORTATION

The Regional Transit Authority (RTA) provides bus service and three subway lines. RTA **buses** travel on 100 routes. Fares are $1.25 for local and $1.50 for express service (50¢ for seniors), payable in exact change or RTA passes; children under 5 ride free. The **Rapid Transit train** runs on the Green Line (which runs between Green and Shaker Sts), the Red Line (between the airport and Windermere Station), and the Blue Line (between Van Aken and Warrensville Rd). Fare is $1.50. Call 216/621-9500 for information.

HOTELS 🏨

📊📊📊 Cleveland Marriott Society Center

127 Public Square, 44114; tel 216/696-9200 or toll free 800/MARRIOT; fax 216/696-8615. Newer (1991) hotel off Public Square in downtown Cleveland. Near the Flats, nightclubs, restaurants, shopping. Huge lobby. **Rooms:** 400 rms and stes. Executive level. CI 1pm/CO noon. Nonsmoking rms avail. Rooms decorated in light, warm colors. **Amenities:** 🛁 🐧 🍹 A/C, cable TV w/movies, dataport, voice mail. All units w/minibars. **Services:** ✕ ☞ 🆅🅿 🛄 🛎 🛍 Babysitting. **Facilities:** 🏋 🏊 🏧 🔑 🔓 1 restaurant, 1 bar, sauna, whirlpool, washer/dryer. Fitness center has large array of equipment. **Rates:** Peak (Apr–Nov) $159 S; $169 D; $380 ste. Extra person $10. Children under age 12 stay free. Min stay peak and special events. Lower rates off-season. Parking: Indoor, $12/day. Weekend Getaway packages avail. AE, CB, DC, DISC, EC, ER, JCB, MC, V.

UNRATED Glidden House

1901 Ford Dr, 44106 (University Circle); tel 216/231-8900; fax 216/231-2130. Elegant 1910 mansion (listed on National Register of Historic Places), renovated and furnished with period furnishings. Original building was owned by founder of Glidden Paint Co. Beautiful grounds and views. Close to Cleveland Garden Center. **Rooms:** 62 rms and stes. CI 4pm/CO noon. Nonsmoking rms avail. **Amenities:** 🛁 🐧 A/C, cable TV. **Services:** 🚐 🛄 🛎 **Facilities:** 🏧 1 bar. **Rates (CP):** $99–$119 S; $105–$129 D; $150–$165 ste. Extra person $10. Children under age 18 stay free. Parking: Outdoor, free. AE, DC, DISC, MC, V.

📊📊 Holiday Inn Airport

4181 W 150th St, 44135 (Cleveland Hopkins Int'l Airport); tel 216/252-7700 or toll free 800/HOLIDAY; fax 216/252-3850. Located off freeway, near airport, with minimal landscaping and small lobby. Elevators to rooms are located a substantial distance from check-in. Typical family-style hotel.

Rooms: 146 rms. CI 3pm/CO noon. Nonsmoking rms avail. **Amenities:** ⚟ ⚏ ▣ A/C, cable TV w/movies. **Services:** ✕ 🚐 ⬜ ⌫ Twice-daily maid svce. Kids 12 and under eat free. Friendly and helpful staff. **Facilities:** ⛹ ⟦275⟧ 🖵 ♿ 1 restaurant, 2 bars, games rm. Sports Bar downstairs, Billiards Bar on sixth floor. Free access to Bally's Health Spa. **Rates:** $83 S; $88 D. Extra person $5. Children under age 18 stay free. Parking: Outdoor, free. Special family rates avail. AE, CB, DC, DISC, JCB, MC, V.

≣≣ Holiday Inn Lakeside

1111 Lakeside Ave, 44114 (Downtown); tel 216/241-5100 or toll free 800/HOLIDAY; fax 216/241-7437. Basic, no-frills hotel, with a small lobby. Located downtown, close to shopping, waterfront, Rock and Roll Hall of Fame, stadium, city hall, and convention center. **Rooms:** 370 rms and stes. Executive level. CI 3pm/CO noon. Nonsmoking rms avail. **Amenities:** ⚟ ⚏ A/C, cable TV w/movies. Some units w/minibars, some w/whirlpools. **Services:** ⦿ VP 🚐 ⬜ ⌫ ⌫ **Facilities:** ⛹ ⟦550⟧ 1 restaurant, 1 bar, sauna. **Rates:** $109 S or D; $250 ste. Extra person $10. Children under age 18 stay free. Parking: Indoor/outdoor, free. AE, CB, DC, DISC, MC, V.

≣≣≣ Marriott Cleveland Airport

4277 W 150th St, 44135; tel 216/252-5333 or toll free 800/MARRIOT; fax 216/251-1508. Located off the freeway, close to the airport, this hotel has been undergoing major renovations. The lobby has marble floors, brass, mahogany wood surroundings, and a quiet area with desks. **Rooms:** 374 rms and stes. Executive level. CI 3pm/CO noon. Nonsmoking rms avail. **Amenities:** ⚟ ⚏ A/C, cable TV w/movies, dataport, voice mail. Concierge rooms have two phones. **Services:** ✕ ⦿ 🚐 ⬜ ⌫ ⌫ Babysitting. Front desk staff greets incoming guests promptly. **Facilities:** ⛹ 🍴 ⟦400⟧ 🖵 ♿ 2 restaurants, 2 bars (1 w/entertainment), sauna, whirlpool. **Rates:** Peak (Apr–Nov) $134 S or D; $250–$350 ste. Children under age 12 stay free. Min stay peak. Lower rates off-season. Parking: Outdoor, free. Weekend packages avail. AE, CB, DC, DISC, MC, V.

UNRATED Omni International Hotel

2065 E 96th St, 44106; tel 216/791-1900 or toll free 800/THE-OMNI; fax 216/231-3329. At Cleveland Clinic. Elegant 17-story building (built 1975), close to Cleveland Playhouse, Case Western Reserve University, and museums. Live jazz in huge, oval, two-story atrium lobby, which features floor-to-ceiling windows, trees, ferns, and large flower arrangements. **Rooms:** 274 rms and stes. Executive level. CI 3pm/CO noon. Nonsmoking rms avail. All rooms completely renovated recently. **Amenities:** ⚟ ⚏ ▣ ⚐ A/C, cable TV w/movies, dataport, voice mail. All units w/minibars, some w/fireplaces, some w/whirlpools. **Services:** ✕ ⦿ VP ⬜ ⌫ Twice-daily maid svce, car-rental desk, babysitting. Fax, copying, and secretarial services available. **Facilities:** ⟦350⟧ ♿ 3 restaurants (see "Restaurants" below), 1 bar (w/entertainment). Local health club privileges. **Rates:** $150 S; $175 D; $225–$1,300

ste. Extra person $10. Children under age 18 stay free. AP and MAP rates avail. Parking: Indoor/outdoor, $8/day. AE, DC, DISC, MC, V.

≣≣≣ Radisson Plaza Suites Hotel

1701 E 12th St, 44114 (Downtown); tel 216/523-8000 or toll free 800/333-3333; fax 216/523-1698. Relatively new, this hotel is downtown, within a corporate apartment complex. Lobby with library lounge is on the fifth floor, furnished with mahogany. A sophisticated decor. Close to shopping and major attractions. **Rooms:** 268 stes. Executive level. CI 3pm/CO noon. Nonsmoking rms avail. **Amenities:** ⚟ ⚏ ▣ A/C, cable TV w/movies, dataport, voice mail. All units w/minibars, some w/terraces. **Services:** ✕ ⦿ VP ⬜ ⌫ ⌫ Fresh apples offered on check-in. **Facilities:** ⛹ ⚐1 🍴 ⟦140⟧ ♿ 1 restaurant, 1 bar, basketball, sauna, beauty salon, washer/dryer. Outdoor patio, indoor pool with view of lake. Hotel is associated with a Market Square, which has a coffee shop, beauty salon, and grocery. **Rates:** $139 ste. Extra person $15. Children under age 18 stay free. Parking: Indoor/outdoor, $3.50–$12/day. AE, CB, DC, DISC, JCB, MC, V.

≣≣≣ Renaissance Cleveland Hotel

24 Public Square, 44113 (Downtown); tel 216/696-5600 or toll free 800/HOTELS-1; fax 216/696-0432. A charter member of Historic Hotels of America, in the heart of downtown Cleveland. Connected to the Avenue at Tower City Center. Marble floors, crystal chandeliers. **Rooms:** 491 rms and stes. Executive level. CI 3pm/CO 1pm. Nonsmoking rms avail. **Amenities:** ⚟ ⚏ ⚐ A/C, cable TV w/movies, refrig, in-rm safe. All units w/minibars, some w/terraces, some w/whirlpools. TVs in all bathrooms. **Services:** ⦿ ⦿ VP ⬜ ⌫ Babysitting. **Facilities:** ⛹ 🍴 ⟦2000⟧ 🖵 ♿ 2 restaurants (see "Restaurants" below), 1 bar (w/entertainment), sauna, beauty salon. Indoor swimming pool and fitness center with bistro tables and trees, 3 ballrooms, 27 meeting rooms. **Rates:** Peak (Apr–Oct) $109–$169 S; $109–$169 D; $225–$450 ste. Children under age 18 stay free. Min stay peak and special events. Lower rates off-season. Parking: Indoor, $12/day. AE, CB, DC, DISC, JCB, MC, V.

≣≣≣≣ The Ritz-Carlton Cleveland

1515 W 3rd St, Tower City Center, 44113 (Downtown); tel 216/623-1300 or toll free 800/241-3333; fax 216/623-1492. Part of the beautifully restored Terminal Tower Rail Station, in the heart of Cleveland's business district. It is connected to the Avenue at Tower City, Gund Arena, Jacobs Field, and rapid transit terminal in Tower City. Traditional Ritz Carlton understated elegance—fresh flowers, oil paintings, comfortable cherry and upholstered furniture, and marble floors. Expansive windows overlook waterfront. **Rooms:** 208 rms and stes. Executive level. CI 3pm/CO noon. Nonsmoking rms avail. **Amenities:** ⚟ ⚏ ⚐ A/C, cable TV w/movies, bathrobes. All units w/minibars, 1 w/whirlpool. **Services:** ⦿ ⦿ VP 🚐 ⬜ ⌫ ⌫ Twice-daily maid svce, masseur, babysitting. Lobby lounge offers traditional afternoon tea, with harp music. Attentive staff. **Facilities:** ⛹ 🍴 ⟦300⟧ ♿ 2 restaurants (see

"Restaurants" below), 2 bars (w/entertainment), spa, sauna, whirlpool. Atrium skylight over Roman spa pool and Jacuzzi. **Rates:** $139 S or D; $300–$450 ste. AP and MAP rates avail. Parking: Indoor, $14/day. Christmas packages avail. AE, CB, DC, DISC, MC, V.

≣≣≣ Sheraton City Center

777 St Clair Ave, 44114 (Downtown); tel 216/771-7600 or toll free 800/321-1090; fax 216/771-5129. Ideal location for visitors to Cleveland's major attractions. Great views of city from upper windows. **Rooms:** 470 rms and stes. Executive level. CI 3pm/CO 11am. Nonsmoking rms avail. **Amenities:** ⛉ ⏀ 🖭 A/C, cable TV w/movies, dataport. **Services:** ✕ 🗝 🍴 🖾 🛏 Babysitting. **Facilities:** 🏋 🛗 🏊 🖥 ⟨⟩ 1 restaurant, 2 bars, games rm, beauty salon. **Rates:** Peak (Apr–Dec) $145 S; $160 D; $300–$850 ste. Extra person $10. Children under age 17 stay free. Lower rates off-season. Parking: Indoor, $9/day. AE, DC, DISC, MC, V.

≣≣≣ Sheraton Hopkins Airport

5300 Riverside Dr, 44135 (Cleveland Hopkins Int'l Airport); tel 216/267-1500 or toll free 800/362-2244; fax 216/265-3177. Located at the entrance to Hopkins Int'l Airport. Impressive atrium-style lobby, with waterfall over marble backdrop. Specifically designed for business travelers. **Rooms:** 268 rms and stes. Executive level. CI 3pm/CO noon. Nonsmoking rms avail. **Amenities:** ⛉ ⏀ 🖭 A/C, cable TV w/movies, dataport, voice mail. Some units w/minibars, 1 w/whirlpool. **Services:** ✕ 🗝 🍴 🖾 🛏 Babysitting. Kitchen/lounge area outside business suites. Coffee, pastries, fresh fruit available Sun–Thurs. **Facilities:** 🏋 🛗 🏊 🖥 ⟨⟩ 1 restaurant, 2 bars, sauna, whirlpool. Large pool, fitness center with locker rooms. **Rates:** $135 S; $145 D; $165–$185 ste. Extra person $10. Children under age 18 stay free. Parking: Outdoor, free. Special weekend rates are generally offered. AE, CB, DC, DISC, MC, V.

MOTELS

≣≣ Budgetel Inn

4222 W 150th St, 44135 (Cleveland Hopkins Int'l Airport); tel 216/251-8500 or toll free 800/428-3438; fax 216/251-4117. Located off freeway in commercial/industrial area, close to airport. Built in 1992, the place is immaculate and welcoming. Good for the money. **Rooms:** 122 rms and effic. CI 3pm/CO noon. Nonsmoking rms avail. **Amenities:** ⛉ 🖭 🍴 A/C, cable TV w/movies, refrig, dataport. **Services:** ✕ 🍴 🖾 ⟨⟩ 🛏 Babysitting. **Facilities:** 🔟 ⟨⟩ Washer/dryer. **Rates (CP):** $48–$51 S; $55–$58 D; $54–$61 effic. Extra person $7. Children under age 21 stay free. Parking: Outdoor, free. AE, DC, DISC, MC, V.

≣ Budget Inns of America

14043 Brookpark Rd, 44135 (Cleveland Hopkins Int'l Airport); tel 216/267-2350 or toll free 800/381-9825; fax 216/267-9237. Exit 12 off I-480 E; exit W 150th St off I-480 W. Located in commercial/industrial area off freeway, near airport, this motel caters largely to truck drivers. Lobby area is plain and a little cluttered. Hotel security could be better. A place for those on a budget. **Rooms:** 125 rms. CI open/CO noon. Nonsmoking rms avail. **Amenities:** ⛉ ⏀ A/C, cable TV w/movies. **Services:** ✕ 🍴 ⟨⟩ **Facilities:** 🔟 ⟨⟩ 1 restaurant, games rm, washer/dryer. **Rates:** $47 S; $50 D. Children under age 21 stay free. Parking: Outdoor, free. AE, DC, DISC, MC, V.

≣≣ Comfort Inn

17550 Rosbough Dr, 44130 (Cleveland Hopkins Int'l Airport); tel 216/234-3131 or toll free 800/391-1112; fax 216/234-6111. All furnishings are new and in excellent condition. Located off freeway to airport. **Rooms:** 136 rms and stes. CI 3pm/CO noon. Nonsmoking rms avail. **Amenities:** ⛉ ⏀ 🖭 🍴 A/C, cable TV w/movies. 1 unit w/whirlpool. **Services:** ✕ 🍴 🖾 ⟨⟩ 🛎 Twice-daily maid svce, babysitting. *USA Today* delivered to room Mon–Fri. Free airport shuttle 6am–1am daily. **Facilities:** 🏋 🔟 🖥 ⟨⟩ Free access to Scandinavian Health Spas on Snow Rd. **Rates (CP):** Peak (May–Sept) $79 S; $84 D; $119–$124 ste. Extra person $5. Children under age 18 stay free. Lower rates off-season. Parking: Outdoor, free. AE, DC, DISC, MC, V.

RESTAURANTS 🍴

Balaton

12523 Buckeye Rd; tel 216/921-9691. Between 116th and 130th Sts. **Hungarian.** Family-owned and -operated, this restaurant has an old-world atmosphere in an older neighborhood. Breaded veal cutlet, wiener schnitzel, and goulash are among the house specialties. **FYI:** Reservations accepted. Children's menu. No liquor license. **Open:** Tues–Wed 11:30am–8pm, Thurs–Sat 11:30am–9pm. **Prices:** Main courses $7–$12. No CC. 🍴

The Baricelli Inn

2203 Cornell Rd (University Circle); tel 216/791-6500. **Italian.** Fine dining in a landmark turn-of-the-century brownstone mansion. Antiques and stained-glass highlight the original parlor, dining rooms, lobby, and bistro areas. The gourmet Italian menu features pastas and breads made in-house. **FYI:** Reservations recommended. No smoking. **Open:** Fri–Sat 5:30–11pm, Mon–Thurs 5:30–10pm. **Prices:** Main courses $20–$30. AE, MC, V. ❤ 🍴 ⚱ 🆚

Classics

In Omni International Hotel, 2065 E 96th St (University Circle); tel 216/791-1300. **Continental.** Very elegant hotel dining. The excellent service includes tableside preparation of steak Diane and rack of lamb. There is a health-conscious menu, too. **FYI:** Reservations recommended. Blues/jazz/piano. Jacket required. **Open:** Lunch daily 11:30am–2:30pm; dinner Mon–Thurs 5:30–9:30pm, Fri 5:30–10pm, Sat 5–10pm. **Prices:** Main courses $18–$25. AE, DC, DISC, MC, V. ❤ 🆚

★ Great Lakes Brewing Company

2516 Market St (Ohio City); tel 216/771-4404. 3 mi W of downtown. **Eclectic.** Many original fixtures are still in use at this, the oldest working bar in Cleveland (dating from 1870). The menu is filled with simple, satisfying foods that go along with beer: bratwurst, burgers, a tasty sausage sampler, cheddar cheese soup, Market St ribs, spicy artichoke crock, and Brewmaster's Pie (Italian sausages, spinach, mozzarella, and ricotta, all baked in a flaky piecrust and topped with marinara sauce). Daily tours of the award-winning microbrewery are available. **FYI:** Reservations recommended. **Open:** Mon–Thurs 11:30am–10:30pm, Fri–Sat 11:30am–11:30pm, Sun 3–8pm. **Prices:** Main courses $9–$15. AE, CB, DC, MC, V. 🍴 🍽 👥

Hofbrau Hauss

1400 E 55th St; tel 216/881-7773. Off I-90. **German/Polish.** There is a polka-party atmosphere in this Bavarian beer hall restaurant, with its handpainted countryside scenes on the walls. Family-style buffets are served in the large main dining room. The food is not fancy, but it is plentiful and very satisfying: stuffed cabbage, fish, stuffed peppers, breaded veal, goulash, spaetzels, and much more. **FYI:** Reservations recommended. Big band/polka. Children's menu. **Open:** Lunch Mon–Fri 11am–3pm; dinner Mon–Fri 4–9:30pm, Sat 4–10pm, Sun 11:30am–8pm. **Prices:** Main courses $12–$14. AE, DC, MC, V. 👥

Hyde Park Grille

1823 Coventry Rd; tel 216/321-6444. Between Cedar and Mayfield. **Steak.** Popular chophouse known for its sophisticated decor, award-winning wine list, and hefty portions of steak, seafood, and chicken. **FYI:** Reservations recommended. Jazz/piano. Dress code. **Open:** Mon–Thurs 5:30–10pm, Fri–Sat 5–11pm. **Prices:** Main courses $15–$48. AE, CB, DC, DISC, MC, V. 🍴 VP

Lopez y Gonzalez

2066 Lee Rd, Cleveland Heights; tel 216/371-7611. N of Cedar Rd. **Mexican.** An upscale taqueria serving generous servings of Mexican lasagna, fajitas, and other popular favorites. **FYI:** Reservations accepted. **Open:** Mon–Thurs 5:30–10pm, Fri–Sat 5:30–11:30pm, Sun 5–9pm. **Prices:** Main courses $12–$19. AE, DC, DISC, MC, V. 🍴 👥

♣ The Riverview Room

In Ritz-Carlton Cleveland, 1515 W 3rd St; tel 216/623-1300. **New American.** The service is impeccable at this romantic rooftop restaurant, where large windows afford panoramic views of the Cuyahoga River and Collision Bend. The food is surprisingly good and only the freshest ingredients are used. (Seafood is flown in fresh daily; vegetables are purchased from local farms.) A Grand Brunch is served on Sun, featuring a lavish buffet and entertainment by a classical ensemble. "Children's tea" is served each Sunday afternoon. **FYI:** Reservations recommended. Harp/piano. Children's menu. Dress code. **Open:** Breakfast Mon–Sat 6:30–11:30am; lunch Mon–Sat 11:30am–2:30pm, Sat 2:30–5:30pm; dinner Mon–

Thurs 5–10:30pm, Fri–Sat 5–11pm, Sun 5–10pm; brunch Sun 10am–2pm. **Prices:** Main courses $16–$45. AE, CB, DC, DISC, MC, V. 🍴 🍽 🖼 🍷 VP ♿

Sammy's

1400 W 10th St (The Flats); tel 216/523-5560. **New American.** Popular with a young, business-type clientele, who come here for the contemporary decor and spectacular views of the Cuyahoga River. Cozy and romantic seating areas provide a great venue for a dinner for two. The menu is heavy on seafood, including a raw bar; there's also a vegetarian menu and an award-winning wine list. Chocolate swans are popular for dessert. **FYI:** Reservations recommended. Jazz. Dress code. **Open:** Mon–Thurs 5:30–10pm, Fri–Sat 5:30pm–midnight. **Prices:** Main courses $22–$29. AE, CB, DC, DISC, MC, V. 🍴 🖼 VP ♿

♣ Sans Souci Mediterranean Cuisine

In Renaissance Cleveland Hotel, 24 Public Sq; tel 216/696-5600. **Mediterranean.** There is a quiet French-countryside ambience in this restaurant off the lobby of the hotel. Each table is private and cozy, and the walls are covered by murals painted by French artists. Roman pillars, marble floors, and beautiful views from every table complement the dining experience. Menu highlights include sautéed snapper, grilled salmon, veal, and Black Angus strip steak. **FYI:** Reservations recommended. Piano. Dress code. No smoking. **Open:** Lunch Mon–Fri 11:30am–2:30pm; dinner Sun–Thurs 5:30–10pm, Fri–Sat 5:30–11pm. **Prices:** Main courses $9–$18. AE, CB, DC, DISC, MC, V. 🍴 ♿

Sfuzzi, An Italian Bistro

In the Avenue at Tower City, 230 Huron Rd NW (Downtown); tel 216/861-4141. **Italian.** Brick and stucco walls make an attractive background for the black bistro tables and secluded booths, and there's an open kitchen so that diners may watch their meals being prepared. Favorite dishes—all of them made with the freshest ingredients—include oven-baked focaccia, veal picatta, and salmon. Cappuccino ice cream pie is a great way to top off your meal. **FYI:** Reservations recommended. **Open:** Lunch Mon–Sat 11am–4pm, Sun 10:30am–3pm; dinner Sun 4–8pm, Mon–Thurs 4–9pm, Fri–Sat 4–10pm; brunch Sun 10:30am–3pm. **Prices:** Main courses $9–$18. AE, DC, MC, V. 👥 VP ♿

600 St Clair

700 W St Clair Ave; tel 216/696-4488. At E 6th St. **Eclectic.** The decor is contemporary and minimalist, and corner tables offer great views of the evening cityscape. Crayons are provided for "table-top self-expression." Menu specialties include Black Angus steak, peppercorn fettuccine with smoked bacon–mushroom sauce, and the 12-oz veal chop. Jazz club and bar downstairs features entertainment on summer weekends. **FYI:** Reservations recommended. Jazz. **Open:** Lunch Mon–Fri 11:30am–4pm; dinner Mon–Tues

5:30–10pm, Wed–Thurs 5:30–11pm, Fri–Sat 5:30pm–midnight. **Prices:** Main courses $9–$20. AE, DISC, MC, V. ♥ ⛴ 🖼

Sterle's Slovenian Country House
1401 E 55th; tel 216/881-4181. Off I-90. **German.** An authentic Central European beer hall, with a large, open dining room, hand-hewn beams, hand-painted murals, and the occasional live polka band. Generous portions of wiener schnitzel and other veal dishes, pierogi, and strudel will fill up the hungriest patron. **FYI:** Reservations recommended. Big band/polka. **Open:** Lunch daily 11:30am–3pm; dinner Tues–Sat 3:30–9pm, Sun 3:30–8pm. **Prices:** Main courses $6–$11. MC, V. 🖼 &

Swingos on the Lake
In Carlyle Towers, 12900 Lake Ave, Lakewood; tel 216/221-6188. **Continental.** A romantic atmosphere prevails at this classy rooftop dining room, with large windows overlooking Lake Erie, candlelit tables, and a welcoming wooden dance floor next to the piano bar. (The rather dated decor was undergoing renovation at time of inspection.) The emphasis is on classic preparations of seafood, steak, and pasta; there's an extensive wine list. **FYI:** Reservations recommended. Dancing/live band. Children's menu. No smoking. **Open:** Lunch daily 11:30am–4pm; dinner Mon–Wed 4–10pm, Thurs–Sat 4pm–midnight, Sun 1–8pm. **Prices:** Main courses $15–$25. AE, DC, DISC, MC, V. ♥ 🆅🅿

ATTRACTIONS 🏛

The Rock and Roll Hall of Fame and Museum
1 Key Plaza; tel 216/781-7625. This magnificent seven-story glass-and-porcelain structure, designed by world-renowned architect I M Pei, houses a chronicle of rock 'n' roll to be experienced through interactive exhibits, archives, and memorabilia of the artists, songwriters, producers, and disc jockeys who created this art form. And of course there's the music itself, captured on state-of-the-art sound and video systems and presented in the context of the sociology of the times. **Open:** Peak (Mem Day–Labor Day) Mon–Tues 10am–5:30pm, Wed–Sun 10am–9pm. Reduced hours off-season. $$$$

Cleveland Museum of Art
11150 East Blvd (University Circle); tel 216/421-7340. Located in a marble Greek Revival building. From *The Treasure of the Guelphs* to Rauschenberg, this exemplary regional collection boasts a sumptuous panorama of Oriental, European, and American art. Some of the best-known works include El Greco's *Christ on the Cross,* Velázquez's *The Clown Calabazas,* Rembrandt's *The Jewish Student,* Cézanne's *Mont Sainte-Victoire,* and two famous Picassos, *Life* and *Harlequin with Violin.* **Open:** Tues–Fri 10am–5:45pm, Sat 9am–4:45pm, Sun 1–5:45pm. **Free**

Oberlin College
Jct OH 511/58, Oberlin; tel 216/775-8411. Located 25 mi SW of Cleveland. Founded in 1833, this liberal arts school was the first college in the world to offer equal co-educational degrees; today, the student population is 2,750. The **Allen Memorial Art Museum** features more than 14,000 works, with a focus on 17th-century Dutch paintings, 19th- and 20th-century European art, contemporary works, and Japanese woodcuts. There's also a music conservatory and a library with more than one million volumes. Campus tours begin at the admissions office in the Carnegie Building. **Open:** Call for tour information. **Free**

Cleveland Museum of Natural History
1 Wade Oval Dr (University Circle); tel 216/231-4600. Fascinating array of fossils, dinosaurs, mammals, birds, and geological specimens, with a special emphasis on the geology of prehistoric Ohio. Native American artifacts and displays of live animals are also popular. Library and planetarium. **Open:** Mon–Sat 10am–5pm, Sun 1–5:30pm. $$

Cleveland Metroparks Zoo
3900 Brookside Park Dr; tel 216/661-6500. One of the oldest zoos in the country, Cleveland Metroparks has more than 3,300 animals in residence including red pandas, snow leopards, rhinos, and cheetahs. **The RainForest,** a recent $30-million addition, is a simulated biosphere with over 600 animals and insects from seven continents (everything from Madagascar hissing cockroaches to Bornean orangutans); a 25-foot waterfall; and a tropical rainstorm exhibit with thunder, lightning, and rain. **Open:** Daily 9am–5pm. $$$

Steamship *William G Mather* Museum
1001 E 9th St Pier (Waterfront); tel 216/574-6262. Now a floating maritime museum, this 618-foot ship was originally built in 1925 to carry millions of tons of iron ore, stone, coal, and grain through the Great Lakes. Visitors can tour the cavernous cargo holds, elegant staterooms, and massive four-story engine room. Guided and self-guided tours available. **Open:** Peak (June–Sept) Mon–Sat 10am–5pm, Sun noon–5pm. Reduced hours off-season. $$

USS *COD*
1089 N Marginal Dr; tel 216/566-8770. During its service in the Pacific, the *COD* is credited with sinking nearly 30,000 tons of Japanese sea vessels. Tours of this famous World War II submarine are led by Navy veterans, and include all areas of the unaltered ship. **Open:** May 1–Labor Day, daily 10am–5pm. $$

Rockefeller Park
Liberty Blvd. A 296 acre oasis between Lake Erie and Case Western Reserve University. Highlights of the park include Japanese gardens, greenhouses, and a Cultural Garden adorned with sculptures and architectural designs from 24 different countries. **Open:** Daily sunrise–sunset. **Free**

The Health Museum
8911 Euclid Ave; tel 216/231-5010. More than 150 permanent hands-on exhibits dramatize the workings of the human body. Favorites include Juno, the transparent talking woman; the Giant Tooth; the Family Discovery Center; and the theaters of Hearing, Sight and Social Concerns. **Open:** Mon–Fri 9am–5pm, Sat 10am–5pm, Sun noon–5pm. **$$**

Inland Seas Maritime Museum
480 Main St, Vermilion; tel 216/967-3467. Located 15 mi W of Cleveland. The maritime history of the Great Lakes is documented here through ship models, paintings, exhibits, and artifacts such as engines and machines. Among the most impressive exhibits is a full-size replica of the 1877 Vermilion lighthouse. Tours of World War II submarine the USS *COD* also available. **Open:** Daily 10am–5pm. **$$**

Lake Erie Nature and Science Center
28728 Wolf Rd, Bay Village; tel 216/871-2900. Programs and services on a wide range of nature, science, ecological, and environmental topics and issues, with Lake Erie and the Lake Erie region as the primary focus. Fishing seminars, wildlife presentations, hikes, and bird walks help bring the area to life. The Schuele Planetarium offers laser shows and astronomy programs. Gift shop. **Open:** Peak (June–Oct) daily 10am–5pm. Reduced hours off-season. **Free**

Playhouse Square Center
1519 Euclid Ave (Downtown); tel 216/241-6000. A symbol of Cleveland's cultural renaissance, this urban-renewal project cost $20 million and endowed the city with one of the largest performance and concert hall complexes in the country. Three theaters (the Ohio, the State, and the Palace) and an elegantly restored cabaret present theatrical performances, ballet, opera, and classical and pop concerts. **Open:** Call for schedule. **$$$$**

Cleveland Play House
8500 Euclid Ave; tel 216/795-7000. Established in 1915, this regional repertory theater is the oldest of its kind in the country. The professional company presents a repertoire of classic and contemporary American theater in three auditoriums. Call for performance schedule. **$$$$**

Jacob's Field
2401 Ontario St; tel 216/420-4200. Home of the 1995 American League champion Cleveland Indians, Jacob's Field seats approximately 42,000 people and hosts the occasional concert in addition to baseball games. **$$$$**

Cleveland Stadium
Lakeside Ave and W 3rd St; tel 216/891-5000. The 80,000-seat home of the Cleveland Browns of the National Football League. Call for schedule. **$$$$**

Cleveland Heights

See Cleveland

Columbus

See also Delaware

Seat of Franklin County, in central part of state. Founded in 1812, its early growth was stimulated when the then-new National Road reached it in 1833. Government and education are still the city's main emphases. The huge Ohio State University is but one of 13 colleges and universities in Columbus; the city also has its own symphony, ballet, and opera. **Information:** Greater Columbus Convention & Visitors Bureau, 10 W Broad St, #1300, Columbus, 43215 (tel toll free 800/354-2657 or 800/3454-FUN).

PUBLIC TRANSPORTATION
The Central Ohio Transit Authority (COTA) provides local and express **bus service.** Fare is $1 for the local, $1.35 for the express. No weekend express service. For information call 614/228-1776.

HOTELS 🏨

≣≣≣ Concourse Hotel & Conference Center
4300 International Gateway, 43219; tel 614/237-2515 or toll free 800/541-4574; fax 614/237-6134. Airport exit off I-670. Excellent accommodations with many extras, especially for business travelers. **Rooms:** 147 rms and stes. CI 4pm/CO noon. Nonsmoking rms avail. **Amenities:** 🕾 ⚄ A/C, cable TV w/movies, refrig, voice mail, bathrobes. All units w/minibars. **Services:** ✕ ⌁ 🚐 🛆 ♺ Car-rental desk, social director, masseur, children's program, babysitting. **Facilities:** 🔁 🏋 300 💻 1 restaurant, 1 bar (w/entertainment), spa, sauna, steam rm, whirlpool, day-care ctr, playground. In-house Athletic Club offers many fitness programs for adults and children and has top-notch equipment, lap-pool, and massage therapy. **Rates:** $88–$108 S; $99–$113 D; $111–$121 ste. Extra person $10. Children under age 18 stay free. Parking: Outdoor, free. Free seven-day parking for all traveling guests. AE, CB, DC, DISC, MC, V.

≣≣≣ DoubleTree Guest Suites Columbus
50 S Front St, 43215 (Downtown); tel 614/228-4600 or toll free 800/222-8733; fax 614/228-0297. 2 blocks N of city hall. Elegant facility in the heart of Columbus. Especially nice for business travelers in need of long-term accommodations. **Rooms:** 194 stes. CI 3pm/CO noon. Nonsmoking rms avail. Upper-level rooms offer beautiful view of downtown area. **Amenities:** 🕾 ⚄ 🚐 ♩ A/C, cable TV w/movies, refrig, dataport. All units w/minibars. **Services:** ✕ 🛆 ♺ Babysitting. Complimentary cookies at check-in. Caring staff. **Facilities:** 🏋 80 💻 ⛆ 1 restaurant, 1 bar, spa. Guests get discount rate ($10) at nearby health club. **Rates:** $89–$199 ste. Extra person $20. Children under age 18 stay free. Min stay special events. Parking: Indoor, $15/day. AE, CB, DC, DISC, MC, V.

≣≣≣ Holiday Inn

175 Hutchinson Ave, Worthington, 43235; tel 614/885-3334 or toll free 800/465-4329; fax 614/846-4353. This comfortable facility gets you away from the heart of the city, but not too far. It's 20 minutes from OSU campus, downtown, Columbus Zoo, and fairgrounds. **Rooms:** 316 rms and stes. CI 3pm/CO noon. Nonsmoking rms avail. **Amenities:** 🗄 🐦 📶 A/C, cable TV. Some units w/whirlpools. **Services:** ✕ 🚐 🖼 🔄 🗲 **Facilities:** 🍴 🏓 🔲600 👍 1 restaurant, 1 bar, basketball, spa, sauna, steam rm, whirlpool, washer/dryer. Kids under 12 eat free in restaurant. **Rates:** $95 S or D; $189 ste. Children under age 18 stay free. Parking: Outdoor, free. AE, CB, DC, DISC, EC, ER, JCB, MC, V.

UNRATED Holiday Inn

328 W Lane Ave, 43201; tel 614/294-4848 or toll free 800/465-4329; fax 614/294-3901. Across the street from Ohio Stadium, one block from St John's Arena and ice rink, and only a few blocks from the other athletic facilities, this is definitely the spot for the true Buckeye fan. It's often the place for pre- and post-game tailgate parties. Early reservations are necessity for big games and other OSU special events. **Rooms:** 243 rms and stes. Executive level. CI 3pm/CO noon. Nonsmoking rms avail. **Amenities:** 🗄 🐦 📶 A/C, cable TV w/movies, dataport. **Services:** ✕ 🗝 🖼 🚐 🖼 🔄 🗲 Social director, babysitting. **Facilities:** 🍴 🏓 🔲1000 👍 1 restaurant, 1 bar (w/entertainment), spa, whirlpool, playground, washer/dryer. Guests have privileges at many of the university's health and fitness facilities. **Rates:** Peak (July–Aug) $74–$104 S or D; $150 ste. Children under age 18 stay free. Lower rates off-season. Parking: Indoor, free. AE, CB, DC, DISC, EC, ER, JCB, MC, V.

≣≣≣ Hyatt on Capitol Square

75 E State St, 43215; tel 614/228-1234 or toll free 800/233-1234; fax 614/469-9664. Connected to City Centre Mall; across from state capitol. **Rooms:** 400 rms and stes. Executive level. CI 3pm/CO noon. Nonsmoking rms avail. **Amenities:** 🗄 🐦 📶 A/C, satel TV w/movies, dataport, voice mail. Some units w/whirlpools. **Services:** ✕ 🗝 🆅🅿 🚐 🖼 🔄 Social director, babysitting. **Facilities:** 🏓 🔲350 👍 1 restaurant (see "Restaurants" below), 1 bar (w/entertainment). **Rates:** $99–$194 S; $99–$219 D; $215–$650 ste. Extra person $25. Children under age 16 stay free. AE, CB, DC, DISC, EC, ER, JCB, MC, V.

≣≣≣ Hyatt Regency

350 N High St, 43215; tel 614/463-1234 or toll free 800/233-1234; fax 614/463-1026. At the convention center, 6 blocks N of state capitol. **Rooms:** 631 rms and stes. Executive level. CI 3pm/CO noon. Nonsmoking rms avail. **Amenities:** 🗄 🐦 A/C, cable TV w/movies. **Services:** ✕ 🗝 🆅🅿 🚐 🖼 🔄 Babysitting. **Facilities:** 🍴 🏓 🔲1200 👍 2 restaurants, 1 bar. **Rates:** $99–$169 S; $99–$189 D; $525–$750 ste. Extra person $20. Children under age 18 stay free. Min stay special events. Parking: Indoor/outdoor, $6–$13/day. AE, CB, DC, DISC, EC, JCB, MC, V.

≣≣≣ Renaissance Dublin Hotel

600 Metro Place N, Dublin, 43017; tel 614/764-2200 or toll free 800/468-3571; fax 614/764-1213. Exit 17A off OH 161. Beautiful, well-tended flowers and trees in courtyard and fountain in lobby are a few of the many extras that set this facility above many others. Excellent business/conference facilities. **Rooms:** 217 rms and stes. CI 3pm/CO 1pm. Nonsmoking rms avail. **Amenities:** 🗄 🐦 📶 A/C, cable TV w/movies, dataport. Some units w/terraces. **Services:** 🍽 🖼 🔄 🗲 Babysitting. Complimentary shuttle service within five-mile radius, which includes Columbus Zoo and Wyandot Lake Amusement Park. **Facilities:** 🍴 🏓 🔲600 🖥 👍 1 restaurant, 1 bar, sauna. Complimentary pass to full-service health club next door. "Library style" arrangement of lounge makes it an excellent spot for private conversations or business meetings while unwinding with refreshments. **Rates:** $94–$150 S; $104–$160 D; $200 ste. Extra person $10. Children under age 18 stay free. Parking: Outdoor, free. AE, CB, DC, DISC, ER, JCB, MC, V.

MOTELS

≣ Best Western University Inn

3232 Olentangy River Rd, 43202; tel 614/261-7141 or toll free 800/528-1234. Exit 114 off I-71. Easy access, close to Ohio State University campus. Excellent for family, business, or school-related travel. **Rooms:** 94 rms and stes. CI 3pm/CO 11am. Nonsmoking rms avail. **Amenities:** 🗄 📶 A/C, satel TV w/movies, dataport. Some units w/terraces, some w/whirlpools. Suites have refrigerators. **Services:** 🔄 🗲 **Facilities:** 🍴 🔲200 👍 1 restaurant (lunch and dinner only), 1 bar, games rm, sauna, whirlpool, washer/dryer. Beautiful pool area has lush landscaping and extra large patio area. **Rates (CP):** Peak (May–Oct) $47 S; $54 D; $90 ste. Extra person $6. Children under age 12 stay free. Min stay special events. Lower rates off-season. Parking: Outdoor, free. AE, CB, DC, DISC, MC, V.

≣ Clarmont Motor Inn

650 S High St, 43215; tel 614/228-6511. 7 blocks S of the state capitol, 1 mi from convention center. Low cost, no-frills accommodations in German Village. Close to downtown. **Rooms:** 58 rms. CI 1pm/CO noon. **Amenities:** 🗄 A/C, cable TV. Some units w/terraces. **Services:** 🚐 🖼 🔄 **Facilities:** 🍴 1 bar. **Rates:** $28–$34 S or D. Extra person $4. Children under age 12 stay free. Parking: Outdoor, free. AE, CB, DC, DISC, MC, V.

≣≣ Cross Country Inn

4240 International Gateway, 43219; tel 614/237-3403 or toll free 800/621-1429; fax 614/237-2173. Very comfortable rooms at very reasonable rates. Close to airport. **Rooms:** 120 rms. CI 1pm/CO noon. Nonsmoking rms avail. **Amenities:** 🗄 🐦 A/C, cable TV w/movies. **Services:** 🚐 🔄 Drive-through check-in/out. **Facilities:** 🍴 🏓 👍 **Rates:** $44–$58 S or D. Extra person $7. Children under age 18 stay free. Parking:

Outdoor, free. Senior citizen discount is 25%. Stay, Park, and Fly—stay one night and park free for up to seven days. AE, CB, DC, DISC, EC, ER, JCB, MC, V.

≣≣ Cross Country Inn

6225 Zumstein Dr, 43229; tel 614/431-3670 or toll free 800/621-1429; fax 614/848-6980. Exit 117 off I-71. Economical accommodations next to the Continent Shopping Plaza and French Market. **Rooms:** 143 rms. CI 1pm/CO noon. Nonsmoking rms avail. **Amenities:** 🛏 A/C, cable TV w/movies. **Services:** ⌂ ⌂ Drive-through check-in/out. **Facilities:** ⌂ ⌂ ⌂ **Rates:** $35–$40 S; $41–$48 D. Extra person $7. Children under age 18 stay free. Parking: Outdoor, free. AE, DC, DISC, MC, V.

≣≣ Days Inn Fairgrounds

1700 Clara St, 43211; tel 614/299-4300 or toll free 800/329-7466; fax 614/299-0058. Exit 111 off I-71. Basic accommodations, particularly convenient for visitors to fairground activities. **Rooms:** 116 rms. CI 3pm/CO noon. Nonsmoking rms avail. **Amenities:** 🛏 ⌂ A/C, cable TV, in-rm safe. **Services:** ⌂ ⌂ **Facilities:** ⌂ ⌂ **Rates (CP):** $36–$42 S; $39–$48 D. Extra person $5. Children under age 18 stay free. Parking: Outdoor, free. Rates affected by activities at fairgrounds. AE, DC, DISC, MC, V.

≣ Days Inn University

3160 Olentangy River Rd, 43202; tel 614/261-0523 or toll free 800/329-7466; fax 614/261-0523. Just off OH 315, 1 block S of Ohio State University campus. Plain, simple, comfortable. Good for one-night stays. **Rooms:** 98 rms and effic. CI 3pm/CO noon. Nonsmoking rms avail. **Amenities:** 🛏 ⌂ ⌂ A/C, satel TV w/movies. **Services:** ⌂ ⌂ **Rates:** $35–$39 S; $42–$48 D; $47–$52 effic. Extra person $3. Children under age 18 stay free. Parking: Outdoor, free. AE, DC, DISC, MC, V.

≣≣ Fairfield Inn

887 Morse Rd, 43229; tel 614/262-4000 or toll free 800/228-2800. Morse Rd exit off I-71. Average, clean, neat. Close to Northland Mall. **Rooms:** 135 rms. CI 3pm/CO noon. Nonsmoking rms avail. **Amenities:** 🛏 ⌂ A/C, cable TV w/movies. **Services:** ⌂ ⌂ **Facilities:** ⌂ ⌂ **Rates (CP):** Peak (May–Oct) $49–$65 S or D. Extra person $3. Children under age 18 stay free. Min stay special events. Lower rates off-season. Parking: Outdoor, free. AE, DC, DISC, MC, V.

≣ German Village Inn Motel

920 S High St, 43206; tel 614/443-6506; fax 614/443-5663. Close to many historic shops and restaurants. **Rooms:** 44 rms. CI 2pm/CO noon. **Amenities:** 🛏 A/C, cable TV. **Services:** ⌂ ⌂ ⌂ **Facilities:** 1 bar (w/entertainment). **Rates:** $32–$50 S or D. Extra person $6. Children under age 12 stay free. Parking: Outdoor, free. AE, DC, DISC, MC, V.

≣≣ Hampton Inn North

1100 Mediterranean Ave, 43229; tel 614/848-9696 or toll free 800/426-7866; fax 614/848-5292. Exit 117 off I-71. Within 30 minutes of Columbus Zoo, OSU, and downtown.

Rooms: 117 rms. CI 2pm/CO noon. Nonsmoking rms avail. **Amenities:** 🛏 ⌂ A/C, cable TV w/movies, dataport. **Services:** ⌂ ⌂ ⌂ **Facilities:** ⌂ ⌂ ⌂ Whirlpool. Reduced price ($4) pass available to nearby Continent Athletic Club. **Rates (CP):** $50–$55 S; $55–$64 D. Children under age 18 stay free. Min stay special events. Parking: Outdoor, free. AE, CB, DC, DISC, MC, V.

≣≣ Holiday Inn Express

4530 W Broad St, 43228; tel 614/870-3700 or toll free 800/465-4329; fax 614/870-3333. At I-270. Beautiful furnishings. Near shopping, restaurants, golf course. **Rooms:** 49 rms and stes. CI 3pm/CO noon. Nonsmoking rms avail. **Amenities:** 🛏 ⌂ A/C, cable TV. Some units w/whirlpools. **Services:** ⌂ ⌂ **Facilities:** ⌂ ⌂ ⌂ **Rates (CP):** $54–$59 S; $59–$64 D; $110–$150 ste. Children under age 18 stay free. Parking: Outdoor, free. AE, CB, DC, DISC, MC, V.

≣≣ Knights Court Suites Hotel

1001 Schrock Rd, 43229; tel 614/431-0208 or toll free 800/543-5644; fax 614/431-0208. Exit 117 off I-71. Spacious lobby with beautiful, lush trees and plants surrounding fountain and garden pool. Across the road from popular shopping plaza and very close to Anheuser Busch Brewery. Thirty minutes from downtown Columbus. A good mid-range value with easy access off the major interstate. **Rooms:** 50 rms and stes. CI 3pm/CO noon. Nonsmoking rms avail. **Amenities:** 🛏 ⌂ ⌂ ⌂ A/C, satel TV, refrig. **Services:** ⌂ ⌂ ⌂ **Facilities:** ⌂ ⌂ ⌂ Whirlpool. **Rates (CP):** Peak (Apr–Nov) $60–$65 S or D; $65–$90 ste. Extra person $5. Children under age 18 stay free. Lower rates off-season. Parking: Outdoor, free. AE, DISC, MC, V.

≣≣≣ Parke University Hotel

3025 Olentangy River Rd, 43202; tel 614/267-1111 or toll free 800/344-2345; fax 614/267-0904. Just off OH 315; 6 mi N of downtown. This older, remodeled, chalet-type building offers more spacious rooms than others at similar rates. Beautiful, well-landscaped courtyard. Excellent for meetings. **Rooms:** 203 rms, stes, and effic. Executive level. CI 4pm/CO noon. Nonsmoking rms avail. **Amenities:** 🛏 ⌂ ⌂ A/C, cable TV w/movies. Some units w/terraces, some w/whirlpools. **Services:** ⌂ ⌂ ⌂ ⌂ ⌂ Extremely warm and friendly staff. **Facilities:** ⌂ ⌂ ⌂ 2 restaurants (lunch and dinner only), 2 bars (1 w/entertainment), washer/dryer. Video conferencing capabilities in one of the meeting rooms. Damon's Restaurant is called the "Place For Ribs" and Damon's Clubhouse the "Place For Sports"—it has several wide-screened TVs and is decorated with autographed pictures of famous college and professional athletes who have stayed here. Free passes to nearby Scandinavia Health and Fitness Center. **Rates (CP):** $60–$77 S; $65–$78 D; $68–$98 ste; $80 effic. Extra person $10. Children under age 12 stay free. Parking: Outdoor, free. AE, CB, DC, DISC, MC, V.

≡≡≡ Radisson Airport

1375 Cassady Ave, 43219; tel 614/475-7551 or toll free 800/333-3333; fax 614/476-1476. Cassady Rd exit off I-270 W. Excellent accommodations close to airport with easy access off highway. Great for conferences and business meetings. Beautiful recessed lobby is easily sectioned off for conversations. **Rooms:** 247 rms and stes. CI 3pm/CO noon. Nonsmoking rms avail. **Amenities:** 🛋 📞 📧 A/C, cable TV w/movies, dataport. Some units w/whirlpools. **Services:** ✗ 🚐 🖼 ↵ **Facilities:** 🍴 🏋 800 💻 ᕪ 1 restaurant, 1 bar, spa, sauna. **Rates (BB):** $87–$99 S or D; $175–$235 ste. Children under age 18 stay free. Parking: Outdoor, free. AE, DC, DISC, MC, V.

≡≡≡ Ramada Inn West

4601 W Broad St, 43228; tel 614/878-5301 or toll free 800/228-2828; fax 614/878-6661. Exit 7B off I-270 S; exit 7 off I-270 W. Nice mid-range facility with easy access off interstate. **Rooms:** 110 rms and stes. CI 2pm/CO noon. Nonsmoking rms avail. **Amenities:** 🛋 📞 A/C, cable TV w/movies. Some units w/whirlpools. Business kings and suites have dataports. **Services:** ✗ 🖼 ↵ **Facilities:** 🍴 🏋 30 ᕪ 1 restaurant, 1 bar (w/entertainment), games rm, washer/dryer. **Rates:** $45–$59 S or D; $75–$100 ste. Children under age 12 stay free. Parking: Outdoor, free. AE, CB, DC, DISC, MC, V.

≡≡ Signature Inn North

6767 Schrock Hill Court, 43229; tel 614/890-8111 or toll free 800/822-5252; fax 614/890-8111. Excellent business stop with many extras to complement its meeting facilities. Amenities, such as extra long phone cord, spacious corner desk with additional extensions (for spreading out paperwork), and interview cubicles in lobby and balcony area, make it perfect for corporate travelers. Guests can use their discount at the driving range across the street or take a walk, jog, or run on the four-mile nature trail in Sharon Woods (across the highway). **Rooms:** 125 rms and stes. CI 3pm/CO noon. Nonsmoking rms avail. **Amenities:** 🛋 📞 A/C, cable TV w/movies, dataport. 1 unit w/whirlpool. **Services:** 🖼 ↵ **Facilities:** 🍴 100 💻 ᕪ Small but immaculate pool received 1995 award for the "Best Kept Pool in Columbus" from the Columbus Board of Health. **Rates (CP):** $59–$62 S or D; $84 ste. Extra person $7. Children under age 18 stay free. Min stay special events. Parking: Outdoor, free. AE, DC, DISC, MC, V.

≡≡ Travelodge

7480 N High St, 43235; tel 614/431-2525 or toll free 800/578-7878; fax 614/431-0272. Easy access off highway and 15 minutes to downtown or OSU campus. **Rooms:** 108 rms. CI 3pm/CO noon. Nonsmoking rms avail. **Amenities:** 🛋 📧 A/C, cable TV, dataport. **Services:** 🖼 ↵ 🚐 Hotel is a regular airport shuttle stop. **Facilities:** 20 ᕪ Games rm. **Rates:** Peak (June–Sept) $36–$38 S; $39–$41 D. Extra person $6. Children under age 18 stay free. Lower rates off-season. Parking: Outdoor, free. AE, DC, DISC, JCB, MC, V.

≡≡≡ Trueman Club Hotel

900 E Dublin-Granville Rd, 43229; tel 614/888-7440 or toll free 800/477-7888; fax 614/888-7879. Exit 117 off I-71 S. Beautiful facility is especially nice for business travelers. Enormous lobby has lots of separate sitting areas for small conferences. **Rooms:** 182 rms and stes. CI 3pm/CO noon. Nonsmoking rms avail. **Amenities:** 🛋 📞 A/C, cable TV w/movies, dataport, voice mail. Some units w/whirlpools. **Services:** ✗ 🚐 🖼 ↵ Reception every weekday with hot and cold snacks and complimentary beverage (5–7pm). **Facilities:** 🍴 🏋 200 ᕪ 1 bar, whirlpool, washer/dryer. Free passes to nearby Continental Athletic Club. **Rates (BB):** $115–$125 S or D; $136–$146 ste. Extra person $10. Children under age 18 stay free. Parking: Outdoor, free. AE, DC, DISC, MC, V.

RESTAURANTS 🍴

A La Carte

2333 N High St; tel 614/294-6783. 3½ blocks N of Ohio State University campus. **Mediterranean.** The surrounding area seems somewhat rundown, but the interior here is quite elegant, as is the menu. Locals like to start a meal here with the Greek shrimp and feta (tossed in a white wine and feta cheese sauce and served over fettuccine) or the sautéed portobello mushroom salad (made with spinach and roasted red peppers and topped with warm extra-virgin olive oil and balsamic vinegar). Pasta alla Romana (fettuccine tossed with spinach, roasted red peppers, black olives, artichoke hearts, and melted blue cheese) is a popular Italian entree. The notable wine cellar has more than 12,000 bottles, with vintages dating back to the late 1960s. Diners can enjoy a bottle with dinner, or take a bottle home from the on-site retail wine shop. **FYI:** Reservations accepted. **Open:** Tues–Thurs 11am–9:30pm, Fri 11am–11pm, Sat 5–11pm, Sun 5–9pm. **Prices:** Main courses $8–$11. AE, CB, DC, DISC, MC, V.

Alex's Bistro

In Arlington Square Shopping Center, 4681 Reed Rd; tel 614/457-8887. **French/Italian.** A trendy bistro in northwest Columbus with an extensive international wine list encompassing over 90 labels. The "wine of the week" highlights a special brand not included on the regular list. **FYI:** Reservations accepted. Children's menu. Dress code. **Open:** Lunch Mon–Fri 11:30–2pm; dinner Mon–Sat 5:30–10pm. **Prices:** Main courses $10–$19. AE, CB, DC, DISC, MC, V. ♥ ᕪ

Bexley's Monk

2232 E Main St; tel 614/239-6665. Just off I-70. **New American.** This trendy East Side spot is a relaxing place for dining on gourmet pasta, fresh seafood, and wood-fired pizza. **FYI:** Reservations recommended. Jazz/piano. **Open:** Lunch Mon–Fri 11:30am–2:30pm; dinner Sun–Thurs 5:30–10pm, Fri–Sat 5:30–11pm. **Prices:** Main courses $14–$24. AE, DC, DISC, MC, V. ♥ 🎵 ᕪ

Chili Verde Café

In Carriage Place Shopping Center, 4852 Sawmill Rd; tel 614/442-6630. **Southwestern.** Specializing in Mexican and American Southwestern foods, this is a great place for those with spicy cravings. Along with the weekly chef's specials, big burritos and enchiladas are favorites. **FYI:** Reservations not accepted. Children's menu. **Open:** Peak (June–Sept) Mon–Thurs 11am–9:30pm, Fri–Sat 11am–10:30pm, Sun 4–9pm. **Prices:** Main courses $5–$13. AE, DISC, MC, V. 👪 ♥ ♿

♥ ★ Engine House No 5

121 Thurman Ave; tel 614/443-4877. 3 blocks E of High St. **Seafood.** This 100-year-old restored fire station is a must-see spot for those visiting the city. Antique fire-fighting equipment (including a brass pole that staff members slide down) decorates the restaurant. Seafood is the main specialty; especially noteworthy are broiled Maryland crab cakes and Charley's Bucket—whole Maine lobster, Dungeness crab, mussels, clams, redskin potatoes, and corn on the cob, all steamed together and served in a replica of a fireman's brigade bucket. **FYI:** Reservations recommended. Piano. Children's menu. Dress code. **Open:** Lunch Mon–Fri 11:30am–4pm; dinner Mon–Thurs 4–10pm, Fri–Sat 4–11pm, Sun 4–9pm. **Prices:** Main courses $11–$30. AE, DC, DISC, MC, V. 🍴 👪 ♿

Figlio Wood-Fired Pizza

1369 Grandview Ave; tel 614/481-8850. Between 3rd and 5th. **Pizza.** A small, lively Short North eatery offering gourmet wood-fired pizzas and pastas like angel hair with shrimp and scallions. **FYI:** Reservations not accepted. Dress code. No smoking. **Open:** Mon–Thurs 5–9pm, Fri–Sat 5–10pm. **Prices:** Main courses $7–$10. DISC, MC, V. ♥ 🍽 ♿

55 at Crosswoods

55 Hutchinson Ave; tel 614/846-5555. Jct I-270/US 23. **New American/Seafood.** This pricey spot for special occasions is well regarded for its Maryland crab cakes and other seafood. Meals can also be taken in the more casual cafe/lounge. **FYI:** Reservations recommended. Children's menu. Dress code. **Open:** Lunch Mon–Fri 11am–2:30pm; dinner Mon–Sat 5–10pm; brunch Sun 10:30am–2:30pm. **Prices:** Main courses $8–$21. AE, DC, DISC, MC, V. ♥ ♿

Florentine Restaurant

907 W Broad St; tel 614/228-2262. 2 blocks from High St, near downtown. **Italian.** A nice, simple spot for Italian basics: lasagna, spaghetti, rigatoni, stuffed shells. **FYI:** Reservations accepted. Children's menu. Dress code. No liquor license. **Open:** Mon–Thurs 11am–9pm, Fri 11am–10pm, Sat 4–10pm. **Prices:** Main courses $8–$15. AE, CB, DC, DISC, MC, V. 👪

Fujiyama Steakhouse

5755 Cleveland Ave; tel 614/891-2224. Across from Northland Mall, ½ mi E of OH 161. **Japanese.** The freshest of vegetables, beef, chicken, pork, and seafood are sliced, diced and cooked at your table by an entertaining chef who likes to

astound with his juggling of utensils and ingredients—and, finally, with his delicious creations. **FYI:** Reservations recommended. Dress code. **Open:** Lunch Mon–Fri 11:30am–1:30pm; dinner Mon–Thurs 5–9:30pm, Fri–Sat 5–10:30pm, Sun 4–9pm. **Prices:** Main courses $8–$20. AE, DC, DISC, MC, V. ♥ 👪 ♿

♥ Handke's

520 S Front St (Brewery District); tel 614/621-2500. 1 block W of High St and German Village. **Eclectic.** World-renowned Hartmut Handke, the only certified master chef in Columbus, has brought his fine cuisine to this elegant "beer cellar" (a long stairway leads to the entrance). Its formal ambience makes it perfect for quiet, special dinners. Menu changes with the seasons and includes a wide variety of seafood, beef, veal, pork, and poultry dishes. Cornish game hen and buffalo sometimes make an appearance on the menu. **FYI:** Reservations recommended. No smoking. **Open:** Mon–Sat 5:30–10pm. **Prices:** Main courses $8–$25. AE, CB, DC, DISC, MC, V. ♥ 🍴 👪 VP

★ Jai Lai Prime Rib

1421 Olentangy River Rd; tel 614/421-7337. At 5th Ave; 1 block S of Ohio State University campus. **American.** Listed by a local critic as one of the "top ten places in Columbus for prime rib," the Jai Lai's on-site butcher shop may be the reason why people keep coming back for it, as well as for the very popular beef stew. The restaurant also has a full bakery on site, which is why the breads and rolls are so fresh and the pies—especially the key lime—are so popular. Homemade blue cheese dressing tops the house salad. Half portions are available for all menu items. "Murder Mystery Dinner Theater" is held in one of the banquet rooms every Friday and Saturday night. **FYI:** Reservations accepted. Piano. Dress code. **Open:** Lunch Sun–Fri 11am–4pm; dinner Mon–Thurs 4–10pm, Fri–Sat 4–11pm, Sun 4–9pm. **Prices:** Main courses $8–$20. AE, CB, DC, DISC, MC, V. ♥ ♥ VP ♿

Lindey's Restaurant

169 E Beck St (German Village); tel 614/228-4343. At Mohawk. **New American.** Favorites at this fun, popular bistro include marinated center-cut pork chops or rack of lamb served with garlic mashed potatoes; angel hair pasta with garlic-butter sauce; and gourmet pizza. Terrace dining available. **FYI:** Reservations recommended. Jazz. Dress code. **Open:** Sun–Wed 11:30am–10pm, Thurs–Sat 11:30am–midnight. **Prices:** Main courses $8–$20. AE, CB, DC, DISC, MC, V. VP

Mohawk Bar & Grill

821 Mohawk St (German Village); tel 614/444-7024. **American.** Small, cozy spot popular for business lunches and pre- and post-theater dining. Varied menu includes many interesting items: white lasagna, spinach fettucine with pesto, turtle soup, quesadillas. **FYI:** Reservations not accepted. Dress

code. **Open:** Mon 11am–11pm, Tues–Thurs 11am–midnight, Fri 11am–1am, Sat 9am–1am, Sun 9am–11pm. **Prices:** Main courses $6–$9. AE, MC, V.

Nancy's Home Cooking Restaurant

3133 N High St; tel 614/265-9012. 2 mi N of Ohio State University campus. **Diner.** This rundown and slightly tacky diner has only one table, six small booths, and a counter—but the unpretentious food is a big hit with OSU students. For breakfast, try a "garbage" omelette (filled with bacon, sausage, onions, peppers, and cheese), served with home fries and toast, for only $2.50. Lunch is mainly burgers, plus items like fried bologna and tuna salad sandwiches. There are no menus; daily dinner entrees (usually two) are posted on the blackboard, and regulars seem to know what's served each day of the week. Wednesday's meat loaf is very popular. Be prepared to stand in a line a block long for Thursday's chicken and noodles. Dessert—your choice of pie or cake—adds just 50¢ to the tab. **FYI:** Reservations not accepted. No liquor license. **Open:** Breakfast Mon–Fri 6–10:30am, Sat 6am–noon, Sun 7am–1pm; lunch Mon–Fri 10:30am–2pm; dinner Mon–Thurs 4–7pm. **Prices:** Main courses $3. No CC.

♛ One Nation

1 Nationwide Plaza (Downtown); tel 614/221-0001. 6 blocks from City Centre Mall. **American.** Dine in beautiful surroundings at this elegant restaurant atop of one of downtown Columbus's tallest buildings. Traditional American cuisine—prime rib and Georgia pork loin in peach sauce, served with pecan rice and mixed greens, are favorites. **FYI:** Reservations recommended. Piano. Children's menu. Dress code. **Open:** Lunch Mon–Fri 11:30am–2:30pm; dinner Mon–Thurs 5:30–10pm, Fri–Sat 5:30–11pm; brunch Sun 10am–2:30pm. **Prices:** Main courses $16–$23. AE, CB, DC, DISC, MC, V. ♥ ▲ ♥ ♿

Paul's Pantry

1565 W 5th Ave; tel 614/481-8848. At North Star Blvd. **American/Italian.** Popular spot featuring mainly Italian fare. Mama Panzera's Famous Lasagna is a wonderful family recipe. Many traditional American dishes also served—liver and onions is the Thursday special. **FYI:** Reservations not accepted. Dress code. **Open:** Mon–Thurs 6am–10pm, Fri–Sat 6am–11pm, Sun 8am–9pm. **Prices:** Main courses $7–$16. No CC. ▦ ♿

The Plaza Restaurant

In Hyatt on Capitol Square, 75 E State St (Downtown); tel 614/365-4550. **American.** New York strip steak tops the list of favorites at this typical American restaurant that is popular for its business lunches and Sunday brunch. Fresh seafood, salad entrees, pastas. **FYI:** Reservations recommended. Guitar/harp/piano. Children's menu. **Open:** Breakfast Mon–Fri 6:30–11:30am, Sat–Sun 6:30am–1pm; lunch Mon–Sat 11:30am–2pm; dinner Sun–Thurs 5:30–10pm, Fri–Sat 5:30–11pm; brunch Sun 10:30am–2pm. **Prices:** Main courses $4–$17. AE, CB, DC, DISC, MC, V. ▦ ♥ ♿

Red Door Tavern

1736 W 5th Ave (Grandview); tel 614/488-5433. 2 mi W of OH 315. **American.** A low-key, unpretentious neighborhood restaurant popular for business lunches. Traditional sandwiches; spaghetti on Wednesday and Thursday. Own pies. **FYI:** Reservations not accepted. Children's menu. Additional location: 6360 Frantz Rd, Dublin (tel 791-8191). **Open:** Mon–Sat 8:30am–10pm. **Prices:** Main courses $7–$11. AE, DISC, MC, V. ▮ ▦ ♿

♛ ★ The Refectory Restaurant

1092 Bethel Rd; tel 614/451-9774. At Kenney. **French.** This elegantly beautiful, award-winning French restaurant is perennially ranked as one of the top two in Columbus and should be part of any extended stay in the city. Located in a restored 19th-century church, the unique interior is enhanced by meticulous details, such as the handmade lamps and candle holders designed by a local artist and fine, imported German china. Wines are from every corner of the globe and together represent one of the finest collections in Ohio. **FYI:** Reservations recommended. **Open:** Mon–Thurs 5:30–10pm, Fri–Sat 5–10:30pm. **Prices:** Main courses $15–$24. AE, CB, DC, DISC, MC, V. ♥ ▮ ▣

Rigsby's Cuisine Volatile

698 N High St; tel 614/461-7888. 4 blocks N of statehouse. **Mediterranean.** Upbeat, stylish restaurant offering a range of Mediterranean dishes. Shrimp à la diavola; rack of lamb with citrus, mint, and port; chicken breast stuffed with sun-dried tomatoes and prosciutto. **FYI:** Reservations recommended. Jazz. Dress code. No smoking. **Open:** Mon–Sat 11am–11pm. **Prices:** Main courses $12–$20. AE, DC, DISC, MC, V. ♥ 𝗩𝗣 ♿

♛ ★ Seven Stars Restaurant

In Worthington Inn, 649 High St, Worthington; tel 614/885-2600. 1 block S of center of town. **Regional American.** The menu here changes with the seasons. A spring favorite is the rack of lamb served with mint pesto and red potatoes, while summer brings lots of seafood (salmon served with sesame sauce and julienned vegetables is especially well liked). For the winter months diners will find duck and venison, and a variety of pork dishes are available year-round. Each season also offers at least one vegetarian entree, such as pasta with vegetables. Smoking allowed in the bar, which also has tables for dining. Half-portions available. **FYI:** Reservations recommended. Jazz. Dress code. No smoking. **Open:** Breakfast daily 7–10am; lunch daily 11am–3pm; dinner Mon–Thurs 5:30–10pm, Fri–Sat 5:30–11pm, Sun 5:30–9pm. **Prices:** Main courses $10–$24. AE, DC, DISC, MC, V. ▮

⑤ Siam Oriental Restaurant

855 Bethel Rd; tel 614/451-1109. At Olentangy River Rd. **Chinese/Thai.** Chinese and Thai cuisine in northwest Columbus. Many regulars swear by the General Tso's chicken. **FYI:** Reservations accepted. **Open:** Mon–Thurs 11:30am–10pm, Fri 11:30am–11pm, Sat noon–11pm, Sun noon–9pm. **Prices:** Main courses $7–$13. AE, DISC, MC, V. ▦ ♿

★ Spagio
1295 Grandview Ave; tel 614/486-1114. 2 blocks S of 5th Ave. **International.** Close to the Short North strip, this popular dining spot offers a European/Pacific Rim–influenced menu featuring seafood, game, and gourmet wood-fired pizzas. Some special favorites include cold pizza with salmon and sour cream, spicy shrimp pasta, and smoked chicken pasta. Spagio's occasionally teams up with the wine shop next door for cooking demonstrations and wine tastings. **FYI:** Reservations not accepted. Jazz. Dress code. **Open:** Mon 11am–10pm, Tues 11am–11pm, Wed–Thurs 11am–10pm, Fri–Sat 11am–11pm. **Prices:** Main courses $7–$20. AE, MC, V. ♨

Tony's
16 W Beck St (German Village); tel 614/224-8669. **Italian.** The star dish at this popular Italian is homemade fettucine topped with shrimp, scallops, and crabmeat and blended in a rich cream sauce. Menu also includes several vegetarian entrees. **FYI:** Reservations recommended. Piano. Dress code. **Open:** Lunch Mon–Thurs 11:30am–4pm, Fri 11:30am–4pm; dinner Mon–Thurs 4–10pm, Fri 4–11pm, Sat 5:30–11pm. **Prices:** Main courses $9–$16. AE, CB, DC, MC, V. ♥ &

ATTRACTIONS 🏛

Ohio Historical Center
I-71 at 17th Ave; tel 614/297-2300. The state's repository of more than two million items relating to its political and natural history, from prehistoric times through the present. Displays include interactive kiosks, dioramas, and a mastodon skeleton. The center also runs Ohio Village, a replica of small-town life in the 1860s with more than a dozen period buildings. **Open:** Mon–Sat 9am–5pm, Sun 10am–5pm. **$$**

Ohio State Capitol
Broad and High Sts; tel 614/752-6350. Affectionately called the "Hat Box Capitol" because of its distinctive rotunda, this building is an excellent example of 19th-century Greek Revival architecture. Its impressive public halls house significant items from Ohio history, including the chair Abraham Lincoln sat in when he learned that his presidential victory was confirmed. Guided and self-guided tours available. **Open:** Mon–Fri 7am–9pm, Sat–Sun 9am–5pm. **Free**

Columbus Museum of Art
480 E Broad St; tel 614/221-6801. The collections housed in this Renaissance Revival-style building focus on North American modernism (with paintings by Maurice Prendergast, Charles Demuth, and Charles Sheeler) and works by European masters (Picasso, Degas, Braque, and Matisse). Sculpture garden, cafe. Free guided tours on Fridays and Sundays at noon and 2pm. **Open:** Tues 10am–8:30pm, Weds–Sun 10am–5:30pm. **$**

Columbus *Santa Maria*
109 N Front St (Downtown); tel 614/645-8760. An authentic, museum-quality re-creation of Christopher Columbus' flagship, built from the original plans. Tours dramatize the conditions under which the explorers sailed, and displays provide historical background on Columbus and his era. **Open:** Apr–Dec. Call for hours. **$$**

Coshocton

Seat of Coshocton County, in east-central part of state. Founded in 1802 at the confluence of the Muskingum, Tuscarawas, and Walhonding Rivers, Coshocton was an important stop along the Ohio and Erie Canal. The Coshocton Canal Festival celebrates this heritage and is held every August. **Information:** Coshocton County Chamber of Commerce, 124 Chestnut St, Coshocton, 43812 (tel 614/622-5411).

MOTELS 🏨

▤▤▤ Roscoe Village Inn
200 N Whitewoman St, 43812; tel 614/622-2222 or toll free 800/237-7397; fax 614/623-6568. Just off OH 16, minutes from Roscoe Village. The beautiful working fireplaces in the lobby, lounge, and restaurant, and the period costumes of the staff all make you feel like a part of Ohio's rich history; however, the inn also offers modern conveniences. Nearby are a golf course, fishing, nature walks on the tow path, museums, shops, and historic Roscoe Village. **Rooms:** 51 rms. CI 3pm/CO noon. Nonsmoking rms avail. Rooms are spacious and cozy with Shaker-style furnishings. **Amenities:** A/C, cable TV w/movies. **Services:** Discounts for living history tours at Roscoe Village; canal boat rides; and other area attractions available to guests. **Facilities:** 1 restaurant, 1 bar (w/entertainment). **Rates:** Peak (May–Oct) $79–$89 S or D. Children under age 18 stay free. Lower rates off-season. Parking: Outdoor, free. Golf and New Year's Eve packages avail, as well as the ever-popular "Murder Mystery" weekend package. AE, DC, DISC, MC, V.

▤▤ Travelodge
275 S Whitewoman St, 43812; tel 614/622-9823 or toll free 800/255-3050. 2 mi from center of town. Basic, clean, and comfortable facility. Minutes from the many historic sites in town. **Rooms:** 50 rms, stes, and effic. CI 2pm/CO noon. Nonsmoking rms avail. **Amenities:** A/C, cable TV w/movies. **Services:** **Facilities:** 1 restaurant. **Rates:** Peak (May–Oct) $48–$52 S; $58 D; $68 ste; $52–$62 effic. Extra person $5. Children under age 18 stay free. Lower rates off-season. Parking: Outdoor, free. AE, CB, DC, DISC, MC, V.

Dayton

See also Miamisburg, Vandalia

Seat of Montgomery County, in southwest part of state. The Miami, Stillwater, Mad, and Wolf Rivers flow through this city of 28 bridges. Long a center of industry and inventions, Dayton is where the Wright Brothers experimented with their early flying machines. Dayton International Airport is the site of the US Air and Trade Show, held in late July. **Information:** Dayton/Montgomery County Convention & Visitors Bureau, 1 Chamber Plaza, 5th and Main, Dayton, 45402-2400 (tel toll free 800/221-8234 or 800/221-8235).

MOTELS 🏨

≣ Best Inn
5551 Springfield Pike, 45431; tel 513/258-2233. Near Wright-Patterson Air Force Base. A motel for one-night's sleep, as services are sparse. It lies within the shadow of the Dayton Int'l Airport. Guests must drive a ways to find food. **Rooms:** 43 rms. CI 2pm/CO 11am. Nonsmoking rms avail. **Amenities:** 🛏 A/C, cable TV. **Facilities:** 🏊 🕭 **Rates:** $30–$32 S or D. Extra person $5. Children under age 5 stay free. Parking: Outdoor, free. Rates higher during the air show and special events in the area. AE, CB, DC, DISC, MC, V.

≣≣ Comfort Inn
7125 Miller Lane, 45415; tel 513/890-9995 or toll free 800/221-2222; fax 513/890-9995. Exit 60 off I-75; left at first light. Clean and neat, but somehow uninspiring. **Rooms:** 56 rms. CI 3pm/CO 11am. Nonsmoking rms avail. **Amenities:** 🛏 👤 A/C, cable TV w/movies. **Services:** 🖼 🕭 🕭 **Facilities:** 🕭 🏊 🕭 Games rm, whirlpool. **Rates (CP):** Peak (June–Aug) $49–$55 S or D. Extra person $5. Children under age 18 stay free. Lower rates off-season. Parking: Outdoor, free. AE, CB, DC, DISC, JCB, MC, V.

≣≣ Econo Lodge North
2221 Wagoner Ford Rd, 45414; tel 513/278-1500 or toll free 800/424-4777; fax 513/299-3093. Exit 57B off I-75. Attractive and clean. Nearby golf, bowling, and fishing. **Rooms:** 108 rms. CI 11am/CO 11am. Nonsmoking rms avail. Rooms are bright and inviting. **Amenities:** 🛏 A/C, cable TV. **Services:** 🕭 **Facilities:** 🕭 🏊 🕭 Large pool area. **Rates:** $32–$45 S; $41–$49 D. Extra person $4. Children under age 18 stay free. Parking: Outdoor, free. Rates higher during special events such as air show and annual national trap shoot. AE, DC, DISC, MC, V.

≣≣ Fairfield Inn
6960 Miller Lane, 45414; tel 513/898-1120 or toll free 800/228-2800; fax 513/898-1120. Exit 60 off I-75. Offers good-size rooms. Bright and cheery lobby with comfortable lounge. Nice touch: flower arrangements throughout interior public areas. **Rooms:** 135 rms. CI 3pm/CO noon. Nonsmoking rms avail. **Amenities:** 🛏 👤 A/C, cable TV w/movies, dataport. **Services:** 🖼 🕭 **Facilities:** 🕭 🕭 Impressive pool area with

wide sun deck. **Rates (CP):** Peak (June 15–Sept 15) $52 S or D. Children under age 18 stay free. Lower rates off-season. Parking: Outdoor, free. Rates are for four persons per room. AE, CB, DC, DISC, MC, V.

≣≣≣ Holiday Inn Dayton South
2455 Dryden Rd, Moraine, 45439; tel 513/294-1471 or toll free 800/HOLIDAY; fax 513/294-4282. Features Holidome multi-use recreation facility with South Seas motif. Wide lobby with several seating areas, hanging baskets, and small wall mirrors. **Rooms:** 203 rms. CI 3pm/CO noon. Nonsmoking rms avail. **Amenities:** 🛏 👤 A/C, cable TV w/movies, dataport. **Services:** ✕ 🖼 🕭 🕭 **Facilities:** 🕭 🕭 🕭 1 restaurant, 1 bar, games rm, whirlpool, playground. Two slides for kids; table tennis. Lower level of Holidome has large area for receptions, special dinners, etc. **Rates:** Peak (Mem Day–Labor Day) $75 S or D. Children under age 12 stay free. Lower rates off-season. Parking: Outdoor, free. Packages include Valentine's Day, Heart-to-Heart, New Year's Eve. AE, CB, DC, DISC, MC, V.

≣≣ Knights Inn North
3663 Maxton Rd, 45414; tel 513/898-1212 or toll free 800/843-5644; fax 513/898-7354. Exit 60 off I-75; left at first light. Very ordinary, but not a bad deal for families on a one-night stay. **Rooms:** 103 rms and effic. CI 3pm/CO noon. Nonsmoking rms avail. Attractive artwork and murals adorn the walls. **Amenities:** 🛏 A/C, satel TV. Efficiency units have microwaves and refrigerators. **Services:** 🕭 **Facilities:** 🕭 🏊 🕭 **Rates:** $31–$45 S or D; $38–$45 effic. Extra person $5. Children under age 17 stay free. Parking: Outdoor, free. Rates higher during special events, such as the airshow. AE, DC, DISC, MC, V.

UNRATED Motel 6
7130 Miller Lane, 45414; tel 513/898-3606; fax 513/890-3898. Spotless property. **Rooms:** 98 rms. Executive level. CI open/CO noon. Nonsmoking rms avail. **Amenities:** 🛏 A/C, satel TV, dataport. **Services:** 🕭 🕭 Only small pets allowed. Staff is constantly at work on repair, upkeep, and renovation. **Facilities:** 🕭 🕭 Washer/dryer. **Rates:** Peak (Mem Day–Labor Day) $28–$34 S or D. Extra person $3. Children under age 17 stay free. Lower rates off-season. Parking: Outdoor, free. AE, CB, DC, DISC, MC, V.

≣≣≣ Ramada Inn
4079 Litte York Rd, 45414; tel 513/890-9500 or toll free 800/860-7666; fax 513/890-8525. Exit 60 off I-75; right at first light. Made up of two large buildings. Recommended for small groups—it's popular for local meetings. Nearby golf, bowling, and fishing. **Rooms:** 139 rms and stes. CI 3pm/CO noon. Nonsmoking rms avail. **Amenities:** 🛏 👤 A/C, cable TV w/movies. Some units w/whirlpools. **Services:** ✕ 🚐 🖼 🕭 🕭 Champagne and flowers can be arranged for any room at any time for $30. **Facilities:** 🕭 🏊 🕭 🕭 🕭 1 restaurant, 1 bar (w/entertainment), playground, washer/dryer. Entertainment in lounge includes a DJ and karaoke. **Rates (CP):** $52–

$60 S or D; $110–$130 ste. Extra person $10. Children under age 18 stay free. Parking: Outdoor, free. Rates higher during special events, such as the air show or Grand National Trap Shoot. Three-day golf package costs $220/person. AE, CB, DC, DISC, MC, V.

≡ Super 8 Motel
8110 Old Troy Pike, Huber Heights, 45424; tel 513/237-1888 or toll free 800/800-8000; fax 513/237-2033. Clean, family-managed chain motel offering few frills. Located across from large shopping center. **Rooms:** 66 rms and stes. CI 2pm/CO 11am. Nonsmoking rms avail. **Amenities:** 🛁 A/C, cable TV. **Services:** 🗘 **Facilities:** ⅍ ⅃ Washer/dryer. **Rates:** Peak (Apr–Sept) $39–$45 S or D; $59 ste. Extra person $3. Children under age 6 stay free. Lower rates off-season. Parking: Outdoor, free. AE, DC, DISC, MC, V.

≡≡ Super 8 Motel
2450 Dryden Rd, Moraine, 45439; tel 513/298-0380 or toll free 800/800-8000; fax 513/298-0380 ext 140. ¼ mi N of I-75 exit 50A. Undergoing a slow renovation. Carpet shows wear, but interior is clean. **Rooms:** 72 rms. CI 11am/CO 11am. Nonsmoking rms avail. **Amenities:** 🛁 A/C, cable TV. **Services:** 🚗 🗘 🗘 VCRs for rent at desk. $10 deposit for pets. **Facilities:** 🛗 ⅍ ⅃ Playground. **Rates:** $40–$50 S or D. Extra person $5. Children under age 18 stay free. Parking: Outdoor, free. AE, DC, DISC, MC, V.

≡≡ Travelodge
7911 Brandt Pike, Huber Heights, 45424; tel 513/236-9361 or toll free 800/578-7878; fax 513/236-9361 ext 170. ¼ mi S of I-70 exit 37 on OH 201. Comfortable motel with wide, well-lit hallways and inside stairways. Nearby golf, bowling, and fishing. **Rooms:** 51 rms and stes. CI noon/CO noon. Nonsmoking rms avail. **Amenities:** 🛁 🧊 📺 A/C, satel TV w/movies. **Services:** 🗘 🗘 **Facilities:** 🛗 ⅍ ⅃ **Rates:** Peak (Mem Day–Labor Day) $42–$51 S or D; $61 ste. Extra person $6. Children under age 18 stay free. Lower rates off-season. Parking: Outdoor, free. Rates increase during holidays and special events. AE, CB, DC, DISC, MC, V.

RESTAURANTS 🍴

Anticoli's
3045 Salem Ave; tel 513/277-2264. 3 mi N of downtown Dayton on OH 49. **American/Italian.** Statuary and sculpture, flowers and plantings adorn this upscale family-run restaurant. The sophisticated, red decor features subdued lighting, murals, ceiling fans, and chandeliers. The bar is separated by panels and mirrors from the dining room. Homemade pastas and sauces and veal scaloppine, chicken piccata, and other classics are made from old family recipes. Efficient, friendly, professional service. **FYI:** Reservations recommended. **Open:** Lunch Tues–Sun 11am–2pm; dinner Tues–Thurs 4:30–10pm, Fri–Sat 4:30–11pm. **Prices:** Main courses $9–$15. AE, DC, DISC, MC, V. 🍷 📷 ⅃

⑤ ★ Bob Evans Restaurant
7400 Miller Lane; tel 513/890-5333. ¼ mi off I-75 exit 60; right at 1st traffic light. **American.** You can get breakfast anytime, and the lunch and dinner menus are quite extensive. The favorites are dishes including Bob Evans Farms sausages and the trademark biscuits and honey. Waffles and pancakes topped with fruit are especially delicious. **FYI:** Reservations not accepted. Children's menu. No liquor license. Additional location: 220 Byers Rd, Miamisburg (tel 866-4222). **Open:** Sun–Thurs 6am–10pm, Fri–Sat 6am–11:30pm. **Prices:** Main courses $5–$8. MC, V. 📷 ♥ ⅃

★ Elinor's Amber Rose
1400 Valley St; tel 513/228-2511. 3 mi from downtown; at Stanley Ave. **Continental.** Steeped in European tradition, this former general store and home (some 100 years ago) is now one of the older restaurants in Old North Dayton, originally settled by German immigrants. A wide, grand stairway leads up from the entrance; the cheery dining area has a rustic wood decor and stained-glass panels above the windows. Specially made potato salads, sauerkraut, roast beef, and steaks from the broiler. Delicatessen located in back. **FYI:** Reservations recommended. **Open:** Mon 11am–2pm, Tues–Thurs 11am–9pm, Fri–Sat 11am–10pm. **Prices:** Main courses $9–$13. MC, V. ■ ⅃

♣ 4 Riverplace
4 Riverplace; tel 513/224-0535. **American.** An upscale facility located on the banks of the Great Miami River, with great views and dependably high-caliber food. Signature entrees include Black Forest filet (beef tenderloin filled with sweet bing cherries and topped with ham and sauce béarnaise) and fresh Norwegian salmon du jour (broiled and served with the sauce of the day, such as a strawberry glaze). **FYI:** Reservations recommended. Piano. **Open:** Lunch Mon–Fri 11:30am–2pm; dinner Mon–Thurs 5–9pm, Fri–Sat 5–11pm. **Prices:** Main courses $15–$40. AE, DC, DISC, MC, V. ♥ ⅃

♣ King Cole
In Kettering Tower, 40 N Main St (Downtown); tel 513/222-6771. **Continental.** Chandeliers, candelabra, mirrors, and plush seating areas set the mood at this upscale French dining room. Private nooks and crannies provide the perfect venue for a "secluded" romantic dinner, or for high-powered deal making at lunch. All sauces are made from scratch and only the freshest produce and the best grades of meat are used. In accordance with the classical French tradition, the menu changes seasonally but will include innovative entrees such as grilled swordfish with tomato coulis sauce, New Zealand rack of lamb with pistachio and mint crust, and breast of Muscovy duck in a plum sauce. Each entree is served with the vegetable of the day. **FYI:** Reservations recommended. Jacket required. **Open:** Lunch Mon–Fri 11:30am–2pm; dinner Tues–Sat 5–10pm. **Prices:** Main courses $16–$27; prix fixe $26. AE, CB, DC, DISC, MC, V. ♥ ⅃

★ **Kitty's**

In Citizens Federal Centre, 110 N Main St; tel 513/228-3333. **New American.** Upscale eatery popular with a young and hip crowd. Chef John Schwab says one of his most-requested specialties is pork chops served with spicy chipotle barbecue sauce glaze. Portobello mushrooms, grilled with asparagus and served with balsamic vinaigrette, are among the vegetarian choices. Service is good and friendly. **FYI:** Reservations recommended. **Open:** Lunch Mon–Fri 11am–2pm; dinner Mon–Thurs 5–10pm, Fri–Sat 5–11pm. **Prices:** Main courses $8–$20. AE, CB, DC, DISC, MC, V. 🗹 &

♥★ **The Paragon Club**

797 Miamisburg-Centerville Rd; tel 513/433-1453. **Seafood/Steak.** The cozy dining room is subtly lit by chandeliers, and the private booths along the walls add to the intimate feel. Broiled filet mignon; broiled lamb chops with mint jelly; poached salmon in white sauce with fresh chives and rosemary. **FYI:** Reservations not accepted. Dress code. **Open:** Mon–Thurs 5–10pm, Fri–Sat 5–11pm, Sun 5–9pm. **Prices:** Main courses $12–$26. DC, MC, V. 🔵 &

Peasant Stock

In Town & Country Shopping Center, 424 E Stroop Rd, Kettering; tel 513/293-3900. **New American.** Popular with shoppers, this restaurant features timbered decor, display cupboards of dishes, and stained-glass accents. At the front is a small atrium dining room. Specialties include marinated sesame chicken, chargrilled and served with fresh spinach and topped with an orange-cashew sauce; and spicy New Orleans crabcakes in a pool of beurre vin blanc, topped with a julienne of vegetables. **FYI:** Reservations recommended. Guitar/piano. Children's menu. **Open:** Mon–Thurs 11am–10pm, Fri–Sat 11am–11pm, Sun 10:30am–2:30pm. **Prices:** Main courses $12–$20. AE, CB, DC, DISC, MC, V. 🖼️ &

★ **The Stockyards Inn**

1065 Springfield St; tel 513/254-3576. **American.** This structure has been here since 1900, serving the public as Dayton's oldest inn. The historical ambience is reinforced by the decades worth of letters, photos, and artwork that cover the walls of the entry hall, dining room, and bar. The dining room itself is a relaxed, friendly atmosphere in which to enjoy specialties like barbecued ribs, charbroiled steak, and prime rib. Tender baby back ribs are baked for several hours, and then broiled, before the award-winning Stockyards barbecue sauce is added. The kitchen staff bakes its own key lime and peanut butter pies. **FYI:** Reservations recommended. **Open:** Lunch Mon–Fri 11am–3pm; dinner Mon–Thurs 3–10pm, Fri–Sat 5–11pm, Sat 3–11pm, Sun noon–9pm; brunch Sat 11am–3pm, Sun noon–3pm. **Prices:** Main courses $9–$23. AE, DC, DISC, MC, V. 🍴 &

Welton's

In Wilmington Heights Shopping Center, 4614 Wilmington Pike, Kettering; tel 513/293-2233. 1 mi N of I-675. **American.** An upscale restaurant decorated in pastels, with artwork and mirrors on the walls. The large dining room with a wall of windows is bright and cheery; the small, inner room is more subdued. Filet mignon and carefully trimmed sirloin are favorites on the American menu. **FYI:** Reservations accepted. **Open:** Mon–Thurs 5–10pm, Fri–Sat 5–11pm. **Prices:** Main courses $11–$17. AE, DISC, MC, V. &

ATTRACTIONS 🏛️

Dayton Museum of Natural History

2600 DeWeese Pkwy; tel 513/275-7431. Exhibits include the Charles E Exley Jr Wild Ohio Zoo (which displays the wildlife of Ohio's woodlands, grasslands, and wetlands); the Caryl D Philips Space Theater and Planetarium; and the Bieser Discovery Center, with hands-on exhibits for children of all ages. **Open:** Tues–Thurs 9am–5pm, Fri 9am–9pm, Sat 9am–5pm, Sun noon–5pm. **$**

Dayton Art Institute

456 Belmonte Park N; tel 513/223-5277. European and American art and sculpture are the chief focus here, along with pre-Columbian arts and decorative arts. Also contains an Asian Gallery, the Experiencenter (a participatory exhibition that explores different aspects of art), and a reference library. **Open:** Tues–Sun noon–5pm. **$$**

SunWatch Prehistoric Indian Village

2301 W River Rd; tel 513/268-8199. This National Historic Landmark is a reconstruction of the Fort Ancient Indian settlement established along the banks of the Great Miami River over 800 years ago. Exhibits and displays offer a glimpse into the community's way of life, from their houses to their systems of charting time to the tools that they used. Group tours, workshops, and classes available. **Open:** Peak (Apr–Oct) Mon–Sat 9am–5pm, Sun noon–5pm. Reduced hours off-season. **$$**

United States Air Force Museum

Wright-Patterson Air Force Base; tel 513/255-3286. One of the world's largest museums of military aviation. More than 200 aircraft are on permanent display, from the Wright Brothers' glider to the huge B-52 bomber to the most up-to-date space rockets. (The graves of Orville and Wilbur Wright are in neighboring Woodland Cemetary.) IMAX films are shown for an additional fee. **Open:** Daily 9am–5pm. **Free**

Carillon Historical Park

2001 S Patterson Blvd; tel 513/293-2841. Situated on 65 landscaped acres in the heart of town, the park depicts the history of Dayton and the Miami River valley. Twenty buildings house exhibits such as trains, antique automobiles, bicycles, and a 1796 log house. An original section of the Miami and Erie canal is on the site, fitted with an original lock. Wright Hall pays tribute to Dayton natives Orville and Wilbur Wright with a display of a 1905 Wright Flyer III, the world's first practical airplane. Museum shop; picnic area. **Open:** Tues–Sat 10am–6pm, Sun and hols 1–6pm. **$**

Defiance

Seat of Defiance County, in northwest part of state. Named for Fort Defiance, which in turn was named after Gen "Mad Anthony" Wayne's statement, "I defy the English, the Indians, and all the devils in hell to take it." According to legend, Johnny Appleseed grew his first apple orchards in this Maumee River city. **Information:** Defiance Area Chamber of Commerce, 615 W 3rd St, PO Box 130, Defiance, 43512 (tel 419/782-7946).

MOTELS 🏨

≣≣ Comfort Inn
1900 N Clinton St, 43512; tel 419/784-4900 or toll free 800/221-2222; fax 419/784-5555. OH 66 N of US 24. Fairly new motel, clean and bright. Several restaurants and fast food facilities within half a mile. Fishing, golf, and tennis facilities nearby. Good value. **Rooms:** 62 rms and stes. CI 2pm/CO 11am. Nonsmoking rms avail. **Amenities:** 🐎 A/C, cable TV. **Services:** 🛎 **Facilities:** 🛠 🏌 ♿ Games rm, whirlpool, washer/dryer. **Rates (CP):** $51-$95 S; $61-$95 D; $95 ste. Children under age 18 stay free. Parking: Outdoor, free. AE, CB, DC, DISC, JCB, MC, V.

≣≣ Days Inn Defiance
1835 N Clinton St, 43512; tel 419/782-5555 or toll free 800/726-7502; fax 419/782-8085. Off OH 66 1 block S of US 24. Good reputation. Clean and airy. Lackluster decor in public areas. **Rooms:** 121 rms and stes. CI noon/CO 11am. Nonsmoking rms avail. Rooms are dimly lit. **Amenities:** 🐎 🅟 A/C, satel TV. **Services:** ✕ 🖨 🛎 🐾 Dogs are the only pets accepted. **Facilities:** 🛠 🏌 🅟 ♿ 1 restaurant, 1 bar, whirlpool. **Rates (CP):** $42-$51 S or D; $85 ste. Children under age 12 stay free. Parking: Outdoor, free. AE, CB, DC, JCB, MC, V.

Delaware

Seat of Delaware County, in central part of state. Mineral springs persuaded Native Americans to camp here. Now a sedate college town, Ohio Wesleyan University was founded here in 1842. **Information:** Delaware Area Chamber of Commerce, 27 W Winter St, Delaware, 43015 (tel 614/369-6221).

MOTEL 🏨

≣≣ Travelodge
US 23 N, 43015; tel 614/369-4421 or toll free 800/578-7878; fax 614/369-4421. 2 mi N of Delaware on US 23. Small but clean and cozy motel with basic accommodations. Located right next to Delaware County Fairgrounds, home of the famous Little Brown Jug harness race held every September. Alum Creek Lake State Park is 10 minutes away. **Rooms:** 31 rms. CI noon/CO noon. Nonsmoking rms avail.

Amenities: 🐎 🅟 ▣ A/C, cable TV w/movies. **Services:** 🖨 🛎 🐾 **Facilities:** 65 **Rates:** Peak (Apr-Sept) $45 S; $53-$65 D. Extra person $6. Children under age 18 stay free. Lower rates off-season. Parking: Outdoor, free. AE, DC, DISC, MC, V.

RESTAURANTS 🍴

The Branding Iron
1400 Stratford Rd; tel 614/363-1846. 1 mi E of OH 23. **American/Steak.** Located in an out-of-the-way, rustic spot two miles south of town, this steakhouse has won several awards in past years. Apart from steak, menu standouts include stuffed flounder, swordfish steak, and salmon steak. **FYI:** Reservations recommended. Children's menu. **Open:** Tues-Thurs 5-9:30pm, Fri-Sat 5-10:30pm, Sun noon-8pm. **Prices:** Main courses $8-$21. MC, V. �

⑤ ✦ Bun's of Delaware
6 W Winter St (Downtown); tel 614/363-3731. **American.** Originally a bakery in the early days of Delaware, this restaurant still bakes all its own breads, rolls, pastries, and other desserts. The regional American fare features Copper Mountain quiche, swiss steak, roast turkey with sage dressing, and barbequed ribs. Recommended desserts are chocolate fudge cake, apple dumplings, and chappel pie (with cherries, apples, pecans, and raisins). **FYI:** Reservations recommended. Children's menu. Dress code. Beer and wine only. **Open:** Peak (Mar-Dec) Tues-Thurs 7:30am-8pm, Fri-Sat 7:30am-9pm, Sun 11am-8pm. **Prices:** Main courses $6-$15. AE, DISC, MC, V. ▮ �

ATTRACTION 🏛

Olentangy Indian Caverns
1779 Home Rd; tel 614/548-7917. This maze of natural passages and rooms occupying three levels of natural limestone caverns 55-105 feet below ground once served as a haven for the Wyandotte tribe. Other attractions on the site include re-creations of a 19th-century frontier camp and a Native American village. Indian Museum, campsites, swimming pool, and snack bar. Guided half-hour cavern tours available. **Open:** Apr-Oct, daily 9:30am-5pm. $$$

Dublin

See Columbus

Eastlake

A Cleveland suburb. **Information:** Eastlake Chamber of Commerce, 35150 Lake Shore Blvd, Eastlake, 44095 (tel 216/951-3600).

HOTEL ▥

≣≣≣ Clarion Hotel & Conference Center

35000 Curtis Blvd, 44095; tel 216/953-8000 or toll free 800/ 221-2222; fax 216/953-1706. Conveniently situated in a commercial area, near major interstates; 15 minutes from downtown Cleveland, 30 minutes from airport. Lobby has light, cheerful colors, fresh flowers, contemporary decor. Caters to business travelers. **Rooms:** 115 rms and stes. Executive level. CI noon/CO noon. Nonsmoking rms avail. **Amenities:** ▦ ⓘ A/C, cable TV w/movies, refrig, dataport. **Services:** ✕ ▭ ▣ ▦ ▣ ↵ ⟳ Babysitting. Golf, tennis, and racquetball can be arranged through the conference planning department. **Facilities:** ▣ ▦ ▣ ☐ ⅙ 1 restaurant, 1 bar (w/entertainment), sauna. Exceptional meeting facilities. Restaurant has DJ entertainment on weekends. Yesterday's nightclub is popular with guests. **Rates:** $89 S; $99 D; $125–$225 ste. Extra person $10. Children under age 18 stay free. AP rates avail. Parking: Outdoor, free. AE, CB, DC, DISC, EC, ER, JCB, MC, V.

Elyria

Seat of Lorain County, in north part of state. Retailing and industrial city at junction of east and west branches of the Black River. Plastics, automobile parts, and tools are the city's chief products. **Information:** Lorain County Chamber of Commerce, 6100 S Broadway, #201, Lorain, 44053 (tel 216/ 233-6500 or 323-9424).

HOTEL ▥

≣≣≣ Holiday Inn

1825 Lorian Blvd, 44035; tel 216/324-5411 or toll free 800/ 321-7333; fax 216/324-2785. Clean, new looking, six-story building with standard lobby and comfortable furnishings. **Rooms:** 250 rms and stes. CI 3pm/CO noon. Nonsmoking rms avail. **Amenities:** ▦ ⓘ A/C, cable TV w/movies. Some units w/terraces. **Services:** ✕ ▦ ▣ ↵ ⟳ Babysitting. **Facilities:** ▣ ▦ ▣ ⅙ 1 restaurant, 3 bars, washer/dryer. Cabana Bar and Grille at poolside. Children with parents eat free. **Rates:** Peak (mid-June–Labor Day) $89 S; $99 D; $125 ste. Extra person $10. Children under age 19 stay free. Lower rates off-season. Parking: Outdoor, free. Bed-and-breakfast special. AE, DC, DISC, MC, V.

MOTELS

≣≣ Comfort Inn

739 Leona St, 44035; tel 216/324-7676 or toll free 800/ 228-5150; fax 216/324-4046. Standard two-story motel with ordinary exterior. Large lobby has skylights, brass rails, and nice furnishings. **Rooms:** 66 rms. Executive level. CI 2pm/ CO 11am. Nonsmoking rms avail. **Amenities:** ▦ A/C, cable TV. Some units w/minibars, some w/whirlpools. **Services:** ▣ ↵ ⟳ Pet fee $5. **Facilities:** ▣ ⅙ Washer/dryer. Free use

of Scandinavian health spa next door for adults 18 and over. **Rates (CP):** Peak (June–Aug) $40–$90 S or D. Extra person $6. Children under age 18 stay free. Lower rates off-season. Parking: Outdoor, free. AE, DC, DISC, MC, V.

UNRATED Days Inn

621 Midway Blvd, 44035; tel 216/324-4444 or toll free 800/ DAYS-INN; fax 216/324-2065. Exit 8 off OH Tpk, ¼ mi N on OH 57. Attractive lobby with tile floor and large staircase. **Rooms:** 101 rms. CI 3pm/CO noon. Nonsmoking rms avail. Some family-style rooms have two double beds and double sofa. **Amenities:** ▦ ⓘ A/C, cable TV w/movies. 1 unit w/whirlpool. **Services:** ▣ ↵ Twice-daily maid svce. **Facilities:** ▣ ▦ ⅙ Games rm, sauna, washer/dryer. **Rates (CP):** Peak (May–Aug) $40–$82 S; $50–$90 D. Extra person $8. Children under age 13 stay free. Lower rates off-season. Parking: Outdoor, free. AE, DISC, MC, V.

≣≣ Econo Lodge

523 Griswold Rd, 44035; tel 216/324-3911 or toll free 800/ 553-2666; fax 216/324-3911. At the Midway Mall. Fully remodeled and renovated with nice, clean lobby. **Rooms:** 120 rms. CI 3pm/CO noon. Nonsmoking rms avail. **Amenities:** ▦ ⓘ A/C, satel TV. **Services:** ▣ ↵ Cedar Point discounts. **Facilities:** ▣ ▦ ⅙ Games rm, washer/dryer. **Rates:** Peak (May–Sept) $34–$91 S or D. Lower rates off-season. Parking: Outdoor, free. AE, DISC, MC, V.

Englewood

MOTELS ▥

≣≣ Cross Country Inn

9325 N Main St, 45415; tel 513/836-8339 or toll free 800/ 621-1429. Well maintained, with spotless, comfortable rooms. **Rooms:** 120 rms. CI 1pm/CO noon. Nonsmoking rms avail. **Amenities:** ▦ A/C, satel TV w/movies. **Services:** ↵ Drive-through window for registration and checkout. **Facilities:** ▣ ⅙ **Rates:** $34–$48 S or D. Extra person $7. Children under age 18 stay free. Parking: Outdoor, free. AE, CB, DC, DISC, MC, V.

≣≣≣ Hampton Inn Northwest

20 Rockridge Rd, 45322; tel 513/832-2222 or toll free 800/ HAMPTON; fax 513/832-3859. Offers comfortable, standard rooms and a bright, open lobby. **Rooms:** 130 rms and stes. CI 4pm/CO noon. Nonsmoking rms avail. Rooms with king-size beds have sofa beds. **Amenities:** ▦ ⓘ A/C, satel TV w/movies, dataport. Suite has mini-kitchen. **Services:** ▦ ▣ ↵ **Facilities:** ▦ ▣ ⅙ **Rates:** Peak (Mem Day–Labor Day) $51–$60 S or D; $65 ste. Children under age 18 stay free. Lower rates off-season. Parking: Outdoor, free. AE, CB, DC, DISC, MC, V.

RESTAURANT ⑪

♥★ Shades of Ruby

555 W National Rd; tel 513/832-3922. On US 40. **American/Continental.** Owner Ruby Meyers takes pride in the gracious atmosphere of her restaurant. The dining room is dimly lit, with a raised dining area and several (very in-demand) booths. Kitchen specialties include Black Forest fillet (beef tenderloin filled with red bing cherries and topped with ham and béarnaise sauce) and chicken Wellington (boneless breast of chicken served with special seasoning and a supreme sauce). Corn fritters with maple syrup are served with all meals. **FYI:** Reservations accepted. Piano/singer. Children's menu. **Open:** Mon–Thurs 5–9pm, Fri–Sat 5–10:30pm. **Prices:** Main courses $9–$16. AE, DISC, MC, V. ♥ ⬛⬛♥&

Findlay

Seat of Hancock County, in northwest part of state. Many elaborate Victorian mansions were built in the town's brief oil and gas boom in the late 19th century, of which several examples still remain. **Information:** Findlay-Hancock County Chamber of Commerce, 123 E Main Cross St, Findlay, 45840-4816 (tel 419/422-3313).

HOTEL 🏨

≣≣≣ Findlay Inn

200 E Main Cross St, 45840; tel 419/422-5682 or toll free 800/825-1445; fax 419/422-5581. Exit 157 off I-75. One block west of the Blanchard River. Comprised of three floors with grand, open staircase and glass elevator. Attracts business travelers, locals, couples, and students. Ambience is one of quiet elegance. YMCA, two blocks away, allows guests to use its Olympic-size pool, racquetball courts, weight room, and video game room. **Rooms:** 80 rms and stes. CI 3pm/CO noon. Nonsmoking rms avail. Suite has two large rooms. **Amenities:** 🛁 & ♦ A/C, cable TV. **Services:** ✕ ☑ 🚐 ☒ ⇦ Twice-daily maid svce, babysitting. Mon–Fri, complimentary continental breakfast and newspaper delivered to room at time requested by guest. Also a shoe-shine token (shoe-shine area just off lobby) is included. Complimentary shuttle service provided anywhere in the city; a fee is charged for stops outside the city. **Facilities:** 🛐 ⚓ 🏌 ⛱ & 1 restaurant, 1 bar (w/entertainment), sauna, steam rm, whirlpool. Jacques Restaurant is tastefully done in pink and black, with a raised area for booths along one side. The lounge offers a prime rib buffet and a soup and salad bar—both quite popular with guests and locals. A 4½-mile running trail along Blanchard River and through parks begins and ends at motel; maps at front desk. **Rates (CP):** $50–$95 S or D; $125–$150 ste. Extra person $6. Children under age 10 stay free. Parking: Outdoor, free. AE, CB, DC, DISC, MC, V.

MOTELS

≣≣ Cross Country Inn

1951 Broad Ave, 45840; tel 419/424-0466 or toll free 800/621-1429; fax 419/424-1043. ½ mi E of exit 159 off I-75. Exceptionally spotless interior and grounds. Three floors, and all rooms entered from parking lot; no interior hallways. Housekeeping and maintenance program are hallmarks. **Rooms:** 120 rms. CI noon/CO noon. Nonsmoking rms avail. Clean rooms. **Amenities:** 🛁 ♦ A/C, satel TV w/movies. **Services:** 🚐 ⇦ Drive-through registration and checkout window. Shuttle to Findlay airport or car rental can be arranged. Nearby restaurants provide room service. **Facilities:** 🛐 ⚓ 🏌 & **Rates:** $33–$47 S or D. Children under age 18 stay free. Parking: Outdoor, free. Senior discount 25%. Stays of five days or more, $28/day. AE, DC, DISC, MC, V.

≣≣≣ Days Inn Findlay

1305 W Main Cross St, 45840; tel 419/423-7171 or toll free 800/DAYS-INN; fax 419/423-8013. Exit 157 off I-75. Located on the northwest edge of Findlay just off I-75, the building is 30 years old, but is in excellent condition inside and out. **Rooms:** 113 rms and stes. Executive level. CI 3pm/CO 11am. Nonsmoking rms avail. **Amenities:** 🛁 & 📞 A/C, satel TV w/movies, dataport, in-rm safe. Some units w/terraces, 1 w/whirlpool. **Services:** ✕ ☒ ⇦ Children's program, babysitting. Masseur can be arranged. Children's program in summer only. **Facilities:** 🛐 ⚓ 🏌 ☕ 🏊 🖥 & 1 restaurant, 1 bar (w/entertainment), games rm, spa, playground. Fitness center next door is owned by the motel and is free to guests. **Rates:** Peak (May–Oct) $48–$75 S or D; $114 ste. Extra person $6. Children under age 18 stay free. Lower rates off-season. Parking: Outdoor, free. Valentines Day and New Year's Eve packages. AE, CB, DC, DISC, JCB, MC, V.

≣≣ Knights Inn

1901 Broad Ave, 45840; tel 419/424-1133 or toll free 800/843-5644; fax 419/425-9810. Complete renovation underway. Good value. **Rooms:** 100 rms and effic. CI 2pm/CO 11am. Nonsmoking rms avail. All beds are either king-size or queen-size. **Amenities:** 🛁 & A/C, cable TV. **Services:** ☒ ⇦ **Facilities:** 🛐 ⚓ 🏌 & Pool is small and shallow. **Rates (CP):** Peak (June–Sept) $33–$40 S or D; $42 effic. Extra person $6. Children under age 18 stay free. Lower rates off-season. Parking: Outdoor, free. AE, CB, DC, DISC, MC, V.

Fremont

Seat of Sandusky County, in north part of state. This small industrial town has also played an important role in American history: it was the site of the Battle of Fort Stephenson during the War of 1812, and Rutherford B Hayes lived and is buried here. **Information:** Fremont/Sandusky County Convention & Visitors Bureau, 1510 E State St, PO Box 643, Fremont, 43420 (tel 419/332-4470 or toll free 800/255-8070).

MOTELS 🏨

▤ The Great Lakes Motel

1737 E State St, 43420; tel 419/334-9797. 1 mi E of Sandusky. Somewhat off the beaten path, a mile from downtown, this Mom-and-Pop operation appeals to families due to the large play area for small children. It's an old property, but has been kept in very good repair. **Rooms:** 18 rms. CI 11am/CO 11am. Nonsmoking rms avail. Small but clean. Furnishings in good repair; however, some bathrooms have the old-style linoleum on the floors. **Amenities:** 🛎 🕎 A/C, cable TV w/movies. **Services:** 🍴 **Facilities:** 🏃 🕭 Playground. **Rates:** $22–$54 S; $28–$64 D. Extra person $4. Children under age 14 stay free. Parking: Indoor/outdoor, free. DISC, MC, V.

▤▤▤ Holiday Inn

3422 Port Clinton Rd, 43420; tel 419/334-2682 or toll free 800/HOLIDAY; fax 419/334-4086. Exit 6 off US 53, S of OH Tpk. Comfortable motel offering upscale service. **Rooms:** 159 rms. CI 3pm/CO 11am. Nonsmoking rms avail. Cheery rooms have king-size beds or double beds. Views are not the best—rooms overlook a truck stop and highways. **Amenities:** 🛎 🕎 📺 A/C, satel TV w/movies, dataport. **Services:** ✕ 🖨 🍴 Babysitting. **Facilities:** 🗗 🏃 🔲 🕭 1 restaurant, 1 bar, games rm, washer/dryer. Whitaker's is an action bar, with TVs and pool tables. The restaurant, open 6am–10pm daily, is very neat and tastefully done. An outside putt-putt golf course is in the courtyard near the pool. Guests can use the local YMCA, about 2 miles south of the property. **Rates:** Peak (June–Aug) $80–$119 S or D. Children under age 18 stay free. Lower rates off-season. Parking: Outdoor, free. AE, CB, DC, DISC, JCB, MC, V.

▤▤ Travelodge

1750 Cedar St, 43420; tel 419/334-9517 or toll free 800/578-7878. 1st traffic light S of US 20 bypass on OH 19. This is a good-looking property, located behind a Denny's Restaurant. **Rooms:** 50 rms, stes, and effic. CI 11am/CO 11am. Nonsmoking rms avail. The bathrooms are very bright. Each room has a recliner. **Amenities:** 🛎 🕎 📺 A/C, cable TV w/movies, dataport. **Services:** 🖨 🍴 **Facilities:** 🗗 🏃 🕭 **Rates:** Peak (June–Aug) $51–$61 S; $57–$67 D; $63–$73 ste; $57–$67 effic. Extra person $6. Children under age 18 stay free. Lower rates off-season. Parking: Outdoor, free. Senior discounts. CB, DC, DISC, MC, V.

Gallipolis

Seat of Gallia County, in south part of state. This "City of the Gauls" was founded by French settlers in 1790, making it the second permanent settlement in the state. **Information:** Gallia County Chamber of Commerce, 16 State St, PO Box 465, Gallipolis, 45631-0465 (tel 614/446-0596).

MOTELS 🏨

▤ Best Western Inn

918 2nd Ave, 45631; tel 614/446-3373 or toll free 800/528-1234; fax 614/446-1337. OH 7 exit off I-35; 3 mi S. Basic accommodations. **Rooms:** 56 rms. CI 2pm/CO 11am. Nonsmoking rms avail. **Amenities:** 🛎 A/C, cable TV. **Services:** 🍴 🖨 Warm, friendly hospitality; family owner/managers live on premises. **Rates:** $35 S; $40–$55 D. Extra person $5. Children under age 12 stay free. Parking: Outdoor, free. AE, CB, DC, DISC, MC, V.

▤▤ Econo Lodge Holzer Medical Center

260 Jackson Pike, 45631; tel 614/446-7071 or toll free 800/553-2666; fax 614/446-7071. Jct OH 160/US 35. Good family value 8 miles from Bob Evans Farm, which features horseback riding, hay rides, canoeing, museum, gift shops, and restaurant. There's a Bob Evans Festival in mid-Oct. **Rooms:** 48 rms. CI 2pm/CO 11am. Nonsmoking rms avail. **Amenities:** 🛎 A/C, cable TV. **Services:** ✕ 🍴 **Facilities:** 🕭 **Rates:** Peak (May–Oct) $46–$60 S or D. Extra person $5. Children under age 12 stay free. Lower rates off-season. Parking: Outdoor, free. AE, DC, DISC, JCB, MC, V.

▤▤ Super 8 Motel

321 Upper River Rd, 45631; tel 614/446-8080 or toll free 800/800-8000; fax 614/446-8080. Jct OH 160/US 35. A good value for families with easy access off highway. **Rooms:** 49 rms and stes. CI 1pm/CO 11am. Nonsmoking rms avail. **Amenities:** 🛎 🕎 A/C, cable TV. 1 unit w/whirlpool. **Services:** 🍴 Very friendly and helpful staff. **Facilities:** 🗗 🔲 🕭 Whirlpool. Beautiful glass-enclosed pool area. **Rates (CP):** $40–$50 S or D; $65–$80 ste. Extra person $5. Children under age 12 stay free. Parking: Outdoor, free. AE, CB, DC, DISC, JCB, MC, V.

Geneva-on-the-Lake

See also Ashtabula

ATTRACTIONS 🏛

Erieview Park "Rides and Slides"

Tel 216/466-8650. A small amusement park with nine adult rides, nine children's rides, and a giant two-flume water slide. Picnic areas, restaurant, and nightclub also on site. **Open:** Mem Day–Labor Day, daily sunrise–sunset. **$$$$**

Old Firehouse Winery

5499 Lake Rd; tel 216/466-9300 or toll free 800/862-6751. Unique winery located on the Lake Erie shoreline in the village's first fire station. Award-winning wines are made on the premises and sold by the glass, bottle, or case. Visitors can see "Old Betsy," the village's first fire truck, and survey the collection of fire paraphernalia. **Open:** Peak (mid-May–Sept) daily noon–midnight. Reduced hours off-season. **Free**

Hamilton

Seat of Butler County, in southwest part of state. Originally founded in 1791 as Fort Hamilton, a Northwest Territory outpost on the Great Miami River. A variety of restored homes and several historic districts preserve much of the city's 19th-century heritage. **Information:** Greater Hamilton Chamber of Commerce, 201 Dayton St, Hamilton, 45011 (tel 513/844-1500).

HOTEL

☰☰☰ The Hamilton Hotel & Meeting Center

One Riverfront Plaza, 45011; tel 513/896-6200 or toll free 800/522-5570, 800/552-5570 in OH; fax 513/896-9463. 1 block N of courthouse on Riverfront Plaza; E side of river. Near banks of Great Miami River, this 11-year-old brick building is imposing from a distance and up close. Very neat, clean, upscale hotel with lots of frills. **Rooms:** 124 rms and stes. Executive level. CI 3pm/CO noon. Nonsmoking rms avail. **Amenities:** A/C, cable TV w/movies. **Services:** Free transportation to Cincinnati airport can be arranged. Travel agency located just off hotel lobby. **Facilities:** 1 restaurant, 1 bar. Pool area with wide sun deck surrounded by 4′ sculptured brick wall. Alexander's Grille is very popular locally. Guests may use facilities of nearby YMCA and Racquetball Club. **Rates:** $69–$77 S or D; $120 ste. Extra person $8. Children under age 18 stay free. Parking: Outdoor, free. AE, CB, DC, DISC, MC, V.

RESTAURANT

ⓢ ★ The Academy

343 N 3rd St; tel 513/868-7171. At Village St. **Regional American.** You'll find romantic yet homey ambience at this local hangout. Two functional marble fireplaces, timbered rafters, a chandelier, lots of windows, and mirrors make this an attractive dining room. Shrimp marinara and chicken pasta (chicken breast tenders served with seasoned pasta and white sauce) are favorites. **FYI:** Reservations accepted. Karaoke/piano. Children's menu. **Open:** Lunch Mon–Fri 11am–2pm; dinner Mon–Thurs 5–10pm, Fri–Sat 5–11pm. **Prices:** Main courses $13–$16. AE, MC, V.

ATTRACTION

Americana Amusement Park

5757 Middletown-Hamilton Rd, Middletown; tel 513/539-7339. An 80-acre park with more than 100 rides and attractions. Highlights include two roller coasters, a log flume, puppet shows, and a petting zoo. There's also a swimming lake and several picnic areas. **Open:** Peak (Mem Day–Labor Day) Mon–Thurs 11am–9pm, Fri–Sat 11am–11pm, Sun 11am–10pm. Reduced hours off-season. $$$$

Holland

See Toledo

Huber Heights

See Dayton

Kelleys Island

For lodgings and dining see Port Clinton, Sandusky

ATTRACTION

Kelleys Island State Park

Tel 419/746-2546. Located in the Lake Erie Islands, approximately 10 mi NE of Port Clinton and accessible by ferry from Sandusky or Marblehead. The park offers a campground with 129 nonelectric sites, picnic areas (one with a shelter), boat ramps, fishing, and 100-foot swimming beach. Five miles of hiking trails. Two Rent-A-Camp units (furnished with tent, picnic table, cooler, cook stove, and lantern) available during summer season; call for details. **Open:** Daily 24 hours. **Free**

Kent

Manufacturing city near the northeastern edge of Akron. Founded in 1805 as Franklin Mills, Kent is now best known as the home of Kent State University. **Information:** Kent Area Chamber of Commerce, 152 Franklin Ave, Kent, 44240 (tel 330/673-9855).

HOTEL

☰☰ University Inn

540 S Water St, 44240; tel 330/678-0123; fax 330/678-7356. On OH 43, 3 mi N of I-76. Seven-story building with remodeled lobby. Good budget hotel for traveling families. **Rooms:** 100 rms, stes, and effic. CI 9/CO 11am. Nonsmoking rms avail. Some one- and two-bedroom family units available. **Amenities:** A/C, cable TV, refrig. Some units w/terraces. **Services:** Sea World and Geauga Lake discounts available. **Facilities:** Washer/dryer. **Rates:** Peak (June–Aug) $35–$75 S; $45–$125 D; $45–$125 ste; $45–$125 effic. Extra person $5. Children under age 16 stay free. Lower rates off-season. Parking: Outdoor, free. AE, CB, DC, DISC, MC, V.

MOTELS

☰☰ Days Inn

4422 Edson Rd, 44240; tel 330/677-9400 or toll free 800/DAYS-INN; fax 330/677-9456. Gray stone building just off highway with outside walkways. Minimal lobby. **Rooms:** 67

rms and stes. CI 3pm/CO 11am. Nonsmoking rms avail. **Amenities:** ⬜ A/C, cable TV. 1 unit w/whirlpool. **Services:** ⬜ Late check-in at drive-through window. **Facilities:** ⬜ ⬜ **Rates (CP):** Peak (May–Sept) $63 S; $69 D; $129 ste. Extra person $6. Children under age 18 stay free. Lower rates off-season. Parking: Outdoor, free. Sea World and Geauga Lake packages avail. AE, DC, DISC, JCB, MC, V.

≣≣≣ Holiday Inn
4363 OH 43, 44240; tel 330/678-0101 or toll free 800/ HOLIDAY; fax 330/677-5001. At I-76. Nice landscaping, with brick and glass blocks. Lobby has traditional furnishings. Holideck with canopied bar. **Rooms:** 153 rms. CI 3pm/CO noon. Nonsmoking rms avail. Outside corridors to rooms. **Amenities:** ⬜ ⬜ A/C, cable TV w/movies, voice mail. **Services:** ✕ ⬜ ⬜ ⬜ Car-rental desk. Breakfast included in winter. Deposit required for pets. Exceptionally friendly and helpful staff. **Facilities:** ⬜ ⬜ ⬜ ⬜ 1 restaurant, 1 bar (w/entertainment), games rm, whirlpool, washer/dryer. Restaurant and lounge in atrium off lobby; children eat free when adult purchases an entree. **Rates:** Peak (June–Aug) $69–$89 S or D. Children under age 19 stay free. Lower rates off-season. AP and MAP rates avail. Parking: Outdoor, free. AE, DC, DISC, MC, V.

≣≣≣ The Inn of Kent
303 E Main St, 44240 (Kent State University); tel 330/ 673-3411; fax 330/673-9878. Modest motel set back beyond Side Door Restaurant parking lot. Exterior walkways. **Rooms:** 57 rms and effic. CI 2pm/CO noon. Nonsmoking rms avail. **Amenities:** ⬜ A/C, cable TV. **Services:** ✕ ⬜ ⬜ ⬜ **Facilities:** ⬜ ⬜ ⬜ 1 restaurant (see "Restaurants" below), 1 bar (w/entertainment), washer/dryer. Fully enclosed pool adjacent to lobby. **Rates:** Peak (June–Sept) $45–$65 S; $48–$75 D; $45–$75 effic. Extra person $3. Children under age 18 stay free. Lower rates off-season. Parking: Outdoor, free. AE, CB, DC, DISC, MC, V.

UNRATED Knights Inn
4423 OH 43, 44240; tel 330/678-5250 or toll free 800/ 843-5644; fax 330/678-7014. At I-76. Very modest low-rise facility with exterior walkways, set back from highway. Good buy for budget travelers. **Rooms:** 100 rms and effic. CI 3pm/ CO noon. Nonsmoking rms avail. **Amenities:** ⬜ A/C, cable TV w/movies. **Services:** ⬜ ⬜ **Facilities:** ⬜ ⬜ Pool is very private, surrounded by high fence and trees. **Rates:** Peak (May–Labor Day) $34–$43 S; $38–$49 D; $38–$49 effic. Extra person $5. Children under age 18 stay free. Lower rates off-season. Parking: Outdoor, free. AE, DC, DISC, MC, V.

RESTAURANTS 🍴

Akropolis Family Restaurant
707 N Mantua St; tel 330/678-2981. **Greek/Italian.** A small fountain adds a welcoming charm to the dining room. Greek salads and gyros as well as full meals (including some vegetarian options, like falafel) are offered. **FYI:** Reservations recom-

mended. Children's menu. Beer and wine only. **Open:** Mon–Thurs 6am–9pm, Fri–Sat 6am–10pm, Sun 7am–4pm. **Prices:** Main courses $4–$13. No CC. 🚹 🔳

Pufferbelly Ltd
152 Franklin Ave; tel 330/673-1771. **Eclectic.** Restored to its original Tuscan Revival design, this 1875 two-story brick train depot boasts high ceilings, distinctive windows and woodwork, and a display of historical artifacts. The food is not old-fashioned, however. The house special is a California Dagwood: grilled eggplant, tomato, zucchini, red onions, and alfalfa sprouts, topped with mozzarella and served on a multigrain bun. Espresso and cappuccino available. **FYI:** Reservations accepted. Children's menu. Additional location: 30 Depot St, Berea (tel 216/234-1144). **Open:** Mon–Thurs 11am–10pm, Fri–Sat 11am–11pm, Sun 11am–9pm. **Prices:** Main courses $4–$15. AE, DISC, MC, V. 💗 🔳 🔺 🚹

The Side Door Restaurant
In the Inn of Kent, 303 E Main St; tel 330/678-5542. 1 block from Kent State University. **American.** An extensive menu includes Heart Healthy and vegetarian selections and a quiche of the day. Chicken breast fillet sautéed with green pepper, onion, mushrooms, and almonds, served over a bed of long-grain and wild rice, is a house specialty. **FYI:** Reservations accepted. Karaoke/rock/singer. Children's menu. **Open:** Sun–Mon 7am–2:30pm, Tues–Sat 7am–9pm. **Prices:** Main courses $4–$16. AE, DISC, MC, V. 💗 ⬜ 🚹 🔳

ATTRACTION 📷

Kent State University
Main St; tel 330/672-2444 or toll free 800/988-5368. Established in 1910, this university consists of 20 schools and colleges, and approximately 33,000 students. A memorial to the four students killed and nine injured by National Guard troops during an anti–Vietnam War protest overlooks the University Commons. Nonacademic campus tours can be arranged by the University News and Information Office. **Open:** Mon–Fri 8am–5pm. **Free**

Kettering
See Dayton

Lakewood
See Cleveland

Lancaster
Seat of Fairfield County, in south-central part of state. A quaint downtown square includes 19 historic buildings, with walking tour tape available from the local visitors bureau. Union Gen William Tecumseh Sherman was born here in

1820. **Information:** Lancaster-Fairfield County Chamber of Commerce, 1 N Broad, PO Box 2450, Lancaster, 43130-5450 (tel 614/653-8251).

MOTELS

≣≣ AmeriHost

1721 River Valley Circle N, 43130; tel 614/654-5111; fax 614/654-5108. Very nice accommodations, with easy access off major highway. Located right next to River Valley Mall's shops and eateries and just north of historic section of Lancaster. Several golf courses are within minutes; a putt-putt course is right next door. **Rooms:** 60 rms and stes. CI 3pm/CO noon. Nonsmoking rms avail. **Amenities:** 🔒 ⚓ A/C, cable TV w/movies, in-rm safe. Some units w/terraces, some w/whirlpools. **Services:** ⌷ ⌷ Twice-daily maid svce, car-rental desk. **Facilities:** 🛋 🖳 🕦 ⅍ Sauna, whirlpool. **Rates (CP):** $60 S; $65 D; $90–$115 ste. Extra person $5. Children under age 18 stay free. Parking: Outdoor, free. AE, DC, DISC, MC, V.

≣≣≣ Best Western

1858 N Memorial Dr, 43130; tel 614/653-3040 or toll free 800/528-1234; fax 614/653-1172. Excellent mid-range accommodations located two miles from historic downtown area of Lancaster and close to many restaurants and lounges. **Rooms:** 168 rms and effic. CI 4pm/CO noon. Nonsmoking rms avail. **Amenities:** 🔒 ⚓ A/C, satel TV w/movies. **Services:** ✗ ⌷ ⌷ ⚓ **Facilities:** 🛋 🖳 ⅍ 1 restaurant, 1 bar (w/entertainment). Small putting green on premises. **Rates:** $50–$55 S; $52–$55 D; $62–$65 effic. Extra person $7. Children under age 19 stay free. Parking: Outdoor, free. AE, CB, DC, DISC, JCB, MC, V.

RESTAURANT

★ Shaw's Restaurant

123 N Broad St; tel 614/654-1842. In the historic section. **American.** Located in the center of the historic section of town, near the Sherman House, this restaurant serving American cuisine with a French accent is a historic site in its own right. Sunday brunch, offering the likes of eggs Benedict and raisin bread French toast, is very popular. Dinner favorites are barbeque baby back ribs with Shaw's special recipe sauce, swordfish with shiitake mushrooms, and veal and lamb chops. **FYI:** Reservations accepted. Children's menu. Dress code. **Open:** Breakfast Mon–Sat 7am–10:30pm, Sun 7am–11:30pm; lunch Mon–Sat 11:30am–2:30pm, Sun 11:30am–3pm; dinner Mon–Sat 5–10pm, Sun 3–9pm. **Prices:** Main courses $9–$22. MC, V. 🍴 ⅍

ATTRACTIONS

The Georgian

105 E Wheeling St; tel 614/654-9923. Completed in 1832, this two-story Georgian mansion with many Regency features—such as curved bays and a massive portico with five fluted Ionic columns—is an important part of Lancaster's Square 13 Historic District. Furnishings are from the 1830s. Gift shop. **Open:** Apr–Nov, Tues–Sun 1–4pm. **$**

Sherman House

137 E Main St; tel 614/687-5891. Built in 1811, this modest frame house was the birthplace of Civil War Gen William Tecumseh Sherman and Sen John Sherman. The original 1811 section portrays the home as it was when the Shermans lived here; a Victorian addition houses Civil War exhibits and family memorabilia. Open January, February, and March by appointment only. **Open:** Apr–Nov, Tues–Sun 1–4pm. **$**

Lebanon

MOTELS

≣≣ Houston Inn

4026 OH 42, 45036; tel 513/398-7277 or toll free 800/732-4741. 2 mi N of Mason on OH 42. A 40-year-old building that is now being renovated, this is fast becoming a solid, comfortable lodging. Nearby shopping malls, antique shops, and museums. **Rooms:** 48 rms and stes. CI 2pm/CO 11am. Nonsmoking rms avail. Renovated rooms are in excellent shape; others are in good shape as far as comfort and cleanliness. Suites have sofa beds. **Amenities:** 🔒 A/C, cable TV. **Services:** ⌷ ⌷ **Facilities:** 🛋 🕴 1 restaurant (see "Restaurants" below). **Rates:** Peak (June–Aug) $62–$70 S or D; $65–$70 ste. Extra person $6. Children under age 11 stay free. Lower rates off-season. Parking: Outdoor, free. AE, CB, DC, DISC, MC, V.

≣≣ Shaker Inn

600 Cincinnati Ave (US 42 S), 45036; tel 513/932-7575 or toll free 800/752-6151. A quality mom-and-pop operation with well-tended grounds. Very personable. Near shopping malls, antique shops, and museums. **Rooms:** 24 rms and stes. CI 2pm/CO 11am. Nonsmoking rms avail. Immaculate rooms with large welcome mats in front of each. **Amenities:** 🔒 A/C, cable TV, refrig. Microwaves in some rooms and available on request. Suites have kitchenettes or full kitchens. **Services:** ⌷ Babysitting. **Facilities:** 🛋 🕴 ⅍ **Rates:** Peak (June–Aug) $57–$62 S or D; $75–$85 ste. Extra person $6. Children under age 12 stay free. Lower rates off-season. Parking: Outdoor, free. Rates sometimes increased during special events, such as jazz festival. AE, DISC, MC, V.

RESTAURANTS

★ Golden Lamb Inn

27 S Broadway; tel 513/932-5065. At Main St. **American.** Open since 1803, this one takes diners back to the years when Ohio represented the western frontier. Servers are dressed in Shaker-style costumes and walls are lined with pictures, antique utensils, and old wicker chairs. Chandeliers and wall lanterns provide warm, subtle light. Highlighted appetizers

include tomato-celery soup, sauerkraut balls with spicy cocktail sauce, and country pâté with black peppercorns. Roast leg of spring lamb with mint jelly, roast Long Island duckling with orange sauce and wild rice dressing, and braised lamb shank are some favored entrees. **FYI:** Reservations recommended. Piano. Children's menu. Dress code. **Open:** Lunch daily 11am–3pm; dinner Mon–Sat 5–9pm, Sun noon–8pm. **Prices:** Main courses $14–$19. AE, CB, DC, DISC, MC, V. ♥ ▬▮⬛✅♿

⑤ ✹ Houston Inn
4026 US 42; tel 513/398-7377. 2 mi N of Mason on OH 42. **American.** The impressive dining room is divided by half-walls into cubicles of four to six tables, making for more cozy dining. Tiffany-style hanging lamps add a warm touch. The 32-item salad bar is popular, and the kitchen is known for its prime rib (roasted overnight and served au jus) and battered frogs' legs. Each entree comes with two side dishes and a salad. **FYI:** Reservations recommended. Dress code. **Open:** Tues–Thurs 3:30–10pm, Fri–Sat 3:30–10:30pm, Sun 11am–8pm. **Prices:** Main courses $9–$15. AE, DC, DISC, MC, V. ♥ ⬛♿

ATTRACTIONS 🏛

Fort Ancient State Memorial
OH 350; tel 513/932-4421. Located on a 245-foot bluff on the banks of the Little Miami River, this is an important North American archeological site for two prehistoric Native American cultures, the Hopewell and Fort Ancient. Fort Ancient's earthworks, spanning 120 acres with earthen walls up to 23 feet high, are the second-largest in the nation. An onsite museum displays archeological finds from the site, along with other Native American artifacts. **Open:** Peak (Mem Day–Labor Day) Wed–Sun 10am–8pm. Reduced hours off-season. **$$**

Warren County Historical Society Museum
105 S Broadway; tel 513/932-1817. The heritage of Warren County is documented via seven rooms of fossil exhibits, Native American artifacts, authentic Shaker furnishings, and local historical archives. **Open:** Tues–Sat 9am–4pm, Sun noon–4pm. **$**

Lexington

See Mansfield

Lima

Seat of Allen County. The Ottawa River meanders through this northwestern Ohio industrial and agricultural center. In October 1933, members of the notorious Dillinger gang murdered the town sheriff during a jail delivery. The nationwide manhunt led to Dillinger's death and the end of the gang. **Information:** Lima/Allen County Convention & Visitors Bureau, 147 N Main St, Lima, 45801 (tel 419/222-6045).

MOTELS 🏨

▤▤ Econo Lodge
1210 Neubrecht Rd, 45801; tel 419/222-0596 or toll free 800/55-ECONO; fax 419/229-9235. Exit 127 of I-75. This property faces OH 81, but the entrance is off Neubrecht Rd. **Rooms:** 130 rms and stes. CI 2pm/CO noon. Nonsmoking rms avail. Rooms are clean, snug, and quite ordinary. **Amenities:** 🛁 A/C, cable TV w/movies, dataport, voice mail. **Services:** ✕ 🖼 🛏 🐾 VCRs may be rented at the desk. **Facilities:** 🏊 🏋 🛋 💯 ♿ 1 restaurant, 1 bar, playground, washer/dryer. The pool area has an enclosed lounge/sunning area within a courtyard. Choices Bar and Restaurant faces OH 81. **Rates:** $43–$48 S; $48–$53 D; $85–$90 ste. Extra person $5. Children under age 18 stay free. Parking: Outdoor, free. Honeymoon and golf packages avail. AE, CB, DC, DISC, JCB, MC, V.

▤▤▤ Holiday Inn Lima
1920 Roschman Ave, 45804; tel 419/222-0004 or toll free 800/HOLIDAY; fax 419/222-2176. Exit 125 off I-75. This is an upscale, posh facility. **Rooms:** 150 rms. CI 3pm/CO noon. Nonsmoking rms avail. Rooms are a good size, but not especially large. Comfortable. **Amenities:** 🛁 ☕ A/C, satel TV w/movies. Some units w/terraces. **Services:** ✕ 🖼 🛏 🐾 **Facilities:** 🏊 🏋 🛋 💯 ♿ 1 restaurant, 1 bar, games rm, sauna, whirlpool, playground. Indoor playground open 10am–10pm with swings, games, slides, and monkey bars; children under 12 must be supervised by an adult. Also a Ping-Pong table. The Metropole bar is large and rich looking, with subdued lighting. The Pavilion dining room is quite elegant. **Rates:** $82–$87 S; $90–$95 D. Extra person $8. Children under age 19 stay free. Parking: Outdoor, free. Honeymoon package avail. AE, CB, DC, DISC, JCB, MC, V.

RESTAURANTS 🍴

✹ Mark Pi's China Gate
702 W North St; tel 419/224-4645. 7 blocks W of City Square on OH 81, exit 127 off I-75. **Chinese.** Cantonese, Mandarin, and Szechuan dishes are available at this ordinary-looking eatery set back from the street near downtown. Popular locally, with good food. Subdued lighting. **FYI:** Reservations accepted. Children's menu. **Open:** Lunch Mon–Sat 11:30am–2:30pm; dinner Mon–Thurs 4:30–9:30pm, Fri–Sat 4:30–10:30pm. **Prices:** Main courses $6–$10. AE, MC, V. ⬛♿

✹ Milano Club
415 W Market St; tel 419/229-9731. 4 blocks W of Courthouse, off I-75 exit 125. **Italian.** The Gujenti family, in the restaurant business for many years, runs the premier dining spot in Lima in an old house near the city square. The lobby is lined with autographed menus, family history, and photos,

and throughout the restaurant are stained-glass windows and sculpture. The Italian specialties are "made to order," and all sauces are prepared from scratch. Crisp, efficient service. **FYI:** Reservations recommended. Karaoke/band. Children's menu. **Open:** Mon–Sat 11am–2:30am. **Prices:** Main courses $8–$14. AE, DC, DISC, MC, V. ♥ 🆅🅿 ♿

⑤ Old Barn Out Back
3175 W Elm St; tel 419/991-3075. 3½ mi W of downtown. **American.** Actually, the old barn burned down several years ago, but the rebuilt version still retains lots of authentic items, from farm tools and milk cans to the lamps perched on wagon wheels suspended from the ceiling. The highlight of the room is the old Conestoga covered wagon converted into a salad bar. Traditional American fare: broiled steak served with an onion sauce and au gratin potatoes; thick-sliced prime rib in its own juice. All baked goods, from breads to donuts and sweet rolls, are made on the premises. Arts-and-crafts gift shop by the entrance. **FYI:** Reservations not accepted. Children's menu. Beer and wine only. **Open:** Tues–Thurs 11am–8pm, Fri–Sat 11am–9pm, Sun 10:30am–6pm. **Prices:** Main courses $5–$12. DISC, MC, V. 🍴 👪 ♿

Tudor's
2383 Elida Rd; tel 419/331-2220. ⅛ mi W of Cable Rd. **American/Italian.** A typical neighborhood restaurant, with ordinary decor and dim lighting, located on a busy highway. Its primarily a steak house, but there are also Italian dishes and a salad bar. Offers good value for families. **FYI:** Reservations accepted. Karaoke. Children's menu. **Open:** Daily 11am–11pm. **Prices:** Main courses $8–$16. AE, CB, DC, DISC, MC, V. 👪 ♿

ATTRACTIONS 💼

Allen County Museum
620 W Market St; tel 419/222-9426. Early 20th-century vehicles, a steam and electric railroad collection, an Oriental Room containing a rare gold household shrine, old firearms, pioneer room settings, and rare glass and china are among the exhibits here. Guided tours available. **Open:** Peak (June–Aug) Tues–Sat 10am–5pm, Sun 1–5pm. **Free**

MacDonell House
622 W Market; tel 419/222-9426. Listed on the National Register of Historic Places, this elaborate Victorian mansion was built in 1893. Its 17 rooms are decorated to reflect a variety of periods and styles, with features ranging from original Victorian chandeliers to ornate hand-carved woodwork, a vivid two-story stained glass window, and other decorative arts and furniture. **Open:** Peak (June–Aug) Tues–Sat 10am–5pm, Sun 1–5pm. Reduced hours off-season. **$**

Mansfield

Seat of Richland County, in north-central part of state. The world heard of this town in the foothills of the Appalachians through the novels of Pulitzer Prize–winning author Louis Bromfield. **Information:** Mansfield/Richland County Convention & Visitors Bureau, 52 Park Ave W, Mansfield, 44902 (tel 800/642-8282).

HOTELS 🏨

🏨🏨 Comfort Inn South
855 Comfort Plaza Dr, Bellville, 44813; tel 419/886-4000 or toll free 800/221-2222; fax 419/886-3813. Excellent accommodations within 15 minutes of Mid-Ohio Sports Car Track, historic Malabar Farm, Mohican State Park, and Snow Trails Ski Resort. **Rooms:** 100 rms. CI 3pm/CO noon. Nonsmoking rms avail. **Amenities:** 🛁 ♨ A/C, cable TV w/movies. Some units w/whirlpools. **Services:** ⛵ 🐾 **Facilities:** 🏋 🛝 🎯 🖤 🏊 ♿ Games rm, spa, whirlpool, washer/dryer. **Rates (CP):** Peak (May–Sept) $52–$115 S or D. Extra person $6. Children under age 18 stay free. Min stay special events. Lower rates off-season. Parking: Outdoor, free. AE, CB, DC, DISC, ER, JCB, MC, V.

🏨🏨 Holiday Inn
116 Park Ave W, 44902; tel 419/525-6000 or toll free 800/465-4329; fax 419/525-0197. 4 blocks W of town square. Perfect for business travelers because of excellent conference and meeting facilities. Within five blocks of Carousel District and Kingwood Center, seven miles to ski areas, and 20 minutes to Mid-Ohio Sports Car Course and Malabar Farm. **Rooms:** 160 rms. Executive level. CI 3pm/CO noon. Nonsmoking rms avail. **Amenities:** 🛁 ♨ 🖥 🍷 A/C, satel TV w/movies, dataport. Some units w/minibars. **Services:** ✕ 🚗 ⛵ 🐾 Babysitting. Some dinner-theater packages for shows at neighboring Renaissance Theater. **Facilities:** 🏋 🛝 🎯 🖤 🏊 ♿ 1 restaurant, 1 bar (w/entertainment), sauna, whirlpool. Beautifully decorated pool area with both indoor and outdoor patios. **Rates:** $69–$89 S; $77–$97 D. Extra person $8. Children under age 20 stay free. Parking: Outdoor, free. Rates increase for peak race weekends. AE, CB, DC, DISC, EC, ER, JCB, MC, V.

MOTELS

🏨🏨🏨 Best Western Inn
880 Laver Rd, 44905; tel 419/589-2200 or toll free 800/528-1234; fax 419/589-5624. Exit 176 off I-71, OH 30 W to Laver Rd, motel at exit. Much nicer than exterior suggests. Close to OH 30, and 20 minutes to Mid-Ohio Sports Car Course, Malabar Farm, Clearfork Reservoir, and Charles Mill Lake (swimming and boating areas). **Rooms:** 105 rms. CI 3pm/CO noon. Nonsmoking rms avail. King rooms have king-size bed and foldout sofa. **Amenities:** 🛁 A/C, cable TV w/movies. **Services:** ✕ ⛵ 🐾 🍽 Copying and fax services available on request. **Facilities:** 🏋 🛝 🎯 🗓 ♿ 1 restaurant (bkfst and dinner only), 1 bar (w/entertainment), games rm. **Rates (BB):** Peak (May–Sept) $49–$150 S or D. Children under age 18 stay free. Lower rates off-season. Parking:

Outdoor, free. Rates increase on peak race weekends. Special packages available for some holidays. AE, CB, DC, DISC, MC, V.

≣≣ Comfort Inn North
500 N Trimble Rd, 44906; tel 419/529-1000 or toll free 800/918-9189; fax 419/529-2953. Exit 176 off I-71, take OH 30 W 8 mi to Trimble Rd. Newly remodeled. Especially good for business travel—excellent conference and meeting facilities. Located right off highway, 1 mile from county fairgrounds, 15 miles from ski areas and Mid-Ohio Sports Car Course, and close to variety of restaurants. **Rooms:** 114 rms and stes. CI noon/CO noon. Nonsmoking rms avail. Executive apartment available. **Amenities:** 🛏 🔦 🍴 A/C, cable TV w/movies, dataport. Some units w/whirlpools. **Services:** ✕ ⛷ 🔄 🐾 Buffet breakfast at Damon's (next door) included in rates. **Facilities:** 🏋 💻 ₺ Games rm, sauna, whirlpool, washer/dryer. Guests receive free pass to nearby private health club. **Rates (BB):** Peak (May–Nov) $62 S; $67 D; $80 ste. Extra person $5. Children under age 18 stay free. Lower rates off-season. Parking: Outdoor, free. Rates increase for peak race weekends. Packages include honeymoon and some holidays. AE, CB, DC, DISC, EC, JCB, MC, V.

≣ Knights Inn
555 N Trimble Rd, 44906; tel 419/529-2100 or toll free 800/722-7220; fax 419/529-6679. Exit 176 off I-71; go 8 mi W on OH 30 to Trimble Rd. Newly redecorated. Close to highway; 1 mile to county fairgrounds; ½-hour to ski areas, Mid-Ohio Sports Car Course, and Malabar Farm. **Rooms:** 110 rms and effic. CI 3pm/CO noon. Nonsmoking rms avail. **Amenities:** 🛏 A/C, cable TV w/movies. **Services:** ✕ ⛷ 🔄 🐾 **Facilities:** 🏋 💻 ₺ Free privileges at nearby private health club. Separate parking lot available for semis. **Rates (CP):** Peak (May–Nov) $43 S; $54 D; $65 effic. Extra person $5. Children under age 18 stay free. Lower rates off-season. Parking: Outdoor, free. 20% discount for four or more days; 25% discount for 30 days. Packages for newlyweds and some holidays. AE, CB, DC, DISC, MC, V.

RESTAURANTS 🍴

★ Brunches Restaurant and Gourmet Coffee
103 N Main St; tel 419/526-2233. 1 block N of the square. **American.** A small, charming cafe with outdoor seating available, this is a great place for breakfast or lunch, as many local businesspeople have discovered. The daily quiche, assorted salads, and specialty sandwiches are good choices. Desserts are wonderful, especially the chocolate peanut butter pie and the cappuccino floats. **FYI:** Reservations not accepted. Children's menu. No liquor license. No smoking. Additional location: 220 N Center Rd, Ashland (tel 281-2233). **Open:** Mon–Sat 7am–3pm, Sun 9am–8pm. **Prices:** Lunch main courses $3–$9. AE, DISC, MC, V. ▮ 🍴 ₺

⑤ ★ Buck's Restaurant
26 E Main, Lexington; tel 419/884-0807. ½ block W of I-97. **American.** Don't let the shabby exterior or the plain, simple decor deter you from this great restaurant. A fun, casual place to enjoy lots of delicious food at very reasonable prices. Steak and seafood are available, but the most popular items are gourmet burgers, huge pizzas piled high with your choice of toppings, and the chef and seafood salads. **FYI:** Reservations not accepted. Children's menu. Jacket required. **Open:** Mon–Thurs 10:30am–midnight, Fri–Sat 10:30am–1am. **Prices:** Main courses $7–$13. AE, CB, DC, DISC, MC, V. 🎱 ₺

ATTRACTIONS 🏛
Oak Hill Cottage
310 Springmill St; tel 419/524-1765. Built in 1847, this is considered one of the most perfect examples of Gothic residential architecture in the United States. The house features seven gables, five double chimneys and seven marble fireplaces, as well as a collection of Victorian furnishings. **Open:** Apr–Dec, Sun 2–5pm. **$**

Kingwood Center
900 Park Ave W; tel 419/522-0211. The centerpiece of this 47-acre estate (the former home of industrialist Charles Kelley King) is a French provincial mansion containing art, original furnishings, and a horticultural library. The gorgeously landscaped gardens include more than 500 varieties of perennials, which are accented by peacocks that roam the grounds and swans gliding across ponds. **Open:** Daily 8am–dusk. **Free**

Richland Carousel Park
75 N Main St; tel 419/522-4223. The focal point of this downtown park is its turn-of-the-century carousel, which features 52 hand-carved, wooden animals and two chariots. **Open:** Peak (June–Sept) Mon–Thurs and Sat 10am–6pm, Fri 10am–9pm, Sun 11am–6pm. Reduced hours off-season. Closed Jan. **Free**

Marblehead
See Port Clinton

Marietta
Seat of Washington County, in southeast part of state. Founded at the confluence of the Ohio and Muskingum Rivers in 1788, Marietta is Ohio's oldest city. Extensive, well-preserved mounds prove the existence of a Native American village long before white settlement. The Ohio River Sternwheel Festival takes place here every September. **Information:** Marietta Area Chamber of Commerce, 316 3rd St, Marietta, 45750 (tel 614/373-5176).

HOTEL 🏨

≣≣≣ Lafayette Hotel

101 Front St, 45750; tel 614/373-5522 or toll free 800/ 331-9336, 800/331-9337 in OH; fax 614/373-4684. 1½ mi W of US 77, at Green St. On America's registry as a historic hotel, this luxurious establishment offers elegance and old-fashioned charm and hospitality not found in newer establishments. The main building was built in 1892, and a wing was added in 1937. It's an official stop of the Delta Queen Steamboat Company, so guests have the occasional pleasure of watching the huge paddleboats come and go, or boarding one for a tour—such as the covered bridge or fall foliage tours. Rooms are booked for years in advance for the Sternwheel Festival, held the week after Labor Day. Nearby boat rental service. **Rooms:** 79 rms and stes. CI 3pm/CO noon. Nonsmoking rms avail. Room sizes range from small, efficient single to two-bedroom suites. **Amenities:** 🛏 ⚬ A/C, cable TV, dataport. Some units w/terraces. Penthouse suites have balconies/decks with tables and chairs and exquisite views of Ohio River. **Services:** ✕ 🚐 🖼 🍴 🦮 **Facilities:** 500 ⚬ 1 restaurant (*see* "Restaurants" below), 1 bar (w/entertainment). Passes to nearby YMCA sports and health center. **Rates:** Peak (Apr–Oct) $60–$65 S or D; $80–$300 ste. Extra person $5. Children under age 18 stay free. Min stay special events. Lower rates off-season. Parking: Outdoor, free. Captain's Club, a frequent stay program, offers special rates, some meals, and discounts at many area sites and restaurants. AE, CB, DC, DISC, MC, V.

MOTELS

≣≣ Best Western Inn

279 Muskingum Dr, 45750; tel 614/374-7211 or toll free 800/528-1234; fax 614/374-7211. Exit 6 off US 77. Clean and comfortable, this basic establishment is right on the Ohio River. **Rooms:** 47 rms and stes. CI noon/CO noon. Nonsmoking rms avail. **Amenities:** 🛏 A/C, cable TV, refrig, dataport. Some units w/terraces. **Services:** 🖼 🍴 Car-rental desk. **Facilities:** Boat dock. Passes to YMCA fitness center. **Rates (CP):** Peak (June–Oct) $40 S; $48–$58 D; $75–$80 ste. Extra person $5. Children under age 12 stay free. Lower rates off-season. Parking: Outdoor, free. Boater and golf packages avail. AE, DC, DISC, MC, V.

≣≣≣ Comfort Inn

700 Pike St, 45750; tel 614/374-8190 or toll free 800/ 537-6858; fax 614/374-3649. Exit 1 off US 77. Newly remodeled and exquisite landscaping. At mid-range rates, it offers much for the family or business traveler. **Rooms:** 120 rms and stes. Executive level. CI 4pm/CO 11am. Nonsmoking rms avail. **Amenities:** 🛏 ⚬ A/C, cable TV, dataport. **Services:** 🖼 🍴 **Facilities:** 🏋 25 🖥 ⚬ 1 restaurant (lunch and dinner only), 1 bar, sauna, steam rm, whirlpool. Jogging/ walking track on premises. Passes to sports and fitness facility at nearby YMCA. **Rates (CP):** Peak (May–Oct) $54–$70 S or

D; $65–$75 ste. Extra person $4. Children under age 12 stay free. Lower rates off-season. Parking: Outdoor, free. Golf packages in conjunction with nearby course avail. AE, CB, DC, MC, V.

≣≣≣ Holiday Inn

701 Pike St, 45750; tel 614/374-9660 or toll free 800/ HOLIDAY; fax 614/373-1762. Exit 1 off US 77. In an attractive setting with well-tended landscaping, this motel is right next to a beautiful golf course. Easy access off highway. Handy for business meetings. **Rooms:** 109 rms. CI 2pm/CO noon. Nonsmoking rms avail. **Amenities:** 🛏 ⚬ A/C, cable TV w/movies, dataport. **Services:** ✕ 🖼 🍴 **Facilities:** 🏋 175 ⚬ 1 restaurant, 1 bar (w/entertainment). Passes to local YMCA sports and fitness facility. **Rates:** Peak (May–Oct) $58–$75 S or D. Children under age 18 stay free. Min stay wknds. Lower rates off-season. Parking: Outdoor, free. Golf packages avail. AE, CB, DC, DISC, EC, ER, JCB, MC, V.

≣ Knights Inn

506 Pike St, 45750; tel 614/373-7373 or toll free 800/ 526-5947; fax 614/374-9466. Exit 1 off US 77. Economical, with easy access off highway. Good for family travel or one-night business stops. **Rooms:** 111 rms and effic. CI 3pm/CO noon. Nonsmoking rms avail. **Amenities:** 🛏 A/C, cable TV w/movies. **Services:** 🖼 🍴 **Facilities:** 🏋 ⚬ **Rates:** $42 S; $47–$49 D; $48–$53 effic. Extra person $5. Children under age 18 stay free. Parking: Outdoor, free. Golf packages avail. AE, DC, DISC, MC, V.

RESTAURANTS 🍴

Betsey Mills Club Dining Room

300 4th St; tel 614/373-3804. At Putnam; 2 blocks from center of town. **American.** The solid, home-style cooking available here is no secret to folks in this residential neighborhood. Homemade soups and stews, a variety of salads, and scrumptious cream pies keep the loyal clientele coming back for more. Sunday buffet is also very popular. **FYI:** Reservations accepted. Children's menu. Dress code. No liquor license. **Open:** Lunch Mon–Sat 11:30am–2:30pm, Sun 11am–2:30pm; dinner Mon–Sat 5–8:30pm. **Prices:** Main courses $4–$7. AE, DC, DISC, MC, V. 🍴 ⚬

♦ The Gun Room

In Lafayette Hotel, 101 Front St (Downtown); tel 614/ 373-5522. At Green St; 1½ mi W of I-77. **American.** In the elegant Lafayette, the dining room has a wonderful view of the city and the Ohio River. The house special is prime rib, said to be the best in town. Seasoned, baked chicken and broiled seafood are frequent choices made from the typically American menu. **FYI:** Reservations recommended. Blues/ comedy/jazz/reggae. Children's menu. **Open:** Breakfast daily 7:30–11am; lunch daily 11am–2pm; dinner daily 4–9pm. **Prices:** Main courses $9–$29. AE, DC, DISC, MC, V. 🍴 🖼 ⚬ ⚬

Marion

Seat of Marion County, in central part of state. Named for Gen Francis Marion of Revolutionary War fame, this small city is at the center of a major popcorn-producing area. Warren G Harding lived here and was editor of the Marion *Star* before he ran for president in 1920. Popcorn Festival held here every September. **Information:** Marion County Convention & Visitors Bureau, 206 S Prospect St, Marion, 43302 (tel 614/389-9770 or toll free 800/371-6688).

MOTELS 🏨

⊨⊨⊨ Fairfield Inn
227 Jamesway, 43302; tel 614/389-6636 or toll free 800/228-2800; fax 614/389-6636. Jct US 23/OH 95. Four miles from town square. Minutes from Warren G Harding Home and Memorial, Popcorn Museum, and many antique shops and displays. Car rental facility next door. **Rooms:** 57 rms and stes. CI 3pm/CO 11am. Nonsmoking rms avail. **Amenities:** 🛁 ♨ A/C, cable TV w/movies, dataport. **Services:** ⛾ ⟲ ⟳ Car-rental desk. Copy and fax equipment available. Meals at nearby Bucky's Restaurant can be charged to room. **Facilities:** 🏋 🔲 ♿ Games rm, whirlpool. **Rates (CP):** Peak (June–Aug) $55–$64 S; $57–$63 D; $68–$74 ste. Children under age 18 stay free. Lower rates off-season. Parking: Outdoor, free. AE, DC, DISC, ER, JCB, MC, V.

⊨⊨ Travelodge
1952 Marion-Mount Gilead Rd, 43302; tel 614/389-4671 or toll free 800/578-7878; fax 614/389-4671. Jct US 23/OH 95. Economical and comfortable, minutes from OSU branch campus and Marion Technical College. **Rooms:** 92 rms and stes. Executive level. CI 2pm/CO noon. Nonsmoking rms avail. **Amenities:** 🛁 ♨ 📺 A/C, cable TV w/movies, dataport. Suites have refrigerators. **Services:** ⛾ ⟲ ⟳ Fax and copy equipment available. Guests receive 10% discount at neighboring Bucky's Restaurant. **Facilities:** 🏋 🔲 ♿ Guests receive free passes to YMCA sports and fitness facility two miles away. **Rates:** $43–$60 S; $48–$65 D; $60–$80 ste. Extra person $6. Children under age 18 stay free. Parking: Outdoor, free. Golf packages avail. AE, CB, DC, DISC, JCB, MC, V.

RESTAURANT 🍽

Ⓢ Bucky's An Extraordinary Eatery
1960 Marion-Mount Gilead Rd; tel 614/389-5456. Jct US 23/OH 95. **American.** An excellent, economical eatery, great for business or family dining. The lunch buffet (Mon–Fri) offers a wide selection of salads, soup, and entrees at a very reasonable price ($5). The lounge has displays of auto-racing memorabilia. **FYI:** Reservations accepted. Blues/country music/karaoke/rock. Children's menu. Dress code. **Open:** Mon 11am–10pm, Tues–Sun 11am–12:30am. **Prices:** Main courses $7–$15. AE, CB, DC, DISC, MC, V. 📶 ♿

ATTRACTION 🖼

President Warren G Harding Home and Memorial
380 Mount Vernon Ave; tel 614/387-9630. During the 1920 presidential campaign, Harding addressed voters from the front porch of this house. Today visitors can take a guided tour of the completely restored home which is decorated with original period furnishings. Also on the property is the **Harding Museum** which displays memorabilia such as the podium used at Harding's inauguration. **Open:** Peak (Mem Day–Labor Day) Wed–Sat 9:30am–5pm. Reduced hours off-season. $

Mason

Located 10 miles northeast of Cincinnati. This small town is a major tourist destination, with family-oriented theme parks galore. The Indiana & Ohio Old Time Passenger Train offers scenic railway excursion between Mason and Lebanon. **Information:** Mason Area Chamber of Commerce, 110 W Main, PO Box 93, Mason, 45040-1699 (tel 513/398-2188).

MOTEL 🏨

⊨⊨⊨ Holiday Inn
9845 Escort Dr, 45040; tel 513/398-8015 or toll free 800/HOLIDAY; fax 513/398-0822. ¼ mi NE of I-71 exit 19; left at first traffic light. Clean, basic. Golf, bowling, and fishing facilities available. Downtown Cincinnati is about 15 minutes away. Shopping malls, College Football Hall of Fame, Beach Water Park, and Kings Island Theme Park are all nearby. **Rooms:** 104 rms. CI 2pm/CO noon. Nonsmoking rms avail. **Amenities:** 🛁 ♨ 📺 A/C, satel TV, dataport. **Services:** ✕ ⛾ ⟲ ⟳ Babysitting. **Facilities:** 🏋 ♨ 🔲 ♿ 1 restaurant, 1 bar, games rm, playground. Pool area is small, but neat and serviceable. **Rates:** Peak (May–Sept) $36–$79 S or D. Extra person $7. Children under age 18 stay free. Lower rates off-season. Parking: Outdoor, free. Rates often increase during special events. AE, DC, DISC, MC, V.

ATTRACTIONS 🖼

Paramount's Kings Island
6300 Kings Island Dr; tel toll free 800/288-0808. Built on 1,600 acres in the northern Cincinnati suburbs, this ultra-modern amusement park features more than 40 attractions, five thrill rides (including the Beast—billed as the world's longest wooden roller coaster—and two log flumes), a mini-zoo, several reconstructions of old villages, and a miniature Eiffel Tower that towers 330 feet over the park. **Hanna-Barbera Land** has kid-sized rides and costumed cartoon characters. The 15-acre **WaterWorks** area features The Plunge (a body slide with a 70-foot drop) and King Mill Run (a lazy river inner tube ride). Live entertainment, Broadway-

style shows, and concession areas also available. **Open:** Peak (Mem Day–Labor Day) daily 9am–dusk. Reduced hours off-season. **$$$$**

Beach Waterpark

2590 Waterpark Dr; tel toll free 800/886-SWIM. Located across from Paramount's Kings Island, this park is home to 2,500 tons of sand and almost 2 million gallons of water. The Thunder Beach Wavepool produces oceanlike surf, while the Pearl entertainment area boasts a swimming pool, hot tubs, and poolside lounging places for adults. Visitors can float through the entire park on the Lazy Miami River, a mile-and-a-half-long ride with a riverboat motif. Two children's areas—Dolphin Bay and Penguin Bay—offer an otter slide and other tot-sized rides. **Open:** Mem Day–Labor Day, daily 10am–dusk. **$$$$**

Mentor

Founded in 1799, southeast of Cleveland. James A Garfield lived here before he took office as President in 1881. **Information:** Mentor Area Chamber of Commerce, 7547 Mentor Ave, #302, Mentor, 44060 (tel 216/946-2625).

HOTEL 🏨

≣≣≣ Travelodge Hotel

7701 Reynolds Rd, 44060; tel 216/951-7333 or toll free 800/255-3050; fax 216/951-7333. Jct US 2/306. Renovation in progress. **Rooms:** 141 rms. Executive level. CI 3pm/CO 11am. Nonsmoking rms avail. **Amenities:** 🛎 A/C, cable TV w/movies. **Services:** 🚐 🗄 🛏 Local phone calls cost 50 cents each. Cribs $5. **Facilities:** 🔧 🏋️ 🏊 ⬜ 🚴 1 restaurant (bkfst only), 1 bar, games rm, washer/dryer. **Rates:** Peak (May 15–Sept 15) $55–$70 S or D. Extra person $5. Children under age 17 stay free. Lower rates off-season. Parking: Outdoor, free. AE, DC, DISC, MC, V.

MOTELS

≣≣ Knights Inn

7677 Reynolds Rd, 44060; tel 216/946-0749 or toll free 800/843-5644; fax 216/946-0925. Jct US 306/2. Basic motel, convenient from interstate. Good value. **Rooms:** 113 rms and effic. CI 4pm/CO noon. Nonsmoking rms avail. **Amenities:** 🛎 A/C, cable TV w/movies. **Services:** 🗄 🛏 🐾 Pets stay free. No charge for cribs. Guests can catch airport shuttle at hotel next door. **Facilities:** 🏊 🚴 **Rates:** $35–$48 S or D; $51–$56 effic. Extra person $6. Children under age 18 stay free. Parking: Outdoor, free. AE, DC, DISC, MC, V.

≣≣ Knights Inn Cleveland East Mentor

8370 Broadmoor Rd, 44060; tel 216/953-8835 or toll free 800/THE-KNIGHTS. On US 306 at I-90. Basic motel in need of some renovation. **Rooms:** 103 rms and effic. CI 4pm/CO noon. Nonsmoking rms avail. Rooms need better lighting. **Amenities:** 🛎 A/C, cable TV. **Services:** 🗄 🛏 🐾

Refundable deposit for free local calls. Outgoing fax service. Free cribs. **Facilities:** 🔧 🏊 **Rates:** Peak (May–Sept) $35–$45 S or D; $51–$54 effic. Extra person $6. Children under age 18 stay free. Lower rates off-season. Parking: Outdoor, free. AE, CB, DC, DISC, ER, JCB, MC, V.

Miamisburg

Four Pennsylvania Dutchmen laid out the town in 1818. It is now a suburb of Dayton. **Information:** South Metro Area Chamber of Commerce, 1410-B Miamisburg-Centerville Rd, PO Box 123, Centerville, 45459 (tel 513/433-2032 or 433-6113).

HOTEL 🏨

≣≣≣ Residence Inn by Marriott

155 Prestige Place, 45342; tel 513/434-7881 or toll free 800/321-2211; fax 513/434-9308. An upscale lodging that resembles a group of condominiums with Tudor architecture; the buildings connect, but the units do not. To get to any one unit, one must climb at least two stairways. The estatelike landscaping is in good condition and includes benches. About two blocks from Dayton Mall. **Rooms:** 96 stes. CI 2pm/CO noon. Nonsmoking rms avail. All units are cheerful studio suites. Most have views of landscaped areas from wide windows. Large pictures on walls. Linen and dishes are far better than average. **Amenities:** 🛎 ❄ 🛏 🍽 A/C, satel TV w/movies, refrig, dataport, voice mail. Some units w/terraces, some w/fireplaces. All units have complete kitchens, irons, ironing boards, and ice makers. **Services:** 🗄 🛏 🐾 Children's program, babysitting. VCRs may be rented. Logs for fireplaces available at front desk for small fee. Room service available from several nearby restaurants. Hospitality hour in Gatehouse Mon–Thurs 5:30–7pm. **Facilities:** 🔧 🏋️ 🚴 Basketball, volleyball, whirlpool, washer/dryer. Upscale pool area with umbrella tables. Access to two health spas. **Rates (BB):** Peak (June–Aug) $79–$135 ste. Lower rates off-season. Parking: Outdoor, free. Children of any age stay free with parents. AE, CB, DC, DISC, JCB, MC, V.

MOTELS

≣≣ Best Western Continental Inn

155 Monarch Lane, 45342; tel 513/866-5500 or toll free 800/528-1234; fax 513/866-8270. ½ mi from I-75 exit 44 on OH 725. Comfortable and clean motel, with grand lobby two stories high. Fine for overnight, or longer. Nearby golf, bowling, and fishing. Several nearby restaurants. **Rooms:** 60 rms. Executive level. CI 2pm/CO noon. Nonsmoking rms avail. Bright and clean rooms. **Amenities:** 🛎 A/C, cable TV w/movies, dataport, VCR. **Services:** ✕ 🗄 🛏 **Facilities:** 🏋️ 🏊 🚴 1 restaurant (dinner only), 1 bar. **Rates (CP):** $45–$55 S or D. Extra person $5. Children under age 18 stay free. Parking: Outdoor, free. Rates higher on weekends. AE, DC, DISC, MC, V.

🏨🏨 Country Hearth Inn

1944 Miamisburg-Centerville Rd, 45459; tel 513/435-1550; fax 513/435-1550. Bright, clean, and homey. **Rooms:** 73 rms, stes, and effic. Executive level. CI 2pm/CO noon. Nonsmoking rms avail. Each room has an upholstered recliner chair, a reading lamp, a large coffee table, and a partial drape at one side of the bed. **Amenities:** 🛏 🅿 A/C, cable TV. Some units w/whirlpools. **Services:** 🛎 ⌂ Babysitting. Guests enjoy full breakfast, watch TV, or read from books on shelves in dining/lounge area. **Facilities:** 🔥 🕴 🕭 Health spa nearby for use by guests. **Rates (BB):** $53–$73 S or D; $62–$68 ste; $67–$73 effic. Extra person $6. Children under age 18 stay free. Parking: Outdoor, free. Packages include Valentine's Day, wedding parties, and New Year's Eve. AE, CB, DC, DISC, MC, V.

🏨🏨🏨 Courtyard by Marriott

100 Prestige Place, 45342; tel 513/433-3131 or toll free 800/638-8108; fax 513/433-0285. Off OH 741 just S of 725; E of I-75 exit 44. Clean, attractive facility, about two blocks from Dayton Mall. Nearby golf, bowling, and fishing. **Rooms:** 146 rms and stes. CI 3pm/CO 1pm. Nonsmoking rms avail. Half the rooms overlook well-landscaped courtyard. **Amenities:** 🛏 🅿 📺 A/C, satel TV w/movies, dataport. Ironing boards and irons in rooms. **Services:** ✕ 🛎 ⌂ Babysitting. Polite and prompt service. **Facilities:** 🔥 🕴 🏊 📅 🕭 1 restaurant (bkfst only), 1 bar, washer/dryer. Spacious pool area with whirlpool, outdoor sun deck, and gazebo with table and chairs. Access to nearby Vic Tanny spa. **Rates:** $69–$83 S or D; $99 ste. Extra person $10. Children under age 12 stay free. Parking: Outdoor, free. Rates higher for special events, such as air show. AE, CB, DC, DISC, MC, V.

🏨🏨🏨 Holiday Inn Dayton Mall

31 Prestige Place, 45342; tel 513/434-8030 or toll free 800/HOLIDAY; fax 513/434-6452. Off OH 725 at OH 741; just W of Dayton Mall. Posh hotel, with two glass elevators. Views are of the atriumlike area where special events are held, as well as the Holidome sports area. **Rooms:** 197 rms. CI 3pm/CO 11am. Nonsmoking rms avail. King bed rooms face the Holidome. Each has a sofa bed. **Amenities:** 🛏 🅿 📺 A/C, cable TV w/movies, dataport, voice mail. **Services:** ✕ 🚐 🛎 ⌂ Car-rental desk, babysitting. **Facilities:** 🔥 🕴 🏊 📅 🕭 1 restaurant, 1 bar (w/entertainment), games rm, sauna, whirlpool, playground, washer/dryer. Ping-Pong, coin-operated basketball game, putting green. Area for children's parties behind pool in Holidome. Small fitness area, but guests may use nearby fully equipped health spas. Ballroom is largest in any Dayton area motel. **Rates:** $90 S or D. Children under age 19 stay free. Parking: Outdoor, free. Priority Club Package includes full breakfast buffet and evening hors d'oeuvres; Bed-and-Breakfast Package includes full breakfast buffet. AE, CB, DC, DISC, JCB, MC, V.

🏨🏨 Knights Inn

185 Byers Rd, 45342; tel 513/859-8797 or toll free 800/843-5644; fax 513/859-5254. ¼ mi W of I-75; exit 44 off OH 725. A solid overnight motel. Well landscaped. Nearby golf, bowling, and fishing. Restaurant next door. **Rooms:** 150 rms and effic. CI 2pm/CO noon. Nonsmoking rms avail. **Amenities:** 🛏 A/C, satel TV. **Services:** ✕ ⌂ ⌂ **Facilities:** 🔥 🕴 📅 🕭 Access to nearby fitness center. **Rates:** $35–$43 S or D; $46 effic. Children under age 18 stay free. Parking: Outdoor, free. AE, DC, DISC, MC, V.

🏨 Motel 6

8101 Springboro Pike, 45342; tel 513/434-8750; fax 513/434-6734. ½ mi S of OH 725 on OH 741; ½ E of I-75 exit 44. Basic motel for an economical price, near Dayton Mall. Restaurant in front of motel. Nearby golf, bowling, and fishing. **Rooms:** 134 rms and stes. CI 2pm/CO noon. Nonsmoking rms avail. Good, clean rooms. Walls are painted, concrete block—bright but not aesthetic. **Amenities:** 🛏 A/C, satel TV. **Services:** ⌂ ⌂ Free coffee in lobby. **Facilities:** 🔥 🕴 🕭 **Rates:** Peak (May–Sept) $28–$34 S or D; $40 ste. Extra person $3. Children under age 17 stay free. Lower rates off-season. Parking: Outdoor, free. AE, CB, DC, DISC, MC, V.

RESTAURANTS 🍴

★ Alex's Continental Restaurant

125 Monarch Lane; tel 513/866-2266. **Continental.** Liberal use of stained-glass windows adds to the ambience of this well-lit dining room. The general decor is international in flavor, in keeping with the restaurant's name, with an abundance of pedestals, flowers, and sculpture. Chicken Fillet Alex's Way (flattened chicken breast rolled in a special breading then sautéed, broiled, and served in a light wine sauce) is the signature entree. Another favorite of diners is the veal Parmesan. **FYI:** Reservations recommended. Piano. Children's menu. **Open:** Mon–Thurs 5–10pm, Fri–Sat 5–11pm. **Prices:** Main courses $8–$15. AE, DC, MC, V. ❤ 🍽 🕭

🍷★ Peerless Mill Inn

319 S 2nd St; tel 513/866-5968. 2 blocks S of OH 725 (Central Ave); 3 mi W of I-75. **American.** Established in 1929 in a former lumber mill dating from 1828, this handsome restaurant with a brick and stone exterior serves up carefully prepared traditional American and country dishes. Large, oblong flagstones form the floors of this rambling structure constructed of hand-hewn timbers and sturdy beams and decorated with flower arrangements and showcases of glassware and dolls, wagon wheels, and other antiques. Five dining rooms on two levels can seat up to 325 diners. Fresh chowders, aged steaks, roasts, and chops, and seafood flown in from Boston twice a week await diners; roast duckling is a house specialty. Lunch is served only during the two weeks prior to Christmas. **FYI:** Reservations recommended. Piano. Children's menu. **Open:** Tues–Thurs 5–9pm, Fri–Sat 5–10pm, Sun 10am–7pm. **Prices:** Main courses $13–$19. AE, CB, DC, MC, V. ❤ 🍴 🕭

Ruby Tuesday

In Dayton Mall, 4700 Miamisburg-Centerville Rd; tel 513/438-8080. **American.** Located in the Dayton Mall, this attractive and well laid out family eatery has an eclectic decor, with Tiffany-style lamps and other faux-Victorian touches throughout. Best known for its quite extensive salad bar. Popular items include "roll-your-own" fajitas and tender barbecued ribs. **FYI:** Reservations accepted. Children's menu. **Open:** Mon–Thurs 11am–10pm, Fri–Sat 11am–11pm, Sun 11am–9pm. **Prices:** Main courses $5–$14. AE, CB, DC, DISC, MC, V. 🖼️ &

Samurai Sword–Japanese American Steak House

150 Monarch Lane; tel 513/866-9148. 1 mi W of Dayton Mall. **Japanese.** Specializing in Osaka-area cuisine, the meals at this authentic Japanese steak house are prepared right at your table. Customers sit in low chairs in a semicircle around a large grill, as the chef prepares the meal—from chopping the vegetables with a flourish to frying the meat—before their eyes. Hibachi chicken or beef—served with fried rice and a veritable garden of sautéed onions, peppers, and potatoes—are the most popular (and entertaining) menu options. Full service bar highlights South Pacific and Asian drinks. **FYI:** Reservations accepted. **Open:** Mon–Thurs 4–10pm, Fri–Sat 4–11pm. **Prices:** Main courses $8–$31. AE, DC, DISC, MC, V. 🖼️ &

★ Steve Kao's Chinese Cuisine

8270 Springboro Pike; tel 513/433-2556. **Chinese.** Award-winning eatery offering Szechuan, Mandarin, and Hunan specialties. Chinese red predominates in the dining room, and there are huge vases and planters throughout. Peking duck, with its very tender meat and crispy skin, is served with Hoisin sauce and Chinese crepes for wrapping; while sautéed salmon is served over noodles and broccoli covered with garlic sauce. **FYI:** Reservations recommended. Karaoke. **Open:** Mon–Thurs 11:30am–10pm, Fri–Sat 11:30am–11pm, Sun 12–10pm. **Prices:** Main courses $5–$15. AE, DC, DISC, MC, V. 🖼️ &

TW's

67 S Main St; tel 513/859-7782. At Linden Ave. **American.** Casual dining beside the Great Miami River. Several large framed mirrors, available for purchase, hang on the walls of the dining room, which is lit by chandeliers and table lamps. The bar is long and narrow. Broiled steaks and chops are mainstays of the menu; the chef uses a minimum of sauces and spices. Grilled turkey steak with cranberry-apple relish is a house specialty. **FYI:** Reservations recommended. Jazz. Children's menu. Dress code. **Open:** Mon–Thurs 5–9pm, Fri–Sat 5–10pm. **Prices:** Main courses $12–$20. AE, CB, DC, MC, V. &

Milan

Located in northwest part of state. The mark of New England is seen in many of the older homes in this small town settled in 1817. Thomas A Edison spent his first seven years here; his childhood home is just south of town. **Information:** Milan Chamber of Commerce, PO Box 544, Milan, 44846 (tel 419/499-2100).

MOTELS 🛏️

UNRATED Comfort Inn Cedar Point South

110202 US 250, 44846; tel 419/499-4681 or toll free 800/4-CHOICE; fax 419/499-3159. Modest exterior, small lobby. **Rooms:** 100 rms and stes. CI 4pm/CO noon. Nonsmoking rms avail. **Amenities:** 🛏️ ⚒️ A/C, cable TV. Some units w/whirlpools. **Services:** ⬛ 🛎️ Pet fee $25. **Facilities:** 🏋️ 🏊 & Games rm, sauna, whirlpool, washer/dryer. **Rates (CP):** Peak (May–Sept) $78 S or D; $118 ste. Extra person $4. Children under age 18 stay free. Lower rates off-season. Parking: Outdoor, free. Weekend getaway packages avail. AE, CB, DC, DISC, MC, V.

🏨🏨 Super 8 Motel

11313 Milan Rd, 44846; tel 419/499-4671 or toll free 800/800-8000; fax 419/499-4671. Basic, two-story budget motel with family atmosphere. Small lobby. **Rooms:** 69 rms. Executive level. CI 3pm/CO noon. Nonsmoking rms avail. **Amenities:** 🛏️ ⚒️ A/C, cable TV w/movies. **Services:** ✗ 🛎️ Twice-daily maid svce. **Facilities:** 🏋️ 🏊 & 1 restaurant (bkfst and dinner only), 1 bar, games rm, washer/dryer. **Rates (CP):** Peak (May–Sept) $34–$109 S or D. Extra person $10. Children under age 16 stay free. Min stay wknds. Lower rates off-season. Parking: Outdoor, free. AE, DC, DISC, MC, V.

RESTAURANT 🍴

Homestead Inn

12018 US 250; tel 419/499-4271. Exit 7 off US 250. **American.** Patrons enjoy elegant dining in a preserved 1883 country mansion with intricately carved ceilings and original Italian marble fireplace. The health-conscious menu includes specialty salads, seafood, beef, pork, and poultry entrees. The Rathskeller downstairs has a private entrance and offers a cozy, intimate setting with the same menu as the Victorian Room above, plus snacks and large salad bar. **FYI:** Reservations recommended. Children's menu. **Open:** Mon–Thurs 11am–9pm, Fri–Sat 7am–10pm, Sun 7am–8pm. **Prices:** Main courses $9–$14. AE, DC, DISC, MC, V. ❤️ 🍴 🖼️

ATTRACTION 🏛️

Milan Historical Museum

10 Edison Dr; tel 419/499-2968. Best known for its impressive collection of American art glass, including over 1,300 rare pieces of flint and pattern glass in addition to Tiffany, Durand, Aurene, and Steuben glass. The museum also includes century-old room settings depicting daily life of Milan's first settlers in the 1800's, along with a collection of artifacts from the Revolutionary and Civil War eras, and a display of china dolls. Gift shop and visitors center. **Open:** Peak (June–Aug) Tues–Sat 10am–5pm, Sun 1–5pm. Reduced hours off-season. **Free**

Moraine

See Dayton

Moreland Hills

RESTAURANTS 🍴

Hyde Park Chop House
34205 Chagrin Blvd; tel 216/464-0688. **Steak.** This New York–style chophouse specializes in "the classics," like steak Oscar, steak au poivre, and steak Diane. Seafood—including tank-fresh lobster—is also available, and there's an award-winning wine list. **FYI:** Reservations recommended. Jazz/piano/singer. Dress code. **Open:** Mon–Thurs 5:30–9:45pm, Fri–Sat 5–11:15pm. **Prices:** Main courses $15–$48. AE, CB, DC, DISC, MC, V. ♥ 🖼 🆅🅿 &

Wards' Inn
34105 Chagrin Blvd; tel 216/595-1954. **Regional American.** Intimate dining in cozy dining rooms with comfortable furniture and paneled walls. The husband-and-wife team who run the place prepare innovative dishes of venison, lamb, and salmon. Desserts (including ice cream and sorbets) are made on premises. Restaurant adjoins the Western Reserve wine shop. **FYI:** Reservations recommended. Dress code. **Open:** Mon–Thurs 5:30–10pm, Fri–Sat 5:30–11pm. **Prices:** Main courses $15–$26. AE, CB, DC, DISC, MC, V. ♥ 🆅🅿

Newark

Industrial city on the Licking River. The Hopewell tribe inhabited this area for approximately 1,000 years; the mounds they left behind were used for social, religious and ceremonial purposes. **Information:** Newark Area Chamber of Commerce, 50 W Locust St, PO Box 702, Newark, 43058-0702 (tel 614/345-9757).

MOTELS 🛏

🟰🟰🟰 Holiday Inn
733 Hebron Rd, 43055; tel 614/522-1165 or toll free 800/HOLIDAY; fax 614/522-1165. Exit 129B off I-70; 7 mi N on OH 79. Very nice, comfortable facility. Indian Mound Shopping Mall with shops and several large department stores is three blocks away. Several golf courses nearby. **Rooms:** 107 rms. CI 2pm/CO noon. Nonsmoking rms avail. **Amenities:** 🛏 🛇 🖥 🍽 A/C, cable TV w/movies, dataport. **Services:** ✕ 🚗 🔄 🔄 🔄 **Facilities:** 🚲 🔟🔟 & 1 restaurant, 1 bar (w/entertainment). **Rates:** Peak (May–Aug) $74 S or D. Children under age 19 stay free. Min stay special events. Lower rates off-season. Parking: Outdoor, free. AE, CB, DC, DISC, JCB, MC, V.

🟰🟰 Howard Johnson
775 Hebron Rd, 43055; tel 614/522-3191 or toll free 800/446-4656; fax 614/522-4396. Exit 129B off I-70; 7 mi N on OH 79. Very clean and neat, basic accommodations. **Rooms:** 72 rms. CI 3pm/CO noon. Nonsmoking rms avail. **Amenities:** 🛏 🛇 A/C, cable TV w/movies. Some units w/terraces, some w/whirlpools. **Services:** 🔄 🔄 🔄 **Facilities:** 🚲 🛁 🔟🔟 & 1 restaurant (lunch and dinner only), games rm, sauna, whirlpool. **Rates (CP):** Peak (Apr–Oct) $60 S; $65 D. Extra person $8. Children under age 18 stay free. Lower rates off-season. Parking: Outdoor, free. AE, CB, DC, DISC, MC, V.

RESTAURANT 🍴

★ Natoma
10 N Park; tel 614/345-7260. On the square. **American.** Located on the square in downtown Newark, this local favorite features basic American fare, including baby beef tenderloin and 8-oz fillet. **FYI:** Reservations not accepted. **Open:** Mon–Thurs 11am–9:30pm, Fri 11am–10pm, Sat 5–10pm. **Prices:** Main courses $8–$18. AE, CB, DC, DISC, MC, V. 🖼 &

ATTRACTIONS 🏛

Moundbuilders State Memorial
99 Cooper Ave; tel 614/344-1920. Located on the site of the ancient Newark earthworks—geometric enclosures built by the prehistoric Hopewell tribe between 100 BC and AD 400—this 66-acre park contains the Great Circle Earthworks (approximately 1,200 feet in diameter and 8–14 feet high) and the Ohio Indian Art Museum, the nation's first museum devoted to prehistoric Native American art. **Open:** Peak (Mem Day–Labor Day) Wed–Sat 9:30am–5pm, Sun and hols noon –5pm. Reduced hours off-season. **$**

Licking County Historical Society Museum
6th and Main Sts; tel 614/345-4898. Housed in the restored 1815 Sherwood-Davidson house, these displays of local history include period furnishings and historical artifacts. The society also maintains the adjacent Buckingham Meeting House (circa 1835), and the 1907 Webb House at 303 Granville St. Guided tours available. **Open:** Mar–Dec, Tues–Sun 1–4pm. **$**

New Philadelphia

Seat of Tuscarawas County, in eastern part of state. Founded in 1804 by German-Swiss religious pilgrims from Pennsylvania. A Separatist commune is located just south of town. **Information:** Tuscarawas County Chamber of Commerce, 1323 4th St NW, PO Box 232, New Philadelphia, 44663-1205 (tel 330/343-4474).

MOTELS 🏨

≡≡≡ Days Inn

1281 W High Ave, 44663; tel 330/339-6644 or toll free 800/329-7466; fax 330/339-3774. Exit 81 off I-77, OH 39 E ¼ mi. Excellent accommodations for price. Within minutes of seven major golf courses. **Rooms:** 104 rms and stes. CI 3pm/CO 11am. Nonsmoking rms avail. Large, comfortable rooms have two entrances: one to outdoor courtyard and one to inside corridor. **Amenities:** 🔒 A/C, cable TV, in-rm safe. 1 unit w/whirlpool. Some rooms have dataports. **Services:** ✗ 🖨 🍽 **Facilities:** 🛗 📶 🏊 300 ♿ 1 restaurant (dinner only), 1 bar (w/entertainment), games rm, whirlpool. **Rates (CP):** Peak (May–Oct) $45–$50 S; $55–$70 D; $95–$100 ste. Extra person $6. Children under age 18 stay free. Lower rates off-season. Parking: Outdoor, free. Golf packages avail. AE, CB, DC, DISC, JCB, MC, V.

≡≡≡ Holiday Inn

131 Bluebell Dr SW, 44663; tel 330/339-7731 or toll free 800/465-4329; fax 330/339-1565. Exit 81 off I-77, ¼ mi E on OH 39. Five miles to Schoenbrunn Village and "Trumpet in the Land" outdoor drama. Popular with business travelers. **Rooms:** 149 rms, stes, and effic. CI 2pm/CO 11am. Nonsmoking rms avail. Spacious rooms, with recently purchased, elegant, cherry furniture. King rooms have lounge chair, desk, and king-size bed. **Amenities:** 🔒 🐾 🖨 A/C, cable TV w/movies, dataport. 1 unit w/whirlpool. **Services:** ✗ 🖨 🍽 🛎 **Facilities:** 🛗 📶 450 ♿ 1 restaurant, 1 bar, sauna, whirlpool, playground. **Rates:** Peak (June–Oct) $75–$125 S or D; $160 ste; $150 effic. Children under age 19 stay free. Lower rates off-season. Parking: Outdoor, free. AE, CB, DC, DISC, MC, V.

≡ Motel 6

181 Bluebell Dr SW, 44663; tel 330/339-6446; fax 330/339-7436. Exit 81 off I-77, ¼ mi W on OH 39, left on Bluebell. Small, economical, and simply furnished, but very clean. Good for one-night stays when cost-saving is important. **Rooms:** 83 rms. CI noon/CO noon. Nonsmoking rms avail. Small, comfortable, no-frills rooms. **Amenities:** 🔒 A/C, cable TV w/movies. **Services:** 🍽 🛎 **Facilities:** 🛗 ♿ Washer/dryer. **Rates:** Peak (May–Oct) $36 S; $42 D. Extra person $3. Children under age 17 stay free. Lower rates off-season. Parking: Outdoor, free. AE, CB, DC, DISC, MC, V.

ATTRACTIONS 🏛

Schoenbrunn Village State Memorial

E High Ave; tel 330/339-3636. Founded in 1772 as a Moravian mission to the Delaware tribe, this was the first Christian settlement in Ohio. It has been restored to appear as it did 200 years ago. Many log structures have been reconstructed, and are now open to the public; the original cemetery and 2½ acres of planted fields are also on the grounds. Costumed volunteers serve as guides. Museum nearby tells the story of the village. **Open:** Peak (Mem Day–Labor Day) Mon–Sat 9:30am–5pm, Sun noon–5pm. Reduced hours off-season. $$

Zoar Village State Memorial

OH 212, Zoar; tel 330/874-3011. Located 9 mi N of New Philadelphia. The village of Zoar was founded in 1817 by a group of German Separatists fleeing religious persecution. Many of the original buildings here have been restored or reconstructed, included the two-story Georgian house of original leader Joseph Baumeler (built in 1835), the Bimeler museum (1868), the Biblically inspired Zoar Gardens (1835), and the village bakery (1845). Several museums maintained by the Ohio Historical Society within the twelve block historic district exhibit furniture, photos, and other historical artifacts. Group tours available. **Open:** Peak (Mem Day–Labor Day) Weds–Sat 9:30am–5pm, Sun and hols noon–5pm. Reduced hours off-season. Closed Nov–Mar. $$

Fort Laurens State Memorial

11067 Fort Laurens Rd NW, Bolivar; tel 330/874-2059. Located 11 mi N of New Philadelphia. Site of the only American fort built in Ohio during the Revolutionary War. Now maintained by the Ohio Historical Society, the site includes a museum and the Tomb of the Unknown Patriot of the American Revolution. The museum features artifacts found in archaeological digs, re-created scenes of fort life, weapons and accouterments of the Revolutionary War period, and an audiovisual program. Reenactments of the Revolutionary War are periodically staged on the picnic area surrounding the museum. Group tours available. **Open:** Apr–Oct, daily 9:30am–sunset. $

North Canton

See Canton

Oxford

Small town in southwest Ohio, less than five miles from Indiana state line. Site of Miami University (founded in 1809); William Holmes McGuffey (of *McGuffey Reader* fame) was one of the university's first instructors. **Information:** Oxford Chamber of Commerce, 118 W High St, Oxford, 45056 (tel 513/523-8687).

MOTEL 🏨

≡≡ Scottish Inn

5235 College Corner Rd, 45056; tel 513/523-6306 or toll free 800/251-1962; fax 513/523-9693. Clean motel good for one or two nights, 1 mile from downtown Oxford. Comfortable but without frills. Hueston Woods State Park, 5 miles north on OH 732, has a number of recreational facilities. **Rooms:** 30 rms. CI noon/CO 11am. Nonsmoking rms avail.

Amenities: A/C, cable TV w/movies. **Services:** **Facilities:** **Rates (CP):** Peak (June–Aug) $36–$48 S or D. Extra person $4. Children under age 10 stay free. Lower rates off-season. Parking: Outdoor, free. Fri–Sat rates higher than Sun–Thurs rates. AE, CB, DC, DISC, MC, V.

Perrysburg

See Toledo

Piqua

MOTEL

Knights Inn
9060 Country Club Rd, 45356; tel 513/773-6275 or toll free 800/843-5644; fax 513/773-0817. Grounds are clean and neat, but entrance and lobby are small and show wear. Even so, it's a pretty good one-night stop. **Rooms:** 50 rms. CI 11am/CO 11am. Nonsmoking rms avail. Carpet shows wear, but housekeeping is good. **Amenities:** A/C, cable TV. **Services:** Babysitting. **Facilities:** 1 restaurant. JJ's Restaurant located in front of motel. **Rates (CP):** Peak (June–Aug) $56–$67 S or D. Extra person $3. Children under age 12 stay free. Lower rates off-season. Parking: Outdoor, free. AE, DC, DISC, MC, V.

Port Clinton

Seat of Ottawa County, in northern Ohio. Scottish immigrants bound for Chicago were shipwrecked here in 1828, and they decided to stay. **Information:** Ottawa County Visitors Bureau, 109 Madison St, Port Clinton, 43452 (tel 419/734-4386 or toll free 800/441-1271)

MOTELS

Comfort Inn
1723 E Perry St, 43452; tel 419/732-2929 or toll free 800/221-0622; fax 419/734-5108. OH 163. Located on northeast edge of city on Lake Erie shore. Clean and bright motel with no beach—too many rocks and riprap placed there to keep the lake at bay. **Rooms:** 52 rms and stes. CI 3pm/CO 11am. Nonsmoking rms avail. Average-size rooms with comfortable furnishings; clean and in good repair. Some Jacuzzi rooms face the lake. **Amenities:** A/C, satel TV. Some units w/terraces. **Services:** VCR rentals. **Facilities:** **Rates (CP):** Peak (Apr–Sept) $100–$120 S or D; $130–$170 ste. Extra person $10. Children under age 18 stay free. Min stay special events. Lower rates off-season. Parking: Outdoor, free. AE, DC, DISC, MC, V.

Fairfield Inn
3760 E State Rd, 43452; tel 419/732-2434 or toll free 800/228-2800; fax 419/732-2434. On OH 53 N at OH 2 bypass. Bright, airy rooms. Near Cedar Point Amusement Park, East Harbor State Park, swimming beaches. **Rooms:** 64 rms. CI 3pm/CO noon. Nonsmoking rms avail. Upholstered chair and reading lamp in one corner of rooms. **Amenities:** A/C, cable TV, dataport. Hair dryers available on request. **Services:** **Facilities:** Games rm, sauna, washer/dryer. **Rates (CP):** Peak (Apr–Sept) $69–$129 S or D. Extra person $6. Children under age 18 stay free. Lower rates off-season. Parking: Outdoor, free. AE, DC, DISC, MC, V.

Phil's Inn Motel
1704 E Perry St, 43452; tel 419/734-4446 or toll free 800/354-7445; fax 419/732-3370. OH 163, ½ mi E of downtown. One block from city swimming/sunning beach, motel sits back from street, with small parking area. Lobby is large with a profusion of flowers and a chandelier. **Rooms:** 38 rms, stes, and effic. CI 2pm/CO noon. Rooms are average, but very well furnished, comfortable, and clean. Not much of a view. **Amenities:** A/C, cable TV, dataport. **Services:** **Facilities:** 1 restaurant (lunch and dinner only), 1 bar. **Rates (CP):** Peak (Mem Day–Labor Day) $60–$90 S or D; $110–$135 ste; $81–$115 effic. Extra person $10. Lower rates off-season. Parking: Outdoor, free. Summer and winter theater packages avail. AE, DISC, MC, V.

RESTAURANTS

$ Cisco & Charlie's Restaurant & Cantina
In Port Clinton Plaza, 1632 E Perry St; tel 419/732-3126. E of downtown. **American/Mexican.** Features lavish south-of-the-border decor with baskets and tapestries, and a dimly lit dining room with wall sconces and a circular fountain. Several booths set in niches provide romantic privacy. Mexican dishes are generally not spicy, but hot peppers are available on request. Traditional American fare is mainly steaks and chops with potatoes. **FYI:** Reservations not accepted. Dancing. Children's menu. **Open:** Peak (June–Aug) Sun–Thurs 11am–10pm, Fri–Sat 11am–11pm. **Prices:** Main courses $7–$20. AE, DISC, MC, V.

Garden at the Lighthouse
226 E Perry St; tel 419/732-2151. **Continental.** Fronted by a colorful garden and overlooking Lake Erie, this fine restaurant is housed in a local landmark—the first lighthouse keeper's house in the city, built in 1832. The main dining room, an atrium with skylights and large windows, is decorated with flowers, wreaths, and latticework. The restaurant's signature entree is poulet d'elegance—lobster tail and swiss cheese wrapped in a breast of chicken and baked in a puff pastry shell. **FYI:** Reservations recommended. Children's menu. **Open:** Peak (Mem Day–Labor Day) Mon–Thurs 10am–10pm, Fri–Sat 10am–11pm. **Prices:** Main courses $10–$20. AE, CB, DC, DISC, MC, V.

Mon Ami

3845 E Wine Cellar Rd; tel 419/797-4445. **Regional American.** Some 100 years ago, much of the land around the old Mon Ami winery near the shores of Lake Erie was devoted to the growing of grapes. Over the years, the winery's companion restaurant has built a reputation for gracious service and exceptional food. The dark wood richness of the main dining room is complemented by the antique chandeliers hanging from the timbered ceiling. Sculpture is displayed along the rock walls of the room. The restaurant specializes in juicy steaks and chops served with chef Robert Szabo's subtly herbed sauces. Each entree is paired with a wine; Mon Ami offers some 26 varieties and is perhaps best known for its sparkling wines, which are available in the small gift shop. Daily tours of the underground cellars provide a glimpse of the wine-making process. **FYI:** Reservations recommended. Dancing/jazz. Children's menu. **Open:** Lunch Mon–Sat 11am–3pm; dinner Mon–Thurs 5–10pm, Fri–Sat 5–11pm, Sun noon–9pm; brunch Sun 11am–3pm. **Prices:** Main courses $13–$19. AE, DISC, MC, V. 🍴 👥

Phil's Inn Restaurant

1708 E Perry St; tel 419/734-4446. **American.** Pleasant mom-and-pop eatery offering tasty meat-and-potatoes fare (steaks and chops) with few frills and few sauces. **FYI:** Reservations not accepted. Children's menu. **Open:** Daily 11am–11pm. **Prices:** Main courses $8–$13. AE, DISC, MC, V. 👥 ♿

REFRESHMENT STOP 🥤

Cheese Haven Restaurant

OH 163/53, Marblehead; tel 419/734-2611. **Burgers/Pizza.** A landmark since 1949, near the shores of Lake Erie. This popular short-order restaurant is adjacent to the Cheese Haven stores, which sell a variety of local and imported cheeses, local wines, smoked meats, and souvenirs to travelers who return to the area year after year. The basic menu offers pizza, burgers, and sandwiches. **Open:** Wed–Sun 11:30am–7pm. MC, V.

ATTRACTIONS 🏛

African Safari Wildlife Park

Lightner Rd; tel 419/732-3606. Visitors can get a up-close look at a menagerie of unusual animals—including llamas, alpacas, and white zebra—from this drive through safari. Camel rides available. **Open:** Mem Day–Labor Day, daily 9am–5pm. $$$

Heineman Winery and Crystal Cave

Catawba St, Put-in-Bay; tel 419/285-2811. Located in the Lake Erie Islands, approximately 10 mi N of Port Clinton. A unique opportunity to get a cave tour and a winery tour at the same location. Crystal Cave is part of a substantial system of caverns on this small island (accessible by ferry from Port Clinton and Catawba Point) in Lake Erie. The area is also known for its wines, and guests are invited to taste a sampling before or after a tour. **Open:** May–Sept, daily 11am–5pm. $$

Perry's Victory and International Peace Memorial

Put-In-Bay; tel 419/285-2184. This memorial in commemoration of Commodore Oliver Hazard Perry's decisive defeat of the British at the Battle of Lake Erie in 1813 consists of a Doric column rising 350 feet in the air. At 317 feet, an observation platform offers spectacular views that extend all the way to Canada. **Open:** Peak (Mem Day–Labor Day) Daily 10am–5pm. Reduced hours off-season. $

Port Jefferson

See Sidney

Portsmouth

Seat of Scioto County, in southern Ohio. Located at the confluence of the Ohio and Scioto Rivers, 100 miles east of Cincinnati. The former brewery town is now a center of iron, brick, and plastic manufacturing. **Information:** Portsmouth Area Chamber of Commerce, 1020 7th St, PO Box 509, Portsmouth, 45662 (tel 614/353-7647).

HOTEL 🏨

🏨🏨🏨 Ramada Inn

711 2nd St, 45662; tel 614/354-7711 or toll free 800/272-6232; fax 614/353-1539. 1 block from the Ohio River. Elegant facility just two blocks from the Murals, beautiful depictions of historic events and people of Portsmouth painted on the flood wall of the Ohio River—a must-see for visitors to the area. **Rooms:** 108 rms. CI 3pm/CO noon. Nonsmoking rms avail. **Amenities:** 🛁 🗜 📺 A/C, cable TV w/movies, dataport. **Services:** ✗ 🛏 🗗 🛎 **Facilities:** 🛗 🎳 🏊 ♿ 1 restaurant, 1 bar (w/entertainment), whirlpool. Beautiful atrium/patio and pool area is focal point of hotel; lush plants and trees give indoor pool an outdoor look. Free access to nearby Shawnee State University sports and fitness facility. **Rates:** $56–$59 S; $63–$70 D. Extra person $7. Children under age 18 stay free. Parking: Outdoor, free. AE, CB, DC, DISC, MC, V.

MOTEL

🏨🏨🏨 Holiday Inn

US 23 N, 45662; tel 614/354-2851 or toll free 800/465-4329; fax 614/353-2084. 1½ mi N of US 52. Within minutes of Shawnee State Forest, this facility offers a lot for a reasonable price. **Rooms:** 100 rms. CI 2pm/CO noon. Nonsmoking rms avail. **Amenities:** 🛁 🗜 A/C, cable TV. **Services:** ✗ 🛏 🗗 🛎 **Facilities:** 🛗 🏊 ♿ 1 restaurant, 1 bar (w/entertainment). Access to nearby Shawnee State University fitness center. **Rates:** $55 S or D. Children under age 18 stay free. Parking: Outdoor, free. AE, CB, DC, DISC, JCB, MC, V.

Sandusky

Seat of Erie County, in northern Ohio. The town, stretching six miles along Sandusky Bay, has an old seaside flavor. The 18-mile-long bay is nearly landlocked by Cedar Point and Marblehead peninsulas, making it one of the finest natural harbors on Lake Erie. **Information:** Erie County Chamber of Commerce, 1610 Cleveland Rd, PO Box 620, Sandusky, 44870 (tel 419/625-6421).

HOTEL 🛏

≣≣≣ Hotel Breakers
1 Causeway Dr, PO Box 5006, 44871; tel 419/626-0830; fax 419/627-2267. Cedar Point. 364 acres. The year 1905 marked the beginning of a long and outstanding vacation tradition at Cedar Point. In 1995, a new $10 million wing (Breakers East) was opened. Updated often, the sprawling hotel overlooking Lake Erie has retained much of its turn-of-the-century charm. Stained-glass windows grace the spacious main lobby, and some of the original wicker furniture (imported from Austria-Hungary in the early 1900s) is used throughout the hotel. Such luminaries as Annie Oakley, Abbot and Costello, Theodore Dreiser, John Philip Sousa, and six US presidents have been guests; opera stars were known to have given impromptu performances from the balcony of a room in the five-story rotunda. **Rooms:** 496 rms and stes. Executive level. CI 3pm/CO 11am. Nonsmoking rms avail. All rooms are comfortable, but some are small. Suites are spacious. **Amenities:** 🛁 🌀 A/C, cable TV w/movies. Some units w/terraces, some w/whirlpools. Suites have bathrobes, complimentary box of chocolates, whirlpools, in-room safes, and closed-in balconies overlooking pool and beach. **Services:** ✕ 🗝 🍸 Social director, babysitting. Shuttle service to Cedar Point attractions and Sandusky Airport (mainly for private planes). **Facilities:** 🖼 🏊 ⌨200 3 restaurants, 1 bar, 1 beach (lake shore), lifeguard, games rm, whirlpool, playground, washer/dryer. Two large pools overlook Lake Erie beach and have huge sun decks lined with lounges and umbrella-topped tables. **Rates:** $110–$130 S or D; $260–$275 ste. Extra person $11. Children under age 5 stay free. Parking: Outdoor, free. Packages include coupons for park rides plus some meals. Closed Oct 1–mid-May. DISC, MC, V.

MOTELS
≣≣ Comfort Inn
5909 Milan Rd, 44870; tel 419/621-0200 or toll free 800/228-5150; fax 419/621-0060. Opened in 1994, this gleaming white building still looks new. The high-ceilinged lobby features a marble floor and windows on two sides. Located on four-lane highway, often heavily trafficked during summer

months. Convenient to local attractions and activities. **Rooms:** 210 rms and stes. CI 4pm/CO noon. Nonsmoking rms avail. **Amenities:** 🛁 A/C, cable TV. Some rooms have radios. **Services:** 🍽 🐾 Pet deposit $20. **Facilities:** 🖼 ⌨125 🏊 Games rm, spa, sauna, whirlpool. Spacious indoor pool with tables and lounges on wide deck. **Rates (CP):** Peak (May 15–Sept 15) $78–$250 S or D; $160–$300 ste. Extra person $6. Children under age 12 stay free. Lower rates off-season. Parking: Outdoor, free. Packages include weekend getaways, Valentine's Day, New Year's Eve, and sweetheart weekend. AE, CB, DC, DISC, MC, V.

≣≣ Econo Lodge Cedar Point
1904 Cleveland Rd, 44870; tel 419/627-8000 or toll free 800/424-4777; fax 419/627-8944. On US 6 across from Cedar Point entrance. Solid overnight motel. Low on flair and amenities, but clean and comfortable. **Rooms:** 118 rms. CI 3pm/CO 11am. Nonsmoking rms avail. **Amenities:** 🛁 🌀 A/C, cable TV. **Services:** ✕ 🍸 **Facilities:** 🖼 **Rates:** Peak (June–Aug) $60–$125 S or D. Extra person $5. Children under age 18 stay free. Lower rates off-season. Parking: Outdoor, free. AE, DISC, MC, V.

≣≣≣ Fairfield Inn
6220 Milan Rd, 44870; tel 419/621-9500 or toll free 800/228-2800; fax 419/621-9500. Clean and bright, near attractions and activities. **Rooms:** 63 rms and stes. CI 3pm/CO noon. Nonsmoking rms avail. **Amenities:** 🛁 🌀 A/C, cable TV w/movies, dataport. Some units w/whirlpools. **Services:** 📠 🍸 **Facilities:** 🖼 🏊 ⌨ ⌨20 🏊 Games rm, sauna, washer/dryer. Large pool area with wide sun deck. **Rates (CP):** Peak (May–Aug) $103–$129 S or D; $129–$139 ste. Extra person $6. Children under age 18 stay free. Lower rates off-season. Parking: Outdoor, free. AE, CB, DC, DISC, MC, V.

≣≣≣ Holiday Inn
5513 Milan Rd, 44870; tel 419/626-6671 or toll free 800/HOLIDAY. On US 250 6 mi N of OH Tpk exit 7. Considered a motel, but operated more like a resort. Clean, bright, and in good repair, with plenty of facilities for the entire family. **Rooms:** 175 rms and stes. CI 4pm/CO 11am. Nonsmoking rms avail. Average size rooms, with good quality, sturdy, tasteful furniture. Tinted glass walls add to color and rich decor. **Amenities:** 🛁 🌀 📺 A/C, cable TV w/movies. Dataports in some rooms. **Services:** ✕ 📠 🍸 Babysitting. **Facilities:** 🖼 ⌨ ⌨300 🏊 1 restaurant, 1 bar, games rm, spa, sauna, whirlpool, playground, washer/dryer. **Rates:** Peak (June–Sept) $99–$189 S or D; $109–$209 ste. Children under age 18 stay free. Lower rates off-season. Parking: Outdoor, free. Heart-to-Heart, Valentine's Day, New Year's Eve, getaways, and Cedar Point packages avail. AE, CB, DC, DISC, MC, V.

≣≣ Holiday Inn Express
5513½ Milan Rd, 44870; tel 419/624-0028 or toll free 800/HOLIDAY; fax 419/624-0098. On US 250 6 mi N of OH Tpk exit 7. Holiday Inn facility minus frills. Built in 1995.

Rooms: 40 rms. CI 4pm/CO 11am. Nonsmoking rms avail. Clean and bright rooms furnished in oak. Upholstered recliner and reading lamp in all rooms. 40 rooms have Murphy beds (in wall). **Amenities:** 🖥 🕭 A/C, cable TV, dataport. **Services:** 🖾 🍽 Babysitting. Guests may use adjoining Holiday Inn pool and Holidome facilities at no extra charge. **Facilities:** 🏊10 🛦 **Rates (CP):** Peak (June–Sept) $99–$189 S or D. Extra person $5. Children under age 18 stay free. Lower rates off-season. Parking: Outdoor, free. AE, CB, DC, DISC, JCB, MC, V.

≡≡≡ Ramada Inn

5608 Milan Rd, 44870; tel 419/626-9890 or toll free 800/2-RAMADA; fax 419/626-0996. On US 250 6 mi N of OH Tpk exit 7. Solid overnighter in summer resort area. Two-story lobby with mirrors on balcony. Next door to shopping mall. **Rooms:** 100 rms. CI 3pm/CO noon. Nonsmoking rms avail. Well-kept rooms with blond, sturdy furnishings and pastel decor. Some rooms have sofa beds; all have floor-style reading lamps. **Amenities:** 🖥 🕭 A/C, cable TV. **Services:** ✕ 🖾 🍽 Babysitting. **Facilities:** 🗐 🏃 🛦 1 restaurant (lunch and dinner only), 1 bar, games rm. Pool in courtyard makes for picturesque setting. **Rates (CP):** Peak (May–Sept) $89–$189 S or D. Extra person $8. Children under age 18 stay free. Lower rates off-season. Parking: Outdoor, free. Rates are for four persons; extra charge for fifth person. Rollaway bed $8. AE, CB, DC, DISC, MC, V.

≡≡ Rodeway Inn Cedar Point

2905 Milan Rd, 44870; tel 419/625-1291 or toll free 800/228-2000. On US 250 3 mi N of jct OH 4. Clean and comfortably furnished rooms. **Rooms:** 113 rms. CI 4pm/CO noon. Nonsmoking rms avail. **Amenities:** 🖥 A/C, cable TV. **Services:** 🍽 🖾 **Facilities:** 🗐 🏃 🏊25 🛦 1 bar (w/entertainment), games rm, washer/dryer. **Rates:** Peak (May 15–Sept 15) $34–$98 S or D. Children under age 18 stay free. Lower rates off-season. Parking: Outdoor, free. Refundable key deposit $5. AE, DC, DISC, JCB, MC, V.

≡≡ Travelodge

5906 Milan Rd, 44870; tel 419/627-8971 or toll free 800/578-7878. Solid overnight facility, close to area attractions and activities. **Rooms:** 92 rms and stes. CI 4pm/CO noon. Nonsmoking rms avail. **Amenities:** 🖥 A/C, cable TV. **Services:** 🍽 🖾 Pet deposit $20. **Facilities:** 🗐 🏃 🛦 Games rm, sauna, whirlpool, washer/dryer. **Rates:** Peak (May 15–Sept 15) $78–$250 S or D; $180–$250 ste. Extra person $10. Children under age 13 stay free. Lower rates off-season. Parking: Outdoor, free. Rollaway bed $10. AE, DISC, MC, V.

RESORT

≡≡≡ Radisson Harbour Inn

2001 Cleveland Rd, 44870; tel 419/627-2500 or toll free 800/333-3333; fax 419/627-0745. At Cedar Point Causeway. 30 acres. Location is excellent—at end of Cedar Point Causeway. Large, tastefully decorated lobby with windows providing much of the light. Has its own pier and water sport rentals and facilities; visiting boaters can tie up their boats at the Radisson pier. **Rooms:** 237 rms and stes. Executive level. CI 4pm/CO noon. Nonsmoking rms avail. Especially comfortable, upscale furnishings; decor is bright, with pastel colors. Many rooms have views of pier area, bay, and Lake Erie. **Amenities:** 🖥 🕭 🖵 A/C, cable TV w/movies. All units w/terraces, some w/whirlpools. **Services:** 🍴 🚗 🖾 🍽 🛎 Children's program. VCR rentals. Pet limit 15 pounds. Golf at three courses can be arranged, along with charter boat fishing in Lake Erie—known for walleye, perch, and smallmouth bass. Hotel is well staffed. **Facilities:** 🗐 🛆 🗀 🥪 🏊500 🛦 1 restaurant, 1 bar (w/entertainment), games rm, whirlpool, washer/dryer. Pool has wide sun deck lined with lounges and chairs. The Bay View Grille, a bright dining room with a wall of windows and excellent views of the bay, offers a prime rib buffet Fri–Sun and a dinner buffet Mon–Thurs; it emphasizes Ohio wines during dinner hours. **Rates:** Peak (Mem Day–Labor Day) $99–$199 S or D; $129–$319 ste. Children under age 18 stay free. Min stay wknds. Lower rates off-season. Parking: Outdoor, free. Valentine's Day, getaway, romance, and "two-for-two" packages avail. Packages to Cedar Point also avail. Minimum stay during summer weekends. AE, DC, DISC, MC, V.

RESTAURANT 🍴

Cedar Villa

1918 Cleveland Rd; tel 419/625-8487. On US 6 across from Cedar Point Causeway. **American/Italian.** This restaurant is located on the corner across from the causeway to Cedar Point Amusement Park; keep an eye out for it as you're driving, or you'll miss it with little chance to turn back. A good stop for lunch or dinner after visiting the park, it offers a basic American-Italian menu. **FYI:** Reservations not accepted. Children's menu. No smoking. **Open:** Peak (June–Aug) daily 11am–11pm. Closed Sept 19–Oct 10. **Prices:** Main courses $6–$10. AE, CB, DISC, MC, V. 🅿🅿

Sidney

Seat of Shelby county in west central Ohio, on the Great Miami River. Refrigerator parts and aluminum products are manufactured here. **Information:** Sidney-Shelby Chamber of Commerce, 100 S Main Ave, Sidney, 45365 (tel 513/492-9122).

MOTELS 🏨

≡≡ Comfort Inn

1959 W Michigan Ave, 45365; tel 513/492-3001 or toll free 800/221-2222; fax 513/497-8150. Exit 92 off I-75. Located off main street on lane that runs along I-75; near Lake Loramie fishing, hiking, swimming, and nature study facilities and near Piqua Historical Park. **Rooms:** 72 rms. Executive level. CI 3pm/CO 11am. Nonsmoking rms avail. **Amenities:** 🖥 A/C, cable TV. Some units w/whirlpools. **Services:** ✕ 🖾

Facilities: ⬚ ⬚ ⬚35 ⬚ Whirlpool. **Rates (CP):** Peak (Apr–Oct) $48–$61 S or D. Extra person $5. Children under age 18 stay free. Lower rates off-season. Parking: Outdoor, free. AE, CB, DC, DISC, JCB, MC, V.

≣ ≣ Econo Lodge

2009 W Michigan St, 45365; tel 513/492-9164 or toll free 800/55-ECONO; fax 513/492-9164 ext 153. Clean and in good repair. Two-story lobby is impressive with large paintings and chandelier; one wall of lobby has second-floor balcony effect. Good for families or couples. Near fishing, bowling, golfing, and the *Titanic* Memorial Museum (many of those who died on the *Titanic* are buried here). **Rooms:** 98 rms and effic. Executive level. CI 1pm/CO 11am. Nonsmoking rms avail. Some large, suite-like rooms are suitable for families. **Amenities:** ⬚ A/C, cable TV, voice mail. **Services:** ✗ ⬚ ⬚ **Facilities:** ⬚ ⬚ ⬚50 ⬚ 1 restaurant, 1 bar, washer/dryer. **Rates (CP):** Peak (July–Aug) $36–$48 S or D; $36–$48 effic. Extra person $5. Children under age 16 stay free. Lower rates off-season. Parking: Outdoor, free. AE, CB, DC, DISC, ER, JCB, MC, V.

≣ ≣ ≣ Holiday Inn Sidney

400 Folkerth Ave, 45365; tel 513/492-1131 or toll free 800/HOLIDAY; fax 513/498-4655. A typical clean and shining Holiday Inn, near a shopping mall. Good for families, couples, and seniors. Nearby are fishing, bowling, golfing, and the *Titanic* Memorial Museum. **Rooms:** 134 rms and stes. CI 3pm/CO noon. Nonsmoking rms avail. **Amenities:** ⬚ ⬚ A/C, satel TV w/movies. **Services:** ✗ ⬚ ⬚ ⬚ Children's program, babysitting. **Facilities:** ⬚ ⬚ ⬚ ⬚300 ⬚ 1 restaurant, 1 bar, games rm, sauna, washer/dryer. Beauty salon is behind and affiliated with motel. **Rates:** $57 S or D; $64 ste. Extra person $5. Children under age 19 stay free. Parking: Outdoor, free. AE, DC, DISC, JCB, MC, V.

RESTAURANTS

The Fairington

In Fairington Park, 1103 Fairington Dr; tel 513/492-6186. **Seafood.** An upscale eatery located in a woodsy setting, perfect for a romantic evening for two. The ambience is rich and relaxing, with windows looking out into the trees and landscaped grounds lining two sides of the large dining room. Flowers decorate the entrance, and the dining room is lit by large chandeliers. Signature entrees include Black Forest filet (filet mignon filled with sweet cherries and topped with ham and béarnaise sauce) and shrimp Catalina (jumbo shrimp stuffed with crabmeat and wrapped in bacon). **FYI:** Reservations recommended. Piano. Children's menu. **Open:** Lunch Mon–Fri 11am–2pm; dinner Mon–Thurs 4:30–9pm, Fri 4:30–9:30pm, Sat 5–9:30pm. **Prices:** Main courses $14–$38. AE, DC, DISC, MC, V. ⬚ ⬚ ⬚

Hussey's Restaurant

8760 S Broad St, Port Jefferson; tel 513/492-0038. **American.** Hard by the Great Miami River, this restaurant's dining room has great views of the river and of the ducks and Canadian geese who call this area home. No wonder the interior decor has a wild-duck theme. Chicken is the most popular entree; charbroiled steak is a close second. **FYI:** Reservations recommended. Children's menu. **Open:** Tues–Fri 4–10pm, Sat 4–10:30pm. **Prices:** Main courses $5–$16. AE, MC, V. ⬚ ⬚ ⬚

ATTRACTION

Titanic Memorial Museum

Russell Rd; tel 513/492-7762. Memorabilia from the ill-fated cruise ship, including original blueprints and photographs of the ship, artifacts, scale models, and actual clothing worn by survivors of the 1912 disaster. **Open:** Mon–Wed 10am–4:30pm, Sat 9am–4:30pm, Sun 1–5pm. $$

Springfield

Seat of Clark County, in western Ohio. Named for the springwater flowing down the cliffs bordering the little valley of Buck Creek to the west. Pennsylvania House (built in 1824) was a tavern and stagecoach stop on the Old National Road. **Information:** Springfield-Clark County Convention & Visitors Bureau, 333 N Limestone St, #201, Springfield, 45503 (tel 513/325-7621).

MOTELS

≣ ≣ ≣ Days Inn

1715 W North St, 45504; tel 513/324-5561 or toll free 800/DAYS-INN; fax 513/324-5845. US 40; 1 mi W of courthouse. Simple, clean motel undergoing a full renovation. Near Cedar Bog Nature Preserve, Springfield Museum of Art, and Weaver Chapel, just off the Wittenberg College campus. **Rooms:** 129 rms. CI 4pm/CO noon. Nonsmoking rms avail. **Amenities:** ⬚ A/C, cable TV. **Services:** ⬚ ⬚ **Facilities:** ⬚ ⬚ ⬚100 ⬚ 1 restaurant, 1 bar. **Rates (CP):** $41–$45 S; $48–$52 D. Extra person $4. Children under age 12 stay free. Parking: Outdoor, free. Children 13–18 are charged $1 to stay in room with parents. AE, DC, DISC, JCB, MC, V.

≣ ≣ ≣ Holiday Inn

383 E Leffel Lane, 45505; tel 513/323-8631 or toll free 800/HOLIDAY; fax 513/323-5389. Exit 54 off I-70. Clean facility offering large rooms. Near Madonna of the Trail Memorial, and Buck Creek State Park fishing, swimming, and hiking. **Rooms:** 150 rms. CI 3pm/CO noon. Nonsmoking rms avail. Some rooms have upholstered chairs and reading lamps. **Amenities:** ⬚ ⬚ A/C, satel TV w/movies, dataport. Some units w/terraces. **Services:** ✗ ⬚ ⬚ Overnight dry cleaning service Mon–Thurs; one-day service Fri. **Facilities:** ⬚ ⬚ ⬚ ⬚500 ⬚ 1 restaurant, 1 bar, games rm, playground. Holidome has play area for youngsters with two slides and monkey bars. **Rates:** $69–$85 S or D. Children under age 18

stay free. Parking: Outdoor, free. Packages include honeymoon, bed-and-breakfast, Valentine's Day, and New Year's Eve. AE, CB, DC, DISC, JCB, MC, V.

RESTAURANTS 🍽️

Casey's

2205 Park Rd; tel 513/322-0397. ½ mi E of US 68 on US 40. **Continental.** Soft overhead lighting, artwork on the walls, tasteful furnishings, and a large aquarium add to the atmosphere at this pleasant bistro. The kitchen churns out chargrilled and broiled steaks, but lighter fare (sandwiches, burgers) is also available. **FYI:** Reservations accepted. Dress code. **Open:** Lunch Mon–Sat 11:30am–2pm; dinner Mon–Sat 5–10pm. **Prices:** Main courses $9–$15. AE, CB, DC, DISC, MC, V. ♥ 🏩 ♿

⑤ ★ The Mill

3404 W National Rd; tel 513/324-4045. ¼ mi W of US 68 on US 40. **Seafood/Steak.** Opened as a gristmill in 1825 and later used as a stagecoach stop, the building's massive timbered construction and the genuinely rustic wood decor give this restaurant a pioneer ambience. The main dining room is in the original mill building, but other dining rooms have been added over the years. The kitchen here has long been known for its slow-roasted prime rib, steaks, and South African lobster tails. All meals come with choice of potato, such as the popular home fries prepared in large, decades-old cast-iron skillets. **FYI:** Reservations recommended. Children's menu. **Open:** Mon–Thurs 11am–10pm, Fri–Sat 11am–11pm. **Prices:** Main courses $8–$33. AE, CB, DC, DISC, MC, V. ⬛ 🏩 ♥ ♿

Toledo

Seat of Lucas County, in northwest part of state. The city's large, excellent harbor makes it an important port on Lake Erie. Everything from glass to spark plugs to paint is produced here. The city is also home to the University of Toledo and numerous cultural institutions. **Information:** Greater Toledo Convention & Visitors Bureau, 401 W Jefferson Ave, Toledo, 43604 (tel 419/321-6404).

HOTELS 🏨

⬌⬌⬌ Clarion Hotel Westgate

3536 Secor Rd, 43606; tel 419/535-7070 or toll free 800/424-6423; fax 419/536-4836. Under new management, the hotel is undergoing a full redecoration of all rooms and public areas. Nearby facilities for tennis, golf, hiking, bicycling, fishing, volleyball, and racquetball. **Rooms:** 309 rms and stes. CI 3pm/CO noon. Nonsmoking rms avail. Rooms are bright and have full-length mirrors. **Amenities:** 🔒 ❄️ A/C, cable TV w/movies. Some units w/whirlpools. Suites have refrigerators. **Services:** ✕ 🚐 🔼 ➥ 🦮 The free parking garage has a clearance of 6' 4", which excludes most full-size

vans and RVs. Extra charge for pets. Massage service available. **Facilities:** 🛎️ 🏋️ 🧖 ⬛ 7500 ♿ 2 restaurants, 1 bar (w/entertainment), games rm, whirlpool, washer/dryer. Coffee shop/lounge open in afternoon. Full-service restaurant rated one of the better establishments in Toledo area. **Rates:** $69–$99 S or D; $225–$275 ste. Extra person $10. Children under age 12 stay free. Parking: Indoor/outdoor, free. AE, CB, DC, DISC, JCB, MC, V.

⬌⬌⬌ Crowne Plaza Hotel

2 Seagate, 43604; tel 419/241-1411 or toll free 800/2-CROWNE; fax 419/241-8161. on Maumee River opposite Owens Illinois Building. The 12-floor structure overlooks the Maumee River and International Park and has its own entrance to the science and industry museum building next door. **Rooms:** 241 rms and stes. Executive level. CI 3pm/CO noon. Nonsmoking rms avail. All rooms have a view of the river; some also have a view of a landscaped reflection pool with waterfall. **Amenities:** 🔒 ❄️ ⬛ A/C, satel TV w/movies, refrig, dataport, voice mail. 1 unit w/whirlpool. Irons and ironing boards, Nintendo. **Services:** ✕ 🔑 VP 🔼 ➥ Babysitting. Sightseeing cruise on river offered at pier behind hotel. Masseur can be arranged. Car-rental desk located just outside hotel. **Facilities:** 🛎️ 🧖 ⬛ 1000 🖥️ ♿ 1 restaurant, 1 bar (w/entertainment), spa, sauna, whirlpool. **Rates:** $89–$119 S or D; $349 ste. Children under age 19 stay free. Parking: Indoor/outdoor, $7–$9/day. Weekend packages include a "Romance Weekend," a "Breakfast Package," and a "New Year's Eve Package." AE, CB, DC, DISC, JCB, MC, V.

⬌⬌⬌ Hilton Hotel

3100 Glendale Ave, 43614; tel 419/381-6800 or toll free 800/HILTON; fax 419/389-9716. An impressive hotel on the campus of the Medical College of Ohio in western Toledo. The lobby is bright, white, and two stories with skylights. Near Toledo sights and attractions. **Rooms:** 213 rms and stes. Executive level. CI 3pm/CO 11am. Nonsmoking rms avail. King rooms have recliners, reading lamps, irons, and ironing boards. **Amenities:** 🔒 ❄️ ⬛ 🍴 A/C, satel TV w/movies, dataport. Refrigerators and makeup mirrors available on request. **Services:** ✕ 🚐 🔼 ➥ Babysitting. Messenger service for one- and two-bedroom suites. HHonors (Hilton program) rooms located on two floors; all have new 25" TVs. **Facilities:** 🛎️ 🏋️ 🧖 📺 3 500 ♿ 1 restaurant, 1 bar (w/entertainment), basketball, volleyball, games rm, racquetball, sauna, steam rm, whirlpool. Pool area, with two walls of windows, wide lounging deck, and some tables with umbrellas, is not large; pool is under cover. The restaurant, a very good one, is open for breakfast, lunch, dinner, and Sun brunch. Occasional entertainment in lounge. Guests have access to 32,000-square-foot Morse Fitness Center on college campus with workout equipment, basketball court, volleyball court, running/walking track, racquetball court, and a masseur. **Rates:** $104–$134 S or D; $150–

$390 ste. Extra person $10. Children under age 18 stay free. Parking: Outdoor, free. Valentine's Day, wedding, family, and romance packages. AE, CB, DC, DISC, MC, V.

≡≡≡ Radisson Hotel

101 N Summit St, 43604 (Downtown); tel 419/241-3000 or toll free 800/333-3333; fax 419/321-2099. Hotel is connected to Seagate Centre, which faces Jefferson Ave. Lobby is bright, with highly polished marble floors. Bar/lounge can be used for special meetings or pre-convention functions. **Rooms:** 400 rms and stes. Executive level. CI 3pm/CO noon. Nonsmoking rms avail. **Amenities:** 📶 A/C, cable TV w/movies, dataport. 1 unit w/terrace, 1 w/whirlpool. Suites have wet bars. **Services:** ✕ ☛ VP ⟋ ⊷ ⬹ Car-rental desk. **Facilities:** ⟦ ⟧ ⟦700⟧ ⬚ ⟋ 1 restaurant, 1 bar, sauna, whirlpool. **Rates:** $69–$109 S; $79–$119 D; $175–$500 ste. Extra person $10. Children under age 5 stay free. Min stay special events. Parking: Indoor/outdoor, $4–$8/day. Packages might include Romantic Adventure, Getaway Adventure, Valentine's Day, and New Year's Eve. AE, CB, DC, DISC, MC, V.

MOTELS

≡≡ Best Western Executive Inn

27441 Helen Dr, Perrysburg, 43551; tel 419/874-9181 or toll free 800/528-1234; fax 419/874-9181 ext 155. 1 block E of US 20 at exit 193 off I-75. Nice family motel near entertainment, physical fitness gym, and several restaurants. Good value. **Rooms:** 102 rms. CI 2pm/CO noon. Nonsmoking rms avail. **Amenities:** 📶 A/C, satel TV. **Services:** ⟋ ⬹ Continental breakfast served Mon–Fri only. A local restaurant will deliver to guest rooms. **Facilities:** ⟦ ⟧ ⟦75⟧ Sauna, whirlpool, washer/dryer. **Rates:** Peak (Apr–Oct) $45–$60 S or D. Children under age 12 stay free. Lower rates off-season. Parking: Outdoor, free. AE, CB, DC, DISC, MC, V.

≡≡ Comfort Inn

3560 Secor Rd, 43606; tel 419/531-2666 or toll free 800/221-2222; fax 419/531-4757. S of I-475. A clean facility with a fitness/workout trail behind it. Hotel next door is under same management and offers restaurant and bar services and pool and weight room privileges. Golf courses, bowling alleys, and racquetball courts nearby. **Rooms:** 70 rms. CI 3pm/CO noon. Nonsmoking rms avail. Corner mirrors give added depth and brightness, as well as additional makeup area. **Amenities:** 📶 A/C, cable TV. **Services:** ⟋ ⟋ ⬹ Massage service can be arranged. **Facilities:** ⟦ ⟧ ⟦ ⟧ **Rates (CP):** $49 S or D. Children under age 18 stay free. Lower rates off-season. Parking: Indoor/outdoor, free. Quoted rates are for up to four persons in room. AE, CB, DC, DISC, JCB, MC, V.

≡≡≡ Courtyard by Marriott

1435 E Mall Rd, 43528; tel 419/866-1001 or toll free 800/321-2211; fax 419/866-9869. Airport Hwy (US 2) and I-475. Furnishings are high quality. Several restaurants and fast food facilities and a large park with fishing, hiking, bicycling, and horseback riding are all nearby. **Rooms:** 149 rms and

stes. CI 3pm/CO 1pm. Nonsmoking rms avail. Very pleasant rooms, average to large, some with courtyard views. **Amenities:** 📶 ⟋ A/C, satel TV w/movies, dataport. Some units w/terraces. Suites have king-size or double beds, sofa bed, and refrigerators. **Services:** ⟦ ⟧ ⟋ ⟋ Babysitting. Transportation to the Toledo Express Airport for car rental can be provided. **Facilities:** ⟦ ⟧ ⟦ ⟧ ⟦80⟧ ⟋ 1 restaurant (bkfst only), 1 bar, whirlpool, washer/dryer. Full bar service Mon–Fri. Restaurant open for breakfast only. Lifeguard at the pool on Sat only. **Rates:** $78–$88 S or D; $95–$105 ste. Children under age 18 stay free. Parking: Outdoor, free. Quoted rates are for up to four persons per room. Some fall and winter weekend packages. Senior discount. AE, DC, DISC, MC, V.

≡≡ Cross Country Inn

1201 E Mall Dr, Holland, 43528; tel 419/866-6565 or toll free 800/621-1429; fax 419/866-6608. E of I-475 exit 8. A clean motel in good repair, across the street from the Spring Meadows Shopping Mall. Near Toledo sights and attractions. **Rooms:** 128 rms. CI 1pm/CO noon. Nonsmoking rms avail. Rooms have recliners with reading lamps in one corner. Bathrooms are well lighted and bright; sinks are separate from showers and toilets. **Amenities:** 📶 A/C, satel TV w/movies. **Services:** ⟋ Free coffee, tea, and hot chocolate in lobby. Drive-up window for registration and/or checkout. **Facilities:** ⟦ ⟧ ⟦ ⟧ **Rates:** $33–$45 S or D. Extra person $7. Children under age 18 stay free. Parking: Outdoor, free. AE, DC, DISC, MC, V.

≡ Crown Inn

1727 W Alexis Rd, 43613; tel 419/473-1485. Bright, clean motel with good living space. The one-story structure compares favorably with other lodgings in the area. The motel is hard to see from the highway, and the sign is not prominent. **Rooms:** 40 rms and effic. CI 3pm/CO noon. Nonsmoking rms avail. Some rooms look out on the new pool area. **Amenities:** 📶 A/C, cable TV. Some rooms have hair dryers. **Services:** ⟋ ⬹ VCR rentals at the office. Deposit required at check-in for pets. **Facilities:** ⟦ ⟧ ⟦ ⟧ Whirlpool. Hot tub. **Rates (CP):** $38–$44 S or D; $43–$49 effic. Extra person $5. Children under age 16 stay free. Parking: Outdoor, free. First two children under 16 stay free, each one thereafter is charged $5. AE, CB, DC, DISC, MC, V.

≡≡≡ Days Inn

10667 Fremont Pike, Perrysburg, 43551; tel 419/874-8771 or toll free 800/DAYS-INN; fax 419/874-8771. E of I-75 exit 193 on US 20. An attractive, clean facility near some 18 restaurants, shopping malls, bowling, and golf facilities. The connecting hallways between buildings and building wings have walls of windows, which add to the brightness and pleasant ambience. Near lots of Toledo sights and attractions. **Rooms:** 124 rms and stes. CI 3pm/CO 11am. Nonsmoking rms avail. **Amenities:** 📶 ⟋ ⟦ ⟧ A/C, cable TV. King rooms have dataports. **Services:** ✕ ⟦ ⟧ ⟋ ⟋ ⬹ Pets $5. **Facilities:** ⟦ ⟧ ⟦ ⟧ ⟦100⟧ ⟋ Washer/dryer. Working fireplace in sunken area of bar/lounge. Nice sun deck at pool, with umbrellas on tables and plenty of chaise lounges. Fitness for a fee at nearby health spa, with masseur on duty. **Rates (CP):** Peak (June–Aug) $55–$80 S or D; $100 ste. Extra person $4. Children under age 12 stay free. Lower rates off-season. Parking: Outdoor, free. AE, CB, DC, DISC, MC, V.

≣≣≣ Econo Lodge
1800 Miami St, 43605; tel 419/666-5120 or toll free 800/242-6446; fax 419/666-4298. Exit 199 off I-75. Clean interior, light and airy hallways. Minimal landscaping; exterior is primarily parking lot. Good value. **Rooms:** 145 rms. CI 3pm/CO noon. Nonsmoking rms avail. **Amenities:** 📺 A/C, cable TV w/movies. Some units w/terraces. **Services:** ✕ 🖼 ⤶ **Facilities:** 🏋 🛝 🍽 🏊 2 restaurants (lunch and dinner only), 1 bar, sauna, whirlpool, playground, washer/dryer. Olympic-size swimming pool. Gloria's Restaurant open 11am–2:30pm and 5–10pm. Coffee shop open 6:30–11am. **Rates:** $54–$49 S or D. Children under age 12 stay free. Parking: Outdoor, free. The 32 efficiency units cost $115 weekly, $595 monthly. AE, CB, DISC, MC, V.

≣≣ Fairfield Inn
1401 E Mall Dr, Holland, 43528; tel 419/867-1144 or toll free 800/228-2800; fax 419/867-1144. This three-story, strikingly white building, trimmed in blue, is a good, solid motel in keeping with Marriott's standards. Lobby is small but bright. Spring Meadows Shopping Mall is across the street. Near Toledo sights and attractions. **Rooms:** 135 rms. CI 3pm/CO noon. Nonsmoking rms avail. Rooms are clean and kept in good repair. **Amenities:** 📺 🔌 A/C, satel TV w/movies, dataport. **Services:** 🖼 ⤶ Babysitting. **Facilities:** 🏋 🛝 ♿ **Rates (CP):** Peak (June–Aug) $48–$80 S or D. Extra person $7. Children under age 17 stay free. Lower rates off-season. Parking: Outdoor, free. AE, DC, DISC, MC, V.

≣≣≣ Holiday Inn French Quarter
10630 Fremont Pike, Perrysburg, 43551; tel 419/874-3111 or toll free 800/HOLIDAY. W of I-75 exit. Recently underwent $2 million renovation. Statuary, an antique car, skylights, and New Orleans decor in lobby. Atrium with raised bar. **Rooms:** 311 rms and effic. Executive level. CI 4pm/CO 11am. Nonsmoking rms avail. Rooms have large wall mirrors, tall chests that house the TV, and sofa beds. Some rooms have balconies overlooking Holidome. **Amenities:** 📺 🔌 A/C, satel TV w/movies, dataport. Some units w/terraces. **Services:** ✕ 🚐 🖼 ⤶ Babysitting. Social director and children's program in summer. **Facilities:** 🏋 🛝 🍽 ♿ 1 restaurant, 2 bars (w/entertainment), games rm, sauna, whirlpool, playground, washer/dryer. One indoor/outdoor pool for adult swimmers; all pools have sun decks. Holidome has large putting green, pool tables, soccer game, and table tennis. Sun brunch has become extremely popular. Gift shop in lobby. **Rates:** Peak (Mar–Nov) $96–$129 S; $109–$135 D; $135 effic. Extra person $10. Children under age 19 stay free. Min stay special events. Lower rates off-season. Parking: Outdoor, free. Pack-

ages include Slipaway Weekends, Sweetheart Concierge, Mem Day, and New Year's Eve. AE, CB, DC, DISC, JCB, MC, V.

RESTAURANTS 🍴

Aztec Grille
In Owens-Illinois Bldg, 1 Seagate; tel 419/255-1116. **American.** This Southwest-inspired restaurant, located in the Owens-Illinois office building, overlooks the Maumee River and International Park across the river. Some tables have a view of a landscaped reflecting pool with waterfall. The specialty is Certified Angus beef, but the very fresh seafood is also popular. Three sauces—béarnaise, au poivre, and bleu cheese/mustard—are always available. Service is gracious and prompt. Complimentary valet parking for dinner hours only. **FYI:** Reservations recommended. Children's menu. **Open:** Mon–Thurs 11am–10pm, Fri 11am–11pm, Sat 5–11pm. **Prices:** Main courses $16–$18. AE, DC, DISC, MC, V. ♥ 🏔 VP ♿

⑤ Bob Evans Restaurant
In Spring Meadows Mall, 6435 Centers Dr, Holland; tel 419/865-7119. **American.** Part of the popular Midwestern chain with the familiar red-barn exterior. Breakfast is the meal Bob Evans does best, and it's available all day. Sausages, biscuits and honey, pancakes topped with fruit, omelettes, and gravy are all superb. **FYI:** Reservations not accepted. Children's menu. No liquor license. Additional locations: 2141 South Reynolds Rd, Toledo (tel 381-1422); 304 East Alexis Rd, Toledo (tel 476-2711). **Open:** Sun–Thurs 6am–10pm, Fri–Sat 6am–11:30pm. **Prices:** Main courses $4–$8. MC, V. 🎮 ♿

♟ Georgio's
426 N Superior St (Downtown); tel 419/242-2424. **International.** Very popular, a favorite of the business crowd as well as couples and families that want to celebrate a special occasion. The preferred dining room has an elevated dining area along one side, mirrors along the entire wall on the other side, and small lamps on each table. Service is gracious and prompt. Though it boasts an international menu, it's best known for fresh seafood. Ample parking nearby—much of it free after 5pm. **FYI:** Reservations recommended. **Open:** **Prices:** Main courses $13–$23. AE, MC, V. ♥ ♿

Mancy's
953 Phillips Ave; tel 419/476-4154. Off I-75. **American.** Popular, award-winning restaurant operated by the Mancy family for over 70 years. Antique furnishings and excellent service—along with the steaks and prime rib—make this an impressive choice. **FYI:** Reservations recommended. Children's menu. **Open:** Lunch Mon–Fri 11am–1:30pm; dinner Mon–Thurs 5–9:30pm, Fri–Sat 5–10pm. **Prices:** Main courses $10–$20. AE, CB, DC, DISC, MC, V. ♥ 🍷 🎮 ♿

⑤★ Tony Packo's Cafe
1902 Front St (East Side); tel 419/691-6054. Front and Fassett at the Maumee River. **Hungarian.** Under the guidance of the Packo family, this has been a favorite with locals and business groups for many years. Known for good food and family fun—and its framed hot dog buns, autographed by celebrities, which line the walls. A specialty is the Hungarian hot dog. Limited American menu also available. Most travelers to Toledo visit Packo's at least once. **FYI:** Reservations accepted. Blues/jazz/piano/magician. Children's menu. Additional location: 5827 Monroe St, Sylvania (tel 885-4500). **Open:** Mon–Thurs 11am–10pm, Fri–Sat 11am–midnight, Sun noon–9pm. **Prices:** Main courses $7–$10. AE, DISC, MC, V. ▇ ▦

REFRESHMENT STOP ▱

Original Pancake House
3310 W Central Ave; tel 419/535-5927. At Secor Rd across from Westgate Mall. **American.** Famous for specialty pancakes and crepes with a variety of toppings. Sandwiches and short orders also served. Limited children's menu. Often long wait for seating, especially on weekends. Closes at 4pm on Sun, June–Aug. **Open:** Sun–Thurs 6:30am–8pm, Fri–Sat 6:30am–9pm. DISC, MC, V. ♥ ▦ ▼ �

ATTRACTIONS ▦

The Toledo Museum of Art
2445 Monroe St; tel 419/255-8000. Permanent exhibits include notable collections of glass, Greek vases, and decorative and graphic arts. The TMA also maintains an impressive array of works by such masters as El Greco, Rubens, Rembrandt, Gainsborough, Turner, Van Gogh, Degas, Monet, Matisse, Picasso, Remington, and Hopper. **Open:** Tues–Thurs 10am–4pm, Fri 10am–9pm, Sat 10am–4pm, Sun 1–5pm. **Free**

SS *Willis B Boyer*
International Park; tel 419/936-3070. Moored alongside the rolling landscape of International Park is the "king of the lake freighters." Built in 1911 and "retired" in 1980, the restored boat now houses a nautical museum containing memorabilia, photography, and artifacts maintained by the Western Lake Erie Historical Society. Guided tours available. **Open:** Peak (May–Sept) daily 10am–5pm. Reduced hours off-season. **$$**

Toledo Botanical Gardens
5403 Elmer Dr; tel 419/536-8365. Large collections of herbs, azaleas, rhododendrons, roses, and wildflowers. Fragrance gardens, art galleries, glassblowing studios. Gift shop. **Open:** Peak (Apr–Sept) daily 8am–9pm. Reduced hours off-season. **Free**

Toledo Zoo
OH 25; tel 419/385-5721. Most of the zoo's buildings are built in Spanish Colonial Revival style, as a subtle salute to Toledo's namesake city in Spain. The animals—hippos, apes, elephants, birds, and more—come from all over the world. Exotic fish from five continents and three oceans in one of North America's largest fresh and saltwater aquariums. For some unusual human surroundings, go to the Carnivore Cafe; there you can dine in the actual animal cages where bears and cats once lived. **Open:** Peak (Apr–Sept) daily 10am–5pm. Reduced hours off-season. **$$**

Troy

Seat of Miami county in west central Ohio, on the Great Miami River. A disastrous flood here in 1913 resulted in the creation of the first flood protection district in the US. **Information:** Troy Area Chamber of Commerce, 305 ½ SE Public Sq, PO Box 218, Troy, 45373 (tel 513/339-8769).

MOTEL ▦

▤▤▤ Days Inn
1610 W Main St, 45373; tel 513/339-7571 or toll free 800/DAYS-INN; fax 513/339-6756. ¼ mi E of I-75 exit 74. Mexican/southwestern motif throughout. Undergoing complete renovation. The Eldean bridge (a truss bridge) and the Brukner Nature Center also nearby. **Rooms:** 74 rms. CI 2pm/CO noon. Nonsmoking rms avail. Rooms are clean and tidy. **Amenities:** ▦ A/C, cable TV. **Services:** ▨ ▱ ▱ VCRs available. **Facilities:** ▦ ▱ 325 ▱ 1 restaurant (lunch and dinner only), 1 bar. Lounge is dimly lit, but quaint. Pool is 45' by 120'. Shuffleboard and horseshoe facilities. **Rates (CP):** Peak (June–Aug) $39–$56 S or D. Extra person $5. Children under age 17 stay free. Lower rates off-season. Parking: Outdoor, free. AE, CB, DC, DISC, MC, V.

RESTAURANT ▦

⑤★ La Piazza Pasta & Grill
2 N Market St; tel 513/339-5553. On the town square. **American/Italian.** Located in the midst of a historic district in a building dating from 1850, this local favorite offers four dining rooms plus a cheery patio room with windows all around. Made-from-scratch pastas receive top billing, but the chicken piccata is also a favorite. **FYI:** Reservations recommended. Guitar/piano. Children's menu. **Open:** Lunch Mon–Fri 11am–2pm; dinner Mon–Thurs 4:30–10pm, Fri–Sat 4–11pm, Sun 4–9pm. **Prices:** Main courses $9–$15. AE, MC, V. ▇ ▦ ▱

Vandalia

Located in west-central Ohio. According to legend, the last time Annie Oakley ever picked up a gun in public was at a trapshoot here in 1925. (Even at age 65, she hit 97 out of 100 targets.) The Trapshooting Hall of Fame and Museum sponsors a world trapshooting tournament every August.

Information: Vandalia-Butler Chamber of Commerce, 59A N Dixie Dr, PO Box 224, Vandalia, 45377 (tel 513/898-5351).

MOTELS 🏨

≡≡ Cross Country Inn

550 E National Rd, 45377; tel 513/898-7636 or toll free 800/621-1429; fax 513/898-0630. Clean, well-maintained property. **Rooms:** 94 rms. CI 1pm/CO noon. Nonsmoking rms avail. Rooms are spotless and comfortable. **Amenities:** 🛏 A/C, satel TV w/movies. **Services:** 🛎 Drive-through window for registration and checkout. **Facilities:** 🛝 🏃 25 🛗 Rates: $36–$51 S or D. Extra person $7. Children under age 18 stay free. Parking: Outdoor, free. AE, CB, DC, DISC, MC, V.

≡≡≡ Dayton Airport Inn

Dayton Int'l Airport, 45377; tel 513/898-1000 or toll free 800/543-7577; fax 513/898-3761. An upscale facility geared more to business and airline personnel than to leisure travelers; however, it's perfect for anyone catching an early plane. Lobby has working fireplace, round leather seats, and large chandelier. Hallways lined with paintings and pictures. **Rooms:** 156 rms and stes. CI 2pm/CO 2pm. Nonsmoking rms avail. Suites are three-room units. **Amenities:** 🛏 🍴 A/C, cable TV. Some units w/whirlpools. **Services:** ✗ 🚗 🛆 🛎 🛎 Twice-daily maid svce. Not only is property patrolled by airport police, but private motel guards patrol halls and lobby. **Facilities:** 🛝 🏃 200 🛗 1 restaurant, 1 bar (w/entertainment). Guests can use Vic Tanny health spa, about 10 minutes away. **Rates:** $85–$95 S or D; $170 ste. Extra person $10. Children under age 10 stay free. Parking: Outdoor, free. AE, CB, DC, DISC, MC, V.

≡≡ Park Inn International

75 Corporate Center Dr, 45377; tel 513/898-8321; fax 513/898-6334. The motel is within sight of Dayton International Airport, across US 40. **Rooms:** 100 rms, stes, and effic. CI noon/CO noon. Nonsmoking rms avail. **Amenities:** 🛏 🍴 📺 A/C, cable TV. **Services:** ✗ 🚗 🛆 🛎 🛎 Room service can be arranged with nearby restaurants. Small pets permitted for $5. **Facilities:** 🛝 🏃 🛥 100 🛗 Rates (CP): $30–$75 S or D; $50–$80 ste; $40–$46 effic. Extra person $6. Children under age 18 stay free. Parking: Outdoor, free. AE, CB, DC, DISC, MC, V.

≡ Scottish Inn

845 E National Rd, 45377; tel 513/898-5871 or toll free 800/251-1962. ¼ mi E of I-75 exit 63. An economical stop, especially for families. However, it's showing wear. **Rooms:** 84 rms. CI 11am/CO 11am. Nonsmoking rms avail. Rooms are quite clean, but there are some maintenance problems, such as badly stained upholstery. **Amenities:** 🛏 A/C, satel TV. **Services:** VCRs for rent. **Facilities:** 🛝 🏃 🛗 Swimming pool in front of motel near street. **Rates:** $21–$27 S or D. Extra person $4. Children under age 3 stay free. Parking: Outdoor, free. $3 key deposit. AE, CB, DC, DISC, MC, V.

Wapakoneta

Seat of Auglaize County, in western Ohio. Plain, substantial houses attest to this town's mostly German heritage. **Information:** Wapakoneta Area Chamber of Commerce, 8 N Blackhoof St, PO Box 208, Wapakoneta, 45895 (tel 419/738-2911).

MOTELS 🏨

≡≡ Budget Host Inn

505 E State St, PO Box 478, Botkins, 45306; tel 513/693-6911 or toll free 800/309-0039; fax 513/693-8202. Clean and well-maintained motel offering no frills. Near the Neil Armstrong Air and Space Museum and between Lake St Marys and Indian Lakes. **Rooms:** 50 rms and effic. CI open/CO 11am. Nonsmoking rms avail. Walls are painted concrete block. **Amenities:** 🛏 A/C, cable TV w/movies. **Services:** ✗ 🛎 🛎 Small pets only. **Facilities:** 🛝 🏃 🍴 1 150 1 restaurant (dinner only), 1 bar (w/entertainment), basketball, games rm, playground, washer/dryer. **Rates (CP):** Peak (Apr–Aug) $26–$31 S; $32–$40 D; $16 effic. Extra person $3. Children under age 12 stay free. Lower rates off-season. Parking: Outdoor, free. Rollaway bed $7. AE, CB, DC, DISC, MC, V.

≡≡≡ Holiday Inn

1510 Bellefontaine Rd, PO Box 1980, 45895; tel 419/738-8181 or toll free 800/HOLIDAY; fax 419/738-6478. The lobby is small, but tidy and bright. Near the Neil Armstrong Air and Space Museum; and Lake St Marys and Indian Lake for fishing, boating, and swimming. **Rooms:** 100 rms and stes. CI 2pm/CO noon. Nonsmoking rms avail. Rooms with king-size beds have desks and upholstered chairs. **Amenities:** 🛏 🍴 📺 A/C, cable TV w/movies. **Services:** ✗ 🛆 🛎 🛎 Babysitting. Same-day laundry service, two-day dry cleaning service. **Facilities:** 🛝 🏃 🍴 300 🛗 2 restaurants, 1 bar, washer/dryer. Very clean and tidy pool with covered seating areas and wide sun deck. Paintings on wall of restaurant entryway are for sale. All restaurants closed Sun. **Rates (CP):** $58 S or D; $65 ste. Extra person $5. Children under age 19 stay free. Parking: Outdoor, free. Packages include Heart-to-Heart, Valentine's Day, and New Year's Eve. AE, CB, DC, DISC, JCB, MC, V.

≡≡ Super 8 Motel

511 Lunar Dr, 45895; tel 419/738-8810 or toll free 800/800-8000; fax 419/738-8810 ext 500. Fairly new motel, clean and in excellent repair. No frills. **Rooms:** 38 rms, stes, and effic. CI 1pm/CO 11am. Nonsmoking rms avail. **Amenities:** 🛏 A/C, cable TV. **Services:** 🛎 **Facilities:** 🏃 🛗 Rates (CP): Peak (Mem Day–Labor Day) $40–$46 S or D; $86 ste; $40–$46 effic. Extra person $4. Children under age 12 stay free. Lower rates off-season. Parking: Outdoor, free. AE, CB, DC, DISC, MC, V.

ATTRACTION 🏛

Neil Armstrong Air and Space Museum

Exit 111 off I-75; tel 419/738-8811 or toll free 282-5393. A tribute to the hometown astronaut who became the first man to set foot on the moon; also commemorates the history of flight and space exploration with exhibits and audiovisual presentation. **Open:** Mar–Nov, Mon–Sat 9:30am–5pm, Sun noon–5pm. **$$**

Warren

Seat of Trumbull County, in northeast part of state. Warren was founded in 1799, and in the following year it became the seat of the Western Reserve. In its early years, coal was the predominant industry, but now steel and auto parts manufacturing have taken over that role. **Information:** Youngstown Warren Region Chamber of Commerce, 160 E Market St, PO Box 1147, Warren, 44482 (tel 330/393-2565).

HOTEL 🏨

⬛⬛⬛ Avalon Inn and Resort

9519 E Market St, 44484; tel 330/856-1900 or toll free 800/828-2566; fax 330/856-2248. A traditional country inn with elegant furnishings and a relaxing atmosphere. **Rooms:** 144 rms. Executive level. CI 3pm/CO noon. Nonsmoking rms avail. **Amenities:** 🛁 ⬜ 🍴 A/C, cable TV, voice mail. Some units w/terraces. **Services:** ✗ 🍽 🚐 📷 🧺 Twice-daily maid svce, social director, babysitting. **Facilities:** 🏊 ▶36 🏋 🏈 🎳 1050 ⬛ 3 restaurants (see "Restaurants" below), 2 bars (1 w/entertainment), basketball, volleyball, games rm, lawn games, racquetball, spa, sauna, whirlpool, playground. Olympic-size indoor pool, driving range, challenging golf courses, pro shop. Tennis courts enclosed in winter. Sunday golf and dinner specials. **Rates:** $68 S; $78–$88 D; $90–$150 ste. Extra person $10. Children under age 16 stay free. AP and MAP rates avail. Parking: Outdoor, free. Getaway, golf, and group packages avail. AE, CB, DC, DISC, MC, V.

MOTEL

⬛ Scottish Inn

4258 Youngstown Rd SE, 44484; tel 330/369-4100 or toll free 800/251-1962; fax 330/369-4100. On US 422. Older building, in need of renovation. **Rooms:** 54 rms. CI noon/CO 11am. **Amenities:** 🛁 A/C, cable TV w/movies. **Services:** 🧺 Twice-daily maid svce. Free coffee in lobby. Free local calls. Airport shuttle available at hotel next door. **Facilities:** 🏊 20 **Rates:** $35 S; $42 D. Extra person $5. Children under age 10 stay free. Parking: Outdoor, free. AE, DISC, MC, V.

RESTAURANTS 🍽

★ Abruzzi's Cafe 422

4422 Youngstown Rd SE; tel 330/369-2422. E of Warren. **American/Italian.** This 56-year-old, family-owned and -operated landmark is famous for homemade pastas, breads, and pies. **FYI:** Reservations recommended. Children's menu. **Open:** Sun–Thurs 11am–10pm, Fri–Sat 11am–11pm. **Prices:** Main courses $8–$28. AE, CB, DC, DISC, MC, V. ♥ 🍴

Fiore's Ristorante

4256 Youngstown Rd SE; tel 330/369-2711. **American.** Seafood, hearty rib dinners, chicken Françoise, and chicken Marsala are the favorites at this cozy trattoria. **FYI:** Reservations recommended. Children's menu. **Open:** Fri–Sat 11am–1am, Sun–Thurs 11am–midnight. **Prices:** Main courses $5–$14. AE, DC, DISC, MC, V. 🍴 ⬛ &

G's Golden Gate

2186 Parkman Rd; tel 330/399-8972. On US 422 E of US 82 exit. **American.** A pleasant dining room in an older urban area, where diners enjoy prime rib dinners and Italian specialties such as eggplant Parmesan. All pasta sauces are made on the premises. **FYI:** Reservations recommended. **Open:** Mon–Thurs 11am–9:30pm, Fri 11am–11pm, Sat 4–11pm. **Prices:** Main courses $7–$20. AE, CB, DC, DISC, MC, V. 🍴

R J Panhandler's & The Cool Oldies Lounge

In Hotel Regency, 4322 Youngstown Rd SE; tel 330/369-8824. **Seafood/Steak.** Locally popular chef Bob Carrol prepares a wide variety of meals, using traditional New England recipes for beef and seafood specialties. **FYI:** Reservations recommended. Piano. Children's menu. Dress code. **Open:** Tues–Sat 5pm–2:30am. **Prices:** Main courses $9–$20. AE, DISC, MC, V. ♥ 🍴

Tall Oaks Restaurant

In Avalon Inn and Resort, 9519 E Market St; tel 330/856-1900. **New American.** The emphasis here is on American classics with a progressive twist. Typical offerings might include beef Wellington, grilled salmon and halibut, or herb-roasted chicken breast. All beef dishes are certified Black Angus. **FYI:** Reservations recommended. Jazz/piano. Children's menu. **Open:** Mon–Thurs 5–10pm, Fri–Sat 6–11pm, Sun 4–10pm. **Prices:** Main courses $11–$25. AE, CB, DC, DISC, MC, V. ♥ 🍽 🎨 🍴 &

Wauseon

Seat of Fulton County, in northwest part of state. This small town located west of Toledo is the site of a re-created 1860 farmstead and pioneer village. **Information:** Wauseon Chamber of Commerce, 115 N Fulton St, PO Box 217, Wauseon, 43567 (tel 419/335-9966).

MOTELS 🏨

⬛⬛ Arrowhead Motel

8225 OH 108, 43567; tel 419/335-5811. This one-story motel is eye-catching from the highway. A mom-and-pop operation with immaculate grounds. Good value. Across from full-service restaurant; convenient to shopping, various attractions, public golf. **Rooms:** 34 rms. CI 1pm/CO 11am. Rooms are generally small, but very clean and with good views of the large, well-manicured green in front of the motel. **Amenities:** 🛗 ⚘ A/C, cable TV. **Services:** ⇦ **Facilities:** ⚘ ⚘ Playground. **Rates:** $30–$36 S; $42–$52 D. Extra person $4. Children under age 12 stay free. Parking: Outdoor, free. AE, DISC, MC, V.

≡≡ Best Western Del-Mar

8319 OH 108, 43567; tel 419/335-1565 or toll free 800/528-1234; fax 419/335-1828. OH 108 just N of OH Tpk exit 3. One-story brick motel. Well-groomed front yard. Very clean. Full-service restaurant across highway. **Rooms:** 40 rms and effic. CI 2pm/CO 11am. Nonsmoking rms avail. Bright decor. View of motel green from all rooms. **Amenities:** 🛗 ⚘ ⚘ A/C, cable TV, refrig, VCR. 1 unit w/whirlpool. **Services:** ⇦ ⇦ **Facilities:** ⚘ ⚘ ⚘ Playground. **Rates (CP):** Peak (June–Aug) $48–$56 S; $58–$66 D; $99–$109 effic. Children under age 12 stay free. Lower rates off-season. Parking: Outdoor, free. AE, CB, DC, DISC, JCB, MC, V.

Willoughby

Near Lake Erie. Nearby is Kirtland Temple, a Mormon Church. **Information:** Willoughby Area Chamber of Commerce, 28 Public Sq, PO Box 44, Willoughby, 44094 (tel 216/942-1632).

HOTEL 🏨

≡≡≡ Harley Hotel East

6051 SOM Center Rd, 44094; tel 216/944-4300 or toll free 800/321-2323; fax 216/944-5344. A favorite with celebrities, according to photographs lining the hallway. Located in residential and commercial area with easy access to Cleveland's eastern suburbs. Close to shopping, golf, Sea World, Geauga Lake. **Rooms:** 146 rms and stes. CI 4pm/CO 11am. Nonsmoking rms avail. **Amenities:** 🛗 ⚘ A/C, cable TV w/movies. All units w/terraces. **Services:** ✕ ⚘ ⚘ ⇦ Babysitting. Hors d'oeuvres served in lounge on weekdays. **Facilities:** ⚘ ⚘ ⚘ 1 restaurant, 1 bar (w/entertainment), volleyball, games rm, sauna, steam rm, washer/dryer. Access to Bally's Scandinavian Health Spa. **Rates:** $108 S; $113 D; $175 ste. Extra person $5. Children under age 18 stay free. AP and MAP rates avail. Parking: Outdoor, free. AE, CB, DC, DISC, MC, V.

Wooster

Seat of Wayne County, in northeast part of state. This small agricultural town also produces rubber, paper, and furniture. Ohio State University has its agricultural research and devel-

opment center one mile south of town. **Information:** Wayne County Convention & Visitors Bureau, 237 S Walnut, PO Box 77, Wooster, 44691 (tel 330/264-1800).

MOTELS 🏨

≡≡ Econo Lodge

2137 Lincoln Way E, 44691; tel 330/264-8883 or toll free 800/248-8341; fax 330/264-8883. On OH 30, 2 mi E of town square. No frills, yet clean and neat. **Rooms:** 98 rms and effic. CI 1pm/CO 11am. Nonsmoking rms avail. **Amenities:** 🛗 ⚘ A/C, cable TV w/movies. **Services:** ⚘ ⚘ ⇦ ⚘ **Facilities:** ⚘ ⚘ ⚘ ⚘ Whirlpool, washer/dryer. **Rates (CP):** Peak (May–Oct) $37 S; $43 D; $55 effic. Extra person $4. Children under age 18 stay free. Lower rates off-season. Parking: Outdoor, free. AE, DC, DISC, MC, V.

≡≡≡ Holiday Inn Express

2055 Lincoln Way E, 44691; tel 330/262-5008 or toll free 800/465-4329; fax 330/262-5084. 2 mi E of town square on OH 30. New, beautifully decorated. In the heart of Amish country, within minutes of several Amish restaurants. Also many nearby antique/collectible shops. **Rooms:** 58 rms and stes. CI 3pm/CO noon. Nonsmoking rms avail. The loftlike whirlpool suite has king-size bed and cozy sitting area. **Amenities:** 🛗 ⚘ A/C, cable TV w/movies, dataport, in-rm safe. 1 unit w/terrace, 1 w/whirlpool. **Services:** ✕ ⚘ ⇦ **Facilities:** ⚘ ⚘ ⚘ Sauna, whirlpool. **Rates (CP):** $58 S; $66 D; $95–$110 ste. Extra person $8. Children under age 18 stay free. Parking: Outdoor, free. AE, CB, DC, DISC, JCB, MC, V.

RESTAURANT 🍽

★ TJ's Restaurant

359 W Liberty St; tel 330/264-6263. 3 blocks W of square. **American/Steak.** Relaxing yet elegant atmosphere. Five separate dining rooms of various sizes make party accommodations pleasant and private. The "library" has one large, elegant table that seats up to 16, perfect for business dining or special family occasions. Entrees include fresh seafood, veal, chicken, and steak; prime rib is the house specialty. **FYI:** Reservations recommended. Children's menu. Dress code. **Open:** Mon–Fri 11am–10pm, Sat 4:30–10pm. **Prices:** Main courses $10–$18. AE, CB, DC, DISC, MC, V. 🈺 🈯

Worthington

See Columbus

Youngstown

Seat of Mahoning County, in northeast part of state. In 1797, James Young and a party of settlers from New York state arrived in what would soon be known as "Young's Town." Coal and steel have dominated the local economy for nearly

200 years. **Information:** Youngstown Warren Region Chamber of Commerce, 1220 Stambaugh Building, Youngstown, 44503-1604 (tel 330/744-2131).

HOTEL 🛏

≣≣≣ Comfort Inn
4055 Belmont Ave, 44505; tel 330/759-3180 or toll free 800/860-7829; fax 330/759-7713. Stucco exterior. Spacious lobby with contemporary furnishings accented with brass and glass. **Rooms:** 150 rms and stes. Executive level. CI 3pm/CO noon. Nonsmoking rms avail. **Amenities:** 🛁 A/C, cable TV w/movies. All units w/terraces, some w/whirlpools. **Services:** ✕ 🍴 🖨 🔁 Twice-daily maid svce. **Facilities:** 🏋 🏊 1 restaurant (lunch and dinner only), games rm, sauna, whirlpool. Full access to Club V health club. **Rates (CP):** Peak (June–Sept 4) $55–$75 S; $60–$85 D; $125–$175 ste. Extra person $10. Children under age 18 stay free. Lower rates off-season. Parking: Outdoor, free. Special Sea World and Geauga Lake packages avail. AE, CB, DC, DISC, JCB, MC, V.

MOTELS

≣≣ Knights Inn
5431 76th Dr, 44515; tel 330/793-9305 or toll free 800/843-9644. Small, next to truck stop. Good value. **Rooms:** 126 rms and effic. CI 3pm/CO noon. Nonsmoking rms avail. **Amenities:** 🛁 A/C, cable TV. **Services:** 🖨 🔁 🍹 **Facilities:** 🏋 🏊 **Rates:** Peak (May–Sept) $33–$37 S; $35–$39 D; $48–$54 effic. Extra person $5. Children under age 18 stay free. Lower rates off-season. Parking: Outdoor, free. Efficiency units rented by day, week, or month. AE, CB, DC, DISC, MC, V.

≣≣ Ramada Inn
4255 Belmont Ave, 44505; tel 330/759-7850 or toll free 800/272-6232; fax 330/759-7850. Elaborate lobby with double staircase and chandelier, but rather tacky furnishings. **Rooms:** 140 rms and stes. CI 2pm/CO noon. Nonsmoking rms avail. **Amenities:** 🛁 A/C, satel TV. Some units w/whirlpools. **Services:** ✕ 🍴 🖨 🔁 Babysitting. **Facilities:** 🏋 🏊 1 restaurant, 1 bar (w/entertainment), beauty salon. **Rates:** Peak (May 1–Sept 12) $59–$64 S; $64–$69 D; $110 ste. Extra person $7. Children under age 18 stay free. Lower rates off-season. AP and MAP rates avail. Parking: Outdoor, free. AE, CB, DC, DISC, EC, JCB, MC, V.

UNRATED Super 8 Motel
5280 76th Dr, 44515; tel 330/793-7788 or toll free 800/800-8000. Basic and modest. Tudor brick exterior and exterior corridors. Tiny lobby. **Rooms:** 63 rms. CI 1pm/CO 11am. Nonsmoking rms avail. **Amenities:** 🛁 A/C, cable TV w/movies. **Services:** 🔁 🍹 Free coffee 24 hours in lobby. **Facilities:** 🏊 **Rates:** Peak (June–Aug) $38 S; $44 D. Extra person $6. Children under age 12 stay free. Lower rates off-season. Parking: Outdoor, free. AE, CB, DC, DISC, EC, MC, V.

RESTAURANTS 🍽

The Moonraker Restaurant
1275 Boardman Poland Rd; tel 330/726-8843. **International.** International buffets and live entertainment on weekends attract people to this restaurant. A Mediterranean buffet is served at lunch on weekdays, along with a limited sandwich menu. Original sauces and baked goods prepared on the premises. Two to four chef's specials are prepared each day for dinner, in addition to the regular menu. The house specialty is Moonraker Combo (shrimp scampi and steak Diane). **FYI:** Reservations accepted. Cabaret/dancing/rock. Children's menu. **Open:** Lunch Mon–Fri 11:30am–2pm; dinner Mon–Thurs 4–10pm, Fri–Sat 4pm–midnight; brunch Sun 11am–2:30pm. **Prices:** Main courses $10–$23. AE, DC, DISC, MC, V. ❤ 🏔 👥 💟 VP &

Our Place Restaurant
725 McCartney Rd; tel 330/743-7954. **International.** A family-run restaurant in an old section of the city, across from the farmers' market. The lamb dinner is the house specialty. **FYI:** Reservations not accepted. Children's menu. **Open:** Mon–Thurs 7am–10pm, Fri–Sat 24 hrs, Sun 7am–3pm. **Prices:** Main courses $5–$11. AE, MC, V. 👥 🈩

ATTRACTIONS 🎟

Butler Institute of American Art
524 Wick Ave; tel 330/743-1107. Founded in the early 1900s, this was the first structure in the United States built for the specific purpose of displaying American art. Its extensive permanent collection encompasses 300 years of the nation's art and includes major works by Thomas Eakins, Mary Cassatt, Edward Hopper, John Steuart Curry, and Roy Lichtenstein, as well as Winslow Homer's famous painting *Snap the Whip*. Also includes a gallery of American sports art. **Open:** Tues–Sat 11am–4pm, Sun noon–4pm. **Free**

Youngstown Historical Center of Industry and Labor
151 W Wood St; tel 330/743-5934. A unique museum depicting Youngstown's history as a major center of the iron and steel industries. The main permanent exhibit, "By the Seat of their Brow: Forging the Steel Valley," re-creates life and work in the early mill towns of eastern Ohio. **Open:** Wed–Sat 9:30am–5pm, Sun noon–5pm. **$$**

Zanesville

Seat of Muskingum County, in the Appalachian foothills in the southeastern part of the state. Zanesville was founded in 1797 by the great-grandfather of novelist Zane Grey. Today, the town is a center of pottery making and high-tech industry. **Information:** Zanesville-Muskingum Convention & Visitors Bureau, 205 N 5th St, PO Box 3396, Zanesville, 43702-3396 (tel 614/454-8687 or toll free 800/743-2303).

RESTAURANTS 🍴

Old Market House Inn
424 Market St; tel 614/454-2555. ½ block from courthouse; across from city hall. **Continental/Italian.** Although the menu lists a variety of seafood and steak entrees, this place is best known for its pasta dishes. House specialties include lasagna, seafood Alfredo, and pasta marinara. All pastas, sauces, and breads are homemade. **FYI:** Reservations not accepted. Children's menu. Dress code. **Open:** Mon–Sat 5–10:30pm. **Prices:** Main courses $8–$25. AE, CB, DC, DISC, MC, V. ♥ 🏛

Zak's Restaurant
32 N 3rd St; tel 614/453-2227. 2 blocks from center of town. **Mexican.** The owners have turned the historic Wiles Warehouse into a fun and colorful spot for dining. Patrons may be seated in either of two indoor dining rooms or the sidewalk cafe. The menu in all rooms features a wide variety of spicy Mexican dishes cooked to please the American palate. Chicken fajita salad, served with cheesy quesadillas and topped with homemade ranch dressing, is a popular lunch option, while the chimichangas platter is a dinner favorite. **FYI:** Reservations recommended. Children's menu. Dress code. **Open:** Mon–Thurs 11am–10pm, Fri 11am–11pm, Sat 5–11pm, Sun 5–10pm. **Prices:** Main courses $4–$12. AE, CB, DC, DISC, MC, V. 🏖 ♿

WISCONSIN

The Definitive Melting Pot

STATE STATS

CAPITAL
Madison

AREA
56,154 square miles

BORDERS
Minnesota, Iowa, Illinois, Michigan, and Lakes Michigan and Superior

POPULATION
4,891,769 (1990)

ENTERED UNION
May 29, 1848 (30th state)

NICKNAMES
Badger State,
Copper State

STATE FLOWER
Wood violet

STATE BIRD
Robin

FAMOUS NATIVES
Laura Ingalls Wilder,
Liberace, Nick Nolte,
Harry Houdini,
Vince Lombardi,
Frank Lloyd Wright

License plates proclaim Wisconsin "America's Dairyland." That image—of tawny Jersey cows and black-and-white Holsteins grazing in sweet-scented meadows, of cheese factories and freshly churned butter, of neat farms and quiet, hidden valleys—is not far from reality. Much of Wisconsin *is* rural and charmingly "small town." It's the sort of place you might expect to run into a latter-day Norman Rockwell, sketchbook at the ready.

But life in Wisconsin has always been more diverse than it appears at first glance. The state's scenery is rugged as well as pastoral. Many parts escaped the great Ice Age glaciers that steamrolled through the Midwest and remain craggy, with rocky bluffs and escarpments that challenge climbers and hills that entice skiers. Other areas are covered with vast primeval forest.

Wisconsin's people are a motley bunch, too. On a map of Wisconsin, the distance between Switzerland and Norway is only about 15 miles. New Glarus, founded in 1845 by 108 immigrants from the Swiss canton of Glarus, is as Swiss as a cuckoo clock. The neighboring community of Mount Horeb maintains strong Norwegian roots in food, custom, and an authentic replica of a 12th-century stave church. The state's surprisingly rich ethnic mix includes an Icelandic community at the tip of scenic Door County, the Germans and Irish whose ancestors settled in Milwaukee, the Cornish who mined lead at Mineral Point (and left a legacy of sturdy stone cottages and savory meat-and-vegetable filled pasties), and the Welsh farmers who worked the land around Spring Green.

Wisconsin has always had a diverse political life as well. The Republican Party was born in a one-room schoolhouse in the small town of Ripon in 1854. Wisconsin also was the home of social pioneer Robert Marion La Follette Sr, a fiery reformer and champion of Wisconsin's flood of immigrants. "Fightin' Bob" La Follette was an advocate of child-labor laws, a minimum wage for women and children, and financial aid to seniors. One of the most important figures in Israeli history—prime minister Golda Meir—grew up in Milwaukee. On the other hand, rabidly anticommunist Senator Joseph McCarthy was born in Grand Chute, and the right-wing John Birch Society still has its headquarters there.

All in all, Wisconsin natives are a fiercely independent bunch, with one thing in common: love of their picturepostcard home state. Have a glass of fresh Wisconsin milk, or a traditional German brew in Milwaukee, and they'll be glad to tell you all about it.

A Brief History

Land of Many Tribes   In the early decades of the 17th century, there were an estimated 100,000 Native Americans living in the upper Great Lakes, about one-fifth of them occupying what now is Wisconsin. The name Wisconsin is popularly believed to be derived from a Chippewa word meaning "gathering of the waters." The land was populated mainly by the agricultural Hurons and the hunting Chippewa, with smaller numbers from the Winnebago, Menominee, Oneida, Pottawatomi, Sauk, and Fox tribes.

In Search of the Northwest Passage   Colonization, which eventually carried the territorial ambitions of the French and the British, got its start in 1634 when Jean Nicolet landed along the shore of Green Bay. The French explorer had been sent by Samuel de Champlain, governor of New France, to find the mysterious Northwest Passage that would open up the riches of the Orient.

Although the mission of reaching China failed, the landfall—with Nicolet in full Oriental regalia—began a long period of French domination, by trappers, traders, and missionaries. France laid claim to Wisconsin as part of its territory in the New World in 1672.

> ## Fun Facts
>
> • "America's Dairyland" makes more cheese and butter than any other state. In an effort to protect butter sales, Wisconsin outlawed the sale of artificially colored margarine until the mid-1960s.
> • In 1856, the first kindergarten in the nation was started by Margaretha Schurz in Watertown, for the children of German immigrants.
> • Wisconsin gained its nickname the Badger State in 1827, when miners built their homes by digging into the hillsides like badgers.
> • The typewriter was invented by a Milwaukee native, Christopher Sholes, in 1868.

The French, who ruled Wisconsin for close to 100 years, engaged in a series of brutal Indian wars, notably against the Iroquois, Miami, Sauk, and Fox. After surrender to the British in Montreal in 1760, French garrisons withdrew along the Fox-Wisconsin river route to Illinois.

Rise & Fall of British Rule   French dominion over Wisconsin endured until 1763, when Wisconsin became part of the territory ceded by France to Great Britain in the Treaty of Paris. But British rule was short-lived. Twenty years later, again at a negotiating table in Paris, the British relinquished their claim to Wisconsin and it became part of the United States.

In 1787, under the Northwest Ordinance, Wisconsin became part of the great territory north and west of the Ohio River out of which Ohio, Indiana, Illinois, Michigan, and Wisconsin were created. In 1836, the Wisconsin territory was organized, including what now are the states of Wisconsin, Iowa, Minnesota, and parts of the Dakotas. The first territorial legislature met at Belmont (about 5½ miles north of Plattesville). The two-story frame building and grounds surrounding the first capitol are now a state park.

In 1832, the Fox-Sauk chief Black Hawk—who had successfully led his people against American forces in the War of 1812—led a small band of followers against the militia in a series of bloody skirmishes known as the Black Hawk War. Outnumbered more than 10 to 1, the small band of renegades was cut down and vanquished—although the chief, then in his 60s, escaped and went on to become a national folk hero.

Mining Boom   In the 1830s, Mineral Point in southwestern Wisconsin became a mining boomtown. Rich lead deposits attracted speculators and a hardy breed of miners from Cornwall in western England known for their skills in hard-rock mining. Also experts in stonecutting and masonry, these Cornishmen used native limestone to build sturdy cottages similar to those they had left behind. Until they were able to build these permanent homes, the miners took shelter in holes burrowed badgerlike into hillsides—thus giving the Badger State its sobriquet. But the boom was short-lived. Over the next decade, production declined. Then came wildfire news of the California gold strike and Mineral Point's boom days were over. In a single day, 60 wagons pulled out, westward ho. Today, Mineral Point includes a restored state historical site and is a major center for artisans and their studios.

Statehood & Settlement On May 29, 1848, Wisconsin became the 30th state accepted into the Union, the last to be formed from the old Northwest Territory. Nelson Dewey, a Democrat and Connecticut Yankee, was the first governor, serving two terms. Soon after, waves of immigrants from northern Europe began to flood into the state, looking for land and a fresh start in America. They brought many of their ways with them.

A Closer Look

GEOGRAPHY

Wisconsin's diverse topography ranges from the craggy coastline of Lake Superior to the sweeping limestone bluffs high above the Mississippi River to the marshlands of the southeast. In between these two extremes are thousands of lakes, miles of meandering streams, and vast stretches of forest.

In northern Wisconsin, the **Apostle Islands** are an archipelago of 22 islands about 70 miles east of Superior, in Lake Superior. The islands—together with the rugged forested country strung around Chequamegon Bay—offer boating, fishing, pristine North Woods scenery, sandy beaches, nature trails, and tent camping. All of the islands except one (Madeline, with a permanent population of 180) are part of the Apostle Island National Lakeshore.

Wisconsin abounds in such common glacial features as drumlins, eskers, till plains, marshes, and moraines. Kanes, conical hills created eons ago by debris boring through weak points in the ice cover,

DRIVING DISTANCES
Milwaukee
47 mi E of Madison
93 mi NW of Chicago, IL
114 mi SE of Green Bay
181 mi SE of Wausau
204 mi SE of LaCrosse
225 mi SE of Escanaba, MI
322 mi SE of St Paul, MN
389 mi SE of Superior/Duluth, MN
Madison
47 mi W of Milwaukee
129 mi SE of LaCrosse
132 mi SW of Green Bay
140 mi SE of Wausau
146 mi NW of Chicago, IL
243 mi SE of Escanaba, MI
258 mi SE of St Paul, MN
325 mi SE of Superior/Duluth, MN
Superior/Duluth, MN
162 mi NE of St Paul, MN
223 mi NW of Wausau
234 mi NW of LaCrosse
279 mi NW of Escanaba, MI
310 mi NW of Green Bay
325 mi NW of Madison
389 mi NW of Milwaukee
463 mi NW of Chicago, IL

rise to more than 350 feet today. Kettles are pit-like depressions in the earth that resulted when the huge blocks of ice buried under the glacial debris melted away. The **Kettle Moraine** area in the southeastern portion of the state carries the most dramatic imprint of Wisconsin's glacial origins, while about 15,000 square miles of the state, mostly in the southwest, were missed by the glaciers altogether.

The state occupies a sizable portion of **Lake Michigan** shoreline—providing charter-boat salmon fishing as well as power-boating and sailing (including "bareboat" and "captained" yacht charters). The rocky shorelines and treacherous waters of Lakes Michigan and Superior have claimed many ships. Scattered along these shores, about 30 historic and picturesque lighthouses now draw visitors, with several lighthouses open for tours.

The state contains about 15,000 lakes altogether, offering a variety of recreational opportunities, from sailing and ice-boating to angling for brown trout, trolling for the legendary muskellunge, and fishing through the ice. Inland lakes include such bodies of water as **Lake Geneva,** a popular retreat with Chicagoans since the late 19th century, and sprawling **Lake Winnebago.** One of the deepest and clearest lakes within Wisconsin is **Green Lake,** a favorite of sailors, ice-boaters, and divers.

Waterfalls are another of Wisconsin's scenic topographical features. Some of the most spectacular falls are located along the Lake Superior shore in Douglas, Bayfield, Ashland, and Iron Counties, and in Marinette County on the western shore of Green Bay. Iron County alone has 15 waterfalls, while Marinette County has a dozen. **Big Manitou Falls** in Douglas County is the state's highest cataract, at 165 feet.

CLIMATE

Summer weather in northern Wisconsin is pleasant,

thanks to refreshing breezes off the Great Lakes and the area's vast expanses of cool northern forest and shady glens. Contrast this with the open farmland and meadows of the south—thestate's celebrated "dairyland"—which often bake in the relentless midday sun and where groves of trees provide the only welcome shade. Differences in temperatures between Milwaukee and Superior can vary by as much as 20°F.

Winter is a different matter. It often hits the Badger State hard and heavy, with prodigious amounts of snowfall and long stretches of below-zero temperatures. But many of these cold winter days are also sunny, and Wisconsin folk make the most of them by touring the snowy countryside in their snowmobiles and heading out to their ice fishing huts and to the downhill ski slopes and cross-country ski trails.

Spring can come early to the south, bringing warm days in March, buds to trees and bushes, and sap to the maples. At the same time, winter lingers in the north, and the ice often doesn't move out of the Lake Superior harbors until well into May. A springtime drive from Madison to the Apostle Islands could begin in warm sunshine and end in a snow squall.

Fall is the time to see nature paint Wisconsin's woodlands with splashy autumnal hues of red, yellow, amber, and gold. This is the season of festivals celebrating the harvest, of apple cider and pumpkin pie. Contact a state tourism office for brochures suggesting fall color tours.

WHAT TO PACK

If you're heading into Wisconsin in the dead of winter, you can be pretty sure what to take along: down jacket, ski pants, sturdy waterproof boots (perhaps felt-lined), a warm head covering, insulated mittens, and thermal underwear. For the remainder of the year, it really depends on where you're going and when. Spring and fall can be unpredictable. Summer can linger before the first cold snap—then it can turn warm again with a brief-but-glorious Indian summer. The answer is to dress in layers—pack a sweater or two, plus a light jacket, and per-

haps wool and cotton shirts and blouses. Most Wisconsin resorts—even the fanciest—are extremely casual. If you are driving in winter, it is prudent to carry an emergency kit (including blankets and extra clothing) in the trunk of your car.

TOURIST INFORMATION

The **Wisconsin Department of Tourism** (tel 800/432-TRIP ext 56T) offers free state road maps and a number of colorful and useful brochures, including calendars of seasonal events and festivals, a guide to Wisconsin state parks, and a directory of B&Bs and historic inns. They also publish *Wisconsin Auto Tours*, a book describing 24 road adventures and interesting attractions to visit along the way. The Department also maintains a World Wide Web page (http://badger.state.wi.us/agencies/tourism) with information on state parks, campgrounds, destinations, lodgings, and more.

Contact information for local tourist bureaus is listed under specific cities in the listings section of this book.

AVG MONTHLY TEMPS (°F) & RAINFALL (IN)		
	Milwaukee	**Green Bay**
Jan	19/1.6	16/1.3
Feb	23/1.5	20/1.1
Mar	33/2.7	31/2.1
Apr	44/3.5	43/2.7
May	55/2.8	54/3.0
June	65/3.2	64/3.4
July	71/3.5	70/3.2
Aug	69/3.5	68/3.6
Sept	62/3.4	60/3.7
Oct	50/2.4	49/2.5
Nov	38/2.5	36/2.3
Dec	24/2.3	22/1.7

DRIVING RULES AND REGULATIONS

Minimum driving age is 16. Speed limits in Wisconsin are strictly enforced, with radar-equipped highway patrols supplemented by aircraft surveillance. Unless otherwise noted, the speed limit is 55 mph on state highways; 65 mph on rural interstates. All adults are required to wear seat belts and all children up to age four must be in a child safety seat. A law enforcement official may stop you if you are traveling with a child under age eight who is not buckled up or in a safety seat. Unless otherwise posted, Wisconsin allows right turns on red and left turns on red from a one-way street onto a one-way street. Motorcyclists under age 18 must wear helmets.

Wisconsin is tough on drunk drivers and warns motorists that they will lose their licenses on the spot if arrested for drunk driving. If you refuse a breath test, you could lose your license for one year. In an effort to curb the incidence of alcohol-related boating accidents, the state also applies its drunk driving laws to its waterways.

RENTING A CAR

The following national rental agencies have offices in Wisconsin. Before you leave, check with your insurance company to see if you are insured while driving a rental car.

- **Alamo** (tel 800/327-9633)
- **Avis** (tel 800/831-2847)
- **Budget** (tel 800/527-0700)
- **Discount** (tel 800/231-7368)
- **Dollar** (tel 800/365-5276)
- **Enterprise** (tel 800/325-8007)
- **Hertz** (tel 800/654-3131)
- **National** (tel 800/227-7368)
- **Thrifty** (tel 800/367-2277)

ESSENTIALS

Area Codes: Wisconsin has three area codes. For the southeastern region of the state (including Milwaukee and Green Bay), the area code is **414.** For the southwestern region (including Madison and La Crosse), the area code is **608.** For the northern region (including Eau Claire and Superior), the area code is **715.**

Emergencies: For the police, an ambulance, or the fire department, dial **911.**

Liquor Laws: Alcoholic beverages may be purchased by anyone 21 years or older, with proof of age. Ordinances governing licensing hours vary by city and county.

Road Info: For the latest road conditions, call 800/ROAD-WIS. For copies of *On the Road Again* (a brochure listing some of the larger summer construction zones) or *Driving Your Way Through a Wisconsin Winter,* call the Wisconsin Department of Transportation (tel 800/242-2514).

Smoking: Officially, Wisconsin is aggressively anti-smoking, though local ordinances vary widely. Smoking is not allowed on public transportation nor in public buildings. Many restaurants maintain separate smoking and smoke-free sections and many hotels provide blocks of smoke-free rooms.

Taxes: Wisconsin's base statewide sales tax is 5%, with the option of an additional 0.5% at local discretion. Hotel taxes vary by municipality (in Milwaukee County, room tax is 14.5%).

Time Zone: Wisconsin is in the central time zone.

Best of the State

WHAT TO SEE AND DO

Below is a general overview of some of the top sights and attractions in Wisconsin. To find out more detailed information, look under "Attractions" for individual cities in the listings portion of this book.

Parks, Forests & Refuges Evidence of Wisconsin's ice-age origins is protected in the **Ice Age National Scientific Refuge,** a huge swath of land that is jointly administered by the state and federal governments. Individual units within the reserve include **Kettle Moraine State Forest,** where the Glacial Hiking Trail allows visitors to get an up-close look at the dramatic hills carved out by the last Ice Age.

The 661,000-acre **Nicolet National Forest,** in the northern part of the state, is named after the French explorer who came to this land in 1634. To the west is the 850,000-acre **Chequamegon National Forest,** home to more than 400 lakes. Both of these North Woods areas offer world-class canoeing routes (many of Wisconsin's rivers originate in the Nicolet territory), miles of hiking trails, camping, and cross-country skiing.

Natural Wonders Contained within a peninsula jutting thumblike into Lake Michigan, Door County has been dubbed "the Cape Cod of the Midwest." Cottage resorts, picturesque fishing villages, artist colonies, fish boils, cherry orchards, wineries, and rugged limestone cliffs, and pretty lighthouses are just a few of the region's delights. It is easy to see why Door County attracts droves of weekenders and vacationers, nature lovers and fishermen. Ferries run from the peninsula to **Washington and Rock Islands** The latter, one of America's first Icelandic communities, is popular with hikers and campers, who enjoy exploring meadows carpeted with wildflowers, foraging for berries, and tramping white beaches circled by swallows and herring gulls.

Historic Sites & Towns In the 1830s, when Chicago was still a mud flat, Mineral Point was a mining boomtown. **Pendarvis** is a restoration of Cornish miners' houses, authentically furnished, including a rowhouse with a traditional kiddlywink, a cozy pub where miners quaffed their Saturday pints. Wisconsin's diverse ethnic heritage is showcased at **Old World Wisconsin** at Eagle. This outdoor "living museum," sprawling over 600 acres, includes more than 50 historic buildings—Finnish homesteads, German farmhouses, a Norwegian schoolhouse, barns, village shops—relocated from around the state. At Greenbush, the **Old Wade House and Wisconsin Carriage Museum** is an old stagecoach inn built in 1851 when horses' hoofs pounded the old plank road connecting Sheboygan and Fond du Lac. On site is a blacksmith shop, smokehouse, and a museum with a display of more than 100 carriages, wagons, and sleighs. Horse-drawn carriage rides are offered.

The **Great River Road** (aka WI 35) traces the banks of the mighty Mississippi River for some 300 miles. Marked by green pilot-wheel signs, the road passes backwaters with lotus beds, century-old farmhouses, and special places to gather morels and wild ginseng and observe herons and thousands of migrating tundra swans. Towns along the road include historic **Alma,** with its terraced rock gardens, stone walls, and stairs that connecting the upper and lower main streets, and Trempealeau, once a fur traders' stop and now one of many places to rent a Mississippi houseboat. At **Pepin,** a museum marks the birthplace of Laura Ingalls Wilder, author of the *Little House* books.

Family Favorites Although some decry the heavily touristed **Wisconsin Dells,** the bustling resort does have a lot going for it. Its towering sandstone cliffs and cool, fern-filled gullies remain relatively unspoiled, despite the never-ending flood of sight-seeing boats and careening amphibious "ducks" (landing craft from World War II). Perennial family attractions at the Dells include Tommy Bartlett's well-produced water, sky, and stage show, go-carts, water parks, shoot-outs, miniature golf, dress-up vintage photo studios, and plenty of the Dells' trademark fudge. At Baraboo, **Circus World Museum** pays homage to the birthplace of the some of the greatest shows on earth. Once headquarters of major circuses, including Ringling Brothers, the museum is a storehouse of gilded wagons, calliopes, clown costumes, and other circus memorabilia. Daily events include performances in the big top, a high-wire act across the Baraboo River, the unloading of a circus train, and a parade.

The **House on the Rock** almost defies description. Built as a retreat atop a 60-foot rock chimney, the house has always been an architectural curiosity, with its massive fireplaces, pools of running water, and spectacular views of the surrounding rugged landscape. It has evolved into an unusual museum, with collections of scrimshaw, model ships, weapons and armor, miniature circuses, doll houses, and theater organs. Outside is the world's largest carousel, with more than 20,000 lights and 269 hand-crafted animals—not one of them a horse.

Your kids might like to milk a cow, pick a pail of fresh raspberries, dine on home-grown vegetables, and see how buffalo are raised. If so, you might want to think about a farm vacation. Accommodations might be in a century-old farmhouse or rustic cabin. Activities may include hay rides and sleigh rides, horseback riding, fishing, canoeing, rafting, cross-country skiing, and snowmobiling. You can obtain details on over two dozen farm vacations from the **Wisconsin Department of Tourism** (tel 800/432-TRIP).

Architecture The Welsh, with their lyrical speech and strong work ethic, settled in the rural countryside surrounding **Spring Green.** Among them was Lloyd Jones, grandfather of renowned architect Frank Lloyd Wright. Today, the Frank Lloyd Wright Visitors Center occupies the former Spring Green Restaurant. Nearby is Wright's famous house and school, built on the brow of a hill facing the Wisconsin River and called **Taliesin,** Welsh for "shining brow." Visitors can observe architects and apprentices at work in the massive drafting studio, which was likened by Wright to "an abstract forest with light pouring in from the ceiling." They also may inspect Wright-designed furniture and take a 90-minute, two-mile country walking tour past gardens, ponds, and other major buildings on the estate.

EVENTS AND FESTIVALS

- **World Championship Snowmobile Derby,** Eagle River. More than 300 professional racers battle it out. Mid-January. Call 800/359-6315.
- **Northern Exposure–Wolf River Rendezvous,** Shawano. Dog sled races, lumberjack competitions. Mid-January. Call 800/235-8528.
- **American Birkebeiner,** Hayward to Cable. North

America's biggest cross-country ski marathon. Late-February. Call 800/872-2753.

- **Reynolds Sugarbush,** Aniwa. Guided tours of maple sugaring areas. Late March through April. Call 715/449-2057.
- **Door County Festival of Blossoms,** Door County. One million daffodils plus apple and cherry blossoms. Every weekend in May. Call 800/52-RELAX.
- **Prairie Villa Rendezvous,** Prairie du Chien. Historic re-enactment of 18th-century fur-trading camp. Mid-June. Call 608/375-4758.
- **Summerfest,** Milwaukee. 10-day outdoor music festival, 11 stages. Begins late June. Call 800/837-FEST.
- **Bristol Renaissance Faire,** Bristol. Jousting, food, crafts, entertainment in a re-created 16th-century English village. Weekends late June to mid-August.
- **Great Circus Parade,** Milwaukee. Recreation of 19th-century parade with wagons, horses, clowns, marching bands. Mid-July. Call 414/273-7877.
- **Annual Experimental Aircraft Association International Fly-In,** Oshkosh. World's largest aviation event, with over 15,000 planes of every size, shape, and description. Late July. Call 414/426-4818.
- **Lumberjack World Championships,** Hayward. Logrolling, speed sawing, chopping, pole-climbing. Late July. Call 715/634-2484.
- **Wilhelm Tell Festival,** New Glarus. Since 1938, English and German performances of drama of Swiss independence. Labor Day weekend. Call 608/527-2095.
- **Indian Summer,** Milwaukee. Native American ceremonies, crafts, food. Early September. Call 800/837-FEST.
- **Annual Cranberry Festival,** Warrens. Tours of colorful cranberry bogs, arts, crafts, parade. Late September. Call 608/378-4388.
- **Apple Festival,** Bayfield. Orchard tours, food, crafts. Early October. Call 715/779-3335.
- **Oktoberfest,** La Crosse. German-style entertainment, arts, crafts along the Mississippi. Late September. Call 608/784-3378.
- **Holiday Folk Fair,** Milwaukee. Nation's biggest multiethnic indoor festival with dance, music, food, crafts. Mid-November. Call 414/225-6220.
- **Display of 6,000 Santas,** Spring Green. Santas from around the world at House on the Rock.

Mid-November through December. Call 608/935-3639.

SPECTATOR SPORTS

Auto Racing   Road America (tel 414/892-4576), the four-mile road-racing facility at Elkhart Lake, is open May through September and has drawn such famous drivers as Mario Andretti, Al Unser, and actor Paul Newman. In late May, the Miller Genuine Draft 200 for Indy cars is held at **State Fair Park** at the Milwaukee suburb of West Allis (tel 414/273-7222).

Baseball   Wisconsin's professional baseball team, the **Milwaukee Brewers,** play their American League games at County Stadium on the city's west side (tel 414/933-9000).

Basketball   Two of Wisconsin's premier professional and collegiate basketball teams share a stadium in Milwaukee. Both the NBA **Milwaukee Bucks** and the **Marquette University Warriors** play home games at the Bradley Center (tel 414/227-0500). The **University of Wisconsin Badgers** of the Big Ten Conference play at the UW Field House in Madison (tel 608/262-1440).

College Football   In fall, the **University of Wisconsin Badgers** football team competes at Camp Randall Stadium (tel 608/262-1440) in Madison.

Pro Football   Wisconsin sports fans are fanatical about their **Packers,** filling Green Bay's Lambeau Field no matter how cold the temperatures nor how deep the snow (tel 414/496-7722). The history of the fabled team is chronicled at the Green Bay Packers Hall of Fame (tel 414/499-4281), just down Lombardi Ave from Lambeau Field. Four out-of-state NFL teams stage their summer training camps in Wisconsin: the Chicago Bears at Platteville (tel 608/342-1496); the New Orleans Saints at La Crosse (tel 608/789-4550); the Kansas City Chiefs at River Falls (tel 715/425-2533); and the expansion Jacksonville Jaguars at Stevens Point (tel 715/344-2556). Practices and scrimmages are open to the public.

Hockey   The **Milwaukee Admirals** of the International Hockey League skate at the multipurpose Bradley Center (tel 414/227-0500)

Greyhound Racing   Wisconsin has four state-of-the-art, climate-controlled greyhound racing parks offering pari-mutuel wagering: Geneva Lakes Kennel Club in Delavan (tel 414/728-8000); St Croix Meadows Greyhound Racing Park in Hudson (tel 715/386-6800); Dairyland Greyhound Park in Kenosha (tel 414/657-8200); and Wisconsin Dells Greyhound Park in Wisconsin Dells (tel 608/253-3647).

Ice Skating Visitors can watch Olympic-caliber skaters perform at Milwaukee's **Petit National Ice Center** at Wisconsin State Fair Park (tel 414/266-0100). This ice center, the only one of its kind in the nation and one of only five in the world, features an enclosed ice training and competition center for speedskating, hockey, and figure skating. Admission is free.

Soccer Professional soccer retains its loose grip in Wisconsin with the **Milwaukee Wave.** The club competes in the National Professional Soccer League and plays its home games at Bradley Center. Call 414/962-WAVE for tickets.

ACTIVITIES A TO Z

Bicycling Wisconsin and bicycles were made for each other. In addition to providing a system of scenic rural roads that take riders through cool forests, into lush valleys, and past glacial lakes, the state is a pioneer of "rails-to-trails," converting abandoned railroad right-of-way into recreational routes. Popular among these trails is the **Elroy-Sparta Trail,** a 33-mile roll through wooded valleys and small towns and the **Cheese Country Recreation Trail,** a 47-mile corridor in the heart of dairy country. More than 10,000 miles of recommended roads are listed in the Wisconsin Bicycle Map, available free from the **Wisconsin Division of Tourism** (tel 800/432-TRIP).

Bird Watching Wisconsin abounds with birding sites, including the famed **Horicon National Wildlife Refuge** (tel 414/387-2658), northeast of Beaver Dam, known worldwide for its spring and fall migrations of Canada geese. Migratory and shorebirds also are attracted to Oconto Marsh, wetlands located on the west shore of Green Bay.

Gordon Bubolz Nature Preserve at Appleton (tel 414/731-6041) is a 762-acre white cedar swamp that provides habitat for a variety of woodland species, including the great horned owl. At Baraboo, the **International Crane Foundation** (tel 608/356-9462) protects cranes and their wetland homes, and **Wyalusing State Park** (tel 608/996-2261), atop the

Mississippi bluffs near Prairie du Chien, is the spot to watch for Kentucky warblers, Acadian flycatchers, red-shouldered hawk, and other spring migrants—and for the raptors that migrate along the bluffs in fall. Also along the Mississippi, bluffs near Stockholm provide a major wintering area for bald eagles January through March.

Canoeing & Kayaking True to its heritage of Native Americans, fur traders, and pioneer settlers plying rivers in birchbark canoes, Wisconsin is a magnet for latter-day paddlers. Its rivers come in all shapes and sizes: some gentle and meandering, others churning with turbulent whitewater. Popular areas include lower stretches of the 430-mile-long Wisconsin River, where numerous islands and sandbars are popular for overnight camping, and the Flambeau River, offering some of the best whitewater paddling in the Midwest. Several Wisconsin outfitters provide professionally-guided canoe trips.

Fishing With its abundant lakes and rivers, Wisconsin attracts anglers of every stripe. Pick up a charter fishing boat at Two Rivers (and other ports) for an outing onto Lake Michigan. In recent years, the Wisconsin Department of Natural Resources has restocked the lake with more than two million coho and chinook salmon, one million lake trout, and almost two million brook, brown, and steelhead trout. Hooking into one of these scrappy game fish can signal the beginning of an exhilarating, arm-tiring struggle. In 1994, a state record 44-pound chinook salmon was landed by a 16-year-old angler at Sturgeon Bay.

Trout fishermen—and especially fly casters—head for the icy, spring-fed streams of **Langlade County** in northeastern Wisconsin. The county has 418 lakes, 225 streams, and more than 200 spring ponds, containing a variety of fish ranging from bluegills to rainbow trout. Native and stocked brook, brown, and rainbow trout are plentiful, and a world-record splake (a hybrid created to combine the fighting qualities of the speckled trout with the large size of the lake trout) weighing 16 pounds 14 ounces was taken from Ada Lake.

Fishing licenses are required for both residents and nonresidents age 16 or older. In addition, trout and salmon stamps must be purchased by persons intending to fish for those species in the Great Lakes as well as in inland waters. Short-term and annual licenses are available, and are sold at most DNR offices, all county clerk offices, and at many bait shops, sporting goods stores, and marinas. For more information, contact the **Wisconsin Department of Natural Resources,** License Section, PO Box 7921, Madison 53707 (tel 608/266-2621).

Golf Wisconsin is a destination for serious and recreational golfers, with more than 425 courses, both private and public. At the renowned **American Club** at Kohler, Blackwolf Run offers two 18-hole courses and one of the toughest tests of golf in the Midwest. The winding Sheboygan River separates the two courses, which offer a level of challenge and strategy reminiscent of the great Scottish links. Green Lake offers 72 challenging holes at three renowned courses: **Tuscumbria** is Wisconsin's oldest golf course; **Mascoutin** is rated among the state's Top Ten links; **Lawsonia** has a national reputation as one of the toughest public golf courses.

Houseboating Imagine a vacation home that floats, with you at the wheel as captain and pilot to chart your own course and set your own pace, stopping on whim for a shore luncheon or to fish backwaters. That is the appeal of a houseboat vacation, especially popular along the Mississippi. La Crosse is a major center of rental firms, with others at Alma, Cassville, Hudson, and Trempealeau. Another option is houseboating on the Eagle River. Houseboats typically sleep up to eight people and are fully equipped with kitchen, toilet, and shower.

Rafting Coursing through Langlade County, the **Wolf River** is perfect for a family rafting adventure. More than a dozen rafting outfitters dot the river's edge in the hamlets of White Lake and Langlade, about 20 miles east of Antigo. Rapids, stretching from one-half to three-quarters of a mile, spill over boulders and ledges. By summer, the turbulent river mellows, making it ideal for novices who often raft in swimsuits and take an occasional dip in clear water averaging in depth little more than two to three feet.

Skiing Nordic skiing is Wisconsin's strength, with more than 350 cross-country ski centers offering a wide variety of trails—from atop limestone bluffs to depths of pristine forests, past glittering frozen waterfalls and across vast frozen lakes. Cross-country ski racing has become a popular sport, with events ranging from the 10 races of the Great Lakes Challenge series to the magic of the "Birkie"—the **American Birkebeiner** cross-country ski race between Hayward and Cable that draws more than

---

SELECTED PARKS & RECREATION AREAS

- **Chequamegon National Forest,** 1170 4th Ave S, Park Falls 54552 (tel 715/762-2461)
- **Nicolet National Forest,** 68 S Stevens St, Rhinelander 54501 (tel 715/362-3415)
- **Apostle Islands National Lakeshore,** Rte 1, Box 4, Bayfield 54814 (tel 715/779-3397)
- **Amnicon Falls State Park,** 6294 S WI 35, Superior 54880-8326 (tel 715/399-8073)
- **Big Foot Beach State Park,** 1452 Hwy H, Lake Geneva 53147 (tel 414/248-2528)
- **Buckhorn State Park,** W8450 Buckhorn Park Ave, Necedah 54646-2789 (tel 608/565-2789)
- **Chippewa Moraine State Recreation Area,** Box 13394, County Hwy M, New Auburn 54757 (tel 715/967-2800)
- **Devil's Lake State Park,** S5975 Park Rd, Baraboo 53913-9299 (tel 608/356-6618)
- **Governor Dodge State Park,** 4715 WI 23, Dodgeville 53533 (tel 608/935-2315)
- **Harrington Beach State Park,** 531 Hwy D, Belgium 53004 (tel 414/285-3015)
- **Heritage Hill State Park,** 2640 S Webster Ave, Green Bay 54301 (tel 414/448-5150)
- **High Cliff State Park,** N7475 High Cliff Rd, Menasha (tel 414/989-1106)
- **Hoffman Hills State Recreation Area,** Rt 6, Box 1, Menomonie 54751 (tel 715/232-2631)
- **Kohler-Andrae State Park,** 1520 Old Park Rd, Sheboygan 53081 (tel 414/451-4080)
- **Lake Kegonsa State Park,** 2405 Door Creek Rd, Stoughton 53589 (tel 608/873-9695)
- **Merrick State Park,** S2965 State Rd, Fountain City 54629-7814 (tel 608/687-4936)
- **Mirror Lake State Park,** E10320 Fern Dell Rd, Baraboo 53913 (tel 608/254-2333)
- **Newport State Park,** 475 Cty Rd NP, Ellison Bay 54210 (tel 414/854-2500)
- **Peninsula State Park,** Box 218, Fish Creek 54212-0218 (tel 414/868-5791)
- **Potawatomi State Park,** 3740 Park Dr, Sturgeon Bay 54235 (tel 414/746-2891)
- **Yellowstone Lake State Park,** 7896 Lake Rd, Blanchardville 53516 (tel 608/523-4427)

6,000 participants nationwide and from more than a dozen foreign countries.

Popular downhill areas include **Telemark** (tel 715/798-3811) at Cable in northern Wisconsin (10 runs, and a full range of lifts and support facilities). In the southern region of the state—and convenient for Chicago skiers—are **Alpine Valley** at East Troy (tel 414/642-7374) and **Grand Geneva Resort and Spa** at Lake Geneva (tel 414/248-8811).

Sleigh Rides   Rides on horse-drawn sleighs, with hardworking Belgians and Percherons in harness, are a charming part of Wisconsin's winter landscape. State tourism offices offer a listing of close to 75 ranches, farms, and stables that provide hayrides, many with such perks as rustic warming lodges with stone fireplaces and catering ranging from hot cider to steak dinners. During warmer months, many of these same operators offers hay rides.

Snowmobiling   Wisconsin is a snowmobiler's Avalon, with nearly 20,000 miles of trails linking every corner of the state. Trails are well marked and methodically groomed by hundreds of local snow-mobile clubs. County trail systems are linked to thousands of miles of trails in state and national forests. **Eagle River** calls itself the "Snowmobile Capital of the World" and every January hosts the World Championship Snowmobile Derby.

Tubing   There's nothing quite like floating down a lazy river on a hot summer's day, legs dangling from an inner tube into the cool water. Head for the **Apple River** near Somerset in St Croix County close to the Minnesota line for the Midwest's most popular tubing spot. No fewer than eight liveries provide rental tubes and shuttles to and from the river. "Bobbing the Apple" involves a three-hour float down a meandering 4½-mile stretch of the river. A shorter trip (about 45 minutes) negotiates swifter water with mild rapids.

SOUTHWESTERN WISCONSIN

Start	New Glarus
Finish	Wyalusing
Distance	Approximately 130 miles
Time	1–3 days
Highlights	Rolling countryside and farms, a "Swiss" village, the Troll Capital of the World, finery and kitsch at the House on the Rock, masterworks by Frank Lloyd Wright, bluffs and caves

The biggest myth of the Midwest is that it is flat—but this winding, climbing, dipping drive through the woods and valleys of southwestern Wisconsin should convince you otherwise. This area is so varied because the glaciers of the last Ice Age did not flatten the terrain as it did in other parts of the Midwest. Some of Wisconsin's finest state parks are here, and so are a number of wildlife viewing areas.

This is also a place rich with the diversity of Midwestern history and heritage. There's New Glarus, originally settled by Swiss pioneers in 1845; Little Norway, a Norwegian homestead dating back to the 1860's; Taliesin, a collection of Frank Lloyd Wright structures designated a National Historic Landmark; and Villa Louis, a Victorian country estate. It's a trip that could take five hours or a week, depending upon your interests and your schedule.

For additional information on accommodations, restaurants, and attractions in the region covered by the tour, look under specific cities in the listings portion of this chapter.

This tour begins about 30 miles SW of Madison. If starting out from Madison, take US 18/151 west for 5 miles to Verona, then head south on WI 69 for about 20 miles to the community of New Glarus. Continue on for 6 miles to:

1. **New Glarus Woods State Park,** WI 69 and County Trunk NN (tel 608/527-2335). The best way to see what these 350 acres have to offer is by parking and walking the 0.3-mile Basswood Nature Trail and the 4.1-mile Havenridge Trail. The nature trail is marked with interpretive signs to help you to recognize the oak, basswood, elm, hickory, and black walnut trees, while self-guided tour brochures (available at the park office) explain the open fields and thickly wooded ridges and valleys of the Havenridge Trail. Camping and picnicking areas are also available.

Take County Trunk NN back to WI 69 and head about 6 miles north to:

2. **New Glarus.** Known as America's Little Switzerland, New Glarus is a town proud of its beginnings. More than a hundred pioneers from Glarus, Switzerland, settled in New Glarus in 1845, and their influence is still very apparent in the town's architecture, shops, and restaurants. **Mrs Lackovich's Christmas House and Gifts** (tel 608/527-5106), at the corner of 1st St and 6th Ave, has a huge selection of holiday ornaments and collectibles. **Roberts European Imports** (tel 608/527-2517 or toll free 800/968-2517), at 102 5th Ave, features all things Swiss, including chimes, nutcrackers, and genuine Swiss Army Knives. There are gift shops and specialty shops galore, as well as places to sit and partake of Old World specialties such as schnitzels and fondues; and Old World entertainment like polka dancing and yodeling.

New Glarus hosts a number of Swiss-themed festivals throughout the year. From May through October, guests can get a taste of the past at the **Swiss Historical Village,** (tel 608/527-2317) located at 612 7th Ave. The village consists of 12 buildings, including a *schmiede* (blacksmith shop), a *feuer wehr haus* (fire station), and a *druckerei* (print shop), as well as other businesses and dwellings preserved and re-created to show life as it was in the original New Glarus.

Leave New Glarus by way of WI 69 N, and go about 4 miles to WI 92. (You will be heading north, even though the route sign says west.) Follow WI 92 west for approximately 14 miles to:

3. **Mount Horeb.** Follow WI 92 west to Bus US 18/151 and turn left (west) to follow Main St, otherwise known as **The Trollway.** Mount Horeb proudly claims the title of the Troll Capital of the World. These hand carved, four-foot-tall wooden trolls are said to be there to welcome visitors to the shops and restaurants and entertainment spots of the area.

Another unique local attraction is the **Mount Horeb Mustard Museum,** 109 E Main St. You can learn everything you ever wanted to know about mustard from the orientation video (called "Mustard Piece Theater"), then try a sample or two of the real thing after consulting with the museum's trained "condiment therapists."

Continue on your way west, following Bus US

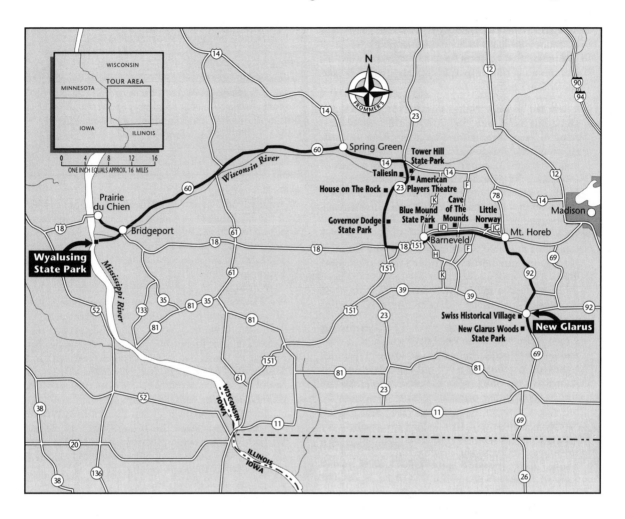

18/151 until it turns into County ID, then take that to County JG (about 3 miles west of Mount Horeb). On County JG, turn right (north) and watch for signs to:

4. **Little Norway** (tel 608/437-8211), a Norwegian pioneer homestead settled in 1856. Guides in Norwegian costume will walk you through the property and provide information about the original farm buildings, and will show off the extensive collection of Norwegian hand tools, arts and crafts, and antique furnishings. Visitors are invited to walk through a replica of a Norwegian Stave Church, poke around the gift shop, or sit by the trout pond.

From Little Norway, drive back south on County JG to County ID. Take a right (west) on County ID. Signs will direct you to:

5. **Cave of the Mounds** (tel 608/437-3038), which has been called the most significant cave in the upper Midwest. Guided tours (which take about an hour)

allow visitors to walk deep into the recesses of the caverns, where they can see first hand why this place is often referred to as the "jewel box" of America's major caves. Stalactites and stalagmites glimmer, and crystallized rock formations are highlighted by shimmering pools. The original rock from which this beauty was formed is believed to be over 400 million years old.

Once back on County ID signs will direct you to:

6. **Blue Mound State Park** (tel 608/437-5711). The highest spot in all of southern Wisconsin, the park is atop the west Blue Mound, some 1,700 feet above sea level. Two 40-foot observation towers let you see practically all of southern Wisconsin. Several nature trails meander through sugar-maple forests, past springs, and up to spectacular vistas; and designated camping and picnicking areas are available.

It's just a couple of miles west on County ID

back to US 18/151 (just past Barneveld). Once on it, follow US 18/151 west just over 11 miles to where US 18 splits off from US 151 (exit 60). Continue on US 18 to WI 23, which you will take north for 7 miles to:

7. **Governor Dodge State Park,** 4175 WI 23 in Dodgeville (tel 608/935-2315). This 5,000-acre park is filled with natural wonder: valleys, sandstone bluffs, prairies, thick woods, pristine lakes, and waterfalls. Watch for deer, wild turkeys, ruffed grouse, red and gray fox, beaver, wood chucks, muskrats and raccoons. You can swim here, boating is permitted on the lakes, and there are many trails for hiking, cross-country skiing, biking, and horseback riding. Although there are more than 200 campsites available, Governor Dodge is a popular place in the summertime so reservations are a good idea.

Continue 5½ miles north on WI 23, to one of the most visited attractions in southern Wisconsin:

8. **The House on the Rock,** 5754 WI 23 in Spring Green (tel 608/935-3639). Fifty years ago, a man named Alex Jordan built a house in the Wyoming Valley of Wisconsin on a sandstone outcropping known as Deer Shelter Rock. People who passed by the 14-room house often stopped by to see if they might get a closer look or perhaps a quick peek inside. Jordan began to charge these visitors 50 cents apiece for a house tour. Many buildings have since been added to the original house in order to house all of Jordan's collections: the Music of Yesterday exhibit (with music machines from all over the world) and the Infinity Room (with more than 3,200 windows) are among the most popular. The grounds also feature over 100,000 flowers and the World's Largest Carousel. The full walking tour is 2½ miles long and takes from two to five hours, but there are designated spots where you can leave and come back in again if you do not want to do the whole tour in a day.

Spring Green has a number of lodging choices, but an exceptional one is **The Silver Star** (tel 608/935-7297), a country inn high in the hills with 10 impeccably appointed rooms and a cozy fireplace in the lobby. The rates are moderately expensive but include a full home-cooked breakfast for two.

Continue for 14 miles north on WI 23 to the next stop:

9. **Frank Lloyd Wright Visitors Center and Taliesin** (tel 608/588-7900). The famous architect used this complex as his summer residence and workshop for nearly 50 years. Eight structures make up the community, including **Hillside Studio,** the building

---

Take a Break

The Silver Star, 3852 Limmex Hill Rd in Spring Green (tel 608/935-7297). This bright, log inn, just 2 miles north of The House on the Rock, is a good choice for a full meal or a light treat. Fresh ingredients are used for the salads and entrees; and fresh baked, wonderful cakes, tarts, and pastries are the perfect on the road snack. Entrees are $9–$13; baked goods are under $5.

---

originally designed as the Hillside Home School for Wright's aunts. (It is still in use as an architectural educational facility.) A variety of tours, lasting from one to four hours and ranging in price from $7 to $50, allow visitors to explore this National Historic Landmark.

Within a mile of Taliesin is the **American Players Theatre,** an outdoor amphitheater where you can watch very fine classical theater productions. There are grills and picnic tables for carry-in picnickers, and gourmet box meals are available for purchase. Down the road just a bit you will find **Tower Hill State Park** (tel 608/588-2116). This lovely little place on the Wisconsin River is a popular spot for canoeing and camping.

Three miles north from the Frank Lloyd Wright Visitors Center, over the broad, lushly bordered Wisconsin River, is the junction of US 14. Take US 14 west to WI 60. Keep going west on WI 60 for a 60-mile drive through rolling countryside, hills, designated wildlife viewing areas, and a handful of small towns. Keep your eyes open for animals, big and small. You're likely to see many deer, lots of racoons, and maybe even a bald eagle. This long stretch is quite winding, not heavily traveled, and very dark at night, so you might want to make sure there is still daylight left before you make your way west toward the Mississippi River.

At US 18 W, head into **Prairie du Chien,** the second-oldest city in the state. Approximately 6 miles west of town, off US 18 W, is:

10. **Villa Louis,** 521 Villa Louis Rd (tel 608/326-2721). A Victorian country estate owned and operated by the State Historical Society of Wisconsin, Villa Louis sits on top of an ancient Native American burial mound on St Feriole Island. Tours take in the mansion, with its authentic Victorian furnishings, as well as the **Museum of Prairie du Chien** and the **Fur Trade Museum.**

If Prairie du Chien finds you in need of a place to sleep, you might try the moderately priced theme suites at the **Best Western Quiet House Suites** (tel 608/326-4777 or toll free 800/528-1234), the well-

---

Take a Break

The Dew Drop Inn, County C and County X (tel 608/996-2243). You can't get anymore Wisconsin than The Dew Drop: deer heads on the wood panelled walls, pool tables and pinball machines, and basic, hearty food. Try the burgers, or the deep fried side dishes like cheddar crisps. There's even a veggie burger for non-meat eaters. Most entrees are under $5.

---

kept, conveniently located, and affordable **Super 8 Motel** (tel 608/326-8777) is managed by the same husband-and-wife team who run the Best Western. Backtrack on US 18 W to County C, just past WI 60 and over the Wisconsin River. At County C go west about 3 miles to County X, take a right (west again), and follow the signs to:

11. **Wyalusing State Park,** 13342 County Hwy C near Bagley (tel 608/996-2261). Wyalusing (named for a Munsee-Delaware word meaning "home of the warrior") has 2,674 acres of hills, forest, trails, prairies, and scenic overlooks that peer down onto both the Mississippi and the Wisconsin Rivers. Come fall, this park is one of the most breathtaking spots in Wisconsin. Its 11 trails draw hikers of varying ability; there's even a trail designed for those with mobility impairments. In the spring, Wyalusing is a stopover for over 200 species of migratory birds.

Canoeists will find a designated canoe trail that takes about two and a half to three hours to float. Campsites are available by reservation and on a first come, first served basis. The park is also open for winter camping, and the area is known for its fine cross-country ski trails.

Once you've had your fill of Wyalusing, retrace your path out of the park and east along County X then County C to US 18. This major highway can take you back toward Madison or to one of the interstates to pick up your trip where you left off before the tour.

Wisconsin Listings

Algoma

Small town on the Lake Michigan side of the Door Peninsula, in the eastern part of the state. Algoma (which means "park of flowers") is home to 140-year-old Von Stiehl Winery. Tours end with samples of wine, cheese, and jelly made from Door Peninsula fruit. **Information:** Algoma Area Chamber of Commerce, 1226 Lake St, Algoma, 54201 (tel 414/487-2041).

MOTELS

Algoma Beach Motel

1500 Lake St, 54201; tel 414/487-2828. Located on Lake Michigan, close enough to hear the sound of waves on the beach. Plenty of green space for children, and connected to beachfront park. **Rooms:** 29 rms, stes, and effic. CI 11am/CO 2pm. Nonsmoking rms avail. Country inn–style rooms, each with different homey decor. Beachfront units available. **Amenities:** A/C, cable TV. Some units w/terraces, 1 w/whirlpool. **Services:** Babysitting. Pets with approval only. Freezer service for storing catch from fishing trips. **Facilities:** 1 beach (lake shore). **Rates:** Peak (July–Labor Day) $53–$57 S; $57–$67 D; $95 ste; $75 effic. Extra person $5. Children under age 16 stay free. Lower rates off-season. Parking: Outdoor, free. Weekly rates for kitchenettes. Discounts on stays of multiple nights. Spring packages avail. Closed Nov–Mar 15. AE, DISC, MC, V.

Scenic Shore Inn

2221 Lake St, 54201; tel 414/487-3214. Lake view, plus sunsets across tranquil farm fields. Family owned and operated, on three acres. Located four miles from Door County line and three miles from Ahnapee State Trail, a 15-mile hiking, biking, snowmobiling, cross-country skiing, and horseback riding trail. **Rooms:** 13 rms. CI 1pm/CO 11am. Nonsmoking rms avail. All rooms face Lake Michigan and feature fresh, neutral decor. **Amenities:** A/C, cable TV w/movies, dataport. Some units w/terraces. **Services:** Complimentary coffee. Small pets only. TDD available. Friendly atmosphere. **Facilities:** **Rates (AP):** Peak (June 20–Sept 5) $39 S; $50 D. Extra person $5. Children under age 16 stay free. Lower rates off-season. Parking: Outdoor, free. 10% discount for stays of one week or longer. Corporate rates avail. AE, CB, DC, DISC, MC, V.

RESTAURANT

⑤ Captain's Table

133 N Water St; tel 414/487-5304. From WI 42, take County Rd "S" E, then N across bridge. **Regional American.** A popular spot with local dairy farmers and Lake Michigan boaters who know good value. Wines are from the local Von Stiehl winery and all fish are caught locally. The Friday and Saturday night trout boils pack 'em in, as does the Sunday breakfast buffet. Full salad bar (including various casseroles) and daily sandwich specials round out the menu. **FYI:** Reservations accepted. Children's menu. **Open:** Peak (June–Oct) daily 5am–9:30pm. **Prices:** Main courses $5–$9. No CC.

Antigo

Seat of Langlade County, in northeast part of state. Antigo, which is Chippewa for "spring river," hosts the Wisconsin State Maple Syrup Festival and Pancake Day on the last Sunday in May. **Information:** Antigo Area Chamber of Commerce, 329 Superior St, PO Box 339, Antigo, 54409 (tel 715/623-4134).

MOTEL

Super 8 Motel

535 Century Ave, 54409; tel 715/623-4188 or toll free 800/800-8000; fax 715/623-5787. Jct I-45 N/WI 64. Adjacent to Antigo's largest shopping center, a few restaurants, and a snowmobile trail, this motel suits nearly every traveler's needs. **Rooms:** 52 rms and stes. CI 2pm/CO 11am. Nonsmoking rms avail. Rooms are clean and decorated in soft pastels. **Amenities:** A/C, cable TV. Some units w/whirlpools. **Services:** **Facilities:** Games rm, sauna, whirlpool. **Rates (CP):** Peak (Apr–Oct) $36–$39 S; $51–$54 D; $54–$75 ste. Extra person $5. Children under age 12 stay free. Lower rates off-season. Parking: Outdoor, free. AE, DC, DISC, MC, V.

RESTAURANT

⑤ Black Jack Steak House
800 S Superior St; tel 715/623-2514. **American/Seafood.**
The food is fine and the maroon-and-green plaid decor is
charming. Nightly specials often include lobster, chicken, and
shrimp entrees; sirloin steaks and a number of sandwiches are
the standard fare. On the downside, service can be somewhat
apathetic, and there's no nonsmoking section. **FYI:** Reservations accepted. Children's menu. **Open:** Lunch daily 11am–
2pm; dinner daily 5–11pm. **Prices:** Main courses $5–$23.
AE, DISC, MC, V.

Appleton

Seat of Outagamie County, in eastern Wisconsin. This paper-
manufacturing center on the Fox River was the first US city
to use hydroelectric power (1882); today, it is the site of
Lawrence University. Novelist Edna Ferber spent her girl-
hood here, and magician Harry Houdini was a native.
Information: Fox Cities Convention & Visitors Bureau, 110
Fox River Dr, Appleton, 54915 (tel 414/734-3358).

RESTAURANTS

♥ Christie's
In Paper Valley Hotel, 333 W College Ave; tel 414/
733-8000. College Ave E exit off US 41. **Seafood/Steak.** An
elegant place for a pretheater dinner (the Attic and the
Lawrence are both nearby). The inventive menu changes
weekly to allow the chef to take advantage of the freshest
ingredients. Entrees often incorporate game, such as boar,
pheasant, and quail. **FYI:** Reservations recommended. Children's menu. Dress code. **Open:** Lunch Mon–Fri 11:30am–
2pm; dinner Mon–Sun 5:30–10pm; brunch Sun 10am–2pm.
Prices: Main courses $14–$25. AE, CB, DC, DISC, MC, V. ♥
&

George's Steak House
2208 Memorial Dr; tel 414/733-4939. S Oneida St E exit off
US 441. **Seafood/Steak.** Basic steak house with friendly
neighborhood atmosphere. A variety of hand-cut chops are
available; all come with choice of soup, salad, and potato.
Broiled seafood (shrimp, scallops, pike) and chicken round
out the menu. **FYI:** Reservations recommended. Piano.
Open: Lunch Mon–Fri 11am–2pm; dinner Mon–Sat 5–
10:30pm. **Prices:** Main courses $8–$30. AE, DC, DISC, MC,
V.

ATTRACTIONS

Outagamie Museum and Houdini Historical Center
330 E College Ave; tel 414/733-8445. Permanent exhibits at
this local museum deal with the role of technology in the
region from 1840–1950. Five historic re-created work places,

ranging from a 1896 wire weaving loom and a 1930s burglar-
proof bank to a 1920s newspaper composing room, are
featured.

Illusionist Harry Houdini spent his early childhood in
Appleton. The museum's Houdini collection includes over
150 personal photographs, 120 artifacts (such as the hand-
cuffs, leg irons, and lock picks he used for his show), and
other documents. The center also offers a walking tour of
downtown Appleton historic sites; magic shows, and family
programs. Gift shop sells magic-related souvenirs. **Open:**
Peak (June–Aug) Mon–Sat 10am–5pm, Sun noon–5pm. Reduced hours off-season. **$**

Wriston Art Center Galleries
613 E College Ave, Lawrence University; tel 414/832-6621.
Built in 1989, this unique structure combines postmodern
glass walls with the classic turrets and curves of Gothic
architecture. Recent exhibitions have focused on the textiles
of India and American-made weathervanes. An outdoor
amphitheater hosts summertime concerts and performances.
Galleries only open to public during exhibitions; call for
schedule. **Open:** Peak (Sept–May) Tues–Fri 10am–4pm, Sat–
Sun noon–4pm. Reduced hours off-season. **Free**

Mossholder Farms Cheese Factory
4017 N Richmond St; tel 414/734-7575. For over 70 years,
this family-owned and -operated dairy farm has been producing a variety of cheeses using fresh, unpasturized milk from
its own cows. Although there are no factory tours, there is an
on-site retail shop if you'd like to sample the wares. **Open:**
Mon–Fri 9am–5pm, Sat 9am–noon. **Free**

The Charles A Grignon Mansion
1313 Augustine St, Kaukauna; tel 414/766-3122. Built in
1837 by Charles Grignon, an interpreter for the government
and scion of a fur trading family. Costumed guides lead tours
of this "mansion in the woods" and discuss everyday life on
the Wisconsin frontier from the 1830s to the 1860s. An
interactive exhibit describes the building of the mansion;
visitors may also browse through the apple orchard and
gardens. Annual Civil War Encampment features narrated
skirmishes between the North and South, live music, historic
foods, crafts, and games. **Open:** Peak (June–Aug) Mon–Sat
10am–5pm, Sun noon–5pm. Reduced hours off-season. **$**

Ashland

Seat of Ashland County, in northern Wisconsin. This port city
on Lake Superior's Chequamegon Bay is home to Sigurd
Olson Environmental Institute, on the campus of Northland
College. **Information:** Ashland Area Chamber of Commerce,
320 4th Ave W, PO Box 746, Ashland, 54806 (tel 715/
682-2500).

MOTELS 🏨

▐ Ashland Motel
2300 W Lakeshore Dr, 54806; tel 715/682-5503. On US 2; the southeastern edge of town. Family-owned motel occupies two separate buildings on main thoroughfare. **Rooms:** 34 rms. CI 10am/CO 10am. Nonsmoking rms avail. Wide variety of room options. Drab decor, but majority of rooms face Lake Superior. **Amenities:** 🏠 🛁 A/C, cable TV. **Services:** ↻ 🛎 **Facilities:** 🏋 🍽 **Rates:** Peak (May–Sept) $30–$52 S; $44–$52 D. Extra person $5. Children under age 16 stay free. Lower rates off-season. Parking: Outdoor, free. AE, DISC, MC, V.

▐▐▐ Best Western Inn
Rte 3, Box 24, 54806; tel 715/682-5235 or toll free 800/528-1234; fax 715/682-4730. Comfortable lobby. Motel owners also run restaurant with full bar next door. **Rooms:** 65 rms and stes. CI 1pm/CO 11am. Nonsmoking rms avail. Poolside and lake-view rooms available for additional charge. **Amenities:** 🏠 🛁 🖥 🍽 A/C, cable TV. 1 unit w/minibar, some w/terraces. **Services:** ↻ 🛎 **Facilities:** 🏋 🍽 1 restaurant (bkfst and lunch only), games rm, sauna, whirlpool. Convenient coffee shop. **Rates:** Peak (May 20–Oct 14) $44–$90 S; $48–$90 D; $84–$90 ste. Extra person $5. Children under age 12 stay free. Min stay special events. Lower rates off-season. Parking: Outdoor, free. AE, CB, DC, DISC, MC, V.

▐▐ Super 8 Motel
1610 W Lakeshore Dr, 54806; tel 715/682-9377 or toll free 800/800-8000; fax 715/682-5593. On US 2. A good choice for families traveling through Ashland. Very clean. **Rooms:** 70 rms and stes. CI 3pm/CO 11am. Nonsmoking rms avail. All rooms recently remodeled. **Amenities:** 🏠 🛁 A/C, cable TV. **Services:** ↻ 🛎 Friendly and helpful front desk staff. **Facilities:** 🏋 🍽 🏋 30 ♿ Whirlpool, washer/dryer. **Rates:** Peak (May 16–Oct 9) $49–$54 S; $56–$66 D; $71–$77 ste. Extra person $5. Children under age 12 stay free. Lower rates off-season. Parking: Outdoor, free. AE, DC, DISC, MC, V.

Bagley

See Prairie du Chien

Baileys Harbor

Range lights have guided ships into harbor since 1870, in this oldest village in Door County. A replica of a 15th-century Norwegian chapel sits at Bjorklunden, a 325-acre estate owned by Lawrence University.

MOTEL 🏨

▐▐ The Petry Place
8040 WI 57, PO Box 345, 54202 (Downtown); tel 414/839-2345 or toll free 800/503-5959. Older but well-maintained, family-owned and -operated property located directly on Lake Michigan, on the "quiet side" of Door County. Waterfront deck off lobby. **Rooms:** 39 rms and stes. CI 2pm/CO 10am. Nonsmoking rms avail. Some rooms have lake view, all have pleasant neutral decor. Lake breeze cools rooms without air conditioning. **Amenities:** TV. No A/C or phone. **Services:** ↻ Morning coffee. **Facilities:** 🏋 🏋 1 beach (lake shore), sauna. Sand beach with beach chairs. Picnic tables. **Rates:** Peak (July–Aug) $60–$90 S or D; $130 ste. Extra person $7. Min stay peak and wknds. Lower rates off-season. Parking: Outdoor, free. Suite rate based on quad occupancy. Midweek, off-season discounts for seniors. Discounts for stays of multiple nights. Closed Nov–Apr. DISC, MC, V.

RESORT

▐▐ Gordon Lodge
1420 Pine Dr, 54202; tel 414/839-2331 or toll free 800/830-6235; fax 414/839-2450. 130 acres. Traditional resort offers secluded, wooded location on bay. Somewhat dated, but well maintained. Lobby features conversation pit around circular fireplace. Golf, summer stock theater, shopping, and galleries 10 minutes away. **Rooms:** 20 rms; 20 cottages/villas. CI 3:30pm/CO noon. Room options include villas, cottages, and main lodge rooms with choice of outside porches with wooded view, patios with water view, and one or two bedrooms. **Amenities:** 🏠 🛁 🖥 A/C, satel TV, refrig. Some units w/terraces, some w/fireplaces, some w/whirlpools. **Services:** ✕ 🛎 ↻ TDD available. **Facilities:** 🏋 ⛰ 🛶 🏌 🏋 🎿 🏓 20 ♿ 2 restaurants (see "Restaurants" below), 3 bars (1 w/entertainment), 1 beach (bay). Row boats, lighted badminton courts, 18-hole putting green, hiking trail, fishing pier, dock. Top Deck cocktail area features water view. **Rates (BB):** Peak (mid-June–mid-Oct) $154 S or D; $100–$212 cottage/villa. Extra person $29. Min stay peak. Lower rates off-season. Parking: Outdoor, free. Discounts and packages avail include senior, multiple night stays, and midweek. Closed mid-Oct–late May. AE, DISC, MC, V.

RESTAURANTS 🍴

♥ The Common House
8041 WI 57 (Downtown); tel 414/839-2708. **New American.** The pressed-tin ceiling of this eatery dates from its original incarnation as a turn-of-the-century hardware store. Today, the beautifully restored building is the setting for casual fine dining with a skylight, wooden floors, and lots of greenery. Original creations of the chef include chicken dredged in cinnamon and cayenne pepper with a sauce of roasted garlic and goat cheese; sea bass with basil fettuccine; and home-smoked salmon salad with aioli mayonnaise. **FYI:** Reserva-

tions recommended. Children's menu. **Open:** Peak (May–Oct) lunch daily 11:30am–2pm; dinner daily 5:30–9pm. Closed Nov–Dec. **Prices:** Main courses $10–$28. DISC, MC, V. ♥ ⅙

Florian II
WI 57 (Downtown); tel 414/839-2361. **Regional American/Seafood.** Diners can take advantage of the beautiful Lake Michigan view from the solarium dining room. Popular menu items include barbecued pork back ribs with house sauce, baked whitefish with lemon butter, and steak barbare (rib eye rolled in bread crumbs and garlic butter). Sunday evening diners can enjoy the Western Barbecue Buffet: barbecued beef and ribs, oven baked chicken, potato, corn-on-the-cob, and tossed salad. **FYI:** Reservations not accepted. Children's menu. **Open:** Breakfast daily 8–11am; dinner daily 4–9pm. Closed Nov–Mar. **Prices:** Main courses $10–$17. MC, V. ▨

Gordon Lodge Dining Room
1420 Pine Dr; tel 414/839-2331. **Continental.** Lots of windows allow diners to enjoy the pine woods setting of this off-the-beaten-path eatery. Eggs Benedict are a breakfast specialty, with evening fare featuring veal Alexandra with brandy cream sauce and asparagus; rack of lamb; and jambalaya. Homemade key lime pie and tiramisù. **FYI:** Reservations recommended. Children's menu. **Open:** Breakfast daily 7:30–10am; dinner daily 5:30–9pm. Closed mid-Oct–late May. **Prices:** Main courses $15–$22. AE, DISC, MC, V. ▨

♣ Maxwelton Braes
In Maxwelton Braes Resort Golf Club, 7670 WI 57; tel 414/839-2321. South end of Bailey's Harbor on WI 57. **Regional American.** Named for a love song about a Scottish lass, Maxwelton Braes is located in a venerable old lodge with huge stone fireplace, vaulted ceilings, and huge wooden beams. The German chef focuses on fresh local fare prepared with a European touch: pan-fried or broiled whitefish, poached or broiled salmon with dill sauce, scallops with caper butter. A slice of homemade cherry pie or apple strudel rounds out the meal. **FYI:** Reservations recommended. Big band/organ. Children's menu. Dress code. **Open:** Breakfast daily 8–9:30am; dinner daily 5:30–8:30pm. Closed Nov–May 15. **Prices:** Main courses $10–$20. AE, CB, DC, DISC, MC, V. ▨

Baraboo

Seat of Sauk County. This small south-central Wisconsin town was the original winter quarters of Ringling Brothers Circus. Devils Lake is three miles south of town. **Information:** Baraboo Area Chamber of Commerce, 124 2nd St, PO Box 442, Baraboo, 53913-0442 (tel 608/356-8333 or toll free 800/BARABOO).

HOTEL ▨

▤▤▤ Quality Inn
630 W Pine St, PO Box 84, 53913; tel 608/356-6422 or toll free 800/355-6422; fax 608/356-6422. Connected to a bar and restaurant that serves breakfast, lunch, and dinner. Handy for families. **Rooms:** 84 rms and stes. CI 2pm/CO 11am. No smoking. **Amenities:** ▨ ⅙ A/C, satel TV w/movies. Some units w/whirlpools. **Services:** ✕ ⅋ Car-rental desk, babysitting. **Facilities:** ▨ ⅙ ▨ ▨ ▨ ⅙ 1 restaurant, 1 bar, games rm, sauna, whirlpool, washer/dryer. Stair stepper and weight machines available to guests. **Rates (CP):** Peak (June–Aug) $65–$145 S; $70–$150 D; $125–$150 ste. Extra person $5. Children under age 18 stay free. Lower rates off-season. Parking: Outdoor, free. Casino package (Ho-Chunk) avail. DC, DISC, JCB, MC, V.

MOTEL

▤ Thunderbird Motel
1013 8th St, 53913; tel 608/356-7757. Very convenient for families, with Circus World Museum within six blocks; casinos and Devil's Lake within 10 miles. **Rooms:** 31 rms. CI 1pm/CO 11am. Nonsmoking rms avail. **Amenities:** ▨ A/C, cable TV w/movies, refrig. **Services:** ⅋ ▨ **Facilities:** ⅙ ▨ ⅙ **Rates:** Peak (June–Aug) $39–$75 S or D. Extra person $5. Children under age 18 stay free. Lower rates off-season. Parking: Outdoor, free. AARP discount 10%. Corporate discounts vary. AE, DISC, MC, V.

ATTRACTIONS ▨

Circus World Museum
426 Water St; tel 608/356-0800. Located on the original winter quarters of the Ringling Bros Circus. The Irvin Feld Exhibit Hall and Visitors Center (open year-round) houses exhibits such as "The Story of the Ringlings," "Art of the American Circus," and "A Century of Spectacle." Live circus performances, magic shows, and concerts are presented on the grounds throughout the summer. **Open:** Peak (June–Aug) daily 9am–6pm. Reduced hours off-season. **$$$$**

Wisconsin Opry
E10964 Moon Rd; tel 608/254-7951. This 80-acre farm in the heart of the Wisconsin Dells aims to be a Midwestern version of Nashville's Grand Ol' Opry. A variety of country music and comedy acts appear here during the season; special Sunday shows feature stars from Nashville. **$$$$**

Mirror Lake State Park
E10320 Fern Dell Rd; tel 608/254-2333. Much of the lakeshore in this 2,050-acre park is formed by sandstone cliffs up to 50 feet high. Pine and oak woods surround the lake and beyond there are sandy prairies and fields of trees, shrubs, and wildflowers. Numerous recreational opportunities include picnicking, boating, camping (144 family campsites, 7 group sites), hiking (with 20 miles of trails), mountain biking, and cross-country skiing. **Open:** Daily 8am–4pm. **$$**

Bayfield

This small northern town on Lake Superior is the gateway to Apostle Islands National Lakeshore, and cruises to offshore islands in the warmer months. Mount Ashwabay Ski Area is three miles south of town. **Information:** Bayfield Area Chamber of Commerce, 42 S Broad St, PO Box 138, Bayfield, 54814 (tel 715/779-3335 or toll free 800/447-4094).

MOTELS

The Bayfield Inn

20 Rittenhouse Ave, PO Box 810, 54814; tel 715/779-3363; fax 715/779-3363. On the shore of Lake Superior, off WI 13. Charming, red-brick motel offers prime location and large windows to enhance view of Memorial Park. Perennial garden is small but well designed around benches and waterfront walk. **Rooms:** 21 rms. CI 2pm/CO 11am. Nonsmoking rms avail. All rooms have ceiling and portable fans. **Amenities:** Cable TV. No A/C. 1 unit w/fireplace. **Services:** Twice-daily maid svce, babysitting. **Facilities:** 1 restaurant (lunch and dinner only), 1 bar, sauna. Restaurant features variety of seafood and grilled food—either indoors or on rooftop cafe. **Rates (CP):** Peak (June–Sept) $65–$85 S or D. Extra person $15. Children under age 12 stay free. Min stay wknds. Lower rates off-season. Parking: Outdoor, free. Senior rates avail in fall. MC, V.

Winfield Inn

Rte 1, Box 33, 54814; tel 715/799-3252; fax 715/799-5180. 4 blocks N of downtown on WI 13. Two separate buildings located on 3½ acres of lakefront property; the older of the two buildings needs some renovation and updating. **Rooms:** 31 rms, stes, and effic. CI 2pm/CO 11am. Nonsmoking rms avail. All rooms have view of Lake Superior. Suites with kitchenettes perfect for groups or families on longer stays. **Amenities:** A/C, cable TV. Some units w/terraces. **Services:** **Facilities:** **Rates:** Peak (June–Oct 15) $52–$105 S or D; $85–$105 ste; $90–$110 effic. Children under age 6 stay free. Lower rates off-season. Parking: Outdoor, free. AE, DISC, MC, V.

INN

Old Rittenhouse Inn

301 Rittenhouse Ave, PO Box 584, 54814; tel 715/779-5111; fax 715/779-5887. On WI 13. This beautiful facility is actually three historic homes in Bayfield that were transformed into the most beautiful rooms in town. Stunning decorations and amazing food are the standard. It's the perfect place for couples on vacation or honeymoon (though kids are welcome, too). Inquire about their calendar of events—you may be able to reserve a room during a Mystery Weekend or the Wassail Dinner Concert Weekend. If you cannot get reservations, consider stopping by for a tour. **Rooms:** 21 rms and stes. CI 3:30pm/CO noon. Nonsmoking rms avail. **Amenities:** No A/C, phone, or TV. Some units w/terraces, some w/whirlpools. **Services:** Babysitting, afternoon tea and wine/sherry served. **Facilities:** 1 restaurant (bkfst and dinner only), guest lounge w/TV. **Rates (CP):** $99–$229 S or D; $119–$129 ste. Extra person $15. Children under age 5 stay free. Min stay wknds. MAP rates avail. Parking: Outdoor, free. MC, V.

ATTRACTIONS

Madeline Island Historical Museum

At the Ferry Landing; tel 414/747-2415. Operated by the State Historical Society, this museum rests on the former site of an American Fur Company trading post. The history of the Apostle Islands is illustrated through exhibits on trapping, logging, Native American cultures, and early settlers. Four pioneer log structures are also on the grounds. **Open:** June–Oct, daily 10am–5pm. **$**

Lake Superior Big Top Chautauqua

Mount Ashwabay, Ski Hill Rd, Washburn; tel 715/373-5552. Located on Mount Ashwabay, overlooking Lake Superior, this 750-capacity, all-canvas, all-professional tent theater produces and presents a 60-plus-night summer season of concerts, plays, live original historical musicals, and lectures. In the past, performers have included Garrison Keillor, Emmylou Harris, Robert Bly, Taj Mahal, Richie Havens, Leon Russell, and the National Shakespeare Company. Food and bar services on premises. **Open:** Mid–June–Labor Day, performances Tues–Sat at 8:15pm. **$$$**

Beaver Dam

Located 30 miles NE of Madison. On the west edge of town is 14-mile-long Beaver Dam Lake, a popular spot for catching crappie and perch. Dodge County Fair lasts for five days in August. **Information:** Beaver Dam Area Visitor & Hospitality Council, 127 S Spring St, Beaver Dam, 53916-2175 (tel 414/887-8879).

MOTEL

Super 8 Motel

711 Park Ave, PO Box 778, 53916; tel 414/877-8880 or toll free 800/800-8000; fax 414/877-8880. Spacious, inviting lobby in a sparkling clean, well-maintained establishment. Located 20 minutes from major attractions in Wisconsin Dells. **Rooms:** 50 rms. CI 2pm/CO 11am. Nonsmoking rms avail. All rooms recently redecorated. **Amenities:** A/C, cable TV w/movies. **Services:** **Facilities:** Washer/dryer. **Rates (CP):** $42–$53 S; $51–$58 D. Extra person $5. Children under age 13 stay free. Parking: Outdoor, free. Rates increase during the EAA Fly-In in Oshkosh. AE, CB, DC, DISC, EC, ER, JCB, MC, V.

Beloit

Located just north of the Wisconsin/Illinois border. Beloit College was founded by New England settlers in 1846; two dozen Native American burial mounds are scattered around the campus grounds. Explorer and adventure writer Roy Chapman Andrews was born here. **Information:** Beloit Convention & Visitors Bureau, 1003 Pleasant St, Beloit, 53511 (tel 608/365-4838).

MOTELS

Comfort Inn

2786 Milwaukee Rd, 53511; tel 608/362-2666 or toll free 800/221-2222; fax 608/362-2666. Exit 185A off I-90, ½ mi W on WI 81. The pleasant exterior of this motel, located on a commercial strip, includes hanging potted plants and planters. Inside, the lobby is clean and functional. **Rooms:** 56 rms and stes. CI 3pm/CO 11am. Nonsmoking rms avail. Smell of smoke is heavy in designated smoking rooms. **Amenities:** A/C, cable TV w/movies. **Services:** Comfort Inn Guest of the Day program awards goodies to a guest chosen at random. **Facilities:** Games rm, whirlpool. **Rates (CP):** Peak (May–Sept) $48–$60 S; $56–$70 D; $58–$80 ste. Extra person $5. Children under age 18 stay free. Lower rates off-season. Parking: Outdoor, free. Thirteenth night free. AE, DC, DISC, JCB, MC, V.

Holiday Inn Express

2790 Milwaukee Rd, 53511; tel 608/365-6000 or toll free 800/HOLIDAY; fax 608/365-1974. Exit 185A off I-90. Works hard at being different from all the other nearby chain properties. A bright green parrot lives in a spacious cage in the lobby and is allowed out at times to visit with the guests. Popular with business travelers. **Rooms:** 73 rms and stes. CI 2pm/CO noon. Nonsmoking rms avail. Some one-room suites available, including a honeymoon suite with a king-size waterbed. **Amenities:** A/C, cable TV w/movies, dataport. Some units w/whirlpools. **Services:** Lobby has a separate cafe area where continental breakfast is served; free coffee, juice, and cookies are available at all times; and the hospitality hour is held Sun–Thurs 5–7pm with soft drinks, chips, crackers, and cheese. **Facilities:** Rates (CP): Peak (June–Sept) $50–$56 S; $55–$62 D; $120 ste. Extra person $6. Children under age 19 stay free. Lower rates off-season. Parking: Outdoor, free. AE, CB, DC, DISC, MC, V.

UNRATED Super 8 Motel

3002 Milwaukee Rd, 53511; tel 608/365-8680 or toll free 800/800-8000; fax 608/365-2411. Exit 185A off I-90. Small, functional property close to interstate and food chains. Suitable for overnight. **Rooms:** 64 rms. CI 2pm/CO 11am. Nonsmoking rms avail. **Amenities:** A/C, cable TV. Free local calls. **Facilities:** Rates (CP): Peak (June–Sept) $42–$52 S or D. Children under age 15 stay free. Lower rates off-season. Parking: Outdoor, free. Super 8 VIP Club discounts and AARP rates avail. AE, DC, DISC, MC, V.

Black River Falls

Seat of Jackson County, in west-central part of state. One of the state's first sawmills was built here. Winnebago Indian Pow-Wow is held at Red Cloud Memorial Pow-Wow Grounds. **Information:** Black River Falls Area Chamber of Commerce, 336 N Water St, Black River Falls, 54615 (tel 715/284-4658 or toll free 800/404-4008).

MOTELS

American Budget Inn

9191 WI 54, 54615; tel 715/284-4333 or toll free 800/356-8018; fax 715/284-9068. Sparkling clean lobby with comfortable chairs and sofas. **Rooms:** 86 rms and stes. CI 3pm/CO noon. Nonsmoking rms avail. **Amenities:** A/C, cable TV. Some units w/whirlpools. Coffeemakers in king rooms and suites. Rental refrigerators available for fee. **Services:** Pets in smoking rooms only. **Facilities:** Sauna, whirlpool, washer/dryer. Pool open 24 hours; games in pool area. **Rates (CP):** Peak (May–Oct) $40–$50 S; $53–$63 D; $95–$110 ste. Extra person $4. Children under age 12 stay free. Lower rates off-season. Parking: Outdoor, free. AE, CB, DC, DISC, EC, MC, V.

Best Western Inn

600 Oasis Rd, 54615; tel 715/284-9471 or toll free 800/284-9471; fax 715/284-9664. 1 block N of I-94. Extensive landscaping includes several ponds and statues of leaping deer. Lobby has vaulted ceiling and fireplace as center point, surrounded by chairs and sofas. Adjacent to Black River Crossing gas station/shop oasis. Expect 90–100% occupancy during autumn foliage season. **Rooms:** 144 rms and stes. CI 3pm/CO noon. Nonsmoking rms avail. **Amenities:** A/C, satel TV w/movies. Some units w/fireplaces, some w/whirlpools. **Services:** Facilities: 1 restaurant, 1 bar, basketball, volleyball, games rm, sauna, whirlpool, washer/dryer. Live country music in bar Sat night. Art shop/gallery on grounds. Large picnic area and camping behind main building. One-mile nature trail through adjoining woods. **Rates:** Peak (Apr–Oct) $49–$59 S; $65–$69 D; $89–$99 ste. Extra person $5. Children under age 12 stay free. Lower rates off-season. Parking: Outdoor, free. AE, CB, DC, DISC, EC, MC, V.

Pines Motor Lodge

Rte 4, Box 297, 54615; tel 715/284-5311 or toll free 800/345-7463; fax 715/284-7002. Jct US 12/I-94. A good value, this complex consists of three main units, with parking near individual units. You can expect almost full occupancy during fishing season and autumn foliage season. No landscaping to speak of, and no hallways, except in the lobby, and no elevators. It's a pickup site for Greyhound buses. **Rooms:** 84 rms. CI 11am/CO 11am. Nonsmoking rms avail. Main building has several guest rooms; all others are in separate buildings. **Amenities:** 🛏 📺 A/C, satel TV w/movies. **Services:** 🍴 🛎 Morning coffee in lobby. **Facilities:** 🎿 ⛷ 🏊 🍴 130 1 restaurant, 1 bar (w/entertainment), games rm, sauna. **Rates:** $36 S; $43 D. Extra person $4. Children under age 12 stay free. Parking: Outdoor, free. DISC, MC, V.

Boulder Junction

Located in north-central Wisconsin, near the Upper Peninsula of Michigan. This secluded village—known as "Muskie Capital of the World"—is a gateway to several national forests and dozens of lakes. The Musky Jamboree is held here in early August. **Information:** Boulder Junction Chamber of Commerce, 5352 Hwy M, PO Box 286, Boulder Junction, 54512 (tel 715/385-2400).

RESORTS 🏨

⬌⬌ Wildcat Lodge

P 6500, PO Box 138, 54512; tel 715/385-2421; fax 715/385-2421. 4 mi N of Boulder Junction on WI M. 55 acres. Summer is peak season, but fall foliage shouldn't be missed. Many repeat guests love the beautiful location, great accommodations, and family-like greeting. **Rooms:** 16 cottages/villas. CI 2pm/CO 10am. Nonsmoking rms avail. Cottages have screened-in porches overlooking Little Kitten Lake. **Amenities:** ♨ 📺 Refrig. No A/C, phone, or TV. All units w/terraces, some w/fireplaces. Two cottages have kitchens and outdoor grills. Some cabins have their own dock. **Services:** 🚗 🍴 🛎 Babysitting. **Facilities:** ⛷ 🏊 🚣 🛶 50 🔥 1 restaurant (bkfst and dinner only), 1 beach (lake shore), basketball, volleyball, games rm, lawn games, playground. Restaurant open to resort guests only. Lots to do—shuffleboard, badminton, foosball—in addition to usual resort entertainment. **Rates:** Peak (June–Aug) $830–$1,150 cottage/villa. Children under age 2 stay free. Min stay special events. Lower rates off-season. MAP rates avail. Parking: Outdoor, free. Rates are per cottage per week. After eight persons, you pay $10 each additional person in cottages. MC, V.

UNRATED Zastrow's Lynx Lake Lodge

County Rd B, PO Box 277, 54512; tel 715/686-2249 or toll free 800/882-5969; fax 715/686-2257. 75 acres. An excellent choice for a long weekend on the lake to enjoy the fall foliage. The lake tapers off slowly (good for young swimmers), and the fishing is fine. Snowmobiling, hiking, and canoeing are some popular pastimes. **Rooms:** 12 cottages/villas. CI 2pm/CO 10am. Nonsmoking rms avail. **Amenities:** ♨ 📺 Refrig. No A/C or phone. Some units w/fireplaces. **Services:** 🍴 🛎 Babysitting. **Facilities:** ⛷ 🏊 🚣 170 🔥 1 restaurant (bkfst and dinner only), 1 bar, 1 beach (lake shore), games rm, lawn games, playground. **Rates (MAP):** Peak (June

16–Aug) $325–$500 cottage/villa. Extra person $40. Min stay. Lower rates off-season. Parking: Outdoor, free. Rates are per person per week. No CC.

RESTAURANT 🍴

♣ The Guide's Inn

Hwy M; tel 715/385-2233. **American.** Award-winning eatery offering exceptional cuisine in a beautiful garden setting. The winding stone path, wildflower garden, and gazebo make the wait for a table entirely enjoyable. Owner/gardener/chef Jimmy Dean Van Rossum is known for making the best walleye and veal around, and his Shrimp St James (made with mushrooms and herbs in a puffed pastry) brings people in time after time. All soups are homemade. **FYI:** Reservations not accepted. Children's menu. **Open:** Daily 5–10pm. **Prices:** Main courses $9–$40. MC, V. 🔥

Brookfield

A suburb of Milwaukee. **Information:** Greater Brookfield Chamber of Commerce, 405 N Calhoun #106, Brookfield, 53005 (tel 414/786-1886).

HOTEL 🏨

⬌⬌⬌ Hampton Inn

575 N Barker Rd, 53045; tel 414/796-1500 or toll free 800/HAMPTON; fax 414/796-0977. Exit 297 off I-94. This well-appointed hotel located in an expanding commercial area offers plenty for the weary traveler. Lobby is airy and comfortable; staff is cordial. **Rooms:** 120 rms. CI 2pm/CO noon. Nonsmoking rms avail. Fresh-smelling, comfortable rooms. **Amenities:** 🛏 ♨ 📺 A/C, cable TV w/movies, refrig, dataport. **Services:** 🛎 🍴 Crayons and coloring books available for children. **Facilities:** 🎿 🏊 🏋 🍴 10 🔥 Whirlpool. **Rates (CP):** $59–$69 S; $67–$77 D. Children under age 18 stay free. Parking: Outdoor, free. Many weekend packages avail. AE, CB, DC, DISC, MC, V.

MOTEL

⬌⬌⬌ Fairfield Inn

20150 W Bluemound Rd, 53045; tel 414/785-0500 or toll free 800/228-2800; fax 414/785-0500. Pleasant, clean motel located one mile east of Brookfield Square mall. Spacious lobby with chairs and couches for quick meetings. Economy lodging equipped for business traveler. **Rooms:** 135 rms. CI 2pm/CO noon. Nonsmoking rms avail. **Amenities:** 🛏 ♨ A/C, cable TV w/movies, dataport. All units w/terraces. **Services:** 🛎 🍴 Free local calls. **Facilities:** 🎿 10 🔥 Discounts to Waukesha Athletic Club. **Rates (CP):** Peak (May–Aug) $44–$86 S; $50–$86 D. Extra person $5–$10. Children under age 18 stay free. Min stay special events. Lower rates off-season. Parking: Outdoor, free. AE, CB, DC, DISC, EC, ER, JCB, MC, V.

Cedarburg

Many lovely 19th-century homes grace this town in the heart of the fruit-growing and wine-making region of central Wisconsin. On the first weekend in February, a Winter Festival features bed and barrel races, a snow goose egg hunt, ice sculpture contests, and sleigh rides. **Information:** Cedarburg Visitors Center, W63 N645 Washington Ave, PO Box 104, Cedarburg, 53012-0104 (tel 414/377-9620).

ATTRACTIONS 🏛

Cedar Creek Winery
N70 W6340 Bridge Rd, in the Cedar Creek Settlement; tel 414/377-8020. This noted regional winery offers tours and tastings in addition to shops, restaurants, and a museum of wine-making equipment. **Open:** Mon–Sat 10am–5pm, Sun 11am–5pm. **$**

The Brewery Works Fine Arts Complex
Riveredge Dr; tel 414/377-8230. Sculptor Paul J Yank has converted this 1843 brewery into a working studio and gallery, where he displays his own work as well as that of other local artisans and craftspeople. Exhibits change every six weeks. **Open:** Tues–Sun 1–5pm. **Free**

Chippewa Falls

See also Eau Claire

Seat of Chippewa County, in western Wisconsin. French-Canadian lumberjacks settled the town in the early 19th century and built a sawmill and dam here. Hydroelectric power is still important to the area economy. **Information:** Chippewa Falls Area Chamber of Commerce, 811 N Bridge St, Chippewa Falls, 54729-1814 (tel 715/723-0331).

MOTELS 🏨

AmericInn Motel
11 W South Ave, 54729; tel 715/723-5711; fax 715/723-5711. On WI 124. Fireplace in lobby makes for pleasant entryway. No elevators. **Rooms:** 62 rms and stes. CI 2pm/CO 11am. Nonsmoking rms avail. **Amenities:** 🛁 🕐 🖭 A/C, cable TV w/movies. Some units w/whirlpools. **Services:** 🛆 🛒 🐾 **Facilities:** 🏢 🏋 🚻 Sauna, whirlpool, washer/dryer. Free pass to YMCA (three miles away). **Rates (CP):** $48–$104 S; $56–$104 D; $104 ste. Extra person $6. Children under age 13 stay free. Parking: Outdoor, free. AE, CB, DC, DISC, EC, JCB, MC, V.

Indianhead Motel
501 N Summit Ave, 54729; tel 715/723-9171 or toll free 800/341-8000; fax 715/723-6142. Well maintained and clean, with a friendly staff. **Rooms:** 27 rms. CI open/CO 11am. Nonsmoking rms avail. All rooms face parking area. **Amenities:** 🛁 A/C, cable TV w/movies, dataport. **Services:** 🛆 🛒 🐾 Babysitting. Complimentary coffee and tea 7am–

11pm. **Facilities:** 🏋 🚻 **Rates:** $28–$35 S; $35–$42 D. Extra person $5. Children under age 10 stay free. Parking: Outdoor, free. AE, CB, DC, DISC, EC, JCB, MC, V.

RESTAURANT 🍽

★ Fill Inn Station, Saloon and Restaurant
104 W Columbia St; tel 715/723-8282. **Eclectic.** In a residential neighborhood at the edge of downtown, this restaurant is popular with local families. Two dining rooms; more casual seating in the bar area. A jukebox, darts, and newspapers complete the comfortable decor. Same menu for lunch and dinner, with steak, chicken, and sandwiches; Canadian walleye pike is a favorite dish. Buckets of chicken are available to go. The bar offers a happy hour Mon–Fri. **FYI:** Reservations accepted. **Open:** Mon–Sat 11am–10pm. **Prices:** Main courses $6–$11. AE, DISC, MC, V. 🛗 🚻

ATTRACTION 🏛

Jacob Leinenkugel Brewing Co
1 Jefferson Ave; tel 715/723-5557. Founded by its namesake in 1867, Leinenkugel now produces nine brands of quality beer. Visitors can tour the brewery to see how the beer is brewed and bottled. Gift shop. **Open:** Gift shop: Mon–Fri 9am–5pm, Sat 9am–4pm. **Free**

Crandon

Seat of Forest County, in northeast part of state. This former logging town is perched between the Wolf and Peshigo Rivers, and is just west of Nicolet National Forest. **Information:** Crandon Area Chamber of Commerce, 201 S Lake Ave, PO Box 88, Crandon, 54520 (tel 715/478-3450).

MOTEL 🏨

Four Seasons Motel
304 W Glen, 54520; tel 715/478-3377 or toll free 800/341-8000; fax 715/478-3785. Jct WI 32/55/8W. A member of the Independent Motels of America Association, this one-story motel is a sure bet for a clean room and friendly greeting. **Rooms:** 20 rms. CI noon/CO 11am. Nonsmoking rms avail. While cleanliness is a top priority, the decor could use a little updating. **Amenities:** 🛁 🖭 A/C, cable TV. **Services:** 🐾 **Facilities:** 🏋 🏀 🚻 Basketball. **Rates:** Peak (July) $32–$38 S; $38–$42 D. Extra person $3. Children under age 5 stay free. Lower rates off-season. Parking: Outdoor, free. AE, DISC, MC, V.

ATTRACTION 🏛

Nicolet Scenic Rail
Jct WI 8/32, Laona; tel 715/674-6309 or toll free 800/752-1465. Diesel-powered railroad offering 18-mile and 60-mile trips through the Nicolet National Forest. Both routes

depart from Laona; the long route goes to Tipler while the shorter one ends at a logging camp at Wabeno. **Open:** June–Oct, call for schedule. **$$**

Delafield

MOTEL 🏨

🏨🏨 Country Pride Inn
2412 Milwaukee St, 53018; tel 414/646-3300; fax 414/646-3491. Clean establishment adjacent to Shoney's restaurant. **Rooms:** 60 rms and stes. CI 2pm/CO 11am. Nonsmoking rms avail. Comfortable rooms with pleasant seating arrangement for four people. **Amenities:** 🛏 👗 A/C, cable TV w/movies. Some units w/whirlpools. **Services:** 🖐 **Facilities:** 🏊 👟 [24] 👗 Sauna, whirlpool. **Rates:** Peak (May–Sept) $43–$55 S; $48–$62 D; $85–$125 ste. Extra person $5. Lower rates off-season. Parking: Outdoor, free. AE, DC, DISC, MC, V.

Delavan

Located in southeast part of state. A town of flowering crabapple trees, it was headquarters for more than two dozen circuses between 1847 and 1894. Many circus members from the old colonies are buried here. **Information:** Delavan-Delavan Lake Area Chamber of Commerce, 52 E Walworth Ave, Delavan, 53115 (tel 414/728-5095).

HOTEL 🏨

🏨 Delavan House Hotel
215 E Walworth Ave, 53115 (Downtown); tel 414/728-9143; fax 414/728-1444. Family-owned and -operated older property with low-key atmosphere. Downtown location is within walking distance of shops, restaurants, and Clown Hall of Fame. **Rooms:** 55 rms and stes. CI 2pm/CO 11am. Nonsmoking rms avail. Decor somewhat dated. King suites have sofas. **Amenities:** 🛏 A/C, cable TV. Some units w/whirlpools. Microwaves and refrigerators available for nominal charge. **Services:** ✗ 🚐 Babysitting. **Facilities:** 🏋 📺 [150] 👗 1 restaurant (lunch and dinner only; see "Restaurants" below), 1 bar. Tanning salon on premises. **Rates:** Peak (May 1–Sept 15) $45–$65 S or D; $65–$150 ste. Extra person $5. Children under age 13 stay free. Lower rates off-season. Parking: Outdoor, free. AARP discounts and weekly rates avail. Packages offered periodically. AE, DISC, MC, V.

RESTAURANTS 🍴

Delavan House Hotel Restaurant
215 E Walworth Ave (Downtown); tel 414/728-9143. **American/Polish.** Originally called the Barnum & Bailey Restaurant in this town where the circus giants got their start, this family-owned restaurant serves up good, basic food. Generous portions of prime rib, fish, ribs, and Polish specialties such as pierogis and stuffed cabbage at reasonable prices ensure good value. **FYI:** Reservations accepted. Children's menu. **Open:** Lunch Mon–Fri 11am–2pm, Sat–Sun 11am–8pm; dinner Mon–Fri 5–8pm. **Prices:** Main courses $5–$14. AE, DISC, MC, V. 🎦 👗

★ Hernandez El Serape
212 S 7th St; tel 414/728-6443. **Mexican.** Colorful serapes, piñatas, and sombreros greet diners at this relaxed, authentic Mexican restaurant. Homemade chips, salsas, and guacamole set the stage for generous portions of fajitas, chiles rellenos, poblano peppers filled with meat, and chimichangas. Diners can choose from among 10 flavors of Mexican pop, nine Mexican beers, and margaritas. **FYI:** Reservations not accepted. Beer and wine only. **Open:** Peak (May–Sept) daily 11am–10pm. **Prices:** Main courses $4–$8. AE, DISC, MC, V. 👗

ATTRACTION 📷

The Clown Hall of Fame and Research Center
114 N 3rd St; tel 414/728-9075. In the 19th century, Delavan was home to many circus troupes, including the famous P T Barnum Circus. This center is dedicated to preserving and advancing the clown tradition via a living history museum, resident clown performers, and a national archive of clown artifacts and history. The Clown Hall is a multipurpose facility that houses a fully equipped exhibition center with a theater and auditorium, research center, and educational accommodations for clown workshops and seminars. **Open:** Mon–Sat 10am–4pm, Sun noon–4pm. **$$**

Detroit Harbor

See Washington Island

Dodgeville

Seat of Iowa County, in southwest part of state. Seven state parks are within a half-hour drive. To the east is Little Norway, an 1856 Norwegian pioneer farmstead with several buildings of Norse antiques, trolls, and *nissa*, as well as a *stavkirke* built for the World's Columbian Exposition in Chicago. **Information:** Dodgeville Chamber of Commerce, PO Box 141, Dodgeville, 53533 (tel 608/935-5557).

MOTELS 🏨

🏨🏨 The New Concord Inn
3637 WI 23 N, 53533; tel 608/935-3770 or toll free 800/348-9310; fax 608/935-9605. N of jct US 18/151 and WI 23. Low-rise, red brick building with bright white pillars and flowering shrubs beautifying the grounds. Recently redone lobby has sunken seating area with fireplace, cafe-like area with tables and chairs, and fine view of sparkling indoor swimming pool. **Rooms:** 64 rms and stes. CI 3pm/CO 11am.

Nonsmoking rms avail. Two-room family suites available. **Amenities:** 🛏 🕐 A/C, satel TV w/movies. Some units w/whirlpools. **Services:** 🛎 Front desk staff is knowledgeable about local attractions, restaurants, and shopping. **Facilities:** 🔥 🏊 ♿ Games rm, whirlpool. Outdoor lounge area located off indoor pool for summertime sunning. **Rates (CP):** Peak (Mem Day–Oct 21) $47–$82 S or D; $80–$115 ste. Extra person $6. Children under age 12 stay free. Lower rates off-season. Parking: Outdoor, free. AE, DISC, MC, V.

🬰 **Super 8 Motel**
1308 Johns St, 53533; tel 608/935-3888 or toll free 800/800-8000; fax 608/935-3888. Fine, no-frills motel offering clean, standard accommodations. Close to local attractions and right next to car-rental facility. **Rooms:** 43 rms. CI 3pm/CO 11am. Nonsmoking rms avail. **Amenities:** 🛏 🕐 A/C, cable TV w/movies. **Services:** 🛎 🐾 Pet deposit required. Manager eager to provide assistance. **Facilities:** 🏊 [20] ♿ **Rates (CP):** Peak (May–Oct) $38–$70 S or D. Extra person $5. Children under age 12 stay free. Lower rates off-season. Parking: Outdoor, free. AE, CB, DC, DISC, JCB, MC, V.

Eagle River

Seat of Vilas County, in northern Wisconsin. Set amidst a chain of 28 freshwater lakes, this tourist town draws participants in both summer and winter sports. The World Championship Snowmobile Derby is held here in January. **Information:** Vilas County Chamber of Commerce, PO Box 369, Eagle River, 54521-0369 (tel 715/479-3649).

MOTELS 🛏

🬰🬰 **American Budget Inn**
780 US 45 N, PO Box 995, 54521; tel 715/479-5151 or toll free 800/356-8018; fax 715/479-8259. 1 mi N of WI 70 on US 45. If you're looking for the dependability of a chain motel and a good deal in Eagle River, this is the place for you. It's located a few blocks from the main street, so it's less noisy than some of the other options. **Rooms:** 97 rms. CI 3pm/CO 11am. Nonsmoking rms avail. **Amenities:** 🛏 🕐 A/C, cable TV w/movies. Some units w/whirlpools. **Services:** 🛎 🐾 **Facilities:** 🔥 🏊 ♿ Sauna, whirlpool, washer/dryer. **Rates (CP):** Peak (June–Sept) $51–$72 S; $61–$80 D. Extra person $10. Children under age 17 stay free. Min stay wknds. Lower rates off-season. Parking: Outdoor, free. MC, V.

🬰 **The Edgewater Inn Motel and Resort**
5054 WI 70 W, 54521; tel 715/479-4011. 1 mi E of WI 17. Easy to find (right on the highway). The interior design could use a little updating. Nothing to write home about. **Rooms:** 14 rms; 6 cottages/villas. CI 2pm/CO 10am. Nonsmoking rms avail. **Amenities:** 🛏 🕐 📺 Cable TV. No A/C. All units w/terraces. **Services:** 🛎 🐾 Very friendly and helpful front desk staff. **Facilities:** 🏊 📶 Basketball, volleyball, playground. **Rates (CP):** Peak (June–Aug) $35–$41 S; $40–$49

D; $255–$495 cottage/villa. Extra person $5. Children under age 10 stay free. Min stay peak and wknds. Lower rates off-season. Parking: Outdoor, free. AE, DISC, MC, V.

🬰🬰 **Traveler's Inn Motel**
309 Wall St, PO Box 1175, 54521; tel 715/479-4403 or toll free 800/344-1194. In the shopping district. In addition to offering the most affordable rooms in Eagle River, this motel also boasts a great location. It is surrounded by gift shops, banks, and ice cream shops. Since it's not on a highway, it's harder to find, but there's less traffic and noise pollution. **Rooms:** 26 rms and effic. CI 1pm/CO 11am. Nonsmoking rms avail. **Amenities:** 🛏 A/C, cable TV. 1 unit w/whirlpool. **Services:** 🛎 **Facilities:** 🏊 ♿ **Rates (CP):** Peak (June 15–Oct 15) $29–$57 S; $39–$70 D; $51–$73 effic. Extra person $4. Children under age 11 stay free. Min stay special events. Lower rates off-season. Parking: Outdoor, free. AE, DISC, MC, V.

UNRATED **White Eagle Motel**
4948 WI 70 W, 54521; tel 715/479-4426 or toll free 800/782-6488. One-story, mom-and-pop motel. A lawn separates the motel from the highway, so noise is kept to a minimum. **Rooms:** 22 rms. CI 1pm/CO 10am. Nonsmoking rms avail. **Amenities:** 🛏 🕐 Cable TV. No A/C. **Services:** 🛎 🐾 **Facilities:** 🔥 🏊 Sauna, whirlpool. **Rates:** Peak (July–Sept 15/Dec 25–Feb 28) $45–$70 S; $50–$70 D. Extra person $5. Children under age 5 stay free. Min stay peak and wknds. Lower rates off-season. Parking: Outdoor, free. DISC, MC, V.

RESORT

UNRATED **Chanticleer Inn**
1458 E Dollar Lake Rd, 54521; tel 715/479-4486 or toll free 800/752-9193; fax 715/479-0004. 3 mi E of Eagle River off WI 70E. 40 acres. Beautiful resort on Lake Voyager is excellent choice for a vacation. Swimming, waterskiing, and fishing available. Snowmobile and cross-country ski trails begin at resort. **Rooms:** 37 rms, stes, and effic; 8 cottages/villas. Executive level. CI 3pm/CO 10:30am. Offers cottages, villas, motel rooms, townhouses, and condominiums. **Amenities:** 🛏 A/C, satel TV. Some units w/terraces, some w/fireplaces, some w/whirlpools. **Services:** 🛎 🐾 Babysitting. **Facilities:** ⛺ 🗺 🏊 🎣 🍴 🚣 [80] 1 restaurant, 1 bar, 2 beaches (lake shore), basketball, volleyball, games rm, playground, washer/dryer. Restaurant and beer garden recommended even if you're not staying at resort. **Rates:** Peak (July–Labor Day) $85–$125 S or D; $125 ste; $125–$205 effic; $131–$195 cottage/villa. Extra person $10. Children under age 16 stay free. Min stay peak and special events. Lower rates off-season. AP and MAP rates avail. Parking: Outdoor, free. July–Labor Day, cottages and villas weekly rentals only. AE, DC, DISC, MC, V.

Eau Claire

See also Chippewa Falls

Seat of Eau Claire County, in western Wisconsin. This town on the Eau Claire and Chippewa Rivers began life as a lumber camp and sawmill; today, it is home to the University of Wisconsin–Eau Claire. **Information:** Eau Claire Area Convention & Visitors Bureau, 3625 Gateway Dr, #F, Eau Claire, 54701 (tel 715/831-2345 or toll free 800/344-3866).

HOTELS 🏢

≣≣≣ Holiday Inn Campus

2703 Craig Rd, 54702; tel 715/835-2211 or toll free 800/472-3297. Exit 65 (WI 37) off I-95. Large lobby with plenty of sitting and assembly space. Low window and counter at front desk accommodates those in wheelchairs. **Rooms:** 137 rms and stes. CI 3pm/CO 11am. Nonsmoking rms avail. **Amenities:** 🛅 🕗 A/C, cable TV w/movies, refrig, dataport. 1 unit w/whirlpool. Some rooms have coffeemakers, irons, and hair dryers. **Services:** ✕ 🚗 🖼 🗗 🖘 Babysitting. VCR, movie rentals, board games available. Pets allowed in smoking rooms only. **Facilities:** 🔳 🏊 🔲 ৬ 1 restaurant, 1 bar, games rm, whirlpool, washer/dryer. Children ages 1–12 eat free in restaurant. **Rates:** $59–$69 S or D; $69–$99 ste. Children under age 19 stay free. Parking: Outdoor, free. AE, CB, DC, DISC, EC, JCB, MC, V.

≣≣≣ Holiday Inn Convention Center

205 S Barstow St, 54701 (Downtown); tel 715/835-6121 or toll free 800/950-6121; fax 715/835-3592. Well-decorated, clean, neat hotel in downtown area surrounded by shops and offices. **Rooms:** 124 rms. CI 3pm/CO 11am. Nonsmoking rms avail. **Amenities:** 🛅 🕗 A/C, satel TV w/movies, voice mail. Some units w/whirlpools. **Services:** ✕ 🚗 🖼 🗗 🖘 Coffee in lobby. **Facilities:** 🔳 🏊 🔲 ৬ 1 restaurant, 1 bar (w/entertainment). **Rates:** Peak (Apr–Sept) $59 S; $69 D. Extra person $10. Children under age 19 stay free. Lower rates off-season. Parking: Indoor/outdoor, free. AE, CB, DC, DISC, EC, MC, V.

MOTELS

≣≣ Antlers Motel

2245 S Hastings Way, 54701; tel 715/834-5313 or toll free 800/423-4526. Clean, pleasant motel with lots of sunlight in front office lobby, adjacent to Embers Restaurant. **Rooms:** 33 rms. CI 11am/CO 11am. Nonsmoking rms avail. Queen-size beds in most rooms. **Amenities:** 🛅 🕗 A/C, cable TV w/movies. Some units w/terraces. **Services:** 🗗 🖘 **Facilities:** 🏊 ৬ Playground. **Rates (CP):** Peak (May–Oct) $36–$45 S; $46–$50 D. Extra person $5. Children under age 12 stay free. Lower rates off-season. Parking: Outdoor, free. AE, CB, DC, DISC, EC, MC, V.

≣≣≣ Best Western Midway Hotel

2851 Hendrickson Dr, 54701; tel 715/835-2242 or toll free 800/728-1234; fax 715/835-1027. Exit 65 off I-94. Paintings and sofas in lobby provide comfortable ambience. Running trails near motel. **Rooms:** 110 rms and stes. Executive level. CI 3pm/CO 11am. Nonsmoking rms avail. Four family suites have double beds and pullout sofa beds. Bridal suite has king-size bed and round bathtub. **Amenities:** 🛅 🕗 🖩 A/C, cable TV w/movies, dataport. **Services:** ✕ 🚗 🖼 🗗 Children's program. Movie and cookie night for kids at 6 and 8pm Fri–Sat, poolside. **Facilities:** 🔳 🏊 🖮 🔲 ৬ 1 restaurant, 1 bar (w/entertainment), games rm, sauna, whirlpool, playground. Bar offers comedy club, DJ. **Rates (BB):** $55–$70 S; $67–$82 D; $67–$79 ste. Extra person $12. Children under age 18 stay free. Parking: Outdoor, free. Bridal package, including champagne and $10 coupon toward dinner, costs $85; two-night package is $141–$171. AE, CB, DC, DISC, EC, JCB, MC, V.

≣≣ Comfort Inn

3117 Craig Rd, 54701; tel 715/833-9798 or toll free 800/221-2222. Exit 65 off I-95. Basic motel; underwent major renovation in 1994. **Rooms:** 56 rms and stes. CI 3pm/CO noon. Nonsmoking rms avail. **Amenities:** 🛅 🕗 A/C, cable TV w/movies. **Services:** 🖼 🗗 🖘 One-time charge of 75 cents for local calls. **Facilities:** 🔳 🏊 🔲 ৬ Games rm, whirlpool. Small meeting area in lobby. **Rates (CP):** Peak (Apr–Aug) $32–$55 S; $40–$65 D; $60–$80 ste. Extra person $5. Children under age 18 stay free. Lower rates off-season. Parking: Outdoor, free. AE, CB, DC, DISC, EC, JCB, MC, V.

≣≣ Exel Inn

2305 Craig Rd, 54701; tel 715/834-3193 or toll free 800/356-8013; fax 715/839-9905. Exit 65 off I-95. Clean and comfortable motel has spacious lobby with plenty of sofas and chairs. **Rooms:** 101 rms and stes. CI 3pm/CO noon. Nonsmoking rms avail. **Amenities:** 🛅 🕗 🖩 ☕ A/C, cable TV w/movies, dataport. 1 unit w/whirlpool. **Services:** 🖼 🗗 🖘 **Facilities:** 🏊 ৬ Games rm, whirlpool, washer/dryer. **Rates (CP):** Peak (May–Oct) $32–$73 S; $40–$73 D; $99 ste. Extra person $4. Children under age 18 stay free. Lower rates off-season. Parking: Outdoor, free. AE, CB, DC, DISC, EC, JCB, MC, V.

≣≣≣ Hampton Inn

2722 Craig Rd, 54701; tel 715/833-0003 or toll free 800/426-7866; fax 715/833-0915. Exit 65 off I-95. Well-decorated and well-maintained inn, with nice ambience. **Rooms:** 106 rms. CI 3pm/CO noon. Nonsmoking rms avail. Artwork in guest rooms. **Amenities:** 🛅 🕗 A/C, cable TV w/movies, dataport. Coffeemakers available for $1/day; irons and ironing boards in all rooms. **Services:** 🚗 🖼 🗗 Coffee in lobby 24 hours. **Facilities:** 🔳 🏊 🖮 🔲 ৬ Steam rm, whirlpool. **Rates (CP):** $49–$55 S; $57–$63 D. Children under age 18 stay free. Parking: Outdoor, free. AE, CB, DC, DISC, EC, JCB, MC, V.

≣≣ Heartland Inn

4075 Commonwealth Ave, 54701; tel 715/839-7100 or toll free 800/334-3277; fax 715/839-7050. Surrounded by shopping malls and outlet shops. **Rooms:** 89 rms. CI 3pm/CO noon. Nonsmoking rms avail. Eight deluxe rooms with recliners, desks, and two double beds. **Amenities:** 🛅 👶 A/C, satel TV w/movies. **Services:** ✗ 🚐 📠 🗗 🏧 Free coffee delivered to room with wake-up call, Sun–Thurs. Friendly, outgoing front desk staff. **Facilities:** 🏋 🈛 👶 Sauna, whirlpool. TV in lobby. Discount pass ($4.20) to fitness center, a three-minute drive away. **Rates (CP):** $37–$41 S; $44–$49 D. Children under age 16 stay free. Parking: Outdoor, free. Free roll-aways for extra guests. AARP gets 10% discount. Enchanted Evening getaway with champagne, chocolate, and silk rose costs $65 plus tax. AE, CB, DC, DISC, EC, MC, V.

≣≣ Heritage Motel

1305 S Hastings Rd, 54701; tel 715/832-1687. I-94 to US 53 N to Clairemont exit. Not part of a chain, this clean, comfortable motel across the street from a high school is within walking distance of numerous restaurants, a mall, and a grocery store. Two blocks east is a jogging path through woods along Otter Creek. **Rooms:** 30 rms and effic. CI 2pm/CO 11am. Nonsmoking rms avail. All rooms open onto parking area with space in front of each unit. **Amenities:** 🛅 A/C, cable TV w/movies. **Services:** 📠 Masseur. **Facilities:** 🏋 **Rates:** Peak (May–Sept) $31–$44 S or D; $165–$185 effic. Extra person $5. Children under age 12 stay free. Lower rates off-season. Parking: Outdoor, free. AE, CB, DC, DISC, EC, MC, V.

≣≣ Maple Manor Motel

2507 Hastings Way, 54701; tel 715/834-2618 or toll free 800/624-3763; fax 715/834-1148. I-94 to US 53 N to Clairemont exit. Picnic tables under trees in front welcome guests to this attractive, older motel with a pleasant staff. Caters to motor coach groups and workers, plus regular travelers. No hallways, no elevators. **Rooms:** 34 rms. CI noon/CO 11:30am. Nonsmoking rms avail. All rooms renovated by local decorator with themes featuring Chippewa River Valley craftspeople and artists. Antiques provided by Chippewa Valley Museum and Paul Bunyan Park. **Amenities:** 🛅 📺 A/C, cable TV w/movies, refrig, VCR, CD/tape player. **Services:** ✗ 📠 🗗 🏧 **Facilities:** 🏋 👶 (bkfst and lunch only) **Rates (BB):** Peak (June–Sept) $29–$39 S; $34–$49 D. Extra person $5. Children under age 12 stay free. Lower rates off-season. Parking: Outdoor, free. Rates increased for Country Jam, Country Fest, and Country Thunder music festivals in summer. AE, CB, DC, DISC, EC, JCB, MC, V.

≣≣≣ Quality Inn

809 W Clairemont, 54702; tel 715/834-6611 or toll free 800/221-2222; fax 715/834-6611 ext 172. Well-maintained motel. **Rooms:** 120 rms and stes. CI 3pm/CO noon. Nonsmoking rms avail. **Amenities:** 🛅 👶 A/C, cable TV w/movies, dataport. Some units w/terraces, some w/whirlpools. **Services:** ✗ 📠 🗗 🏧 Social director. **Facilities:** 🎰 🏋 🏊 👶

1 restaurant, 1 bar (w/entertainment), games rm, sauna, whirlpool. O'Leary's bar has DJ and sing-along machine. Outside sun deck accessible from pool. Pass available to Eau Claire Athletic Club, a five-minute drive away, for $5. **Rates:** $54–$62 S; $64–$68 D; $89–$99 ste. Extra person $10. Children under age 18 stay free. Parking: Outdoor, free. AE, CB, DC, DISC, EC, JCB, MC, V.

≣≣ Road Star Inn

1151 MacArthur Ave, 54702; tel 715/832-9731 or toll free 800/445-INNS. Exit 65 off I-94. Small, well-maintained motel. **Rooms:** 62 rms. CI 2pm/CO noon. Nonsmoking rms avail. Four theme rooms (one with a waterbed); two executive king rooms. **Amenities:** 🛅 A/C, satel TV w/movies. **Services:** 🗗 🏧 Pet deposit $25. **Facilities:** 🏋 **Rates (CP):** Peak (May–Sept) $30–$35 S; $37–$42 D. Extra person $5. Children under age 15 stay free. Lower rates off-season. Parking: Outdoor, free. During special events, children do not stay free and AARP discounts do not apply. AE, CB, DC, DISC, EC, MC, V.

≣≣ Super 8 Motel

6260 Texaco Dr, 54703; tel 715/874-6868 or toll free 800/800-8080. Exit 59 off I-94. A neat, clean motel at a truck stop along the interstate. **Rooms:** 31 rms. CI 2pm/CO 11am. Nonsmoking rms avail. **Amenities:** 🛅 👶 A/C, cable TV w/movies. **Services:** 🗗 🏧 **Facilities:** 🏋 👶 Playground. **Rates (CP):** Peak (Apr–Sept) $40 S; $45 D. Extra person $4. Children under age 16 stay free. Lower rates off-season. Parking: Outdoor, free. AE, CB, DISC, MC, V.

RESTAURANTS 🍴

★ Fanny Hill Dining Room

In Victorian Inn, 3919 Crescent Ave; tel 715/836-8184. On County Rd EE. **Eclectic.** A pink ranch-style building overlooking the Chippewa River valley houses this delightful restaurant, bed-and-breakfast, and dinner theater—popular for weddings, anniversaries, and romantic getaways. The chef, formerly of Lafitte's Crossing in the New Orleans area, combines Wisconsin game and fish with French cooking technique for many of his dishes. Two menu possibilities are tournedos Veronique (sautéed beef medallions with red and green grapes served over eggplant, with applejack brandy sauce) and rack of lamb. Extensive, sophisticated wine list, plus vast array of single-malt scotches. The dinner theater, separate from the main restaurant, features solo musicians and revues. Guests can purchase Fanny Hill products, including jars of its poppy-seed dressing. **FYI:** Reservations recommended. Cabaret. Children's menu. No smoking. **Open:** Dinner Sun–Mon 5–8pm, Tues–Thurs 5–9pm, Fri–Sat 5–10pm; brunch Sun 10am–2pm. **Prices:** Main courses $13–$24. AE, CB, DC, DISC, MC, V. 💟 🈚 🏞 💟 👶

★ Woo's Pagoda

1700 S Hastings Way; tel 715/832-6431. US 12/53. **Chinese.** Easily identified by its pagoda tower, this popular place is located on busy strip packed with auto repair shops and outlet malls. Tasty Szechuan and Mandarin cooking is the draw, with cashew chicken the most popular dish. Locals line up for take-out. **FYI:** Reservations recommended. **Open:** Mon–Fri 11am–11pm, Sat 4:30pm–midnight, Sun 11am–10pm. **Prices:** Main courses $6–$12. DISC, MC, V. 🖼️ &

ATTRACTION 🏛️

Paul Bunyan Logging Camp of Eau Claire
1110 Carson Park Dr; tel 715/835-6200. An authentic replica of a logging camp from the 1890s. Interpretive Center features a movie, photographs, artifacts, and exhibit rooms documenting logging history. The camp itself contains a bunkhouse, blacksmith shop, ox barn, and cook's shanty. Guided tours available. **Open:** Mar–Nov, daily 10am–4:30pm. $

Egg Harbor

A charming town on the Green Bay shore of Door County, known for its water activities and tasty fish boils. A buffalo hide robe painted by Sacajawea is featured among the artifacts at Chief Oshkosh Indian Museum.

MOTELS 🏨

≡≡≡ Ashbrook Suites
7942 Egg Harbor Rd, 54209; tel 414/868-3113; fax 414/868-2837. Owner-built and -operated, with wicker, dried flowers, and luxuriant drapes and quilts throughout. Lobby features marble fireplace and vaulted ceiling. Easy walking distance to shops, restaurants, galleries. Children must be 13 or older. **Rooms:** 28 rms and stes. CI 3pm/CO 11am. No smoking. Plush interiors with views of woods or landscaped lawn and flowers. **Amenities:** 🛗 🌀 📺 A/C, cable TV, refrig, VCR. Some units w/terraces, some w/fireplaces, some w/whirlpools. All rooms have microwaves. **Services:** Morning coffee and bakery items served in lobby. Friendly, competent staff. **Facilities:** 🏋️ 🏊 🖼️ & Sauna, whirlpool. Pool solarium capped with cupola-like ceiling in blond wood. Sun deck off pool. **Rates:** Peak (July–Oct 22) $95–$125 S or D; $120–$175 ste. Extra person $25. Min stay peak. Lower rates off-season. Parking: Outdoor, free. Off-season packages avail. AE, MC, V.

≡≡≡ The Baypoint Inn
7933 WI 42, PO Box 287, 54209; tel 414/868-3297; fax 414/868-2876. Smaller property in excellent condition with "family" atmosphere. Award-winning accommodations and staff. Within easy walking distance to shops, galleries, and restaurants; 1 mile to beach, 7 miles to Peninsula State Park. **Rooms:** 10 stes. CI 3pm/CO 11am. Nonsmoking rms avail. All rooms have pleasant, freshly updated decor, outside entrances, and bay views. Some rooms with king-size beds. **Amenities:** 🛗 🌀 📺 A/C, TV, refrig, VCR, CD/tape player. All units w/terraces, some w/fireplaces, 1 w/whirlpool. All

have kitchenettes. **Services:** ✕ 🍴 Babysitting. Continental breakfast during off-season. Competent, friendly staff can accommodate most special requests. **Facilities:** 🏋️ 🏊 & Whirlpool. Small pool and sunning area overlook bay. Grill, picnic area. **Rates:** Peak (June 23–Aug 26) $140–$165 ste. Extra person $12. Min stay peak. Lower rates off-season. Parking: Outdoor, free. Variety of special packages avail during off-season. AE, CB, DC, DISC, MC, V.

≡≡≡ Egg Harbor Lodge
7965 WI 42, PO Box 57, 54209; tel 414/868-3115. Situated on a bluff overlooking Egg Harbor, the family-owned and -operated lodge bills itself as having "the best water view in Door County." Caters to adults only and is within easy walking distance to Egg Harbor shops, restaurants, and galleries. **Rooms:** 25 rms and stes. CI 2pm/CO 11am. Nonsmoking rms avail. Continual updates have kept room decor fresh. All have water view. Access to all rooms from outside corridor. **Amenities:** 🛗 🌀 📺 A/C, TV, refrig, dataport. All units w/terraces, 1 w/fireplace, some w/whirlpools. Some have connecting balconies. **Services:** Friendly, capable staff. **Facilities:** 🏋️ 🏊 & Whirlpool. Putting green (balls and clubs). **Rates:** Peak (late June–Aug) $103–$128 S or D; $200 ste. Extra person $25. Min stay wknds. Lower rates off-season. Parking: Outdoor, free. Discounts on stays of five nights or longer. Closed Nov–Apr. AE, MC, V.

≡≡ Mariner Motel
7505 Mariner Rd, 54209; tel 414/868-3131. 40 acres. Secluded, quiet setting, with a north woods feel to it. Ideal for families, with lots of running/play room for children. Family owned and operated. **Rooms:** 22 rms and stes; 4 cottages/villas. CI 2pm/CO 10:30am. Nonsmoking rms avail. Rooms are either air conditioned or have ceiling fans. Views are poolside, wooded, or water. Two- and three-bedroom units available. **Amenities:** 📺 TV, refrig. No A/C or phone. Some units w/terraces. Some rooms have private balconies overlooking Green Bay; kitchenettes available. **Services:** 🍴 Twice-daily maid svce, babysitting. **Facilities:** 🏋️ 🚴 🏊 & 1 beach (lake shore). Grills, picnic tables, rafts, rowboats, fishing pier. Walking trails through 40 acres of woods. **Rates:** Peak (mid-June–Labor Day) $52–$91 S or D; $80–$95 ste; $620–$800 cottage/villa. Extra person $7. Children under age 3 stay free. Min stay wknds and special events. Lower rates off-season. Parking: Outdoor, free. Cottage rates are weekly. Closed Nov–Apr. AE, DISC, MC, V.

≡≡≡ The Shallows
7353 Horse Shoe Bay Rd, 54209; tel 414/868-3458. Quiet, secluded location with a pleasant, relaxed atmosphere. Ideal for families, with lots of running and playing room for children. Located on Horse Shoe Bay, a short drive away from horseback riding, golf, restaurants, shops, and Peninsula State Park. **Rooms:** 32 rms and stes; 4 cottages/villas. CI 2pm/CO 10am. Nonsmoking rms avail. Rooms have wooded or water view. **Amenities:** 🌀 A/C, TV, refrig. No phone.

Some units w/terraces, some w/fireplaces. All rooms have microwaves. Cottages have full kitchens and fireplaces. **Services:** Babysitting. Continental breakfast served in breakfast room, which is also open for cards and board games. Tennis rackets and balls available. **Facilities:** 1 beach (bay), playground. Fishing pier. Beach has stony bottom. **Rates (CP):** Peak (Late June–Aug) $80–$100 S or D; $130 ste; $170 cottage/villa. Extra person $15. Children under age 1 stay free. Min stay peak. Lower rates off-season. Parking: Outdoor, free. $5 for children during summer only. Closed Nov–mid-Apr. AE, MC, V.

RESORT

Landmark Resort

7643 Hillside Rd, 54209; tel 414/868-3205; fax 414/868-2569. S of Egg Harbor on WI 42. 42 acres. The largest resort in Door County is located atop a wooded bluff within short driving distance to Egg Harbor shops, restaurants, boat launch, galleries, and Peninsula State Park. Four buildings each have their own lobby with fireplace and amenity floor, including whirlpool and sauna. Full range of facilities makes it ideal for families. Adjacent to 27-hole golf course. **Rooms:** 293 rms and stes. CI 3pm/CO 11am. All rooms have woodland or water view, each with private veranda. Options include one-, two-, or three-bedroom lofted suites. **Amenities:** A/C, cable TV, refrig, VCR. All units w/terraces. Suites equipped with fully stocked kitchens, microwaves, and dishwashers. **Services:** Social director, children's program, babysitting. Masseuse on call. Video rental center. Comprehensive activity schedule for children and adults. Staff readily accommodates needs of business travelers. **Facilities:** 5 250 1 restaurant, 1 bar, basketball, volleyball, games rm, lawn games, sauna, whirlpool, playground. Three outdoor heated pools plus large indoor pool. Extensive health club. Grills, bluff-side picnic areas, shuffleboard, horseshoes. Boat and RV parking. **Rates:** Peak (late June–mid-Aug) $120–$250 S or D; $120–$250 ste. Extra person $15. Children under age 12 stay free. Min stay peak. Lower rates off-season. Parking: Outdoor, free. Seasonal and other packages avail include golf, theater, and family packages. Group discounts with 10 rooms or more. AE, CB, DC, DISC, MC, V.

RESTAURANTS

Casey's Inn

7855 WI 42; tel 414/868-3038. **Seafood/Steak.** Comfortable and casual "Wisconsin Roadhouse" atmosphere. Steaks, local whitefish, veal. **FYI:** Reservations accepted. **Open:** Peak (May–Oct) lunch daily 11am–2:30pm; dinner daily 5–9pm. **Prices:** Main courses $13–$23. AE, CB, DC, DISC, MC, V.

★ Olde Stage Station

WI 42 (Downtown); tel 414/868-3247. **Diner/Italian.** Built around the turn of the century, this former stagecoach stop serves up hearty, reliable fare. Chicken or seafood pot pie, baked in puff pastry and chock-full of vegetables, tops the lunch menu. Italian specialties—fettuccine primavera, lasagna al forno, and pizza topped with seven Wisconsin cheeses—are served at dinner. Over 150 bottled beers (imports and local microbreweries) and 13 beers on tap should satisfy any beer connoisseur. **FYI:** Reservations accepted. Children's menu. Dress code. **Open:** Peak (late May–mid-Oct) daily 8am–10pm. **Prices:** Main courses $5–$15. MC, V.

The Village Cafe

WI 42; tel 414/868-3342. **Cafe.** A pleasant eatery with red painted chairs, colorful tablecloths and curtains, and bright table service. Daily breakfast specialties include home-baked coffee cakes and muffins, quiches, and potatoes spiked with paprika. During July and August, a fish boil is also served on weekend nights and is accompanied by the Boilmaster's monologue on local history and traditions. **FYI:** Reservations not accepted. Children's menu. Beer and wine only. No smoking. **Open:** Daily 7am–3pm. Closed late Oct–early May. **Prices:** Lunch main courses $4–$7. DISC, MC, V.

ATTRACTION

Birch Creek Music Center

County Rd E; tel 414/868-3763. Located 3 mi E of Egg Harbor. A rustic "concert hall in a barn," hosting a full summer schedule of pop, light classical, and big-band performances. **Open:** June–Aug, call for schedule. $$

Elkhorn

Seat of Walworth County, in southern Wisconsin. Alpine Valley Ski Resort is nearby. Walworth County Fair, held in late August, is one of the state's largest. **Information:** Elkhorn Area Chamber of Commerce, 9 S Broad St, PO Box 41, Elkhorn, 53121 (tel 414/723-5788).

MOTEL

AmericInn

210 E Commerce Court, 53121; tel 414/723-7799 or toll free 800/634-3444; fax 414/723-7799. Elkhorn exit off I-43. The lobby of this newer property features high ceilings, a stone fireplace, and upholstered sofas and chairs. Lots of green space; guests can watch nesting waterfowl from side patio. Located within minutes of Walworth County Fairgrounds, Geneva Lakes Kennel Club, and Alpine Valley. **Rooms:** 42 rms, stes, and effic. CI 3pm/CO 11am. Nonsmoking rms avail. **Amenities:** A/C, cable TV. Some units w/whirlpools. **Services:** **Facilities:** 15 Sauna, whirlpool. Pool and whirlpool in pleasant cedar-paneled solarium. **Rates (CP):** Peak (May–Sept) $63–$67 S; $68–$75 D; $105–$132 ste; $75 effic. Extra person $6. Children under age 12 stay free. Lower rates off-season. Parking:

Outdoor, free. Rates increase for County Fair, July 4, and Mem Day weekend. Discounts include AARP and WI state employees. AE, DC, DISC, MC, V.

Ellison Bay

Resort near the northern tip of Door County. A ferry to Washington Island departs year-round from Gills Rock. In late June, Old Ellison Bay Days features a parade, fishing contests, fish boil, bazaars, and fireworks.

RESTAURANTS 🍽

★ The Viking

WI 42; tel 414/854-2998. On the N side of Ellison Bay. **American.** One of the original purveyors of the Door County fish boil, this family-style restaurant also features breakfast, lunch, and dinner specials. The fish boil dinner of whitefish, new potatoes, onions, coleslaw, bread, and cherry pie is served picnic style. Breakfast fare includes Swedish and buttermilk pancakes, while lunchtime soup seekers can dive into a bowl of lentil, bean, or pea soup. **FYI:** Reservations not accepted. Children's menu. Beer and wine only. **Open:** Peak (May–Oct) daily 6am–8pm. **Prices:** Main courses $8–$15. AE, DISC, MC, V. ♿

Voight Supper Club

12010 WI 42; tel 414/854-2250. **American.** Diners can choose between intimate red-leather booths or tables at this establishment, which has been a supper club since the 1950s. Signature dishes include prime rib, broiled whitefish, and roast duck with orange/cherry sauce. **FYI:** Reservations accepted. Children's menu. Dress code. **Open:** Peak (May–Oct) lunch Mon–Sat 11:30am–4pm; dinner daily 5–9pm; brunch Sun 10am–2pm. **Prices:** Main courses $10–$15. AE, CB, DISC, MC, V.

Wagon Trail Resort Dining Room

In Wagon Trail Resort, 1041 County ZZ (Rowley's Bay); tel 414/854-2385. E of WI 42. **American/Swedish.** Dinner buffets at this family-owned and -operated eatery feature a different ethnic cuisine each night, such as Swedish smorgasbord and Italian Night. Swedish bakery items are a particular specialty, and a full dessert table is always piled high with homemade pies, bread pudding, and apple crisp for diners who manage to save a little room. Wagon Trail pecan rolls and cherry pies are so popular that they are sold wholesale to other area restaurants. **FYI:** Reservations not accepted. Children's menu. No liquor license. No smoking. **Open:** Peak (July 15–Aug 15/Sept 15–Oct 15) daily 6am–11pm. **Prices:** Main courses $8–$15. AE, DISC, MC, V. 👪

Ephraim

Founded in 1853 by Moravian settlers, this village on the Green Bay shore of the Door Peninsula is now a popular resort. Fyr-Bal Fest, three days in June, is a Scandinavian welcome to summer, with fish boil, Blessing of the Fleet, art fair, and bonfires on the beach at dusk.

MOTELS 🏨

☰☰☰ Edgewater

10040 Water St (WI 42), PO Box 143, 54234 (Downtown); tel 414/854-2734; fax 414/868-3350. Bills itself as having "the best view in Ephraim" for sunsets across the harbor. The three inn buildings were built in 1901 and 1906 with the third added in the 1970s—all originally owned and operated separately. Carefully maintained flower gardens and buildings. Charming courtyard with porch swing. Lots of green space for children makes it popular with families. **Rooms:** 39 rms and stes; 2 cottages/villas. CI 2pm/CO 11am. No smoking. Front rooms have porches and overlook pool and bay; other rooms have garden/courtyard view. New furnishings in 1995. Whirlpool suites feature iron frame beds. **Amenities:** 🛁 ♨ A/C, cable TV, refrig. Some units w/terraces, some w/whirlpools. **Services:** ⌟ Babysitting. Long-term staff provides consistency of service and welcoming faces for returning guests. **Facilities:** 🏠 🕴 ♿ 1 restaurant (bkfst and dinner only; see "Restaurants" below), 1 beach (bay), playground. Private pier, beach, and sunning area on bay. Picnic tables, grill. **Rates:** Peak (June 23–Aug 19) $62–$98 S or D; $128–$166 ste; $92–$104 cottage/villa. Extra person $10. Children under age 2 stay free. Min stay peak. Lower rates off-season. Parking: Outdoor, free. Weekly rates for cottages. Breakfast specials for returning guests. Closed Nov–Apr. DISC, MC, V.

☰☰ Ephraim Shores Motel

10407 WI 42, PO Box 166, 54211; tel 414/854-5959; fax 414/854-4926. On Eagle Harbor. Owned and operated by original builder of this 1967 motel. Unobstructed view of Eagle Harbor allows for enjoying nightly sunsets. In the heart of Ephraim on (sometimes busy) WI 42, steps from shopping and restaurants. **Rooms:** 46 rms and effic. CI 3pm/CO 10:30am. No smoking. Furnishings in some rooms are rather dated. **Amenities:** 🛁 ♨ 🖭 A/C, cable TV w/movies, refrig. Some units w/terraces, some w/whirlpools. **Services:** ⌟ Babysitting. Door County dried cherries on pillow. Playing cards and books available. **Facilities:** 🏠 🕴 ♿ 1 restaurant (see "Restaurants" below), 1 beach (bay), games rm, sauna, whirlpool, playground, washer/dryer. Sun deck, sand beach, and pier directly on Eagle Harbor. Pool table, video games. **Rates:** Peak (mid-June–mid-Aug) $77–$97 S or D; $87–$107 effic. Extra person $10. Children under age 5 stay free. Min stay peak. Lower rates off-season. Parking: Outdoor, free. Closed Nov–mid-May. MC, V.

☰☰ Evergreen Beach Motel

German Rd, PO Box 170, 54211 (Downtown); tel 414/854-2831. At WI 42. Well-maintained, family-owned and -operated, with view of bay. Wide sweeping treed lawn fronts property on bay side. Main lodge building built in 1897 as a hotel and has large covered porch. Within easy walking or biking distance to area shops, restaurants, galleries; 1 mile to golf course, ¼ mile to public beach. **Rooms:** 30 rms. CI 2pm/ CO 10:30am. No smoking. Delightful, fresh decor in rooms, with furniture from original hotel in main lodge rooms. Beach units available, as are two-bedroom units. **Amenities:** 📺 A/C, cable TV, refrig. All units w/terraces, 1 w/fireplace. **Services:** 🛎 Babysitting. **Facilities:** 🖼 🚣 🛇 1 beach (bay), playground. **Rates (CP):** Peak (July–Aug) $89–$102 S or D. Extra person $15. Min stay peak. Lower rates off-season. Parking: Outdoor, free. Extra charge for children. Closed late Oct–mid-May. AE, DISC, MC, V.

≋≋≋ Pine Grove Motel

WI 42, PO Box 94, 54211 (Downtown); tel 414/854-2321 or toll free 800/292-9494; fax 414/854-2511. Modern-looking motel situated on bay, within easy walking or biking distance to Ephraim's shops, restaurants, galleries, and other attractions. **Rooms:** 44 rms and stes. CI 2pm/CO 11am. Nonsmoking rms avail. All rooms have water or wooded view. **Amenities:** 📺 🛇 A/C, cable TV, refrig. All units w/terraces, some w/whirlpools. **Services:** 🛎 Babysitting. **Facilities:** 🖼 🚣 🛶 🛇 1 beach (bay), basketball, games rm, sauna, whirlpool, washer/dryer. Sand beach. Indoor pool features wood-and-glass solarium. **Rates:** Peak (June 21–Sept 5) $78–$95 S or D; $145–$165 ste. Extra person $8–$12. Min stay wknds. Lower rates off-season. Parking: Outdoor, free. Single rates avail during off-season. Closed Nov–Mar. DISC, MC, V.

≋≋≋ Somerset Inn & Suites

WI 42, PO Box 555, 54211; tel 414/854-1819; fax 414/ 854-9087. N of downtown. Newer establishment adjacent to mini-golf and short walk or drive to shops, restaurants, galleries, and beach facilities. Wide hallways with stenciling. **Rooms:** 38 rms and stes. CI 3pm/CO 11am. No smoking. Attractive room decor with country flavor. View is of pool or woodland. **Amenities:** 📺 🛇 📺 A/C, cable TV, refrig. All units w/terraces, some w/fireplaces, 1 w/whirlpool. All rooms have microwaves. **Services:** 🛎 **Facilities:** 🖼 🚣 🛇 Whirlpool, playground. Gas grills. Fireplace lounge overlooks pool and whirlpool. **Rates:** Peak (Mem Day–Aug) $84 S or D; $130 ste. Extra person $12. Children under age 2 stay free. Min stay wknds and special events. Lower rates off-season. Parking: Outdoor, free. Seasonal holiday packages avail. DISC, MC, V.

≋≋ Trollhaugen Lodge

10176 WI 42, PO Box 142, 54211; tel 414/854-2713 or toll free 800/484-1577 ext 2713. New owners have given this facility, located on 1¾ wooded acres, a fresh look. Within walking or biking distance to Ephraim shops, restaurants, galleries, and waterfront. Family owned and operated. **Rooms:** 16 rms; 1 cottage/villa. CI 2pm/CO 10am. Nonsmoking rms avail. Three types of accommodations: lodge, motel units, and authentic log cabin. Most have wooded view; all have fresh, comfy decor. **Amenities:** 📺 🛇 A/C, cable TV, refrig. Some units w/terraces, some w/fireplaces. Some units have microwaves. Log cabin has fully stocked kitchen.

Facilities: 🚣 Gas grill. **Rates (CP):** Peak (July–Aug) $67–$75 S or D; $100–$145 cottage/villa. Extra person $7. Min stay peak. Lower rates off-season. Parking: Outdoor, free. Spring and fall packages avail. Boat cruise and dinner packages avail. AE, DISC, MC, V.

≋≋≋ Village Green Lodge

Cedar St, PO Box 21, 54211; tel 414/854-2515. E of WI 42. On quiet side of street away from traffic, this family-owned and -operated facility features a secluded garden setting. Lobby has a brick fireplace, hardwood floors, stuffed chairs, and shelves full of books. Easy walking distance to waterfront, shops, restaurants, and galleries. No children. **Rooms:** 15 rms. CI 2pm/CO 11am. No smoking. Rooms have pool, wooded, or garden view. Many feature stenciling. **Amenities:** 📺 🛇 A/C, cable TV, refrig. **Services:** Afternoon coffee, tea, and cookies in lobby. **Facilities:** 🖼 🚣 📺 🛇 Picnic table. **Rates (CP):** Peak (July–Aug) $88 S or D. Extra person $15. Min stay peak. Lower rates off-season. Parking: Outdoor, free. Closed Nov–Apr. AE, MC, V.

RESTAURANTS 🍴

Edgewater Dining Room

10040 Water St (WI 42) (Downtown); tel 414/854-4034. **Regional American.** The Edgewater's bright and sunny dining room features a view of Eagle Harbor. Freshly baked muffins and coffeecakes complement cherry pancakes and hash browns for breakfast, while a Door County fish boil (consisting of fresh whitefish, potatoes, onions, coleslaw, pumpkin and lemon breads, and cherry pie) is the only item available in the evening. **FYI:** Reservations recommended. Children's menu. No liquor license. No smoking. **Open:** Breakfast daily 7:30–11am; dinner daily 5:30–8pm. Closed Nov–Apr. **Prices:** Main courses $13. No CC. 🏞 🛇

Paulson's Old Orchard Inn

10341 WI 42; tel 414/854-5717. 1½ mi N of Ephraim Visitor Center. **American/Swedish.** The setting for this family-owned and -operated Victorian-theme restaurant includes a stone fireplace, large windows, and cottage garden. The on-site bakery turns out enough rhubarb custard pies, cherry-nut bread pudding, and other goodies to supply a steady stream of customers. Eggs Benedict on a croissant and authentic Swedish meatballs are special dishes. Sandwiches and salads available during lunch and dinner hours. **FYI:** Reservations not accepted. Guitar. Children's menu. No liquor license. No smoking. **Open:** Peak (Mother's Day–Oct) breakfast daily 8–11:30am; lunch Mon–Sat 11:30am–2:30pm, Sun 11:30am–1:30pm; dinner Mon–Sat 4:30–8pm. Closed Dec–Jan. **Prices:** Main courses $8–$15. DISC, MC, V. 🖼 🍴 🛇

The Second Story

In Ephraim Shores Motel, 10407 WI 42; tel 414/854-2371. **Regional American.** Every table has a commanding view of Eagle Harbor. The cherry pie has been rated as one of the five best in Door County (a major cherry region). Besides dessert, diners can feast on Cajun whitefish, chicken caesar salad or the salad bar, which is available all day. Breakfast muffins and rolls are baked fresh daily. **FYI:** Reservations accepted. Children's menu. No liquor license. No smoking. **Open:** Daily 8am–8pm. Closed Oct 31–May 5. **Prices:** Main courses $8–$13. MC, V.

Fennimore

ATTRACTIONS

Fennimore Railroad Historical Society Museum

1130 Lincoln Ave; tel 608/822-6144 or 822-6319. Artifacts include a ticket office complete with telegraph machine and telephone switchboard, a restored 15-gauge steam locomotive, and two G-scale model trains with replicas of Fennimore buildings circa 1900. A 15-gauge train operating on 700 feet of track takes visitors around the complex. **Open:** Peak (Mem Day–Labor Day) daily 10am–4pm. Reduced hours off-season. Closed Nov–May. **$**

Fennimore Doll and Toy Museum

1140 Lincoln Ave; tel 608/822-4100 or toll free 800/822-1131. Displays at this comprehensive collection of dolls and toys (ranging from the 19th century to the present) include an array of toy buses, cars, and John Deere tractors; circus memorabilia; a papier-mâché doll made in 1850; advertising dolls representing various commercial products; and dolls of Hollywood stars. Many visiting exhibits; gift shop. **Open:** Mem Day–late Dec, daily 10am–4pm. **$**

Fish Creek

Small but popular Door Peninsula resort on the shore of Green Bay. Several resident theater companies perform contemporary and historical plays during the summer season, while nearby Peninsula State Park draws hikers, bikers, and cross-country skiers.

MOTELS

Beowulf Lodge

3775 WI 42, 54212; tel 414/868-2046 or toll free 800/433-7592; fax 414/868-2381. 10 acres. Geared toward families, located just north of Fish Creek adjacent to amusement park. Comfortable lobby with wood stove and board games. Four buildings separated by lots of lawn and play space for children. Peninsula State Park hiking and biking trails directly across road; snowmobile trails out back door. **Rooms:** 60 rms, stes, and effic. CI 3pm/CO 11am. Nonsmoking rms avail. Rooms have either wooded or lawn view. Suites available with woodburning stoves. Honeymoon and deluxe family suites also available. **Amenities:** A/C, cable TV. Some units w/terraces, some w/fireplaces. **Services:** Children's program, babysitting. Craft classes. Video game units and

cartridges for rent. Extensive directory of Door County activities, shops, and restaurants. **Facilities:** Basketball, volleyball, games rm, whirlpool, playground, washer/dryer. Picnic areas with grills, basketballs, tennis rackets and balls. Pool inside wood-paneled solarium. **Rates:** Peak (late June–late Aug) $83 S or D; $79–$106 ste; $89 effic. Extra person $10. Min stay peak. Lower rates off-season. Parking: Outdoor, free. Rates based on quad occupancy. Off-season and mid-season packages avail, including senior discount. Discounts for stays of seven nights or more. MC, V.

By-The-Bay

WI 42, PO Box 367, 54212; tel 414/868-3456; fax 414/868-1604. Family-owned and -operated; well maintained; located in the middle of Fish Creek shops, restaurants, and attractions; across the street from beach. Little green space. **Rooms:** 16 rms and stes. CI 2pm/CO 10:30am. No smoking. Each room features unique, fresh decor. Views are of streetside/water, a quiet residential street, or other units. **Amenities:** A/C, cable TV. No phone. All units w/terraces, 1 w/fireplace. **Facilities:** **Rates:** Peak (June–Aug) $79 S or D; $110 ste. Extra person $8. Min stay wknds. Lower rates off-season. Parking: Outdoor, free. Closed Nov–Apr. AE, DISC, MC, V.

Cedar Court

9429 Cedar St, PO Box 94, 54212 (Downtown); tel 414/868-3361. W of WI 42. One of the first resorts in Door County, painstakingly renovated and restored. Located on quiet side of street between downtown and harbor. Walking distance to shops and restaurants; short drive or bike ride to entrance of Peninsula State Park. **Rooms:** 12 rms; 9 cottages/villas. CI 2pm/CO 10am. Nonsmoking rms avail. Choice of motel rooms, inn rooms, and guest houses. Country motif featuring pine furnishings. Most rooms have courtyard or wooded bluff view. Units are situated around central lawn and garden area and outdoor pool. **Amenities:** A/C, cable TV, refrig. No phone. Some units w/terraces, some w/fireplaces, some w/whirlpools. **Services:** **Facilities:** **Rates:** Peak (July–Aug) $74–$115 S or D; $115–$235 cottage/villa. Extra person $10. Children under age 12 stay free. Min stay wknds and special events. Lower rates off-season. Parking: Outdoor, free. High-season weekly rates avail for some accommodations. Off-season packages avail. MC, V.

The Homestead Motel

4006 Main St, 54212; tel 414/868-3748; fax 414/868-2874. Located at the entrance to Peninsula State Park, in the midst of Fish Creek attractions. Family-owned and -operated. **Rooms:** 33 rms and stes. CI 3pm/CO 11am. No smoking. Rooms have street, wooded, or lawn views and inside or outside corridor entrances. **Amenities:** A/C, cable TV. Some units w/terraces, some w/fireplaces, some w/whirlpools. **Services:** **Facilities:** Basketball, games rm, sauna, whirlpool, playground. **Rates (CP):** Peak

(July–Aug) $89 S or D; $159 ste. Extra person $10. Children under age 2 stay free. Min stay peak. Lower rates off-season. Parking: Outdoor, free. Fall and spring packages avail. DISC, MC, V.

≣≣ Peninsula Motel

4020 WI 42, PO Box 246, 54212; tel 414/868-3281. At entrance to Peninsula State Park. Nicely maintained, family-owned and -operated, older motel located a half-block from public beach. The U-shaped facility surrounds a courtyard with porch swings and gazebo. Reasonably priced accommodations for those who use motel as a base from which to explore Door County. **Rooms:** 12 rms. CI 3pm/CO 10am. No smoking. Spotless housekeeping and painstaking care have kept the vintage 1950s bathrooms in excellent shape. All rooms except one have courtyard view. **Amenities:** ⚿ A/C, cable TV w/movies. No phone. **Services:** ⊖ Morning coffee and rolls. **Facilities:** ⚑ 1 restaurant (dinner only). Bike rentals across street. **Rates:** Peak (June 23–Aug 24) $68 S or D. Extra person $10. Min stay peak. Lower rates off-season. Parking: Outdoor, free. Closed Nov–Mar. DISC, MC, V.

≣≣≣ Settlement Courtyard

WI 42, PO Box 729, 54212; tel 414/868-3524. 240 acres. Comfortable innlike lobby with fieldstone fireplace, stuffed chairs, and hardwood floors. Within walking distance to Settlement shops; short drive or bike ride to Fish Creek. Tranquil atmosphere away from hustle and bustle of town. **Rooms:** 33 rms, stes, and effic. CI 3pm/CO 10:30am. Nonsmoking rms avail. Country decor with oak detailing has been kept fresh with continual updates. Rooms have meadow or wooded view. **Amenities:** ⚿ ⚑ A/C, TV, refrig. All units w/fireplaces. Kitchenettes with icemakers in all rooms. **Services:** ⊖ Masseur, babysitting. "Art in April" classes. Early May: Mountain Bike Madness. Thanksgiving Dinner served for guests. **Facilities:** ⚑ ⚹ Lawn games. Grills, outdoor picnic areas, horseshoes. Hiking, biking, and ski trails through woods and around pond on property; on-site trails connect directly to Peninsula State Park. **Rates (CP):** Peak (mid-June–Oct) $93 S or D; $109 ste; $150–$160 effic. Extra person $10. Children under age 4 stay free. Min stay wknds. Lower rates off-season. Parking: Outdoor, free. Mid-week, off-season discount for stays of multiple nights. Seventh night is free during high season. AE, DISC, MC, V.

RESTAURANTS 🍴

♣ The Black Locust

4020 WI 42; tel 414/868-2999. At entrance to Peninsula State Park. **Eclectic.** Diners are greeted by a simple but elegant dining atmosphere in this converted 100-year-old house. Unique entrees feature fresh fish and game prepared in innovative ways: veal chop with sage sauce, pan-roasted duck breast with wilted mixed greens and cherry-mushroom jus, and lamb loin in mustard crust with roasted rosemary and garlic jus. Desserts such as basil-pistachio ice cream and chocolate cheesecake with macadamia-nut crust are as crea-

tive as the main courses. **FYI:** Reservations recommended. Beer and wine only. **Open:** Peak (May–Oct) daily 5:30–9:30pm. **Prices:** Main courses $15–$26. DISC, MC, V. ⚑ ⚹

★ C & C Supper Club

WI 42 (Downtown); tel 414/868-3412. **Regional American.** This family-owned and -operated eatery claims to have the largest selection of fresh seafood north of Green Bay. The kitchen uses healthy cooking techniques to turn out fresh and delicious main courses such as broiled Atlantic salmon with lemon-caper butter, and sautéed chicken breast with pasta in garlic, white wine, and lemon sauce. All entrees come with salad bar. Homemade soups (tomato bisque, beefy mushroom with barley) and desserts round out the menu. Watch out for the frozen turtle sundae pie with hot fudge sauce. **FYI:** Reservations recommended. Children's menu. **Open:** Lunch daily 11:30am–2pm; dinner Sun–Thurs 4:45–9pm, Fri–Sat 4:45–10pm. **Prices:** Main courses $10–$20. DC, DISC, MC, V. ⚑ ⚹

The Cookery

4135 WI 42; tel 414/868-3634. **Regional American.** The comfortable interior includes hardwood floors, Windsor chairs, and wood beams. Many of the recipes were formulated in consultation with nutritionists. Favorites with diners include walnut-crusted chicken breast with fresh cilantro and cherry salsa, buttermilk pancakes topped with cherry sauce, and a variety of open-faced sandwiches and burgers. Rich desserts include tollhouse-cookie pie and bread pudding with caramel sauce. **FYI:** Reservations not accepted. Children's menu. Beer and wine only. No smoking. **Open:** Peak (May–Nov) daily 7am–9pm. **Prices:** Main courses $7–$10. MC, V. ⚑ ⚹

English Inn

Rte 1, WI 42; tel 414/868-3076. **American.** Cottage garden, Windsor chairs, and brick fireplace all add to the publike atmosphere that the owners of this restaurant have worked hard for two generations to create and maintain. Roasted rack of lamb with a Dijon crumb crust, Beef Wellington, veal specialties, and fresh fish of the day are just some of the treats here. **FYI:** Reservations accepted. Children's menu. No smoking. **Open:** Daily 5:30–9:30pm. Closed Nov–Apr. **Prices:** Main courses $14–$26. DC, MC, V. ⚑ ⚑ ⚹

★ Pelletier's

4199 Main St; tel 414/868-3313. **Regional American/Cafe.** The fish boil has been a tradition at this family-owned and -operated eatery for three generations. French-style crepes featured for breakfast and lunch. **FYI:** Reservations recommended. Children's menu. Beer and wine only. **Open:** Breakfast daily 7:30am–2:30pm; dinner daily 5–8pm. Closed Nov–mid-May. **Prices:** Main courses $10. No CC. ⚑ ⚑ ⚹

Summertime Restaurant

1 N Spruce St; tel 414/868-3738. **International.** Diners can take a tour of several continents when sampling the eclectic offerings here: Greek lemon chicken, South African–style

barbecued pork ribs, jambalaya, Mediterranean salad. All baked goods and desserts (fruit pies, carrot cake, German chocolate cake) and all soups (black bean with bacon, sauerkraut and dumpling) are made on premises. Outdoor seating is available in a pleasant garden setting. **FYI:** Reservations accepted. Children's menu. Dress code. Beer and wine only. **Open:** Peak (mid-May–Oct) Sun–Thurs 7:30am–10pm, Fri–Sat 7:30am–11pm. **Prices:** Main courses $11–$19. AE, MC, V. ⛴ &

White Gull Inn

4225 Main St (Downtown); tel 414/868-3517. **Regional American.** This popular vacation inn, first opened in 1896, offers informal dining for breakfast, lunch, and fish boils, but things get a bit fancier on those evenings when candlelight dinners are served. Cherry-stuffed french toast, beef Wellington, and other popular entrees utilize as much fresh produce and local products as possible. **FYI:** Reservations recommended. Children's menu. Beer and wine only. No smoking. **Open:** Peak (May–Oct) breakfast daily 7:30am–noon; lunch daily noon–2:30pm; dinner Mon–Tues 5–8:30pm, Wed 5:45–8pm, Thurs 5–8:30pm, Fri–Sun 5:45–8pm. **Prices:** Main courses $14–$20. AE, CB, DC, DISC, MC, V. ▮ &

ATTRACTIONS 🏛

Peninsula State Park and Golf Course

WI 42; tel 414/868-3258. Wisconsin's second-oldest state park makes the most of its scenic location with an abundance of recreational facilities. Guided tours of **Eagle Lighthouse** are given daily early June to mid-October (extra fee), while 75-foot **Eagle Tower** provides scenic views of surrounding Green and Nicolet Bays. **American Folklore Theater** offers concerts and historical re-enactments (late June–late August). In addition, the park boasts 469 campsites; 35 miles of hiking, biking, and nature trails; and boat launch ramps and a swimming beach at Nicolet Bay. The scenic 18-hole golf course (reservations recommended) offers food service and a pro shop. In winter, the park is a haven for cross-country skiing, sledding (on the golf course's fairway), snowmobiling, snowshoeing, primitive camping, and ice fishing. **Open:** Daily 6am–11pm. **$$**

Thumb Fun Park and Waterworks

WI 42; tel 414/868-3418. Over two dozen rides and attractions, including water slides, high-speed go-carts, bumper cars, bumper boats, miniature golf, a haunted mansion, and other fast-moving rides. There's also a golf driving range, a video game center, a restaurant, and snack stands. **Open:** Mem Day–Labor Day, daily 10am–9pm. **$$$$**

Fond du Lac

Seat of Fond du Lac County, in eastern Wisconsin. Fond du Lac (French for "foot of the lake") was founded in 1835 at the southern shore of Lake Winnebago. The 19th-century fur trade and lumbering industries have given way to 20th-century tourism. Sturgeon-spearing festival takes place in late February, and there's a walleye tournament every June. The museum at nearby Kettle Moraine State Forest shows how glaciers molded the area's terrain. **Information:** Fond du Lac Convention & Visitors Bureau, 19 W Scott St, Fond du Lac, 54935-2342 (tel 414/923-3010).

MOTELS 🏨

≣≣ Budgetel Inn

77 Holiday Lane, 54937; tel 414/921-4000; fax 414/921-4472. Landscaping of flowers and bushes complements the white building on US 41. Two-story lobby has comfortable breakfast room. Guests can walk to several restaurants. **Rooms:** 80 rms. CI 3pm/CO 11am. Nonsmoking rms avail. **Amenities:** 🛏 ⟁ 🖪 A/C, cable TV. Some units w/terraces. **Services:** ⟲ Microwave and vending machines available in a common area. Pleasant staff. **Facilities:** 🔓 🏋 🏊 & Whirlpool, washer/dryer. Beautifully maintained pool and whirlpool. **Rates (CP):** Peak (July–Aug) $43–$63 S or D. Extra person $5. Children under age 12 stay free. Lower rates off-season. Parking: Outdoor, free. MC, V.

≣≣ Super 8 Motel

391 N Pioneer Rd, 54935; tel 414/922-1088 or toll free 800/800-8000; fax 414/922-1088. Jct WI 23/US 41. Located next door to Forest Mall and near the airport and Lake Winnebago. Nicely landscaped with many flowers. **Rooms:** 48 rms and stes. CI 3pm/CO 11am. Nonsmoking rms avail. **Amenities:** 🛏 ⟁ A/C, cable TV w/movies. **Services:** ⟲ ⟲ ⟲ Car-rental desk. Coffee, tea, cookies, and fruit offered 24 hours. Microwave available for guest use. Fax and copy services. **Facilities:** 🏋 🏊 📺 & Games rm, washer/dryer. **Rates (CP):** Peak (June–Sept) $37–$48 S; $47–$56 D; $57 ste. Extra person $5. Children under age 13 stay free. Lower rates off-season. Parking: Outdoor, free. AE, CB, DC, DISC, JCB, MC, V.

RESTAURANTS 🍽

★ Petrie's Restaurant

84 N Main St (Downtown); tel 414/921-9150. **American.** Since 1937, Petrie's has been serving up hearty, basic meals to the people of the Fond du Lac area. With its authentic, warm Bavarian atmosphere, it has remained a local family favorite. Buffets are offered twice daily. Mrs Petrie, the manager's mother, plays the organ during the week. **FYI:** Reservations accepted. Children's menu. **Open:** Tues–Thurs 5:30am–9pm, Fri–Sat 5:30am–10pm, Sun 5:30am–7:30pm. **Prices:** Main courses $8–$13. DISC, MC, V. 🍴 &

Salty's Seafood & Spirits

503 N Park; tel 414/922-9940. At Scott St. **Seafood/Steak.** Nautical decor complements the extensive seafood menu at this popular local eatery. Diners can pick their own live Maine lobster from Salty's lobster tank, or order cold-water lobster from South Africa and Australia or warm-water lobster from

the Caribbean. Other seafood entrees include prawns, Alaskan snow-crab legs, and combination platters. Prime rib, steak, and pastas also available. **FYI:** Reservations not accepted. Children's menu. **Open:** Sun–Thurs 11am–10pm, Fri–Sat 11am–11pm. **Prices:** Main courses $9–$22. AE, DISC, MC, V. 🅿️ ♿

★ Schreiner's Restaurant

168 N Pioneer Rd; tel 414/922-0590. Johnson St exit E off US 41. **German.** Since 1938, Schreiner's has been providing home-cooked meals and friendly service. (Paul Cunningham, the current owner, worked for the Schreiner family for 23 years before buying the restaurant in 1992.) Staples like stewed chicken and dumplings, ham loaf with horseradish sauce, German-style pork chops, spareribs and sauerkraut with German potato salad, and roast loin of pork are offered along with soups and baked goods. **FYI:** Reservations not accepted. Children's menu. **Open:** Peak (mid-July–mid-Aug) daily 6:30am–10pm. **Prices:** Main courses $5–$9. AE, DISC, MC, V. 🅿️ ♿

ATTRACTIONS 🏛️

Historic Galloway House and Village

336 Old Pioneer Rd; tel 414/922-6390. Built in 1847 and remodeled in 1880, this Midwest version of an Italianate villa has four fireplaces, hand-carved pine, stenciled ceilings, a total of 30 rooms, and one of the first indoor bathrooms to appear in Wisconsin. The surrounding village is comprised of 22 restored turn-of-the-century buildings, including a one-room schoolhouse, a print shop, a general store, and a gristmill. The Blakely Museum holds a collection of Native American artifacts, American war memorabilia, guns, and early industrial tools. **Open:** Peak (Mem Day–Labor Day) daily 10am–4pm. Reduced hours off-season. Closed Oct–Mem Day. $$

Wade House and Wesley Jung Carriage Museum State Historic Site

W7747 Plank Rd, Greenbush; tel 414/526-3271. Starting in the 1850s, Wade House was a popular stopover for people traveling between Sheboygan and Fond du Lac. Costumed guides provide a sense of life in mid-19th-century Wisconsin; tours include the kitchen (where cooks still prepare meals over a wood-fired stove), the communal dining room and tap room, and the blacksmith's shop outside. The nearby museum houses Wisconsin's largest collection of hand- and horse-drawn carriages, commercial wagons, and other vehicles of the day. **Open:** May–Oct, daily 9am–5pm. $$

Fort Atkinson

Small town 30 miles west of Milwaukee. Birthplace of the Wisconsin Dairyman's Association and, by extension, the state's status as a center of dairy production. In nearby Lake Ripley, Ole Evinrude invented the outboard boat motor in 1908. **Information:** Fort Atkinson Area Chamber of Commerce, 244 N Main St, Fort Atkinson, 53538 (tel 414/563-3210 or 563-1870).

MOTELS 🏨

≡≡ Best Western Courtyard Inn

1225 Janesville Ave, 53538; tel 414/563-6444 or toll free 800/992-6789; fax 414/563-6444. Near US 12 and WI 26. Relatively new property located right next door to locally well-known Fireside Dinner Theater. Courtyard has gazebo with tables and chairs, and grill available for guests' cookouts. Popular stopover for families as well as for theater guests. Close to municipal park, golf, fishing, and boat launch area. **Rooms:** 60 rms and stes. CI 2pm/CO 11am. Nonsmoking rms avail. **Amenities:** 🛏️ ♨️ A/C, cable TV w/movies. Some units w/whirlpools. **Services:** 🛎️ 🚗 Car-rental desk. Exercise equipment (barbells, dumbbells, exercycle) available for use in rooms. **Facilities:** 🏋️ 🅿️ ♿ Whirlpool, washer/dryer. **Rates (CP):** $50–$70 S; $60–$70 D; $75–$109 ste. Extra person $10. Children under age 12 stay free. **Parking:** Outdoor, free. AE, DC, DISC, MC, V.

≡ Super 8 of Fort Atkinson

225 S Water St E, 53538; tel 414/563-8444 or toll free 800/800-8000; fax 414/563-8444. US 12 to Water St, E 2 blocks. A solid, old building of white-washed bricks adorned with black, wrought-iron window decorations, this does not look like a typical Super 8. It sits on Rock River, so you can drop a fishing line in right on-site. **Rooms:** 40 rms and stes. CI 2pm/CO 11am. Nonsmoking rms avail. **Amenities:** 🛏️ A/C, cable TV w/movies. 1 unit w/terrace. **Services:** 🛎️ 🚗 Masseur. **Facilities:** 🏋️ 🅿️ ♿ 1 bar. **Rates (CP):** $47–$49 S; $52–$55 D; $75 ste. Extra person $5. Children under age 16 stay free. **Parking:** Outdoor, free. AE, CB, DC, DISC, MC, V.

Glendale

HOTEL 🏨

≡≡≡ Woodfield Suites

5423 N Port Washington Rd, 53217; tel 414/962-6767 or toll free 800/338-0008; fax 414/962-8811. This newer property located 10 minutes north of downtown features a large lobby with fireplace and lots of sofas and chairs. **Rooms:** 109 rms, stes, and effic. CI 2pm/CO noon. Nonsmoking rms avail. Pleasant decor. Double-paned windows suppress road noise from freeway. Views of pool area or cityscape. **Amenities:** 🛏️ ♨️ 📺 A/C, cable TV w/movies, refrig, VCR, voice mail. Some units w/whirlpools. **Services:** 🛎️ 🚗 Car-rental desk. Complimentary cocktails during hospitality hour. Video rental center. **Facilities:** 🏋️ 🅿️ ♿ Games rm, whirlpool, washer/dryer. Toddler playroom with toys and climbers. **Rates (CP):** $80 S; $90 D; $90–$126 ste; $110 effic. Extra person $10. Children under age 17 stay free. **Parking:** Outdoor, free. AE, DC, DISC, MC, V.

MOTEL

≝≝ Exel Inn

5485 N Port Washington Rd, 53217; tel 414/961-7272 or toll free 800/356-8013. Located 10 minutes north of downtown and lakeside festival grounds. Though sandwiched bewtween freeway and busy street, extra soundproofing makes road noise undetectable. Car rental across the street. **Rooms:** 125 rms. CI 3pm/CO noon. Nonsmoking rms avail. Nicely updated room decor. **Amenities:** 🛅 🕭 A/C, satel TV w/movies, dataport. **Services:** 🔌 🖘 Free local calls. **Facilities:** 🏋 🕹 Games rm, washer/dryer. **Rates (CP):** Peak (mid-June–mid-Sept) $47–$64 S; $57–$64 D. Children under age 17 stay free. Min stay peak. Lower rates off-season. Parking: Outdoor, free. Chainwide frequent traveler program. Senior rates for 55 and older. AE, DC, DISC, MC, V.

RESTAURANT 🍴

★ Kopp's Frozen Custard

5373 N Port Washington Rd; tel 414/961-3288. **Burgers/Custard.** A Milwaukee tradition since 1950, the popularity of this strictly carry-out eatery is based on the fact that they serve up "fast food that is not too fast": flavorful jumbo burgers, grilled chicken fillets, onion rings. The special custard made here is used in the malts, shakes, and sundaes. **FYI:** Reservations not accepted. No liquor license. Additional locations: 76th and Layton, Greenfield (tel 282-4312); 189th and Bluemound, Brookfield (tel 789-9490). **Open:** Peak (June–Aug) daily 10:30am–11:30pm. **Prices:** Lunch main courses $1–$4. No CC. 🅿️ 🕭

Green Bay

Seat of Brown County, in eastern Wisconsin. The oldest settlement in Wisconsin (founded sometime early in the 17th century), Green Bay is known today as a center of paper and cheese production, and as the home of the Green Bay Packers of the National Football League. **Information:** Green Bay Area Visitors & Convention Bureau, 1901 S Oneida St, PO Box 10596, Green Bay, 54307-0596 (tel 414/494-9507).

HOTELS 🏨

≝≝≝ Best Western Downtowner Inn

321 S Washington, 54301; tel 414/437-8771 or toll free 800/252-2952; fax 414/437-3839. At Main St and Port Plaza. Brick building located in heart of downtown Green Bay. Not much landscaping because of location, but parking lot and building are clean and well maintained. **Rooms:** 140 rms. CI 2pm/CO 11am. Nonsmoking rms avail. **Amenities:** 🛅 🕭 A/C, cable TV w/movies. Some units w/terraces. **Services:** 🛆 🔌 🖘 Pets accepted in first floor smoking room only, if available. Friendly and helpful front desk staff. **Facilities:** 🛗 🏋 🏊 250 🕭 1 restaurant, games rm, spa, sauna, whirlpool. Pool table, shuffleboard, Ping-Pong, put-

ting green. **Rates (CP):** $52–$65 S; $67–$75 D. Extra person $8. Children under age 12 stay free. Parking: Outdoor, free. Rates of pool area rooms are higher. One-night family special rates and mini-vacation rates avail. AE, DC, DISC, MC, V.

≝≝≝ Days Inn Downtown

406 N Washington St, 54301; tel 414/435-4484 or toll free 800/DAYS-INN; fax 414/435-3120. White building with turquoise trim overlooking the Fox River. Newly redecorated, with friendly atmosphere. Conveniently located downtown, across from Regency Conference Center, adjacent to Port Plaza Mall, and six miles from airport. **Rooms:** 98 rms and stes. CI 3pm/CO noon. Nonsmoking rms avail. **Amenities:** 🛅 🕭 A/C, cable TV, in-rm safe. **Services:** ✕ 🚐 🛆 🔌 🖘 **Facilities:** 🛗 🏋 🏊 300 🕭 1 restaurant, 1 bar. **Rates:** Peak (July–Aug) $58–$68 S; $63–$73 D; $68–$78 ste. Extra person $5. Children under age 18 stay free. Lower rates off-season. Parking: Indoor/outdoor, free. AE, CB, DC, DISC, JCB, MC, V.

≝≝≝ Holiday Inn City Centre

200 Main St, 54301; tel 414/437-5900 or toll free 800/457-2929; fax 414/437-1199. Located in the heart of Green Bay's business and entertainment center, the white high-rise building has blue trim and is tastefully landscaped. Lobby has small sitting area with television, library, and fireplace. Nautical decor in lobby, restaurant, and bar. Across the street is Port Plaza, Green Bay's largest shopping mall. In back of the hotel is the City Centre Marina. **Rooms:** 149 rms and stes. Executive level. CI 3pm/CO noon. Nonsmoking rms avail. **Amenities:** 🛅 🕭 A/C, cable TV w/movies. Some units w/minibars. **Services:** ✕ 🚐 🛆 🔌 🖘 Car-rental desk. **Facilities:** 🛗 🏋 🏊 250 🕭 1 restaurant (see "Restaurants" below), 1 bar (w/entertainment), sauna, whirlpool, washer/dryer. Health club privileges. **Rates:** $66 S; $76–$95 D; $75–$93 ste. Extra person $5. Children under age 12 stay free. Parking: Outdoor, free. AE, CB, DC, DISC, JCB, MC, V.

≝≝≝ Ramada Inn

2750 Ramada Way, 54304; tel 414/499-0631 or toll free 800/272-6232; fax 414/499-5476. Lovely hotel with chandeliers, paintings, and chairs in lobby, which also features a bookcase of paperback books to buy or trade. **Rooms:** 156 rms. CI 3pm/CO noon. Nonsmoking rms avail. **Amenities:** 🛅 🕭 🖥 A/C, cable TV w/movies, dataport, voice mail. Some units w/terraces. **Services:** ✕ 🚐 🛆 🔌 Car-rental desk, babysitting. Friendly staff. **Facilities:** 🛗 🏋 🏊 500 🖥 🕭 1 restaurant, 1 bar (w/entertainment), basketball, games rm, sauna, whirlpool. **Rates (BB):** Peak (July 15–Nov 15) $70–$90 S; $80–$100 D. Extra person $10. Children under age 19 stay free. Lower rates off-season. MAP rates avail. Parking: Outdoor, free. Two weekend packages avail—Friday's First Class, one room for two for one night; and an escape package, one room for two nights. AE, CB, DC, DISC, EC, ER, JCB, MC, V.

Regency Suites

333 Main St, 54301; tel 414/432-4555 or toll free 800/236-3330; fax 414/432-0700. Lovely hotel in a convenient downtown location. Attractive lobby with red brick pillars and ceiling, Queen Anne chairs, green carpet, and small fountain. Luxuriant plants everywhere. Indoor access to Port Plaza shopping mall. Indoor parking available. **Rooms:** 242 stes. CI 3pm/CO noon. Nonsmoking rms avail. **Amenities:** A/C, cable TV w/movies, refrig, dataport, voice mail. Some units w/terraces. **Services:** Car-rental desk. Guests receive free newspapers, and two hours of complimentary beverages each evening. **Facilities:** 1 restaurant, 1 bar, games rm, sauna, steam rm, whirlpool. **Rates (BB):** $92–$153 ste. Extra person $15. Children under age 18 stay free. Min stay special events. Parking: Indoor/outdoor, free. AE, DC, DISC, MC, V.

MOTELS

Budgetel Inn

2840 S Oneida, 54304; tel 414/494-7887 or toll free 800/428-3438; fax 414/494-3370. Tasteful brown and beige building surrounded by green bushes located on west side of Green Bay. **Rooms:** 80 rms and stes. CI 1pm/CO 11am. Nonsmoking rms avail. **Amenities:** A/C, cable TV w/movies. **Services:** Continental breakfast can be delivered to your room. Friendly and accommodating staff. **Facilities:** Games rm. **Rates (CP):** $49–$59 S; $55–$65 D; $55–$68 ste. Extra person $7. Children under age 18 stay free. Parking: Outdoor, free. AE, CB, DC, DISC, MC, V.

Comfort Inn

2842 Ramada Way, 54304; tel 414/498-2060 or toll free 800/221-2222; fax 414/498-2060. White mid-rise building pleasantly landscaped with green bushes and flowering plants. **Rooms:** 60 rms and stes. CI 3pm/CO 11am. Nonsmoking rms avail. Queen- or king-size beds in all rooms. **Amenities:** A/C, cable TV w/movies. **Services:** Coffee, tea, cookies, and fruit available 24 hours. Microwave available for guest use. Fax and copy services available. Pleasant staff. **Facilities:** Games rm, whirlpool. **Rates (CP):** Peak (May 15–Oct) $47–$62 S; $53–$72 D; $62–$72 ste. Extra person $5. Children under age 18 stay free. Lower rates off-season. Parking: Outdoor, free. AE, CB, DC, DISC, ER, JCB, MC, V.

Exel Inn

2870 Ramada Way, 54304; tel 414/499-3599 or toll free 800/356-8013; fax 414/498-4055. Sand-colored building with brick-red trim and minimal landscaping on the west side of Green Bay. Good for budget-minded travelers. **Rooms:** 105 rms. CI 3pm/CO noon. Nonsmoking rms avail. **Amenities:** A/C, cable TV. **Services:** **Facilities:** Washer/dryer. **Rates (CP):** $39–$49 S; $48–$58 D. Extra person $4. Children under age 18 stay free. Parking: Outdoor, free. AE, CB, DC, DISC, MC, V.

Road Star Inn

1941 True Lane, 54304; tel 414/497-2666 or toll free 800/445-INNS; fax 414/497-4754. Located across the street from Lambeau Field, this yellow and white motel is the perfect choice during football season for Packer fans. During the rest of the year, its niche is basic accommodations for senior citizens and other travelers who are price-conscious and want proximity to the downtown area. **Rooms:** 63 rms. CI 2pm/CO 11am. Nonsmoking rms avail. **Amenities:** A/C, satel TV w/movies. **Services:** **Facilities:** Games rm. **Rates (CP):** $32–$40 S; $38–$46 D. Children under age 15 stay free. Parking: Outdoor, free. AE, CB, DC, DISC, MC, V.

RESTAURANTS

Dragonwyck

1992 Gross Ave; tel 414/498-9836. **Chinese.** Statues of foo dogs and a red-lacquered door greet diners. Besides standard Chinese options, there are hamburgers and sandwiches. Imported beers available. **FYI:** Reservations accepted. **Open:** Mon–Thurs 11am–10pm, Fri–Sat 11am–11pm, Sun 11am–9pm. **Prices:** Main courses $6–$10. MC, V.

★ Eve's Supper Club

2020 Riverside Dr; tel 414/435-1571. **American.** Serving locals and visitors for more than 25 years. The menu offers a wide variety of seafood (including fresh whitefish and salmon), combination platters (seafood and beef, beef and lamb), prime rib, steaks, and sandwiches. After dinner, you can enjoy the views of the Fox River while you savor your favorite ice cream drink. **FYI:** Reservations recommended. **Open:** Lunch Mon–Sat 11am–2pm; dinner Mon–Sat 5–10pm. **Prices:** Main courses $6–$30. AE, DC, DISC, MC, V.

The River Room

In Holiday Inn City Centre, 200 Main St; tel 414/437-5900. Jct US 141/WI 29. **American.** Bright decor and a tranquil riverside setting make this one of the most popular spots in town. Dinner features Wisconsin veal (prepared Oscar, scaloppine marsala, or parmigiana); other options include chicken (cordon bleu, parmigiana, amaretto), prime rib, steaks, and seafood. Heart Healthy options available. On summer Sunday evenings, the River Room sponsors a Dixieland barbecue on the banks of the river (ribs, grilled chicken, baked beans, corn muffins, and salads, plus live entertainment). **FYI:** Reservations accepted. **Open:** Daily 6am–10pm. **Prices:** Main courses $7–$16. AE, CB, DC, DISC, MC, V.

★ Rock Garden Supper Club

1951 Bond St; tel 414/497-4701. **American/Steak.** Diners here can choose from steaks, seafood, pasta, ribs, orange roast duckling, and chicken Oscar. All entrees include soup, salad bar, choice of potato or rice, warm bread, and beverage. There's a special brunch on Sundays when the Green Bay Packers are home. A Polish-American buffet—complete with

Polish sausage, sauerkraut, pierogi, potato soup, and blood sausage—is featured on Thursdays. **FYI:** Reservations recommended. Children's menu. **Open:** Mon–Thurs 11am–11pm, Fri–Sat 11am–1am, Sun 11am–10pm. **Prices:** Main courses $8–$15. AE, MC, V. &

♥★ The Wellington

1060 Hanson Rd; tel 414/499-2000. **American.** A red carpet ushers diners into a wood-paneled foyer; in here stands a cabinet filled with dolls, which are presented to little ladies celebrating special events. Appetizers such as escargot, oysters Rockefeller, and shrimp de jonge are a great segue into the featured main courses: fresh yellowfin tuna dusted in ground pine nuts and served with anchovy-caper mayonnaise, chorizo chicken, chicken saltimbocca, Jamaican pork tenderloin served with kiwi-pineapple salsa, and veal strip loin (stuffed with Asiago cheese, spinach, and roasted red peppers, and served with Madeira demiglace). **FYI:** Reservations recommended. Children's menu. **Open:** Lunch Mon–Sat 11am–2pm; dinner Mon–Sat 5–10pm. **Prices:** Main courses $12–$20. AE, DC, MC, V. ♥ ⚓ &

ATTRACTIONS 📷

Bay Beach Wildlife Sanctuary

Sanctuary Rd; tel 414/391-3671. This 700-acre wildlife refuge supports a substantial waterfowl flock, including 4,300 geese and 3,000 ducks, plus birds of prey, reptiles, deer, timber wolves, fish, and various other animals in natural landscapes. A 6.2-mile nature trail system runs through forest, field, and marsh, and connects with the University Cofrin Arboretum trail system to offer a total of 12 miles of hiking and cross-country skiing trails. Nature Education Center offers interactive educational exhibits and programs. **Open:** Peak (June–Aug) daily 8am–8pm. Reduced hours off-season. $$

Hazelwood Historic Home Museum

1008 S Monroe Ave (Astor Historic District); tel 414/437-1840. Constructed in 1837 on a hillside overlooking the Fox River, Hazelwood is a fine example of Greek Revival architecture. Home to three generations of the influential 19th-century Martin family, it is filled with many of their original furnishings, works of art, and memorabilia. **Open:** Mem Day–Labor Day, Fri–Mon 1–4pm. $

Green Bay Packer Hall of Fame

855 Lombardi Ave; tel 414/499-4281. State-of-the-art exhibits, including seven video theaters and numerous multimedia shows and interactive displays, illustrate the history of the only team to win ten NFL championships. Trophies, old photos, and a collection documenting the career of legendary coach Vince Lombardi are among the highlights. Gift shop stocks a huge selection of Packer souvenirs. **Open:** Daily 10am–5pm. $$$

Neville Public Museum of Brown County

210 Museum Place (Downtown); tel 414/448-4460. The history and art of the Green Bay region are the focus of this 58,000-square-foot facility. The museum's permanent exhibit, "On the Edge of the Inland Sea," examines 12,000 years of natural history beginning with a simulated glacier. The current temporary exhibition (through 1998) is "Whodunit? The Science of Solving Crime," an exploration of the scientific principles, methods, and technologies (such as fingerprinting and DNA profiling) used by criminal investigators. **Open:** Tues–Sat 9am–4pm, Sun–Mon noon–4pm. **Free**

National Railroad Museum

2285 S Broadway; tel 414/435-7245 or 437-7623. One of the largest rail museums in America, featuring more than 70 railroad cars and locomotives. Highlights include Gen Dwight D Eisenhower's World War II staff car, the Rock Island Aerotrain, and a Union Pacific "Big Boy'—the world's largest steam locomotive. Tours include a 20-minute train ride. Library, multimedia orientation, gift shop. **Open:** May–Oct, daily 9am–5pm. $$$

Oneida National Museum

866 EE Rd; tel 414/869-2768. The heritage of the "People of the Standing Stone," who came to Wisconsin in the 1880s, is the focus here. Authentic clothing, tools, and structures tell the story of the tribe's history. **Open:** Tues–Fri 9am–5pm, Sat–Sun 10am–2pm. $

Bay Beach Amusement Park

1313 Bay Beach Rd; tel 414/448-3365. Adjacent to the Wildlife Sanctuary, the amusement park offers a dozen rides, including merry-go-round, miniature train, Ferris wheel, and bumper cars. **Open:** Peak (Mem Day–mid-Aug) daily 10am–9pm. Reduced hours off-season. **Free**

Green Lake

ATTRACTION 📷

Larson's Famous Clydesdales

W12654 Reeds Corner Rd, Ripon; tel 414/748-5466. Located 20 mi SE of Green Lake. Guided 90-minute tours of this ranch—home to 14 champion Clydesdales—include a performance of the national champion six-horse hitch as well as a collection of antique hitch wagons, harnesses, and equipment. Souvenir shop. **Open:** May–Oct, Mon–Sat 1pm. $$$

Hayward

Seat of Sawyer County, in northwest part of state. Site of the Lumberjack World Championship—with logrolling, tree climbing, and sawing competitions—in late July. **Information:** Hayward Area Chamber of Commerce, PO Box 726, Hayward, 54843 (tel 715/634-8662).

MOTELS

≣≣ Cedar Inn Motel
Rte 7, Box 7148, 54843; tel 715/634-5332 or toll free 800/776-2478. Jct US 63/WI 77. True to its name, this family-owned, one-story building is all cedar. Perfect for couples, business travelers, or families. **Rooms:** 22 rms. CI 2pm/CO 10:30am. Nonsmoking rms avail. Honeymoon suites available. **Amenities:** A/C, cable TV w/movies, refrig, dataport. 1 unit w/fireplace, some w/whirlpools. **Services:** **Facilities:** Sauna, whirlpool. **Rates (CP):** $46–$56 S; $51–$130 D. Extra person $5. Children under age 5 stay free. Parking: Outdoor, free. AE, MC, V.

≣≣ Super 8 Motel
317 WI 27, 54843; tel 715/634-2646 or toll free 800/800-8000; fax 715/634-6482. Easy to find, occupying two separate buildings. One of few motels in Hayward with indoor pool, so it attracts families. Near chain restaurants and "main drag." **Rooms:** 46 rms. CI 2pm/CO 11am. Nonsmoking rms avail. **Amenities:** A/C, cable TV. Some units w/whirlpools. **Services:** **Facilities:** Games rm, whirlpool. **Rates:** Peak (Apr–Sept) $48–$53 S; $53–$59 D. Extra person $6. Children under age 12 stay free. Lower rates off-season. Parking: Outdoor, free. AE, CB, DC, DISC, MC, V.

RESORT

≣≣≣ Ross' Teal Lake Lodge
Ross Rd, 54843; tel 715/462-3631. 20 mi NE of Hayward on WI 77 E. 220 acres. One of a kind, full-service resort in north woods. Year after year, families come back; in fact, it may be difficult to get reservations. **Rooms:** 25 stes; 25 cottages/villas. CI 2pm/CO 11am. Nonsmoking rms avail. Cabins located along a half mile of private shoreline. **Amenities:** TV w/movies, refrig. No A/C or phone. Some units w/terraces, some w/fireplaces. Nearly all of the cabins have full kitchens. **Services:** Social director, babysitting. **Facilities:** 1 restaurant (bkfst and dinner only), 1 bar, 1 beach (lake shore), basketball, games rm, sauna, whirlpool, playground, washer/dryer. **Rates:** Peak (July 16–Aug 20) $120–$140 ste; $190–$420 cottage/villa. Extra person $10–$20. Children under age 2 stay free. Min stay peak. Lower rates off-season. AP and MAP rates avail. Parking: Outdoor, free. MC, V.

RESTAURANTS

Chippewa Inn
County Rds A and B; tel 715/462-3648. **German.** This supper club, one of the first in the area, has been serving solid German food for more than 35 years. Set in a German-style chalet, it's out of the way, but worth the trip. The house specialty is the Wiener schnitzel; the restaurant is also known for its walleye and for its excellent Norwegian *torsk* served on Friday evenings. Numerous beef, chicken, and pork options

as well. **FYI:** Reservations accepted. Children's menu. **Open:** Mon 4–10pm, Wed–Sat 4–10pm, Sun noon–10pm. **Prices:** Main courses $10–$25. MC, V.

★ Famous Dave's BBQ Shack and Resort
Rte 5, Box 5167; tel 715/462-3352. **Barbecue.** Nearly 3,000 people are served in a single weekend at this unique spot, a real hit with vacationers (the town only has 2,000 residents!). The easily accessible lakeside location allows patrons to drive, swim, ski, windsurf, sail, or snowmobile up to the door. Pleasant outdoor dining is available on the deck. The dining room contains wonderful antiques and knickknacks, while a large, lively bar contributes to the fun. Hickory-smoked ribs are the main draw; barbecued chicken and steak are excellent as well. **FYI:** Reservations not accepted. Children's menu. **Open:** Peak (June–Aug) Wed–Fri 4–10pm, Sat–Sun 11am–10pm. **Prices:** Main courses $6–$38. MC, V.

The Maximillian Inn
Rte 2, Box 38; tel 715/865-2080. Jct WI 70/2; on Sand Lake. **American/German.** This award-winning restaurant—great for families and large groups—has won a following for its authentic fare prepared by the German chef-owner who lends his name to the place. The large dining room has a stone fireplace and a view of Sand Lake; a mural of Maximillian's homeland is painted on the wall. Veal is a specialty here. Four times a year, the restaurant opens at noon for a special brunch; the Octoberfest brunch (fourth Saturday in September) brings Bavarian food and dancing. **FYI:** Reservations recommended. Children's menu. **Open:** Peak (June–Aug) daily 4–10pm. **Prices:** Main courses $9–$22. DISC, MC, V.

ATTRACTIONS

National Fresh Water Fishing Hall of Fame
1 Hall of Fame Dr; tel 715/634-4440. Built in the shape of a giant muskellunge fish (popularly called a muskie), this walk-through museum is half a block long. Guests enter through the "belly" of the fish, walk through exhibits of fishing equipment and mountings of record catches, and end up at the five-story-high observation deck in the muskie's mouth. **$$**

Chippewa Queen Tours
WI 4; tel 715/462-3874. Visitors can enjoy a two-hour scenic cruise aboard the 40-foot, glass-enclosed *Denum Lacey*. On shore, a main lodge sells cocktails, soft drinks, and ice cream before departure. Three-hour dinner cruises also available; must reserve 24 hours in advance. **Open:** Mem Day–early Oct. Call for schedule. **$$$**

Hudson

Seat of St Croix County, in western Wisconsin on the Minnesota border. **Information:** Hudson Area Chamber of

Commerce & Tourism Bureau, 421 2nd St, PO Box 438, Hudson, 54016 (tel 715/386-8411 or toll free 800/657-6775).

MOTELS 🏨

≡≡≡ Best Western Inn
1616 Crestview Dr, 54016; tel 715/386-2394 or toll free 800/528-1234; fax 715/386-3167. Exit 2 off I-94. Homelike, pleasant atmosphere. **Rooms:** 102 rms and stes. CI 3pm/CO 11am. Nonsmoking rms avail. **Amenities:** 🎂 🛁 A/C, satel TV w/movies, dataport. Some units w/whirlpools. **Services:** ✕ 🛄 🍽 Breakfast included in room rate Mon–Fri for each paying adult. **Facilities:** 🏋 🏊 🎾 🎱 📦 🛗 1 restaurant, 1 bar (w/entertainment), sauna, steam rm, whirlpool. **Rates:** $47–$58 S; $55–$66 D; $77–$160 ste. Extra person $6. Children under age 12 stay free. Parking: Outdoor, free. Corporate and AARP discounts avail. AE, CB, DC, DISC, MC, V.

≡≡ Comfort Inn
811 Dominion Dr, PO Box 719, 54016; tel 715/386-6355 or toll free 800/221-2222; fax 715/386-9778. Exit 2 off I-94. Clean establishment on a hill overlooking the St Croix River not far from downtown. **Rooms:** 60 rms and stes. CI 2pm/CO 11am. Nonsmoking rms avail. **Amenities:** 🎂 🛁 A/C, cable TV w/movies, dataport. Some units w/whirlpools. **Services:** 🚐 🛄 🍽 🍷 **Facilities:** 🏋 🏊 🎾 📦 🛗 Games rm, whirlpool. **Rates (CP):** $48–$59 S; $53–$64 D; $67–$100 ste. Extra person $5. Children under age 17 stay free. Parking: Outdoor, free. AE, DC, DISC, MC, V.

≡≡ Super 8 Motel
808 Dominion Dr, 54016; tel 715/386-8800 or toll free 800/800-8000; fax 715/386-3805. Exceptionally clean, very basic rooms. **Rooms:** 60 rms and stes. CI 2pm/CO 11am. Nonsmoking rms avail. **Amenities:** 🎂 🛁 A/C, cable TV w/movies, dataport. **Services:** 🚐 🍽 🍷 **Facilities:** 🏊 🎾 📦 🛗 Games rm, whirlpool, washer/dryer. **Rates (CP):** Peak (June–Sept) $50–$73 S; $55–$95 D; $68–$73 ste. Extra person $5. Children under age 17 stay free. Lower rates off-season. Parking: Outdoor, free. Corporate and AARP discounts avail. AE, DC, DISC, V.

ATTRACTION 🏛

Phipps Center for the Arts
109 Locust St; tel 715/386-8409. One of the principal centers devoted to the visual and performing arts in the St Croix Valley. The $7 million state-of-the-art facility houses a 243-seat proscenium theater (site of theater, music, and dance performances), a Wurlitzer pipe organ, and three galleries housing paintings, sculpture, photographs, and mixed-media exhibits by local artists. **Open:** Mon–Fri 8am–4:30pm. **$$$$**

Hurley

Seat of Iron County, in northern Wisconsin. Winter sports and tourism have taken the place of lumbering and mining in the economic life of this town near the Upper Peninsula of Michigan. **Information:** Hurley Area Chamber of Commerce, 110 Iron St, Hurley, 54534 (tel 715/561-4334).

MOTEL 🏨

≡≡ American Budget Inn
850 10th Ave, 54534; tel 715/561-3500 or toll free 800/356-8018; fax 715/561-3236. Good choice for one- or two-night stay. **Rooms:** 70 rms. CI 2pm/CO noon. Nonsmoking rms avail. Clean rooms. **Amenities:** 🎂 🛁 A/C, cable TV w/movies. Some units w/whirlpools. **Services:** 🛄 🍽 🍷 Helpful front desk staff. **Facilities:** 🏋 🏊 🎾 Games rm, sauna, whirlpool, washer/dryer. **Rates (CP):** Peak (May–Oct) $37–$62 S; $42–$67 D. Extra person $5. Children under age 18 stay free. Lower rates off-season. Parking: Outdoor, free. AE, CB, DC, DISC, MC, V.

ATTRACTION 🏛

Iron County Museum
303 Iron St; tel 715/561-2244. Three floors of exhibits on the history of Iron County and its industries include early working looms (finished woven products are on display and for sale), miners' equipment, a model saloon from Hurley's days of as a center of gambling, and old wine-making equipment. Other displays feature late-19th-century home furnishings, the town's original courthouse clock, and 19th-century clothing and photographs. **Open:** Mon–Wed and Fri–Sat 10am–2pm. **Free**

Janesville

Seat of Rock County, in southern Wisconsin. Founded in 1836, the town is often called the "bower city" because of its many shade trees. Abraham Lincoln weekended here in 1859. **Information:** Forward Janesville, Incorporated, 20 S Main St, PO Box 8008, Janesville, 53545 (tel 608/757-3160).

MOTELS 🏨

≡≡≡ Hampton Inn Janesville
2400 Fulton St, 53546; tel 608/754-4900 or toll free 800/HAMPTON; fax 608/754-4980. Exit 171A (WI 26 N) off I-90. Newer property built in 1993 has bright clean look. Spacious lobby with a larger-than-average-screened television available for guests' viewing. For business travelers and/or families. **Rooms:** 99 rms and stes. CI 3pm/CO noon. Nonsmoking rms avail. Rooms have double, queen-size, or king-size beds. **Amenities:** 🎂 🛁 A/C, cable TV w/movies, dataport. Some units w/whirlpools. **Services:** ✕ 🛄 🍷 Local restaurant delivers and lets you charge your meals to your room.

Facilities: 🚹 🛝 🖵30 ♿ Whirlpool. Video games. Hospitality room, used for small meetings, available by hour or overnight. **Rates (CP):** Peak (June–Aug) $44–$70 S or D; $79–$109 ste. Children under age 18 stay free. Lower rates off-season. Parking: Outdoor, free. Special rating system in effect for National Water Ski Show that comes through town in Aug; rooms are often booked a year in advance for this time. AE, CB, DC, DISC, MC, V.

UNRATED **Select Inn of Janesville**
3520 Milton Ave, 53545; tel 608/754-0251 or toll free 800/641-1000; fax 608/754-0251. Exit 171 A off I-90. Functional and convenient. Small landscaped area in front of building has picnic table in shade. Popular with value-conscious business travelers and families. **Rooms:** 63 rms. CI 2pm/CO 11am. Nonsmoking rms avail. **Amenities:** 🛏 A/C, cable TV w/movies. **Services:** ⤸ 🍽 Microwave in lobby for guests' use. **Facilities:** ♿ **Rates (CP):** $30 S; $36 D. Extra person $6. Children under age 13 stay free. Parking: Outdoor, free. Senior discounts for those over 55. Select Traveler Club discounts. AE, CB, DC, DISC, MC, V.

⬛ **Super 8 Motel**
3430 Milton Ave, 53545; tel 608/756-2040 or toll free 800/800-8000; fax 608/756-2040. Exit 171A off I-90. Located in a commercial row, close to restaurants and other conveniences. **Rooms:** 48 rms and stes. CI 1pm/CO 11am. Nonsmoking rms avail. Most rooms have queen-size beds. **Amenities:** 🛏 A/C, cable TV, dataport. Some alarms and radios in rooms. **Services:** ⤸ 🍽 Advanced permission required for pets. **Facilities:** 🛝 🖵8 ♿ **Rates:** Peak (Apr–Sept) $38–$45 S; $44–$52 D; $62–$72 ste. Extra person $5. Children under age 12 stay free. Lower rates off-season. Parking: Outdoor, free. AE, CB, DC, DISC, MC, V.

ATTRACTION 🏛

Lincoln-Tallman Restorations
440 N Jackson St; tel 608/756-4509. Built between 1855 and 1857, the home of William M Tallman has been regarded as a monument to Italianate architecture. It is also historically significant as the only remaining Wisconsin home to have hosted Abraham Lincoln. Recently restored, it offers a view of life during the middle to late 1800s. More than three-quarters of the home's furnishings are original, including the bed in which Lincoln slept. Group tours available. **Open:** Peak (June–Sept) Tues–Sun 11am–4pm. Reduced hours off-season. $$

Kenosha

Seat of Kenosha County, in southeast corner of state. Most of this port city's Lake Michigan frontage is devoted to parks. Orson Welles was born here in 1915. Bristol Renaissance Fair, just north of the Illinois border, is the site of a medieval marketplace on most summer weekends. **Information:** Kenosha Area Chamber of Commerce, 5455 Sheridan Rd, #101, PO Box 518, Kenosha, 53141-0518 (tel 414/654-2165).

HOTEL 🏨

⬛⬛⬛ **Best Western Inn**
7220 122nd Ave, 53142; tel 414/857-7699 or toll free 800/438-3932; fax 414/857-2698. I-94 exit off WI 50. This new facility is probably the best hotel at this interstate junction. Near restaurants, family attractions, and outlet malls; 10 miles from Great America Theme Park and Gurnee Mills shopping. **Rooms:** 115 rms and stes. Executive level. CI 2pm/CO noon. Nonsmoking rms avail. All rooms have reclining chairs and feature new decor. Harborside views available. **Amenities:** 🛏 ♿ 📺 A/C, cable TV. 1 unit w/terrace, some w/whirlpools. **Services:** 🖊 ⤸ VCRs and movies available for rent. **Facilities:** 🚹 🖵50 ♿ 1 bar, whirlpool. Free passes to Gold's Gym. **Rates (CP):** Peak (May–Aug) $63–$65 S or D; $125–$200 ste. Children under age 18 stay free. Lower rates off-season. Parking: Outdoor, free. Discounts: AARP, government contractors, military on leave, and Holiday Inn Mature Seniors program. Special packages avail with area attractions and meals. AE, DC, DISC, MC, V.

MOTELS

⬛ **Budget American Motel, Inc**
1800 60th St, 53140; tel 414/658-2361; fax 414/658-1626. I-94 exit off WI 50. Off 60th St near uptown shopping area in a residential neighborhood, 2 miles from downtown Kenosha. **Rooms:** 82 rms. CI 2pm/CO 11am. Nonsmoking rms avail. Furnishings are somewhat tired. **Amenities:** 🛏 A/C, cable TV. TV reception not sharp, even with cable. **Services:** ⤸ 🍽 **Facilities:** 🚹 🖵50 ♿ 1 restaurant (lunch and dinner only), 2 bars. **Rates:** Peak (Apr–Sept) $44–$45 S. Extra person $5. Children under age 18 stay free. Lower rates off-season. Parking: Outdoor, free. Weekly and monthly rates avail. AE, DC, DISC, MC, V.

⬛⬛⬛ **Holiday Inn**
5125 6th Ave, 53140 (Harborside); tel 414/658-3281 or toll free 800/465-4329; fax 414/658-3420. Exit 158 off I-94. Downtown location directly on Kenosha Harbor, with sport fishing nearby. Within 15 miles of outlet shopping and Bristol Renaissance Faire; midway point between Milwaukee and O'Hare airports. **Rooms:** 110 rms. CI 3pm/CO 11am. Nonsmoking rms avail. All rooms have reclining chairs and feature new decor. Harborside views available. **Amenities:** 🛏 ♿ A/C, satel TV, dataport. **Services:** 🚐 🖊 ⤸ 🍽 Car-rental desk, babysitting. Pet deposit required. **Facilities:** 🚹 🛝 🖵50 ♿ Games rm, sauna, whirlpool. Complimentary use of local health club. Pool depth is three feet. Inside solarium with harbor view. **Rates (CP):** Peak (May–Oct) $79–$100 S or D. Children under age 18 stay free. Min stay peak. Lower rates off-season. Parking: Outdoor, free. Discounts: AARP, gov-

ernment contractors, military on leave, and Holiday Inn Mature Seniors program. Special packages avail with area attractions and meals. AE, DISC, MC, V.

⧉⧉ Knights Inn

7221 122nd Ave, 53142; tel 414/857-2622 or toll free 800/ 843-5644; fax 414/857-2375. I-94 exit off WI 50. Clean, quiet, no-frills, family accommodation. Convenient access from expressway; near restaurants, family attractions, and outlet malls; 10 miles from Great America Theme Park and Gurnee Mills shopping. **Rooms:** 113 rms and effic. CI 4pm/ CO noon. Nonsmoking rms avail. **Amenities:** 🛋 A/C, cable TV w/movies. **Services:** 🛎 🕸 **Facilities:** 🛏 🕭 **Rates:** Peak (May–Aug) $43–$44 S; $44–$45 D; $53 effic. Extra person $4. Children under age 18 stay free. Lower rates off-season. Parking: Outdoor, free. Special rates for stays of seven days or more. AE, DC, DISC, MC, V.

RESTAURANTS 🍴

★ Ray Radigans

11712 S Sheridan Rd; tel 414/694-0455. **American.** Located on an underdeveloped strip of scenic Sheridan Road, this eatery has been famous for its T-bone steaks, quiet elegance, and fine service since 1933. Children's portions are available (dishes can even be altered to suit a child's tastes) and the staff is extremely accommodating. **FYI:** Reservations recommended. **Open:** Tues–Thurs 11am–10pm, Fri–Sat 11am–11pm, Sun noon–10pm. **Prices:** Main courses $12–$27. AE, CB, DC, DISC, MC, V.

Taste of Wisconsin

7515 125th Ave; tel 414/857-9110. Exit 344 (WI 50) off I-94; 2 blocks W. **Regional American.** Under skylights and high, beamed ceilings, diners may choose from regional specialties such as Wisconsin sausage kabobs, fresh Wisconsin veal, and homemade beef stew New Berliner–style. Wisconsin wines are available, as are freshly baked cream puffs from the restaurant's spotless bakery. Takeout counters offer regional deli specialties. **FYI:** Reservations not accepted. Children's menu. **Open:** Daily 7:30am–10pm. **Prices:** Main courses $7–$12. AE, MC, V. 🛋 🏖 🕭

ATTRACTIONS 🏛

Kemper Center

6501 3rd Ave; tel 414/657-6005. Included in this complex of mid-19th-century buildings located on the Lake Michigan shore are the Anderson Arts Center (a regional gallery specializing in contemporary works), an Italianate Victorian mansion originally built in 1860, and Kemper Pier (a large fishing pier). The complex also boasts more than 100 different trees, a rose collection, outdoor tennis courts, a mural, and a picnic area. Guided tours by appointment. Donation suggested. **Open:** Daily sunrise–sunset. **Free**

Kenosha Public Museum

5608 10th Ave; tel 414/653-4140. On display are priceless ivory, Oriental art, rare African masks and carvings, and Pacific Island and Native American artifacts (including masks, jewelry, and weapons). The Wisconsin natural history exhibit includes mounted mammals, birds, fish, insects, reptiles, and amphibians, as well as minerals and prehistoric fossils. The new life-size *Deinonychus* dinosaur model and the exhibit of mammals from around the world are especially popular. Gallery shop. **Open:** Peak (May–Oct) Mon–Fri 9am–5pm, Sat 9am–4pm. Reduced hours off-season. **Free**

The Frank A Palumbo Civil War Museum

2001 Alford Dr; tel 414/551-5801 or toll free 800/ 351-4058. Located at Carthage College, this museum houses a rare collection of artwork, photos, weapons, uniforms, currency, and personal papers from the Civil War era. Letters of commission signed by President Lincoln are prominently featured. **Open:** Sept–June, daily 11am–5pm. **Free**

Kenosha County Historical Society Museum

6300 3rd Ave; tel 414/654-5770. Local and Wisconsin history is represented through Native American artifacts, folk and decorative art, and various dioramas. Research library. **Open:** Tues–Sat 2–4:30pm. **Free**

Kohler

See Sheboygan

Lac du Flambeau

Located in north-central part of state. Chippewas used to fish and canoe at night by the light of birch bark torches, so the French named the village "Lake of the Torch." Today, the area still features several Chippewa craft workshops. **Information:** Lac du Flambeau Chamber of Commerce, PO Box 158, Lac du Flambeau, 54538 (tel 715/588-3346).

ATTRACTION 🏛

Lac du Flambeau Chippewa Museum and Cultural Center

Tel 715/588-3333. Ojibwe culture is the focus here, with exhibits such as a 24-foot Ojibwe dugout canoe, smaller birch-bark canoes, Ojibwe arts and crafts, and traditional clothing. There's also a French fur-trading post and a world-record sturgeon taken from one of Flambeau's many beautiful lakes. Year-round programs, workshops, and special events offered. Group tours available. **Open:** Peak (May–Oct) Mon–Sat 10am–4pm. Reduced hours off-season. **$**

La Crosse

Seat of La Crosse County, in western Wisconsin. Granddad Bluff provides a panoramic view of this tree-shaded city at the confluence of the Mississippi, Black, and La Crosse Rivers. **Information:** La Crosse Area Convention & Visitors Bureau, 410 E Veterans Memorial Dr, Riverside Park, 54601 (tel 608/782-2366 or toll free 800/658-9424).

HOTELS 🏨

≣≣ Days Inn Hotel & Conference Center

101 Sky Harbour Dr, 54603; tel 608/783-1000 or toll free 800/DAYS-INN; fax 608/783-2948. Exit 2 off I-90. Pretty, quiet place located at the edge of town. Lobby flanked with two curved staircases that make their way up to second floor; central courtyard offers benches and other outdoor seating. Popular with tour groups, conferences, and families. **Rooms:** 148 rms and stes. CI 3pm/CO 11am. Nonsmoking rms avail. **Amenities:** 🛁 ⚬ 📻 A/C, cable TV w/movies. Some units w/whirlpools. **Services:** ✕ 🚐 🖂 ⇄ ⇱ Children's program. **Facilities:** 🛗 🏋 🏖 🖾 👤 1 restaurant (*see* "Restaurants" below), 1 bar (w/entertainment), games rm, sauna, whirlpool. **Rates:** $49–$85 S; $59–$95 D; $150–$180 ste. Extra person $10. Children under age 17 stay free. Parking: Outdoor, free. Many packages and discounts avail, including a referral discount. Corporate Connection includes free breakfast and lunch. Days Inn Family Vacation Club provides other savings. AE, CB, DC, DISC, JCB, MC, V.

≣≣≣ Radisson Hotel La Crosse

200 Harborview Plaza, 54601; tel 608/784-6680 or toll free 800/333-3333; fax 608/784-6694. At 2nd and Main Sts. Located right across from the Mississippi River and a lovely river walk and park area is this shiny, elegant hotel. Huge lobby offers couches and comfortable chairs. Next to La Crosse's exhibition center, connected by walkway to the hotel. **Rooms:** 170 rms. Executive level. CI 3pm/CO noon. Nonsmoking rms avail. Some rooms afford city and bluff view, others offer river view. **Amenities:** 🛁 ⚬ 📻 A/C, cable TV w/movies. **Services:** ✕ 🖉 🚐 🖂 ⇄ ⇱ Car-rental desk, babysitting. Highly efficient, helpful staff. **Facilities:** 🛗 🚹 🏖 🏋 🏖 🖾 👤 ⛶ 2 restaurants (*see* "Restaurants" below), 1 bar (w/entertainment), games rm, whirlpool. The mid-rise section has a wide sidewalk area that in summer is lined with tables and chairs; food service provided in good weather. **Rates:** $79–$119 S; $89–$129 D. Extra person $10. Children under age 17 stay free. Parking: Outdoor, free. Ask about the Bed and Breakfast Breakaway, a special package available a few months out of the year. AE, CB, DC, DISC, JCB, MC, V.

MOTELS

≣≣≣ Hampton Inn

2110 Rose St, 54603; tel 608/781-5100 or toll free 800/HAMPTON; fax 608/781-3574. Exit 3 off I-90, S on US 53. Easy-to-find motel on commercial row. Really clean and polished inside, with classical music softly piped into the lobby. Popular in fall and winter months with local athletic teams. **Rooms:** 101 rms and stes. CI 2pm/CO noon. Nonsmoking rms avail. **Amenities:** 🛁 ⚬ A/C, satel TV w/movies, dataport. **Services:** ✕ 🖂 ⇄ Exceptional reception staff, full of information about restaurants and attractions. Expect a call from front desk to make sure you are satisfied with your accommodations. **Facilities:** 🛗 🏋 🏖 🖾 👤 ⛶ Whirlpool. Indoor pool; outdoor lounging area open in summer. **Rates (CP):** $55–$79 S; $59–$79 D; $99 ste. Children under age 18 stay free. Min stay special events. Parking: Outdoor, free. Senior discounts avail. AE, CB, DC, DISC, MC, V.

UNRATED Holiday Inn

529 Park Plaza Dr, 54603; tel 608/784-9500 or toll free 800/HOLIDAY; fax 608/784-7562. Cass St W from downtown to Mississippi River. From the outside parking lot, it's hard to tell that this popular motel is so pleasant inside. Located right on the Mississippi River and complete with a Holidome Recreation Center, it has a lot to offer. **Rooms:** 277 rms and stes. CI 4pm/CO noon. Nonsmoking rms avail. Poolside rooms can get noisy. **Amenities:** 🛁 ⚬ 🍷 A/C, cable TV w/movies, dataport. **Services:** ✕ 🚐 🖂 ⇄ Car-rental desk, social director, children's program, babysitting. **Facilities:** 🛗 ▲ 🎿 🏖 🏋 🏖 🖾 👤 1 restaurant, 2 bars (1 w/entertainment), basketball, games rm, sauna, whirlpool, washer/dryer. Holidome has indoor resort feel to it with cafe-style seating on one side of pool and plenty of tables and chairs all around. Outdoor pool is next to Mississippi River. Bikini Yacht Club is outdoor bar on river with small souvenir and sundries shop. Some dinner and party cruises on river use this as their port of departure. **Rates:** Peak (June–Oct) $59–$85 S; $69–$95 D; $135 ste. Extra person $10. Children under age 19 stay free. Lower rates off-season. Parking: Outdoor, free. AE, CB, DC, DISC, EC, ER, JCB, MC, V.

≣ Road Star Inn

2622 Rose St, 54603; tel 608/781-3070 or toll free 800/445-4667; fax 608/781-5114. Exit 3 off I-90, S on US 53 1 block. Located on a commercial strip off I-90. Functional lobby has racks of information about the area. A restaurant and ice cream parlor are practically next door. **Rooms:** 110 rms. CI open/CO noon. Nonsmoking rms avail. Theme rooms. Some rooms have recliners. **Amenities:** 🛁 A/C, satel TV w/movies. **Services:** 🖂 ⇄ ⇱ Complimentary cookies and coffee in lobby. Managers live here, and are always available to assist guests. **Facilities:** 🏋 🏖 👤 Rates **(CP):** Peak (Apr–Oct) $35–$41 S; $41–$47 D. Extra person $5. Children under age 15 stay free. Lower rates off-season. Parking: Outdoor, free. Preferred Guest Club membership offers 13th night free. AE, CB, DC, DISC, MC, V.

UNRATED Super 8 Motel

1625 Rose St, 54603; tel 608/781-8880 or toll free 800/800-8000; fax 608/781-4366. Exit 3 off I-90, 1 mi S on US 53. One of the newer properties on this commercial strip, this Super 8 is exceptionally clean, inside and out. **Rooms:** 82

rms. CI 2pm/CO 11am. Nonsmoking rms avail. **Amenities:** A/C, cable TV w/movies. Some units w/whirlpools. **Services:** **Facilities:** Whirlpool. Large indoor pool and whirlpool located in bright atrium-style facility. **Rates (CP):** $53–$61 S or D. Extra person $5. Children under age 17 stay free. Parking: Outdoor, free. AE, CB, DC, DISC, MC, V.

RESTAURANTS

Adam's Rib & Apple Cellar Lounge
In Days Inn Hotel & Conference Center, 101 Sky Harbour Dr; tel 608/783-1000. **American.** Bright, colorful chain place with brass fixtures, framed prints on the walls, mirrors, vinyl-benched booths, and a fireplace. Lunch and dinner items include sandwiches, salads, ham, steak, pork chops, and fish. **FYI:** Reservations not accepted. Country music/rock. Children's menu. **Open:** Peak (Mar–Nov) daily 6:30am–10pm. **Prices:** Main courses $7–$16. AE, CB, DC, DISC, MC, V.

The Boat Works
In the Radisson Hotel La Crosse, 200 Harborview Plaza; tel 608/784-6680. Jct Main and 2nd Sts. **American/Seafood.** A top spot for special occasions, it offers fine cuisine in a subtly elegant room providing a beautiful view of the Mississippi River. Excellent menu specialties are New York sirloin with cabernet and shallot butter, swordfish with fresh tomato salsa and chive cream sauce, and chicken breast with apple chutney. The buffet brunch is very popular. **FYI:** Reservations recommended. **Open:** Breakfast Mon–Fri 6:30–11am, Sat 7–11am, Sun 7–10am; lunch Mon–Fri 11am–2pm; dinner Mon–Thurs 5:30–10pm, Fri–Sat 5:30–11pm; brunch Sun 10am–2pm. **Prices:** Main courses $11–$30. AE, CB, DC, DISC, ER, MC, V.

The Freighthouse Restaurant
107 Vine (Downtown); tel 608/784-6211. W of 3rd St. **American.** Housed in an old freighthouse that is a National Historic Site, this is one of La Crosse's most popular fine dining spots. The huge space features brick walls adorned with historic railroad photos and posters; tall, beamed ceilings; and chandeliers that look like clusters of lanterns. The zigzag bar area is grand. Hand-cut, aged prime rib and porterhouse steak and crab legs are some of the favorites; chicken and fish selections are also available. **FYI:** Reservations not accepted. Blues/folk/jazz. **Open:** Mon–Thurs 4–10pm, Fri–Sat 4–10:30pm, Sun 4:30–9:30pm. **Prices:** Main courses $8–$33. AE, CB, DC, DISC, MC, V.

The Haberdashery Restaurant & Pub
In the Radisson Hotel La Crosse, 200 Harborview Plaza; tel 608/784-6680. Jct Main and 2nd Sts. **Burgers/Pub.** This festive spot has a fun publike atmosphere. Buffet features chicken, beef, fish, soup, and a batch of salads. The "Five & After" menu includes grilled Thai chicken served with lo mein noodles, roast prime rib of beef, pizza, pasta, and fish. Video trivia games and interactive football amuse revelers. **FYI:** Reservations not accepted. Comedy/country music/ karaoke/rock. Dress code. **Open:** Peak (Mar–Nov) daily 11am–2am. **Prices:** Main courses $5–$16. AE, CB, DC, DISC, ER, MC, V.

ATTRACTIONS

Hixon House
429 N 7th St; tel 608/782-1980. Built in 1859, this graceful Italianate house exemplifies elegant Victorian living. Its 15 rooms feature original 19th-century furnishings, as well as five fireplaces and gardens true to the period. A "Turkish Nook" is filled with exotic Near East artifacts. **Open:** Mem Day–Labor Day, daily 1–5pm. **$**

Riverside Museum
Riverside Park; tel 608/782-1980. This museum focuses on the importance of the Mississippi River in the development of La Crosse. Exhibits include prehistoric artifacts, large collections of area birds and freshwater clams, slide shows and photographs from the riverboat era, and artifacts from the steamer *War Eagle*. Group tours by appointment. **Open:** Mem Day–Labor Day, daily 10am–5pm. **Free**

Pump House Regional Arts Center
119 King St; tel 608/785-1434. Three galleries feature works by local and regional visual artists, while concerts (from folk to classical) and theater productions are presented most weekend evenings in the 140-seat Dayton Theater. Home to the local arts council, the center is also an excellent source for information about cultural events happening throughout the area. **Open:** Tues–Sat 9am–5pm. **Free**

G Heileman Brewery
1111 S 3rd St; tel 608/782-BEER or toll free 800/433-BEER. One hour guided tours of the brewery are followed by beer sampling. Of special interest is "The World's Largest Six-Pack" (a 60-foot replica of Heileman's Old Style brand). Gift shop located on premises. **Open:** Mon–Sat 8am–3pm. **Free**

Lake Geneva

Popular four-season vacation destination in the southeast corner of state. Flatiron Park hosts the Venetian Festival every August. **Information:** Lake Geneva Convention & Visitors Bureau, 201 Wrigley Dr, Lake Geneva, 53147 (tel 414/248-4416).

MOTELS

Ambassador Inn
415 Wells St, 53147; tel 414/248-3452; fax 414/248-0605. S on Wells St from WI 50. Comfortable lobby with skylight, fireplace, and easy chairs. Located on seven wooded acres, three blocks from public beach and boat launch. Within walking distance of shops and restaurants. No alcohol permitted on premises. **Rooms:** 18 rms. CI 2pm/CO 11am. No smoking. Views of wooded or landscaped parking lot.

Amenities: 🛏 🔥 A/C, cable TV. Some units w/terraces, some w/whirlpools. **Services:** 🍽 Books available in lobby. **Facilities:** 🎣 🏃 🏊 �⊃1 🛏50 🚹 Basketball, sauna, whirlpool. Horseshoe pits; outdoor patio and sitting area. **Rates (CP):** Peak (May 24–Sept 15) $65–$135 S or D. Extra person $10. Children under age 18 stay free. Min stay peak. Lower rates off-season. Parking: Outdoor, free. Closed Thanksgiving– Dec 31. AE, DISC, MC, V.

≋ ≋ Budget Host Diplomat Motel

1060 Wells St, 53147; tel 414/248-1809 or toll free 800/ 264-5678; fax 414/248-1809. S on Wells St from WI 50. Quiet location with lots of green space away from traffic and hustle and bustle of downtown. Family owned and operated. **Rooms:** 23 rms. CI 2pm/CO 11am. Nonsmoking rms avail. Access from outdoor corridor. **Amenities:** 🛏 🔥 A/C, cable TV. Some units w/terraces. **Services:** 🍽 🐾 Pets allowed with approval. **Facilities:** 🎣 🏃 🏊 🚹 Basketball. Picnic area. **Rates:** Peak (early June–mid-Sept) $36–$71 S; $41–$89 D. Extra person $10. Children under age 12 stay free. Min stay peak. Lower rates off-season. Parking: Outdoor, free. AARP and corporate discounts avail. Winter ski packages avail. AE, DISC, MC, V.

INN

≋ ≋ ≋ French Country Inn

W4190 West End Rd, 53147; tel 414/245-5220; fax 414/ 245-9060. I-94 to WI 50 W. 5 acres. This one-time speakeasy and gambling casino is now a charming, quiet getaway popular with honeymoon and anniversary couples. Hand-carved oak staircase and inlaid parquet floor in guest and main houses were imported from Denmark as the Danish Pavilion for Chicago's 1893 Columbian Exposition. On Lake Como, near Lake Geneva's beach and attractions. Unsuitable for children under 12. **Rooms:** 24 rms and stes. CI 3pm/CO noon. French country decor in each uniquely furnished room. Queen- or king-size beds, with sofa beds in king rooms. All rooms have lake views. **Amenities:** 🛏 🔥 A/C, cable TV w/movies, VCR. All units w/fireplaces. **Services:** 🍽 After-noon tea and wine/sherry served. **Facilities:** 🎣 🏃 🏊 🚹 1 restaurant, 1 bar, guest lounge. Entertainment in bar on Sun. Boaters can dock at pier, but not launch. **Rates (BB):** Peak (May–Oct) $75–$135 S; $155 ste. Extra person $10. Min stay wknds. Lower rates off-season. Higher rates for special events/hols. Parking: Outdoor, free. MC, V.

RESORT

≋ ≋ ≋ Grand Geneva Resort & Spa

7036 Grand Geneva Way, 53147; tel 414/248-8811 or toll free 800/558-3417; fax 414/292-4763. At WI 50 and US 12. 1,300 acres. Former Playboy Club built in 1968 and fully renovated in 1994. Comfortable ambience in lobby suggests a lodge, with a chandelier made of elks' horns, skylight, fire-place, grand piano, bar, and puffy leather armchairs. **Rooms:** 355 rms and stes. Executive level. CI 4pm/CO 2pm. Non-

smoking rms avail. Above-average comfort and muted colors and patterns. Large bathrooms. Stunning views from every room. **Amenities:** 🛏 🔥 📺 🍽 A/C, cable TV w/movies, dataport, VCR, voice mail. All units w/terraces, some w/fire-places, some w/whirlpools. Call waiting. **Services:** ✕ 🗝 VP 🚗 📠 🍽 Twice-daily maid svce, car-rental desk, social director, masseur, children's program, babysitting. Full spa services, tennis director, $25 shuttle to Chicago and Milwau-kee airports, safe at desk. Grand Adventure Kids Club entertains kids for a few hours or all day. **Facilities:** 🎣 🚴 ⛷ ⛳36 ⛵ 🎿 🏃 🏊 🌊6 ⛄4 🎾 🛏1500 💻 🚹 3 restaurants, 3 bars (2 w/entertainment), basketball, volleyball, games rm, rac-quetball, spa, sauna, steam rm, whirlpool, day-care ctr, play-ground. 12 runs of downhill skiing with 211-foot vertical drop, private airstrip, grand ballroom, theater company, gift and specialty shops. **Rates:** Peak (May 15–Oct 15) $155–$185 S or D; $195–$750 ste. Extra person $15. Children under age 12 stay free. Lower rates off-season. Parking: Outdoor, free. AE, CB, DC, DISC, MC, V.

RESTAURANTS 🍽

The Red Geranium Restaurant

7194 WI 50E; tel 414/248-3637. **American.** Red geraniums against a crisp, white backdrop brighten the landscaping and decor, while fresh steaks and seafood sizzle on the grill in the open kitchen. Some dining rooms offer quiet garden views, enclosed porches, or a player piano. Fashion and art shows held during Thursday luncheon. **FYI:** Reservations recom-mended. Piano. Dress code. **Open:** Lunch Mon–Sat 11:30am–2:30pm; dinner Mon–Sat 5–10pm. **Prices:** Main courses $14–$26. AE, DISC, MC, V. 🚹

♣ St Moritz

327 Wrigley Dr; tel 414/248-6680. **Continental.** Situated in a huge Victorian structure that is on the National Register of Historic Places. Seating is in one of the gracious rooms featuring a fireplace, or on a veranda with a lake view. Signature dishes include Brie, wild mushrooms, and spinach in puff pastry, served with port wine sauce; salmon Polignac, sautéed with onions, tomatoes, white wine, garlic, and topped with steamed shrimp; and veal piccata ticinese, marinated veal sautéed with sage, prosciutto, artichoke hearts, and wild mushrooms. **FYI:** Reservations recommended. Dress code. **Open:** Tues–Sun 5:30–10pm. **Prices:** Main courses $14–$22. AE, DC, DISC, MC, V. ♥ 🍴 🖼 🚹

Land O'Lakes

Fishing and boating draw many visitors to this tiny village in the heart of Wisconsin dairy country. **Information:** Land O'Lakes Chamber of Commerce, US 45 N, PO Box 599, Land O'Lakes, 54540-0599 (tel 715/547-3432 or toll free 800/236-3432).

RESORT

Sunrise Lodge

5894 W Shore Rd, 54540; tel 715/547-3684 or toll free 800/221-9689; fax 715/547-6110. 26 acres. Easily one of the best places for a family vacation in northern Wisconsin. The resort, which sits on a beautiful lake, plans a plethora of activities and treats guests like visiting family. The lawns and 750 feet of lakeshore property offer a great location for a pickup game of softball or frisbee. **Rooms:** 21 cottages/villas. CI 2pm/CO 11am. Nonsmoking rms avail. **Amenities:** TV, refrig. No A/C or phone. Some units w/terraces, some w/fireplaces. **Services:** Children's program, babysitting. **Facilities:** 1 restaurant, 1 beach (lake shore), basketball, volleyball, games rm, lawn games, playground. Miniature golf. **Rates (AP):** Peak (June 24–Aug) $385–$485 cottage/villa. Children under age 1 stay free. Lower rates off-season. MAP rates avail. Parking: Outdoor, free. Rates are per person per week. Rates for children and extra adults vary—call for details. DISC, MC, V.

Madison

Seat of Dane County. Wisconsin's attractive capital city lies on an isthmus between Mendota and Monona Lakes. The white granite State Capitol dominates the downtown area, and the University of Wisconsin-Madison dominates the cultural and economic life of the city. Half a dozen buildings provide classic examples of Frank Lloyd Wright's Prairie School period. **Information:** Greater Madison Convention & Visitors Bureau, 615 E Washington Ave, Madison, 53703 (tel 608/255-2537).

HOTELS

Best Western Inn on the Park

22 S Carroll St, 53703; tel 608/257-8811 or toll free 800/279-8811; fax 608/257-5995. Great downtown location on Capitol Square—across street from capitol building. Extremely friendly and professional staff. **Rooms:** 213 rms and stes. CI 3pm/CO noon. Nonsmoking rms avail. One-room suites with decorative mirrors and local artwork. Upper floors boast great views of capitol building and Lake Mendota. Rooms available off pool area. **Amenities:** A/C, cable TV, dataport. **Services:** Car-rental desk. **Facilities:** 2 restaurants (see "Restaurants" below), 2 bars (1 w/entertainment), games rm, sauna, whirlpool. Large pool area is pretty enough for weddings, receptions, and luncheons. **Rates (CP):** Peak (June–Aug) $76–$124 S; $84–$132 D; $114–$124 ste. Extra person $8. Children under age 12 stay free. Lower rates off-season. Parking: Indoor/outdoor, free. AE, CB, DC, DISC, MC, V.

Best Western InnTowner

2424 University Ave, 53705; tel 608/233-8778 or toll free 800/258-8321; fax 608/233-1325. Just minutes west of the UW campus, it's tucked away off the busy street and offers great facilities. The UW Badgers prepare here the night before home football games. Near two beautiful fitness trails—Military Ridge trail and Lake Mendota trail. **Rooms:** 179 rms and stes. Executive level. CI 3pm/CO noon. Nonsmoking rms avail. **Amenities:** A/C, satel TV w/movies, dataport. Some units w/whirlpools. **Services:** Car-rental desk. **Facilities:** 1 restaurant (see "Restaurants" below), 1 bar, games rm, whirlpool. **Rates:** $75–$105 S; $85–$115 D; $145–$175 ste. Extra person $10. Children under age 12 stay free. Parking: Outdoor, free. AARP rates avail, plus special rates for football weekends and other school events. AE, DC, DISC, MC, V.

East Towne Suites Hotel

4801 Annamark Dr, 53704; tel 608/244-2020 or toll free 800/950-1919; fax 608/244-3434. Mid-rise, all-suite building in heart of one of Madison's commercial areas, close to shopping and restaurants. Exterior of building is nothing special, but high-ceilinged lobby is surprisingly well appointed and comfortable, with leather couches, fresh flowers, and decorative screens. **Rooms:** 123 stes. CI 2pm/CO noon. Nonsmoking rms avail. Rooms are spacious. **Amenities:** A/C, cable TV w/movies, refrig, dataport. Some units w/terraces, some w/whirlpools. **Services:** Babysitting. Breakfast served buffet-style in dining room. T-shirts, mugs for sale at front desk. Extremely polite and helpful manager and front desk personnel. **Facilities:** Volleyball, lawn games, whirlpool. **Rates (BB):** Peak (Feb–Oct) $49–$71 ste. Extra person $7. Children under age 14 stay free. Lower rates off-season. Parking: Outdoor, free. AE, CB, DC, DISC, MC, V.

Hampton Inn

4820 Hayes Rd, 53704; tel 608/244-9400 or toll free 800/HAMPTON; fax 608/244-9400. Quiet location on a beautiful hilltop, just off a busy highway. **Rooms:** 116 rms. CI 2pm/CO noon. Nonsmoking rms avail. Rooms are quiet and provide nice views. **Amenities:** A/C, cable TV w/movies, dataport. **Services:** **Facilities:** Whirlpool. **Rates (CP):** Peak (June–Aug) $69 S or D. Children under age 18 stay free. Lower rates off-season. Parking: Outdoor, free. Club rates with 12th night free. AE, CB, DC, DISC, MC, V.

Holiday Inn Madison East Towne

4402 E Washington, 53704; tel 608/244-4703 or toll free 800/HOLIDAY; fax 608/244-7829. Exit 135A off I-90/94. Winner of a 1995 Holiday Inn World Inn World Service Award for its outstanding staff. Airy, glass-ceilinged lobby with marble floors has beautiful island plants complete with faux parrots on branches. **Rooms:** 227 rms and stes. CI 4pm/CO noon. Nonsmoking rms avail. **Amenities:** A/C, cable TV w/movies, dataport, voice mail. Some units w/whirlpools. Irons and ironing boards in every room. **Services:** Car-rental desk. **Facilities:** 1 restaurant, 1 bar (w/entertainment), games rm, sauna, whirlpool, washer/dryer. **Rates:** $88–$95 S; $95–$105 D; $99–$108 ste. Extra person $7. Children under age 19 stay free. Parking: Outdoor, free. AE, DC, DISC, MC, V.

≡≡ Ivy Inn Hotel & Restaurant

2355 University Ave, 53705; tel 608/233-9717; fax 608/233-2660. At Highland Ave. Located on University of Wisconsin's campus, this privately owned hotel—owned and operated by the same family for some 40 years—is solidly built and extremely well kept. A small but comfortable lobby has couches and fireplace. Prints line hallway walls. Visiting faculty sometimes stay here, as do other long-term guests. **Rooms:** 57 rms and stes. CI 2pm/CO noon. Nonsmoking rms avail. Three-room suite available. **Amenities:** 🐘 🕹 A/C, cable TV. **Services:** ✕ 🖼 ⊷ 🐦 Babysitting. Efficient, friendly service. **Facilities:** 🏊 ⬜85 🕹 1 restaurant (see "Restaurants" below), 1 bar. Pretty, parlorlike restaurant. **Rates:** $58–$68 S; $65–$73 D; $106–$113 ste. Extra person $7. Children under age 13 stay free. Parking: Outdoor, free. AE, CB, DC, MC, V.

≡≡ Madison Inn

601 Langdon St, 53703; tel 608/257-4391; fax 608/257-2832. 5 blocks NW of Capitol Square. Located right between downtown and UW campus, hotel is popular with seminar attendees and guest lecturers at the school. **Rooms:** 75 rms. CI 2pm/CO noon. Nonsmoking rms avail. **Amenities:** 🐘 🕹 A/C, cable TV. **Services:** 🖼 ⊷ **Facilities:** 🏊 1 restaurant (lunch only), 1 bar. Passes to nearby health club available for $5. **Rates (CP):** $48–$65 S; $53–$70 D. Extra person $5. Children under age 18 stay free. Parking: Indoor/outdoor, free. AE, CB, DC, DISC, MC, V.

≡≡≡ Sheraton Inn and Conference Center

706 John Nolen Dr, 53713; tel 608/251-2300 or toll free 800/325-3535; fax 608/251-1189. Off US 12-18 (Beltline Hwy). Located across from Dane County Expo Center, minutes from state capitol and UW. Modern entrance opens to lobby with large columns and beautiful stairwell. Property was once owned by Leona Helmsley. **Rooms:** 236 rms and stes. Executive level. CI 3pm/CO noon. Nonsmoking rms avail. King- and queen-size rooms available with very fine patterned fabric headboards. **Amenities:** 🐘 🕹 📺 🍴 A/C, satel TV w/movies, dataport, voice mail. Irons and ironing boards in rooms. **Services:** ✕ 🍽 🚗 🖼 ⊷ Car-rental desk, babysitting. Professional staff is helpful and friendly. **Facilities:** 🏊 🏊 🎱 ⬜600 🖥 🕹 2 restaurants, 1 bar, games rm, sauna, whirlpool. Pretty glassed-in pool area and outside sun deck with changing rooms and showers and towel service. **Rates:** $129 S; $139 D; $175–$350 ste. Extra person $10. Children under age 18 stay free. Parking: Outdoor, free. AARP rates avail. AE, CB, DC, DISC, MC, V.

MOTELS

≡≡≡ Budgetel Inn Budgetdome

8102 Excelsior, 53717; tel 608/831-7711 or toll free 800/428-3438; fax 608/831-1942. Old Sank Rd exit of West Beltline Hwy (US 12). From the outside, this place looks like a brand-new office building, but inside it gets warmer. The lobby is built for comfort, with lots of cushy seating, plants, indirect lighting, and a loftlike balcony that extends over the reception desk. An open-air courtyard provides tables and chairs. **Rooms:** 130 rms and stes. CI 2:30pm/CO noon. Nonsmoking rms avail. Pleasant poolside rooms have sliding glass doors that open directly onto pool deck, but they might get noisy, since game room is also located in pool area (but recreational facilities do close at 11pm). **Amenities:** 🐘 🕹 📺 A/C, cable TV w/movies, voice mail. Some units w/whirlpools. **Services:** 🚗 🖼 ⊷ 🐦 Car-rental desk, masseur. Fax and copy services can be provided. One complimentary evening cocktail in the Old Sauk Lounge (except Sun). **Facilities:** 🏋 🏊 🎱 ⬜65 🕹 1 bar, games rm, sauna, whirlpool, washer/dryer. Fitness center has good selection of cardiovascular equipment. Comfortable pool area with wide deck areas and lounge chairs. Game room is extensive, with air hockey machine, pool table, video games. Grill available for outdoor cooking. **Rates (CP):** $55–$75 S; $63–$86 D; $80–$123 ste. Extra person $10. Children under age 18 stay free. Parking: Outdoor, free. Special rates avail, including corporate and AARP rates, Sam's Club discounts, and Road Runner privileges (12th night free). AE, CB, DC, DISC, MC, V.

≡ Budget Host Aloha Inn

3177 E Washington, 53704; tel 608/249-7667 or toll free 800/825-6420; fax 608/249-7669. On US 151, 3 mi S of I-90/94. Don't let the rundown exterior or the lobby discourage you: This is a cozy, comfortable motel good for value-conscious travelers (though why it's called "Aloha" is not clear). The same family has owned and operated the property for over 35 years. **Rooms:** 39 rms and stes. CI 2pm/CO noon. Nonsmoking rms avail. **Amenities:** 🐘 A/C, cable TV w/movies, dataport. **Services:** ⊷ **Facilities:** 🏋 🏊 Sauna, whirlpool. **Rates (CP):** $34 S; $37–$41 D; $36–$64 ste. Extra person $5. Parking: Outdoor, free. AE, DISC, MC, V.

≡≡≡ Comfort Suites Madison

1253 John Q Hammons Dr, 53717; tel 608/836-3033 or toll free 800/221-2222; fax 608/836-0949. Old Sauk Rd exit off West Beltline Hwy (US 12). Fresh, new property with the feel of a resort, with rust-tone walls and hunter green roofs, but the surrounding area is mostly commercial. Lobby decorated like a library—two elevated sitting areas have stuffed bookshelves and fireplaces. Attracts corporate guests during the week, and the getaway crowd on weekends. **Rooms:** 95 stes. CI 3pm/CO noon. Nonsmoking rms avail. All rooms are suites, but not all are alike. Two-story suites are like loft apartments, with sleeping quarters upstairs and living area down. **Amenities:** 🐘 🕹 📺 🍴 A/C, cable TV w/movies, refrig, dataport, voice mail. Some units w/whirlpools. **Services:** 🚗 🖼 ⊷ Car-rental desk, masseur. Overnight guests get one complimentary cocktail Mon–Sat. Enthusiastic and always available personnel. **Facilities:** 🏋 🏊 🎱 ⬜90 🕹 1 bar, games rm, whirlpool, washer/dryer. Complete fitness center offers resistance and cardiovascular equipment. Indoor pool area is huge. **Rates (CP):** $71–$159 ste. Extra person $10. Children under age 18 stay free. Parking: Outdoor, free. AARP, corporate, and special weekday rates avail. AE, CB, DC, DISC, MC, V.

≣≣ Days Inn

4402 E Broadway Service Rd, 53716; tel 608/223-1800 or toll free 800/DAYS-INN; fax 608/223-1800. 1 mi W of I-90; exit 266 off US 12/18. Opened in 1995. Cozy lobby with fireplace and glass block decor. Efficiencies offer exceptional value. **Rooms:** 68 rms, stes, and effic. Executive level. CI 3pm/CO 11am. Nonsmoking rms avail. **Amenities:** 🛁 🖳 A/C, cable TV w/movies. Some units w/whirlpools. **Services:** 🛏️ 🛎️ Travel packages for children. Refundable pet deposit $50. Friendly and helpful staff. **Facilities:** 🎮 🏊 🍴 🏊 50 ⅊ Games rm, whirlpool, washer/dryer. Sun deck in pool area. **Rates (CP):** Peak (May–Sept) $52–$57 S; $56–$65 D; $89–$103 ste; $74–$78 effic. Extra person $5. Children under age 12 stay free. Lower rates off-season. Parking: Outdoor, free. AARP rates avail. AE, CB, DC, DISC, MC, V.

≣≣ Quality Inn South

4916 E Broadway, 53716; tel 608/222-5501 or toll free 800/221-2222; fax 608/222-0859. Situated on a very quiet piece of property, with most rooms connected to the quaint, landscaped courtyard. **Rooms:** 156 rms. CI 2pm/CO noon. Nonsmoking rms avail. **Amenities:** 🛁 🖳 A/C, cable TV w/movies. **Services:** ✕ 🖂 🛏️ 🛎️ Drive-up window for express check-in/out. **Facilities:** 🎮 🏊 400 1 restaurant, 1 bar, games rm, whirlpool, washer/dryer. Surprisingly large pool. **Rates:** $61–$67 S or D. Extra person $5. Children under age 18 stay free. Parking: Outdoor, free. AE, DC, DISC, JCB, MC, V.

UNRATED Red Roof Inn

4830 Hayes Rd, 53704; tel 608/241-1787 or toll free 800/THE-ROOF; fax 608/241-7034. A steep driveway leads up to these two buildings adorned with flowering plants and well-kept bushes and trees. It's a clean place with plenty of parking and not much else—adequate for short-term stay. **Rooms:** 108 rms. CI 2pm/CO noon. Nonsmoking rms avail. **Amenities:** 🛁 A/C, cable TV w/movies. **Services:** 🛏️ 🛎️ Free morning coffee in lobby. **Facilities:** 🏊 ⅊ **Rates:** Peak (June–Aug) $28–$50 S; $35–$68 D. Extra person $6. Children under age 18 stay free. Lower rates off-season. Parking: Outdoor, free. AE, DC, DISC, MC, V.

≣≣ Road Star Inn

6900 Seybold Rd, 53719; tel 608/294-6900 or toll free 800/445-4667; fax 608/274-6900. Located on a hilltop off US 12-14, offering efficiency and quality. Great rates for caliber of rooms. **Rooms:** 95 rms and stes. Executive level. CI 2pm/CO noon. Nonsmoking rms avail. Large one-room suites have king-size bed and pull-out sofa bed in a somewhat confused decor. **Amenities:** 🛁 A/C, cable TV w/movies. One-room suites have microwave and large dinner table. **Services:** 🛏️ 🛎️

Pet deposit of $50. Very helpful and courteous staff. **Facilities:** 🏊 ⅊ Washer/dryer. **Rates (CP):** $36–$51 S; $44–$59 D; $48–$79 ste. Extra person $7. Children under age 15 stay free. Min stay special events. Parking: Outdoor, free. Preferred guests receive 10% discount with 13th night free. AARP rates avail. AE, CB, DC, DISC, MC, V.

RESTAURANTS 🍴

★ Antonio's

1109 S Park St; tel 608/251-1412. **Italian.** Rated Madison's best Italian restaurant by a local magazine for seven years straight. The undistinguished decor is made up for by the healthy-size portions of special Southern Italian cuisine. The house specialty is spiedini, rolls of sirloin stuffed with bread crumbs, tomato sauce, romano cheese, and herbs, and served with linguine. Another good bet is lobster with porcini-mushroom ravioli. **FYI:** Reservations recommended. Children's menu. No smoking. **Open:** Tues–Sat 4–9pm. **Prices:** Main courses $7–$17. AE, MC, V. ⅊

Botticelli's Restaurant & Bar

107 King St; tel 608/257-1110. 2 blocks W of State Capitol building. **Italian.** Elegant and inviting restaurant with rich wood furnishings and windows that admit lots of sun. Dishes include fettuccine conchiglia with scallops in champagne sauce, and shrimp scampi. Breads and pastries are made in house. Friendly service. **FYI:** Reservations recommended. No smoking. **Open:** Sun–Thurs 7am–9pm, Fri–Sat 7am–10pm. **Prices:** Main courses $6–$17. DISC, MC, V.

★ Ella's Deli & Ice Cream Parlor

2902 E Washington Ave; tel 608/241-5291. 3½ mi E of downtown. **Deli/Ice cream.** A fun place for kids, this could double as a museum of toys and children's artifacts. You can't miss the place—there's a brightly colored, flashy carousel out front. Most of the square, hollow tables with glass tops hold toys, games, or model towns that can be activated by the push of a button or with magnets that enable you to guide the displays. Automated toys fly overhead and up the walls. The lengthy deli menu includes hoagies, stuffed potatoes, turkey and gravy, meatloaf, and breakfast plates. A favorite, scrumptious dessert is the hot fudge sundae with grilled poundcake. **FYI:** Reservations not accepted. Children's menu. No liquor license. No smoking. Additional location: 425 State St (tel 257-8611). **Open:** Peak (June–Aug) Sun–Thurs 10am–11pm, Fri–Sat 10am–midnight. **Prices:** Main courses $6–$9. MC, V. 👨‍👩‍👧 ⅊

Francie's Casual Cafe

In Best Western InnTowner, 2424 University Ave; tel 608/233-8778. Just W of UW campus. **American.** Popular with university students, this cafe features a gardenlike setting. Hot items include pot pies, Friday night all-you-can-eat fish fry, and Sunday brunch. **FYI:** Reservations accepted. Children's menu. **Open:** Breakfast Mon–Sat 6:30–11am; lunch

Mon–Sat 11am–2pm; dinner Mon–Sat 5–10pm, Sun 5–9pm; brunch Sun 10am–2pm. **Prices:** Main courses $7–$17. AE, DC, DISC, MC, V. 🖤 ♿

Great Dane Pub & Brewing Co

123 E Doty; tel 608/284-0000. 1 block W of State Capitol building and Capitol Square. **American/Cajun.** Nestled in the heart of downtown, this business district favorite features local microbrews on tap daily. The complete microbrewery is located behind clear glass walls, making for a unique dining experience. Marble-inlay booths with rich mahogany furnishings lend polish. Notable are the North Woods cottage pie, cheese artichoke dip, and homemade sodas. **FYI:** Reservations accepted. Blues/jazz. Children's menu. **Open:** Sun–Thurs 11am–2am, Fri–Sat 11am–2:30am. **Prices:** Main courses $8–$13. AE, DC, MC, V. ♿

Imperial Garden East

4214 E Washington Ave; tel 608/249-0466. On US 151 S; exit 135A off I-90/94. **Chinese.** Enter into this inviting Chinese restaurant and you'll be transported far from Madison. An opulent wooden tiger stands in the lobby and intricate wood carvings and traditional Chinese light fixtures grace the richly decorated dining room and bar. **FYI:** Reservations accepted. **Open:** Peak (June–Aug) lunch Mon–Fri 11:30am–2pm, Sun 11:30am–4pm; dinner Mon–Thurs 4–9:30pm, Fri–Sat 4–10:30pm, Sun 4–9pm. **Prices:** Main courses $6–$23. AE, DISC, MC, V. 👪 ♿

Ivy Inn Restaurant

2355 University Ave; tel 608/233-9717. **American/Vegetarian.** This local lunch favorite has the feel of an extra-large dining room in someone's home. The food is pretty standard, except for the popular vegetarian brunches held every other weekend, for which folks come from miles around to sample fresh vegetables and salads, meatless pastas and casseroles, and a bounty of baked goods. **FYI:** Reservations accepted. **Open:** Breakfast Mon–Sat 7–11am, Sun 7–10am; lunch Mon–Sat 11am–2pm; dinner Mon–Thurs 5–8pm, Fri 5–9pm, Sat 5–8pm; brunch Sun 10am–2pm. **Prices:** Main courses $6–$14. AE, CB, DC, MC, V. ♿

JJ's

In Best Western Inn on the Park, 22 S Carroll St; tel 608/257-8811. Across from the State Capitol building. **American.** Convenient location makes this a frequent stop for everyone from tour groups to business district folks. Pleasant, upbeat atmosphere, polite and helpful waitstaff. Pot roast is a favorite. **FYI:** Reservations accepted. Piano. No smoking. **Open:** Mon–Fri 6am–9pm, Sat–Sun 7am–9pm. **Prices:** Main courses $9–$16. AE, CB, DC, DISC, MC, V. VP

Ⓢ Kabul's Restaurant

541 State St (Downtown); tel 608/256-6322. 4 blocks from Capitol. **Mediterranean.** This small storefront restaurant contains lots of little touches to make dining here comfortable and pleasant: chairs and booths draped with custom-made slipcovers, posters of Middle Eastern wonders and historic moments, Mediterranean music, and very solicitous service. Spicy specialties include koftachalow, Afghan-style meatballs with a sauce of onions, tomatoes, and yellow split peas, and Tunisian spinach stew. Lots of vegetarian fare on the menu, as well as beef, lamb, chicken, and fresh fish. **FYI:** Reservations accepted. No smoking. **Open:** Mon–Thurs 11am–10:30pm, Fri–Sat 11am–11pm, Sun 11am–10pm. **Prices:** Main courses $7–$10. AE, CB, DC, MC, V. 🍰

★ The Mariner's Inn

5339 Lighthouse Bay Dr; tel 608/246-3120. **Seafood/Steak.** Located on the waterfront, this is one of the most popular places in Madison for steak and seafood. The boathouse motif is carried out with the buoys and heavy ropes wrapped around pilings outside, and an interior featuring more elegant touches like shiny brass nautical instruments and antiques. The smoked salmon spread makes a nice opening for lobster (available at market price) and prime cuts of beef. **FYI:** Reservations accepted. No smoking. **Open:** Sun–Thurs 4:30–10:30pm, Fri–Sat 4:30–11pm. **Prices:** Main courses $8–$30. MC, V. 🏔 🖤

Nau-ti-gal

5360 Westport Rd; tel 608/246-3130. **American.** Located on the waterfront (near Cherokee Lake), this casual restaurant is popular for lunch and dinner and is a fun stop for refreshments. The outdoor seating provides views of the marina. Inside, the nautical motif (stuffed fishes, life preservers, etc.) goes well with such playfully named, filling-if-nothing-else menu selections as Shark Bites (marinated shark breaded and deep-fried) and Ragin' Cajun Gator (real alligator). Hamburgers and chicken plates also available. **FYI:** Reservations accepted. Children's menu. **Open:** Peak (June–Aug) Mon–Sat 11:30am–11:30pm, Sun 10am–10pm. **Prices:** Main courses $4–$14. MC, V. 🍰 🏔 ♿

★ Quivey's Grove Stable Grill

6261 Nesbitt Rd; tel 608/273-4900. **Regional American.** The Stable Grill was a working stable when it was built in 1855; today, its hard wood floors and stone walls make a setting for enjoying well-prepared, hearty entrees and sandwiches. Cornish hen is grilled with peppers and served with zucchini fries; boneless trout fillets are baked with dill, green onion, and mustard-butter; and pork ribs come with "smashed" potatoes. The Lady Godiva—coffee ice cream, Godiva Chocolate Liqueur, hot fudge, roasted hazelnuts, and whipped cream—is a hard-to-resist dessert. **FYI:** Reservations not accepted. Children's menu. No smoking. **Open:** Daily 11am–10pm. **Prices:** Main courses $5–$15. MC, V. ▮

★ Quivey's Grove Stone House

6261 Nesbitt Rd; tel 608/273-4900. **Regional American.** Listed in the National Register of Historic Places, this beautiful mansion dating from the mid-1800s is surrounded by a white picket fence, extensive grounds with paths lined with old fashioned gaslights, and outbuildings. Two floors are divided into six dining rooms (with names like Grandmother's

Garden, Valentine Room, and the Nursery) appointed with antiques, quilts, and collectibles and artwork; a small, private dining room for two is at the front of the house. Intent on promoting Wisconsin traditions and history, the restaurant serves many dishes made from regional ingredients. Wisconsin pheasant breast is sautéed with a variety of vegetables and served with pasta, while trout fillets are pan-fried with black walnuts and served with sweet corn relish. After dinner, stroll the grounds or perhaps request a tour of The Tunnel, a more recent addition to the grounds that leads from the Stone House to the Stable Grill. **FYI:** Reservations recommended. Piano. Children's menu. No smoking. **Open:** Tues–Sat 5–9pm. **Prices:** Main courses $15–$24. MC, V. ♥ ▮

★ **Smokey's Club**
3005 University Ave; tel 608/233-2120. Just W of Capitol Square and UW campus. **Seafood/Steak.** Specializing in steaks, seafood, and homemade soups, this award-winning establishment is known as Madison's best steak house. Decor is wonderfully eclectic and richly tacky; walls are covered with souvenirs from around the world. Large bar. **FYI:** Reservations accepted. **Open:** Mon 5–9:45pm, Wed–Fri 5–9:45pm, Sat 4:30–10pm. Closed late July–early Aug. **Prices:** Main courses $5–$18. No CC. ♿

White Horse Inn
202 N Henry; tel 608/255-9933. Across from Madison Civic Center; 2 blocks W of Capitol Square. **Creole/Seafood/Steak.** Located across from the Madison Civic Center, this is the place for elegant dining downtown. The bi-level dining area with decorative fabric curtains, brass banisters, and mahogany woodwork provides an intimate, inviting setting. The diverse menu includes prime rib steak and great salad selections. Over 80 wines from around the world. **FYI:** Reservations recommended. Children's menu. **Open:** Lunch Mon–Fri 11am–2pm; dinner Mon–Fri 5–10pm, Sat 5–11pm, Sun 5–9pm; brunch Sun 9am–2pm. **Prices:** Main courses $12–$22. AE, MC, V. ♿

ATTRACTIONS 🏛

Wisconsin State Capitol
Capitol Square; tel 608/266-0382. Set on the highest point of land on the isthmus, this white-granite structure dominates the local skyline for miles and is flooded with light at night. The dome, which culminates in Daniel Chester French's gilded bronze statue *Wisconsin*, features an observation platform. Guided tours available. On Saturday mornings, the capitol is the site of the Madison Farmers' Market, one of the oldest of its kind in the Midwest. **Open:** Mon–Sat 9am–3pm, Sun 1–3pm. **Free**

State Historical Museum
30 N Carroll; tel 608/264-6555. Located on Capitol Square, this museum features permanent and changing exhibits on many aspects of US and Wisconsin history, ranging from

prehistoric Native American culture to contemporary social issues. Theater. **Open:** Tues–Sat 10am–5pm, Sun noon–5pm. **Free**

Geology Museum at the University of Wisconsin–Madison
1215 W Dayton St; tel 608/262-2399. Many facets of rocks, minerals, and fossils are explored here. Highlights among the vertebrate displays include a 33-foot-long duck-billed dinosaur, a mastodon, a 918-foot-long marine lizard, a saber-toothed cat, and a horselike *mesohippus*. There's also a model of a limestone cave (complete with stalactites and stalagmites, drips, and echoes) and a piece of native copper weighing 1,300 pounds. Guided tours should be arranged at least 10 days in advance. **Open:** Mon–Fri 8:30am–4:30pm, Sat 9am–1pm. **Free**

Elvehjem Museum of Art
800 University Ave; tel 608/263-2246. Located on the U of W campus, this museum's permanent collection includes paintings, sculpture, and decorative arts from 2,300 BC to the present. Asian, Egyptian, Greek, and Roman antiquities are a standout. Changing exhibits; 80,000-volume research library. **Open:** Daily 9am–5pm. **Free**

Madison Art Center
211 State St; tel 608/257-0158. Three floors of galleries display works by artists such as Alexander Calder, Jim Dine, Roy Lichtenstein, and Cindy Sherman. In the past there have been exhibitions of Georgia O'Keeffe, Richard Avedon, and Frank Lloyd Wright. Educational programs and lectures also offered. Group tours available; gallery shop. **Open:** Tues–Thurs 11am–5pm, Fri 11am–9pm, Sat 10am–5pm, Sun 1–5pm. **Free**

Olbrich Botanical Gardens
3330 Atwood Ave; tel 608/246-4550. More than 14 acres of outdoor specialty gardens, including rose, herb, and rock gardens. The Bolz Conservatory—a sunny, 50-foot-high glass pyramid—houses a diverse collection of ferns, palms, and flowering plants in a tropical setting complete with a rushing waterfall, bamboo arbors, wooden bridges, and free-flying birds. Meeting rooms, a horticultural library, and gift shop also on the grounds. **Open:** Conservatory: Mon–Sat 10am–4pm, Sun 10am–5pm. Gardens: Peak (June–Aug) daily 8am–8pm. Reduced hours off-season. **$**

Madison Civic Center
211 State St; tel 608/257-0158. Live music and theater (including top-ranked entertainers and Broadway shows) are presented at this restored movie theater. The Civic Center is also home to the Madison Repertory Theatre, Madison Symphony Orchestra, and CTM Productions. **Open:** Call for schedule. **$$$$**

Capital Brewery Co
7734 Terrace Ave, Middleton; tel 608/836-7100. The home of Garten Brau beer, this microbrewery specializes in German-style lager. Guided tours include a walk through the

brewhouse, fermenting and aging cellars, and kegging area, followed by a beer tasting. Gift shop. **Open:** Mon–Fri 9am–5pm, Sat noon–5pm. **$**

Manitowish Waters

Set in the Northern Highlands–American Legion State Forest amid 14 lakes, this tiny northern town is a popular destination for canoeists and campers. **Information:** Manitowish Waters Chamber of Commerce, US 51 and Airport Rd, PO Box 251, Manitowish Waters, 54545-0251 (tel 715/543-8488).

RESTAURANT 🍴

Little Bohemia Lodge

US 51 S; tel 715/543-8433. **American.** John Dillinger, Baby Face Nelson, and their gang stayed here in 1934, at a time when young FBI director J Edgar Hoover was itching to catch these notorious criminals. When the G-Men moved in, Dillinger got away and the FBI agents shot up the joint. Today, one can dine in rooms with bullet holes still in the walls or with original newspapers bearing headlines like DILLINGER ESCAPES; TWO SLAIN. The vaulted ceilings with wooden beams, walls, and floors are typical of North Woods lodges. There is a large fireplace and a screened-in porch with panoramic views of Little Star Lake. The menu relies heavily on hearty fare: steak, ribs, roast duck. **FYI:** Reservations recommended. Children's menu. Jacket required. **Open:** Peak (May 25–Sept 5) lunch Thurs–Tues 11:30am–2pm; dinner Thurs–Tues 5–10pm. Closed Jan 15–Apr 15. **Prices:** Main courses $9–$21. DISC, MC, V. 🍺 🔥

REFRESHMENT STOP 🍵

Fireplace Inn Supper Club

Corner of County Rd W and Tower Rd; tel 715/543-2464. **French/Greek.** Award-winning Greek recipes and excellent Angus beef steaks have earned this restaurant a far-reaching reputation. Also known for its unique selection of French and Italian gourmet entrees. A snowmobile route leads directly to the Inn. **Open:** Daily 5–10pm. Closed Mar. MC, V.

Manitowoc

See also Two Rivers

Seat of Manitowoc County, in eastern Wisconsin. An excellent harbor has made this an important ship-building center through the years. The Lake Michigan Car Ferry travels daily between Manitowoc and Ludington, MI. **Information:** Manitowoc Visitor & Convention Bureau, 4221 Calumet Ave, PO Box 966, Manitowoc, 54221-0966 (tel 414/683-4388 or toll free 800/627-4896).

HOTEL 🏨

≡≡≡ Inn on Maritime Bay

101 Maritime Dr, PO Box 7000, 54220; tel 414/682-7000 or toll free 800/654-5353; fax 414/682-7013. Manitowoc's only lakefront hotel and restaurant, this mid-rise red brick building is just two blocks from downtown. Lobby features red and blue nautical theme, with rowboat hanging below large skylight. Downhill and cross-country skiing and hiking are minutes away. Charter fishing for coho salmon, lake trout, rainbow trout, and Chinook salmon is also available. **Rooms:** 107 rms. CI 4pm/CO 11am. Nonsmoking rms avail. **Amenities:** 📺 ☕ 🎬 A/C, cable TV w/movies, dataport. **Services:** ✕ 🚗 🖨 🍽 🛎 **Facilities:** 🏠 🏃 🎣 ⛳ ♿ 1 restaurant (see "Restaurants" below), 1 bar, games rm, sauna, whirlpool. Nautilus center, indoor tennis and racquetball courts, swimming pools, running track, and weight rooms available at adjacent YMCA on daily basis. Sailing instructions and sailboat rental available. **Rates:** Peak (June–Oct) $94 S or D. Extra person $10. Children under age 18 stay free. Lower rates off-season. Parking: Outdoor, free. AE, DC, DISC, MC, V.

MOTELS

≡≡ Comfort Inn

2200 S 44th St, 54220; tel 414/683-0220 or toll free 800/221-2222; fax 414/683-0220. Jct I-43/US 151. Creamy white building with green trim, green benches, and green plants. Clean and well maintained; very friendly, helpful staff. Convenient to many nearby restaurants. **Rooms:** 47 rms. CI 2pm/CO 11am. Nonsmoking rms avail. Queen- or king-size beds in all rooms. **Amenities:** 📺 ☕ A/C, cable TV w/movies. **Services:** 🖨 🛎 🐾 **Facilities:** 🏃 🎣 ♿ Games rm, whirlpool. **Rates (CP):** Peak (May 31–early Sept) $49–$59 S or D. Extra person $5. Children under age 18 stay free. Lower rates off-season. Parking: Outdoor, free. AE, DC, DISC, JCB, MC, V.

≡ Super 8 Motel

4004 Calumet Ave, 54220; tel 414/684-7841 or toll free 800/800-8000; fax 414/684-8873. White shingled building with green trim and green shrubs. Just completed full renovation. **Rooms:** 81 rms. CI 1pm/CO 11am. Nonsmoking rms avail. **Amenities:** 📺 A/C, cable TV w/movies. **Services:** 🖨 🛎 **Facilities:** 🏃 🎣 ♿ **Rates (CP):** Peak (Apr–Sept) $40 S; $56 D. Extra person $6. Children under age 12 stay free. Lower rates off-season. Parking: Outdoor, free. AE, DC, DISC, MC, V.

RESTAURANTS 🍴

Ⓢ ★ The Breakwater

In the Inn on Maritime Bay, 101 Maritime Dr; tel 414/682-7000. **American.** Diners are treated to a scenic shoreline view of Lake Michigan, with sailboats and the huge car ferry steaming into the harbor. The decor is cozy: green-striped awning, green walls and carpet, and blond wood. The luncheon menu offers soups, salads, sandwiches, and chicken and seafood entrees. For dinner, you can start with carpaccio, oysters Rockefeller, baked Wisconsin brie, or escargot and move onto any of a variety of seafood and beef, veal, and chicken specialties. Heart Healthy and "lighter fare" selections available. Friday night features a seafood buffet with shrimp, catfish, mussels, crab legs, seafood croquettes, gumbo, and more. **FYI:** Reservations recommended. Children's menu. **Open:** Peak (July–Aug) Mon–Thurs 6am–10pm, Fri 6am–11pm, Sat 7am–11pm, Sun 7am–10pm. **Prices:** Main courses $10–$18. AE, DC, DISC, MC, V. 🍴 🖼 👥 ♿

Luigi's Pizza Palace III

6124 US 151; tel 414/684-4200. **Italian.** Traditional, pan, or stuffed pizzas can be topped with anything from Canadian bacon to hot peppers. Italian pasta dinners; veal, chicken, swordfish, and steak entrees, and hot and cold sandwiches round out the menu. **FYI:** Reservations not accepted. **Open:** Tues–Sat 11am–11pm, Sun 11am–10pm. **Prices:** Main courses $6–$11. MC, V. 👥 ♿

ATTRACTIONS 🏛

Wisconsin Maritime Museum

75 Maritime Dr; tel 414/684-0218. Over 100 years of Great Lakes maritime history and treasures are documented at this $2 million state-of-the-art museum. A re-created Great Lakes port tells the story of Great Lakes shipbuilding and commerce over the last century, with a model ship gallery and video presentations on maritime history. Moored next to the museum is the World War II submarine USS *COBIA*. This National Historic Landmark is also open for tours. **Open:** Peak (Mem Day–Labor Day) daily 9am–6pm. Reduced hours off-season. **$$$**

Pinecrest Historical Village

924 Pine Crest Lane; tel 414/684-5110. This 60-acre complex re-creates a turn-of-the-century rural village, with over 20 authentically restored buildings, gardens, and nature trails. There are also special events and changing gallery exhibits exploring Manitowoc County history. Gift shop. **Open:** Peak (May–Labor Day) daily 9am–4:30pm. Reduced hours off-season. Closed Dec–May. **$$**

Rahr-West Art Museum

610 N 8th St; tel 414/683-4501. The 15 rooms of this late Victorian mansion feature collections of 19th-century American paintings and furniture, Chinese ivory carvings, Boehm porcelains, art glass, prehistoric relics, and antique dolls. One wing holds a permanent collection of contemporary American art. Educational programs and events offered, along with guided group tours. **Open:** Mon–Tues and Thurs–Fri 10am–4pm, Wed 10am–8pm, Sat– Sun 11am–4pm. **Free**

Zunker's Antique Car Museum

3722 MacArthur Dr; tel 414/684-4005. Over 40 antique and special interest cars—ranging from a 1915 Ford Model-T pickup truck to a 1965 Corvair Corsa Convertible—are on display here. **Open:** May–Sept, daily 10am–5pm. **$**

Marinette

Seat of Marinette County, in northeast part of state. This industrial city is located on the south bank of the Menominee River, where it flows into Green Bay. **Information:** Marinette Area Chamber of Commerce, 601 Marinette Ave, PO Box 512, Marinette, 54143-0512 (tel 715/735-6681 or toll free 800/236-6681).

HOTEL 🏨

≡≡≡ Best Western Riverfront Inn

1821 Riverside Ave, 54143; tel 715/732-0111 or toll free 800/338-3305; fax 715/732-0800. On US 41 in uptown Marinette. Great for business travelers. Four floors of rooms and multiple meeting facilities can accommodate large groups. Located at bridge between Marinette and Menominee, MI, so many touring and restaurant options. **Rooms:** 117 rms and stes. CI 3pm/CO noon. Nonsmoking rms avail. **Amenities:** 🛁 ❄ 🖥 A/C, cable TV w/movies. Some units w/whirlpools. **Services:** ✕ 🚗 ⌧ 🛎 **Facilities:** 🏋 🌊 ♿ 1 restaurant, 1 bar, games rm, washer/dryer. Restaurant is said to be an excellent place for fine dining. Bar features Fri night karaoke. **Rates (BB):** Peak (May–Oct) $63–$71 S; $67–$75 D; $104–$107 ste. Extra person $6. Children under age 18 stay free. Lower rates off-season. Parking: Outdoor, free. AE, DC, DISC, MC, V.

MOTEL

≡ Super 8 Motel

1508 Marinette Ave, 54143; tel 715/735-7887 or toll free 800/800-8000; fax 715/735-7455. On WI 41; ½ mi S of WI 64. Clean, comfortable place to stay for a night or two. Hallways redecorated in 1995. **Rooms:** 68 rms. CI 2pm/CO 11am. Nonsmoking rms avail. **Amenities:** 🛁 A/C, cable TV. **Services:** 🛎 🐾 **Facilities:** 🏋 🌊 ♿ Sauna, whirlpool. **Rates (CP):** Peak (Apr–Sept) $38–$42 S; $42–$47 D. Extra person $4. Children under age 12 stay free. Lower rates off-season. Parking: Outdoor, free. AE, DISC, MC, V.

RESTAURANTS 🍴

Memories Restaurant

1378 Main St; tel 715/735-3348. **Diner.** Memorabilia and music from the 1950s and 1960s add to the pink and black decor at this hip little diner. Patrons can sit at the counter and chat with the friendly wait staff. (For fun, see if you can get your coffee in a Howdy Doody mug.) Burgers of all sorts dominate the menu, but the famous big Sunday breakfast is also a winner. **FYI:** Reservations accepted. Children's menu. No liquor license. **Open:** Mon–Sat 6am–7pm, Sun 7am–7pm. **Prices:** Main courses $2–$7. MC, V. ♿

The Rail House Brewing Company

W 1130 Old Peshtigo Rd; tel 715/735-9800. Jct I-41/Old Peshtigo Rd/Cleveland Ave. **Pizza/Pub.** Four main brews and one seasonal brew are on tap at this popular place for pizza or Friday fish fry. One of the offerings, Rail House Red, is a smooth, medium-bodied, malty ale brewed with caramel and chocolate malts. Beer alternatives include home-brewed iced tea and root beer. Brewery tours given Sat at 3pm. **FYI:** Reservations not accepted. **Open:** Mon–Thurs 11am–11pm, Fri–Sat 11am–midnight, Sun 11am–10:30pm. **Prices:** Main courses $3–$9. AE, DC, DISC, MC, V.

Marshfield

Located in central Wisconsin. A dairy center, the city sponsors Dairyfest, 1st weekend June, and Central Wisconsin State Fair, six days ending Labor Day. **Information:** Marshfield Visitors & Promotional Bureau, 700 S Central, PO Box 868, Marshfield, 54449 (tel 715/384-3454).

MOTELS 🏨

≣≣≣ Best Western Marshfield Innkeeper

2700 S Roddis Ave, 54449; tel 715/387-1761 or toll free 800/227-1761. On WI 13. Clean, neat motel at south edge of town, not far from Wildwood Park. **Rooms:** 100 rms. CI 3pm/CO noon. Nonsmoking rms avail. **Amenities:** 🛁 🕃 A/C, cable TV w/movies, dataport. **Services:** ✕ 🚐 🖼 🛏 🛎 Manager on duty 24 hours. **Facilities:** 🔧 🖈 🏊 [250] 1 restaurant, 1 bar, games rm, whirlpool, washer/dryer. **Rates:** $54 S; $58 D. Children under age 12 stay free. Parking: Outdoor, free. Bridal packages avail. AE, CB, DC, DISC, EC, MC, V.

≣≣ Comfort Inn

114 E Upham St, 54449; tel 715/387-8691 or toll free 800/221-2222. At Central Ave. Standard facility. Lobby updated in 1995. **Rooms:** 46 rms and stes. CI 2pm/CO 11am. Nonsmoking rms avail. **Amenities:** 🛁 🕃 A/C, cable TV w/movies, refrig. **Services:** 🛏 **Facilities:** 🔧 🖈 [45] 1 bar, whirlpool. **Rates:** $48 S; $52 D; $65–$70 ste. Extra person $5. Children under age 18 stay free. Parking: Outdoor, free. AARP, corporate, military, and senior supersaver discounts. AE, CB, DISC, MC, V.

≣ Park Motel

1806 Roddis Ave, 54449; tel 715/387-1741. On WI 13 S. Neat, clean, family-owned property. **Rooms:** 20 rms. CI 1pm/CO 11am. Nonsmoking rms avail. All rooms open to parking lot, with lawn chairs in front of each one. **Amenities:** 🛁 A/C, cable TV w/movies. **Services:** 🆅🅿 **Facilities:** 🖈 **Rates:** $34–$46 S; $38–$46 D. Extra person $4. Children under age 12 stay free. Parking: Outdoor, free. AE, DISC, MC, V.

≣ Super 8 Motel

1651 N Central Ave, 54449; tel 715/387-2233 or toll free 800/800-8000; fax 715/384-8366. On WI 97 N. Typical Super 8, close to Marshfield Clinic and St Joseph's Hospital, as well as shopping and restaurants. **Rooms:** 105 rms and stes. CI 3pm/CO 11am. Nonsmoking rms avail. **Amenities:** 🛁 🕃 A/C, cable TV w/movies. **Services:** 🛏 **Facilities:** 🔧 🖈 🏊 ♿ Sauna, whirlpool. **Rates (CP):** $48 S; $52 D; $58–$65 ste. Extra person $5. Children under age 16 stay free. Parking: Outdoor, free. Higher rates for special events. AE, CB, DC, DISC, MC, V.

ATTRACTIONS 🎫

New Visions Gallery at Marshfield Clinic

1000 N Oak Ave; tel 715/387-5562. Nonprofit community organization that promotes public awareness and appreciation of the visual arts. The 1,500-square foot gallery has several permanent exhibits (including posters by Marc Chagall and models of the inventions of Leonardo da Vinci); recent traveling exhibits have featured Australian Aboriginal art, art with agricultural themes, and works from some of the country's best-known watercolorists. **Open:** Mon–Fri 9am–5:30pm, Sat 11am–3pm. **Free**

Foxfire Gardens

M220 Sugarbush Lane; tel 715/387-3050. These unique gardens offer many different settings, from willow-lined walkways, ponds, and waterfalls, to a specially designed firepit, tea house, water lily lagoon, and gazebo. Formal English gardens are perfect for a contemplative mood. Open by special arrangement for group tours. **Open:** May–Sept, Mon–Fri noon–5pm, Sun noon–sunset. **Free**

Wildwood Zoo

Jct WI 13/S Roddis Ave; tel 715/384-4642. A 60-acre zoo that houses a variety of over 200 animals and birds from all over the world. The wildlife trail features buffalo, elk, and white tail deer, as well as sheep and wild timber wolves in their natural habitat. The main zoo area showcases grizzly bears, Japanese snow monkeys, and swans. **Open:** Peak (May–Sept) daily 8am–8pm. Reduced hours off-season. **Free**

Menomonie

Seat of Dunn County, in western Wisconsin. This former lumbering town is located on the Red Cedar River. **Information:** Greater Menomonie Area Chamber of Commerce, 533 N Broadway, PO Box 246, Menomonie, 54751 (tel 715/235-9087).

MOTELS 🏨

≣≣ Best Western Holiday Manor

1815 N Broadway, 54751; tel 715/235-9651 or toll free 800/622-0504. Jct I-94/WI 25. Sofas and chairs in lobby lend themselves to comfortable gatherings. TV in lobby. Everything on one floor. Lobby open 24 hours. **Rooms:** 138 rms and stes. CI 2pm/CO 11am. Nonsmoking rms avail. Tables can be used as desks. **Amenities:** 🛏 🍽 A/C, cable TV w/movies, dataport. Some units w/whirlpools. **Services:** 🛎 🧺 🧺 Babysitting. **Facilities:** 🏋 🏊 100 ♿ 1 bar, games rm, whirlpool, washer/dryer. **Rates (CP):** $41–$46 S; $54–$74 D; $80–$99 ste. Extra person $2–$4. Children under age 12 stay free. Parking: Outdoor, free. AE, CB, DC, DISC, EC, JCB, MC, V.

☰☰ Super 8 Motel

1622 N Broadway, 54751; tel 715/235-8889 or toll free 800/800-8000; fax 715/235-9127. On US 12. On a very heavily traveled street, this motel has a large, bright lobby (that is locked 11:15pm–5:30am). No elevators. **Rooms:** 81 rms. CI 2pm/CO noon. Nonsmoking rms avail. **Amenities:** 🛏 ♿ A/C, cable TV w/movies. **Services:** 🧺 🧺 **Facilities:** 🏋 🏊 20 ♿ Whirlpool, washer/dryer. **Rates (CP):** Peak (May–Sept) $45–$50 S; $55–$65 D. Extra person $5. Children under age 12 stay free. Lower rates off-season. Parking: Outdoor, free. AE, CB, DC, DISC, EC, JCB, MC, V.

ATTRACTIONS 🏛

Hoffman Hills State Recreation Area

921 Brickyard Rd; tel 715/232-2631. A nature reserve area with self-guided nature trail, hiking and ski trails, 60-foot-tall observation tower, and picnicking area. Visitors are free to wander the marshes, ponds, prairies, and coniferous woods. **Open:** Daily 7am–9pm.

Red Cedar State Trail

WI 29; tel 715/232-2631. Nestled in the heart of western Wisconsin, this trail passes through wooded sandstone bluffs, prairies, and wetlands for over 14 miles along the Red Cedar River. Picnicking, biking, hiking, cross-country skiing, and fishing are available all along the route. **Open:** Daily sunrise–sunset.

Pepin Historical Museum

306 3rd St, Pepin; tel 715/442-3161. Located 30 mi SW of Menomonie. Also known as the Laura Ingalls Wilder Museum, it features artifacts from Pepin's history, as well as items relating to the famed author Laura Ingalls Wilder (who was born in Pepin). Gift shop on the grounds. The Laura Ingalls Wilder Memorial Society also runs the "Little House Wayside," a log cabin constructed on the site of Laura's birthplace one mile north of town. **Open:** Mid-May–mid-Oct, daily 10am–5pm. **Free**

Milwaukee

See also Brookfield, Glendale, Waukesha, Wauwatosa

Known by original Native American inhabitants as Millioki ("gathering place by the waters") and colonized by the French in 1822, Wisconsin's largest city is most commonly associated with German-American culture. Local and national beer breweries thrive here, including Pabst and Miller (both of which give tours). Metropolitan center of five counties, Milwaukee has a lively cultural life and celebrates its cultural diversity with many ethnic festivals throughout the summer. **Information:** Greater Milwaukee Convention & Visitors Bureau, 510 W Kilbourn Ave, Milwaukee, 53203 (tel 414/273-3950 or toll free 800/231-0903).

PUBLIC TRANSPORTATION

The Milwaukee County Transit System provides **bus service.** Fare is $1.25 (60¢ for senior citizens and children 6–11), payable with exact change; a weekly pass ($10) can be purchased at any local bank or post office. Call 414/344-6711 for information.

HOTELS 🏨

☰☰☰ Best Western Midway Hotel Airport

5105 S Howell Ave, 53207; tel 414/769-2100 or toll free 800/528-1234; fax 414/769-0064. Exit 318 off I-94. Set back from main thoroughfare away from traffic and noise. **Rooms:** 143 rms and stes. Executive level. CI 3pm/CO noon. Nonsmoking rms avail. Poolside rooms available. **Amenities:** 🛏 ♿ 📺 A/C, satel TV w/movies, refrig, dataport, voice mail. Some units w/whirlpools. **Services:** ✕ 🚐 🧺 🧺 **Facilities:** 🏋 🏊 🏊 🏋 325 ♿ 1 restaurant (*see* "Restaurants" below), 1 bar, games rm, whirlpool, beauty salon, washer/dryer. **Rates:** $63–$77 S; $69–$83 D; $110–$150 ste. Extra person $6. Children under age 12 stay free. Parking: Outdoor, free. AARP, corporate, and government discounts. Weekend and bridal packages. AE, DC, DISC, MC, V.

☰☰☰ The Grand Milwaukee Hotel

4747 S Howell Ave, 53207; tel 414/481-8000 or toll free 800/558-3862; fax 414/481-8065. Exit 318 off I-94. Across major thoroughfare from Mitchell Int'l Field Airport, but set back and landscaped so property is separated from traffic and noise. Close to family restaurants; 10 minutes from downtown; 20 minutes to Wisconsin State Fair Park. **Rooms:** 510 rms and stes. CI 2pm/CO noon. Nonsmoking rms avail. Color and style of rooms differ by wing. **Amenities:** 🛏 ♿ A/C, cable TV w/movies, dataport, voice mail. Some units w/terraces, some w/whirlpools. **Services:** ✕ 🚐 🧺 🧺 Car-rental desk, social director. Turndown service available upon request, as are wine and cheese baskets. Barber and travel agency on premises. **Facilities:** 🏋 🏊 🏊 🏋 8 🏋 1500 ♿ 2 restaurants, 2 bars (1 w/entertainment), games rm, racquetball, spa, sauna, steam rm, whirlpool. Gourmet restaurant, plus indoor and outdoor pools. **Rates:** Peak (Mar–Oct) $85–$150 S or D; $225–$295 ste. Extra person $10. Children under age 16 stay free. Lower rates off-season. Parking: Outdoor, free. AARP, corporate, and government discounts. Special packages include Summer Festivals, State Fair, and Labor Day. AE, DC, DISC, MC, V.

Hampton Inn Northwest

5601 N Lovers Lane Rd, 53225; tel 414/466-8881 or toll free 800/426-7866; fax 414/466-3840. Very impressive, comfortable lobby with nice greeting. **Rooms:** 108 rms. CI 2pm/CO noon. Nonsmoking rms avail. **Amenities:** A/C, satel TV w/movies, dataport. **Services:** **Facilities:** Whirlpool. Access to North Hills Athletic Club $5/day. **Rates (CP):** Peak (May 26–Sept) $59–$89 S; $67–$89 D. Extra person $8. Children under age 18 stay free. Min stay special events. Lower rates off-season. Parking: Outdoor, free. Travelers over 50 years old stay free with other guests. AE, DC, DISC, MC, V.

Hilton Inn Milwaukee River

4700 N Port Washington Rd, 53212; tel 414/962-6040 or toll free 800/445-8667; fax 414/962-6166. Located 10 minutes north of downtown via easy access to freeway. Within ½-mile of bicycle and running path, Lincoln Park golf course, tennis courts, and area shopping mall. **Rooms:** 164 rms and stes. CI 2pm/CO noon. Nonsmoking rms avail. Views of Milwaukee River or parking lot. **Amenities:** A/C, cable TV w/movies, dataport, voice mail. **Services:** Babysitting. **Facilities:** 1 restaurant, 1 bar. Restaurant offers seasonal outdoor riverfront dining. **Rates:** $79–$114 S; $94–$129 D; $190–$370 ste. Extra person $15. Children under age 18 stay free. Parking: Outdoor, free. AARP and government discounts. Off-season Bounce Back weekend rates include continental breakfast. AE, CB, DC, DISC, ER, MC, V.

Hotel Wisconsin

720 N Old World 3rd St, 53203 (Downtown); tel 414/271-4900; fax 414/271-9998. An older hotel (built in 1913) that has not had the advantage of a total restoration. Adjacent to Grand Avenue Mall and skywalk system connecting to convention center, river-walk system. Short walk to theater district and lakefront. Easy freeway access. **Rooms:** 100 rms and stes. CI 1pm/CO 11am. Nonsmoking rms avail. Views of cityscape or neighboring buildings. **Amenities:** A/C, cable TV, refrig. **Services:** Twice-daily maid svce, car-rental desk. Discount tickets sold for area attractions and advance festival tickets. Friendly, accommodating service. **Facilities:** 2 restaurants, 1 bar (w/entertainment), washer/dryer. **Rates:** Peak (May–Sept) $62–$75 S; $66–$75 D; $75 ste. Extra person $8. Children under age 18 stay free. Min stay peak. Lower rates off-season. Parking: Indoor/outdoor, free. Discounts include AARP, military, government, and corporate. AE, CB, DC, DISC, ER, MC, V.

Hyatt Regency

333 W Kilbourn Ave, 53203 (Downtown); tel 414/276-1234 or toll free 800/233-1234; fax 414/276-6338. Award-winning hotel with cosmopolitan atmosphere. Lobby includes 18-floor atrium. Located in heart of downtown, connected to convention center and Grand Avenue Mall by skywalk system. Convenient to Bradley Center and area restaurants. Short drive to lakefront. **Rooms:** 484 rms and stes. CI 3pm/CO noon. Nonsmoking rms avail. Rooms open off lobby atrium; most feature cityscape view. Fresh decor. **Amenities:** A/C, cable TV w/movies, dataport. Some units w/minibars. **Services:** Car-rental desk, social director, babysitting. **Facilities:** 3 restaurants, 3 bars. Revolving restaurant, Polaris, on top floor. Gourmet restaurant and cafe, also post–sports events sundae bar. **Rates:** Peak (May–Oct) $145 S; $170 D; $275–$750 ste. Extra person $25. Children under age 18 stay free. Lower rates off-season. Parking: Indoor, $7.50/day. Discounts include senior, corporate, travel industry, and government upon availability. Special summer festival packages avail. AE, CB, DC, DISC, MC, V.

UNRATED Milwaukee Hilton Downtown

509 W Wisconsin Ave, 53203 (Downtown); tel 414/271-7250 or toll free 800/558-7708; fax 414/271-1039. Built in 1928, it recently underwent a complete restoration to its original grandeur. The elegant lobby has chandeliers and marble floors. Located in the heart of downtown, within walking distance of convention center, Grand Ave, and connecting skywalk system. **Rooms:** 500 rms and stes. Executive level. CI 3pm/CO 11am. Nonsmoking rms avail. Cityscape views. **Amenities:** A/C, cable TV w/movies, dataport, voice mail. **Services:** Car-rental desk, babysitting. Midwest Express Airlines desk on premises. **Facilities:** 2 restaurants (see "Restaurants" below), 2 bars, sauna, beauty salon. Pool surrounded by glass dome and tropical plants, adjoined by sun deck. Locker and dressing rooms in pool area. **Rates:** Peak (May–Oct) $145 S; $165 D; $190–$500 ste. Extra person $20. Children under age 18 stay free. Lower rates off-season. Parking: Indoor, $7.25/day. Discounts include AARP, senior, corporate, government, groups, and Hilton Honors. AE, CB, DC, DISC, MC, V.

Park East Hotel

916 E State St, 53202; tel 414/276-8800 or toll free 800/328-7275; fax 414/765-1919. Located immediately northeast of downtown, within easy walking distance to lakefront and restaurants. Spacious lobby with contemporary furnishings. **Rooms:** 159 rms, stes, and effic. CI 2pm/CO noon. Nonsmoking rms avail. Some rooms have lake view and sofas. **Amenities:** A/C, cable TV w/movies, dataport, VCR. Some units w/minibars, some w/whirlpools. **Services:** Complimentary shuttle to downtown cultural, entertainment, and sporting events. **Facilities:** 1 restaurant, 1 bar, washer/dryer. Passes to nearby health club. **Rates:** Peak (May–Sept) $86 S; $96 D; $100–$210 ste. Extra person $10. Children under age 18 stay free. Min stay wknds. Lower rates off-season. Parking: Outdoor, free. Discounts include corporate, AARP, military, government, and university. AE, DC, DISC, MC, V.

Pfister Hotel

424 E Wisconsin Ave, 53202 (Downtown); tel 414/273-8222 or toll free 800/558-8222; fax 414/273-8222. Built in the

tradition of the "grand hotels," the Pfister, located in the heart of downtown, has housed every president since McKinley and continues to provide guests with the experience of European hotels and service. On the National Historic Register, it recently underwent an extensive restoration for its 100th year. Houses the largest collection of Victorian art of any international hotel; the stunning lobby features a barrel vaulted ceiling three stories high painted with a mural and accented with gold leaf. Tower is 23 floors, Pfister building is 8 floors. **Rooms:** 307 rms and stes. CI 2pm/CO noon. Nonsmoking rms avail. English country decor complements the crown moldings and full marble bathrooms. Cityscape views from Pfister building; city and lake views from tower. **Amenities:** 🛗 ⚲ 🖺 A/C, cable TV w/movies, dataport, voice mail. All units w/minibars, some w/whirlpools. **Services:** ⦿ ⬛ 🆅🅿 🛆 🛁 Twice-daily maid svce, car-rental desk, social director, masseur, babysitting. Award-winning concierge services available to all guests. Historical tours of Victorian artwork collection provided after Sun brunch. **Facilities:** 🎣 🎿 ⛷ 🎱 🔲 ⚲ 3 restaurants (*see* "Restaurants" below), 2 bars (1 w/entertainment), sauna, beauty salon. **Rates:** $189–$209 S; $209–$229 D; $209–$429 ste. Extra person $20. Min stay special events. Parking: Indoor, $8/day. AE, CB, DC, DISC, MC, V.

≣≣≣ Sheraton Mayfair

2303 N Mayfair Rd, 53226; tel 414/257-3400 or toll free 800/325-3535; fax 414/257-0900. Across from Mayfair Mall. Beautiful, large, comfortable hotel located across the street from Mayfair mall. **Rooms:** 108 rms. CI 3pm/CO noon. Nonsmoking rms avail. **Amenities:** 🛗 ⚲ 🖳 A/C, cable TV w/movies, refrig. **Services:** ✕ ⦿ 🚗 🛆 🛁 🛎 Social director, babysitting. Caged pets accommodated on request. Large staff. **Facilities:** 🎣 🔲 ⚲ 1 restaurant, 1 bar (w/entertainment), sauna. Very nice pool. Different dinner buffet five nights/week. Entertainment Fri nights. Access to Highlander Elite health club. **Rates (CP):** Peak (May 26–Sept) $59–$89 S; $67–$89 D. Extra person $8. Children under age 18 stay free. Min stay special events. Lower rates off-season. Parking: Outdoor, free. Bridal package and weekend escape package avail. AE, DC, DISC, MC, V.

MOTELS

≣≣ Exel Inn of Milwaukee South

1201 W College Ave, 53221; tel 414/764-1776 or toll free 800/356-8018; fax 414/762-8009. College Ave exit off I-94. Located 7 miles from downtown, 1¼ miles from Mitchell Int'l Airport, next door to family-style restaurant. City bus stop with direct route to downtown in front of motel. **Rooms:** 110 rms and stes. CI 2pm/CO noon. Nonsmoking rms avail. Fresh decor maintained by renovation every three years. **Amenities:** 🛗 ⚲ A/C, satel TV w/movies, dataport. 1 unit w/whirlpool. **Services:** 🚗 🛆 🛁 🛎 Pets free, but must be attended at all times. Rental car companies will deliver on-site. Very knowledgeable and competent staff. **Facilities:** 🎿

🐾 ⚲ Games rm, washer/dryer. **Rates (CP):** Peak (June–Oct) $38–$48 S; $53–$60 D; $100–$150 ste. Extra person $5. Children under age 18 stay free. Lower rates off-season. Parking: Outdoor, free. Discounts include AARP and Park and Ride Program—stay one night and leave car parked for entire week for $10 (including airport transportation). AE, CB, DC, DISC, MC, V.

≣≣ Golden Key Motel

3600 S 108th St, 53228; tel 414/543-5300. Exit WI 100 S off I-94. Pleasant, treed setting. Large yard space next to play area for children. Located on commercial strip, with many restaurants nearby. Approximately 5 minutes from Wisconsin State Fair, 10 minutes from zoo, 15 minutes from downtown and lakefront. Close to two major shopping malls. **Rooms:** 23 rms. CI 11am/CO 11am. No rooms face roadway. **Amenities:** 🛗 ⚲ A/C, cable TV, refrig. Some units w/terraces. **Services:** 🛆 🛁 Babysitting. **Facilities:** 🎣 🎿 🐾 Playground. **Rates:** Peak (May 15–Sept 15) $35–$50 S; $45–$60 D. Extra person $5. Children under age 10 stay free. Min stay peak. Lower rates off-season. Parking: Outdoor, free. AARP and commercial discounts. AE, MC, V.

≣≣≣ Holiday Inn Airport

6331 S 13th St, 53221; tel 414/764-1500 or toll free 800/465-4329; fax 414/764-6531. College Ave exit off I-94. Pool/Holidome area opens off lobby area—smell of chlorine hits one in the face upon entering. Ideal facility for families, with lots of open common areas in the Holidome. Located approximately 10 minutes from Mitchell Int'l Airport. **Rooms:** 159 rms. CI 2pm/CO 11am. Nonsmoking rms avail. **Amenities:** 🛗 ⚲ A/C, satel TV w/movies, dataport. All units w/terraces. Rooms are either poolside or have patios that open onto outside. **Services:** ✕ 🚗 🛆 🛁 🛎 Car-rental desk. Faxing and copying services available. Pets must be on leash or in cage at all times. Nintendo and Trivia available for extra charge. **Facilities:** 🎣 🎿 🐾 🎱 🔲 ⚲ 1 restaurant, 1 bar, games rm, sauna, washer/dryer. Table tennis, jungle gym in Holidome. **Rates:** Peak (June–Aug) $84–$93 S; $91–$100 D. Extra person $7. Children under age 19 stay free. Lower rates off-season. Parking: Outdoor, free. Discounts include Great Rates, AARP, and Best Breaks (which includes breakfast). AE, CB, DC, DISC, ER, JCB, MC, V.

≣≣≣ Hospitality Inn

4400 S 27th St, 53221; tel 414/282-8800 or toll free 800/825-8466; fax 414/282-7713. Two buildings of different ages, though both interiors show same care. Spacious lobby in newer building features fireplace and sitting area. Located 10 minutes from airport, downtown, lakefront. Close to St Luke's Hospital. **Rooms:** 167 rms and stes. CI 3pm/CO noon. Nonsmoking rms avail. Freshly updated decor. Some special theme suites. **Amenities:** 🛗 A/C, cable TV w/movies, dataport. Some units w/whirlpools. **Services:** ✕ 🚗 🛆 🛁 Car-rental desk. Free shuttle to St Luke's Hospital. Fax and copy service available. Competent, efficient staff. **Facilities:** 🎣 🎿 🐾 🎱 🔲 ⚲ 1 restaurant, games rm, sauna, whirlpool, washer/dryer. Two indoor pools. **Rates (CP):** Peak (June 1–Sept 8) $55–$80 S or D; $125 ste. Extra person $10. Children under age 12 stay free. Min stay peak. Lower rates off-season. Parking: Outdoor, free. Discounts include AARP, corporate, military, and government. AE, CB, DC, DISC, MC, V.

▦▦ Howard Johnson Plaza Hotel

1716 W Layton Ave, 53221; tel 414/282-7000 or toll free 800/446-4656; fax 414/282-7000. Layton Ave exit off I-94. Older property under new ownership. Lobby smelled of smoke. Some freeway noise in building. Restaurant next door caters to families. **Rooms:** 96 rms. CI 3pm/CO noon. Nonsmoking rms avail. Poolside rooms available, as well as rooms with double vanities. Rooms show heavy use. **Amenities:** 🛁 ♨ ☎ ♫ A/C, satel TV, VCR. All units w/terraces. **Services:** ✗ 🚐 ⛱ ⌂ ♨ Children's program. "Oops Program" for forgotten toiletries. Pets allowed upon signature of damage contract. Children's program: play SEGA free and also receive a HOJO FunPack with crayons and activities. Shuttle service on call 24 hours. Very accommodating service. **Facilities:** ⛴ 🏃 ⛱ 🏊65 ♿ 1 restaurant (bkfst and dinner only), 1 bar, games rm, washer/dryer. Delightful pool area. **Rates:** Peak (June–Aug) $49–$70 S; $54–$75 D. Extra person $5. Children under age 12 stay free. Lower rates off-season. Parking: Outdoor, free. Room guarantee: sleep tight or it's free (any valid complaint with notice to corporate office has a full refund). AARP, senior citizen, and medical discounts. Summer festivals special packages include transportation. AE, CB, DC, DISC, MC, V.

▦▦ Manchester Suites Airport

200 W Grange Ave, 53207; tel 414/744-3600 or toll free 800/723-8280; fax 414/744-4188. Airport exit 318. Newer property with a roomy, plush lobby. Located across from airport, though airport noise is not noticeable. **Rooms:** 100 stes. CI 3pm/CO noon. Nonsmoking rms avail. **Amenities:** 🛁 ♨ A/C, cable TV w/movies, refrig, dataport, voice mail. All have microwaves and wet bars. **Services:** 🚐 ⛱ ⌂ Car-rental desk. Service very friendly and extremely helpful. **Facilities:** 🏃 ⛱ 🏊15 ♿ Passes available to local health club. No room for children to run or play. **Rates (BB):** Peak (June–Sept 15) $65–$76 ste. Extra person $8. Children under age 14 stay free. Lower rates off-season. Parking: Outdoor, free. AARP and Corporate Client frequent stayer program discounts. AE, CB, DC, DISC, MC, V.

▦ Motel 6 Airport

5037 S Howell Ave, 53207; tel 414/481-7800; fax 414/482-1089. Exit 318 off I-94. A bare-bones motel good for a cheap sleep. Hallways not carpeted, so can be noisy. **Rooms:** 118 rms. CI noon/CO noon. Nonsmoking rms avail. **Amenities:** 🛁 A/C, cable TV w/movies. **Services:** ⌂ ♨ Free coffee in lobby 7am–noon. Free local phone calls, HBO, and ESPN. Pets must be registered upon check-in. **Facilities:** ⛴ 🏃 ⛱ ♿ **Rates:** Peak (May 18–Oct 31) $29 S; $33 D. Extra person $2. Children under age 17 stay free. Lower rates off-

season. Parking: Outdoor, free. AARP and Motel 6 Welcome Card discounts. No personal checks accepted. AE, DC, DISC, MC, V.

▦▦▦ Quality Inn Airport

5311 S Howell Ave, 53207; tel 414/481-2400 or toll free 800/221-2222; fax 414/481-4471. Attractive southwestern decor in lobby, which faces glassed-in pool area. Recent addition of 45 guest rooms. Located directly across from Mitchell Int'l Airport. **Rooms:** 180 rms and stes. CI 2pm/CO noon. Nonsmoking rms avail. **Amenities:** 🛁 A/C, satel TV w/movies, refrig, voice mail. Some units w/whirlpools. Super Nintendo and pay-per-view in all rooms. **Services:** ✗ 🚐 ⛱ ⌂ Free baggage service. Turndown service available. Sun–Thurs complimentary manager's reception for guests staying at corporate rate. Long-term parking for guests flying out of Mitchell Field $5/day. **Facilities:** ⛴ 🏃 ⛱ 🏊1700 ♿ 1 restaurant, 1 bar, sauna, washer/dryer. Recently redecorated bar and restaurant. **Rates (CP):** Peak (July–Aug) $61–$75 S or D; $79–$149 ste. Extra person $5. Children under age 18 stay free. Lower rates off-season. Parking: Outdoor, free. AARP, corporate, and government discounts. Wintertime weekend packages avail. AE, CB, DC, DISC, MC, V.

▦▦▦ Ramada Inn Convention Center South

6401 S 13th St, 53221; tel 414/764-5300 or toll free 800/228-2828; fax 414/764-5300. College Ave exit off I-94. Large, dated lobby showcases African trophies, including an elephant head over the front desk. Located approximately two miles from airport. Lots of green space outside for children to play. **Rooms:** 190 rms. CI 2pm/CO noon. Nonsmoking rms avail. Newly decorated rooms feature pleasant colors and furniture. **Amenities:** 🛁 ♨ A/C, cable TV. Some units w/terraces. Dataports available. **Services:** ✗ 🚐 ⛱ ⌂ ♨ VCR rentals available. Pets welcome with advance notice. Airport shuttle 6am–10pm on demand. Desk staff not very knowledgeable about property, and therefore not very helpful. **Facilities:** ⛴ 🏃 ⛱ 🏊2000 ♿ 1 restaurant, 1 bar (w/entertainment), sauna, whirlpool. Large indoor pool area with pool table; video games in adjacent area. **Rates:** Peak (June–Aug) $85–$105 S or D. Extra person $10. Children under age 18 stay free. Lower rates off-season. Parking: Outdoor, free. Super Saver, AARP, senior, corporate, and military discounts upon availability. AE, CB, DC, DISC, JCB, MC, V.

▦▦ Super 8 Motel Airport

5253 S Howell Ave, 53207; tel 414/481-8488 or toll free 800/800-8000; fax 414/481-8086. Exit 318 from I-94. Located approximately five minutes from Mitchell Int'l Airport. High ceiling gives spaciousness to cozy lobby. **Rooms:** 116 rms and stes. CI 3pm/CO 11am. Nonsmoking rms avail. Rooms with recliners available, as well as sofas and stuffed chairs. **Amenities:** 🛁 ♨ A/C, cable TV. **Services:** 🚐 ⌂ ♨ Pets allowed with permission. Airport shuttle on demand 24 hours. Service very friendly and accommodating. **Facilities:** 🏃 ⛱ 🏊12 ♿ Whirlpool, washer/dryer. **Rates (CP):** Peak (May 15–Sept 15) $48–$53 S; $56–$61 D; $65–$71 ste.

Extra person $5. Children under age 18 stay free. Lower rates off-season. Parking: Outdoor, free. Senior citizen, AARP, corporate, and government discounts. Packages avail for "Park and Stay"—stay one night, leave car parked for $5 for entire week; includes airport transport. AE, CB, DC, DISC, MC, V.

RESTAURANTS 🍴

African Hut Restaurant & Bar
1107 N Old World 3rd St (Downtown); tel 414/765-1110. **African.** No menu item takes less than three hours' preparation here, but don't worry—the work is almost done by the time you sit down at your table. Handmade bamboo lamps, batik prints, preserved palm trees, and taped music from many countries on the African continent provide a delightful atmosphere. Authentic Nigerian recipes and imported spices are featured, and heavy emphasis is placed on non–red meat dishes and lots of vegetables. Peanut stew Banfi has a raw peanut base cooked with onions, tomatoes, and chicken or vegetables, and Cameroonian-style collard greens show off Chef Adedoicun's skills. Sweet potato pie and mindin mindin are satisfying traditional desserts. **FYI:** Reservations recommended. **Open:** Mon–Thurs 11:30am–10pm, Fri–Sat 11:30am–11pm. **Prices:** Main courses $7–$12. AE, MC, V. &

Antonino's
8412 W Morgan Ave; tel 414/321-6365. **Sicilian.** Having learned the culinary trade in Sicily, Chef Antonino brought his talents to the Milwaukee area in 1980. House specialties include seafood Antonino (scallops, crab, and/or shrimp in Alfredo sauce), chicken Capri served in lemon sauce, and veal Française in egg batter with lemon butter. Breads are baked fresh daily, and homemade desserts include cannoli and cheesecakes. **FYI:** Reservations accepted. Children's menu. Dress code. **Open:** Mon–Thurs 4:30–10pm, Fri–Sat 4:30–11pm, Sun 4–9pm. **Prices:** Main courses $7–$13. AE, DISC, MC, V. ♥ &

★ Beans & Barley
1901 E North Ave (East Side); tel 414/278-7878. **Eclectic/Vegetarian.** After a devastating 1993 fire, this popular eatery reopened in 1994 in a new building with a 20-foot glass wall to let in the sunshine. Mealtimes are busy, so expect to wait unless you grab a stool at the lunch counter. Freshness of ingredients is emphasized, as evidenced by the homemade desserts, soups, dressings, muffins, and cookies on the menu. Beans' signature burritos are chock-full of cheese, tomatoes, onions, avocado, and sour cream. Changing exhibits highlight the work of local artists, and there's an adjacent health food market and deli. **FYI:** Reservations not accepted. Beer and wine only. No smoking. **Open:** Peak (Mem Day–Labor Day) Mon–Thurs 9am–9pm, Fri–Sat 9am–10pm, Sun 9am–8pm. **Prices:** Main courses $7–$10. MC, V. &

★ Benjamin's Deli Restaurant
4156 N Oakland, Shorewood; tel 414/332-7777. Capitol Dr exit off I-94. **Deli/Kosher.** Diners can either sit at tables or grab a seat at the counter at this bustling kosher deli. Homemade soups and carrot cake round out a menu featuring meats and bakery items from local and Chicago purveyors. Corned beef tops the list of favorites, followed by matzo ball soup and hoppel. More substantial offerings include roast chicken, brisket dinner, and fish fry. **FYI:** Reservations not accepted. **Open:** Daily 7am–8pm. **Prices:** Lunch main courses $4–$10. MC, V. ▨

Benson's Steak House
In Milwaukee Hilton, 509 W Wisconsin Ave (Downtown); tel 414/271-7250. **Steak.** Attractive setting in one of Milwaukee's landmark hotels. Wait staff are schooled in enology, so they can assist patrons in making the best wine selection to complement their food. Items topping the menu include beer-and-cheddar soup, mixed grill, and creamed spinach. Soups, dressings, breads, and sauces are all made on premises. Chocolate Suicide cake, loaded with sauce and espresso, is the most popular dessert. **FYI:** Reservations recommended. Children's menu. **Open:** Lunch Mon–Fri 11:30am–2pm; dinner daily 5–10pm. **Prices:** Main courses $16–$30. AE, CB, DC, DISC, MC, V. &

★ Boulevard Inn
In Cudahy Towers Condominiums, 925 E Wells St (Lakefront); tel 414/765-1166. **American/German.** Located in a former hotel built in the 1920s, this quaint eatery specializes in inventive cuisine, tastefully and dramatically presented. Partly boned honey duck is brought to the table, then flamed with curaçao, honey, and butter. There's also swordfish, served over angel-hair pasta with tomato-basil sauce; and marinated sauerbraten served with gingersnap gravy and potatoes. (Vegetarian menu also offered.) All desserts, breads, sauces, and dressings prepared fresh daily. **FYI:** Reservations recommended. Piano. Children's menu. Dress code. No smoking. **Open:** Mon–Thurs 11:30am–9pm, Fri–Sat 11:30am–10pm, Sun 10:30am–2pm. **Prices:** Main courses $16–$40. AE, CB, DC, DISC, MC, V. ♥ VP &

Clock Steak House
720 N Plankinton Ave; tel 414/272-1278. **Continental.** Steaks are definitely the focus here, with methods of preparation including Cajun prime, fillets, and strip cut to any size requested. Surf-and-turf entrees also available, and all main dishes come with homemade bread and sauces. Killer Cake (chocolate cake with crème de cocoa and vanilla ice cream) is a great way to finish a meal. The interior has streetside views with cherry wood furnishings and detailing. **FYI:** Reservations recommended. **Open:** Peak (Sept–May) lunch Mon–Fri 11:30am–2pm; dinner Mon–Fri 5–9pm, Sat 5–11pm. **Prices:** Main courses $15–$21. AE, CB, DC, DISC, MC, V. ♥

Crawdaddy's
6501 W Greenfield, West Allis; tel 414/778-2228. **Cajun/Seafood.** Diners are treated to the earthy, down-home feel of New Orleans at this eatery, where the cooking is a crossover between Cajun fusion and island Creole. There are so many

hot sauces offered here that the proprietors developed a separate hot sauce menu. Diners can treat their tastebuds to spicy jambalaya, Creole ribeye—hand-cut, rubbed, and blackened—and the weekend crawfish and shrimp boil. Nightly specials feature fresh seafood and soups (alligator and turtle) that are anything but mundane. **FYI:** Reservations not accepted. **Open:** Lunch Tues–Fri 11:30am–2pm; dinner Tues–Fri 4:30–10pm, Sat 3:30–10pm. **Prices:** Main courses $5–$15. AE, MC, V.

★ **Dos Bandidos**
5932 N Green Bay Ave; tel 414/228-1911. **Mexican.** Brightly colored Mexican-style tiles and upholstery complement the authentic south-of-the-border menu. Popular items include fajitas (served sizzling at the table) and flautas (meat and onion wrapped in corn tortillas and served with sour cream and guacamole); the chile verde and carne asada provide extra-spicy alternatives. Tortilla chips are made on premises, as are the red and green salsas. **FYI:** Reservations not accepted. Children's menu. **Open:** Mon–Tues 11am–10pm, Wed–Thurs 11am–10:30pm, Fri–Sat 11am–11:30pm, Sun 4–10pm. **Prices:** Main courses $6–$17. AE, DISC, MC, V.

English Room
In Pfister Hotel, 424 E Wisconsin Ave (Downtown); tel 414/273-8222. **New American/Continental.** Original works of 19th-century art, leaded glass, Waterford sconces, and tapestried wall coverings grace this elegant dining room. The menu is changed seasonally to take advantage of the freshest ingredients, but typical creations include garlic-crusted shrimp with Spanish sherry and thyme, grilled Muscovy duck with Riesling and sage jus, and grilled veal chops with cranberry demiglacé. Crème brûlée and Godiva chocolate mousse are two of the temptations from the dessert tray. Complimentary limousine will pick diners up and deliver them home again. **FYI:** Reservations accepted. Guitar. **Open:** Lunch Mon–Fri 11:30am–2pm; dinner Mon–Fri 5:30–10pm, Sat 5:30–11pm, Sun 5–10pm. **Prices:** Main courses $17–$29. AE, CB, DC, DISC, MC, V.

Gil's Cafe
2608 N Downer (East Side); tel 414/964-4455. **Eclectic.** Exposed brick and a hardwood floor and ceiling provide a warm, welcoming atmosphere at this establishment housed in a 1912 building. California-style pizzas include the Provençal and sweet red onion; also, original chicken caesar sandwich. **FYI:** Reservations not accepted. Folk/jazz/gospel music. Beer and wine only. **Open:** Mon–Thurs 8am–11pm, Fri 8am–midnight, Sat 9am–midnight, Sun 9am–10pm. **Prices:** Main courses $6–$9. MC, V.

♥ **Grenadier's**
747 N Broadway (Downtown); tel 414/276-0747. **French.** Crystal chandeliers and pewter service plates set the elegant and formal tone at this award-winning establishment. Diners are presented with a selection of 15 to 20 pieces of fresh seafood and a choice of preparation. (Sea scallops with lamb ragout is a standout.) Organically grown vegetables and herbs, breads baked on the premises, and Chef Knut's 40 years of experience ensure a memorable dining experience. The extensive wine list features a short narrative on each category of wine and its suggested food complements. Limousine service provided free of charge for the downtown area. **FYI:** Reservations recommended. Piano. Jacket required. **Open:** Lunch Mon–Fri 11:30am–2:30pm; dinner Mon–Sat 5:30–10:30pm. **Prices:** Main courses $18. AE, CB, DC, DISC, MC, V.

★ **Heinemann's Restaurant**
In Dr Jennings Plaza, 317 N 76th St; tel 414/258-6800. At Blue Mound Rd. **American.** Great value for the money at this quaint diner with old-time atmosphere. (Senior citizens can take advantage of the many discounted rates here.) Hummus on homemade Welsh rye bread is popular; familiar favorites include meat loaf and chicken primavera. **FYI:** Reservations accepted. Children's menu. No liquor license. No smoking. **Open:** Mon–Sat 7am–8pm, Sun 7am–2:30pm. **Prices:** Main courses $4–$7. MC, V.

Izumi's
2178 N Prospect Ave; tel 414/271-5278. **Japanese.** There is no doubting the absolute freshness of ingredients at an eatery like this authentic sushi bar. Cho Chin paper ceiling lights, Japanese artwork, and a simple color scheme set the tone. Specialties include an extensive offering of sushi, beef or chicken teriyaki, and delicately battered tempura. **FYI:** Reservations accepted. Beer and wine only. **Open:** Lunch Mon–Fri 11:30am–2pm; dinner Mon–Thurs 5–10pm, Fri–Sat 5–10:30pm, Sun 4–9pm. **Prices:** Main courses $9–$22. AE, DC, MC, V.

John Ernst's Restaurant
600 E Ogden Ave (Lower East Side); tel 414/273-1878. **German.** German beer hall ambience pervades the dining room and a huge stone fireplace adds to the *gemutlichkeit* ("welcoming feeling"). Diners most often clamor for sauerbraten with sweet-and-sour gravy, Wiener schnitzel, and schaum torte. Soups, dressings, and desserts are all made on premises. **FYI:** Reservations recommended. Children's menu. **Open:** Tues–Sun 11:30am–10pm. **Prices:** Main courses $13–$43. AE, CB, DC, DISC, MC, V.

★ **Karl Ratzsch's Restaurant**
320 E Mason St (Downtown); tel 414/276-2720. **German.** At its present location since 1929, Ratzsch's has been owned and operated by the same family for three generations. Hearty fare such as Wiener schnitzel with fresh lemon; sauerbraten with gingersnap gravy, red cabbage, and potato dumpling; and roast duck in gravy with wild rice and red cabbage are served amid beer steins and European glass. Hot bacon dressing is a tasty salad complement, and cherry strudel and Viennese chocolate torte are good reasons for diners to loosen their belts a notch or two. **FYI:** Reservations recom-

mended. Piano. Children's menu. Dress code. **Open:** Mon–Fri 4–9:30pm, Sat 4–10:30pm, Sun 4–9pm. **Prices:** Main courses $14–$23. AE, CB, DC, DISC, MC, V. ▪ ▾ VP

★ King and I

823 N 2nd St (Downtown); tel 414/276-4181. **Thai.** The fiery cuisine is complemented by the authentic Thai costumes worn by the wait staff. Fresh fish, chicken, pork, and vegetables form the basis of most entrees, and diners can choose their preferred degree of spiciness (mild, medium, or hot). Favorites here include volcano chicken in garlic sauce, pad thai, and the spicy combination plate (tenderloin steak and shrimp in garlic sauce). **FYI:** Reservations recommended. **Open:** Mon–Fri 11:30am–10pm, Sat 5–11pm, Sun 4–9pm. **Prices:** Main courses $9–$17. AE, DC, DISC, MC, V. &

Lauer's

In Best Western Midway Hotel Airport, 5105 S Howell Ave (Airport); tel 414/769-2100. Exit 318 off I-94. **American.** Located close to several airport motels and hotels and also not far from the Skyway Cinema. A fireplace, plants, and lots of windows make for a peaceful meal—whether it's the Fri night fish fry, Sat night all-you-can-eat prime rib, or shrimp, beef, or chicken stir-fries. Senior citizen discounts available. **FYI:** Reservations accepted. Children's menu. **Open:** Breakfast Mon–Fri 6:30–11am, Sat–Sun 7–11am; lunch Mon–Fri 11am–1:30pm, Sat 11am–1pm; dinner Mon–Thurs 5–9:30pm, Fri–Sat 5–10pm. **Prices:** Main courses $10–$17. AE, CB, DC, DISC, MC, V. ▦ &

★ Mader's German Restaurant

1037 N Old World 3rd St; tel 414/271-3377. **German.** In its current location since 1902, Mader's has been owned and operated by four generations of the Mader family. Leaded glass and hardwood floors grace the four dining rooms. Bavarian-style sauerbraten is marinated for 10 days, then served with gingersnap sauce and dumplings. Other favorites include pork shank seasoned with caraway seeds and sautéed Wiener schnitzel served with noodles. All desserts (including linzer torte and Black Forest cake) are made on the premises. Over 210 beers are featured (including German, English, Irish, French, and Polish imports), with nine on tap. Adjacent gift shop/art gallery features German imports. **FYI:** Reservations recommended. Children's menu. **Open:** Mon 11:30am–9pm, Tues–Thurs 11:30am–10pm, Fri–Sat 11:30am–11:30pm, Sun 10:30am–9pm. **Prices:** Main courses $14–$22. AE, CB, DC, DISC, MC, V. ▪ ▾ VP &

❦ Mike & Anna's

2000 S 8th St; tel 414/643-0072. **Eclectic.** The chic decor here is a real surprise in this modest neighborhood. The classy interior features stunning gladiola table centerpieces and a granite and marble bar accented with black and rose decor, dramatic lighting, and ethereal "cloud trees." (Even the bathrooms are stunning!) The menu, which changes daily, might have rack of lamb, fresh seafood, or steer tenderloin. Veteran waitstaff promises impeccable service. **FYI:** Reserva-

tions recommended. Dress code. **Open:** Sun–Thurs 5:30–9pm, Fri–Sat 5:30–10pm. **Prices:** Main courses $18–$25. AE, MC, V. &

O'Donoghue's

5108 W Bluemound Rd (Stadium); tel 414/774-9100. **Irish.** The Waterford crystal in the bar is the perfect backdrop for this restaurant, whose owner was born and raised in Killarney, Ireland. Menu changes seasonally, although daily specials usually include a plate of traditional corned beef and cabbage. Prime rib sandwich is a popular menu item, as are Friday fish fry and prime-cut steaks. **FYI:** Reservations accepted. Jazz. **Open:** Lunch Mon–Fri 11am–2:30pm; dinner Tues–Sun 5–9pm. **Prices:** Main courses $6–$19. AE, DC, MC, V. ▦ &

★ Old Towne Serbian Gourmet House

522 W Lincoln Ave; tel 414/672-0206. **Serbian.** At this family-owned and -operated establishment, diners can start their meal with a roasted red bell pepper salad, followed by one of the many entrees featuring freshly cut meats: goulash (beef simmered in its own juice with paprika and dumplings), chicken paprikash (simmered with vegetables and paprika), or roast suckling lamb (covered and baked with green peppers, tomatoes, leeks, and rosemary). **FYI:** Reservations recommended. Dress code. **Open:** Lunch Tues–Sun 11:30am–2:30pm; dinner Tues–Sun 5–11pm. **Prices:** Main courses $5–$16. AE, CB, DC, DISC, MC, V. &

Osteria Del Mondo

In Knickerbocker Hotel, 1028 E Juneau Ave; tel 414/291-3770. **Italian.** Diners may eat alfresco, or amid the blond wood floors, alabaster light fixtures, and arched columns of the dining room. The menu changes seasonally, but highlights include *dentice con funghi* (sautéed red snapper on a bed of shiitake mushrooms with roasted-garlic and parsley broth); grilled halibut with sautéed asparagus and red-wine sauce; and *vitello saltimbocca* (veal wrapped with prosciutto and sage, and sautéed in white-wine sauce). Fresh seafood is served daily and all pastas are made on the premises. High-quality Italian wines of the finest vintage complement the entrees. **FYI:** Reservations recommended. Children's menu. Dress code. No smoking. **Open:** Lunch Mon–Fri 11:30am–2:30pm; dinner Mon–Thurs 5–10:30pm, Fri–Sat 5–11pm. Closed Jan 1–7. **Prices:** Main courses $12–$21; prix fixe $35–$55. AE, MC, V. ● VP &

Safe House

779 N Front St (Downtown); tel 414/271-2007. **American.** Diners must find their way past a "front" (International Exports Ltd) to get to the interior of this unique espionage-themed restaurant and bar. Established in the 1960s during the James Bond craze, the Safe House has succeeded in outlasting typical theme bars by continuing to incorporate new gimmicks and entertainment for diners' enjoyment. Specialties of the kitchen include slow-cooked barbecued ribs served in a spicy house sauce, homemade soups (Wisconsin

cheese, cream of turkey with wild rice), and Bond's Bomb—mint chocolate chip ice cream dipped in chocolate, and served with a "fuse." If that's not enough, try one of the house drinks bearing spy-inspired names while figuring out the nightly magician's tricks. **FYI:** Reservations accepted. Magician. **Open:** Lunch Mon–Sat 11:30am–2:30pm; dinner Mon–Thurs 5–9pm, Fri–Sat 5–10pm, Sun 4–8pm. **Prices:** Main courses $11–$17. AE, MC, V.

♣ Sanford

1547 N Jackson; tel 414/276-9608. **New American.** Elegant, intimate award-winning restaurant located in a former grocery store. Chef Sanford, a graduate of the Culinary Institute of America, specializes in contemporary American food with various ethnic influences. Signature dishes include cumin wafer appetizers, elk loin with sweet-potato gnocchi and black currant sauce, and snapper with crab hash. Eighteen desserts are made to order each night. Maximum of eight per party. **FYI:** Reservations recommended. Dress code. Beer and wine only. No smoking. **Open:** Mon–Thurs 5:30–9pm, Fri–Sat 5:30–10pm. **Prices:** Main courses $27–$30. AE, CB, DC, DISC, MC, V.

★ Saz's Steak House

5539 W State St (Miller Valley); tel 414/453-2410. **American.** Visiting professional sports teams often find their way here after games and events—possibly because of the mozzarella marinara (served in won ton skins instead of breading). The barbecue sauce used on Saz's award-winning ribs and rib sandwich is so popular that it is bottled and marketed outside the restaurant. Appetizers, sandwiches, and entrees are named after celebrities. Late night menu offered from 9pm to midnight. **FYI:** Reservations not accepted. Country music/karaoke/rock. Children's menu. **Open:** Mon–Thurs 11am–9pm, Fri–Sat 11am–11pm, Sun 10:30am–9pm. **Prices:** Main courses $7–$15. AE, MC, V.

★ Three Brothers

2414 S St Clair St (Bay View); tel 414/481-7530. **Serbian.** Old-world charm—in the form of wood ceilings and Serbian artwork—pervades this family-owned and -operated establishment. Serbian salad (tomatoes, onions, and green pepper, topped with Serbian cheese and dressing) is a refreshing appetizer. Also popular are the *bureks:* phyllo dough filled with choice of beef and cheese or spinach and cheese. The lamb entree is slow roasted with vegetables and served au jus. If you have room, be sure to try the *palacinka* (Serbian crepes filled with preserves) or one of the homemade strudels or tortes. Serbian beer available. **FYI:** Reservations recommended. **Open:** Tues–Thurs 5–10pm, Fri–Sat 4–11pm, Sun 4–10pm. **Prices:** Main courses $11–$15. No CC.

♣ Weissgerber's Third Street Pier

1110 N Old World 3rd St; tel 414/272-0330. **Seafood/Steak.** The award-winning wine list and picturesque riverfront views are two of the reasons that visiting celebrities dine at this classy eatery. Caribbean-style bouillabaisse with spicy tomato base makes a great starter for entrees such as Dover sole served with honey butter and pistachio sauce and prime rib prepared with garlic-herb rub. Desserts worth saving room for include Chocolate Decadence with raspberry sauce, and honey-almond crumble. **FYI:** Reservations recommended. Piano. Dress code. **Open:** Lunch Mon–Fri 11:30am–2pm; dinner Mon–Sat 5–10pm, Sun 4–9pm. **Prices:** Main courses $11–$25. AE, DISC, MC, V.

Yen Ching

7630 W Good Hope Rd; tel 414/353-6677. At N 76th St. **Chinese.** Quiet and beautifully furnished, good for romantic dining. The large selection of ornately presented Mandarin dishes is matched by a great variety of wines. **FYI:** Reservations recommended. **Open:** Lunch Mon–Fri 11:30am–2pm, Sun 11:30am–2:30pm; dinner Mon–Thurs 4:30–9:30pm, Fri–Sat 4:30–10pm, Sun 4:30–9pm. **Prices:** Main courses $7–$10. AE, CB, DC, DISC, ER, MC, V.

ATTRACTIONS

MUSEUMS

Discovery World Museum of Science, Economics, and Technology

712 W Wells St; tel 414/765-0777. An interactive museum with exhibits emphasizing science, economics, and technology. Hour-long laser show explains light waves and laser phenomenon; high voltage electrical displays illuminate principles of electricity; the "Health is Wealth" display provides information on nutrition, fitness, the cardiopulmonary system, and the senses. In other exhibits, you can test your business skills managing a robot store or selling lemonade; bend a tornado with your own breath; blend colors using your shadow; and feel the force of a giant gyroscope. Assistants are on hand to help, explain, and demonstrate. Live theater shows and workshops also offered. **Open:** Mon–Sat 9am–5pm, Sun 11am–5pm. $$

Milwaukee Public Museum

800 W Wells St; tel 414/278-2700. One of the country's largest natural history museums, housing more than 4½ million specimens. Besides important zoological and geological exhibits (a life-size reconstruction of a *Tyrannosaurus rex* is one of the highlights), there are replicas of old Milwaukee, a European village, a Costa Rican rain forest, a Hopi pueblo, a New Delhi bazaar, and a Mexican Street scene. The "Wizard Wing" will appeal to budding scientists. Workshops and lectures offered. Gift shop. **Open:** Daily 9am–5pm. $$$

Milwaukee Art Museum

750 N Lincoln Memorial Dr; tel 414/224-3200. Located downtown on the lakefront, the collection comprises more than 20,000 pieces, with an emphasis on contemporary European and American works. The permanent collection includes works from Picasso, Warhol, O'Keeffe, Homer, Degas, Monet, Miró, and Rodin, among others. Also features one of the world's premier collections of Haitian art; and The

Frank Lloyd Wright School Collection of decorative art and design. Gift shop. **Open:** Tues–Wed 10am–5pm, Thurs noon–9pm, Fri–Sat 10am–5pm, Sun noon–5pm. **$$**

Charles Allis Art Museum

1801 N Prospect Ave; tel 414/278-8295. The extensive collection of the late "king of farm machinery" Charles Allis, housed in a beautiful 1909 Tudor-style mansion. Strong points include Asian art (from China, Korea, Japan, and Persia) and French and contemporary American paintings. **Open:** Wed 1–9pm, Thurs–Sun 1–5pm. **$**

Betty Brinn Children's Museum

929 E Wisconsin Ave (O'Donnell Park); tel 414/390-5437. Interactive exhibits and programs offer a variety of hands-on activities. Young children are given the opportunity to crawl through an oversized ear (to learn how we hear) and to explore musical instruments from around the world via a special computer program. **Open:** Tues–Sat 9am–5pm. **$**

HISTORIC BUILDINGS

Pabst Mansion

2000 W Wisconsin Ave; tel 414/931-0808. Completed in 1893, the home of Pabst brewery founder Captain Frederick Pabst is a tribute to opulence. The Flemish Renaissance–style building contains 37 rooms, 12 baths, and 14 fireplaces. The scrupulously restored interior is graced with handsome, carved wooden cabinets, ornamental iron work, and carved panels imported from a 17th-century Bavarian castle. Guided tours available. **Open:** Mon–Sat 10am–3:30pm, Sun noon–3:30pm. **$$$**

Villa Terrace

2220 N Terrace Ave; tel 414/271-3656. Charming Italian Renaissance–style villa designed in 1923 by architect David Adler, with terraces and gardens overlooking Lake Michigan. Furnishings include sculpture, 18th-century furniture, Shaker handicrafts, and antique porcelain. **Open:** Wed–Sun noon–5pm. **$**

St Joan of Arc Chapel

14th St and Wisconsin Ave; tel 414/288-6873. A remarkable example of Gothic architecture, this authentic 15th-century French chapel was transported and re-erected in 1965—stone by stone—on the campus of Marquette University. According to legend, Joan of Arc prayed here before going to the stake. **Open:** Daily 10am–4pm. **Free**

PARKS & GARDENS

Boerner Botanical Gardens

5879 S 92nd St, Hales Corner; tel 414/425-1130. Formal and informal gardens surrounded by an arboretum. Elegant rose gardens contain over 4,000 rose plants with 450 different varieties. The Plant Doctor Program provides advice on gardening problems and is offered from May through October. Outdoor concerts in the gardens, walking tours, and lectures offered. **Open:** Gardens: Apr–Oct, daily 8am–sunset. Garden House: year-round 8am–4pm. **Free**

Mitchell Park Conservatory (The Domes)

524 S Layton Blvd; tel 414/649-8126. Thoroughly unique horticultural structures, The Domes lets visitors experience tropical, arid, and seasonal displays in three glass domes which are each seven stories high. The Show Dome houses five floral shows each year. Picnic area, gift shop. **Open:** Daily 9am–5pm. **$**

Milwaukee County Zoological Park

10001 W Blue Mound Rd; tel 414/771-3040. This world-renowned zoo is known for its wide variety of animals, many of which are on the endangered species list. It offers a one-hour guided tour on the Zoomobile and a sea lion show. Two miles of cross-country ski trails. Picnic area, gift shops. **Open:** Peak (May–Labor Day) Mon–Sat 9am–5pm, Sun and hols 9am–6pm. Reduced hours off-season. **$$**

Schlitz Audubon Center

1111 E Brown Deer Rd, Bayside; tel 414/352-2880. Fox, deer, and other wild animals roam through this 185-acre wooded park. Visitors center offers guided tours through some of the park's many terrains: prairies, forest, ponds, and Lake Michigan's shore. Seasonal activities include an art fair, cross-country skiing, and maple sugaring. Bookstore on the grounds. **Open:** Tues–Sun 9am–5pm. **$**

BREWERIES

Miller Brewing Company

4251 W State St; tel 414/931-2337. Miller—the second-largest brewery in the world—offers free hour-long guided tours of its main plant as well as a free beer tasting. The Caves Museum is housed in a restored portion of the original Plank-Road Brewery that was used for storing beer, and displays a collection of authentic brewing implements from the last century. **Open:** Peak (May–Sept) Mon–Sat 10am–3:30pm. Reduced hours off-season. **Free**

Pabst Brewing Company

915 W Juneau Ave; tel 414/223-3709. Established in 1844, Pabst was the first of the great Milwaukee brewers. Free tours include viewing of the Brew House, with its copper brew kettles dating from the 1890s; the Packaging Center; and the ultramodern Shipping Center. Half-hour guided tours given daily April–November. Gift shop. **Open:** Call for schedule. **Free**

Sprecher Brewing Company

701 W Glendale Ave, Glendale; tel 414/964-2739. Microbrewery located in a former elevator car factory. Guided tours introduce visitors to the traditional seven step brewing process. Some of the products available for sampling are a German style amber beer, a wheat flavored Weiss, and a Bavarian style lager, as well as root beer and cream sodas. **Open:** Office: Mon–Fri 9am–5pm. Retail: Mon–Fri 11am–6pm, Sat 11am–4pm. **$**

OTHER ATTRACTIONS

Harley-Davidson Transmission and Engine Plant

11700 W Capitol Dr; tel 414/535-3666. Fans of the classic American motorcycles can see the production of Harley-Davidson transmissions and engines from start to finish. **Open:** Mon–Fri 9am–12:30pm. **Free**

Milwaukee Repertory Theater

108 E Wells; tel 414/224-1761. Presents traditional and contemporary theater in a new performing-arts complex with three adjacent auditoriums: the Mainstage Theater, the Stienke Theater, and the Stackner Cabaret. **Open:** Sept–May, call for schedule. **$$$$**

Performing Arts Center

929 N Water St; tel 414/273-ARTS or 273-7206 (box office). This group of ultramodern buildings is home to the Milwaukee Symphony Orchestra, under principal conductor Zdenek Macal (Sept–June); the Pennsylvania-Milwaukee Ballet (Sept–May): the First Stage Milwaukee Theater (a children's theater): and the Florentine Opera Company and Bel Canto Chorus, under music director Richard Hinson (Nov–May). **Open:** Call for schedule. **$$$$**

Potawatomi Bingo Casino

1721 W Canal St; tel toll free 800/PAYS-BIG. Bingo casino which includes 200 Las Vegas–style slot and poker machines. Full-service restaurant. **Open:** Daily 8am–3pm.

Mineral Point

Located southwest of Madison, near several state forests. Cornishmen from England came in the 1830s to mine lead. The mines were in sight of the homes, and wives called men to meals by shaking rags. Thus the town was called "Shake Rag." Shake Rag Under the Hill is a restored craft community, with traditional marketplace. Six restored log and limestone homes of Cornish miners comprise Pendarvis, Cornish Restoration. **Information:** Mineral Point Chamber of Commerce, PO Box 78, Mineral Point, 53565 (tel 608/987-3201).

MOTEL 🏨

UNRATED Redwood Motel

US 151, 53565; tel 608/987-2317 or toll free 800/321-1958; fax 608/987-2317. Somewhat run down, but inexpensive and accommodating. Located next door to its restaurant of the same name. **Rooms:** 28 rms. CI 2pm/CO 11am. Nonsmoking rms avail. **Amenities:** 🛏 🅟 A/C, cable TV. **Services:** 🍴 **Facilities:** 🔥 🅖 1 restaurant (bkfst and lunch only). **Rates:** Peak (May–Oct) $33–$48 S; $44–$48 D. Extra person $5. Lower rates off-season. Parking: Outdoor, free. DISC, MC, V.

Minocqua

A popular four-season resort area, this "Island City" is surrounded by Lake Minocqua. The area's 2,000 lakes contain every major freshwater fish found in Wisconsin. There's clear water diving in summer, and groomed cross-country and snowmobile trails in winter. Minocqua Winter Park Nordic Center is southwest. **Information:** Minocqua-Arbor Vitae-Woodruff Area Chamber of Commerce, US 51 and Front St, PO Box 1006, Minocqua, 54548 (tel 715/356-5266).

MOTELS 🏨

🏅🏅 Best Western Lakeview Motor Lodge

US 51 N, PO Box 575, 54548; tel 715/356-5208 or toll free 800/852-1021; fax 715/356-1412. Popular because it's located on Minocqua Lake and on main tourist strip. Great restaurants across the street and down a block or two. **Rooms:** 41 rms. CI 1pm/CO 11am. Nonsmoking rms avail. Many rooms have view of lake. **Amenities:** 🛏 🅟 A/C, cable TV. Some units w/terraces, some w/whirlpools. **Services:** 🍴 🛎 Guests can enjoy breakfast either in front of large stone fireplace or in lounge chair by hotel's private dock. **Facilities:** 🅰 1 beach (lake shore), playground. **Rates (CP):** Peak (June 26–Sept 6) $67–$93 S; $82–$99 D. Extra person $6. Children under age 12 stay free. Min stay wknds. Lower rates off-season. Parking: Outdoor, free. Business traveler's rate avail Mon–Thurs. AE, CB, DC, DISC, MC, V.

🏅🏅 Comfort Inn

8729 US 51 N, 54548; tel 715/358-2588 or toll free 800/876-8422. At WI 70 W. Located at intersection of two major highways, it attracts vacationing families. **Rooms:** 51 rms and stes. CI 3pm/CO 11am. Nonsmoking rms avail. **Amenities:** 🛏 A/C, cable TV w/movies. Some units w/whirlpools. **Services:** 🍴 🛎 **Facilities:** 🔥 🅰 📺 🅖 Games rm, whirlpool. **Rates (CP):** Peak (June 15–Sept 4) $67–$85 S; $73–$91 D; $100 ste. Extra person $6. Children under age 17 stay free. Min stay peak and wknds. Lower rates off-season. Parking: Outdoor, free. AE, DC, DISC, JCB, MC, V.

🏅🏅 New Concord Inn of Minocqua

320 Front St, 54548; tel 715/356-1800 or toll free 800/356-8888; fax 715/356-6955. Relatively new to Minocqua, motel is conveniently located near many shops and restaurants and across from a park with playground equipment and tennis courts. **Rooms:** 53 rms and stes. CI 3pm/CO 11am. Nonsmoking rms avail. Many rooms have great view of lake. **Amenities:** 🛏 🅟 A/C, cable TV. Some units w/whirlpools. **Services:** 🍴 **Facilities:** 🔥 🅰 📺 🅖 1 bar, games rm, whirlpool. Boat slips available. **Rates (CP):** Peak (Jan–Mar/June–Oct) $83–$115 S or D; $102–$124 ste. Extra person $7. Children under age 12 stay free. Min stay peak and wknds. Lower rates off-season. During fall and winter weekdays, rooms are $50. Group rates avail. AE, CB, DC, DISC, MC, V.

⬢ Super 8 Motel

Jct US 51 N/WI 70 W, PO Box 325, 54548-0325; tel 715/ 356-9541 or toll free 800/800-8000; fax 715/358-2152. One-story motel right off two major highways, but noise isn't too bad. **Rooms:** 34 rms and stes. CI 2pm/CO noon. Nonsmoking rms avail. Clean and comfortable rooms recently redecorated and recarpeted. **Amenities:** � 📞 A/C, cable TV. 1 unit w/fireplace. **Services:** 🛎 🐾 Motel staff frequently rents snowmobiles and jet skis from dealer in town for guests. **Facilities:** 🏃 🕹 **Rates (CP):** Peak (May 28–Oct) $43–$50 S; $58 D; $50–$65 ste. Extra person $4. Children under age 12 stay free. Min stay wknds. Lower rates off-season. Parking: Outdoor, free. AE, DC, DISC, MC, V.

RESTAURANTS 🍴

⑤ Bosacki's Boat House

305 Oneida St; tel 715/356-5292. **American.** Great-grandfather Bosacki founded this family-oriented restaurant and marina before the bridge was built; today it's a very popular ice cream and sweet shop, restaurant, bar, and boat rental center. Its location on Minocqua Lake enables boaters to arrive by water for lunch on the porch. The huge bar is decorated with a mantle from 1903; the dining room has vaulted ceilings typical of the region, with wooden beams running across the top. Friday fish fry. **FYI:** Reservations recommended. Children's menu. **Open:** Daily 11am–midnight. **Prices:** Main courses $3–$16. AE, CB, DC, DISC, MC, V. 👥

Little Swiss Village

7650 Blue Lake Rd; tel 715/356-3675. **American.** Although it may be difficult to find in the woods of Minocqua, this curious Swiss village is well worth the trouble. Set amidst hundreds of pines beside beautiful Blue Lake and surrounded by flower beds, this locale features excellent, reasonably priced food in addition to unusual wildlife "theater." While the huge cowbells and the Swiss music are enchanting, the real draw is the chipmunks outside the windows. The waitstaff, dressed in traditional Swiss costume, feeds them over 800 pounds of peanuts every summer! Food for paying customers includes waffles, crepes, and pancakes, plus sandwiches made with fresh-baked German rye bread. Gift shops, numerous family photo opportunities. **FYI:** Reservations accepted. No liquor license. No smoking. **Open:** Daily 8am–3pm. Closed Oct 10–May 15. **Prices:** Lunch main courses $3–$8. DISC, MC, V. ▮ 👥

♣ Norwood Pines Supper Club

10171 WI 70W; tel 715/358-2702. **American.** Hidden down a long, winding drive is a quaint and homey supper club with rolling lawns and a lively bar. Built in the 1920s, this stone-and-log lodge features a small, intimate, original dining room; structural additions are a second dining room with views of Lake Patricia and a screened-in porch often used for parties. Chef Pam Stevens is always creating new recipes for nightly seafood specials; excellent steaks and pastas are

served as well. Ideal atmosphere for couples or for get-togethers with friends. **FYI:** Reservations accepted. Children's menu. No smoking. **Open:** Mon–Sat 5–10pm. **Prices:** Main courses $7–$25. CB, DC, MC, V.

⑤ Paul Bunyan's Logging Camp Cook Shanty

8653 US 51 N; tel 715/356-6270. **American.** You can't miss the huge statue of the famous North Woods logger and his blue ox, Babe. Inside the shanty, you will find two dining rooms, a small sweet shop, and a gift shop. The dining rooms continue the logging theme with long tables, wooden benches, red-and-white-checkered tablecloths, and stainless steel plates and cups. There's even an old wagon suspended from the ceiling. The food is advertised as an all-you-can-eat buffet, but there is table service as well. Three or four main entree selections each day please the hearty appetite. **FYI:** Reservations not accepted. No smoking. Additional location: 411 WI 13, Wisconsin Dells (tel 608/254-8717). **Open:** Mon–Sat 7am–9pm, Sun 7am–8:30pm. Closed Oct–May 15. **Prices:** Main courses $7–$10. DC, DISC, MC, V. 👥

Spang's Italian Restaurant

318 Milwaukee St; tel 715/356-4401. **Italian.** Tasty standbys in an Italian villa atmosphere. The dining room ceiling is circled with white lights, vines, and bunches of grapes. Booths in little nooks offer intimate dining, while there are large tables to accommodate families. Classical Italian music adds the finishing touch. The menu includes lasagna, chicken cacciatore, hearth-baked pizza, and an all-you-can-eat spaghetti special. **FYI:** Reservations not accepted. Children's menu. Additional location: WI 70 E, St Germain (tel 479-9400). **Open:** Peak (July–Aug) daily 5–10pm. **Prices:** Main courses $6–$18. AE, DISC, MC, V.

Monroe

Seat of Green County, in southern Wisconsin. The courthouse in this dairy town of Swiss heritage has a 120-foot tall clock tower. Self-guided tours of Alp and Dell Cheesery to see the making of cheese. Cheese Days, third weekend September. **Information:** Monroe Area Chamber of Commerce, 1516 11th St, Monroe, 53566 (tel 608/325-7648).

MOTEL 🏨

⬢⬢ Alphorn Inn

250 N 18th Ave, 53566; tel 608/325-4138 or toll free 800/ 448-1805; fax 608/329-4804. 18th Ave exit off WI 69. A quiet, privately owned lodging with annexes two blocks from main property, this motel is a delightful find. Annexes are 12-plexes, almost like studio apartments (without the kitchens) in a tree-lined, parklike setting. Some views are of farmland, so noise is almost nonexistent. Walking distance to fine dining. A truly exceptional value. **Rooms:** 63 rms. CI 2pm/CO 11am. Nonsmoking rms avail. Annex rooms are called executive rooms, perhaps because of their larger size, work areas,

dressing areas, and real closets. **Amenities:** 🛏 A/C, cable TV w/movies. **Services:** 🚗 🍴 🛎 Twice-daily maid svce. On-site owners are eager to provide services and information. Prior permission requested for pets. **Facilities:** 🛝 🔲 Basketball. **Rates (CP):** $26–$39 S; $38–$47 D. Extra person $3. Children under age 12 stay free. Parking: Outdoor, free. AE, DISC, MC, V.

New Glarus

Located 20 miles south of Madison. Window boxes, lace curtains, Swiss flags, folk art, and re-created Alpine chalets set the mood at this village founded by Swiss immigrants in 1845. Swiss Volksfest, held in early August, includes Swiss-style yodeling and dancing. **Information:** New Glarus Chamber of Commerce, PO Box 713, New Glarus, 53574-0713 (tel 608/527-2095).

MOTELS 🏨

🏨🏨🏨 Chalet Landhaus
Jct WI 69/39, PO Box 801, 53574; tel 608/527-5234 or toll free 800/944-1716; fax 608/527-2365. Swiss-looking lodging right on highway and on the Sugar River State Trail, a national recreational trail. Property is well tended and adorned with flowers and outdoor seating. Across the street from a miniature golf course complete with miniature Swiss Alps and live goats for viewing and feeding. Octoberfest and Wilhelm Tell Festival are very popular, and motel fills in advance. **Rooms:** 64 rms and stes. CI 2pm/CO 11am. Nonsmoking rms avail. Rooms designated for families have up to four beds. **Amenities:** 🛏 🕭 A/C, cable TV w/movies, VCR. Some units w/terraces, some w/whirlpools. **Services:** 🍴 🛎 Swiss cookouts offered by restaurant during summer months. Bike storage provided. Staff is eager to be helpful. **Facilities:** 🛝 🔲 🕭 1 restaurant (bkfst and dinner only), 1 bar. **Rates:** Peak (May–Oct) $54–$74 S or D; $90–$135 ste. Extra person $8. Children under age 13 stay free. Lower rates off-season. Parking: Outdoor, free. Special packages include Winter Packages, and Bike Packages for those touring on the Sugar River State Trail, and provide special coupons for a variety of merchants in New Glarus. AE, MC, V.

🏨 Swiss-Aire Motel
1200 WI 69, 53574; tel 608/527-2138 or toll free 800/798-4391. 4 blocks S of WI 39. A one-floor motel owned and managed by a family, within strolling distance of New Glarus and its chalet-style architecture, museums, and shops. **Rooms:** 26 rms. CI 2pm/CO 11am. Nonsmoking rms avail. **Amenities:** 🛏 🕭 🍴 A/C, cable TV. **Services:** 🍴 🛎 Babysitting. Extra charge for pets. Offers plenty of local tourism information. **Facilities:** 🔲 📷 🛝 🔲 Basketball. Outdoor pool is appealing to kids. **Rates (CP):** Peak (May–Oct) $40–$51 S; $50–$67 D. Extra person $6. Children under age 5

stay free. Min stay special events. Lower rates off-season. Parking: Outdoor, free. Some off-season discounts avail. DISC, MC, V.

ATTRACTION 🏛

New Glarus Historical Museum
612 7th Ave; tel 608/527-2317. Situated on a hilltop in the heart of America's Little Switzerland, this museum is comprised of 13 buildings, each representing a facet of everyday life in the 19th-century Midwest. The Hall of History offers educational displays describing the Swiss immigration to New Glarus. Other buildings include a print shop, newspaper office, a replica of New Glarus's first log church, an authentic log cabin settler's home, a blacksmith shop, cheese factory, schoolhouse, general story, fire house, farm implement building, and a Swiss-type bee house. Several times during the season, demonstrations, such as cheesemaking, are offered. Guided tours available. **Open:** May–Oct, daily 9am–5pm. **$$**

Nicolet National Forest

One of two national forests in Wisconsin, this huge (657,000 acres) forest is the starting point for many of Wisconsin's major wild rivers, including the Pine, Pike, Popple, Peshtigo, and Wolf Rivers. Not surprisingly, enthusiasts of canoeing, kayaking, and fishing flock here. There are a wide variety of camping opportunities in the forest, ranging from developed sites in the Anvil Lake Campground (with a swimming beach, picnic shelter, and boat landing) to backcountry sites with little but solitude. The 12-mile Anvil National Recreation Trail and the Lauterman Lake National Recreation Trail are popular with hikers and cross-country skiers. The approximately 400-year-old "MacArthur Pine," named for General Douglas MacArthur, is one of the larger white pine trees in the nation, standing 148 feet tall with a circumference of 17 feet.

Interesting attractions can be found in and around the numerous towns located within the forest: St Paul's Evangelical Lutheran Church in Tipler is believed to be one of the few log churches in this country still used for regular services; in Long Lake, you'll find an inn that was used to house prisoners of war during World War II.

For more information contact the Nicolet National Forest, Eagle River District, PO Box 1809, Eagle River, WI 54521 (tel 715/479-2827); or Florence District, HC 1, Box 83, Florence, WI 53121 (tel 715/528-4464).

Oconomowoc

RESORT 🏨

🏳🏳🏳 Holiday Inn Sun Spree Resort

1350 Royale Mile Rd, 53066; tel 414/567-0311 or toll free 800/558-9573; fax 414/567-5934. 220 acres. Beautiful resort located on large pond with many activities. A ski hill, visible from I-94, towers above the flat farmland. A quiet forest getaway. **Rooms:** 370 rms and stes; 117 cottages/villas. CI 4pm/CO noon. Nonsmoking rms avail. Spacious rooms. **Amenities:** 🛁 🕹 A/C, cable TV w/movies. Some units w/terraces, some w/fireplaces. **Services:** ✕ 🚐 ⬜ ↩ Masseur, babysitting. **Facilities:** 🏌 ♿▶18 🏖 🚣 🎣 🎱2 🏊2 ⚒🍴 ⬜ & 2 restaurants, 2 bars (1 w/entertainment), 1 beach (lake shore), basketball, volleyball, games rm, lawn games, racquetball, spa, sauna, steam rm, whirlpool, beauty salon, washer/dryer. **Rates:** Peak (May–Oct) $89–$119 S or D; $179 ste; $98–$170 cottage/villa. Extra person $10. Children under age 18 stay free. Min stay wknds. Lower rates off-season. Parking: Indoor/outdoor, free. AE, CB, DC, DISC, MC, V.

RESTAURANT 🍴

♥ ✦ Golden Mast Inn

1270 Lacy Lane, Okauchee; tel 414/567-7047. **American/German.** The specialties in this attractive family-operated restaurant are the German dishes: roast loin of veal with dill sauce and spaetzle, Wiener schnitzel, sauerbraten, roast duck, and stuffed pork chops. Fairy tale paintings on the sides of buildings near the restaurant will enchant the kids, while adults will enjoy the outdoor patio overlooking a dreamy lake. **FYI:** Reservations recommended. Children's menu. **Open:** Peak (May–Oct) Mon–Sat 5–11pm, Sun 11am–9pm. **Prices:** Main courses $17–$50. AE, MC, V. 💗 🍺 🏞 🎦 &

ATTRACTIONS 🏛

Octagon House and the First Kindergarten

919 Charles St, Watertown; tel 414/261-2796. Completed in 1854, the house is one of the largest, single-family residences of the pre-Civil War period in Wisconsin. It features conveniences that were modern for the period, such as central heating, running water, and ventilating systems. Also on the grounds are the first kindergarten in the United States, built in 1856 (the interior depicts a class in session), and the Plank Road Barn, which now houses a collection of pioneer tools and farm implements. **Open:** Peak (Mem Day–Labor Day) daily 10am–4pm. Reduced hours off-season. $$

Honey of a Museum at Honey Acres

WI 67 N, Ashippun; tel 414/474-4411. The Honey Acres are owned by the Diehnelts, beekeepers and honey packers since 1852. Exhibits include a bee tree providing a close-up view of bees' activities; a 20-minute multimedia presentation on honey; displays on beekeeping around the world, as well as pollination and beeswax; and a quarter-mile nature walk that leads to a lookout tower which offers view of the surrounding countryside. Honey tasting offered; gift shop in the tower. **Open:** Peak (mid-May–Oct) Mon–Fri 9am–3:30pm, Sat–Sun noon–4pm. Reduced hours off-season. **Free**

Kettle Moraine Scenic Steam Train

WI 83, North Lake; tel 414/782-8074. An eight-mile round trip is offered on a full-size, old-time steam engine. The route begins at the North Lake Depot, travels over the Oconomowoc River and through West Merton, and returns. **Open:** June–Oct. Call for schedule. $$$

Okauchee

See Oconomowoc

Oshkosh

On the west shore of Lake Winnebago, this midsized city is now synonymous with the company that produces Oshkosh B'Gosh overalls. The EAA International Fly-In Convention, held every summer, draws in thousands of aircraft. Home of University of Wisconsin-Oshkosh. **Information:** Oshkosh Convention & Visitors Bureau, 2 N Main St, Oshkosh, 54901-4897 (tel 414/236-5250).

HOTELS 🏨

🏳🏳 Budgetel Inn

1950 Omro Rd, 54901; tel 414/233-4190 or toll free 800/4-BUDGET; fax 414/233-8197. White two-story building with green accents and minimal landscaping. **Rooms:** 100 rms. CI 4pm/CO 11am. Nonsmoking rms avail. **Amenities:** 🛁 🕹 A/C, cable TV w/movies. **Services:** ↩ Friendly and efficient staff. **Facilities:** 🚣 🎣 & Games rm. **Rates (CP):** $35 S or D. Extra person $5. Children under age 12 stay free. Parking: Outdoor, free. AE, DC, MC, V.

🏳🏳🏳 Fairfield Inn by Marriott

1800 S Koehler St, 54901; tel 414/233-8504 or toll free 800/228-2800; fax 414/233-8504. Three-story hotel with tidy landscaping near airport and Lake Winnebago. **Rooms:** 57 rms and stes. CI 3pm/CO 11am. Nonsmoking rms avail. Rooms tastefully decorated with functional furniture. **Amenities:** 🛁 🕹 A/C, cable TV w/movies. **Services:** ⬜ ↩ ⬙ **Facilities:** 🏊 🚣 🎣 📺20 & Games rm, whirlpool. **Rates (CP):** Peak (May 14–Nov 4) $62 S; $67 D; $62–$68 ste. Extra person $6. Children under age 18 stay free. Lower rates off-season. Parking: Outdoor, free. AE, DC, DISC, MC, V.

UNRATED Holiday Inn

500 S Koehler St, 54901; tel 414/233-1511 or toll free 800/465-4329; fax 414/233-1909. Near the downtown area. Undergoing major renovation of lobby and rooms. **Rooms:** 132 rms. CI 3pm/CO noon. Nonsmoking rms avail. **Amenities:** 🛁 🕹 A/C, cable TV w/movies, in-rm safe.

Services: 🛎 **Facilities:** 🛗 🏊 📷 💼 📶 ♿ Games rm, sauna, whirlpool. Three-hole putting green (with plastic golf balls), shuffleboard, Ping-Pong. **Rates:** $40 S; $55–$80 D. Extra person $5. Children under age 12 stay free. Parking: Outdoor, free. AE, CB, DC, DISC, JCB, MC, V.

MOTEL

🏨 Super 8 Motel
1581 W South Park Ave, 54903 (Wittman Regional Airport); tel 414/426-2885 or toll free 800/808-6200; fax 414/426-5488. Conveniently located motel has bright flowers and tall evergreens, with a ground cover of juniper berries. **Rooms:** 61 rms and stes. CI 2pm/CO 11am. Nonsmoking rms avail. **Amenities:** 📺 🍴 A/C, cable TV w/movies. **Services:** 🛎 🍴 **Facilities:** 🏊 📷 🔲 ♿ Sauna, whirlpool, washer/dryer. **Rates (CP):** Peak (June–Sept) $40–$43 S; $50–$53 D; $57 ste. Extra person $5. Children under age 12 stay free. Lower rates off-season. Parking: Outdoor, free. AE, DC, DISC, MC, V.

RESTAURANTS 🍴

Butch's Anchor Inn
225 W 20th Ave; tel 414/232-3742. At Oregon St. **American.** Black Angus steaks, pastas, and seafood highlight the extensive menu in this family-owned and -operated restaurant replete with fish tanks and sailing memorabilia collected by owner/chef Butch Arps (who, along with son John, is a graduate of the Culinary Institute of America). Diners can request more intimate dining in private "huts." All pastas, breads, soups, and pastries are homemade. A special feature is the Treasure Island buffet, which features five "islands" of food. **FYI:** Reservations accepted. **Open:** Mon–Sat 11am–10pm, Sun 8:30am–2pm. **Prices:** Main courses $12–$26. AE, MC, V. 🖼 ♿

The Granary Restaurant
50 W 6th Ave; tel 414/233-3929. At Oregon St. **American.** Located in a renovated late-19th-century stone flour mill. (Upon entering the restaurant, you can look up into the towering four-story chutes that once held wheat and barley.) A grand staircase leads to the balcony-level dining room. Prime rib and steaks are naturally aged and hand-cut daily, while seafood includes Alaskan king crab, Gulf shrimp, Canadian scallops, and cold-water Australian lobster. Lunch is a variety of salads, soups, pasta, sandwiches, burgers, and seafood. **FYI:** Reservations recommended. Country music/folk/jazz. Children's menu. **Open:** Lunch Mon–Fri 11am–2pm; dinner Sun–Thurs 5–10pm, Fri–Sat 5–10:30pm. **Prices:** Main courses $8–$19. AE, DC, DISC, MC, V. 🍷 ♿

★ Robbins
1018 Omro Rd; tel 414/235-2840. **American.** Soups, smoked meats, and homemade sausages have been a tradition at Robbins since it opened in 1928. Dinner might include smoked barbecued spare ribs with homemade sauce, Bavarian plate (with homemade bratwurst, cheddarwurst, Wiener schnitzel, potato dumplings, and red cabbage), Cajun-style blackened prime rib, or grilled smoked pork chops with potato dumplings and red cabbage. Takeout available. **FYI:** Reservations recommended. **Open:** Sun–Thurs 11am–10pm, Fri–Sat 11am–11pm. **Prices:** Main courses $9–$19. AE, DISC, MC, V. 🖼 ♿

Wisconsin Farms
2450 Washburn; tel 414/233-7555. Jct US 41/WI 44. **American.** A family of fiberglass cattle greets diners as they drive up to this dairy country diner, a popular place with parents and their young children. The extensive menu focuses on steaks, sandwiches, burgers, and soups; homemade cheesecakes and pies satisfy sweet tooths. A gift shop sells T-shirts and sweatshirts adorned with cows, cow dolls dressed in country attire, and the "original cow pie." **FYI:** Reservations accepted. Children's menu. Beer and wine only. **Open:** Mon–Thurs 5am–8pm, Fri–Sun 9am–8pm. **Prices:** Main courses $4–$16. MC, V. 🖼 ♿

ATTRACTIONS 🏛

EAA Air Adventure Museum
3000 Poberezny Rd; tel 414/426-4818. Located at the EAA Aviation Center in east-central Wisconsin, the museum contains some of the most significant and spectacular contributions to the world of aviation. It has aircraft displays encompassing the history of aviation, dynamic theater and video presentations, and galleries. An exhibit on jet fighters features American F-86 Sabres, Soviet-bloc MiGs and British-built fighters. The Eagle Hangar showcases WWII planes such as the B-17 Flying Fortress, the XP-51 Mustang and a P-38 Lightning. Numerous vintage aircraft such as an original Ford Tri-Motor and a flying replica of Lindbergh's *Spirit of St Louis* are displayed. Aerial demonstrations of some of these rare airplanes also provided when weather permits. **Open:** Mon–Sat 8:30am–5pm, Sun 11am–5pm. $$$

Paine Art Center and Arboretum
1410 Algoma Blvd; tel 414/235-4530. Housed in an elegant Tudor Revival mansion, the center offers exquisitely crafted period rooms reflecting 300 years of English architectural history, a world-class permanent collection of art, traveling exhibitions, and six colorful garden displays in the arboretum, including a Rose Garden. The permanent collection features landscape paintings by French Barbizon masters and important 19th-century American painters such as George Inness and Ralph Albert Blakelock, as well as Oriental rugs, porcelain, silver, and a sculpture collection of the works of Oshkosh-born Helen Farnsworth Mears. Tours, demonstrations, lectures, and musical performance offered. **Open:** Tues–Fri 10am–4:30pm; Sat–Sun 1–4:30pm. $

Platteville

Located in southwest part of state, just east of the Mississippi River. Lead and zinc mining were key in the development of the town, and the University of Wisconsin-Platteville is one of the country's top schools for mining engineering. Sport fishing is popular, due to the area's many streams. **Information:** Platteville Chamber of Commerce, 275 US 151 W, PO Box 16, Platteville, 53818 (tel 608/348-8888).

MOTELS 🏨

≡≡ Best Western Governor Dodge Motor Inn

US 151, PO Box 658, 53818; tel 608/348-2301 or toll free 800/528-1234; fax 608/348-8579. Near jct WI 80/81 and US 151. This bright white, two-story building with pillars adorning the entrance is less than a mile from some of Platteville's top attractions, such as the Mining Museum and Chicago Bears' training camp. The lobby is cozy but somewhat worn. Motel fills up for special events during the school year. **Rooms:** 74 rms and stes. CI 2pm/CO noon. Nonsmoking rms avail. **Amenities:** 🖥 🍴 A/C, cable TV w/movies. Some units w/whirlpools. **Services:** ⬠ ⬠ **Facilities:** 🖼 🏃 🍴 🎱 ⅃ 1 restaurant (*see* "Restaurants" below), 1 bar, games rm, whirlpool. Restaurant is across the parking lot from building. Pool, in separate building, is quite large, with plenty of deck chairs. **Rates:** Peak (June–Oct) $56–$61 S; $67–$72 D; $100–$120 ste. Extra person $5. Children under age 12 stay free. Lower rates off-season. Parking: Outdoor, free. AE, CB, DC, DISC, MC, V.

≡ Super 8 Motel

100 WI 80/81 S, 53818; tel 608/348-8800 or toll free 800/800-8000. Near jct US 151. Located at major highway intersection, so parking lot and surrounding area get a lot of traffic, but property is kept quite clean. Lobby is appointed with antiques and knickknacks, a bit cluttered in the small space. **Rooms:** 46 rms and stes. CI 3pm/CO 11am. Nonsmoking rms avail. **Amenities:** 🖥 A/C, cable TV w/movies. Some units w/terraces, some w/whirlpools. **Services:** ⬠ ⬠ Pets $10 per night. **Facilities:** 🏃 🔟 ⅃ Sauna, steam rm, whirlpool, washer/dryer. **Rates (CP):** Peak (July–Oct) $39–$62 S or D; $75–$125 ste. Extra person $5. Children under age 12 stay free. Lower rates off-season. Parking: Outdoor, free. AE, CB, DC, DISC, MC, V.

RESTAURANTS 🍽

Governor's Cafe

In Best Western Governor Dodge Motor Inn, US 151; tel 608/348-3778. **American.** This family restaurant has the feel of a chain, though it's not quite so plastic and slick. The standard American fare is decent, and the service is efficient. Croissant with ham, egg, and cheese is a breakfast favorite. Sandwiches, steaks, and Mexican and Italian dishes also available. **FYI:** Reservations not accepted. Children's menu.

No liquor license. **Open:** Mon–Thurs 6am–8pm, Fri–Sat 6am–9pm, Sun 6am–7pm. **Prices:** Main courses $6–$9. AE, CB, DC, DISC, MC, V. 👓

★ The Timbers Supper Club

670 Ellen St; tel 608/348-2406. Near jct US 151/WI 81. **International.** Located on a small hill overlooking a busy intersection, the building's angles and many windows evoke the designs of Frank Lloyd Wright. Inside you'll find the largest theater electronic organ ever built. Among the elegant dishes available is blackened rib eye and shrimp sautéed in the shell with garlic, Worcestershire sauce, and beer. Game dishes also offered, including hard-to-find Peking duck. Special desserts. **FYI:** Reservations accepted. Organ concerts. Children's menu. **Open:** Lunch Mon–Sat 11am–1:30pm; dinner Mon–Sat 5–10pm, Sun 3–9pm; brunch Sun 10:30am–2pm. **Prices:** Main courses $8–$20. AE, DC, DISC, MC, V. ♥ ⅃

ATTRACTION 🏛

The Mining Museum and Rollo Jamison Museum

405 E Main; tel 608/348-3301. The Mining Museum traces the development of lead and zinc mining in the Upper Mississippi Valley through models, dioramas, artifacts, and photographs. A guided tour includes a walk down into the Bevans Lead, an 1845 lead mine, a visit to a head-frame which shows how zinc ore was hoisted from a mine and hand sorted, and a train ride around the museum grounds in ore cars pulled by a 1931 mine locomotive. Rollo Jamison was a collector who accumulated over 20,000 items in his lifetime. The museum features turn-of-the-century displays from his collection; farm implements, carriages, tools, a tavern/general store, a kitchen and parlor, musical instruments, and mechanical music boxes, among many others. **Open:** Peak (May–Oct) daily 9am–5pm. Reduced hours off-season. **$$**

Portage

Seat of Columbia County in south-central Wisconsin. Fort Winnebago formerly occupied this site on a narrow strip of land between the Fox and Wisconsin Rivers; several of its buildings still remain. Pulitzer Prize–winning author Zona Gale was born here in 1874. **Information:** Portage Area Chamber of Commerce, 301 W Wisconsin St, Portage, 53901-2191 (tel 608/742-6242 or toll free 800/474-2525).

MOTELS 🏨

≡≡ Ridge Motor Inn

2900 New Pinery Rd, 53901; tel 608/742-5306; fax 608/742-5306. Comfortable, spacious lobby. Next door to McDonald's. **Rooms:** 113 rms and stes. CI 2pm/CO 11am. Nonsmoking rms avail. **Amenities:** 🖥 📺 A/C, cable TV w/movies. Some units w/whirlpools. **Services:** ✕ ⬠ ⬠ ⬠ Masseur, babysitting. **Facilities:** 🖼 🏃 🎿 🔲 ⅃ 1 restaurant,

1 bar, volleyball, sauna, whirlpool, day-care ctr. Tanning salon. **Rates:** Peak (June–Aug/Dec 25–Apr) $45–$55 S; $55–$75 D; $75–$125 ste. Extra person $5. Children under age 12 stay free. Lower rates off-season. Parking: Outdoor, free. Ski packages at Devils Head Mountain and casino packages at Ho-Chunk casino avail. AE, CB, DC, DISC, EC, ER, JCB, MC, V.

≣≣ Super 8 Motel
3000 New Pinery Rd, 53901; tel 608/742-8330 or toll free 800/800-8000; fax 608/742-8330 ext 305. Sparkling clean, comfortable establishment with tree-lined parking lot. Wisconsin Dells attractions are 20 minutes away. **Rooms:** 61 rms and stes. CI 2pm/CO 11am. Nonsmoking rms avail. Recently remodeled rooms, some with sofa sleepers and recliners. **Amenities:** 🛏 ♨ A/C, cable TV w/movies. **Services:** ⇨ ⇦ **Facilities:** 🏃 30 ♿ Washer/dryer. **Rates (CP):** Peak (June 16–Sept 16) $49–$68 S; $59–$68 D; $50–$75 ste. Extra person $5. Children under age 18 stay free. Lower rates off-season. Parking: Outdoor, free. Rates increase for the EAA Fly-In. AE, CB, DC, DISC, MC, V.

ATTRACTION 🎪
Zona Gale House–The Women's Civic League of Portage
506 E Edgewater St; tel 608/742-7744. Portage native Zona Gale rose to prominence as a playwright, author, and suffragette. (She won a Pulitzer Prize in 1921 for her stage comedy *Miss Lulu Bett*.) This Greek-Revival house was built in 1906 and houses original furnishings and memorabilia from Gale's literary and political careers. **Open:** Mon–Fri, call for schedule. $

Port Washington

Seat of Ozaukee County, in eastern Wisconsin. Many pre-Civil War homes grace this town on the shore of Lake Michigan. A fine marina affords excellent fishing and boating. **Information:** Port Washington Chamber of Commerce, PO Box 514, Port Washington, 53074 (tel 414/284-0900).

MOTEL 🏨
≣≣≣ Best Western Harborside Motor Inn
135 E Grand Ave, 53074 (Downtown); tel 414/284-9461 or toll free 800/528-1234; fax 414/284-3169. Well maintained. Comfortable lobby has view of indoor swimming pool. Located directly on Port Washington Harbor, with docking space nearby. Within walking distance of charter fishing, marina, shops, and restaurants. **Rooms:** 96 rms and stes. CI 2pm/CO noon. Nonsmoking rms avail. Many rooms newly redecorated. Views of Lake Michigan, street, or harbor. **Amenities:** 🛏 ♨ A/C, satel TV, dataport. Some units w/whirlpools. **Services:** 📠 ⇨ ⇦ Pets allowed on limited basis. **Facilities:** 🏊 🏃 100 ♿ 1 restaurant (bkfst only), 1 bar, games rm, sauna, whirlpool, washer/dryer. **Rates:** Peak (Mem Day–Labor Day)

$72–$102 S; $82–$112 D; $102–$132 ste. Extra person $10. Children under age 12 stay free. Lower rates off-season. Parking: Outdoor, free. AARP discounts avail. Special packages avail Oct 15–May 15. AE, CB, DC, DISC, MC, V.

RESTAURANTS 🍽
★ Buchel's Colonial House
1000 S Spring St; tel 414/284-2212. **American/German.** This family-owned and -operated restaurant continues the tradition of culinary excellence established by the founder's father, who served as personal chef to the prince of Lichtenstein. The enchanting Early American decor provides a perfect backdrop for homemade desserts, interesting soups (red-pepper bisque with scallops and shrimp, pumpkin soup), and entrees such as boned whitefish broiled on a maple plank and served with piped mashed potatoes, tender lamb shanks braised with vegetable gravy, and beef rouladen with spaetzel. **FYI:** Reservations recommended. Children's menu. **Open:** Tues–Sun 5–10pm. **Prices:** Main courses $10–$22. MC, V. ♿

Smith Bros "Fish Shanty" Restaurant
100 N Franklin St (Downtown); tel 414/284-5592. **American/Seafood.** Specializing in fish, this eatery has a commanding view of Lake Michigan and the Port Washington harbor. Booth and table seating are available, as is seating on a screened-in deck. Diners at Smith Bros most frequently treat themselves to the planked fish, and a variety of pastas with seafood. "Mile-High" lemon meringue pie is a winning dessert. Operated by a successful Milwaukee restaurateur, the Fish Shanty also has a brightly tiled fish market featuring fresh fish, seasonings, sandwiches, and appetizers. **FYI:** Reservations recommended. Karaoke. Children's menu. **Open:** Peak (Mem Day–Labor Day) Sun–Thurs 11am–10pm, Fri–Sat 11am–11pm. **Prices:** Main courses $9–$28. AE, DC, DISC, MC, V. 🏞 ♿

ATTRACTION 🎪
Washington County Historical Society Museum
340 S 5th Ave, West Bend; tel 414/335-4678. Located 10 mi W of Port Washington. Museum consists of the 1886 county sheriff's home and jail. It includes many artifacts from Washington County early settler life, and is presently renovating the 1889 county courthouse. **Open:** Apr–mid-Dec, Tues and Thurs 1–4pm. **Free**

Prairie du Chien

Seat of Crawford County, in southwest part of state. Founded by French traders in 1673, this town is one of the oldest European settlements in the region. Hercules Dousman, an agent for the American Fur Trade Company and the state's first millionaire, built his fortune here in the 1870s.

Information: Prairie du Chien Chamber of Commerce, 211 S Main St, PO Box 326, Prairie du Chien, 53821 (tel 608/ 326-8555 or toll free 800/732-1673).

MOTELS

UNRATED **Best Western Quiet House Suites**
US 18 and WI 35 S, 53821; tel 608/326-4777 or toll free 800/528-1234. Well-tended, unpretentious property. Families are welcome, but some of the suites cater to couples. Lobby is cozy and homey. **Rooms:** 42 stes. CI 2pm/CO 11am. Nonsmoking rms avail. All-suite lodging prides itself on its "theme suites." **Amenities:** A/C, cable TV w/movies, dataport. 1 unit w/fireplace, some w/whirlpools. **Facilities:** Whirlpool. **Rates (CP):** $70–$130 ste. Extra person $7. Children under age 3 stay free. Parking: Outdoor, free. AE, CB, DC, DISC, MC, V.

Brisbois Motor Inn
533 N Marquette Rd, PO Box 37, 53821; tel 608/326-8404 or toll free 800/356-5850; fax 608/326-8404 ext 501. A low-rise building located on one of the main commercial drags in town, this well-tended property is run (and has been for more than 40 years) by a family set on making your stay comfortable. John and Jacqueline Kennedy stayed here in 1959, and there is now a suite named after them. A good deal. **Rooms:** 46 rms and stes. Executive level. CI 2pm/CO 11am. Nonsmoking rms avail. All rooms are simply yet tastefully appointed. Rooms with individual entrances directly off parking lot are worn; request a renovated room. **Amenities:** A/C, cable TV w/movies. **Services:** X ☕ ⇦ **Facilities:** Basketball, playground. Fish cleaning table. **Rates:** Peak (June–Oct) $34–$69 S or D; $44–$69 ste. Extra person $5. Children under age 16 stay free. Lower rates off-season. Parking: Outdoor, free. Extended-stay and other packages avail. Tenth night free. AE, DC, DISC, MC, V.

UNRATED **Prairie Motel**
1616 S Marquette Rd, 53821; tel 608/326-6461 or toll free 800/526-3776. A shady property close to downtown, this inexpensive little place is on one floor, with individual entrances to each room. Located next to bowling alley and sports bar; miniature golf course adjacent to property. **Rooms:** 32 rms. CI 2pm/CO 11am. Nonsmoking rms avail. **Amenities:** A/C, cable TV w/movies. **Services:** ☕ ⇦ Free casino shuttle service to nearby gaming facilities. **Facilities:** Basketball, playground. **Rates:** Peak (May–Oct) $35–$49 S; $49–$59 D. Children under age 10 stay free. Lower rates off-season. Parking: Outdoor, free. AE, DC, DISC, MC, V.

UNRATED **Super 8 Motel**
US 18 and WI 35 S, 53821; tel 608/326-8777 or toll free 800/800-8000; fax 608/326-4787. This clean property close to attractions is managed by a couple with lots of experience and a real interest in the area. **Rooms:** 30 rms. CI 2pm/CO 11am. Nonsmoking rms avail. **Amenities:** A/C, cable TV w/movies, dataport. **Services:** Free coffee in lobby.

Facilities: ⚓ & **Rates:** $39–$49 S; $51–$57 D. Extra person $5. Children under age 12 stay free. Parking: Outdoor, free. AE, CB, DC, DISC, MC, V.

RESTAURANT

⑤ **Dew Drop Inn**
12761 County Rd, Bagley; tel 608/996-2243. At County Rd C. **American/Burgers.** This friendly, dimly lit place has the feel of a well-kept country tavern, with its wood paneling, deer's head on the wall, and long bar decorated with bumper stickers, pennants, and an extensive knife collection. Menu offers good, mostly fried or grilled food: burgers, deep-fried onion rings and mushrooms, fried egg sandwich, and—this being Wisconsin—deep-fried cheese curds. Takeout available. **FYI:** Reservations not accepted. **Open:** Mon–Sat 9am–2am, Sun 10am–2am. **Prices:** Main courses $4–$6. No CC.

ATTRACTIONS

Villa Louis Historic Site
521 N Villa Louis Rd; tel 608/326-2721. The site of three National Registered Landmarks, this mansion overlooks some of Wisconsin's most historic grounds. Just a few miles to the south, the first European explorers arrived by canoe from Lake Michigan in 1673 and made the area the hub of the fur trade. Where the Villa now stands, American and British-Canadian troops clashed for control of Forth Shelby in the only battle of the War of 1812 fought in Wisconsin. The elegant Villa mansion stands as the legacy of the pioneering Dousman family, and is one of the most authentically furnished Victorian houses in the nation. The site also includes a general store built in the 1850s that houses a museum documenting the fur trade on the Upper Mississippi River Valley, and a museum of Prairie du Chien history. Group tours available. **Open:** May–Oct, daily 9am–5pm. **$$**

Fort Crawford Medical Museum
717 S Beaumont Rd; tel 608/326-6960. The museum is housed in a national historic landmark, the reconstructed military hospital at Fort Crawford. It documents the history of Wisconsin medicine. Exhibits include relics of 19th-century medicine, such as displays of Native American herbal remedies, a replica of an 1890s pharmacy, a dentist and physicians' offices, and dioramas illustrating the progress of surgery during the last century. Picnic area. **Open:** May–Oct, Wed–Sun 10am–5pm. **$**

Kickapoo Indian Caverns
WI 60, Wauzeka; tel 608/875-7723. These onyx caverns, the largest that are open to the public in Wisconsin, were used for centuries by Native Americans as a shelter. The site houses a unique collection of hundreds of tribal artifacts. Guided tours available. **Open:** Daily 9am–4:15pm. **$$$**

Racine

Seat of Racine County, in southeast part of state. This midsized city lies on a peninsula of land jutting into Lake Michigan. World headquarters of SC Johnson Wax (designed by Frank Lloyd Wright) is located here. Zoofari Day takes place at Racine Zoological Gardens in late June. **Information:** Racine County Convention & Visitors Bureau, 345 Main St, Racine, 53403 (tel 414/634-3293 or toll free 800/272-2463).

HOTEL 🏨

≣≣≣ Holiday Inn Riverside

3700 Northwestern Ave, 53405; tel 414/637-9311 or toll free 800/HOLIDAY; fax 414/637-4575. Looks like a motel, but offers a hotel's range of amenities and services. **Rooms:** 112 rms. Executive level. CI 2pm/CO noon. Nonsmoking rms avail. First-floor rooms open both onto parking lot or outdoor pool, and into indoor hallway. Pleasant, clean rooms. **Amenities:** 🛁 🔊 📺 🍷 A/C, satel TV w/movies, dataport. **Services:** ✗ 🛆 🖐 🖐 Car-rental desk. **Facilities:** 🛠 125 🚹 1 restaurant, 1 bar, washer/dryer. Contract with Flex Gym, about two blocks away. **Rates:** Peak (Apr 15–Labor Day) $71–$77 S or D. Extra person $6. Children under age 18 stay free. Lower rates off-season. Parking: Outdoor, free. Bed-and-breakfast packages avail through Holiday Inn Corporation. AE, CB, DC, DISC, JCB, MC, V.

MOTEL

≣≣ Comfort Inn

1154 Prairie Dr, 53406; tel 414/886-6055 or toll free 800/221-2222; fax 414/886-1117. Off WI 50, 4 miles from downtown Racine. Modern exterior, two stories. Country Kitchen Restaurant adjacent to motel. **Rooms:** 81 rms and stes. CI 2pm/CO noon. Nonsmoking rms avail. Quiet decor with pastel-colored paintings. Hospitality suite sleeps four, with pull-out bed and sleeper sofa. **Amenities:** 🛁 🔊 A/C, cable TV w/movies, VCR. 1 unit w/minibar. **Services:** 🛆 🖐 **Facilities:** 10 🚹 Exercise room includes stair-stepper, treadmill, exercise bike, and TV; children under 18 must be accompanied by an adult. **Rates (CP):** Peak (May–Oct) $59–$80 S or D; $75–$85 ste. Children under age 18 stay free. Lower rates off-season. Parking: Outdoor, free. AE, DC, DISC, MC, V.

RESTAURANTS 🍴

★ Corner House

1521 Washington Ave (Uptown); tel 414/637-1295. On WI 20 E. **American.** An extensive poster collection, dark woods, and muted lighting give this dining room a very cozy feel. The staff likes to boast that patrons come here from around the world to enjoy the great American meat-and-potatoes menu, which is now complemented by seafood and other lighter fare. **FYI:** Reservations recommended. **Open:** Mon–Sat 5–10:30pm, Sun 4–9:30pm. **Prices:** Main courses $8–$22. AE, CB, DC, DISC, MC, V. 🚹

Great Wall

6025 Washington Ave; tel 414/886-9700. Exit 333 off I-94; 4 mi E. **Chinese/Thai.** The plain exterior should not discourage you. Inside, charming Chinese decorations fill the simple dining room, lanterns hang from the ceiling, and a painting of the Great Wall fills the back wall. The menu contains dependable Szechuan and Mandarin favorites. Takeout available. **FYI:** Reservations recommended. **Open:** Sun–Thurs 11am–8:30pm, Fri 11am–9:30pm, Sat 4–9:30pm. **Prices:** Main courses $8–$10. AE, DISC, MC, V.

Old Country Buffet

In Westgate Mall, 4901 Washington Ave; tel 414/634-5122. Exit 333 off I-94; 5 mi E. **American/Cafeteria.** A casual, family-style cafeteria with simple and durable decor. The menu changes nightly, but there's always a bustle around the buffet tables as patrons scoop up entrees like fried chicken and meat loaf, and side dishes of potato salad and macaroni and cheese. Special discount for seniors. **FYI:** Reservations accepted. No liquor license. **Open:** Mon–Thurs 11am–9pm, Fri 11am–10pm, Sat 8am–10pm. **Prices:** Main courses $8. MC, V. 👶 🚹

Valentyne's

1675 Douglas Ave; tel 414/633-7500. On WI 32. **American/French.** The unassuming exterior leaves diners unprepared for the eclectic, thoughtful collection of antique fixtures contained in the dining room. Leaded glass and Tiffany stained-glass windows, a hand-carved fireplace, and heavy brass chandeliers create a heady, romantic ambience. Look for pleasant surprises: hand-painted ceilings in the private dining rooms; once gas-lighted chandeliers over the piano and in the board room; and cupids painted on the bathroom stall doors. The owner, proudly residing as host, chef, and designer, recommends the chateaubriand and two-pound Australian lobster tails. **FYI:** Reservations recommended. **Open:** Peak (Nov–Mar) Tues–Sun 5–10pm. **Prices:** Main courses $16–$25. AE, CB, DC, DISC, MC, V. 🍷 🍴 🖼 🚹

ATTRACTIONS 🏛

Golden Rondelle Theater

14th and Franklin Sts; tel 414/631-2154. Moved from New York to Racine at the close of the 1964 World's Fair, this futuristic-looking structure now serves as the visitor center for the SC Johnson Wax Company complex. The theater offers an extensive film program and is the departure point for tours of the Frank Lloyd Wright–designed Johnson world headquarters (reservations required). **Open:** Tues–Fri 10am–3pm. **Free**

Racine County Historical Museum

701 Main St; tel 414/636-3926. Housed in the former Andrew Carnegie public library, this museum chronicles the

cultural history of the county through permanent and changing exhibits including a collection of vintage photographs and historical archives. **Open:** Tues–Fri 9am–5pm, Sat–Sun 1–5pm. **Free**

Charles A Wustum Museum of Fine Arts

2519 Northwestern Ave; tel 414/636-9177. Permanent and changing exhibits feature painting, graphics, crafts, photography, and sculpture from local, regional, and nationally known artists. Park and formal gardens on the premises. **Open:** Tues–Wed and Fri–Sun 1–5pm, Mon and Thurs 1–9pm. **$**

Racine Zoo

2131 N Main St; tel 414/636-9189. Located on 32 acres along the Lake Michigan shoreline, the zoo houses over 300 animals. Picnic area. **Open:** Peak (Mem Day–Labor Day) daily 9am–8pm. Reduced hours off-season. **Free**

Reedsburg

Located in south-central part of state, just north of Wisconsin River and surrounded by lakes. Home of Wisconsin Dairies, one of the largest butter producing plants in the world; the Nishan Park Butter Festival is held here in late June. **Information:** Reedsburg Area Chamber of Commerce, 240 Railroad St, PO Box 142, Reedsburg, 53959 (tel 608/524-2850 or toll free 800/844-3507).

ATTRACTIONS 🏛

Museum of Norman Rockwell Art

227 S Park St; tel 608/524-2123. Features more than 4,000 magazine covers, calendars, story illustrations, and advertisements designed by Rockwell. Video program shown hourly. **Open:** Mon–Sat 9am–5pm. Sun 10am–5pm. **$$**

Park Lane Model Railroad Museum

S 2083 Herwig Rd; tel 608/254-8050. Large collection of model trains and scenic operating layouts as well as miniature farm tractors, cars, and trucks. **Open:** May 15–Sept 15, daily 10am–5pm. **$$**

Rhinelander

Seat of Oneida County, in northern Wisconsin. This popular vacation destination is surrounded by more than 200 lakes, 11 trout streams, and 2 rivers, along with miles of old logging roads and paved bicycle trails. The logging industry, long the dominant economic force in the area, is now taking a back seat to tourism. The Hodag Country Music Festival is held here every July. **Information:** Rhinelander Area Chamber of Commerce, PO Box 795, Rhinelander, 54501-0795 (tel 715/362-7464 or toll free 800/236-4386).

MOTELS 🏨

≡≡≡ Best Western Claridge Motor Inn

70 N Stevens St, 54501; tel 715/362-7100 or toll free 800/528-1234; fax 715/362-3883. Known for two things: the motel mascot, a yellow Labrador named Austin, and an excellent restaurant called the Cavalier. **Rooms:** 81 rms, stes, and effic. CI 2pm/CO 11am. Nonsmoking rms avail. **Amenities:** 📻 ⚱ A/C, cable TV. Some units w/terraces. **Services:** ✗ 🍴 ⇔ ⇔ **Facilities:** ⚐ 🏊 ⚱ 🛏 ⚱ 1 restaurant, 1 bar, whirlpool, washer/dryer. **Rates:** Peak (June 15–Oct 15) $47–$65 S; $49–$80 D; $90–$120 ste; $73–$76 effic. Extra person $8. Children under age 18 stay free. Lower rates off-season. Parking: Outdoor, free. Special group and vacation packages avail. AE, DC, DISC, MC, V.

≡≡≡ Holiday Inn

668 W Kemp St, PO Box 675, 54501; tel 715/369-3600 or toll free 800/465-4329; fax 715/369-3600. Jct WI 47/US 8. The cream of the crop of Rhinelander lodging options. Business travelers and families stay at this conveniently located motel. **Rooms:** 101 rms. CI 3pm/CO noon. Nonsmoking rms avail. Rooms renovated in 1995. **Amenities:** 📻 ⚱ 🍴 A/C, cable TV w/movies, dataport. **Services:** ✗ 🍴 ⚱ ⇔ **Facilities:** ⚐ 🏊 🛏 ⚱ 1 restaurant, 1 bar (w/entertainment), games rm, sauna, whirlpool, washer/dryer. **Rates:** Peak (May–Aug) $63 S; $71 D. Extra person $8. Children under age 19 stay free. Lower rates off-season. Parking: Outdoor, free. Sign up for Priority Club discount at front desk or through toll-free number. For $10/year, you are eligible for a variety of discounts. At this location, your room will cost $58, regardless of number of persons. AE, DC, DISC, JCB, MC, V.

≡ Super 8 Motel

667 W Kemp St, ; tel 715/369-5880 or toll free 800/800-8000; fax 715/369-2312. Jct US 8/WI 47. Clean motel with convenient location. Good for a night. **Rooms:** 43 rms. CI 1PM/CO 11am. Nonsmoking rms avail. **Amenities:** 📻 ⚱ A/C, cable TV. **Services:** ⚱ ⇔ Friendly staff. **Facilities:** ⚱ **Rates:** Peak (May–Oct) $36–$46 S; $47–$58 D. Children under age 12 stay free. Min stay special events. Lower rates off-season. Parking: Outdoor, free. AE, CB, DC, DISC, MC, V.

RESTAURANTS 🍴

★ The Rhinelander Cafe and Pub

33 N Brown (Downtown); tel 715/362-2918. **American/Greek.** A fixture in the heart of downtown for over 85 years, now in its third generation of owners. While the decor could use a some updating, the locals still flock here for steak and seafood. **FYI:** Reservations accepted. Children's menu. **Open:** Peak (July–Oct 21) breakfast Mon–Fri 7am–11pm, Sat–Sun 7am–2pm; lunch daily 11am–4:30pm; dinner Fri 4–11pm, Sat–Thurs 4:30–11pm. **Prices:** Main courses $5–$20. AE, DISC, MC, V.

Ⓢ **Tula's**
232 S Courtney; tel 715/369-5248. **American.** Comfortable family restaurant with a clean, bright dining room, attentive staff, and a varied menu. Highlights are its excellent breakfast choices and Friday fish fry. In season, patrons can dine outdoors beside the Wisconsin River. **FYI:** Reservations recommended. Children's menu. Additional location: 1123 E Wall St, Eagle River (tel 479-4592). **Open:** Mon–Fri 6am–9pm, Sat–Sun 6am–10pm. **Prices:** Main courses $3–$14. DISC, MC, V. 🖼 ⚫

ATTRACTION 🏛

Logging Museum Complex
Oneida Ave, in Pioneer Park; tel 715/362-2193. The Rhinelander Logging Museum preserves the heritage of Wisconsin's early lumber days. A true-to-life replica of a lumber camp of the 1870s can be viewed, as well as tools and equipment pertaining to the early logging days and photographs. The complex also includes a replica of the Civilian Conservation Corps camp building; a restored blacksmith shop; a one-room schoolhouse; a building that houses restored old-time fire engines used by Rhinelander in the past; the restored red "Soo Line Caboose" from 1913; the "Soo Line Depot" from 1894; narrow-gauge railroad engine, and other equipment used by loggers. Another feature is the Animal and Indian Display. Gift shop. **Open:** Mem Day–Labor Day, daily 10am–5pm. **Free**

Rice Lake

Located in northwest part of state. Rice Lake was named for the nearby rice sloughs that served as a food source for the Chippewa and Sioux. Today, the town is a focal point of a major recreation area. **Information:** Rice Lake Area Chamber of Commerce, 37 S Main St, Rice Lake, 54868-2299 (tel 715/234-2126 or toll free 800/523-6318).

MOTELS 🏨

≡≡ Currier's Lakeview Resort Motel
2010 E Sawyer, 54868; tel 715/234-7474 or toll free 800/433-5253. Peaceful wooded setting, on east side of Rice Lake. **Rooms:** 19 rms and effic. CI 1pm/CO 11am. Nonsmoking rms avail. Rooms have different decorations, amenities, and rates. All have views of lake. The Bay House, a two-story A-frame located on property, also available for rent. **Amenities:** 🔒 ⚫ A/C, cable TV, refrig. **Services:** 🍴 🍴 Babysitting. **Facilities:** ⚠ 🔳 👤 Basketball. **Rates (CP):** Peak (May–Sept) $41–$49 S; $49–$75 D; $56–$75 effic. Extra person $4. Min stay peak. Lower rates off-season. Parking: Outdoor, free. AE, DISC, MC, V.

≡≡ Super 8 Motel
2401 S Main St, 54868; tel 715/234-6956 or toll free 800/800-8000; fax 715/234-6956. US 53 to Main St. In heart of Rice Lake, 1 mile off US 53, near restaurants and shopping.

Rooms: 48 rms and stes. CI 2pm/CO 11am. Nonsmoking rms avail. All rooms redone with new carpeting, draperies, and televisions. **Amenities:** 🔒 ⚫ A/C, cable TV. **Services:** 🍴 🍴 **Facilities:** 👤 ⚫ Games rm, washer/dryer. **Rates (CP):** Peak (June–Sept) $47–$55 S; $50–$69 D; $65–$79 ste. Extra person $6. Children under age 12 stay free. Lower rates off-season. Parking: Outdoor, free. 10% discount with Super 8 VIP. AE, CB, DC, DISC, MC, V.

ATTRACTION 🏛

Hunt Hill Audubon Sanctuary
Audubon Rd, Sarona; tel 715/635-6543. Nestled in the hills of Washburn County, a 400-acre sanctuary of maple, basswood, and oak forest, white pine groves, meadows, and black spruce and tamarack bogs. Two small lakes support loons and ospreys. The unique 80-acre bog and wetlands provide habitats to sundew and pitcher plants, bald eagles, and bears. Other nearby attractions include the scenic Namekagon River, Lake Superior's South Shore, the Apostle Islands National Lakeshore, and the Chequamegon National Forest. The facility has lodging for up to 75, a dining hall, lecture hall, and gift shop. **Open:** Mar–Oct, daily 9am–5pm. **Free**

St Croix Falls

A popular year-round resort area, with great fishing in St Croix River and many area lakes. The Gorge of the St Croix River forms the Dalles of the St Croix, with sheer rock walls of volcanic formation. **Information:** St Croix Falls Chamber of Commerce, PO Box 178, St Croix Falls, 54024 (tel 715/483-3929).

ATTRACTION 🏛

Interstate State Park
US 35; tel 715/483-3747. Wisconsin's oldest state park offers a view of the state's glacial history via the unique geological formations along the bluffs of the St Croix River. The Dalles of the St Croix, a deep gorge cut by the river, features volcanic-rock formations, sheer rock walls (some over 200 feet tall), and potholes drilled in rock by glacial waters. An Ice Age Interpretive Center includes photographs and murals, and an orientation film with information about the age of glaciers. Recreational activities include hiking, fishing, swimming, boating, canoeing, and cross-country skiing. Picnic areas, campsites, naturalist-led tours. **Open:** May–Oct, daily 6am–11pm. **$$**

St Germain

RESTAURANTS 🍴

Eliason's Some Place Else Supper Club

WI 70 E and WI 155; tel 715/542-3779. **American.** The Eliasons have run this welcoming supper club for 30 years now and don't show any signs of slowing down. The dimly lit dining room is the setting for popular nightly specials such as chicken Kiev, pot roast, prime rib, and a Friday fish fry. A big draw is the organ bar where patrons participate in sing-a-longs and dancing on weekends. Adjoining gift shop. **FYI:** Reservations not accepted. Dancing/singer. **Open:** Tues–Sun 5–9pm. Closed Nov. **Prices:** Main courses $6–$20. MC, V.

♥ Whitetail Inn

WI 70 E and Country Rd C; tel 715/542-2541. **American.** This very beautiful restaurant is a must if you're anywhere near the area. Two-hundred-year-old logs were cut to build this stunning cabin; the result is a dining room with beautifully knotty pine ceilings and walls. The custom carpeting, laser-engraved bar, deer-antler chandeliers and massive, double-sided fieldstone fireplace complete the interior. With its location on the St Germain Golf Course, the view is beautiful, too. Known for its excellent Sunday brunch and delicious entrees like garlic-stuffed tenderloin. **FYI:** Reservations accepted. Children's menu. No smoking. **Open:** Lunch Mon–Sat 11am–3:30pm; dinner Mon–Sat 4:30–10pm, Sun 4–9pm; brunch Sun 10am–2pm. Closed 1st week in Dec. **Prices:** Main courses $11–$39. MC, V. 🖼️ ⑇

Sheboygan

See also Kohler, Sheboygan Falls

Located on Lake Michigan north of Milwaukee. Dairying and beer brewing are important industries, along with manufacture of plastics, stainless-steel products, leather and paper goods, enamelware, and furniture. **Information:** Sheboygan County Chamber of Commerce, 712 Riverfront Dr, #101, Sheboygan, 53081 (tel 414/457-9491).

MOTELS 🏨

≡≡ A Harbor Inn

905 S 8th St, 53081 (Riverfront); tel 414/452-2424; fax 414/452-0239. This family-owned and -operated facility carries a nautical theme throughout. Observation deck for harbor viewing has benches and deck chairs. Adjacent to riverfront shops, restaurants, and charter fishing. Short drive to Kohler Arts Center, public beach, and marina. **Rooms:** 29 rms and stes. CI 2pm/CO 11am. Nonsmoking rms avail. Rooms have views of river or street. Some suites feature sofas and/or king-size beds. **Amenities:** 🛁 A/C, cable TV. 1 unit w/whirlpool. **Services:** 🖼️ ⑇ Morning coffee and fresh bakery items in lobby. **Facilities:** 🏖️ ⑇ **Rates (CP):** Peak

(May–Oct) $52–$57 S; $57–$62 D; $135–$175 ste. Extra person $5. Children under age 12 stay free. Lower rates off-season. Parking: Outdoor, free. Government discounts avail. AE, DC, DISC, MC, V.

≡≡ Budgetel Inn

2932 Kohler Memorial Dr, 53081; tel 414/457-2321 or toll free 800/428-3438; fax 414/457-0827. Nicely maintained and updated, with pleasant lobby and entrance. This property marks the halfway point between Milwaukee and Green Bay; 15 miles to Road America. **Rooms:** 97 rms. CI 1pm/CO noon. Nonsmoking rms avail. Rooms feature newly updated decor. View is of parking lot or neighboring buildings. **Amenities:** 🛁 📺 A/C, cable TV w/movies, dataport. **Services:** 🖼️ ⑇ 🍷 Juice and muffin/roll delivered to room before 8am every morning. Small pets only. Friendly, competent staff. **Rates (CP):** Peak (Apr–Oct) $39–$43 S; $46–$50 D. Children under age 18 stay free. Min stay special events. Lower rates off-season. Parking: Outdoor, free. Discounts include AARP, senior, Sam's Club, and corporate with stays of multiple nights. AE, CB, DC, DISC, MC, V.

≡≡≡ Ramada Inn

723 Center Ave, 53081 (Downtown); tel 414/458-1400 or toll free 800/672-6232; fax 414/458-6767. This Gold Key hotel (Ramada's designation for its top 10% properties) is within walking distance to shopping, restaurants, beach, marina, and Kohler Art Center. Glassed-in stairwells provide view of downtown shops. **Rooms:** 54 rms. CI 3pm/CO noon. Nonsmoking rms avail. Rooms feature updated decor, and all have views of downtown area. Suites feature sofas and larger room. **Amenities:** 🛁 ⑇ A/C, cable TV. Some units w/whirlpools. **Services:** ✕ 🚗 🖼️ ⑇ 🍷 Babysitting. **Facilities:** 🏊 ⑇ 1 restaurant, 1 bar (w/entertainment), whirlpool. Bar and restaurant feature happy hour, Fri fish fry, and Sat prime rib buffet. **Rates:** $65 S or D. Extra person $6. Children under age 18 stay free. Min stay special events. Parking: Outdoor, free. AARP, corporate, military, and senior citizen discounts avail. Super Saver weekend rates offered year-round. AE, DC, DISC, MC, V.

≡≡ Select Inn

930 N 8th St, 53081 (Downtown); tel 414/458-4641 or toll free 800/641-1000; fax 414/458-4641. Exterior appears somewhat neglected, but interior is well maintained. Conveniently located—six blocks to public beach, Harbor Center restaurants and gift shops; across the street from city park; 6 miles to golf courses; 10 miles to Road America race track. **Rooms:** 53 rms. CI 3pm/CO 11am. Nonsmoking rms avail. Updated rooms feature dark carpeting, which makes existing lighting insufficient. Views are of parking lot. Access rooms from outside corridors. **Amenities:** 🛁 A/C, cable TV. **Services:** 🖼️ ⑇ 🍷 **Facilities:** ⑇ 1 restaurant, 1 bar. **Rates (CP):** Peak (June–Aug) $35–$40 S; $40–$45 D. Extra person $5. Children under age 13 stay free. Lower rates off-season. Parking: Outdoor, free. AARP, corporate, military, and travel agents' discounts avail. AE, DC, DISC, MC, V.

≣≣ Super 8 Motel

3402 Wilgus Rd, 53081; tel 414/458-8080 or toll free 800/800-8000; fax 414/458-8013. Well-maintained, with easy on/off freeway access. Located close to restaurants, movie theater, shopping; 1½ miles to Lake Michigan, Sheboygan Harbor and Marina. **Rooms:** 60 rms. CI 2pm/CO 11am. Nonsmoking rms avail. Updated rooms with fresh decor; access from inside corridor. View is of either parking lot or office complex. **Amenities:** 🛍 🔥 A/C, cable TV. **Services:** ⚲ 🗗 Complimentary morning doughnuts and coffee served year-round. Friendly, accommodating service. **Facilities:** 🛝 🔲₁₂ 🔥 **Rates:** Peak (Apr–Sept) $44 S; $54 D. Extra person $5. Children under age 12 stay free. Lower rates off-season. Parking: Outdoor, free. AARP and Super 8 VIP discounts avail. AE, CB, DC, DISC, MC, V.

RESORT

≣≣≣≣ The American Club

Highland Dr, Kohler, 53044; tel 414/457-8000 or toll free 800/344-2838; fax 414/457-0299. 1,000 acres. Built in 1918 as a dormitory for immigrant workers for Kohler (the folks who make the bathroom fixtures) and converted in 1981 into this luxury country inn offering extensive recreational facilities. The English Tudor, red brick main structure is now on the National Register of Historic Places. Popular for business conferences. **Rooms:** 234 rms and stes. CI 4pm/CO noon. Nonsmoking rms avail. Rooms, located in two wings around a flowered courtyard and in a nearby annex, are distinguished, not surprisingly, by their bathrooms, all of which are equipped with single or double whirlpool tubs. Lots of oak paneling, brass fixtures, crown moldings, and louvered wood shutters, oak desks, and armoires (all by Baker or McGuire, both Kohler companies). **Amenities:** 🛍 🔥 🍽 A/C, cable TV w/movies, dataport, in-rm safe, bathrobes. Some units w/minibars, some w/terraces, some w/fireplaces, all w/whirlpools. Some rooms have wet bars, all have speakerphones. **Services:** ✕ ➤━ VP 🚐 ⚲ 🗗 Twice-daily maid svce, car-rental desk, masseur, children's program, babysitting. Staff of 1,000 (for 234 rooms!). **Facilities:** 🔄 🚲 ⚓ ▶₃₆ ♣ 🖼 🛝 🐟₆ 🐟₆ 🎳 🔲₇₅₀ 🔥 9 restaurants (*see* "Restaurants" below), 7 bars (1 w/entertainment), 2 beaches (lake shore), racquetball, spa, sauna, steam rm, whirlpool, beauty salon. Extraordinary variety of recreational facilities (even if most of them have to be shared with club members or local residents), among them indoor and outdoor tennis courts, a 500-acre game preserve, trap shooting, 30 miles of hiking trails, two outstanding (and public) golf courses designed by Pete Dye, 1½-mile parcourse trail with 15 stations. Also carriage and sleigh rides. **Rates:** $160–$410 S; $190–$440 D; $595 ste. Extra person $15. Children under age 10 stay free. Min stay peak, wknds, and special events. Parking: Indoor/outdoor, free. Published rates may go up for special sporting events; special packages (for golfers, romantics, seniors, and mothers) can save $100 or more. AE, CB, DC, DISC, MC, V.

RESTAURANTS 🍽

Ⓢ City Streets Riverside

In Riverfront Centre, 712 Riverfront Dr; tel 414/457-9050. **American/Seafood.** Friendly place that caters to families—witness the "child-designed" children's menu and coloring books. Skylights and a view of the riverfront provide an open, airy atmosphere. Prime rib served with choice of baked potato, garlic pasta, or rice pilaf; whitefish baked in sour cream, bread crumbs and onions; and seafood with angel-hair pasta Alfredo top the menu. Lighter fare includes homemade soups: corn and sausage chowder, calico bean and ham, chilled melon, double-baked french onion. **FYI:** Reservations recommended. Children's menu. **Open:** Lunch Mon–Fri 11am–2pm; dinner Mon–Thurs 5–9pm, Fri–Sat 5–10pm. **Prices:** Main courses $8–$17. AE, DC, MC, V. 👥 🔥

♛ Richard's

501 Monroe St; tel 414/467-6401. **American.** An out-of-the-way yet elegant eatery, housed in a colonial frame structure that was built in the 1840s as a stagecoach stop for travelers making their way across the wilds of Wisconsin. The award-winning executive chef emphasizes fresh ingredients, locally grown beef and produce, and health-conscious preparation. Favorites include baked salmon with cucumber-dill sauce, prime veal medallions in marsala sauce, and oysters Rockefeller. **FYI:** Reservations recommended. **Open:** Lunch Tues–Fri 11:30am–2pm; dinner Tues–Thurs 5–9pm, Fri–Sat 5–10pm. **Prices:** Main courses $13–$36. MC, V. ♥ 🔥

★ Rupp's Lodge Restaurant

925 N 8th St (Downtown); tel 414/459-8155. **American/Steak.** This family-owned and -operated restaurant features a vintage 1939 carved-oak bar, and a beveled-glass enclosure that allows diners to view goings-on in the kitchen. Diners can choose from bratwurst (a Sheboygan specialty), prime rib, duck, and a Friday perch fry with all the trimmings. Don't forget to try a "popper" (a deep-fried, cheese-covered appetizer). **FYI:** Reservations recommended. Piano. Additional location: 5008 S 12th St (tel 457-6444). **Open:** Lunch Mon–Fri 11am–2pm; dinner Mon–Fri 4–10pm, Sat 4:30–10pm, Sun 2–10pm; brunch Sun 10:30am–2pm. **Prices:** Main courses $8–$20. AE, DC, DISC, MC, V. 👥 💟 🔥

The Wisconsin Room

In The American Club, Highland Dr, Kohler; tel 414/457-8000. **American/Continental.** Among the many dining spots available at the American Club, the most appealing for setting, service, and price is this 140-seat gem. Leaded-glass windows, antique chandeliers, custom-designed tapestries and fine oak paneling create a baronial air. If the village of Kohler is a bit off the beaten path, Chef David Esau's inventive dishes reward the journey—appetizers like eggplant cannelloni and oriental-style potato cakes with seared rock shrimp; and entrees like herb-grilled tenderloin of beef with charlotte of asparagus and red onion risotto, and seared walleye pike with braised vegetables in red wine chanterelle. Service is warm, friendly, and knowledgeable. Tip: have your after-dinner coffee or espresso in The Greenhouse, a birdcage of an ice cream parlor in the patio garden. **FYI:** Reservations recommended. Children's menu. Dress code. **Open:** Daily 6am–10pm. **Prices:** Main courses $14–$23. AE, CB, DC, DISC, ER, MC, V. 🆅🅿 ♿

ATTRACTIONS 🏛

John Michael Kohler Arts Center
608 New York Ave; tel 414/458-6144. Located in an impressive Italianate villa built in 1882, the center is a nationally recognized visual and performing arts center that is committed to showcasing new directions in contemporary American art. Dubbed "a national treasure" by the Wisconsin Arts Board, it has concentrated on temporary exhibitions rather than the acquisition of a permanent collection. Its unique residency program brings professional visual and performing artists from around the country to the center for a limited period of time. Over the years, renowned exhibitions have included "Hmong Art: Tradition and Change," which was the most extensive exhibition and catalogue ever organized in this country of Hmong artifacts; "Structure and Surface: Beads in Contemporary American Art," which also displayed at the Smithsonian; and "From Hardanger to Harleys: A Survey of Wisconsin Folk Art." The Footlights subscription series brings acclaimed professional performers to the center for performances and residencies. Lectures, demonstrations, workshops, and guided tours offered. **Open:** Mon–Wed 10am–5pm, Thurs 10am–9pm, Fri 10am–5pm, Sat–Sun noon–5pm. **Free**

Sheboygan County Historical Museum
3110 Erie Ave; tel 414/458-1103. This museum chronicles the history of Sheboygan County. The David Taylor house from the early 1850s is the core exhibit space and houses artifacts relevant to Sheboygan's history; the Weinhold log cabin of 1864 portrays early German living experience; the Bodenstab Cheese Factory (built in 1867) and the Schuchardt barn are other original structures that showcase the local heritage. Guided tours available. **Open:** Apr–Oct, Tues–Sat 10am–5pm, Sun 1–5pm. **$**

Kohler-Andrae State Park
1520 Old Park Rd; tel 414/451-4080. Located on Lake Michigan, this 1,000-acre park featuring woods and sand dunes offers 105 camping sites, 3½ miles of hiking trails, one mile of nature trails, and 2½ miles of trails for mountain biking and horse riding. Fishing, picnic areas, and nature programs available. **Open:** Daily 8am–11pm. **Free**

Sheboygan Falls
See Sheboygan

Shorewood
See Milwaukee

Sister Bay
Many visitors say this pretty, northern Door Peninsula village is reminiscent of Cape Cod. Sister Bay Fall Festival (held every October) offers a fish boil and a parade.

MOTELS 🏨

🗖🗖 Bluffside
403 Bluffside Lane, 54234; tel 414/854-2530. Older but well maintained, and located on a quiet side street away from main traffic. Built on a wooded bluff, it is within easy walking distance to village beach and park, shops, restaurants, and galleries. Family owned and operated. **Rooms:** 18 rms and stes. CI noon/CO 10am. Room options include motel units or cottage suites with two bedrooms, screened-in porches, and sitting areas. **Amenities:** 🗄 ⚙ 🔲 A/C, cable TV, refrig. Cottage suites have kitchens. **Services:** ⤵ Babysitting. Microwave in common area. **Facilities:** 🛝 ♿ Picnic tables, grills. **Rates:** Peak (July 1–Aug 21) $58–$64 S or D; $105–$115 ste. Extra person $6. Min stay wknds. Lower rates off-season. Parking: Outdoor, free. Spring special: stay two nights, the third night is free. Closed Nov–Apr. MC, V.

🗖🗖 Coachlite Inn
WI 42, PO Box 316, 54234; tel 414/854-5503 or toll free 800/745-5031. On the S side of Sister Bay. Located in a pine grove, within easy walking distance of restaurants, shops, and golf. **Rooms:** 14 rms. CI 3pm/CO 10am. Nonsmoking rms avail. All rooms face wooded and landscaped lawn area and feature pleasant neutral decor. **Amenities:** A/C, cable TV. No phone. Some units w/terraces. Upper level has wood deck. **Services:** ⤵ **Facilities:** 🛝 ♿ Picnic tables, lawn chairs, fire ring in pine woods. **Rates:** Peak (June 30–Aug 20) $65–$69 S or D. Extra person $7. Children under age 4 stay free. Min stay special events. Lower rates off-season. Parking: Outdoor, free. 50% deposit required to hold reservation. Senior discount avail. 10% discount for stays of one week or longer. MC, V.

🗖🗖🗖 Country House Resort
715 N Highland Rd, 54234; tel 414/854-4551 or toll free 800/424-0041; fax 414/854-9809. W on N Highland Rd off WI 42. 16 acres. Situated on 16 secluded wooded acres, the main building of this comfortable facility was built in 1907. No children under 13 allowed at this family-owned and -operated gem. **Rooms:** 45 rms and stes. CI 2pm/CO 11am.

Nonsmoking rms avail. Variety of room sizes and types available, including queen-size brass beds, extra bathrooms, and sofa sleepers. Some rooms have water view. **Amenities:** ☎ ⚷ A/C, cable TV, refrig. All units w/terraces, some w/fireplaces, some w/whirlpools. **Services:** Masseur. Staff can accommodate business needs and will customize weekend stays as per special requests. **Facilities:** 🛒 🛏 🛏 ⚐₁ 🎱 ⚷ Volleyball, lawn games, whirlpool. Nature trail, dock/pier, gazebo, sun deck adjacent to pool and whirlpool, horseshoe pits, shuffleboard, rowboats. **Rates (CP):** Peak (June 15–Oct 15) $93–$121 S or D; $148–$193 ste. Extra person $22. Min stay peak. Lower rates off-season. Parking: Outdoor, free. Spring and fall packages. AE, DISC, MC, V.

≣ Edge of Town

11092 WI 42, 54234; tel 414/854-2012. On the N side of Sister Bay. Older lodging on three acres of woods, within short driving or biking distance from area restaurants and shops. Pleasant outdoor sitting area. **Rooms:** 9 rms. CI 2pm/CO 11am. Nonsmoking rms avail. Rooms accessed from outdoor corridor. **Amenities:** A/C, cable TV, refrig. No phone. Rooms available with microwaves. **Services:** ⚐ 🐾 Pets must be small and attended at all times. Board full of notes from satisfied customers attests to friendly, accommodating service. **Facilities:** 🛏 **Rates:** Peak (mid-June–mid-Oct) $56 S; $62 D. Extra person $6. Children under age 3 stay free. Lower rates off-season. Parking: Outdoor, free. 5% discount for stays of four nights or longer. DISC, MC, V.

≣≣ Helm's 4 Seasons

414 Mill Rd, PO Box 255, 54234; tel 414/854-2356. W on Mill Rd off WI 42 in downtown Sister Bay. Located in heart of Sister Bay, yet on quiet side street. Within easy walking distance to shops, restaurants, and playground. Ideal for families—children can feed the ducks. **Rooms:** 43 rms, stes, and effic. CI 1:30pm/CO 10am. Rooms are either waterfront or poolside; some have skylights. **Amenities:** ☎ ⚷ A/C, cable TV, refrig. Some units w/terraces, some w/fireplaces. **Services:** ⚐ Babysitting. Continental breakfast Labor Day–Mem Day. Pleasant, relaxed service. **Facilities:** 🛒 🛏 🏖₈₀ ⚷ 1 beach (bay), whirlpool, washer/dryer. Sun deck and peaceful lakefront area with sandy bottom swimming area. Docking available. Charcoal grills, lounge chairs. **Rates (CP):** Peak (June 23–Oct 15) $81–$87 S; $89–$95 D; $120–$180 ste; $100–$120 effic. Extra person $8. Min stay peak. Lower rates off-season. Parking: Outdoor, free. Senior citizen discount for guests 65 and over. Winter packages avail. MC, V.

≣≣≣ Inn at Little Sister Hill

2715 Little Sister Hill Rd, 54234; tel 414/854-2328 or toll free 800/768-6317. W on Little Sister Hill Rd off WI 42. Country furnishings, a large stone fireplace, and a vaulted wood ceiling grace the lobby of this facility, located in a wooded setting away from the road. **Rooms:** 26 stes and effic. CI 3pm/CO 10am. Nonsmoking rms avail. One- and two-bedroom units available, all with sleeper sofas in living rooms. All rooms have woods view. **Amenities:** ⚷ 📺 A/C, cable TV,

refrig, VCR. No phone. All units w/terraces. Kitchens are fully stocked. **Services:** ⚐ Babysitting. Low key, friendly service. **Facilities:** 🛒 🛏 ⚷ Playground, washer/dryer. Pool area separated from three main buildings, also in wooded setting. Grills available. **Rates:** Peak (June 24–Aug 26) $99–$129 ste; $99–$129 effic. Extra person $10. Children under age 6 stay free. Min stay. Lower rates off-season. Parking: Outdoor, free. 10% discount for stay of seven nights or longer. Fall specials avail. MC, V.

≣≣≣ Nordic Lodge

2721 Nordic Dr, 54234; tel 414/854-5432. On the S end of Sister Bay on WI 42. Family-owned and -operated, with roomy, sunny corridors. Located away from hustle and bustle of downtown, but within short drive to area shopping and restaurants. **Rooms:** 33 rms and effic. CI 3pm/CO 11am. No smoking. Thanks to continued updates, the colors and furnishings are very fresh. Some rooms face road, so are noisy during heavy traffic hours. **Amenities:** ☎ ⚷ A/C, cable TV. All units w/terraces, 1 w/fireplace. Each room has private porch with chairs that overlook wooded area. Suites available with fully equipped kitchen, fireplace, and recliners. **Services:** ⚐ Social director, babysitting. Staff is happy to provide information on area and restaurants. **Facilities:** 🛒 🛏 ⚷ Whirlpool. An L-shaped sun deck adjacent to pool overlooks woods. Wood interior of pool and whirlpool area softens usually noisy swimming areas. Grills and picnic tables. **Rates:** Peak (July–Aug) $72–$78 S or D; $125–$140 effic. Extra person $10. Lower rates off-season. Parking: Outdoor, free. Closed Nov–Apr. MC, V.

≣≣≣ Open Hearth Lodge

1109 S Bay Shore Dr, 54234; tel 414/854-4890. On the S side of Sister Bay on WI 42. Set back from road and surrounded by 6½ acres of trees and wildflowers. Large stone fireplace and sitting area in lobby. Fresh colors and furnishings with stenciling throughout lobby, corridors, and rooms. Ideal for families. **Rooms:** 32 rms and stes; 2 cottages/villas. CI 3pm/CO 11am. Nonsmoking rms avail. Separate cottage and villa available during high season only. **Amenities:** ☎ A/C, cable TV, refrig. **Services:** ⚐ Babysitting. Complimentary coffee and doughnuts (plus hot apple cider in winter). Games and books in lobby for kids. **Facilities:** 🛒 🛏 ⚷ Whirlpool, playground. Pool in glass solarium, whirlpool in glass gazebo; outdoor patio off pool and whirlpool area. Sandbox adjacent to playground. Grills and picnic tables. **Rates:** Peak (June 23–Aug 26) $74–$84 S or D; $104–$114 ste; $650–$1,750 cottage/villa. Extra person $10. Min stay special events. Lower rates off-season. Parking: Outdoor, free. Infants stay free; $3/child. Cottage rates are weekly. Special seasonal packages. AE, DISC, MC, V.

≣≣ Voyager

232 WI 57, 54234; tel 414/854-4242. 1 mi SE of Sister Bay. Situated outside town on six acres of woods and wildflowers. **Rooms:** 28 rms. CI 3pm/CO 11am. Nonsmoking rms avail. Fresh, light decor. **Amenities:** ☎ ⚷ A/C, cable TV, refrig.

Some units w/terraces. **Services:** Complimentary coffee and doughnuts. Swedish massage available. Separate pool and sauna towels. Relaxed, friendly service. **Facilities:** Lawn games, sauna, steam rm, whirlpool. Bicycle storage. Outside whirlpool. Indoor sitting/social room adjacent to pool area with fireplace and cooking facilities for late night snacks or card games. Picnic tables, barbecue grills, horseshoe pits. Ample room for boat or bus parking. **Rates:** Peak (July–Aug) $69–$72 S or D. Extra person $7. Min stay wknds and special events. Lower rates off-season. Parking: Outdoor, free. Packages in fall and spring include dinner and golf at area's finest facilities. Closed Nov–Apr. DISC, MC, V.

LODGE

⊨⊨⊨ Hotel Du Nord

11000 Bayshore Dr, PO Box 408, 54234; tel 414/854-4221 or toll free 800/582-6667; fax 414/854-2710. On the N side of Sister Bay. Hardwood floors, a huge stone fireplace, and heavy wood rocking chairs grace the lobby of this newer inn. Restaurants, shopping, and the harbor are only steps away. **Rooms:** 50 rms and stes; 5 cottages/villas. CI 2pm/CO 11am. Nonsmoking rms avail. All rooms in main building overlook bay. Woods-side suites available, as are cottages or rooms in separate lodge building. **Amenities:** A/C, cable TV. Some units w/terraces, 1 w/fireplace, some w/whirlpools. **Services:** Children's program, babysitting. VCRs and movies available. Continental breakfast Mon–Sat only. Children's program includes games, nature crafts, and other activities with on-staff coordinator. **Facilities:** 1 restaurant (lunch and dinner only; see "Restaurants" below), 1 bar (w/entertainment), whirlpool, playground, washer/dryer. Lunch served in restaurant July–Aug only; dinner served nightly. Docking space. Boat house on water offers sandwiches and beverages. Sun deck. **Rates (CP):** Peak (June 23–Aug 20) $83–$99 S; $109 D; $99–$165 ste; $100–$135 cottage/villa. Children under age 15 stay free. Min stay peak. Lower rates off-season. Parking: Outdoor, free. Discounts for seniors (65+). Family, theater, and winter packages avail. AE, DISC, MC, V.

RESTAURANTS

Cherrywood Inn

321 Country Walk Dr; tel 414/854-9590. E on Country Walk Dr from WI 42; S end of Sister Bay. **Regional American.** Cozy high-backed booths and country charm are the setting for this Door County eatery, where even the ice cream is homemade. Baked lemon chicken with linguine is a favorite here as are the slow-cooked barbecue ribs and Door County fish boil. The extensive list of pies and desserts is notable: peanut butter pie, chocolate cheesecake, caramel flan, passion pie, and—of course—ice cream pies. **FYI:** Reservations accepted. Children's menu. Beer and wine only. **Open:** Lunch daily 11:30am–3pm; dinner daily 5–9pm. Closed Nov. **Prices:** Main courses $12–$16. MC, V.

Door Deli

WI 42; tel 414/854-4514. **Regional American/Deli.** A cozy atmosphere prevails in the dining room, with high-backed wooden booths along the walls. Tables near the windows give diners a comfortable spot to watch pedestrian traffic while munching on a submarine sandwich, bratwurst, or rib-eye sandwich. Twenty flavors of ice cream, specialty sundaes, gourmet coffees, and cappuccino are available to top off a meal. **FYI:** Reservations accepted. Children's menu. Beer and wine only. **Open:** Peak (July 1–Aug 20) daily 6am–10pm. Closed Nov–Apr. **Prices:** Main courses $5–$11. DISC, MC, V.

Hotel Du Nord Dining Room

11000 N Bayshore Dr; tel 414/854-4221. On WI 42. **Seafood.** With a view of Sister Bay and a vaulted wood ceiling, this elegant restaurant is flooded with sunlight during the day. Breads, desserts, soups, sauces, and cheesecakes are made daily on the premises. Among entrees, salmon with lemon tarragon and tenderloin á la Oscar are particular standouts. **FYI:** Reservations recommended. Guitar. Children's menu. No smoking. **Open:** Peak (July–Aug) lunch Tues–Fri 11am–2pm; dinner daily 5:30–9:30pm; brunch Sun 9:30am–12:30pm. **Prices:** Main courses $16–$23. AE, DISC, MC, V.

Spring Green

Located just north of the Wisconsin River, in south-central Wisconsin. Frank Lloyd Wright home and studio may be toured at Taliesin. South of town, Alexander Jordan's House on the Rock houses an eclectic collection of antique furniture and oddities. Summer and early fall sees drama at American Players Theatre. **Information:** Spring Green Area Chamber of Commerce, PO Box 3, Spring Green, 53588 (tel 608/588-2042).

INN

⊨⊨⊨ The Silver Star

3852 Limmex Hill Rd, 53588; tel 608/935-7297. 340 acres. This new, huge, log building rises up through a clearing on top of a hill after a winding, four-mile drive. A wide porch and deck curves around half the structure, while flower gardens are bright and colorful against the backdrop of woods and farmlands. Walk through the door into a cozy cafe that leads into a sitting area with a fireplace—like a big, friendly living room. Jean Langer, one of the innkeepers, displays her photographs throughout, and suites are named for things and people pertinent to photography. A Land's End catalog was photographed here. Definitely a place for grown-ups. **Rooms:** 10 rms and stes. CI 4pm/CO 11am. No smoking. All rooms are called suites, but some are a bit small. Each is individually decorated with a mix of antiques and contemporary furnishings. **Amenities:** A/C. No phone or TV. 1 unit w/terrace, 1 w/whirlpool. **Services:** Masseur. When cafe is not open, guests can help themselves to refreshments on honor system. Owners live on premises and treat inn like home and guests like friends. **Facilities:** ⚓ 🛏 ⅙ 1 restaurant (*see* "Restaurants" below), guest lounge w/TV. **Rates (BB):** $95–$125 D; $125–$135 ste. Extra person $12.50. Parking: Outdoor, free. MC, V.

RESTAURANT 🍽

The Silver Star
3852 Limmex Hill Rd; tel 608/935-7297. **New American.** A log inn houses this new cafe featuring well-chosen furnishings and original art (photos, paintings, textiles) by local artists. The good taste of the decor is matched by the food: boneless trout amandine in champagne sauce, pork loin with brandied apples and onions, and chicken piccata. The winter menu includes ragouts, goulashes, and stews. Dessert favorites are lemon blintz, fresh berry torte, and cheesecake. **FYI:** Reservations accepted. Children's menu. BYO. No smoking. **Open:** Peak (May–Oct) Tues–Thurs 11am–7pm, Fri–Sat 11am–9pm, Sun 9am–3pm. **Prices:** Main courses $9–$13. MC, V. 🍴 📷 ⅙

ATTRACTIONS 🏛

Taliesin
Jct WI 23 and County Rd C; tel 608/588-7900. Frank Lloyd Wright's primary residence for nearly 50 years. There are five major designs on the 600 acres of Taliesin, representing work from every decade of Wright's 73-year career. The estate includes a romantic windmill of unusual construction, homes, a farm, a school, a theater, and a waterfall on the parklike grounds. The Taliesin Preservation Commission operates four unique guided tours. **Open:** May–Oct, Mon–Fri 8:30am–5:30pm, Sat–Sun 8:30am–6:30pm. **$$$**

House on the Rock
5754 WI 23; tel 608/935-3639. Designed and built by architect Alex Jordan, this architectural marvel hangs 450 feet above the Wisconsin River. Waterfalls, pools, and trees have been integrated into the design of the building. The "Infinity Room" was built with walls of glass, and projects 218 feet over the Wyoming Valley. With 3,264 windows incorporated into its design, visitors are afforded a unique view of the forest floor 156 feet below. **Open:** Peak (June–Aug) daily 9am–7pm. Reduced hours off-season. Closed Jan–Mar. **$$$$**

Wisconsin Artists Showcase/Jura Silverman Gallery
143 S Washington; tel 608/588-7049. Housed in an early 1900s cheese warehouse, this artist-owned and -operated gallery focuses on outstanding art and fine crafts by over 150 Wisconsin artists and artisans working in all media. The gallery works with clients on special requirements and commissions, and offers consultations in both home and business

environments. The season is year-round, with shows changing every six to eight weeks. **Open:** Peak (May–Oct) Wed–Sun 10am–5:30pm. Reduced hours off-season. **Free**

Stevens Point

Seat of Portage County, in central Wisconsin. This small city on the Wisconsin River is mainly an agricultural and dairy center. Home of the University of Wisconsin-Stevens Point. **Information:** Stevens Point Area Convention & Visitors Bureau, 23 Park Ridge Dr, Stevens Point, 54481-4432 (tel 715/344-2556 or toll free 800/236-4636).

MOTELS 🏨

≣≣ Budgetel Inn
4917 Main St, 54481; tel 715/344-1900 or toll free 800/428-3438; fax 715/344-1254. Exit 158 off US 51, at Jct US 10A and US 51. Three miles from airport, UW Stevens Point, and downtown's Center Point Mall. **Rooms:** 79 rms. CI 1pm/CO noon. Nonsmoking rms avail. Pleasant, contemporary colors. Rooms in back of motel face quiet wooded area and are away from street noise. **Amenities:** 🛏 📺 A/C, satel TV w/movies. **Services:** 🛎 ⬅ ⬥ Service is extremely accommodating. **Facilities:** ⚓ 🛏 ⅙ Washer/dryer. **Rates (CP):** $38–$47 S; $45–$54 D. Children under age 18 stay free. Parking: Outdoor, free. Rate discounts include AARP, Allstate Motor Club, and Sam's Wholesale Club members. AE, DC, DISC, MC, V.

≣≣≣ Comfort Suites
300 N Division St, 54481; tel 715/341-6000 or toll free 800/221-2222; fax 715/341-8908. Exit 161 off US 51. The winner of awards two years in a row, placing it in the top 4% of 1,000 competing hotels and motels—and it's only two years old. Facility in excellent condition, with light, airy decor throughout. Three miles from downtown and UW Stevens Point. **Rooms:** 105 rms and stes. CI 3pm/CO noon. Nonsmoking rms avail. **Amenities:** 🛏 ♨ 📺 A/C, cable TV w/movies, refrig, VCR. Some units w/whirlpools. **Services:** 🛎 ⬅ Cashless video rental machines accept credit cards. Well-run property with an efficient, competent staff. **Facilities:** 🏊 ⚓ 🍴 🛏 ⅙ Whirlpool, washer/dryer. Noise from adjoining pool spills over into lobby. **Rates (CP):** Peak (May–Aug) $59–$69 S; $69–$79 D; $99 ste. Children under age 18 stay free. Lower rates off-season. Parking: Outdoor, free. Senior, corporate, and government/military discounts. AE, CB, DC, DISC, MC, V.

≣≣≣ Holiday Inn
1501 North Point Dr, 54481; tel 715/341-1340 or toll free 800/922-7880; fax 715/341-9446. Exit 161 off US 51. With the recent addition of its convention center, this has become a convention workhorse. It may take some time to get oriented to this facility's extensive layout. Located along one of the major commercial strips in Stevens Point, not far from

downtown shopping areas. **Rooms:** 295 rms and stes. CI 3pm/CO 11am. Nonsmoking rms avail. Rooms have more of a view than in a traditional low-rise motel. Updating needed in bathrooms to bring decor in sync with more contemporary colors in sleeping areas. To avoid Holidome noise, steer clear of poolside rooms. **Amenities:** 🛏 🕓 A/C, cable TV w/movies, VCR. Some units w/terraces. **Services:** ✗ 🚐 📷 🛏 🐕 Babysitting. Pets accommodated with prior arrangement. Free airport shuttle to both regional airports. Staff can sometimes be very busy handling requests of convention guests, causing delays in service. **Facilities:** 🔥 🏊 🛎 2800 🚹 1 restaurant (see "Restaurants" below), 1 bar (w/entertainment), games rm, sauna, whirlpool, washer/dryer. The Holidome is a child's paradise with video game pits, air hockey, sand pits, and a full-sized pool. Poolside location of the exercise room makes it susceptible to wet floors. **Rates:** $70–$79 S; $80–$89 D; $90–$130 ste. Extra person $5. Children under age 18 stay free. Parking: Outdoor, free. Discounts offered periodically. Golf packages avail with SentryWorld Golf, rated one of the top 25 golf courses in the United States. AE, CB, DC, DISC, JCB, MC, V.

RESTAURANTS 🍴

Hot Fish Shop
1140 Clark St; tel 715/344-4252. 1 block S of Center Point Mall. **Seafood/Steak.** Fresh seafood is trucked in daily to this nautical-themed eatery. Specialties include seafood fettuccine, walleye pike and shrimp platter, and New York strip. Owners take visible pride in customers' satisfaction. **FYI:** Reservations accepted. Children's menu. **Open:** Mon–Thurs 11am–9:30pm, Fri–Sat 11am–10pm. **Prices:** Main courses $10–$17. AE, DC, DISC, MC, V.

Mesquite Grill & Restaurant
In Holiday Inn, 1501 North Point Dr; tel 715/341-1340. **Barbecue/Steak/Tex-Mex.** Features a full salad bar and a "show grill," where diners can watch food preparation. Specialities include mesquite-grilled barbecue ribs, steaks, and pastas. Diners can create their own omelettes during the Tex-Mex brunch (Sun). A full-time pastry chef bakes all breads, pastries, and desserts. No sound barrier between restaurant and bar, so noise levels can be high when bar features evening entertainment. **FYI:** Reservations recommended. Blues/cabaret/comedy/country music/rock. Children's menu. **Open:** Sun–Thurs 6:30am–10pm, Fri–Sat 6:30am–11pm. **Prices:** Main courses $8–$20. AE, DC, DISC, MC, V. ♿

The Restaurant
In Sentry Insurance World Headquarters, 1800 North Point Dr; tel 715/346-6010. **American/Italian.** A display of historic miniature buggies and carts greets diners upon entering the building from the parking ramp. The dining area features a vaulted ceiling and a wall of windows affording a view of a wooded preserve where deer feed. **FYI:** Reservations recom-

mended. **Open:** Lunch Mon–Thurs 11am–2pm; dinner Mon–Thurs 3:30–9:30pm, Fri–Sat 4–10pm. **Prices:** Main courses $6–$19. AE, MC, V. ▲

ATTRACTION 🏛

Stevens Point Brewery
2617 Water St; tel 715/344-9310. Founded in 1857, Stevens Point is Wisconsin's oldest family-owned brewery still in existence. Guided tours; gift shop. **Open:** Peak (June–Aug) Mon–Sat 11am–1:30pm. Reduced hours off-season. **Free**

Sturgeon Bay

See also Bailey's Harbor, Egg Harbor, Ephraim, Fish Creek, Sister Bay, Washington Island

Seat of Door County. Situated at the base of the Door Peninsula, the name of this village derived from the swarms of sturgeon that were once caught here. Although fruit growing and processing has somewhat replaced maritime industry in the economic life of Door County, there are still three active shipyards here. **Information:** Door County Chamber of Commerce, 1015 Green Bay Rd, PO Box 406, Sturgeon Bay, 54235 (tel 414/743-4456).

MOTELS 🏨

🎖🎖🎖 Bay Shore Inn
4205 Bay Shore Dr, 54235; tel 414/743-4551; fax 414/743-3299. N from Sturgeon Bay on 42/57 to County BB; W to County B; N 1 mi. 3 acres. The main building of this award-winning inn was built in 1922. Ideal for families during the summer, it is situated on the water and is close to golf courses and horseback riding. **Rooms:** 29 stes. CI 3pm/CO 11am. All have water views and king-size beds. **Amenities:** 🛏 🕓 📞 A/C, cable TV w/movies, refrig, VCR. All units w/terraces, all w/whirlpools. **Services:** 📷 🐕 Babysitting. Video delivery available. **Facilities:** 🔥 🏊 🛎 🏊 🎣 🎣 1 📏 80 🚹 1 restaurant (dinner only), 1 beach (bay), basketball, games rm, whirlpool, playground, washer/dryer. Restaurant on premises serves dinner nightly May–Oct. Boat parking at pier; boat launches one mile to north and south. Rowboats. Grills and picnic tables. Nature trail, 850 feet of shoreline. **Rates:** Peak (July–Aug) $160–$260 ste. Extra person $15. Children under age 6 stay free. Min stay peak. Lower rates off-season. Parking: Outdoor, free. Corporate/group discount avail during off season. AE, DISC, MC, V.

🎖🎖 Best Western Maritime Inn
1001 N 14th Ave, 54235; tel 414/743-7231 or toll free 800/528-1234; fax 414/743-9341. On the N end of Sturgeon Bay on Business 42. Large wood-beamed lobby with stone fireplace and social area. Ideal for families. Close to shopping and restaurants; short drive to downtown and shipyards. **Rooms:** 90 rms, stes, and effic. CI 3pm/CO 11am. Nonsmoking rms avail. Back rooms face wooded area. **Amenities:** 🛏

A/C, cable TV w/movies, refrig. Some units w/whirlpools. **Services:** 🏊 🍴 **Facilities:** 🎣 🚶 🎿 ♿ Games rm, whirlpool. Pool area features vaulted wood ceiling and wall of windows; large recreation room off pool with sitting area. **Rates (CP):** Peak (July–Aug) $45–$79 S; $50–$86 D; $130 ste; $99 effic. Extra person $7. Children under age 12 stay free. Lower rates off-season. Parking: Outdoor, free. Gold Crown discount 10%. Spring and winter packages avail. AE, CB, DC, DISC, MC, V.

≣ Chal-A Motel
3910 WI 42/57, 54235; tel 414/743-6788. Situated on 11 acres of trees and meadow, this economical stopover is located along a cross-country ski and snowmobile trail. The real highlight here is the on-premise doll and antique car museum that features rooms of mechanical animal displays, antique dolls, 1,000 Barbie dolls, and vintage cars ($1 charge). Plenty of running room for children. **Rooms:** 20 rms. CI 11am/CO 10:30am. **Amenities:** 📺 ♨ A/C, TV w/movies. **Services:** 🍴 **Facilities:** 🚶 🎿 ♿ Picnic table, sandbox. Boat parking, cleaning station, and freezer space for fish. **Rates:** Peak (July–Aug) $44 S; $49 D. Extra person $4. Lower rates off-season. Parking: Outdoor, free. MC, V.

≣≣≣ The Cliff Dwellers
3540 N Duluth Ave, 54235; tel 414/743-4260. Main building is built into cliff that rises abruptly from driveway. Across the bay from the city of Sturgeon Bay, with a fascinating view of the shipbuilding yards for which this city is famous. Adjacent to Potawatomi State Park; short drive to restaurants and shopping. **Rooms:** 16 rms; 13 cottages/villas. CI 3pm/CO 11am. No smoking. All rooms and cottages have water view. Some cottages have screened-in porches and private waterside sitting areas. Furnishings a little funky, but view is worth it. **Amenities:** ♨ TV. No A/C or phone. Some units w/terraces, some w/fireplaces. Main building has air conditioning, cottages do not. Some cottages have kitchenettes. **Services:** 🍴 Babysitting. Wake-up tray delivered to each room. Lending library with books, games, and puzzles. Accommodating staff provides personalized service. **Facilities:** 🎣 🏊 🎿 🚶 🎿 ♨2 ♿ Lawn games, sauna, whirlpool. Pleasant pool area has adjacent waterfront sunning and picnic area. Rowboats, horseshoe pit. Covered parking available. **Rates (CP):** Peak (July–Aug) $89–$95 S or D; $95–$165 cottage/villa. Extra person $20. Min stay special events. Lower rates off-season. Parking: Outdoor, free. Discount on stays of six or more nights during high season. Midweek specials offered during off-season. Closed Nov–Apr. AE, DISC, MC, V.

≣≣ Comfort Inn
923 Green Bay Rd, 54235; tel 414/743-7846 or toll free 800/221-2222. On WI 42/57 at first stop light in town. Newer property located on south edge of town on busy roadway. Popular with tour groups and visiting sports teams. **Rooms:** 52 rms and stes. CI 3pm/CO 11am. Nonsmoking rms avail. Fresh decor in rooms, which either face parking lot or wooded area. **Amenities:** 📺 A/C, cable TV. Some units

w/whirlpools. **Services:** 🍴 Efficient staff. **Facilities:** 🎣 🚶 ♿ Whirlpool, washer/dryer. Pool is small. **Rates (CP):** Peak (July–Aug) $79–$81 S; $86–$87 D; $88–$122 ste. Extra person $7. Children under age 18 stay free. Min stay special events. Lower rates off-season. Parking: Outdoor, free. Corporate rates during week. AE, CB, DC, DISC, ER, JCB, MC, V.

≣ Super 8 Motel
409 Green Bay Rd, 54235; tel 414/743-9211 or toll free 800/800-8000; fax 414/743-4143. Well maintained, with full-sized informal lobby with wood stove. Easy access to main highways. Short drive to downtown. **Rooms:** 62 rms. CI 3pm/CO 11am. Nonsmoking rms avail. Views from most rooms are of parking lot or roadways; road noise is apparent. **Amenities:** 📺 A/C, cable TV, refrig. 1 unit w/whirlpool. **Services:** 🏊 🍴 Babysitting. Friendly staff. **Facilities:** 🎣 🚶 🎿 ♿ Whirlpool. **Rates (CP):** Peak (July–Oct 15) $69–$74 S; $76–$81 D. Extra person $7. Children under age 12 stay free. Lower rates off-season. Parking: Outdoor, free. Winter packages avail. AE, CB, DC, DISC, MC, V.

≣≣ White Birch Inn
1009 S Oxford Ave, 54235; tel 414/743-3295. Located away from the main Sturgeon Bay traffic, this family-owned and -operated.property gets its name from the stand of birch trees located in front. The high-ceilinged lobby features southwestern decor with wooden rockers and tile floor. **Rooms:** 16 rms and stes. CI 2pm/CO 11am. Nonsmoking rms avail. Rooms have individual decor, such as southwestern and country with wicker and antique furniture. **Amenities:** 📺 ♨ A/C, TV. Some units w/terraces, some w/fireplaces, some w/whirlpools. Patios available with wooded view. **Services:** ✕ 🏊 🍴 **Facilities:** 🚶 🎿 20 ♿ 1 restaurant (lunch and dinner only; see "Restaurants" below), 1 bar. **Rates (CP):** Peak (June–Sept) $75–$95 S or D; $135–$150 ste. Extra person $10. Min stay peak. Lower rates off-season. Parking: Outdoor, free. Senior and government discounts. AE, MC, V.

RESORT

≣≣≣ Cherry Hills Lodge
5905 Dunn Rd, 54235; tel 414/743-4222 or toll free 800/545-2307; fax 414/743-4222. N from Sturgeon Bay 1½ mi to Dunn Rd; W to lodge. Newer place ideal for golf enthusiast. Lobby features stone fireplace. Cherry orchards nearby. Toll-free number for Midwestern calls only. **Rooms:** 31 rms and stes. CI 3pm/CO 11am. Nonsmoking rms avail. Four room options, all of which overlook golf course. **Amenities:** 📺 ♨ A/C, TV, refrig. All units w/terraces, some w/whirlpools. **Services:** 🍴 Social director. Accommodating staff meets special requests. **Facilities:** 🎣 ⛳18 🚶 🎿 25 ♿ 1 restaurant (see "Restaurants" below), 1 bar (w/entertainment), whirlpool. Golf course is 6,192 yards, par 72. Locker and shower facilities; fully equipped pro shop with on-staff PGA pro located on lower level; snack shop at ninth hole; valet service for clubs. Outdoor whirlpool. **Rates:** Peak (mid-June–early

Sept) $96–$111 S or D; $132–$137 ste. Extra person $15. Min stay wknds. Lower rates off-season. Parking: Outdoor, free. Winter theme weekend packages. Golf packages include lodging, unlimited golf, cart, range balls, breakfast, and complimentary cocktails. Closed Nov–Mar. AE, CB, DC, DISC, MC, V.

RESTAURANTS ⑪

★ **Mill Supper Club**
4128 WI 42/57; tel 414/743-5044. **American.** For three generations, the Mill's owners have been serving up satisfying fare in their 1930 vintage dining room. Knotty-pine paneling, moose and deer trophies, and a 40-foot-long bar contribute to the rustic atmosphere. Besides homemade breads and rolls, desserts, and soups, diners can enjoy the special oven-baked chicken with potatoes, stuffing, and cole slaw; summer-time fish boils; and an array of Friday night seafood specials. **FYI:** Reservations accepted. Children's menu. **Open:** Peak (Mem Day–Labor Day) Tues–Sun 5–10pm. **Prices:** Main courses $9–$23. MC, V. 🍴 &

The Nautical Inn
234 Kentucky St (Downtown); tel 414/743-3399. **Regional American.** Built in 1886, this former boarding house has undergone several incarnations. The dining room is comfortable thanks to a stone fireplace, wood paneling,and cozy booths. Lunchtime sandwich board includes a Monte Cristo, charbroiled chicken breast croissant, and tasty soups like wild rice and mushroom and french onion au gratin. Evening specials include broiled whitefish with paprika butter, barbecued baby back boneless ribs with homemade sauce, and tenderloin or rib eye steaks topped with mushrooms and onions. **FYI:** Reservations accepted. Piano. **Open:** Lunch daily 11am–2pm; dinner daily 5–9pm. **Prices:** Main courses $9–$17. AE, MC, V. 🍴 &

★ **Perry's Cherry Diner**
230 Michigan St; tel 414/743-9910. **Burgers/Diner.** The popularity of this '50s-style diner is evidenced by a packed dining room even in mid-afternoon, so expect a wait if you come during traditional dining hours. Perry bases his reputation on his old-fashioned malts and shakes, homemade pies, and gyros and burgers. **FYI:** Reservations not accepted. Children's menu. No liquor license. No smoking. **Open:** Mon–Sat 6am–9pm, Sun 8am–3pm. **Prices:** Main courses $5–$6. No CC. 🍴

The Restaurant at Cherry Hills
In Cherry Hills Lodge, 5905 Dunn Rd; tel 414/743-4222. N from Sturgeon Bay on WI 42; 1½ mi to Dunn Rd; W to lodge. **Regional American.** This is a perfect place to unwind after playing a round of golf at Cherry Hills Lodge. Besides featuring Wisconsin and regional products this restaurant prides itself on its dessert buffet at Sunday brunch, herb crusted prime rib served with horseradish and mashed potatoes, and cobb salad with cold cucumber soup. Special-event weekends during the winter include a Mozart weekend that features a performance of the composer's music followed by a multicourse Viennese meal. **FYI:** Reservations recommended. Piano. No smoking. **Open:** Breakfast daily 7–10:30am; lunch Mon–Sat 11am–2:30pm; dinner daily 6–9pm; brunch Sun 11am–1:30pm. Closed Nov–Mar. **Prices:** Main courses $9–$17. AE, CB, DC, DISC, MC, V. 🍴 🏞 &

White Birch Inn
1009 S Oxford Ave; tel 414/743-3295. **American.** A view of birch trees greets diners at this family-owned and -operated dining room. The dish that packs them in here is the family-style baked chicken with mashed potatoes and gravy, cranberry dressing, and all the trimmings. Other popular favorites include barbecued ribs and baked perch. Strawberry shortcake for dessert. **FYI:** Reservations accepted. Children's menu. **Open:** Lunch Wed–Mon 11:30am–1:30pm; dinner Wed–Mon 5:30–9:30pm. **Prices:** Main courses $8–$29. MC, V. 🍴 &

ATTRACTIONS 🎫

Door County Museum
18 N 4th Ave; tel 414/743-5809. The museum focuses on the history of Door County and the ethnic heritage of the Scandinavian and Belgian settlers, as well as early businesses and vocations common to most Wisconsin counties. The lower-level wing is devoted to artifacts related to agriculture, dairying, logging, fishing, and blacksmithing. Also included are a model general store, early settlers log house, and numerous storefronts from "small town" Wisconsin. The recreated Pioneer Fire Station houses several original fire trucks and other fire fighting equipment from the original fire department. **Open:** May–Oct, daily 10am–4:30pm. **Free**

Door County Maritime Museum
101 Florida; tel 414/743-8139. Located 10 mi N of Sister Bay. Small local museum documenting the importance of commercial fishing to the area economy. Among the exhibits are several old tugboats and Coast Guard craft, as well as a re-created sea captain's office. **Open:** Peak (Mem Day–Labor Day) Sun–Thurs 9am–6pm, Fri–Sat 9am–8pm. Reduced hours off-season. Closed Nov–Mem Day. **$**

Miller Art Center
107 S 4th Ave; tel 414/746-0707. The permanent collection of this nonprofit museum includes more than 250 paintings, drawings, and graphics, with a major emphasis on contemporary local artists. A performing arts series has recently presented selections from Rachmaninoff, chamber music, and Czech folk music. Guided tours available. **Open:** Mon–Thurs 10am–5pm and 7–9pm, Fri–Sat 10am–5pm. **Free**

Door Peninsula Winery
5806 WI 42, Carlsville; tel 414/743-7431 or toll free 800/551-5049. Located 8 mi N of Sturgeon Bay. Housed in a renovated 1868 schoolhouse, this winery has been producing award-winning fruit wines for over 20 years. Specialties include Montmorency cherry, plum, pear, and apple fruit

wines, and mulled Christmas wines. Twenty-minute guided tours are followed up by a free tasting; an orientation video explains the winemaking process. **Open:** Peak (June–Nov) daily 9am–6pm. Reduced hours off-season. **$**

Superior

Seat of Douglas County, in northwest corner of state. Superior-Duluth, at the head of Lake Superior, has for years been one of the leading ports in the country because of its fine natural harbor. Three state parks are within a half-hour drive from town. **Information:** Superior-Douglas County Convention & Visitors Bureau, 305 Harbor View Pkwy, Superior, 54880 (tel 715/392-2773 or toll free 800/942-5313).

MOTELS 🏨

≣≣ Barker's Island Inn and Conference Center
300 Marina Dr, 54880; tel 715/392-7152 or toll free 800/344-7515; fax 715/392-1180. 2 blocks E of I-2. Although the motel caters to business travelers and conventioneers, it is perfectly suited for vacationing families as well. Within walking distance of public playground and beach. **Rooms:** 114 rms and stes. CI 3pm/CO 11am. Nonsmoking rms avail. **Amenities:** 🛁 A/C, cable TV. 1 unit w/whirlpool. **Services:** ✗ ⚐ ⛵ Guests can have a Nordic Track delivered to room. **Facilities:** 🛦 🏊 🎣 ❸ 🏊 🖥 ৬ 1 restaurant, 1 bar, games rm, sauna, whirlpool, washer/dryer. **Rates:** Peak (June–Sept) $65–$250 S or D; $135–$250 ste. Children under age 18 stay free. Min stay special events. Lower rates off-season. Parking: Outdoor, free. AE, CB, DC, DISC, MC, V.

≣≣ Days Inn
110 Harborview Pkwy, 54880; tel 715/392-4783 or toll free 800/DAYS-INN; fax 715/392-2068. Across from the visitor's center. Large motel conveniently located across from visitor's center and lakefront walk. **Rooms:** 110 rms and stes. CI 2pm/CO noon. Nonsmoking rms avail. **Amenities:** 🛁 A/C, cable TV. **Services:** ✗ ⚐ Helpful and courteous staff. **Facilities:** 🛦 🎣 🚭 ৬ Games rm, sauna, whirlpool, washer/dryer. **Rates (CP):** Peak (July–Sept) $58–$98 S; $63–$98 D; $85–$105 ste. Extra person $5. Children under age 17 stay free. Min stay special events. Lower rates off-season. Parking: Outdoor, free. AE, DC, DISC, MC, V.

≣ Superior Inn
525 Hammond Ave, 54880; tel 715/394-7706 or toll free 800/777-8599; fax 715/394-7708. At the foot of the Blatnik Bridge. Brightly painted motel located downtown, within walking distance of some great restaurants. **Rooms:** 67 rms and stes. CI 3pm/CO noon. Nonsmoking rms avail. View is nothing to brag about, and decor is drab. **Amenities:** 🛁 🍴 A/C, cable TV, refrig. 1 unit w/terrace, 1 w/whirlpool. **Services:** ⚐ ⛵ Upon request, front desk staff will cook a frozen pizza for you to pick up. **Facilities:** 🛦 🎣 🚭 ৬ Games rm, sauna, whirlpool. **Rates (CP):** Peak (June–Aug)

$55–$69 S; $60–$69 D; $100–$135 ste. Extra person $4. Children under age 18 stay free. Lower rates off-season. Parking: Outdoor, free. AE, DISC, MC, V.

RESTAURANTS 🍽

The Library
1410 Tower Ave; tel 715/392-4821. Off I-2 and 53; 2 blocks N on Tower Ave. **American.** This setting of extraordinary woodwork and shelf after shelf of beautiful antique books possesses a quietly elegant, romantic ambience. Unique oil paintings complete the decor. A large salad bar and significant wine list complement the menu offerings. **FYI:** Reservations recommended. Children's menu. **Open:** Peak (May–Oct) Mon–Sat 11am–10pm, Sun 10–9pm. **Prices:** Main courses $8–$37. AE, DC, DISC, MC, V. 🍷 🗪

The Shack Supper Club
3301 Belknap St; tel 715/392-9836. **American.** By no means a shack, this supper club catering to an older crowd can be counted on for good seafood and steaks and attentive service. **FYI:** Reservations recommended. Dinner theater. **Open:** Lunch Mon–Sat 11am–2:30pm; dinner Mon–Thurs 4:30–9pm, Fri–Sat 4:30–10pm, Sun 11:30am–8pm. **Prices:** Main courses $9–$17. DC, DISC, MC, V. ৬

★ Zona Rosa Restaurante Mexicano
1410 Tower Ave; tel 715/392-4161. **Mexican.** A popular local choice for a burrito or enchilada. The restaurant is partitioned into three semi-separate dining rooms whose peach stucco walls are covered with framed photos of Mexican generals, gunfighters, politicians, and families. Large portions and an extensive menu. Every meal begins with a basket of warm, freshly baked tortilla chips and salsa. The attentive wait staff dresses in traditional Mexican attire. **FYI:** Reservations recommended. Children's menu. Beer and wine only. **Open:** Peak (May–Oct) Mon–Fri 11am–10pm, Sat 11am–10:30pm, Sun 11am–9pm. **Prices:** Main courses $4–$25. AE, DC, DISC, MC, V. 🗪

ATTRACTIONS 🏛

SS *Meteor* Maritime Museum
US 2/53 and MI 13; tel 715/392-5742 or 392-1083. The engine room, pilothouse, and crew's quarters of this last remaining whaleback freighter (built in 1896) are now open to the public. Also of special interest are the *Col DD Gaillard* (a dipper-dredge vessel used to widen the St Lawrence Seaway) and a statue paying tribute to the men lost in the famed wreck of the *Edmund Fitzgerald*. **Open:** Peak (July–Aug) daily 10am–7pm. Reduced hours off-season. **$$**

Fairlawn Mansion and Museum
906 E 2nd St; tel 715/394-5712. This 42-room Victorian mansion on the waterfront, built in 1890, is now a museum that interprets the history of Douglas County. All the rooms on the first floor are restored to Victorian-era decor; featured on the second floor are exhibits of the prehistoric

Native American cultures of the Lake Superior region, the Sioux and Ojibwe cultures, the Yankee settlers and the European immigrant cultures; third-floor exhibits showcase the heritage of the region and its industries. **Open:** Daily 9am–5pm. **$$**

Tomah

Located 30 miles west of La Crosse. This central Wisconsin town is the gateway to cranberry country. Lake Tomah, on west edge of town, offers boating and ice-fishing. **Information:** Greater Tomah Area Chamber of Commerce, 708 Superior Ave, PO Box 625, Tomah, 54660-0625 (tel 608/372-2166 or toll free 800/368-3601).

MOTELS

Budget Host Daybreak Inn

US 12 and WI 16, 54660; tel 608/372-5946 or toll free 800/999-7088; fax 608/372-5947. Exit 43 off I-90, US 12 W 1½ mi. Four buildings—three for lodging and one with lobby and living quarters of owners—make up this facility. Most of the rooms are on ground level with parking outside each room's entrance. A bright red barn stands at one end of the property, which is highlighted with trees, bushes, and a large yard with picnic tables. Close to municipal swimming pool that guests can use in summer. **Rooms:** 32 rms. CI noon/CO 10:30am. Nonsmoking rms avail. Southwestern Wisconsin history is focus of theme rooms (Amish, Frank Lloyd Wright, Laura Ingalls Wilder). Patchwork quilts, rag dolls, and country-kitsch wall decorations are mixed in with functional, well-worn motel furnishings. Rooms in back building have view of open field, sometimes visited by a deer or two. **Amenities:** A/C, cable TV w/movies. **Services:** Owners are always around to cheerfully take care of guest requests. **Facilities:** Basketball. **Rates:** Peak (May 16–Oct 15) $32–$48 S; $45–$58 D. Extra person $5. Children under age 17 stay free. Lower rates off-season. Parking: Outdoor, free. AE, CB, DC, DISC, MC, V.

Holiday Inn Tomah

WI 21, PO Box 845, WI; tel 608/372-3211 or toll free 800/HOLIDAY; fax 608/372-3243. Exit 143 off I-94. Older motel in need of some upgrading, but still comfortable and professionally staffed. Lobby is somewhat dark, with couches, coffee tables, and a colorful aquarium. **Rooms:** 100 rms. CI 3pm/CO noon. Nonsmoking rms avail. **Amenities:** A/C, cable TV w/movies, dataport. **Services:** Coffee available in lobby after restaurant is closed. Board games available at front desk. Knowledgeable staff is eager to provide assistance and/or tourist information. **Facilities:** 1 restaurant, 1 bar (w/entertainment), volleyball, games rm, sauna, steam rm, whirlpool, washer/dryer. Indoor swimming pool, with table tennis and pool tables in pool area. Kids under 12 eat free in restaurant when accompanied by adult. **Rates:** Peak (May 24–Sept 2) $55–$68

S; $61–$74 D. Extra person $6. Children under age 19 stay free. Lower rates off-season. Parking: Outdoor, free. Bed-and-breakfast package avail. AE, CB, DC, DISC, JCB, MC, V.

Super 8 Motel

I-94 and WI 21, PO Box 48, 54660; tel 608/372-3901 or toll free 800/800-8000; fax 608/372-5792. Exit 143 off I-94. Clean and service-oriented. A small but comfortable lobby features indirect lighting, couches, and tables. Close to golfing and snowmobile trails. **Rooms:** 64 rms and stes. CI 2pm/CO 11am. Nonsmoking rms avail. Clean and functional. King rooms have recliners and king-size beds. **Amenities:** A/C, cable TV w/movies. 1 unit w/whirlpool. Dataports available in some rooms. **Services:** **Facilities:** Washer/dryer. **Rates (CP):** Peak (Mem Day–Sept) $44–$58 S; $50–$65 D; $65–$105 ste. Extra person $7. Children under age 18 stay free. Lower rates off-season. Parking: Outdoor, free. Snowmobile and other winter packages avail. AE, CB, DC, DISC, MC, V.

ATTRACTIONS

Wisconsin National Guard Memorial Library and Museum

101 Independence Dr, Volk Field, Camp Douglas; tel 608/427-1280. Located at historic Camp Williams-Volk Field and housed in a restored 1896 log lodge, the museum documents the history of the Wisconsin National Guard, and chronicles its military engagements since its founding. It contains 3,000 square feet of exhibits, including full-scale and miniature dioramas, video and slide programs, and a light map of a battlefield. Aircraft, artillery, and tanks are also on display. The library contains books, diaries, personal histories, scrap books, photos, slides, videos, and maps. **Open:** Tues–Sat 9am–4pm, Sun noon–4pm. **Free**

Cranberry Expo Ltd

Exit 135 off I-94, Warrens; tel 608/378-4878. A unique and interesting look at all aspects of the Wisconsin cranberry industry, from its heritage, to the equipment used and the cultivation methods employed. Exhibits feature hand rakes, horse clogs, water reels, and harvest boats. Gift shop carries the area's largest display of cranberry glass, as well as refreshments such as cranberry candies, pie, and ice cream. Picnic area; group tours available. **Open:** Apr–Oct, daily 10am–4pm. **$$**

Two Rivers

ATTRACTIONS

Historic Washington House

1622 Jefferson St; tel 414/793-2490. According to legend, Two Rivers resident Ed Berners invented the ice cream sundae in 1881. This museum, which was originally an immigrant hotel built around 1850, houses a replica of Berners' Ice Cream Parlor and offers 18 different sundaes, as well as cokes and root beers served from an old fashioned ice cream fountain. Six rooms display local history and artifacts; the dance hall, the huge murals it contains, and original hotel rooms, are presently being restored. **Open:** Peak (May–Oct) daily 9am–9pm. Reduced hours off-season. **Free**

Point Beach Energy Center

6600 Nuclear Rd; tel 414/755-6400. Located on the shore of Lake Michigan, the center offers displays and programs about the era of electricity and nuclear energy. Visitors can tour a simulated nuclear reactor, play energy computer games, and view exhibits on solar and wind energy. There is also a half-mile nature trail, an observation tower, and picnic areas. Special programs and tours available by reservation. **Open:** Peak (Apr–Oct) daily 9am–4:30pm. Reduced hours off-season. **Free**

Great Lakes Coast Guard Museum

2022 Jackson St; tel 414/793-5905. The spirit of the "always ready" US Coast Guard is displayed via exhibits of uniforms, navigational and search-and-rescue equipment, and the recovered cabin of the *Chinook*. **Open:** May–Sept, daily 9am–5pm. **$**

Point Beach State Forest

Headquarters, 9400 County Trunk O; tel 414/794-7480. This 2,843-acre forest boasts a variety of landscapes, including sand dunes, a lakefront beach, and a northern pine forest. Hiking, cross-country skiing, snowmobiling, and ice skating are among the recreational activities featured; campsites, picnic areas, playgrounds, nature center, and concession site also available. **Open:** Daily sunrise–sunset. **$**

Washington Island

Six miles off the coast of Door County, this tiny island was settled in 1869 by Icelandic immigrants. Scandinavian Festival, held every August, celebrates local heritage with smorgasbord and dance. The island is accessible by half-hour ferry trip from Gills Rock. **Information:** Washington Island Chamber of Commerce, Rte 1, Box 222, Washington Island, 54246 (tel 414/847-2179).

HOTEL 🏨

≡≡≡ Findlay's Holiday Inn

Main Rd, Detroit Harbor, 54246; tel 414/847-2526. Located on Detroit Harbor, the original inn (which burned in 1989) was built in 1895. Close proximity to beaches; very little road traffic makes for bucolic setting. **Rooms:** 28 rms, stes, and effic. CI 1pm/CO 10am. Nonsmoking rms avail. Three buildings provide variety of room options with lake or wooded views. Quaint furnishings include chenille bedspreads and Battenburg lace table coverings; individual furniture and wallpaper treatments in each room. **Amenities:** Satel TV. No A/C or phone. Some units w/fireplaces. **Services:** ✕ ⌂ Twice-daily maid svce, babysitting. Guests receive 10%

discount on dinner at restaurant. **Facilities:** 🔲 🛶 🛏 🔟 🕹 ᕕ 1 restaurant (*see* "Restaurants" below). Grills and firewood. Pool, exercise room, and whirlpool located ¼ mile away at island's recreation center. Library/sitting area in two of three buildings. Observation deck with sitting area for viewing wildlife. Telephone in foyer. **Rates:** Peak (July–Aug/Oct–Nov) $55–$80 S; $63–$94 D; $60–$85 ste; $80–$110 effic. Extra person $5. Children under age 8 stay free. Lower rates off-season. Parking: Outdoor, free. 10% discount on stays of one week or longer. MC, V.

RESTAURANT 🍴

Findlay's Holiday Inn

Main Rd, Detroit Harbor; tel 414/847-2526. On Main Rd S of jct with Detroit Harbor Rd. **American.** Polished wood floors and a wall of windows grace the interior of this eatery. Breads, jams, dessert, soups, and dressings are all made on the premises. Prime rib, broiled whitefish, and a fresh perch fry top the dinner menu. **FYI:** Reservations recommended. Piano/organ. Children's menu. Beer and wine only. No smoking. **Open:** Breakfast daily 7–10:30am; lunch daily 11:30am–2pm; dinner daily 5:30–7:30pm. Closed Oct 16–Apr. **Prices:** Main courses $6–$12. MC, V. 🏔 💟 ᕕ

ATTRACTION 🏛

Jacobsen's Museum

Little Lake Rd; tel 414/847-2213. Native American relics and antiques from the area's early days are housed in a recreation of a 19th-century log cabin. **$**

Waukesha

Seat of Waukesha County, in southeast part of state. Many parks and wooded areas run through this city, which is located along the Waukesha River. The nearby mineral springs were a popular 19th-century resort destination. **Information:** Waukesha Area Tourism, 223A Wisconsin Ave, Waukesha, 53186 (tel 414/542-4249 or toll free 800/366-VISIT).

MOTEL 🏨

≡≡≡ Holiday Inn

2417 W Bluemound Rd, 53186; tel 414/786-0460 or toll free 800/HOLIDAY; fax 414/786-1599. Clean and comfortable motel on a commercial strip with numerous businesses and fast food restaurants. **Rooms:** 117 rms. CI 3pm/CO noon. Nonsmoking rms avail. **Amenities:** 🛏 🔥 🖵 A/C, satel TV w/movies. **Services:** ✕ ⌂ ⌔ ⌕ Babysitting. Coffee in lobby 24 hours. Fax machines available. **Facilities:** 🔟 🔟 ᕕ 1 restaurant, 1 bar, games rm, playground, washer/dryer. Waukesha Athletic Club nearby. **Rates:** Peak (June–Sept 15)

$74–$99 S or D. Children under age 18 stay free. Lower rates off-season. Parking: Outdoor, free. AE, CB, DC, DISC, JCB, MC, V.

RESTAURANT 🍽

♥★ Weissgerber's Gasthaus

2720 N Grandview Blvd; tel 414/544-4460. **American/German.** This beautiful restaurant is situated by a large lake in a quiet residential area; outdoor dining is a treat on warm summer nights. Large storybook paintings cover the exterior of the restaurant, while interior decorations are old country German. Fine home-cooked cuisine awaits hungry guests; pork shank is the specialty. **FYI:** Reservations recommended. Piano. Children's menu. **Open:** Mon–Fri 11:30am–10pm, Sat 5–10pm, Sun 4–9pm. **Prices:** Main courses $13–$38. AE, MC, V. 🟣 🛗 🛋 🖼 🎮 ♿

ATTRACTION 💼

Waukesha County Museum

101 W Main St; tel 414/548-7186. This museum documents the history and culture of Waukesha County through exhibits of a wide variety of artifacts from the earliest settler days to the present; from agricultural tools, Victorian period rooms and memorabilia, Native American items, and historic photographs, to modern technological appliances. There are slide shows on architecturally significant homes and businesses, and various aspects of pioneer and Victorian life, as well as videos of antiques and their preservation. Lectures, workshops, demonstrations, and walking and driving tours offered. Guided tours available by reservation. **Open:** Tues–Sat 9am–4:30pm. **Free**

Wausau

Seat of Marathon County, in central Wisconsin. Paper products are the chief industry in this midsized city, called "Faraway Place" by Native Americans. **Information:** Wausau Area Convention & Visitors Council, 300 3rd St, #200, PO Box 6190, Wausau, 54402-6190 (tel 715/845-6231 or toll free 800/236-9728).

HOTEL 🏨

🏨🏨🏨 Ramada Inn and Conference Center of Wausau

201 N 17th Ave, PO Box 1224, 54402; tel 715/845-4341 or toll free 800/754-9728; fax 715/845-4990. Exit 192 off I-51. This round tower of a motel can be seen from I-51 and throughout Wausau. It caters to business travelers but is also well suited for families or large groups. **Rooms:** 235 rms and stes. Executive level. CI 3pm/CO 11am. Nonsmoking rms avail. **Amenities:** 🛖 ♨ A/C, cable TV w/movies, dataport. Some units w/minibars, some w/whirlpools. **Services:** ✕ 🛏 🕹 Continental breakfast Mon–Fri only. **Facilities:** 🎰 🏊 🏋 ⛳ 💻 ♿ 1 restaurant, 1 bar, games rm, sauna, whirlpool,

playground, washer/dryer. Nine banquet rooms available. **Rates (CP):** $54–$89 S; $89–$175 ste. Extra person $10. Children under age 19 stay free. Parking: Outdoor, free. AE, DC, DISC, MC, V.

MOTELS

🏨 Budgetel Inn

1910 Stewart Ave, 54401; tel 715/842-0421 or toll free 800/428-3428; fax 715/845-5096. Exit 192 off I-51; follow signs. Located in a commercial district. **Rooms:** 99 rms. CI noon/CO noon. Nonsmoking rms avail. **Amenities:** 🛖 🖥 A/C, cable TV w/movies. **Services:** 🛏 🕹 ⛳ **Facilities:** 🏊 🏋 ♿ **Rates (CP):** $40–$44 S; $47–$51 D. Children under age 18 stay free. Parking: Outdoor, free. AE, CB, DC, DISC, MC, V.

🏨 Exel Inn

116 S 17th Ave, 54401; tel 715/842-0641 or toll free 800/356-8013; fax 715/848-1356. Often full for two good reasons: it's conveniently located, and it's the most affordable stay in Wausau. Decor could use some updating. **Rooms:** 123 rms and effic. CI 3pm/CO noon. Nonsmoking rms avail. **Amenities:** 🛖 ♨ A/C, cable TV w/movies. 1 unit w/whirlpool. **Services:** 🛏 🕹 ⛳ **Facilities:** 🏊 🏋 ♿ Games rm. **Rates (CP):** Peak (June–Oct) $34–$44 S; $43–$51 D; $40–$50 effic. Extra person $4. Children under age 17 stay free. Min stay special events. Lower rates off-season. Parking: Outdoor, free. Ski packages avail for groups. AE, DC, DISC, MC, V.

🏨 Super 8 Motel

2006 W Stewart Ave, 54401; tel 715/848-2888 or toll free 800/800-8000; fax 715/842-9578. Clean and pleasant in convenient location, although street has plenty of traffic. Fast food nearby. **Rooms:** 88 rms. CI 2pm/CO noon. Nonsmoking rms avail. All rooms recently redecorated. **Amenities:** 🛖 ♨ A/C, cable TV. **Services:** 🛏 🕹 ⛳ **Facilities:** 🎰 🏊 🏋 ♿ Whirlpool. **Rates (CP):** Peak (June–Oct) $48–$61 S; $55–$61 D. Children under age 12 stay free. Lower rates off-season. Parking: Outdoor, free. AE, DC, DISC, MC, V.

RESTAURANTS 🍽

Gulliver's Landing

2204 Rib Mountain Dr; tel 715/842-9098. **American/Seafood.** This nautically-themed restaurant is a favorite among vacationing families and businesspeople entertaining guests. The atmosphere is warm and inviting, with great lake views and unusual, decorative artifacts and antiques. **FYI:** Reservations recommended. Children's menu. No smoking. **Open:** Sun–Thurs 4:30–10pm, Fri–Sat 4:30–11pm. **Prices:** Main courses $5–$22. DC, DISC, MC, V. ♿

Michael's

2901 Rib Mountain Dr; tel 715/842-9856. **American.** Owner and head chef Michael Myers offers fine dining and quiet sophistication in an unlikely location. Features steaks and other basic American fare **FYI:** Reservations accepted. Children's menu. **Open:** Mon–Sat 5–10pm. **Prices:** Main courses $8–$29. AE, CB, DC, MC, V.

2510 Restaurant

2510 Stewart Ave; tel 715/845-2510. **American.** There is more than meets the eye when you drive up to this ever-expanding restaurant. This large facility manages to provide intimate dining by separating the dining area into small sections, each with its own fireplace. Every day, fresh breads, soups, and salads are prepared for sale in the deli/bakery and the restaurant. **FYI:** Reservations recommended. Children's menu. No smoking. **Open:** Daily 11am–10am. **Prices:** Main courses $4–$22. AE, DC, DISC, MC, V. 🖼 &

Wausau Mine Co

3904 Stewart Ave; tel 715/845-7304. **American.** Home of the Motherlode Eatery and the Rusty Nail Saloon, this miners' shack might be in an out-of-the-way location, but it's well worth the trip. Broiled, baked, and charbroiled food is prepared with fresh ingredients according to "secret recipes." Well regarded for Italian baked potato fries, served with a red sauce and cheese. Also pizza, burgers, sandwiches, and Italian entrees. **FYI:** Reservations accepted. Children's menu. **Open:** Daily 11am–midnight. **Prices:** Main courses $3–$13. CB, DC, DISC, MC, V.

ATTRACTIONS 🏛

Rib Mountain State Park

5301 Rib Mountain Dr; tel 715/842-2522. At 1,940 feet, the summit of Rib Mountain is one of the highest points in the state. There are seven miles of hiking trails, 1½ miles of snowmobile trails, and 30 camping sites within the 940-acre park. There is a picnic area (accessible to the disabled) as well as a concessions spot. **Open:** Daily 6am–11pm. **$$**

Grand Theater

415 4th St; tel 715/842-0988. Built in 1927 as a movie palace and vaudeville house, this magnificently restored Greek Revival theater now hosts a full season of national touring productions and local concerts, drama, and dance. **Open:** Call for schedule. **$$$**

Wauwatosa

This pleasant western Milwaukee suburb is the site of the area's oldest home. **Information:** Wauwatosa Area Chamber of Commerce, 7707 W State St, Wauwatosa, 53213 (tel 414/453-2330).

HOTELS 🏨

🎗🎗🎗 Best Western Midway Hotel

251 N Mayfair Rd, 53226; tel 414/774-3600 or toll free 800/528-1231; fax 414/774-3929. On WI 100, 2 mi S of Mayfair Mall. Near Mayfair Mall along busy commercial strip, this is a nice, clean establishment with a comfortable lobby. **Rooms:**

116 rms and stes. Executive level. CI 3pm/CO noon. Non-smoking rms avail. **Amenities:** 🔒 🅰 🗂 A/C, satel TV w/movies, refrig, dataport. Some rooms have hair dryers. **Services:** ✗ 🍽 🖼 🛎 Children's program. **Facilities:** 🏋 🏌 🎣 🐴 🚲 & 1 restaurant, 2 bars (1 w/entertainment), games rm, sauna, steam rm, whirlpool, playground, washer/dryer. Very nice pool, video games, and table tennis in same room. Exercise equipment available. **Rates:** Peak (June–Aug) $78–$92 S or D; $84–$94 ste. Extra person $10. Children under age 18 stay free. Lower rates off-season. Parking: Outdoor, free. Weekend and family packages avail. AE, CB, DC, DISC, EC, ER, JCB, MC, V.

🎗🎗 Holiday Inn Mayfair

11111 W North Ave, 53226; tel 414/778-0333 or toll free 800/HOLIDAY; fax 414/778-0331. Located on a major street across from Mayfair Mall, this is a clean, basic establishment. **Rooms:** 122 rms and stes. CI 2pm/CO noon. Non-smoking rms avail. **Amenities:** 🔒 🅰 A/C, satel TV w/movies, refrig, dataport. Some units w/terraces, 1 w/whirlpool. **Services:** 🖼 🛎 Children's program. Free local phone calls. **Facilities:** 🎣 & Children eat free for entire stay. **Rates (CP):** Peak (May 15–Sept 30) $59–$70 S or D; $85 ste. Extra person $6. Children under age 18 stay free. Lower rates off-season. Parking: Outdoor, free. AE, CB, DC, DISC, EC, ER, JCB, MC, V.

RESTAURANTS 🍴

Alioto's

3041 N Mayfair Rd, Wauwatosa; tel 414/476-6900. 3 blocks N of Mayfair Mall. **Italian.** This candlelit, family-friendly Italian restaurant serves up some of the richest pastas in the area; the creamy pasta primavera in particular is a big hit. Chateaubriand for two, served tableside, is a center cut of tenderloin accompanied by onion rings, button mushrooms, and vegetables. **FYI:** Reservations accepted. Children's menu. **Open:** Closed July 1–7. **Prices:** Main courses $7–$34. AE, CB, DC, DISC, MC, V. 🖼 🚗 &

★ Jake's

6030 W North Ave, Wauwatosa; tel 414/771-0550. **American.** The wood-planked interior looks out onto newly landscaped North Ave. Roast duck with orange sauce, poached salmon, and fresh-roasted prime rib are the most-requested entrees. Onion rings are a favorite—Jake's claims to have served over four million pounds of them since 1960. Loyal cooking staff, wait staff, and management—some have been here 20 years or more—assure that quality service remains consistent. The award-winning wine list is translated into Japanese, German, Spanish, and Braille, as is the menu. **FYI:** Reservations accepted. Children's menu. No smoking. Additional location: 21445 W Capital Dr, Brookfield (tel 781-7995). **Open:** Mon–Sat 5–10pm, Sun 5–9pm. **Prices:** Main courses $15–$20. AE, CB, DC, MC, V.

West Allis

See Milwaukee

Whitefish Bay

RESTAURANT 🍴

★ Jack Pandl's Whitefish Bay Inn
1319 E Henry Clay St; tel 414/964-3800. **American/German.** The third generation of the Pandl family now owns and operates this restaurant originally built in 1915, when the surrounding area was still countryside. Knotty-pine paneling, an extensive beer stein collection, and historic photos decorate the dining room and bar. German pancakes—plate-sized puff pastry that must be seen to be believed—are served with syrup, powdered sugar, and seasonal fruit sauces and can be ordered for breakfast or dessert. Boned whitefish is lightly oiled and salted, then broiled and skinned to make a simple yet tasty entree. The ribs are marinated and grilled in the house sauce. **FYI:** Reservations recommended. Children's menu. Dress code. **Open:** Lunch Mon–Sat 11:30am–2:30pm; dinner Mon–Thurs 5–9pm, Fri–Sat 5–11pm, Sun 4–8pm; brunch Sun 10:30am–2:30pm. **Prices:** Main courses $13–$20. AE, CB, DC, DISC, MC, V.

Wisconsin Dells

The Wisconsin River flowed through a new channel to carve out the nearby Dells, which are now the state's foremost tourist attraction. The Great Wisconsin Dells Balloon Rally is held here in early June. **Information:** Wisconsin Dells Visitors & Convention Bureau, 701 Superior St, PO Box 390, Wisconsin Dells, 53965-0390 (tel 608/254-8088).

HOTELS 🏨

≡≡≡ Holiday Inn
655 Frontage Rd N, PO Box 236, 53965; tel 608/254-8306 or toll free 800/543-3557; fax 608/254-8306. A very family-oriented facility in a cluster of other hotels. Denny's Restaurant and First Station Pizza Arcade are across the street. Near Rocky Arbor cross-country skiing and Christmas Mountain downhill skiing. **Rooms:** 228 rms and stes. Executive level. CI 4pm/CO 10:30am. Nonsmoking rms avail. **Amenities:** 🛏 🌣 📺 A/C, satel TV, refrig, dataport. **Services:** ✗ 🖼 ⛐ Car-rental desk, children's program, babysitting. **Facilities:** 🛝 🏊 🌊 🎳 🏊 1 restaurant, 1 bar (w/entertainment), games rm, sauna, whirlpool, washer/dryer. Children 12 and under eat free in adjoining restaurant when dining with an adult. Complimentary passes to Tamarach Health Club available. Poolside snack bars, water slides. **Rates:** Peak (May–Sept)

$100–$112 S or D; $135–$150 ste. Extra person $4. Children under age 19 stay free. Lower rates off-season. Parking: Outdoor, free. AE, DISC, MC, V.

≡≡ Mayflower
910 Wisconsin Dells Pkwy, 53965; tel 608/253-6471 or toll free 800/345-7407; fax 608/253-7617. One of the largest motels in the area, located on the entertainment strip. **Rooms:** 75 rms and stes. CI 3pm/CO 11am. **Amenities:** 🛏 🌣 A/C, cable TV w/movies, refrig. Some units w/terraces, some w/whirlpools. **Services:** ⛐ **Facilities:** 🛝 🏊 🌊 🎳 Games rm, sauna, whirlpool, playground, washer/dryer. **Rates:** Peak (July–Aug) $38–$78 S; $44–$94 D; $78–$110 ste. Children under age 18 stay free. Min stay wknds. Lower rates off-season. Parking: Outdoor, free. Closed late Oct–Apr. AE, DC, DISC, MC, V.

MOTELS

≡≡ Black Hawk
720 Race, PO Box 15, 53965; tel 608/254-7770. At Broadway. Opened in 1945, this is the oldest family-owned motel in Wisconsin Dells. Still family oriented. **Rooms:** 75 rms, stes, and effic. CI 3pm/CO 11am. Nonsmoking rms avail. One room is large enough for three queen-size beds. **Amenities:** 🛏 A/C, cable TV w/movies. All units w/terraces, some w/whirlpools. **Services:** ⛐ Babysitting. **Facilities:** 🛝 🏊 🌊 🎳 Games rm, sauna, whirlpool, playground, washer/dryer. **Rates:** Peak (June 15–Aug) $55–$85 S; $75–$95 D; $125–$160 ste; $95–$165 effic. Extra person $5. Children under age 18 stay free. Lower rates off-season. Parking: Outdoor, free. Closed Nov–Mar. AE, CB, DC, DISC, JCB, MC, V.

≡≡ Chippewa
1114 E Broadway, 53965; tel 608/253-3982 or toll free 800/756-2447. 4 blocks E of downtown. Attractive, well-maintained property located on major street near attractions, hotels, water slides, museums, and deer park. Across the street from Family Chef Restaurant. **Rooms:** 58 rms and stes. CI 1pm/CO 10am. Nonsmoking rms avail. **Amenities:** 🛏 A/C, cable TV w/movies, refrig. All units w/terraces, some w/whirlpools. **Services:** ⛐ **Facilities:** 🛝 🏊 🌊 🎳 Games rm, sauna, whirlpool, playground, washer/dryer. **Rates:** Peak (June 20–Sept 7) $28–$88 S; $32–$88 D; $95–$150 ste. Children under age 12 stay free. Lower rates off-season. Parking: Outdoor, free. AE, DISC, MC, V.

≡≡ Days Inn
944 US 12, PO Box 381, 53965; tel 608/254-6444 or toll free 800/DAYS-INN. At WI 16. Conveniently located in center of town, along the entertainment strip. **Rooms:** 100 rms, stes, and effic. CI 4pm/CO 11am. Nonsmoking rms avail. Large, impressive rooms with comfortable furniture, including easy chairs and sofas in some rooms. **Amenities:** 🛏 A/C, cable TV, dataport. Some units w/terraces, 1 w/whirlpool. **Services:** ⛐ **Facilities:** 🛝 🏊 🌊 🎳 🏊 Games rm, sauna, whirlpool. Tanning beds. **Rates:** Peak (June 23–Sept 3) $30–$95 S; $50–$110 D; $70–$160 ste; $36–$95

effic. Extra person $5. Children under age 12 stay free. Min stay wknds. Lower rates off-season. Parking: Outdoor, free. AARP and government discount is 10%. Special July 4th rate and discounts to area attractions. AE, DC, DISC, MC, V.

≣≣ International

1311 E Broadway, 53965; tel 608/254-2431. Clean establishment on quiet side of town, five blocks from main entertainment strip. **Rooms:** 45 rms, stes, and effic. CI noon/CO 11am. Nonsmoking rms avail. **Amenities:** A/C, cable TV. No phone. Some units w/terraces. **Services:** Social director, babysitting. **Facilities:** 🚣 🏊 🎾 👌 Basketball, games rm, playground. **Rates:** Peak (July–Aug) $30–$55 S; $30–$85 D; $45–$120 ste; $60–$120 effic. Extra person $5. Min stay wknds. Lower rates off-season. Parking: Outdoor, free. Group rates for 20 or more avail. Closed Oct–May. AE, CB, DC, MC, V.

≣≣ Skyline

1970 Wisconsin Dells Pkwy, 53965; tel 608/253-4841 or toll free 800/759-8475; fax 608/253-4841. Exit 87 off I-90. Located on one of the major entertainment strips of the area, near water slides, museums, and deer park. Very handy and well-maintained property. **Rooms:** 53 rms and stes. CI 2pm/CO 10:30am. Nonsmoking rms avail. **Amenities:** 🛗 A/C, cable TV w/movies, refrig. Some units w/terraces, some w/whirlpools. **Services:** **Facilities:** 🚣 🏊 🎾 👌 Basketball, volleyball, games rm, sauna, whirlpool, playground. Pools: two kiddie, one indoor, one outdoor, and two indoor whirlpools. **Rates:** Peak (June 23–Aug 26) $40–$74 S; $40–$79 D; $79–$189 ste. Extra person $5. Children under age 16 stay free. Min stay wknds. Lower rates off-season. Parking: Outdoor, free. AARP discounts offered in off-season. Casino, Jacuzzi, and ski packages avail. AE, DISC, MC, V.

RESTAURANTS 🍴

Cheese Factory, The Restaurant

521 Wisconsin Dells Pkwy S; tel 608/253-6065. Just off I-90/94 on WI 12. **American.** On the banks of the Wisconsin River between Lake Delton and Mirror Lake stands this charming restaurant with a 1950s-style appeal. Comfortable ambience, complete with a flower garden out front and a white picket fence, makes this a good spot for a romantic evening. Two non-alcoholic bars specialize in cappuccino; a stage for live entertainment is next to the upstairs bar. **FYI:** Reservations not accepted. Blues/comedy/country music/jazz/rock. Children's menu. No liquor license. No smoking. **Open:** Peak (June 15–Aug 15) Wed–Mon 9am–9pm. Closed Jan–Mar. **Prices:** Main courses $5–$12. AE, MC, V. 💟 🍽 📷

Country Kitchen

US 12 and WI 16; tel 608/254-2593. **American.** Family restaurant offering traditional no-frills meals: meat loaf, steaks, stir-fries. Fruit pies and, every now and then, a surprise such as cappuccino and coconut cream pie are available for dessert. Good for families and late-night partygoers who need some hearty fare. **FYI:** Reservations not accepted. Children's menu. No liquor license. **Open:** Daily 24 hrs. **Prices:** Main courses $6–$10. AE, MC, V. 📷 🍴 👌

ATTRACTIONS 📷

Noah's Ark Waterpark

1410 Wisconsin Dells Pkwy; tel 608/254-6351. Claiming to be America's largest water park, Noah's Ark boasts two wave pools, two "Lazy River" inner-tube rides, 31 water slides, four children's water play areas, bumper boats, go-carts, and miniature golf on its 65 acres. Restaurants, shops, and picnic areas. **Open:** Mem Day–Labor Day, call for hours. $$$$

Family Land

Wisconsin Dells Pkwy; tel 608/254-7766. A 60-acre water park with water slides, miniature golf, and a tidal wave pool. Also shops, restaurants, games, and arcades. **Open:** May–Aug, daily. Call for hours. $$$$

Tommy Bartlett's Ski, Sky, and Stage Show

560 Wisconsin Dells Pkwy; tel 608/254-2525. Variety of entertainment acts including a waterskiing show, a contortionist, super stunt boats, the "Juggling Jokester," and a laser/water spectacular (after dark). **Open:** June–Aug, daily. Call for hours. $$$$

Winnebago Indian Museum

3893 N River Rd; tel 608/254-2268. This 42-year-old family-operated museum documents the cultural histories of local Native American tribes, as well as general Native American arts and crafts. It offers cultural presentations and educational workshops. **Open:** May–Oct, Mon–Sat 9am–8pm, Sun 9am–6pm. $

Ripley's Believe It or Not! Museum

115 Broadway; tel 608/253-7556. Extensive assortment of strange and unusual items, pictures, and drawings which continue the legacy of the popular adventurer/cartoonist Robert Ripley's lifelong obsession to find incredible oddities. **Open:** Apr–Oct, daily. Call for hours. $$$

Wax World of the Stars

105 Broadway; tel 608/254-2184. More than 100 life-size wax figures are on display here representing personalities from screen, stage, and music. Immortalized in wax are Arnold Schwarzenegger, Marilyn Monroe, Bill Cosby, the Three Stooges, and Lucille Ball, just to name a few. **Open:** May–Sept, daily. Call for hours. $$

Biblical Gardens

441 Clara Ave, Lake Delton; tel 608/253-5091. More than a dozen life-size sculptures of Biblical scenes are placed in this wooded sandstone canyon. Wild and cultivated flowers, ferns, and fragrant pines provide the garden atmosphere. **Open:** May–Sept, daily 9am–8pm. $$

Dells Auto Museum

591 Wisconsin Dells Pkwy; tel 608/221-1964 or 608/254-2008. This museum showcases a wide range of cars from 1901 to through the present, including early automotive

prototypes, novelty cars, and convertibles. Exhibits change regularly. The Antique Shoppe features glassware, furniture, jewelry, period clothing, and a display of over 200 antique dolls and toys. **Open:** Mem Day–Labor Day, daily 9am–9pm. **$$**

OK Corral Riding Stable

WI 16; tel 608/254-2811. Guided horseback tours of the area lead visitors past Boot Hill, a western cemetery, and a Native American camp on their 50-minute rides. Free pony rides for children, petting zoo. **Open:** Apr–Nov, daily 9am–7pm. **$$$$**

Wisconsin Dells Greyhound Racing

Winners Way; tel 608/253-DOGS. All-weather greyhound racing offered from February through November. Matinee and evening racing, and pari-mutuel betting featured. Indoor/outdoor seating available, as well as restaurant and bar serving lunch and dinner. **Open:** Feb–Nov. Call for schedule. **$**

Index

Listings are arranged alphabetically, followed by a code indicating the type of establishment, and then by city, state, and page number. The codes for type of establishment are defined as follows: (H) = Hotel, (M) = Motel, (I) = Inn, (L) = Lodge, (RE) = Resort, (R) = Restaurant, (RS) = Refreshment Stop, (A) = Attraction.

10 % OFF
TIME & MILEAGE

Terms and Conditions
- Offer includes 10% discount off all time and mileage charges
  on Cruise America or Cruise Canada vehicles only.
- Offer not available in conjunction with other discount offers or promotional rates.
- Excludes rental charges, deposits, sales tax, amd fuels.
- Normal rental conditions and customer qualification procedures apply.
- Members must reserve through Central Reservations only, at least one week in
  advance of pick up and mention membership affiliation at time of reservation.
  For reservations, call: 1-800-327-7799 US and Canada
- By acceptance and use of this offer, member agrees to the above conditions.
- Offer expires December 31, 1997.

Save 10%   **Save 10%**

Sleep   Comfort   Quality   Clarion

CHOICE HOTELS
I N T E R N A T I O N A L

Rodeway   Econo Lodge   MainStay Suites

Offer expires December 31, 1997.

Savings are subject to certain restrictions and availability.
Valid for flights on most airlines.

Minimum Ticket Price	Save
$200.00	$25.00
$250.00	$50.00
$350.00	$75.00
$450.00	$100.00

TRAVEL DISCOUNTERS
DISCOUNTING THE WORLD OF TRAVEL

Terms and Conditions
1. Advance reservations required.
2. Coupon must be presented at check-in.
3. Coupon cannot be combined with any
   other special offers, discounted rates.
4. Subject to availability.
5. Valid through December 31, 1997.
6. No photo copies allowed.

Travelodge.

For reservations, call 1-800-578-7878 or your travel agent and ask for the 5CPN discount.

All reservations must be made by calling our toll free reservation system, Superline. Any reservation requiring a guarantee must be guaranteed with the corporate V.I.P. identification number and the individual traveler's major credit card. If a guaranteed reservation is made and subsequently neither used nor cancelled, the corporate traveler will be billed for the one night's room charge plus tax.

expires December 31, 1997

Redeemable at participating Dollar® locations only.

This coupon entitles you to a one class upgrade from a compact or economy car to the next higher car group at no extra charge. Simply make a reservation for a compact or economy class car, then present this coupon to any Dollar rental agent when you arrive. You'll receive an upgrade to the next car class at no additional charge. Upgrade subject to vehicle availability. Renter must meet Dollar age, driver and credit requirements. This coupon must be surrendered at time of rental and may not be used in conjunction with any other offer and has no cash value. **EXPIRES 12/15/97.**

For worldwide reservations, call your travel agent or
800-800-4000

D●LLAR
RENT A CAR
DOLLAR MAKES SENSE.

PAUL BUNYAN LOGGING CAMP

Authentic 1890's Logging Camp

Interpretive Center Introducing the Visitor To:
- Local History of the Lumbering Industry
- Bunkhouse and Cooks' Shanty
- Heavy Logging Equipment
- Blacksmith Shop & Barn
- Tools & Artifacts

10% Discount
on Merchandise

A Lasting Tribute to the Pioneers of the Lumber Era.

Valid through December 31, 1997

10% OFF

DAYS INN
Follow the Sun

- Available at participating properties.
- This coupon cannot be combined with any other special discount offer.
- Limit one coupon per room, per stay. Expires December 31, 1997.
- Not valid during blackout periods or special events.
- Void where prohibited.
- No reproductions accepted.

1-800-DAYS INN

THE DETROIT INSTITUTE OF ARTS

Hours:

Wednesday–Friday 11.1.m.-4 p.m.; Weekends 11 a.m.-5 p.m.
Closed Mondays, Tuesdays and some holidays.

5200 Woodward Avenue, Detroit, Michigan 48202
313-833-7900

Tommy Bartlett Thrill Show

Enter his incredible thrill zone. Witness legendary Tommy Bartlett's spectacular
two-hour live outdoor entertainment show featuring daredevil waterskiers and
worldwide entertainers Mr. Sound Effects Wes Harrison, the amazing
Ashton family and the Nerveless Nocks Sway Poles. See the incredible
laser light and fireworks extravaganza at the 8:30 p.m. show.

Valid during 1997 season. Offer may be redeemed at any Tommy Bartlett ticket outlet.
Coupon must be presented at time of purchase and is not valid
in conjunction with any other discount, promotion or group rate.
Not redeemable for cash. Coupon code: FRM97

Tommy Bartlett's Robot World & Exploratory

Enter the next level of interactivity. A hands–on experience with
virtual reality and simulator excitement that involves you in
space adventure and futuristic encounters. 90 interactive exhibits.
All new robot activities in 1997. Entirely new command module.
Open year–round, 8 a.m. to 10 p.m. Spring, fall & winter hours vary.

Valid during 1997 season. Offer may be redeemed at any Tommy Bartlett ticket outlet.
Coupon must be presented at time of purchase and is not valid
in conjunction with any other discount, promotion or group rate.
Not redeemable for cash. Coupon code: FRM97

THE KALAMAZOO AIR ZOO

3101 E. MILHAM KALAMAZOO, MI I-94 EX. 78 SOUTH

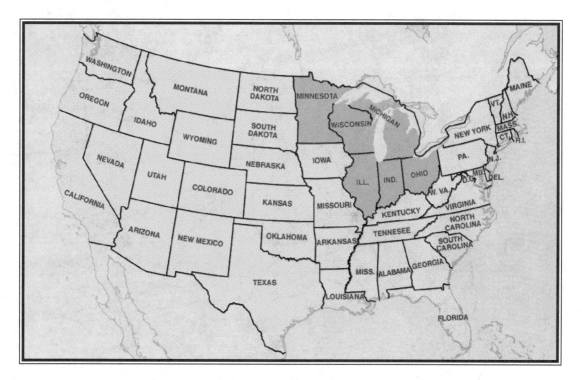

CONTENTS

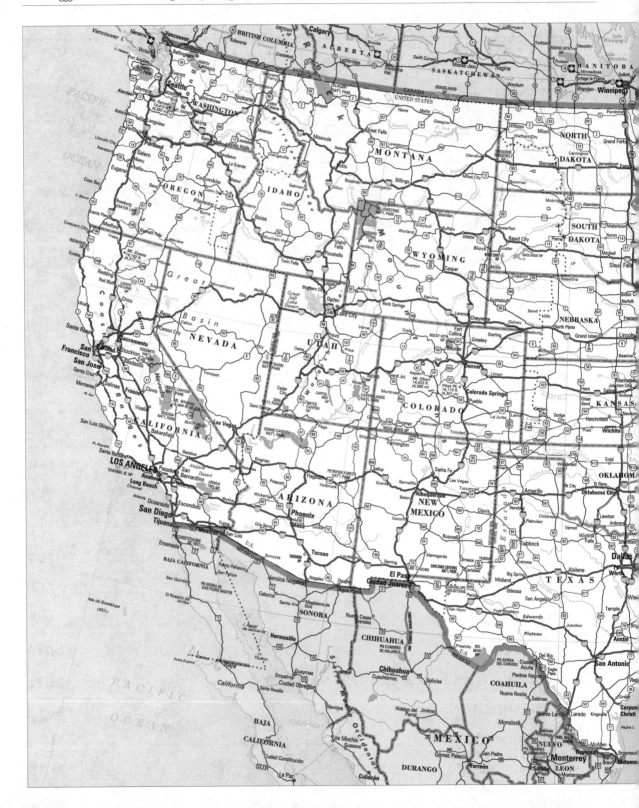

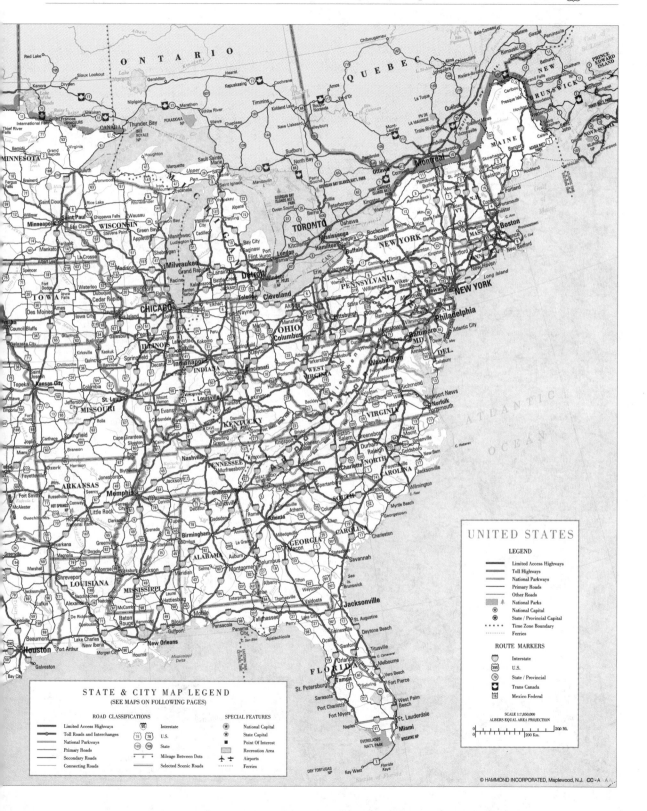

UNITED STATES

LEGEND

- Limited Access Highways
- Toll Highways
- National Parkways
- Primary Roads
- Other Roads
- National Parks
- National Capital
- State / Provincial Capital
- Time Zone Boundary
- Ferries

ROUTE MARKERS

- Interstate
- U.S.
- State / Provincial
- Trans Canada
- Mexico Federal

SCALE 1:7,850,000
ALBERS EQUAL AREA PROJECTION

0   200 Mi.
0   200 Km.

STATE & CITY MAP LEGEND
(SEE MAPS ON FOLLOWING PAGES)

ROAD CLASSIFICATIONS

- Limited Access Highways
- Toll Roads and Interchanges
- National Parkways
- Primary Roads
- Secondary Roads
- Connecting Roads
- Interstate
- U.S.
- State
- Mileage Between Dots
- Selected Scenic Roads

SPECIAL FEATURES

- National Capital
- State Capital
- Point Of Interest
- Recreation Area
- Airports
- Ferries

Akron . . . . F 2	Canton . . . . . . F 2	East Liverpool . . F 2	Kettering . . . . D 3	Middletown . . . D 3	Saint Marys . . . D 2	Troy . . . . D 3	Westerville . . . . E 3
Alliance . . . . . F 2	Celina . . . . . . D 2	Elyria . . . . . . E 1	Lakewood . . . . F 1	Mount Vernon . . E 3	Salem . . . . . . F 2	Uhrichsville . . F 3	Whitehall . . . . E 3
Archbold . . . . D 1	Chillicothe . . . E 3	Euclid . . . . . . F 1	Lancaster . . . . E 3	Napoleon . . . . D 2	Sandusky . . . . E 2	Urbana . . . . . . D 3	Wickliffe . . . . F 1
Ashland . . . . . E 2	Cincinnati . . . . D 4	Findlay . . . . . D 2	Lebanon . . . . D 3	New Philadelphia F 2	Shaker Heights . F 1	Vandalia . . . . D 3	Willoughby . . . F 1
Ashtabula . . . . F 1	Circleville . . . E 3	Fostoria . . . . . E 2	Lima . . . . . . D 2	Newark . . . . . E 3	Sidney . . . . . . D 3	Van Wert . . . . D 2	Wilmington . . . D 3
Athens . . . . . E 3	Cleveland . . . . F 1	Franklin . . . . . D 3	Logan . . . . . . E 3	Niles . . . . . . F 2	Springfield . . . D 3	Wapakoneta . . . D 2	Wooster . . . . . E 2
Aurora . . . . . F 2	Cleveland Heights F 1	Fremont . . . . E 2	Lorain . . . . . . E 2	Norwalk . . . . . E 2	Steubenville . . . F 3	Warren . . . . . F 2	Worthington . . . E 3
Barberton . . . . F 2	Columbus . . . . E 3	Galion . . . . . . E 2	Mansfield . . . . E 2	Oberlin . . . . . E 1	Tiffin . . . . . . E 2	Washington C.H. . E 3	Xenia . . . . . . D 3
Bellaire . . . . . F 3	Conneaut . . . . F 1	Gallipolis . . . . E 4	Marietta . . . . F 3	Oregon . . . . . E 1	Toledo . . . . . . D 1	Wauseon . . . . D 1	Youngstown . . . F 2
Bellefontaine . . D 3	Coshocton . . . E 3	Geneva-on-the-	Marion . . . . . E 2	Oxford . . . . . D 3	Toronto . . . . . F 2	Wellsville . . . . F 3	Zanesville . . . . E 3
Bellevue . . . . E 2	Cuyahoga Falls . F 2	Lake . . . . . F 1	Martins Ferry . . F 3	Painesville . . . F 1			
Bowling Green . . D 2	Dayton . . . . . D 3	Greenville . . . D 3	Massillon . . . . F 2	Parma . . . . . . F 2			
Brunswick . . . . F 2	Defiance . . . . D 2	Hamilton . . . . D 3	Maumee . . . . D 2	Piqua . . . . . . D 3			
Bryan . . . . . . D 2	Delaware . . . . E 3	Ironton . . . . . E 4	Medina . . . . . E 2	Port Clinton . . E 2			
Bucyrus . . . . . E 2	Delphos . . . . . D 2	Jackson . . . . . E 4	Mentor . . . . . F 1	Portsmouth . . . E 4			
Cambridge . . . F 3	Dover . . . . . . F 2	Kenton . . . . . D 2	Miamisburg . . . D 3	Ravenna . . . . F 2			

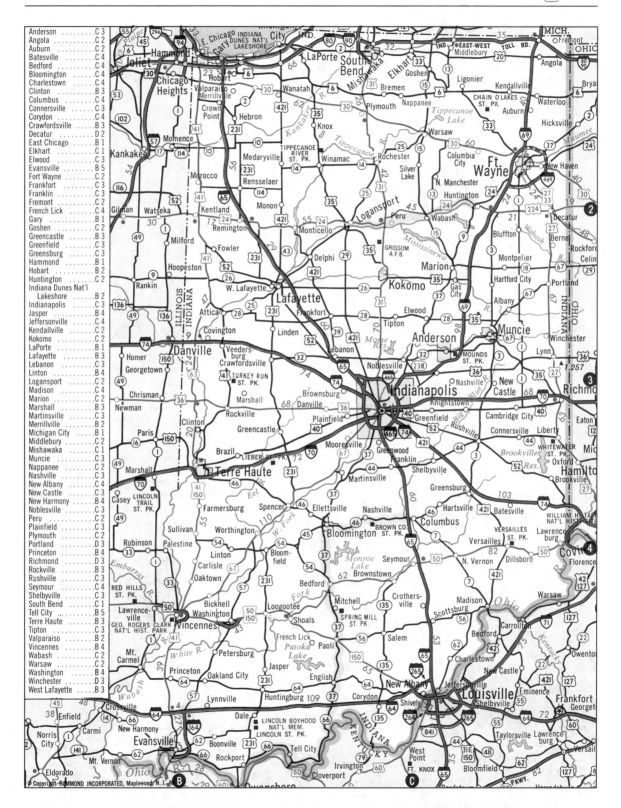

Anderson ....C 3
Angola ....C 2
Auburn ....C 2
Batesville ....C 4
Bedford ....C 4
Bloomington .....C 4
Charlestown .....C 4
Clinton ....B 3
Columbus ....C 4
Connersville ....C 3
Corydon ....C 4
Crawfordsville ..B 3
Decatur ....D 2
East Chicago ....B 1
Elkhart ....C 1
Elwood ....C 3
Evansville ......B 5
Fort Wayne ......C 2
Frankfort ....C 3
Franklin ....C 3
Fremont ....C 2
French Lick .....C 4
Gary ....B 1
Goshen ....C 2
Greencastle .....B 3
Greenfield ......C 3
Greensburg ......C 3
Hammond ....B 1
Hobart ....B 2
Huntington ......C 2
Indiana Dunes Nat'l
  Lakeshore .....B 2
Indianapolis ....C 3
Jasper ....B 4
Jeffersonville ..C 4
Kendallville ....C 2
Kokomo ....C 2
LaPorte ....B 1
Lafayette ....B 3
Lebanon ....C 3
Linton ....B 4
Logansport ......C 2
Madison ....C 4
Marion ....C 2
Marshall ....B 3
Martinsville ....C 3
Merrillville ....B 2
Michigan City ...B 1
Middlebury ......C 2
Mishawaka ....C 1
Muncie ....C 3
Nappanee ....C 2
Nashville ....C 4
New Albany ......C 4
New Castle ......C 3
New Harmony .....B 4
Noblesville .....C 3
Peru ....C 2
Plainfield ......C 3
Plymouth ....C 2
Portland ....D 3
Princeton ....B 4
Richmond ....D 3
Rockville ....B 3
Rushville ....C 3
Seymour ....C 4
Shelbyville .....C 3
South Bend ......C 1
Tell City ....B 5
Terre Haute .....B 3
Tipton ....C 3
Valparaiso ......B 2
Vincennes ....B 4
Wabash ....C 2
Warsaw ....C 2
Washington ......B 4
Winchester ......D 3
West Lafayette ..B 3

© Copyright RAMMOND INCORPORATED, Maplewood, N.J.

© Copyright HAMMOND INCORPORATED, Maplewood, N.J.

MICHIGAN (Upper Peninsula)

MICHIGAN (Lower Peninsula)
(See map on p.6)

© Copyright HAMMOND INCORPORATED, Maplewood, N.J.

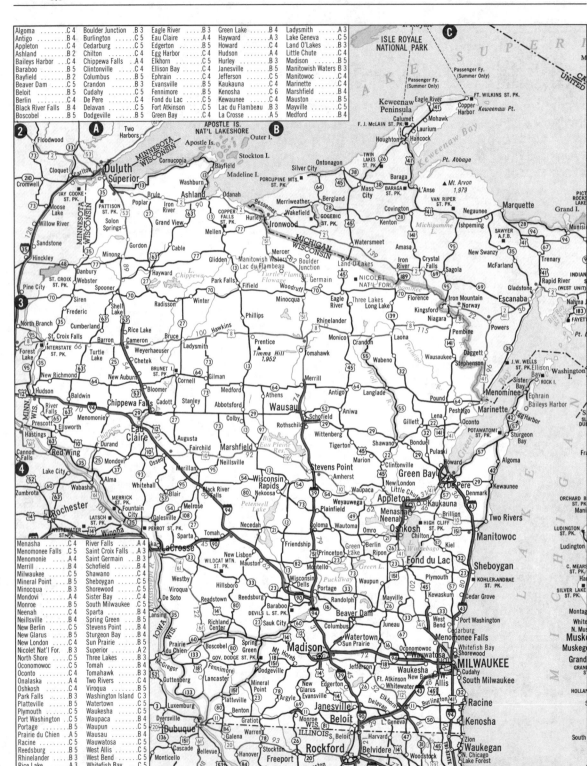

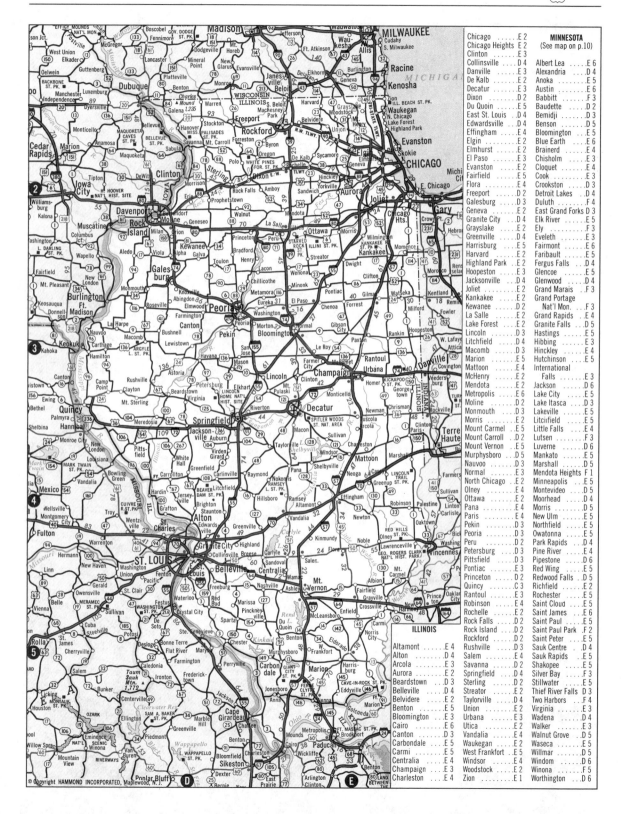

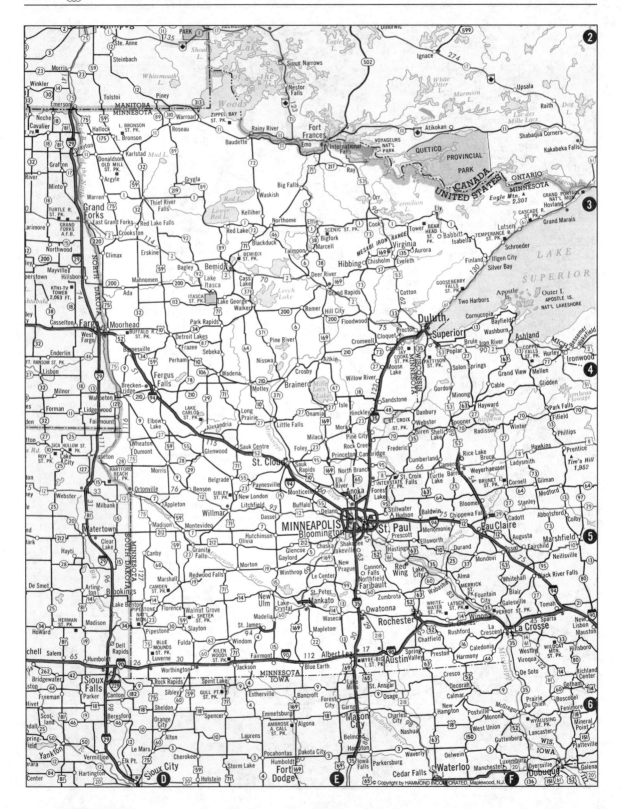

Key to Points of Interest Map

1. BELLE ISLE AQUARIUM
   & CONSERVATORY (F-3)
2. CHRYSLER CORP. (E-2)
3. COBO HALL (E-3)
4. DOSSIN GREAT LAKES
   MUSEUM (F-3)
5. FISHER BUILDING (E-3)
6. FORD MOTOR CO. (D-3)
7. HENRY FORD MUSEUM &
   GREENFIELD VILLAGE (D-3)
8. HISTORICAL MUS. (F-3)
9. INSTITUTE OF ARTS (F-3)
10. MATTHAEI BOTANICAL
    GARDENS (A-3)
11. OLYMPIA STADIUM (F-3)
12. U. OF MICH.-DEARBORN (D-3)

| 0 | 1 | 2 | 3 | 4 | 5 | | 10 | | 15 MILES |

| 0 | | 5 | | 10 | | 15 | | 20 | | 25 KILOMETERS |

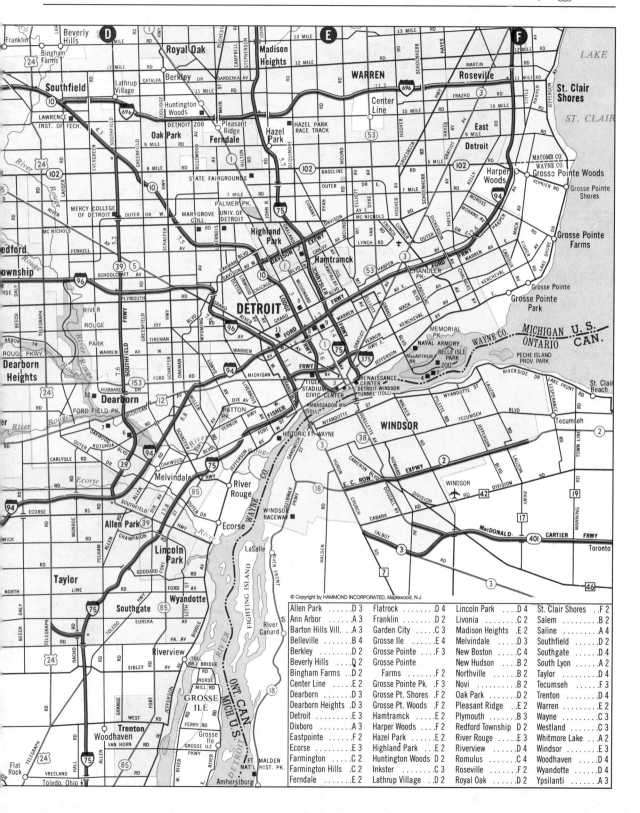

© Copyright by HAMMOND INCORPORATED, Maplewood, N.J.

Allen Park	D 3	Flatrock	D 4	Lincoln Park ....D 4	St. Clair Shores ..F 2
Ann Arbor	A 3	Franklin	D 2	Livonia ....C 2	Salem ....B 2
Barton Hills Vill.	A 3	Garden City	C 3	Madison Heights .E 2	Saline ....A 4
Belleville	B 4	Grosse Ile	E 4	Melvindale ....D 3	Southfield .....D 2
Berkley	D 2	Grosse Pointe	F 3	New Boston ....C 4	Southgate .....D 4
Beverly Hills	Q 2	Grosse Pointe		New Hudson ...B 2	South Lyon ....A 2
Bingham Farms	D 2	Farms	F 2	Northville ....B 2	Taylor ....D 4
Center Line	E 2	Grosse Pointe Pk.	F 3	Novi ....B 2	Tecumseh ......F 3
Dearborn	D 3	Grosse Pt. Shores	F 2	Oak Park ......D 2	Trenton ....D 4
Dearborn Heights	D 3	Grosse Pt. Woods	F 2	Pleasant Ridge .E 2	Warren ....E 2
Detroit	E 3	Hamtramck	E 2	Plymouth ......B 3	Wayne ....C 3
Dixboro	A 3	Harper Woods	F 2	Redford Township D 2	Westland ......C 3
Eastpointe	F 2	Hazel Park	E 2	River Rouge ...E 3	Whitmore Lake .A 2
Ecorse	E 3	Highland Park	E 2	Riverview .....D 4	Windsor ....E 3
Farmington	C 2	Huntington Woods	D 2	Romulus ......C 4	Woodhaven ....D 4
Farmington Hills	C 2	Inkster	C 3	Roseville ......F 2	Wyandotte .....D 4
Ferndale	E 2	Lathrup Village	D 2	Royal Oak .....D 2	Ypsilanti ......A 3

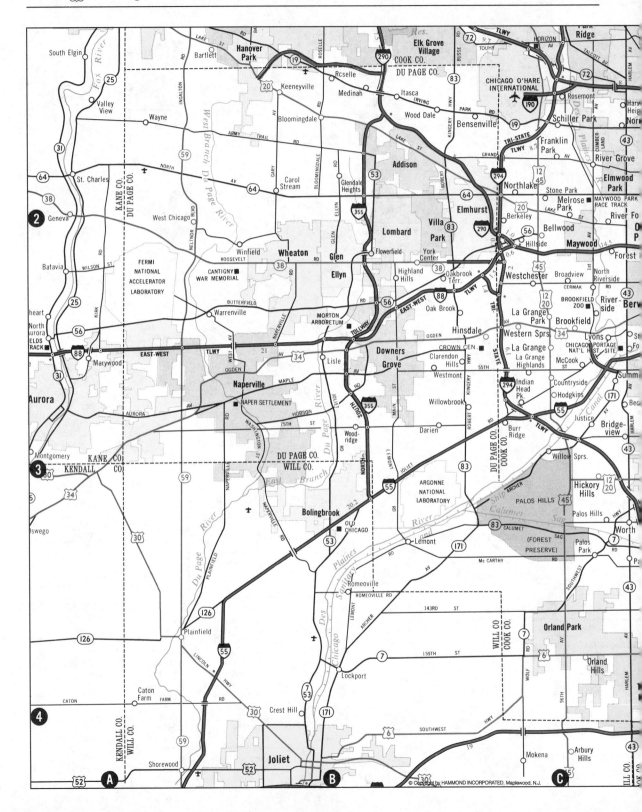

© Copyright by HAMMOND INCORPORATED, Maplewood, N.J.

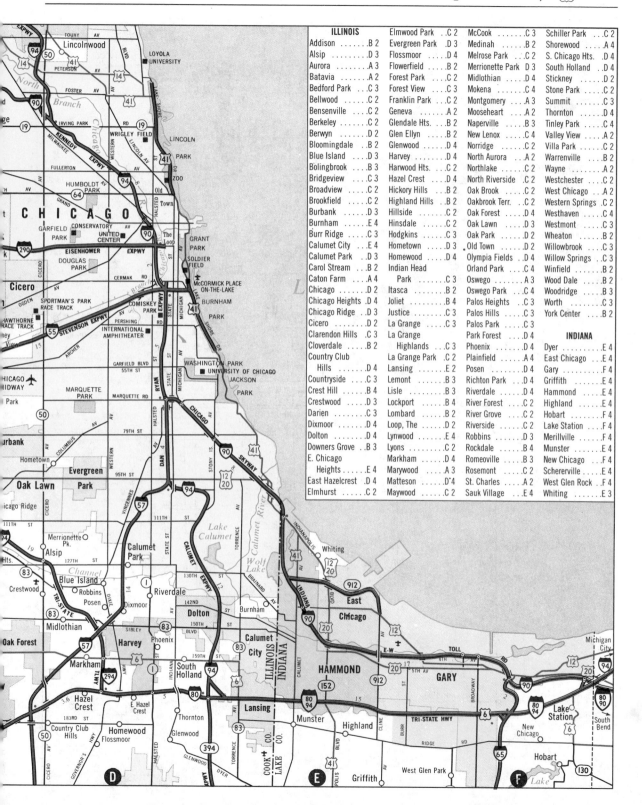

ILLINOIS

Addison ....B 2	Elmwood Park ..C 2	McCook ....C 3	Schiller Park ...C 2
Alsip ....D 3	Evergreen Park .D 3	Medinah ......B 2	Shorewood .....A 4
Aurora ....A 3	Flossmoor ......D 4	Melrose Park ...C 2	S. Chicago Hts. .D 4
Batavia ....A 2	Flowerfield .....B 2	Merrionette Park D 3	South Holland ..D 4
Bedford Park ..C 3	Forest Park ....C 2	Midlothian .....D 4	Stickney ......D 2
Bellwood .....C 2	Forest View ....C 3	Mokena ....C 4	Stone Park .....C 2
Bensenville ...C 2	Franklin Park ...C 2	Montgomery ....A 3	Summit ......C 3
Berkeley .....C 2	Geneva ....A 2	Mooseheart ....A 2	Thornton ......D 4
Berwyn ....D 2	Glendale Hts. ...B 2	Naperville .....B 3	Tinley Park ....C 4
Bloomingdale ..B 2	Glen Ellyn ....B 2	New Lenox ....C 4	Valley View ....A 2
Blue Island ...D 3	Glenwood .....D 4	Norridge ......C 2	Villa Park .....C 2
Bolingbrook ...B 3	Harvey ....D 4	North Aurora ...A 2	Warrenville ....B 2
Bridgeview ....C 3	Harwood Hts. ..C 2	Northlake ......C 2	Wayne ....A 2
Broadview ....C 2	Hazel Crest ...D 4	North Riverside .C 2	Westchester ....C 2
Brookfield ....C 2	Hickory Hills ...C 3	Oak Brook ....C 2	West Chicago ...A 2
Burbank ......D 3	Highland Hills ..B 2	Oakbrook Terr. .C 2	Western Springs .C 2
Burnham ......E 4	Hillside ......C 2	Oak Forest ....D 4	Westhaven .....C 4
Burr Ridge ....C 3	Hinsdale ......C 2	Oak Lawn .....D 3	Westmont .....C 3
Calumet City ..E 4	Hodgkins .....C 3	Oak Park .....D 2	Wheaton ......B 2
Calumet Park ..D 3	Hometown .....D 3	Old Town .....D 2	Willowbrook ...C 3
Carol Stream ..B 2	Homewood ....D 4	Olympia Fields .D 4	Willow Springs .C 3
Caton Farm ...A 4	Indian Head	Orland Park ...C 4	Winfield ......B 2
Chicago ....D 2	Park ....C 3	Oswego ....A 3	Wood Dale ....B 2
Chicago Heights .D 4	Itasca ....B 2	Oswego Park ...C 4	Woodridge ....B 3
Chicago Ridge ..D 3	Joliet ....B 4	Palos Heights ..C 3	Worth ....C 3
Cicero ....D 2	Justice ....C 3	Palos Hills ....C 3	York Center ...B 2
Clarendon Hills .C 3	La Grange .....C 3	Palos Park ....C 3	
Cloverdale ....B 2	La Grange	Park Forest ...D 4	**INDIANA**
Country Club	Highlands ...C 3	Phoenix ......D 4	Dyer ....E 4
Hills ....D 4	La Grange Park ..C 2	Plainfield .....A 4	East Chicago ..E 4
Countryside ...C 3	Lansing ....E 2	Posen ....D 4	Gary ....F 4
Crest Hill .....B 4	Lemont ....B 3	Richton Park ..D 4	Griffith ....E 4
Crestwood ....D 3	Lisle ....B 3	Riverdale ......D 4	Hammond .....E 4
Darien ....C 3	Lockport ......B 4	River Forest ...C 2	Highland ......E 4
Dixmoor ......D 4	Lombard ......B 2	River Grove ...C 2	Hobart ....F 4
Dolton ....D 4	Loop, The .....D 2	Riverside ......C 2	Lake Station ...F 4
Downers Grove .B 3	Lynwood ......E 4	Robbins ....D 3	Merrillville .....F 4
E. Chicago	Lyons ....C 2	Rockdale ......B 4	Munster ....E 4
Heights ....E 4	Markham ......D 4	Romeoville ....B 3	New Chicago ...F 4
East Hazelcrest .D 4	Marywood ....A 3	Rosemont .....C 2	Schererville ...E 4
Elmhurst ......C 2	Matteson .....D 4	St. Charles ...A 2	West Glen Rock .F 4
	Maywood .....C 2	Sauk Village ...E 4	Whiting ....E 3

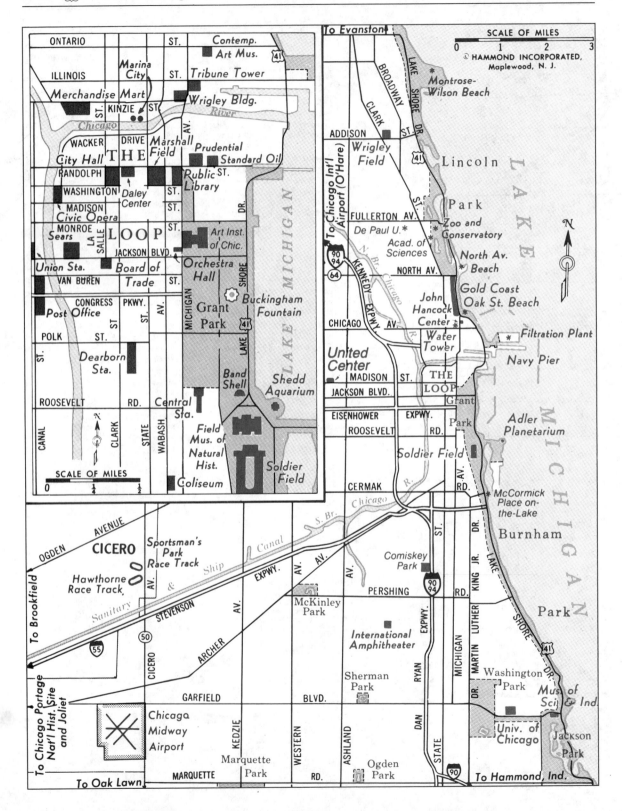

SCALE OF MILES
0   1   2   3
© HAMMOND INCORPORATED,
Maplewood, N. J.

To Evanston

ONTARIO   ST.
Contemp.
Art Mus.

ILLINOIS   ST.
Marina
City
Tribune Tower

Merchandise Mart
Wrigley Bldg.
KINZIE   ST.
River
Chicago

WACKER
DRIVE
Marshall
Field
Prudential
Standard Oil

City Hall
THE
AV.

RANDOLPH
Public
Library
ST.

WASHINGTON
Daley
Center
ST.

MADISON
ST.
Civic Opera
MONROE
Sears
LOOP
ST.
Art Inst.
of Chic.

JACKSON   BLVD.
Orchestra
Hall
Union Sta.
Board of
VAN BUREN
Trade   ST.

CONGRESS   PKWY.
Post Office
Grant
Park
MICHIGAN
AV.
LAKE
SHORE
DR.
Buckingham
Fountain
POLK   ST.

Dearborn
Sta.
CANAL
CLARK
STATE
WABASH
Band
Shell
Shedd
Aquarium

ROOSEVELT   RD.
Central
Sta.
Field
Mus. of
Natural
Hist.
Soldier
Field
SCALE OF MILES
0
Coliseum

LAKE MICHIGAN

Broadway
Clark
Lake Shore Dr.
Montrose-
Wilson Beach

ADDISON
Wrigley
Field
Lincoln

To Chicago Int'l
Airport (O'Hare)
FULLERTON AV.
De Paul U.
Acad. of
Sciences
Park
Zoo and
Conservatory
North Av.
Beach

90
94
64
KENNEDY EXPWY.
N. Br. Chicago R.
NORTH AV.
Gold Coast
Oak St. Beach
John
Hancock
Center

CHICAGO
AV.
Water
Tower
Filtration Plant
Navy Pier

United
Center
MADISON   ST.
THE
LOOP
JACKSON BLVD.
Grant

EISENHOWER
EXPWY.
Park
Adler
Planetarium
ROOSEVELT   RD.
Soldier Field

CERMAK   RD.
Chicago R.
McCormick
Place on-
the-Lake

N

LAKE MICHIGAN

Burnham

OGDEN   AVENUE
CICERO
Sportsman's
Park
Race Track
Canal
Ship
Comiskey
Park

Hawthorne
Race Track
Sanitary
&
STEVENSON
EXPWY.
McKinley
Park
PERSHING
90
94
RD.
Park

55
50
ARCHER
AV.
International
Amphitheater
DAN
RYAN
MICHIGAN
MARTIN LUTHER KING JR.
LAKE SHORE DR.
Washington
Park
Mus. of
Sci. & Ind.

To Brookfield
CICERO
AV.
Sherman
Park
GARFIELD   BLVD.

To Chicago Portage
Nat'l Hist. Site
and Joliet
Chicago
Midway
Airport
KEDZIE
WESTERN   RD.
ASHLAND
Ogden
Park
STATE
Univ. of
Chicago
Jackson
Park

MARQUETTE
Marquette
Park
To Oak Lawn
41
90
To Hammond, Ind.